ALL · IN · ONE

Linux+™ Certification

EXAM GUIDE

Jeff W. Durham

Osborne / McGraw-Hill

New York • Chicago • San Francisco • Lisbon
London • Madrid • Mexico City • Milan • New Delhi
San Juan • Seoul • Singapore • Sydney • Toronto

Osborne/**McGraw-Hill**
2600 Tenth Street
Berkeley, California 94710
U.S.A.

To arrange bulk purchase discounts for sales promotions, premiums, or fund-raisers, please contact Osborne/**McGraw-Hill** at the above address. For information on translations or book distributors outside the U.S.A., please see the International Contact Information page immediately following the index of this book.

The Linux+™ Certification All-In-One Exam Guide

1234567890 DOC DOC 01987654321

Book p/n 0-07-219369-7 and CD p/n 0-07-219370-0
parts of

ISBN 0-07-219368-9

Publisher
Brandon A. Nordin

Vice President & Associate Publisher
Scott Rogers

Acquisitions Editor
Michael Sprague

Project Editor
Jenn Tust

Acquisitions Coordinator
Alex Corona

Technical Editor
Chris Hare

Compositor
MacAllister Publishing Services, LLC

Cover Design
Greg Scott

This book was composed with QuarkXPress™.

DEDICATION

To Willie, for her boundless understanding and support
through the writing of this volume.

ACKNOWLEDGMENTS

Writing is never the sole operation of one individual or organization. So here's the short list of those who got this book out the door and onto the shelf:

To Emmett Dulaney, Jon Holman, Tara Lankford, and all the other trainers and support staff at Mercury Technical Solutions: Do I still have to wear this Plus Boy sign around on my back all day, or can I finally take it off?

To my acquisitions editor, Michael Sprague: Thanks for the understanding, the extensions, and the absolute professionalism that carried me through this writing process. Thanks to Paulina, Alexander, Robin, and Barbara for everything you've done.

To Molly Applegate at MacAllister Publishing Services: Thanks for being able to spot when the little things are turning into big things.

And finally, to CertificationCorner.com: Thanks for providing the perfect vehicle for me to receive invaluable comments and suggestions from true certification candidates.

ABOUT THE AUTHOR

Jeff W. Durham is one of the industry's leading authorities on CompTIA certifications. He is the Director of CompTIA Training and Development as well as the co-founder of Mercury Technical Solutions, LLC, which specializes in CompTIA certification training.

Jeff is the author of the monthly "On The Plus Side" column for *CertCities.com* and a frequent contributor to *Certification Magazine*.

BRIEF CONTENTS

CONTENTS

INTRODUCTION

It seems as though CompTIA is rapidly moving into a position where they offer an exam and certification for everyone. One of their newer exams, Linux+, is aimed at the entry-level Linux administrator. The exam costs $190 ($140 for CompTIA members), features 95 questions, and is available through Prometric and VUE testing centers.

The Linux+ exam is comprised of seven major objective categories called *domains*. A weighting is assigned to each category to determine how many questions will come from each category. The categories and the weightings employed are as follows:

- Planning the Implementation—4%

- Installation—12%

- Configuration—15%

- Administration—18%

- System Maintenance—14%

- Troubleshooting—18%

- Identify, Install, and Maintain System Hardware—19%

Although there are no prerequisites for this certification, the last domain should clue you in to the fact that A+ (hardware) certification is strongly recommended. In addition to the 19 percent of the exam specifically listed as covering hardware as a top-level domain, hardware topics also appear within objectives throughout the other domains. Indeed, a solid understanding of hardware is essential for approximately 35 to 40 percent of the exam.

All questions are either multiple-choice with at least four possible choices or point-and-click graphics questions. Of the multiple-choice questions, there are a mixture of "choose one" and "choose more than one" questions. The grading scale is between 100 and 900, with a passing score being above 655.

The components of the Linux+ exam can be classified in one of three ways: good, bad, and so-so. On the good side, it is the only Linux certification that requires only one exam. CompTIA has proven time and time again that there is a need for verification of a person's skills with a single exam, and this is another excellent opportunity put to good use. I've run into dozens of people proclaiming that they know Linux — *really* know Linux. What that really translates into, though, is different for everyone. Whereas one person interprets "knowing Linux" as being able to recompile the kernel on-the-fly, another thinks it merely means knowing the difference between the **grep** and **diff** utilities. Linux+ certifies that a person knows the basics of the operating system on a level platform and can operate as an entry-level administrator.

Now to the bad side. Because of its advertised experience level (six months), you can easily be lulled into a false sense of confidence. Try to pass the exam without studying and you'll likely leave the test center $190 poorer and with a severe blow to your pride. The six-months-experience target audience for this exam is more for someone who eats and sleeps in the server room, and who clips his pager around the neck of his T-shirt because his cell phone and other devices are occupying all the available belt room. You need to study for this exam as you would any other.

The so-so portion of the exam is more a personal preference of mine than anything else. Instead of the exam asking 95 questions, I'd prefer to see fewer, more difficult questions. Everyone knows that Linux is a case-sensitive operating system and that so much of its power lies at the command line. It seems a waste to not have fill-in-the-blank questions testing comprehension of common commands (change the password to . . . , kill a process, and so on). When you have 95 multiple-choice questions, you border on questions that have to be in a simplistic, multiple-choice format in order for candidates to be able to answer all of them in the allotted time.

Planning an Implementation

This chapter covers the following competencies required to master the Linux+ certification exam:

- Identifying the purpose of Linux machine
- Identifying required system hardware
- Determining required software and services
- Allocating storage space to filesystems
- Comparing Linux licensing methods
- Identifying the function of Linux services
- Identifying the strengths and weaknesses of different distributions
- Comparing functions, features, and benefits of Linux versus other operating systems
- Understanding Linux kernel version numbering
- Identifying where to obtain software and other resources
- Analyzing customer resources for solutions

Understanding Linux

Unlike traditional operating systems, it is not necessary to purchase a copy of the Linux operating system. Linux is known as open-source software and is not subject to the rules of proprietary software products. Traditional software results in the user buying the product with no ability to change or alter it and no access to the product source code. This copyright and protected software is how companies like Microsoft operate their businesses. Products like Microsoft Windows are licensed to the end user, who has limited specific rights to the product.

Using the open-source approach, any user or developer can obtain the source code and extend the capabilities of the operating system. Their enhancements, or *bug fixes*, can then be provided back to the community for implementation in the operating system itself or to be used by other Linux users. Although Linux is often considered free, this does not necessarily refer to the cost. Even though many Linux distributions can be downloaded from the Internet, the concept of free actually refers to the ability to alter the code and distribute it if desired.

 NOTE The terms "free software" and "open-source software" are often used interchangeably. The terms "free software" and "freeware" are not interchangeable. Freeware refers to programs that are available at no cost.

There are disadvantages to using open-source software, as you must be willing and able to support the environment yourself, unless you want to pay one of the few companies available that offer support for their own distributions.

Linux is free thanks to the GNU General Public License (GPL). The full context of the license is beyond the scope of this book. However, the GPL instructs distributors of GPL-protected programs that they must provide the same rights to the recipients that you have. This means people must have access to your source code, and you must provide the terms of the GPL so they can understand their rights. The GPL copyright ensures you have continued free access to the software and the associated source code, while granting the legal permission to copy, distribute, and/or modify the software. This can be construed as giving authors artistic license over the code to do what they want with it.

Through the GPL, software authors are also protected. A software author who modifies and redistributes an existing program uses the GPL to specify that there is no warranty for the software. Once a program is covered under the GPL, the program authors are prohibited from seeking a software patent that would make the program proprietary. The GPL addresses this by stating that the patent must be free for everyone's use or not patented at all.

Caldera introduced their OpenLinux Operating System with limitations under the GNU licensing scheme. This enables them to make companies buy individual licenses and even gives them the ability to close some of the code that they feel is proprietary. When it comes down to where the rubber hits the road, the GNU GPL license is just another legal document that can be manipulated to serve a purpose. Anyone who modifies and redistributes open-source code under the GNU license must want to stay within the intent of the GNU license to keep GNU/Linux free.

Microsoft, in contrast, maintains closed-source software. You cannot modify, use, or in any way tamper with their code and redistribute it as you can with GNU/Linux.

You can see the GPL license on Linux.ORG at **http://www.linux.org/info/gnu.html.**

Running Linux

What do you want your Linux to do? Do you want to implement a server or a workstation solution? These are some of the questions we will answer. Major distributions of Linux divide the operating system into three generic categories:

- Server

- Workstation

- Custom install (pieces of both the previous categories)

A server operates just as its name sounds; it serves files and applications for other computers to access. Servers are usually stronger than normal desktop models. They are built with larger hard drives, more memory, and faster, easier access. The applications that run on a server are designed for others to connect to.

A workstation usually is on the receiving end of things in the computer world. It will ask the server for files and applications and be redirected to the needed resources.

A custom install can involve both server and workstation applications that accept incoming connections and also connect to other computers.

Linux is a versatile and robust operating system that can be customized to almost any situation. We can break down servers into more distinct categories. Linux is able to serve as a mail server with the appropriate software such as Sendmail or other third-party software. It can be configured to go out to the Web and get the mail and distribute it to the appropriate mailboxes. *MySQL* is database software that is used on Web servers all over the world to accumulate and distribute information. Red Hat Linux has a department dedicated to distributing its Linux to embedded applications for smart appliances such as Web-browsing cell phones.

The beauty of running Linux in the command line is that it only needs 4MB of RAM to operate. Of course, when you add the Xserver and other programs we have come to know and can't function without, the RAM requirements run upwards of 64MB as in SuSE Linux, which is based on a graphical (X Window) installation method.

Introducing the Operating System

A number of popular Linux distributions are available for the user to choose from. Aside from the vendors involved, the user must decide if he or she needs a server or a workstation system, as these are the major distinctions between the distributions. The Linux workstation is intended for a multiuser, multitasking environment, where each user accesses the system by providing a username and password.

The Linux server is known to run for longer periods of time than other operating systems. They have been known to run for months without restarting the system. Contrast this to the known problems with Microsoft Windows servers, which need to be rebooted on a regular basis. Unix, upon which many facets of Linux is based, has long been the operating system of choice for large-scale systems and Internet-based Web servers. It is worth noting that even Microsoft uses Unix to run the servers associated with their popular Web-based e-mail system.

The kernel is considered by many to be the core of the Linux operating system. Although many other applications and programs make up the operating system, the kernel provides control of the system hardware, memory management, system and process scheduling, and other low-level system management tasks. Every request to access a file or interact with a system on the network is processed through the kernel. Without the kernel, there would be no operating system.

Linus Torvalds developed the original Linux kernel, which has undergone many extensions and revisions thanks to the legions of worldwide developers who have taken on the task of creating the implementations of Linux we see today.

System Architecture

Linux was originally developed on the Intel computing platform, and has since been ported to other system architectures as well. Each system architecture offers its own advantages and challenges due to differing device, memory, and configuration management issues.

Linux is most commonly found running on the Intel processor family, including the 80386 and higher processors. Linux ports have also been developed for Compaq (formerly DEC) Alpha, RISC-based processors, Motorola 68K processors, and the PowerPC processor found in the PowerMac.

After the processor type, the next challenge is the system bus architecture. The specific bus architecture supported by the processor is typically included; however, the Intel and similar processor family has a wide range of bus types available. Linux support for various bus architectures includes

- Industry Standard Architecture (ISA), VESA local bus (VLB), Extended Industry Standard Architecture (EISA), and Peripheral Component Interconnect (PCI)

- PS/2 Micro Channel Architecture (MCA)

- VersaModule Eurocard (VME)

Often support for these bus architectures is limited to specific Linux ports due to the association with a specific processor type. It is recommended that you review the specific requirements for your hardware type prior to installing Linux.

With the predominance of Intel-based processors, this chapter focuses on this processor family, primarily because this is also the focus of the exam.

The customized hardware found in laptop systems poses a special problem for the Linux administrator. The specialized hardware might not be supported on Linux, thereby reducing the overall capabilities of the laptop. Problems are typically found with customized video, sound, modems, and power management systems. Additionally, the use of PCMCIA cards in laptops can be an issue due to different levels of support for the various cards. Important information on the system configuration is found in the /proc filesystem.

BIOS

The interface between the computer hardware and the operating system is controlled at the hardware level using the Basic Input/Output System (BIOS). All operating system requests to access specific hardware, such as the floppy disk or reading a file, are given to the BIOS for processing.

Each computer type has its own system BIOS. The capabilities of today's BIOS have significantly expanded from those of a BIOS one year ago. ISA, EISA, and PCI bus architectures all introduce specific BIOS configurations that are different from each other. Consequently, BIOS configuration can be a challenge and is best performed with a copy of the BIOS documentation specific to your BIOS and system mainboard.

Changing BIOS configuration information affects the system hardware and subsequently the operation of both the hardware and the operating system. For example, changing the time of the hardware clock affects how the operating system reports the time.

Setting the Clock

Linux uses the hardware clock built on the system mainboard to track the actual time of day. Consequently, adjustments to the hardware clock affect how Linux interprets and reports the actual time.

Configuring the Linux clock requires the definition of the time zone to report the correct local time, and the correct date and time must be established. Having the correct time zone is important to ensure that messages received from other systems are shown at the correct time. From a security perspective, having the correct, and ideally synchronized time, means the time of specific events can be accurately determined.

Linux supports all of the available time zones based upon the geographical areas and distance from Greenwich Mean Time (GMT), which is also known as the Universal Time Clock (UTC). Both GMT and UTC are used interchangeably and refer to the time at Greenwich, England.

The **timeconfig** command prompts the administrator to select the appropriate time zone and select an option to specify if the hardware clock on the system is set to GMT. If your system clock is set to GMT, select this option; otherwise, leave it blank.

Once the time zone is properly defined, we can then set the correct time using the **date** command. **date** is most commonly used to display the system date, as

```
[root@mercury.technical /bin]# date

Sat Jul 21 11:36:18 CDT 2001
```

The **date** command has a wide array of options to print the command in multiple formats or extract specific information from the date. However, the administrator, or root user, has the ability to define a new date and time on the command line, thereby changing the system clock.

```
[root@mercury.technical /bin]# date
Sat Jul 21 11:36:18 CDT 2001
[root@mercury.technical /bin]# date 072214052001.34
Sun Jul 22 14:05:34 CDT 2001
[root@mercury.technical /bin]#
```

When setting the current date and time, the new time must be provided using the format

```
MMDDhhmmCCYY.ss
```

The parameters are

MM   Two-digit month

DD   Two-digit day of the month

hh   Two-digit hour in 24-hour clock format

mm   Two-digit minutes

CC Two digits of the year (century)

YY Current year

ss The number of seconds to be applied

If the requirement is to only change the system date or the time, the values for the century, year, and seconds are optional. The century and year are applied from the current values, and the seconds are set to zero. However, the minimum acceptable argument must include MMDDhhmm. This means that even if you only want to change the numerical value of the date, you must still provide the minimum details.

```
[root@mercury.technical /bin]# date 07230923
Mon Jul 23 09:23:00 CDT 2001
[root@mercury.technical /bin]#
```

While the clock has been set, most systems suffer from *clock drift*, which affects the accuracy of the clock. If it is critical to the system operation that the clock drift be minimized, configuring a time synchronization service such as Network Time Protocol (NTP) is highly recommended. NTP uses a highly reliable clock source to detect clock drift and reset system clocks to the correct time.

Using I/O Communication Ports

The commonly available serial, parallel, and joystick ports found on today's computer systems are all supported under Linux. Even the most basic kernel includes support for the 8250, 16450, 16550, and 16550A universal asynchronous receiver-transmitters (UARTs) used for serial communications. Default support is included in the kernel for single and multiport serial cards. Traditional serial ports require the CPU to process all data received and transmitted through the serial port, which is accomplished using Interrupt Requests (IRQs) and I/O ports.

Be careful not to confuse I/O ports and memory addresses, as they are not the same. The I/O address is used to store the actual information being transferred to or from the serial device. Due to the sometimes significant CPU load associated with serial cards, systems that must support more than four can choose between a dumb or intelligent serial interface. Interfaces that require the main CPU to perform the processing are called dumb, whereas multiport serial cards that provide their own CPU for faster processing of the serial data are called intelligent serial controllers.

There are two primary varieties for dumb serial controllers. One uses the AST Four-Port approach, assigning a block of memory addresses for the IRQ, which then distinguishes between the ports on the card. The second format requires four IRQ values, one for each port. This consumes a lot of CPU resources, as it consumes virtually all of the free IRQ channels available.

Serial ports on a Linux system are named ttyS followed by a number corresponding to the actual DOS COM port. For example, ttyS0 corresponds to COM1, ttyS1 corresponds to COM2, and so on. The /dev/ directory, which is discussed in the "The /dev Directory" section later in this chapter, holds the device files for access to the serial ports. When listing the serial ports, use the following command:

```
[root@mercury.technical /root]# ls -l /dev/ttyS*
crw-------  1 root    tty    4, 64 May 5 1998 /dev/ttyS0
crw-------  1 root    tty    4, 65 May 5 1998 /dev/ttyS1
crw-------  1 root    tty    4, 66 May 5 1998 /dev/ttyS2
crw-------  1 root    tty    4, 67 May 5 1998 /dev/ttyS3
[root@mercury.technical /root]#
```

The device files typically exist even if the hardware is not installed. Consequently, the administrator cannot use the assumption that the hardware is there just because the device file exists.

The kernel serial port driver keeps a list of the I/O addresses for each serial port and maps the physical device to the associated name. The command **setserial** lists and modifies the serial port configurations.

The **setserial** command prints the configuration information for the configured serial ports by specifying the serial port you want the information on:

```
[root@mercury.technical /root]# setserial -g /dev/ttyS*
/dev/ttyS0, UART: 16550A, Port: 0x03f8, IRQ: 4
/dev/ttyS1, UART: unknown, Port: 0x02f8, IRQ: 3
/dev/ttyS2, UART: unknown, Port: 0x03e8, IRQ: 4
/dev/ttyS3, UART: unknown, Port: 0x02e8, IRQ: 3
```

This output tells us that there is a serial port at IRQ 4 (COM1 in DOS/Windows). We know this because the UART is identified. On the other ports if the UART is unknown, it doesn't mean that there isn't a serial port there; it only means that the UART cannot be identified. Some low-cost serial ports won't identify themselves.

If your system came preconfigured with two serial ports, they will likely be detected by the system without requiring **setserial** to configure the appropriate support. However, changes to the IRQ or I/O address must be specified with **setserial**.

Unlike many commands, **setserial** does nothing to validate that the I/O address and IRQ are valid and not already in use. Although **setserial** accepts the values and configures the serial driver, the serial port will still not function due to the invalid configuration.

If you must make changes to your serial port driver, it is essential that you record the configuration changes for future reference. This is most easily done by saving the output of **setserial** to a file, sending it via e-mail to the administrator account, or if you have a printer, creating a hardcopy. Commands used to do this are the following:

```
setserial -g /dev/ttyS* | lp
setserial -g /dev/ttyS* > /tmp/serial.configuration
setserial -g /dev/ttyS* | mail root
```

Using Parallel Ports

Linux also supports the common parallel ports, which are recognized without additional configuration. Like the serial ports, the parallel devices are found in the /dev/ directory and will exist even if the associated hardware is not installed. The parallel port device names start with the prefix *lp*:

```
crw-rw----  1 root    daemon   6,  0 May 5 1998 lp0
crw-rw----  1 root    daemon   6,  1 May 5 1998 lp1
crw-rw----  1 root    daemon   6,  2 May 5 1998 lp2
```

There is no effective way for Linux to find the parallel ports, because there is no command similar to **setserial** for parallel devices. Checking for the parallel ports is most easily done by reviewing the system startup messages using the **dmesg** command:

```
dmesg | more
...
parport0: PC-style at 0x3bc (0x7bc) [SPP,ECP,ECPPS2]
parport0: detected irq 7; use procfs to enable interrupt-driven operation.
parport0: no IEEE-1284 device present.
lp0: using parport0 (polling).
```

If there are no parport lines reported during the system initialization, there are no parallel ports configured. Like the serial ports, the printer port is detected automatically during system bootup.

Linux kernels after version 2.2. provide support for a lot of parallel devices other than line printers, including Zip drives, parallel port Integrated Device Electronic (IDE) drives, and CD-ROM drives.

Using Hard Disks

Linux detects and supports virtually all common disk controllers and disks without additional device drivers. Linux supports

- IDE

- Enhanced-IDE (E-IDE)

- Modified frequency modulation (MFM)

- Enhanced Small Device Interface (ESDI) when configured for ST-506 MFM/RLL/IDE
- Generic 8-bit XT
- Run-length limited (RLL)
- Various Small Computer System Interface (SCSI) controllers

The use of the ext2fs filesystem is highly recommended to ensure that disk interfaces that support bad block checking are properly analyzed to prevent data loss by eliminating the chance of writing the data to the bad blocks.

Linux will support multiple disk controllers, including a mixture of disk types. However, when combining SCSI and IDE devices, the IDE devices will typically boot first. Furthermore, Linux supports multiple IDE controllers and multiple disk drives. For example, each IDE interface supports two IDE devices, and Linux supports two IDE controllers, for a maximum of four IDE devices including disk drives and CD-ROM drives.

A problem with earlier BIOS versions is the 1,024-cylinder boundary, which requires the operating system to be installed in the first 1,024 cylinders on the disk. This is not a problem with boot manager systems like LILO or with newer versions of system BIOS software. However, if your system requires the use of special software to translate the disk geometry to something DOS understands, or for limitations of your BIOS, you should upgrade your BIOS prior to installing Linux. Upgrading the BIOS should only be done if you are very comfortable with and understand installation routines. Even then you should contact the manufacturer of the motherboard for specific instructions as to how they want you to perform the action.

The Linux kernel supports a wide range of SCSI controller cards, although differences in implementation and configurations limit the options and level of support. It is also important to note that not all SCSI controllers are intended to support disk drives. Lower-cost interface cards are intended for SCSI disk drives or removable disks and do contain a BIOS. Additionally, the lower throughputs provide no performance gain over the standard IDE controller.

SCSI cards that contain a BIOS can boot the system or load a program from the device such as LILO. The exact method of loading and configuring the BIOS depends upon the controller card, manufacturer, and specific BIOS revision. However, Linux detects most SCSI adapters on system startup and properly configures them.

Configuring SCSI Devices

Apple popularized the SCSI with the development of the Apple Macintosh computer. SCSI provides many advantages including a high degree of flexibility and data transfer speeds on the SCSI bus.

Each SCSI device on the bus is assigned an SCSI ID, which is unique to that interface. The SCSI controller itself uses an SCSI ID, typically ID 7. If a device is configured with ID 7, the controller is confused and lists the device on every SCSI ID. This prevents the system from operating correctly, if it will even start at all. Consequently, it is important to determine what SCSI IDs are available on the SCSI bus prior to installing the new device.

The SCSI ID numbers are typically reported by the SCSI controller during system startup. If your SCSI controller does not have a BIOS, you must manually determine the IDs for each device by looking in the system startup messages using **dmesg**:

```
dmesg | more
.....
aha152x: BIOS test: passed, auto configuration: ok, detected 1 controller(s)
aha152x0: vital data: PORTBASE=0x340, IRQ=11, SCSI ID=7, reconnect=enabled,
parity=enabled, synchronous=disabled, delay=100, extended translation=
disabled
aha152x: trying software interrupt, ok.
scsi0 : Adaptec 152x SCSI driver; $Revision: 1.7 $
scsi : 1 host.
 Vendor: PIONEER  Model: CD-ROM DR-U12X  Rev: 1.06
 Type:  CD-ROM                ANSI SCSI revision: 02
Detected scsi CD-ROM sr0 at scsi0, channel 0, id 2, lun 0
sr0: scsi3-mmc drive: 12x/12x xa/form2 cdda tray
```

In this example, the system has an Adaptec 152x SCSI controller with one device connected (an SCSI CD-ROM). From this output, we can see—as revealed by the shaded areas—that the SCSI ID of the controller is ID 7 and that the SCSI ID for the CD-ROM is ID 2.

The major system devices are disk controllers and drives, serial and parallel ports, and system processors.

Linux Hardware

Hardware is the biggest factor in deciding to run Linux. Among the items to consider are the video hardware, sound card, and any network adapters. If you want to run Linux with the graphical user interface (GUI), the choice of which video card to use becomes more important. Not to worry though, low-cost video cards can be purchased that will display Linux GUI very well.

Today's popular Linux distributions provide support for a myriad of systems and hardware. If you are unsure about your system's capability to run Linux, several books are available that take an in-depth look at hardware. A good updated hardware list exists on the Web at **http://www.linux.org/hardware/index.html**. Some of the links at the end of the chapter will help you decide on the right hardware for your Linux installation.

The Linux Filesystem

During the installation process, a number of directories are created to hold system files. The following sections discuss each of the directories.

The / Directory

The path through the Linux directory structure always begins at the / directory. When specifying the location of a file using absolute pathnames, the / is the first component because the root directory is the ultimate origin as there is no directory above it.

The /bin Directory

The /bin directory holds system binaries or programs used to operate the system. On today's implementations, the /bin directory holds commands available to all users, whereas the system administrations typically found in bin on Unix implementations are now found in /sbin. Additionally, application programs or binaries that are not critical to the operation of the system are found in /usr/bin.

The /boot Directory

The /boot directory holds all the files needed to boot the system, except for configuration files. These include the kernel, boot loaders, and message files defining the text printed on the screen at system boot. Most new implementations of Linux store the kernel in /boot, whereas some still place the kernel in the /root directory as a holdover from traditional Unix.

The /dev Directory

As discussed earlier, the /dev directory stores all devices files used to access the various hardware components on the system. Clicking on the graphical representation of the CD-ROM works because there is an association between the icon and the CD-ROM device file in the /dev directory. Regardless of the device type, there is a file for it, including disk drives, floppy disks, tape drives, terminals, the console, serial ports, parallel ports, and the sound card.

```
brw-rw-rw-   1 root    root        2,  4 March 23  2001 floppy
brw-r-----   1 root    operator    3,  1 March 23  2001 drive1
crw-rw----   1 root    lp          6,  0 March 23  2001 lp0
crw-rw----   1 root    lp          6,  1 March 23  2001 lp1
crw-rw----   1 root    lp          6,  2 March 23  2001 lp2
brw-rw-r--   1 root    disk       23,  0 March 23  2001 cd
crw-r-----   1 root    kmem        1,  1 March 23  2001 mem
```

```
crw-rw-rw-   1 root     root       1,    3 March 23   2001 null
crw-rw-rw-   1 root     root      10,    1 Sep 27 15:34 mouse
brw-------   1 root     root       1,    0 March 23   2001 ram0
brw-------   1 root     root       1,    1 March 23   2001 ram1
brw-------   1 root     root       1,    2 March 23   2001 ram2
brw-------   1 root     root       1,    3 March 23   2001 ram3
brw-------   1 root     root      31,    0 March 23   2001 rom0
brw-------   1 root     root      31,    1 March 23   2001 rom1
br--------   1 root     root      31,    8 March 23   2001 rrom0
br--------   1 root     root      31,    9 March 23   2001 rrom1
brw-rw-r--   1 root     disk      15,    0 March 23   2001 sonycd
crw--w--w-   1 root     root       4,    0 March 23   2001 tty0
crw-rw----   1 root     tty        4,    1 March 23   2001 tty1
crw-rw----   1 root     tty        4,   10 March 23   2001 tty10
crw-rw----   1 root     tty        4,   11 SEP 27 10:00 tty11
crw-rw----   1 root     tty        4,   12 March 23   2001  tty12
crw-rw----   1 root     tty        4,   13 March 23   2001 tty13
crw-rw----   1 root     tty        4,   14 March 23   2001 tty14
crw-rw----   1 root     tty        4,   15 March 23   2001 tty15
```

The results of the ls -lk listing in the /dev directory shows several important things. First, the files are either type *b* or *c*, denoting either a character or block device. Character devices are modems, terminal ports, and transmit or receive data one character at a time. Block devices, such as disk drives, work on blocks of data for higher data transfer capabilities.

Second, the files do not illustrate the size of the device driver or physical device in bytes. The numbers represent the kernel driver used to interact with the device. This is useful information, but beyond the scope of the actual exam.

The /etc Directory

The /etc directory contains a suite of system configuration files used to control the system initialization and configuration parameters for networking, network services, e-mail, and many other subsystems. The /etc directory files are often readable by all users on the system; however, any commands found in this directory are executable only by the system administrator.

The /home Directory

The /home directory is the default location for storing the user's home directory. Each user has a directory from /home for the storage of his or her personal configuration and data files. Some other services, such as File Transfer Protocol (FTP) and Hypertext Transfer Protocol (HTTP), also create directories in the user's /home directory. It is important to note that the root user is the exception to this rule. For the protection of the root account, the root user's /home directory is found under /root.

The /lib Directory

Many of the Linux operating system commands use shared libraries, allowing the executable files to be smaller and use new features in the library without needing to be recompiled. The shared libraries are typically written in the C programming language and found in the /lib directory.

The /mnt Directory

This is a directory used to mount other external filesystems or devices. Although the /mnt directory often contains entries, these are not used to store data directly, but are reference points to external filesystems or devices.

The common directories in /mnt are cdrom, floppy, and so on. There is a tmp directory often found in /mnt for temporary file storage, but the use of /tmp is the preferred location.

The /opt Directory

The /opt directory is the storage place for additional or add-on software. Not every application installs itself in this location, but any application that does creates a subdirectory with the application name. There is no definitive standard stating that applications must install in this directory, but it is a holdover from traditional Unix.

The /proc Directory

The virtual filesystem, /proc, is dynamically generated to hold information processes, the kernel, network devices, and other system information. Each process is a folder with permissions to control access to the process environment.

Processes are depicted as folders, each having permissions and variables associated with them. Other system information is most commonly depicted as files, as shown in the following:

```
# ps
  PID T7TY           TIME CMD
15193 pts/0     00:00:00 bash
15220 pts/0     00:00:00 sleep
15222 pts/0     00:00:00 sleep
15236 pts/0     00:00:00 ps
# ls -l
dr-xr-xr-x    3 root      root        0 Sep 20 08:34 15193
dr-xr-xr-x    3 root      root        0 Sep 20 08:34 15220
dr-xr-xr-x    3 root      root        0 Sep 20 08:34 15222
dr-xr-xr-x    4 root      root        0 Sep 20 08:34 bus
```

```
-r--r--r--   1 root      root            0 Sep 20 08:34 cmdline
-r--r--r--   1 root      root            0 Sep 20 08:34 cpuinfo
-r--r--r--   1 root      root            0 Sep 20 08:34 devices
-r--r--r--   1 root      root            0 Sep 20 08:34 dma
-r--r--r--   1 root      root            0 Sep 20 08:34 fb
-r--r--r--   1 root      root            0 Sep 20 08:34 filesystems
dr-xr-xr-x   2 root      root            0 Sep 20 08:34 fs
dr-xr-xr-x   4 root      root            0 Sep 20 08:34 ide
-r--r--r--   1 root      root            0 Sep 20 08:34 interrupts
-r--r--r--   1 root      root            0 Sep 20 08:34 ioports
-r--------   1 root      root     67112960 Sep 20 08:34 kcore
-r--------   1 root      root            0 Sep 20 08:16 kmsg
-r--r--r--   1 root      root            0 Sep 20 08:34 ksyms
-r--r--r--   1 root      root            0 Sep 20 08:34 loadavg
-r--r--r--   1 root      root            0 Sep 20 08:34 locks
-r--r--r--   1 root      root            0 Sep 20 08:34 mdstat
-r--r--r--   1 root      root            0 Sep 20 08:34 meminfo
-r--r--r--   1 root      root            0 Sep 20 08:34 misc
-r--r--r--   1 root      root            0 Sep 20 08:34 modules
-r--r--r--   1 root      root            0 Sep 20 08:34 mounts
dr-xr-xr-x   4 root      root            0 Sep 20 08:34 net
dr-xr-xr-x   3 root      root            0 Sep 20 08:34 parport
-r--r--r--   1 root      root            0 Sep 20 08:34 partitions
-r--r--r--   1 root      root            0 Sep 20 08:34 pci
-r--r--r--   1 root      root            0 Sep 20 08:34 rtc
dr-xr-xr-x   2 root      root            0 Sep 20 08:34 scsi
lrwxrwxrwx   1 root      root           64 Sep 20 08:34 self -> 15252
-r--r--r--   1 root      root            0 Sep 20 08:34 slabinfo
-r--r--r--   1 root      root            0 Sep 20 08:34 sound
-r--r--r--   1 root      root            0 Sep 20 08:34 stat
-r--r--r--   1 root      root            0 Sep 20 08:34 swaps
dr-xr-xr-x  10 root      root            0 Sep 20 08:34 sys
dr-xr-xr-x   4 root      root            0 Sep 20 08:34 tty
-r--r--r--   1 root      root            0 Sep 20 08:34 uptime
-r--r--r--   1 root      root            0 Sep 20 08:34 version
#
```

The /root Directory

Not to be confused with the / directory, which is the top-level directory containing all of the directories discussed in this chapter, the /root directory is the home directory for the root user. In traditional Unix systems, the root user's home directory is /. This was changed in later Unix versions and carried to Linux where the root user has his or her home directory as /root. This was done for security purposes, although improved security is achieved by moving the /root directory to an alternate location on the system and by renaming it to something less obvious.

The /sbin Directory

The /bin directory holds standard executables that most users utilize; the /sbin directory holds binary executables for system administration. Many of these utilities are used for booting the system and once resided in the /etc directory.

The /tmp Directory

The /tmp directory is used to hold temporary files. Many applications, including compilers, create temporary files for specific purposes. These files are generally short lived; for example, they might not last longer than your current session. By storing them in the /tmp directory, the filesystem can be better managed, as these files are deleted on the next system restart.

The /usr Directory

The /usr directory is an enormous directory with a directory structure of its own. The term "/usr" originally denoted user-specific resources, although today that meaning has been lost for the most part.

Subdirectories beginning with *X* define the X Window environment. The bin subdirectory contains user binary (executable) files. The binary files in the /usr/bin directory are not critical to the operation of the system, even though many of them are used on a regular basis by users. Commands essential to the operation of the system are stored in /bin, whereas system administration commands are found in /sbin.

Files for the spell-checking commands are found in the /dict directory, whereas the game directory may contain only a few commands, such as banner, or be empty. The /usr/game directory does not generally hold third-party games.

If the C compiler is installed on your system, you will find that the support files in the directories /usr/include and /usr/lib for the C language include and library files. Even if the C compiler is not installed, many libraries will be found in /usr/lib due to the dynamic library support found in Linux.

The /tmp directory is typically empty except for times during the installation process, and the man directory holds the online manual pages, which form part of the documentation set if they are installed.

Unlike the /sbin directory, which stores system administration commands, the /usr/sbin directory holds system-specific binaries. The commands in /usr/sbin are not critical to the operation of the system, but they do make things easier for the administrator. The administrator can in fact care for the system without the binaries in /usr/sbin, although it will be more difficult and time consuming. The /share directory stores specific information about the machine, including additional documentation and the Linux HOWTO series at the time the system was published. Of special mention is the /src directory, which is typically empty unless you install support to create your own kernels.

The /var Directory

The /var directory contains variable information, which is where the name is derived from. Typically, the files and directories located here include user mailboxes, system log files, and spool logs.

The principle directories include

- **lock**   Lock files for system processes
- **log**   Log files for login/logout, current users, syslog, httpd, ftpd, mail, and spool files
- **run**   Files created for the current system run level
- **spool**   Data that has been spooled for subsequent processing, such as print jobs
- **state**   System state variables

Other Directories

This is by no means an exhaustive or complete list of all directories found under /, as the administrator can create additional directories for other purposes. The lost+found directory, which exists in the top-level directory on every distinct filesystem, is used to store files and directories when filesystem corruption occurs.

Maintaining Filesystem Integrity

Day-to-day management of these systems is performed using the commands **df**, **du**, and **fsck**. The **df** and **du** commands only display information about the filesystem, and do not make any changes to the information or filesystem structure. The **fsck** command is used to restore the filesystem tables after a system crash or when some form of corruption has damaged the filesystem structure.

To see the amount of free space on any given filesystem, use the **df** command. Table 1-1 shows the various options available with **df**.

Table 1-1 Options for the **df** Utility

Option	Description
-a	Lists all filesystems, including those with no blocks allocated.
-h	Displays the space variables in human readable form.
-l	Lists only local filesystems—does not include NFS or other remote filesystems.
-m	Displays the disk space in megabytes.
-t	Shows only the filesystems with the specified type.
-T	Includes the filesystem type in the output.

The **df** command normally reports the number of 1K blocks available in the filesystem, as well as the number used and the remaining available:

```
# df
Filesystem              1k-blocks    Used Available Use% Mounted on
/dev/hda1                1980969    573405  1305178  31% /
/dev/hda3                5871498      5212  5562198   0% /home
#
```

Like many Linux commands, the options can be combined to alter the information displayed with **df**:

```
# df -am
Filesystem              1M-blocks    Used Available Use% Mounted on
/dev/hda1                   1934      560     1275  31% /
/dev/hda3                   5734        5     5432   0% /home
devpts                         0        0        0   -  /dev/pts
/proc                          0        0        0   -  /proc
noname:(pid12019)              0        0        0   -  /auto
#
```

Whereas the **df** command displays disk usage information on a filesystem basis, the **du** command displays the disk usage for files and directories. For example, the **df** command reports the amount of disk space used on the filesystem, but does not indicate where the space is actually consumed. The **du** command displays the number of disk blocks used for each file and directory, starting from the specified location. If you start at the root directory, **du** lists the disk space used for each file and directory on the system.

```
14     ./.seyon
2      ./Desktop/Autostart
2      ./Desktop/Trash
8      ./Desktop/Templates
```

```
20     ./Desktop
22     ./.kde/share/config
1      ./.kde/share/apps/kfm/tmp
1      ./.kde/share/apps/kfm/bookmarks
8      ./.kde/share/apps/kfm
6      ./.kde/share/apps/kdewizard/Work/Windows
7      ./.kde/share/apps/kdewizard/Work
1      ./.kde/share/apps/kdewizard/Themes
9      ./.kde/share/apps/kdewizard
1      ./.kde/share/apps/kpanel/applnk
1      ./.kde/share/apps/kpanel/pics
3      ./.kde/share/apps/kpanel
3      ./.kde/share/apps/kdisknav
5      ./.kde/share/apps/kwm/pics
6      ./.kde/share/apps/kwm
1      ./.kde/share/apps/kdisplay/pics
2      ./.kde/share/apps/kdisplay
2      ./.kde/share/apps/kdehelp
34     ./.kde/share/apps
1      ./.kde/share/icons/mini
2      ./.kde/share/icons
2      ./.kde/share/applnk
1      ./.kde/share/mimelnk
1      ./.kde/share/sounds
63     ./.kde/share
64     ./.kde
119    .
```

The **du** command has a number of options, listed in Table 1-2, modifying the actual information printed.

Table 1-2   Options for the **du** Utility

Option	Description
-b	Shows the file size in bytes.
-c	Prints a grand total.
-h	Prints the file size in human readable form.
-k	Displays the file size in kilobytes.
-l	Prints the number of links to the file or directory.
-m	Shows the space used in megabytes.
-s	Prints only a total.
-x	Lists only the files on the current/same filesystem. This means if the file or directory is on another filesystem, the file is skipped.

The **fsck**, or **filesystem check** command, is a major utility system that administrators are concerned with. This command verifies the filesystem structure and if damaged, repairs it. **fsck** uses the entries in the /etc/fstab file to determine which filesystems must be checked during system startup if **fsck** has been configured to run automatically using the -A option.

 NOTE Many commands read the /etc/fstab file; however, no command actually edits the contents. Administrators regularly update this file as they make changes to the filesystems installed on the system.

The **fsck** command determines the type of filesystem and runs the correct version of **fsck** for the specific filesystem being checked. **fsck** runs through several phases to analyze the filesystem structure. The following shows a sample of **fsck** output for the ext2 filesystem:

```
# fsck -A
Parallelizing fsck version 1.14 (9-Jan-1999)
E2fsck 1.14, 9-Jan-1999 for EXT2 FS 0.5b, 95/08/09
/dev/hda1 is mounted.

WARNING!!! Running e2fsck on a mounted filesystem may cause
SEVERE filesystem damage.

Do you really want to continue (y/n)? y
Pass 1: Checking inodes, blocks, and sizes
Pass 2: Checking directory structure
Pass 3: Checking directory connectivity
Pass 4: Checking reference counts
Pass 5: Checking group summary information
/dev/hda3: 927/1521664 files (0.3% non-contiguous), 215482/6081768
blocks
#
```

Phases 2 through 5 verify and correct the actual directory structures, whereas Phase 1 requires additional explanation. Every file on the system has an inode, which is stored in the inode table. You can think of the inode table as synonymous with the file allocation table (FAT) under DOS and Windows systems. The inode stores all the information about the file with the exception of the actual data.

Every file and directory on the system has an inode associated with it. The inode includes the

- Inode number
- Type of file
- Permissions
- Size of the file
- Number of links or references
- User ID (UID) of the file's owner
- Group ID (GID) of the group owning the file
- Inode update/creation, modification, and access times
- Locations of the data on the disk

Inode numbers are unique to each filesystem and always start with inode 2, which is the root directory of the filesystem. Inodes 0 and 1 are reserved. Typically, files created earlier on the filesystem have smaller numbers. The system will reuse inodes when a file is deleted according to an algorithm in the kernel file management routines.

When the filesystem becomes corrupted, **fsck** attempts to recover the file and save the data, assuming the problem is associated with the directory entry for the file.

There are a wide variety of types of filesystem corruption, not all of which can be corrected by **fsck** without data loss.

When **fsck** attempts to recover a file whose directory entry is damaged, it creates a new entry in the lost+found directory, using the file's inode number as the name. This is important to remember because the filename is not stored in the inode, but in the directory where the file is to be located on the disk.

The information found in the inode is commonly viewed using the **ls** command. Printing the inode numbers is done using the -i option to the **ls** command:

```
# ls -l
drwx------ 5      root root              1024 Sep 22 23:57 Desktop
-rw-r--r-- 1      root root                81 Sep 23 00:25 Monday
-rw-r--r-- 1      root root               152 Sep 23 00:26 Tuesday
-rw-r--r-- 1      root root                38 Sep 23 00:26 Wednesday
#
# ls -li
18471 drwx------ 5      root root         1024 Sep 22 23:57 Desktop
18535 -rw-r--r-- 1      root root           81 Sep 23 00:25 Monday
18536 -rw-r--r-- 1      root root          152 Sep 23 00:26 Tuesday
18537 -rw-r--r-- 1      root root           38 Sep 23 00:26 Wednesday
#
```

Moving the file does not affect the inode number, as moving the file doesn't create a new file. Rather, the **mv** command results in moving the file one directory to another, while retaining the inode information. When a file is copied, a new inode and data block are allocated for the copy:

```
# mv monday Friday
# ls -li
18471 drwx------ 5      root root      1024 Sep 22 23:57 Desktop
18535 -rw-r--r-- 1      root root        81 Sep 23 00:25 Friday
18536 -rw-r--r-- 1      root root       152 Sep 23 00:26 Tuesday
18537 -rw-r--r-- 1      root root        38 Sep 23 00:26 Wednesday
# cp friday Monday
# ls -li
18471 drwx------ 5      root root      1024 Sep 22 23:57 Desktop
18535 -rw-r--r-- 1      root root        81 Sep 23 00:25 Friday
18538 -rw-r--r-- 1      root root        81 Sep 23 00:38 Monday
18536 -rw-r--r-- 1      root root       152 Sep 23 00:26 Tuesday
18537 -rw-r--r-- 1      root root        38 Sep 23 00:26 Wednesday
#
```

Finding Files

Finding a particular file or directory on any computer system can be a challenging task due to the nature of our systems, the innocuous places they store our files, and because sometimes we just are not paying attention. There are several utilities available in Linux to make it easier to find the files, including

- locate
- update
- which
- find (and a companion, xargs)

The **locate** command does not search the directory tree to locate the file. Rather, it reviews a database of file locations to find instances of the specified file. The database is typically found in /var/state or /var/lib and is maintained using the **updatedb** command. The **updatedb** command can be run manually even though it runs automatically, generally twice a day, to update the database.

The **locate** command runs much faster than the **find** command to search for a file, although because it is driven by a database, any files created after the last database update will not be found until **updatedb** is executed again.

The **updatedb** command creates a database entry for a file no matter where it is found. This behavior can be controlled using the /etc/updatedb.conf file to limit the directories included in the locate database.

Using the **locate** command is as simple as specifying the name of the file to search for

```
# locate grep
/opt/kde/share/apps/kmail/pics/kmmsgreplied.xpm
/usr/bin/egrep
/usr/bin/fgrep
/usr/bin/grep
/usr/bin/zgrep
/usr/bin/zipgrep
/usr/doc/dosemu-0.98.5/bugreports.txt
/usr/doc/grep-2.2
/usr/doc/grep-2.2/ABOUT-NLS
/usr/doc/grep-2.2/AUTHORS
/usr/doc/grep-2.2/INSTALL
/usr/doc/grep-2.2/NEWS
/usr/doc/grep-2.2/README
/usr/doc/grep-2.2/THANKS
/usr/doc/grep-2.2/TODO
/usr/lib/python1.5/grep.pyc
/usr/lib/python1.5/grep.pyo
/usr/lib/xemacs-20.4/lisp/efs/dired-grep.elc
/usr/lib/xemacs-20.4/lisp/packages/igrep.elc
/usr/man/de/man1/egrep.1.gz
/usr/man/de/man1/grep.1.gz
/usr/man/man1/egrep.1.gz
/usr/man/man1/fgrep.1.gz
/usr/man/man1/grep.1.gz
/usr/man/man1/zgrep.1.gz
/usr/man/man1/zipgrep.1.gz
/usr/share/locale/de/LC_MESSAGES/grep.mo
/usr/share/locale/es/LC_MESSAGES/grep.mo
/usr/share/locale/fr/LC_MESSAGES/grep.mo
/usr/share/locale/ko/LC_MESSAGES/grep.mo
/usr/share/locale/nl/LC_MESSAGES/grep.mo
/usr/share/locale/no/LC_MESSAGES/grep.mo
/usr/share/locale/pl/LC_MESSAGES/grep.mo
/usr/share/locale/ru/LC_MESSAGES/grep.mo
/usr/share/locale/sl/LC_MESSAGES/grep.mo
/usr/share/locale/sv/LC_MESSAGES/grep.mo
/usr/share/vim/bugreport.vim
#
```

The **which** command does not use a database like **locate**, but searches the directories specified in your PATH variable to find the files. When **which** finds a match, it stops searching. Using the PATH variable to provide the search directories is useful as it identifies the exact location of the command or file found during the PATH search. If the file specified is a command, it clearly identifies which version of the command is executed when you enter only the command name:

```
# which grep
/usr/bin/grep
#
```

The find Utility

The **find** command is an extremely powerful search utility. It performs a full filesystem search for the specified files and displays every file meeting the specified criteria. However, the vast array of options that can be combined to create powerful searches is what makes this such a powerful and useful tool. The command syntax for **find** is simply

```
find [starting point] [criteria]
```

Although this looks simple, it can be a challenge to master the first few times you use **find**. If the starting point is not specified, **find** starts searching at the current working directory for the specified files, although you can specify any directory on the system as your starting point. When **find** starts, it searches the starting point directory and any subdirectories below it.

The available options that establish the search criteria are listed in Table 1-3.

For example, to find all the files on the system named "date" starting at the root directory, use the following command:

```
# find / -name "date"
/usr/bin/grep
#
```

find will by default print the path and filename of any matching files, even if the -print option is omitted, as printing the filename is the default action. Unlike the **locate** command, the **find** command will list only an exact match unless you provide wildcard characters in the name to search for.

You can combine your search with executing specific actions including changing the permissions, ownership, or listing the details of the file:

```
# find / -name "date" -exec ls -l {} \;
-rwxr-xr-x 1 root     root       70652  Aug 11 1999 /usr/bin/grep
#
```

Table 1-3 Options for the **find** Utility

Option	Purpose
-atime *days*	True if the file was accessed within the specified number of days.
-ctime *days*	True if the file was changed within the specified number of days. This is not the same as modified as it identifies changes to the inode.
-exec *command*	Executes the named command. Using this option requires you specify the command execution is for a group using {}, and is followed by a \, indicating the search is to continue.
-group *name*	True if the specified GID matches the file's GID.
-inum *number*	True if the file has the specified inode number.
-links *number*	True if the file has the specified number of links.
-mount	Limits the search to only the specified filesystem. Using the -mount options prevents other filesystems from being checked.
-mtime *days*	True if the file was modified within the specified number of days. This means the contents of the file were changed.
-name *file*	True if the filename matches the specified name.
-perm *permission*	True if the file has the specified permissions.
-print	Instructs **find** to print the name of the matching files.
-size *number*	True if the file has the specified number of blocks or characters.
-type *type*	True if the file is of the specified type, where type is a file (f), directory (d), block device (b), character device (c).
-user *name*	True if the named user owns the file.

NOTE Exercise caution when using the -exec option, as you can specify any valid command, including mv, rm, and so on. You are not prompted to confirm the action you are requesting unless you specify the -ok option.

Files can be found using other specifications besides the filename. For example, to locate all files accessed five or more days ago, use the following command:

```
# find . -atime +5
```

With the date options, mtime, ctime, and atime, the plus sign (+) preceding the number of days indicates that the file must have been accessed five or more days ago. If the minus (−) sign is used, the file must have been accessed within the specified number of days:

```
# find . -atime -5 .
```

To find which files have been accessed, you use the -atime option. If the number following -atime is preceded by a plus sign (+), then **find** returns entries in which the access day was more than the number of days given. If the number following is preceded by a minus sign (−), then **find** returns entries in which the access day was less than the number of days given: for example, to find files in the current directory that have not been accessed for ten days or more.

To find all the files on the system not owned by a valid user, meaning a user not found in the /etc/passwd file, use the following command:

```
# find / -nouser
/home/trainer
/home/trainer/.bash_logout
/home/trainer/.bashrc
/home/trainer/.cshrc
/home/trainer/.inputrc
/home/trainer/.login
/home/trainer/.logout
/home/trainer/.profile
/home/trainer/.tcshrc
/home/trainer/.seyon
/home/trainer/.seyon/phonelist
/home/trainer/.seyon/protocols
/home/trainer/.seyon/script.CIS
/home/trainer/.seyon/script.PCBoard
/home/trainer/.seyon/script.QWK
/home/trainer/.seyon/script.unix
/home/trainer/.seyon/startup
/home/trainer/fileone
/home/trainer/filethree
/home/trainer/filetwo
/home/trainer/.bash_history
#
```

A final note on **find**: It pays no attention to the existence of a leading period (.) in the filename, so it will list all files, even those normally hidden when using the **ls** command.

xargs

The **find** command locates files within the filesystem and can perform some basic functions on them. However, the **find** command cannot easily search the contents of a file for specific text. This function is actually performed by the **grep** command, which accepts a list of filenames as its input.

Searching for text in a file using **find** can only be done using the following command:

```
# find / - .rhosts -exec grep -i hostname {} \;
stored in the refrigerator overnight will be thrown out
#
```

This example finds all .rhosts on the system and prints the lines containing the string hostname. However, this has the effect of printing the text if found, but not the filename. Consequently, you have no idea which .rhosts file actually contains the text.

The **xargs** command is used to pipe the results of one command to the input of another, achieving the same effect as a pipe. **xargs** performs no processing on the input it receives. Using **xargs**, our command to search for text in the .rhosts files now is

```
# find / - .rhosts | xargs grep -i hostname
PRINT RESULTS
```

```
Now, the filename and the text are displayed, allowing you to take the
 appropriate action.
```

The desired file is indicated, so you can print it for the new employees.

It was presented that **xargs** works like a pipe. If that is the case, why does the command

```
# find / - .rhosts | xargs grep -i hostname
```

not produce the same results? This doesn't so much have to do with the **xargs** command, but has to do with how **grep** operates. The **grep** command searches for the specific pattern in the provided text. The previous **find** command prints a list of filenames. These are passed through the pipe to the **grep** command, which then looks for the pattern in the list of filenames, and the search text is not found.

When using **xargs**, the **grep** operation is started with the filename to process; hence, **grep** opens the file and searches for the specified text in the contents.

Configuring inetd and Related Services

The init daemon on Linux systems is responsible for bringing up the various system services required at specific run levels and maintaining system integrity. The init daemon starts and stops other system daemons including syslogd (the system logger), kswapd (the swapper), and inetd (the Internet Super Daemon).

NOTE As a general rule, any process with a last character of d is a daemon.

When started, inetd reviews the configuration file /etc/inetd.conf and determines what network services are to be operational and are managed by inetd. If you do not want to offer any network services, do not remove /etc/inetd.conf—simply comment out the entries in the file.

There is sufficient documentation within the /etc/inetd.conf file itself to make it easy to understand. Each entry is divided into several sections, all separated by spaces or tabs. Taking a sample line from /etc/.inetd.conf

```
#systat    stream    tcp    nowait    nobody    /usr/sbin/tcpd    /bin/ps    -auwwx
telnet     stream    tcp    nowait    root      /usr/lbin/tcpd    telnetd
```

you can see the seven components, as illustrated in Table 1-4.

Changing the contents of /etc/inetd.conf does not mean that the changes are immediately available. It is necessary for you to allow inetd to reread the configuration file.

Table 1-4   The Seven Components of the Default File

Component	Value in Example	Comment
Service	telnet	This is the name of the service.
Socket	stream	This is the socket type. Transmission Control Protocol (TCP) generally uses stream sockets, whereas User Datagram Protocol (UDP) uses dgram.
Protocol	tcp	This can be TCP or UDP.
Flags	nowait	This can be wait or nowait. As a general rule, stream-type sockets use nowait, and dgram-type sockets use wait.
User	root	This is the name of the user the daemon runs as. A nonroot daemon provides lower privilege.
Program	/usr/sbin/tcpd	This is the name of the actual executable to run. If you look through the file, you will see that it is almost always /usr/sbin/tcpd.
Arguments	telentd	These are the command and options to execute.

This can be done by rebooting the system, which is a very drastic method to get a configuration change performed. Rather, you can stop and restart networking, or use the preferred method of sending the inetd daemon a signal to reread the file, using either

```
kill -1 inetd
```

or

```
kill -SIGHUP inetd
```

When the signal is received by inetd, it rereads the configuration file and enables or disables the appropriate services.

The /etc/services File

The /etc/services file provides a mapping between a service name and the associated network port. The real value from /etc/services is realized in conjunction with the /etc/inetd.conf file. When /etc/inetd.conf says a service is to be started, inetd checks /etc/services to see what port it should be running on. /etc/services is an ASCII file that appears on every Linux or Unix system. Each line in the file has three components:

- Service (whatever name also appears in the /etc/inetd.conf file)
- Port (what port to use)
- Alias(es) (optional and constitute other names the service is known as)

The ports listed in the /etc/services file are the common port assignments for those services, which are typically referred to as well-known ports. You can change the port the service runs at for security or other reasons, and while the service still runs, the user must now know the port to connect to.

The easiest example to demonstrate this is the World Wide Web (WWW). The WWW service is commonly available on port 80, which makes the service available to anyone with the requirement to know the port number to connect to. If you build a Web site at the address **http://www.certificationcorner.com**, then anyone in the world can use the Web site because it is at port 80 by default.

If, on the other hand, you want to make your Web site available to only those people you tell the correct port number to, you can change the service from port 80 to port 2800. Now, anyone connecting to **www.certificationcorner.com** does not see the Web page, whereas connecting to it using **www.certificationcorner.com:2800** enables him or her to see the information.

NOTE It is very important you become familiar with the services and configuration of /etc/inetd.conf. Many methods to access your system remotely are configured in this file.

Samba

Samba is used much like a Windows server for interconnectivity between the Windows and Linux platforms. Microsoft uses Server Message Blocks (SMBs) to send data across the network. Linux uses the Network File System (NFS). These are incompatible with each other: hence, Samba. More information can be found at **http://samba.org**.

Apache

Apache is the world's most widely used Web server. Apache is run almost exclusively on the Unix/Linux platform. It is a highly configurable, complex piece of open-source software. A person can make a career out of running Apache. People who can run Apache and run it well are in high demand. More information can be found at **http://apache.org**.

Squid

Squid is a high-performance proxy-caching server for Web clients, supporting FTP, gopher, and HTTP data objects. Squid keeps Web page data cached in RAM. It also caches Domain Name System (DNS) lookups and supports nonblocking DNS lookups. Squid is compatible with the Secure Sockets Layer (SSL). In short, Squid keeps all of the data that you download off the Web so you don't have to go out to a Web site every time to retrieve information. Squid makes Web browsing faster.

BIND

BIND stands for the Berkeley Internet Name Domain and is an implementation of the DNS. BIND provides an openly redistributable reference implementation of the major components of the DNS. BIND enables you to implement your own DNS services for a large network.

ipchains

Linux **ipchains** is a rewrite of the Linux IPv4 firewalling code. **ipchains** came from the rewrite of the **ipfwadm** code, which came from BSD's **ipfw**. It is required to administer the IP packet filters in Linux kernel versions 2.1.102 and above. With the implementation of kernel 2.4, **ipchains** became the standard for Linux packet-filtering firewalls.

Red Hat Package Management

Despite the popularity of tarball distributions for Unix and Linux applications, more and more software is being deployed using packages. There are two principle methods of package management: the Red Hat package manager (RPM) and Debian's **dpkg**.

RPM, as developed by Red Hat, is an open-source system for package management and distribution. Although most commonly seen on Linux systems, RPM has also been compiled and implemented on other Unix platforms. Using RPM, the developer can build both source and binary distributions of their package, manage dependencies, and automate the installation process if desired.

Aside from managing the actual software components for distribution, RPM also provides a powerful database to track the software installed on your system, manage version numbers, provide a query method to determine what software is in fact installed, and provide a method of removing those packages when they are no longer needed.

Using the query options, a user or administrator can search the RPM databases for specific packages to see what files are in a package, or to determine what package a file is from. The RPM distributions are compressed images with a custom binary header, allowing for quick retrieval of information from the package describing its contents.

The package verification options in RPM determine if a package complete, and if not, determine what components are missing. Missing components can be easily reinstalled without affecting any modified files.

Installing and Removing Software Using RPM

The simplest command to install new software using RPM is

```
rpm -i rpm-name.rpm
```

For example, to install <INSERT-PACKAGE-NAME>, use the following command:

```
# rpm -i <INSERT PACKAGE NAME>
```

rpm reads the specified RPM file, extracts the files, and installs them into the correct locations as defined in the RPM header. Any pre- or postinstall scripts are also executed.

NOTE Most software components are installed in the system directories; therefore, the package must be installed by the root user.

Removing a package uses the -e, or erase, option:

```
rpm -e <INSERT PACKAGE NAME>
```

The previous install and remove commands expect the RPM file to be local to your system, either on the hard disk or a CD-ROM. However, one of the powerful features with rpm is its capability to download from the Internet and install the package. The RPM source file is not installed on your system. To install a package from an RPM on an FTP site, you must know the source path to the RPM file, and enter it on the command line:

```
rpm -i ftp://ftp.site.com/pub/package-name.rpm
```

To use this remote installation feature, you must be connected to a network and have access to the remote site; otherwise, the connection will fail. rpm establishes a connection to the remote site and installs the package. The RPM is not transferred to your system.

rpm has an extensive array of option, which we will only examine the major sets. To see a complete list of options, use rpm -help, or check the documentation using the **man** command or in the /usr/doc directory.

Verifying a Package Using RPM

From time to time, files get accidentally erased on a running system, and no one notices until a command does not work right. The verification options in rpm can identify the packages that are installed, and what, if any, components of those packages are missing.

Verifying all the packages installed on the system is accomplished with the following command:

```
# rpm -Va
```

When verifying the installed packages, rpm compares the installed package information from the rpm database with the files actually installed on the system. The verification process checks the file size, Message Digest 5 (MD5) checksum, permissions, file type, and the owner and group for each file. Every discrepancy identified is reported to the user.

MD5 provides a highly reliable checksum, which can be used to validate the integrity of the file. If the MD5 checksums differ between the file on the disk and the file in the RPM package, the disk version has likely been modified.

Getting Information: RPM Query

The RPM file format structure provides the capability to query or extract information from the RPM file. The query facility can identify what package a given file belongs to and to even print information about the package.

To query the RPM database to determine what package a given file belongs to, use the options -qf to the **rpm** command and provide the filename:

```
[root@mercury.technical RPMS]# rpm -qf /sbin/insmod
modutils-2.3.14-3
[root@mercury.technical RPMS]#
```

In this case, the /sbin/insmod program is part of the modutils package.

The query option also prints information about the rpm file itself. The extent of the information printed through this facility is dependent upon the level of detail provided by the developer or distributor.

To retrieve the package information from the module, use the -qpi options to rpm. For example, to see the information for the <PACKAGE>, execute the following command:

```
[root@mercury.technical RPMS]# rpm -qpi zip-2.3-8.i386.rpm
Name      : zip        Relocations: /usr
Version   : 2.3        Vendor: Red Hat, Inc.
Release   : 8          Build Date: Thu 24 Aug 2000 11:16:53 AM EDT
Install date: (not installed)        Build Host: porky.devel.redhat.com
Group     : Applications/Archiving   Source RPM: zip-2.3-8.src.rpm
Size      : 271467              License: distributable
Packager  : Red Hat, Inc. <http://bugzilla.redhat.com/bugzilla>
Summary   : A file compression and packaging utility compatible with PKZIP.
Description :
The zip program is a compression and file packaging utility. Zip is
analogous to a combination of the UNIX tar and compress commands and
is compatible with PKZIP (a compression and file packaging utility for
MS-DOS systems).

Install the zip package if you need to compress files using the zip program.
```

The -i option instructs rpm to list the information in the package, whereas the -l option lists the files in the package:

```
[root@mercury.technical RPMS]# rpm -qpl zip-2.3-8.i386.rpm
/usr/bin/zip
/usr/bin/zipcloak
/usr/bin/zipnote
```

```
/usr/bin/zipsplit
/usr/share/doc/zip-2.3
/usr/share/doc/zip-2.3/BUGS
/usr/share/doc/zip-2.3/CHANGES
/usr/share/doc/zip-2.3/MANUAL
/usr/share/doc/zip-2.3/README
/usr/share/doc/zip-2.3/TODO
/usr/share/doc/zip-2.3/WHATSNEW
/usr/share/doc/zip-2.3/WHERE
/usr/share/doc/zip-2.3/algorith.txt
/usr/share/man/man1/zip.1.gz
[root@mercury.technical RPMS]#
```

For many system administrators, they will not need to perform any additional work with rpm files. However, for some, or some who will develop a tool and want to distribute it, a review of package construction using RPM is required.

Building a Package Using RPM

Building a package with RPM can be as simple or as a complex as required for your unique situation. However, if you are working to build a package for a binary program, it is best if you can obtain the source code and build it yourself. This provides the maximum flexibility during the RPM construction process.

There are five major steps to building an RPM package:

1. Obtain the source code for the package if you don't already have it.

2. If required, construct a patch of the changes you made to the original source code.

3. Create an RPM spec file for the package.

4. Ensure that all files are in their proper locations.

5. Create the RPM package.

The RPM spec file provides the specification on the package, including the instructions on how to build it and the list of files. You cannot build an RPM without a spec file. The spec file is named using the following convention:

```
Package name - version number - release number . spec
```

Using this format enables multiple versions of the same package to exist without conflicts (which would be wumpus-1.3-A.spec for our Wumpus example). This provides multiple versions of the same package, and the spec file remains intact. The following is a sample spec file:

```
[root@mercury.technical wumpus]# more *.spec
summary: Hunt the wumpus
```

```
Name: wumpus
Version: 1.3
Release: A
Copyright: GPL
Group: Amusement/Games
Source: http://a-URL-pointing-to-the-source
Patch:
Buildroot: /var/tmp/%name-buildroot

%description
This is a true implementation of the classic mainframe computer game, wumpus.

%prep
%setup -q
%patch -p1 -b .buildroot

%build
make RPM_OPT_FLAGS="$RPM_OPT_FLAGS"

%install
rm -rf $RPM_BUILD_ROOT
mkdir -p $RPM_BUILD_ROOT/usr/local/games
mkdir -p $RPM_BUILD_ROOT/usr/man/man1

install -s -m 755 eject $RPM_BUILD_ROOT/usr/local/games/wumpus

%clean
rm -rf $RPM_BUILD_ROOT

%files
%defattr(-,root,root)
%doc README TODO COPYING ChangeLog

/usr/local/games/wumpus

%changelog
Sat Dec 2 15:24:30 EST 2000 Jon Howe root_cissp@hotmail.com
- created RPM from wumpus tarball
[root@mercury.technical wumpus]#
```

The space files have a consistent structure, as explained in Table 1-5.

Aside from the header, the %prep section, as listed in Table 1-6, contains the macros used in the compilation and setup of the package.

All commands in the %prep section including the %setup and %patch macros are executing the shell. The %build section doesn't really have any macros, but is used to provide the commands to actually build the software. This section should include the appropriate commands to extract the source and apply relevant patches if required. Any legal shell commands can be executed here as the shell processed the commands in the %build section.

Table 1-5 RPM Headers

Section	Description
Summary	A one-line description of the package.
Name	This is the name of the package you are creating. It must be the same as the file-name you are using for your package.
Version	This is the version of your RPM. It must match the version included in the file-name.
Release	The release number for packages of the same version.
Copyright	This describes the copyright type, namely GPL, BSD, MIT, public domain, distrib-utable, or commercial.
Group	This identifies the group the package belongs to.
Source	This is the home location of the original source file. This is used if you want the source again or want to check for a newer version.
Patch	The location of the patch file.
Buildroot	This is the root directory for building and installing the new package. This can be used to test the new package by installing it on your system.
%description	This is a multilane field used to give a comprehensive description of the package.

Table 1-6 %prep Macros

Macro Name	Description
%setup	Defines the process to unpack the source and enter the directory tree. Using the -q option sets the name of the directory tree to the value set by %name.
%patch	This macro applies the patches to the source.

The next step in the process is installation. The %install section contains the commands required to install the software, which are executed by the shell. If a makefile is used to build the software, a make install section can be added to the makefile using a patch, or the appropriate commands can be included by hand.

The final section is the %clean macro. This is used in the spec file to provide a clean source tree for the build. It is important to verify the directory prior to executing commands, as the imprudent package maintainer could remove his or her entire Linux distribution by executing the wrong commands as root in the / directory.

The %changelog section identifies the changes for each version and release of the package. Each change starts with an asterisk (*) and includes the date and time and the maintainer's e-mail address. The remainder of the text area is free form, but should be written to provide some form of readability.

Once the spec file has been defined, the package is ready to build.

The RPM Build Tree

The build tree is typically defined in /etc/rpmrc or /usr/slib/rpm/rpmrc and can be modified by the package maintainer to suit his or her particular requirements. Most people use the /usr/src directory to construct and build their packages. If necessary, you may need to create some directories for your package construction:

- **BUILD**   Where the package is built
- **SOURCE**   The location of the source files
- **SPECS**   The location of the spec files
- **RPMS**   The location of the assembled binary RPM files
- **SRPMS**   The location of the source RPM files

With the directory tree assembled, compile the source code and review it for the files it creates and installs, their locations, and what additional commands were necessary to compile them, such as create a patch or enter additional commands. Using the spec file, you are now ready to build the package with the following command:

```
# rpm -ba filename.spec
```

rpm then creates the source and binary RPM files using the definitions in the spec file. The best method of testing the newly created RPM is to install it on a different system. Because you have just installed it on your own system, it will be difficult to test that the build and resulting RPM files were in fact properly constructed. If you missed a file in your build process, you will not know by testing it on your system.

As the package maintainer, you will be using the following command:

```
# rpm -ba package-name
```

but the people installing your package will be executing

```
# rpm -i package name
```

Consequently, it is very important to include all the steps required to construct the package. In the event you want to distribute your package to other users, you can then upload it to an Internet site such as **ftp.redhat.com**.

The Graphical Side of Red Hat Package Management

Red Hat has a GUI for the front end of its package manager. It is accessible by going to the K Development Environment (KDE) menu systems and choosing Package Manager. Figure 1-1 shows the default view of Package Manager. The figure shows the GUI and all of the packages available to it.

Packages are installed and uninstalled by highlighting the package name and pressing one of the buttons marked install marked/uninstall.

Figure 1-2 shows the categories of packages that can be installed.

The Red Hat package manager is not intuitive enough for the beginner and is still in development. The command line is still the strongest point from which to install new

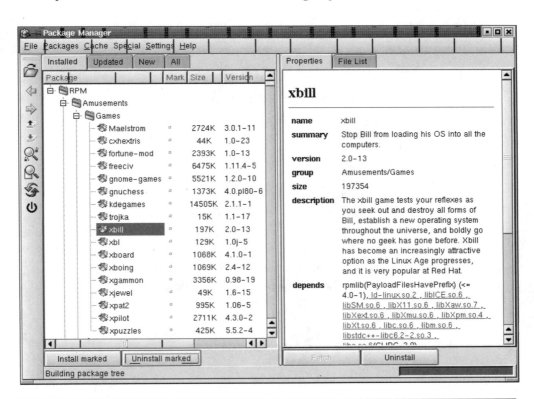

Figure I-I   The Package Manager default view

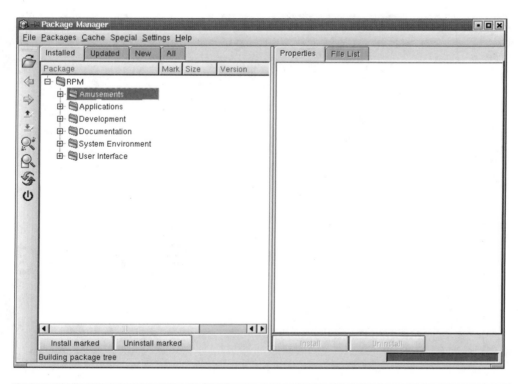

Figure I-2 The various packet categories available

packages. The package manager is an excellent point of information for querying packages. Figure 1-3 shows properties of the XFree86 package. Note the description and dependencies.

Using the Debian Package Management System

The Debian package management system is very different from that used by Red Hat and other Linux distributions. The Debian system uses a facility called **dpkg**. The **dpkg** man page is vague enough that it states, "This man page should not be used by package maintainers wishing to understand how **dpkg** will install their packages." Other references for information on **dpkg** and how to use it to construct packages are provided for the reader.

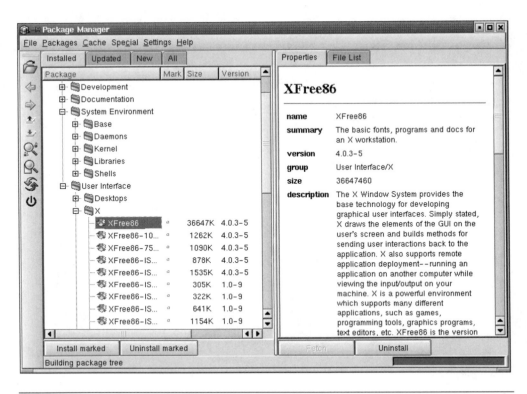

Figure 1-3 The XFree86 package properties

The primary method for package management is through **dselect**, which in turn uses **dpkg** to execute the actual commands. **dselect** provides a user-friendly interface, whereas **dpkg** is an entirely command-line-based tool. **dpkg** actions consist of one action and zero or more options to define what **dpkg** is to do and how to do it.

dpkg maintains information about the installed packages, much like RPM does. However, the information maintained consists of the package state, selection states, and flags, each modified using **dselect**.

dselect and **dpkg** states indicate if the package is installed or not, as outlined in Table 1-7.

Although **dselect** is not required to install package, many people use it over the command-line interface of **dpkg**. **dpkg** uses the command

```
# dpkg -i | --install package_file...
```

Table 1-7   Debian Package States

Package State	Description
Installed	The package is fully installed and configured.
Half-installed	The installation has been started, but not completed.
Not-installed	The package is not installed.
Unpacked	The package has been unpacked, but not yet installed.
Half-configured	The package is unpacked, but configuration and installation has not been completed.
Config-files	The configuration files are the only component from the package found on the system.

to install the software associated with the named package. For example, installing the wu-ftp package from the distribution is done using the following command:

```
# dpkg wu-ftpd_2.6.0-5.1.deb
```

The naming convention for Debian packages is similar to the RPM format, using the following syntax:

```
package name-package version-deb version.deb
```

dpkg also enables multiple versions of the package to exist on the system. Installation of any package consists of the same steps:

1. Extract the files from the package.

2. If you are replacing an existing package, run the prerm script from the old package.

3. If the new package provides one, run the preinst script.

It is important to run the prerm script prior to removing the old package version and the preinst script if provided by the new package. Table 1-8 shows several **dpkg** command examples.

The Debian packages are prioritized to determine the need for the package in the operating system. The priorities are

- **Required**   The package must be installed for the system to operate properly.

- **Important**   The package is typically found on all Unix systems.

Table 1-8   Example **dpkg** Commands

Command Example	Function
dpkg -i package.deb	Installs the package named package.deb
dpkg -I package.deb	Shows information about the package named package.deb (rpm -qpi)
dpkg -c package.deb	Lists the files in package.deb (rpm -qpl)
dpkg -l	Shows all installed packages
dpkg -r package-name	Removes the named package from the system (the name used is the name shown in the output of by **dpkg -l**)

- **Standard**   The package is part of the text-based Debian system.

- **Optional**   Additional components are not required for the operation of the system. This includes utilities such as the X Window System.

- **Extra**   The package is for a small group of people and is interest-specific or specialized in nature. They are not required for system operation.

Installing and Removing Packages Using Debian

In the following example, we want to install the package inn2_2.2.2.2000.01.31-4.deb:

```
debian:/cdrom/dists/potato/main/binary-i386/news# dpkg -i inn2_2.2.2.2*.deb
Selecting previously deselected package inn2.
(Reading database ... 31440 files and directories currently installed.)
Unpacking inn2 (from inn2_2.2.2.2000.01.31-4.deb) ...
dpkg: dependency problems prevent configuration of inn2:
 inn2 depends on inn2-inews; however:
 Package inn2-inews is not installed.
dpkg: error processing inn2 (--install):
 dependency problems - leaving unconfigured
Errors were encountered while processing:
 inn2
debian:/cdrom/dists/potato/main/binary-i386/news#
```

This output reports that a dependency error was encountered while executing the **dpkg** command. This means that the packages that this one depends upon must be installed before inn2 can be installed:

```
debian:/cdrom/dists/potato/main/binary-i386/news# dpkg -i inn2-inews*
Selecting previously deselected package inn2-inews.
(Reading database ... 31670 files and directories currently installed.)
```

```
Unpacking inn2-inews (from inn2-inews_2.2.2.2000.01.31-4.deb) ...
Setting up inn2-inews (2.2.2.2000.01.31-4) ...

debian:/cdrom/dists/potato/main/binary-i386/news#
```

With the dependent package installed, we can execute the same command with the desired package again:

```
debian:/cdrom/dists/potato/main/binary-i386/news# dpkg -i inn2_2.2.2.2*.deb

(Reading database ... 31685 files and directories currently installed.)
Preparing to replace inn2 2.2.2.2000.01.31-4
(using inn2_2.2.2.2000.01.31-4.deb)
...
Unpacking replacement inn2 ...
Setting up inn2 (2.2.2.2000.01.31-4) ...
installing initial content for /var/lib/news/active
installing initial content for /var/lib/news/newsgroups
building history database in /var/lib/news...
mv: history.n.hash: No such file or directory
mv: history.n.index: No such file or directory
chown: history*: No such file or directory
chmod: history*: No such file or directory
done
Starting innd.
Scheduled start of /usr/lib/news/bin/innwatch.

debian:/cdrom/dists/potato/main/binary-i386/news#
```

Removing packages is also performed with the **dpkg** command using the -r option. However, we frequently do not know the exact name of the package we want to remove, and so we must use the **dpkg -l** command to determine the package name:

```
debian:/cdrom/dists/potato/main/binary-i386/news# dpkg -l | more
Desired=Unknown/Install/Remove/Purge/Hold
| Status=Not/Installed/Config-files/Unpacked/Failed-config/Half-installed
|/ Err?=(none)/Hold/Reinst-required/X=both-problems (Status,Err:
uppercase=bad)
||/ Name          Version        Description
+++-==============-===============-
=============================================
ii  adduser      3.11.1     Add users and groups to the system.
ii  ae           962-26     Anthony's Editor -- a tiny full-screen editor
ii  anacron      2.1-5.1    a cron-like program that doesn't go by time
ii  apmd         3.0final-1 Utilities for Advanced Power Management (APM)
ii  apt          0.3.19     Advanced front-end for dpkg
ii  at           3.1.8-10   Delayed job execution and batch processing
--More--
```

However, the large number of packages makes it difficult to find the ones you are looking for. You can search for the desired packages by sending the output of **dkpg -l** into **grep**:

```
debian:/cdrom/dists/potato/main/binary-i386/news# dpkg -l | grep inn
ii inn2      2.2.2.2000.01. News transport system 'InterNetNews' by the
ii inn2-inews  2.2.2.2000.01. NNTP client news injector, from InterNetNews
debian:/cdrom/dists/potato/main/binary-i386/news#
```

Once you've located the desired packages, use the **dpkg -r** command to remove them:

```
debian:/cdrom/dists/potato/main/binary-i386/news# dpkg -r inn2
(Reading database ... 31685 files and directories currently
installed.)
Removing inn2 ...
Stopping news server: innd
dpkg - warning: while removing inn2, directory '/var/log/news'
not empty so not
removed.
dpkg - warning: while removing inn2, directory '/var/lib/news'
not empty so not
removed.
dpkg - warning: while removing inn2, directory '/var/run/news'
not empty so not
removed.
dpkg - warning: while removing inn2, directory
'/usr/lib/news/bin/rnews.libexec'
 not empty so not removed.
dpkg - warning: while removing inn2, directory
'/usr/lib/news/bin/filter' not empty so not removed.
dpkg - warning: while removing inn2, directory
'/usr/lib/news/bin/control' not empty so not removed.
dpkg - warning: while removing inn2, directory '/usr/lib/news/bin'
not empty so
not removed.
dpkg - warning: while removing inn2, directory '/usr/lib/news' not
empty so not
removed.
debian:/cdrom/dists/potato/main/binary-i386/news#
```

In the output of **dpkg -r**, directories that aren't empty aren't removed. These directories typically contain files that are created by the application and that hold important data that should not be arbitrarily erased. If the data isn't required, you'll need to remove the directories manually.

Querying Packages Using Debian

Aside from querying for the installed packages, **dpkg** is also used to list the files in a specific package. This is accomplished with the **dpkg -c** command, as illustrated in the following example:

```
debian:/cdrom/dists/potato/main/binary-i386/news# dpkg -c inn2_2* | more
drwxr-xr-x root/root        0 2000-05-27 01:56:08 ./
drwxr-xr-x root/root        0 2000-05-27 01:56:10 ./etc/
drwxr-sr-x news/news        0 2000-05-27 01:56:08 ./etc/news/
-rw-r--r-- news/news     5018 2000-05-27 01:56:02 ./etc/news/newsfeeds
-rw-r----- news/news     5145 2000-05-27 01:56:02 ./etc/news/incoming.conf
-rw-r----- news/news     1017 2000-05-27 01:56:02 ./etc/news/nnrp.access
-rw-r----- news/news      516 2000-05-27 01:56:02 ./etc/news/nnrpd.track
--More-
```

As seen in this example, the **dpkg -c** command is used to list the files in the package, not the files installed on the system as part of the package. The **dpkg** command has an additional argument to query information about the package itself. The **dpkg -I** command prints information about the package including the section of the Debian system, the version number, and any package dependencies that exist. It also identifies the package maintainer and prints a description of what the package is for.

```
debian:/cdrom/dists/potato/main/binary-i386/sound# dpkg -I esound_0*.deb
 new debian package, version 2.0.
 size 48692 bytes: control archive= 1053 bytes.
    422 bytes,  11 lines    control
    701 bytes,  13 lines    md5sums
    249 bytes,   8 lines  * postinst        #!/bin/sh
    190 bytes,   6 lines  * prerm          #!/bin/sh
 Package: esound
 Version: 0.2.17-7
 Section: sound
 Priority: optional
 Architecture: i386
 Depends: libaudiofile0, libc6 (>= 2.1.2), libesd0 (>= 0.2.16) |
libesd-alsa0 (>= 0.2.16), esound-common
 Installed-Size: 132
 Maintainer: Brian M. Almeida <bma@debian.org>
 Description: Enlightened Sound Daemon - Support binaries
 This program is designed to mix together several digitized
 audio streams for playback by a single device.
debian:/cdrom/dists/potato/main/binary-i386/sound#
```

As a command-line utility, **dpkg** is accepted as more difficult to use than rpm. Consequently, **dselect** was developed to provide a front-end interface. The **dselect** menu commands are

- **Access**   Selects the method to obtain and installs the select packages
- **Update**   Using the package database, creates a list of updates applicable to your system
- **Select**   Selects the package
- **Install**   Processes and installs all selected packages

Through the access option, several access methods are available to the administrator. These include FTP, HTTP, floppy diskette, CD-ROM, and NFS. The access method depends upon where the packages to install are located.

The update option checks the currently installed packages against a list of new packages when used with an access method of HTTP and FTP. A new package list is retrieved and a list of applicable updates are compiled. The administrator can then select the desired packages for installation.

The administrator selects the packages to process using the select option; however, no action is taken using this function itself. Pressing ENTER selects the desired package. **dselect** then performs a dependency check, determining if there are other packages that must be installed. The **dpkg** command, if used directly, reports the dependency problem, but performs no other actions.

Once the packages are installed, selecting the install option causes **dselect** to execute the appropriate commands to load and configure the selected packages. Once the packages are installed, selecting Quit exits **dselect** and returns the administrator to the command line.

Understanding the Linux Kernel

The system supervisor in Unix and Linux systems is known as the kernel. As the supervisor, it is responsible for providing all users with access to system services and executing the commands submitted by users. The kernel allocates CPU time and handles memory management, disk access, and the hardware installed in the system. The user is typically not aware of the kernel or the services it provides as they interact with the command interpreter or a specific application. However, the system administrator is very aware of the kernel in performing his or her responsibilities.

Without realizing it, users interact with the kernel when they execute commands such as **ps**. The kernel loads the command, accesses the required resources on the user's behalf, and then prints the data for the user to see. Unlike users, however, system administrators interact with the kernel to install new hardware, such as printers, application software, or new operating system components or features.

All Linux kernel version numbers contain three numbers separated by periods. The first number is the kernel version. The most recent release is the third kernel, version 2. Some of you may be running a version 1 kernel.

The second number is the kernel major number. Major numbers, which are even numbers, are said to be stable. That is, these kernels should not have any crippling bugs, as they have been heavily tested. Although some contain small bugs, they can usually be upgraded for hardware compatibility or to armor the kernel against system crackers. The kernels with odd major numbers are developmental kernels. These have not been tested as often and will not break. Occasionally, one works well enough that users needing the latest and greatest support before the next stable release will adopt it. This is the exception rather than the rule, and it requires substantial changes to a system.

The last number is the minor number and is increased by one for each release. If you see kernel version 2.0.8, you know it is a kernel 2.0, stable kernel, and it is the ninth release because you begin counting with zero.

Using Local Documentation

Any user or administrator's ability to successfully use a system can be impacted by the level of available online documentation. There are several documentation types available including man pages, info pages, and the help documentation built into the command itself.

The Man Pages

The man, or manual pages, are online documentation, which is often what you find in the printed manuals shipped with your Unix system. The **man** command displays the online documentation for the specified command. However, Unix was historically not good at having man pages for all of the commands. This has improved dramatically on Linux.

The **man** command works by displaying the documentation on the user's terminal using a program like more, so the user can see the information in manageable pieces.

Table 1-9 Subdirectories for **man** Files

Subdirectory	Descriptions Contained Within
man1	Utilities typically executed by all users
man2	System calls
man3	C language library functions
man4	Device descriptions
man5	Configuration files
man6	Games
man7	Linux system files
man8	Root user/system administration utilities

The actual command that displays the text is controlled by the environment variable PAGER or MANPAGER. This is typically set to either more or less.

Two other variables affect the operation of the **man** command: namely MANPATH to define the directories to search for man pages and MANSECT to define the sections in the man pages.

The man pages themselves are found under the directory /usr/man, although additional utilities may install their man pages in other locations, such as /usr/local/man. Table 1-9 lists the subdirectories in /usr/man and what command groups are found there.

When entering a command name for **man** to locate, the directories in /usr/man are searched until the first match is found. For example, when entering a command such as

```
man nice
```

the /usr/man directories are searched until the first match for date is found. The man page is displayed using the program specified by the PAGER variable. The output of **man** is shown in the following example, along with line numbers for discussion purposes:

```
[root@mercury.technical root]#man nice

1    NICE(1)                                                      NICE(1)
2
3
4    NAME
5         nice - run a program with modified scheduling priority
6
7    SYNOPSIS
```

```
 8      nice  [-n  adjustment]  [-adjustment]  [--adjustment=adjust_
 9      ment] [--help] [--version] [command [arg...]]
10
11 DESCRIPTION
12      This documentation is no longer being maintained and may
13      be inaccurate or incomplete. The Texinfo documentation is
14      now the authoritative source.
15
16      This manual page documents the GNU version of nice. Note
17      that most shells have a built-in command by the same name
18      and with similar functionality.
19
20      If no arguments are given, nice prints the current
21      scheduling priority, which it inherited. Otherwise, nice
22      runs the given command with its scheduling priority
23      adjusted. If no adjustment is given, the priority of the
24      command is incremented by 10. The superuser can specify a
25      negative adjustment. The priority can be adjusted by nice
26      over the range of -20 (the highest priority) to 19 (the
27      lowest).
28
29      OPTIONS
30        -n adjustment, -adjustment, --adjustment=adjustment
31             Add adjustment instead of 10 to the command's pri_
32             ority.
33
34        --help Print a usage message on standard output and exit
35             successfully.
36
37          --version
38             Print version information on standard output then
39             exit successfully.
40
41
...
66 FSF                    GNU Shell Utilities                    1
```

The output of the man pages follows a defined format, consisting of the command name and a set of common sections used for readability. In the command name in Line 1, the (1) indicates this is from section 1 of the manual and is a common command available to all users. There may be other entries in the manual for the **nice** command, but they are not displayed due to the man's configuration to display only the first match.

There may be more than one entry in the man pages for time, which can be found using the **whatis** command:

```
# whatis nice
nice (1)      - run a program with modified scheduling priority
nice (2)      - change process priority
(END)     (press q}
#
```

The **whatis** command lists all entries in the man pages with the specified name. The **whatis** command is similar to the **locate** command in that it uses a database to look for entries, which is created with /usr/sbin/makewhatis.

Because **man** prints the first match, reading man pages from other sections of the manual is done by including the section number you want the man page from:

```
man 2 nice
```

This format instructs **man** to show the man page from section 2 of the manual, which is found in /usr/man/man2. Similarly, use 3 for man3, 4 for man4, and so on.

The man pages follow a defined format for consistency and ease of use. The common sections are

- **Name**   The name of the command
- **Synopsis**   A short description of what the command does (matches the text returned by **whatis**)
- **Description**   A more detailed description of what the command does
- **Options**   The available options and what they are used for

The man page may include additional sections depending upon the complexity of the command and other features. Additional sections commonly seen are

- **See also**   References to other commands or documentation
- **Diagnostics**   Error messages and return code
- **Bugs**   Known problems or future enhancements
- **History**   Where the command is derived from

The man pages are stored in a compressed format to conserve disk space. However, each time a new man page is accessed, an uncompressed version of the page is written to the var/catman directory. This enables **man** to more quickly display the command the next time you request the man page. Like /usr/man, /var/catman contains subdirectories for each manual section.

The **man** command also has a man page, accessed using **man man**, identifying the options available, including

-a   Displays all matches in the man pages for the command.

-C   Uses alternate display configuration parameters.

-K   Searches all man pages for specified text and shows the title page of each found. This is the extent of the search capabilities.

-k   Displays all man pages with the same name, as found in the whatis database.

-M   Specifies the search path, as opposed to /usr/man.

-P   Specifies the pager program to display the man page.

Using --help

Many commands in Linux also include help messages accessed using the --help option on their command line. Whether the command supports this feature or not is up to the original programmers. Generally, this provides only a brief description of the syntax for the command and the options. For example,

```
# man --help
man, version 1.5h

Usage: man [-adfhtwW] [section] [-M path] [-P pager] [-S list]
       [-m system] [-p string] name ...

  a : find all matching entries
  c : do not use cat file
  d : print gobs of debugging information
  D : as for -d, but also diplay the pages
  f : same as whatis(1)
  h : print thid gelp message
  k : same as apropos(1)
  K : search for a string in all pages
  t : use troff to format pages for printing
  w : print pages of man pages that would be displayed
      (if no name given: print directories that would be searched)
  W : as for -w, but display filenames only

  C file    : use 'file' as configuration file
  M path    : set search path for manual pages
  P pager   : use program 'pager'to display pages
  S list    : colon seperated section list
  m system  : search for alternate systems man pages
  P string  : string tells which preprocessors to run
                e - [n]eqn(1)    p - pic(1)    t - tbl(1)
                g - grap(1)      r - refer(1) v - vgrind(1)
```

This is a listing of the information on the options available with the man page. Most of the newer commands, including GNU, do include the --help option, but it is not standard. It will not be found on the older commands and is not available with application software. When looking for information on a command, try all avenues.

Getting info

An additional help facility called **info** is available for documentation on the GNU utilities. Accessing the info database is done using the following command:

```
info
```

or

```
info {utility name}
```

Calling **info** with no utility name shows a main menu screen similar to the following:

```
File: dir,   Node: Top

Info main menu
==============

   A few useful info commands are:
     h    Enter a short tutorial on info.
     d    Return to this menu.
     ?    List all info commands.
     q    Quit info.

Not all of the topics shown below may be available on your system.

   * Menu:


Miscellaneous:
==============

   * As: (as).                The GNU assembler.
   * Bash:(bash).             The GNU Bash Features Guide.
   * Bfd: (bfd).              The Binary File Descriptor library.
   -----Info: (dir)Top, 205 lines --Top-------------------------
```

The **info** command opens a file (in this case, dir) and displays information in the file. When requesting information on a specific topic, **info** checks its database to determine which file it is in and opens the file to the correct place. The database and the related info files are found in /usr/info.

The dir file lists all utilities, programming languages, miscellaneous, and so on, and lists the text to type to display the item. For example, if you want **info** on the **time** command, type

```
# info time
```

Because **info** is a full-screen display program, you can enter commands without exiting. For example, typing *m* displays a menu prompt at which point you can enter the name of the command you want to see information on (in this case, **time**). When start-ing **info**, the first screen displays the commonly used keys for navigating in the tools and their functions.

Movement through the display is done using the arrow keys, whereas pressing ENTER selects the item where your cursor is. As the files use a hypertext format, making one selection can lead you to another menu.

To illustrate, start the utility without any parameters:

```
# info
```

Using the down arrow to scroll through the list to

```
* gzip:(gzip).                 The GNU compression utility.
```

and pressing ENTER invokes the menu of options specific to it:

```
File: gzip.info,  Node: Top,  Up: (dir)

This file documents the `gzip' command to compress files.

* Menu

* Copying::          How you can copy and share 'gzip'.
* Overview::          Preliminary information.
* Sample::          Sample output from 'gzip'.
* Invoking gzip::     How to run 'gzip'.
* Advanced usage::    Concatenated files.
* Environment::     The 'GZIP' environment variable
* Tapes::           Using 'gzip' on taps.
* Problems::          Reporting bugs.
* Concept Index::     Index of concepts.
```

With a list of items displayed, make your selection and **info** will display the requested data. Pressing Q at any time quits the **info** application; the SPACEBAR scrolls down and DELETE scrolls up in the display.

Other Local Documentation

There is other online documentation in other locations on the system, including **whereis** and **apropos**. The **whereis** utility finds all locations of a file including the com-mand location and documentation. For example,

```
# whereis time
time: /usr/bin/time /usr/man/man1/time.1.gz
.../usr/man/man2/time.2.gz
#
```

The search that **whereis** performs is limited to specific directories, so catman entries are not identified. In our previous example, the first entry is the command, and the remaining entries are the man entries. If there is no documentation, but other files such as source code or library files exist, these are also listed.

Similar to **whatis**, **apropos** searches the whatis database and identifies all entries that match the specified name. All entries, both exact and approximate accesses, are found using **apropos**, whereas **whatis** returns only an exact match. For example, searches for "time" produces the following:

```
# whereis time
Time::Local       {3pm} - efficiently compute time from local and GMT time
Time::gmtime      {3pm} - by-name interface to perl's built-in
  gmtime()function
Time::localtime   {3pm} - by-name interface to perl's built-in localtime()
  function
Time:tm           {3pm} - internal object used by Time:gmtime and
  time::localtime
time              (1) - time a simple command or give resource usage
time              (2) - get time in seconds
time              (n) - Time the execution of a script
#
```

An additional online resource is /usr/doc. This location includes additional documentation on specific packages or elements of the software included in the Linux distribution, as well as Linux itself. The major subdirectories under /usr/doc are

- **FAQ** This directory contains documents of frequently asked questions regarding Linux, security, and other topics.

- **HOWTO** This is sometimes a link to /pub/Linux/docs/HOWTO; it stores detailed information on how to configure or use a Linux component or system.

- **{application name}** These directories contain information on the configuration and use of specific applications installed in your system. The directory name typically consists of the application name and version number.

Budget, Staffing, and Resources

When determining a solution for a customer, you have to look at these items. Some businesses have only one person to perform IT work and he or she may not even be dedicated to IT concerns. If you are about to suggest a major overhaul of all of the systems and software because you feel that they are behind the times, IT may not have the time and money to perform this. Simply suggesting a minor upgrade of a few select programs at a time is the way to go. It is different for a large corporation with the resources to perform independent testing and verification of new software.

Finding Remote Resources

Aside from the large amount of documentation available locally on the Linux system, there is a vast amount of resources available on the Internet. Each Linux implementation has its own Web site and online documentation. Aside from the vendors, other resources include newsgroups and implementation-independent Web sites.

Web sites provide relatively static information accessed on an as-needed basis by the Internet user community. Newsgroups provide an online discussion forum where any user can pose a question to the newsgroup and all people who are interested can provide a response.

Table 1-10 provides a listing of some common Web sites providing Linux or utility-specific information. Because the Internet is a constantly evolving entity, some sites listed in Table 1-10 may no longer be available, while other new ones may have emerged. When you are looking for information on the Internet, remember to consider the use of a good search engine to aid you in your search.

Table 1-10   Linux Information Sites

Category	Site	Description
Documentation	**www.kde.org**	The organization behind the KDE interface
Documentation	**www.linuxdoc.org**	Linux Documentation Project (LDP)— invaluable for finding HOWTO information
Documentation	**www.linuxlookup.com**	LinuxLookup—HOWTOs and reviews
Documentation	**www.linuxnewbie.com**	Generic information for new users
Exam	**www.lpi.org**	Linux Professional Institute
Exam	**www.lpi.org/faq.html**	Frequently asked questions about the LPI exams
Exam	**www.lpi.org/p-glossary.html**	All the terms needed for the LPI exam
News	**webwatcher.org**	Linux Webwatcher
News	**www.embedded.com**	Linux News
News	**www.linux.com**	Linux.com
News	**www.linux.org**	Linux Online
News	**www.linuxgazette.com**	Linux Gazette

(continued)

Table 1-10   Linux Information Sites *(continued)*

Category	Site	Description
News	**www.linuxjournal.com**	Linux Journal
News	**www.linuxplanet.com**	LinuxPlanet
News	**www.linuxtoday.com**	LinuxToday
News	**www.lwn.net**	Linux Weekly News
News	**www.maximumLinux.com**	Maximum Linux Magazine
News	**www.slashdot.org**	Slashdot
News	**www.ugu.com**	Unix Guru's Universe
Software	**www.Linuxtapecert.org**	Enhanced Software Technologies
Software	**www.freshmeat.com**	Freshmeat
Software	**www.linuxapps.com**	LinuxApps
Software	**www.linuxmall.com**	Linux Mall
Standards	**www.fsf.org**	Free Software Foundation
Standards	**www.li.org**	Linux International
Standards	**www.usenix.org**	Usenix
Vendor	**linux.corel.com**	Corel
Vendor	**www.calderasystems.com**	Caldera OpenLinux
Vendor	**www.debian.org**	Debian
Vendor	**www.linuxcare.com**	LinuxCare
Vendor	**www.linux-mandrake.com**	Mandrake
Vendor	**www.redhat.com**	Red Hat
Vendor	**www.slackware.com**	Slackware
Vendor	**www.suse.com**	SuSE
Vendor	**www.turbolinux.com**	TurboLinux

Even if the site is for an implementation of Linux you are not using, you should consider reviewing it for the information you desire. Many of the Linux sites post FAQ listings and information that is not specific to their implementation, but for the operating system in general.

As the number and location of Web sites changes on a frequent basis, the same is true for newsgroups. The names, for the most part, explain the major topic or discussion area for the newsgroup, which is intended to assist you in posting your question to the correct group:

- comp.os.linux.advocacy
- comp.os.linux.announce.html
- comp.os.linux.answers
- comp.os.linux.development.apps
- comp.os.linux.development.system
- comp.os.linux.hardware
- comp.os.linux.misc
- comp.os.linux.networking
- comp.os.linux.setup
- comp.os.linux.x

Many newsgroup FAQs recommend you check the newsgroup archives prior to submitting a new question. Both AltaVista and Deja.com archive the news groups for later review. Alternatively, you can also subscribe to a wide variety of mailing lists on Linux topics. To subscribe to one of the more popular mailing lists, send a message to **majordomo@vger.rutgers.edu** with the topic "subscribe" and the name of the mailing list. The names are self-explanatory:

- linux-admin
- linux-alpha
- linux-apps
- linux-c-programming
- linux-config
- linux-doc
- linux-kernel
- linux-laptop
- linux-newbie
- linux-sound
- linux-standards

Chapter Summary

This is the most basic of chapters, although many, many new ideas and applications are covered. First, we looked at the GNU/Linux licensing scheme and compared it internally between Linux distributions and externally with closed-source software.

We covered hardware, what is valid for a Linux installation, and how some of the hardware works with the operating system. We looked at filesystems and how Linux allocates and uses space on a hard disk after installation. Linux kernel and services were covered as to how they interact and that the main component of Linux is the kernel, although we could never use the kernel if it weren't for other applications like the shell.

We compared distributions and talked about what it takes for making recommendations for a customer. Last but not least, we looked at resources to find information on the Net and some books to peruse. Getting information on the Web is the way to go. Linux development is happening on the Web all the time, so the information is being shared constantly and the best thing about it is that you can download it for free.

In Chapter 2 we go over the actual installation of Linux and ways to implement it.

Questions

1. The command to set the system clock is:
   a. date
   b. date 07311432
   c. time 07311432
   d. time

2. The command **setserial -g /dev/ttyS1**:
   a. Configures the serial port on COM2
   b. Prints the serial port configuration for COM3
   c. Configures the serial port on COM3
   d. Prints the serial port configuration on COM1

3. How do you tell the difference between Red Hat package management and Debian package management packages?
   a. Upon execution of the package, it will tell you.
   b. The .deb and .rpm extensions.
   c. By invoking the -p option to query the package.
   d. By querying the package and looking at the author's comments.

4. What command checks all filesystems?
   a. fsck
   b. fsck -y
   c. fsck -A
   d. fsck -a

5. Where does **fsck** attempt to restore files when the corresponding directory entry has been corrupted?
   a. /tmp
   b. lost+found
   c. /dev
   d. /var/log

6. Which of the following commands is not used to find a file on the disk?
   a. find
   b. locate
   c. whatis
   d. which

7. What command is used to create the filesystem on a partition?
   a. mount
   b. mkfs
   c. format
   d. fdisk

8. What **find** command is used to list all files on the root filesystem that have not been accessed in the last 15 days?
   a. find / -atime +15
   b. find / -atime −15
   c. find / -mtime +15
   d. find / -mtime −15

9. What environment established the directories to search for man pages?
   a. PAGER
   b. PATH
   c. MANSECT
   d. MANPATH

10. Which device represents the first IDE hard disk on the second IDE controller?
    a. /dev/hda
    b. /dev/hdd
    c. /dev/hdb
    d. /dev/hdc

Answers

1. **B.** The command to set the system clock is date 07311432.

2. **D.** The command **setserial -g /dev/ttyS1** prints the serial port configuration on COM1.

3. **B.** The extension denotes the package type.

4. **A.** The **fsck** command checks all filesystems.

5. **B.** The **fsck** command attempts to restore files in lost+found when the corresponding directory entry gets corrupted.

6. **C.** The **whatis** command is the only command listed that is not used to find a file on the disk.

7. **B.** The **mkfs** command is used to create the filesystem on a partition.

8. **A.** The **find / -atime +15** command is used to list all files on the root filesystem that have not been accessed in the last 15 days.

9. **D.** MANPATH is the environment variable that establishes the directories that search for man pages.

10. **D.** /dev/hdc is the device that represents the first IDE hard disk on the second IDE controller.

Installation

In this chapter, covers the following competencies required to master the Linux+ certification exam:

- Choosing the method installation method based on the environment
- Understanding the different types of Linux installation for varied situations
- Choosing correct installation parameters
- Selecting the best Linux package based on machine function
- Choosing partition options
- Using fdisk for drive partitioning
- Implementing filesystems
- Choosing networking protocols and configuration strategies
- Choosing security settings
- Creating users and passwords
- The x86server
- Video card support
- Monitor information and settings
- Selecting an appropriate desktop environment
- Kernel compilation
- Installing the boot loader
- Installing and uninstalling applications and programs
- Making sense of logfiles
- Testing installed applications

Installation

In the previous chapter, we dealt with understanding Linux and the way it is should be installed. In this chapter, we will cover installing Linux as laid out in Domain 2.0 by CompTIA for the Linux+ examination.

When the install script is running, it will cover all aspects of configuring your computer to run as a system. All of the hardware in your computer will be probed and set. This process happens each step of the way with your approval. If for some reason it is not correctly probed, you will need to change it to the correct hardware that is in your system. Your keyboard and mouse will be found, and most of the time, the hardware will be found correctly.

The first question upon installing Linux is which language you want to install Linux in. The default here is English because it is the most common language out there. There are many languages to choose from.

You will be asked which time zone you live in. The default for this is usually something crazy like Tijuana or Costa Rica. I guess it wouldn't be so crazy if you lived there; 100 percent of the time, you will have to go look for the city or area that you live in and choose it.

Identifying Your Environment

We start by looking at the elements within our network that will enable us to install Linux onto a system. Can we install over the network? Linux has the ability to install several different ways. We can install Linux over the network with a variety of different protocols, such as FTP, HTTP, NFS, and SMB.

If your network has an active File Transfer Protocol (FTP) server with Linux installation files on it, you can link to it as in Figure 2-1.

Network File System (NFS)

The *Network File System* (NFS) is a system-independent method of mounting or sharing disks among systems. Commonly found in Unix and Linux implementations, NFS has been ported to other operating systems. NFS uses two daemons to provide its services: **rpc.nfsd** and **rpc.mountd**. When started, **nfsd** reads the contents of the /etc/exports file to see which filesystems are to be exported or shared to other systems. Although the file exists by default, it is empty; therefore, it exports no filesystems.

The **rpc.mountd** daemon is used to mount filesystems from remote systems for use on the local system. The **rpc.nsfd** offers filesystems to other systems, while **rpc.mountd**

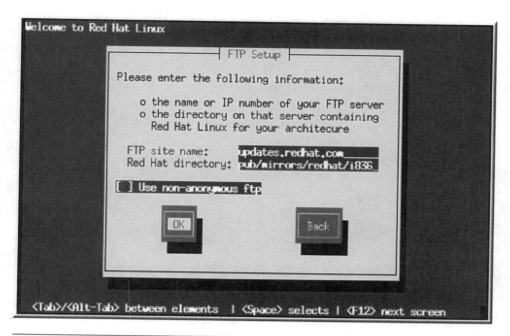

Figure 2-1   FTP Setup dialog

uses filesystems from other systems. The third service, which is not specifically a part of NFS, but one that must be running, is the RPC portmapper. The **portmap** daemon must be running to translate Transmission Control Protocol (TCP) ports into their corresponding RPC ports. If the **portmap** daemon is not running, NFS will not work.

Difficulties encountered with NFS typically involve problems with either the /etc/exports or file with the daemons. Errors with the configuration files are corrected by editing them and making the corrections. Daemon-related problems often are a result of the fact that not all daemons are running or that they have been started in the incorrect order. The **portmap** daemon must be started first for the other RPC services to register and accept requests.

NOTE   NFS mounts can also be performed using the **mount** command.

Linux can be loaded using an NFS server at installation time, as Figure 2-2 shows.

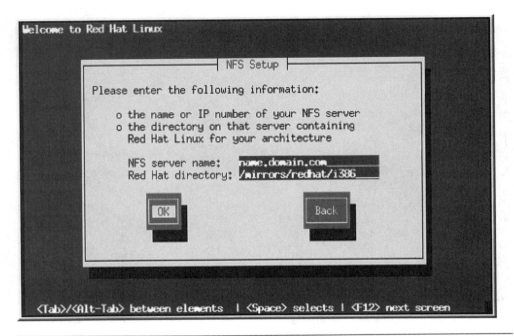

Figure 2-2 NFS Setup dialog

NetBIOS Message Block (NMB)

Windows networks use NetBIOS names to identify computers that Linux cannot interact with natively. The NetBIOS Message Block (NMB) service resolves the NetBIOS names to actual systems for the resources to be found and used. Linux uses the **nmbd** daemon to translate the NetBIOS names to something Linux understands and, in so doing, makes the Windows network resources transparent to Linux.

The service known as *Samba* provides the **smbd** and **nmbd** daemons both to serve resources to other systems and to use resources. Windows users can click the Network Neighborhood icon or My Network Places to see the resources that exist on a Linux system as if they were on a Windows-based system.

Next we look at how Linux is to be used. Will we use the X Window GUI or a straight command-line environment? This still has the aura of pre-installation, but it falls under the guise of installation. Your role as an administrator of a system requires you to think of all the possible options, from installation to daily administration.

Make a list of all the technology in your computer or network. This includes the ability to install from a CD and if your machine is part of a network (LAN or WAN). You need to remember to include the type of keyboard, mouse, and internal components that comprise your system. All of these factors are involved in deciding which direction to implement Linux.

Current versions of Linux are more than a product for which you prepare to install. Linux is a fully involved teaching tool also. Recent distributions of Linux will walk you through the installation, giving you the freedom and the knowledge to use different utilities to partition your hard disk and install software. One very intuitive brand of partitioning software is Disk Druid used by Red Hat. Disk Druid is a powerful graphical tool for partitioning drives and configuring RAID arrays in Red Hat. With Disk Druid, you can add, delete, edit, and write partitions to a disk.

You will be installing software that will perform a specific function. Each function is based on the role a machine will play in a network. Each role is a specific installation of software. The three generic installations of a Linux system are

- Server

- Workstation

- Custom

Your installation will always fit into one of these categories. The server serves files to workstations. The workstation receives files from the server. A custom system is one designed as a hybrid fit for smaller companies that want the security of a centralized network, but do not have the need or the resources for a separate server.

The first thing we will look at is the hard disk layout and how the disk is to be partitioned with Linux.

Sizing the Partitions

Many administrators consider the process of sizing the partitions to be the most difficult part of the installation process. If you estimate incorrectly, you may have to reinstall your system because you may be too short of disk space to operate correctly.

Designing the disk layout is best done with paper and pencil. List each of the filesystems you want to have and identify if you want them configured as a primary or extended partition.

Determining the amount of swap is driven by how much physical RAM you have in your system. It is recommended you have no less than 16MB of swap or virtual memory space. It is often considered a general guideline to add the equivalent amount of swap space as you have physical RAM. For example, 64MB of RAM in your system means you should add 64MB of swap. This gives a total of 128MB of virtual memory on your system. This may be sufficient unless you are running extremely resource-intensive

Table 2-1   Disk Partition Worksheet Example

Disk	Partition #	Name	Prim/Ext	Size
1	1	/boot	Primary	50MB
1	2	/	Primary	1GB
1	3	/usr	Primary	2GB
2	1	Swap	Primary	128MB
2	2	/tmp	Primary	500MB
3	1	/var	Primary	2GB
3	4	/home	Extended	9GB
3	4-1	/tools	Extended	2GB

applications, at which point you may want to add additional swap partitions. Adding additional swap partitions can be done at any time.

The worksheet illustrated in Table 2-1 provides a sample to use for calculating the amount of disk space for each partition. Because Linux supports multiple disks, you may wish to split the data across multiple disks for performance. Additionally, if you will have more than one Linux system on your network, you may want to install the documentation and man pages on one system and make those accessible through NFS to other Linux systems. This decreases the amount of disk space required on each system.

All that being said, the actual amount of disk space you have available plays a major factor in the design of your disk layout.

Using the worksheet, you can work with your partition and determine what works best for you without having to reinstall over and over again. The extended partitions on disk 3 shows the actual partition number and logical division.

For most installations, the first disk partition is /boot. Using /boot addresses, the BIOS 1,024 cylinder limitation is approxiamately 8GB if you are using LILO. Because the boot partition contains the kernel image and needed files to boot the system, the partition doesn't have to be large. However, even though there are not a lot of files in this partition, the size of the kernel images can easily fill the available space if the partition is too small.

The swap space is on disk 2 of our example to capitalize on the difference between the slow mechanical systems in a disk drive and the faster electronics in the computer.

By putting the swap partition on the second disk, you can speed up your system by loading the data from one disk and swapping to the second. This improves the speed at which files can be opened and loaded.

> **NOTE**   The root filesystem should be as small as you can make it, unless you are planning on running within as few partitions as possible.

Consider our example in the following. When comparing against a running system, we see

```
[root@mercury.technical root]# df
filesystem 1k-blocks Used Available Use% Mounted on
/dev/sda5 704448 75596 689884 10% /
/dev/sda1 49913 5948 41388 13% /boot
/dev/sdb1 396623 77079 299060 21% /home
/dev/sdb5 98551 31583 61880 34% /tmp
/dev/sda7 1046648 906668 86812 92% /usr
/dev/hdb1 1056192 353184 703008 34% /u01
[root@mercury.technical root]#
```

We can see that the root partition is 700MB, and the /usr/partition is 1GB. The root partition could have been smaller and /usr/ could have been bigger. In fact, if we had made / 400MB, it still would be only about 20 percent used.

Other than the output of the **df** command, there are four important things to consider in designing your disk layout:

- Are you planning for a workstation or a server?
- What software packages are you installing?
- What other applications and software will be installed?
- What disk space requirements do your applications have?

Assembling a multi-partition system creates a great deal of flexibility later on should your requirements change and you need more disk space for certain areas. The sample layout in Table 2-2 can easily handle the full installation of Linux and still leave room on your disk for other filesystems or data.

Many distributions of Linux will give you the option of performing automatic partitioning for you or letting you do it manually as shown in Figure 2-3.

Table 2-2 Sample Layout

Partition/filesystemsystem	Size
/boot	25MB
/	400MB
Swap	64MB
/usr	1400MB

 ALERT Automatic partitioning will not lay out an optimum disk as shown in Table 2-2; for that you would need to perform a custom install.

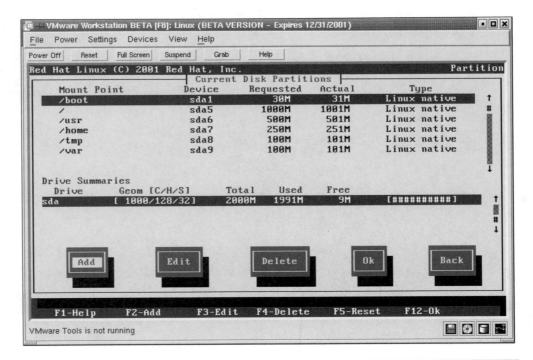

Figure 2-3 Partitioning with Red Hat

fdisk is used to create or modify the disk partitions.

ALERT If you are modifying the disk partitions on a running system, any changes will result in data loss and require a recovery from a backup tape to restore your data.

The **fdisk** command must be executed as root using the syntax:

```
# fdisk /dev/disk-name
```

where disk-name identifies the device you want to partition such as /dev/had or /dev/sdb. **fdisk** has a very comprehensive list of commands as listed in the help section of **fdisk**, but the most commonly used commands are

a   Toggles a bootable flag

p   Prints the partition table

d   Deletes a partition

l   Lists known partition types

m   Prints this menu

t   Changes a partition's system ID

n   Creates a new partition

d   Deletes a partition

q   Quits without saving changes

w   Writes the new partition table and exits

fdisk stores the partition table in internal memory and verifies the layout while you design it. When you are ready to actually store the partition table, the **w** command in **fdisk** writes the partition table and alters the disk layout.

```
[root@mercury.technical root]# fdisk /dev/hdb

The number of cylinders for this disk is set to 1900.
There is nothing wrong with that, but this is larger than 1024,
and could in certain setups cause problems with:
1) software that runs at boot time (e.g., old versions of LILO)
2) booting and partitioning software from other OSes (e.g., DOS
FDISK, OS/2 FDISK)

Command (m for help): p
```

```
Disk /dev/hdb: 16 heads, 63 sectors, 1900 cylinders
Units = cylinders of 1008 * 512 bytes

Device Boot Start End Blocks Id System

Command (m for help): n
```

In the previous listing, we see that no partitions are defined on this disk. The **n** command instructs **fdisk** to create a new partition:

```
Command action
 e extended
 p primary partition (1-4)
p
Partition number (1-4): 1
First cylinder (1-1900, default 1):
Using default value 1
Last cylinder or +size or +sizeM or +sizeK (1-1900, default 1900):
+200M
```

Here, we have instructed **fdisk** to create a new partition that is 200MB in size. This is the first partition, and so it is named /dev/hdb1. We will repeat this process for partitions 2 and 3. However, partition 4 will be an extended partition so we can create more filesystems on this disk:

```
Command (m for help): p

Disk /dev/hdb: 16 heads, 63 sectors, 1900 cylinders
Units = cylinders of 1008 * 512 bytes

Device Boot Start End Blocks Id System
/dev/hdb1 1 407 205096+ 83 Linux
/dev/hdb2 408 814 205128 83 Linux
/dev/hdb3 815 1221 205128 83 Linux

Command (m for help): n
Command action
 e extended
 p primary partition (1-4)
e
Partition number (1-4): 4
First cylinder (1222-1900, default 1222):
Using default value 1222
Last cylinder or +size or +sizeM or +sizeK (1222-2100, default
1900):
Using default value 1900

Command (m for help):
```

Now we have four partitions defined: three primary and one extended. We will now create some logical partitions in the extended partition:

```
Command (m for help): n
First cylinder (1222-1900, default 1222):
Using default value 1222
Last cylinder or +size or +sizeM or +sizeK (1222-2100, default
   1900): +200M
```

Notice that **fdisk** was aware that we are adding new logical entries in the extended partition. We repeat this process once more to add one more logical partition. This now gives us six partitions on the disk, which are each approximately 200MB:

```
Command (m for help): p

Disk /dev/hdb: 16 heads, 63 sectors, 1900 cylinders
Units = cylinders of 1008 * 512 bytes

Device Boot Start End Blocks Id System
/dev/hdb1 1 407 205096+ 83 Linux
/dev/hdb2 408 814 205128 83 Linux
/dev/hdb3 815 1221 205128 83 Linux
/dev/hdb4 1222 2100 443016 5 Extended
/dev/hdb5 1222 1628 205096+ 83 Linux
/dev/hdb6 1629 2100 237856+ 83 Linux

Command (m for help): w
The partition table has been altered!

Calling ioctl() to re-read partition table.

WARNING: If you have created or modified any DOS 6.x
partitions, please see the fdisk manual page for additional
information.
Syncing disks.
[root@mercury.technical root]#
```

Once the partition table is created, the new partitions must be formatted with the appropriate filesystem structure before data can be stored on them. There are three basic filesystems in use with Linux:

- ext2fs

- ext3fs

- Reiserfs

The most popular being, of course, the ext2fs filesystem. It has been around for quite some time and is small and stable. It is only recently that you start seeing large amounts of data that need to be categorized or journalized by the filesystem. The ext2 filesystem does not categorize any of the data or where it is stored. It must be done manually and on a large filesystem, a tremendous amount of downtime could be incurred. This is where the ext3 and reiser filesystems come in to play. The ext3 is an extension of the ext2 filesystem that enables journalizing. The reiserfs filesystem is a whole new filesystem that is a journaling filesystem. Generally, you would use the **mke2fs** to format the filesystem in a ext2 style.

To create the fs or e2fs on the new partitions, use the command **mke2fs**:

```
# mke2fs /dev/hdb1
```

This step must be repeated for each newly created partition, with the exception of any extended partitions. The extended partition itself is not formatted, but all of the logical partitions must be

```
[root@mercury.technical root]# mke2fs /dev/hdb1
mke2fs 1.18, 28-aug-2000 for EXT2 FS 0.5b, 95/08/09


filesystem label=
OS type: Linux
Block size=1024 (log=0)
Fragment size=1024 (log=0)
51400 inodes, 204801 blocks
10254 blocks (5.01%) reserved for the super user
First data block=1
25 block groups
8192 blocks per group, 8192 fragments per group
2056 inodes per group
Superblock backups stored on blocks:
  8193, 24577, 40961, 57345, 73729

Writing inode tables: done
Writing superblocks and filesystem accounting information: done
[root@mercury.technical root]#
```

Because the disk partitions have been modified, we must update our LILO configuration, which is discussed in detail in Chapter 3.

 TIP   At install time, most major distributions of Linux will do everything for you, including make and write the partition for you. All you have to do is specify the size. It is best to understand the processes that the installation program is doing so you get a better handle on how Linux actually performs tasks.

TCP/IP Background

The *Transmission Control Protocol/Internet Protocol* (TCP/IP) is a suite of protocols designed to be routable and efficient. Originally designed as a set of WAN protocols, TCP/IP has developed into an industry standard, supporting communication from the desktop through global WANs. Since the initial government-sponsored development of TCP/IP, continuous improvements have been made to the protocol suite.

The evolution of the TCP/IP protocols—from the small four-site Defense Advanced Research Projects Agency (DARPA) to the global nature of the Internet—has been remarkable. TCP/IP development started more than 25 years ago, and although many improvements have been made and new functionality added in response to the data-networking explosion, the initial spirit of the original design is intact.

As a protocol suite, TCP/IP has several advantages over other network protocols, including

- No single company controls the protocol suite. The Internet community as a whole determines how the protocol suite will develop and mature. Therefore, the protocols are not subject to vendor-specific compatibility issues.

- TCP/IP is not operating system-dependent; it connects heterogeneous operating systems and hardware platforms. Protocols, such as the FTP and the Terminal Emulation Protocol (Telnet), have been written to support heterogeneous implementations.

- As a cross-platform protocol, TCP/IP enables vendors to develop client/server applications such as SQL and SNMP. Because the specifications are public and available for comments, the protocols for those applications are universally available for many different operating environments and platforms.

- TCP/IP has developed into the de facto protocol of the Internet and enables access to hundreds of thousands of systems and information repositories around the world. To connect to the Internet, however, a valid IP address is required.

The Four Layers of TCP/IP

While the International Standards Organization (ISO) was developing the Open Systems Interconnect (OSI) protocol suite as a formal standard, TCP/IP surged ahead as the industry-independent de facto standard. The OSI model has seven layers, whereas TCP/IP has four layers: the network interface, Internet, transport, and application layers. These four layers form the basis of the Internet protocol suite and correspond to one or more layers of the OSI model (which the TCP/IP model predates). Table 2-3

Table 2-3   The Corresponding Layers of the TCP/IP and OSI Models

TCP/IP layer	OSI layer
Network interface	Physical Data link
Internet	Network
Transport	Transport
Application	Session Presentation Application

illustrates how the four layers of the TCP/IP model correspond to the seven layers of the OSI model.

The network interface layer handles the communication with the network hardware and the underlying physical network. This layer must understand the network architecture—such as fiber optics, token ring, or Ethernet—and provide an interface for the Internet layer to communicate with it.

The three basic physical transport methods are as stated previously:

- **Fiber optics**   Digital signal transferred using light on glass strands. Very dependable and the fastest of the three. Very secure, cannot be tampered with or eavesdropped on very well.

- **Ethernet**   Digital signal transported over four or eight strands of copper wire. Limitations on length of cable although fast and dependable. Not very secure.

- **Token ring**   Almost totally outdated. Very slow. Troubleshooting can be very involved. Involves computers hooked in a ring. If separation occurs in the ring, the system goes down.

The Internet layer communicates with the network interface layer for the routing and delivery of packets through the IP. All of the protocols in the transport layer must use IP to communicate with the network, as IP establishes the rules for packet delivery, addressing, packet fragmentation and reassembly, security, and protocol identification. Because IP is a connectionless protocol, it cannot guarantee the delivery of any particular packet. The packet might be lost, damaged, or received out of order. Ensuring the delivery of the packet is the responsibility of the higher protocol layers. In addition to

IP, the Internet layer includes the Internet Control Message Protocol (ICMP), the Internet Group Management Protocol (IGMP), and the Address Resolution Protocol (ARP).

The transport layer provides communications between systems for applications, and maps to the OSI model's transport layer. The transport layer services include both connection-based and connectionless services. As with IP, connectionless services using the User Datagram Protocol (UDP) do not ensure the packet has been received by the remote system. Connection-based services, however, do provide a method for guaranteeing delivery to the remote destination using the TCP.

The highest layer of the Internet protocol suite is the application layer, which maps to the session, application, and presentation layers in the OSI model. Many protocols interact at this layer, providing an interface to text- or graphics-based user interfaces and an access method to the network. Some protocols in the application layer include the Simple Network Management Protocol (SNMP), the FTP, and the Simple Mail Transfer Protocol (SMTP).

It is important to remember that each layer has a defined interface and associated rules for passing information between layers. If information does not conform to these rules, the receiving layer does not know how to process the data. The interface between the network interface and Internet layers, for example, must listen to all broadcasts on the network and send the rest of the data in the frame to the Internet layer for processing. If the network interface layer receives a non-IP frame type, the frame must be discarded without notification to the upper layers.

The Internet layer interface must provide information, such as the source and destination address, protocol types, and other information, to the transport Layer. Remember, the protocol type indicates whether the packet is a TCP or UDP packet. The interface rules also enable the transport layer the ability to change any parameters or to pass parameters from the application layer to the Internet layer.

Primary Protocols

The following six primary protocols comprise the TCP/IP suite:

- TCP
- UDP
- IP
- ICMP
- ARP
- IGMP

Transmission Control Protocol (TCP)

The TCP is probably the most visible of the protocols in the transport layer. TCP is a connection-based protocol that requires a session be established before data is transmitted between the systems. During the connection process, TCP uses a port or socket to transmit and receive information and uses a defined method to ensure the successful delivery and acknowledgement of the packet. The session tracks the progress of the individual packets and ensures they arrive in sequence to provide the data in a coherent fashion to the upper layers.

Once the session is established, the two systems communicate back and forth. If information is lost or garbled during the transmission across the network, the session protocol indicates it did not successfully receive the packet and requests the information be retransmitted.

When initializing a TCP session (through what is often referred to as a three-way handshake), the two systems must agree on the best method to synchronize the communication and how much data is sent at any given time. The two systems also establish the acknowledgement numbers to transmit upon receiving data from the other system.

Data can be transmitted across the connection only after the handshake is complete. Reliable delivery is accomplished by putting the packets into a sequence and sending them in order. For each packet transmitted, the sender expects an acknowledgement that the packet was received. Only when the acknowledgement is received is more data transmitted. TCP is used in two common situations: when the application requires confirmation that the packet was received or when transferring large amounts of data.

TCP uses the concept of *sliding windows* (or *streams*, in Linux/Unix vernacular) to provide a buffer, or window, for transmitting and receiving data. Each side of the connection has both a send window and a receive window. As these windows are used to buffer the data, the communication between the systems is more efficient. The send window contains a portion of the data being transmitted to the remote system; the receive window contains the data being received. Because not all data will be successfully delivered to the remote system, both systems keep track of the data flow and continue to stream data to the remote end without having to wait for an acknowledgement for every packet.

With the sliding window, the receiving computer does not send an acknowledgement for every packet, but sends an acknowledgement referencing a particular sequence number; the transmitting system assumes everything up to that number was properly received.

User Datagram Protocol (UDP)

The *User Datagram Protocol* (UDP) is a connectionless protocol that does not establish a session between the two systems before data is transmitted. UDP packets are still delivered to sockets or ports, as they are in TCP. Because there is no session, however, UDP cannot guarantee the delivery of the packets or that they are delivered in the correct sequence. Any lost packets are not retransmitted because there is no indication that they have been lost.

UDP datagrams constitute a popular method of communication because they require very little system overhead. (There is no session to manage and no synchronization parameters or options.) The datagram contains only the destination IP address, the source and destination ports, the length of the data, a checksum to verify the header, and the data. Because UDP doesn't establish a session, it also doesn't have to manage sequence numbers, retransmit frames, *delayed-acknowledgement timers*, and the *retransmission of packets*. This makes UDP a very fast and streamlined protocol; delivery is just not guaranteed. Thus, UDP is the protocol of choice for broadcasting packets to the entire network, or real-time data.

UDP is also the protocol of choice for delivering streaming audio and video. The lack of a delivery guarantee does not affect the experience in this case because retransmitting the packets would be pointless. In most cases, unless the number of packets lost is severe, the user does not notice. If there is a requirement to use UDP for its speed, but you still require some delivery guarantee, the verification can be included in a higher layer such as transport.

Internet Protocol

The first of several protocols found in this suite is the IP. IP is an essential component, as the transport layer cannot communicate at all without IP at the Internet layer.

The most important IP element is the address space that IP uses. Each machine is given a unique 32 bit-address called an *Internet* (or *IP*) *address*. Addressing is divided into five address classes, which are discussed later in this chapter.

IP receives packets of data from either TCP or UDP in the transport layer and sends datagrams to the network interface layer. The size of a datagram depends on the characteristics of the physical network (such as Ethernet or token ring). If the packet has too much information to be transmitted in one datagram, the packet is fragmented into the required number of datagrams, each of which then must be reassembled on the receiving end by either TCP or UDP.

NOTE The 32-bit IP addresses mentioned here commonly are referred to as IPv4 addresses—as in IP version 4. IPv6, which has not yet gained widespread acceptance, uses 128-bit address space in which eight fields are separated by colons instead of periods to resolve a potential shortage of IP addresses.

Internet Control Message Protocol

The ICMP is responsible for reporting errors and messages regarding the delivery of IP datagrams. ICMP is the protocol used with the **ping** and **traceroute** commands. ICMP can optimize the connection between two machines by sending source quench and other self-tuning signals during data transfers. ICMP is the service that reports when the destination host in unreachable or how long it took to contact the remote host.

There are two basic categories of ICMP messages: the reporting of errors and the sending of queries. Error messages include the following:

- Destination unreachable
- Redirect
- Source quench
- Time exceeded

The most commonly used general message queries are

- Echo request
- Echo reply

The Packet Internet Groper (**ping**) utility uses the echo request and echo reply messages to verify whether there is a host at the specified IP address. The echo request query is a directed datagram that asks the target host for a response indicating it is connected to the network. If the remote host with the specified IP address is on the network and receives the request, ICMP responds with an echo reply to the originating system. The information from the **ping** command identifies that the host is present on the network and the amount of time it took to contact and receive a response from the remote system.

Internet Group Management Protocol (IGMP)

The *Internet Group Management Protocol* (IGMP) is a protocol and set of specifications that enables hosts to be added and removed from IP address groups using the class D address range. Using IGMP, groups of machines can receive broadcast data as one functional unit. A system can belong to one or more groups or can be excluded.

Most implementations of TCP/IP support class D addressing on the local system, but many routers that broadcast IGMP messages from one network to another are still in the experimental stage. As specialized computers, routers are designed to transmit data for multicast groups on a local segment only if there is a system that is part of that group. The router queries the systems on the local network segment for IGMP membership. If a system responds that it is a member, the router processes the datagrams and broadcasts them on the segment.

Address Resolution Protocol (ARP)

Although IP is used for broadcasting messages on the network, it is more common to see packets destined for a specific system. IP addresses identify the path to deliver the datagram to the target host. When the datagram reaches the network where the host is connected, the IP address must be translated to the physical address of the system for delivery. IP relies on the ARP to perform this IP to physical address translation. Using ARP, IP keeps track of the systems it knows the physical address for in the ARP cache.

> **NOTE** ARP is used only on the local network. A system that is not on the local network cannot determine the physical address of a remote system, as ARP is not routed through the network.

The ARP cache, used to store the IP to physical address translation, is maintained for a defined period of time, and then each entry is expired. If this query is not performed, a system that had the network interface card replaced would not receive any datagrams unless the originating system's ARP cache was cleared.

Protocols and Well-Known Ports

Port numbers or sockets are actually used to transfer data to the application layer. These sockets or ports enable a host machine to support and track simultaneous sessions with other hosts on the network. Table 2-4 lists some of the more commonly known ports. There are approximately 65,535 definable ports.

> **TIP** For the exam, be sure to memorize the ports that appear in Table 2-4.

Table 2-4   Common Port Assignments

Port	Service	Purpose
20, 21	FTP	Transfers files from one host to another
23	Telnet	Connects to a host as if on a dumb terminal for administrative purposes
25	SMTP	Simple Mail Transfer Protocol
53	DNS	Domain Name System
80	WWW	The World Wide Web service
110	POP3	The Post Office Protocol (version 3) for retrieving e-mail
119	NNTP	The Network News Transfer Protocol
143	IMAP	The Internet Mail Access Protocol, which can be used in place of POP3
161	SNMP	The Simple Network Management Protocol

The /etc/services file is an ASCII file that maps services to ports. The Internet Assigned Numbers Authority (IANA) assigns ports with lower numbers. Administrators may freely assign higher port numbers to processes and protocols.

 ALERT   Check to be sure that a process you are assigning to a port will not be a breach of security on your system leaving a backdoor for crackers to come in. For instance, leaving finger running on a port will enable outsiders to gather information about accounts inside the organization.

Using Network Adapters

Ethernet adapters vary greatly in performance, price, and to the extent that they are supported by Linux. Many low-cost network cards are available and can be found in many computers. Whichever card you decide on, you should check the supported hardware list before buying it.

The common network adapters, including PCMCIA cards, are found at installation time and during initial configuration. The user is prompted to select the card manufacturer and type, or the card is sensed during the installation.

On occasion, the NIC doesn't respond to the defaults and must be enabled using the additional options for the card, including the IRQ and the I/O and memory addresses.

These values inform the kernel how to communicate with the NIC and enable networking.

Once the system is operational, the network module loaded for the interface can be seen in the boot messages displayed by the **dmesg** command:

```
eth0: 3Com 3c589, io 0x300, irq 3, hw_addr 00:A0:24:64:6A:49
8K FIFO split 5:3 Rx:Tx, auto xcvr
eth0: flipped to 10baseT
```

Once the installation is completed and the system is rebooted, the kernel initializes the NIC and enables networking. Proper configuration of the NIC is done using the **ifconfig** command, which is used to display and change the actual network parameters.

If the NIC doesn't function under Linux, you must boot the system into a Windows environment and use the troubleshooting and diagnostic tools from the vendor to determine if the card works under Windows and if the settings used in Linux are correct.

You check the operation of the NIC using the **ifconfig** command, which reports and can change the network interface configuration. The –*a* parameter shows all of the information about networking devices attached to your system. In most Linux distributions, the –*a* parameter is automatically added so you do not need to add to the command. Consider the following example:

```
[root@mercury.technical root]# ifconfig -a
eth0 Link encap:Ethernet HWaddr 00:A0:24:64:6A:49
 inet addr:192.168.0.221 Bcast:192.168.0.255 Mask:255.255.255.0
 UP BROADCAST NOTRAILERS RUNNING MTU:1500 Metric:1
 RX packets:1869 errors:0 dropped:0 overruns:0 frame:0
 TX packets:1308 errors:0 dropped:0 overruns:0 carrier:0
 collisions:1 txqueuelen:100
 Interrupt:3 Base address:0x300

lo Link encap:Local Loopback
 inet addr:127.0.0.1 Mask:255.0.0.0
 UP LOOPBACK RUNNING MTU:3924 Metric:1
 RX packets:38 errors:0 dropped:0 overruns:0 frame:0
 TX packets:38 errors:0 dropped:0 overruns:0 carrier:0
 collisions:0 txqueuelen:0

[root@mercury.technical root]#
```

In the previous example, the system has one physical NIC (eth0) and the loopback adapter (lo). The eth0 settings inform us of the IP address configuration for the interface and whether it is running or not:

```
eth0 Link encap:Ethernet HWaddr 00:A0:24:64:6A:49
 inet addr:192.168.0.4 Bcast:192.168.0.255 Mask:255.255.255.0
 UP BROADCAST NOTRAILERS RUNNING MTU:1500 Metric:1
```

The IP address for the interface is 192.168.0.221, and the interface is running. We can verify this using several commands such as **arp** and **ping**. Using **arp**, we can determine what other network devices are visible on the LAN:

```
[root@mercury.technical root]# arp -a
win2k03 (192.168.0.3) at 00:80:C6:F1:FA:C9 [ether] on eth0
win2k04 (192.168.0.2) at 00:60:97:59:53:B8 [ether] on eth0
train7 (192.168.0.1) at 00:00:81:F3:05:9A [ether] on eth0
```

With this information, we know that the eth0 interface is receiving packets properly. The output of the **arp** command shows the hostname and its IP and MAC addresses. We can further validate the proper operation of the card by using the **ping** command to contact another system on the network:

```
[root@mercury.technical root]# ping 192.168.0.221
PING 192.168.0.221 (192.168.0.221): 56 data bytes
64 bytes from 192.168.0.221: icmp_seq=0 ttl=128 time=2.8 ms
64 bytes from 192.168.0.221: icmp_seq=1 ttl=128 time=0.9 ms

--- 192.168.0.221 ping statistics ---
2 packets transmitted, 2 packets received, 0% packet loss
round-trip min/avg/max = 0.9/1.8/2.8 ms
```

This confirms the proper operation of our NIC and its ability to transmit and receive data on the network.

Modems

A large number of modems rely on Windows software to download the control program at runtime. The devices are known as *winmodems*. Many manufacturers have recognized the Linux as a valid OS and are writing drivers for their hardware to run under Linux. These modems may or may not run properly on a Linux machine. You will have to check with the manufacturer or look at the list at **http://www.linux.org/hardware/components.html**.

You must validate the existence of the new serial port to which the modem is connected after the modem is physically installed. This is done using the **setserial** command, as described earlier:

```
 [root@mercury.technical root]# setserial -g /dev/ttyS*
/dev/ttyS0, UART: 16550A, Port: 0x03f8, IRQ: 4
/dev/ttyS1, UART: unknown, Port: 0x02f8, IRQ: 3
/dev/ttyS2, UART: 16550A, Port: 0x03e8, IRQ: 4
/dev/ttyS3, UART: unknown, Port: 0x02e8, IRQ: 3
[root@mercury.technical root]#
```

We know from the previous example that /dev/ttyS0 is equivalent to COM1 and that /dev/ttyS2 is equivalent to COM3. The modem itself is installed at COM3 (or /dev/ttyS2 in this system). We can work with this as the device name for the modem, but Linux systems generally link this to the /dev/modem file; if not, we are able to manually link it using the **ln** command:

```
[root@mercury.technical root]# ls -l /dev/ttyS2
crw------- 1 root tty 4, 66 Nov 12 19:59 /dev/ttyS2
[root@mercury.technical root]# ls -l /dev/modem
ls: /dev/modem: No such file or directory
[root@mercury.technical root]# ln /dev/ttyS2 /dev/modem
[root@mercury.technical root]# ls -l /dev/modem
crw------- 2 root tty 4, 66 Nov 12 19:59 /dev/modem
[root@mercury.technical root]#
```

The **minicom** program is capable of communicating with a modem. To be sure that the modem is truly responding, connect a phone line to it and try to dial a remote system. If the modem responds by trying to dial the remote system, your modem is configured correctly.

To use SLIP or PPP for dial-in or dial-out support is the primary reason for configuring a modem. You must have your modem manual handy to check the commands that will enable particular features while configuring the modem for PPP. These features include

- Hardware flow control (RTS/CTS) (&K3 on many Hayes modems)
- E1 Command/usr/src/linux-2.0.27/include/linux/serial.h Echo ON (required for **chat** to operate)
- Q0 Report result codes (required for **chat** to operate)
- S0=0 Auto Answer OFF (unless you want your modem to answer the phone)
- &C1 Carrier Detect ON only after connect
- &S0 Data Set Ready (DSR) always ON
- (depends) Data Terminal Ready

With the modem configuration saved and **minicom** able to talk to the modem, we can proceed with configuring the PPP connection.

Establishing the connection to your ISP is important so you can see what the prompts are. These prompts are important because you need them to build a chat script, which is the program that the PPP client uses to interface with the server at login.

The directory /etc/ppp contains all the files used to configure the PPP client and server. These files may include

- chap-secrets
- ioptions
- options
- options-full
- options-old
- options-no-pap-chap
- pap-secrets

PPP uses a number of files to set up a PPP connection. These files differ in name and location between PPP 2.1.2 and PPP 2.2 and 2.3. For PPP 2.1.2, the files are

- **/usr/sbin/pppd**   The PPP binary
- **/usr/sbin/ppp-on**   The dialer/connection script
- **/usr/sbin/ppp-off**   The disconnection script
- **/etc/ppp/options**   The options that pppd uses for all connections
- **/etc/ppp/options.ttyXX**   The options that are specific to a connection on this port

For PPP 2.2 and 2.3, the files are

- **/usr/sbin/pppd**   The PPP binary
- **/etc/ppp/scripts/ppp-on**   The dialer/connection script
- **/etc/ppp/scripts/ppp-on-dialer**   Part 1 of the dialer script
- **/etc/ppp/scripts/ppp-off**   The actual chat script itself
- **/etc/ppp/options**   The options pppd uses for all connections
- **/etc/ppp/options.ttyXX**   The options specific to a connection on this port

The options file typically contains all of the options available for the PPP connection. If for any reason your installation is missing this file, check the PPP-HOWTO to get a good working copy for yours to function with. You must carefully read through the options in the file, and it can take some effort and research with the system administrator of the target system to find the correct set of options.

The typical options (as listed in the following) will function. One option worth identifying is auth/noauth. The auth parameter requires the remote connection to authenticate itself, even if the Linux system is the client. The noauth directive can be disabled. If you appear to authenticate successfully but cannot get a connection established, add noauth, which should address the problem. The parameters in a sample options file are shown in the following:

```
[root@mercury.technical ppp]# more options
# /etc/ppp/options (NO PAP/CHAP)
#
# Prevent pppd from forking into the background
-detach
#
# use the modem control lines
modem
# use uucp style locks to ensure exclusive access to the serial device
# lock
# use hardware flow control
# crtscts
# create a default route for this connection in the routing table
# defaultroute
# do NOT set up any "escaped" control sequences
asyncmap 0
# use a maximum transmission packet size of 552 bytes
mtu 552
# use a maximum receive packet size of 552 bytes
mru 552
#
#-------END OF SAMPLE /etc/ppp/options (no PAP/CHAP)
#
#
# force pppd to use your ISP user name as your 'host name' during the
# authentication process
name jholman-1 # you need to edit this line
#
# If you are running a PPP *server* and need to force PAP or CHAP
# uncomment the appropriate one of the following lines. Do NOT use
# these is you are a client connecting to a PPP server (even if it #
# uses PAP
# or CHAP) as this tells the SERVER to authenticate itself to your
# machine (which almost certainly can't do - and the link will fail).
#+chap
#+pap
#
# If you are using ENCRYPTED secrets in the /etc/ppp/pap-secrets
# file, then uncomment the following line.
# Note: this is NOT the same as using MS encrypted passwords as can be
# set up in MS RAS on Windows NT.
#+papcrypt
noauth
[root@mercury.technical ppp]#
```

When using the **minicom** program to connect to the target system, disconnect from the remote system once PPP is running without resetting the modem line. This will retain the connection and enable you to start the pppd daemon by hand using the following command:

```
pppd -d -detach /dev/ttySx 38400
```

where x is the number of the serial port to which the modem is connected. Alternatively, you could use the device /dev/modem. Once done, you can test the operation of the PPP link using the **ifconfig** command:

```
[root@mercury.technical ppp]# ifconfig ppp0
ppp0 Link encap:Point-to-Point Protocol
  inet addr:147.129.10.110 P-t-P:47.129.8.102 Mask:255.255.255.255
  UP POINTOPOINT RUNNING NOARP MULTICAST MTU:552 Metric:1
  RX packets:7 errors:0 dropped:0 overruns:0 frame:0
  TX packets:7 errors:0 dropped:0 overruns:0 carrier:0
  collisions:0 txqueuelen:10
```

The output from **ifconfig** shows that there is a working PPP connection from the client to the server. However, we want to automate the PPP connection so that it dials and connects automatically when we want it to. This is done using the files in the /etc/ppp/scripts directory.

NOTE If you don't find the files there, look in the /usr/doc/ppp* directory.

```
[root@mercury.technical scripts]# pwd
/etc/ppp/scripts
[root@mercury.technical scripts]# ls -l
total 40
-rw-r--r-- 1 root root 3644 Nov 20 20:30 README
-rw-r--r-- 1 root root 2301 Nov 20 20:30 callback
-rw-r--r-- 1 root root 2795 Nov 20 20:30 chat-callback
-rw-r--r-- 1 root root 548 Nov 20 20:30 ip-down.local.add
-rw-r--r-- 1 root root 734 Nov 20 20:30 ip-up.local.add
-rw-r--r-- 1 root root 967 Nov 20 20:30 ppp-off
-rw-r--r-- 1 root root 1642 Nov 20 20:32 ppp-on
-rw-r--r-- 1 root root 397 Nov 20 20:30 ppp-on-dialer
-rw-r--r-- 1 root root 2237 Nov 20 20:30 redialer
-rw-r--r-- 1 root root 2376 Nov 20 20:30 secure-card
[root@mercury.technical scripts]#
```

We're interested in the ppp-on and ppp-on-dialer scripts at this point. The ppp-on script contains the information that's required to make the call to the target PPP server. This includes the telephone number, user name, and password. To prevent people from seeing your account information, you are strongly encouraged to restrict the permissions on this file.

```
[root@mercury.technical scripts]# more ppp-on
#!/bin/sh
#
# Script to initiate a ppp connection. This is the first part of the
# pair of scripts. This is not a secure pair of scripts as the codes
# are visible with the 'ps' command. However, it is simple.
#
# These are the parameters. Change as needed.
TELEPHONE=555-1212 # The telephone number for the connection
ACCOUNT=neo # The account name for logon
PASSWORD=geek # The password for this account
LOCAL_IP=0.0.0.0 # Local IP address if known. Dynamic = 0.0.0.0
REMOTE_IP=0.0.0.0 # Remote IP address if desired. Normally 0.0.0.0
NETMASK=255.255.255.0 # The proper netmask if needed
#
# Export them so that they will be available at 'ppp-on-dialer' time.
export TELEPHONE ACCOUNT PASSWORD
#
# This is the location of the script which dials the phone and logs
# in. Please use the absolute file name as the $PATH variable is not
# used on the connect option. (To do so on a 'root' account would be
# a security hole so don't ask.)
#
DIALER_SCRIPT=/etc/ppp/ppp-on-dialer
--More--(62%)
```

Change the phone number, account name, and password to configure the script. With this information, the ppp-on script then calls the pppd program with the name of the dialer script: ppp-on-dialer. The ppp-on-dialer script establishes the connection with the remote PPP server, which is why tracking the keystrokes to establish the connection is so important.

The most difficult part of the actual PPP configuration can be the chat process. Assuming that your PPP server doesn't require anything extra to establish a connection, the default ppp-on-dialer script establishes the connection with no problem. However, you may need to enter a command like **ppp** to get the server to start. Change the script to include the additional commands required:

```
#!/bin/sh
#
# This is part 2 of the ppp-on script. It will perform the connection
```

```
# protocol for the desired connection.
#
exec chat -v \
 TIMEOUT 3 \
 ABORT '\nBUSY\r' \
 ABORT '\nNO ANSWER\r' \
 ABORT '\nRINGING\r\n\r\nRINGING\r' \
 " \rAT \
 'OK-+++\c-OK' ATH0 \
 TIMEOUT 30 \
 OK ATDT$TELEPHONE \
 CONNECT " \
 login:--ogin: $ACCOUNT \
 password: $PASSWORD     \
 command:      ppp
[root@mercury.technical scripts]#
```

Once you have defined your chat negotiation, you must test your connection with ppp-on. You can add start-up scripts to your system to establish your connection on every boot up. Remember, you will have to make the ppp-on and ppp-on-dialer scripts executable.

NOTE Look at the read permissions on the file and make necessary changes to prevent unauthorized access to the username and password information.

Creating and Managing Users

During the installation process, the root user, or superuser, is added to the system. As the most powerful user on the system, root can perform any function available and override some of the security features that prevent other users from doing things they should not. Every individual user can't be allowed to use the root account to access the system and run applications, however. With the newest distributions, an extra user is required to be added, as shown in Figure 2-4. Consequently, we add users to the system to allow them private access to the system and engage the security functions available within Linux. The administrator's ability to add users to the system is enhanced with an understanding of the files that hold the user account and password information.

The first of these files is /etc/passwd. This is a colon-delimited file that contains seven fields. Linux adds at least one user (root/superuser) to the system. Root is the most powerful user on the system, able to do almost anything. After the installation, it is

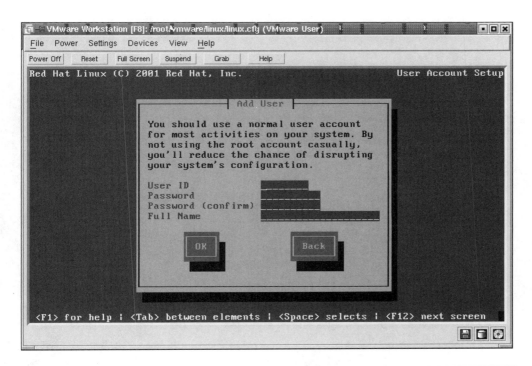

Figure 2-4 Adding a user during installation of Red Hat

often necessary to add users and modify the variables associated with existing ones. This section examines both tasks. Figure 2-4 shows adding a user at install time.

To understand what is involved, it is important to know the files the operating system uses to deal with users. The first file of importance is the /etc/passwd file. Fields are delimited by colons. For example

```
root:x:0:0:root:/root:/bin/bash
bin:x:1:bin:/bin:
daemon:x:2:2:daemon:/sbin:
adm:x:3:4:adm:/var/adm:
lp:x:4:7:lp:/var/spool/lpd:
sync:x:5:0:sync:/sbin:/bin/sync
shutdown:x:6:0:shutdown:/sbin:/sbin/shutdown
halt:x:7:0:halt:/sbin:/sbin/halt
mail:x:8:12:mail:/var/spool/mail:
news:x:9:13:news:/var/spool/news:
uucp:x:10:14:uucp:/var/spool/uucp:
operator:x:11:0:operator:/root:
games:x:12:100:games:/usr/games:
```

```
gopher:x:13:30:gopher:/usr/lib/gopher-data:
ftp:x:14:50:FTP User:/var/ftp:
nobody:x:99:99:Nobody:/:
nscd:x:28:28:NSCD Daemon:/:/bin/false
mailnull:x:47:47:/var/spool/mqueue:/dev/null
ident:x:98:98:pident user:/:/bin/false
rpc:x:32:32:Portmapper RPC user:/:/bin/false
rpcuser:x:29:29:RPC Service User:/var/lib/nfs:/bin/false
xfs:x:43:43:X Font Server:/etc/X11/fs:/bin/false
gdm:x:42:42:/home/gdm:/bin/bash
apache:x:48:48:Apache:/var/www:/bin/false
jhowe:x:500:500:Jon Howe:/home/jhowe:/bin/bash
jhweb:x:501:501:Jon Howe, web interface:/var/www/jhowe:/bin/bash
webcam:x:502:502:Jon Howe, web cam:/var/www/webcam:/bin/bash
cdupuis:x:503:503:Clement Dupuis, FTP ONLY:/var/ftp/cdupuis:/bin/false
seal:x:1001:1001:SEAL Audit FTP Account:/var/www/seal:/bin/false
mailman:x:1002:1002:Mailing List Administrator:/home/mailman:/bin/bash
```

Each of the seven fields holds information of importance to the system:

- **User name** This is a text value that must be unique per system. The user name can be changed by adjusting the values in /etc/passwd and related files. Of the preceding list, bin typically owns the operating system executables; daemon is used for the system services; adm owns the log files; and apache owns the Web server. Other accounts, such as cdupuis and chare, are FTP only and individual user accounts.

- **Password** The field can contain the encrypted value of the user's password or the letter *x*, which indicates the password is stored in the /etc/shadow file. Inserting any other letter besides the one displayed will disable the account.

NOTE The /etc/shadow file enhances system security by restricting who can see the encrypted password values. By restricting their visibility, it is harder for an attacker to obtain them and crack the passwords.

- **UID** This is the numerical representation the system really knows the user as. The UID must be unique on the system. The root account is always 0; system accounts typically run to 99. The number assignment for user accounts differs from one Linux vendor to another, but generally start at 500 or 1000.

- **Group ID (GID)** The group ID establishes the default or login group for the user. The lower numbers represent system groups, which the users should not generally be members of. The regular users are assigned groups starting with the number in the /etc/login.defs file.

- **Comment or description**   This field, which typically has been known as the comment field, is used to provide information about the owner of the account. Such information can include his or her real name, telephone number, and so forth. This is a free-form field, commonly used by the **finger** command to print information about the user.

- **User's home directory**   This is the location in the filesystem where the user is placed when she logs in. The user has permission to add, modify, and delete files in this area.

> **TIP**   Within several shells, including bash, the home directory can be referenced using the tilde (~) character. If a user is in a different directory and wants to list the contents of his home, he can use the command ls ~.

- **Login shell**   This field defines the particular shell used for the user when she logs in. If no shell is specified, the default, bash, is used.

If the encrypted password is not stored in the /etc/passwd file, it is found in the /etc/shadow file:

```
root:$1$nS26huxt$eSAcLvTa.zHs2pq1s2A6M.:11468:0:99999:7::
bin:*:11468:0:99999:7::
daemon:*:11468:0:99999:7::
adm:*:11468:0:99999:7::
lp:*:11468:0:99999:7::
sync:*:11468:0:99999:7::
shutdown:*:11468:0:99999:7::
halt:*:11468:0:99999:7::
mail:*:11468:0:99999:7::
news:*:11468:0:99999:7::
uucp:*:11468:0:99999:7::
operator:*:11468:0:99999:7::
games:*:11468:0:99999:7::
gopher:*:11468:0:99999:7::
ftp:*:11468:0:99999:7::
nobody:*:11468:0:99999:7::
nscd:!!:11468:0:99999:7::
mailnull:!!:11468:0:99999:7::
ident:!!:11468:0:99999:7::
rpc:!!:11468:0:99999:7::
rpcuser:!!:11468:0:99999:7::
xfs:!!:11468:0:99999:7::
gdm:!!:11468:0:99999:7::
apache:!!:11468:0:99999:7::
jhowe:$1$.4tzBwJg$ET1PcOHzlvycJ0WHrxCnJ1:11468:0:99999:7::
jhowe:$1$btF2E1gy$nDOu2ajX17i7WrNv3LMg50:11469:0:99999:7::
```

```
webcam:$1$btF2E1gy$nDOu2ajX17i7WrNv3LMg50:11469:0:99999:7::
cdupuis:$1$YOobcaUK$LFD1DiTn4x4euNhK1Fbwl1:11478:0:99999:7::
seal:z3Dbt1Okq.u/M:11479:0:7::0
mailman:f/cuNS2gH4fhQ:11482:0:7::0
```

The eight fields in /etc/shadow are as follows:

- **User name**   This matches the entry in /etc/passwd.

- **Encrypted password hash**   If no password is assigned, this field contains an asterisk. The encrypted password value can be either an MD5 hash or a DES crypt hash. This field must not be blank.

- **Last password change date**   The date the password changed, expressed in the number of days since January 1, 1970.

- **Minimum password age**   The number of days the user must wait before she can change her password.

- **Maximum password age**   The number of days the password is valid before the user must change it.

NOTE   An empty field indicates there is no restriction.

- **Warning days**   The number of days before the password expires, and the system starts to warn the user to change his password.

- **Grace period**   The number of days after the password expires that the system waits before disabling the account from login.

- **The expiration date for the password**   The date the password expires, expressed in days since 1/1/1970.

NOTE   The shell prompts in this chapter are the pound sign (#), as most of the security and user-management commands must be executed as root. The only exception is if the user is executing them to affect his or her own account.

Creating User Accounts

User accounts can either be created manually or by using one of the many utilities provided with each Linux implementation. If you are not using the shadow file, you can insert your entry into the password file by using **cat**.

> **NOTE**   Creating a user account manually is not the recommended approach. Regardless of the method, if you are adding a user manually, you should create a backup copy of the /etc/passwd file first.

If you decide to create the password manually, you can append an entry to the password file, leaving the password blank (as it can be assigned using the **passwd** command):

```
# cat >> /etc/passwd
mcote:2000:2000:Mignona C:/home/mcote:/bin/bash
{Press Ctrl-D}
#
# passwd mcote
New user password: {Enter password}
Retype new user password: {Enter password again}
passwd: all authentication tokens updated successfully
#
# tail -1 /etc/passwd
mcote:petKv.fLWG/Ig:2000:2000/home/mcote:/bin/bash
#
```

> **TIP**   Any user can use the passwd command to change his or her own password. Only the root user can change the password for any user.

This method puts the account information at the end of the password file. The example here creates the password in the /etc/passwd file and does not utilize the /etc/shadow file. If the home directory exists and the user is its owner, he or she can now log into the system.

An alternative to using the **cat** command is the **vipw** command. Using **vipw** requires an understanding of the vi editor. With **vipw**, a backup of the password file (and /etc/shadow) is made. **vipw** opens the password file for the administrator to add the entry. If the /etc/shadow file is used on the system, the administrator is prompted to add the user to the shadow file as well.

```
# vipw
(the editor window opens to add the user information)
#
```

Most Linux implementations also provide the **useradd** command aside from their own utilities. **useradd** requires a number of options; a principal one is **–D**, which displays the default settings:

```
# useradd -D
GROUP=200
HOME=/home/%s
SHELL=/bin/bash
SKEL=/etc/skel
PASS_MIN_DAYS=0
PASS_MAX_DAYS=-180
PASS_WARN_DAYS=7
PASS_INACTIVE=-1
PASS_EXPIRE=-1
SKEL=/etc/skel
#
```

The defaults, as found in /etc/login.defs, are used to create the account with the **useradd** command, unless they are provided on the command line. For example, the following sequence is possible:

```
# useradd lisaf
# tail -1 /etc/passwd
lisaf:x:2001:2001:/home/lisaf:/bin/bash
# tail -1 /etc/shadow
lisaf:!!:11486:1:180:10::
#
# passwd lisaf
New user password: {Enter password}
Retype new user password: {Enter password again}
passwd: all authentication tokens updated successfully
# tail -1 /etc/shadow
lisaf:$1$bnAp/sDx$yZJanHcD3Cev6O7aOgs5M/:11486:1:180:10::
#
```

This example uses the /etc/shadow file to store the password.

 NOTE The system is either configured to use /etc/shadow for passwords or it is not. The methods are not combined.

This example shows how the /etc/shadow file would be utilized. The parameters in /etc/login.defs are listed in Table 2-5.

Table 2-5   Values Used To Create New Accounts

Default	Result in /etc/passwd and /etc/shadow
GROUP	The default numerical group to add users to
HOME	The base path for the user's home directory
SHELL	Defines the user's login shell
SKEL	Defines the location of the default files added to the user's home directory
PASS variables	Establishes the default values for the /etc/shadow entry

The skeleton (*SKEL*) variable provides the location of the files to be copied into each user's home directory when his account is created. By default, **useradd** does not create the home directory unless the -m option is specified. If the home directory is created, the files in /etc/skel are copied as well. In typical implementations, /etc/skel holds the following files:

- .bash_logout
- .bashrc
- .cshrc
- .inputrc
- .login
- .logout
- .profile
- .seyon
- .tcshrc

All the files in this directory are used for setting up the environment and variables for the various shells.

There are a number of options to **useradd** that override the default settings:

-c   Provides the text for the fifth field of the password file, commonly called the *comment*. Most implementations default to an empty entry or some derivation of the user name.

-d   Instructs **useradd** to use a home directory different from /home/{*username*}.

-e   Alters the expiration date for the account using the format *mm/dd/yyyy*.

-f   Defines how many days after expiration the account can function before being disabled. The default of -1 prevents the account from being disabled.

-g   Uses the specified GID for the login group.

-r   Switches to a root directory.

-s   Uses the indicated shell.

-u   Specifies a UID. Normally, **useradd** will compute the next highest available UID. If you attempt to use a number already in use, **useradd** reports an error message indicating the UID is already in use.

Switching Between the passwd and Shadow Files

Earlier examples showed the password stored in the /etc/passwd file and later in the /etc/shadow file. The **pwconv** and **pwunconv** commands will convert your system one way or the other. The **pwconv** command takes a system that is only using the /etc/passwd file and moves the passwords and associated defaults into the /etc/shadow file. The opposite of **pwconv** is **pwunconv**, which converts the system from storing the password hashes in the /etc/shadow file and moves them to the /etc/passwd file. Once the conversion is complete, **pwunconv** removes the /etc/shadow file.

The su Utility

Once a valid entry for a user has been established in the /etc/passwd file, the user can log in and authenticate to the system. If the user knows the password for another account, he or she can use the **su** command to become that user without having to log out and log in again. This creates a *subshell* with the new user's identity. The user can then return to his or her own identity by typing the **exit** command.

There are many legitimate and not so legitimate reasons why a user would want to become another. The command **su,** without specifying a username, tries to make the user the root user. Remember, the user must know the root password to do so. Using the **su** command enables each administrator to have his or her own account and become root only when needed. All **su** attempts, successful and unsuccessful, are logged to the system log in /var/log/messages. Working in this manner can be a blessing in disguise, as it means it is much harder for the administrator to unintentionally damage the system. It still provides the ability to become root and solve problems within a system, when necessary.

NOTE   As an alternative to su, you should consider the sudo command, which enables you to grant command rights to users for other accounts, such as root, without them having to know the password for that account. Because they are restricted to the commands they can actually execute, they are permitted to perform only the tasks for which they are authorized.

Creating User Accounts

During installation, users can be added on the newest distributions as shown in Figure 2-5 Multiple users can be added at this time for a multiuser system.

To create new users manually or by using utilities, simply append an entry to the /etc/passwd file.

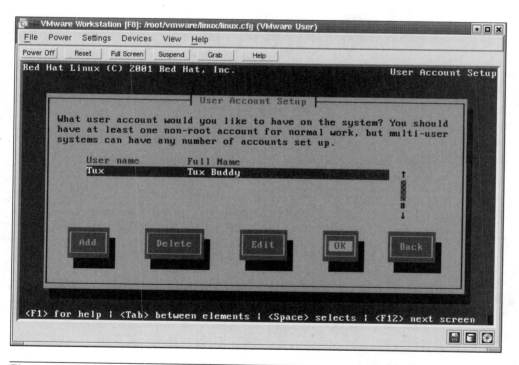

Figure 2-5   Adding a user

NOTE It is strongly recommended that you make a backup copy of the file before changing it.

You can leave the password field blank and then assign a password using the **passwd** utility. If you simply leave it blank, it is a valid account without a password:

```
# cat >> /etc/passwd
JoniH:504:100:JoniH:/home/evan:/bin/bash
{Press Ctrl+D}
#
# passwd evan
New user password: {Enter password}
Retype new user password: {Enter password again}
passwd: all authentication tokens updated successfully
#
# tail -1 /etc/passwd
JoniH:petKv.fLWG/Ig:504:100/home/evan:/bin/bash
#
```

Notice that this method places the encrypted password in the /etc/passwd file itself and does not utilize the /etc/shadow file. If the user is the owner of the home directory, (see the discussion of **chown** in Chapter 4), the user being added becomes an authenticated user.

A utility to simplify this process is **useradd**, which is provided with Linux (most vendors also have their own utilities as well). You must use options with the utility, and a key one is **–D** to display default settings:

```
# useradd -D
GROUP=100
HOME=/home/%s
SHELL=/bin/bash
SKEL=/etc/skel
PASS_MIN_DAYS=0
PASS_MAX_DAYS=-1
PASS_WARN_DAYS=7
PASS_INACTIVE=-1
PASS_EXPIRE=-1
#
```

You can use these defaults to create a new user with this utility. The defaults come from the text file /etc/login.defs. Therefore, the following sequence is possible:

```
# useradd rascal
# tail -1 /etc/passwd
```

```
rascal:x:508:100:Caldera OpenLinux User:/home/kerby:/bin/bash
# tail -1 /etc/shadow
rascal:*not set*:11213:0:-1:7:-1:-1:
#
# passwd rascal
New user password: {Enter password}
Retype new user password: {Enter password again}
passwd: all authentication tokens updated successfully
# tail -1 /etc/shadow
rascal:M3cMnQDwHjRD6:11213:0:-1:7:-1:-1:
#
```

NOTE This code uses the /etc/shadow file.

The values used to create the entries in the two files come directly from the defaults shown in Table 2-6.

By default, **useradd** makes the entries in the passwd and shadow files but does not create the home directory for the user. By using the -m option, **useradd** also creates the home directory for the user and copies files from the **SKEL** location (a skeleton, or template of files that you want copied for every new user) into the new directory. In typical implementations, /etc/skel holds the following files:

- .bash_logout
- .bashrc
- .cshrc
- .inputrc
- .login
- .logout
- .profile
- .seyon
- .tcshrc

All the files are hidden files used for processing how the user is authenticated on the system and how they interact with the various shells.

Table 2-6 Values Used To Create New Accounts

Default	Result in /etc/passwd and /etc/shadow
GROUP	Becomes the fourth field of passwd
HOME	Becomes the sixth field of passwd, with the %s variable becoming the name given on the command line (which becomes the first field of both passwd and shadow)
SHELL	Becomes the seventh field of passwd
PASS variables	Entered into appropriate fields of shadow

To override default settings, you can use a number of options with **useradd**:

-c Specifies the free text (the fifth field of passwd) associated with the user. Most Linux implementations default to an empty entry here or a deviation of the name.

-d Specifies a home directory different from /home/{*username*}.

-e Changes the expiration date (with the format *mm/dd/yyyy*).

-f Sets the variable defining how many days after expiration the account becomes disabled. The default of **-1** prevents it from being disabled even after expiration.

-g Specifies a different GID.

-r Switches to a root directory.

-s Chooses a different shell.

-u Specifies a UID: By default, the next available number is used. If you try to use a number already in use, the utility fails and identifies which user already has that number.

The X Window System

Developed at the Massachusetts Institute of Technology as the display component of Project Athena, the X Window System provides a large and powerful graphics display and management system environment for Unix systems. Since its development, many commercial Unix vendors have ported the X Window System to their platform, since making it the industry standard graphical interface for Unix systems. It is safe to say that almost every Unix variant in the world has some form of the X Window System as its display manager.

Unlike the commercial versions that use a royalty-based X Window license, Linux uses the freely distributable X Window implementation. Titled XFree86, it is based upon the X Window System version 11 release 6, commonly referred to as X11R6. The XFree86 implementation for the 80386/80486 and Pentium processor families has since been ported to many other Unix systems, including System V/386 and 386BSD. As it is based upon the freely distributable port, the XFree86 implementation includes all source code, binaries, libraries, and tools available in the X11R6 distribution.

Before looking at the details, first some clarification on terminology. Unlike the common terminology, the X server runs on the local workstation, where the user wants to display the graphics. The X server itself is responsible for the screen and display management. The X client is an application that wants to display information on the X server. The X client establishes a communication path to the server and sends the information and formatting instructions to the server, which in turn displays it so the user can see it.

Figure 2-6 illustrates the components provided by the X server and the clients.

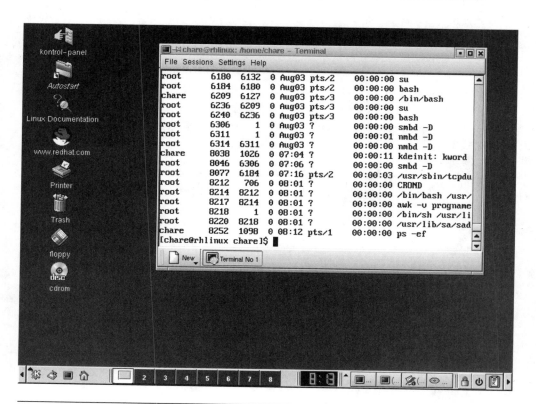

Figure 2-6   Sample X display

The X Window System is mostly invisible because it provides the communications path and ability to display the graphics the user sees. The actual graphics come from the X clients. The X client can be an application program, such as Kword, a shell, or the file manager. The user has the ability to manage the display windows using the window manager, which in Figure 2-6 is KDE. It is important to stress that due to the networked nature of the X Window System, the X client can be on the local or a remote workstation.

Hardware Requirements

Due to the varying hardware used in today's computer graphic displays, the X Window System is highly specific to the components used. Incorrect configurations can still damage your video card and monitor, however most of today's multisync monitors are more difficult to damage as they adjust to the sync and refresh rates from the video card.

Despite these improvements, caution is required when configuring or adjusting the video settings to prevent damage to one of the most expensive components in your system.

During the Linux installation process, the X Window installation program determines the system video configuration and verifies it with the user. Typically, the installation program is very accurate when determining the available hardware configuration. You should only correct it if you are sure it is wrong. Of particular concern is the chipset used on the video card, which determines which X server is used. Most video card manufactures develop proprietary chipsets, which are used to provide their individual characteristics. If the chipset is not specifically identified in the document, verify it with the manufacturer.

NOTE www.xfree86.org/4.0/Status.html lists the supported video cards and monitors.

For reasonable performance, the system should have a minimum 80486 processor with supported video chipsets and a minimum of 8MB of RAM. For good performance, a faster processor, more memory, and an accelerated video card is highly recommended. However, before buying your video adapter, you should verify it is supported by XFree86 by reviewing the supported hardware list at **www.xfree86.org/4.0/ Status.html**. Because X Window adds a higher degree of load to the system, additional memory is recommended to reduce swapping. With X Window running, a system with only 4MB of RAM will up to ten times slower than a system with 8MB. For better performance, you should have more than 16MB of RAM.

Installing XFree86

Most Linux implementations today include the X Window System as a component. There are differences in the installation program, however, as both Mandrake and Red Hat now use X Window as the graphical display engine for the installation program. If you have problems with the display during installation, you can choose a text-based install until the system is running, and then correct the X Window installation later.

If there are no problems during the graphical installation, the Linux distribution will optimize the graphical configuration. Configuring X Window in this manner rarely requires additional editing of the configuration files after installation.

Because X Window is generally included in the Linux distribution, you will not normally need to download the X Window source and compile it. However, the X Window binary distributions are found on numerous FTP sites on the Internet, with the definitive reference found on the XFree86 site: **ftp://ftp.xfree86.org/pub/XFree86/ 4.0.2//binaries/**. Specifically, your download must include the Linux-axp-glibc21, Linux-ix86-glibc20, or the Linux-ix86-glibc21 subdirectories, depending on your processor type (axp=alpha, ix86=Intel 80x86) and Gnu C library version.

Once you have retrieved the binaries, you must execute the Xinstall.sh script to determine if there are other system dependencies to resolve before continuing the installation. You can find the complete instructions for installing the XFree86 binary distribution at **www.xfree86.org/4.0/Install2.html**.

It is advisable to use FTP and not your web browser to retrieve the X Window files as there are a number of them, and using the Web will take far longer than you are prepared to spend. This list of files is as follows:

```
[root@localhost X]# ls -l
total 32808
-rw-rw-r-- 1 root root 1047 Dec 28 09:20 BugReport
-rw-rw-r-- 1 root root 416171 Dec 28 09:20 FILES
-rw-rw-r-- 1 root root 15776 Dec 28 09:20 Install
-rw-rw-r-- 1 root root 4451 Dec 28 09:20 README
-rw-rw-r-- 1 root root 47206 Dec 28 09:20 RELNOTES
-rw-rw-r-- 1 root root 1517 Dec 28 09:20 SUMS.md5
-rw-rw-r-- 1 root root 1307 Dec 28 09:20 SUMS.md5sum
-rw-rw-r-- 1 root root 6521206 Dec 28 09:21 Xbin.tgz
-rw-rw-r-- 1 root root 261268 Dec 28 09:21 Xdoc.tgz
-rw-rw-r-- 1 root root 130655 Dec 28 09:21 Xetc.tgz
-rw-rw-r-- 1 root root 1245569 Dec 28 09:21 Xf100.tgz
-rw-rw-r-- 1 root root 368706 Dec 28 09:21 Xfcyr.tgz
-rw-rw-r-- 1 root root 237548 Dec 28 09:21 Xfenc.tgz
```

```
-rw-rw-r-- 1 root root 1645274 Dec 28 09:22 Xflat2.tgz
-rw-rw-r-- 1 root root 2212102 Dec 28 09:22 Xfnon.tgz
-rw-rw-r-- 1 root root 2768773 Dec 28 09:22 Xfnts.tgz
-rw-rw-r-- 1 root root 1517403 Dec 28 09:22 Xfscl.tgz
-rw-rw-r-- 1 root root 65267 Dec 28 09:22 Xfsrv.tgz
-rw-rw-r-- 1 root root 841857 Dec 28 09:22 Xhtml.tgz
-rw-rw-r-- 1 root root 23079 Dec 28 09:22 Xinstall.sh
-rw-rw-r-- 1 root root 105680 Dec 28 09:22 Xjdoc.tgz
-rw-rw-r-- 1 root root 452962 Dec 28 09:22 Xlib.tgz
-rw-rw-r-- 1 root root 605644 Dec 28 09:23 Xman.tgz
-rw-rw-r-- 1 root root 5146667 Dec 28 09:23 Xmod.tgz
-rw-rw-r-- 1 root root 456815 Dec 28 09:23 Xnest.tgz
-rw-rw-r-- 1 root root 3615902 Dec 28 09:23 Xprog.tgz
-rw-rw-r-- 1 root root 1067064 Dec 28 09:24 Xprt.tgz
-rw-rw-r-- 1 root root 618320 Dec 28 09:24 Xps.tgz
-rw-rw-r-- 1 root root 617 Dec 28 09:24 Xvar.tgz
-rw-rw-r-- 1 root root 1510249 Dec 28 09:24 Xvfb.tgz
-rw-rw-r-- 1 root root 867685 Dec 28 09:24 Xxserv.tgz
-rw-rw-r-- 1 root root 317738 Dec 28 09:24 extract
-rw-rw-r-- 1 root root 317738 Dec 28 09:24 extract.exe
```

For example, running Xinstall.sh results in the following output:

```
[root@localhost root]# sh Xinstall.sh
Welcome to the XFree86 4.0 installer
You are strongly advised to backup your existing XFree86 installation
before proceeding. This includes the /usr/X11R6 and /etc/X11
directories. The installation process will overwrite existing files
in those directories, and this may include some configuration files
that may have been customised.
Do you wish to continue? (y/n) [n] y
Checking which OS you're running...
uname reports 'Linux' version '2.2.16-22smp', architecture 'i586'.
Object format is 'ELF'. libc version is '6.1'.
Checking for required files ...
You need to download the 'extract' (or 'extract.exe') utility
and put it in this directory.
When you have corrected the problem, please re-run 'sh Xinstall.sh'
to proceed with the installation.
```

In this example, the Xinstall.sh script identifies some missing components, specifically the extract program. All that is required to install XFree86 is to obtain the binary distribution, create the directory /usr/X11R6 (as root), and unpack the files from /usr/X11R6.

After unpacking the binary files into the /usr/X11R6 directory, add the directory /usr/X11R6/bin to your PATH, using the appropriate command for the shell you are using. You should also add it to the system profile because making changes to your environment only affects the current session. Edit the system profile using the commands

```
$ vi /etc/profile
$ . /etc/profile
```

NOTE When editing the .profile, add the directory /usr/X11R6/bin to your PATH.

Although the system profile /etc/profile is specifically identified, you should alter the system startup file to whatever shell the users on your system will be using.

If the line /usr/X11R6/lib is not already in the /etc/ld.so.conf file used by the dynamic linker to find the X Window shared libraries, add it using the commands

```
$ vi /etc/ld.so.conf
```

With the preceding steps complete, you can now configure the X Window System for your Linux workstation. Remember, if your Linux distribution includes the X Window System as a component, you will not need to perform much additional configuration.

X Window System Configuration

Earlier versions of the X Window System were difficult to configure, even after the different Unix vendors made their specific customizations. On some systems, such as those with a finite number of hardware options like Sun or Hewlett-Packard systems, the level of configuration required was minimal. On those environments, such as PC based Unix systems that support a wide range of graphics cards, the configuration could be quite challenging. However, the XFree86 environment has matured to the point that most users can install the X Window System with few problems.

Initial versions of the X server required a different server to manage each video card. Recent changes in the X server to support loadable modules, depending upon the video card and the chipset used, have made the installation and configuration of the server much easier to manage. Typically the commands **XF86Setup** or **xf86config** are used to perform the configuration. Different Linux implementations have made specific changes to accommodate their own customizations. For example, Red Hat Linux uses Xconfigurator, while Mandrake uses Xfdrake.

Regardless of the command used, all serve the same purpose: to configure the X Window System to function correctly with the installed video hardware. Each configuration program works with the file /etc/X11/XF86Config, which stores the configuration information for the X server, including file locations, font definitions, screen resolutions, and monitor configurations.

TheXF86Setup program initializes a VGA 16-bit color server and works with the user to verify the different configuration parameters and test the selected X server. The Red

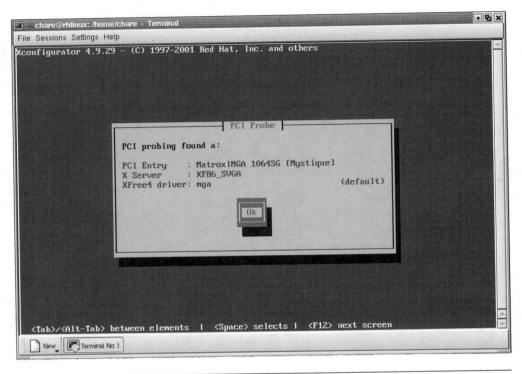

Figure 2-7   Xconfigurator main display

Hat and Debian versions of Xconfigurator do not start the server until sufficient information has been collected to select the appropriate server, and it is ready to test the configuration. Figure 2-7 illustrates the Red Hat Xconfigurator confirming the installed video hardware.

The XF86Setup and Xconfigurator tools are enhanced versions of xf86config, which is entirely text based, and less user friendly. The Xconfigurator program is an enhanced version of xf86config, which is entirely text based, as seen in Figure 2-8.

Each of the X Window configuration programs work through a series of configuration items including video hardware, monitor, mouse video resolution, and color depth as illustrated in Figure 2-9. With each new piece of information, the number of choices for the correct X server is reduced until there is really only one to try. Once the configuration program determines which is the best option, the user must test it to verify it works correctly.

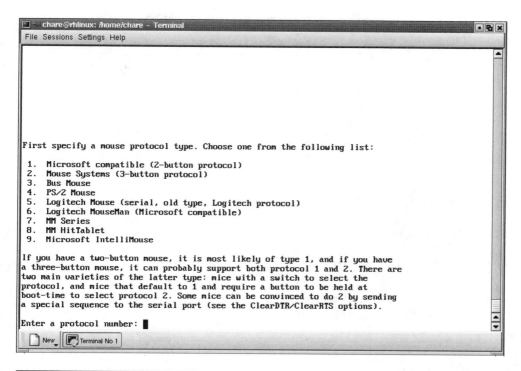

Figure 2-8   xf86config mouse selection

As previously discussed, monitor selection is a critical element to proper configuration of the X server. Most modern multisync monitors are capable of adjusting to almost any setting provided by the video card, so it is more difficult to damage the monitor. If you are not sure what your monitor is, or it is not listed, try the generic monitor type first. Then, try the monitors from your specific manufacturer. If necessary, you have to contact your manufacturer to determine the settings for your monitor to choose the best match from the supported list.

During the configuration process, some X configuration programs start a program called *xvidetune* to adjust the display settings to get the configuration correct, as seen in Figure 2-10. Xvidtune is not very user friendly, and although it is more difficult to damage your monitor, it is still possible using xvidtune inappropriately.

The X configuration programs assume the mouse is connected to /dev/mouse, which should be correct because it is normally defined when Linux is installed. If the configuration option is not correct, you may need to determine what port the mouse is connected to and create a link from that port to /dev/mouse.

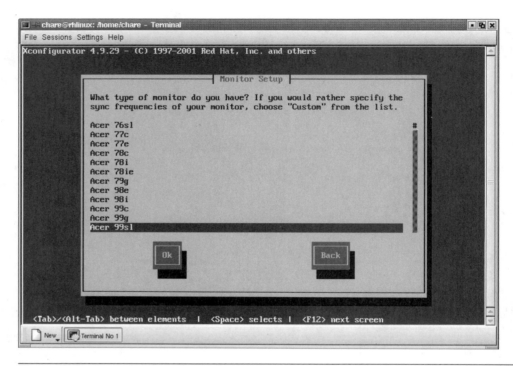

Figure 2-9 Example of monitor selection

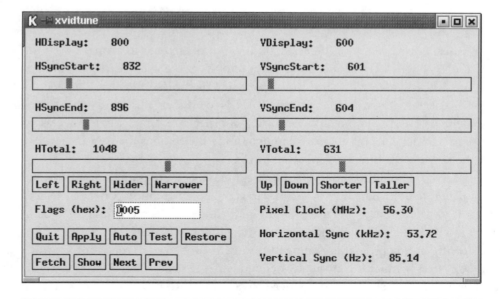

Figure 2-10 xvidtune display

The XF86Config File

The XF86Config file is located in /etc/X11 and is read by the X server during startup to get its configuration. The X server checks the following directories, looking for the XF86Config file:

- /usr/X11R6/etc/X11/<cmdline>
- /etc/X11/$XF86CONFIG
- /usr/X11R6/etc/X11/$XF86CONFIG
- /etc/X11/XF86Config-4
- /etc/X11/XF86Config
- /etc/XF86Config
- /usr/X11R6/etc/X11/XF86Config.<hostname>
- /usr/X11R6/etc/X11/XF86Config-4
- /usr/X11R6/etc/X11/XF86Config
- /usr/X11R6/lib/X11/XF86Config.<hostname>
- /usr/X11R6/lib/X11/XF86Config-4
- /usr/X11R6/lib/X11/XF86Config

Like other configuration files, the XF86Config file contains sections with specific configuration information relating to the server components. These sections are shown in Table 2-7.

Two additional sections, Keyboard and Pointer, may still be found in some configuration files. However, these sections are obsolete, and although still recognized for compatibility reasons, the InputDevice section is to be used instead.

Binding the input and output devices together in a session is accomplished by the server with the ServerLayout section. The input devices, including the keyboard and mouse, are defined in the InputDevices section. The distinct components that make up the output device, such as the graphics card and monitor, are described in the Device and Monitor sections, respectively. Binding the output devices is done in the Screen section, defining the resolution and color depth is referenced in the ScreenLayout section.

There is extensive documentation on the format and contents of the Xfconfig86 file in the Linux man pages. However, if you must make changes to the XF86Config file by hand, carefully review the documentation for the section you are going to change. It is not uncommon to find XF86Config files with more than 400 lines, although they are well commented for readability.

Table 2-7 XF86Config Sections

Files	File pathnames
ServerFlags	Server flags
Module	Dynamic module loading definitions
InputDevice	Input devices
Device	Graphics devices
VideoAdaptor	X video adapter
Monitor	Monitor description
Modes	Video mode descriptions
Screen	Screen configuration
ServerLayout	Overall layout
DRI	DRI-specific configuration
Vendor	Vendor-specific configuration

Displaying the fonts is performed by the X font server. The font server has traditionally be part of the X server itself; however, it is unbundled on some X servers such as Red Hat. Consequently, the XF86config file has a font server section defining the location of the fonts on the system, as illustrated in the following extract:

```
# Multiple FontPath entries are allowed (they are concatenated together)
# By default, Red Hat 6.0 and later now use a font server independent of
# the X server to render fonts.

 FontPath "unix/:7100"

EndSection
```

The FontPath directive indicates to the X server where to find the fonts on the system. It can contain a list of font directories or the instructions to connect to a font server that may or may not be on the same system. Font server specifications have the syntax:

```
<trans>/<hostname>:<port-number>
```

The trans component is either unix for Unix domain sockets or tcp for TCP connections. Hostname is the name of the server where the font server is running, and the port number is the network port to connect to, which is usually 7100. You can find the hostname of the system you are on by using the command **hostname**.

Looking at the specific example again

```
FontPath "unix/:7100"
```

tells us the connection is using Unix domain sockets as the transport. With no host-name to the left of the colon, the X server will attempt to contact the font server on the local system. The port number following the colon is the port to contact the font server. Using the font server on a different host would have an entry resembling

```
FontPath "unix/fontserver.mydomain.com:7100"
```

If there is no FontPath entry in your XF86Config file, the X server uses the default locations specified when the X server was built. These default locations are

- /usr/X11R6/lib/X11/fonts/misc/
- /usr/X11R6/lib/X11/fonts/Speedo/
- /usr/X11R6/lib/X11/fonts/Type1/
- /usr/X11R6/lib/X11/fonts/CID/
- /usr/X11R6/lib/X11/fonts/75dpi/
- /usr/X11R6/lib/X11/fonts/100dpi/

If you are going to configure a set of directories, the recommended list of font directories are

- /usr/X11R6/lib/X11/fonts/local/
- /usr/X11R6/lib/X11/fonts/misc/
- /usr/X11R6/lib/X11/fonts/75dpi/:unscaled
- /usr/X11R6/lib/X11/fonts/100dpi/:unscaled
- /usr/X11R6/lib/X11/fonts/Type1/
- /usr/X11R6/lib/X11/fonts/CID/
- /usr/X11R6/lib/X11/fonts/Speedo/
- /usr/X11R6/lib/X11/fonts/75dpi/
- /usr/X11R6/lib/X11/fonts/100dpi/

Any directory in the font path that does not exist or does not contain any fonts is automatically removed from the font path when the server starts up. As you add new directories with fonts, you must add them to the FontPath directive, or they are not used. However, if you are using the separate X font server as with Red Hat 6.0 and later, changes to XF86config do not affect the X font server.

The X font server is automatically started at system startup. The font server reads the configuration file found at /etc/X11/fs/config. A sample configuration file is shown in the following:

```
#
# Default font server configuration file for Red Hat Linux
#

# allow a max of 10 clients to connect to this font server
client-limit = 10

# when a font server reaches its limit, start up a new one
clone-self = on

# alternate font servers for clients to use
#alternate-servers = foo:7101,bar:7102

# where to look for fonts
#
catalogue = /usr/X11R6/lib/X11/fonts/misc:unscaled,
 /usr/X11R6/lib/X11/fonts/75dpi:unscaled,
 /usr/X11R6/lib/X11/fonts/100dpi:unscaled,
 /usr/X11R6/lib/X11/fonts/misc,
 /usr/X11R6/lib/X11/fonts/Type1,
 /usr/X11R6/lib/X11/fonts/Speedo,
 /usr/X11R6/lib/X11/fonts/75dpi,
 /usr/X11R6/lib/X11/fonts/100dpi,
 /usr/share/fonts/default/Type1,
 /usr/share/fonts/ja/TrueType

# in 12 points, decipoints
default-point-size = 120

# 100 x 100 and 75 x 75
default-resolutions = 75,75,100,100

# use lazy loading on 16 bit (usually Asian) fonts
deferglyphs = 16

# how to log errors
use-syslog = on

# don't listen to TCP ports by default for security reasons
no-listen = tcp
```

The catalogue keyword defines the directories where the font server looks for the font files and is analogous to the FontPath keyword in the XF86Config file. Consequently, if you make changes to the FontPath in XF86config, you should make the same changes to the catalogue keyword in the font server configuration file.

As mentioned, the font server is started at system startup as defined in the file /etc/nit.d/xfs. If you require additional information on the operation of the font server, consult the xfs man page.

Controlling X

The .Xresources file, if it exists, is found in the user's home directory and is not automatically created when a new user is added unless you modify the user creation scripts. This is not a major concern because each X client can have its own default configuration file to provide the same information.

.Xresources are issued to customize the appearance and behavior of an X client to suit a particular user. Each X client reads the .Xresources file from the user's home directory when it initializes and alters its configuration accordingly. The following extract from a .Xresources file shows how to modify the colors for an Xterm:

```
xterm_color*background: DarkBlue
xterm_color*foreground: Yellow
xterm_color*cursorColor: Orchid
xterm_color*reverseVideo: false
xterm_color*scrollBar: true
xterm_color*saveLines: 5000
xterm_color*reverseWrap: true
xterm_color*font: fixed
xterm_color.geometry: 80x25+20+20
xterm_color*fullCursor: true
xterm_color*scrollTtyOutput: off
xterm_color*scrollKey: on
xterm_color*VT100.Translations: #override\n\
 <KeyPress>Prior : scroll-back(1,page)\n\
 <KeyPress>Next : scroll-forw(1,page)
xterm_color*titleBar: false
```

Each entry in the .Xresources file is a directive altering how the client is displayed. Each line consists of the client name, an asterisk, the parameter name, a colon, and the new value.

As the user makes careful changes to their .Xresources file, the configuration can be modified on a per client basis. Once defined, other users on the system can use the same file by copying the .Xresources file to their home directory, by applying the changes to the client defaults as defined in the /usr/lib/X11/app-defaults directory.

Starting X

There are two methods to starting an X session. The first method is by logging into a text-based environment and having the user's shell startup files configure the environment and start the X session. The second is to use the graphical login facilities provided by XDM.

For the user to access the X server and related clients, the path /usr/lib/X11R6/bin must be in the user's *PATH* variable.

Starting the X session from the command line is done by invoking the command **startx**, which in turn calls the necessary programs to configure the environment and start the X server. Once the X server is initialized, it reads the .xinitrc file found in the user's home directory. If there is no .xinitrc file in the user's home directory, the system default, /usr/X11R6/lib/X11/xinit/xinitrc is processed.

A sample system xinitrc file contains the following commands:

```
xclock -geometry 100x100-5+5 &
xterm -geometry 80x50-50+150 &
if [ -f /usr/X11R6/bin/fvwm2 ]; then
exec fvwm2
else
exec twm
fi
```

This part of the xinitrc script starts two X clients, namely xclock and xterm, and then initializes the window manager, either fvwm2 or twm. Note that the window managers are started with the shell exec statement, which replaces the xinit process with the window manager. This approache causes the user to be logged out when they exit the window manager. When the window manager is terminated, the X server shuts down, and the getty process restarts for the next login.

There are several window managers available, of which twm and fvwm2 are only two. The window managers are discussed in more detail later in the chapter. The last command in the xinitrc file must be started using the shell exec statement and not started in the background. Should the window manager be started in the background, it causes the X server to exit once the clients are finished executing.

Using XDM

Aside from the text-based login and initiating the X Window session once the user logs in, another method is to use the X display manager, *XDM*. XDM provides a graphical login, collects the user's login name and passwords, authenticates the user, and then initiates the user's session.

XDM uses the XDM Control Protocol (XDMCP) to establish the login session. This process also enables remote X servers to connect to the system and establish an X Window session and connect to X clients. XDM itself is controlled by several configuration files as listed in Table 2-8.

Table 2-8 XDM Control Files

File	Purpose
Xaccess	How hosts can connect to this host
Xservers	Specify local and remote Xservers without XDMCP support
Xresources	Initial resources for Xlogin window
Xdm-config	Configuration file for XDM

Several files must be reviewed and edited to provide for XDM support for remote devices. All of the XDM files are located in /usr/lib/X11/xdm. If you want to enable XDM for only the graphical login on the console, the effort is minimal. The Xaccess file, shown in the following, controls how remote clients can access this host:

```
# $XConsortium: Xaccess,v 1.5 91/08/26 11:52:51 rws Exp $
#
# Access control file for XDMCP connections
#
# To control Direct and Broadcast access:
#
# pattern
#
# To control Indirect queries:
#
# pattern    list of hostnames and/or macros ...
#
# To use the chooser:
#
# pattern    CHOOSER BROADCAST
#
# or
#
# pattern    CHOOSER list of hostnames and/or macros ...
#
# To define macros:
#
# %name list of hosts ...
#
# The first form tells xdm which displays to respond to itself.
# The second form tells xdm to forward indirect queries from hosts matching
# the specified pattern to the indicated list of hosts.
# The third form tells xdm to handle indirect queries using the chooser;
# the chooser is directed to send its own queries out via the broadcast
# address and display the results on the terminal.
# The fourth form is similar to the third, except instead of using the
# broadcast address, it sends DirectQuerys to each of the hosts in the list
#
```

```
# In all cases, xdm uses the first entry which matches the terminal;
# for IndirectQuery messages only entries with right hand sides can
# match, for Direct and Broadcast Query messages, only entries without
# right hand sides can match.
#
# * #any host can get a login window
#
# To hardwire a specific terminal to a specific host, you can
# leave the terminal sending indirect queries to this host, and
# use an entry of the form:
#
#terminal-a host-a
#
# The nicest way to run the chooser is to just ask it to broadcast
# requests to the network - that way new hosts show up automatically.
# Sometimes, however, the chooser can't figure out how to broadcast,
# so this may not work in all environments.
#
* CHOOSER BROADCAST #any indirect host can get a chooser
#
# If you'd prefer to configure the set of hosts each terminal sees,
# then just uncomment these lines (and comment the CHOOSER line above)
# and edit the %hostlist line as appropriate
#
#%hostlist host-a host-b
#* CHOOSER %hostlist #
```

There are several methods of connecting to XDM available, although the most commonly used is the *chooser*. The chooser regularly broadcasts its availability on the network, enabling X terminals and other X servers to connect and establish an X session. The previous Xaccess listing indicates the chooser is available with the line

```
* CHOOSER BROADCAST #any indirect host can get a chooser
```

If you prefer to limit the hosts that can connect to XDM by commenting out the chooser BROADCAST line shown previously and using the line

```
#%hostlist host-a host-b
#* CHOOSER %hostlist #
```

and changing the *%hostlist* parameter in the preceding line to the hosts you wish to authorize connections to XDM. Both of these lines are commented by default, so you must remember to remove the comments as XDM is not capable of supporting both access methods. It is not necessary to edit the Xaccess file if you will not be allowing other hosts to connect—the default file is acceptable.

However, the Xaccess file on its own does not provide the console with a graphical login. Providing the graphical login requires the use of the Xservers file, also found in the /etc/X11/xdm directory. The Xservers file typically resembles

```
# $XConsortium: Xserv.ws.cpp,v 1.3 93/09/28 14:30:30 gildea Exp $
#
# Xservers file, workstation prototype
#
# This file should contain an entry to start the server on the
# local display; if you have more than one display (not screen),
# you can add entries to the list (one per line). If you also
# have some X terminals connected which do not support XDMCP,
# you can add them here as well. Each X terminal line should
# look like:
# XTerminalName:0 foreign
#
:0 local /usr/X11R6/bin/X
```

The last line in the previous Xservers file is what provides the graphical login on the console. By commenting out this line, the graphical login is replaced with the text-based login. If you are supporting remote Xservers, you will want to provide them with a login prompt. This is done by adding lines to the Xservers file for those devices capable of supporting XDMCP. Adding a line such as

```
remote-host:0    foreign
```

tells XDM to display the graphical interface for login on the remote device.

What the user actually sees is controlled by the /etc/X11/xdm/Xresources files, which is similar to the .Xresources file discussed earlier in the chapter. In this case, Xresources controls the login information presented to the user. Usually, there is no requirement to edit this file.

The last file used by XDM to configure the X interface is xdm-config. The following is an example:

```
! $XConsortium: xdm-conf.cpp /main/3 1996/01/15 15:17:26 gildea $
! $XFree86: xc/programs/xdm/config/xdm-conf.cpp,v 1.6 2000/01/31 19:33:43
dawes Exp $
DisplayManager.errorLogFile: /var/log/xdm-errors
DisplayManager.pidFile: /var/run/xdm-pid
DisplayManager.keyFile: /etc/X11/xdm/xdm-keys
DisplayManager.servers: /etc/X11/xdm/Xservers
DisplayManager.accessFile: /etc/X11/xdm/Xaccess
DisplayManager.willing: su nobody -c /etc/X11/xdm/Xwilling
! All displays should use authorization, but we cannot be sure
! X terminals will be configured that way, so by default
! use authorization only for local displays :0, :1, etc.
DisplayManager._0.authorize: true
DisplayManager._1.authorize: true
! The following three resources set up display :0 as the console.
DisplayManager._0.setup: /etc/X11/xdm/Xsetup_0
DisplayManager._0.startup: /etc/X11/xdm/GiveConsole
DisplayManager._0.reset: /etc/X11/xdm/TakeConsole
!
```

```
DisplayManager*resources: /etc/X11/xdm/Xresources
DisplayManager*session: /etc/X11/xdm/Xsession
DisplayManager*authComplain: false
! SECURITY: do not listen for XDMCP or Chooser requests
! Comment out this line if you want to manage X terminals with xdm
DisplayManager.requestPort: 0
```

Like other X configuration files, xdm-config alters the operation of XDM itself. If you are using the KDE interface to X, it is likely that KDM is managing the graphical login and not XDM, just to complicate things. If KDM is the display manager, you can change its behavior by editing the file /etc/X11/xdm/kdmrc, which is shown here:

```
# KDE Config File
[Desktop0]
BackgroundMode=VerticalGradient
BlendBalance=100
BlendMode=NoBlending
ChangeInterval=60
Color1=56,96,136
Color2=56,96,136
CurrentWallpaper=0
LastChange=0
MultiWallpaperMode=NoMulti
Pattern=
Program=
ReverseBlending=false
Wallpaper=
WallpaperList=
WallpaperMode=Tiled
[KDM]
GreetString=Red Hat Linux (HOSTNAME)
#Users=root,johndoe
NoUsers=adm,amanda,apache,bin,bind,daemon,exim,falken,ftp,games,gdm,gopher,
halt,http
d,ingres,kmem,lp,mail,mailnull,man,mta,news,nobody,nscd,operator,pop,postfix,
postgre
s,reboot,rpc,rpcuser,sendmail,shutdown,sync,tty,uucp,xfs,xten,ident,named
#ShowUsers=All/Selected/None
ShowUsers=None
#MinShowUID=1000
SortUsers=true
#ShutdownButton=All/ConsoleOnly/RootOnly/None
ShutdownButton=ConsoleOnly
FailFont=helvetica,12,5,0,75,0
GreetFont=charter,24,5,0,50,0
StdFont=helvetica,12,5,0,50,0
SessionTypes=default,kde,gnome,failsafe
#GUIStyle=KDE/Windows/Platinum/Motif/Motif+/CDE/SGI
GUIStyle=KDE
#LogoArea=KdmLogo/KdmClock/None
LogoArea=KdmLogo
#LogoPixmap=/dev/null
```

```
#EchoMode=NoEcho/OneStar/ThreeStars
EchoMode=OneStar
Restart=/sbin/reboot
Shutdown=/sbin/poweroff
ConsoleMode=/sbin/init 3
#AllowConsoleMode=false
#GreeterPosFixed=true
#GreeterPosX=200
#GreeterPosY=100
#AutoLoginEnable=false
#AutoLoginUser=fred
#AutoLogin1st=false
#NoPassEnable=false
#NoPassUsers=fred,ethel
#AutoReLogin=false
#ShowPrevious=false
#[Locale]
#Country=C
#Language=C
[Lilo]
Lilo=true
LiloCommand=/sbin/lilo
LiloMap=/boot/map
#Lilo=false
```

In this file, it is possible to change a number of things KDM displays, including the login banner. Other than this one configuration file, KDM works like and uses the same configuration files as XDM.

Choosing a Window Manager

The display component the user interacts with is commonly referred to as the *desktop*. However, using X Window terminology, this area is called a *screen*. The screen itself is composed of several components, namely the root window, which is the background of your screen, and the window manager, which provides the window interaction and management with the user.

The root window, or background, doesn't really behave like a window because you cannot resize it or adjust its position on the screen. However, it can be configured to display color and even pictures of various types. The window manager, as the mechanism of interacting with the window, provides all other controls, including the window title bars, window management commands, and the taskbar displayed on the bottom of the screen. Some window managers also provide virtual desktops, menus, icons, and many advanced customization features. Consequently, with so much of the X Window experience in the control of the window manager, it is virtually impossible to work in X without one.

Users generally interact with the window manager using the keyboard and mouse to select, manipulate, and move windows on the screen. Each window represents an X client, including the clock, the terminal, and the file manager as seen in Figure 2-11.

Window behavior is defined by the customizations applied by the window manager. Window selection, or focus, determines where the input provided by the user is processed. A window is focused if it is selected. The focused window is where keyboard input is directed. The unfocused window can continue to have new information written in the display, but the user cannot direct input there until it has been selected.

Selecting or focusing the window can be done in several ways, depending upon the window manager configuration. The first is to click in the desired window, and the second is to move the mouse pointer into the desired window. A third method, which is a carryover from Microsoft Windows, is to use the ALT+TAB key combination to select the desired window from a list. You can determine which is the active window by looking at the window title bar. If the title bar is colored or textured differently from the others, as in Figure 2-11, this is the active window.

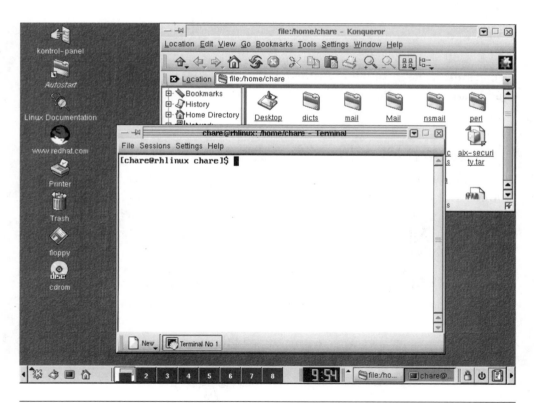

Figure 2-11   The Windows desktop

The window manager, as the definitive interface the user interacts with, affects your overall impression of the operating system. There are many die-hard Macintosh users in the world simply because of the user interface provided by the Macintosh window manager. Consequently, the more obscure the window manager that you choose is, the less likely you will be as productive as you can be and the more frustration you will experience as a user.

There are a wide variety of window managers available to the Linux community today. These include fvwm, twm, and kwm. Some window managers are part of an overall display management environment, such as GNOME or KDE, while others stand on their own, such as twm. Consequently, choosing an overall environment, such as GNOME or KDE, can add other benefits, as discussed later in the chapter.

Today, the fvwm and fvwm2 window managers are the most popular. The fvwm window manager is based upon the more cumbersome twm. Fvwm is easier to use than twm, consumes fewer system resources, and is considered more user friendly. However, the new standard window manager is fvwm2 and closely resembles the window manager made popular by Microsoft Windows 95 and 98.

fvwm2 will run in a 256-color display environment, which is something few other window managers will tolerate gracefully. Fvwm2 also provides dynamic menus and themes, so it can be made took almost exactly like Microsoft Windows 95 with little effort. Most of the window managers available on Linux are configured in the same way, and the idiosyncrasies of each window manager are not discussed here. Table 2-9 lists many of the window managers available for Linux.

The window manager's Web site is located at **www.PLiG.org/xwinman**. It provides more information about the latest window managers, enhancements, and features, while Linux implementations of these window managers can generally be found at **ftp://metalab.unc.edu/pub/Linux/X11/window-managers**.

Aside from the window manager in use, including support from a desktop environment, such as GNOME or KDE, provide additional enhancements including applications, games, and configuration tools for the system. Although some of these services will run under other environments and window managers, the overall functionality is reduced due to the dependency on the desktop environment.

Configuring the Window Manager

Each window manager is capable of various specific customizations, but all understand and interpret the .xinitrc file if it exists in the user's home directory. The global file /usr/lib/X11/xinit/xinitrc can be used to provide a consistent look and feel across all users who connect to the system. Many administrators who must use the .xinitrc file to provide user-specific customizations will test it in their home directory until it is the

Table 2-9 Window Managers

Name	Description
Fvwm	Highly extensible manager
Icewm	Window manager capable of emulating multiple environments, including OS/2
AmiWM	Amiga workbench window manager
Mlvwm	Macintosh-style window manager
Dfm	A desktop and file manager that resembles the OS/2 workplace shell
Olwm	Sun's Open Look Window Manager
Olvwm	Open Look Window manager with a virtual desktop
Mwm	Motif Window Manager from OSF
Window Maker	Provides a NextStep environment
AfterStep	A NextStep window manager
Enlightenment	The default window manager for the GNOME environment

way the user wants it. If desired, the .xinitrc file can then be copied to the system Xinitrc. Using the global file does not preclude the use of a .xinitrc file if so desired. However, if you have a large number of users to support, you do not want to be in a position of having to create one for each user!

Consider the following example .xinitrc:

```
#!/bin/sh
xsetroot -solid darkgreen
# start some basic applications
xclock -geometry 96x96+2+2 -bg grey40 -fg black -hl white &
xload -geometry 120x96+2+147 -bg grey40 -fg white -hl darkred -update 4 &
xterm -sb -ls -geom 80x25-2+2 -title "shell" &
xterm -sb -ls -geom 80x25-2-2 &

# start the window manager
exec /usr/X11R6/bin/twm
```

The success you have with this example depends upon the window managers on your system. Our discussion will focus on the twm window manager as it should exist on all Linux implementations. To see what window managers your system has installed, look in /usr/X11R6/bin/*wm*. If you don't have twm, you can select an alternate window manager.

As mentioned previously in the chapter, the .xinitrc is a shell script executed when the user runs the **startx** command. It starts the desired X clients and customizations. The last list line of the .xinitrc must always be the window manager, and it must start with the **exec** command or the X server exits once the window manager loads.

Figure 2-12 shows how the desktop looks after you've logged in and started X.

In Figure 2-12, the clients specified in the .xinitrc file are started, followed by the window manager. Because the .xinitrc file is a shell script, any valid shell command can be executed, enabling for specific customizations based upon the user or the system.

The X Window System geometry enables the user to place the client on the screen anywhere they desire. With most window managers, it is more guesswork to find the correct location than being able to get the location of the window from the window manager. However, once the location is determined, very precise settings can be achieved, because almost every X client responds to the geometry definitions.

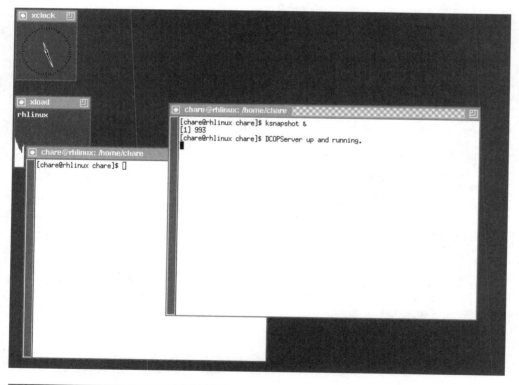

Figure 2-12   The desktop after running .xintrc

As mentioned before, each window manager has its own specific configuration settings, and as such, our discussion focuses on the twm window manager. Every window manager has a configuration file like system.mwrc or some similar named file which it uses to hold its configuration details. The twm window manager uses the file system.twmrc, which is found in /usr/lib/X11/twm. A sample system.twmrc file is shown in the following:

```
# $XConsortium: system.twmrc /main/9 1996/10/16 16:14:38 kaleb $
#
# Default twm configuration file; needs to be kept small to conserve string
# space in systems whose compilers don't handle medium-sized strings.
#
# Sites should tailor this file, providing any extra title buttons, menus,
etc.
# that may be appropriate for their environment. For example, if most of the
# users were accustomed to uwm, the defaults could be set up not to decorate
# any windows and to use meta-keys.
#
# $XFree86$
#

NoGrabServer
RestartPreviousState
DecorateTransients
TitleFont "-adobe-helvetica-bold-r-normal--*-120-*-*-*-*-*-*"
ResizeFont "-adobe-helvetica-bold-r-normal--*-120-*-*-*-*-*-*"
MenuFont "-adobe-helvetica-bold-r-normal--*-120-*-*-*-*-*-*"
IconFont "-adobe-helvetica-bold-r-normal--*-100-*-*-*-*-*-*"
IconManagerFont "-adobe-helvetica-bold-r-normal--*-100-*-*-*"
#ClientBorderWidth

Color
{
 BorderColor "slategrey"
 DefaultBackground "rgb:2/a/9"
 DefaultForeground "gray85"
 TitleBackground "rgb:2/a/9"
 TitleForeground "gray85"
 MenuBackground "rgb:2/a/9"
 MenuForeground "gray85"
 MenuTitleBackground "gray70"
 MenuTitleForeground "rgb:2/a/9"
 IconBackground "rgb:2/a/9"
 IconForeground "gray85"
 IconBorderColor "gray85"
 IconManagerBackground "rgb:2/a/9"
 IconManagerForeground "gray85"
}

#
# Define some useful functions for motion-based actions.
```

```
#
MoveDelta 3
Function "move-or-lower" { f.move f.deltastop f.lower }
Function "move-or-raise" { f.move f.deltastop f.raise }
Function "move-or-iconify" { f.move f.deltastop f.iconify }

#
# Set some useful bindings. Sort of uwm-ish, sort of simple-button-ish
#
Button1 = : root : f.menu "defops"

Button1 = m : window|icon : f.function "move-or-lower"
Button2 = m : window|icon : f.iconify
Button3 = m : window|icon : f.function "move-or-raise"

Button1 = : title : f.function "move-or-raise"
Button2 = : title : f.raiselower

Button1 = : icon : f.function "move-or-iconify"
Button2 = : icon : f.iconify

Button1 = : iconmgr : f.iconify
Button2 = : iconmgr : f.iconify

#
# And a menus with the usual things
#
menu "defops"
{
"Twm" f.title
"Iconify" f.iconify
"Resize" f.resize
"Move" f.move
"Raise" f.raise
"Lower" f.lower
"" f.nop
"Focus" f.focus
"Unfocus" f.unfocus
"Show Iconmgr" f.showiconmgr
"Hide Iconmgr" f.hideiconmgr
"" f.nop
"Xterm" f.exec "exec xterm &"
"" f.nop
"Kill" f.destroy
"Delete" f.delete
"" f.nop
"Restart" f.restart
"Exit" f.quit
}
```

The color section defines the colors used by the window manager. Colors are defined using either their name of the color definition, both of which are stored in the rgb.txt

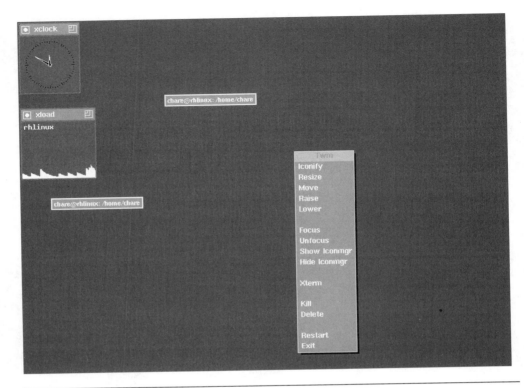

Figure 2-13 Default twm menu

file found in /usr/lib/X11. From Figure 2-13 and the BorderColor statement in the system.twmrc file, we see the color definition is slategrey. This can be changed to blue by changing the BorderColor line from

```
BorderColor "slategrey"
```

to

```
BorderColor "blue"
```

NOTE Using this approach, we can completely modify the color scheme of the window manager. Most window managers have a similar scheme, although newer implementations, such as fvwm2, KDE, and GNOME, have a simpler configuration approach.

It is also possible to specify the actual color definitions using the standard RGB syntax consisting of a one to four digit hexadecimal number. For example, the color blue in RGB notation is rgb:0/0/ffff or using the older syntax, #00000000ffff. The syntax to written in the system.twmrc file consists of

```
rgb:<red>/<green>/<blue>
```

With the ability to change the screen layout and color scheme, we can also change the window manager menu displayed when the user presses the left mouse button on the root window. The default twm menu is displayed in Figure 2-13.

The menu presented in Figure 2-13 is defined in the system.twmrc, where each menu item has a defined function or command to execute. Each menu item is defined using the format:

```
Menu-text Command
```

Command items beginning with the letter f are built-in functions and specify the command action to perform. A complete list of the available functions is available in the documentation specific to the window manager. For example, the f.exec function in the twm window manager enables a command external to the window manager to be executed, such as an X client. Using the f.menu item, nested menus can be created, increasing the functionality of the window manager itself.

For example, we can add a new menu item called clients to the root menu using the command

```
"Commands" f.menu "Clients"
```

in the system.twmrc. From there we can add a new menu listing the X clients we want to allow the user to execute. Now our menu sections in the system.twmrc look like

```
menu "defops"
{
"Twm" f.title
"Iconify" f.iconify
"Resize" f.resize
"Move" f.move
"Raise" f.raise
"Lower" f.lower
"" f.nop
"Focus" f.focus
"Unfocus" f.unfocus
"Show Iconmgr" f.showiconmgr
"Hide Iconmgr" f.hideiconmgr
"" f.nop
"Clients" f.menu "Clients"
"" f.nop
```

```
"Kill" f.destroy
"Delete" f.delete
"" f.nop
"Restart" f.restart
"Exit" f.quit
}
```

and the new client's menu definition as

```
Menu Clients
{
"Xterm" f.exec "exec xterm &"
"Snapshot" f.exec "exec ksnapshot &"
}
```

Finally, each user can create a file called .Xdefaults in their home directory used to store settings on an application-by-application basis. This enables the same settings to be applied each time the application is started. For example, if you want every xterminal to be started using a blue background and yellow text, you can execute the command

```
xterm -fg yellow -bg blue &
```

However, you must use this command each time you run an xterm. If you want the xterm to always be the same, you can add the lines

```
[root@mercury /root]# more .Xdefaults
xterm*foreground: yellow
xterm*background: blue
[root@mercury /root]#
```

In the future, all xterm clients will start using a yellow text on a blue background. Alternatively, you can edit the files found in /usr/lib/X11.app-defaults, which provides system-wide defaults for the various X clients. The typical X client configurations in /usr/lib/X11/app-defaults are

```
Beforelight Viewres Xedit Xloadimage Xpdf
Bitmap XCalc Xedit-color XLogo Xplaycd
Bitmap-color XCalc-color XF86Cfg XLogo-color Xplaymidi
Chooser XClipboard Xfd Xmag XscreenSaver
Clock-color XClock XFontSel Xman XSm
Editres XConsole Xgc Xmessage Xterm
Editres-color Xditview XISDNLoad XMixer XTerm-color
GV Xditview-chrtr XLoad XPaint Xvidtune
```

The appropriate app-defaults file is loaded before the .Xdefaults file in the user's home directory. Some of the app-defaults files are very complex, with the one of the largest being the configuration for the Xcalc application. If you wish your changes to apply to all users, modify the configuration in app-defaults, whereas the .Xdefaults file is used to configure changes for a specific user.

Kernel Construction

Building new kernels is not done on a daily basis as it is only required to provide support for features not available as modules and found directly in the kernel itself. Often new kernels have other improvements, including improved process and memory management, speed, and stability. A kernel reconfiguration does not always mean a complete new revision, but may only be a series of patches and updates to the existing kernel release.

Before embarking on a kernel installation, you should have a thorough knowledge of the system hardware and services required. A C compiler and the kernel development libraries, as required by your Linux vendor, are also required, in addition to the appropriate kernel source code as identified in the kernel development documentation. Generally, if you installed the kernel source code from your distribution CD, you have the necessary elements.

Obtaining the Kernel Source Code

Even if you are only adding a single new feature to your existing kernel, it may be appropriate to ensure you have the latest kernel release from your Linux vendor or direct from the kernel sources archive found at **ftp.funet.fi** or any number of locations that serve as Linux mirrors. The kernel software is typically named linux-x.y.z.tar.gz where x.y.z is the version number. The highest even number is the latest stable version, while the highest odd number is considered a test version. If you're expecting your system to be stable, for example on a production system, then don't use the latest odd-numbered kernel.

Once you have retrieved the new source code, you must unpack and install it. If you're not using new source code, this is already done, provided you installed the Linux kernel source code from your distribution CD.

The Linux Loader (LILO)

LILO enables Linux to coexist on your machine with other operating systems: up to 16 images can be swapped back and forth to designate what operating system is loaded on the next boot.

By default, LILO boots the default operating system each time, but you can enter the name of another operating system at the BOOT: prompt or force the prompt to appear by pressing SHIFT, CTRL, or ALT during the boot sequence. Entering a question mark (or pressing TAB) shows the available operating systems as defined in the /etc/lilo.conf file: this text file can range from simple to complex based upon the number of operating systems you have.

NOTE In order to boot your Linux system, you usually need to install LILO. During installation, you are given the option to install LILO in one of two places: In the Master Boot Record of the first sector of your rout partition.

The Master Boot Record (MBR)

This is the recommended place to install LILO, unless the MBR already starts another operating system loader, such as System Commander or OS/2's Boot Manager. The MBR is a special area on your hard drive that is automatically loaded by your computer's BIOS and is the earliest point at which LILO can take control of the boot process. If you install LILO in the MBR, when your machine boots, LILO will present a LILO: prompt. You can then boot Linux or any other operating system that you have configured LILO to boot.

The First Sector of Your Root Partition

This is recommended if you are already using another boot loader on your system (such as OS/2's Boot Manager). In this case, your other boot loader will take control first. You can then configure that boot loader to start LILO (which will then boot your flavor of Linux).

Installing Software

In the Linux community are several primary methods of software distribution. One is to use one of the package management systems, which we will look at later. The second is to use a tarball file. The tarball is a single compressed file containing a tar image of a set of files.

Using tar

Aside from the package management utilities, Linux provides several commands for backup management, including **tar** and **cpio**. **tar**, or tape archiver, reads a list of files and writes them to a single file. Because Linux makes no distinction between a device and a file, **tar** can be used to write to a device or another file on the disk. The syntax for it is

```
tar {options} {target_file} {source_files}
```

Both the target and source files can be a full pathname. **tar's** options include

c   Create a new tar image

d   Compare the target and source

f   Specify the output file

p   Maintain the file permissions

r   Append the new archive to an existing archive

t   Print the names of the files in the archive

u   Add only new files to the archive

v   Print additional information during the operation

x   Extract the files from a tar archive

z   Process the output through gzip or gunzip

For example, the command

```
tar cvf /dev/rmt0 {files}
```

creates a new tar archive, prints additional information during processing, and writes the archive to the tape device, /dev/rmt0.

The **cpio** command, **CoPy In, Out**, performs a similar function to **tar**. However, a distinction worth noting: **tar** will copy device files, those in /dev, and empty directories; **cpio** will not.

When using **cpio**, you must specify an action:

-i   Extract files from an archive

-o   Create or copy out to an archive

-p   Print the contents of the archive

Additional options change how **cpio** operates. It is not a requirement to use any additional options, but frequently, one or more of the following options are used in conjunction with the action:

d   Create directories as required

f   Indicate a file

t   Show the contents

u   Overwrite existing files

v   Print additional information during processing

For example, reading the data from a tape device, or file, is done using the command

```
cpio -iv < /dev/rmt0
```

cpio can also be used to copy files located in different directories on the filesystem. For example, to find all the files own by the user sql and copy them to a new directory, use the command

```
find / -owner sql | cpio -pdv /home/sql-files
```

You'll know you are working with a tarball or compressed tarball because the file name has a .tar or .tar.gz extension. For example,

```
program-1-2-3.tar.gz
program-1-2-3.tar
```

are tarballs. If a file is named

```
program-1.2.3.rpm
```

it is an RPM file. Tarballs are the preferred file format for downloading Linux software. When you've identified the software that you wish install, you'll need to obtain it from a provider. For example, to get tester from ftp.certificationcorner.org, use **ftp** as shown in the following:

```
ftp> bin
200 Type set to I.
ftp> get tester-2.4.tar.gz
local: tester-2.4.tar.gz remote: tester-2.4.tar.gz
227 Entering Passive Mode (192,190,237,102,12,145)
150 Opening BINARY mode data connection for tester-2.4.tar.gz
  (9293 bytes).
226 Transfer complete.
9293 bytes received in 0.207 secs (44 Kbytes/sec)
ftp>
```

This results in retrieving tester-2.4.tar.gz to your system. Next, you must uncompress and untar the file. You can do this in one or two steps. The traditional two-step approach involves uncompressing the file and then untarring the files. This is done using the commands

```
# gzip -d FILE
# tar xvf FILE
```

The first command uncompressed the file, and the second performed the extraction. Because tar files have been such a common way of distributing software, the GNU version of **tar** that's included with Linux uncompresses the archive and extracts the files in one step. This is done using the command

```
# tar zxvf FILE
```

The v option to **tar** lists all the files in the archive as they are extracted. If you prefer not to see the files listed, simply omit the v. The x informs **tar** to extract the files, while the f identifies the file to extract the files from

```
[root@mercury.technical root]# tar zxf tester*
[root@mercury.technical root]# ls -l
total 42
drwxr-xr-x 5 jholman jholman 1024 Nov 26 16:01 Desktop
-rw-r--r-- 1 104 bin 359 Aug 20 1994 Makefile
-r--r--r-- 1 104 bin 307 Apr 25 1994 READ.ME
-r--r--r-- 1 104 bin 10084 Apr 25 1994 Supertest.c
-rw-rw-r-- 1 root root 9293 Nov 26 16:22 tester-2.4.tar.gz
-r--r--r-- 1 104 bin 17883 Apr 25 1994 tester.c
[root@mercury.technical root]#
```

We have just extracted the files from the tarball. Tester is simple in that it comprises only a few files. We compile Tester using the **make** command. (Note that you must have the development tools installed to be able to compile any software on your system.) The **make** command relies upon a specification file to define what it needs to do. This is called a *makefile* and is illustrated in the following:

```
#
# Makefile for 'Pass the Tester' and 'Supertest' games
#

CC=gcc
CFLAGS=-g

all: tester Supertest

tester: tester.c
 $(CC) $(CFLAGS) tester.c -o tester
```

```
Supertest: Supertest.c
 #(CC) $(CFLAGS) Supertest.c -o Supertest

clean:
 rm -f tester tester.o Supertest Supertest.o TAGS

TAGS:
 etags tester.c

tar:
 tar -cvf tester.tar READ.ME Makefile tester.c Supertest.c
[root@mercury.technical tester]#
```

This is a very simple makefile, but it is suitable for our discussion. With the makefile, you may have to change parameters or options to get the program compiled on your environment. The makefile is structured with options, such as CC=gcc, and with objects such as all. The object all is dependent upon the objects tester and Supertest.

We can see that the object tester is dependent upon the object tester.c. This tells **make** that, to make the object all, it must first make the object tester. Compiling tester.c makes the object tester. **make** performs the same process on the other objects that all is dependent upon. The first object is typically the default. This means typing make with no argument results in make building all. Typing make tester results in make building only the components necessary to build tester:

```
[root@mercury.technical tester]# make
cc -g tester.c -o tester
cc -g Supertest.c -o Supertest
[root@mercury.technical tester]# ls -l
total 109
-rw-r--r-- 1 104 bin 359 Aug 20 1994 Makefile
-r--r--r-- 1 104 bin 307 Apr 25 1994 READ.ME
-rwxrwxr-x 1 root root 35127 Nov 26 16:25 Supertest
-r--r--r-- 1 104 bin 10084 Apr 25 1994 Supertest.c
-rwxrwxr-x 1 root root 31460 Nov 26 16:25 tester
-rw-rw-r-- 1 root root 9293 Nov 26 16:22 tester-2.4.tar.gz
-r--r--r-- 1 104 bin 17883 Apr 25 1994 tester.c
[root@mercury.technical tester]#
```

We can now test tester by running the compiled program:

```
[root@mercury.technical tester]# ./tester
INSTRUCTIONS (Y-N)
?y
RUN THE TESTER

ARE YOU PREPARED FOR THE TEST
TEST WILL TAKE APPROXIMATELY 1.5 HOURS

TEST OR QUIT (T OR Q) [T]
?
```

Typically, editing the makefile is required to alter parameters like the C compiler to be used, or the path specifications to find programs. You may have to edit the libraries included during the compile. However, more complex software no longer relies upon the user to edit the makefile, because there can be simply too many options to wrestle with, which have results in the development of configure. Looking at a more complex situation, we want to install the latest version of Perl (which we can download from **ftp.perl.org**):

```
ftp> bin
200 Type set to I.
ftp> get perl-5.6.0.tar.gz
local: perl-5.6.0.tar.gz remote: perl-5.6.0.tar.gz
227 Entering Passive Mode (209,85,3,25,12,163).
150 Opening BINARY mode data connection for perl-5.6.0.tar.gz
  (5443601 bytes).
226 Transfer complete.
5443601 bytes received in 148 secs (36 Kbytes/sec)
ftp>
```

We again uncompress and unpack

```
[root@mercury.technical root]# tar zxf perl*
```

This gives us a new directory: perl-5.6.0. In this directory, you'll find a command, **configure**. This script is common to many GNU utilities and configures the software for the environment:

```
[root@mercury.technical perl-5.6.0]# ls -l configure
-r-xr-xr-x 1 504 1001 346347 Mar 22 2000
 Configure
[root@mercury.technical perl-5.6.0]# ./Configure

Sources for perl5 found in "/home/jon1/perl-5.6.0".

Beginning of configuration questions for perl5.

Checking echo to see how to suppress newlines...
...using -n.
The star should be here-->*

First let's make sure your kit is complete. Checking...
Looks good...
This installation shell script will examine your system and ask
 you questions to determine how the perl5 package should be installed.
 If you get stuck on a question, you may use a ! shell escape to
 start a subshell or execute a command. Many of the questions will
 have default answers in square brackets; typing carriage return
 will give you the default.
```

```
On some of the questions which ask for file or directory names
 you are allowed to use the ~name construct to specify the login
 directory  belonging to "name",
even if you don't have a shell which knows about that.
 Questions where this is allowed will be marked "(~name ok)".

[Type carriage return to continue]
```

While figuring out the configuration of your system, the **configure** script prompts you to answer some questions. Once the questions are answered, you must run **make** to actually compile the software:

```
[root@mercury.technical perl-5.6.0]# make
'sh cflags libperl.a miniperlmain.o' miniperlmain.c
 CCCMD = cc -DPERL_CORE -c -fno-strict-aliasing -D_LARGEFILE_SOURCE -D
_FILE_OFFSET_BITS=64 -O2
...
[root@mercury.technical perl-5.6.0]#
```

Installation is accomplished using the **make install** command, which installs the binary and additional files into the places designated during the execution of **configure**.

Installing and Removing Software Using RPM

The simplest command to install new software using RPM is

```
rpm -i rpm-name.rpm
```

For example, to install the ftp client for Red Hat 7.1 **ftp-0.17-7.i386.rpm**, use the command:

```
# rpm -i ftp-0.17-7.i386.rpm
```

rpm reads the specified RPM file, extracts the files and installs them into the correct locations as defined in the RPM header. Any pre- or post-install scripts are also executed.

NOTE   Most software components are installed in the system directories and, therefore, the package must be installed by the root user.

Removing a package uses the –e, or erase, option:

```
rpm -e ftp-0.17-7.rpm
```

The previous install and remove commands expect the RPM file to be local to your system, either on the hard disk or a CD-ROM. However, one of the powerful features with rpm is its ability to download from the Internet and install the package. The RPM source file is not installed on your system. To install a package from an RPM on an FTP site, you must know the source path to the RPM file and enter it on the command line:

```
rpm -i ftp://ftp.site.com/pub/package-name.rpm
```

To use this remote installation feature, you must be connected to a network and have access to the remote site; otherwise, the connection will fail. **rpm** establishes a connection to the remote site and installs the package. The RPM is not transferred to your system.

rpm has an extensive array of options, which we will only examine the major sets. To see a complete list of options, use **rpm –help**, or check the documentation using the **man** command or in the /usr/doc directory.

Verifying a Package Using rpm

From time to time, files get accidentally erased on a running system, and no one notices until a command does not work right. The verification options in rpm can identify the packages that are installed, and what, if any, components of those packages are missing.

Verifying all the packages installed on the system is accomplished with the command

```
# rpm -Va
```

When verifying the installed packages, rpm compares the installed package information from the rpm database with the files actually installed on the system. The verification process checks the file size, MD5 checksum, permissions, file type, and the owner and group for each file. Every discrepancy identified is reported to the user.

Message Digest 5, commonly referred to as MD5, provides a highly reliable checksum, which can be used to validate the integrity of the file. If the MD5 checksums differ between the file on the disk and the file in the RPM package, the disk version has likely been modified.

Getting Information: RPM Query

The RPM file format structure provides the ability to query or extract information from the RPM file. The query facility can identify what package a given file belongs to and to even print information about the package.

To query the RPM database to determine what package a given file belongs to, use the options "-qf" to the **rpm** command and provide the filename:

```
[root@mercury.technical RPMS]# rpm -qf /sbin/insmod
modutils-2.3.14-3
[root@mercury.technical RPMS]#
```

In this case, the /sbin/insmod program is part of the modutils package.

The query option also prints information about the RPM file itself. The extent of the information printed through this facility is dependent upon the level of detail provided by the developer or distributor.

To retrieve the package information from the module, use the -qpi options to rpm. For example, to see the information for the <PACKAGE>, execute the command

```
[root@mercury.technical RPMS]# rpm -qpi ftp-0.17-7.i386.rpm
Name : ftp Relocations: (not relocatable)
Version : 0.17 Vendor: Red Hat, Inc.
Release : 7 Build Date: Sat 20 Jan 2001 06:10:06 PM EST
Install date: 07/16/01 Build Host: porky.devel.redhat.com
Group : Applications/Internet Source RPM: ftp-0.17-7.src.rpm
Size : 74617 License: BSD
Packager : Red Hat, Inc. http://bugzilla.redhat.com/bugzilla
Summary : The ftp package provides the standard UNIX command-line ftp
(File Transfer Protocol) for transferrong files over the internet and for
archiving files.
```

The -i option instructs rpm to list the information in the package, while the -l option lists the files in the package:

```
[root@mercury.technical RPMS]# rpm -qpl ftp-0.17-7.i386.rpm
/usr/bin/ftp
/usr/bin/pftp
/usr/share/man/man1/ftp.1.gz
/usr/share/man/man1/pftp.1.gz
/usr/share/man/man5/netrc.5.gz
  [root@mercury.technical RPMS]#
```

For many system administrators, they will not need to perform any additional work with RPM files. However, for some who will develop a tool and want to distribute it, a review of package construction using RPM is required.

Preparing to Build a Package Using RPM

Building a package with RPM can be as simple or as a complex as required for your unique situation. However, if you are working to build a package for a binary program, it is best if you can obtain the source code and build it yourself. This provides the maximum flexibility during the RPM construction process.

There are five major steps to build an RPM package:

1. Obtain the source code for the package if you don't already have it.

2. If required, construct a patch of the changes you made to the original source code.

3. Create an RPM spec file for the package.

4. Ensure all files are in their proper locations.

5. Create the RPM package.

The RPM spec file provides the specification on the package, including the instructions on how to build it and the list of files. You cannot build an RPM without a spec file. The spec file is named using the following convention:

```
Package name - version number - release number . spec
```

Using this format enables multiple versions of the same package to exist without conflicts (which would be tester-1.3-A.spec for our Tester example).

This enables multiple versions of the same package, and the spec file remains intact. Here is a sample spec file:

```
[root@mercury.technical tester]# more *.spec
summary: test the tester
Name: tester
Version: 1.3
Release: A
Copyright: GPL
Group: Exams
Source: http://a-URL-pointing-to-the-source
Patch:
Buildroot: /var/tmp/%name-buildroot

%description
This is an implementation of the RHCE Linux exam, tester.

%prep
%setup -q
%patch -p1 -b .buildroot

%build
make RPM_OPT_FLAGS="$RPM_OPT_FLAGS"

%install
rm -rf $RPM_BUILD_ROOT
mkdir -p $RPM_BUILD_ROOT/usr/local/exams
mkdir -p $RPM_BUILD_ROOT/usr/man/man1

install -s -m 755 eject $RPM_BUILD_ROOT/usr/local/exams/tester
```

```
%clean
rm -rf $RPM_BUILD_ROOT

%files
%defattr(-,root,root)
%doc README TODO COPYING ChangeLog

/usr/local/exams/tester

%changelog
* Sat Dec 2 15:24:30 EST 2000 Jon Holman root_mts@hotmail.com
- created RPM from tester tarball
[root@mercury.technical tester]#
```

The space files have a consistent structure as explained in Table 2-10. Aside from the header, the %prep section, as listed in Table 2-11, contains the macros used in the compilation and setup of the package.

All commands in the %prep section, including the %setup and %patch macros, are executing the shell. The %build section doesn't really have any macros, but is used to provide the commands to actually build the software. This section should include the

Table 2-10   RPM Headers

Section	Description
Summary	A one-line description of the package.
Name	This is the name of the package you are creating. It must be the same as the filename you are using for your package.
Version	This is the version of your RPM. It must match the version included in the filename.
Release	The release number for packages of the same version.
Copyright	This describes the copyright type, namely GPL, BSD, MIT, public domain, distributable, or commercial.
Group	This identifies the group the package belongs to.
Source	This is the HOME location of the original source file. This is used if you want the source again or want to check for a newer version.
Patch	The location of the patch file.
Buildroot	This is the root directory for building and installing the new package. This can be used to test the new package by installing it on your system.
%description	This is a multilane field used to give a comprehensive description of the package.

Table 2-11 %Prep Macros

Macro name	Description
%setup	Defines the process to unpack the source and enter the directory tree. Using the -q option sets the name of the directory tree to the value set by %name.
%patch	This macro applies the patches to the source.

appropriate commands to extract the source and apply relevant patches if required. Any legal shell commands can be executed here as the shell processed the commands in the %build section.

The next step in the process is installation. The %install section contains the commands required to install the software, which are executed by the shell. If a makefile is used to build the software, a make install section can added to the makefile using a patch, or the appropriate commands can be included by hand.

The final section is the %clean macro. This is used in the spec file to provide a clean source tree for the build. It is important to verify the directory prior to executing commands, as the imprudent package maintainer could remove their entire Linux distribution by executing the wrong commands as root in the / directory.

The %changelog section identifies the changes for each version and release of the package. Each change starts with a * and includes the date and time and the maintainer's e-mail address. The remainder of the text area is freeform, but should be written to provide some form of readability.

Once the spec file has been defined, the package is ready to build.

Building a Package Using RPM

The build tree is typically defined in /etc/rpmrc or /usr/slib/rpm/rpmrc and can be modified by the package maintainer to suit their particular requirements. Most people use the /usr/src directory to construct and build their packages. If necessary, you may need to create some directories for your package construction:

- **BUILD**   Where the package is built
- **SOURCE**   The location of the source files
- **SPECS**   The location of the spec files
- **RPMS**   The location of the assembled binary RPM files
- **SRPMS**   The location of the source RPM files

With the directory tree assembled, compile the source code and review it for the file it creates and installs, their locations, and what additional commands were necessary to compile them, such as create a patch or enter additional commands. Using the spec file, you are now ready to build the package using the command

```
# rpm -ba filename.spec
```

rpm then creates the source and binary RPM files using the definitions in the spec file. The best method of testing the newly created RPM is to install it on a different system. Because you have just installed it on your own system, it will be difficult to test that the build and resulting RPM files were in fact properly constructed. If you missed a file in your build process, you will not know by testing it on your system.

As the package maintainer, you will be using the command

```
# rpm -ba package-name
```

However, the people installing your package will be executing

```
# rpm -i package name
```

Consequently, it is very important to include all the steps required to construct the package. In the event you want to distribute your package to other users, you can then upload it to an Internet site such as **ftp.redhat.com**.

Using the Debian Package Management System

The Debian package management system is very different from that used by Red Hat and other Linux distributions. The Debian system uses a facility called dpkg. The dpkg man page is vague enough that is states, "this man page should not be used by package maintainers wishing to understand how **dpkg** will install their packages." Other references for information on dpkg and how to use its construct packages are provided for the reader.

The primary method for package management is through dselect, which in turn uses dpkg to execute the actual commands. Dselect provides user-friendly interface, while dpkg is an entirely command line based tool. Dpkg actions consist of one action and zero or more options to define what dpkg is to do and how to do it.

Dpkg maintains information about the installed packages, much like RPM does. However, the information maintained consists of the package state, selection states, and flags, each modified using dselect.

Table 2-12   Debian Package States

Package state	Description
Installed	The package is fully installed and configured.
Half-installed	The installation has been started, but not completed.
Not-installed	The package is not installed.
Unpacked	The package has been unpacked, but not yet installed.
Half-configured	The package is unpacked, but configuration and installation has not been completed.
Config-files	The configuration files are the only component from the package found on the system.

Dselect and dpkg states indicate if the package is installed or not, as outlined in Table 2-12.

Although dselect is not required to install a package, many people use it over the command line interface of dpkg. Dpkg uses the command

```
# dpkg -i | --install package_file
```

to install the software associated with the named package. For example, installing the ftp package from the distribution is done using the command

```
# dpkg wu-ftpd_2.6.0-5.1.deb
```

The naming convention of Debian packages is similar to the RPM format, using the syntax

```
package name-package version-deb version.deb
```

dpkg also enables multiple versions of the package to exist on the system. Installation of any package consists of the same steps:

1. Extract the files from the package.

2. If you are replacing an existing package, run the prerm script from the old package.

3. If the new package provides one, run the preinst script.

Table 2-13 Example **dpkg** Commands

Command Example	Function
Dpkg -i package.deb	Installs the package named package.deb.
Dpkg -I package.deb	Shows information about the package named package.deb (rpm -qpi).
Dpkg -c package.deb	Lists the files in package.deb (rpm -qpl).
Dpkg -l	Shows all installed packages.
Dpkg -r package-name	Removes the named package from the system. (The name used is the name shown in the output of by dpkg -l.)

It is important to run the prerm script prior to removing the old package version, and the preinst script if provided by the new package. Table 2-13 shows several **dpkg** command examples.

The Debian packages are prioritized to determine the need for the package in the operating system. The priorities are

- **Required** The package must be installed for the system to operate properly.

- **Important** The package is typically found on all Unix systems.

- **Standard** The package is part of the text-based Debian system.

- **Optional** Additional components not required for the operation of the system. Includes utilities such as the X Window System.

- **Extra** The package is for a small group of people, are interest-specific, or specialized in nature. They are not required for system operation.

Installing and Removing Packages Using Debian

In the following example, we want to install the package n_news2.2000.01.31-4.deb:

```
debian:/cdrom/dists/potato/main/binary-i386/news# dpkg -i
n_news2_2.2000*.deb
Selecting previously deselected package n_news2.
(Reading database ... 31440 files and directories currently installed.)
Unpacking n_news (from n_news_2.2.2000.01.31-4.deb) ...
dpkg: dependency problems prevent configuration of n_news:
 n_news depends on n_news-inews; however:
 Package n_news-inews is not installed.
dpkg: error processing n_news (--install):
 dependency problems - leaving unconfigured
```

```
Errors were encountered while processing:
 n_news
debian:/cdrom/dists/potato/main/binary-i386/news#
```

This output reports that a dependency error was encountered while executing the **dpkg** command. This means that the packages that this one depends upon must be installed before n_news can be installed:

```
debian:/cdrom/dists/potato/main/binary-i386/news# dpkg -i n_news-inews*
Selecting previously deselected package n_news-inews.
(Reading database ... 31670 files and directories currently installed.)
Unpacking n_news-inews (from n_news-inews_2.2000.01.31-4.deb) ...
Setting up n_news-inews (2.2000.01.31-4) ...

debian:/cdrom/dists/potato/main/binary-i386/news#
```

With the dependent package installed, we can execute the same command with the desired package again:

```
debian:/cdrom/dists/potato/main/binary-i386/news# dpkg -i n_news_2.2*.deb

(Reading database ... 31685 files and directories currently installed.)
Preparing to replace n_news 2.2000.01.31-4 (using n_news_2.2000.01.31-4.deb)
...
Unpacking replacement n_news ...
Setting up n_news (2.2000.01.31-4) ...
installing initial content for /var/lib/news/active
installing initial content for /var/lib/news/newsgroups
building history database in /var/lib/news...
mv: history.n.hash: No such file or directory
mv: history.n.index: No such file or directory
chown: history*: No such file or directory
chmod: history*: No such file or directory
done
Starting innd.
Scheduled start of /usr/lib/news/bin/innwatch.

debian:/cdrom/dists/potato/main/binary-i386/news#
```

Removing packages is also performed with the **dpkg** command using the -r option. However, we frequently do not know the exact name of the package we wish to remove, and so we must use the **dpkg –l** command to determine the package names:

```
debian:/cdrom/dists/potato/main/binary-i386/news# dpkg -l | more
Desired=Unknown/Install/Remove/Purge/Hold
| Status=Not/Installed/Config-files/Unpacked/Failed-config/Half-installed
|/ Err?=(none)/Hold/Reinst-required/X=both-problems (Status,Err:
uppercase=bad)
||/ Name Version Description
+++-==============-==============-
==========================================
```

```
ii adduser 3.11.1 Add users and groups to the system.
ii ae 962-26 Anthony's Editor -- a tiny full-screen editor
ii anacron 2.1-5.1 a cron-like program that doesn't go by time
ii apmd 3.0final-1 Utilities for Advanced Power Management (APM
ii apt 0.3.19 Advanced front-end for dpkg
ii at 3.1.8-10 Delayed job execution and batch processing
--More--
```

However, the large number of packages makes it difficult to find the ones you are looking for. You can search for the desired packages by sending the output of **dkpg -l** into **grep** to search for the packages:

```
debian:/cdrom/dists/potato/main/binary-i386/news# dpkg -l | grep inn
ii n_news 2.2000.01. News transport system 'InterNetNews' by the
ii n_news-inews 2.2000.01. NNTP client news injector, from InterNetNews
debian:/cdrom/dists/potato/main/binary-i386/news#
```

Once you've located the desired packages, use the **dpkg -r** command to remove them:

```
debian:/cdrom/dists/potato/main/binary-i386/news# dpkg -r n_news
(Reading database ... 31685 files and directories currently installed.)
Removing n_news ...
Stopping news server: innd
dpkg - warning: while removing n_news, directory '/var/log/news' not empty
so not removed.
dpkg - warning: while removing n_news, directory '/var/lib/news' not empty
so not removed.
dpkg - warning: while removing n_news, directory '/var/run/news' not empty
so not removed.
dpkg - warning: while removing n_news, directory
'/usr/lib/news/bin/rnews.libexec'
 not empty so not removed.
dpkg - warning: while removing n_news, directory '/usr/lib/news/bin/filter'
not empty so not removed.
dpkg - warning: while removing n_news, directory
'/usr/lib/news/bin/control' not empty so not removed.
dpkg - warning: while removing n_news, directory '/usr/lib/news/bin' not
empty so not removed.
dpkg - warning: while removing n_news, directory '/usr/lib/news' not empty
so not removed.
debian:/cdrom/dists/potato/main/binary-i386/news#
```

In the output of **dpkg -r**, directories that aren't empty aren't removed. These directories typically contain files that are created by the application and that hold important data that should not be arbitrarily erased. If the data isn't required, you'll need to remove the directories manually.

Querying Packages Using Debian

Aside from querying for the installed packages, **dpkg** is also used to list the files in a specific package. This is accomplished with the **dpkg –c** command as illustrated here:

```
debian:/cdrom/dists/potato/main/binary-i386/news# dpkg -c n_news_2* | more
drwxr-xr-x root/root 0 2000-05-27 01:56:08 ./
drwxr-xr-x root/root 0 2000-05-27 01:56:10 ./etc/
drwxr-sr-x news/news 0 2000-05-27 01:56:08 ./etc/news/
-rw-r--r-- news/news 5018 2000-05-27 01:56:02 ./etc/news/newsfeeds
-rw-r----- news/news 5145 2000-05-27 01:56:02 ./etc/news/incoming.conf
-rw-r----- news/news 1017 2000-05-27 01:56:02 ./etc/news/nnrp.access
-rw-r----- news/news 516 2000-05-27 01:56:02 ./etc/news/nnrpd.track
--More--
```

As seen in this example, the **dpkg –c** command is used to list the files in the package, not the files installed on the system as part of the package. The **dpkg** command has an additional argument to query information about the package itself. The **dpkg –I** command prints information about the package including the section of the Debian system, the version number, and any package dependencies that exist. It also identifies the package maintainer and prints a description of what the package is for:

```
debian:/cdrom/dists/potato/main/binary-i386/sound# dpkg -I esound_0*.deb
 new debian package, version 2.0.
 size 48692 bytes: control archive= 1053 bytes.
 422 bytes, 11 lines control
 701 bytes, 13 lines md5sums
 249 bytes, 8 lines * postinst #!/bin/sh
 190 bytes, 6 lines * prerm #!/bin/sh
 Package: esound
 Version: 0.2.17-7
 Section: sound
 Priority: optional
 Architecture: i386
 Depends: libaudiofile0, libc6 (>= 2.1.2), libesd0 (>= 0.2.16) | libesd-
alsa0 (>
= 0.2.16), esound-common
 Installed-Size: 132
 Maintainer: Brian M. Almeida bma@debian.org
 Description: Enlightened Sound Daemon - Support binaries
 This program is designed to mix together several digitized
 audio streams for playback by a single device.
debian:/cdrom/dists/potato/main/binary-i386/sound#
```

As a command-line utility, **dpkg** is accepted as more difficult to use than **rpm**. Consequently, dselect was developed to provide a curses-based front-end interface. The dselect menu commands are

- **Access**   Select the method to obtain and install the select packages.
- **Update**   Using the package database, create a list of updates applicable to your system.
- **Select**   Select the package.
- **Install**   Process and install all selected packages.

Through the access option, one of several access methods is available to the administrator. These include FTP, HTTP, floppy diskette, CD-ROM, and NFS. The access method depends upon where the packages to install are located.

The update option checks the currently installed packages against a list of new packages when used with an access method of HTTP and FTP. A new package list is retrieved, and a list of applicable updates is compiled. The administrator can then select the desired packages for installation.

The administrator selects the packages to process using the select option; however, no action is taken using this function itself. Pressing the ENTER key selects the desired package. Dselect then performs a dependency check, determining if there are other packages that must be installed. The **dpkg** command, if used directly, reports the dependency problem, but performs no other actions.

Once the packages are installed, selecting the install option causes dselect to execute the appropriate commands to load and configure the selected packages. Once the packages are installed, selecting Quit exists dselect and returns the administrator to the command line.

Related Boot Files and Utilities

You should be aware of a few other files and utilities before walking through a boot. The first of these is the **dmesg** utility, which enables you to display bootup messages generated from LILO (in /var/log/messages). By default, when you type in **dmesg**, the messages are displayed on your screen. If you encounter a problem, however, and you want to save the messages for troubleshooting purposes, you can use the command

```
dmesg > {filename}
```

It generates a file similar to the following:

```
Linux version 2.2.10 (root@tuvok.calderasystems.com)
  (gcc version egcs-2.91.66 20000104 (egcs-1.1.2 release)) _
#1 SMP Tue Aug 10 19:01:45 MDT 2000
mapped APIC to ffffe000 (0024f000)
mapped IOAPIC to ffffd000 (00250000)
Detected 150004465 Hz processor.
Console: colour VGA+ 80x30
Calibrating delay loop... 299.01 BogoMIPS
Memory: 30692k/32768k available (920k kernel code,
  416k reserved, 652k data, 88k init)
VFS: Diskquotas version dquot_6.4.0 initialized
Checking 386/387 coupling... OK, FPU using exception
  16 error reporting
Checking 'hlt' instruction... OK.
Intel Pentium with F0 0F bug - workaround enabled.
POSIX conformance testing by UNIFIX
per-CPU timeslice cutoff: 1.56 usecs.
CPU0: Intel Pentium MMX stepping 04
SMP motherboard not detected. Using dummy APIC emulation.
PCI: PCI BIOS revision 2.10 entry at 0xf0200
PCI: Using configuration type 1
PCI: Probing PCI hardware
Linux NET4.0 for Linux 2.2
Based upon Swansea University Computer Society NET3.039
NET4: Unix domain sockets 1.0 for Linux NET4.0.
NET4: Linux TCP/IP 1.0 for NET4.0
IP Protocols: ICMP, UDP, TCP, IGMP
|Initializing RT netlink socket
Starting kswapd v 1.5
vesafb: framebuffer at 0x000a0000, mapped to 0xc00a0000,
  size 128k
vesafb: mode is 640x480x4, linelength=80, pages=50719
vesafb: scrolling: redraw
Console: switching to colour frame buffer device 80x30
fb0: VESA VGA frame buffer device
Detected PS/2 Mouse Port.
Serial driver version 4.27 with no serial options enabled
ttyS00 at 0x03f8 (irq = 4) is a 16550A
pty: 256 Unix98 ptys configured
Real Time Clock Driver v1.09
RAM disk driver initialized: 16 RAM disks of 4096K size
PCI_IDE: unknown IDE controller on PCI bus 00 device 11,
  VID=10b9, DID=5219
PCI_IDE: not 100% native mode: will probe irqs later
PCI_IDE: simplex device: DMA disabled
ide0: PCI_IDE Bus-Master DMA disabled (BIOS)
PCI_IDE: simplex device: DMA disabled
ide1: PCI_IDE Bus-Master DMA disabled (BIOS)
hda: IBM-DTNA-22160, ATA DISK drive
hdc: UJDCD8730, ATAPI CDROM drive
```

```
ide0 at 0x1f0-0x1f7,0x3f6 on irq 14
ide1 at 0x170-0x177,0x376 on irq 15
hda: IBM-DTNA-22160, 2067MB w/96kB Cache, CHS=525/128/63
hdc: ATAPI 8X CD-ROM drive, 128kB Cache
Uniform CDROM driver Revision: 2.55
Floppy drive(s): fd0 is 1.44M
FDC 0 is a National Semiconductor PC87306
md driver 0.90.0 MAX_MD_DEVS=256, MAX_REAL=12
raid5: measuring checksumming speed
raid5: MMX detected, trying high-speed MMX checksum routines
pII_mmx : 229.362 MB/sec
p5_mmx : 275.844 MB/sec
8regs : 112.776 MB/sec
32regs : 76.200 MB/sec
using fastest function: p5_mmx (275.844 MB/sec)
md.c: sizeof(mdp_super_t) = 4096
Partition check:
hda: hda1 hda2
VFS: Mounted root (ext2 filesystem) readonly.
Freeing unused kernel memory: 88k freed
parport0: PC-style at 0x378 [SPP,PS2]
Linux PCMCIA Card Services 3.0.14
kernel build: 2.2.10 #1 SMP Thu Aug 5 20:42:02 MDT 1999
options: [pci] [cardbus]
Intel PCIC probe:
TI 1131 PCI-to-CardBus at bus 0 slot 4, mem 0x68000000,
 2 sockets
host opts [0]: [isa irq] [no pci irq] [lat 32/176] [bus 32/34]
host opts [1]: [isa irq] [no pci irq] [lat 32/176] [bus 35/37]
ISA irqs (scanned) = 5,7,10,11,12 status change on irq 11
cs: IO port probe 0x1000-0x17ff: clean.
cs: IO port probe 0x0100-0x04ff: excluding 0x178-0x17f
 0x378-0x37f 0x408-0x40f 0x480-0x48f 0x4d0-0x4d7
cs: IO port probe 0x0a00-0x0aff: clean.
VFS: Disk change detected on device fd(2,0)
```

Notice the order of operations as the system comes up. Other files to be aware of are

- /var/log/messages

- /etc/conf.modules

- /etc/modules.conf

- utmp

- wtmp

cron and other processes write messages to the first file that can be useful in troubleshooting problems. Some of the contents of this file are displayed by the **dmesg** command. The second and third files differ according to the vendor, but are one and the same.

NOTE   Some systems use conf.modules, and others use modules.conf.

This file holds information used by the kernel to identify the machine. The file is a C++ source file and usually not accessed by administrators unless corruption has occurred.

I mentioned the utmp and wtmp files earlier in the chapter. They are log files that are counterparts of each other and exist in either /etc or elsewhere. If elsewhere, then utmp is beneath /var/run, and wtmp is beneath /var/log. By default, when the system starts, entries are written to utmp; when the system is properly shutdown, entries are written to wtmp.

You can use the **last** command to look at the most recent entries in wtmp— showing users and system state changes:

```
# last
root pts/0 Mon Oct 9 14:58 still logged in
root :0 Mon Oct 9 14:21 still logged in
reboot system boot 2.2.10 Mon Oct 9 14:15 (03:01)
root pts/1 Mon Oct 9 11:35 - down (02:15)
root pts/0 Mon Oct 9 11:35 - down (02:15)
root :0 Mon Oct 9 11:34 - down (02:16)
reboot system boot 2.2.10 Mon Oct 9 11:33 (02:16)
root pts/0 Tue Oct 3 11:18 - crash (6+00:15)
root :0 Mon Oct 2 16:31 - 11:28 (6+18:56)
reboot system boot 2.2.10 Mon Oct 2 16:23 (6+21:26)
root :0 Mon Sep 25 16:32 - 17:20 (00:48)
reboot system boot 2.2.10 Mon Sep 25 16:29 (00:51)
root :0 Mon Sep 25 16:18 - 16:25 (00:06)
reboot system boot 2.2.10 Mon Sep 25 16:06 (00:18)

wtmp begins Mon Sep 25 16:06:45 2000
```

Putting It All Together

Having looked at different elements of the boot, you can put it all together and run through the steps of a boot from start to finish:

1. When any machine starts, it first performs a power-on self test (POST) to verify that all is internally present that should be. This occurs regardless of operating system.

2. The boot loader for the operating system begins. With Linux, that is LILO. By default, it waits 50 deciseconds (five seconds) for you to press a key and identify

another operating system you want to boot. If you press no key, the default of Linux is loaded.

3. The kernel is loaded from the hard drive, floppy drive, or other specified location into memory. By default, it is located within the /boot directory and exists in compressed state. As it loads into memory, it uncompresses.

4. The kernel is booted, and messages are written to /var/log/messages.

5. The system loads modules, defaults, and others from /etc/modules.conf or /etc/conf.modules.

6. The kernel passes control to the **init** daemon, which begins reading the /etc/inittab file. Because of this, the **init** daemon always has a process ID of 1 and is the parent of many other daemons.

7. Normally, a check of the filesystem (**fsck**) is carried out, and the local filesystem is mounted. Other operations can include mounting remote filesystems and cleaning up temporary files.

8. The system begins changing to the runlevel specified by the *initdefault* parameter. In so doing, it runs scripts beneath the /etc/rc.d directory and usually starts other processes or daemons, such as a print server, **cron**, **sendmail**, and so on.

9. The terminals become active for login (getty has initiated), and the boot process is finished.

Chapter Summary

In this chapter, we covered Domain 2.0 for the Linux+ exam according to CompTIA. This domain relies heavily on the newer Linux distributions ability to walk the user through the installation. The install script usually configures the X server and will set parameters for windows managers. We also gave you the commands that the install script runs so you may become adept at using them should the occasion arise. We looked at package management and manipulated packages from different vendors.

Questions

1. What does the **dmesg** utility provide?
   a. Messages created at boot time by the system
   b. A way to send messages across the network
   c. Instant Message capabilities for the Internet
   d. Messages about failed daemons and processes

2. Which Internet protocol provides echo request and echo reply queries?
   a. ARP
   b. IP
   c. IGMP
   d. ICMP

3. Which layer of the IP protocol suite communicates with the physical network?
   a. Application
   b. Transport
   c. Internet
   d. Network interface

4. The ARP protocol _____.
   a. Routes traffic across the network
   b. Translates IP addresses to physical network addresses
   c. Transfers data from one system another
   d. Pings network devices

5. At which port does FTP operate?
   a. 23
   b. 110
   c. 25
   d. 21

6. What is the simplest way to install new software using RPM?
   a. rpm -i rpm-name.rpm
   b. rpm -e rpm-name.i386.rpm
   c. rpm -q rpm-name.1386.rpm
   d. rpm -ivh rpm-name.i386.rpm

7. The command **hostname** _____.
   a. Prints the name of the host
   b. Prints the domain name for the host
   c. Configures the network card
   d. Starts a telnet session

8. The file /etc/services maps
   a. Hostnames to IP addresses
   b. IP to RPC ports
   c. Service names to port numbers
   d. Network names to network addresses

9. I want to set the configuration for the xload application to display with specific colors. Which file do I edit?
   a. /etc/profile
   b. .Xdefaults
   c. /etc/inittab
   d. /usr/lib/X11/rgb.txt

10. Which file is used to configure the window manager?
    a. .xinitrc
    b. system.wmrc
    c. .Xdefaults
    d. startx

Answers

1. **A.** Messages created at boot time by the system are displayed by **dmesg**.

2. **D.** The ICMP Internet protocol provides echo request and echo reply queries.

3. **D.** The Network interface layer of the IP protocol suite communicates with the physical network.

4. **B.** The ARP protocol translates IP addresses to physical network addresses.

5. **D.** FTP operates at port 21.

6. **A.** rpm -i rpm-name.rpm is the simplest way to install an RPM software package.

7. **A.** The hostname command prints the name of the host.

8. **C.** The file /etc/service maps service names to TCP port numbers.

9. **B.** Edit the .Xdefaults file if you want to set the configuration for the xload application to display with specific colors.

10. **B.** system.wmrc is the file that is used to configure the window manager.

Configuring the Linux System

This chapter covers the following competencies required to master the Linux+ certification exam:

- Using automated utilities to reconfigure the X Window System
- Configuring remote access for the client's workstation
- Setting environmental variables
- Configuring basic network services
- Configuring server services
- Configuring Internet services
- Identifying swap space requirements
- Installing and configuring printers
- Installing and configuring add-in hardware
- Reconfiguring the boot loader
- Understanding configuration files
- Editing configuration files
- Configuring list modules
- Documenting the operating system installation and configuration
- Configuring access privileges

Reconfiguring the X Window System

If you made a mistake in your original configuration or just want to learn the nuances of the X Window System back end, there are a couple of tools that will guide you in choosing the proper settings for your hardware. The X Window System consists of several configuration files that will do a portion of starting and configuring X.

In Chapter 2, we covered the initial installation of the XFree86 server and the files that make the configuration happen. Here we are going to reapply those utilities on a running system using Red Hat's Xconfigurator. Before starting, save a backup of your XF86Config file.

The first step to configure a running X Window is by knowing exactly what hardware you have in your machine and what it is doing. The second is knowing what to put in the XF86Config file. The second part we don't have to know very well because we are going to let the Xconfigurator write the file for us.

We start by typing **Xconfigurator** at the command-line prompt. We see the first screen shown in Figure 3-1. This screen gives us all the places to look for the XF86Config file and a choice to cancel the manipulation or go on with it. Choose OK.

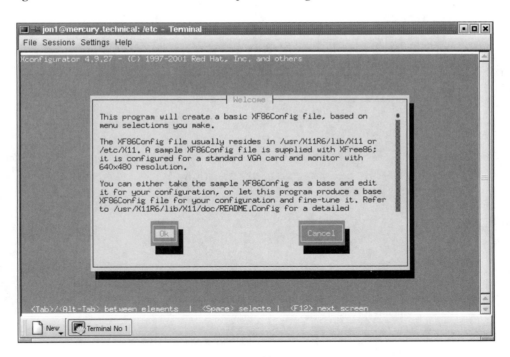

Figure 3-1 Welcome Screen for Red Hat's Xconfigurator

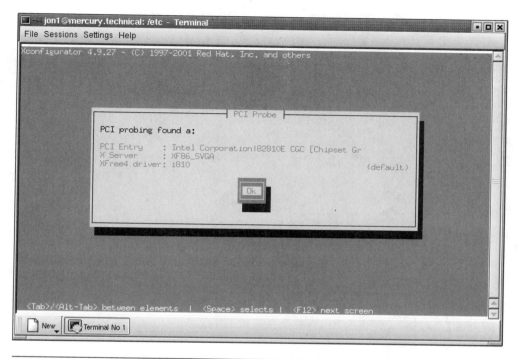

Figure 3-2   Red Hat's Xconfigurator probing for a video card

The second screen probes the PCI bus for a video card, and we see the results in the Figure 3-2.

The third screen shows Xconfigurator looking for the monitor. If the monitor is new enough, information sent back to the application will be displayed, as shown in Figure 3-3. If you have an older monitor, the application will ask you for the details concerning the type of monitor you are running.

Xconfigurator will then ask you how much memory your video adapter has. Again, if yours is a newer system, the card will reveal itself to the application.

NOTE   Make sure that all of the information reported by the Xconfigurator command is valid and relevant to your system.

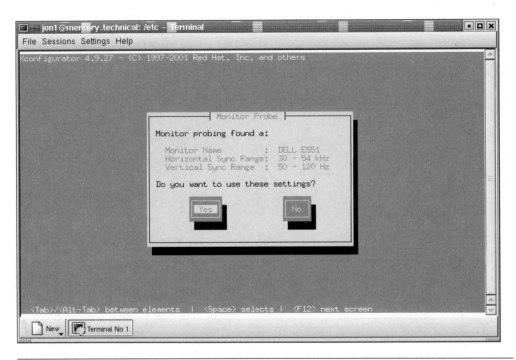

Figure 3-3   Red Hat's Xconfigurator probing for the monitor type

In Figure 3-4, notice that the application goes as far as predetermining the amount of video memory in the system.

The next section is where it gets tricky. The clock chip is being set (see Figure 3-5). The recommended setting is no clockchip. You should set this manually only if you know the exact chip of your board.

Next, the video modes you would like to run are being set (see Figure 3-6). Common sense applies here. If you have a 15-inch monitor, you do not want to run at a anything higher than a 800×600 resolution. If you do, everything will be very small.

You will see a screen similar to the one in Figure 3-7. Don't start X yet; select the skip option. This screen is a congratulatory screen. Remember that the application has written a new configuration file for you. Before rebooting the X server, you should take a look at both files to ensure that they are both the same (they should be).

You have been working in the command line and graphical user interface. When you work in the text user interface (TUI), you are interacting with the shell to execute commands.

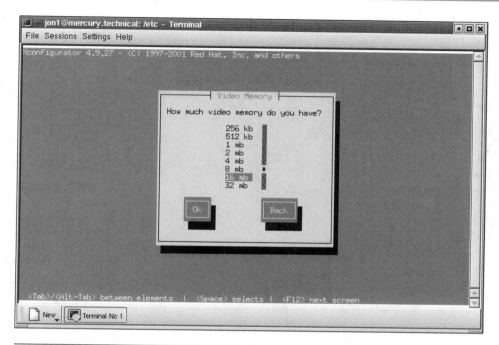

Figure 3-4   Red Hat's Xconfigurator probing for the amount of memory on the video card

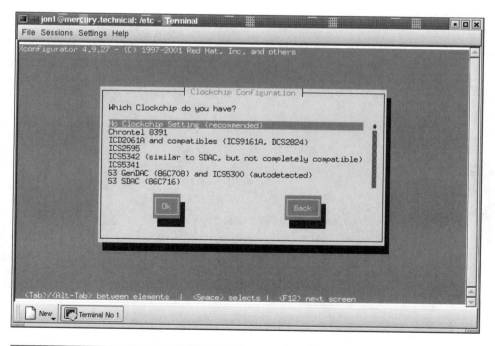

Figure 3-5   Clockchip setting under Red Hat's Xconfigurator

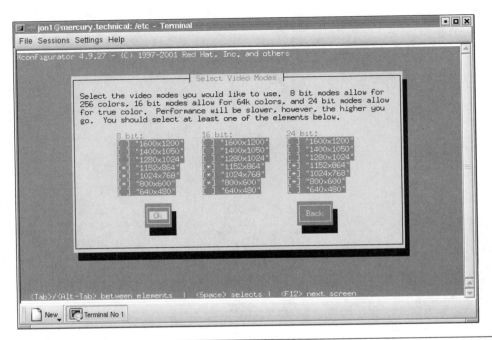

Figure 3-6 User-definable video resolutions under Red Hat's Xconfigurator

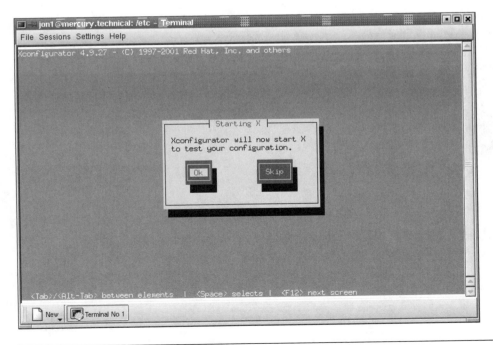

Figure 3-7 Xconfigurator screen to test or skip video settings

Basic Server Services

Some of the basic server services, such as NFS and NMB, were explained in Chapter 2. Here, we look at the configuration of these services plus another application included on every major distribution of Linux.

In a very large or enterprise network, these services will occupy their own server. That is why they are called *server services*. Many people and processes are able to use these services at the same time.

NFS

There are three main configuration files you will need to edit to set up a Network File System (NFS) server: /etc/exports, /etc/hosts.allow, and /etc/hosts.deny.

For a bare bones minimum, you only need to edit /etc/exports to get NFS to work, but you would be left with an extremely insecure setup. /etc/exports will let other people see your files, and if you edit only these files, everybody will have access to it. After this step is done, you need to secure it by either allowing people or disallowing people to access to the accessible data.

The /etc/exports file contains a list of entries; each entry indicates a volume that is shared and how it is shared. An entry in /etc/exports will typically look like this:

```
directory machine1(option 1,option 2) machine2(option 1,option 2)
```

The line shows some options that need explaining. Above the directory option is the directory that you want to share. It may be an entire filesystem or disk, though it need not be. If you share a directory, then all directories under it within the same filesystem will be shared as well.

Machine1 and machine2 are the client machines that will have access to the directory that you are sharing. The machines may be listed by their DNS address (**machine.company.com***)* or IP address (**192.168.0.8**). Using IP addresses is more reliable and more secure.

For simplicity's sake, I will cover the basic options for NFS exports. Using **ro** when exporting a drive means that you are sharing it as a read-only volume. This should be done when sharing anything that you don't want overwritten. Using **rw** in the options means that the volume of data that you want to share will have a read-write permission applied to it; anyone you let into this data will have the capability to read it and overwrite it. Home directories on a remote server are shared in this manner so that users can place data in them.

To supply more security for the data you want to share, the /etc/host.allow and /etc/host.deny files should be edited. The host.deny file should contain "all" in the open text. "All" will not let anybody view your shared data. I can hear your questions. What good is shared data if no one can view it? This is where the hosts.allow file comes in. The hosts.allow file contains entries of specific machines or users who are allowed to view the shared information. The entries in the hosts.allow file take precedent over the files in the host.deny file. When these three files are configured properly, your data can be shared in a safe and efficient manner.

SMB and NMB

As stated in Chapter 2, SMB (Samba) provides the functionality to integrate Linux and Windows. Samba configuration on a Linux machine is controlled by a single file, /etc/smb.conf. We are going to look at the formatting of smb.conf and at the simpler side of configuring it.

This file determines which system resources you want to share with the outside world and the restrictions you want to place on them.

Because the following sections will address sharing Linux drives and printers with Windows machines, the smb.conf file shown in this section is as simple as you can get, just for introductory purposes.

Each section of the file starts with a section header such as [global], [homes], [printers], and so on. The [global] section defines a few variables that Samba will use to define sharing for all resources. The [homes] section enables remote users to access their (and only their) home directory on the local (Linux) machine. That is, users trying to connect to this share from Windows machines will be connected to their personal home directories. Note that to do this, they must have an account on the Linux box.

The following sample smb.conf file enables remote users to get to their home directories on the local machine and to write to a temporary directory. For a Windows user to see these shares, the Linux box has to be on the local network. Then, the user simply connects a network drive from the Windows file manager or Windows Explorer.

```
; /etc/smb.conf

[global]
# Uncomment this if you want a guest account
# guest account = nobody
log file = /var/log/samba-log.%m
lock directory = /var/lock/samba
share modes = yes

[homes]
comment = Home Directories
browseable = no
```

```
read only = no
create mode = 0750

[tmp]
comment = Temporary file space
path = /tmp
read only = no
public = yes
```

Look for thses headers in your own smb.conf file. Having written a new smb.conf, it is useful to test it to verify its correctness. You can test the correctness of a smb.conf file by using the **testparm** utility; if **testparm** reports no problems, smbd will correctly load the configuration file and give you the chance to view the changes through a dump file.

Transfer Protocols

The transfer protocols are FTP and SMTP. File transfer protocol (FTP) is the *de facto* standard of uploading and downloading files over the Internet. Simple Mail Transfer Protocol (SMTP) is the most widely used mail protocol for sending e-mail.

FTP

The FTP protocol is designed to enable transferring data between hosts that use dissimilar file systems. Although the protocol provides a lot of flexibility for transferring data, it does not attempt to preserve file attributes that are specific to a particular file system (for example, the permissions of a file).

SMTP

SMTP is a simple ASCII protocol. After establishing the TCP connection to port 25, the sending machine, operating as the client, waits for the receiving machine, operating as the server, to talk first. The server starts by sending a line of text giving its identity and telling whether it is prepared to receive mail. If it is not, the client releases the connection and tries again later.

In your computer, an e-mail daemon that "speaks" SMTP is listening to port 25. This daemon accepts incoming connections and copies messages from them into the appropriate mailboxes. If a message cannot be delivered, an error report containing the first part of the undeliverable message is returned to the sender.

The Shell

The *shell* is the command interpreter, or command-line interface to Linux. It accepts commands, interprets them, issues commands to the kernel, starts commands, and provides the results to the user. It also understands input and output redirection, file-name generation, variable substitution, and piping. These facilities, combined with a built-in programming language, make the shell one of the administrator's most powerful allies.

More shells are available now than ever before, and different Linux vendors provide different combinations of shells with their implementations. The most common and simplest of all the shells is the Bourne shell (/bin/sh), which been around since the inception of Unix. Because it was one of the first shells, it has the smallest number of features. The Korn shell (ksh) expanded upon the capabilities of the /bin/sh and included a much larger number of options and a more complete programming language.

The Bourne Again shell (/bin/bash) took the new functionality in the ksh, added a host of new features and combined them with sh. This new shell is closer in operation to the original /bin/sh while supporting a stronger programming language. The Z shell is more closely based upon the ksh and added extensive functionality. Figure 3-8 shows the /bin/sh as a terminal.

Users who are familiar with the C programming language can use the C shell. The intent of this shell was to provide a command environment that is friendlier for C programmers as it added C language features to the shell. Unfortunately, it also deviated greatly from the /bin/sh. Development of the C shell has progressed and is available in Tom's C shell (tcsh).

Typically, each Linux vendor provides more than one shell to address the preferences of their users. Rarely do they provide all available shells. For example, Caldera provides bash, tcsh, and zsh, while Red Hat provides ash, bash, and tcsh. Incidentally, ash is very similar to the system V Unix /bin/sh.

For compatibility with existing shell scripts and programs, Linux vendors provide links to the historical names. For example, when a user executes the command **sh**, they are executing bash. Similarly, requests for **csh** are satisfied with tcsh. Figure 3-9 of the shell shows an application being executed.

 NOTE All the shells are found in the /bin/directory. The shell started for users on login is specified for them in their /etc/passwd file entry.

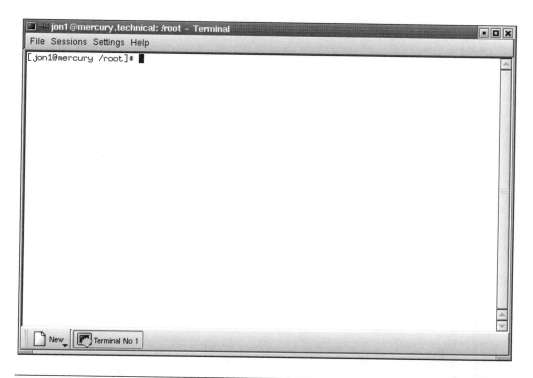

Figure 3-8   A typical terminal showing a bash prompt

Although each shell performs its tasks with some minor differences, each supports a core set of functionality. A solid understanding of the bash shell is necessary in preparing for the exam, and you should understand the various configuration files that affect the operation and configuration of the shell.

Shell Variables

Shell variables are keywords defined with a value for processing by the shell. They can be used in shell scripts to hold information for processing in the script, or they can form part of the environment, which affects the configuration and operation of the shell. Shell variables are case-sensitive. This means the variable names *STUFF* and *stuff* do not refer to the same variable. Although there are a number of shell variables built-in, the variable that can most significantly affect command processing is *PATH*.

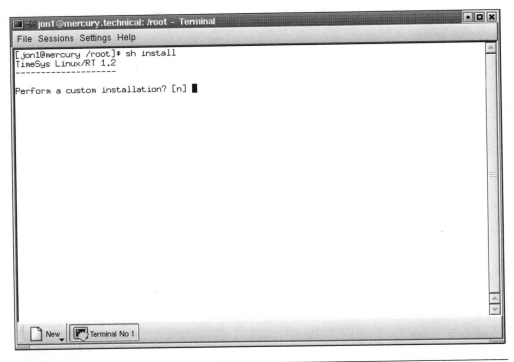

Figure 3-9   An application being executed from the command line

The shell doesn't know where to find the commands the user types unless they are built-in to the shell itself. External commands must be located on the filesystem and executed for the user. The shell does this by searching the directories specified in the *PATH* variable, looking for the command to execute. When it finds a match, the command is loaded and executed. If no match is found after processing each directory, the shell responds with an error message:

```
bash: <name>: command not found
```

The *PATH* variable can be viewed using the following command:

```
echo $PATH
```

Although this is true for all shell variables, there are some other issues regarding the *PATH* variable of which you must be aware.

First, the path does not include the current working directory by default. This is a security measure to prevent the unexpected execution of a program. Suppose you can see an executable file in your working directory using the **ls** command. When you type its name, the shell reports that the command cannot be found. Working around this is accomplished by entering the full path to the file, adding the specific directory to the *PATH* variable, or by adding the current directory (.) to the *PATH*.

Secondly, each directory in the *PATH* variable is separated with a colon, and the order of the directories in the *PATH* should include the most-common directories first and any user specified directories at the end. Ordering the directories in this manner can dramatically speed up command execution.

When adding a new directory to the *PATH*, you can either redefine the entire *PATH*, or simply add the new directory. Assigning a complete new *PATH* is done using the command

```
PATH=/bin:/usr/bin:<directory-name>
```

Simply adding a new directory to the currently defined *PATH* variable is done using the syntax

```
PATH=$PATH:<directory-name>
```

Thus, to add the directory /home/jon1 to the *PATH* using the second example, the command would be

```
PATH=$PATH:/home/jon1
```

The syntax as shown is important when defining any shell variable. There can be no spaces between the variable name and the equal sign, or between the equal sign and the value. For example,

```
PATH=<path> OK
PATH =<path> No
PATH= <path> No
PATH = <path> No
```

If you feel the need to add the current working directory to the *PATH*, you can add the (.) using the command

```
PATH=$PATH:./
```

 ALERT As mentioned previously, it is recommended for security reasons not to include the current directory in the **PATH** variable. If you feel the need to do so, make sure you include it as the very last component. It is also highly recommended you do not include the (.) in root's **PATH**.

Common Variables

As mentioned earlier, there are a number of defined variables in the shell, and users can create any number of variables for their own use. Any variable can be viewed using the **echo** command, followed by the variable name. The syntax is

```
echo ${variable name}
```

Therefore, to see the value associated with the variable *MAIL*, the command is

```
echo $MAIL
```

Figure 3-10 shows the path as displayed in a terminal window.

This command shows the location of the user's mailbox, $HOME, the user's home directory. There are two commands available to display the currently defined variables: **env** and **set**. The **env** command is used to display variables that are part of the environment, whereas **set** displays the local variables. It is important to know the dif-

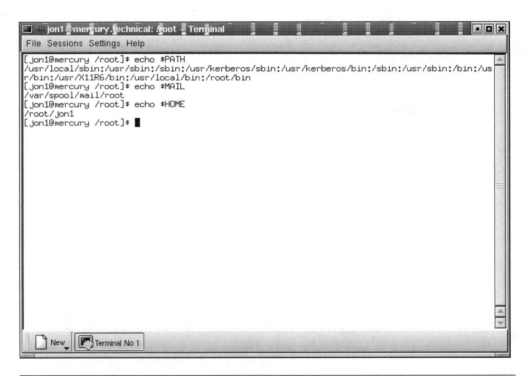

Figure 3-10 PATH as shown in a terminal window—also note use of "$" parameter to display paths to the MAIL and HOME directories

ference between the two commands. Typically, the output of the **env** command is a subset of the variables shown in the **set** output.

The most-common variables displayed using the **env** command are

- **HOME**   The user's home directory. The initial value of this variable is the home directory defined in the /etc/passwd file.

- **LINES**   The number of lines in the display (used by commands like **more** or **less**).

- **LOGNAME**   Whom the user is logged in as.

- **PWD**   Where you are currently working—the Present Working Directory.

- **SHELL**   The full pathname of the shell you are using.

- **TERM**   The terminal emulation or type currently used.

- **USER**   The name of the user, which is rarely different from the value of *LOG-NAME*.

- **PATH**   The search path for commands. It is a colon-separated list of directories in which the shell looks for commands.

NOTE   Although any variable can be either upper- or lowercase, the environment or predefined system variables are generally uppercase only.

At any time you can define your own variables, or redefine an existing one using the same format, as illustrated when changing the *PATH* variable. To create a new variable called *PROGRAMS*, use the syntax

```
PROGRAMS=/home/jon1/bin
```

You can now see the value of the variable by using the command

```
echo $PROGRAMS
```

which results in /home/jon1/bin. Now use the **set** command to display the defined variables:

```
set
```

The variable we defined, *PROGRAMS*, appears in the list. The **env** command

```
env
```

however, does not display the *PROGRAMS* variable. This is because *PROGRAMS* is a local variable—that is, local to our shell. No other shell or program executed can see the *PROGRAMS* variable. For executed commands to access the variable, it must be declared in the shell environment using the **export** command:

```
export PROGRAMS
```

Once the variable is moved into the environment, it is accessible to the current shell and any new processes started. The variable and its value can be changed at any time and are available until the user logs out. To make this variable available in future sessions, it must be added to either the system or user profiles.

Typically, the value of a variable is not static. Redefining the value is accomplished by simply assigning the new value:

```
PROGRAMS=/usr/local/bin
```

Once the variable has been exported to the environment, there is no need to do it again. The new value is applied in both the local shell and the environment. Removing a defined variable is done using the **unset** command:

```
unset PROGRAMS
```

The shell has built-in knowledge of variables that control the interface presented at the command line, also known as the *prompt*. The prompt is the shell's method of communicating with the user that it is ready to accept, process, and input. Each shell has a default prompt—something people use to immediately identify the shell in use:

- $ As the last character for Bourne, bash, and Korn shells
- %   As the last character for C shell and Z shell
- >   As the last character for tcsh

The configuration of the command-line prompt is not consistent among the shells. The primary prompt is either PS1 or prompt, depending upon the shell you are using. This is the prompt typically displayed when the user is working at the command line. In the bash shell, a typical PS1 value is defined as

```
[\u@\h \W]\$
```

Dissected into its components, PS1 is equal to the following:

- The left bracket ([)
- The name of the current user

- The at symbol (@)
- The name of the current host
- A space
- The present working directory
- The right bracket (])
- The dollar sign ($)

Each time you press RETURN, the shell computes the prompt to display based upon the defined values. Using the prompt definition just presented, the prompt is displayed as

```
[root@mercury.technical /tmp]#
```

In the prompt definition previously presented, the backstroke character (\) is used several times. This signifies to the shell that the following character is special. In the case of the prompt, the following character identifies a string the character should be replaced with. The different values used in the prompt are shown in Table 3-1.

Most shells include several levels of prompts as the shell has multiple input layers. For example, if you want to enter a complex command and have it easy for you to read

Table 3-1   Partial List of Shell Parameters

Value	Result
\d	The current system date
\h	The hostname without the domain
\n	New line
\s	The name of the shell
\t	The current system time
\u	Username
\W	Current working directory
\!	History number (see history discussed later in this chapter)
\#	Command number
\$	Default prompt—$ for standard users and # for root
\\	An actual backstroke is to appear (literal)
ABC	ABC (the value of that text)

as you type, you can enter line continuation characters. These line continuation characters are also the backstroke. Strictly speaking, they tell the shell not to interpret the carriage return as the end of the command.

Now, using the backstroke to indicate we have not finished entering our input is

```
[root@mercury.technical /tmp]# ls *.c \
> *.o \
> *.tar
```

Notice the prompt change from our initial setting to the greater than sign (>). This indicates the shell is still accepting input and is called the secondary prompt or PS2. Had the shell not changed its prompt, we would not know it was still accepting input and confuse the user. Like PS1, you can change the value of PS2 to suit your particular requirements in the same manner. Due to the complexities of today's shells, most typically have three or four layers of prompts.

Other Variables

From the previous discussions, you should have realized the dollar sign ($) is used to identify a keyword as a variable. If you have a variable called *MYHOME*, you view its contents using the syntax **$MYHOME**. There are several other variables that are useful for determining your environment. The *$$* variable shows the process number of the shell that is currently executing:

```
echo $$
```

Each command executed by the shell provides a return code to signify success or failure of the command. Success is signified with a return code of 0. Any other value signifies failure. For example, the **pwd** command is used to display the current working directory. It will return success after printing the directory name. If the file does not exist, it returns an error code that can be checked using the $? syntax. With this information, you can test for the successful completion of a command:

```
[root@mercury.technical /tmp]# pwd
/tmp
[root@mercury.technical /tmp]# echo $?
0
[root@mercury.technical /tmp]# pwd-z
bash: pwd: illegal option: -z
pwd: usage: pwd [-PL]
[root@mercury.technical /tmp]# echo $?
1
[root@mercury.technical /tmp]#
```

The next variable, *$!*, displays the process number for the last child process started in the background. If no processes have been started in the background, this variable will be empty. A thorough discussion of processes is covered in Chapter 4, but for our discussion it is important to know the ampersand (&) signifies the process is to be started in the background. For example

```
[root@mercury.technical /tmp]# echo $!

[root@mercury.technical /tmp]# date &
[1] 10470
[root@mercury.technical /tmp]# Sat May 19 10:01:00 EDT 2001

[1]+ Done date
[root@mercury.technical /tmp]# echo $!
10470
[root@mercury.technical /tmp]#
```

The first time we look at *$!*, it has no value, indicating no background processes have been initiated. Executing the **date** command with the ampersand runs the command in the background. This prints the process ID and runs the command. When we look at *$!* again, we see the process ID for our last background task.

Configuration Files

Variables exist for a defined lifetime: until they are explicitly unset, the user logs off, or the shell they were created in is terminated. Remember, when you export a variable to the environment, it is only provided to the child processes—the parent never sees them. This means that as you exit shells, and only the default variables remain. Redefining variables each time you log in can become tiresome. Fortunately, the configuration files used by the shell at startup provide a method for addressing this.

Before looking at the files, a quick review of the login process is beneficial to the discussion. Recall that when a user sits at a keyboard and enters his or her username, the program getty starts the **/bin/login** utility. The **login** program prompts the user for his or her password. The terminal settings are adjusted so the characters entered by the user are not displayed on the screen. This is a security feature to prevent the disclosure of the user's authentication information.

Once the user has entered the password, **login** encrypts it using the same process as the **password** command. This newly encrypted password is verified against the encrypted password stored in the /etc/passwd file. If the password is correct, the user is allowed access; otherwise, he is greeted with a Login incorrect response. A second security feature with **login** is the user is not informed if it is the username or password that is incorrect. Despite common assumptions, the **login** program cannot decrypt the password stored in /etc/passwd.

With the password entered and accepted, the system files utmp and wtmp are updated to reflect the login. The **login** program finally starts the shell specified in the user's /etc/passwd file entry, then initiates the shell.

The login shell, identifiable in a process listing as-sh, executes the /etc/profile for configurations applicable to all users. Once /etc/profile is finished, the configuration files in the user's home directory are then executed. This provides the administrator with the ability to establish a system-wide environment and allow the users to customize it, as applicable. The bash shell looks for .bash_profile in the user's home directory and executes it if found. If .bash_profile doesn't exist, bash then searches for .bash_login and finally .profile. There is no requirement that a user must have any of these files, but if one is found, it will be processed. Similarly, when the user logs out, bash looks for .bash_logout in the user's home directory and executes the commands found prior to terminating the session. However, not all shells are started at login, as the login shell will spawn many child processes and shell during the session. The new shell can have additional customizations applied by using the .bashrc file found in the user's home directory. Finally, .inputrc, if found, is used to configure specific key bindings. The .inputrc file is not required for proper operation of the shell.

Two parameters exist, *noprofile* and *norc*, to prevent the execution of the customization files when a shell is started. The *noprofile* parameter prevents the execution of both /etc/profile, .bash_login, .bash_profile, and .profile. Similarly, the parameter *norc* prevents the execution of the .bashrc file when a new shell is created.

When a new user is added, all of the files we have discussed are copied to the user's home directory automatically, if you are using a program such as useradd or userconf. The default versions of these files are found in /etc/skel, should you need to make changes to the default version provided. If you manually create a user by editing the /etc/passwd file, you must manually copy the default files from /etc/skel to the user's home directory.

Sample Files

The files illustrated here are from Red Hat Linux 7. Each Linux vendor has made his or her own configuration files that are specific to how he or she has addressed his or her Linux implementations.

The following is a sample /etc/profile and is similar to what you find on your system. Remember, this file contains or runs scripts to initialize the environment for every user:

```
# /etc/profile

# System wide environment and startup programs
# Functions and aliases go in /etc/bashrc

PATH="$PATH:/usr/X11R6/bin"

ulimit -S -c 1000000 > /dev/null 2>&1
if [ 'id -gn' = 'id -un' -a 'id -u' -gt 14 ]; then
 umask 002
else
 umask 022
fi

USER='id -un'
LOGNAME=$USER
MAIL="/var/spool/mail/$USER"

HOSTNAME='/bin/hostname'
HISTSIZE=1000

if [ -z "$INPUTRC" -a ! -f "$HOME/.inputrc" ]; then
 INPUTRC=/etc/inputrc
fi

export PATH USER LOGNAME MAIL HOSTNAME HISTSIZE INPUTRC

for i in /etc/profile.d/*.sh ; do
 if [ -x $i ]; then
 . $I
 fi
done

unset I
```

Once the /etc/profile has completed executing, the user's .profile in their home directory is executed. Like /etc/profile, the .profile is executed only on login to the system:

```
# .bash_profile

# Get the aliases and functions
if [ -f ~/.bashrc ]; then
 . ~/.bashrc
fi
```

```
# User specific environment and startup programs

PATH=$PATH:$HOME/bin
BASH_ENV=$HOME/.bashrc
USERNAME=""

export USERNAME BASH_ENV PATH
```

However, unlike the previous two files, .bashrc is executed for every shell started after you login. This may be different for each user.

```
# .bashrc

# User specific aliases and functions

# Source global definitions
if [ -f /etc/bashrc ]; then
 . /etc/bashrc
fi
```

Red Hat Linux does not include a .inputrc file by default. The Caldera Linux implementation does provide one, however, and as it is found in the user's home directory, it can be customized for each user. A sample .inputrc file is illustrated here:

```
set meta-flag on
set output-meta on
set convert-meta off
#set bell-style visible
#set show-all-if-ambiguous on
```

Finally, when the user logs out, the shell executes .bash_logout, if found, from the user's home directory:

```
# ~/.bash_logout

clear
```

Defining Shell Scripts

A *shell script*, in its simplest form, is a series of commands entered at the command line for processing by the shell. Typically, however, the commands are placed in a file for execution again and again. You can write a shell script to do just about anything you can at a command line. For example, if it is important, I have a script to regularly check for FTP sessions in the system log file.

The command amounts to

```
[root@mercury.technical /root]# grep ftpd /var/log/messages
May 20 08:14:48 mercury ftpd[17976]: getpeername (in.ftpd):
Transport endpoint is not connected
May 20 08:26:25 mercury ftpd[17982]: getpeername (in.ftpd):
Transport endpoint is not connected
May 20 11:11:38 mercury ftpd[18056]: FTP LOGIN FROM 192.168.0.16
[192.168.0.16], chweb
May 20 11:57:06 mercury ftpd[18056]: FTP session closed
May 20 12:02:24 mercury ftpd[18741]: FTP LOGIN FROM 192.168.0.16
[192.168.0.16], root
May 20 12:25:57 mercury ftpd[18741]: User root timed out after 900
seconds at Sun May 20 12:25:57 2001
May 20 12:25:57 mercury ftpd[18741]: FTP session closed
May 20 17:03:59 mercury ftpd[19014]: getpeername (in.ftpd):
Transport endpoint is not connected
May 20 20:49:13 mercury ftpd[19103]: getpeername (in.ftpd):
Transport endpoint is not connected
[root@mercury.technical /root]#
If there are not ftp transfers recorded in the log file, there
will be no results from the grep.
[root@mercury.technical /root]# grep ftpd /var/log/messages
[root@mercury.technical /root]#
```

This is an extremely simplistic example, but it serves the point we are discussing. Placing this single command line into a file creates a shell script, which we can execute time and time again. Our one line command is found in *f* to make it simple to type the name of the command. In actuality, you will want to make your script names at least as meaningful as the Linux command names. As simple as this command is, it can be placed into a file and executed from there. To save me from having to type the command in every five minutes to see whether or not she has come in yet, it can be placed into a file of any name; we'll use *x* to make it very simple:

```
[root@mercury.technical /root]# cat f
grep ftpd /var/log/messages
[root@mercury.technical /root]#
```

Rather than having to type the full commands each time we want them, we can simply run our shell script:

```
[root@mercury.technical /root]# sh f
May 20 11:11:38 mercury ftpd[18056]: FTP LOGIN FROM 192.168.0.16
[192.168.0.16], chweb
May 20 11:57:06 mercury ftpd[18056]: FTP session closed
May 20 12:02:24 mercury ftpd[18741]: FTP LOGIN FROM 192.168.0.16
[192.168.0.16], root
```

```
May 20 12:25:57 mercury ftpd[18741]: User jon1 timed out after 900
seconds at Sun May 20 12:25:57 2001
May 20 12:25:57 mercury ftpd[18741]: FTP session closed
[root@mercury.technical /root]#
```

However, we can also take advantage of Unix file permissions and make the file executable. Bear in mind, a shell script is interpreted by the shell, and therefore, must be readable by all users who will be executing it. If you don't want anyone else to execute your script, use the appropriate permissions. For now, we will allow any user to run our script and set our permissions as

```
[root@mercury.technical /root]# chmod 755 f
$ ls -l f
-rwxr-xr-x 1 jon1 jon1 28 May 21 09:11 f
[root@mercury.technical /root]# f
May 20 11:11:38 mercury ftpd[18056]: FTP LOGIN FROM 192.168.0.16
[192.168.0.16], jon1
May 20 11:57:06 mercury ftpd[18056]: FTP session closed
May 20 12:02:24 mercury ftpd[18741]: FTP LOGIN FROM 192.168.0.16
[192.168.0.16], jon1
May 20 12:25:57 mercury ftpd[18741]: User jon1 timed out after 900
seconds at Sun May 20 12:25:57 2001
May 20 12:25:57 mercury ftpd[18741]: FTP session closed
[root@mercury.technical jon1]#
```

It is necessary to change the file permissions to add the execute bit. The default file permissions for regular files is 666 and then the umask is applied. The default file permissions are typically 644 (-rw-r--r--) after the umask of 022 is applied, making the files nonexecutable.

The permissions we assign are critical. If we assign 777 to the permissions, we are allowing any user to change or destroy our shell script. This is a very bad practice to create a world-writable file and must be discouraged.

Sprucing Up the Basic Script

Our shell script is very simple, and any command executable from the command line can be executed in the shell script. As we will see, there are some things we do in shell scripts that are not as easy from the command line.

For the next part of our discussion, let's consider a different shell script example. At any given time we want to see how many processes a given user is running on the system. We can do that using

```
[root@mercury.technical /root]# ps -ef | grep -c jon1
15
[root@mercury.technical /root]#
```

If the user is not currently logged in, then no data is returned:

```
[root@mercury.technical /root]# ps -ef | grep jon1
root 22969 18755 0 09:24 pts/2 00:00:00 grep jon1
[root@mercury.technical /root]#
```

That was not quite a true statement. The **grep** command is still returned because it matches the parameter given to it. Let's correct that by putting in a second **grep** to eliminate the appearance of **grep** in the process list:

```
[root@mercury.technical /root]# ps -ef | grep jon1 | grep -v grep
[root@mercury.technical /root]#
```

This is now in our shell script called p. However, the silent output can sometimes be confusing. The Unix command philosophy of "say nothing on success" is not always user-friendly. Sometimes no output can be interpreted as a failed or incomplete operation when it was working correctly, even though there were no values in the output to display.

We learned at the beginning of the chapter about return codes and testing them for successful completion. If the operation was successful, then a 0 is returned to the shell. Another value constitutes a failure.

```
[root@mercury.technical /root]# p
15
[root@mercury.technical /root]# echo $?
0
[root@mercury.technical /root]#
```

Remembering how this works, we can add it to the shell script. The x script can be modified to the following:

```
[root@mercury.technical /root]# cat p
ps -ef | grep root | grep -v grep-c
echo "command returns $?"
[root@mercury.technical /root]#
```

It is important in this script to add some text to the return code because the script is already returning a numerical value, and it may be confusing otherwise.

```
[root@mercury.technical /root]# sh p
15
command returns 0
[root@mercury.technical /root]#
```

With the addition of the comment in the output, the actual text value we want is not all that intuitive. We can add this into the script:

```
[root@mercury.technical /root]# cat p
#
# This script prints the total number of processes a user is running,
# and then print the return code from the grep command.
# we use back ticks around the grep command to execute it and then print
# the result in the echo
echo "root is running 'ps -ef | grep root | grep -v grep -c' processes"
echo "command returns $?"
[root@mercury.technical /root]#
```

The preceding illustration demonstrates the use of comments in the shell script. A comment is denoted by a pound sign (#). This instructs the shell to ignore all characters behind the #. Comments are important as they allow you and anyone else to understand what the program is doing when you have forgotten what it did.

The very first line of the script should contain the correct interpreter for the shell script. This is advisable because the shell will run the command interpreter specified and then give control of the script to that interpreter. The interpreter specification is done using #! followed by the correct pathname for the desired shell, as illustrated here:

```
#!/bin/sh
```

By adding this line, the shell can invoke the correct interpreter. Now our shell script looks like

```
[root@mercury.technical /root]# cat p
#! /bin/sh
#
# This script prints the total number of processes a user is running,
# and then print the return code from the grep command.
# we use back ticks around the grep command to execute it and then print
# the result in the echo
echo "root is running 'ps -ef | grep root | grep -v grep -c' processes"
echo "command returns $?"
[root@mercury.technical /root]#
```

We have seen how we can get the shell to provide us with information. How can we ask the user to provide the shell with information?

Accepting Input

The shell script p that we have been looking at is not terribly useful, as it can only look for processes running by user root. Having the ability to accept input on the command line or by prompting the user will greatly extend the value of the scripts. This is nothing new, as almost every utility we have looked at in this book does the same thing.

For example, when using the command

```
cat /etc/profile /etc/passwd
```

the **cat** command sees two arguments, both of which are files for **cat** to process. The shell understands the concept of passing arguments to a script and uses positional parameters to pass arguments. These positional parameters or variables are defined as

- *$0* is the name of the command being executed.

- *$1* is the first argument.

- *$2* through *$9* are the other initial arguments.

- *$** represents all arguments, regardless of number.

- *$#* shows the number of arguments provided.

Consider the following example:

```
$ cat parms
parms $1 $2 $3 $4
#
# parms one two three four
one two three four
#
```

The parms script takes the first four variables and prints them back to the user. If more than four arguments were given to parms, it would still only print the first four. If fewer than four arguments are provided, parms will only print those.

With this information, we can go back and modify the p script to search for any user's processes.

```
[root@mercury.technical /root]# cat p
#! /bin/sh
#
# This script prints the total number of processes a user is running,
# and then print the return code from the grep command.
# we use back ticks around the grep command to execute it and then print
# the result in the echo
echo "$1 is running 'ps -ef | grep $1 | grep -v grep -c' processes"
[root@mercury.technical /root]#
```

By changing the word "root" to $1, we can now run the command and see how many jobs are executed by each user:

```
[root@mercury.technical /root]# p root
root is running 16 processes
[root@mercury.technical /root]# p root
root is running 41 processes
[root@mercury.technical /root]# p jhowe
fhare is running 0 processes
[root@mercury.technical /root]#
```

Representing the Variables

Understanding the subtle differences between the $* (all arguments) and $# (how many arguments) is important in scripting. On the one hand, $* enables you to address all command-line arguments, while $# enables you to perform some testing to see if there are enough arguments.

Looking at the following example, what can we expect?

```
[root@mercury.technical /root]# cat parms1
echo there are $# arguments
echo they are $*
[root@mercury.technical /root]#
```

The script will print the total number of arguments entered on the command line, and then print all of those arguments.

```
[root@mercury.technical /root]# parms1 a b c d 1 2 3 4 live free or die
there are 12 arguments
they are a b c d 1 2 3 4 live free or die
[root@mercury.technical /root]#
```

As we saw earlier, the shell only knows how to specially address the first ten variables, $1 to $9. If that is the case, what do we do to process the others?

The shift Command

The **shift** command is used to shift the parameter on the command line or, as we will see later, a variable after we separate it into multiple components. This takes the variables $1 to $9 and shifts them one position to the left. Doing so affects the value and makes other parameters available, making the value associated with $2 now $1, $3 becomes $2, and so on. This is repeated each time **shift** is called, as illustrated with our modified version of parms1:

```
[root@mercury.technical /root]# cat parms1
echo there are $# arguments
echo they are $*
shift
echo now they are $*
shift
echo now they are $*
echo and we finish with $# arguments
[root@mercury.technical /root]# parms1 a b c d 1 2 3 4 live free or die
there are 12 arguments
they are a b c d 1 2 3 4 live free or die
now they are b c d 1 2 3 4 live free or die
now they are c d 1 2 3 4 live free or die
and we finish with 10 arguments
[root@mercury.technical /root]#
```

The **shift** command does not know how many values there are to shift. If there are a large number of values to process, this is not a problem. However, if there are too few values, it becomes possible for **shift** to start nonexistent variables and can result in error messages. If there are too few values, some version of **shift** will generate an error message similar to

```
shift: shift count must be <= $#
```

Other versions of **shift** will not complain at all.

Adding Logic

The ability to test and implement logic is where any programming language proves its value. The shell is no different, having the **test** command and the ability to evaluate expressions. The **test** command has numerous options defining the actual test to be evaluated, as shown in Table 3-2.

Table 3-2 **test** Options

Option	Purpose
=	True, if the two strings are equal.
!=	True, if the two strings are not equal.
-a	(AND) Both tests to be evaluated must be true.
-b	True, if the file is a block special file.

(continued)

Table 3-2   **test** Options *(continued)*

Option	Purpose
-c	True, if the file is a character special file.
-d	True, if the name specified is a directory.
-e	True, if the file exists.
-eq	Two values are equal—typically used to evaluate numbers.
-f	True, if the file exists and is a regular file.
-G	True, if the file belongs to the user's group.
-g	True, if the file exists and has SGID set.
-ge	True, if the first value is greater than or equal to the second value.
-gt	True, if the first value is greater than the second.
-k	The named file exists and the sticky bit is set.
-L	The file must exist and is a symbolic link.
-le	True, if the first value is less than or equal to the second value.
-lt	True, if the first value is less than the second value.
-n	True, if the length of the string is greater than zero.
-ne	True, if the two values are not equal to each other.
-nt	True, if the first file is newer than the second file.
-O	True, if the file is owned by the user.
-o	True, if only one condition of two or more is true.
-ot	True, if the first file is older than the second file.
-p	True, if the file exists and is a named pipe.
-r	True, if the file exists and is readable.
-s	True, if the named file exists and has more than zero characters in it.
-u	True, if the file has the SUID bit set.
-w	True, if the named file is writable.
-x	True, if the named file is executable.
-z	True, if the string is null.

The real value of **test** is found when creating shell scripts, although you can also execute it on the command line. **test** always returns 0 for success and 1 if unsuccessful. This can be tested in the script or on the command line using the *$?* (return code) variable. For example, to see if the file /etc/bash.rc exists, use the following command:

```
[root@mercury.technical /root]# test -f /etc/bash.rc
[root@mercury.technical /root]# echo $?
1
[root@mercury.technical /root]# test -f /etc/bashrc
[root@mercury.technical /root]# echo $?
0
[root@mercury.technical /root]#
```

The first **test** fails because the file is not called /etc/bash.rc, but /etc/bashrc. To see if the sticky bit is set on the /tmp directory, use

```
[root@mercury.technical /root]# test -k /tmp
[root@mercury.technical /root]# echo $?
0
[root@mercury.technical /root]#
```

The **test** passes because the sticky bit is in fact set on the /tmp/ directory.

Using [

The **test** command has been around since the earliest days of Unix and exists on every Linux implementation. The [is a synonym for **test**, as most people do not use the **test** command specifically in their shell scripts because of the popularity associated with the [command.

If we take a quick look at the **test** and [commands,

```
[root@mercury.technical /root]# ls -li /usr/bin/test /usr/bin/[
 193136 lrwxrwxrwx 1 root root 4 May 12 04:34 /usr/bin/[ -> test
 193152 -rwxr-xr-x 1 root root 17540 Jul 12 2000 /usr/bin/test
[root@mercury.technical /root]#
```

we see [is a symbolic link pointing to **test**.

Because [is a command, it must be followed by a space, then the condition to be evaluated, and finally with a]. The closing] signifies the entire condition has been specified and instructs [to perform the evaluation. This is important because [file is not a command.

For example, we can expand our :p script to report an error if no arguments are given on the command line.

To see if root is logged in, the command would be

```
[root@mercury.technical /root]# [ 'who | grep root' ]
[root@mercury.technical /root]# echo $?
1
[root@mercury.technical /root]#
```

This indicates root is not logged onto the system, based upon the return code from the [command. The [command, when coupled with the $#, can ensure there are more arguments to process before executing the **shift** command. However, testing a variable is only useful if you can actually make a decision with it.

If I Must, Then I Must

Everything we do is based upon a test and then a decision. If the phone rings, I answer it. If I am late, I miss the bus. What we have seen so far with the shell and its ability to process commands is no different. Evaluating variables to make a decision using the [or **test** commands leads to the decision-making process associated with the following: "if a condition exists, then perform an action."

The shell script syntax to selectively perform a set of commands is based upon the **if** construct. Essentially, this is written:

```
if {some condition exists}
then {perform some action}
fi
```

The format is always **if-then-fi**. The **fi** command, "if" spelled backwards, signifies the end of the **if** block. There is no definitive style for shell programs—indentation is purely up to the programmer writing the code, but indentation does it make it easier to follow the logic. Typically, shell programs are written so the commands following the **then** statement are indented some arbitrary amount for readability.

As you will surmise, there is no limited number of conditions that can be nested within the **if-then-fi**. When doing so, the clear levels of indentation make it easier to determine which commands belong to which block of code. For example

```
if {condition one exists}
then
if {condition two exists}
then
{perform some action}
fi
fi
```

It cannot be stressed enough that there must be a matching **fi** for every **if** statement. Failing to balance the results in the shell will result in a syntax error. Some shell programmers will include the **then** statement on the same line as the **if**, which is possible only if you include a semicolon after the test. There is syntactically no difference between the two, and there is no difference in performance of the shell script. Through the coming examples, we will see both methods of describing the statements.

Looking back at the p script, we can test to see if an argument was given by the user and print a usage message if he or she forgot the argument. The p script with the **if** statement to perform the test looks like

```
[root@mercury.technical /root]# cat p
#! /bin/sh
#
# This script prints the total number of processes a user is running,
# and then print the return code from the grep command.
# we use back ticks around the grep command to execute it and then print
# the result in the echo
if [ $# -lt 1 ]
then
 echo "usage: $0 user"

 fi
echo "$1 is running 'ps -ef | grep $1 | grep -v grep -c' processes"
[root@mercury.technical /root]#
```

Now running the **p** command with no arguments on the command line results in

```
[root@mercury.technical /root]# p
usage: p user
Usage: grep [OPTION]... PATTERN [FILE]...
Try 'grep --help' for more information.
 is running 0 processes
[root@mercury.technical /root]# p root
root is running 16 processes
[root@mercury.technical /root]#
```

With the ability to test for and evaluate both variables and arguments, we are well on our way to building more complicated shell scripts. How do we pass a return code back to the shell from which our script was called?

Taking the Exit

We need to exit our script at the right time to stop execution and potentially generate more errors the user must then interpret. The **exit** command enables us to stop processing at the point where the **exit** command is in the script and provide a return code back to the parent shell.

```
[root@mercury.technical /root]# cat p
#! /bin/sh
#
```

```
# This script prints the total number of processes a user is running,
# and then print the return code from the grep command.
# we use back quotes around the grep command to execute it and then print
# the result in the echo
if [ $# -lt 1 ]
then
 echo "usage: $0 user"
 exit
 fi
echo "$1 is running 'ps -ef | grep $1 | grep -v grep -c' processes"
[root@mercury.technical /root]#
```

Now our script will exit when the error condition is encountered and processing stops. The commands following the **if-then-fi** block are never executed. However, the **exit** command itself doesn't guarantee the parent shell will see a non-zero return code, unless we specifically instruct **exit** to provide one. Running the script as it is right now will give you something you don't expect:

```
[root@mercury.technical /root]# sh p
usage: p user
[root@mercury.technical /root]# echo $?
0
[root@mercury.technical /root]#
```

The return code the parent received is zero, meaning success, even though an error was generated, and the script didn't run to completion. We can alter this behavior by specifying the return code we want the **exit** command to give back to the shell.

The **exit** command accepts an argument, which is the exit code. If we change the previous **exit** line from

```
exit
```

to

```
exit 1
```

the parent shell receives a failure error code:

```
[root@mercury.technical /root]# cat p
#! /bin/sh
#
# This script prints the total number of processes a user is running,
# and then print the return code from the grep command.
# we use back ticks around the grep command to execute it and then print
# the result in the echo
if [ $# -lt 1 ]
then
 echo "usage: $0 user"
 exit 1
```

```
    fi

    echo "$1 is running 'ps -ef | grep $1 | grep -v grep -c' processes"
[root@mercury.technical /root]# sh p
usage: p user
[root@mercury.technical /root]# echo $?
1
[root@mercury.technical /root]#
```

If you want to signify an error, you must provide a non-zero return code as the argument for **exit**. Using different return codes provides other shells the ability to determine what caused the error and to handle it appropriately if needed.

Decisions, Decisions

The **if** command has several variations enabling for multiple decision branches to be taken. The first is **if-then-else-fi**, and the second is **if-then-elif**. The first of these provides both a positive and negative command path, depending on the results of the test.

The steps around the **if-then-else** resemble the following:

```
if test is true
then
 execute commands
else
 execute commands
fi
```

The **if-then-else** construct enables us to make some complicated decisions and execute very different code branches, depending on the results of the test. In the situation where we have multiple conditions to test, we can use the **if-then-elif** construct. The flow of this construct looks like

```
if test is true
then
 execute commands
elif second test is true
 execute commands
else
 execute commands
fi
```

We can modify the p script to use **if-then-else** as shown here:

```
[root@mercury.technical /root]# cat p
#! /bin/sh
#
# This script prints the total number of processes a user is running,
# and then print the return code from the grep command.
# we use back ticks around the grep command to execute it and then print
```

```
# the result in the echo
if [ $# -lt 1 ]
then
 echo "usage: $0 user"
else
 echo "$1 is running 'ps -ef | grep $1 | grep -v grep -c' processes"
fi
[root@mercury.technical /root]#
```

This script prints the error message if there are no arguments; otherwise, it prints the processes running for the specified user. Assume we want to change the message delivered to the user and tell him or her who he or she can call for support based upon who is logged into the system? If root is logged in, tell the user to contact them. If root is not, but user root is, then have the user see if he or she should contact root. Finally, if neither root nor root is online, advise the user that no online support is available at this time.

```
! /bin/sh
#
# This script prints the total number of processes a user is running,
# and then print the return code from the grep command.
# we use back ticks around the grep command to execute it and then print
# the result in the echo
if [ $# -lt 1 ]
then
 echo "usage: $0 user"
 ROOT='who | grep root'
 USER='who | grep root'
 if [ "$ROOT" ]
 then
 echo "contact the system administrator for support"
 elif [ "$USER" ]
 then
 echo "contact Jon Howe for support"
 else
 echo "support is not available at this time."
 fi
else
 echo "$1 is running 'ps -ef | grep $1 | grep -v grep -c' processes"
fi
```

With the preceding script, one of two messages will be displayed along with the usage message, indicating who the user should contact if he or she needs support. The message is based upon the value of two variables, set with the **who** command.

NOTE Remember, when you use multiple if-then statements, you must end each with an "fi," as they are independent blocks. When using if-then-else or if-then-elif statements, only one fi is required.

Conditional Execution

We have seen how the **if-then-else** construct can establish conditional execution and then run a series of commands. Similar results can be found using the && and || operators to establish a logical Boolean execution method. These operators work based upon the exit code of the first command and will execute the second appropriately. The operators mean

- **&&**   Execute the second command only if the exit status of the first is zero.

- **||**   Execute the second command only if the exit status of the first is above zero.

This is often used as a shortcut to the **if** statement, as in

```
[ '$LOGNAME' = root ] && echo "Welcome Chris"
```

If the user logs in and the value of LOGNAME is root, the second command executes, and I see "Welcome Chris". If the value of $LOGNAME is something different, the **echo** command will not execute.

I can write the same thing using the || operator:

```
[ "$LOGNAME" = root ] || echo :Welcome other user"
```

The second example isn't very friendly, but it illustrates the point. If the value of $LOGNAME is not root, the **echo** command is executed and the associated text is printed.

Looping Around

Sometimes you need to run the same series of commands over and over again. This can be done by adding the same step to the script as many times as needed. Unless you can anticipate every iteration, however, it gets tedious to maintain. The better solution is to use loops. This section discusses the following three topics:

- while
- until
- for

Using the while Loop

The **while** loop evaluates the condition at the top of the loop and executes the instructions in the block until the test fails. The syntax for the **while** loop is

```
while {condition evaluates true}
do
 (execute the commands)
done
```

A common use for this type of loop is to continue to process variables as long as variables exist (in other words, to continue to shift while variables remain). For example

```
! /bin/sh
#
# This script prints the total number of processes a user is running,
# and then print the return code from the grep command.
# we use back ticks around the grep command to execute it and then print
# the result in the echo
if [ $# -lt 1 ]
then
 echo "usage: $0 user"
else
 echo "$1 is running 'ps -ef | grep $1 | grep -v grep -c' processes"
fi
[root@mercury.technical /root]
```

We can modify our script to use a **while** loop and process each user name on the command line:

```
$
#! /bin/sh
#
# This script prints the total number of processes a user is running,
# and then print the return code from the grep command.
# we use back ticks around the grep command to execute it and then print
# the result in the echo
if [ $# -lt 1 ]
then
 echo "usage: $0 user"
else
 while [ $# -ge 1 ]
 do
 echo "$1 is running 'ps -ef | grep $1 | grep -v grep -c' processes"
 shift
 done
fi
[root@mercury.technical /root]# sh p root root oracle
root is running 15 processes
root is running 41 processes
oracle is running 0 processes
[root@mercury.technical /root]#
```

By looping in this manner, we do not have to worry about how many arguments the user gives on the command line; we can process all of them. Notice the **while** loop requires the keywords *do* and *done* to signify the top and bottom of the **while** loop. The *do* and *done* keywords, like **if** and **fi**, must appear as pairs. The same holds true for the **until** and **for** commands, which use the same keywords.

Using the until Loop

The **while** loop evaluates the condition at the top of the loop, and consequently, the instructions in the loop may never be executed. The same is true for the **until** loop, but it executes the instructions in the block until the test is true. That is to say, the loop will execute as long as the test is false. The syntax for this is

```
until {condition exists}
do
  (series of commands)
done
```

For example, the following script will execute the users logged on the system until root logs on:

```
[root@mercury.technical /root]# cat r
until [ 'who | cut -d" " -f1 | grep root' ]
do
echo "root is not online"
sleep 10
done
echo "root is online"
[root@mercury.technical /root]# sh r
root is not online
root is not online
root is online
[root@mercury.technical /root]#
```

The test fails on the initial evaluation because root is not logged in. Once root logs in, the loop exists. Worth mentioning here is the **sleep** command, which pauses execution for the number of seconds specified, in this case, ten. Remember, the **while** command will execute the commands in the loop as long as the test is true. The **until** command executes the commands in the loop as long as they are false.

Using the for Loop

The final method of looping, the **for** command, does not depend upon the evaluations of a test. Rather, it works on a set of data values you want to work with. For each value in the set, **for** assigns the value to a variable, which is then processed in the loop instructions.

The syntax for the command is

```
for {variable} in {set}
do
{commands}
done
```

The following script combines several constructs we have seen so far. It accepts a command-line argument, which is then evaluated to see if it is a file or a directory:

```
[root@mercury.technical /root]# cat I
for file in 'ls $1'
do
 if [ -f $file ]
 then
 echo "$file is a regular file"
 elif [ -d $file ]
 then
 echo "$file is a directory"
 fi
done
[root@mercury.technical /root]#
```

The **for** loop is useful for any activity that requires repetitive operations on an unknown number of variables. The one thing to remember is the **for** loop operates on a set of values that are in a set.

Revisiting Input

We have seen a lot of shell scripting up to this point, but we have yet to actually collect input from the user or look at how to build a script that can accept data from a pipe. This is accomplished with the **read** command. The syntax is

```
read {variable names}
```

You can specify one or more variable names on the **read** command line. Each variable is split at the first whitespace character and assigned to the corresponding variable. If there are not enough variables, all text is assigned to the last variable named. An example of this command within a script would be

```
[root@mercury.technical /root]# cat r
#!/bin/sh

if [ $# -lt 1 ]
then
 while [ "$want" = "" ]
```

```
 do
 echo "Enter the name of the user to watch for"
 read want
 done
else
 want=$1
fi
until [ 'who | cut -d" " -f1 | grep $want' ]
do
echo "$want is not online"
sleep 10
done
echo "$want is online"

[root@mercury.technical /root]#
```

In our script, the user is prompted to enter a username if he or she does not supply one on the command line. The **read** command does not provide a prompt, which explains why one is necessary before issuing the command.

When the user enters the name, it is assigned to the variable *want*, and the script continues to execute. If the user were to enter **root chweb root**, the value of *want* is equal to root chweb root. If more than one variable is identified on the **read** command line, each word is assigned to a separate variable. For example, assume we have our file of employee names:

```
[root@mercury.technical /root]# cat employee.list
OTTON1510510 Jon Howe
RTPNC1637921 Jeff Durham
MORNJ1437246 John Sleeva
NATLA2039485 Keith Carlson
DALTX3558734 Jeff Sweeten
BRAON1243956 Pat Yahner
SHRLA3448902 Jon Holman
[root@mercury.technical /root]#
[root@mercury.technical /root]# more x
cat employee.list | while read number name
do
echo "name=$name number=($number)"
done
[root@mercury.technical /root]#
[root@mercury.technical /root]# sh x
name=Jon Howe number=(OTTON1510510)
name=Jeff Durham number=(RTPNC1637921)
name=John Sleeva number=(MORNJ1437246)
name=Keith Carlson number=(NATLA2039485)
name=Jeff Sweeten number=(DALTX3558734)
name=Pat Yahner number=(BRAON1243956)
name=Jon Holman number=(SHRLA3448902)
[root@mercury.technical /root]#
```

When the script x runs, it reads the information from the file, assigns the first field to the variable *number*, and the second field to the variable *name*. As the names have two space-separated fields, both words are assigned to the last variable, *name*.

Working with the case Command

If you are in the situation where there are a lot of **if-then-fi** blocks to be coded or you need more functionality with less code, there is the **case** statement. The syntax for this is

```
case {variable} in
{first choice}) {commands} ;;
{first choice}) {commands} ;;
{first choice}) {commands} ;;
esac
```

With the **case** command, each code block is executed based on the named variable matching one of the available choices. When a match is found, the commands in that code block are executed. When the final command is reached, the execution continues at the first command following the esac statement, which closes the case section.

Each code block is terminated with two semicolons, which must be present or the shell reports an error when processing the script. Like the **if** statement, there is no defined format for indentation. However, the choices are generally one indent, and the commands are two indents. For example

```
[root@mercury.technical /root]# cat c
#!/bin/sh
# case illustration

echo "
 Select an option and press ENTER

 1 - date
 2 - who

 -> \c"

read OPTION

case $OPTION in
 1)
 date
 ;;
 2)
 who
 ;;
 *)
 echo "you were supposed to make a choice!"
```

```
 ;;
esac
[root@mercury.technical /root]#
```

After the user enters his or her selection in our example, the value is assigned to the variable *OPTION*. When the case statement is reached, it evaluates the value of *OPTION* and selects the correct match and executes the commands in the block. The use of the asterisk (*) denotes "match any value." This is typically used in the case statement as the default should no value match in the case statements. With this in mind, you can see how the asterisk would be a good thing to use for catching errors in selection or variable assignment elsewhere in the script.

```
case $OPTION in
Q||q)
 exit
 ;;
esac
```

This is not say you can't duplicate the code; there is just a better solution. Finally, if you are so inclined, you can use the **tr** command to convert the lowercase values to uppercase, and then only provide options matching the uppercase value.

It is also possible to match on more than a single character. Suppose you want to exit the script when a user presses any of a, b, c, or d. The case statement is then written:

```
case $OPTION in
 [a-d])
 exit
 ;;
esac
```

This illustrates using a range of values and having them all execute the same code block. Finally, you can match on words or partial words using the asterisk:

```
case $OPTION in
 exit|ex*)
 exit
 ;;
esac
```

The pattern matching in **case** provides the administrator with a great deal of flexibility in writing his or her script.

Not Quite an exit

The **exit** command has been used extensively in this chapter. However, from time to time, there is valid reason for exiting a loop or **case** statement and continue execution at the command following the loop or **case**. The **exit** command will not do this for you. Rather, we turn to the **break** command. The **break** command is useful, particularly in large scripts, to bypass sections of code when it is no longer necessary to execute them:

```
[root@mercury.technical /root]# cat b
#!/bin/sh
# demonstrating break

if [ $# -lt 1 ]
then
 echo "you must enter a series of words"
 exit 1
fi

for word in $*
do
 if [ "$word" = "exit" ]
 then
 break
 fi
 echo "the word is $word"
done

echo "finished"
[root@mercury.technical /root]#
```

In this example, the user enters a series of words on the command line. If one of the words is "exit," the **if-then** test is true, and the break is executed. The next command executed is the first following the done statement in the **for** loop. The user sees

```
[root@mercury.technical /root]# sh b hello bye exit done
the word is hello
the word is bye
finished
[root@mercury.technical /root]#
```

The script prints the words "hello" and "bye," but does not print the words "exit" and "done" because the command to do so is not executed.

Working with Numbers

The shell considers all variables to be strings, even if we are working with numbers. In most situations, this is acceptable because we often don't care what the shell thinks the value is.

For example

```
[root@mercury.technical /root]# z=18
[root@mercury.technical /root]# y=2
[root@mercury.technical /root]# echo $z
18
[root@mercury.technical /root]# echo $y
2
[root@mercury.technical /root]# echo $z + $y
18 + 2
[root@mercury.technical /root]#
```

Because the shell treats everything as a string, attempting to perform arithmetic operations appears to be difficult. However, the **expr** command provides the ability to do just that:

```
[root@mercury.technical /root]# echo $z
18
[root@mercury.technical /root]# echo $y
2
[root@mercury.technical /root]# echo 'expr $z + $y'
20
[root@mercury.technical /root]# echo 'expr $z / $y'
9
[root@mercury.technical /root]#
```

This is a very portable method and works in any shell. However, if you are writing scripts that will be run in the Korn shell or bash environments, you can also use the command **typeset** to declare the variable as a number:

```
[root@mercury.technical /root]# typeset -i z=18
[root@mercury.technical /root]# echo $z
18
[root@mercury.technical /root]# echo 'expr $z / 3'
6
[root@mercury.technical /root]#
```

The -i option informs **typeset** to declare the following variable as an integer. **typeset** can also define a variable as an array. The following is an example of a script file that will accept a number as input and on the command line and then increment to that number by one:

```
[root@mercury.technical /root]# cat e
#!/bin/sh

x=1
while [ $x -le 10 ]
do
 echo $x
 x='expr $x + 1'
done
[root@mercury.technical /root]# sh e
```

```
1
2
3
4
5
6
7
8
9
10
[root@mercury.technical /root]#
```

The **expr** command adds one to the value, and the control returns to the top of the **while** loop. When the value becomes greater than ten, the loop exits. As there are no other commands after the loop, the script exists.

TCP/IP Host Configuration

To configure TCP/IP on a host, you must know three values: the host's IP address, the subnet mask, and the default gateway. Each of these values is discussed in the following sections.

IP Address

Every host on a TCP/IP network must have a unique IP address that comprises values from a 32-bit binary number. Typically, hosts using IPv6 support both 32- and 128-bit IP addresses. Because it can be difficult to remember a 32-bit binary number, the IP addressing format uses four decimal-number octets. The first octet identifies the address class and determines the number of hosts available on the network. You can modify the actual number of hosts by using the subnet mask (discussed in the following section). Table 3-3 lists the class of address and the number of available host addresses.

Many new system administrators incorrectly assume that class B starts with the octet 127. The address 127.0.0.1 is reserved for a loopback address to always signify the current host. The second, third, and fourth octets in all address classes identify the network and the host. Figure 3-11 shows the **ifconfig-a** command, which tells all of the IP addresses on the system.

You should understand that each host in a given address space or realm must have a unique address. If two or more hosts attempt to share the same IP address, the network does not know which system the packet is for. IP has tests to identify this type of problem and inform the system manager. If there are 20 hosts on a network, for example, each host must have a unique IP address on the network. If the system is directly connected to the Internet, the system must have the only occurrence of the address in the entire Internet.

Table 3-3   Classes, Addresses, Hosts, and Subnet Masks

Class	Address	Number of hosts available per address	Default subnet mask
A	01–126	16,777,214	255.0.0.0
B	128–191	65,534	255.255.0.0
C	192–223	254	255.255.255.0
D	224–239	Used only for multicasting; cannot be assigned to individual hosts	
E	240–255	Reserved addresses; cannot be issued	

Figure 3-11   The **ifconfig -a** command, as seen in a terminal window

Three address ranges have been designated as private addresses for networks not connected to the network or protected using technologies such as firewalls or routers using network address translation. There is one in each of the A, B, and C address ranges. Within the class A addresses, the range 10.x.x.x is available, wherein each of the *X*s can be any number up to 255. Class B addresses reserve the range 172.16.x.x to 172.31.x.x for private use, and the class C address segment reserves 192.168.x.x.

Subnet Mask

The subnet mask determines whether the network has been further divided into smaller networks (called *subnets*) or whether all the hosts can be found on one wire. The default value is based on the class of the network, as shown in Table 3-3. Deviating from the default value divides the total number of hosts on a network into a smaller number of hosts on more networks. Although the division of your network into subnets increases your ability to isolate systems, it can significantly impact the number of hosts available on each network. Table 3-4 illustrates this trade-off.

When a subnet value is used, it limits the possible IP address values by removing some of the values that could have been used. For example, if you are using a class C address of 205.120.10 and are not using subnets, the fourth field can have values from 1 to 254. If you change the subnet mask from 255.255.255.0 to 255.255.255.192, only six bits are left for the IP address. This creates two subnets, each with 62 hosts and IP ranges of 65 to 126 for one network, and 129 to 190 for the second network.

Default Gateway

The default gateway defines the route off your network if no other route is found. Typically, it is the IP address of the router. If you are connecting to an ISP, the ISP typically

Table 3-4 The Trade-Off of Using Values Other Than the Default

Additional bits required	Subnet address	Maximum number of subsets	Minimum number of hosts: C network	Maximum number of hosts: B network	Maximum number of hosts: A network
0	0	0	254	65,534	16,777,214
1	128	2	126	32,766	8,388,606
2	192	4	62	16,382	4,194,302
3	224	8	30	8,190	2,097,150
4	240	16	14	4,094	1,048,574
5	248	32	6	2,046	524,286
6	252	64	2	1,022	262,142

provides these values. Even though the IP address must be unique for every host on the network, each host shares the same default gateway to connect to hosts beyond the local network.

Supplying Values

When configuring TCP/IP on Linux and other workstation operating systems, you can either manually specify the IP address information establishing a static assignment, or you use a dynamic address allocation using the Dynamic Host Configuration Protocol (DHCP).

Using DHCP requires that a DHCP server, or a system running the DHCP daemon (dhcpd), be on the network. The DHCP server has a known range of addresses—known as a *scope*—and can lease IP addresses to other systems on the network. You can configure the duration of the lease—from a short period to forever. Provided that the forever option is not used, the client will attempt to periodically renew its lease from the server. If the server isn't available, the client continues to make requests until the lease expires. Once the lease expires, the server puts the IP address back into the assignable pool, and the client must request a new lease. After every expiration, the client always requests the same IP address as previously leased (if it's not already in use). Figure 3-12 shows a network adapter configured for DHCP in **linuxconf**.

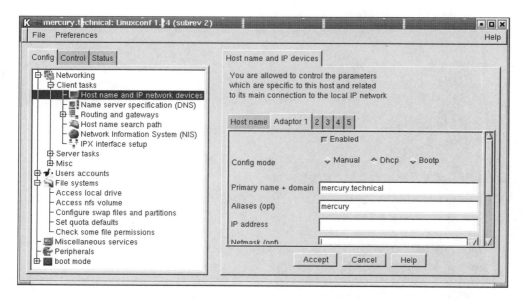

Figure 3-12   An example of a network card using DHCP to set the IP address and subnet mask

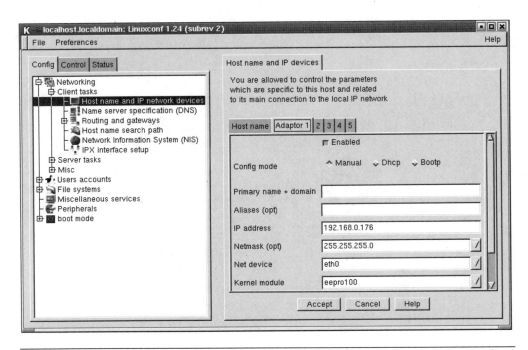

Figure 3-13 An example of an adapter card using a manually set IP address and subnet mask via **linuxconf**

All the values for setting configuration files for connectivity with TCP/IP can be set via **linuxconf**. **linuxconf** is a viable, strong graphical configuration tool. Some of the settings shown in Figure 3-13 are discussed here within the TCP/IP portion of this chapter. Figure 3-14 shows an expanded view of variables that can be set using **linuxconf**.

Other TCP/IP Configurations

When preparing for the Linux+ exam, make sure you are familiar with the following configuration files and utilities:

- **/etc/hostname** This file holds the name of the host on a single line. If networking is not configured, the entry will read

```
noname nodomain nowhere
```

On some implementations, this is /etc/hostname.

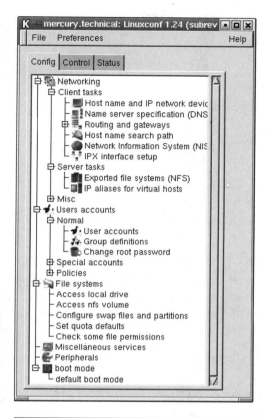

Figure 3-14   The expanded menu of **linuxconf**

- **/etc/hosts**   This file is used to list IP addresses and corresponding system names. Because it must be manually updated to maintain the list of all hosts, the file should be used only on small networks. The preferred method for resolving host-name to IP addresses is to use DNS (discussed in the next chapter).

- **/etc/networks**   This file lists the known networks with which the host can communicate.

You should also be familiar with the following utilities when studying for the exam:

- **arp**   The **arp** command prints the entries in the system's ARP table, listing the IP and physical addresses for each entry.

- **domainname**   Similar to **hostname**, this utility shows the Network Information Service (NIS) domain name used by the host.

- **dnsdomainname** Similar to **hostname**, the **dnsdomainname** command prints the DNS domain name used by the host.

- **ftp** The file transfer program relies upon the FTP to transfer data between the local and remote systems.

- **hostname** A simple utility, it shows the name of the host.

- **ifconfig** Using the syntax **ifconfig interface options**, this command configures the TCP/IP parameters on the command line. Configuring the first Ethernet interface with an IP address of 205.110.20.3, for example, would use the command **ifconfig eth0 205.110.20.3**. If the subnet mask is not specified, the default for the address class is used. Configuring the same network interface with a subnet mask of 255.255.255.192 uses the command **ifconfig eth0 205.110.20.3 255.255.255.192**.

- **netstat** The **netstat** command prints the network statistics for the TCP and UDP protocols. When used without any options, **netstat** prints the protocol statistics and current TCP/IP connections. **netstat** can also provide information about routing tables and interfaces—similar to what can be obtained from /sbin/route and from **ifconfig**.

- **ping** The **ping** command sends ICMP echo-request commands to a remote host to determine whether the host is connected to the network and responding. If the target host doesn't respond, **ping** prints an error message that indicates the host is unreachable. Figure 3-15 shows the **ping** command in a typical terminal window.

- **route** The **route** command is used to configure routing and to print the contents in the route table. New routes are added using the command **route add**, whereas using **route** without any arguments prints the contents of the route table.

- **telnet** The **telnet** command establishes an interactive terminal session with the remote host. This is typically used for administration, but can also be used by any user who requires command-line access.

- **traceroute** This command prints the path taken to reach a specific host, including each hop in the network path. The **traceroute** command is often used as a replacement for **ping**, but takes longer to execute because of the additional overhead. **traceroute** will show each stop your data makes on its way and can also show how routing tables change. A couple of typical examples using the **traceroute** command are shown in Figure 3-16.

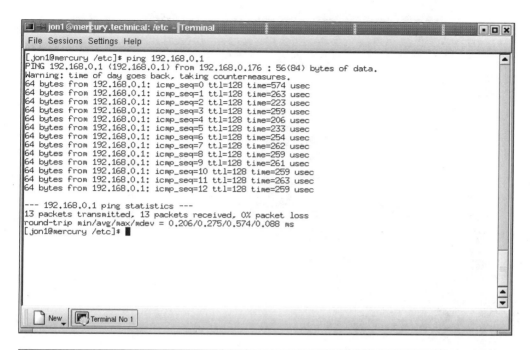

Figure 3-15 An example of the **ping** command in a terminal window

Moving on to DNS

In the early days of the Internet, the HOSTS file was updated by a single source, and all Internet connection systems received continuous updates to keep with the rate of growth. However, this meant an organization that wanted to add a new host to its network must first contact the registration authority to have them add the system to the master HOSTS file.

This lack of flexibility and the growing size of the HOSTS file resulted in the development of the Domain Name Systems (DNS) in 1984. Instead of putting every host in a single file, DNS enables an organization to manage the IP addresses for the systems within their own environment. This creates a multiserver, distributed database, with the master knowing where to ask for information it does not have. This approach distributes the processing load on thousands of systems and enables the database size to grow as required.

For a system to be DNS-aware, it must be configured with the IP address of the DNS server offering the service. Most Unix systems use the file /etc/resolv.conf to store the default configuration for the DNS client.

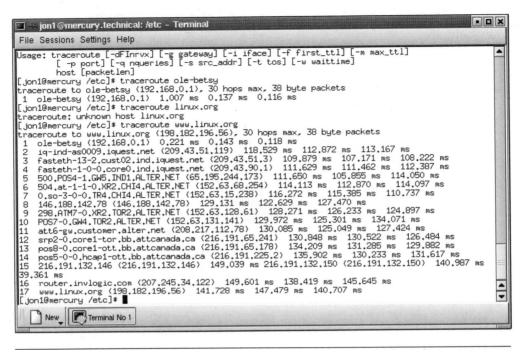

Figure 3-16 An example of the **traceroute** command in a terminal window

DNS Structure

The naming system used in DNS is based on a tree-type directory structure (see Figure 3-17). At the top is the root of the tree or the root nameservers. As you progress lower in the tree, the organization's domain name becomes more specific and unique.

The tree-type structure enables an organization to take responsibility for defining any subdomains and the names of the systems within their enterprise. Without the tree structure, there could have only been one system in the entire Internet called *sales*.

The resolution of domain names to IP addresses is done through a series of nameservers. Any organization can run a nameserver that is responsible for its domain, but only authorized agencies can run a nameserver responsible for a top-level domain, like .com. The following are the most common top-level domains:

- **com**   Commercial enterprise
- **edu**   Educational institution
- **gov**   Government

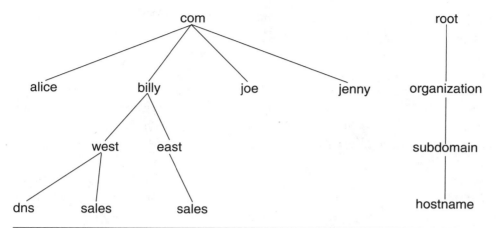

Figure 3-17 The DNS tree

- **mil**   Military
- **net**   Network provider
- **org**   Organization/original/not-for-profit

Typically, the preceding domains represent organizations located in the United States. If the organization is outside of the United States, the top-level domain becomes the two-letter abbreviation of the country. These country codes are the International Standard country code designations. Dozens of such country abbreviations exist, and some of those most used include

- **au**   Australia
- **de**   Germany
- **ca**   Canada
- **es**   Spain
- **fr**   France
- **uk**   United Kingdom

An organization has the ability to further divide its domain (billy.com) into subdomains. Grouping systems into subdomains enables an organization to compartmentalize or isolate systems and possibly reuse system names within the different subdomains. If you have two subdomains in billy.com, one being east.billy.com and the other west.billy.com., and both subdomains contain a host called sales, these two hostnames do not point to the same system: one is sales.east.billy.com and the other is sales.west. billy.com. They can be two distinctly different systems. When working with fully qualified domain names, always start from the right to break it into its components.

As previously mentioned, name resolution is accomplished using a series of name servers as the different layers in the tree structure. With the proliferation of hosts on the Internet, it would be possible for a single system to store all the names. Furthermore, this system would be so busy answering queries that it would never be able to satisfy the demand on it.

Consequently, DNS servers are responsible for *zones*—the area in which they are considered the authority to answer requests. Through the zone model, the administrative burden of maintaining the database and the system impact of answering DNS queries is shared across the Internet. Each zone will have a primary server and at least one secondary to answer queries, should the primary or zone master be unavailable.

All changes to the DNS database to add/change/remove a host is done on the primary nameserver. Changes should not be made on the secondary nameserver, as this is read-only data and is overwritten each time the secondary replicates the data from the zone master. The replication process is called a *zone transfer*.

A third DNS server, known as a *caching-only server*, is used to provide quick answers to information it already knows. This server type does not have a zone file and, as such, can only answer queries from its cache. The caching-only server must ask another nameserver for every lookup unless it is in the cache.

DNS Records

The DNS database consists of a number of records defining the information about the DNS zone and other records to define the hostnames and IP addresses for each host in the database. The records in the DNS database, called *resource records*, vary slightly depending on the type of information they contain. The most common record types are

- **SOA record**   Start of Authority
- **NS record**   Nameserver
- **A record**   Address
- **CNAME record**   Canonical Name
- **MX record**   Mail Exchanger
- **HINFO record**   Host Information
- **PTR record**   Pointer

Every DNS zone must contain an SOA record. The SOA record identifies the zone and establishes the namerserver's responsibility for the zone. The SOA record also contains the following parameters that affect how the zone operates:

- **Source host**   The primary name server.

- **Contact e-mail**   The e-mail address of the domain administrator. This is often hostmaster@domain to prevent a single person from becoming known as the DNS contact.

- **Serial number**   The incrementing version number of the database.

- **Refresh time**   The number of seconds that a secondary server waits before checking for changes to the database file.

- **Retry time**   The number of seconds that a secondary server waits before another attempt if replication fails.

- **Expiration time**   The number of seconds before the old zone information is deleted from secondary servers. As a minor point, all DNS servers (not just caching-only) cache entries; the difference is that caching-only servers do only that (unless the TTL is zero).

- **Time To Live (TTL)**   The number of seconds that a caching-only server can cache resource records from this database file before discarding them and performing another query.

The NS record identifies the primary server and all other DNS servers that can answer queries for the domain. When registering a new domain, the top-level domain authorities generally require at least one secondary name server.

The MX record identifies how mail is routed to systems in this domain. There must be at least one MX record regardless of who is actually hosting your organization's e-mail.

The A record identifies the hostname and the corresponding IP address. When the DNS server receives a query to find an IP address, it checks the A records for a host with the specified name. If one is found, the IP address is returned. If not, an error is returned.

The CNAME record enables you to specify more than one host name for a given IP address. This establishes aliases for the host.

The HINFO record also provides host information, typically the operating system type, CPU, and any other information. For security reasons, you should not use this record, as it can identify information about your system environment to enable an attacker to find and exploit a weakness.

Finally, the PTR record is used to translate an IP address back to a hostname, using what is known as a *reverse lookup*.

Utilities to Use with DNS

Most applications that users interact with perform the name resolution themselves using a facility call the *resolver*. Through the resolver facility, the application can get the IP address for a named server transparently to the user. If the local server doesn't know the answer, the question is asked until the response is no host found.

We discussed the **hostname** command as a method of finding the name of the local host. The **nslookup** command is used to query DNS and perform both name and IP address resolution. If started without any arguments, **nslookup** begins an interactive session. The typical argument is a fully qualified domain name. If the FQDN provided is found in the DNS database, the IP address is provided. There are a number of commands and options for **nslookup** that affect both the command line and interactive versions. The **nslookup** command is a deprecated command on Red Hat 7.1. The commands **dig** and **host** are the preferred method of querying DNS for resolution. Shown in Figure 3-18 is the **nslookup** command.

As mentioned earlier, DNS can also accept an IP address and perform a reverse lookup to attempt to find the hostname assigned to that IP address.

When finding an IP address for www.billy.com, DNS asks the following questions:

1. Is this my domain? If so, simply give back the address.

2. Do I already know the IP address for www.billy.com? Is it in my cache?

3. Who is the .com nameserver or who is authoritative for billy.com?

4. Can I find the hostname www.billy.com by contacting the authoritative name server billy.com?

5. What do I do when I receive the IP address or a "host not found" error?

The process of looking for the correct host always starts from the top-level domain. The same is true for performing a reverse lookup using the IP address. When giving an IP address to **nslookup** to search for, you must provide it in reverse—the name reverse lookup. For example, you want to find the hostname for IP address 24.112.10.10. When you provide this to **nslookup**, you must provide the address 10.10.112.24.in-addr.arpa. The reverse format with the domain in-addr.arpa informs DNS to perform a reverse lookup and get the hostname from the PTR records.

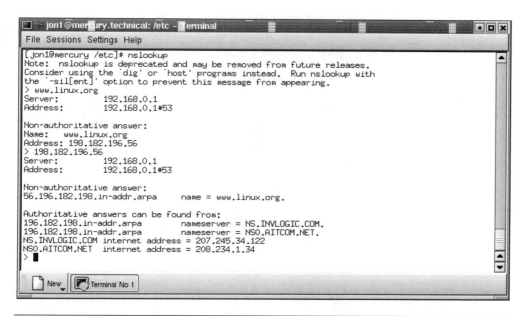

Figure 3-18   **nslookup** resolves names to and from IP address.

When DNS processes the reverse lookup requests, the nameserver goes through a similar process as with a hostname:

1. Where is network 24 assigned?

2. Does the owner of network 24 also own network 24.112?

3. Who owns network 24.112.10, and what nameservers are present?

4. Ask the nameserver with authority for network 24.112.10 what the hostname is for the requested system.

Like performing a hostname or forward lookup, if there is a corresponding entry in DNS mapping the IP to a hostname, the hostname is returned.

The Berkeley Internet Name Domain (BIND) is the Linux implementation of DNS. The BIND package includes the actual name server, named, a resolver library and tools for interaction. As of this writing, BIND 9.1.3 is the latest release. You can read more about BIND at **http://www.isc.org/products/BIND/bind-history.html**, and an unofficial FAQ is located at **http://www.intac.com/~cdp/cptd-faq/**.

Figure 3-19 shows a DNS setup screen via **linuxconf**.

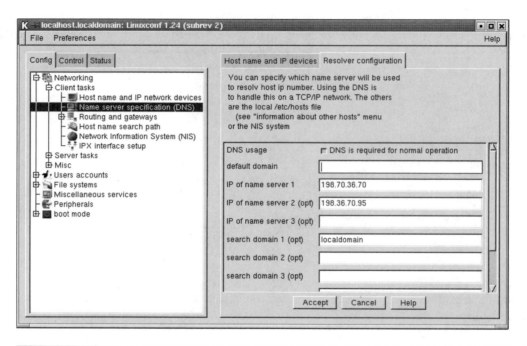

Figure 3-19   An example of **linuxconf** being used to set the IP addresses of DNS servers

Two Helpful Utilities

Two additional utilities can be extremely helpful when working with the Linux network configuration: **netconfig** and **linuxconf**. However, these commands are not included on all versions of Linux. You can easily find out if they are included in your distribution using the command

```
which netconfig [linuxconf]
```

netconfig

Aside from configuring the networking basics such as IP address, subnet mask, and so on, **netconfig** can also be used to configure the TCP maximum window size for network performance improvements. If you have a low-speed network connection, you might want to decrease your TCP window for smaller packets, while a faster, dedicated connection yields improved network performance from a larger TCP window size. **netconfig** is commonly found in /usr/sbin and uses the /etc/netconfig file to store the networking

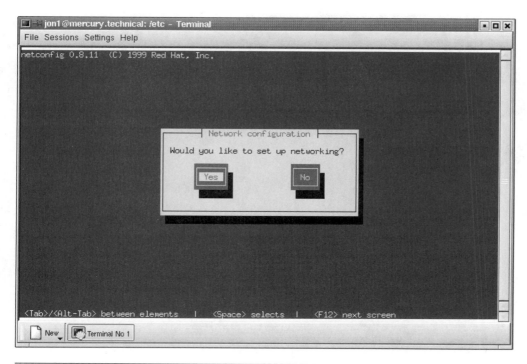

Figure 3-20   Red Hat's netconfig used to set up networking

configuration information. Figure 3-20 shows the initial screen of **netconfig** and can be invoked by typing **netconfig** at the command-line prompt.

linuxconf

linuxconf has been almost exclusively found in Red Hat distributions, although it works with most other Linux distributions as well. **linuxconf** is intended as an all-inclusive system management tool, which interacts with many of the networking components, including Samba, sendmail, and squid.

Both text and graphical interfaces are included, enabling administration through the X Window interface, the popular command line, or as an automatic administrator from the autopilot model.

linxconf can determine which daemons need to be started or stopped and restarted based upon the configuration changes. **linuxconf** can interact directly with network cards, daemons, disks, and mount/unmount volumes.

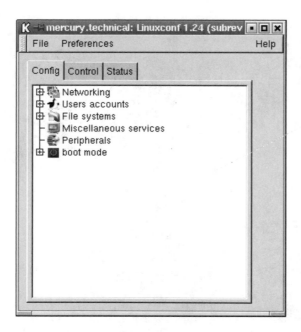

Figure 3-21   The default view of **linuxconf**

Several pictures of the **linuxconf** graphical interface have been inserted throughout this chapter showing the versatility and strength of this configuration tool. Figure 3-21 shows the default view of **linuxconf**.

Reconfiguring LILO

Reconfiguring the bootloader requires that we alter the LILO configuration. We can either manually edit the /etc/lilo.conf file, or we can use a system tool such as **linux-conf**. The /etc/lilo.conf configuration is plain text and viewable using the **cat**, **more**, or **vi** commands:

```
[root@mercury.technical /root]# more /etc/lilo.conf
boot=/dev/had
map=/boot/map
install=/boot/boot.b
prompt
timeout=50
message=/boot/message
default=linux
```

```
image=/boot/vmlinuz-2.4.2-2
 label=linux
 read-only
 root=/dev/hda1
[root@mercury.technical /root]#
```

As seen in the illustration, the /etc/lilo.conf file has a global or defaults section at the top of the file and image specific sections for each kernel on the system. Any parameter specified in an image section overrides the value defined at the top of the file in the global section. Note, however, there is no label for the global section. The options for the global section are listed in Table 3-5.

Table 3-5   Options for /etc/lilo.conf Global

Keyword	Description
Backup=backup-file	Where the boot-sector is copied (Boot=/dev/???). The hard disk partition where the boot sector is. Omitting this parameter indicates to LILO that the root file system is located on the boot device.
Compact	Attempts to merge adjacent read requests into a single read request.
Delay=tsecs	The time period, in tenths of a second, that LILO waits before booting the default kernel image. This is not the same as timeout.
Disk=/dev/name	The disk device you must include specific parameters for.
Disktab=file-name	A disk table with specific disk information. Use of a disktab file is highly discouraged.
Ignore-table	Instructs LILO to ignore corrupt partition tables.
Install=boot-file	Installs the specified file as the boot sector.
Lock	Has the effect of recording the boot command lines, locking LILO onto a specific image until it is later changed.
Message=message-file	The named file contains a text message printed before the boot: prompt. No additional messages are printed while LILO waits for a shift key to be pressed after printing LILO.
Map=map-file	The location of the map file.
Default=image-name	This is the kernel image loaded if no kernel is specified before the delay period is reached.
Prompt	This prints the boot: prompt without any prior key presses. Unattended reboots are only possible with the prompt parameter if the timeout parameter is used.
Timeout	The time in seconds that LILO waits before booting loading the default kernel image.

The .etc/lilo.conf file supports multiple images, each starting with the image= identifier. Image-specific parameters can be defined for that image. If a parameter is missing, the default value is used. If the default kernel is not identified using the default parameter in the global section, the first image specified is started by default. The image section options are listed in Table 3-6.

Adding the kernel we compiled earlier in the chapter is accomplished by copying the lines from another kernel section in /etc/lilo.conf and modifying them to match our new kernel. However, the changes to the /etc/lilo.conf file do not become active until LILO is rerun to create the new LILO map:

```
[root@mercury.technical /root]# /sbin/lilo-v
LILO version 21.4-4, Copyright (C) 1992-1998 Werner Almesberger
'lba32' extensions Copyright (C) 1999,2000 John Coffman

Reading boot sector from /dev/had
Merging with /boot/boot.b
Mapping message file /boot/message
Boot image: /boot/vmlinuz-2.4.2-2
Added linux *
Boot other: /dev/fd0, loader /boot/chain.b
Added floppy
/boot/boot.0300 exists - no backup copy made.
Writing boot sector.
[root@mercury.technical /root]#
```

Running the **lilo** command installs the new LILO information and activates the kernel for the next reboot. There is a KDE implementation of **lilo** called *klilo*, using the X Window System to provide a graphical interface to the **lilo** command. The **klilo** command has less functionality than the command-line tool, particularly around error

Table 3-6   The /etc/lilo.conf Image Options

Keyword	Description
Image=file	The path and filename of the image to load.
Label=text	The test description to show in the boot list.
Root=device	The disk partition containing the root file system.
Initrd=image	Where the initial RAM disk image is found.
Append	Adds the specified parameters to the kernel command line. This is useful for devices that cause system failures when probed.
Read-only	Indicates the root file system is mounted in read-only mode.

messages if there is a problem. Aside from the missing diagnostic messages, **klilo** has an excellent interface.

With the new kernel added to the LILO configuration, you can reboot and select your new kernel from the boot menu. This is important, as you should thoroughly test your new kernel before making it your default.

> **ALERT**   Incomplete testing of your new kernel may leave your system non-operational or lead to data loss or corruption.

When thoroughly tested, install the new kernel as the default by changing the default parameter in the global section or by making the new kernel the first image section in your /etc/lilo.conf file.

Adding and Configuring a Printer

Many administrators, regardless of the operating system involved, often spend more time configuring printers than actually configuring the most complex of networks. Perhaps the preceding statement is an exaggeration, but it is indicative of how simple the network has become and how complex printing in a network is. The recent standardization in printer technology and operating system features has improved the printing subsystem, but it is still much more complicated than necessary.

Compared to some operating systems, Linux is more straightforward in approach and configuration of the printer subsystems. The quickest introduction to the printing subsystem is to look at the simplest of operations and proceed from there.

Printing a File

The printing services are provided through **lpd**—the line printer daemon. **lpd** has traditionally been in the realm of BSD-based Unix systems since its inception. The functionality of **lpd** has been largely unchanged since then. The initial command used to submit print requests, or jobs, to **lpd** is the **lp** command. However, **lpr** is more commonly used today because it supports features not typically found in **lp**.

You can print files from the command line or through the graphical interface, as shown in Figure 3-22.

Figure 3-22 Most GUIs include a graphical icon to represent the printer.

Because most system administrators tend to be working at the command line and must be able to support utilities and programs that initiate print requests in this manner, we will focus our discussion there. In its simplest form, **lpr** is executed as follows:

```
lpr {filename}
```

For example, to print a file called employee.list, the command is

```
lpr employee.list
```

When initiating a print request, **lpr** checks for the *LPDEST* and *PRINTER* environment variables. If either exists, it identifies the default printer to use. Because no destination printer is provided in our example, the print request for employee.list is sent to the default printer.

Neither of these environment variables is defined by default. If the administrator wants to define them globally, he or she must add them to /etc/profile. If there are requirements for user-specific defaults, they should be set in the .bashrc found in their home directory.

After checking for the *LPDEST* or *PRINTER* environment variables, the print job is sent to the queue for that printer. The **lpd** daemon removes the job from the printer and produces the finished output.

Once everything is working correctly, getting output to the printer is as simple as it sounds. You can change the printer destination or how the output is processed by using the wide array of available options, including the following:

-b   Does not print a banner or header.

-F   Indicates the file has a particular format and processes it accordingly. The following options must be used in conjunction with -F:

    -b   Does not process this binary file.

    -d   Used with tex editor files.

    -l   The same as -b.

    -n   Accepts output from **troff**.

    -p   Uses **pr** to format the file before printing.

    -r   Deletes the file after spooling.

    -t   The same as -n.

    -v   Assumes a raster image.

-K   Specifies the number of copies to print.

-m   Identifies e-mail addresses to send error messages to.

-P   Specifies the destination printer.

-Q   Specifies the spool queue.

-R   Specifies the remote account name for remote print jobs.

-T   Specifies text for the title page (added by **pr**).

-w   Defines the page width.

Formatting a File

The **pr** command (**/bin/pr**) is used to perform many of the page and text formatting functions required by **lpr**. The **pr** command is also used to process a text file prior to printing. The output from **pr** includes a header (consisting of the date and time of last modification), the file name, and page numbers.

You can alter the default header by using the -h option with the **pr** command. The default page size for **pr** is 72 characters and 66 lines. You can customize these settings by using the -w and -l options, respectively.

Basic Configuration

Three principle files are required for the print service to work: lpd.conf, lpd.perms, and printcap. **lpd** uses a printer-capability database, stored in /etc/printcap, to establish the functionality and capabilities for each printer. The following is a default version of the /etc/printcap file:

```
# /etc/printcap
#
# Please don't edit this file directly unless you know what you are doing!
# Be warned that COAS requires a very strict format!
# Other applications (like WordPerfect) cannot cope with LPRng-extensions
# to the syntax (those are best hidden in a 'lpd-printcap')
#
# The preferred method to modify this file is COAS.

lp:\
  :lp=/dev/lp0:\
  :br#57600:\
  :rm=:\
  :rp=:\
  :sd=/var/spool/lpd/lp:\
  :mx#0:\
  :sh:\
  :if=/var/spool/lpd/lp/printfilter:
```

The warning at the top of the file is there for a reason. Although you *must* know about this file for the exam, you don't have to know how to edit it. Linux implementations typically provide tools to create printer configurations far easier than the traditional trial-and-error methods.

When **lpd** starts, it reads the /etc/printcap to determine what printers are available and then processes the printer queues looking for unfinished print jobs to complete. It is important to remember the purpose of printcap is to hold the definitions for the connected printers. You can use the definitions to alter the settings and operation of the printer. For example, if a printer is remote to the local system, the path to that printer will be entered in /etc/printcap.

The permissions for the various printer services, including **lpr, lpq,** and basic spooling operations are found in /etc/lpd.perms. The documentation in the file is extensive and some of the best found in any utility. The default version of the file is shown here, with some of the comments shortened to preserve space:

```
####################################################################
# LPRng - An Extended Print Spooler System
# Copyright 1988-1995 Patrick Powell, San Diego, CA
# papowell@astart.com
# See LICENSE for conditions of use.
####################################################################
```

```
# MODULE: TESTSUPPORT/lpd.perms.proto
# PURPOSE: prototype printer permissions file
# lpd.perms,v 3.7 1998/03/24 02:43:22 papowell Exp
######################################################################
# Printer permissions data base
## LPRng - An Enhanced Printer Spooler
## lpd.perms file
## Patrick Powell <papowell@astart.com>
## Access control to the LPRng facilities is controlled by entries
## in a set of lpd.perms files. The common location for these files
## are: /etc/lpd.perms, /usr/etc/lpd.perms, and /var/spool/lpd/lpd.perms.
## The locations of these files are set by the perms_path entry
## in the lpd.conf file or by compile time defaults in the
src/common/defaults.c
## file. In addition to the global permissions files, each spool queue
## can also have a permissions file. This file is searched when information
## or operations on a specific printer is requested.
##
## Each time the lpd server is given a user request or carries out an
unspooling
## operation, it searches to the perms files to determine if the action
## is ACCEPT or REJECT. The first ACCEPT or REJECT found terminates the
search.
## If none is found, then the last DEFAULT action is used.
##
## Permissions are checked by the use of 'keys' and matches. For each of
## the following LPR activities, the following keys have a value.
##
## Key Match Connect Job Job LPQ LPRM LPC
## Spool Print
## SERVICE S 'X' 'R' 'P' 'Q' 'M' 'C,S'
## USER S - JUSR JUSR JUSR JUSR JUSR
## HOST S RH JH JH JH JH JH
## GROUP S - JUSR JUSR JUSR JUSR JUSR
## IP IP RIP JIP JIP RIP JIP JIP
## PORT N PORT PORT - PORT PORT PORT
## REMOTEUSER S - JUSR JUSR JUSR CUSR CUSR
## REMOTEHOST S RH RH JH RH RH RH
## REMOTEGROUP S - JUSR JUSR JUSR CUSR CUSR
## REMOTEIP IP RIP RIP JIP RIP RIP RIP
## CONTROLLINE S - CL CL CL CL CL
## PRINTER S - PR PR PR PR PR
## FORWARD V - SA - - SA SA
## SAMEHOST V - SA - SA SA SA
## SAMEUSER V - - - SU SU SU
## SERVER V - SV - SV SV SV
##
## KEY:
## JH = HOST host in control file
## RH = REMOTEHOST connecting host name
## JUSR = USER user in control file
## CUSR = REMOTEUSER user from control request
## JIP= IP IP address of host in control file
```

```
## RIP= REMOTEIP IP address of requesting host
## PORT= connecting host origination port
## CONTROLLINE= pattern match of control line in control file
## FW= IP of source of request = IP of host in control file
## SA= IP of source of request = IP of host in control file
## SU= user from request = user in control file
## SA= IP of source of request = IP of server host
##
## Match: S = string with wild card, IP = IPaddress[/netmask],
## N = low[-high] number range, V= matching or compatible values
## SERVICE: 'X' - Connection request; 'R' - lpr request from remote host;
## 'P' - print job in queue; 'Q' - lpq request, 'M' - lprm request;
## 'C' - lpc spool control request; 'S' - lpc spool status request
## NOTE: When printing (P action), the remote and job check values
## (i.e. - RUSR, JUSR) are identical.
##
## The SAMEHOST match checks to see that one (or more) of the
## IP addresses of the host originating the request are the
## same as one or more of the IP addresses of the host whose
## hostname appears in the control file.
## The SERVER match checks to see if one (or more) of the
## IP addresses of the host originating the request are the
## same as one or more of the IP addresses of the server or
## match the localhost's IP address. Note that in IPV6, there may
## be multiple IP addresses for a single host.
## The FORWARD checks to see that all of the IP addresses of the
## IP addresses of the host originating the request are not the
## same as one or more of the IP addresses of the host whose
## hostname appears in the control file. This is equivalent to
## NOT SAMEHOST
##
## The special key letter=patterns searches the control file
## line starting with the (upper case) letter, and is usually
## used with printing and spooling checks. For example,
## C=A*,B* would check that the class information (i.e. - line
## in the control file starting with C) had a value starting
## with A or B.
##
## A permission line consists of list of tests and an a result value
## If all of the tests succeed, then a match has been found and the
## permission testing completes with the result value. You use the
## DEFAULT reserved word to set the default ACCEPT/DENY result.
## The NOT keyword will reverse the sense of a test.
##
## Each test can have one or more optional values separated by
## commas. For example USER=john,paul,mark has 3 test values.
##
## The Match type specifies how the matching is done.
## S = string type match - string match with glob.
## Format: string with wildcards (*)
## * matches 0 or more chars
## Character comparison is case insensitive.
## For example - USER=th*s matches uTHS, This, This, Theses
```

```
##
## IP = IP address and submask. IP address must be in dotted form.
## Format: x.x.x.x[/y.y.y.y] x.x.x.x is IP address
## y.y.y.y is optional submask, default is 255.255.255.255
## Match is done by converting to 32 bit x, y, and IP value and using:
## success = ((x ^ IP ) & y) == 0 (C language notation)
## i.e. - only bits where mask is non-zero are used in comparison.
## For example - REMOTEIP=130.191.0.0/255.255.0.0 matches all address
130.191.X.X
##
## N = numerical range - low-high integer range.
## Format: low[-high]
## Example: PORT=0-1023 matches a port in range 0 - 1023 (privileged)
##
## The SAMEUSER and SAMEHOST are options that form values from information
## in control files or connections. The GROUP entry searches the user group
## database for group names matching the pattern, and then searches these
## for the user name. If the name is found, the search is successful.
## The SERVER entry is successful if the request originated from the current
## lpd server host.
##
## Note carefully that the USER, HOST, and IP values are based on values
found
## in the control file currently being checked for permissions. The
## REMOTEUSER, REMOTEHOST, and REMOTEIP are based on values supplied as part
## of a connection to the LPD server, or on the actual TCP/IP connection.
##
## Example Permissions
##
# All operations allowed except those specifically forbidden
## DEFAULT ACCEPT
##
#Reject connections from hosts not on subnet 130.191.0.0
## # or Engineering pc's
## REJECT SERVICE=X NOT REMOTEIP=130.191.0.0/255.255.0.0
## REJECT SERVICE=X NOT REMOTEHOST=engpc*
##
## #Do not allow anybody but root or papowell on
## #astart1.astart.com or the server to use control
## #facilities.
## ACCEPT SERVICE=C SERVER REMOTEUSER=root
## ACCEPT SERVICE=C REMOTEHOST=astart1.astart.com REMOTEUSER=papowell
##
## #Allow root on talker.astart.com to control printer hpjet
## ACCEPT SERVICE=C HOST=talker.astart.com PRINTER=hpjet REMOTEUSER=root
## #Reject all others
## REJECT SERVICE=C
##
## #Do not allow forwarded jobs or requests
## REJECT SERVICE=R,C,M FORWARD
##
# allow root on server to control jobs
ACCEPT SERVICE=C SERVER REMOTEUSER=root
```

```
# allow anybody to get status
ACCEPT SERVICE=S
# reject all others, including lpc commands permitted by user_lpc
REJECT SERVICE=CSU
#
# allow same user on originating host to remove a job
ACCEPT SERVICE=M SAMEHOST SAMEUSER
# allow root on server to remove a job
ACCEPT SERVICE=M SERVER REMOTEUSER=root
REJECT SERVICE=M
# all other operations allowed
DEFAULT ACCEPT
```

The third file, /etc/lpd.conf, is extremely lengthy, and all of the configuration options are disabled by default. Each entry in the file takes two lines. The first line consists of a comment describing the parameter; the second line is the command itself. There are approximately 180 different configuration parameters available to optimize the **lpd** service. Items affected include banners, the default job format, temporary file directories, and more.

Although you are not required to know all 180 options in the /etc/lpd.conf file, a review of the file from your own system is advisable because you must understand the purpose of the configuration file.

As with most other utilities, there is a graphical utility that can be used to add a printer to your system. **printtool** can simplify the process of adding a printer to your system. Figure 3-23 shows the default view of **printtool**.

The r Utilities

A number of commands written at the University of California at Berkley are known as the **r** commands. The **r** commands exist in many Unix and some Linux implementations, but were not ported to other TCP/IP implementations (such as the one provided by Microsoft). The **r** commands include

- **rwho**
- **ruptime**
- **rlogin**
- **rcp**

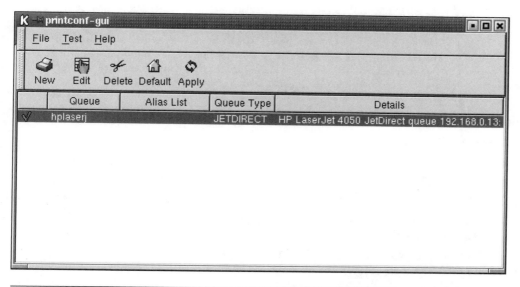

Figure 3-23   **printtool** shown with a Hewlett Packard LaserJet 4050 installed

Using rwho

Similar to the **who** command, **rwho** displays the users who are logged in on the various systems on the network. For this service to operate, the **rwhod** daemon must be running on the system. By default, the command lists only the users who have been idle on the system for less than one hour. The idle time is shown in the right-most column of the display. If no information is printed in the last column, the user is actively working at his or her session. Using the -a option instructs **rwho** to list all the users, regardless of idle time.

Using ruptime

The **ruptime** command provides information for all systems in the network much like the **uptime** command provides for the local system. Each system's name is printed, along with the time the system has been on the network, in days and hours. As with the **uptime** command, **ruptime** also prints the users logged in and the system load averages for the last 1, 5, and 15 minutes.

NOTE   Both the ruptime and rwho commands rely on the rwhod daemon process running on each machine. If the daemon is not running, the two commands won't print any information for that system. The rwhod daemon updates the information for the local system, broadcasts its information to the network, and listens for other rwhod broadcasts from other systems.

Using rlogin

The **telnet** command commonly is used to establish an interactive session with a remote host. The **rlogin** command provides similar functionality by establishing a connection to the remote host—as though physically connected. The **rlogin** command, however, does not support the same type of terminal-negotiation protocol defined in **telnet**. Once logged in, you can run any standard Linux command.

The advantage of **rlogin** is that it tries to connect to the remote system with the same username as the one you are logged in as on the local system. If the account exists on the remote system, you may be granted access without having to provide a password. If the account does not exist, however, you are prompted for a password. You must then log in as normal.

You can also use **rlogin** to access the system with an alternate username, by providing it as an argument on the command line. To access the system daffy with the username billy, for example, the syntax is

```
$ rlogin daffy -l billy
```

The -l followed by the username instructs **rlogin** to access the system as the specified user. Once the connection is made and the user logs in, the **rlogin** process appears in the process table as the **rlogind** command. The argument on the command line in the **ps** listing is the hostname of where the connection is from, not the name of the connected user.

You can execute commands within **rlogin** on the local system by using the command tilde (~) followed by the letter z. The ~z sequence suspends your **rlogin** session and returns you to the local system. You can return to your **rlogin** session by typing the **exit** command.

NOTE   rlogin has been replaced in popularity by telnet.

Using rcp

Although Linux still offers the **rcp** (remote copy) command, many users choose to move data using the **ftp** command. The **rcp** command copies files from one system to another, much like the **cp** command. It is a much less efficient protocol for moving large quantities of data than **ftp**, however. A less capable version of FTP is the Trivial File Transfer Protocol (TFTP).

Kernel Modules

Traditional Unix implementations require the kernel to have all required device driver software loaded at all times, whether the device is being used at that time or not. If a new device was installed, the kernel was recompiled to install support for that device. Linux, on the other hand, uses the concept of a loadable module to implement new hardware support or other functionality.

A *loadable module* is a separate component available to provide specific features or functionality. They are not compiled or linked into the kernel, but loaded only when the specific support is required. This approach enables Linux to be as small as possible, saving memory resources and making it a faster kernel. When developers create new functionality or device driver software, they compile it separately, allowing the system administrator to load them as runtime, if required. The number of available modules has increased significantly and includes Ethernet interfaces, tape drives, PCMCIA devices, parallel ports, printer devices, and sound cards. Interacting with loadable modules is done using the commands listed in Table 3-7.

Table 3-7 Commands for Loadable Modules

Command	Description
lsmod	Lists the loaded modules
insmod	Installs a module
rmmod	Removes a module
modinfo	Prints information about a module
modprobe	Probes and install a module and its dependents
depmod	Determines module dependencies

The commands affect modules being placed into the kernel, as well as those already installed. The loaded modules are included in the information stored in the /proc file system. Listing the currently loaded modules is done using the **lsmod** command:

```
[root@mercury.technical root]# lsmod
Module Size Used by
autofs 11136 1 (autoclean)
ne 7104 1 (autoclean)
8390 6752 0 (autoclean) [ne]
3c59x 25312 1 (autoclean)
ipchains 38944 0 (unused)
[root@mercury.technical root]#
```

The file /proc/modules is maintained by the kernel and includes information about the currently loaded modules:

```
[root@mercury.technical root]# cat /proc/modules
autofs 11136 1 (autoclean)
ne 7104 1 (autoclean)
8390 6752 0 (autoclean) [ne]
3c59x 25312 1 (autoclean)
ipchains 38944 0 (unused)
[root@mercury.technical root]#
```

The **lsmod** output includes column headings to identity the information reported and lists the information in columns.

Each module may be specifically referenced by another module, such as nfs, which is referenced by the lockd module. Module references typically mean that the referenced module is required before the dependent module can be loaded. This means before the lockd module is used, the nfs module must have already been loaded.

Consider this example. We want to use loadable modules to access our sound card, an Ensoniq AudioPCI., which uses the es1371 sound module. As we can from our **lsmod** example, the sound card is not loaded:

```
[root@mercury.technical root]# insmod es1371
```

 NOTE In many cases, more than one module is required when enabling a device. Sound cards typically require several modules, including soundcore, and the appropriate audio codecs. Although we illustrate using loadable modules with a sound card, the command sndconfig is best used to configure the sound card and to resolve any module dependencies.

After loading the es1371 module, we can check to see if it is loaded using the **lsmod** command:

```
[root@mercury.technical sound]# lsmod
Module Size Used by
es1371 25968 1
soundcore 4432 4 [es1371]
ac97_codec 8704 0 [es1371]
autofs 11136 1 (autoclean)
ne 7104 1 (autoclean)
8390 6752 0 (autoclean) [ne]
3c59x 25312 1 (autoclean)
ipchains 38944 0 (unused)
[root@mercury.technical sound]#
```

With the modules loaded, our sound card is ready for use.

The opposite of **insmod** is **rmmod**, to remove modules no longer required. For example, **lsmod** reports the following:

```
[root@mercury.technical sound]# lsmod
Module Size Used by
es1371 25968 0
soundcore 4432 4 [es1371]
ac97_codec 8704 0 [es1371]
autofs 11136 1 (autoclean)
ne 7104 1 (autoclean)
8390 6752 0 (autoclean) [ne]
3c59x 25312 1 (autoclean)
ipchains 38944 0 (unused)
[root@mercury.technical sound]#
```

Assume we now want to remove the soundcore modules from our system using the command **rmmod soundcore**:

```
[root@mercury.technical sound]# rmmod soundcore
soundcore: Device or resource busy
[root@mercury.technical sound]#
```

Carefully reviewing the **lsmod** output again shows us the soundcore module is being used by the es1371 module:

```
[root@mercury.technical sound]# lsmod
Module Size Used by
es1371 25968 0 (unused)
soundcore 4432 4 [es1371]
ac97_codec 8704 0 [es1371]
autofs 11136 1 (autoclean)
ne 7104 1 (autoclean)
8390 6752 0 (autoclean) [ne]
3c59x 25312 1 (autoclean)
ipchains 38944 0 (unused)
[root@mercury.technical sound]# rmmod soundcore
```

Because the soundcore module is busy servicing the es1371 module, we cannot remove it without first removing the modules depending upon it:

```
[root@mercury.technical sound]# rmmod es1371
[root@mercury.technical sound]# rmmod soundcore
[root@mercury.technical sound]# lsmod
Module Size Used by
ac97_codec 8704 0
autofs 11136 1 (autoclean)
ne 7104 1 (autoclean)
8390 6752 0 (autoclean) [ne]
3c59x 25312 1 (autoclean)
ipchains 38944 0 (unused)
[root@mercury.technical sound]#
```

The modules have now been removed from the kernel, and the services provided are no longer available to the system users until the module is reloaded.

Frequently, we want to get information on what the module is so we can choose the correct module to load. This is accomplished using the **modinfo** command. **modinfo** can report the following information:

- The author

- The module description

- The parameters the modules accepts

The information is only available if the module author included it when the module was created. For example, to see the descriptions of sound modules available in the /lib/modules/<kernel>/sound directory, use the command **modinfo-d**:

```
[root@mercury.technical sound]# modinfo -d * | grep -v "none" | more
Audio Excel DSP 16 Driver Version 1.3
SB AWE32/64 WaveTable driver
CMPCI Audio Driver
Cirrus Logic CS4281 Driver
Crystal SoundFusion Audio Support
Creative EMU10K1 PCI Audio Driver v0.7
Copyright (C) 1999 Creative Technology Ltd.
ES1370 AudioPCI Driver
ES1371 AudioPCI97 Driver
ESS Solo1 Driver
Intel 810 audio support
ESS Maestro3/Allegro Driver
ESS Maestro Driver
Turtle Beach MultiSound (Classic/Monterey/Tahiti) Linux Driver
Turtle Beach MultiSound Driver Base
Turtle Beach MultiSound (Pinnacle/Fiji) Linux Driver
Module for OPL3-SA2 and SA3 sound cards (uses AD1848 MSS driver).
```

```
Soundblaster driver
S3 SonicVibes Driver
Core sound module
OSS Sound subsystem
Trident 4DWave/SiS 7018/ALi 5451 PCI Audio Driver
DSP audio and mixer driver for Via 82Cxxx audio devices
Turtle Beach WaveFront Linux Driver
Yamaha YMF7xx PCI Audio
[root@mercury.technical sound]#
```

Modules can also be loaded using the **depmod** and **modprobe** commands. As there is often a dependency between modules, it is necessary to understand how Linux determines and resolves those dependencies. The **depmod** command determines the dependencies between the various modules and is run at system startup to create a Makefile type dependency list that is used by the **modprobe** command. Running **depmod** with the -a and -v options instructs **depmod** to touch each module and be verbose about what it is doing. A sample of the **depmod-a-v** output is shown here:

```
[root@mercury.technical root]# depmod -av | more
type 2 /lib/modules/2.4.2-2/kernel/drivers/sound
xftw_readdir /lib/modules/2.4.2-2/kernel/drivers/sound
user function /lib/modules/2.4.2-2/kernel/drivers/sound
user function /lib/modules/2.4.2-2/kernel/drivers/sound/ac97.o
user function /lib/modules/2.4.2-2/kernel/drivers/sound/ac97_codec.o
user function /lib/modules/2.4.2-2/kernel/drivers/sound/aci.o
user function /lib/modules/2.4.2-2/kernel/drivers/sound/ad1816.o
user function /lib/modules/2.4.2-2/kernel/drivers/sound/ad1848.o
user function /lib/modules/2.4.2-2/kernel/drivers/sound/adlib_card.o
user function /lib/modules/2.4.2-2/kernel/drivers/sound/aedsp16.o
user function /lib/modules/2.4.2-2/kernel/drivers/sound/awe_wave.o
user function /lib/modules/2.4.2-2/kernel/drivers/sound/cmpci.o
user function /lib/modules/2.4.2-2/kernel/drivers/sound/cs4232.o
type 2 /lib/modules/2.4.2-2/kernel/drivers/sound/cs4281
xftw_readdir /lib/modules/2.4.2-2/kernel/drivers/sound/cs4281
user function /lib/modules/2.4.2-2/kernel/drivers/sound/cs4281
user function /lib/modules/2.4.2-2/kernel/drivers/sound/cs4281/cs4281.o
user function /lib/modules/2.4.2-2/kernel/drivers/sound/cs46xx.o
type 2 /lib/modules/2.4.2-2/kernel/drivers/sound/emu10k1
xftw_readdir /lib/modules/2.4.2-2/kernel/drivers/sound/emu10k1
user function /lib/modules/2.4.2-2/kernel/drivers/sound/emu10k1
user function /lib/modules/2.4.2-2/kernel/drivers/sound/emu10k1/emu10k1.o --
More--
```

The **modprobe** command uses the output of **depmod** to load a set of modules, a single module or a set of dependent modules. **modprobe** will automatically load all the modules required for a particular service based upon the module dependency file created from **depmod**. If loading one of the modules in the dependency chain fails, all modules loaded to that point are removed.

modprobe loads modules using a probe, where it tries to load the modules. If successful, the service is now available on the system, and if not, it reports that the device is not installed or available on the system. This is useful if you don't know what kind of Ethernet card you have—you can use **modprobe** to load a series of Ethernet modules to see which one loads. The second method is to load all the modules from a defined list.

Module management using the **depmod** and **modprobe** services uses a text-based, human-readable file called /etc/conf.modules, or /etc/modules.conf depending upon your Linux vendor, which stores information affecting the operation of the **depmod** and **modprobe** commands. The format of the file is shown here:

```
[root@mercury.technical sound]# cat /etc/modules.conf
alias eth0 3c59x
alias parport_lowlevel parport_pc
alias sound-slot-0 es1371
post-install sound-slot-0 /bin/aumix-minimal -f /etc/.aumixrc -L >/dev/null
2>&1 || :
pre-remove sound-slot-0 /bin/aumix-minimal -f /etc/.aumixrc -S >/dev/null
2>&1 || :
alias eth1 ne
[root@mercury.technical sound]#
```

The /etc/conf.modules file has three characteristics you should remember when reading or editing:

- All empty lines and all text on a line after a # are ignored.
- Lines may be continued by ending the line with a \.
- The lines specifying the module information must fall into one of the following formats listed in Table 3-8.

Each parameter is processed by the command interpreter, enabling the use of shell tricks like wildcards and commands enclosed in back-quotes (`) during module processing.

If the configuration file /etc/conf.modules is missing, or if any parameter is not overridden, the following defaults are assumed:

```
depfile=/lib/modules/'uname -r'/modules.dep
path[boot]=/lib/modules

path[fs]=/lib/modules/'uname -r'
path[misc]=/lib/modules/'uname -r'
path[net]=/lib/modules/'uname -r'
path[scsi]=/lib/modules/'uname -r'
path[cdrom]=/lib/modules/'uname -r'
path[ipv4]=/lib/modules/'uname -r'
```

Table 3-8   The Enabled Parameters for /etc/conf.modules

Parameter	Description
Keep	Finding the word "keep" before any lines containing a path adds the following paths to the default path. Otherwise, the default path is replaced with those defined in the configuration file.
depfile=DEPFILE_PATH	This defines the location of the dependency file created by **depmod** and used by **modprobe**.
path=SOME_PATH	Specifies a directory location to search for modules.
path[tag]=SOME_PATH	The optional tag to the path parameter provides information on the purpose of the modules and enables some automated operations by **modprobe**. The tag is appended to the path keyword enclosed in square brackets. If the tag is missing, the misc tag is assumed. One very useful tag is boot, which can be used to mark all modules that should be loaded at boot time.
Options	Defines module specific options.
alias	Specifies an alternate name for the module.
Pre-install module command	Identifies a command to be executed before loading the module.
Install module command	Installs the named module.
Post-install module command	Executes a command once the module is loaded.
Pre-remove module command	Executes a command prior to removing the module.
Remove module command	Removes the named module.
Post-remove module command	Executes a command once the module has been removed.

```
path[ipv6]=/lib/modules/'uname -r'
path[sound]=/lib/modules/'uname -r'

path[fs]=/lib/modules/default
path[misc]=/lib/modules/default
path[net]=/lib/modules/default
path[scsi]=/lib/modules/default
path[cdrom]=/lib/modules/default
path[ipv4]=/lib/modules/default
path[ipv6]=/lib/modules/default
path[sound]=/lib/modules/default

path[fs]=/lib/modules
path[misc]=/lib/modules
path[net]=/lib/modules
path[scsi]=/lib/modules
```

```
path[cdrom]=/lib/modules
path[ipv4]=/lib/modules
path[ipv6]=/lib/modules
path[sound]=/lib/modules
```

Using the default options enables the /etc/conf.modules to be very simple and only contain the entries different from the defaults.

The *option* parameter specifies the default options for the named modules. For example, if a parameter must be provided when loading a module, the parameter can be specified in the /etc/conf.modules file using the options keyword. For example, when loading the **ne** module, we run

```
modprobe ne bnc=1
```

and then add the entry

```
options ne -o bnc=1
```

to the /etc/conf.modules file. Although the options are saved in /etc/cconf.modules, any options provided on the command lines of the various module utilities override those found in the /etc/conf.modules file.

The alias lines are used to assign an alternate name to a module. Recalling the /etc/conf.modules file, we see

```
alias eth0 3c59x
alias parport_lowlevel parport_pc
```

which establishes the alias eth0 for the module 3c59x, and parport for the parallel port module. Using aliases means the administrator can establish alternate names instead of having to remember the actual module name, allowing the use of commands like **modprobe eth0** command even though no such module exists.

modprobe first examines the modules directory compiled for the current release of the kernel, and if not found, looks in the release specific directory. As previously mentioned, the current kernel release is determined using the command **uname-r**.

```
[root@mercury.technical net]# uname-r
2.4.2-2
[root@mercury.technical net]#
```

When installing a new Linux kernel, the modules should be moved to a directory related to the release and version of the kernel that you're installing. Then you should create a symbolic link from this directory to the default directory. Each time you compile a new kernel, the **make modules_install** command creates a new directory, but it won't change the default.

Chapter Summary

This domain is the heart of how your system operates. We have dealt with the configuration and operation of all of the major systems: network, Internet kernel, and hardware.

We created extra functionality by writing shell scripts to make your job easier. These are one of the most important tools to have. If you can think of a shortcut, there can be a script to support it.

The most important piece of the system is the documentation of all of your efforts. As each piece of your system is being put in place, a list needs to be made. What you configured and when you configured it needs to be in this list. This may be the only safety net that you have. When something goes wrong, and it will, this could be the difference of finding the answer quickly or merely guessing at the answer.

Questions

1. There are several different methods of looping. One method tests for the condition to be true before the commands in the loop are executed. The loop command is:
   a. until
   b. for
   c. case
   d. while

2. The **pr** command is used to:
   a. Filter content
   b. Add headers and file names to the print job
   c. Format text
   d. Append to the printer database

3. The **expr** command is used to:
   a. Concatenate strings together.
   b. Perform arithmetic operations on shell variables.
   c. Export a variable.
   d. Configure a prompt.

4. The initial command used to submit print requests to an off-line printer is
   a. lpr
   b. lp
   c. lpd
   d. lpdest

5. How many positional parameters does the shell know?
   a. 11
   b. 9
   c. 8
   d. 10

6. What does the **route** command do?
   a. Uses the OSPF model to deliver packets
   b. Configures the routing of packets
   c. Creates the routing table based on commands that you create
   d. Uses the ICMP protocol to send messages back to the sender

7. There are several special parameters the shell understands. Which one specifies the name of the script being executed?
   a. $*
   b. $$
   c. $0
   d. $1

8. Which command exits the shell script?
   a. **break**
   b. **exit**
   c. **done**
   d. **fi**
   e. **join**

9. **linuxconf** and **netconfig** are examples of:
   a. Text-based configuration tools
   b. Graphical configuration tools
   c. r utilities
   d. Internet providers

10. The bash shell is based on which older shell?
    a. Tom's c-shell
    b. Korn shell
    c. Tortilla shell
    d. Bourne shell

Answers

1. **D.** The **while** loop tests for the condition to be true and then executes the commands specified in the loop.

2. **C.** The **pr** command formats text for printing.

3. **B.** **Expr** is used to signal that an arithmetic function is to performed on a variable instead of the default string interpretation.

4. **A.** **Lpr** sends commands to an off-line printer.

5. **B.** The shell knows positional parameters *$1* to *$9*.

6. **B.** The **route** command is used to manipulate the routing of packets.

7. **C.** *$0* is a special parameter that signifies the name of the script currently being executed.

8. **B.** A simple **exit** will get you out of a shell script.

9. **B.** **linuxconf** and **netconfig** are graphical configuration tools.

10. **D.** The bash shell is based on the Bourne shell.

Administration

This chapter covers the following competencies required to master the Linux+ certification exams:

- Managing users
- Modifying current users
- Managing groups
- Identifying and changing file permissions
- Understanding the Linux hierarchy
- Understanding the Linux filesystem
- Performing administrative tasks
- Installing and managing filesystems and devices
- Using command utilities to connect to and administer remote systems
- Using **tar** to manipulate file and tape archives
- Using **init** and **shutdown** to manage runlevels
- Stopping, starting, and restarting services
- Managing print spools and queues
- Using vi to create, edit, and save files
- Navigating the Graphical User Interface (GUI)
- Using common shell commands to program the basic shell scripts

Creating Users

To create a user, invoke the **useradd** command. You have to specify some options. The easiest way to g about it is to use the skeleton directory located in /etc/skel. The syntax will look like the following:

```
[root@mercury.technical /root]# useradd -m -k /etc/skel <username>
```

The -m option will create a directory for the user, and the -k option will use the default directory located in the /etc/skel directory.

To verify this, go to the /home directory, type **ls**, and verify that the user you named was created. Next, to make the account viable, you have to add a password. The syntax will resemble the following:

```
[root@mercury.technical /root]# passwd <username>
Changing password for <username>
New UNIX password:
Retype new UNIX password:
Passwd: all authentication tokens updated successfully
```

When you type the password, you will not see anything on the screen. This is a security measure to keep the password out of the shell history.

Managing User Accounts

Once the account is created, it doesn't magically take care of itself. From time to time, you will need to update information, change parameters associated with the account, and perhaps change the account name. If an employee changes her name, for example, you will want to change her username in /etc/passwd. This can be easily done because the UID remains the same. Once the name change is complete, all of her files are now owned by the new account. This isn't magic because Linux keeps track of the file owner using the UID, not the account name.

Once you change the user's name, you should rename her home directory; the home directory name and the user name should always match for administrative purposes.

If a user changes groups, you need simply to edit /etc/passwd and change the group value to reflect the number of the new group.

A previous section looked at using the **useradd** command to insert a new user account into the /etc/passwd and /etc/shadow files. You can use the **usermod** command to change the existing values to new ones, using a set of flags to select the items you want to change:

-c   Replaces the descriptive text with the new value

-d   Changes the location of the home directory

-e   Updates the password expiration date

-f   Sets the inactive parameter

-G   Adds additional group memberships by inserting the additional groups with comma delimiters

-g   Changes the user's login GID

-l   Change the user's login name

-m   Creates the new home directory (must be used with -d)

-p   Changes the password

-s   Changes to a different shell

-u   Changes the UID

Generally, it's best to perform these activities when the user is not logged in, as it reduces the possibility of user problems as the configuration changes. For example,

```
# grep reg /etc/passwd
reg:petKv.fLWG/Ig:506:100:Reg:/home/reg:/bin/bash
# usermod -l riskit reg
# grep risk /etc/passwd
riskit:petKv.fLWG/Ig:506:100:Reg:/home/reg:/bin/bash
# ls -l /home
drwx------ 19 jholman jholman 4096 Jun 13 18:44 jholman
drwx------ 4 lisaf lisaf 4096 Jun 12 21:46 lisaf
drwxrwxr-x 2 reg reg 4096 Jun 13 18:49 reg
drwxr-x--- 11 jholman jholman 4096 Jun 8 22:36 seal
$ usermod -d /home/riskit -m riskit
# ls -l /home
drwx------ 19 jholman jholman 4096 Jun 13 18:44 jholman
drwx------ 4 lisaf lisaf 4096 Jun 12 21:46 lisaf
drwxrwxr-x 2 riskit riskit 4096 Jun 13 18:49 riskit
drwxr-x--- 11 jholman jholman 4096 Jun 8 22:36 seal
# grep risk /etc/passwd
riskit:petKv.fLWG/Ig:506:100:Reg:/home/riskit:/bin/bash
#
```

usermod can also prompt you to change the password. This should ideally be done using the **passwd** command discussed earlier, however. The **passwd** command is the preferred method because the password is hidden; that is, it is not displayed on the command line like **usermod**, and you must enter it twice to validate it.

 ALERT Using usermod to change the password is dangerous, as the password must be provided on the command line, which adds it to the shell history file.

If you need to change a large number of passwords for some reason, such as a potential system compromise, a batch password change can be performed using the **chpasswd** command. Using **chpasswd** requires you create a colon-delimited file with a username and a password for each user on the system.

```
# cat > changes
jholman:tea42+mug
riskit:good43Guy
lisaf:bio91tech
{Ctrl-D}
#
# chpasswd < changes
#
```

Because the passwords are in clear text, you should make sure the permissions are such that no other user can read the file and remove the file as soon as you are finished with it. An alternative to using clear-text passwords is to encrypt them and use the -e (encrypt) option to **chpasswd**.

 TIP Passwords should consist of at least eight characters, including upper- and lowercase, at least one digit, and a symbol. The Pluggable Authentication Module (PAM) in Linux has a feature to check potential passwords against a list of disallowed words.

Removing Users

Deleting a user from the system is necessary when the account is no longer required. However, the proper method of dealing with the removal depends on the situation. A user who goes on maternity leave, for example, does not need her account deleted.

Rather, you should change her password to something that even she doesn't know until her return. If a user's password may have been compromised, you are not required to delete the account, simply to change the password. Finally, if a user leaves the organization, the account should be deleted.

Deleting the user can be done manually by editing the /etc/passwd and, if necessary, /etc/shadow files directly, or by using the **userdel** command. Regardless of which method you choose, the user's files are not automatically deleted, requiring someone, typically the manager, to review them and determine what should be kept and what should be deleted.

Working with Groups

Group management is important because it enables the administrator to group users into a set and grant them permissions and privileges based on their group rights. The group information is stored in /etc/group, which is a colon-delimited file resembling the following:

```
root:x:0:root
bin:x:1:root,bin,daemon
daemon:x:2:root,bin,daemon
sys:x:3:root,bin,adm
adm:x:4:root,adm,daemon
tty:x:5:
disk:x:6:root
lp:x:7:daemon,lp
mem:x:8:
kmem:x:9:
wheel:x:10:root
mail:x:12:mail0
news:x:13:news
uucp:x:14:uucp
man:x:15:
games:x:20:
gopher:x:30:
dip:x:40:
ftp:x:50:
nobody:x:99:
users:x:100:
floppy:x:19:
nscd:x:28:
slocate:x:21:
utmp:x:22:
mailnull:x:47:
ident:x:98:
rpc:x:32:
rpcuser:x:29:
```

```
xfs:x:43:
gdm:x:42:
apache:x:48:
jholman:x:500:
seal:*:1001:
mailman:*:1002:
lisaf:x:2001:
```

Each of the group file entries has four fields. The first field is the group name, which is limited to a maximum of eight characters. The group name is displayed with a command like **ls -l**. The second field typically is blank, but can contain a password for using the group. The third field is the numerical group ID, which must be unique on the system. The forth field is used to list the users who are members of the group.

Creating a New Group

You can create a group manually either by editing the /etc/group file directly, or by using the **groupadd** command. When adding the group manually, you must use a unique name and group ID number. The **groupadd** command greatly simplifies the operation.

```
# groupadd -g 3002 admin
# tail -1 /etc/group
admin:x:3002:
#
```

```
The -g option instructs groupadd to use the specified number as the GID.
If the number is not unique, groupadd prints an error message and exits.
On most Unix-based systems, including Linux, group IDs 0 through 99 are
reserved for system groups. # groupadd -g 101 admin
groupadd: gid 101 is not unique
#
```

Attempting to use a group name that already exists results in an error message:

```
# groupadd admin
groupadd: group admin exists
#
```

There are no other options for the **groupadd** command aside from -g. If you need to refine the settings around your group, you must either edit the /etc/group file manually, or use the **gpasswd** command. **gpasswd** is used, among other things, to establish a password for the group.

NOTE The gpasswd command does not exist in traditional Unix, which doesn't have a command for adding a password to a group.

Executing **gpasswd** with only a group name causes the password entered to be the group password:

```
# gpasswd admin
Changing the password for group admin
New Password: {Enter value}
Re-enter new password: {Enter value again}
# tail -1 /etc/group
admin:QJHexo2Pbk7TU:3002:
#
```

If you decide to remove the password from the group, the -r (remove) option on **gpasswd** causes the password to be removed. Adding users to the group is either done manually, or by using the -a (add) option on the **gpasswd** command. (The reverse of the -a option is the -d (delete) option, which deletes the named user from the group.)

```
# gpasswd -r admin
# gpasswd -a jholman admin
Adding user jholman to group admin
# grep admin /etc/group
admin:3002:jholman
#
```

Attempting to add a nonexistent user to a group, or a valid user to a nonexistent group, causes **gpasswd** to print an error.

 NOTE The gpasswd command can work with only one user at a time.

If you are willing to act as a group administrator, use the -A option on **gpasswd**. Establishing group administrators requires the use of the group shadow file, /etc/gshadow, which, like /etc/shadow, is readable only by root. The group passwords are stored in /etc/ghsadow and, therefore, are protected.

Like converting /etc/passwd to support the shadow password file /etc/shadow, the **grpconv** command is used to convert /etc/group to support the group shadow file.

grpconv extracts the password, if defined, replaces it with the letter x, and puts the password in the /etc/gshadow file. The gshadow file consists of four fields per entry, in the following format:

```
Group name:password:administrator:users
```

The sequence of events for adding additional users and declaring an administrator is as follows:

```
# gpasswd -r admin
# gpasswd -a jholman admin
# grep admin /etc/group
admin:!:3002:jholman
# gpasswd -a lisaf admin
# gpasswd -a mcote admin
# gpasswd -a riskit admin
# gpasswd admin
Changing the password for group admin
New Password: (Enter password)
Re-enter new password: (Enter password)
# grep admin /etc/group
admin: 08F5sEPR35F96:3002:jholman,lisaf,mcote,riskit

# grpconv
# tail -1 /etc/group
admin::3002:jholman,lisaf,mcote,riskit
[root@mercury.technical /root]# cat /etc/gshadow
root:::root
bin:::root,bin,daemon
daemon:::root,bin,daemon
sys:::root,bin,adm
adm:::root,adm,daemon
tty:::
disk:::root
lp:::daemon,lp
mem:::
kmem:::
wheel:::root
mail:::mail
news:::news
uucp:::uucp
man:::
games:::
gopher:::
dip:::
ftp:::
nobody:::
users:::
floppy:x::
nscd:x::
slocate:x::
```

```
utmp:x::
mailnull:x::
ident:x::
rpc:x::
rpcuser:x::
xfs:x::
gdm:x::
apache:x::
jholman:!::
lisaf:!::
admin:08F5sEPR35F96::jholman,lisaf,mcote,riskit
[root@mercury.technical /root]# gpasswd -A cdupuis admin
[root@mercury.technical /root]# grep admin /etc/group
admin:3002:jholman,lisaf,mcote,riskit
[root@mercury.technical /root]# grep admin /etc/gshadow
admin:08F5sEPR35F96:cdupuis:jholman,lisaf,mcote,riskit
```

The administrator's name does not appear in the /etc/group file, but is in the third field in the /etc/gshadow file. To stop using the /etc/gshadow file, use the **grpunconv** command.

Deleting Groups

Deleting a group is done when the group is no longer a viable entity and is not required for day-to-day operations. To delete a group, use the **groupdel** command. The syntax for the following:

```
[root@mercury.technical /root]# groupdel <groupname>
```

This is not an everyday activity and should be done only with the utmost care.

Identifying and Changing File Permissions

As an administrator, you will have to move files and change permissions when creating new groups and adding users to those groups. When you perform these actions, the file ownership will sometimes need to change also; this is achieved with the **chown** command. With the **chown** command, you will be able to change a file's user and group ownership.

Another command for changing ownership is the **chgrp** command. **chgrp** will enable you to change the group ownership parameter of a file. We will not cover **chgrp** in too much detail because **chown** has superseded **chgrp** and incorporated all of its options.

chown

The syntax most associated with **chown** is

```
chown [options] owner file
```

The options to **chown** are as follows in Table 4-1.

The preceding syntax will change the ownership of the file to the user listed, but the group ownership will remain the same. To change the group ownership along with the owner, we would need to append the group to the owner's name, as shown in the following code:

```
chown -v jhowe.sales salesrec1
```

Not only would this change the ownership of the file to the user jhowe, it would let anyone from the sales group access the file salesrec1. We achieved this by adding the .group extension to the user's name. If we added a dot to the end of the user's name and did not list a group, then that user would be made the owner of the file, and the group ownership would be set to the user's login group.

chgrp

The syntax the **chgrp** command is a little different from that of **chown**. There is not a dot notation form to change anything extra, although one difference with the syntax is the addition of a template, as follows:

```
chgrp -v --reference=rfile salerec1
```

Table 4-1   **chown** Options

Option	Description
-c	Like verbose, but only reports when a change is made
-f	Silent, suppresses most error messages
-R	Operates on files and directories recursively
-v	Prints a diagnostic for every file processed
--help	Displays help and exits
--version	Displays the output version and exits

This syntax uses the rfile as a template and applies it to the file salesrec1. Although the use of **chgrp** has been eliminated for the most part, system administrators may still use it, and you will find it in scripts and makefiles.

NOTE   Only the root user can change file ownership.

chmod

This command changes the permissions of the file according to the mode. There are two modes to get this done:

- Changing the symbolic link
- Changing the octal number representing the new permission

Changing permissions under **chmod** is accomplished by using the following syntax:

```
chmod [option] mode[,mode] file     for symbolic mode
chmod [option] octal-mode file      for octal mode
```

This method of changing permissions can be tough to understand. The format for symbolic mode is [ugoa . . .][+−=][rwxXstugo . . .][. . .][. . .]. Multiple symbolic operations can be given as long as they are separated by commas. The letters *u g o a* change which users access to the file will be changed:

u   The user who owns it

g   Other users in the file's group

o   Other users not in the file's group

a   All users

The second group of symbols (+−=) after ugoa is the operator group. The operators specify whether you are adding (+) permissions, taking away (−) permissions, or causing the permissions listed to be the only ones given (=).

The third group selects the permissions for the affected users as follows:

r   Read

w   Write

x   Execute

X   Execute only if the file is a directory or already has execute permissions

s   Set user or group ID on execution

t   Save program text on swap device

u   Permissions for the user who owns the file currently has for it

g   Permissions that other users in the file's group have for it

o   Permissions that others not in the group have for it

The octal mode follows the numerical system found with setting permissions in other ways in Linux. The format is very close to the Users, Groups, and Others (UGO) way of setting permissions; it also uses a numeric mode. A numeric mode is from one to four octal digits (zero to seven) that are derived from adding up the bits with values four, two, and one. Any digits that are omitted are considered to be 0. The first digit sets the UID (four), the GID (two), and savetext image (one) attributes. The second digit selects attributes for the user who owns the file as follows: read (four), write (two), and execute (one). The third sets permissions for other users in the files group, using the same values. The fourth group sets permissions for other users not in the same group using the same values.

The options are the same as listed in Table 4-1.

 NOTE   Before setting permissions on a file, use mkdir to create the file.

Getting from Here to There

Navigating the Linux hierarchal filesystem via the command line can be cumbersome at times. After logging in and getting to a prompt, you will be in the /root directory by default. To go to any other directory, it is necessary to type the change directory command, which abbreviated is **cd**. For example, to change directories from the /root directory to go to the /etc directory, you would enter

```
[root@mercury.technical /root]# cd /etc
```

NOTE Remember to type the forward-leading slash (/) when changing directories.

This is relatively simple and is the focal point of traversing the Linux filesystem. The second highest-ranking task in Linux is to find out which directory you are in. This is displayed in the prompt in most-current Linux distributions. Some embedded variations of Linux choose to save space by omitting this feature. If you find yourself at a prompt without the current directory listed, simply type **pwd** at the prompt. This stands for "present working directory" and will print the following:

```
[root@mercury.technical /etc]# pwd
/etc
[root@mercury.technical /etc]#
```

Multiple directories can also be dug into. You do not have to type each directory one at a time. Consider the following:

```
[root@mercury.technical /etc]# cd /etc/httpd/conf
[root@mercury.technical /conf]#
```

To take it one step further is to use the **pwd** command. The prompt might tell you that you are in the /conf directory, but it doesn't say which one. Entering **pwd** at the prompt will yield

```
[root@mercury.technical /conf]# pwd
/etc/httpd/conf
[root@mercury.technical /conf]#
```

This will tell you where you are and the parent directories above you.

Manipulating Files

After learning the location of files in Linux, we have to find out what is in them. We do this using the list command **ls**. **ls** is used in many functions in Linux, but the basic usage is

```
[root@mercury.technical /etc]# ls
```

This will return the entire contents of whichever directory you are presently in, as Figure 4-1 shows.

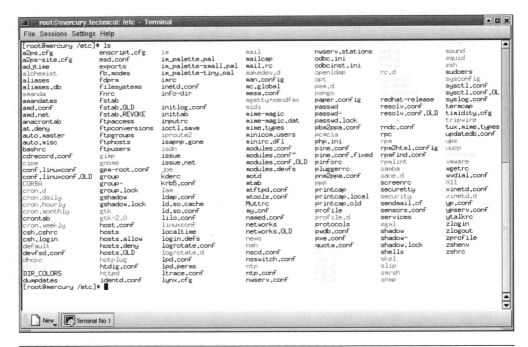

Figure 4-1   The contents of the /etc file on a Red Hat 7.1 machine

mkdir is responsible for creating or making a directory. To create a directory use the following syntax:

```
[root@mercury.technical /etc]# mkdir jon1
```

This will result in a directory named jon1 being created in the /etc file. A directory can be removed using the same syntax, except with the command **rmdir** (remove directory).

NOTE   You will not be able to remove a directory if it contains files; the files will have to be removed first as a safety precaution.

Command History

Command history, which was first introduced with the C shell, provides the user with an easy-to-use method of reexecuting previously entered commands. Bash offers the same functionality and provides a convenient command-line method using the arrow keys to scroll through the previous commands. The traditional method of entering two exclamation marks (!!), called *bangs*, is to rerun the most-recent command.

The command history shows all the commands previously stored, with an incrementing number on the left of the list. To execute a command from the left, the syntax is ! followed by the command number, as in !101.

NOTE The command history prints the entire history list. You can modify this by adding the number of entries to print, as in:

```
history 30
history 5
```

Command history is powerful, but you can make it even more so. Entering a bang followed by a set of characters will rerun the last command executed matching those characters. For example

```
!make
```

reexecutes the most-recent command starting with the word "make."

Command history is impacted by several shell variables:

- **HISTFILE** Identifies the file containing the shell history. This is by default .bash_history in the user's home directory.

- **HISTSIZE** Specifies the number of command entries to track for each session.

NOTE An additional command, fc, can also be used to edit commands in the history and reexecute them.

Using the Common Shell Commands

The Linux+ exam objectives identify specific commands you should be familiar with. The objectives specifically mention **grep**, **find**, **cut**, and the built-in command **if**. However, there is much more to know than this small list. The **grep** command is one of a family, and the value of **cut** is lessened without the knowledge of **paste** and **join**. Because the **if** command is a shell built-in and part of the shell programming language, it is discussed, more appropriately, under scripting.

cut, paste, and join

The **cut** utility extracts fields or columns of data from a file. The default character used by **cut** to separate into fields or columns is the tab; although as we will see, this can be changed by the user. For example, a user has a file named employee.list containing a series of names separated by tabs:

```
Billy Stephen Ethan Tom
Jill Ann Christine Lisa
Mallory Carol Lori Janice
```

It is irrelevant that the columns do not line up. Each column is separated by a tab. The command

```
cut -f1 employee.list
```

returns

```
Billy
Jill
Mallory
```

whereas

```
cut -f2,3 employee.list
```

returns the data from columns 2 and 3:

```
Stephen Ethan
Ann Christine
Carol Lori
```

Notice then, that the -f option enables the user to specify which column of data is retrieved from the file. Specifying columns can be done using the comma to indicate the specific fields or using a dash (-) to signify consecutive field numbers:

```
cut -f2-3 employee.list
```

Aside from the -f options, **cut** has two other important options:

-c Specifies the characters to cut rather than fields

-d Changes the field separator

The first option we will work with is -d to demonstrate how to pull fields of information from a file. We want to get a list of the username and home directories for the system users from /etc/passwd. Remember, the file format for /etc/passwd is username, password marker, UID, GID, comment, home directory, and shell. To get a list of the users and their home directories, use the command

```
cut -f1,6 -d":" /etc/passwd
```

The resulting output lists only the username and his or her home directory, ignoring all other information in the file.

The owner always begins with the 16th character and continues for the length of the name. The command

```
ls -l | cut -c16
```

will return the 16th character—the first letter of the owner's name. If an assumption is made that the most users will use eight characters or less for their name, the command

```
ls -l | cut -c16-24
```

will return those entries in the name field.

The name of the file begins with the 55th character, but it can be impossible to determine how many characters to take after that because some filenames will be considerably longer than others. A solution to this is to begin with the 55th character and not specify an ending character (meaning that the entire rest of the line is taken), as in

```
ls -l | cut -c55-
```

paste

While **cut** extracts fields from a file, **paste** and **join** are used to combine them. The simpler of the two is the **paste** command. **paste** has no real feature sets and simply takes the data from one file and joins it with the data in the second file. It does this on a line-by-line basis. Consider the following two files:

```
Jholman
dsmith
jhweb
```

and

```
/home/jholman
/home/dsmith
/var/www/html/jholman
```

Using the **paste** command, the output from merging these two files becomes

```
[root@mercury.technical /tmp]# paste a b
jholman /home/jholman
dsmith /home/dsmith
jhweb /var/www/html/jholman
[root@mercury.technical /tmp]#
```

The resulting output contains the first entry in file one, a tab, and then the first entry from file two. The tab character is the default delimiter, but when using the -d option, it is possible for the user to specify the field separator:

```
[root@mercury.technical /tmp]# paste -d":" a b
jholman:/home/jholman
dsmith:/home/dsmith
chweb:/var/www/html/jholman
[root@mercury.technical /tmp]#
```

The **paste** command is not capable of doing anything more complicated than merging the files based upon each line. The **join** command provides considerably much better flexibility.

join

The flexibility gained in the **join** command over **paste** makes up for the increased level of complexity in its use. However, **join** can work only if there is a common field or component on each line. Without the common field, or index, the command produces no output. If we used **join** instead of **paste** on the previous files, the resulting output from **join** is

```
$ join a b
$
```

The **join** command assumes that the common index between the files is the first field. If the files are modified to contain

```
jholman Jon Holman
dsmith Dennis Smith
jhweb Web user 1
```

and file b contains

```
jholman /home/jholman
dsmith /home/dsmith
jhweb /var/www/html/jholman
```

then joining these two files results in the following output:

```
[root@mercury.technical /tmp]# join a b
,holman Jon Holman /home/jholman
dsmith Dennis Smith /home/dsmith
jhweb Web user 1 /var/www/html/jholman
[root@mercury.technical /tmp]#
```

The **join** command uses the first field to establish the index or link between the two fields. Although **paste** simply combines each line in the two files together, **join** only matches the lines that have the same index. Of critical importance is the sorting order of the two files: Both must have been sorted into the same order before they are joined, and they must be an exact match. Failing to do so results in **join** printing only the matched lines up to the unmatched line. To illustrate this point, assume file b has an extra line in it:

```
[root@mercury.technical /tmp]# cat b
jholman /home/jholman
dsmith /home/dsmith
smc /home/smc
jhweb /var/www/html/jholman
```

Using the **join** command on these now mismatched files produces the following:

```
[root@mercury.technical /tmp]# join a b
jholman Jon Holman /home/jholman
dsmith Dennis Smith /home/dsmith
$
```

join can only process lines that are an exact match, as it does not scan the entire file —only the current line. If the index field in the two files does not match, the operation prints nothing, despite a match existing in both files. As mentioned, it is very important to ensure that the two files are synchronized and sorted prior to issuing the **join**.

Although **join** uses the first field as the index, it does not have to start in this fashion. The -1 option enables the selection of the field to use as in the index in the first file, while -2 is used for the second file. Assume that two files have the index in a different column, as seen here:

```
[root@mercury.technical /tmp]# cat a
jholman Jon Holman
dsmith Dennis Smith
```

```
jhweb Web user 1
[root@mercury.technical /tmp]# cat b
/home/jholman jholman
/home/dsmith fdsmith
/var/www/html/jholman jhweb
```

Notice in the files, the index is field 1 in the first file and field 2 in the second field. The syntax to join these two files is as follows:

```
$ join -1 1 -2 2 a b
```

The default operation of **join** is to print the entire joined line. This can be changed using the -o option and defining the fields to actually be printed in the resulting output. The -o option requires an option definition in the format of (file.field). To print the first field in the first file and the second field of the second file, the syntax is

```
[root@mercury.technical /tmp]# join -1 1 -2 2 -o 1.1 2.2 a b
jholman jholman
dsmith dsmith
jhweb jhweb
[root@mercury.technical /tmp]#
```

What we have seen with **cut, paste,** and **join** is a set of powerful commands to select, extract, and merge data from files. However, finding the data is sometimes more of a challenge, which is where our discussion now turns.

The grep Family

If you have used Linux for any length of time, the command names are somewhat obvious based on their function, but where developers come up with the command names is questionable. The **grep** family of commands (**grep, egrep,** and **fgrep**) is no different. **grep** is really an acronym for Global Regular Expression Print. **grep** takes a regular expression and a filename as its arguments and searches the file for the given pattern or expression. To be proficient with these commands, you must become proficient with regular expressions.

There are a series of rules when specifying a regular expression. The most important are

1. Any non-special character will be equal to itself. That is, the character a is an a.

2. Any special character in the expression equals itself if preceded by a \. For example, a $ is a dollar sign if preceded by a \.

3. Finding a pattern at the beginning of the line is specified using the carat (^) and at the end of the line with a dollar sign ($).

4. A range of characters is specified in square brackets ([]). This is known as a *character class*.

.5. A carat (^) as the first character in the square brackets ([^]) matches any character *not* in the brackets.

6. A period (.) matches any single character.

7. An asterisk (*) matches everything.

8. Quotation marks (" ") are not always needed, but are recommended to define the pattern.

To clarify the rules offered previously, let's look at some examples shown in Table 4-2.

Table 4-2 **grep** Search Expressions

Rule	Characters	Search result
1	c	Matches c anywhere in the text to be searched.
1	apple	Matches the word apple anywhere.
2	$	Matches every line having a carriage return, which is every line.
2	\$	Every line having a dollar sign.
3	^c	Matches a line starting with the letter c.
3	c$	Matches every line ending with the letter c.
4	[apple]	Matches every word containing either an a, p, l, or e.
4	[a–z]	Matches only lowercase letters.
4	[:lower:]	Matches only lowercase letters. Other available keywords are [:alnum:], [alpha:], [:digit:], and [:upper:].
5	[^a–z]	Matches all text except lowercase letters.
5	[^0–9]	Matches any character except a digit.
6	c.	Matches two-letter words starting with the letter C.
6	c..$	Matches three-letter words appearing at the end of the line. Those words must start with the letter c.
7	c*	Matches any word starting with the letter c. This also matches a single c and any word beginning with a c.
8	"c*"	Matches any word starting with the letter c. This also matches a single c and any word beginning with a c.
8	"c apple"	Matches the letter c followed by the word apple.

To illustrate how **grep** works, we will use the following as our sample text:

```
Did you hear the dogs last night?
One dog howled. Another dog howled,
until the night air was filled with the dog chorus.
And now I am doggone tired.
```

Finding all lines with the word "dog" is as simple as

```
[root@mercury.technical /tmp]# grep dog dogs
Did you hear the dogs last night?
One dog howled. Another dog howled,
until the night air was filled with the dog chorus.
And now I am doggone tired.
[root@mercury.technical /tmp]#
```

Because the word, or rather sequence of characters, "dog" appears on every line in the file, **grep** prints each line. Each line contains an instance of the characters dog: dogs in the first, dog in the second and third, and doggone in the last. What if we only want the word dog?

```
[root@mercury.technical /tmp]# grep "dog " dogs
One dog howled. Another dog howled,
until the night air was filled with the dog chorus.
[root@mercury.technical /tmp]#
```

This example specifically searches for the characters "dog" followed by a space. This is important in this example because we are looking for the word "dog." The space in the expression prevents matches on "dogs" and "doggone."

A different way to handle the same search is to eliminate the specific letters we are concerned with:

```
[root@mercury.technical /tmp]# grep "dog[^sg]" dogs
One dog howled. Another dog holwed,
until the night air was filled with the dog chorus.
[root@mercury.technical /tmp]#
Let's see how many lines have a period in them:
[root@mercury.technical /tmp]# grep "." dogs
Did you hear the dogs last night?
One dog howled. Another dog holwed,
until the night air was filled with the dog chorus.
And now I am doggone tired.
[root@mercury.technical /tmp]#
```

This didn't work because the period (.) is a special character in a regular expression. To accomplish what we specifically want, we must use

```
[root@mercury.technical /tmp]# grep "\." dogs
One dog howled. Another dog howled,
until the night air was filled with the dog chorus.
And now I am doggone tired.
[root@mercury.technical /tmp]#
```

Did this match more than you expected? The first line has a period, even though it is not at the end of the line. To find the lines ending with a period, use the syntax:

```
[root@mercury.technical /tmp]# grep "\.$" dogs
until the night air was filled with the dog chorus.
And now I am doggone tired.
[root@mercury.technical /tmp]#
```

Options for grep

grep is a powerful tool when searching for text in a large display. Administrators will often use **grep** to see the jobs on a system associated with a particular user:

```
[root@mercury.technical /tmp]# ps -ef | grep jholman
jholman 867 854 0 May18 ? 00:00:14 [kwm]
jholman 895 867 0 May18 ? 00:00:00 kbgndwm
jholman 910 867 0 May18 ? 00:00:07 kfm
jholman 911 867 0 May18 ? 00:00:00 krootwm
jholman 912 867 0 May18 ? 00:00:01 kpanel1
jholman 918 867 0 May18 ? 00:00:05 konsole -restore konsolerc.1 -ic
jholman 919 918 0 May18 pts/0 00:00:00 [bash]
jholman 934 1 0 May18 ? 00:00:02 /usr/bin/autorun --interval=1000
jholman 1045 910 0 May18 ? 00:00:03 konsole -icon konsole.xpm -minii
jholman 1046 1045 0 May18 pts/1 00:00:00 [bash]
jholman 9220 910 0 May19 ? 00:00:00 kioslave
/tmp//kio_500_910thumpe
jholman 18755 18754 0 12:21 pts/2 00:00:00 -bash
jholman 18940 18755 0 15:48 pts/2 00:00:00 ps -ef
jholman 18941 18755 0 15:48 pts/2 00:00:00 grep jholman
[root@mercury.technical /tmp]#
```

From all the output of the **ps** command, only the lines matching jholman are displayed. Looking at the output, we may be more interested in what jholman is doing at a specific terminal. We can then combine another **grep** statement:

```
[root@mercury.technical /tmp]# ps -ef | grep jholman | grep "pts/2"
jholman 18755 18754 0 12:21 pts/2 00:00:00 -bash
jholman 18944 18755 0 15:51 pts/2 00:00:00 ps -ef
jholman 18945 18755 0 15:51 pts/2 00:00:00 grep jholman
jholman 18946 18755 0 15:51 pts/2 00:00:00 grep pts/2
[root@mercury.technical /tmp]#
```

We could have just as easily only searched on the terminal location because it is unlikely more than one user ID will be running jobs from that terminal. However, sometimes we are not interested in the actual information itself, but how many jobs that user actually has running:

```
[root@mercury.technical /tmp]# ps -ef | grep -c jholman
14
[root@mercury.technical /tmp]#
```

The -c option to **grep** counts the number of lines and displays that number, rather than the default behavior of printing each matching line. Incidentally, the same output can be obtained using the syntax

```
[root@mercury.technical /tmp]# ps -ef | grep jholman | wc -l
 15
[root@mercury.technical /tmp]#
```

However, this is more expensive from a system resource perspective; it runs one more command. On most systems, this wouldn't be an issue. On a heavily loaded system, however, the fewer command issued, the better the performance.

Other useful options with **grep** include

-f Specifies a file containing the strings to search for.

-H Includes a default header identifying the filename the matches came from, if applicable. The default operation of **grep** is to not print this header information.

-i Causes **grep** to match all occurrences of the string regardless of case. Using -i results in matches on jholman, Jholman, JHOLMAN, and any other possible variation.

-L Causes **grep** to print the filenames not containing a match for the search string, while using -l to print those file containing the match.

-n Used to print the line number of the file where the match occurred. This is based upon the input file and not numbering the output like the **nl** command.

-q Instructs **grep** to perform the search but print nothing. This is useful in shell scripts where you only want to test the return code.

-s Used to silence errors in the search. Using -s prevents **grep** from printing error messages, such as for inadequate permissions.

-v Tells **grep** to print all lines not matching the specified string. Using our **ps** example earlier, ps -ef | grep -v jholman would print all lines not containing the pattern "jholman".

-w Causes **grep** to display matches based upon a strict word match.

-x Tells **grep** to print the line only if there is a complete match.

As long as the options do not conflict or cancel each other, they can be combined as desired. For example, you cannot mix both the -c and -n options to print the final count of matches and the line numbers because these two options are mutually exclusive.

Some examples to demonstrate the functionality associated with **grep** will illustrate these options and expressions. To list all the files in the /etc/ using **ls -l** is a common activity. Suppose you want to know exactly how many files there are, excluding directories and subdirectories. Using the first character of the **ls -l** command output, which is the permissions field and file type, will tell you how many files there are:

```
ls -l | grep -c "^-"
```

Knowing how many users are in the /etc/passwd file on a large system is done using

```
grep -c "." /etc/passwd
```

Suppose you want to know how many FTP transfers have been made to or from your system. You must know where your FTP server logs this data, which is generally /var/log/xferlog by default. We can find out how many files have been transferred using the syntax

```
[root@mercury.technical log]# grep -c "." /var/log/xferlog
1026
[root@mercury.technical log]#
```

What if you want to know how many times your Web site index.html file has been transferred using FTP? The **grep -c** command does this, but we also need to add a pattern:

```
grep -c "index.html" /var/log/xferlog
```

This is one of the many uses for **grep**—finding information and extracting it from log files. At the same time, suppose you want to find all the files transferred that were not HTML files. The syntax

```
grep -v "\.htm" /var/log/xferlog
```

shows you all the lines that do not have .htm in their filename.

Web sites contain a lot of different files, however, so we can use the -f option to **grep** and provide a list of patterns to search for. This method is a lot easier and faster than using multiple **grep** commands. We have a file called *htmlfiles*, containing the following:

```
[root@mercury.technical log]# cat /tmp/htmlfiles
html
gif
[root@mercury.technical log]#
```

By providing this filename to **grep**, we can perform multiple searches in the file and return all the lines that match at least one of the patterns. Using the -f option is shown here:

```
[root@mercury.technical log]# grep -f /tmp/htmlfiles /var/log/xferlog | more
Sun May 20 11:12:37 2001 1 192.168.0.16 626
/var/www/html/jholman/_borders/_vti_cnf/bottom.htm b _ o r chweb ftp 0 * c
Sun May 20 11:12:37 2001 1 192.168.0.16 645
/var/www/html/jholman/_borders/_vti_cnf/left.htm b _ o r chweb ftp 0 * c
Sun May 20 11:12:38 2001 1 192.168.0.16 963
/var/www/html/jholman/_borders/bottom.htm b _ o r chweb ftp 0 * c
Sun May 20 11:12:41 2001 1 192.168.0.16 469
/var/www/html/jholman/_derived/_vti_cnf/download.htm_cmp_zero110_bnr.gif
b _ o r chweb ftp 0 * c
```

Although we can use the -f option to **grep** to perform multiple pattern searches, this option did not exist on the original **grep** implementations. Consequently, administrators used **fgrep**.

fgrep

After **grep** had been available for some time, there was interest in providing a method of easily searching for multiple items at a time. **fgrep** was designed in the early days of Unix, well before Linux was conceived. Although the idea was good in theory, the implementation left something to be desired. The price for multiple search strings was very high: the loss of regular expressions in **fgrep**. Although **fgrep** still exists, it is rarely used because the functionality has been added to the **grep** command.

egrep

There was a subsequent attempt to enhance **grep** again, called extended grep, or **egrep**. This combined the new functionality of **fgrep** with **grep** and maintained regular expressions. Like **fgrep,** you can specify multiple search patterns, but you can specify them in several different manners.

First, you can put the patterns in a file and use the -f option to specify the file. You also can enter them on multiple lines using uneven quotes. Finally, you can use the pipe (|) symbol. For example

```
[root@mercury.technical log]# cat /tmp/data
auth
connect
failed
ftpd?
Login
[root@mercury.technical log]# vi /tmp/data
[root@mercury.technical log]# egrep -f /tmp/data messages | more
```

```
May 20 08:14:48 mercury ftpd[17976]: getpeername (in.ftpd):
Transport endpoint is not connected
May 20 12:21:08 mercury PAM_unix[18754]: (system-auth) session
opened for user jholman by (uid=0)
May 20 12:25:57 mercury ftpd[18741]: FTP session closed
May 20 16:11:43 mercury PAM_unix[18974]: (system-auth) session
opened for user root by jholman(uid=500)
May 20 20:49:13 mercury ftpd[19103]: getpeername (in.ftpd):
Transport endpoint is not connected
[root@mercury.technical log]# [root@mercury.technical log]# egrep
"open|close" messages | more
May 20 11:57:06 mercury ftpd[18056]: FTP session closed
May 20 12:21:08 mercury PAM_unix[18754]: (system-auth) session
opened for user jholman by (uid=0)
May 20 12:25:57 mercury ftpd[18741]: FTP session closed
May 20 16:11:43 mercury PAM_unix[18974]: (system-auth) session
opened for user root by jholman(uid=500)
[root@mercury.technical log]#
```

The new functionality in **egrep** also added two new variables to the regular expression syntax:

?   Shows zero or one instance of the preceding character

+   Shows one or more instances of the preceding character

Our Linux systems have some esoteric names for system components. You are looking for information from the system's log file to troubleshoot a problem with the sound installation. However, you can't remember the name of the driver or if there is underscore (_) in the name. Use the question mark (?) in the search pattern, as follows:

```
[root@mercury.technical log]# egrep "_?audio" messages.1
May 16 21:04:11 mercury kernel: i810_audio: unable to allocate irq 11
May 16 21:04:11 mercury kernel: i810_audio: Found 0 audio device(s).
May 16 21:04:11 mercury kernel: i810_audio: No devices found.
[root@mercury.technical log]#
```

Using the question mark (?) after the underscore (_) instructs **egrep** to look at zero or one instance of the underscore, and if found, it compares against the rest of the string. The result is we know what the name of the audio driver is on our Linux system thanks to **egrep**.

Using the employee.list file shown here, we will look at the + option in the **egrep** pattern:

```
[root@mercury.technical /tmp]# cat employee.list
Joe Smith
Roger Moore
Ethan Hunt
Virginia Woolf
```

```
Annie Hall
Jaime Sommers
Sgt. Bilko
[root@mercury.technical /tmp]#
```

Recall the question mark (?) is used to indicate zero or one instances of the character immediately preceding the question mark. The plus sign (+) means at least one instance of the preceding character. From our employee list, we don't know if Virginia spells her name with one or two O's. Consequently, we can use the plus sign and see what we get:

```
[root@mercury.technical /tmp]# egrep "Woo+" /tmp/employee.list
Virginia Woolf
[root@mercury.technical /tmp]#
```

Had there been only one O in Virginia's name, using the pattern Woo+ would have failed to match.

Remember, **egrep** was created in the Unix environment, prior to Linux. Because most of the features of **egrep** have been incorporated into **grep**, there is little use of this command. You can get most of the functionality associated with **egrep** by using **grep -E**.

What Is a Process?

A *program* is a file residing on a disk, containing instructions for the system to execute. A *process* is any instance of a command or program while it is being executed. When you type a command to the shell, such as **cat**, a program file is loaded into memory and a process created to execute the instructions returns the results to the user.

As everything on the system is a process one way or another, you must realize that even your shell is a process. If you enter a command to the shell that is built-in and doesn't require loading another program, the shell executes the instruction itself.

However, if the user enters a command external to the shell, such as **date**, the shell must initiate another command to perform the task. This results in the shell being the parent process of the command to be executed, while the new command is a child of the parent, as illustrated in Figure 4-2.

Upon completing the task, the child returns a result to the parent and exits. (The kernel has responsibility for adding and removing entries from the process table.) Linux, like Unix, is a multitasking operating system enabling for many child processes related to a single parent. This is important to remember, because if the child process cannot complete the task on its own, it can start new processes to perform additional work. In this way, each child process can itself become a parent, as illustrated in Figure 4-3.

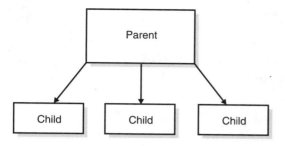

Figure 4-2   The new process is called the child.

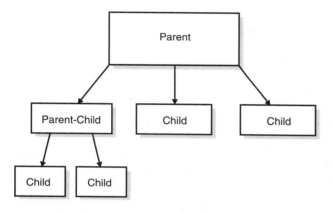

Figure 4-3   Children can also be parents.

   NOTE   Unless specific instructions are designed into a process, such as the restricted shell, every process has the ability to be a parent or a child.

At any given time, the system is running processes on your behalf, for other users, or to provide system services, such as printing. The system services are commonly referred to as *daemons*, and typically do not interact directly with the system users. Common system daemons are **lpd** for printing, **httpd** as the Web server, **cron** for running system jobs, and **sendmail** for processing e-mail.

Viewing the Process Table

The kernel uses the *process table* to keep track of the jobs running on the system at any one time. The **ps** command is the user's view into the process table and lists not only the processes, but also specific information about the process status. When executing **ps** with no options, your currently running commands are listed, including the **ps** command. Remember, because **ps** is a process, it is listed in the process table as well:

```
[root@mercury.technical /root]# ps
 PID TTY TIME   CMD
 2224 pts/6 00:00:00 bash
 2290 pts/6 00:00:01 tar
 2291 pts/6 00:00:00 ps
[root@mercury.technical /root]#
```

ps prints four columns of information by default. The process ID (PID) is printed in the first column. PID identifies each process to the system. The numbering starts at one when the system is booted, and as each new process is created, a new number is assigned. When the system default maximum is reached, the numbering starts over. However, the kernel knows which PID numbers are still in use and will not use them until they become free.

The second column, TTY, identifies the terminal from where the user has executed the command. Because **ps** lists the processes only for the user running the **ps** command, the terminal identifier should always be the same.

The third column, TIME, indicates the amount of CPU time the process is using. Many commands execute very quickly or perform some work and sit idle while waiting for their turn to execute again. Consequently, the TIME field is often 0:00. A large value in the TIME field can indicate a command that is taking a long time to complete or one that is hung and consuming system resources, therefore affecting the performance of the system.

The fourth column, CMD, prints the actual command name the user is executing. The first line is generally the user's shell and is known as the *session leader*. Without it, the user would not be logged on the system. The last line in the **ps** output is the command that has just executed, with all other currently executing processes listed between them.

Like most Linux commands, **ps** has a number of options affecting the information displayed. The -a option instructs **ps** to list all the commands the user is executing, except for the session leaders. The resulting output resembles

```
[root@mercury.technical /root]# ps -a
 PID TTY TIME CMD
 1211 pts/2 00:00:00 su
```

```
1215 pts/2 00:00:00 bash
1864 pts/5 00:00:00 su
1868 pts/5 00:00:00 bash
2334 pts/5 00:03:39 perl
2388 pts/6 00:00:00 ps
[root@mercury.technical /root]#
```

> **NOTE** While ps -a removes the session leaders, it also lists all the commands
> the user is executing, regardless of the terminal they are associated with.

The -A or -e options (all or everything) list every process running on the system, not just those running by the user or for the current terminal. This process listing can be extensive, depending on the number of processes. It resembles the following:

```
[root@mercury.technical /root]# ps -e
PID TTY TIME CMD
1 ? 00:00:04 init
2 ? 00:00:00 keventd
3 ? 00:00:00 kapm-idled
4 ? 00:00:00 kswapd
5 ? 00:00:00 kreclaimd
6 ? 00:00:00 bdflush
7 ? 00:00:00 kupdated
8 ? 00:00:00 mdrecoveryd
429 ? 00:00:00 syslogd
434 ? 00:00:00 klogd
448 ? 00:00:00 portmap
463 ? 00:00:00 rpc.statd
547 ? 00:00:00 apmd
594 ? 00:00:00 automount
606 ? 00:00:00 atd
621 ? 00:00:01 sshd
641 ? 00:00:00 xinetd
681 ? 00:00:00 sendmail
694 ? 00:00:00 gpm
706 ? 00:00:00 crond
742 ? 00:00:03 xfs
767 ? 00:00:00 rhnsd
783 ? 00:00:00 miniserv.pl
786 ? 00:00:00 gdm
794 ? 00:00:34 X
795 ? 00:00:00 gdm
807 ? 00:00:02 ksmserver
906 ? 00:00:00 kdeinit
908 ? 00:00:00 kdeinit
910 ? 00:00:00 kdeinit
912 ? 00:00:00 sshd
```

```
917  ?     00:00:00  kdeinit
928  pts/0 00:00:00  bash
963  ?     00:00:00  kdeinit
968  ?     00:00:01  knotify
971  ?     00:00:03  kdeinit
974  ?     00:00:06  kdeinit
997  ?     00:00:18  kdeinit
1004 ?     00:00:01  autorun
1018 ?     00:00:00  kdeinit
1019 ?     00:00:00  kdeinit
1021 ?     00:00:00  kdeinit
1024 pts/1 00:00:00  cat
1042 ?     00:00:00  smbd
1047 ?     00:00:00  nmbd
1050 ?     00:00:00  nmbd
1065 ?     00:00:02  httpd
1068 ?     00:00:00  httpd
1076 ?     00:00:05  kdeinit
1077 pts/2 00:00:00  bash
1097 pts/3 00:00:00  bash
1117 pts/3 00:00:00  su
1121 pts/3 00:00:00  bash
1142 pts/4 00:00:00  bash
1203 pts/2 00:00:00  su
1207 pts/2 00:00:00  bash
1289 ?     00:00:00  kdeinit
1307 pts/5 00:00:00  bash
1330 pts/2 00:00:11  perl
1346 pts/2 00:00:00  sh
1347 pts/2 00:00:04  find
1349 pts/0 00:00:00  ps
1350 pts/0 00:00:00  mail
```

Some particular items worth mentioning in the **ps** display include

- A number of processes are started when the system initializes to support the proper operation of the system. These processes typically have the lowest number PIDs (see PIDs one through eight). Given the mission critical nature of these processes, should one fail, the system will generally become unusable.

- Many processes are not run on a specified terminal and show up in the display with a ? in the TTY field. The lack of a terminal indicates the process runs without terminal interaction or does not use a terminal as the default standard output for the process.

- Typically, a terminal on which a user is not logged in runs a process called *getty* to display the login prompt and waits for a user to log in. On workstations where the X graphical user interface is used as the default user interface, a getty is not running. Instead, a process called *kdm*, *xdm*, or *gdm* runs to provide the graphical login interface to the user on the console. Other nonconsole terminal devices, like serial ports, will still run a getty if so configured.

Of the many other options commonly used with **ps**, the most commonly used include

-l Displays more information about the process (like **ls -l** does for files)

-u Displays the username and related statistics

-f Displays all process information

The -f option is most favored by administrators because of the information it provides in the output:

```
[root@mercury.technical /root]# ps -f
UID PID PPID C STIME TTY TIME CMD
jholman 928 912 0 21:13 pts/0 00:00:00 -bash
jholman 1426 928 0 22:01 pts/0 00:00:00 find / -name questions
jholman 1427 928 19 22:01 pts/0 00:00:00 ps -f
[root@mercury.technical /root]#
```

Additional columns for UID, PPID, C, and STIME are now printed in the **ps** output. The UID column prints the name of the user running the command. The PPID column identifies the parent PID. This is how you can establish which process started what other processes. The C column indicates if scheduling on the CPU is performed, and STIME specifies when the process started executing.

NOTE The CMD field with the -f option provides additional command-line arguments over the normal ps display. Because this information is visible to any user on the system, arguments, such as passwords, must not be provided on the command line to a program.

The power of **ps** is more fully realized the options are combined, such as -ef, which displays all the running processes in full format:

```
UID PID PPID C STIME TTY TIME CMD
root 1 0 0 21:12 ? 00:00:04 init [5]
root 2 1 0 21:12 ? 00:00:00 [keventd]
root 3 1 0 21:12 ? 00:00:00 [kapm-idled]
root 4 1 0 21:12 ? 00:00:01 [kswapd]
root 5 1 0 21:12 ? 00:00:00 [kreclaimd]
root 6 1 0 21:12 ? 00:00:00 [bdflush]
root 7 1 0 21:12 ? 00:00:00 [kupdated]
root 8 1 0 21:12 ? 00:00:00 [mdrecoveryd]
```

```
root 429 1 0 21:12 ? 00:00:00 syslogd -m 0
root 434 1 0 21:12 ? 00:00:00 klogd -2
rpc 448 1 0 21:12 ? 00:00:00 portmap
rpcuser 463 1 0 21:12 ? 00:00:00 rpc.statd
root 547 1 0 21:12 ? 00:00:00 /usr/sbin/apmd -p 10 -w 5 -W -P
root 594 1 0 21:12 ? 00:00:00 /usr/sbin/automount --timeout 60
daemon 606 1 0 21:12 ? 00:00:00 /usr/sbin/atd
root 621 1 0 21:12 ? 00:00:01 /usr/sbin/sshd
root 641 1 0 21:12 ? 00:00:00 xinetd -stayalive -reuse -pidfil
root 681 1 0 21:13 ? 00:00:00 sendmail: accepting connections
root 694 1 0 21:13 ? 00:00:00 gpm -t ps/2 -m /dev/mouse
root 706 1 0 21:13 ? 00:00:00 crond
xfs 742 1 0 21:13 ? 00:00:04 xfs -droppriv -daemon
root 767 1 0 21:13 ? 00:00:00 rhnsd --interval 120
root 783 1 0 21:13 ? 00:00:00 /usr/bin/perl /usr/libexec/webmi
root 786 1 0 21:13 ? 00:00:00 /usr/bin/gdm -nodaemon
root 794 786 1 21:13 ? 00:00:41 /etc/X11/X -auth /var/gdm/:0.Xau
root 795 786 0 21:13 ? 00:00:00 /usr/bin/gdm -nodaemon
jholman 807 795 0 21:13 ? 00:00:02 ksmserver --restore
jholman 906 1 0 21:13 ? 00:00:00 kdeinit: dcopserver --nosid
jholman 908 1 0 21:13 ? 00:00:00 kdeinit: klauncher
jholman 910 1 0 21:13 ? 00:00:00 kdeinit: kded
root 912 621 0 21:13 ? 00:00:00 /usr/sbin/sshd
jholman 917 1 0 21:13 ? 00:00:00 kdeinit: kxmlrpcd
jholman 928 912 0 21:13 pts/0 00:00:00 -bash
jholman 963 1 0 21:13 ? 00:00:00 kdeinit: Running...
jholman 968 1 0 21:13 ? 00:00:01 knotify
jholman 971 963 0 21:14 ? 00:00:04 kdeinit: kwin
jholman 974 1 0 21:14 ? 00:00:06 kdeinit: kdesktop
jholman 997 1 0 21:14 ? 00:00:19 kdeinit: kicker
jholman 1004 1 0 21:14 ? 00:00:01 /usr/bin/autorun -l --interval=1
jholman 1018 1 0 21:14 ? 00:00:00 kdeinit: klipper -icon klipper -
jholman 1019 1 0 21:14 ? 00:00:00 kdeinit: khotkeys
jholman 1021 1 0 21:14 ? 00:00:00 kdeinit: kwrited
jholman 1024 1021 0 21:14 pts/1 00:00:00 /bin/cat
root 1042 1 0 21:16 ? 00:00:00 smbd -D
root 1047 1 0 21:16 ? 00:00:00 nmbd -D
root 1050 1047 0 21:16 ? 00:00:00 nmbd -D
root 1065 1 0 21:16 ? 00:00:02 /usr/sbin/httpd -DHAVE_PROXY -DH
apache 1068 1065 0 21:17 ? 00:00:00 /usr/sbin/httpd -DHAVE_PROXY -DH
apache 1069 1065 0 21:17 ? 00:00:00 /usr/sbin/httpd -DHAVE_PROXY -DH
apache 1070 1065 0 21:17 ? 00:00:00 /usr/sbin/httpd -DHAVE_PROXY -DH
apache 1071 1065 0 21:17 ? 00:00:00 /usr/sbin/httpd -DHAVE_PROXY -DH
apache 1072 1065 0 21:17 ? 00:00:00 /usr/sbin/httpd -DHAVE_PROXY -DH
apache 1073 1065 0 21:17 ? 00:00:00 /usr/sbin/httpd -DHAVE_PROXY -DH
apache 1074 1065 0 21:17 ? 00:00:00 /usr/sbin/httpd -DHAVE_PROXY -DH
apache 1075 1065 0 21:17 ? 00:00:00 /usr/sbin/httpd -DHAVE_PROXY -DH
jholman 1076 963 4 21:17 ? 00:02:00 kdeinit: konsole -icon konsole -
jholman 1077 1076 0 21:17 pts/2 00:00:00 /bin/bash
jholman 1097 1076 0 21:17 pts/3 00:00:00 /bin/bash
root 1117 1097 0 21:17 pts/3 00:00:00 su
root 1121 1117 0 21:17 pts/3 00:00:00 bash
jholman 1142 1076 0 21:18 pts/4 00:00:00 /bin/bash
root 1203 1077 0 21:19 pts/2 00:00:00 su
```

```
root 1207 1203 0 21:19 pts/2 00:00:00 bash
jholman 1289 1 0 21:38 ? 00:00:00 kdeinit: kio_uiserver
jholman 1307 1076 0 21:42 pts/5 00:00:00 /bin/bash
root 1372 1042 0 21:48 ? 00:00:00 smbd -D
root 1388 1207 12 21:58 pts/2 00:01:06 perl seal.pl
root 1401 1388 0 21:58 pts/2 00:00:00 [perl <defunct>]
root 1403 1388 0 21:58 pts/2 00:00:00 [mount <defunct>]
jholman 1407 963 1 21:58 ? 00:00:09 kdeinit: konqueror --silent
root 1414 1388 0 21:59 pts/2 00:00:00 sh -c find /usr -xdev -print 2>/
root 1415 1414 0 21:59 pts/2 00:00:01 find /usr -xdev -print
root 1419 706 0 22:01 ? 00:00:00 CROND
root 1420 1419 0 22:01 ? 00:00:00 /bin/bash /usr/bin/run-parts /et
root 1422 1420 0 22:01 ? 00:00:00 awk -v progname=/etc/cron.hourly
root 1423 1 0 22:01 ? 00:00:00 /bin/sh /usr/lib/sa/sa1 600 6
root 1425 1423 0 22:01 ? 00:00:00 /usr/lib/sa/sadc 600 6 /var/log/
jholman 1428 928 0 22:06 pts/0 00:00:00 ps -ef
jholman 1429 928 0 22:06 pts/0 00:00:00 mail jholman
```

Working with pstree and top

The **pstree** and **top** commands also interact with the process table to show process and system information. The **pstree** command identifies the relationships between processes using text-based graphics:

```
init-+-apmd
     |-atd
     |-automount
     |-autorun
     |-bdflush
     |-crond---crond---run-parts---awk
     |-gdm-+-X
     |     '-gdm---ksmserver
     |-gpm
     |-httpd---8*[httpd]
     |-kapm-idled
     |-9*[kdeinit]
     |-kdeinit-+-2*[kdeinit]
     |         '-kdeinit-+-bash---su---bash---perl-+-mount
     |         |         |                          |-perl
     |         |         '-sh---find
     |         |-bash---su---bash
     |         '-2*[bash]
     |-kdeinit---cat
     |-keventd
     |-klogd
     |-knotify
     |-kreclaimd
     |-kswapd
     |-kupdated
```

```
|-mdrecoveryd
|-miniserv.pl
|-nmbd---nmbd
|-portmap
|-rhnsd
|-rpc.statd
|-sa1---sadc
|-sendmail
|-smbd---smbd
|-sshd---sshd---bash-+-mail
|   '-pstree
|-syslogd
|-xfs
'-xinetd
```

pstree illustrates the children for each process and identifies where each process is run from. **pstree** provides an easy way of navigating through the process table to see which process is actually the parent or child of another.

The **top** command is shown in Figure 4-4. Unlike **ps**, **top** remains active and shows the running processes and changes in the CPU time and system utilization. There are

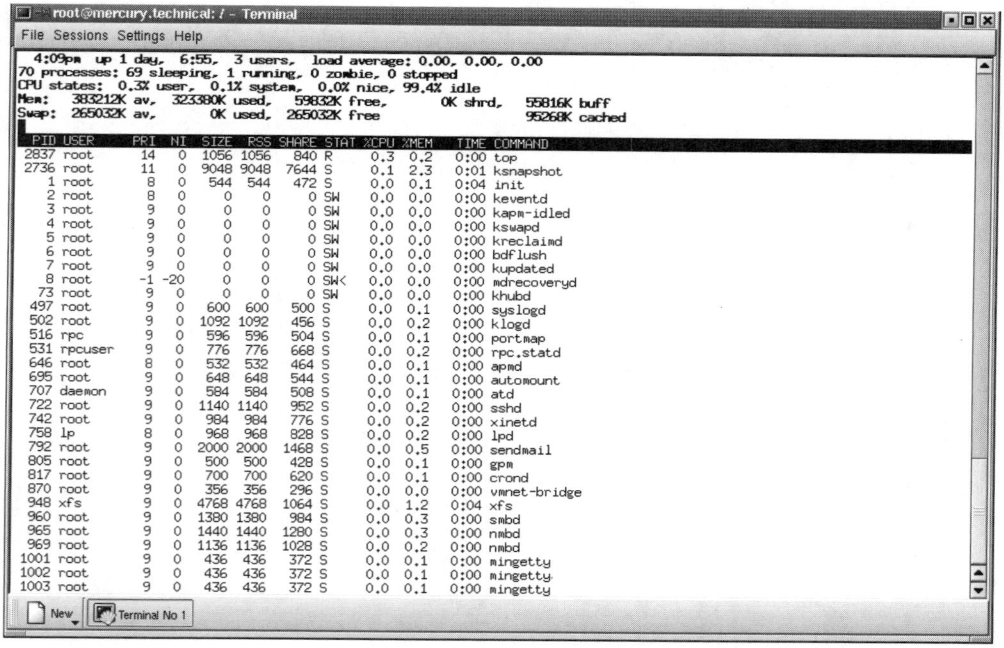

Figure 4-4   The **top** utility shows memory and usage statistics, as well as processes, and continually updates the display.

also X Window implementations of **top**, which provide nice graphics and real-time displays.

When **top** is running, you can press any of the following keys to interact with it:

h	Provides application help
q	Quits top
s	Changes the default refresh delay from five seconds
space bar	Updates the display now
u	Displays information for a single user

Among the columns of information displayed for each process (aside from the standard PID and CMD), the amount of memory used and the CPU resources are also displayed.

Quoting

Quoting is generally accepted as one of the more difficult shell concepts to master, although once you learn it, it is hard to forget. There are three distinct sets of quotes used in the shell, each with a distinct meaning:

- The double quotes (")
- The single quote (')
- The back quote (`)

The double quotes are used to disable all characters except for the backstroke (\), the dollar sign ($), and the single quote ('), whereas the single quote disables all characters but the back quote (`). The back quote is used to execute the command specified and place the results in place of the command.

The quotes must be used in even numbers, or the shell will not understand what it must do. The shell finds an odd number of quotes and assumes you have more input to provide until the matching quote is provided. Because the quotes protect information or perform work, they can be combined together to provide significant flexibility.

The double quotes are used to protect the white space between the words and change the way arguments are presented to the command. For example, assume you have a file in your home directory called My Programs, and you execute the command

```
ls My Programs
```

This has the undesirable effect of instructing **ls** to list a file called My and one called Programs. The shell normally interprets the white space between the words as a *delimiter*, meaning the **ls** command sees two arguments: My and Programs. For the **ls** command to identify the file properly, double quotes are used:

```
ls "My Programs"
```

This has the effect of canceling the effect of the white space and giving the command only one argument—the entire text between the quotes. However, the double quotes do not cancel the effect of all the special characters. Remembering the *$PROGRAMS* variable from earlier in the chapter, which has a value of "/usr/local/bin", the commands

```
echo $PROGRAMS
```

and

```
echo "$PROGRAMS"
```

are equivalent because the double quotes do not remove the meaning of the dollar sign. However, the command

```
echo '$PROGRAMS'
```

results in the text *$PROGRAMS* being printed, as the single quotes do remove the meaning associated with the dollar sign.

Suppose you want to print the results of the **pwd** command in an echo statement or print the assignment to a variable. Using the command

```
echo 'pwd'
```

prints the word *pwd*, whereas, using the back quotes, as in

```
echo `pwd`
```

returns the result of the command. In this manner, we can also assign the output of the command to a variable. To illustrate this, we want to save the output of the **pwd** command to a variable and then print the variable:

```
CWD=`pwd`
echo $CWD
```

The first command executes the **pwd** command and saves the result in the variable *CWD*. The second command then prints the value of *CWD*, which is actually the output of the **pwd** command. This is an important construct to remember when building shell scripts.

As mentioned earlier, the shell expects to find an even number of quotes. Failing to do so causes the shell to replace PS1 with PS2 and continues to do so until an even number of quotes is reached, even if you are not finished entering the entire command, as illustrated here:

```
[root@mercury.technical /tmp]# echo "This is test of the
> shell quoting methods. The current
> date is `date` and my directory is 'pwd'"
This is test of the
shell quoting methods. The current
date is Sat May 19 10:40:06 EDT 2001 and my directory is /tmp
[root@mercury.technical /tmp]#
```

There are situations where you do not want the shell to interpret the meaning associated with the quote characters themselves. This typically occurs when you want to include them in the text as output, such as

```
Welcome "Jon"
```

Using the command

```
echo Welcome "Jon"
```

does not produce the desired result, but rather prints

```
Welcome Jon
```

Remember, the quotes are a special character to the shell, intending the item between the quotes to be taken as a single entry or argument. The shell performs the operation and loses the quotes. This is prevented by using the backstroke (\) character, which cancels the special meaning the shell assigns to the quotes:

```
echo Welcome \"Jon\"
```

Each instance of the character you want to preserve as a literal, or to *escape*, as it is often called, must be preceded by the backstroke. Failing to do so can introduce quoting errors in your command.

Ending a Process

When a child process is created, the child executes a set of instructions on behalf of the parent and returns a result. When the child finishes executing, it exits on its own and is removed from the process table. Occasionally, processes finish executing or become stuck in a processing loop, creating a runaway process. Runaway processes can consume system resources, including CPU time; however, they often just sit as entries in the process table and consume memory.

The parent process cannot exit until the child processes it started have completed executing. This is important, as a child process can also start other processes to complete the desired task. For example, a user starts a shell, which runs the **tar** command, which runs **gzip** to compress the resulting archive. Normally, **gzip** will complete, return processing control to **tar**, which exits and returns control to the shell, which also exits.

In the situation where the final command in the chain does not exit after execution, the parent is not notified and continues to wait. Consequently, three processes are running and consuming resources, when they are actually no longer needed on the system. A runaway is created when all of the parent processes exit, either normally due to the application design, or through a failure of some kind, leaving the last child.

To address problems with runaway processes or to stop processes that are no longer needed before they finish executing, use the **kill** command with the syntax:

```
kill {option} PID
```

To remove the perl process in the processing listing, use the following:

```
[root@mercury.technical /root]# ps -f
UID PID PPID C STIME TTY TIME CMD
jholman 1710 1709 0 09:49 pts/5 00:00:00 -bash
jholman 1747 1710 0 09:49 pts/5 00:00:00 perl
jholman 1756 1710 1 09:50 pts/5 00:00:00 perl
jholman 1757 1710 0 09:50 pts/5 00:00:00 ps -f
[root@mercury.technical /root]#
[root@mercury.technical /root]# kill 1756
[root@mercury.technical /root]#
```

Using **kill** with no options instructs the process to die gracefully and to clean up after itself. However, in many situations, the process ignores the request from the **kill** command and continues processing. There are a total of 32 signals available in Linux, which are sent to a process using the **kill** command, which the process responds to accordingly. The signal is used as the option to the **kill** command, although in practicality, there are only a few signals commonly used. These signals are

-1   Hangup

-2   Interrupt (also generated using CTRL+C)

-3   Quit

-9   Terminate immediately

-15 Terminate (the default signal sent using **kill** with no options)

NOTE The kill -l command will list all the signals known by your operating system.

Assuming the process does not go away politely, the sequence of operations then becomes

```
[root@mercury.technical /root]# ps -f
UID PID PPID C STIME TTY TIME CMD
jholman 1159 1037 0 08:24 pts/0 00:00:00 /bin/bash
jholman 1035 1159 0 08:19 pts/0 00:00:00 /bin/cat
jholman 1896 1159 0 10:36 pts/0 00:00:00 perl
jholman 1900 1159 0 10:37 pts/0 00:00:00 ps -f
[root@mercury.technical /root]#
[root@mercury.technical /root]#kill 1896
[root@mercury.technical /root]# ps -f
UID PID PPID C STIME TTY TIME CMD
jholman 1159 1037 0 08:24 pts/0 00:00:00 /bin/bash
jholman 1035 1159 0 08:19 pts/0 00:00:00 /bin/cat
jholman 1896 1159 0 10:36 pts/0 00:00:00 perl
jholman 1900 1159 0 10:37 pts/0 00:00:00 ps -f
[root@mercury.technical /root]#
[root@mercury.technical /root]# kill -9 1896
Killed
$ ps -f
[root@mercury.technical /root]# ps -f
UID PID PPID C STIME TTY TIME CMD
jholman 1159 1037 0 08:24 pts/0 00:00:00 /bin/bash
jholman 1035 1159 0 08:19 pts/0 00:00:00 /bin/cat
jholman 1900 1159 0 10:37 pts/0 00:00:00 ps -f
[root@mercury.technical /root]#
```

Using **kill** with no options to attempt signal 15 (terminate) first is the preferred approach. If the process will not die, then use signal 9 (**kill**). Signal 15 is the preferred approach because the child will generally remove temporary files, and so on before exiting, whereas signal 9 will not. It is important to verify there are no child processes owned by the process you want to kill. If there are, they should be killed first.

A second approach is to use the **killall** command. This takes a command name and kills all processes with that command name, rather than the PID approach used by **kill**. Using the -w option instructs **killall** to wait for each process to exit. **killall** checks once every second and will only exit if all the named processes have died. There are some instances where you may want to interactively select the processes to be killed using the -I option.

Background and Foreground

Commands can be run in the foreground or the background. Running commands in the foreground is the most-common method, meaning the command runs attached to our terminal, and we must wait for it to complete before we can execute the next command. Background processing disassociates the process from the terminal, so we can perform other work while waiting for the command to finish.

The shell knows we want to run the job in the background when it finds an ampersand (&) following the name of the command:

```
[root@mercury.technical /root]# find /var -print > /tmp/list &
[1] 2084
[root@mercury.technical /root]#
```

The shell prints two pieces of information when you run a job in the background. The first is the job number, which is printed between the square brackets and indicates the number of jobs you are running in the background. The second number is the PID for the child process.

NOTE The PID of the last job placed in the background can also be referenced as $!.

Should a job be started in the background that we must wait for completion, we can use the **wait** command to return the job to the foreground. The **wait** command requires us to provide the PID of the command to wait for. The shell then suspends execution, meaning the prompt does not return, until the specified process completes:

```
[root@mercury.technical /root]# find /var -print > /tmp/list &
[1] 2102
[root@mercury.technical /root]#
[root@mercury.technical /root]#wait 2102
```

Once PID 2102 completes execution, the shell displays the prompt and awaits additional instructions from the user.

jobs

Most shells available today understand the concept of jobs and job control. (A *job* is a process that is running in the background.) The **jobs** command prints a list of all current background jobs:

```
[root@mercury.technical /root]# jobs
[1]+ Stopped perl
[2]- Running find / -print 2>/dev/null >/tmp/listing &
[root@mercury.technical /root]#
```

Terminated jobs are not printed in the list, and recently completed jobs are only printed once. Next, the **find** command finishes execution, the next time we run **jobs**, we see

```
[root@mercury.technical /root]# jobs
[1]+ Stopped perl
[2] Done find / -print 2>/dev/null >/tmp/listing
[root@mercury.technical /root]#
```

A plus sign (+) following a job number indicates the most-recent job that can run or that is currently running. The minus sign (−) is the next most-recent job. If **wd** is printed in the command name, it is followed by the working directory name. The output of **jobs** can be altered using the -l option to include the PID numbers in the display, while the -p option prints only the PID. By default, **jobs** lists all background jobs, but the -n option causes **jobs** to print only the suspended jobs.

fg

The job control command, **fg**, takes the named background job and puts in the foreground to complete execution. The **fg** syntax requires the use of the percent sign (%) followed by the job number. For example, we can start a **find** command and place it in the background:

```
[root@mercury.technical /root]# find / -print 2>/dev/null > /tmp/listing &
[2] 2175
[root@mercury.technical /root]# jobs
[1]+ Stopped perl
[2]- Running find / -print 2>/dev/null >/tmp/listing &
[root@mercury.technical /root]#
```

To move the **find** command to the foreground, use the command **fg** followed by the job number, which in this case is 2:

```
[root@mercury.technical /root]# fg %2
find / -print 2>/dev/null >/tmp/listing
```

When the command is brought to the foreground, the actual command being executed is printed on the display, and the shell waits until the **jobs** command finishes before printing a new prompt. The %2 can also be replaced with two special arguments,

%+ and %-, specifying the two most, recent jobs. The **fg** command has a third substitution method, %?, enabling you to specify the command by a portion of its name:

```
[root@mercury.technical /root]# jobs
[1] Stopped perl
[2]- Stopped vi /tmp/list
[3]+ Stopped cat
[root@mercury.technical /root]# fg %?c
cat
```

bg

Just as we want to bring background commands to the foreground, we also will want to send jobs to the background. This is done using the **bg** command. To get a foreground job to the background, you must first suspend the job using the **susp** signal, generated by CTRL+Z on the keyboard. This stops the job and enables you to interact with it using **fg** and **bg**.

```
[root@mercury.technical /root]# jobs
[1] Stopped perl
[2] Stopped vi /tmp/list
[3]- Stopped cat
[4] Running find / -print 2>/dev/null >/tmp/listing &
[root@mercury.technical /root]#
[root@mercury.technical /root]# find / -print 2>/dev/null
/home/jholman/perl/libnet-1.0703/demos/inetd
/home/jholman/perl/libnet-1.0703/Hostname.pm.eg
/home/jholman/perl/libnet-1.0703/t
/home/jholman/perl/libnet-1.0703/t/nntp.t
/home/jholman/perl/libnet-1.0703/t/ph.t
/home/jholman/perl/libnet-1.0703/t/require.t
Ctrl+Z pressed
[5]+ Stopped find / -print 2>/dev/null
```

With the job suspended using CTRL+Z, you can now put the job in the background and enable it to continue executing:

```
[root@mercury.technical /root]# bg %5
[6]+ find / -print 2>/dev/null >/tmp/listing &
[root@mercury.technical /root]# jobs
[1] Stopped perl
[2] Stopped vi /tmp/list
[3]- Stopped cat
[5] Running find / -print 2>/dev/null >/tmp/listing &
[root@mercury.technical /root]#
```

Getting Your Priorities Straight

When starting a new process, the kernel assigns a default priority of zero to enable all processes to compete at an equal level for the CPU and other system resources. However, sometimes we want to run a very resource-intensive process at a lower priority, or make another process run faster by raising its priority. Changing priority levels is done using the **nice** and **renice** commands.

nice

The **nice** command is used to change the priority of a process when the command is started. It has no effect on running processes. There are 40 different priority levels, half negative and half positive, including:

19   Lowest priority

 0   Default priority

−20   Highest priority

When specifying the **nice** value on the command line, you must use a hyphen followed by the new priority level, and then the command:

```
[root@mercury.technical /root]# nice -20 find / -print 2>/dev/
null > /tmp/listing
[root@mercury.technical /root]#
```

The number on the command line may resemble a negative number, but in fact, is an option and is a positive number. A user can only lower his or her job priority—he or she is prevented from raising it. Therefore, a nice value of 20 changes the priority to the lowest available. The root user can increase priority using the negative numbers:

```
[root@mercury.technical /root]# nice --15 find / -print
2>/dev/null > /tmp/listing
[root@mercury.technical /root]#
```

In this case, root is raising the priority level of the process so it will complete faster. The **nice** command, with no options or arguments, prints the default scheduling priority.

renice

The **renice** command is used when you need to change the priority of a currently running process. The command uses the same priority numbers as **nice**. The **renice** command can affect a process using the -p option and the PID, a process group using -g, and a user using the -u option. A user named jholman on the system can change the priority of his processes using the command:

```
[root@mercury.technical /root]# renice +10 -u jholman
500: old priority 0, new priority 10
[root@mercury.technical /root]#
```

The **renice** command prints the UID of the user, as well as the old and new priorities. Like the **nice** command, a user cannot increase his or her priority—only the root user can.

Understanding Runlevels

Unlike many operating systems that have only two runlevels, running and halted, Linux and other Unix systems have several runlevels, each offering specific services. The available runlevels are described in Table 4-3.

The system is not running at runlevel 0 and requires a reboot to be operational again. When entering this runlevel while performing a shutdown or halt, all open files are synchronized to the disk, and the system is left in a state where it can be safely powered off without damaging the filesystems or data. Single-user or administrative mode is Level 1. This enables a single user, typically root, access to the console, while preventing any other users from accessing the system. When rebuilding the kernel or performing

Table 4-3   Linux System Runlevels

Runlevel	Purpose
0	The systems powered off or down
I	Single-user mode
2	Multiuser mode, no network services
3	Multiuser network mode
4	Differs per implementation
5	The X environment
6	Shut down and reboot
S or s	Single-user mode or runlevel I

other system administrative tasks that require reboots, this is the level you should be working in.

Level 2 is multiuser mode, enabling more than one user access to the system and its resources. The system starts up all system services with the exception of networking. Level 3 provides the same functionality and services as Level 2, but all network services are available. Level 4 varies from vendor to vendor, and Level 5 provides all functionality from Level 3, along with the X Window environment. Level 6 is a special runlevel that causes an automatic reboot of the system. This is equivalent to changing to runlevel 0 and then performing a warm boot of the system. It is a warm boot because the power is not shut off. Likewise, runlevel 0 is considered a cold boot because the system must be powered off in order to restart.

NOTE Runlevels 2, 3, and 5 are the operational level. They provide all system services and enable users access to the system services. All other runlevels are used for maintenance or system shutdown, preventing user access.

The **runlevel** command enables a user to determine the current runlevel of the system:

```
[root@mercury.technical /root]# /sbin/runlevel
N 5
[root@mercury.technical /root]#
```

The output of the **runlevel** command is two values: the previous runlevel, shown here as N for None, and 5, indicating the current runlevel. The values shown by the **runlevel** command are retrieved from the system /var/run/utmp file, where all runlevel changes are stored. If /var/run/utmp is corrupt or does not contain the required information, **runlevel** returns a value of unknown.

Up and Down

There are two commands available to change the runlevel on the system: **shutdown** and **init**. The **shutdown** command is really an interface to **init**, providing some additional features like warning the users that the system services are changing.

The **init** command is found in /sbin and when executed at the command line, must be followed by the runlevel you want to change to. The available runlevels are 0 through 6 and the letters S or s. The numbers identify the new runlevel, while S switches to single-user mode enabling only root, and s is single-user mode, but does not care which user. Changing runlevels is done using the following command syntax:

```
init 2
```

 NOTE There is one more command: telinit, which works exactly like init and is actually a link to init.

The **shutdown** command provides a variety of other options, including user advisories regarding the change in system state and enabling a delay before the shutdown takes place. The option affecting how shutdown works are

-F Forces **fsck** to run after the reboot, which is the default behavior

-f Prevents **fsck** from running after the reboot, thus creating a fast reboot

-h Switches to runlevel 0 after shutdown

-k Sends out a warning to all users, but does not really change state

-r Reboots after shutdown (Level 6)

-t Specifies the number of seconds before the change begins

If no parameters are specified, **shutdown** attempts to change to runlevel 0. The default runlevel **shutdown** attempts is level 0. An example of using the utility is

```
$ shutdown -h -t120 now
```

This forces a change to runlevel 0 (-h) 120 seconds (-t) from the current time (now). When using **shutdown**, you must specify the time for the shutdown to start. Any text following the time is considered by **shutdown** as the message to print to the users. For example

```
# shutdown -h now Emergency Power down in progress
```

results in the user seeing the following on his or her display:

```
[root@mercury.technical /root]# /sbin/shutdown now Emergency
Power down in progress

Broadcast message from root (pts/5) Sat Jun 9 14:23:56 2001...

Emergency Power down in progress
The system is going down to maintenance mode NOW !!
```

The action in this case is to have **shutdown** switch to single-user mode on the console for system management. You can also use the **write** and **wall** commands to send messages to users about the shutdown. It is possible to cancel the shutdown using the -c option, but the shutdown process must not have started already. Once the process has started, it cannot be stopped.

Typically, only root can run the **shutdown** command. However, the /etc/shutdown.allow file is used to list other users who should be able to shut down the system.

Three other commands are also used to shut down the system:

- **halt** Implements **shutdown -h**
- **reboot** Implements **shutdown -r**
- **poweroff** The same as **halt**

You must use the commands we have discussed to shut the system down prior to power off, regardless of which one. Failing to do so can lead to filesystem damage and data loss.

The inittab File

The **init** command is responsible for many things, including the initialization of the system. **init** uses the /etc/inittab file to define what is done at the different runlevels. The file is colon delimited and has four fields per line:

- **Short ID** Unique identifier in the file
- **Runlevel** The runlevels at which this is executed (blank means all)
- **Action** How do we do it
- **Command** What is executed

The following file is representative of what every inittab file looks like, although this one comes from Red Hat Linux 7.1. The line numbers have been added to the listing to facilitate the discussion surrounding the file:

```
1 #
2 # inittab This file describes how the INIT process should set up
3 # the system in a certain run-level.
4 #
5 # Author: Miquel van Smoorenburg, <miquels@drinkel.nl.mugnet.org>
6 # Modified for RHS Linux by Marc Ewing and Donnie Barnes
7 #
```

```
 8 # Default runlevel. The runlevels used by RHS are:
 9 # 0 - halt (Do NOT set initdefault to this)
10 # 1 - Single user mode
11 # 2 - Multiuser, without NFS (The same as 3, if you do not have networking)
12 # 3 - Full multiuser mode
13 # 4 - unused
14 # 5 - X11
15 # 6 - reboot (Do NOT set initdefault to this)
16 #
17 id:5:initdefault:

18 # System initialization.
19 si:sysinit:/etc/rc.d/rc.sysinit

20 l0:0:wait:/etc/rc.d/rc 0
21 l1:1:wait:/etc/rc.d/rc 1
22 l2:2:wait:/etc/rc.d/rc 2
23 l3:3:wait:/etc/rc.d/rc 3
24 l4:4:wait:/etc/rc.d/rc 4
25 l5:5:wait:/etc/rc.d/rc 5
26 l6:6:wait:/etc/rc.d/rc 6

27 # Things to run in every runlevel.
28 ud:once:/sbin/update

29 # Trap CTRL-ALT-DELETE
30 ca:ctrlaltdel:/sbin/shutdown -t3 -r now

31 # When our UPS tells us power has failed, assume we have a few minutes
32 # of power left. Schedule a shutdown for 2 minutes from now.
33 # This does, of course, assume you have powerd installed and your
34 # UPS connected and working correctly.
35 pf:powerfail:/sbin/shutdown -f -h +2 "Power Failure; System Shutting Down"

36 # If power was restored before the shutdown kicked in, cancel it.
37 pr:12345:powerokwait:/sbin/shutdown -c "Power Restored; Shutdown Cancelled"


38 # Run gettys in standard runlevels
39 1:234:respawn:/sbin/mingetty tty1
40 2:234:respawn:/sbin/mingetty tty2
41 3:234:respawn:/sbin/mingetty tty3
42 4:234:respawn:/sbin/mingetty tty4
43 5:234:respawn:/sbin/mingetty tty5
44 6:234:respawn:/sbin/mingetty tty6

45 # Run xdm in runlevel 5
46 # xdm is now a separate service
47 x:5:respawn:/etc/X11/prefdm -nodaemon
```

Line 17 is the first line that is not a comment, and it defines the default runlevel associated with the system, which **init** attempts to establish on every boot. Lines 20 through

26 tell **init** to execute the shell script /etc/rc.d/rc with an argument of the desired runlevel. The rc script looks in the /etc/rc.d directories for other directories based upon runlevel, such as rc1.d, rc2.d, and so on with the rc-runlevel directories as shell scripts starting with an S or a K, to either Start or Kill a specific service. The S files are executed when entering the runlevel, while the K services are executed when leaving that runlevel.

On most systems, the keyboard sequence CTRL+ALT+DEL initiates a reboot. Line 30 of inittab prevents this from occurring, although it does initiate a shutdown. Line 47 starts up the X Window graphical environment and login manager when entering runlevel 5. If the system is not running the X Window graphical environment, terminal sessions are started on the console terminals, as defined in lines 39 to 44. When the user exits his or her session, a new login process is started for the terminal due to the respawn action. Other available actions are

- **boot**   Runs only at boot time
- **bootwait**   Runs at boot time and prevents other processes until finished
- **kbrequest**   Sends a request for keyboard action or inaction
- **off**   Doesn't run the command
- **once**   Only runs the command once
- **ondemand**   Same as respawn
- **powerfail**   Runs in the event of a power failure signal
- **powerokwait**   Waits until the power is okay before continuing
- **sysinit**   Runs before any users can log on
- **wait**   Enables completion before continuing

The **init** daemon is responsible for switching between runlevels and executing the appropriate shell scripts. As one of the first services to be activated during system initialization, **init** reads and processes the commands in the /etc/inittab file. When system initialization is completed, **init** remains active to respawn any processes that terminate and interact with various system log files, including /var/utmp and /var/wtmp.

Changes made to /etc/inittab do not take effect until the next reboot unless you specifically instruct **init** to reread the /etc/inittab file using the command

```
init q
```

And then the User

Once the system boot process has completed, the user can log in and start using the services of the operating system. The **init** process started a getty (get a tty) process for each terminal, which displays a login prompt and awaits a user to login. If you run the **ps -ef** command, you might see getty processes running on your system. If you are using the graphical interface on the console, no getty processes will be running.

The format for login name depends on the organization. Most commonly they are the user's initials, first name, last name, or some variation. Knowing the user's login name is essential to being able to send e-mail or communicate with them. The login name is also visible in directory listings.

When the user enters his or her login name, getty spawns the **/bin/login** command. The **login** command then prompts the user to enter his or her password, which is not displayed on the screen for security reasons. If the user enters an incorrect password, the login name is not valid, and the **/bin/login** command responds with a generic message stating the login is incorrect.

The **login** command then takes the password provided by the user and encrypts it using the same mechanisms as the **passwd** command. If the two encrypted values match, the password is correct, and the user is granted access to the system and updates both the utmp and wtmp files.

The login program starts the user's login shell, which in turn processes the /etc/profile file to configure the shell environment, and the user is placed in his home directory. If there are user-specific customization files, such as .profile, present in the user's home directory, they are executed next. Once complete, the shell prints a command prompt and is ready to accept commands from the user.

Letting the System Do It for You

Linux has the facility to run regularly scheduled jobs on your behalf, regardless of whether you are at work or at home. If the job is to be run only once, the **at** command is the scheduler of choice, whereas running the command more than once on a regular basis requires the use of **cron**.

Using at

Simply speaking, the **at** command enables you to run a job at a specified time. The job is run only once. The syntax is as follows:

```
at {time}
```

You can specify the time in a variety of formats, including

- **19:45**   Runs the job at 7:45 in the evening.
- **now**   Runs the job now.

- **now + 5 days**   Runs the job five days from now at the exact same time.

- **09:30 Aug 29**   Runs the job at 9:30 in the morning on August 29.

- **midnight**   Runs the job at midnight tonight. Other special words are *today, tomorrow*, and *noon*.

The system is initially configured to only enable the root user to use the **at** command. This can be changed by editing either the /etc/at.allow or /etc/at.deny files. The at.deny file typically exists on most systems and has the generic system accounts defined. If at.allow exists, it will list the users allowed to run the **at** command. If the at.deny file exists, then all users but those in the at.deny file are permitted to use **at**.

After entering the time specification on the command line, **at** responds with the shell PS2 (>) prompt so you can list the commands to execute. You can specify as many commands as desired—they will be executed sequentially by **at**. When you have entered all the desired commands, press CTRL+D to signal that you have finished entering data, and it should schedule the jobs.

The commands **atq** or **at -l** enable the user to see his or her own queued jobs. Unless he or she is the root user, he or she cannot see any other user's scheduled jobs.

Each spooled job is saved as a text file in the directory /var/spool/atjobs. These files hold a copy of the environment information applied when the user created the job, and the actual commands to be executed. It is possible to cancel the scheduled job prior to execution by using the **at -d** or **atrm** commands.

The following is an example of scheduling a job to run at a later time. Notes about the action appear as comments:

```
[root@mercury.technical /root]# pwd
/home/jholman
[root@mercury.technical /root]# ls -l runme
-rwxrwxr-x 1 jholman jholman 82 Jun 9 22:19 runme
[root@mercury.technical /root]# cat runme
hostname
date
w
who
df -v
netstat -I
logger -t runme script executed successfully
[root@mercury.technical /root]#
```

The runme script will execute, collect some statistics, and exit after using the **logger** command to save a message in the /var/log/messages file. To rerun this job, we need to know the time and when we want to run it:

```
[root@mercury.technical /root]# date
Sat Jun 9 22:31:32 EDT 2001
```

```
[root@mercury.technical /root]# at 22:35
warning: commands will be executed using (in order) a) $SHELL b)
login shell c) /bin/sh
at> /home/jholman/runme
at> <EOT>
job 1 at 2001-06-09 22:35[root@mercury.technical /root]# atq
1 2001-06-09 22:35 a jholman
[root@mercury.technical /root]#
```

The output from **atq** shows this is the first **at** job scheduled and when it will run. The *a* means it is an **at** job, and the user is jholman. While a job is spooled, there is a file under /var/spool/at or /var/spool/atjobs. The job files have cryptic names, such as a0000100fc507b, and the files are only readable by root:

```
::::::::::::::
a0000100fc507b
::::::::::::::
#!/bin/sh
# atrun uid=500 gid=500
# mail jholman 0
umask 2
PWD=/home/jholman; export PWD
HOSTNAME=mercury; export HOSTNAME
QTDIR=/usr/lib/qt-2.3.0; export QTDIR
LESSOPEN=\|/usr/bin/lesspipe.sh\ %s; export LESSOPEN
KDEDIR=/usr; export KDEDIR
USER=jholman; export USER
LS_COLORS=no=00:fi=00:di=01\;34:ln=01\;36:pi=40\;33:so=01\;35:bd=40\;33\
;01:cd=40\;33\;01:or=0
1\;05\;37\;41:mi=01\;05\;37\;41:ex=01\;32:\*.cmd=01\;32:\*.exe=01\;32:\*
.com=01\;32:\*.btm=01\
;32:\*.bat=01\;32:\*.sh=01\;32:\*.csh=01\;32:\*.tar=01\;31:\*.tgz=01\;31
:\*.arj=01\;31:\*.taz=
01\;31:\*.lzh=01\;31:\*.zip=01\;31:\*.z=01\;31:\*.Z=01\;31:
\*.gz=01\;31:\*.bz2=01\;31:\*.bz=01
\;31:\*.tz=01\;31:\*.rpm=01\;31:\*.cpio=01\;31:\*.jpg=01\;
35:\*.gif=01\;35:\*.bmp=01\;35:\*.xb
m=01\;35:\*.xpm=01\;35:\*.png=01\;35:\*.tif=01\;35:; export LS_COLORS
MACHTYPE=i386-redhat-linux-gnu; export MACHTYPE
MAIL=/var/spool/mail/jholman; export MAIL
INPUTRC=/etc/inputrc; export INPUTRC
BASH_ENV=/home/jholman/.bashrc; export BASH_ENV
LANG=en_US; export LANG
LOGNAME=jholman; export LOGNAME
SHLVL=1; export SHLVL
HOSTTYPE=i386; export HOSTTYPE
OSTYPE=linux-gnu; export OSTYPE
HISTSIZE=1000; export HISTSIZE
HOME=/home/jholman; export HOME
SSH_ASKPASS=/usr/libexec/openssh/gnome-ssh-askpass; export SSH_ASKPASS
PATH=/usr/local/bin:/bin:/usr/bin:/usr/X11R6/bin:/home/jholman/bin;
export PATH
```

```
SSH_TTY=/dev/pts/2; export SSH_TTY
cd /home/jholman || {
 echo 'Execution directory inaccessible' >&2
 exit 1
}
/home/jholman/runme
```

The spool file contains all relevant information required to run the job, including the userID, environment variables, and so on. By including all the appropriate information in the file, **at** can ensure the user is allowed to execute the command. The last line in the spool file is the name of the command to execute. It is important to provide the full path to the command because it will not know where to find it otherwise.

When the command executes, we can see an entry in /var/log/messages.

When the time has elapsed and the command has run, the line will be added to the system log, as shown here:

```
[root@mercury.technical /root]# date +%H:%M
22:36
[root@mercury.technical /root]# atq
[root@mercury.technical /root]#
[root@mercury.technical /root]# su root
Password:
[root@mercury.technical log]#
[root@mercury.technical log]# tail -3 /var/log/messages
Jun 9 22:32:56 mercury su(pam_unix)[5604]: session opened for user root by
jholman(uid=500)
Jun 9 22:35:00 mercury runme: script executed successfully
Jun 9 22:35:00 mercury runme: script executed successfully
[root@mercury.technical log]# exit
[root@mercury.technical /root]#
```

In the runme script, we executed several commands. Because there was no definition in the **at** job or the script regarding where to put the output from the job, **at** mailed it to the user:

```
----- Original Message -----
From: "Jon Holman" <jholman
To: <jholman
Sent: Saturday, June 09, 2001 10:36 PM
Subject: Output from your job 1

mercury
Sat Jun 9 22:36:01 EDT 2001
 10:36pm up 14:18, 7 users, load average: 0.06, 0.04, 0.01
USER TTY FROM LOGIN@ IDLE JCPU PCPU WHAT
jholman pts/0 - 2:28pm 8:07m 0.02s 0.02s /bin/cat
jholman pts/1 - 8:11pm 1:42m 0.39s 0.18s bash
jholman pts/2 vista.jholman-ciss 8:15pm 8.00s 0.41s 0.41s -bash
jholman :0 Jun 9 14:27
```

```
jholman pts/0 Jun 9 14:28
jholman pts/1 Jun 9 20:11
jholman pts/2 Jun 9 08:24
jholman pts/3 Jun 9 08:27
jholman pts/4 Jun 9 08:27
jholman pts/2 Jun 9 20:15
Filesystem 1k-blocks Used Available Use% Mounted on
/dev/hda1 396623 64259 311883 18% /
/dev/hda8 1494204 425680 992620 31% /home
/dev/hda5 3028080 1246352 1627908 44% /usr
/dev/hda6 1011928 174116 786408 19% /var
/dev/hdc 652882 652882 0 100% /mnt/cdrom
Kernel Interface table
Iface MTU Met RX-OK RX-ERR RX-DRP RX-OVR TX-OK TX-ERR TX-DRP TX-OVR Flg
eth0 1500 0 15082 0 0 0 11101 0 0 0 BRU
eth0: 1500 0 - no statistics available - BRU
eth0: 1500 0 - no statistics available - BRU
eth0: 1500 0 - no statistics available - BRU
eth0: 1500 0 - no statistics available - BRU
lo 16436 0 15940 0 0 0 15940 0 0 0 LRU
```

Two options to **at** worth mentioning are

-m   Sends the user an e-mail message when the job is done

-f   Instructs **at** to read the command list from a file

There is a similar command to **at** called **batch**. **batch** works exactly the same as the **at** command, except **batch** will run the commands based upon the system utilization. If the system load is too high, **batch** will not run the command.

The **at** command is great if you need to run a single job only once at a given time. **batch** is the choice if you need to run a job once, but do not really care when that is. However, if you need to run a job at regular intervals, **cron** is the command to use.

Working with cron

The **cron** command runs jobs at regularly scheduled intervals. **cron** reads a file with commands and times named crontab, as in cron table. Each user can have his or her own crontab. However, like the **at** command, the files /etc/cron.allow and /etc/cron.deny determine which users can actually run jobs using **cron**. If the file /etc/cron.allow exists, only the users in the file can use **cron**. If the file /etc/cron.deny exists, all users are allowed **cron** access except those identified in the file. You would not have both files on the same system—it is one or the other.

A user can list the contents of his current crontab using the command

```
crontab -l
```

297

To remove the crontab, use

```
crontab -r
```

 NOTE You should not remove root's crontab file. It is used to run system jobs and removing it not only prevents those jobs from running, but it destroys the crontab.

To edit the crontab entries, use the command

```
crontab -e
```

A user can only see his or her own crontab file. The root user can see any crontab file using the command

```
crontab -u "username"
```

where username is the name of the user whose crontab root wants to see.

The layout of the crontab consists of one set of time and command specifications per line, with a total of six space-separated fields. Because the fields are space-separated, it tends to look very confusing the first time you look at one.

The six fields in the crontab entry are

- Minutes (0 to 59)
- Hours (0 to 23)
- Day of month (1 to 31)
- Month (1 to 12)
- Day of week (0=Sunday, 6=Saturday)
- Command to run

To illustrate

```
[root@mercury.technical /root]#pwd
/home/jholman
[root@mercury.technical /root]#
[root@mercury.technical /root]#crontab -l
no crontab for jholman
[root@mercury.technical /root]#crontab -e 0 2 * * * cd /home/jholman/tmp; rm
-rf /home/jholman/tmp# exit the editor
[root@mercury.technical /root]# [root@mercury.technical /root]# crontab -l
# DO NOT EDIT THIS FILE - edit the master and reinstall.
# (/tmp/crontab.13245 installed on Sun Jun 10 07:55:47 2001)
# (Cron version -- $Id: crontab.c,v 2.13 1994/01/17 03:20:37 vixie Exp $)
```

The **crontab -e** command starts up the vi editor to insert, delete, or modify any existing crontab entries, as well as enter new ones. The command specified in the example instructs **cron** to

- Run the command at zero minutes on the hour.
- Run the command at hour 2 of the day, so when combined with the minutes, this command runs only at 2:00 A.M.
- Run the command on every day of the month.
- Run the command every month of the year.
- Run the command every day of the week.

Each of the time specification fields (the first five on each line) can have a range of possible values:

- A number indicates it must be an exact match.
- A hyphen indicates a range of values, as in 20-30.
- A comma indicates a series of legal values, such as 5, 10, and 15.

Some example crontab time specifications are listed in Table 4-4.

The **cron** daemon is started by **init** on system initialization checks every minute to see if there is a job to be executed. The spooled jobs are stored in /var/spool/cron. The user-specific crontabs should be stored in their home directory, while the system crontabs are stored in /etc/crontab, /etc/cron.d, and other directories in /etc. On some systems, like Red Hat 7.1, the **at** daemon, **atd**, runs the **at** jobs. On other systems, **cron** may start the **atrun** command to look for and execute **at** jobs.

Table 4-4   Examples of **cron** Syntax

Syntax	Result
30 3 * * *	3:30 A.M. every day of the year
45 11 15 * *	11:45 A.M. on the fifteenth day of the month
0,10,20,30,40,50 * * * *	Every 10 minutes
30 8,17 * * *	8:30 A.M. and 5:30 P.M.
0 0 1 1 *	Only on January first at midnight
1 18 * * 2–4	At 6:01 P.M. on Tuesday, Wednesday, and Thursday

Using the HOSTS Files

When TCP/IP was first implemented, the number of networks and hosts on those networks was very small. Most users used a dumb terminal connected to a large, expensive host system. They would perform their work on one system, with little need to connect to other systems.

Because the number of hosts was small, a host table was created to list the name for each host and the IP address. Even with the size of the Internet today, some systems will still use a host file for specific reasons. The /etc/hosts file is an ASCII file that must reside on each host and provide the required information to resolve each hostname to an IP address. You should consider the /etc/hosts file static in nature because of the effort required to keep it updated on all the hosts in your network.

The following is an example of a HOSTS file from a host:

```
[root@mercury.technical /etc]# cat hosts
# Do not remove the following line, or various programs
# that require network functionality will fail.
127.0.0.1 localhost.jon1.com localhost
192.168.0.1 gateway.jon1.com gateway
192.168.0.2 winserv.jon1.com winserv
192.168.0.3 mercury.jon1.com mercury ftp mail www
192.168.0.4 vista.jon1.com vista
[root@mercury.technical /etc]#
```

 NOTE The /etc/hosts file is an ASCII file, which you can edit by using vi or any other text editor. The pound sign (#) is used to indicate a comment and is ignored when the file is processed. In the preceding example, the initial lines are comments, and the remaining lines are hostnames for resolution.

Each line of the file can contain up to 255 characters, and each file can contain an unlimited number of lines. The file itself is either space or tab delimited, with a minimum of three fields per line. The first column of each line is the IP address for the given system. The remaining columns are the text names for the system. The second column generally contains the fully qualified name for the machine. Any subsequent columns establish an alias, or alternative name, for the system. Using the HOSTS file in the previous example, a user that enters the command

```
$ telnet mercury
```

causes Linux to check the HOSTS file for the entry containing "mercury." When found, the IP address is given back to the application to establish the connection to the remote system. However, if you look at the mercury entry, the names *www*, *mail*, and *ftp* all refer to the same system:

```
192.168.0.3 mercury.jon1.com mercury ftp mail www
```

This means the names *mercury*, *www*, *ftp*, and *mail* all point to the same system.

The /etc/hosts file must reside on every system. This can present a significant challenge if there are a large number of hosts to keep updated. Failing to add a new host to the /etc/hosts file makes it impossible to access that host using anything but an IP address. This model severely limits your ability to change the IP address or names of a system in the network. Add to this the performance impact when the file becomes too large.

Performance is also impacted with too many comments or unnecessary entries, as the file is always processed sequentially from top to bottom. Placing the most commonly used entries at the top of the file will speed up the process of finding a match.

Controlling Print Services

There are several utilities for interacting with the printing service. The first of these utilities is the line printer control program (**lpc**), which works on any printer defined in either /etc/printcap or /etc/lpd.conf. **lpc** is used to

- Cancel the active job (using the **abort** command)
- Enable/disable the printer (using the **down** command)
- Enable/disable the spool/queue (using the **disable** or **enable** command)
- Hold/release print jobs (using the **holdall/noholdall** or **hold/release** commands)
- Rearrange jobs within a queue (using the **topq** or **up** command)
- Redirect jobs to another printer (using the **move** or **redirect** command)
- Reprint a job (using the **redo** command)
- See the current status of printers (using the **status** command)
- Start/stop print queues (using the **start** and **stop** commands)

Starting **lpc** with the -P option specifies the printer spool queue to work with. If no printer queue is specified, the default system printer queue is used. Although each of the commands listed previously are possible, the user may be restricted from performing certain tasks based on his or her permissions.

Listing jobs in the print queue is accomplished with **lpq**. Much like the status command with **lpc**, **lpq** gets its information from the daemon directly. Similar to **lpc**, the -P specifies the printer queue to query. Omitting the -P lists the information for the system default printer. Listing the print jobs for all the printers configured in /etc/printcap is done using the -a option. You can modify the output to show a short listing using the -s option, or a long listing using -l. A sample output from **lpq** using the -l option is shown here:

```
Printer: hp880@mercury (printing disabled)
 Queue: 1 printable job
 Server: no server active
 Status: hp880@mercury.hare.home.com: job 'root@mercury+952'
printed at 19:20:05.316
 Status: job 'root@mercury+952' removed at 19:20:05.316
 Rank Owner/ID Class Job Files Size Time
1 root@mercury+316 A 316 /etc/passwd 846 22:00:16
```

NOTE The lpstat utility provides similar functionality to lpq for checking the status of the printer service and listing jobs in the queue waiting to be processed.

You can remove jobs from the print queue by using the **lprm** command. Users typically run it with the job number they want to remove. If they don't provide a job number, **lprm** attempts to remove the last job submitted. If they use the -a option, **lprm** will attempt to remove all the jobs listed in the queue. Like the other commands, the -P option instructs **lprm** to process the specified printer queue. For users who want to display more information, the -V option instructs **lprm** to print verbose output while executing. The following shows **lprm** in verbose mode:

```
LPRng-3.6.24, Kerberos5, Copyright 1988-2000 Patrick Powell,
<papowell@astart.com>
Printer hp880@mercury:
 checking perms 'root@mercury+316'
 dequeued 'root@mercury+316'
```

In the previous example, the most-recent job submitted has been removed. It is possible to specify a username to **lprm**, causing it to delete the jobs submitted by that user.

Additional Configuration Files

Additional configuration or operational support files are created in the configuration process or needed in addition to those described previously. When a printer is added, a subdirectory for the printer is created, called /var/spool/lpd/(printer-name), which is the spool directory. If the printer name is hp880, the spool directory is found at /var/spool/lpd/hp880, with the permissions being drwx--S---. There is also a lock file created called lpd.lock.printer-name.printer used for queue control.

The following files are located within the printer subdirectory:

- **active.printer-name**   The active job (This file exists only while a job is active.)
- **printer-name**   The lock file for queue control
- **control.printer-namen**   The queue control
- **log.printer-name**   The log file
- **status.printer-name**   The current status
- **unspooler.printer-name**   The PID for the command to unspool the job
- **Printfilter or filter**   The filter used to process the print job and generate the output—an example of this file follows:

```
#!/bin/bash
source /etc/sysconfig/printers/lp
if [ "$PAPERSIZE" = "a4" ]; then
 T=A4
else
 T=Letter
fi

enscript -M $T -Z -p - |

if [ "$DOUBLEPAGE" = "true" ]; then
 psnup -d -b0.6cm -p$PAPERSIZE -2
else
 cat -
fi |

if [ "$GSDEVICE" = "PostScript" ]; then
 cat -
elif [ "$GSDEVICE" = "uniprint" ]; then
 exec 3>&1 1>&2
 gs @$UPP.upp -q -sOutputFile="|cat 1>&3"
else
 gs -q $GSOPTIONS -sDEVICE=$GSDEVICE \
 -r$RESOLUTION \
 -sPAPERSIZE=$PAPERSIZE \
```

```
 -dNOPAUSE \
 -dSAFER \
 -sOutputFile=- -
fi

if [ "$SENDEOF" != "" ]; then
 printf "\004"
fi

exit 0
```

Magicfilter and APS Filter are two of the more commonly used print filters. If the file being printed is plain text, neither filter is required to process the file. If the print job is non-ASCII, however, the filters are used to process the file and generate output matched to the printer type. APS Filter is more automated than Magicfilter. Both are available from **http://www.ibiblio.org/pub/Linux/system/printing**.

NOTE If you are adding a printer manually, you will need to add the printer entry in /etc/printcap, and then create the spool directory in /var/spool//lpd. All other files are optional, as they will be created when you use the printer the first time.

Printing PostScript Files

Printing PostScript files has historically been a challenge on various systems. It is generally an issue with making certain that the drivers and printers are capable of handling PostScript files and that they are communicating properly. Today, most business-quality printers are capable of printing PostScript files, although typically inkjet printers are not. If you're experiencing printing problems, you should first check the vendor's Web site for updated drivers.

Additional tools exist to convert files back and forth between PostScript and non-PostScript. These utilities are available for Linux; any Linux Internet library should have them, some for free downloading.

Networking Printers

Two additional files can be of assistance when printing across the network: /etc/hosts.lpd and /etc/hosts.equiv. You must configure these files carefully, as they can provide access to other services aside from printing. The /etc/hosts.lpd file establishes a list of hostnames enabled to access the printer, while /etc/hosts.equiv identifies the systems enabled to access the system as if they were local. Careful configuration of

/etc/hosts.equiv is required to prevent unauthorized access to other components on the system.

Using Graphical Printer Configurations

Thus far, this chapter has focused on the information required for the exam. However, there are many different tools for configuring printers on a Linux system. Consequently, it would be a disservice to fail in presenting the tools used to simplify the tasks a system administrator frequently has to deal with.

From this point, our discussion turns to using the Red Hat Line Printer Manager, **printtool**. Red Hat is not presented here because it offers anything more than any other version of Linux; it simply serves as a good example of what to expect in the real world.

You can start **printtool** at the command line or by choosing Red Hat, followed by System and then Printer Tool from the menu. This displays the printer configuration tool, as illustrated in Figure 4-5.

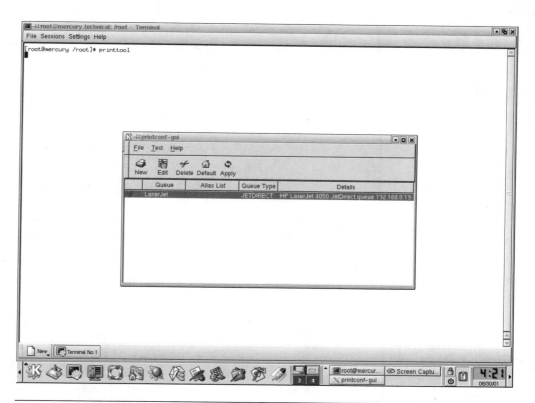

Figure 4-5 The printer configuration tool

To install a new printer, click the New button. This opens a dialog in which you select the type of printer. The available types are

- Local printer

- Remote Unix lpd queue

- SMB Windows 9x/NT printer

- Netware printer

- Direct to port printer

In our example, we will add a local printer. **printtool** examines the local printer ports to see which are available and reports the configured ports. The **printtool** dialog to add the printer information is displayed as illustrated in Figure 4-6.

You might be tempted to use cartoon character names or some other cute naming convention for the printer name. When you are wondering where the printer named "snoopy" is located, however, you will wish you had chosen a better name. After specifying the printer information, you can select the printer model by clicking the Select

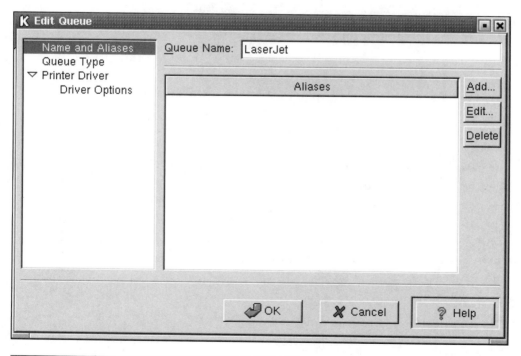

Figure 4-6   Editing the local printer entry

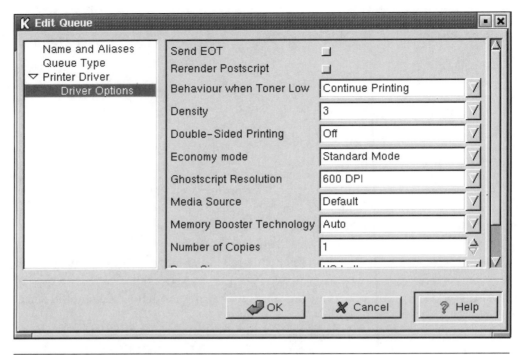

Figure 4-7   Specifying the printer model and attributes

button. This opens a window to select the printer filter based upon the printer model shown in Figure 4-7. In this dialog, you can select the printer model from the available list. Many printer filters are available by default and will often support similar printers even if yours is not directly listed.

After specifying the printer attributes, click the OK button, and then click OK in the Edit Local Printer Entry dialog. This adds the printer and creates the printer queues. At this point, you must restart **lpd** from the **lpd** item on the menu bar. The printer is now configured and ready to use.

Although the rough-and-ready system administrator may prefer to edit the configuration files manually, using the graphical interface is faster and easier.

Chapter Summary

In this chapter, we covered administration of the system. We learned how to create and delete users and groups. We learned about shell scripts and how to make some administration tasks easier. One of the most important skills in this chapter is filesystem navigation. Learning to manage printers and print queues is next. As an administrator, one of your basic duties will to be sure that everyone is able to print.

Questions

1. **grep**, **egrep**, and **fgrep** all have one thing in common. What is it?

2. Which command adds a new group to the /etc/group file?
   a. gpasswd -a
   b. chgrp
   c. groupmod
   d. chown

3. Which command changes the owner of a file to another user?
   a. gpasswd
   b. chmod
   c. chgrp
   d. chown

4. Which command is used to enable the /etc/shadow file to store the encrypted passwords?
   a. passwd
   b. pwconv
   c. grpconv
   d. gpasswd

5. What does the **at** command enable you to do?
   a. Prevent users from scheduling a job
   b. Allow users to schedule a job
   c. Schedule a job to run only once
   d. Schedule a job to run repeatedly

6. You can type _____ at the command prompt to configure a printer.
   a. xf86Config
   b. printtool
   c. print.conf
   d. printconfig

7. When putting a printer on the network, which file enables users to print to it?
   a. /etc/print.conf
   b. /etc/hosts
   c. /etc/hosts.lpd
   d. /etc/hosts.allow

8. Of the commands used to check which processes are active, which one actively uses resources and should be invoked only when needed?
   a. top
   b. pstree
   c. init
   d. yes

9. A good password should be at least _____ characters long.
   a. 5
   b. 6
   c. 7
   d. 8
   e. 9

10. The **ps -e** or **-A** command tells you everything except
    a. How long the system has been up
    b. All of the processes currently running on a system
    c. All PID numbers and TTYs
    d. Which service or daemon the process is associated with

Answers

1. They all use **grep** in one form or another.

2. A. **gpasswd -a** adds a new group to the /etc/group file?

3. D. The **chgrp** command changes the owner of a file to another user.

4. B. **pwconv** is used to enable the /etc/shadow file to store the encrypted passwords.

5. C. The **at** command enables you to schedule a job to run only once.

6. B. You can type printtool at the command prompt to configure a printer.

7. C. The /etc/hosts.lpd file enables users to print to a printer on the network.

8. A. **top** actively uses resources and should be invoked only when needed.

9. D. A good password is at least eight characters long and should contain non-alpha characters.

10. A. The **ps -e** or **-A** command does everything except tell how long the system has been up. It prints all processes.

Maintenance

This chapter covers the following competencies required to master the Linux+ certification exam:

- Creating and managing local storage device and filesystems.
- Understanding the function of **cron**.
- Removing or forwarding core dumps, as needed.
- Running and interpreting **ifconfig**.
- Downloading and installing patches and updates.
- Differentiating core services from noncritical services.
- Identifying, executing, and killing processes.
- Monitoring system log files regularly for errors, logins, and unusual activity.
- Documenting work performed on a system.
- Performing and verifying backups and restores.
- Performing and verifying best security practices.
- Assessing security risks.
- Setting daemon and process permission.

Filesystems

The files that you manipulate everyday on your system are organized into a filesystem. To access files on a device such as a CD-ROM or floppy disk, you attach its filesystem to a specified directory. In this way, the system can read and interpret the file. This is called *mounting the filesystem*. For example, to access files on a floppy disk, you must first mount its filesystem to a particular directory, usually /mnt.

Linux is capable of handling a large number of storage devices connected to it. You can configure your system to access multiple hard drives, different partitions on different hard drives, CD-ROM discs, floppy disks, and even tape archives. These storage devices can be attached manually or they can be set to mount automatically when you boot. The main partition holding your Linux system programs is attached when you boot, but a floppy disk must be manually attached when you put a disk in the floppy drive.

Creating a Filesystem

Two utilities are invaluable for creating a working fiesystem: **fdisk** and **mkfs**.

The **fdisk** utility is used to break apart or partition your hard drive into usable chunks. The purpose of this is to make separate areas for your data to prevent any kind of corruption from happening between filesystems. When you break up the hard drive by partitioning it, you are, in effect, creating a space for your data that is a virtual hard drive unto itself.

When you use **fdisk**, you are wiping out any data that is on the disk. This is the command you would use when rebuilding a filesystem that it too corrupt to bring back with a filesystem checker. You would save the files to a backup tape or other medium, reset the partition with **fdisk**, and then reinstall the data from your backup.

All distributions of Linux come with **fdisk** They also come with their own particular brand of partitioning software. **fdisk** can be difficult to understand and use for the Linux novice, but to understand **fdisk** is to understand how a hard drive operates.

The **mkfs** command makes a filesystem to your specifications. You specify where the fiesystem is to go, and **mkfs** initializes the volume label, filesystem label, and startup block. In other circles, making a filesystem is known as formatting a hard drive. When formatting a hard drive, you are making a blank partition usable by telling the hard drive and the operating system just what type of data is going to be stored on it.

With **mkfs** it is possible to set all of the attributes of the hard drive. Unless you specify individual attributes, **mkfs** will take default attributes contained in /etc/filesystem and build the filesystem. Again, when you make filesystems or format them, you are foregoing all of the data that is contained in the filesystem.

Using Filesystems

Linux files are organized into a filesystem. Linux keeps track of where the files and filesystems are on your system by the use of a directory tree. The files themselves reside on storage devices such as hard drives or CD-ROMs. The Linux directory tree may encompass several filesystems and storage devices. On a hard drive with several partitions, there is a filesystem for each partition. All of the files and filesystems themselves are organized into one seamless tree of directories, beginning from your root (/) directory. This is called a hierarchical filesystem. If you wanted to look for files on a CD-ROM, the root may be located in a filesystem on a hard drive partition, but a pathname that is listed in the filesystem leads directly to files on the disc itself.

A *directory tree* is how the files and filesystems are stored. A filesystem has its files organized into its own directory tree. This can be thought of as a branch on a tree or a subtree that must be attached (mounted) to the main directory tree to be interpreted and read. A floppy disk with Linux files has its own tree of directories. You need to mount this subtree to the main tree on your hard drive partition. If you do not attach or mount these files to the main directory tree, they cannot be read.

To mount a filesystem, you first have to attach the filesystem to the main directory tree. You can then switch to that directory and access those files. The *mountpoint* is where the filesystem is attached to the main directory tree. When you mount a floppy, the mountpoint is in the /mnt directory. Mountpoints for other devices and directories are contained in the mstab or fstab, depending on your distribution. These files are merely a listing or a link to mountable filesystems that are on the system.

To get the most from the **mount** command, it must be used from the command line. Open a shell command line; you can use the **mount** command to mount a filesystem, as shown in Figure 5-1.

The **mount** command syntax is as follows:

```
[root@mercury.technical /root]mount -option device directory
```

Table 5-1 shows some options available to the **mount** command.

For a filesystem to be accessible, it must be mounted. Only the root user can mount filesystems. This is a task to be done by a system administrator and cannot be performed by a regular user except when a system administrator has configured a filesystem to be user-mountable. The filesystem on your hard disk partition must be mounted with a **mount** command. Your system is automatically configured to mount your main filesystem whenever it starts.

When accessing a floppy or CD-ROM, you must tell the system to mount the desired filesystem. Alternately, to demount the media you must use the unmount command, **umount**. If you remove a floppy from the drive without unmounting it first, recently copied files will not be written to the disk. With a CD-ROM, you must use the unmount command, **umount,** before the disc can be taken out of the drive.

Linux is designed to be a conservative filesystem. By conservative, I mean that you allot only as much space to the partition as your filesystem will take up. If you do not anticipate using more than 1.5GB for your root partition, then no more space needs to

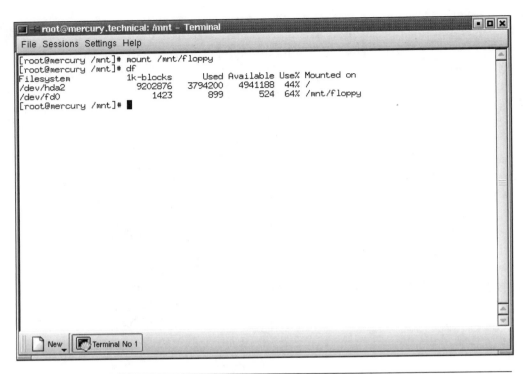

Figure 5-1   The **mount** command followed by **df**, showing all mount devices

be given. The partitions on each hard drive are formatted to take up a specified amount of space. If you have formatted your hard drive partition to take up 1.5GB, the free space will be 1.5GB less than the files installed or created on that filesystem. The space open for use is referred to as *free space.*

Maintaining Filesystems

Filesystems are the heart of your system and have to be looked after. They need to be checked to ensure that the free space is not being consumed to the point of having a full disk. If a disk partition runs out of free space, data corruption occurs. We have two tools at our disposal to ensure that corruption does not happen: the disk-free utility, **df**, and the filesystem checker, **fsck**.

Table 5-1   Partial Listing of **mount** Command Options

Options	Description
-V	Output version
-h	Prints a help message
-v	Verbose mode
-a	Mounts all filesystems of a given type that are listed in fstab
-f	Simulates mounting a filesystem; used with -v to see what **mount** is doing
-l	Adds the ext2 labels in the mount output
-n	Mounts the filesystem without writing in /etc/mtab; used when /etc is read-only
-s	Ignores **mount** options not supported by a filesystem
-r	Mounts the filesystem read-only; can also use -o ro
-L	Mounts partition that has the specified label
-t	Used when indicating filesystem type such as samba, nfs, ncpfs
-o	Other options (see man pages for complete listing)

Using df to Check Free Space

The **df** command is used to check your hard disk for free space. The **df** command lists filesystems and their properties as follows:

- The name of the device

- How much memory they take up

- Percentage of the memory used

- Where they are mounted

The **df** command only shows mounted filesystems. The output of **df** is as follows:

```
[root@mercury.technical /root]# df
Filesystem     1k-blocks     Used Available    Use%   Mounted on
/dev/hda1       1714416   1093916   563412     66%    /
/dev/sda2       8064272   7168948   485672     96%    /usr
/dev/sda1       3028080   1693928  1180332     59%    /bin
/dev/sda3       3028080   1148332  1725928     40%    /home
```

fsck—The Filesystem Checker

You can use **fsck** to check the health of your system. The **fsck** command is also used to repair the damage done to a filesystem. It is a front end for whichever filesystem checker comes with your flavor of Linux. Table 5-2 lists some of the options to be used with **fsck**.

To use **fsck**, enter **fsck** and the device name that references the filesystem. The following examples check the disk in the floppy drive and the primary hard drive:

```
[root@mercury.technical /root]# fsck    /dev/fd0
[root@mercury.technical /root]# fsck    /dev/hda1
```

For Linux ext2 filesystems, another tool is available that **fsck** will call, which is known as **e2fsck**. If you know that you are working with a Linux second extended filesystem, it will give you a little more control over the checking of the filesystem. This comes with a different set of options shown, which are shown in Table 5-3.

For a full explanation of options and what they are for, invoke the manual pages for **e2fsck**.

Occasionally, bits and pieces of files will become detached from the rest of the file. When these lost pieces are found by **fsck**, they are grouped in the /lost+found directory. They are listed by actual inode numbers. When they are found, they should be checked to see where they go and returned to their proper place. The following sample shows the output of a file located in the /lost+found directory:

```
[root@mercury.technical /root]# ls /lost+found/
#518
```

Table 5-2 Options for **fsck**

Options	Description
-a	Automatically repairs filesystem without prompting
-A	Checks all filesystems listed in /etc/fstab file
-V	Produces verbose output
-t	Specifies the type of filesystem to be checked
-a	Automatically repairs any problems
-l	Lists the names of all files in the filesystem
-r	Asks for confirmation before repairing filesystem
-s	Checks more than one filesystem

Table 5-3   Partial Options for **e2fsck**

Options	Description
-c	Causes **e2fsck** to look for bad blocks and mark them so that data will not be written to them
-C	Causes **fsck** to write completion information so that progress may be monitored
-f	Forces checking even if the filesystem seems clean
-n	Opens the filesystem in read-only mode
-p	Automatically repairs (preens) the filesystem without any questions
-v	Verbose mode
-y	Assumes an answer of yes to all questions, noninteractive mode

Mount Configuration: /etc/fstab

We have already described the **mount** command, which is used to make a filesystem part of a Linux system's directory structure. There are ways of making filesystems easier to mount with a particular set of configuration options. These configuration options are specified using the /etc/fstab file. This file is referenced when you use the **mount** command. You can mount a filesystem directly with only a **mount** command. However, it is better to simplify the process by placing mount information directly into the /etc/fstab configuration file. Entries in this file permit certain filesystems to automatically mount at boot time. Otherwise, you would have to automatically enter this information as arguments to the **mount** command.

When you add a new hard disk partition to your Linux system, you will most likely want to have it automatically mounted on startup and unmounted when you shut down. If you didn't, you would have to manually mount and unmount the partition after starting up and before shutting down. To have Linux automatically mount the filesystem on your new hard disk partition, you only need to add its name to the fstab file. You can do this by directly editing the /etc/fstab file to type in a new entry.

An entry in a fstab file contains fields that are separated by a space or tab. The fields are listed in order:

- The name of the filesystem to be mounted. This usually begins with /dev.
- The directory in your file structure where you want the filesystem on this device to be attached.
- The third field is the type of filesystem being mounted.

Table 5-4   A Partial List of Filesystem Types

Type	Description
Minix	A local filesystem, supports long filenames
ext	Filesystem replaced by ext2
ext2	A feature-packed local filesystem
msdos	Filesystems for DOS partitions
HPFS	A local filesystem for High-Performance Filesystem (HPFS) partitions
iso9660	A local filesystem for CD-ROM drives
nfs	A filesystem for mounting partitions from remote systems
Swap	A disk partition to be used for swapping

Table 5-4 provides a list of all the different types you can mount.

- The fourth field is used as the mount options for the filesystem.
- The **dump** command is used for the fifth field, if no value is present (0). The filesystem is not dumped.
- The last field is used by **fsck** to determine which order the filesystems are to be checked.

The options set up in the fourth field are by filesystem. The default filesystem for Linux is the ext2 filesystem.

Using cron

The scheduler **cron** enables you to run jobs, execute commands, and backup data while doing something else. **cron** can perform many tasks such as remove temporary files or parse out modules that have not been used in a while and remove them.

cron has two parts: the application crontab, which supplies the scheduling information, and user files. The actual daemon is named **cron**. Some of the features and options of crontab appear in Table 5-5.

Table 5-5   Options of **crontab**

Option	Description
-a	Installs file as your crontab file. On many systems, this option is automatically appended to the command
-e	Edits a crontab file.
-l	Displays the crontab file.
-r	Removes the crontab file.
-v	Displays the last time you edited the crontab file.
-u	Administrator use only. Usually used in conjunction with other commands to modify or view the crontab file of a user.

The daemon itself is started from the /etc/rc file, which is run at system startup. Scripts in Linux are run line by line. In the following rc file, see if you can pick out what it is doing on each line, such as

- Looks for the run level

- Checks which option is being used and if it is a user-confirmation mode so that it knows whether to run interactive mode or not

- Tells Linuxconf what the run levels are

- Looks for a directory for the new run level

- Kills certain subsystems and brings them up with new processes started

The following is an example of the /etc/rc file:

```
#!/bin/bash
#
#rc    This file is responsible for starting/stopping services when the
#      runlevel changes. It is also responsible fo the very first setup
#      of basic things, such as the hostname.
#
# Original Author
#      Miquel van Smoorenburg, Miquels@drinkel.nl.mugnet.org
#

# Now find out what the current and what the previous runlevel are,
argv1="$1"
set '/sbin/runlevel'
runlevel=$2
previous=$1
export runlevel previous
```

```
# Source function library
. /etc/init.d/functions

# See if we want to be in user confirmation mode
if["$previous" = "N" ]; then
    if frep -i confirm /proc/cmdline >/dev/null
     rm-f /var/run/confirm
     CONFIRM=yes
     echo $"Entering interactive startup"
    else
     CONFIRM=no
     echo $"Entering non-interactive startup"
    fi
fi

export CONFIRM

#Get first argument. Set new runlevel this argument.
[ -n "argv1" ] && runlevel="$argv1"

# Tell Linuxconf what runlevel we are in
[ -d /var/run ] && echo "/etc/rc$runlevel.d" >

# Is there an rc directory for this new runlevel?
if [ -d /etc/rc$runlevel.d ]; then
    # First, run the KILL scripts.
    for i in /etc/rc$runlevel.d/K*; do
        # Check if the script is there,
        [ ! -f $i ] && continue

        # Don't run  [KS]??foo.{pmsave,rpmorig} scripts
        [ "${i%.rpmsave}" !="{i}" ] && continue
        [ "${i%.rpmoriginal}" ] && continue
        %.rpmnew!="{i}" ] && continue

        # Check if the subsystem is already up.
        subsys=${i#/etc/rc$runlevel.d/K??}
        [! -f/var/lock/subsys/${subsys}.init ] && continue

        # If we're in confirmation mode, get user confirmation
        [ -n "$CONFIRM" ] &&
          {
          confirm $? in
          case $? in
            0>
               :
            ;;
            2>
               CONFIRM=
            ;;
            *>
               continue
            ;;
```

```
        esac
    }

    # Bring the subsystem up.
    if egrep -q "{daemon laction >" $ ; then
        $1 start
    else
            if [ "$subsystem" = "halt" -o "$subsys" = reboot" then
                if [ "$subsys" = "halt" -o "$subsys" = "reboot" ]; then
                unset LANG
                unset LC_ALL
                unset TEXTDOMAIN
                unset TEXTDOMAINDIR
                exec $i start
            fi
            $1 start
        else
            action $"Starting $subsys: "$i start
        fi
    fi
    done
fi
```

cron is command-line driven. A user creates a crontab file and **cron** finds this file and executes it according to the specific instructions contained in the file.

Understanding Core Dumps

A *core dump* is a snapshot of the exact moment that a program is aborted by your system. If your system is attempting to write to an illegal memory space and gets a termination signal, Linux will record the event so that later you will be able to interpret the results and fix the problem. Core dumps are very cryptic; they do not give you the information the way you would like it to. A core dump will provide a way to gain some insight in to a problem.

A core dump is usually handled by another application. This application can vary from distribution to distribution. Red Hat uses **crash**, which tells you where to get the core dump and what to do with it. It is generally suggested that you send the instance to the author of the application.

Interpreting ifconfig

ifconfig stands for InterFace Configuration. Linux uses this command to configure the way a computer interfaces with the network. All aspects of the interface can be configured including the IP address, netmask, and gateway.

When initially installing Linux, **netconfig** is invoked to configure your networking. The two screens of **netconfig** are shown in Figure 5-2.

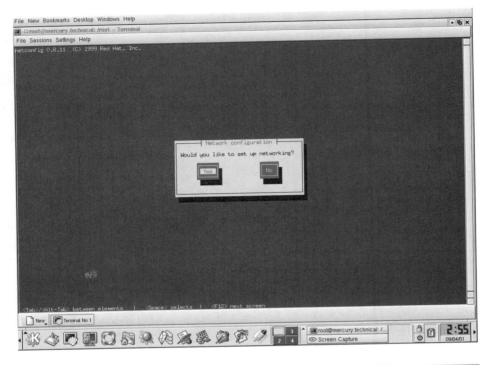

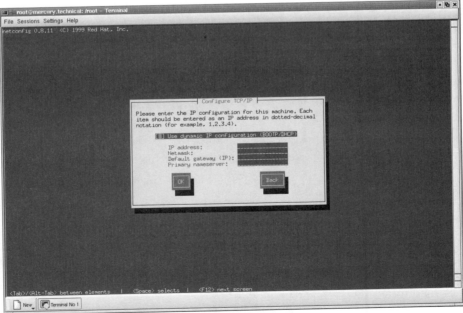

Figure 5-2 The netconfig screen as seen in Red Hat

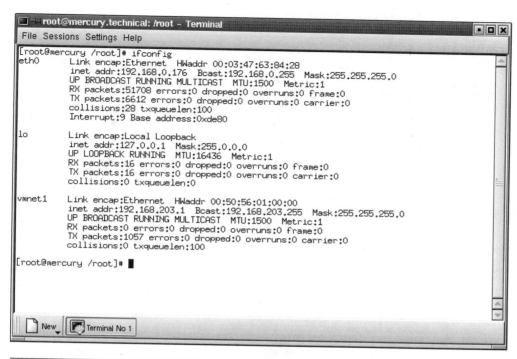

Figure 5-3 Typical **ifconfig** output for a system with one network card

Although **netconfig** is easy to use, it cannot configure all your networking options as well as **ifconfig**; it will get your network adapter configured in the most basic sense to be able to get you connected to the network.

The information contained in the default **ifconfig** screen can be obtained by typing **ifconfig** at the prompt. This is the same information that is given when you type **ifconfig -a**. Figure 5-3 shows a typical **ifconfig** output for a system with one network card.

Notice the virtual machine network adapter in the third paragraph. It is a result of the program VMware and aliases the network card to work on its own private subnet. If you are having trouble with network connections, the first thing to do is to check the **ifconfig** settings. In this example, the first paragraph shows the actual adapter eth0. If there had been another physical adapter, it would have been named eth1 and so on.

ifconfig is a more robust application for setting or adjusting your network interface. To effectively set your interface, we need a laundry list of items to get before we can go any farther:

- Host IP address

- IP broadcast address of your network

- IP network address

- IP netmask

- Addresses of any routers

- Domain Name Server (DNS) addresses

Several options are available for setting IP information on your system. The following shows an example of setting the interface eth0 using **ifconfig**:

```
[root@mercury.technical /root]# ifconfig eth0 192.168.0.165
netmask 255.255.255.0 up
```

We are setting the network interface to the IP address of 192.168.165 with a submask of 255.255.255.0 and we are telling the system that the interface is up. If you wanted to deactivate a network connection, you would simply type

```
[root@mercury.technical /root]# ifconfig eth0 down
```

In Figure 5-4, we see the result of running the above **ifconfig** code. Eth0 is no longer shown because it has been shut down; only the vmnet1 and the loopback are shown.

ifconfig is used to get a response from the networking components in your machine. First, **ifconfig** lists the interfaces that are active and running. It continues to give infor-

Figure 5-4   eth0 is disabled as shown by **ifconfig**.

mation about the interfaces such as the IP address, broadcast address, and netmask. **ifconfig** also gives detailed information about how many other packets have been received and transmitted. In the preceding examples, you can see that the VMware interface has transmitted no packets and has not received any.

ifconfig is one of the most powerful applications that you can use to configure and troubleshoot your network interface. Some of the parameters available for **ifconfig** are shown in Table 5-6.

The routes for your machine are in your routing table and should be in the /proc/net/route file. To display the routing table, enter **route** with no arguments.

```
[root@mercury.technical /root]# route
Kernel routing table
Destination     Gateway      Genmask         Flags  Metric  Ref  Use  Iface
192.168.0.0         *        255.255.255.0   U      0       0    0    eth0
192.168.203.0       *        255.0.0.0       U      0       0    0    vmnet1
127.0.0.1           *        255.255.255.0   U      0       0    0    lo
default         ole-betsy    255.255.255.0   UG     0       0    0    etho
```

It is imperative that you have at least one entry in your routing table for a loopback interface. If one is not configured, you must use the **route** command and the **add** option with the following syntax:

```
route   add   address
```

To actually add the loopback address (which is always 127.0.0.1) to the routing table, use the following:

```
[root@mercury.technical /root]# route add 127.0.0.1
```

Table 5-6   Parameters Available with **ifconfig**

Options	Description
up	Causes the device to be activated
down	Causes a device to be deactivated
[-]arp	Enables or disables ARP for this device
[-]promisc	Enables or disables device to accept all packets
[-]allmulti	Enables or disables to accept all multicast packets
mtu N	Sets the mtu of the device to N
netmask addr	Matches the netmask of the device to addr
address	Sets the IP address for this device

Updates and Patches

We covered updates and package management in Chapters 2 and 3. One topic we have not covered is the **tar** utility, which stands for tape archive.

Aside from the package management utilities, Linux provides several commands for backup management including **tar** and **cpio**. The **tar** command reads a list of files and writes them to a single file. Because Linux makes no distinction between a device and a file, **tar** can be used to write to a drive or another file on the disk. The syntax for it is

```
tar {options} {target_file} {source_files}
```

Both the target and source files can be a full pathname. Options for **tar** include

c   Creates a new **tar** image

d   Compares the target and source

f   Specifies the output file

p   Maintains the file permissions

r   Appends the new archive to an existing archive

t   Prints the names of the files in the archive

u   Adds only new files to the archive

v   Prints additional information during the operation

x   Extracts the files from a tar archive

z   Processes the output through **gzip** or **gunzip**

For example, the command

```
tar cvf /dev/rmt0 {files}
```

creates a new tar archive, prints additional information during processing, and writes the archive to the tape device, /dev/rmt0.

The **cpio** command, which stands for "copy in/out," performs a similar function to **tar**. However, a distinction is worth noting: **tar** will copy device files, those in /dev, and empty directories; **cpio** will not.

When using **cpio**, you must specify an action

-i   Extracts files from an archive

-o   Creates or copies out to an archive

-p   Prints the contents of the archive

Additional options change how **cpio** operates. It is not a requirement to use any additional options, but frequently, one or more of the following options are used in conjunction with the action:

d   Creates directories as required

f   Indicates a file

t   Shows the contents

u   Overwrites existing files

v   Prints additional information during processing

For example, reading the data from a tape device, or file, is done using the following command:

```
cpio -iv < /dev/rmt0
```

cpio can also be used to copy files located in different directories on the filesystem. For example, to find all the files owned by the user sql and copy them to a new directory, use the following command:

```
find / -owner sql | cpio -pdv /home/sql-files
```

Related Utilities

The backup utilities **tar** and **cpio** assemble a backup image of your system. However, not everyone wants to copy data to a tape device, but would rather have a compressed image of his or her data online. The utilities **gzip** and **gunzip** compress and uncompress data, respectively. Once the data is compressed, it is not necessary to uncompress and extract the contents of the archive to view the contents. Rather, the command **zcat** displays the contents of the compressed image. The compressed image created during a kernel build cannot be viewed using these commands. Other compression utilities that may exist on your system include pack and unpack as well as compress and uncompress.

 NOTE   tar is discussed in depth later in the chapter under the "Back Up, Back Up, Back Up" section.

Critical and Noncritical Services

You will not see some of the critical services Linux provides. The system timer coordinates all the action on your computer by telling applications when to make a system call and whether it can access a piece of hardware.

As discussed previously in Chapters 1 and 2, services are applications running on your machine, which provide some kind of functionality for you or give you a service. We have discussed **pstree** and **top** in earlier chapters and how they can show us the processes on our system. Here we will look at critical services, what they are, and how we can identify them.

Critical services are processes with a low process ID (PID) number. They are started first, usually to start other noncritical services or services that you specify. The PPID number specifies which process is the parent process of a process. The PPID number is the process identity (ID) number of the parent process; that is, the process from within which a process with a PID number was created.

Using the **ps** command, we will once again explore some services, how to interpret them, how to kill them, and how to restart them.

First we start out by looking at the processes that are currently running by entering the following command:

```
[root@mercury.technical /root]# ps -e
```

If you recall, the -e option gives us the description of all of the processes that are running on our system. Figure 5-5 shows the top portion of the processes specified with

```
ps -e.
```

Killing a Process

When you run a process in the foreground where you can actively interact with it, quitting the program usually quits the process. Background processes generally do not have an interactive interface and you need a way to stop or **kill** these processes. Also, if an application crashes or stops responding, you need an alternate way of terminating that process or service.

The **killall** command cancels all processes that you started, except those producing the **killall** process. This command is probably the easiest way of canceling all processes created by the shell that you control. When started by a root user, the **killall** command by default cancels all cancelable processes with a **sigkill** or -kill attribute.

The **kill** command provides a way to stop a process on a Linux system that has stopped responding to your commands. The **kill** command works by sending a termination signal to the process in question. These signals provide a mechanism to inter-

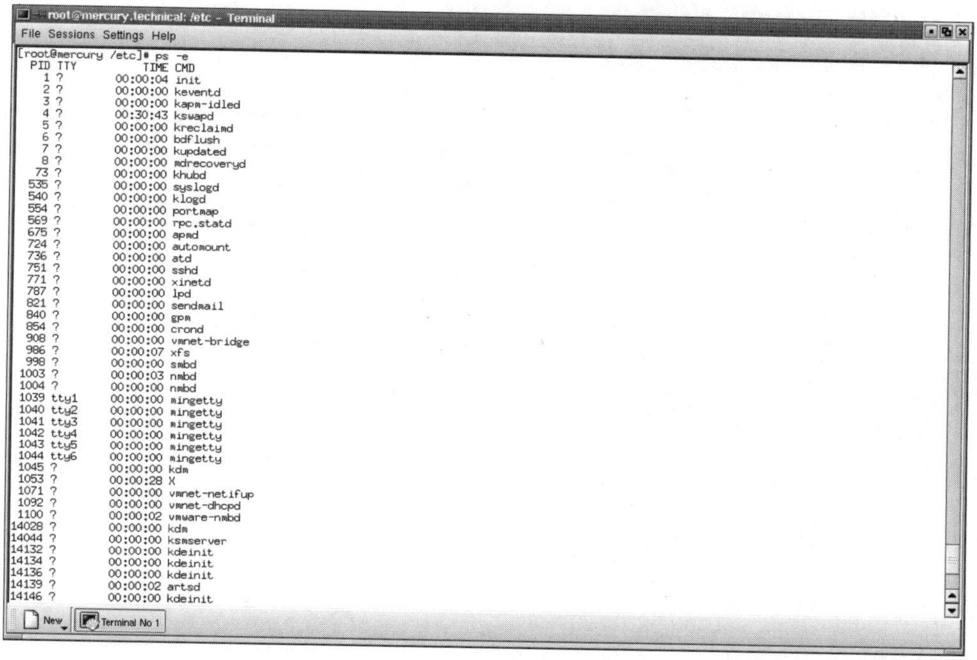

Figure 5-5   Critical and noncritical processes

rupt a process and tell it to respond to the signal. Ultimately, though, it is up to a process to decide if and how it should respond to the signal. There are 32 kill signals listed in Table 5-7.

The basic syntax of the **kill** command is

```
# kill -<signal> <PID>
```

The signal can be the number of the signal or the name above such as -KILL. The PID is the process ID that is the numeric identifier of the process. The PID is the first column displayed when evoking the **ps** command.

```
# ps
  PID TTY          TIME CMD
29298 pts/11   00:00:00 bash
29319 pts/11   00:00:00 ps
```

For instance, to send the terminate signal to the knotify process in the previous **ps** output, you could use the following command:

```
# kill -INT 14153
```

Table 5-7 The 32 Unique **kill** Signals of Linux

Signal	Flag for the kill Command	Numeric Value	Action
SIGHUP	-HUP	1	Hangs up signal (which often restarts a process instead of stopping it).
SIGINT	-INT	2	That's what CTRL-C sends. It's a nice way of ending a process.
SIGQUIT	-QUIT	3	That's what CTRL-D sends.
SIGILL	-ILL	4	Program sends an illegal action.
SIGTRAP	-TRAP	5	Traps signal at ppoint of failure.
SIGABORT	-ABRT	6	Aborts a currently running process.
SIGBUS	-BUS	7	Sent to a program because of a hardware error.
SIGFPE	-FPE	8	Sent when a program executes a floating point error, such as divide by 0.
SIGKILL	-KILL	9	Terminates signal that cannot be ignored by the process.
SIGUSR1	-USR1	10	Used for grouping and terminating child commands.
SIGSEGV	-EGV	11	Sent to a program when it tries to access a portion of memory that is not there or doesn't exist.
SIGUSR2	-USR2	12	Used for grouping and terminating child commands.
SIGPIPE	-PIPE	13	Terminates a process because of a broken pipe command.
SIGALRM	-ALRM	14	Terminates a process when timer value has been exceeded.
SIGTERM	-TERM	15	Terminates signal.
SIGCHLD	-CHLD	17	Used to terminate a process' children.
SIGCONT	-CONT	18	Reawakens a suspended process.
SIGSTOP	-STOP	19	Temporarily halts a process.
SIGTSTP	-TSTP	20	Same as a CTRL-Z.
SIGTTIN	-TTIN	21	Suspends a bg process when it tries to read from its terminal.

Signal	Flag for the kill Command	Numeric Value	Action
SIGTTOU	-TTOU	22	Terminates a bg process when it tries to write to a terminal.
SIGURG	-URG	23	Terminates a process when a file descriptor is bad.
SIGXCPU	-XCPU	24	Signal sent when a CPU time limit has been exceeded.
SIGXFSZ	-XFSZ	25	Terminates a process when application exceeds a block size limit.
SIGVTALRM	-VTALRM	26	Terminates a process after a virtual interval timer expires.
SIGPROF	-PROF	27	Similar to sigbus; terminates a process when a virtual profiling timer expires.
SIGWINCH	-WINCH	28	Suspends signal used to change screen size.
SIGIO	-IO	29	Suspends for an urgent condition on an I/O channel.
SIGPWR	-PWR	30	Terminates processes based on power; usually found on notebooks.
SIGSYS	-SYS	31	Similar to sig xfsz; terminates a signal when an app reaches block size limit.
SIGRTMIN	-RTMIN	32	Exits on first realtime signal.

The **kill** command can also use the numeric signal values as follows. For instance, to use the numeric value of the terminate signal, the previous example could be rewritten as

```
# kill 2 14153
```

The **kill** command uses the SIGTERM terminate signal by default so if no signal is provided, then this signal is used. This means the previous example could be rewritten without an explicitly indicated signal:

```
# kill 14153
```

NOTE The SIGHUP signal is typically used to cause a process to reload its configuration files, but leave the process running.

Managing Logs

The way that you use your logs is of the utmost importance. If you do not use them properly, vital information pertaining to security and troubleshooting can be missed. You can use your logs to look for outside threats as well as internal ones. In short, logs can be an administrator's best friend.

To track users inside of the network, two logs are used. The log /var/log/secure logs successful and unsuccessful attempts by users to log into the system. The log /var/log/sulog records any attempts to become the root user. These logs store information on unsuccessful and successful attempts to log into the system both from the outside and the inside. These files need scrupulous interaction to catch any interlopers on the system and stop their action.

To optimize your logging efforts, most distributions will employ the use of the syslog daemon to manage log files. With syslogd, you have the ability to redirect your log files when they outgrow their current folder. Where, when, and how you log can be determined by syslogd. They can be output to a dedicated server that does nothing but store your log files. Regardless of how you log your messages, you have to know when and why the messages are logged according to syslogd. The configuration file for the syslog daemon is syslog.conf.

Monitoring Files

Earlier in the chapter under logging files, we talked about the scrupulous inspection of system logs. The same applies to your critical system files. You may unwittingly have an interloper with full access to your system and not know it.

Attackers use various means to gain access to a system. One of the means is the Trojan horse or backdoor program. If a hacker gets into your system, one of the first things he or she will do is create a backdoor by which he or she can continue to enter at his or her will. One way to accomplish this is to replace critical system files with ones that will let him continue his covert operations on your system. This may include sending him the password file or even parse out the passwords of any one with superuser permissions.

The most basic way to ensure that your files have not been tampered with is to create a file that holds checksums of the file sizes that you specify. You commonly see this on FTP sites while downloading files. Along with the file, is an md5 checksum that you can use to compare to the file once you have downloaded it. This is used for data corruption in this case.

If a hacker had gained his or her way on to your system, the attacker would be able to change these values to whatever size the values are once he or she found them. Simple physical security takes care of that by storing the values on removable media and securing it. You could go one step further and calculate a mathematical checksum that would make it extremely difficult to recreate a matching checksum.

You can use the sum program to calculate simple checksums for your use. If you wanted to maintain a checksum on any file, the syntax would be

```
# sum <filenamehere>
```

This provides output that looks similar to the following output.

```
03448     40
```

This output consists of the checksum value (03448) and the number of disk block used (40). You can use these figures to periodically check the values of the checksums at a later date to verify their integrity.

Documenting Your Work

Not enough can be said for documenting your work. This is the most crucial step to gaining the best understanding of your system. I not only keep records of simple text files on my computer, but I also document them on a form that I keep handy.

Do yourself a huge favor and try this method of documenting changes to your system. Create a simple form that will let you detail any changes you have made. Let this form be generic to be used on installation also. Some of the items to include are

- Date
- Machine worked on
- Functions performed
- Issue at hand
- Results

I keep these organized in an order that pertains to

- Configuration files
  - Log
  - Web
  - Mail
  - Connectivity, such as Samba, NFS, and so on
- Kernel
  - Current version

- Modules
- Users
  - Not enough can be said for this topic; I have a whole separate folder for these guys.
- Hardware
  - List any anomalous hardware and how it reacts with your system

These can be in any order you want, with as much or as little organization as you can stand.

Back Up, Back Up, Back Up

Almost all backup strategies rely on the three basic of backup types. The only difference is the way that they go about backing up the data. The following is the holy trinity of saving data in case the unthinkable happens:

- **Full** A full backup provides a complete backup of a filesystem. All files belonging to all users on the filesystem being backed up are saved during the backup procedure.
- **Incremental** An incremental backup is usually performed one or more times between full backups and backs up only those files that have changed or been created since the date and time of the last incremental or full backup.
- **Differential** A differential backup can be performed one or more times between full backups and backs up all files that have changed or been created since the date and time of the last full backup regardless of whether or not they have changed since the last differential backup.

A full backup is always the stating point for the administrator of a system. These generally consume a great deal of time and resources to create. As such, it is best to perform these when the system is the least busy, such as nighttime or when network traffic is at a minimum.

An incremental backup backs up only data that has changed since the last backup was run. If you get into the habit of only performing incremental backups, you will be absolutely crushed if a system failure hits. You will have to restore *all* of the incrementals since the last full backup was made.

Differential backups will back up all changes made since the last back up. This will consume more resources than an incremental backup but not as many as a full backup.

This will create a data redundancy and cost a little more, but what price do you have on your data?

NOTE   The first step is to start backing up your data. Make the first full backup and proceed from there.

Backup Strategies

You can arrange backup strategies based on your needs. You choose the amount of work by choosing either incremental or differential backups to be included with a regular full backup. If you choose full backups at a low frequency with higher-frequency incremental backups in between, then you will have to apply each incremental backup in case of a system failure. If you choose full backups at a low frequency with higher-frequency differential backups in between, then you will incur a higher cost because the size of the differential backup will consume more media.

The most common strategy when backing data up is to perform a full backup once a week. This should happen on a weekday or weekend night when there is no user traffic. Incremental backups can be performed during the week to backup data that has been changed or updated.

The most important item to consider is that you should never trust your media. All too often backup tapes can become corrupt or worn out and your data/hard work is all for naught.

NOTE   The best way to archive and store your data is to place one backup per media whether that is tape or disc.

Other Backup Strategies

Backup strategies all take money, time, and extra expense. One of the most effective of back up strategies is to back up your data as soon as it is created. Mirroring your data does this. With mirroring, you are writing to two places instead of just one. These places are usually another hard drive in your computer. All of the changes that you make to the data are saved to two places at once, in real time. This is also called a fault tolerant data solution. If one hard drive fails, the other can pick up and keep going until the failed hard drive can be replaced.

One of the most effective ways to back up data is to implement an archival system of tape or off-site storage of data combined with fault tolerance. This gives you two levels of insurance that your data is safe and can be recovered in the case of an accident or hardware failure.

Disk mirroring is also a form of RAID, which stands for Redundant Array of Inexpensive Disks. Disk mirroring is called RAID level 1. As the name suggests, RAID involves many disks storing the same data to provide a fault tolerant system of storing data. Another benefit of RAID is increased read and write times for your data.

Other levels of RAID commonly used is RAID level 5. This is a set of multiple disks with one of the disks being used for parity so that if one disk fails the data can still be retrieved and the disk replaced. If more than one disk fails at a time, all of the data is then lost.

NOTE Although the cost is higher, combining an archival backup system with RAID 5 provides the highest level of data protection available.

Backup Software and Utilities

Instead of buying a back up solution from a company, many administrators choose to implement their own archival solution. Using **cron**, one can schedule backups to be made through **tar** and **cpio**. These backups, while not providing the bells and whistles that off-the-shelf archival solutions provide, are effective solutions nonetheless.

Backups with Standard Linux Tools   The **tar** utility was originally designed to create archives of files on tape devices. Today it is used to create archive files for the Web and for software storage and retrieval in addition to being a backup utility.

With **tar**, you can easily create an archive of files using the following command:

```
[root@mercury.technical /root]# tar cvf <archive file> <files>
```

The command breaks down as follows:

- c, v, and f are the most commonly used options for the command. c stands for create and indicates that an archive will be created, v will always stand for verbose mode and tells you what is going on during the process by displaying each file that is being archived, and f stands for file and indicates that an new archive file is being created instead of archiving to a device.

- The full path to the archive file and the name of it should be included with the .tar extension.

- The files to be archived or added to an archive are listed here. If you list a single file, it will be archived. If you list a directory, all of the files under it will be archived also.

If you wanted to create an archive file called January in the backup folder that contained all of the data in the /home/sales directory, the command would resemble the following:

```
# tar cvf /backup/january.tar /home /sales
```

To back up the same file to a Small Computer Systems Interface (SCSI) tape device instead of a file, you would change the command to look like this:

```
# tar cv /dev/st0 /home/sales
```

These files are being backed up by using their full size. This is unacceptable because of the sheer volume of tape it takes to store them. **tar** supports compression in the form of **gzip**. To create a compressed version of the same file that we archived, we would add a z to the option list and append .gz to the end of the file name.

```
# tar czvf /backup/january.tar.gz /home /sales
```

NOTE   When you see a file with the .gz or .tgz extension, it is a compressed archive.

You can view a list of files in an archive with the t option:

```
# tar tvf /backup/today.tar
```

Just add the **z** to view the contents of a compressed archive:

```
# tar tzvf /backup/today.tar.gz
```

Finally, you can extract the contents of an archive file relative to the current directory with one of the following commands:

```
# tar xvf /backup/today.tar
# tar xzvf /backup/today.tar.gz
```

If you want to extract specific files from the archive, specify them at the end of the command line:

```
# tar xzvf /backup/today.tar.gz /etc/fstab
```

Given all this, producing a complete compressed backup to the first SCSI tape drive would use the following command:

```
# tar czvf /dev/st0 /
```

Similarly, you can perform the same backup and store it on a removable disk drive containing an ext2 filesystem that is the fourth IDE device with the following command if the partition is mounted at /mnt:

```
# tar czvf /mnt/fullbackup.tar.gz /
```

If you want to use **tar** to perform partial backups such as incremental or differential backups, you can specify that you only want to archive files with date stamps that are more recent than a specified date stamp using the command with the --newer option. For instance, if your last full backup was on July 28, 2001 at 16:00, then you can use the following for and a differential backup:

```
# tar czvf --newer "28-Jul-2001 16:00" /mnt/fullbackup.tar.gz /
```

If you wanted to do an incremental backup, you would just specify the date and time of your last incremental backup.

NOTE You will want to automate these backup processes so that you only need to change media without having to issue backup commands. You can automate these tasks using the cron daemon we learned about earlier in the chapter.

Backup Software Packages

There are backup software and hardware packages available for Linux that you should be aware of. If you need more than basic self-developed backup systems, you should consider an integrated backup solution. Among the packages worth reviewing are

- **Amanda**   Amanda is a backup program that grew out of the Advanced Maryland Automated Network Disk Archiver project. Amanda is free software that uses utilities such as **tar** and **awk**, which are usually on your system to create backups. Amanda is a full-featured archiving solution. One backup server with a multitape drive can provide backups for users across the network. You can download this from **ftp://ftp.amanda.org/pub/amanda**.

- **Time Navigator**   Time Navigator is a global backup and archiving solution. Backup and archiving servers must be independent; however, they share the same graphical interface and the same storage resources. This makes the administrator's job much easier. Provided by Atempo, Time Navigator is a scalable backup tool usable by administrators and end users alike. This is not free software. For more information on availability, go to **http://www.atempo.com/products/html/US/archives.php3**.

- **Taper**   Taper is an alternative to **tar** for producing tape archives or archive files. The advantage of Taper is that information about the files being stored is placed at the start of the archive so it is easy to restore a list of files in an archive without scanning the entire archive as is required with **tar**.

Emergency Recovery Techniques

Eventually, you are going to have problems. Getting down to the bottom of these problems involves some time and effort and a few items you should never be without, such as hardware lists and the all-important rescue disk. Some of the issues include

- Linux loader boot-up sequence

- Single-user rescue boot with read-only boot disk

- Performing a filesystem consistency check

Before jumping into a recovery type situation, make sure you have a list of any important application settings and even copies of configuration files.

Linux Loader Boot-up Sequence

After your computer has finished the Power On Self Test (POST), the BIOS hands the bootup sequence over to LILO, which is located usually in the Master Boot Record (MBR) or the first track of the data storage area. LILO then continues to boot your computer from the /boot/boot.b file. LILO then loads the kernel from the location specified in the file /etc/lilo.conf. LILO is a very powerful program. Some have referred to it as a useful boot sector virus because it almost thinks for itself and is hard to get rid of.

LILO has the ability to read files from the hard drive before any filesystem drivers are intialized. LILO has to know the disk geometry locations of the kernel and the boot.b file in order to boot. If LILO cannot find the boot device, it will go into a loop and display an endless series of binary digits. However, on the other hand, if LILO finds the boot device but cannot discern the location of the kernel, LI will appear to freeze on the display. This indicates a disk geometry problem. Sometimes this can be remedied by allowing the hard disk to spin for a while and warm up.

Single-User Rescue Boot

After LILO loads the kernel and the operating system, the root device is mounted in read-only mode. When initial filesystem checks are made, the root device is mounted in read-write mode. This can be evidenced by watching the script go by during a system startup.

If you have problems with your root device, you can get to a prompt several ways. Some of the options include

- Booting to an alternate root partition, if you have one that will work. To do this, enter *<bootname>* **root=***<root device>* at the LILO prompt. The name of your kernel would be the boot name. In Red Hat, it is **vmlinuz**. This is also known as passing a parameter to the kernel at boot time. For a single drive system, this will not work. This will work for a multiple drive array with an alternate boot source on it.

- Boot to emergency mode. This is done by using the -b option with the kernel name, as in **vmlinuz -b**. This will prompt you for a login and password for the root user.

At least one of these options should provide you with a superuser command prompt from which you can fix any configuration problems and reconfigure and install LILO settings if needed.

Rescue Disks

The first thing to try is the rescue disk you created when installing the system. You did create one, didn't you? I create one for each system using the system it might rescue one day. This ensures that I always have a way in. If the install CD-ROM is bootable, it will use the same code that is on a rescue disk and can then be used to boot the system.

Special Permissions

The three main permissions—read, write, and execute—are joined by three special permissions, which grant more detailed access to files:

- Set user ID (SUID)
- Set group ID (SGID)
- Sticky bit

SUID

The Set User ID (SUID) permission enables a user to run a program that he or she normally cannot. For example, the /etc/passwd file has permissions of

```
-rw-r--r--    1 root     root     1378 Jun 13 18:58 /etc/passwd
```

yet any user can change his or her password using the **passwd** command. Looking at the permissions for the **passwd** command, we see

```
-r-s--x--x    1 root     root     13536 Jul 12  2000 /usr/bin/passwd
```

The SUID permission enables any user on the system to execute the **passwd** command and have the privileges of the root user for the time the **passwd** command is executing. This is how any user can change his or her password.

In Chapter 4, we discussed user and file permissions. The SUID permission is obvious by the *s* in place of the *x* for the owner's execute bit. The numerical representation of the SUID permission is 4000. Setting the SUID permission using the symbolic representation is as follows:

```
chmod u+s filename
```

It is essential to remember the value of this permission as the user running the process has all the privileges associated with the owner of the program.

SGID

The Set Group ID (SGID) permission is similar to SUID, except that the privileges assigned are those corresponding to the group that owns the file. The numerical representation for SGID is 2000, and changes the *x* in the group permissions to an *s* when set.

```
[root@mercury.technical /root]# ls -l sales
-rwxr-xr--    1 jholman    jholman        216 Jun  6 19:20 sales
[root@mercury.technical /root]# chmod 2755 sales
[root@mercury.technical /root]# ls -l rsales
-rwxr-sr-x    1 jholman    jholman        216 Jun  6 19:20 sales
[root@mercury.technical /root]#
```

The SGID permission is represented in symbolic form using **chmod** as

```
chmod g+s filename
```

Sticky Bit

The final permission, the sticky bit, does not work like the other special permissions. The numerical representation is 1000, and the behavior of this permission is different for a file and a directory. When the sticky bit is applied to a directory, it prevents users from deleting files they don't own. This is particularly useful for public or shared directories like /tmp. Users can delete any file they own, but no others.

When the sticky bit is used on a program file, the program is loaded into memory and remains loaded, even when no one is using it. This is why it is called the *sticky bit*. Using the sticky bit carefully can increase the performance of your system by keeping frequently used commands in memory rather than always reading them from the hard drive.

The sticky bit shows as a *t* or a *T* in the execute position of the other user permissions. If the sticky bit is applied to an executable file or to a directory, the last bit is a *t*.

Performing Administrative Security Tasks

Despite the security breaches reported in the news on a regular basis, many organizations don't spend much time thinking about the security of the operating systems on their computers. If you apply too little security, your data is exposed to anyone who wants it. They can modify it, delete it, or give it to your competitors.

Some organizations swing in the opposite direction, however, and apply too much security, making it almost impossible for people to perform their assigned tasks. It has often been said the most secure computer is one that has been smashed to a million pieces, encased in concrete, and buried 50 feet under the ground. Unfortunately, such a system is also unusable.

Somewhere between a complete lack of security and too much security lies the appropriate level—one that enables your business to continue and still protects your data. That level depends on your organization, the type of information you work with, the access methods users will have, and so forth.

Regardless of the particular level of security, you should be working with the following mindset:

- *Maintain physical security*. No matter what level of logical security you install, if attackers have physical access to the system or network components, they can do whatever they want.

- *Monitor the environment*. Many things cause data corruption and loss, including electromagnetic interference (EMI) caused by cabling running too close to fluorescent lighting and electric motors. Other environmental factors include low electricity quality, temperature, and humidity.

- *Verify that all installation media is free from viruses before you install the software.* You can do this by verifying checksums, running antivirus programs, obtaining the software only from trusted sites, or even doing code reviews on the source code. The ideal method, however, is to install the software on a stand-alone system and verify its operation prior to adding it your production environment.

- *Create a password policy and educate the users about password use.* Ensure that the passwords are a minimum of eight characters in length and use the Linux Pluggable Authentication Modules (PAM) to implement the dictionary evaluation of the passwords. Also set expiration dates to force the users to change their passwords periodically.

- *Use the shadow file to protect the encrypted password values.* By making the encrypted passwords unavailable to the system users, they cannot be attacked using programs such as crack.

- *Check the system log files regularly to ensure that users are not suddenly logging in and out at odd times.* If users typically do not work in the middle of the night, investigate suspicious login times when they occur.

- *Disable any accounts that are not needed for user logins.* For example, make sure all system accounts are locked and do not have a valid password—with the obvious exception being the root account.

- *Use good authentication methods for remote access.* Point-to-Point (PPP) supports both Password Authentication Protocol (PAP), which does not encrypt passwords, and Challenge Handshake Authentication Protocol (CHAP), which does.

- *Use other security tools, such as TCP wrappers, to limit where connections are accepted from across the network.* The TCP wrapper control files /etc/hosts.allow and /etc/hosts.deny and work with the wrapper program to establish which machines are allowed to be hosts. If they are specifically listed in the .allow file, then they can be hosts, whereas if they are specifically listed in the .deny file, they cannot.

- *Examine your system on a routine basis for world-writable files and files with SUID and SGID permissions.* Because of the evaluated authorities granted in SUID and SGID programs, there must be a reason for them to exist on your system. World-writable files enable any user on the system to modify or destroy the contents of the file, which could spell disaster for your organization.

- *Verify that all daemons are running with the minimal privileges assigned.* If they don't need root access, then don't run them with root access.

- *If you have a requirement to log into the system over the network, protect the session by using ssh instead of telnet.* Telnet puts the password in the clear on the network, enabling people to obtain it by using sniffer tools. ssh not only encrypts the connection, it uses public and private keys for authentication, providing improved validation that it is an authorized user from an authorized computer. OpenSSH code, although not in all Linux releases, is readily available for download from the Internet, along with SSH clients for Windows and other operating systems.

- *Use an appropriate umask value to make default permissions for newly created files and directories as minimal as possible.*

Many of the preceding issues appear to be common sense. In the real world, however, common sense requires common knowledge. When working on a system, or when taking the exam, always consider both the possibilities and the ramifications when adding security to a host or network.

Setting Up Host Security

The most effective way to secure a system—and the key applications running on it—is to know as much as possible about the purposes of the applications and the issues surrounding them. You set up a Web server, for example, to deliver Web content to users. In such a situation, that host should not be providing Dynamic Host Control Protocol (DHCP) addresses to clients. It shouldn't even be able to do so.

The /etc/inetd.conf file holds a list of the services that will be started on a host when networking is started. You should carefully review the /etc/inetd.conf file on each host and disable any unnecessary services to limit the attack methods available. It is also highly recommended that you review the log files created by the syslog daemon to see which services are starting up and whether they are encountering problems that force them to restart.

Keeping track of the exposures and vulnerabilities found in the various Linux implementations is a daunting but necessary task. You really only need to be concerned about the vendor-specific implementation you are using at your site. New issues are found frequently; having a response plan enables your organization to handle those issues effectively when they arise.

You can keep track of the reported vulnerabilities by joining the Computer Emergency Response Team (CERT) mailing list at **http://www.cert.org**. You can also contact CERT via e-mail at **cert@cert.org**, or through regular mail at the following address:

CERT Coordination Center
Software Engineering Institute
Carnegie Mellon University
Pittsburgh, PA 15213-3890

Other resources include the Computer Security Institute (**http://www.gocsi**) and the BUGTRAQ mailing list. To join BUGTRAQ, send an e-mail to **listserv@securityfocus .com** with a blank subject, and a message of "SUBSCRIBE BUGTRAQ."

The most common way to address security problems is to patch the source code and replace the affected binaries. Most vulnerabilities are not based on malicious intent, but are due to issues missed during the initial design and development of the source code. Consequently, you should be cautious of where you download your applications. If you do not know the site, find out what others think about it and whether anyone you trust has performed a source code review. The only way to deal with a threat is to eliminate it as expeditiously as possible.

TIP   Documentation is always key. Maintain a log of system changes to enable you to correct them and revert to the original settings should an unforeseen problem occur. Remember to always perform a full system backup, including all your data prior to making any major changes to the system.

Setting Up User-Level Security

Regardless of the level of security actually implemented, users are often the weakest link. All users should be configured with the least privilege required for them to perform their job responsibilities. It is always easier to grant additional access than to give them root access and find out later that they have damaged the system. Not only does it create more work for the system administrator, it violates the principle of least privilege, which is a major security principle.

It is not uncommon for system administrators to grant too much privilege, often through group memberships when creating a user simply to make the administrator's job easier. Remember, however, your organization depends on you to act responsibly and in its best interest when establishing and maintaining system security.

It is also important to place other limits on the users. For example, you should

- Use quotas to limit the amount of storage each user has. This prevents them from accidentally, or intentionally, using all available hard disk space and possibly halting the system.

- Use the **ulimit -u** command to restrict the type and number of processes that users can execute at any given time, preventing them from filling the process table.

- Use the **ulimit -v** command to limit the amount of virtual memory available to the shell.

TIP The ulimit specifications should be placed in the /etc/profile to apply to all users.

- Use the /etc/securetty file to identify the terminals from which root can log in. Every terminal device is listed in this file, by default. Ideally, direct root login should be restricted to the console. The usertty file, which does not exist by default, can be used to hold user restrictions. You can specify the terminals and users allowed to log in through the USERS section of the file. The GROUPS section performs the same function, giving users in specific groups access to the system only through specific terminals. An example of this file follows:

```
# cat /etc/usertty
USERS
jholman   tty3
lisaf   tty4 @192.168.0.0/255.255.255.0
#
```

In this example, user jholman is restricted to accessing the system only from tty3, and user lisaf is allowed access only on tty4 or a machine running on the 192.168.0.0 network. To apply a restriction to all users, start the line with an asterisk (*).

You can specify both hard and soft controls using the **ulimit** command. The hard values represent limits that cannot be exceeded, whereas soft values can be exceeded. The options used with **ulimit** (other than those already listed) include

-a   Shows all current limits

-f   Specifies the maximum size of files created by a shell

-t   Specifies the maximum CPU time that can be used (in seconds)

-n   Specifies the maximum number of open files

NOTE On most Linux systems, -n can be viewed, but not set.

The following is an example of the command in action:

```
[root@mercury.technical /tmp]# ulimit -a
core file size (blocks)      1000000
```

```
data seg size (kbytes)         unlimited
file size (blocks)             unlimited
max locked memory (kbytes)     unlimited
max memory size (kbytes)       unlimited
open files                     1024
pipe size (512 bytes)          8
stack size (kbytes)            8192
cpu time (seconds)             unlimited
max user processes             4096
virtual memory (kbytes)        unlimited
[root@mercury.technical /tmp]#
```

Physical Security

Patching the source code and looking for unconventional files is only half the battle. Physical security is still to be looked at. In today's age, we hear about the savvy cracker that comes in through an unprotected port or uses a brute force password cracker to gain entry into a system.

The need to formalize a security policy is of the utmost importance. If you do not have a policy and deal with things only on a per-instance basis, you are in effect telling people that anything goes. You are giving the people on your system permission to do anything they like and only then deciding if they can do it or not. This is a poor policy to have because it is a moral breaker as well as a very permissive statement. A locked door and a secure room is still the best answer to data protection after you have hardened your system to digital attackers.

Consider the people who are around your system while you are not there. I am sure there are cleaning people and or maintenance people around after hours. These are the people who are most likely to simply walk off with a computer or storage device containing your company's data. For whatever purpose it is taken, the data is still gone.

I don't advocate being paranoid—just be aware of all of the dangers that are associated with your system and where attacks can come from.

Chapter Summary

In this chapter, we have moved from the administration side of things into actually maintaining the system. Here we have covered many core services and processes that perform a myriad of functions for us.

Managing the filesystem using **fsck** being one of the most used utilities to verify the integrity of your system and the data it handles along with **df** to check the free space on your system. We performed basic connectivity to a network and used **ifconfig** to set the

IP address and subnet of our system and used syslog to log events associated with security issues and everyday events.

Two major issues surfaced during this chapter: backups and documentation. Not enough can be said for documentation; it is the core of the whole system. To know what you've got, you have to know what you've got. It can't be put any plainer than that. That last phrase can apply to backups also. When you back up, you have to know that when the time comes to use it that your data is actually on the tape.

Questions

1. The configuration file for the logs daemon is _____.
   a. syslogd.conf
   b. syslog.rc
   c. syslog.conf
   d. syslog.cron

2. Which **kill** signal is not trappable?
   a. -STOP
   b. -HUP
   c. -INT
   d. -KILL

3. When documenting work performed on a system, what should you document? (Choose two.)
   a. Number of hours worked
   b. System worked on
   c. Software installed
   d. When you stopped working

4. What does **fsck** stand for?
   a. Filesystem cron+kde
   b. Filesystem corrupted
   c. Filesystem checker
   d. Filesystem core compiler

5. Pick three Linux package management extensions.
   a. .rpm
   b. .zip
   c. .deb
   d. .tar
   e. .pzip
   f. .gzu

6. What is Amanda?
   a. An application to check for correct data
   b. A powerful software backup system
   c. A shell script that seeks out new hardware
   d. LILO boot configuration file

7. What should a secure physical environment encompass?
   a. Limited access
   b. Hardened system software
   c. No Internet access
   d. Background checks

8. The **ifconfig** flag **down** causes what to happen?
   a. The network adapter card not to be recognized
   b. Whatever portion of the networking is named not to be recognized
   c. No Internet access
   d. The network to go down

9. What is the proper syntax to immediately kill a process?
   a. **kill -33 14153**
   b. **kill -9 14153**
   c. **kill -hup 14153**
   d. **kill -48 14153**

10. What is the purpose of **cron**?
    a. To run a scheduled job once
    b. To run a scheduled job many times
    c. To run a scheduled batch of jobs
    d. To run a scheduled job next week

Answers

1. **C.** syslog.conf is the configuration file for the log service.

2. **D.** -**kill** is the only termination signal of the four listed that is not trappable.

3. **B** and **C.** Of the answers listed, the number of hours worked and what you installed are the only relevant answers.

4. **C.** **fsck** is the filesystem checker.

5. **A. C.** and **D.** .rpm is the Red Hat package manager, .deb is the Debian package manager, and .tar is tape archive.

6. **B.** Amanda is a free software archival solution for Linux.

7. **A.** By reducing access, you harden your system physically.

8. **B.** **down** causes the named portion of the networking to not be recognized.

9. **B.** **kill -9 14153** would terminate PID 14153 immediately.

10. **B.** **cron** is a scheduler that will run a job as many times as you ask it to.

## CHAPTER 6

Troubleshooting

This chapter covers the following competencies required to master the Linux+ certification exam:

- Identifying and locating problem type: hardware, OS, application, configuration, or user
- Troubleshooting best practices
- Using system utilities to examine and edit configuration files based on problem signs and symptoms
- Examining processes based on problem symptoms
- Examining system status tools
- Diagnosing filesystems on workstations and servers using system file logs to determine errors
- Solving system problems using disk utilities
- Troubleshooting problems based on user feedback
- Understanding typical errors
- Fixing boot errors
- Identifying backup and restore errors
- Diagnosing application failure at the server level
- Understanding and using troubleshooting commands
- Identifying network problem via network utilities

Troubleshooting

There are many, many avenues to take when troubleshooting a system. When we look at an error on a system, we first have to determine where the error is coming from. It is through years of systems going down and finding problems and fixing them that I have come to the conclusion that 90 percent of all problems on a system is due to a combination of end-user errors and data corruption.

In this chapter, we will cover basic troubleshooting systems that cover most all of the points that a problem can sprout from. We will look at where the largest population of problems occurs—with the end user on a network, which falls under configuration (specifically permissions).

Most of this chapter involves looking at and thinking about a problem, where it lies, and how to apply the proper patch or fix. Diagnostic skills are in the highest demand; hence, CompTia is committed to a chapter devoted to the application of troubleshooting. We will have some utilities that are included with the newest distributions of Linux. In other situations, intuition and knowledge take over to seek a new direction in handling a problem.

Identifying the Problem

Problems with computers have many faces and many solutions. When looking at the problem, are you really seeing the problem or just one of its symptoms? Here we have to decide whether the problem is user related or just a piece of hardware that has gone bad.

Dealing with hardware is pretty simple. A piece of hardware gone bad can appear as something else, but eventually, through reasoning and deduction, you get down to the piece that really is bad. In dealing with people, it is prudent to keep a very open mind because they can send you off in a direction that holds absolutely no clues to the problem at hand.

User-Related Problems

The first place to look for a problem is with any user-configurable settings. A person might tell you what he or she thinks the problem is or is not. The user can be a source of information with which to find an error that was made. Some of the following questions can help define the problem a little more:

- When did the problem first start?

- Have you installed any new software recently?

- Have you made any configuration changes to files such as smb.conf or xf86config?

- Have you installed any new hardware?

Be polite and listen; the user may have a clue for you to start from. If you derive nothing from the user, thank him or her and start the common troubleshooting techniques, as defined later in the chapter under the heading "Configuration."

Hardware

In any troubleshooting role, identifying the problem is the hardest part. There are several solutions. You have a myriad of options to explore here. First, let's take a look at a stand-alone computer—not one connected to a network, just a multimedia workstation with a generic 56K connection to the Internet. We will look at components both inside the case and outside of the case.

Internal

- Motherboard
- Video card
- Modem
- Power supply
- Memory
- Hard drive
- CD-ROM drive
- Floppy disk drive
- Power switch

External

- Monitor
- Keyboard
- Pointing device (mouse)
- Any external drives (Zip or CD-ROM)
- Incoming power source

After looking at all of these components possibly contributing towards an anomaly, the only logical choice is to simplify the problem as much as possible.

To give ourselves a fighting chance, we have to make it more obvious what the problem is. This means that we have to reduce the number of variables down to the least amount possible.

Configuration

In addition to hardware being the problem, the second step is to take a quick look at some configuration-specific problems. Some of the more obvious problems are listed in the following section. They deserve a quick look and I would recommend that they be disabled before proceeding any further with troubleshooting.

- **Beta software**   If you are running beta drivers or other low-level software, it is best to get rid of it and stick with proven software.

- **Overclocked systems or tweaked Basic Input/Output System (BIOS) settings** Overclocking is pushing your system too hard. This occurs if you set the system variable to make your machine run faster than it is supposed to run. Overclocking is usually reserved for a late-night session where you have nothing to do except to see just how fast that hardware will actually run before making funny noises and maybe a little smoke. The first thing I do when working on a system is to set the BIOS back to original conditions. Most system software and hardware is designed around a generic working model. Most BIOS have a Use BIOS Defaults option. When clicked, this returns the BIOS to factory-fresh readiness.

- **Power management**   The only thing that I want my computer to do when I am away is to do whatever I told it to do when I was away. In other words, I am not a big fan of power management. Power management is great if you have software that knows how to deal with it. A hard disk spinning down or a monitor turning off may seem like a hardware error at first. I had a gentleman call me to inform me that a system I had built for him shut off in the middle of a game, only to find out that when the mouse moved, the screen came back on. That is a prime example of software that does not make the proper system calls. Shutting off power management can go along way in troubleshooting a system.

- **Unusual configurations**   I have a friend who gets excited whenever he finds an old piece of hardware such as a 486 motherboard or an 8-bit network card. I always tell him that it is better to go out and spend the extra money to get a quality piece of hardware. The same goes for older utilities that load up a system with a bunch of terminate-and-stay-resident programs. When troubleshooting, it is imperative to disable these and to avoid unusual configurations altogether. It's fine if the whole system is old. You get into trouble when you introduce an old piece of hardware into a newer system.

- **setserial**   This is a program to check the status of serial ports. If you are planning to use an external modem or anything else attached to a serial port, you should know this command. The **setserial** program is designed to set and/or report the configuration information associated with a serial port. This information includes what I/O port and Interrupt Request (IRQ) a particular serial port is using. The following shows an output of **setserial**:

```
[root@mercury.technical root]# setserial -g /dev/ttyS*
/dev/ttyS0, UART: 16550A, Port: 0x03f8, IRQ: 4
/dev/ttyS1, UART: unknown, Port: 0x02f8, IRQ: 3
/dev/ttyS2, UART: 16550A, Port: 0x03e8, IRQ: 4
/dev/ttyS3, UART: unknown, Port: 0x02e8, IRQ: 3
[root@mercury.technical root]#
```

NOTE   For four ports, only two IRQs are used; this can lead to an IRQ conflict and prevent a piece of hardware attached to a serial port from working. The main difference between the ports is the I/O address, which is shown by the 0x0xxx format.

You want to avoid the out of the ordinary altogether when troubleshooting a system. After returning the BIOS of the machine to default settings, the second thing I do is look for any funky software utilities or cute screensavers. If I see Tux run across the screen, he's outta there!

When I first started troubleshooting computers, I had to totally revise my strategy. I had the bad habit of jumping to a conclusion ten minutes after seeing a minor portion of the symptoms the machine was exhibiting. The problem with acting too quickly is that you may apply the wrong fix to a problem and end up making things worse. There is nothing more embarrassing for a tech than making things worse! It will also make things more difficult when re-establishing what the problem really is.

The key to troubleshooting is patience. You want to make sure that you take enough time to find the real problem. With some intermittent problems, the cause is not easily established. Only by taking care of the real or root problem will the problem go away permanently. Often, if you take the time to fully explore the problem, the problem turns out to be just another symptom with the real problem lying much deeper.

There is a theory that asking the question "why" a bunch of times will distill the problem out into the light. Suppose you have just installed that huge, ultrafast hard drive that you have had your eye on for a while and after a week of using it, corrupted data starts showing up. What do you do? The first thing that comes to mind is "Replace the disk; it's bad." What you should be thinking is

"Why is the hard disk showing bad sectors now?"

"Something has changed."

"Why?"

"The hard drive is set to LBA mode."

"Why?"

"I just installed it last week; maybe I didn't install it right."

"Why?"

"The hard drive must not be formatted or partitioned properly."

"Why?"

"The root partition is too small and there is not enough room for data."

If you had returned the drive to the manufacturer, you would have been assessed a penalty of at least 10 percent of the purchase price of a drive's cost for returning a fully functioning drive!

Another situation is data loss. If a hard drive becomes toast because of a naturally occurring disaster, the knee-jerk reaction may be to purchase a surge protector or an uninterruptible power supply (UPS). The situation when examined thoroughly presents the fact that this is the first instance of data loss due to nature in five years. Data loss has always been due to the lack of a backup solution or training to implement it. Maybe a data backup solution and the training to use it are more in order, not to mention a better way to spend the earmarked money.

As you can see, the objective is to isolate the problem. We have looked at things inside the system; now we need to turn our focus to external causes. For instance, one fine day you go to boot your machine and it doesn't turn on. Nothing happens. What is the cause? To go through a troubleshooting scenario would be to

- Check for loose power cables
- Plug the machine into a different power socket
- Bypass the surge suppressor
- Change the power cord

If any of these steps worked, you can take appropriate action to ensure that the same anomaly does not happen again. If these steps don't work, the problem is inside the machine. The key to this form of troubleshooting is to take one step at a time and view the problem to see if it has been corrected. If you snug up the power cord, plug the machine into a different outlet, bypass the surge suppressor, and change the power cord, you will not know which step solved your problem. However, this is a valid way to troubleshoot if you have to get the system up immediately. To know what the problem is, you must retrace the steps it took to encounter the problem. Too many times troubleshooting is done two or three steps at a time, when it needs to be done one step at a time.

Write It Down

The purpose of this section is to familiarize you with some general troubleshooting steps, not to ascertain and focus on a certain problem. The second thing is to document the problem. Whenever you discern a piece of evidence or you figure out something about the current situation your PC is in, document it. Keeping a history of what you discover and what your symptoms are will help you not only with this problem, but also with any future difficulties. A log book is a good idea. The first place I turn for answers is to the file that I have on a certain computer (yes, I said a file). The motherboard book and any other documentation on hardware such as the video card, network card, and modem are in it. I keep my drivers in another place.

Intermittent and Repeatable Problems

Most problems with a PC fall into one of two categories: either they are repeatable or they are intermittent. A repeatable problem is one where the problem occurs all the time or always in response to a specific user action. For example, a PC that has a problem that prevents it from booting will probably always fail to boot no matter how many times you reset it. Or you may have an application that crashes with an error whenever you try to run it. You may find that your PC hangs, but only when you move the mouse at the same time that you are communicating using your modem.

In contrast, some problems are intermittent and not repeatable. In some cases, you may have a PC that will usually boot up fine, but one day a month will fail to boot for some reason. An application may work most of the time but occasionally crash. The PC may lock up at seemingly random intervals. Your mouse may work almost all of the time, but one day out of five or ten, it may give you trouble.

It is helpful to determine if the problem you are experiencing is repeatable, because intermittent difficulties are much more difficult to resolve than repeatable ones. If a problem is repeatable, and there is a specific set of actions that cause the problem, this gives you at least some initial clues about how to find the cause. In addition, you have a way of testing to see if you have resolved the problem when you are trying different solutions. Intermittent problems are much more difficult to deal with.

Determining if a problem is repeatable is pretty simple: Try to duplicate the conditions that caused the problem and see if it happens again.

Intermittent problems are problems that appear to happen spontaneously or randomly. They don't seem to be caused by anything obvious and are not repeatable. They can be extremely difficult and frustrating to diagnose.

Sometimes problems that seem intermittent really aren't; it's just that the specific set of circumstances that cause the problem to occur may be obscure or hard to notice. Spend some time trying to determine what the circumstances are when the problem arises. For example, many problems with crashes or lockups will occur only after the system has been on for more than an hour; some may occur only within the first few minutes that the PC is turned on. You may find that a certain program only crashes when run at the same time as another program, or that a particular behavior is associated with a peripheral of some sort.

You will have to be patient when dealing with these sorts of issues. Because the problem is not something you can duplicate at will, you might not be able to systematically work your way towards the ultimate cause. In this situation, you may have to employ trial-and-error skills, making a change and then waiting to see if the problem recurs. It can take days (or longer) sometimes because you have to wait before seeing if the problem happens again. Be patient.

Data Corruption

Due to the complexity of the filesystem used on modern PCs, there is always the risk that filesystem errors and corruption will develop in the logical structures that control the disk. Most of the time, buggy software, bad drivers, power failures, or human error cause these problems. Rarely, they are the result of actual hardware problems with the PC.

The filesystem checker (**fsck**) is used to check and optionally repair a filesystem that has been corrupted. **fsck** is just a front-end for a various filesystem checkers for Linux. Filesystem integrity problems can occasionally lead to data loss. It is important that any problems be caught as soon as possible to minimize the chances of extensive damage. Fortunately, checking for filesystem problems is very quick and easy to do. I recommend that filesystems be scanned for errors on a daily basis. You can do it less often, but you increase the chances of problems mushrooming exponentially. Use **cron** to schedule **fsck** when network usage is down. With modern drives and filesystems being as big as they are, the ext2 filesystem can take a long time to check a file. The Reiser journaling filesystem is much faster because it keeps a journal of all the files and their location.

Scheduling Jobs

Scheduling jobs is an easy matter. All scheduled jobs are stored in an individual configuration file (known as the crontab file) for the user, with each line representing a job that has been scheduled.

We will start by looking at the format of crontab file entries before moving to how we actually edit the crontab file to create scheduled jobs.

Each entry takes the following form:

```
<time-date> <command>
```

The time-date entry consists of five numeric fields (each separated by spaces), which indicate when a job should be run. The five fields (in order) are

- **Minute** Possible values are 0 through 59.
- **Hour** Possible values are 0 through 23.
- **Day of month** Possible values are 1 through 31.
- **Month** Possible values are 1 through 12 (or the first three letters of the month's name).
- **Day of week** Possible values are 0 through 7 where both 0 and 7 represent Sunday (or the first three letters of the day's name).

For all these fields, several rules provide flexibility:

- Ranges of numbers can be used. For instance, 1 through 3 in the hour field says to schedule the command for 1:00 A.M., 2:00 A.M., and 3:00 A.M. Similarly, 2 through 4 in the day of the week field schedules the job for Tuesday, Wednesday, and Thursday.
- Ranges can be stepped with the increments greater than one. For instance, to indicate every other hour from midnight to midnight, use the range 0 through 23 and combine it with the step of 2, separating them with slashes: 023/2.
- An asterisk (*) indicates the entire range for a field, from smallest value to largest value. Thus, * in the day of the month field is the same as 0 through 31, and in the day of the week field is the same as 0 through 7.

Sample Times and Dates

Table 6-1 lists some examples of time-date fields.

The Command Field

The time-date field is separated from the command field by one or more spaces and runs until the end of the line. The commands are processed by the /bin/sh shell. For instance, the crontab entry

```
0 1 * * *     /usr/local/bin/backup
```

will run the program /usr/local/bin/backup daily at 1:00 A.M.

Table 6-1 **cron** Variables

Variables	Meanings
0 1 * * *	This field indicates a job that should run every day at 1:00 A.M.
30 14 * * 0	This field indicates a job that should run every Monday at 2:30 P.M.
0 12 1 * *	This field indicates a job that should run at noon on the first day of every month.
0 12 * 1 1	This field indicates a job that should run at noon on every Monday in January every year.
0 14 8 2 *	This field indicates a job that should run at noon on February 14 every year.

Sometimes commands (such as the **mail** command) require information to be entered through the standard input. This is achieved using percent signs (%). The first percent sign marks the start of standard input, and each subsequent percent sign serves as a new line character in the standard input.

So, the crontab entry

```
30 8 * * 1    /bin/mail -s "OGIM" root@mercury.technical %Oh
Goodness It's Monday.%
```

will send the following e-mail message:

```
Oh Goodness It's Monday.
```

to root@mercury each Monday morning at 8:30.

Managing the Logs for Errors

One of the benefits of Linux is that it provides standard mechanisms for the logging of an activity from the numerous daemons and programs running on the system. These logs can be used to debug system problems as well as to track usage of the system, covering everything from possible security breaches to advanced warnings of possible hardware failure.

For example, the following extract of the main Red Hat system log file (/var/log/messages) provides numerous pieces of information from a two-minute period:

```
Apr 16 03:55:29 localhost login:  ROOT LOGIN ON tty1
Apr 16 03:55:58 localhost syslog:  Warning - secret file /etc/paus
  (has world and/or group access
```

```
Apr 16 03:55:58 localhost kernel:  CSLIP:  code copyright 1999 Regents
   (of the University of California
Apr 16 03:55:58 localhost kernel:  PPP:  version 2.2.0 (dynamic (channel
   allocation)
Apr 16 03:55:58 localhost kernel:  PPP Dynamic channel allocation (code
   copyright 2000 RedHat, Inc.
Apr 16 03:55:58 localhost kernel:  PPP line discipline registered.
Apr 16 03:55:58 localhost kernel:  registered device ppp0
Apr 16 03:55:58 localhost pppd [207]:  pppd 2.2.0 started by root, uid 0
Apr 16 03:55:59 localhost chat [208]:  send (ATDT8447077^M)
Apr 16 03:56:00 localhost chat [208]:  expect (CONNECT)
Apr 16 03:56:32 localhost chat [208]:  ATDT8447077^M^M
Apr 16 03:56:32 localhost pppd [207]:  Serial connection established.
Apr 16 03:56:32 localhost chat [208]:  CONNECT - got it
Apr 16 03:56:32 localhost chat [208]:  send (^M)
Apr 16 03:56:33 local host pppd [207]:  Using interface ppp0
Apr 16 03:56:33 localhost pppd [207]:  Connect:  ppp-<-> /dev/cual
Apr 16 03:56:36 localhost pppd [207]:  Remote message:
Apr 16 03:56:36 localhost pppd[207]:  local IP address 192.168.0.1
Apr 16 03:56:36 localhost pppd [207]:  remote IP address 192.168.10.1
```

What exactly do we learn in this example? We see the login program informing us that the root user has logged in; we have a warning about the security of information in a file that should be secure; we see the kernel loading its Point-to-Point Protocol (PPP) module successfully; and we see the pppd process establish a connection to the Internet.

What Gets Logged?

It is important to make a distinction between the different types of logs in a Linux system. Basically, there are two types of logs: system logs and application logs. We will be looking at system logs because all systems have them. Application-specific logs are dependent on the applications being run and how these applications are configured to generate their logs.

In system logs, you are likely to find messages and warnings from the kernel that include information about modules that have loaded, data from the **sendmail** daemon that provides a trail of the messages that have been processed in the system, and messages about the success or failure of authentication (login) attempts.

System logs are generated by the **syslogd** daemon, which loads at boot time. The daemon accesses messages at eight levels of severity from various system processes such as the kernel, the mail system, user programs configured to use **syslogd**, and authentication programs such as the **login** program.

In order of increasing severity, these levels of messages are

- debug

- info

- notice

- warning

- err

- crit

- alert

- emerg

These levels are used in the /etc/syslog.conf file to tell **syslogd** where to create logs for different types of information. The /etc/syslog.conf file contains multiple entries, one on each line, each containing two fields separated by one or more spaces: a facility-level list and a log file location.

The facility-level list is a semicolon-separated list of facility-level pairs. Facilities are indicated by facility names such as mail, kern (for the kernel), user (for user programs), and auth (for authentication programs). Sample facility-level pairs include

- **mail.err**   Errors generated by the mail daemon

- ***.info**   All information messages

- **kern.emerg**   Emergency messages from the kernel

Let's look at the default /etc/syslog.conf file that is included with Red Hat Linux to get a sense of how this works:

```
# Log all kernel messages to the console.
# Logging much else clutters up the screen
#kern.*                                    /dev/console

#Log anything (except mail) of level info or higher.
#Don't log private authentication messages!
*.info;mail.none;authpriv.none            /var/log/messages

#The authpriv file has restricted access.
authpriv.*                                /var/log/secure

# Log all the mail messages in one place.
mail.*                                    /var/log/maillog

# Everybody gets emergency messages, plus log them on another machine.
*.emerg                                        *

# Save mail and news errors of level err and higher in a special file

uucp, news.crit                           /var/log/spooler
```

The first important line is

```
*.info;mail.none;authpriv.none          /var/log/messages
```

This line logs information messages from all facilities except mail and authentication (hence, mail.none;authpriv.none) in the file /var/log/message. This is followed by

```
authpriv.*                              /var/log/secure
```

which places all authentication messages in /var/log/secure.

Next we find the following line, which specifies that all mail log messages should be placed in /var/log/maillog:

```
uucp,news.crit                          /var/log/spooler
```

This /var/log/maillog logs certain mail- and news-related messages to /var/log/spooler.

The first thing you will probably notice is that log messages are separated into different files. The goals behind this practice are to keep the size of each log manageable and to keep the information in each log related so that tracking down log messages will be easy. If every message of every level from every facility ended up in a single log file, the information would be practically useless because the volume of information in the file would be unmanageable.

Other Linux distributions may break the messages down differently than the way shown in our example, but it is unlikely that all system log messages would end up in a single log file. You can check /etc/syslog.conf on your system to find out where your messages are being logged.

If you want to change your logging strategy, you can manually edit the syslog.conf file and then tell **syslogd** to reload the configuration with the following command:

```
[root@mercury.technical /root] # kill -HUP 'cat
/var/run/syslogd.pid'
```

Notice the use of the back quotes. These indicate that the command they contain should be run and the resulting standard output should be provided as an argument to the **kill -HUP** command. The -HUP flag of the **kill** command indicates that the process should reread its configuration but keep running.

Network Troubleshooting Utilities

The cause of network problems is inevitably linked to the user not being able to get to the information that he or she desires. If you suspect a network slowdown or failure, there are many tools at your disposal.

ping (Packet Internet Groper)

This utility has been around since the beginning of networking. The **ping** utility uses the Internet Control Message Protocol (ICMP) to contact a host on the network. A small amount of data is sent to a computer on a network to determine connectivity. If the packet is received, you will see an acknowledgement that tells you everything is in order. It is also used to test a network card to see if you have it configured properly.

To see if you have a network card configured properly, **ping** it by using the following code:

```
[root@mercury.technical root]# ping 127.0.0.1
```

This will **ping** the network card itself and will supply the following acknowledgement:

```
[root@mercury.technical root]# ping 127.0.0.1
PING 127.0.0.1 (127.0.0.1) FROM 127.0.0.1 : 56(84) bytes of data
Warning: time of day goes back, taking countermeasures
64 bytes from 127.0.0.1: icmp_seq=0 ttl=225 time=380 usec
64 bytes from 127.0.0.1: icmp_seq=1 ttl=225 time=143 usec
64 bytes from 127.0.0.1: icmp_seq=2 ttl=225 time=143 usec
64 bytes from 127.0.0.1: icmp_seq=3 ttl=225 time=141 usec
--- 127.0.0.1 ping statistics ---
4 packets transmitted, 4 packets received, 0% packet loss
Round trip min/max/mdev = 0.141/0.181/0.380/0.089 ms
[root@mercury.technical root]#
```

If you see anything other than 0 percent packet loss, you have a problem with the network card itself. When you use the **ping** utility to contact other computers on the network, you will see the same display as the previous example; however, a high packet loss number could indicate a problem with the cable, hub router, or switch that you happen to be connected to.

traceroute

traceroute is used to view the computers that your data packet encounters along the way. It is used as follows:

```
root@mercury.technical root]# traceroute 206.8.226.230
```

When using **traceroute**, the jump from server to server is calculated to a maximum of 30 jumps or hops. You can use this command to configure routers to make them more efficient.

telnet

telnet is used to configure computers remotely. This has been a hacker's tool of choice for a long time. If we try to telnet into the same machine as we did the **traceroute**, an interesting thing happens. The connection is refused. If it were not refused, we would be allowed access into their computer and would be able to access their shared files. You can configure your Linux machine to accept a **telnet** connection by specifying incoming telnet connections in the /etc/services folder.

SNMP

The Simple Network Management Protocol (SNMP) has become the de facto standard for network management. Because it is a simple solution, requiring little code to implement, vendors can easily build SNMP agents to their products. SNMP is extensible, enabling vendors to easily add network management functions to their existing products. SNMP also separates the management architecture from the architecture of the hardware devices, which broadens the base of multivendor support.

A network management system contains two primary elements: a manager and agents. The manager is the console through which the network administrator performs network management functions. Agents are the entities that interface to the actual device being managed. Bridges, hubs, routers, or network servers are examples of devices that agents can run on.

netstat

netstat is used to print network connections, routing tables, and interface statistics. All in all, it provides information about the Linux networking subsystem. The command **netstat -route** will display the kernel routing tables. This is very helpful when determining why a network is slow. If a file is taking the long road to your computer, it can be changed by the use of this command.

FTP

File Transfer Protocol (FTP) is the workhorse of the Web. When you download a file from the Web, it is often from an FTP site. FTP works faster than the other protocols and is therefore used for the back end of the Internet. When you are accessing a Web page, you are in effect asking to communicate with port 80 or the http port. FTP operates on port 21 by default. Almost any Web site has a back end that you can access by substituting ftp:// for http:// at the beginning of the Web address. In Linux, ftp in lowercase is the file transfer program that makes use of port 21 for downloads on the Net. More information about ftp can be found in the manual pages.

POP3

Post Office Protocol 3 (POP3) is the most-recent version of a standard protocol for receiving e-mail. POP3 is a client/server protocol in which e-mail is received and held for you by your Internet server. Periodically, you (or your client e-mail receiver) check your mailbox on the server and download any mail. POP3 is built into the Netmanage suite of Internet products and one of the most popular e-mail products, Eudora. It's also built into the Netscape and Microsoft Internet Explorer browsers.

Linux as an Intranet Server

You have probably heard a lot about intranets: Internal corporate networks that use Internet technology such as TCP/IP, Web browsers, and Internet-standard e-mail to share information and applications within an organization.

Many articles discussing intranets and the hardware and software used to deploy them depict intranets as expensive endeavors only suited to large corporations and organizations. This couldn't be further from the truth.

Even in small offices, an intranet can provide a convenient way to publish information to be read by all employees through a Web browser, and with a little ingenuity and some time, paperwork in your office can be eliminated by introducing Web-based forms for everything from leave requests to expense report submissions.

In addition, if you have small databases scattered across your organization, each used on a daily basis by different users, an intranet can provide a common means by which occasional users of the data can access the information contained in a database without needing full access to the database tools used to create, maintain, and update the data. By integrating the database with an intranet Web server, simple Web-based forms can be used to query the database.

Linux, which offers a wealth of powerful, flexible Web servers as well as fully functional relational database systems, can enable the creation of an intranet server without the cost involved in deploying Windows NT, a commercial database such as Oracle, and an expensive Web-database integration tool. There are even some free tools for Linux that make it relatively easy to produce intranet programs and applications that make use of your corporate databases.

Working with Files and Commands

Linux is one of the most flexible editing systems available. You can compare two files by using the **diff** command. The **df** command, which stands for disk free, reports how much free space is left on your hard drive by logical or physical drives. To list all the commands would be beyond the scope of this book. I suggest keeping a newer copy of O'Reilly's *Linux in a Nutshell* next to your computer for quick reference of almost any Linux command. All of the commands listed in this book can be found in your manual pages by typing **man <commandname>**.

Using cat to View a File

For displaying short ASCII files, the simplest command is **cat**, which stands for *concatenate*. The **cat** command takes a list of files (or a single file) and prints the contents unaltered on standard output, one file after another. Its primary purpose is to concatenate files (as in cat file1 file2>file3), but it works just as well to send contents of a short file to your screen.

If you try to display large files by using **cat**, the file scrolls past your screen as fast as the screen can handle the character stream. One way to stop the flow of data is to alternatively press CTRL-S and CTRL-Q to send start and stop messages to your screen, or you can use one of the page-at-a-time commands, **more** or **less**.

Using more to View a File

The **more** and **less** commands each display a screen of data at a time. Although they both do roughly the same thing, they do it differently. The **more** and **less** commands determine how many lines your terminal can display from the terminal database and from your TERM environment variable.

The **more** command is older than **less**, and it's derived from the Berkeley version of Unix. It proved so useful that, like the vi editor, it has become a standard. This section covers just the basics of the command.

The simplest form of the **more** command is

```
more filename
```

You see a screen of data from the file. If you want to go on to the next screen, press the SPACEBAR. If you press RETURN, only the next line is displayed. If you're looking through a series of files (with the command **more file1, file2**, and so on) and want to stop to edit one, you can do so with the **e** or **v** command. Pressing E within **more** invokes whatever editor you've defined in your EDIT shell environment variable on the current file. Pressing V uses whatever editor has been defined in the VISUAL variable. If you haven't defined these variables in your environment, **more** defaults to the ed editor for the **e** command and to the vi editor for the **v** command.

The **more** command has only one real drawback—you can't go backward in a file and redisplay a previous screen. However, you can go backward in a file with **less**.

Using less to View a File

One disadvantage to the **less** command is that you can't use an editor on a file being displayed. However, **less** makes up for the deficiency by enabling you to move forward and backward through a file.

The **less** command works almost the same way that **more** does. To page through a file, type the command

```
less filename
```

One screen of data is displayed. To advance to the next screen, press the SPACEBAR as you did with the **more** command.

To move backward in a file, press B . To go to a certain position expressed as a percentage of the file, press P and specify the percentage at the : prompt.

locate, grep, and tail

These are the most useful of all tools. **locate** uses the directory structure of Linux to find a file for you. The syntax is

```
[root@mercury.technical root]# locate [filename]
```

A wildcard * can be used to find multiple files with the same attributes.

```
[root@mercury.technical root]# locate *.conf
```

This will find all of the files that end with the extension "conf" and will show you the folder they are contained in. This is the fastest of all find commands.

The **tail** command has many useful features. It will print out the last ten lines of a file to any output that you specify. One interesting feature is the ability to monitor a file with the -**f** option. This will follow a file or keep listing data as the file is appended to. A common file to follow would be the /var/log/maillog folder in which **sendmail** keeps all of the details of sending and receiving mail. The syntax would be as follows:

```
[root@mercury.technical root]# cd /var/log
[root@mercury.technical log]# tail -f maillog
```

This will cause the last ten lines of the file to appear. As new lines are added, they will appear in the output until stopped with a CTRL-C.

The **grep** command is used to search for specific lines within a file. Most commonly used with the -**i** option, which ignores case, the **grep** syntax is as follows:

```
[root@mercury.technical log]# grep -i sendmail maillog
```

This will parse through the maillog file and display the output of only the lines that have **sendmail** in them. **grep** is a very powerful tool with many options. You can find out more about it in the manual file by entering

```
[root@mercury.technical log]# man grep
```

This will display the contents of the manual file and give you all of the option and the syntax that is available to **grep**. You can also use the **man** command to get information about **tail** and **locate**.

Solving File Problems

Most file problems come from a lack of permissions on the part of the user trying to view a file. Occasionally, a file will become corrupt. Checking the file with **fsck** while the file is not mounted should solve this problem. If many files are becoming corrupt at one time, the problem most likely centers on something other than the file itself.

Reviewing File Permissions

Setting permissions for a software package usually occurs automatically during installation. The installation script that comes with your application usually installs each file with the proper ownership and permissions. Only when something goes wrong and a user who should be able to access the program can't do so are you required to find the directory the application was copied to and check the permissions.

Typically, the executable file that you run to start the application is installed with permissions that let any user run the file; however, only the superuser can delete or overwrite it. The application usually is installed in a directory with read and execute permissions, but no write permissions.

Solving Problems

A well-written and well-supported application installs onto your system with minimal requests for information from you. It sets permissions properly so that all you have to do is test the program and inform your users—often through e-mail—that the application is now available. However, things can and do go wrong in the installation of programs and their subsequent operation. If, for whatever reason, the program doesn't complete the loading process or fails to operate correctly after installation, it's your responsibility to determine why and to fix the problem.

If a program doesn't install completely, your troubleshooting efforts often require no more than reading the documentation and README files supplied with the application and looking for a list of exceptions or problems and their solutions. However, no one expects you to possess expertise and familiarity with the scores of software packages available for Linux. Occasionally, you'll require outside help.

If you can't solve the problem by using the information that came with the package, you should try looking on the Usenet news to see whether there is any discussion of the package in question. A question posted in the appropriate Linux group on Usenet can solve a lot of problems. If you can't find help on the Net, you can try to contact the application developer, usually via e-mail. Remember, Linux is free, and so are most of the software packages that exist for Linux. Don't expect shrink-wrapped manuals and 24-hour technical support lines.

Version Conflicts

Occasionally, when upgrading a program or application, the newer version will not perform as desired. If you experience problems with diminished performance, the best remedy to the problem is to remove the offending package via the appropriate package manager and reinstall the old version. When installing packages for a particular application, you will see a dependency error. This is a file that is needed by the application but was not installed. This has been a problem with Red Hat package managers (RPMs). Debian has mastered the dependency problem by developing **apt-get**, which is a program that goes to the Debian Web site and retrieves the packages automatically.

Mounting Filesystems and Disks

Managing the Linux filesystem is one of the system administrator's most important tasks. You are responsible for ensuring that users have access to the files and data that they need and that these files and data remain uncorrupted and secure. Administering the filesystem includes tasks such as

- Making local and remote files available to users
- Monitoring and managing the system's (usually) finite disk resources
- Protecting against file corruption, hardware failures, and user errors via a well-planned backup schedule
- Ensuring data confidentiality by limiting file and system access
- Checking for and correcting filesystem corruption
- Connecting and configuring new storage devices

Some of these tasks, such as checking for and correcting filesystem corruption, are usually done automatically at boot time, once the initial setup is done. Others, like backups, are usually done manually on an as-needed basis. We looked at file ownership and protection in Chapter 5. This chapter describes how Linux handles disks and covers such topics as mounting and dismounting them, the filesystem configuration file, checking filesystem integrity, and restoring the filesystem.

Linux uses **mount** to attach a named filesystem (fsname) to the filesystem hierarchy at the pathname location. The directory must already exist. It becomes the name of the newly mounted root. If fsname is of the form

```
host:path
```

the filesystem type is assumed to be **nfs**.

The **unmount** command will unmount a currently mounted filesystem, which can be specified either as a directory mounted within a directory or a filesystem.

mount and **unmount** maintain a table of mounted filesystems in /etc/mtab. If invoked without an argument, **mount** displays the table. If invoked with only one fsname, **mount** searches the file /etc/fstab for an entry whose fsname field matches the given argument. For example, if the following line is in /etc/fstab

```
/dev/usr   usr   xfs   rw   0   0
```

then the commands **mount/usr** and **mount/dev/usr** are shorthand for **mount/dev/usr/usr**.

Restoring the Filesystem

Filesystems such as / and /usr contain operating system files that pose few problems when the backups are intended to restore the occasional accidentally deleted or otherwise lost file. When the file in question is an unmodified system file, you can usually restore it from the operating system installation media, provided you have it and that it is readable under normal system conditions. If either of these conditions is not the case, you should do a full backup of all system filesystems from time to time.

Files that you modify should be backed up regularly. When critical filesystem files need to be completely restored (usually due to hardware problems), some special considerations come into play. There are often two distinct approaches that can be taken:

- Reinstalling from the original operating system installation tapes or CDs and then restoring those files that you have modified. This approach may also involve reconfiguring some subsystems.

- Booting from alternate media and then restoring the filesystems from full backups that you have made.

Which alternative is preferable depends a lot on the characteristics of your particular system, such as how many files have been customized and how widely they are spread across the various filesystems, how much device and other reconfiguration needs to be redone (because all of its results do not reside in files), and similar considerations. If you have to restore multiple partitions, it is usually faster to reinstall the operating system from scratch, unless there is accessible but unbacked up data on a different partition on the same disk.

If you decide to take the first route, you will need to make reliable full backups of the system whenever it changes significantly. Because you are depending on them for a system restoration in an emergency, these backups should be verified or even made in duplicate.

The following is the general procedure for restoring a key filesystem from a backup:

1. Boot off alternate media: either an installation tape or CD, or a special bootable diskette or tape that you have made. At this point, you will be running off an in-memory filesystem (RAM disk) or one based on the boot medium.

2. Create device files for the disks, disk partitions, and/or tape drive that you will need to access if necessary. They may already have been provided for you if you used a system utility to create the bootable tape or diskette.

3. Prepare the hard disk as necessary. This may include formatting (rarely) or partitioning it.

4. Create a filesystem on the appropriate partition.

5. Mount the filesystem (/mnt is the conventional location). Change to the mountpoint.

6. Restore the files from the backup tape.

7. Change back to the root directory and unmount the restored filesystem.

8. Repeat the process for any additional filesystems and then reboot the system.

There is one additional point to consider when using this approach. The filesystem provided by emergency boot tapes or disks is very limited, and only a small subset of the normal system commands are available. You will need to verify that the restoration utility that you need is available after booting from alternate media. In other words, if, for example, the boot diskette provides only **cpio**, then the backup of the root filesystem shouldn't be a tar archive, or you will be in trouble.

LILO Error Messages

There are two places where you might see error messages when using LILO. One is when you type **lilo** and the other when you try to boot with LILO. Errors you receive after running the **lilo** command are fairly self-explanatory, but the LILO bootstrap error codes are very cryptic. The following should help you figure out what your problem is with the boot process:

- **(nothing)**   No part of LILO loaded.
- **L <error>**   LILO started but there is either a media failure or a disk geometry mismatch. The <error> is a two-digit error code.
  - **0x00**   Internal error: usually corrupt LILO install.
  - **0x02**   Address mark not found: media problem.
  - **0x04**   Sector not found: usually a disk geometry mismatch.
  - **0x07**   Invalid Initialization: BIOS failed, used BIOS overrides for LILO.
  - **0x0C**   Invalid media: media error.
  - **0x10**   CRC error: Media error; try rerunning the map installer.
  - **0x20**   Controller error.
  - **0x40**   Seek failure: may be a media problem.
  - **0x80**   Disk timeout: media is bad or the disk isn't spinning.
  - **0xBB**   BIOS error: first reboot; if the problem persists, remove the COMPACT option.
- **LI**   The second part of LILO loaded but could not execute. This is usually caused by a disk geometry mismatch. This can also mean that the /boot/boot.b file was moved and you did not run the map installer.
- **LIL**   The second part of LILO loaded, but the third did not. Again, this is typically caused by a media failure or a disk geometry mismatch.
- **LIL?**   The second stage of LILO loaded but at an incorrect address. This is usually caused by a subtle geometry mismatch or by moving the /boot/boot.b file without running the map installer.
- **LILO**   LILO loaded successfully.

You may also run into a problem if you have a Small Computer System Interface (SCSI) and an Integrated Device Electronic (IDE) hard drive. LILO will not know which drive to attempt to boot with. If the SCSI disk is normally the drive that your BIOS likes to boot from, then consider it the first disk. You need to override the BIOS options with the following lilo.conf BIOS options:

- BIOS = 0x80 for the first disk
- BIOS = 0x81 for the second disk

Choose the disk that the Linux root partition is installed on.

For disk geometry errors, try to use the linear option or specify the heads, cylinders, and sectors within the lilo.conf file.

Using the Boot Disk

There will come a time when you will not be able to boot your system. A system will usually not boot right after you have been editing a configuration file or tweaking lilo.conf.

Linux users, just like Unix users, pride themselves on the amount of time that their system has been up and running between restarts. If you have substantially changed any configuration files, it is fair to assume that there is a chance that your machine will not be able to boot up, and a restart of the system is in order. First, verify that your machine will boot next time you need it to and secondly, if it doesn't boot, you will have the changes that you have made fresh in your mind.

If your system fails to boot, you should have a boot disk handy along with a rescue disk. If you have installed a recent distribution of any popular Linux OS, you should have been asked if you wanted to make a boot disk. If for some reason you didn't, you can use the **mkbootdisk** command to create one.

Go to your /lib/modules directory and look at the kernels contained there. You should see something like 2.2.15-15 or 2.4.2-2. At the prompt, enter the following line:

```
[root@mercury.technical /root]# makedisk 2.4.2-2
```

After this prompt, you will see a warning that all the data on the disk will be lost and to press ENTER to continue or CTRL-C to abort. Insert a new disk and press ENTER. Linux will then format the disk and copy files needed to boot your system from the floppy. Occasionally, you will see an error message stating that the boot process cannot continue. A line in the message states

```
Kernel PanicL VFS: Unable to mount root fs on 00:30
```

This may seem a bit unsettling. The word "panic" is melodramatic. This situation can be fixed with a rescue disk. Your Linux disc should contain the image for a rescue disk.

On Red Hat 7.1, the image is located in /images/rescue.img on the CD-ROM. The easiest way to go about getting it is with the **cat** command, as follows:

```
cat /mnt/cdrom/images/rescue.img > /dev/fd0
```

The rescue disk created will contain a pared-down version of the root operating system, which has a skeleton selection of utilities to repair the system. If by chance you did not think ahead to a time that your system cannot boot and you are not able make a boot disk because your system is not booting, you can still make a boot disk. There is a DOS program in the /dosutils directory on a Red Hat disk that enables you to make a copy of both the boot disk and the rescue disk. To get into rescue mode, you first have to boot your system with the boot floppy. A prompt, type **rescue.** Your kernel will be loaded, and you will be prompted to enter your rescue disk. A RAM disk will be created at this point, and you will be at a system prompt. This is where you will have access to the **skeleton** command set. You will be able to mount and unmount filesystems, move and edit files, and more.

The biggest deterrent while working in the rescue environment is the lack of higher-level commands.

NOTE   If you make changes to files located on the partitions you have mounted from the rescue disk, you will need to use the sync command to manually flush the changes you have made to your hard disk.

Remember to unmount any filesystems before exiting. If you are like me, you are probably used to the system automatically mounting and unmounting filesystems!

Additional Information

More information can be found by accessing the info pages, man pages, and HOWTOs. Info pages can be accessed by typing **info [name of page desired]**. Entering **info man** at the command line will display an info page about the manual pages and give information on how to access them. A HOWTO is a short paper on how to do something. If you go to your favorite search engine and enter **HOWTO**, you will receive hits on everything from how to configure **ppp** to how to set up printing on your computer.

Chapter Summary

Many things can go wrong in a system. The most common hardware problem is a failed hard disk drive. Hardware problems, as noted in the beginning of the chapter, are easy to diagnose. Software problems are a little trickier.

We have recovered some ground here with **mount** and **umount**. We looked at LILO again and learned some new filesystem restoration tips. Learning where to look for a problem is the first step in being able to diagnose it. We learned to ask some of the questions that enable us to narrow down a problem. Because Linux is so configurable, your system will become almost an extension of yourself, so troubleshooting becomes a system-specific task. Presented here are some vendor-neutral, generic guides to helping you look in the right direction for problems on your system.

Questions

1. The **cat** command is short for what?
   a. Categorize
   b. Concatenate
   c. CTRL-C
   d. Configurator

2. System logs are generated by which daemon?
   a. syslogd
   b. pppd
   c. httpd
   d. varlogd

3. What is overclocking?
   a. Installing a faster system clock
   b. Configuring your Apache server to serve pages faster
   c. Configuring BIOS settings to run faster
   d. Upgrading to a new processor

4. Where is the table kept that **mount** and **unmount** use to keep track of mounted files?
   a. /etc/fsname
   b. /etc/mtab
   c. /etc/fstab
   d. /etc/mntconfig

5. What is the one thing that the **less** and **more** commands have in common?
   a. Both use the vi editor to display text.
   b. Both display text in a binary format.
   c. Both display text one screen at a time.
   d. Both use emacs to configure kernel modules.

6. What are the two types of logs installed by default in Linux?
   a. System logs
   b. Security logs
   c. Warning logs
   d. Application logs
   e. Event logs

7. A disk geometry mismatch would keep which program from loading?
   a. vi
   b. X Windows
   c. LILO
   d. vmlinuz

8. What are spontaneous problems also called?
   a. Random
   b. Intermittent
   c. Repeating
   d. Software

9. When troubleshooting a non-booting system, where is the first place you should check?
   a. Faulty motherboard
   b. Blank video card
   c. Dark monitor
   d. Loose power cable

10. Which utility would you use to check a filesystem for corruption?
   a. **mkfs**
   b. **LILO**
   c. **fsck**
   d. **syslog**

Answers

1. **B.** The **cat** command enables you to concatenate commands to define the focal point of your action.

2. **A.** syslogd is the daemon that is responsible for writing the logs. All daemons are characterized by the lowercase *d* at the end of the name.

3. **C.** When you overclock your computer, you set your BIOS to make your computer run faster than it is intended to.

4. **B.** The table that the **mount** and **unmount** commands use to keep track of the filesystem is kept in /etc/mtab.

5. **C.** The **less** and **more** commands both make text appear one screen at a time.

6. **A and D.** The system logs and application logs are the only logs by default if you do not include the installation log, which is not an answer to choose from.

7. **C.** If you have a disk geometry mismatch, LILO will not be able to find the record on the disk of where you installed Linux.

8. **A and B.** Spontaneous problems are also called random or intermittent problems.

9. **D.** Always start with the easiest procedure. Ensuring that a power cord is properly attached is easier than opening the case to test the internal power supply.

10. **C.** You would use the **fsck** command to check for filesystem corruption. (**fsck** stands for filesystem checker.)

Identify, Install, and Maintain System Hardware

This chapter covers the following competencies required to master the Linux+ certification exam:

- Configuring ATA hardware prior to installation
- Configuring SCSI and IEEE hardware prior to installation
- Configuring peripheral hardware prior to installation
- Identifying IRQs, DMAs, and I/O addresses for proper configuration
- Adding and removing field replaceable hardware components
- Understanding basic networking
- Troubleshooting ATA devices
- Troubleshooting SCSI devices
- Troubleshooting core system hardware

System Hardware

Modern PCs are the wonder of the modern world. They have been put in the position to support many of our human systems entirely. Today's computer is a spectacle on our desktops that we take for granted everyday. The individual components that fashion a computer are both simple and complex. The parts used to build the whole are constructed to be a system that is integrated into even bigger systems to provide us with our present-day networking and Internet services. In this chapter, we will give you some brief examples of components inside of a modern PC system, with visual references of each.

Power Supply

Needed to supply electrical power to every part of the PC, the power supply is very important while being the least noticed. Basically, the power supply needs to change the 110v AC wall current into the 3.3v, 5v, and 12v power that the system needs for operation.

Notice the power switch attached to the power supply in Figure 7-1. This is an example of an older AT-style power supply. The newest power supply available that is compatible with Linux is the ATX style. The power supply, while seemingly innocent, can be a common source of intermittent problems.

Motherboard

The motherboard maintains everything in the system; it is the PC. Everything in the working system connects to the motherboard. In Figure 7-2, we see the motherboard of

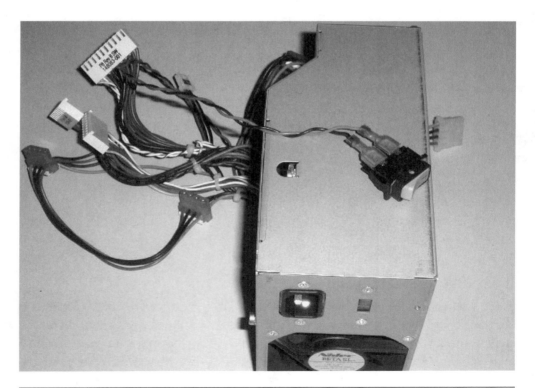

Figure 7-1   Basic AT power supply

Figure 7-2   A proprietary motherboard from a Compaq system

a proprietary system. We know that it is proprietary because of the shape. Industry-standard motherboards must conform to a form or predetermined structure.

Usually contained in the motherboard are the following:

- Bus slots
- Memory Single Inline Memory Module (SIMM) or Dual Inline Memory Module (DIMM) sockets
- Motherboard chipset
- Processor voltage regulators
- Level 2 (L2) cache, usually found in today's CPUs
- Read-Only Memory Basic Input/Output System (ROM BIOS)
- Clock/Complementary Metal Oxide Semiconductor (CMOS) battery
- Super I/O chip
- Processor socket

Containing all the primary circuitry, the chipset is the motherboard. It controls L2 cache and main memory, the CPU or processor bus, the Industry Standard Architecture (ISA) bus, and the Peripheral Component Interconnect (PCI) bus. The chipset dictates the primary features and specifications of the motherboard; it represents the chassis to which the processor of your system is installed.

More modern systems include the L2 cache inside the processor (Pentium Celeron/II/III class), not on the motherboard. Therefore, in the best and newest designs, the L2 cache is part of the processor die, not a separate chip in the processor module. This is how the industry is able to attain higher processor speeds by making the L2 cache faster and faster.

The chipset performs a significant job by shaping the features a system can support. Among the most important of these features are the type of memory that can be installed, how much memory can be installed, which processors you can use, and which type of system buses your system can support. The ROM BIOS contains a system setup program (CMOS setup) for configuring the system, drivers for items that are built into the board of the BIOS code, and the bootstrap loader that loads the operating system CD-ROM.

Optical Drives

DVD drives are removable media optical drives of high capacity and can only read information. Hence, data cannot be altered or rewritten on the discs. The more expensive versions are available to be rewritten but are not included as standard in most PCs. CD-ROMs have become the mainstream standard of storage for removable media because they can hold a great deal of information and are inexpensive. Figure 7-3 shows a CD-ROM drive out of the case.

Processor

Modern processors contain millions of transistors etched into a tiny piece of silicon called a *die*. This tiny but powerful piece of silicon is seen as the engine of a computer. It is the single most important chip, used as the primary circuit that carries out any software's program instructions. As tiny as it is, the processor is the single most expensive part of any computer. The processor may cost as much as two to ten times more than the motherboard of its system. Figure 7-4 shows two Intel Pentium processors. Notice the heatsink attached to the processor on the right. Processors must be kept cool by some means. If they aren't, they will overheat and fail.

Figure 7-3 A CD-ROM drive out of the case

Figure 7-4 Two early Intel Pentium processors

Monitors

Monitors are grouped, most generally, three ways: diagonally in inches, by the resolution in pixels, and by the refresh rate in hertz (Hz). Built into low-cost PCs and portable units, monitors can also be housed in separate and protective cases. Usually ranging from 14 to 21 inches as desktop monitors and 11 to 19 inches as Liquid Crystal Displays (LCDs), monitors are usually smaller than the size advertised. The resolution ranges from 640 × 480 pixels to 1600 × 1200 pixels (horizontal then vertical). Made up of a combination of dots, each pixel uses red, green, and blue colors. The display of the screen is redrawn from the contents of the video adaptive memory on an average of 60 Hz or 60 times per second. Higher-quality monitors refresh at 100 Hz. Tied to the functioning of the system video adapter, the monitor controls the resolution and refresh rates (with the exception of portable LCD screens).

Keyboard

In order to interact with the control system, a keyboard must accompany the PC. Available in many sizes, layouts, and languages, keyboards display several characteristics and functions. The PC was created by IBM and initially used the detached keyboard, enabling the freedom to choose the keyboard that best suits the user's needs. Prior to this innovation of IBM, the keyboard was usually attached to the system with limited versatility. It is now possible for you to connect the keyboard of your choice to the PC, making your system as versatile as you desire. Some of the new ergonomic designs "split" the keyboard, giving you a different posture and potentially reducing repetitive stress injuries. In Figure 7-5, we see a plain old vanilla-flavored keyboard.

Hard Disk Drive

The primary storage facility for a system is the hard disk. Spinning platters of aluminum or ceramic, coated with a magnetic medium, hard disk drives contain all the programs and data that are currently active in the main memory. Most desktop systems use drives with 3 1/2-inch platters, although laptops and notebooks use the smaller size of 2 1/2-inch platter drivers for obvious space-saving reasons. Figure 7-6 shows two hard drives, one Small Computer Systems Interface (SCSI) and one Integrated Development Environment (IDE). See if you can tell the difference. We will get to that later in the chapter.

Memory (RAM)

Random access memory (RAM) is the primary memory, holding the data that the processor is using at a given time. Everything in RAM is emptied when the computer is

Figure 7-5 A common keyboard

Figure 7-6 IDE and SCSI hard drives

turned off because RAM requires power to maintain storage. In order for the processor to run, the memory must be reloaded each time the user turns on the PC.

ROM is the system's memory that is not erased each time the user turns off the PC. The ROM contains information to enable the system to reload or "boot" programs from one of the disk drives to the main RAM memory in order for the PC to perform normal operations and work. If the PC has more memory capacity, the system can perform more programs simultaneously.

In Figure 7-7, three types of memory are shown: (from the top) 168 pin DIMM, 72 pin SIMM, and 30 pin SIMM. The age increases from top to bottom also, with the 30 pin SIMM being the oldest.

Historically, memory has been equal to or greater than the cost of the motherboard. The memory purchased and installed for a system is in either SIMM or DIMM, with the newest style of memory being Rambus Inline Memory Module (RIMM). The significant reduction in prices for purchasing memory has enabled users the ability to upgrade systems and increase their PC speed and productivity.

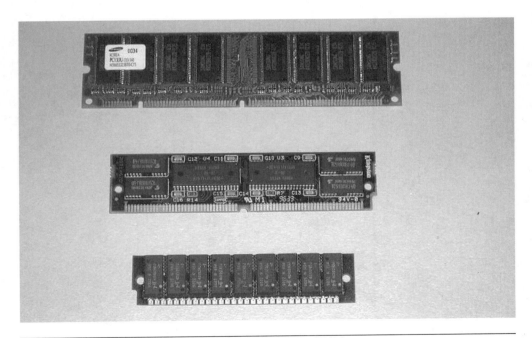

Figure 7-7   168-pin DIMM, 72-pin SIMM, and 30-pin SIMM memory

Video Card

Controlling the information that is shown on the monitor, the video card has four basic parts: a video chip, video RAM, a Digital to Analog Converter (DAC) and a BIOS. As it writes data to the video RAM, the video chip controls the information on the screen. In order to drive the monitor, the DAC reads the video RAM and changes the digital data into the analog signals. Holding the primary video driver, the BIOS enables the display to function during boot time and in basic console mode in Linux. To enable advanced video modes for a Linux GUI, more enhanced drivers are then usually loaded from the hard drive.

Video cards come in three forms that will plug into the busses on a motherboard: ISA, PCI, and Accelerated Graphics Port (AGP). AGP is a special high-speed bus only for video cards. Shown from left to right in Figure 7-8 are two examples of video cards, with the card on the left being the older ISA style. The card on the right is a PCI card and is a little newer.

Figure 7-8   Older ISA- and PCI-style cards

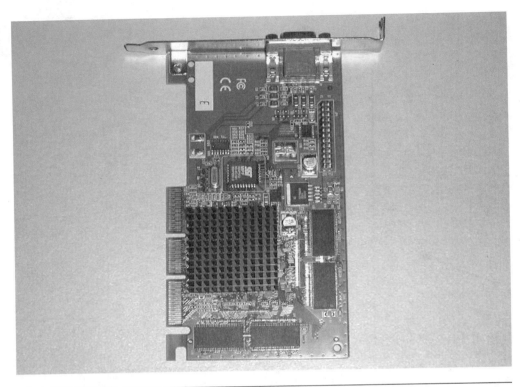

Figure 7-9   A Nvidia 32-MB AGP video card

Figure 7-9 is an example of a new AGP video card with 32MB of RAM. With Red Hat v7.1, sophisticated drivers have been developed to take advantage of these new, high-memory cards.

Case (Chassis)

Containing the motherboard, power supply, disk drives, adapter cards, and other components of the system, the case is available in various sizes to adapt to users' needs. Small and thin versions sit horizontally on desktops (see Figure 7-10), while towers stand vertically on the floor (see Figure 7-11). Others are prepared to be used industrially and are rack-mounted, which is usually how you will find servers mounted.

Some cases are available with features that enable users to add or eliminate components easily. Among these are removable cages or brackets that allow easy access to disk drives, side panels or trays to allow easy motherboard access, and screwless designs that

Figure 7-10 A common desktop computer

require no tools to disassemble. Heavy-duty systems have air filters to ensure the interior will remain clean, or extra fans for cooling. Bare cases and power supplies can be purchased separately.

Mouse

First called a pointing device, the mouse has become an innovative piece of equipment that enables users to point at or select items shown on a screen, and operating systems running a GUI require a mouse. The standard mouse device today has two buttons: one for selecting items under a pointer on the screen and another for activating menus. Other devices have become common, such as the trackball and a mouse that uses a laser to "see" optically and track the pointer across the screen. The pointer is moved

Figure 7-11 A tower design case

across the screen as the mouse is simultaneously moved across a desk or tabletop. This enables the user to more easily select or manipulate items on a screen, rather than using a keyboard alone. Figure 7-12 shows a wheel mouse, which uses the center wheel to scroll through applications and Web browser screens.

Floppy Disk Drive

The floppy drive is not as important as it once was. Floppy disks were once used as the primary software distribution and system backup solution for the PC. Now with the availability of CD-ROM discs, users do not require floppies for installing or loading new software in a system. Every PC made within the last ten years has been made with a 3 1/2-inch, 1.44MB capacity floppy drive, except for the Apple iMac. Advancements in

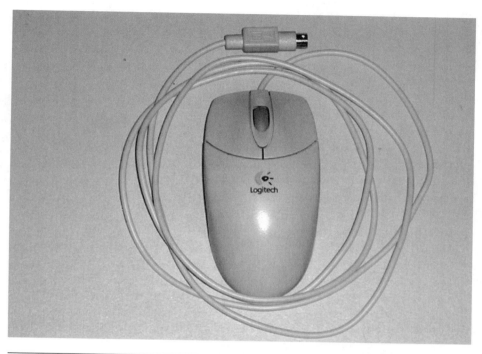

Figure 7-12   A PS2-style Logitech wheel mouse

technology have created new types of floppy drives with up to 120MB or more of storage, enabling temporary backups or files to be moved from system to system. Apple traded in the floppy for a 100MB Zip drive. Figure 7-13 shows a floppy disk drive removed from the case.

Hard Disk Drives

The two main hard drive technologies available today are SCSI and Enhanced Integrated Drive Electronics (EIDE). One of the biggest debates concerning hard disks is the one that exists between the proponents of these two systems. Each technology has its advantages and disadvantages. All modern x86 motherboards include IDE controllers, while SCSI drive controllers are a different story. One must normally purchase a separate SCSI host adapter or a motherboard at an inflated price that has a SCSI chip built-in.

Figure 7-13 A floppy disk drive

EIDE Controllers

It's important to use a motherboard that supports the fastest form of the IDE possible because the IDE controllers are built-in to all motherboards. The interface that you are most likely to see in new motherboards is either the 66 MBps or 100 MBps variants. These variants can be referred to in various ways. The 66 MBps EIDE interface can be referred to as ATA/66, Ultra-66, or Ultra DMA 66. The same goes for the 100 MBps variant, only substitute 100 for 66.

The History of EIDE

The predecessor to EIDE was IDE. EIDE is, as the name implies, an enhancement to IDE, just as IDE was a successor to older hard disk technologies. On older computers, the hard drive connected to a separate controller board. Little electronic circuitry on the older hard disks drives was used in conjunction with these interface boards. The IDE form integrated these two components into one. In Figure 7-14, you can see the electronics on three separate EIDE hard drives. To the motherboard, an IDE drive looks just like a controller card and drive.

Plain IDE drives were quite common in the mid-1990s. Programmed input/output (PIO) was the control method of the day. The computer's CPU had to fetch every byte that was transferred to or from the hard disk. Linux and PIO mode did not agree with

Figure 7-14   Three drives and their control circuits

each other because PIO mode requires a great deal of CPU time and does not interact well with complex multitasking operating systems such as Linux.

Direct Memory Access (DMA) grew from PIO mode. DMA controllers have the capability to transfer data to and from memory directly without using the CPU. This improves overall system performance and greatly reduces the CPU load when accessing disks on multitasking operating systems.

Today's motherboards are capable of operating in both PIO and DMA. Access methods are different for each chipset when operating in DMA mode, but CIO modes can be used with more standardized interface methods. To get the most out of an EIDE controller, you'll need a customized Linux driver.

CAUTION   Experimental drivers are potentially unstable, which means you might lose data if you tend to use them. Some of these drivers are nonetheless quite reliable and you should exercise caution when using them.

Characteristics of EIDE Disks

Little dissimilarity exists between EIDE and SCSI disks. The technology behind modern hard disks is so similar that the only thing different is the interface. EIDE disks do have certain characteristics or leased tendencies (see Figure 7-15):

- **Low cost**   EIDE hard disks cost less and achieve almost the same speed as SCSI disks of the same capacity.

- **Performance**   One of the reasons the IDE hard disks cost less is because of their higher seek times and they don't spin at quite as high a rate. This has more to do with disk manufacturers wanting to sell SCSI drives over EIDE drives.

- **CHS/LBA modes**   CHS stands for Cylinder/Head/Sector. It describes how a hard drive is broken down in to addressable sections. The CHS addressing is a holdover from when hard disks had almost no electronics. The IDE drives now have the LBA (Logical Block Addressing) mode, which is identified by a single number equal to a sector on the hard disk.

- **Device limit**   There's a two-device limit on each EIDE chain. Motherboards today include only two EIDE ports, so that motherboards can support only four EIDE devices total. If you have extra drives on your system, this can be a very restricting limitation to expansion on your computer.

- **Concurrent communication**   A data transfer can take place from only one disk at a time; whichever disk is transferring data owns the bus. Another disk on the same port will have to wait until the port is free to transfer data.

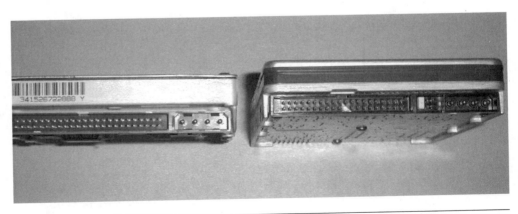

Figure 7-15   The disk on the right is identifiable as an EIDE disk by the white jumper next to the interface pins. The SCSI drive has 50 pins, as compared to the IDE drive's 40 pins.

- **Resource consumption** Each EIDE chain requires the use of one interrupt. These resources are very limited as your computer only has a limited amount of interrupts. The use of one Interrupt Request Line (IRQ) for two devices can be a very serious problem if you plan to have more devices attached to your motherboard.

Characteristics of SCSI Disks

SCSI has always been the choice for high-speed hard disk operations. SCSI hard disk characteristics complement EIDE characteristics:

- **High cost** EIDE drives are typically less expensive than SCSI drives of the same capacity. This is due in part to the SCSI interface, economic factors, and some of it relates to drive performance.

- **Performance** SCSI hard disks do have larger caches, faster rotation rates, and lower seek times than EIDE drives of the same capacity, however.

- **High command latency** SCSI drives are also a bit slower to respond to commands than EIDE drives. This is due to SCSI protocols imposing greater overhead on commands than EIDE protocols.

- **High capacity** You can obtain EIDE drives as large as most SCSI drives sold; however, a few SCSI models exceed the capacity of the highest-capacity EIDE models.

- **LBA mode only** Another drawback may be that x86 operating systems have traditionally used CHS addressing, so SCSI host adapters have to translate LBA to CHS mode. SCSI disks have always communicated with their host adapters by presenting a view of the disk using a single linear block of addresses. This greatly simplifies matters for the computer if the computer understands this view of things. Some may not, as in the case of the x86 operating systems.

At least as important as the differences between the EIDE and SCSI hard disks are the differences between the two types of busses. The characteristics of the SCSI bus that set it apart from the EIDE bus include

- **The 7- to 15-device limit** You should be able to attach up to 7 or 15 devices to each SCSI host adapter, depending on the SCSI variant in use. (Wide SCSI variants support up to 15 devices, whereas narrow varieties support only 7.) In practice, however, cable length limits make it difficult to add more than five or six devices to a narrow chain. Each SCSI device has a unique ID number, which is set by a jumper. Figure 7-16 shows a typical SCSI setting switch. Newer SCSI variants can assign IDs by the host adapter.

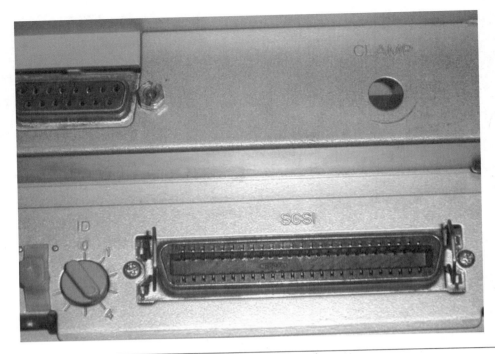

Figure 7-16   A SCSI selector switch on a SCSI-based scanner

- **Device reuse**   Because the limit on SCSI devices is much higher than that of EIDE devices, it is more practical to add hard disks to a SCSI system. This may mean your initial investment in hard drives can last longer.

- **Concurrent communication**   SCSI was designed from the beginning to support concurrent communication. You can begin a transfer with one SCSI device and then start another simultaneously with a device on the same chain. Both transfers will proceed at full speed, provided the sum of the speeds of the individual devices does not equal more than the speed of the original bus. This factor alone gives SCSI a huge advantage if you need a high-performance disk system.

- **Resource consumption**   Each SCSI host adapter requires one IRQ, as does each EIDE controller. Because you can attach so many more SCSI devices to a chain, those devices tend to consume fewer IRQs.

- **Termination**   A SCSI bus consists of several SCSI devices strung in a line, including a host adapter. A jumper or special terminating resistor pack must be set to the SCSI cable in order to appropriately terminate the device on each end of the line.

Figure 7-17   A SCSI cable capable of supporting four devices with a terminator on one end

The host adapter will terminate one end and the ribbon cable will usually have a terminator on the other end, as shown in Figure 7-17. If this is not done, termination problems can account for many of the difficulties that arise with SCSI devices.

• **Driver issues**   Unlike EIDE, SCSI controllers don't operate as clones of the early PC hard disk interfaces. No fallback compatibility mode is available on any SCSI host you may choose, as there is with an EIDE. Therefore, Linux needs specialized drivers for any SCSI host.

If cost is no object, SCSI is the bus of choice for hard disks. However, using SCSI rather than EIDE can add somewhere between $100 to $500 to the cost of a PC, depending on the size of the hard disk, number of devices, and so on. You get more performance for your money with SCSI, but the expense may be prohibitive for low-end or mid-range systems. A recommendation for the use of SCSI is to have SCSI on systems that require several disk-like devices, such as tape backup units, Compact Disc-Recordable (CD-R) drives, zip drives, and so on. These devices, in conjunction with a CD-ROM drive and a single hard disk, require three IRQs and an add-on EIDE controller if bought in EIDE form. In SCSI form, all five devices can be attached to a single host adapter and consume a single IRQ. It is important to point out that the latest SCSI host adapters work best with the latest disk devices when only other high-speed SCSI devices are in use. It may be helpful to have two SCSI host adapters in such systems.

Using EIDE and SCSI in a Single System

SCSI devices are more varied than EIDE devices in that SCSI hard disks are identified much like an EIDE hard disk, except that the device filename takes the form of /dev/sdxy. SCSI CD-ROM device filenames take the form /dev/scdx, where *x* is a number from 0 up. EIDE devices, on the other hand, are accessed as /dev/hdxy, where *x* is a letter (a,b,c . . .) and *y* is a partition number for hard disk partitions or is not there at all for devices such as CD-ROM drives that don't have partitions. In Linux, you access raw devices through these entries in the /dev directory.

It is not difficult to work with a system using both SCSI and EIDE devices under Linux if you use the appropriate device identifiers when you mount the devices. The /etc/fstab file usually contains these identifiers for the most commonly used partitions and devices. An example with a SCSI hard disk and an EIDE CD-ROM drive with the file name /etc/fstab might contain the following entries:

```
/dev/sda6 / ext2 defaults 1 1
/dev/sda5 /home ext2 defaults 1 2
/dev/had /mnt/cdrom iso9660 ro,user,noauto 0 0
```

These entries specify that two SCSI disk partitions (/dev/sda6 and /dev/sda5) will be mounted as / and /home, respectively. The EIDE CD-ROM drive, /dev/had, is mounted as /mnt/cdrom.

Most computers' BIOSs are configured to boot from EIDE devices before SCSI devices. However, you can mix both EIDE and SCSI hard disks if you install LILO (Linux Loader) on the EIDE disk and leave the boot order intact. On most systems, you can still install Linux on the SCSI disk, even when the system begins its boot process and loads LILO from the EIDE disk. If you do change the BIOS boot order, you may need to modify your /etc/lilo.conf file to reflect this fact by using lines such as the following:

```
dis=/dev/sda
  bios-0x80
```

 NOTE   These commands will inform LILO that the BIOS treats /dev/sda as the first disk (code 0x80). Without this command, you probably won't be able to boot Linux using LILO should your BIOS boot from SCSI disks before EIDE disks.

The 1024-Cylinder Limit

Both EIDE and SCSI disks suffer from what's known as the *1024-cylinder limit*. The difficulty arises from the old CHS addressing mode using a 10-bit number to identify the cylinder number of a hard disk. A 10-bit number can hold a value between 0 and 1023, limiting the number of cylinders accessible by the BIOS to 1024. Assorted systems have been developed to get around the problem, however. Many OSs, including Linux, aren't bothered by the 1024-cylinder limit once they have been booted. The problems arise while actually booting because the ancient x86 BIOS is bothered by the 1024-cylinder limit. Given the limits on the number of sectors and heads, the 1024-cylinder limit works out a bit under 8GB with modern hard disks. Earlier BIOSes lacked the features to raise the limit that high, and it could be as low as 504MB on these drives.

It therefore becomes necessary to put the Linux kernel below the limit in order for Linux to boot, regardless of the exact value of the 1024-cylinder limit. The BIOS loads the kernel (under direction from LILO). Once the kernel has been loaded, it can use its own disk drivers, which, as mentioned before, aren't bothered by the 1024-cylinder limit, to continue booting the OS.

Also, as mentioned previously, two good ways around the 1024-cylinder limit are to either create a small /boot partition that falls below the limit and then place the Linux kernel in that directory, or to use a floppy disk for booting purposes. Putting the Linux kernel along with a copy of LOADLIN.EXE on a DOS boot floppy or writing the kernel to the floppy without a filesystem by using a Linux **dd** command will accomplish the latter. You can then boot Linux without using the hard disk to load the Linux kernel.

Evaluating Disk Performance

When shopping for a hard disk, several different measures of performance are important. The three most essential are the disk head seek time, the data transfer rates, and the disk's cache size. The three differ in priority according to how the drive is used. If you frequently access several files, possibly on different partitions, such as when several users read and write multiple files simultaneously, the seek time should be the first consideration. It is most pertinent for multitasking OSs than for single-tasking OSs. The transfer rate becomes more prominent when you routinely read a single, large file straight through, such as a large audio or video file.

Disk Seek Times

The interior of a hard disk is built from one or more circular disk platters on which data are stored. These platters spin at high speeds, and the disk heads ride over and between the platters on arms that can pivot. The arms then bring the heads over any point on the data storage surface. The time it takes to move the head is what we refer to as the *seek time*. The seek time can be measured in several ways, including the time to seek from the center to the outer edge, the time to seek to the midway point, and so forth. The seek time measurement you will most often see is the average time taken to move the head from one location to a randomly selected second location. Statistically, that usually equals the time it takes to seek one-third of the head's range.

Latency is the time it takes the desired sector to come up under the read/write head after the seek is complete. That time averages out to about half the time it takes for the rotation of the disk platter. Both the seek time and latency together are known as the *access time*.

All of these times are measured in milliseconds (ms). Hard disks today have seek times of 5 ms to 10 ms and spin between 5,400 and 10,000 revolutions per minute (rpm) for average latencies of 3 ms to 6 ms. In all three time measurements, the smaller the numbers, the better. You may find one vendor advertising seek times while another promotes access times, but these values are not directly comparable. You need to know the spin rate of the two drives so that you can convert one to the other easily in order to do a comparison.

Disk Transfer Rates

The next consideration in comparing hard disks is how quickly the disk can transfer data to and from the computer, or, in other words, the *disk transfer rates*. Because different data transfer at different rates, the following information is helpful in understanding the term *rates*:

- The disk spins at the same rate no matter which cylinder is being read, but modern hard drive designs place more sectors along outer cylinders than along inner ones. The data read from the outer cylinders therefore transfer faster than the data from the inner cylinder. The internal data transfer rate is variable.

- Also, the data transfer rate from the platters may differ from the data transfer rate between the hard disk and the computer. The data density and the speed with which the platter spins determine the transfer rates from the platters. The transfer rate between the hard disk and the computer is determined by the computer's interface type, such as 66 MBps for an Ultra-66 interface.

The rate of information transfer from the disk platters to the drive electronics, the *internal transfer rate*, is much more important than the external rates. However, hard disk manufacturers may try to confuse you by trying to emphasize the external rates.

To make matters even worse, manufacturers often quote internal data transfer rates in megabits per second (Mbps), but external rates in megabytes per second (MBps). Although the difference in the abbreviations for these terms differs only slightly, the actual difference is a factor-of-eight value. For instance, if an internal rate is reported as 240 Mbps and the external as 66 MBps, it is easy to become confused and believe that the external rate is the bottleneck. In reality, if the internal rate were reported in MBps, it would only equal 30 MBps in such a case.

Troubleshooting Hard Drives

Learning to identify and troubleshoot an ATA (AT Attachment) device, particularly a hard drive, can be quite an undertaking. The most-common sign of an imminent failure associated with hard drives is noise. Common to drives starting to fail is a high-pitched whine that does not quit. This may be accompanied by bumping or banging noises coming from the drive itself. These are impending signs of doom that are telling you to back up your data and get a new drive installed. The worst sign is the black screen telling you "no operating system found."

If you are faced with a machine making noise or giving you a black screen, the first thing you should do is confirm that it is the hard drive. This can be done by removing the case cover, listening to your computer running, and by touching the hard drive itself.

 ALERT   This should be done with the utmost care. If you are not comfortable working around live electronics, you should leave this part to a qualified technician.

When the case cover is removed, the whining sound should get louder. You should be able to physically feel the drive vibrate or thump.

A non-booting hard drive is a different story altogether. A series of steps should be followed when troubleshooting a non-booting disk:

1. The first step in troubleshooting is to think. Think about any changes made to the system and the last thing that was done on your computer. This may account for its behavior. Be sure to take into account any physical movements of the system itself, lightning storms, or changes made to configuration files. If you find that this is the case, try reversing the changes made and restart the system.

2. Make sure a disk is not in the floppy drive. If there is, take it out and reboot. This may clear up the problem. If not, move to step 3.

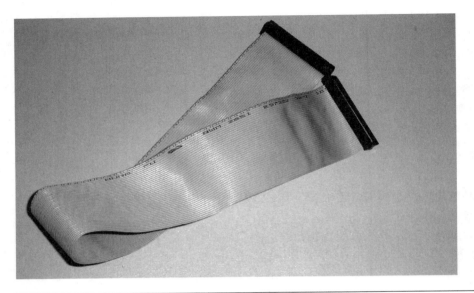

Figure 7-18 IDE ribbon cable

3. Shut down your computer and remove the cover. Check the cabling for any loose connections or severely pinched ribbon cabling. See Figure 7-18 for an example of a ribbon cable.

4. If a cable is loose, try restarting the system. If it starts with no problem, then you know what to watch out for. If the system still does not respond as you think it should, move on to step 5.

5. Every major manufacturer has diagnostic tools available on their site. Go to the manufacturer's Web site on another computer and download a copy that corresponds to your hard drive. The diagnostic software will usually fit on a disk and boot your system into their diagnostic routine. The program will tell you whether the drive is bad.

6. If you have recently installed a new hard drive, you may have configured it wrong. Look at the directions and configure it again. If you still have trouble, the manufacturer will have a number that you can call to have someone help you with installation.

Configuring an ATA system for a single hard drive is a relatively easy task. ATA-style hard drives have jumpers (as shown in Figure 7-19) for configuring up to two drives per IDE port, which is where the hard drive plugs in to the motherboard. If you look closely

Figure 7-19 A jumper on an IDE drive

at Figure 7-19, you can see the positions for Master (MA) and Slave (SL). ATA-style hard drives have three configuration selections available:

- **Single disk on system** Used when running only one disk
- **Master** Used to identify the lead disk on an IDE port when two disks are present on the system
- **Slave** Used to indicate the second disk of two on a system

If the disks are not jumpered correctly, the system will not boot. Disks are very finicky about the order in which they are tethered to the system. The two top problems in diagnosing a non-booting disk are faulty or loose cables and jumpers not being configured correctly.

SCSI Devices

Troubleshooting a SCSI device involves more steps than troubleshooting an ATA device. As with all SCSI devices, a SCSI hard drive relies on a setting called a *SCSI ID number*. This number uniquely identifies the drive to the system. The hard drive should be a low number because it should be one of the first devices involved in the startup of the system. If the ID of the hard drive is set to the same number as another device, the hard drive will not boot.

SCSI drives present some of the same problems as with troubleshooting IDE drives, and you can follow the same troubleshooting guide as with ATA drives. One of the main differences in the interfaces between SCSI and IDE is the width of the cable. A SCSI cable is wider (the connecting end has 50 pins instead of 40 pins), and it will most likely have more than three connectors on it. In Figure 7-20, we see the difference between IDE and SCSI cables and their ends.

The Power-On Self-Test (POST)

In 1981, safety features were integrated into PCs that had not been previously employed. The Power-On Self-Test (POST) and parity-checked memory were among

Figure 7-20   The physical differences between IDE and SCSI cables

the most widely used. Although parity-checked memory is being used less frequently in present-day systems, POST is automatically run when the user initially turns on the system. This way, POST can check all the main system components at one time. This may cause a delay when the system is turned on because the computer hardware is being tested before the user can execute commands or open programs.

What is tested? The purpose of these tests being run on the system is to check various integral parts of the computer, such as motherboard circuitry, CPU, ROM, memory, and important peripherals. Errors are detected and the user may note these as they are detected, although the POST system check is not as complete as other disk-based diagnostics.

Even though it is not as complete as other tests, the POST check is the primary check when looking for problems with the motherboard. Sometimes it is necessary to halt the system and create an error message when a problem has occurred. These kinds of POST-checked errors are considered fatal because you cannot boot the system when they occur. Three types of messages can be seen following a POST check:

- Hexadecimal numeric codes sent to an I/O port address
- Onscreen text messages
- Audio codes

POST audio error codes incorporate a series of audible beeps. A component that is not working properly can be noted as a POST audio error code. As soon as the system is booted up, you should hear a beep or a series of short and long beeps. Usually, the codes specific to your motherboard and BIOS will alert you to the specific audio codes for your system. You can get this information from the BIOS manufacturer.

POST visual error code systems display a variety of messages as the result of checks to the system. You will know approximately where in the system the error is located because the POST memory stops just before the expected total is tested. The number displayed can help locate the faulty module and it proves very important when troubleshooting. An error detected onscreen might be an error that was found during POST procedures. These are generally shown as numeric codes several digits long. `1980 Disk 1 Error` is one example of the way an error might look. Check your motherboard or system BIOS for information concerning these errors. Web sites also contain this type of information.

I/O Port POST Codes

The BIOS conveys test codes to a special I/O port address. These ports are only read by a special adapter card and are utilized at the beginning of each POST. The special adapter card is plugged into one of the system slots. Initially used by system manufacturers for burn-in testing of the motherboard, they eliminate the need for video display adapters. Technicians can access these cards through these marketing companies: Trinitech, Ultr-X, Data Depot, JDR Microdevices, and Micro 2000.

During the POST, you will see two-digit hexadecimal numbers flash on the display of the card. You will be able to note the test in progress when the system inadvertently stops and then note the faulty component. As part of the ISA or EISA bus, these POST cards fit into the 8-bit ISA connector. Most PCI-based motherboards have these ISA connectors and are usable. Eventually, PCs will not have ISA slots and an ISA POST card will not work. Some advanced troubleshooting cards have an ISA and PCI connector on the same board (such as Post Probe from Micro2000) and include a MicroChannel bus adapter. Some systems provide slot adapters that enable their existing ISA cards to work in MCA bus systems. It is recommended that users find POST cards that will work in PCI slots. As PCI-only systems become available, this will happen more frequently. ForeFront Direct has a POSTPlus card, which is ISA/PCI.

Diagnostic Software

Diagnostic functions are incorporated into the PC hardware or into peripheral attributes of the system. Separate software items or system utilities are also used. Troubleshooting your PC can be easier when assisted by software. POST is operable anytime the PC power is on.

Most Linux distributions include operating system diagnostics software for the command-line and X Window System. Manufacturer-supplied diagnostics software from IBM, Compaq, Hewlett-Packard, or Dell incorporates software specifically for their systems. Sometimes users may automatically download this software from a manufacturer's Web site or they may purchase the item through a retailer. Aftermarket packages may be accessible through limited use, or others may employ accessibility on the hard drive through installed software. This way, major companies could make sure that diagnostics software is accessible and usable by the consumer.

Aftermarket diagnostics software is software considered for general usage and may be bundled with other maintenance and repair software. These types of software are free to the user through distribution CDs or the Internet and are most likely written for DOS or Windows.

Peripheral diagnostic software is made to test certain system functions. You can use a keystroke at boot time to access functions in the card's BIOS for host adapters such as

Adaptec SCSI. Some adapters that are network adapters function specifically with their own device driver. Sometimes integrated with the device driver is a diagnostic program or disk.

Networking

A *network* is a group of two or more computer systems that have been linked together by some kind of physical communications medium. What makes a network function is not merely the physical connections, but it is a collection of rules and regulations about how the computers can communicate. These rules are called *protocols*, which are fixed, formalized standards that specify how two dissimilar network components can establish communication. How a network functions depends on how the protocols interact. As we learned in Chapters 1 and 2, TCP/IP is the *de facto* protocol standard for how networks communicate.

Local Area Networks (LANs)

A *local area network* (LAN) is defined as a set of computers connected in series within a building or other defined space. A LAN is defined by its topology or how it is connected. Three main types of LANs exist:

- **Star** This is the most-common type of network topology. In a star network, each computer is connected by a cable to a central device called a *hub*. The biggest disadvantage associated with the star topology is the amount of wiring needed to connect each computer to the hub. On the other hand, a computer can be disconnected or taken off of the network and reconnected without disturbing the network. Star networks are the most popular network topology to implement.

- **Bus** A bus network uses a main trunk to connect computers. One segment of cabling is used to connect many computers as opposed to the star network where one cable connects one computer. A computer cannot be taken off of a bus network without disrupting the entire network. Bus networks require less wiring than other networks, but are more prone to problems with breaks in the cabling.

- **Ring** A ring network operates in much the same fashion as a bus network, with each end connected to form a ring. Ring networks operate by passing a token around the ring with each computer given a chance to acquire it. The computer then attaches data to the token that is bound for a certain computer. The ring topology is limited.

Peer-to-Peer

A peer-to-peer network is one composed of computers that share each other's files and resources. On a peer-to-peer network, no one computer is the boss. Each user on the network makes decisions on which files and resources are to be shared with other users.

Peer-to-peer networks are the easiest to set up. They are easy to maintain if they are small. Linux is not designed to operate in a peer-to-peer fashion.

Client/Server Networks

To implement a client/server network, one must begin with a server. A server can also be called a *dedicated server* or a *file server*. A server is nothing more than a powerful computer. A server does as its name implies; it serves files and applications for client computers. The server contains shared file storage and applications that are accessible to everyone on the network. The server also makes peripherals such as printers and scanners available to the network users.

A *client* is a fully operational workstation capable of storing and manipulating data. This may confuse some people because the only thing different about a server and a client is the level of hardware and the applications that it runs. Programs can be run on either the server or the workstation. It is best to let the application run on the workstation and let the server do the duties it needs to do. Linux is designed for a client/server environment.

Chapter Summary

We have covered CompTia's seventh domain under the Linux+ blueprint. We looked at the boot process of a PC and the hardware involved in it. More importantly, we covered hard drives, their installation, and some of the troubleshooting techniques involved. We looked at networking and some of the topologies and types of networks around us.

Questions

1. List the three types of memory modules.

2. Where is the 1024-cylinder limit on a hard drive in gigabytes?
   A. 2.1GB
   B. 504MB
   C. 8GB
   D. 14GB

3. How are computers in a star topology connected?
   A. All in a series on one cable
   B. Individually, by a cable to a hub
   C. Modem
   D. One hooked to another in a ring

4. What does POST stand for?
   A. Manufacturer of breakfast foods
   B. Preoperative System Test
   C. Power-On Self-Test
   D. Post Compile Silicon Technology

5. What is the term SCSI an acronym for?
   A. Scientific Capsule Shuttle Interface
   B. A really dirty computer
   C. Short Command System Identifiers
   D. Small Computer System Interface

6. Name the two types of keyboard plugs.

7. What does the term seek time refer to?
   A. The time it takes for the read head in a hard drive to position itself over the data
   B. The amount of time it takes to transfer data from the hard drive to the CPU
   C. How long it takes to access data in a specific sector on the hard drive
   D. The time it takes to process data during the initial startup (boot time)

8. What is the most common floppy drive capacity?
   A. 2.88MB
   B. 1.44MB
   C. 768KB
   D. 100MB

9. Linux is designed to operate in what type of environment?
   A. Peer-to-peer
   B. Stand-alone
   C. Client/server
   D. Centralized

10. What is diagnostic software?
    A. Software that probes your computer for an AGP video card
    B. Software that looks at your system hardware
    C. Software that registers you to vote
    D. A program that will make changes to your system to make it run better

Answers

1. **SIMM, DIMM, RIMM**. These are the most widely used memory modules that are commercially available.

2. **C.** The 1,024-cylinder limit is right at the 8GB limit.

3. **B.** Computers in the star topology are connected to a hub by their own separate cable.

4. **C.** Post stands for Power-On Self-Test.

5. **D.** SCSI stands for Small Computer System Interface

6. **PS/2 and AT style**. These are the most popular commercially available interface for keyboards.

7. **A.** The seek time is the amount of time that it takes for the read head in a hard drive to position itself over the data to be read.

8. **B.** Typical floppy drives are produced only in the 1.44MB capacity.

9. **C.** Linux is designed for the client/server environment.

10. **B.** Diagnostic software looks at your system hardware to determine if a problem may exist.

Linux Commands

This appendix provides a reference to some of the more common Linux commands and utilities.

any_command --**help**   Displays a brief list of help on a command.

apropos topic   Displays a list of commands that are related to the topic that is being searched for.

ar -x my_archive.a file1 file2   This utility extracts files file1 and file2 from an archive called my_archive.a. The archiver utility **ar** is mostly used for reserving file libraries.

arch   Displays the current architecture of the machine on which Linux is currently running. In regards to **arch**, i586 will mean Pentium-based machines, i486 will mean 80486 machines, and axp will mean Alpha-based machines.

ark &   A GUI-based archiver application. **gnozip** is an alternative.

arp   Modifies and displays address resolution between IP addresses and MAC addresses.

at 18:00   The **at** command runs a command at a specified time: in this case, 18:00 hours, or 6:00 P.M.

atrm   Deletes the selected run job from the schedule queue.

bg *job_number*   This command restarts a process that has been stopped in the background. This is utilized to decompress a file (*.bz2) zipped with the **bzip2 compression** utility. This command is utilized in conjunction with larger compressed files.

break   Aborts a command or stops a program.

cat   Displays on the standard output a combination of any one or more file sets.

cd   Changes the current working directory to your home directory within the Linux file tree.

cdplay play 2   This command plays the second track from a music CD. You can use **cdplay** if you want to play the entire CD. **cdplay stop** stops the CD from running.

chage -l my_login_name   You can use **chage -l my_login_name** to see any information on password expiration. **chage -M 100** *login_name* sets the password expiry to 100 days for the user named login_name.

checkalias   Checks to see whether or not a specified alias is defined by first checking the user's file and then the system alias file.

chgrp   Alters the group ownership configuration of one or many files and/or file directories.

chmod   Alters any access permissions of one or more files and/or file directories.

chown   Changes either the client or user ownership of files and/or directories.

clear   Erases any terminal screen output and then resets the prompt and cursor location to the first point on the screen.

compress   This command compresses files or any other standard input using the Lempel-Ziv compression procedure. The **convert -geometry** command is used to scale pictures to the needed pixel size. In this case, the pixel size is set to 60 × 80. This command converts an X Windows screen capture (that uses the .xwd file format) and converts it to the .jpg file type.

cp   Simply copies files and/or file directories.

cron   Initiates all timed events in a system.

crontab   Either changes or displays a user's cron table, which is the table that indicates when scheduled actions are performed by the cron daemon.

cut   Removes sections from a line in specified files to a standard output.

date   Either changes or prints the operating system's time and date settings. If you are setting the BIOS clock off of the system clock, then invoke the **setclock** command.

dd   Stands for data duplicator, and is used to create an image of the contents of a floppy to the file called floppy_image in the active directory. After creating floppy_image, **dd** copies the floppy image to another floppy. This is very similar to DISKCOPY that exists in DOS.

df   Prints disk info about all the filesystems (in human-readable form).

dmesg | Prints all kernel messages.

domainname   This sets the Linux network system's NIS domain name. It displays the current NIS domain name as the default unless otherwise specified.

du   Displays the disk usage on the filesystem by directory.

e2fsck   This is the default for Linux partitions. It checks the state of a Linux second extended filesystem.

echo   This command displays a text line.

eject   Simply ejects the CD-ROM tray. Its default is the CD-ROM, but it can also be used to eject other media by specifying the appropriate device.

exit   Exits you from the current shell or program.

fdisk   The tool used to create partitions on a disk.

fg *job_number*   Puts a background or stopped process in the foreground.

file   Displays and determines file types.

find   Locates files that match any criteria indicated at the command line, and then it takes actions that are indicated by certain options.

finger *user_name*   Invokes system information about a particular user.

free   A memory-tracking device. It displays a report of both free and used memory. **giftopnm** *my_file.giff > my_file.pnm* converts a gif graphic into a pnm file for better portability. It then converts pnm files into png, which is a better standard for using them via the Internet.

fsck   Checks file system consistency and interactively repairs the file system.

gpasswd   Allows for a change in the password of a specified group.

grep   This command searches files that match a specified pattern, and then displays the lines that were searched for.

groupadd   Enables the root user to create a new group on the system.

groupdel   Deletes a current group.

groupmod   Modifies an open group.

groups   Lists the groups to which the current user belongs.

grpck   Checks on the integrity of the password and group files.

grpconv   Converts older passwords and group files to more secure shadow-type files.

gunzip filename.gze   You can use the **gz** (or **gunzip**) command to decompress a zipped file (*.gz or *.z). Use **gzip** (also **zip** or **compress**) if you want to compress files to this file format.

halt   Either stops or reboots the machine, and is usually used in remote contexts. Use **halt** if the keyboard will not respond.

head filename   This command prints the first set number of lines of a long text file.

help   The standard **help** command illustrates quick information on a bash shell built-in command. Some standard built-in bash commands are as follows: **alias**, **bg**, **cd**, **echo**, **exit**, **export**, **fg**, **help**, **history**, **jobs**, **kill**, **logout**, **pwd**, **set**, **source**, **ulimit**, **umask**, **unalias**, and **unset**.

history | more   Shows the last set of commands that were run from the command line on the current account. The **| more** component enables the display to stop after each screenful. If you want to check on another user's usage of your system, log in as the root user, and look through the history file. History can be found in the .bash_history in the user's home directory.

hostname   Prints the current name of the local host for the machine you are working on. If you want to change the machine name, use **netconf**.

id username   Prints the user ID (UID), group ID (GID), effective ID, and additional groups.

ifconfig   Displays information on any and all network interfaces such as Ethernet, Token Ring, and PPP. **ifconfig** comes with many options for configuring the interfaces. For a list of them, check out **ifconfig -help**.

ifdown *interface_name*   Shuts down the network interface.

ifport   Sets the type of transceiver required for a chosen network interface.

ifup ppp1   Use **ifup ppp1** to either start up or shut down the ppp interface only when permission is given in ppp setup using the **netconf** command. You can also use KDE's kppp to start a dial-up connection.

info topic   Illustrates the informational content of a particular command. **info** can be used in place of **man** so as to view the most recent changes to the system documentation.

init   This command is used to change a run level.

insmod   Installs a loadable module into the most recent kernel.

insmod ppa   Inserts modules into the kernel (a module is roughly the equivalent of a DOS device driver). You can also use **modprobe** to insert modules into the kernel.

ipchains   This command is used to set up, maintain, and inspect the IP firewall rules in the Linux kernel.

ipfwadm -F -p m   Sets up the firewall IP forwarding policy to the masquerading configuration. (It is not very secure, but it's simple.) It gives the impression to outsiders that all machines on your network are one constantly running machine.

ipfwadm-wrapper -F -a m -S xxx.xxx.xxx.0/24 -D 0.0.0.0/0   This does the same as the previous entry. Here you would substitute the *x*s with the numbers of a class C IP address that is assigned to your network.

iptables -L   This lists the rules of the firewall iptables, which are new to Linux kernel 2.4.x.

jobs   Lists either stopped or background processes, as well as illustrates their corresponding job numbers.

join   Applies the join relational database operator.

kdehelp   The KDE help navigator is a graphical tool used to browse the entire system. KDE can be brought up via the control panel. The GNOME equivalent of KDE would be gnome-help-browser.

kernelcfg   This is a GUI interface that is used to either add or remove kernel modules. A kernel module is similar to a device driver in terms of function with hardware.

kill   Sends a message to one or more application causing them to end all processes.

kill PID   Forces a process shutdown. In order to do this, you must first determine the PID of the process to kill. Use **ps** to do this.

killall *program_name*   Kills any program via its name.

konqueror &   This launches the KDE file manager in Linux. The KDE file manager is superior to MS Windows Explorer in that it embeds Web browsing, pdf viewing, and other tools in the same GUI.

ksnapshot   A GUI-based utility that is used to capture screen grabs. **gtop** and **ktop** are two GUI-based choices for top.

last   Shows the listing of users who were last logged into the system. This command can be used in a security function to periodically check up on the system.

lastb   Illustrates the last unsuccessful login attempts on the system.

ldconfig   Reconfigures the cache so as to load dynamic libraries and subsequent bindings.

lilo   Installs the Linux boot loader.

linuxconf   The root tool for making network system settings and changes.

listalias   This command shows the user and system aliases.

ln   This command is used to create links between existing files.

locate filename   Finds the filename that contains the filename string. **locate filename** is a better choice than the previous command, although it depends on a nightly rebuilding database for proper functioning.

logger   This places an entry into the system log.

login   Logs the user into the system.

logrotate   Rotates log files, and then compresses them for archiving purposes.

lpc   Controls and checks the various printer types available. In order to see the various command options, type **?**.

lpq   Shows the contents of the current printer queue. Correspondingly, you can use the KDE's Printer Queue, which is found under K menu—Utilities.

lpr   Prints any standard file to the associated printer spool. It sends the standard input if nothing is specifically indicated.

lprm *job_number*   This command removes a print job by locating its print job number from the queue.

lpstat   Prints the status of arguments that are request IDs, printer names, or printer classes.

ls   Lists the contents of the currently active directory. **ls** and **dir** (which are found in Microsoft instances) basically do the same thing.

ls -al   Lists all current directory files in long form.

lsmod   Lists the kernel modules that are currently loaded.

mail   Basically sends and receives e-mail messages. **mail** can be set to show different types of information, such as the header information, which is provided in the form of a flag.

make bzImage   Creates the bzImage file, which will be a newly created Linux kernel.

make modules_install   This command installs any new kernel and subsequent modules that have been created. **make modules_install** copies any new files to the /boot directory and also makes changes to the /etc/lilo.conf file.

make xconfig   A front end that is used to configure kernal options in order to have everything ready for any customized kernel.

man   Produces the manual page for a specified command.

man topic   Shows the contents of the system manual pages on the chosen topic area. Pressing Q causes the viewer to quit.

mcd   Changes the directory on a DOS filesystem, such as a CD-ROM drive.

mcopy source destination   This command will copy a file from a DOS-based file structure. Other tools that can access DOS files without mounting include the following: **mdir, mcd, mren, mmove, mdel, mmd, mrd,** and **mformat.**

mdeltree   Deletes one or more specified DOS directories.

messages   Indicates the amount of messages located in a user's inbox, or another folder that is previously specified.

minicom   Configures a modem to work with a line protocol.

mkbootdisk   Can be used to make an emergency boot disk. This is in order to make it after the install prompt has requested that you make one during install. The kernel name can be indicated through either the **-a** or the **ls/lib** command.

mkdir directory   Creates a new directory.

mkdosfs   Formats a DOS filesystem for an indicated device.

mkfs -c -t ext2 /dev/fd0   This command performs a base-level format operation of a floppy disk in the first floppy drive. After this is completed, it creates a Linux filesystem. **mkfs** can also format floppies for different densities. For example, you can format the default density using **fdformat /dev/fd0.**

mkpasswd   Generates a random password and then assigns it to a specific user.

mkswap   Sets up a device as a swap area.

modprobe -l |more   This command shows all the available modules for the kernel you are using. **modprobe sb** simply installs and loads the soundblaster (sb) module.

mount /mnt/cdrom   This enables the user to mount a CD drive. In order to do this, you must have the /etc/fstab file enabled, and the /mnt/cdrom path must not be the current directory.

mount /mnt/floppy   This enables the user to mount a floppy drive. In order to implement this, you must have the /etc/fstab file setup. Also, the /mnt/floppy must not be the current directory.

mount -t auto /dev/fd0 /mnt/floppy   This command mounts the floppy as root. In order to perform this procedure, the directory /mnt/floppy must be created. It also must not be the current directory, and should be clean of any files. Print the Post-

Script file my_file.ps, outputting two logical pages on one physical page. Save the output to the file new_file.ps. mpg123 -w my_file.wav my_file.mp3 enables you to create a wave audio file from an mp3. This is good to use if you want to make an audio CD from an existing mp3, which means converting the mp3 to a .wav format.

mv   Renames or moves files to different directory locations.

netconf   A menu-driven setup for your network.

netstat   Displays information on network properties, configurations, and settings.

newgrp   Logs an indicated user into a new group.

nmblookup -A *ip_address*   Shows the current conditions of a networked Microsoft Windows computer that has a NetBIOS name. This is the equivalent of **nbstat** in Windows.

nslookup *host_to_find*   You can use **nslookup** *host_to_find* in order to query the default domain name server (DNS) for either an IP number or Internet name. Use this to check the status of the DNS. You can also use this to figure out the name for your host when the IP number is all the information you've got.

passwd   Used to change the password on the current account. You can change the password for any user using **passwd** *user_name* if you are the root user.

paste   Performs the paste function, which is merging information from one file into another file, or files.

ping   Sends an echo request packet to a network host to see if it can be accessed via the network.

ping *machine_name*   Pings a particular machine to see if you can establish contact with a host.

play *my_file.wav*   This command plays a wave file.

poweroff   This command powers down the requested hardware component.

pppstats   Displays information regarding PPP activities.

printtool   The administrative tool to use with printers. It is the configuration tool for your printer(s). Settings go to the file /etc/printcap and (strangely) /var/spool/lpd.

./program_name   This command runs an executable in the current directory.

ps   Presents information about the processes/jobs/programs that are running on the server.

pstree   Displays processes in the form of a tree structure.

pwck   Checks the password file for any associated problems or error. **pwck** can check entry format to ensure that the information is valid in each field.

pwconv   **Converts plain-text passwords to encrypted passwords and stores them in /etc/shadow.**

pwd   Displays the absolute path name of the current working directory.

pwunconv   Restores a password from a corresponding shadow password file.

quotacheck   This scans a file's system for the disk usage output by either a user or group of users, and then moves the results to two quota files.

rcp   Remote copies one or more files between corresponding systems.

reboot   Performs the same function as **halt**.

rm files   The **rm** command is used to either remove or delete a file. Ownership must be made towards the file before it can be removed. **rm -f** removes any file in the active directory. You can also use -f if you do not want a confirmation of deletion to be displayed.

rm -r files   Removes directories, subdirectories, and any included files. Watch using this command as root because it can be easy to remove all files on the system. With no undelete feature in Linux, this could prove disastrous. If you truly want to delete all files, then use the **rm -rf/*** command.

rmdir directory   Removes an existing directory.

rmmod   Unloads loaded modules.

rmmod *module_name*   Removes the module called *module_name* from the kernel.

route   Either changes or displays the IP routing table. It displays the routing table by default if nothing else is indicated.

route -n   Shows the kernel routing table.

rpm -e *package_name*   This command uninstalls the package named *package_name*.

rpm -ivh --force --nodep package_name-version.platform.rpm   This command installs the required package and ignores any possible package dependency conflicts.

rpm -ivh package_name-version.platform.rpm   This command installs a package and also prints hashes that show the progress of the active installation routine. The rpm stands for Red Hat Packet Manager.

rpm -qai   The **rpm -qai** command queries all system packages installed to display their info. You can use **rpm -qa | grep -c** if you need to count packages.

rpm -qf a_file   The previous command finds the name of the installed package to which the file a_file belongs. This is helpful if you accidentally erase a file and then need to quickly reinstall the correct package.

rpm -qi package_name   This queries the already installed package so that it displays information about its current status.

rpm -qpi package_name-version.platform.rpm   This query (option q) performs the function of querying the uninstalled package (option p) so that it displays the package info (option i) contained within the package.

rpm -qpl package_name-version.platform.rpm   This queries the uninstalled package so that it displays the listing (indicated as option l) of all the package file contents.

rpm -Uvh package_name-version.platform.rpm   This utility is used when you need to upgrade a package. It also displays appropriate hashes.

rpm -Va   Use this command to verify with the V option all the packages (option a) installed on the current system. This lists files that were modified since the installation. The legend for the output is as follows:

.   Test passed

c   Configuration file

5   MD5 checksum failed

S   Different file size

L   Symbolic link has changed

T   File modification time changed

D   Modified device file

U   User who owns the file has changed

G   Group that owns the file has changed

M   File mode (permissions and/or file type) has been modified

runlevel   Prints all (previous and current) run levels. N5 means no previous level, whereas 5 is the current run level. The following list indicates standard run levels:

0   halt (Do *not* set initdefault to this.)

1   Single-user mode

2   Multi-user mode

3   Full multi-user mode

4   Unused

5   X11

6   Reboot (Do *not* set initdefault to this.)

rwho -a   This stands for remote who, and is used to indicate the range of users who are logged into machines across the network. In order for **rwho -a** to function, the **rwho** service must be enabled.

setclock   Enables your computer hardware clock to set from the current Linux system time and date settings.

set | more   Shows the current user environment. Use setup to configure keyboard, mouse, video, windows, soundcard, and systemwide devices.

setserial   Configures serial ports at runtime.

showmount   Shows the current mount status from an NFS server.

shutdown   This command shuts down the system and stops all logins.

startx   This starts an X Windows server and the default Windows manager. It works like typing **win** under DOS with Win3.1.

startx -- :1   Starts a corresponding X Windows session on the primary display. You can run multiple GUI terminals at once, and switch between them using CTRL-ALT-F7, F8, and so on.

statserial   This command shows any serial port status by displaying signals on the pins of the port, as well as checking the handshake line status.

su   Runs a corresponding shell under different user and/or group IDs.

SuperProbe   This tool is used to check the type of video card installed. It also checks the available video card memory.

sync   Saves the disk cache to the physical disk.

tail   Prints the last ten lines of a longer text file. **tail -f filename** can be used to implement a **tail** that will follow the file as it continues to grow. This helps when log file review is required.

tar   This command creates a tarball file of either files or directories.

tar -xvf filename.tar   This command untars a tarred tarball that has already been uncompressed.

tcpdump -i ppp0 -a -x   This command prints out all current network traffic that is going through the phone as either ASCII or hexadecimal characters. You can utilize **tcpdump** to build more customized network traffic tools.

telnet   This command establishes a connection to a host using the **port** command.

test   Returns true or false according to a conditional expression that is provided.

time   Used to determine how long it takes for any given process to complete.

timed   Used to synchronize the time with the timestamp on other machines in the network.

top   Utilized to keep listing the running processes, sorted by CPU usage. The following is a list of indicators for **top**:

PID	Process identification
USER	Name of user who started the process
PRI	Process priority
NI	Niceness level
SIZE	Kilobytes of code + data + stack taken by the process in memory
RSS	Kilobytes of physical memory taken
SHARE	Kilobytes of memory shared with other processes
STAT	State of the process: S=sleeping, R=running, T=stopped or traced, D=uniterruptable sleep, and Z=zombie
%CPU	Percentage of CPU usage
%MEM	Share of physical memory

> **TIME**   Total CPU time used by the process
>
> **COMMAND**   Command line used to start the task

touch   Changes the date/timestamp on the file to the current time. You can create the empty file if the file does not exist.

traceroute *host_to_trace*   This shows the route in which your messages trace (either via host name or IP number).

true   Returns a successful exit status.

umount   Unmounts any mounted filesystem or directory.

uname -a   This displays information on the local server. You can also use **guname** in an X Window terminal to display the information in a more presentable fashion.

uncompress   This command uncompresses files that are compressed using the **compress** utility.

unzip filename.zip   This is the command used to decompress a file (*.zip) zipped with a compression program that is compatible with PKZIP for DOS.

uptime   Indicates the amount of time since the last reboot.

useradd *user_name*   Used to add a new user.

userconf   Consists of menu-driven configuration tools. Examples include tools for changing password policies, making group modifications, as well as adding users, and so on. **userconf** is part of the **linuxconf** package, although you can run it separately.

userdel *user_name*   Used to remove an account if you are the root user. **groupdel** can be used to delete entire groups.

usermod   Used to modify user accounts without the need to manually edit the following files: /etc/passwd, /etc/shadow, /etc/group, and /etc/gshadow.

vi   Starts the visual display text editor.

vipw   Edits the file that contains the system password, using the editor that is specified in the EDITOR environment.

vmstat   A tool for checking virtual memory.

w   Can be used to find out the following information: who is logged onto the system, their actions, and their processor usage. **w** is used widely in a security capacity to determine covert user activities.

wc   The word count utility that prints the number of words and lines contained within a chosen document. If you choose multiple document filenames, then each is counted and displayed separately and as a sum total.

whatis topic   Displays a short list of commands matching my topic. **whatis** is similar to **apropos** (*see* **apropos topic**)—they both use the same database. However, **whatis** searches keywords, whereas **apropos** also searches the descriptions of the keywords.

whereis   The **whereis** utility prints the locations for all the manual, binary, and source files of the command.

which *executable_name*   Illustrates the full path to the executable that would run if I just typed the name of the executable on the command line. For example, the following command:

```
which redhat
```

would produce the following:

```
/usr/bin/redhat
```

who   Lets the user know who is currently logged into the machine.

whoami   Prints the current login name of the user.

xinit   Starts a completely blank X Windows server.

xkill   This command kills a client by its X resource.

xterm   Can be used to run a basic X Windows terminal.

xvidtune   Used with the monitor to correct resolution and picture problems. It can fix problems such as black bands, display shifts, and other related parameters. You can make settings permanent by transferring settings to the /etc/X11/XF86Config setup file.

ypdomainname   This displays the domain name for the system's NIS.

zcat filename.gz   This command lists the contents of a compressed file. Other utilities such as **zless**, **zmore**, **zgrep**, and others can be used for performing compressed file tasks.

Linux+ Testing Tips

This appendix will cover the following topics:

- Before taking the exam
- Things to consider during the exam
- Tips for taking multiple choice tests
- After taking the Linux+ exam

So you've arrived at the point where you're comfortable with the tasks and procedures required for the Linux+ exam. You're confident that your knowledge combined with what you've learned about the Linux+ exam from this guide is going to pull you through. You're ready to head to the testing center and get on with it. If you're anything like me, you might develop a bit of test-taking anxiety.

I've talked to professionals from all different information technology genres who have taken various certification exams. A lot of those who fail the test blame it on the test engine they used, the boot camp they went to, or the study guide they used to prepare for the test. A quick glance at the reviews on amazon.com will show many people disgruntled that the study guide they used didn't get them through the exam. In a number of cases, it's probably that the candidate knows the material; he or she just has problems taking tests.

This appendix addresses some of the information I've always considered valuable when taking tests, and when studying in general. This comes from spending time training individuals, teaching university classes, and creating testing materials for the certification market. Although all of it might not pertain to your individual circumstance, you'll probably take something from this appendix that pertains to you.

Before Taking the Exam

Before you walk into the testing center, be sure that you've got these bases covered:

- Bring two forms of identification. Be certain that one has your photo on it, such as your company identification badge or driver's license. If you don't have a driver's license, a passport or some other form of documentation should be fine.

- Make sure you know where the testing center is located. I would even suggest driving there before the day of your test. The last thing you need is to be driving around looking for the testing center and burning up time that you could spend going over some test notes. This will also give you an idea of how long it should take to get there, so you can leave with plenty of time to spare.

- Give yourself enough time to get to the testing center. I would suggest arriving 15 to 20 minutes early. This will give you time to get something to drink or just to relax and mentally prepare for what you're about to do.

- Eat breakfast. Countless studies show that cognition and mental performance are significantly improved by eating earlier in the day. Although five cups of coffee before noon might get you through your normal workday, it's not recommended for the day of the test. You want your brain to be working in high gear and be able to think through questions it hasn't encountered before. You don't have to spend two hours at the local diner over eggs and bacon—just make sure you get something in you. You'll be glad you did.

- Wear comfortable clothes. If you've never quite gotten used to wearing a tie everyday at work, take it off before the exam. You don't want to be tugging at your collar while taking the exam.

Once you've signed in and been shown to your test computer, you should be aware of certain things:

- Make sure that the machine is powered on, and that the test you signed up for is on the screen in front of you. This might seem obvious, but everyone makes mistakes. You don't want to realize halfway through the test that you're taking the LPI I exam and not Linux+.

- The test is closed book, so you won't be allowed to take anything into the testing area with you. If you're accustomed to wearing your cell phone, PDA, or anything of that type on your belt for work, take it off and leave it in the car. Many cell phones and other devices come with calculators, so they won't be permitted. If you wear a watch with a calculator, leave it at home. You don't want to walk out of a test with something like this, and be disqualified without ever really having done anything wrong.

- Make sure that the testing center representative answers any questions you might have. Once the test begins, the representative is not allowed to talk to you, so make sure you understand everything before stepping in to take the test.

Things to Consider During the Exam

Unlike a certification exam like Cisco's CCNA, with the Linux+ exam, you will be able to move forward and backward through the exam items. This will enable you to develop a bit of a test-taking strategy so that you can be successful. The following are some things to think about:

1. Begin by moving through the test answering all the items that you are sure you're correct about. Then go back through the exam and work on the harder problems. You have the ability with the test to mark questions and return to them later. Make sure you utilize this function. You will probably encounter a question later in the exam that will spur your thinking about one that you temporarily passed on.

2. Answer all the questions. The Linux+ exam doesn't penalize you for guessing, so taking a chance with something is better than nothing.

3. Don't rush through the test. The exam time is usually more than enough time to complete the entire test.

Tips for Taking Multiple-Choice Tests

The Linux+ exam, like almost every certification exam, at least all or in part, consists of multiple-choice questions. Although you may know the material inside and out, knowing a little about how to answer this type of question will help:

- Think about the key words that exist in the phrase. Try to discern what they are and concentrate on them above the rest.

- If you find two answer choices that are very similar, chances are the answer isn't either one of them.

- If two choices are completely opposite of one another, then one of them is probably the right answer.

- Don't try to read too much into a question. Try to see it for what it is, not what you're trying to make it into.

- In most cases, answers that use words like all, never, always, and none are usually wrong answers. This isn't an absolute, but a tendency you should watch for.

- Answers that tend to be correct will often have words like probably, often, or sometimes. Watch for these.

- Don't rule out a possible answer unless you know what each word in that answer means.

- Like they say in all tests, read each and every test answer. Sometimes you will see decoy answers that are placed as answer choice A or B that could just about be the answer, with the real answer later on.

- If a question is somewhat scenario based, with a long exposition, and then a question, read the question first. That will indicate what you are looking for and will then get your mind ready. This will affect how you read the rest of the passage. After you read the question component, try to figure out what the answer is. If you think you know it at that point, then you probably do. Read the entire question first though to make absolutely certain.

- In most cases, the answer that has either the longest or most complicated answer is usually the correct one. The longest answer means the test creator has had to put as many qualifying statements in as needed so as to make the answer complete.

- If you come across a question that seems just too difficult, try reading it out loud. If that doesn't work, try drawing some sort of picture of the situation. The key here is to get your mind to approach the problem in a different light. Looking at it from another point of view might show you what you were missing to begin with.

- Watch out for questions that seem too obvious. This is another tactic used to psych you out.

After Taking the Linux+ Exam

After you have completed the exam, the following will happen:

- The testing center will give you back immediate results of your score. If you happen to take a beta exam, then you won't know for some time, as the results of the test will be mailed to you.

- You will be presented with a printout of your examination score report. This will indicate whether or not you've passed the exam, your score, as well as your performance for each component objective of the exam.

If you don't pass the exam the first time, try not to be too discouraged. You will be presented with a form that indicates your areas of weakness. Spend time going over that part of the exam objectives using the study guide, any free online study materials you can find, and other materials. You should also try to get more real-world experience in that area as soon as possible. You may consider even taking a course on the subject. The key is to make a plan for getting your knowledge up-to-speed so that you can take the test again while you're in that mode.

The Server+ Short Course

The biggest weakness of the Linux+ exam is that it asks so few questions about actual Linux. Linux questions are sprinkled into this exam along with a compilation of hardware questions from two other CompTIA certifications: A+ and Server+. As an administrator, you are no doubt familiar with the basics of simple hardware; the questions pulled from the A+ exams shouldn't be too difficult. What may be foreign to you, however, are the advanced hardware topics the Server+ exam is targeted for. Advanced hardware topics include such things as redundant array of inexpensive disks (RAID), Small Computer Systems Interface (SCSI), and so on. To help fill in gaps that you may have with such topics, the following is, in its entirety, the *Server+ Short Course*. This document walks through the objectives of the Server+ exam, tests your knowledge, and points you to sites where you can find further information. After reading it, not only will you have a better understanding of the Server+ exam, but, more importantly, you'll be better prepared for the Linux+ exam.

Installation

The following are the objectives for the *Installation* section of the Server+ exam:

- Conduct preinstallation planning activities.
- Install hardware using electronic software distribution (ESD) best practices (boards, drives, processors, memory, internal cable, and so on).

Conducting Preinstallation Planning Activities

When planning a server installation, you need to know the following:

- The entire hardware list for the server
- The exact location where the server is to be installed
- The location of the network connection for the server
- The location of the power outlet for the server
- The server's role in the entire network scheme

To verify your server installation plan, you should

- Ensure the network connection is active and not being used by something else.
- Test the power outlet with a volt/ohm meter.
- Confirm that all hardware has been delivered, is where you need it, and is included in the installation plan.
- Ensure that you have the correct location where the server is to be installed.

All operating system vendors publish a list of hardware that they support as working with their operating system software. To verify hardware compatibility with the operating system, you should check the vendor compatibility list to ensure that all of the hardware for the network server is on the vendor's list, as well as check each vendor's Web site for the most current compatibility list.

When verifying the power source, you need to confirm that the correct uninterruptible power supply (UPS) for the server is available. You also need to make sure that you can monitor the UPS via a serial communication cable. Finally, be sure to verify that power sources have been tested with a voltmeter and that they are not too far away from the server rack.

Also note that you join multiple server racks together to form an installation space for a larger number of servers.

Installing Hardware Using ESD Best Practices

To install hardware using ESD best practices, keep the following points in mind:

- Use antistatic carpeting and antistatic mats, when possible.
- Use antistatic cleaners on carpet and tables in the server room.

- Implement a room humidifier if the humidity level falls below 60 percent. This will decrease the amount of ESD.

- Keep all boards, drives, processors, memory, and internal cables in static bags until you are ready to install them.

- Hold drives and peripherals by their edges. Don't touch the circuit board component.

A standard rack unit is 1.75 inches tall and is designated by the letter *U*. Server racks come in varying sizes and must be mounted in an equipment rack manufactured specifically for rack-mounted hardware. Server racks also have doors and side panels, which can help to keep the equipment secure and cool.

Most networks today are built using unshielded twisted-pair (UTP) cable. The connector on the end of the cable is known as an *RJ-45 connector*. UTP cable has four pairs that have two wires a piece for a total of eight wires. You can connect UTP cable to an RJ-45 connector by using a crimping tool (see Figure C-1).

The UPS is external to the server itself. The UPS is plugged directly into the power source. The server and its components are then plugged into the UPS. A serial cable that runs from the UPS to a serial port on the server enables the network operating system to monitor the UPS so that it will know when the power has failed and the UPS is providing power via batteries. Generally, a rack-mounted UPS is installed as the lowest device in the rack.

Each end of a SCSI bus must be terminated into a component of some type. The SCSI controller is on one end of the bus, with termination being on the motherboard itself. A physical terminator or the register on the last disk drive on the chain ends the other end point.

SCSI-1 (often referred to simply as SCSI) generally supports a single channel per SCSI controller. SCSI is attached to the disk controller via a 50-pin connector. Early SCSI used DB-25 25-pin connectors for external SCSI devices.

Figure C-1   You can connect UTP cable to an RJ-45 connector with a crimping tool.

SCSI-2 is usually found inside a server chassis due to bus length restrictions. With SCSI-2, you need to use either single-ended or differential interfaces. A differential interface enables you to use longer cabling and to connect the server to an external SCSI device.

SCSI-2 uses a 50-pin connector—the same used by SCSI-1. Figure C-2 shows a diagram of a 50-pin connector.

Wide SCSI-2 is a variation of SCSI-2. It can transfer 16 bits at a time, instead of the normal 8 bits permitted by SCSI-1 and SCSI-2.

SCSI-2 permits at least 16 devices on the SCSI-2 channel.

Fast SCSI-2 is another variation of SCSI-2. It doubles the speed from 5 to 10 MHz. The bus length is cut in half (from six meters to three) to facilitate the increase in speed.

Fast-Wide SCSI-2 can transfer data at 20 MHz.

The newest type of SCSI-2 connector is the SCA 80-pin connector (see Figure C-3).

SCSI-3 is the latest standard of the SCSI family, combining all the best features of the previous SCSI standards. It uses Low-Voltage Differential Signaling (LVDS) to support up to 15 devices on a single cable (which can be up to 12 meters long).

SCSI-3 can support three separate bus speeds:

- Ultra (20 MHz)
- Ultra2 (40 MHz)
- Ultra3 (double-clocked 40 MHz)

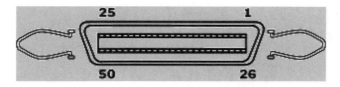

Figure C-2   A 50-pin connector

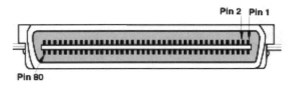

Figure C-3   An SCA 80-pin connector

There are both narrow (8-bit) and wide (16-bit) implementations of the three SCSI-3 bus speeds.

Ultra SCSI-3 and Ultra2 SCSI-3 both use 50-pin connectors. The wide variants (Wide Ultra SCSI-3 and Wide Ultra2 SCSI-3, as well as Ultra3 (also known as Ultra160 SCSI-3) use 68-pin connectors. All versions of SCSI-3 require active termination. Also note that Wide SCSI devices have four jumpers. All other types have three.

The following lists the maximum cable lengths, speed, and number of devices for all SCSI types:

SCSI Type	Cable Length (in meters)	Maximum Speed (MBps)	Number of Devices
SCSI-1	6	5	8
SCSI-2	6	5 to 10	8 or 16
Fast SCSI-2	3	5 to 10	8
Wide SCSI-2	3	20	16
Fast-Wide SCSI-2	3	20	16
Ultra SCSI-3, 8-bit	1.5	20	8
Ultra SCSI-3, 16-bit	1.5	40	16
Ultra-2 SCSI	12	40	8
Wide Ultra-2 SCSI	12	80	16
Ultra-3 (Ultra160/m) SCSI	12	160	16

There are many types of external devices to install:

- **Keyboard**   Plugs the keyboard into the server's keyboard port.

- **Mouse**   Plugs the mouse into the server's PS/2 mouse port.

- **Monitor**   Connects the monitor to the video adapter. Use an HD-15 connector. If space is limited, you can rack-mount the monitor for space requirements.

- **Power supply**   Server hardware can have multiple, hot-swappable power supplies. Having two (or even three) power supplies enables you to balance the electrical load. If one power supply fails, the other power supply can handle the entire electrical load. You can then replace the failed power supply, without having to take the network server offline.

- **Video adapter**   The video adapter can either be built in or connected via an available bus slot.

To verify the power-on sequence,

- Make sure all components are installed into the chassis correctly.

- Power on the external powered devices first, and then power on the server.

The server will go through its startup procedures. Watch for indicators from the SCSI controllers, which locate each SCSI device on the appropriate channel.

Further Reading

SCSI Configuration—**www.pcguide.com/ref/hdd/if/scsi/conf.htm**

SCSI Bus Termination—**www.pcguide.com/ref/hdd/if/scsi/cables_ Adapters.htm**

ESD Precautions—**www.pcguide.com/site/warnESD-c.html**

Test Your Knowledge

1. What rating is used to specify the size of a UPS?
   a. VA
   b. KVM
   c. EIDE
   d. Volt/ohm meter

2. How must memory be installed in network servers?
   a. In 32MB chunks.
   b. In groups of two or four memory modules.
   c. In groups of two or three memory modules.
   d. You cannot install memory in a network server.

3. When installing a network server, a network server specialist should confirm that all the processors on the server are what? (Choose all that apply.)
   a. The same type
   b. The same speed
   c. The same version
   d. The same age

4. To provide peak performance during the backup process, where should you install backup devices on a network server?
   a. On the same controller as the disk drives
   b. On a separate controller from the disk drives
   c. On a UPS with its own backup battery
   d. On a DLL

5. In most cases, how can you identify pin 1 of an internal SCSI adapter?
   a. A colored strip on the edge of the ribbon cable
   b. A black-and-white strip on the edge of the ribbon cable
   c. A colored strip on the edge of the round bundle
   d. A black-and-white strip on the edge of the round bundle

6. Which of the following switches enables one keyboard, one video display, and one mouse to be utilized by multiple network servers that are in a single rack?
   a. RAID
   b. KVM
   c. SCSI-3
   d. Multiple network servers, even on a single rack, cannot utilize just one keyboard, video display, and mouse.

7. Which of the following statements about a server with bridged buses is false?
   a. A server with bridged buses has multiple buses that act as one.
   b. A server with bridged buses is configured as such to increase the number of PCI slots available on a server.
   c. Bridged buses share the available transfer speed.
   d. On a server with bridged buses, you can load balance by placing the disk controller on one bus and the NIC on another bus.

8. Which of the following must you match exactly when adding additional memory to a network server? (Choose all that apply.)
   a. The memory type
   b. The memory speed
   c. The memory N + 1
   d. All of the above

9. Why are IDE or EIDE disks seldom used in network servers? (Choose all that apply.)
   a. Because of the load they put on the processor
   b. Because of the limited number of disk drives that can be installed on a single disk controller
   c. Because they do not allow connections to internal disk drives
   d. All of the above

10. ATA disk drives are limited to how many drives per channel?
    a. One
    b. Two
    c. Three
    d. Four

11. What is the maximum length of an IDE/ATA channel ribbon cable?
    a. 12 inches
    b. 18 inches
    c. 36 inches
    d. 1 meter

12. What does the CSEL option enable an IDE disk controller to do?
    a. The CSEL option enables the IDE controller to have more than two disk drives per channel.
    b. The CSEL option enables the IDE controller to load balance.
    c. The CSEL option enables the IDE controller to select which IDE disk drive will function as master and which IDE disk drive will function as slave.
    d. The CSEL option enables the IDE controller to maintain more than one master drive per channel.

13. How wide is a PCI-64 bus?
    a. 4 bits
    b. 8 bits
    c. 32 bits
    d. 64 bits

14. A server that will be transferring large amounts of data to and from the disk drives as well as transferring large amounts of data to and from the network can have this workload balanced between peer buses. To balance the workload, you place the disk controller on one bus. Where do you place the NIC?

   a.   On the same bus.

   b.   On a different bus.

   c.   It doesn't matter.

   d.   On a PC Card.

Answers

1. **A.** The size of a UPS is specified by a volt-amp (VA) rating. The larger the VA rating of the UPS, the longer the UPS can keep the network server running in the event of a power failure. Answer B is incorrect, as it enables the keyboard, mouse, and video display to be switched among network servers. Answer C is incorrect because EIDE stands for Enhanced IDE, which is a newer version of the IDE mass storage device interface standard. Answer D is incorrect because a volt/ohm meter is used to check the voltage of the power source.

2. **B.** Servers require memory that must be installed in groups of two or four memory modules. (Check the server vendor's documentation to see whether memory modules must be installed in groups of two or four, rather than singly.) Answer A is incorrect because the size of the memory does not necessarily have to be 32MB. Answer C is incorrect because you do not have to install memory in groups of three. Answer D is incorrect, of course, because you can add memory to a network server.

3. **A, B,** and **C.** The server specialist must verify that the processors are of the same type, speed, and stepping (version). Answer D is incorrect because it doesn't matter whether the processors are all the same age (although this might affect whether they are the same version and speed).

4. **B.** The backup devices should be installed on a separate controller from the disk drives of the network server to provide peak performance during the backup process. Answer A is incorrect because your backup devices should not be on the same controller as your disk drives. Answer C is incorrect because a UPS is an uninterruptible power supply, which is a device that enables a computer to keep running for at least a short time after the primary power source has been lost. Answer D is incorrect because DLL is the abbreviation for dynamic link library, which is a file containing small sections of executable code or data that can be used by a Windows application.

5. **A.** Internal SCSI cables are generally ribbon cables, with pin 1 identified by a colored (usually red) strip on the edge of the ribbon cable. Answer B is incorrect because the pin is usually marked with a colored strip, not a black-and-white one. Answers C and D are incorrect because an internal SCSI cable is generally a ribbon cable, not a round bundle.

6. **B.** A rack-mounted network server might include a keyboard/video/mouse (KVM) switch to enable one keyboard, one video display, and one mouse to be utilized by multiple network servers that are in a single rack. Answer A is incorrect because the acronym RAID stands for redundant array of inexpensive disks. Answer C is incorrect because SCSI-3 is a Small Computer Systems Interface standard that uses a 16-bit bus and can support data rates of 160 MBps. Answer D is incorrect because the KVM switch enables a single keyboard, mouse, and video display to be switched (usually from the keyboard) among the network servers in the rack.

7. **D.** On a server with bridged buses, placing the disk controller on one bus and the NIC on the other bus has no load balancing benefit because the buses are essentially one. Answer A is incorrect because it is a true statement: A server with bridged buses has multiple buses that act as one. Answer B is incorrect because it is a true statement: A server with bridged buses is configured as such to increase the number of PCI slots available on a server. Answer C is incorrect because it is a true statement: In a server with bridged buses, both buses share the available transfer speed.

8. **A and B.** The memory type must meet the requirement of the network server hardware. You cannot mix types of memory in a server, even if the memory can be physically installed into the server. Check the memory type required by the network server hardware and make sure that all memory to be installed into the network server is of the correct type. The memory speed must also be the same for all the memory in the network server. Answer C is incorrect because $N + 1$ refers to the requirement that processors in a multiprocessor server vary by no more than one version. Answer D is incorrect because Answer C is a wrong choice.

9. **A and B.** IDE or EIDE disks are seldom used in servers due to the load that they put on the processor and the limited number of disk drives that can be installed on a single disk controller (two disks per channel and two channels per controller). Answer C is incorrect because IDE and EIDE disk controllers are also limited to disk drives that are internal to the network server. (No external connections are allowed.) Answer D is incorrect because Answer C is a wrong choice.

10. **B**. IDE disk drives and controllers (also known as ATA disk drives and controllers) are limited to two channels with a maximum of two disk drives per channel.

11. **B**. The IDE/ATA channel is a 40-conductor ribbon cable that is a maximum of 18 inches long. The short channel length limits IDE/ATA to devices that are internal to the network server.

12. **C**. The Cable Select (CSEL) option enables the IDE adapter to select which IDE disk drive will function as master and which IDE disk drive will function as slave. Answer A is incorrect because IDE disk drives and controllers (also known as ATA disk drives and controllers) are limited to two channels with a maximum of two disk drives per channel. Answer B is incorrect because the CSEL option has nothing to do with load balancing. Answer D is incorrect because you cannot have two drives designated as master. If both IDE disk drives that are on a single channel are set to master, or if both are set to slave, the disk subsystem will not work.

13. **D**. The PCI-64 bus is 64 bits wide, which means that it can transfer eight characters of data per clock cycle.

14. **B**. A server that will be transferring large amounts of data to and from the disk drives, as well as transferring large amounts of data to and from the network, can have the workload balanced between the peer buses. You just place the disk controller on one bus and the NIC on the other bus. Answer A is incorrect because you would achieve no load balancing if you have the disk controller and the NIC on the same bus. Answer C is incorrect because to effectively load balance you need to have the disk controller on one bus and the NIC on another bus. Answer D is incorrect because a PC Card is a credit card-sized adapter card designed to be used with portable computers.

Configuration

The following are the objectives for the *Configuration* section of the Server+ exam:

- Check/upgrade BIOS/firmware levels (system board, RAID, controller, hard drive, and so on).
- ConFigure C- RAID.
- Install NOS.
- ConFigure C- external peripherals (UPS, external drive subsystems, and so on).
- Install NOS updates to design specifications.

- Update manufacturer specific drivers.
- Install service tools (SNMP, backup software, system monitoring agents, event logs, and so on).
- Perform server baseline.
- Document the configuration.

Checking/Upgrading BIOS/Firmware Levels

BIOS Updates

- The BIOS version number displays when the server moves through power up.
- You should keep the latest BIOS version installed on the server at all times.
- BIOS is flashable on most operating systems, enabling it to be easily updated.

SCSI Controller BIOS

- The SCSI controller displays the current version of the BIOS on power up.
- The SCSI controller may require a new chip when you install the latest version of the BIOS, if there is a compatibility issue between the BIOS and the subsequent chip.

RAID Controller BIOS

- The RAID controller displays its BIOS version during power up.
- The RAID controller may require a BIOS chip replacement in order to be upgraded.
- Check the vendor Web site for RAID controller BIOS update information.

Firmware Levels

- All current levels of firmware can be found at the vendor's Web site.
- Firmware level upgrades are usually found on the same page with drivers.
- Firmware comes in two parts: the firmware binary image and the utility used to load the firmware.

Configuring RAID

RAID Level 0

- RAID Level 0 provides disk striping but no redundancy.
- RAID Level 0 is used for increasing the level of input/output but is not fault tolerant.
- RAID Level 0 requires two disk drives to implement.

Although you can use RAID Level 0 in robust workstations, you should not use it in a production server context.

RAID Level 1

- RAID Level 1 can be used for two different implementations: disk mirroring and disk duplexing. With disk duplexing, the single failure capacity does not exist, as it does with mirroring.
- Read-level performance increases via the use of two disks, but write performance stays the same for one disk.
- RAID Level 1 duplicates the data on two separate disk drives that are configured into two separate controllers.
- RAID Level 1 requires two disk drives to implement.

RAID Level 5

- RAID Level 5 consists of date striping with parity.
- With a minimum of three overlapping disks, if one disk fails, data can be retrieved easily from one of the remaining disks.
- As the number of disks in the array increases, your overhead decreases by a factor of the number of those disks. This is best described with the following formula (where x is the number of servers):

```
1/x * 100
```

- RAID Level 5 requires three to five disk drives to implement.

RAID Level 0 + I

- RAID Level 0 + 1 (sometimes called RAID 10) is the process of mirroring (or duplexing) two RAID Level 0 arrays, which then produces a fault tolerance of RAID Level 1 combined with the I/O speed of RAID Level 0.

- RAID Level 0 + 1 equals a greater degree of performance than the other types, but ends up costing more.

- RAID Level 0 + 1 requires four disk drives to implement.

- RAID Level 0 + 1 comes in both software and hardware formats.

Installing NOS

When installing the NOS, keep the following points in mind:

- Utilize the appropriate server software vendor disks, if at all possible.

- Create appropriate boot disks and diagnostic disks during this process.

- The following information is required as part of a network server installation plan:

  - Server name

  - Password for the administrator account

- The majority of networks utilize either IPX/SPX or TCP/IP, or both.

- The frame type is required if you are using the IPX/SPX protocol.

- When using TCP/IP as the network protocol, the following is required:

  - IP domain name

  - IP address

  - Subnet mask

  - Default gateway address

  - Address of DNS server

  - Address of WINS server (Microsoft networks only)

Figure C-4 shows an example of the TCP/IP Properties dialog box in Windows 2000. Network configuration consists of two components:

- Selecting the network protocol to be used

- Configuring it to function correctly on the network for consistent connectivity

The following table shows commands that apply changes to network configurations:

Command	NOS	Description
arp	All	Resolves IP addresses to MAC addresses
config	NetWare	Used to view the IP stack configuration in NetWare networks
ifconfig	Linux/Unix	Used to view the IP stack configuration in Linux/Unix network
ipconfig	NT/2000	Used to view the IP stack configuration in Windows NT/2000 networks
netstat	All	Enables you to view a listing of ports and their status
ping	All	Verifies that a host is reachable by sending ICMP echoes
tracert	NT/2000	Tells whether a host is reachable and the route taken to reach it
winipcfg	WIN95/98	Used to view the IP stack configuration in Windows 95/98 networks

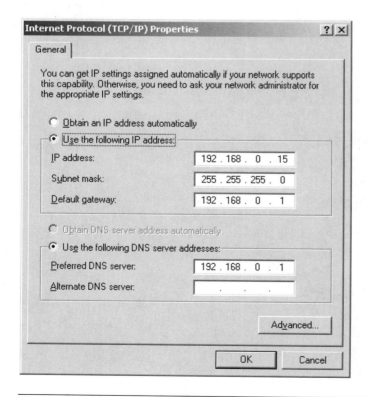

Figure C-4   The TCP/IP Properties dialog box

Configuring External Peripherals

- External disk subsystems can vary anywhere from one disk drive and one power supply to up to 100 disk drives and their subsequent power supplies.

- You can attach external drives to the system via a SCSI or RAID controller.

- Large external systems can utilize their own onboard RAID mechanism for RAID processes.

- You can configure C- external systems to be shared by multiple servers for greater availability.

- Some external CD-ROM systems can take the form of CD libraries, with up to 20 CD-ROM drivers.

- Logical Unit Numbers (LUNs) are part of the SCSI standard and are used in conjunction with large-capacity CD drives. LUNs enable the assignment of smaller SCSI-ID type components.

The UPS requires server-side software in order to detect power failures and supply power to the server. You should conFigure C- UPS software to cover the following:

- The allotted time before sending a battery power warning to clients

- The allotted time before shutting down the server

- Which software or commands to run as part of the shutdown procedure

Installing NOS Updates to Design Specifications

When installing updates, you need to keep a few things in mind. For example, you should keep the current version of the NOS installed on your machine.

You can download NOS updates from vendor Web sites. Updates are known as *patches* in the Linux and Novell community. Windows refers to its updates as *service packs*.

Updating Manufacturer-Specific Drivers

To update manufacturer-specific drivers, you need to

- Access the latest vendor-specific drivers from the vendor's Web site.

- Compare driver versions to ensure that the current one is in place.

- Record the driver version for all drivers.

Installing Service Tools

SNMP

- Simple Network Management Protocol (SNMP) is used to manage network devices such as bridges, routers, and client workstations.
- The SNMP agent is configured with an SNMP community name after installation on the network server software.
- SNMP agents can exchange data with SNMP consoles as long as the community names are synonymous.
- The Management Information Base (MIB) is the database the SNMP agent uses to monitor network devices. MIBs can be supplied for a number of network objects, including routers, bridges, gateways, hubs, and machines.

Backup Software

- Backup software is operating system specific.
- Most operating systems come with some type of backup component.
- If your needs are more specialized in terms of backup type, you might want to go with third-party backup software.

System Monitoring Agents

Major network server hardware vendors often have server monitoring and management software available. In order for this software to monitor the different components of the network server, you need to install the monitoring agents on the network server. This process is usually accomplished automatically when using the network server vendor's setup software. It might be necessary to install these monitoring agents after the network operating system is installed, however. Simply follow the network server vendor's instructions to install the system monitoring agents.

System monitoring agents enable you to monitor all types of network processes, including

- Processor speed and work
- Network utilization
- Hardware temperature

Event Logs

- Event logs are Microsoft service components that catalog any type of event that happens in the network architecture. You can set event logs to monitor specific events.
- Event logs are installed on the network server software, by default.
- The event log size should be set to minimum amounts in order to keep the log capacity stabilized.

Performing Server Baseline

A *server baseline* is a measurement of the server's performance. The purpose of taking a baseline measurement is to log information about the server's tasks. The following are the major network component baselines that you should monitor:

- Processor
- Memory
- Disk subsystem
- Network subsystem

In order to ascertain network server utilization, compare the recorded numbers with the baselines collected over a set period of time. You should consider upgrades as the network component nears its maximum level of utilization.

Documenting the Configuration

Documentation should consist of the following information:

- Server name
- OS version
- RAID configuration
- NIC network address (for each card)
- SNMP group name
- Size and location of swap file(s)
- Monitoring agents installed
- Backup software and version
- Baseline measurements
- System BIOS version

You should change the documentation information whenever major server upgrades are made that will significantly impact the network infrastructure.

Further Reading

Troubleshooting Power Sources and Power Protection Devices — www. pcguide.com/ts/x/comp/power.htm

What Is RAID? — www.adaptec.com/worldwide/product/prodtechindex.html? cat=%2fTechnology%2fRAID

System BIOS — www.pcguide.com/ref/mbsys/bios/index.htm

Network Operating System Comparison — www.openvms.compaq.com/ openvms/whitepapers/nosc/nosc.html

SNMP — www.rad.com/networks/1995/snmp/snmp.htm

Test Your Knowledge

1. Which Linux command enables you to view the network configuration?
   a. ipconfig
   b. inetcfg
   c. ifconfig
   d. ping

2. Which IP address is the best one to ping for network connectivity?
   a. 128.168.1.200
   b. Default gateway IP
   c. Microsoft.com
   d. 207.46.131.91

3. Which of the following pieces or information can be used for configuring IPX/SPX?
   I. Ethernet frame type
   II. IP address
   III. Default gateway
   IV. Token Ring frame type
   a. I only
   b. II and IV only
   c. I, III, and IV
   d. I and IV

4. Which of the following statements best describes an external disk subsystem?
   a. A tower chassis with seven or more CD-ROM drives
   b. A second or third hard disk drive installed on a single server
   c. A jukebox of CD-ROM drives
   d. Hard disk drives that are external to the server chassis

5. When configuring an external disk subsystem, which of the following is good advice regardless of the type of connection you use to connect the subsystem to your server chassis?
   a. Turn on the subsystem before the network server.
   b. Turn off the subsystem, boot the server, and then turn on the subsystem.
   c. Use fiber channel only.
   d. Turn on both the subsystem and server simultaneously.

6. What name is often associated with an external CD-ROM system?
   a. CD-ROM drive network
   b. CD-ROM array
   c. CD-ROM library
   d. CD-ROM jukebox

7. Which of the following statements most closely describes an LUN?
   a. Enables multiple servers to reside on a network
   b. A cable that connects a disk subsystem to a server
   c. Provides a way to remotely administer a LAN
   d. Enables you to assign sub-SCSI IDs to a single SCSI ID

8. What information is needed by the server from a UPS during a power outage?
   I. Which programs to shut down
   II. When there has been a power failure
   III. Amount of time to wait before beginning a shutdown
   IV. When the UPS is providing power to the network from its batteries
   a. I and II
   b. II
   c. II and IV
   d. III

9. Which of the following is generally *not* an item that is configured for UPS software?

   a. Time to wait before sending a warning to clients
   b. Time to wait before beginning a shutdown
   c. Time to wait before software updates
   d. Name of program or commands to run during shutdown

10. What type of software usually lets you check the voltage level entering and leaving the UPS?

   a. NOS
   b. UPS monitoring software
   c. Windows NT/2000
   d. LUN

11. Which name is given to Novell NOS updates?

   a. Patches
   b. Service packs
   c. Fixpacs
   d. Softpacs

12. Where is the best place to find the latest driver for a network server component?

   a. CD-ROM on which the NOS was delivered
   b. Hardware vendor's Web site
   c. Hardware CD-ROM
   d. NOS vendor's Web site

13. Which of the following best describes the purpose of the SNMP community name?

   a. Provides redundant data backup
   b. Provides a primitive form of security
   c. Enables SNMP to monitor network devices
   d. Sets swap file size per volume

14. Which of the following is the Windows NT/2000 swap file?

   a. pagefile.sys
   b. pagefile.com
   c. pagefile.ini
   d. pagefile.cnt

Answers

1. **C.** This command is used by Linux and Unix to view or change the network configuration. Answer A is incorrect, as this is a command for Windows NT/Windows 2000. Answer B is incorrect, as this is a command for Novel NetWare 4.x/5.x. Answer D is incorrect, as this verifies network connectivity.

2. **B.** The default gateway should always be available to return the ping request. Answer A is incorrect, as this address may not always be available. Answer C is incorrect, as microsoft.com may not be available at the time of your ping request. Answer D is incorrect, as this is the microsoft.com IP address and may not be available at the time of your ping request.

3. **D.** These frame types are used for configuring IPX/SPX, depending on the network configuration. Answer A is incorrect because Token Ring frame type is another valid answer. Answer B is incorrect, as IP address is not used for the IPX/SPX protocol. Answer C is incorrect because default gateway is not used for the IPX/SPX protocol.

4. **D.** An external disk subsystem is a set of hard disk drives that are external to the server chassis. Answer A is incorrect, as this defines an external CD-ROM system. Answer B is incorrect, as these hard disks are internal disks, not external. Answer C is incorrect, as this is an external CD-ROM subsystem.

5. **A.** You should be sure the power switch on the external disk subsystem is ON before turning on the network server. Answer B is incorrect, as it's just the opposite of what you should do. Answer C is incorrect, as this is a connection device. Answer D is incorrect, as you want to make sure the subsystem is on first.

6. **C.** External CD-ROM systems are often referred to as a CD-ROM library. Answers A and B are incorrect, as these are not systems. Answer D is incorrect, as this is the name that describes a device that holds a number of CDs.

7. **D.** A LUN is a Logical Unit Number that enables multiple devices to share the same SCSI ID. Answer A is incorrect, as this describes a feature of an NOS. Answer B is incorrect, as this is a standard external SCSI cable or fiber channel. Answer C is incorrect, as this is a utility provided by an NOS.

8. **C.** The network server needs to know when there has been a power failure and that the UPS is supplying power to the network from its batteries. Answer A is incorrect, as choice I describes information that is configured on the server and does not come from the UPS. Answer B is incorrect, as choice IV must be sent to the server as well. Answer D is incorrect, as choice II must be sent to the server as well.

9. **C.** This is not part of configuring the UPS software, although it may be a built-in part of any software (including UPS software). Answers A, B, and D are all things you should consider configuring when setting up UPS software.

10. **B.** UPS monitoring software often includes the capability to check the status of the UPS, such as the voltage level entering the UPS, as well as the voltage level leaving the UPS. Answer A is incorrect, as the NOS does not have the capability to check these levels. Answer C is incorrect, as this is an NOS. Answer D is incorrect, as this is the LUN, which enables multiple devices to share the same SCSI ID.

11. **A.** Novell refers to updates to its NOS as patches. Answer B is incorrect, as this is the name used by Microsoft. Answer C is incorrect, as this is the name for IBM updates. Answer D is incorrect, as this is the name used for Compaq's device driver updates.

12. **D.** You should download the NOS updates from the vendor's Web site. Answer A is incorrect, as the drivers on the CD-ROM may be outdated. Answer B is incorrect, as the hardware vendor's Web site might not have the latest driver for your particular NOS. Answer C is incorrect, as the hardware CD-ROM might have outdated drivers.

13. **B.** The SNMP community is a primitive form of security for the SNMP protocol. Answer A is incorrect, as this is RAID. Answer C is incorrect, as this is the SNMP agent. Answer D is incorrect, as this is pagefile.sys.

14. **A.** The name of the Windows NT/2000 swap file is pagefile.sys. Answers B, C, and D are not valid swap filenames.

Upgrading

The following are the objectives for the *Upgrading* section of the Server+ exam:

- Perform full backup.
- Add processors.
- Add hard drives.
- Increase memory.
- Upgrade BIOS/firmware.
- Upgrade adapters (such as NICs, SCSI cards, RAID, and so on)
- Upgrade peripheral devices: internal and external.

- Upgrade system monitoring agents.
- Upgrade service tools (such as diagnostic tools, EISA configuration, diagnostic partition, SSU, and so on).
- Upgrade UPS.

Performing Full Backups

When performing backups, keep the following in mind:

- Make sure you have more than one copy of the system backup, in case you need to perform the backup more than once.
- There are three basic backup strategies:
  - **Full**   Also known as an archival backup. Backs up all data. Has the longest backup time and the shortest restore time.
  - **Incremental**   Backs up only the files added or changed since the previous backup. Requires multiple tapes to back up (last full backup tape plus all incremental backups).
  - **Differential**   Backs up only the files modified since the last full backup. Do *not* mix incremental backups with differential backups.

Adding Processors

When adding processors, check the following to see whether the motherboard will support a faster processor:

- Clock cycle speed
- Physical requirements

Remember that you should also upgrade the system board's BIOS when upgrading to a faster processor.

To install multiple processors, the following requirements must be met:

- The new processor must be same model as existing one.
- The level 2 cache size must be identical.
- The clock speed must be the same.
- The stepping must match.

To upgrade Windows NT/2000 to support multiple processors, the hardware abstraction layer (HAL) on the network server must be updated to recognize multiple processors.

To enable NetWare 5 to support multiple processors, use NWCONFIG, which will make the necessary modifications to STARTUP.NCF and AUTOEXEC.NCF.

In order for Linux to support multiple processors, you must rebuild the kernel.

Adding Hard Drives

You can upgrade ATA/IDE disk drives in one of the following two ways:

- By adding an extra drive

- By replacing the slower drive with a faster model

Remember that only two disk drives per channel are allowed on ATA/IDE controllers. Use a 40-pin connector on the hard disk drive to attach additional drives. After attaching, select the correct master-slave CSEL roles for the disks.

Disk drive speed is measured in rotational speed—5,400, 7,200, and 10,000 revolutions per minute (RPM). Faster rotational speed equals faster seek time.

When you upgrade from ATA/IDE or ATA-2/EIDE disk drives to SCSI disk drives, you need to remove or disable all ATA/IDE or ATA-2/EIDE drives, and then you can install the SCSI bus controller and SCSI disk drive.

You can upgrade a SCSI disk drive in one of the following two manners:

- By adding a SCSI disk to an existing SCSI channel

- By replacing the existing SCSI disks with a faster disk drive

To add an internal SCSI hard drive, you need to verify the appropriate connectors on the SCSI bus ribbon cable.

External SCSI devices are normally daisy-chained to the SCSI channel.

To replace a SCSI hard disk, perform the following steps:

1. Remove the existing SCSI hard disk.

2. Check the SCSI ID.

3. Set the new SCSI hard disk to match the ID of the previous one, and then install it.

Adding drives to a SCSI-based RAID is the same as adding them to a SCSI channel. With SCSI-based RAID, you must use the RAID **config** utility to add disk drives to the array.

You need to initialize each disk drive when making the SCSI drives part of an existing RAID array. You will lose the data on the existing drives.

Increasing Memory

Check the following before adding memory:

- The number of memory slots available
- The current module's speed and capacity
- The memory module type (SIMM, DIMM, RIMM, buffered, unbuffered, or registered)
- The memory type (DRAM, SDRAM, or RDRAM)
- The error-detection method (parity/non-parity or ECC/non-ECC)

Keep the following in mind when attempting to install memory:

- Install memory in accordance with the manufacturer's specs.
- Memory must be installed in pairings of four.
- Use a continuity module for module slots, as all slots must be filled.

Typical memory choices for servers include

- **SIMMs**   Single inline memory modules
- **DIMMs**   Dual inline memory modules
- **RIMMs**   The name is not an acronym, but a trademark of Rambus Inc.

Upgrading BIOS/Firmware

When upgrading your system's BIOS, keep the following points in mind:

- Determine the current BIOS version by looking through the operating system as it boots to see the current level.
- Do not interrupt the BIOS flashing process.
- You must purchase a new BIOS chip to replace the existing one if the BIOS cannot be upgraded via a flash upgrade mechanism.

The steps to upgrade your system's flash BIOS are as follows:

1. Retrieve the current BIOS from the vendor's Web site.
2. Load the BIOS onto a floppy, and then shut down and reboot from the floppy that contains both the latest BIOS and the upgrade program.
3. Follow the on-screen instructions.

Firmware is the software that gets integrated into a card that enables it to function. Whereas the driver connects the hardware to the operating system, firmware is what actually makes the card run.

To prepare for firmware upgrades

*   Analyze the system to make sure a firmware update is required.
*   Make sure power is continually supplied to the UPS.
*   Make each reboot a cold reboot.
*   Back up the entire system.

Upgrading Adapters

Upgrading adapters takes different forms:

*   Swapping a faster adapter for the existing one
*   Upgrading adapter BIOS and firmware

The following are adapter components that you will eventually have to update:

*   **Network interface cards (NICs)**   NICs may have to be installed when the bandwidth is greater than a single card can handle. If you use more than one card for access, you are getting into the process of load balancing.
*   **SCSI adapter**   A SCSI adapter will use onboard memory for cache between the SCSI drive and server memory. A larger onboard memory buffer means more information.
*   **Video adapter**   A video adapter uses memory to display the current image. More memory equals higher resolution and more colors.
*   **RAID controller**   A RAID controller is backed up by an onboard battery. A RAID controller acts like a SCSI adapter in that it functions as a buffer.

Upgrading Peripheral Devices

There are two types of peripheral devices:

- **Internal**   Examples of internal devices include floppy disk drives, CD-ROM drives, DVD drives, and NICs.
- **External**   External peripherals are defined as components external to the network server chassis. Examples include hot-swap and plug-and-play devices, printers, monitors, keyboards, and mice.

Upgrading System Monitoring Agents

System monitoring agents are vendor-supplied software that monitor network functionality. They keep watch over things such as

- Configuration
- Mass storage
- NICs
- System utilization
- Thermal conditions
- Operating system status

Monitoring agents report to their consoles using standard protocols such as HTTP, SNMP, and DMI. The management console can come in any of the following formats:

- Standard Web browser
- Vendor-supplied management console
- Third-party network management console

Upgrading Service Tools

A service tool is a unique network server component, used to conFigure C- and maintain the network server. It is installed on the network server along with the initial installation of the server operating system. Vendors release new versions of service tools to fix bugs, add new features, or support new hardware.

Types of service tools include the following:

- **Server support tools**   Server support tools perform such functions as backups and antivirus protection.

- **EISA configuration tools** EISA configuration tools are used to conFigure C- the network components of servers with EISA buses.

- **Diagnostic tools** Regular diagnostic tools are network server-specific. Third-party diagnostic tools are also available.

Upgrading UPS

Possible reasons for upgrading the UPS include

- The power provisions from the existing UPS are low.

- The server cannot shut down properly.

- The amount of equipment supported by the UPS has increased.

When upgrading a system's UPS, keep the following points in mind:

- Always shut down the server when replacing a UPS with one with a higher VA rating.

- The charge time for a typical UPS is 12 hours.

- Most UPS models require that you power down the network server when replacing the UPS's battery.

- Some UPS models let you hot swap the UPS's battery while the network server is running.

Figure C-5 shows an example of a rack-mounted UPS.

Further Reading

Backups and Disaster Recovery—**www.pcguide.com/care/bu/index.htm**

Figure C-5 A rack-mounted UPS from American Supply

Non-Parity, Parity, and ECC Memory—**www.pcguide.com/ref/ram/errParity-c.html**

BIOS Upgrades—**www.pcguide.com/ref/hdd/bios/overBIOS-c.html**

Firmware—**www.pcguide.com/ref/hdd/op/logicFirmware-c.html**

Additional Peripheral Installation Procedure—**www.pcguide.com/proc/pcassy/periphs-c.html**

Extended Industry Standard Architecture (EISA) Bus—**www.pcguide.com/ref/mbsys/buses/types/olderEISA-c.html**

Universal Power Supply Overview—**www.pcguide.com/ref/power/ext/ups/over.htm**

Test Your Knowledge

1. What technology lets you replace an adapter without shutting down the server?
   a. Flashable BIOS
   b. EIDE
   c. Hot docking
   d. PCI hot plug

2. Which type of software can sometimes predict the impending failure of a network component?
   a. Network monitoring agent
   b. Network protocol
   c. Office suite
   d. RAM drive

3. Which of the following is not a type of service tool category?
   a. Diagnostic tools
   b. EISA configuration
   c. Diagnostic partition
   d. BIOS support

4. Before installing a new UPS, what should you do?
   a. Upgrade the RAM.
   b. Plug it into AC power.
   c. Install an energy-efficient hard disk.
   d. Discharge all its power.

5. Which of the following is not a step in replacing a UPS?
   a. Shut off the new UPS.
   b. Power off the network server.
   c. Disconnect all power cords from the old UPS.
   d. Turn off the old UPS.

6. How are EPROMs different from EEPROMs?
   a. EPROMS are erased via software.
   b. EPROMS are erased via ultraviolet light.
   c. EPROMS cannot be erased.
   d. EEPROMS are erased via ultraviolet light.

7. When upgrading IDE/ATA/EIDE/ATA-2 disk drives to SCSI drives, what two actions must you take to boot from a SCSI drive? (Choose all that apply.)
   a. Enable BIOS on SCSI bus controller.
   b. Set SCSI ID to one.
   c. Disable BIOS on SCSI bus controller.
   d. Set SCSI ID to zero.

8. What should you remember when upgrading memory in your network server?
   a. Tin and gold can be mixed between memory modules and slot connectors.
   b. Tin cannot be used with memory modules.
   c. Gold cannot be used with memory modules.
   d. Tin and gold cannot be mixed between memory modules and slot connectors.

9. If using RIMM memory modules, what must be done if a memory slot is empty?
   a. Install an SIMM module.
   b. Install a DIMM module.
   c. Install a continuity module.
   d. Leave it empty.

10. Which of the following is generally not a reason to upgrade your network server BIOS?
    a. BIOS expires
    b. Correcting known bugs in the BIOS code
    c. Adding support for newer and/or faster processors
    d. Adding plug-and-play support

Answers

1. **D.** PCI hot plug (or PCI hot swap) enables an adapter to be replaced, upgraded, or added without powering down the network server. Answer A is incorrect, as this technology is for upgrading a BIOS. Answer B is incorrect, as this is a drive type. Answer C is incorrect, as this is a technology for dynamically adding or removing hardware devices.

2. **A.** In some cases, network-monitoring agents are able to predict the impending failure of network server components, such as the processor, the memory, or the hard disk drives. Answer B is incorrect, as this is the type of software that enables network devices to communicate. Answer C is incorrect, as this enables users to perform routine word-processing, spreadsheet, and other user tasks. Answer D is incorrect, as this sets up a virtual drive that is stored in RAM.

3. **D.** This is not a category of service tools. Answers A, B, and C (and server-support utilities) are service tool categories.

4. **B.** You should plug in a new UPS to let its batteries to charge. Answer A is incorrect, as this does not affect UPS systems. Answer C is incorrect, as it is a good idea in case your system does switch over to the UPS during a power outage but does little to the actual UPS prior to installing the UPS. Answer D is incorrect, as you should charge up the UPS.

5. **A.** You should turn on the new UPS when you attach it to the server. Answers B, C, and D are all correct steps you take when replacing a UPS.

6. **B.** Erasable Programmable Read-Only Memory (EPROMs) are erased via exposure to ultraviolet light. They also require a special device to let them be reprogrammed after they have been erased. Answer A is incorrect, as it is EEPROMs that are erased via software. Answer C is incorrect, as you can erase EPROMs. Answer D is incorrect, as it is EPROMs that are erased via ultraviolet light.

7. **A and D.** In order to boot from a SCSI disk drive, the BIOS on the SCSI bus controller must be enabled, and the SCSI ID of the boot disk must be set to zero. Answers B and C are incorrect as the settings must enabled and set to zero.

8. **D.** Do not mix tin and gold between memory modules and memory slot connectors. Answer A is incorrect, as you cannot mix the two metals. Answer B is incorrect, as tin can be used with memory modules. Answer C is incorrect, as gold can be used with memory modules.

9. **C.** If a RIMM memory module is not installed in a slot, then a continuity module must be installed. A continuity module does not contain any memory. Answer A is incorrect, as you cannot use an SIMM module in a RIMM slot. Answer B is incorrect, as you cannot use a DIMM module in a RIMM slot. Answer D is incorrect, as you must populate all RIMM slots with memory modules or a continuity module.

10. The BIOS does not expire. It may grow outdated, however, compared to the software and hardware that becomes available. Answers B, C, and D are all reasons why you might upgrade the server BIOS.

Proactive Maintenance

The following are the objectives for the *Proactive Maintenance* section of the Server+ exam:

- Perform regular backup.
- Create baseline and compare performance.
- Set SNMP thresholds.
- Perform physical housekeeping.
- Perform hardware verification.
- Establish remote notification.

Performing Regular Backups

Backups come in three types:

- **Full**   Backs up all files
- **Differential**   Backs up files modified since the last full backup
- **Incremental**   Backs up files modified since the last full or incremental backup

Other types of backup procedures include the following:

- **Copy**   Copies files to some form of portable storage
- **Daily**   Backs up files every day
- **Partial**   Copies all files within a particular directory

The following are some backup strategies to keep in mind:

- Run a full backup once a week and an incremental backup every other weeknight.

or

- Run a full backup once a week and a differential backup every other weeknight.

Tape is the recommended backup media because it is

- Inexpensive
- Reusable
- Transportable
- Capable of holding a large capacity

The media options for Windows NT backups include tape, high-capacity disk drives, as well as DVD-RAM. Click the Backup button on the Management Console toolbar or use NTBACKUP.EXE from the command line.

To access the Windows 2000 Backup utility, follow this path: select Start | Programs | Accessories | System Tools | Backup | Backup Tab | Start Backup. Figure C-6 shows an example of the Backup utility in Windows 2000 Server.

Creating Baselines and Comparing Performance

A *baseline* consists of a point in time of the server's life cycle running at maximum optimization. When compiling a baseline, keep the following in mind:

- Acquire baseline information from data that exists across a span of resources.
- Update baselines when you make significant changes to the network server system.
- Use the Performance Monitor tool to monitor performance in Windows 2000.

Setting SNMP Thresholds

The SNMP enables you to remotely monitor and troubleshoot network components, such as routers and bridges.

Using SNMP, you can obtain information from each client about the following:

- Hard drive space
- IP addresses and ports

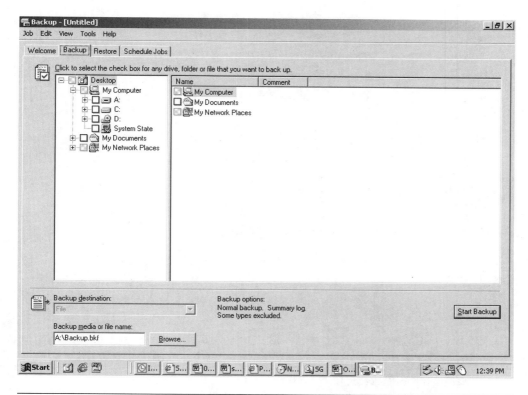

Figure C-6 The Windows 2000 Backup utility

- Host and BIOS versions
- The number of open files

The SNMP Management System is a management console that queries the SNMP agent on a server at periodic times and collects data from those intervals. The statistics can then be displayed graphically or captured in a log file. SNMP Management System commands are as follows:

- **get**   Makes a request for a set value
- **get next**   Makes a request for the value of the next object in the queue
- **set**   Makes a change to the value of an object that has read/write properties

An SNMP community is the group of hosts running the SNMP service to which all groups are a part. Communities are defined by community name.

SNMP agent security options include

- **Accepted community names**   Illustrates the list of accepted community names to which the SNMP agent can respond
- **Accept SNMP packets from any host**   Responds to any query from any internal management system
- **Accept SNMP packets from these hosts**   Responds to listed hosts only
- **Send authentication trap**   Tells the trap initiator that the trap failed

SNMP errors are recorded in the system log.

Performing Physical Housekeeping

- Server rooms should be both temperature and humidity controlled and free of dust.
- Ambient heat factors will affect server performance; do not place a server near ductwork or AC units.
- Do not put a server near electrical appliances (motors, microwaves, or electrical equipment) that generate excessive electromagnetic interference (EMI).
- Lock down the server inside a server closet.
- Make sure cabling run in a drop ceiling has enough space so that air can circulate freely.
- Use plenum-grade PVC coaxial cabling for drop ceiling crawlspaces.

Figure C-7 shows an example of PVC coaxial cabling with an F-type connector.

F-Type

Figure C-7   PVC coaxial cabling with F-type connector

Performing Hardware Verification

Hardware verification is the process of making sure that the hardware is operating and understands the calls the bus processor makes to it. You can verify hardware by using the tools provided by the operating system.

- For Windows NT, use the NT Hardware Query tool.

- For Windows 2000, use the General tab located in System Properties.

- For Linux, check the /roc file structure.

System BIOS information can give you statistics on hard drives and operating system parameters.

Establishing Remote Notification

Use SNMP for remote event notification. Through TCP/IP integration, SNMP can be used in a variety of server environments, including Windows NT/2000 and Linux.

Remote notification can also be obtained by using operating system-specific tools. One such example is the Messenger Service that is included with Windows 2000.

Further Reading

Backups and Recovery—**www.pcguide.com/care/bu/index.htm**

QIC Standards—**www2.qic.org/qic/html/qicstan.html**

SNMP Overview—**www.rad.com/networks/1995/snmp/snmp.htm**

Test Your Knowledge

1. SNMP runs at which port by default?
   a. Port 161
   b. I/O port 060-06F
   c. COM1
   d. RS-232C

2. Why should you not use polyvinyl chloride (PVC) coaxial cable in the space above a drop ceiling (between the ceiling and the floor of a building's next level)?
   a. It has a range of just ten meters.
   b. When on fire, it produces poisonous fumes.

   c. On average, the cable deteriorates yearly, and replacement in such a space is expensive and hazardous.

   d. No reason. You should use PVC cable in the space above a drop ceiling.

3. In Windows 2000, if you set a notification threshold, which service actually provides the notification when the requisite conditions exist?

   a. Bulletin Board Service

   b. Messenger Service

   c. Microsoft Download Service

   d. Windows Naming Service

4. When using the Linux **cpio** backup utility, which option enables you to overwrite existing files?

   a. d

   b. f

   c. t

   d. u

5. In Windows 2000, which tool enables you to monitor system performance?

   a. NTFS

   b. Performance

   c. Network monitor

   d. NTDSUTIL

6. Which Windows NT utility enables you back up the Registry to one floppy disk?

   a. Disk management

   b. REGEDIT.EXE

   c. RDISK.EXE

   d. RJ-45

7. With regard to servers, what is the best definition of a baseline?

   a. A disk or tape that contains a copy of data

   b. A disk that enables you to boot to a basic OS to run repair applications

   c. A snapshot in time of how a server is running

   d. All of the above

Answers

1. **A.** SNMP is the Simple Network Management Protocol. Running at port 161 by default, it is the only way to obtain true statistics of network usage under TCP/IP. Answer B is incorrect because it is the I/O port for a keyboard controller. Answer

C is incorrect because the COM designation refers to serial ports in a computer (1 through 4). Answer D is incorrect because RS-232C is a serial interface standard.

2. **B.** PVC cabling gives off poisonous fumes when it burns. Answer A is incorrect because PVC coaxial cable is not limited to just 10 meters. Answer C is incorrect because PVC coax cable does not deteriorate yearly. Answer D is incorrect because you should definitely not use PVC cabling in the drop space; in fact, fire codes prohibit PVC cabling in the plenum (space above the drop ceiling) because poisonous fumes in the plenum can circulate freely throughout the building.

3. **B.** Within Windows 2000, you can establish thresholds to notify you when conditions exist (such as when the available memory on a machine drops below a specified level). Such notifications are sent via the Messenger Service. Answer A is incorrect because a BBS is an electronic message center serving a specific interest group. Answer C is incorrect because MSDL is an official Microsoft dial-in BBS that contains sample programs, device drivers, patches, and so on. Answer D is incorrect because WINS is the Microsoft-specific naming service that can be used to assign IP addresses to computer domain names within a LAN environment.

4. **D.** You can use the u option with the **cpio** utility to overwrite existing files. Answer A is incorrect because the d option enables you to create directories, if necessary. Answer B is incorrect because the f option enables you to specify a file. Answer C is incorrect because the t option enables you to show the contents.

5. **B.** To monitor system performance in Windows 2000, you can use the Performance tool. Answer A is incorrect because NTFS is the file system in Windows 2000. Answer C is incorrect because the Network Monitor is a troubleshooting utility that enables you to capture and view network traffic. Answer D is incorrect because NTDSUTIL is a utility that enables you to seize a single-operations master and to perform authoritative restores.

6. **C.** Windows NT enables you to make a backup of the Registry that fits on a floppy disk using the **rdisk.exe** utility. This utility compresses the hives that constitute the Registry to where they will fit on a floppy and enables you to recover only the Registry should it become corrupted. Answer A is incorrect because Disk Management is a Windows 2000 tool that enables you to create and delete partitions, format disks using different file systems, create additional primary partitions, and create dynamic disks for RAID arrays and Active Directory services (and replaces the **fdisk** and **format** utilities). Answer C is incorrect because it is the Registry Editor, a Windows 9x utility that enables you to manage the Registry. Answer D is

incorrect because RJ-45 is a type of cable connector associated with twisted-pair network cables.

7. **C.** A baseline is a snapshot in time of how a server is running. A system's baseline should always be a collection of utilization data on a wide range of resources. Answer A is incorrect because it describes a backup. Answer B is incorrect because is describes an emergency start disk.

Environment

The following are the objectives for the *Environment* section of the Server+ exam:

- Recognize and report on physical security issues.
- Recognize and report on server room environmental issues (temperature, humidity/ESD/power surges, and backup generator/fire suppression/flood considerations).

Recognizing and Reporting on Physical Security Issues

When considering physical security issues, you need to look at a couple of things. Make certain that the server is in a lockable server rack, in a lockable room. Also know all of the server room's access points, such as adjoining rooms and ductwork. Check on all other available entry points as well.

You need to take a look at the locks that you can use. Possible lock types consist of the following:

- **Physical locks and keys**   Lock down all physical components.
- **Combination locks**   Dispense with the need for keys.
- **Card readers**   Eliminate the need for keys; they can be centrally controlled as well as access monitored.
- **Biometric key readers**   Completely secure but very expensive.

Locking the physical server protects against computer theft, unwanted tampering, and removal of server peripherals.

Figure C-8 shows an example of a lockable server cabinet from Connect-Tek.

Figure C-8   A lockable server cabinet

Auxiliary physical security for servers includes the following:

- Drive locks for removable media types
- Case locks for servers
- Sensors and alarms

Security options for backup media include the following:

- Have a third-party firm secure backups.
- Keep the media in a locked office/cabinet.
- Keep the media in a local safe.

Figure C-9   A computer media safe

Figure C-9 shows an example of a media safe from Guardall Security.

Recognizing and Reporting on Server Room Environmental Issues

Temperature Considerations

Server rooms need to be kept cool and air-conditioned year round. The room temperature should be between 65 and 70 degrees. Check the server's BTU output to make sure the air conditioning in the server room can adequately handle the heat generated by the unit. Raised floors in the server room act as air-conditioning ventilators in addition to being a housing mechanism for network cabling.

The server room should not be too humid, as excess moisture will damage server components. Conversely, a server room that is too dry will build up excessive electrostatic discharge (ESD). Make sure a dehumidifier is in place if the humidity is not controlled by the air-conditioning system.

Power Considerations

There are three types of power problems that you might encounter:

- **Transient (spikes/surges)**   The line voltage is too high. This is considered a *spike* if measured in nanoseconds and a *surge* if measured in milliseconds.

- **Low voltage (brownouts/sags)**   The line is delivering insufficient power. This can last for extended periods.

- **Outage**   No power is being delivered.

Backup generators supply power requirements to large data systems and primary organizational centers, and are used in conjunction with UPSs. Backup generator features to consider include the following:

- Time to generate power

- Power capacity

- Amount of fuel for generator

Make sure that the generator can support the system for anywhere from 36 to 72 hours.

Fire Considerations

Carbon dioxide-based fire suppression systems are the standard for server rooms. Sprinklers are dangerous as fire-suppression systems for server rooms due to the possibility of electrical fire.

Fire extinguishers are important to have on hand. Their designations are

- **Class A extinguishers**   Used with ordinary combustibles, such as wood, cloth, and paper

- **Class B extinguishers**   Used on fires involving liquids, such as oils, gasoline, and grease

- **Class C extinguishers**   Used for electrically energized fires

- **Class D extinguishers**   Used on fires involving combustible metals, such as magnesium, potassium, and sodium

Flooding Considerations

You should take the following actions in the event the server room becomes flooded:

1. Power down the server.

2. Move the equipment to the highest building point in the building.

3. Remove the hot swap drives and store them in a dry location.

4. Allow any wet components to dry for 48 hours.

Further Reading

Comparison of Power Protection Methods — **www.pcguide.com/ref/power/ext/comp.htm**

Protection Against Power Problems — **www.pcguide.com/ref/power/ext/prot.htm**

External Power Problems—**www.pcguide.com/ref/power/ext/probs.htm**

Media Storage—**www.pcguide.com/care/bu/howStorage-c.html**

Test Your Knowledge

1. Most high-end servers have what security mechanism built in that enables you to secure your hardware?
   a. Biometrics
   b. Case and drive locks
   c. Alarms
   d. All of the above

2. What is a power spike?
   a. An over-voltage measured in milliseconds
   b. An over-voltage measured in nanoseconds
   c. An under-voltage condition corrected in a few milliseconds
   d. An under-voltage that exists for an extended period of time

3. Surge suppressors cannot protect your hardware against what?
   a. Spikes
   b. Surges
   c. Sags
   d. Lightning strikes

4. What is the advantage of using card readers and proximity readers rather than a key system to secure a server environment?
    a. You can authorize and remove access from the central authentication server.
    b. You can implement a card reader for less expense than a key system.
    c. You no longer have to maintain control lists.
    d. Card readers offer no advantage over key systems.

Answers

1. **B.** With most high-end servers, you can lock the case; in many cases, you can lock the drives into the server chassis. Answer A is incorrect because biometrics are authentication techniques that use measurable physical characteristics for authentication; these are expensive, not built in, and are generally used to secure an environment (not the hardware itself). Answer C is incorrect because alarms are generally not built-in to the hardware; they are add-ons.

2. **B.** A *power spike* is a transient over-voltage that is measured in nanoseconds. Answer A is incorrect because an over-voltage measured in milliseconds is known as a *surge*. Answer C is incorrect because an under-voltage that is corrected in a few milliseconds is called a *sag*. Answer D is incorrect because an under-voltage that exists for an extended period of time is called a *brownout*.

3. **C.** A surge suppressor is an inexpensive power-line filter, which filters an incoming power signal to smooth out variations. Surge suppressors are not effective against sags. Answers A, B, and D are incorrect because surge suppressors can be very effective against spikes and surges, and can be a lifesaver in the event of catastrophic power surge, such as a lightning strike.

4. **A.** The advantage of this system over a key system is that you can authorize and remove access from the central authentication server. Instead of having to re-key a lock and redistribute keys, or reset a combination and having to redistribute the combination, you just need to turn off the access card or token. Answer B is incorrect because a card or proximity reader is more expensive to implement than a key system. Answer C is incorrect because you still have to maintain a control list that shows who has an access card or token. Answer D is incorrect because the card or proximity reader does offer an advantage (central authentication server management).

Troubleshooting and Problem Determination

This following are the objectives for the *Troubleshooting and Problem Determination* section of the Server+ exam:

- Perform problem determination.
- Use diagnostic hardware and software tools and utilities.
- Identify bottlenecks (such as processor, bus transfer, I/O, disk I/O, network I/O, and memory).
- Identify and correct misconfigurations and/or upgrades.
- Determine if problem is hardware-, software-, or virus-related.

Performing Problem Determination

You should consider the following information when a network server problem arises:

- Last known time when server was up and running
- Changes made to server since it was last operational
- Hardware that has been added recently and why
- Software that has been added recently and why
- Person who reported the problem
- Impact that server downtime will have on the organization

You should also maintain a contact list of professionals who can assist with problems. The list should contain e-mail addresses, phone numbers, and the type of problems the professional specializes in fixing. People on this list should include

- Building maintenance personnel
- Building personnel responsible for HVAC systems
- Building personnel responsible for electrical systems
- Senior system administrator
- Information Technology director
- Internet service provider contact

When using your senses to determine problems, you should check for the following:

- Alarms sounding (either server or UPS)
- Flashing error lights on hardware
- Network components hot to the touch
- Power cords or network cables disconnected
- External or SCSI devices connected correctly

Using Diagnostic Hardware and Software Tools and Utilities

Both hardware and software diagnostic tools will aid you in locating problems on your sever network system. Diagnostic tools are most likely bundled together with the operating system software.

Windows 2000 Diagnostic Tools

- **Task Manager**   Task Manager is found in both Windows NT and Windows 2000. It displays processor and memory utilization, and enables you to view the processes and applications running on the server (see Figure C-10).

- **Event Viewer**   Same as Windows NT Server's Event Viewer; updated for Windows 2000. Event Viewer maintains files regarding program, security, and system events that occur on the server.

- **Computer Management**   Replaces the Windows NT Diagnostics utility (see Figure C-11). Computer Management enables the administrator to manage both remote and local machines using a single, consolidated desktop interface. It integrates several administration tools into a single console, so that a server's administrative properties can be accessed.

- **Disk Management**   A GUI front end for managing disks and volumes in Windows 2000. It supports partitions, logical drives, new dynamic volumes, and remote disk management.

Windows 2000 Network Diagnostic Utilities

- **ipconfig**   Displays TCP/IP protocol configuration parameters for the server
- **nbtstat**   Illustrates data about sessions using NetBIOS over TCP/IP
- **netstat**   Shows information about current TCP/IP connections

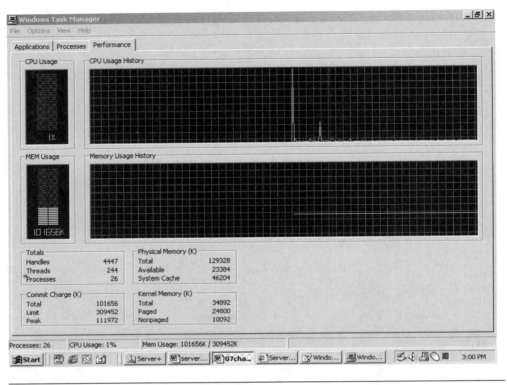

Figure C-10 The Windows 2000 Task Manager

- **nslookup** Uses a DNS server to test host name resolution
- **ping** Tests the network link between two servers
- **tracert** Provides router information through with server communication passes

All previous diagnostic utilities (**IPCONFIG**, **NBTSTAT**, **NETSTAT**, **NSLOOKUP**, **PING**, and **TRACERT**) apply the same in Windows 2000 as in Windows NT.

Novell NetWare

You can use monitor.nlm to display the following:

- Memory utilization
- Processor utilization
- Disk queue length
- Number of logged on users

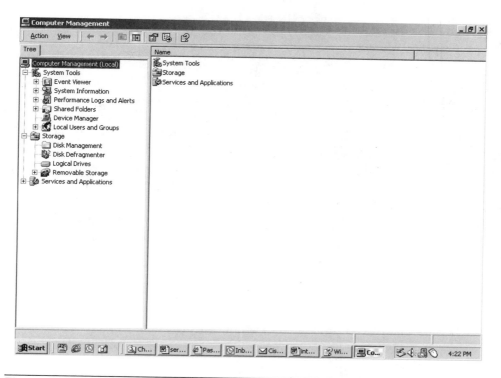

Figure C-11   The Windows 2000 Computer Management console

Linux/Unix

The aforementioned diagnostic tools (**ifconfig**, **netstat**, **nslookup**, **ping**, and **tracert**) also apply to Linux/Unix.

IBM OS/2

Use the standard tools that come bundled with IBM OS/2 (such as Netfinity Manager and Client Services for Netfinity Manager) for server administration.

Shutdown Procedures

- **Windows NT**   Use either Server Manager or the **net send** command.
- **Windows 2000**   Use either Computer Management or the **net send** command.
- **Novell Netware**   Use the **down** command at the command prompt.
- **Unix**   Use the **shutdown** command. Flags are -F (fast); -h (system halt); -k (avoids shutdown), and -r (reboot after shutdown).

- **Linux**   Use the **shutdown** command or press CTRL+D. The flags mentioned previously also apply here.

- **OS/2**   The **shutdown** command runs the **killall** command, which ends any remaining processes. Next, the **sync** command runs to flush all memory-resident disk blocks. From there, system is unmounted using the **halt** command.

Field replaceable units (FRUs) are hardware components that can be easily changed out. These usually require specialized tools or are not integrated into system boards. The following are likely FRUs: keyboards, monitors, mice, power supplies, hard disk drives, floppy drives, CD and DVD-ROM drives, system boards, video and SCSI controllers, NIC cards, processors, fans, and memory.

Logs, errors, and events are various responses by the server that give the administrator an idea as to the current level of server functionality. The following list illustrates the more common types:

- **Error logs**   Show errors that have been generated by the either applications or the operating system itself.

- **OS errors**   Display information concerning the network operating system on the server console.

- **Health logs**   Log specific hardware failures.

- **Critical events**   Show significant events occurring across the network range.

Wake-On-LAN (WOL) enables a remote machine to be powered on by sending a signal to the machine's NIC. Through WOL, the computer can then be diagnosed via remote software or backed up via the network link. WOL is the generic name of AMD's Magic Packet technology.

A *remote alert* is a signal generated by an SNMP agent. The SNMP management console runs the software that allows for SNMP troubleshooting.

Identifying Bottlenecks

A *bottleneck* is defined as an interruption in the information flow of either a microprocessor or a TCP/IP-based network. This occurs when the bandwidth is insufficient to support the amount of data being transmitted at the rate in which it is processed.

You can use performance-monitoring tools to analyze and troubleshoot bottlenecks. The following table indicates the monitoring tools for various operating systems:

Windows NT	Performance Monitor
Windows 2000	Server Performance
NetWare	Managewise
Linux/Unix	sar, iostat, vmstat, and ps
OS/2	System Performance Monitor/2 (SPM/2)

The following describes the Linux monitoring tools previously mentioned:

- **sar**   Reports and contains system activity logs

- **vmstat**   Provides data about virtual memory located on the network server

- **iostat**   Provides information about the disk subsystem's input and output

- **ps**   Creates and displays a one-time image of the processes currently running on the server in standard output mode

The following table indicates bottleneck types and how to resolve them:

Bottleneck Source	Resolution
Processor	Upgrade existing processor. Add more processors. Move resources to another server.
Disk I/O	Add memory.
Network I/O	Replace hub with switches. Eliminate unnecessary protocols.

Identifying and Correcting Misconfigurations and/or Upgrades

Identifying and correcting the various mistakes that can arise is an integral part to good server operations. When troubleshooting disk-drive problems, you should

- Check the power and cable connection.

- Listen for uncommon noises.

- Ensure the hard drive is spinning and operational.

You should check the following things when SCSI problem solving:

- The device should be set firmly in the chassis.
- The device should be connected to the controller and disk drive.
- Both channels should be properly terminated.
- The SCSI channel cable should be the correct length.

TCP/IP troubleshooting commands include

- **hostname**   Indicates the network server's name
- **ipconfig**   Indicates the current TCP/IP configuration
- **ping**   Pings the loopback address
- **ping** *ip name*   Tests TCP/IP communication with the network interface card
- **ping** *remote host ip name*   Checks to see whether the DNS server is resolving the host IP name
- **ping** *remote host*   Verifies that TCP/IP packet forwarding via the router is taking place
- **ping** *default gateway*   Verifies the network's capability to communicate among systems

Determining If Problem Is Hardware-, Software-, or Virus-Related

In order to determine a problem, follow this process:

1. Identify the problem by actively testing each component of the system. If you are having problems with a scanner, for example, you need to identify the various components of the scanning system, including the

   - Scanner application
   - Scanner driver
   - Scanner interface with either the network or a stand-alone machine
   - Scanner application where the scan will materialize

2. Check all hardware specifications and settings to ensure that problem is not hardware-related.

3. Check software for failure.

4. Use virus-checking software to check for network server virus possibilities.

Further Reading

From Power Up to Prompt—**www.linuxdoc.org/HOWTO/From-PowerUp-To-Bash-Prompt-HOWTO.html**

LILO, Linux Crash Rescue HOW-TO—**www.linuxdoc.org/HOWTO/LILO-crash-rescue-HOWTO.html**

Common Performance Issues in Network Applications. Part 1: Interactive Applications—**www.microsoft.com/windows2000/library/operations/communications/netapps.asp**

Managing Windows 2000 Disks and Backup and Restore—**www.microsoft.com/windows2000/library/planning/incremental/managedisks.asp**

Test Your Knowledge

1. What are the basic functions of the Windows NT Task Manager? (Choose all that apply.)
   a. It enables you to view the current processor and memory utilization.
   b. It enables you to view the processes running on the network server.
   c. It enables you to view the applications or programs running on the network server.
   d. It enables you to view a detailed report about the hardware and software installed on the network server.

2. Which of the following is not a Windows NT diagnostic utility?
   a. Task Manager
   b. Event Viewer
   c. Disk Management
   d. Windows NT Diagnostics

3. Which three logs does Windows NT generate?
   a. System, Security, Error
   b. System, Security, Application
   c. Security, Application, Error
   d. System, Performance, Diagnostic

4. Which Windows NT-generated log contains entries about services starting, stopping, or failing to load or start?
   a. The Diagnostic log
   b. The Performance log
   c. The Error log
   d. The System log

5. What does a hygrometer enable a server specialist to measure?
    a. Heat
    b. Cold
    c. Smoke
    d. Humidity

6. Which Windows NT Diagnostics tab displays information about the location and size of the pagefile(s)?
    a. Services
    b. Display
    c. Memory
    d. Drives

7. Which Windows 2000 Server command is used to display the TCP/IP protocol configuration for the network server?
    a. tracert
    b. ipconfig
    c. netdiag
    d. pathping

8. Windows 2000 supports Automatic Private IP Addressing (APIPA) for which of the following Windows clients?
    a. Windows 2000
    b. Windows 98
    c. Windows ME
    d. All of the above

9. Which Windows 2000 command enables you to display information about sessions that are using NetBIOS over TCP/IP?
    a. ping
    b. tracert
    c. netdiag
    d. nbstat

10. Which Windows 2000 Server command tests DNS service IP name resolution?
    a. netstat
    b. nslookup
    c. ipconfig
    d. ping

11. If you want to determine which I/O ports are used on a network server, which tab would you check on the Windows NT Diagnostics utility?
    a. Environment
    b. Resources
    c. Network
    d. Services

12. Which Windows 2000 command runs a standard set of network tests and generates a report of the results?
    a. TRACERT
    b. PING
    c. NETDIAG
    d. PATHPING

13. In which two modes can you use the Windows 2000 Server **nslookup** command?
    a. Command line and interactive
    b. Command line and verbose
    c. Verbose and passive
    d. Interactive and static

14. What is the primary Novell NetWare diagnostic tool?
    a. Performance
    b. Task Manager
    c. Monitor
    d. Registry Editor

15. Which Novell NetWare command enables you to display information about the network configuration on the Novell NetWare network server?
    a. **ipconfig**
    b. **config**
    c. **netdiag**
    d. **netconfig**

16. Which Unix/Linux command enables you to display specific information about the flags used with network performance diagnostic commands on the different versions of Unix/Linux?
    a. **ipconfig**
    b. **man**
    c. **iostat**
    d. **ps**

17. Which Unix/Linux command enables you to test TCP/IP communications between two network servers?
    a. ipconfig
    b. ping
    c. netstat
    d. ps

18. Which command enables you to shut down a Novell NetWare server?
    a. down
    b. end
    c. close
    d. ps

19. What does a clicking noise coming from a hard disk drive usually indicate?
    a. The drive is the designated download drive.
    b. The drive is a shared network drive.
    c. The drive is experiencing a catastrophic failure.
    d. The drive is operating normally.

20. What does the message Request Timed Out indicate?
    a. The pinged computer did not reply to the **ping** command.
    b. There is not a route from the computer issuing the **ping** command to the computer being pinged.
    c. There is a name resolution problem.
    d. The destination host is unreachable.

21. What is a POST diagnostics board?
    a. A Windows 2000 tool designed to replace the FDISK and FORMAT utilities.
    b. A device that plugs into a system's expansion slots and reads the information moving through the system's buses. It is used when not enough of the system is running to support any other type of diagnostic tool.
    c. A device that plugs into any available PCI expansion slot in a network server and tests the operation of the system as it powers up.
    d. All of the above

22. What is the most likely cause of a Destination Host Unreachable message?
    a. The IP name could not be resolved to an IP address by a DNS server.
    b. The computer being pinged is not currently running.
    c. There is not a valid default gateway configured in the TCP/IP configuration of the computer issuing the **ping** command.
    d. The destination host has unrecognized NICs.

Answers

1. **A, B,** and **C.** Task Manager enables you to see the current processor and memory utilization on the Performance tab. It also enables you to see which processes are running on the network server. It also lets you view the applications or programs that are running on the network server. Answer D is incorrect because it is the Windows NT Diagnostics program, not Task Manager, that enables you to view a detailed report about the hardware and software installed on the network server.

2. **C.** Disk Management is a Windows 2000 tool designed to replace the FDISK and FORMAT utilities. Answers A, B, and C are incorrect because they are Windows NT diagnostic utilities.

3. **B.** Windows NT generates three logs (viewable via Event Viewer): the System log, the Security log, and the Application log. Answers A and C are incorrect because Windows NT does not generate an Error log. Answer D is incorrect because Windows NT generates neither a Performance log nor a Diagnostic log.

4. **D.** The System log contains entries about services starting, stopping, or failing to load or start. Answers A, B, and C are incorrect because they are not Windows NT-generated logs.

5. **D.** A server hardware specialist's toolkit should include a hygrometer (humidity meter). The hygrometer can be used to get an exact humidity reading of the server room. Answers A and B are incorrect because heat and cold are measured by a thermometer. Answer C is incorrect because smoke is not measured by a hygrometer; it might be detected (in sufficient density) by a smoke detector/alarm.

6. **C.** The Memory tab displays information about the actual memory installed in the network server and its current utilization. Information about the location and size of the pagefile(s) is also displayed on this tab. Answer A is incorrect because the Services tab displays the name and status of all services currently installed on the network server. Answer B is incorrect because the Display tab contains information about the video adapter that is in the network server and the version of the software driver for the video adapter. Answer D is incorrect because the Drives tab displays information about the drives in the network service.

7. **B.** The Windows 2000 Server IPCONFIG command is used to display the TCP/IP protocol configuration for the network server. Answer A is incorrect because the Windows 2000 Server TRACERT command provides information about the routers that the communications passes through going from the current network server to another server on the network. Answer C is incorrect because the Win-

dows 2000 Server NETDIAG command runs a standard set of network tests and generates a report of the results. Answer D is incorrect because the Windows 2000 Server PATHPING command is a combination of the PING command and the TRACERT command.

8. **D.** Windows 2000 supports Automatic Private IP Addressing (APIPA) for Windows 2000, Windows 98, and Windows ME clients.

9. **D.** The Windows 2000 Server NBTSTAT command is used to display information about sessions that are using NetBIOS over TCP/IP (NBT). Answer A is incorrect because the Windows 2000 Server PING command is used to test communications between the current network server and another server on the network. Answer B is incorrect because the Windows 2000 Server TRACERT command provides information about the routers that the communications passes through going from the current network server to another server on the network. Answer C is incorrect because the Windows 2000 Server NETDIAG command runs a standard set of network tests and generates a report of the results.

10. **B.** The Windows 2000 Server NSLOOKUP command tests DNS service IP name resolution. Answer A is incorrect because the Windows 2000 Server NETSTAT command displays information about current TCP/IP connections to the network server. Answer C is incorrect because the Windows 2000 Server IPCONFIG command is used to display the TCP/IP protocol configuration for the network server. Answer D is incorrect because the Windows 2000 Server PING command is used to test communications between the current network server and another server on the network.

11. **B.** The Resources tab has multiple displays. It can display interrupt requests (IRQs), I/O ports, direct memory access channels (DMAs), memory, and devices. Answer A is incorrect because the Environment tab displays the names and values of the current system or local user environment variables. Answer C is incorrect because the Network tab displays general information about the network to which the server is attached, the transports (protocols and hardware addresses of NICs), network settings, and current network statistics. Answer D is incorrect because the Services tab displays the name and status of all services currently installed on the network server.

12. **C.** The Windows 2000 Server NETDIAG command runs a standard set of network tests and generates a report of the results. Answer A is incorrect because the Windows 2000 Server TRACERT command provides information about the routers that the communication passes through going from the current network server to

another server on the network. Answer B is incorrect because the Windows 2000 Server PING command is used to test communications between the current network server and another server on the network. Answer D is incorrect because the Windows 2000 Server PATHPING command is a combination of the PING command and the TRACERT command.

13. **A.** The Windows 2000 Server NSLOOKUP command can be used in two different modes: command line and interactive.

14. **C.** The primary Novell NetWare diagnostic tool is Monitor (MONITOR.NLM). Answer A is incorrect because Performance is a Windows 2000 tool that enables the user to monitor and view the performance of all parts of a system (but at a very low level). Answer B is incorrect because the Task Manager is a Windows diagnostic utility. Answer D is incorrect because the Registry Editor is a Windows 9x utility used to manage the Registry.

15. **B.** The CONFIG command displays information about the configuration of a Novell NetWare network server. Answer A is incorrect because the Windows IPCONFIG command is used to display the TCP/IP protocol configuration for the network server. Answer C is incorrect because NETDIAG is a Windows 2000 Server command that runs a standard set of network tests and generates a report of the results. Answer D is incorrect because NETCONFIG is not a viable command, neither under Windows nor under Novell.

16. **B.** Use the **man** command to display specific information about the flags used with these commands on the different versions of Unix/Linux. Answer A is incorrect because the **ifconfig** (interface configuration) utility is used to conFigure C- the TCP/IP configuration for a specific NIC or to display the TCP/IP configuration. Answer C is incorrect because the **iostat** command provides information about disk subsystem I/O on a Unix/Linux network server. Answer D is incorrect because the **ps** command lists all the processes running on a Unix/Linux network server.

17. **B.** The **ping** command is used to test TCP/IP communications between two network servers. Answer A is incorrect because the **ifconfig** (interface configuration) utility is used to conFigure C- the TCP/IP configuration for a specific NIC or to display the TCP/IP configuration. Answer C is incorrect because the **netstat** utility is used to display TCP/IP network statistics. Answer D is incorrect because the **ps** command lists all the processes running on a Unix/Linux network server.

18. **A.** To shut down a Novell NetWare server, you must issue the **down** command at the system console. Answers B, C, and D are incorrect because they are not valid NetWare commands.

19. **C.** A clicking noise coming from a hard disk drive is definitely a bad sign. It usually indicates a catastrophic failure of the disk drive. Answer A is incorrect because a designated download drive should not be making any clicking noise. Answer B is incorrect because a shared network drive should not be making a clicking noise. Answer D is incorrect because a normally operating drive should not be making a clicking noise.

20. **A.** The Request Timed Out message indicates that the pinged computer did not reply to the **ping** command. This usually means that the computer being pinged is not currently running. Answer B is incorrect because the message Destination Host Unreachable indicates that there is not a route from the computer issuing the **ping** command to the computer being pinged. Answer C is incorrect because the message Unknown Host indicates that the IP name could not be resolved to an IP address by a DNS server. Answer D is incorrect because it would generate a Destination Host Unreachable message.

21. **C.** A POST diagnostics board is a diagnostic device that plugs into any available PCI expansion slot in the network server and tests the operation of the system as it powers up. Answer A is incorrect because it is the definition of Disk Management, a Windows 2000 utility. Answer B is incorrect because it is the definition of POST cards.

22. **C.** The most likely cause of a Destination Host Unreachable message is that there is not a valid default gateway configured in the TCP/IP configuration of the computer issuing the **ping** command. Answer A is incorrect because if that condition exists, you would receive an Unknown Host message. Answer B is incorrect because if that condition exists, you would receive a Request Timed Out message. Answer D is incorrect because the destination host's NICs have nothing to do with the Destination Host Unreachable message.

Disaster Recovery

The following are the objectives for the *Disaster Recovery* section of the Server+ exam:

- Plan for disaster recovery
- Restoring

Planning for Disaster Recovery

A disaster can be illustrated as an unforeseen problem that results in the server going down. Therefore, disaster recovery is the process of reestablishing the server, bringing it back online, and reintegrating it with the existing network infrastructure.

Redundancy needs to be implemented into the system to ensure high availability. Redundancy is the hardware concept of having multiple servers in place in order to ensure consistent network connections and availability in the case of a server failure.

RAID is a series of components for using smaller hard drives together in a collection to simulate a larger hard drive. By having more than one hard drive, you can still save a majority of data if one is lost.

- **RAID 0**   Also known as *disk striping*, RAID 0 does not truly provide for redundancy, as it is more of the combining of two or more disks for larger storage capacity. In this fashion, data is fragmented into blocks. Each block is then written to a separate disk drive.

- **RAID 1**   This provides redundancy through *mirroring*, which duplicates data on two disks using a single disk controller.

- **RAID 5**   Also known as *striping with parity*, RAID 5 provides redundancy by allowing data to be shared across all the disks in an array.

RAID makes available the option of *hot spare for failover*. This is the process in which if one drive reaches a certain level of threshold error, it automatically loads its data onto another drive in the array, and then shuts itself down. At that point, the bad drive can be taken out of the system for further analysis at a later time.

The following shows redundancy strategies for other components:

- **Power supplies**   Add additional power supplies to shift power in the event of a failure.

- **Fans**   Keep fans well maintained during server operations.

- **NICs**   Use redundant NICs.

- **Processors**   Use multiprocessor servers.

- **UPS**   Add UPSs for power backup. Make sure that you calculate your system's power requirements before purchasing an additional UPS.

Clustering is the process of having several computers working together as one larger entity. This results in greater processing times as well as the capability for another machine to take up the spare work if anther fails.

You need to use various techniques to ensure availability:

- **Hot swap** To remove and replace a component while the power is on and the system is still operating—with no disruption to I/O functions.

- **Warm swap** To replace a component without turning off the power. While the system remains on, the component being replaced must not be in use.

- **Hot spare** A component kept on hand in case a hot swap is required (NIC, controller, and so on). To implement a hot spare, simply select the appropriate drive, and then choose the menu option to make it a hot spare. A hot spare will automatically replace a failing drive.

The next step in this process is to develop and create a disaster recovery plan. To do so,

- Analyze potential risks.
- Measure the impact it will have on the organization.
- Create processes and strategies.
- Create emergency scenarios.
- Train personnel in disaster recovery plans and measures.

Fault tolerance is a system's capability to function uninterrupted in the event of a hardware or software failure. It provides backup in the event of system problems (disk failures, power issues, operating system corruption, and so forth). You should implement fault tolerance in your disaster recovery plan.

Disaster recovery plan guidelines and procedures include

- Identifying risk-generating components.
- Identifying hardware-based risks (for example, the possibility of the server crashing).
- Implementing a fault-tolerant configuration for each component.
- Documenting the configuration of the network server components.
- Keeping spare parts for all components that cannot be organized into a fault-tolerant scheme.
- Documenting the recovery plan.

Backup tape is an inexpensive and reliable backup strategy. The following includes some of the major offerings in this arena:

- **Digital data storage (DDS)**   Developed by Sony and Hewlett Packard in 1989, DDS is a data storage format that evolved from DAT (Digital Audio Tape) technology. It is inexpensive and works well with smaller systems.

- **Digital linear tape (DLT)**   DLT provides faster speed and higher capacity than DDS and is better suited for medium- to large-scale networks.

- **Mammoth**   A tape drive, created by the Exabyte Corporation, with a considerably larger capacity than standard tape drives.

- **Linear tape open (LTO)**   The newest development in high-capacity tape technology. LTO technology is an open-format technology, which means that users have multiple choices for product and media. The open nature of LTO technology also provides a means of enabling compatibility among different vendors' offerings.

- **Advanced intelligent tape (AIT)**   AIT is an intelligent tape technology developed by Sony that offers high-speed, large-capacity storage. AIT features the Memory In Cassette (MIC) architecture, in which a memory chip is built-in to the data cartridge holding the system's log and other user-definable information.

The other type of backup hardware is disk backup. This comes in three different forms:

- **Floppy disks**   A five-inch floppy disk can hold 360K or 1.2MB. A three-inch floppy normally can store 720K, 1.2MB, or 1.44MB of data.

- **Hard disk**   Hard disks can store anywhere from 20MB to more than 10GB. Hard disks are also from 10 to 100 times faster than floppy disks.

- **Removable hard disk**   This is a type of system in which hard disks are enclosed in some sort of cartridge. You can remove them just like a floppy disk. Removable cartridges are very fast, although usually not as fast as fixed hard disks. Removable cartridge examples include such things as Zip, Jaz, and SyJet.

Traditional backup types were discussed in previous chapters. The following two strategies are alternate methods to use:

- **Tower of Hanoi**   A backup rotation scheme based on the Tower of Hanoi mathematical puzzle. Used for multiple tape backups to result in even tape wear.

- **Transactional backup**   Stores a copy of the transactional log readout to a tape medium each time it cycles through any transition.

In terms of options for backup tape storage, three options can be considered:

- Have workers keep them at their homes or some off-site storage of their choosing.
- If you have multiple options, you can swap backup tapes among them.
- Hire an off-site storage company.

Off-site storage provides the best means for ensuring data safety. Most services will come to your facility to pick up backups at regularly scheduled times.

When testing the recovery plan, you should

- Verify the recovery process for each server component.
- Know whom to alert in the event of a problem.
- Verify hot spare and equipment locations.
- Check your components' warranties and service agreements.

Restoring

In the event of a crash resulting from hardware failure, you need to identify the hardware components that need to be replaced. Remember to reference hardware parameters and configurations before restoring, either in the product's documentation or at the vendor's Web site.

Recovery site types include

- **Hot site** A backup facility that aids in restoring mission-critical information. It provides hardware and resources to aid in the complete recovery process.
- **Cold/shell site** A backup facility that is used only for storage, but that has server-room configurations, such as air-conditioning and a raised floor. Critical business processes can be stored here, and then replicated in the event of a complete environmental failure at the primary location.

Further Reading

RAID Levels—**www.acnc.com/raid.html**

Fault Tolerance Concepts with Examples — **hissa.ncsl.nist.gov/chissa/ SEI_Framework/framework_8.html**

Tape Types—**www.pctechguide.com/15tape.htm**

Minicartridge Drive Classes—**www2.qic.org/qic/image/mig/minidr.gif**

Test Your Knowledge

1. Which type of RAID is also known as a striped disk array?
   a. RAID 0
   b. RAID 1
   c. RAID 0/1
   d. RAID 5

2. Which of the following performance advantages does duplexing offer over mirroring?
   a. Only one drive is written to at a time, thereby speeding performance.
   b. Increased redundancy.
   c. You can survive a drive failure, but not a controller failure.
   d. All of the above

3. How many drives are required to implement RAID 5?
   a. Two
   b. Three
   c. Four
   d. Five

4. If you are using software RAID on a Windows NT server, which of the following partitions cannot be part of a striped set? (Choose all that apply.)
   a. Extended partition
   b. Primary partition
   c. System partition
   d. Boot partition

5. Which of the following components can a server specialist conFigure C- in a redundant manner in a server?
   a. Power supplies
   b. Cooling fans
   c. CPUs
   d. All of the above

6. In which server clustering model does one of the servers own the disk resource and the other server take ownership of the resource only if the primary server fails?
   a. Nothing-shared model
   b. Shared-device model
   c. Client/server model
   d. None of the above

7. Which term refers to how well a hardware or software system can adapt to increased demand?
   a. Redundancy
   b. Scalability
   c. Fault tolerance
   d. High availability

8. If you have a 24 × 7 × 365 system and require 99.999 percent availability, how much downtime can you have per year?
   a. 5 minutes
   b. 53 minutes
   c. 44 hours
   d. 88 hours

9. If you experience a memory failure on your network server, what should you check?
   a. That the type of memory is correct
   b. That the speed of the memory is correct
   c. That the form factor of the memory is correct
   d. All of the above

10. In which type of RAID array is the data striped across the disks and each block of data has a parity bit written to a parity drive?
    a. RAID 0
    b. RAID 1
    c. RAID 0/1
    d. RAID 5

Answers

1. **A.** RAID 0 is also known as striped disk array. In a RAID 0 array, the data is broken down into blocks and each block is written to a separate disk drive. Answer B is incorrect because RAID 1 is also known as a mirrored pair. Answer C is incorrect because RAID 0/1 is known as a mirrored, striped array. Answer D is incorrect because RAID 5 is also known as a striped array with parity.

2. **B.** Duplexing offers increased redundancy over mirroring. In a mirrored configuration, you can survive a drive failure, but not a controller failure. In a duplexed configuration, you can survive the loss of a drive or the loss of a controller. Answer A is incorrect because with duplexing, both drives can be written to con-

currently (thereby increasing performance). Answer C is incorrect because in a duplexed configuration, you can survive the loss of a drive or the loss of a controller.

3. **B.** RAID 5 requires a minimum of three drives to implement. Also known as striping with parity, RAID 5 provides redundancy by allowing data to be shared across all the disks in an array.

4. **C and D.** If you are using software RAID on a Windows NT server, the system and boot partitions cannot be a part of a striped set. Answer A is incorrect because an extended partition just refers to a secondary DOS partition that can be created after the drive's primary partition has been established. Answer B is incorrect because a primary partition just refers to the volume you create using unallocated space on a hard disk.

5. **D.** You can conFigure C- a number of server components in a redundant manner, including power supplies, cooling fans, and CPUs. Most high-end servers come with an option to install additional power supplies. This enables the server to shift the power load when a power supply fails. Additional cooling fans are usually part of the server configuration, and are not usually ordered as an option for the server. CPUs are relatively easy components to implement in a fault-tolerant way. If you buy a multiprocessor server from most of the major vendors, the server will continue to run (albeit with a degradation in performance) with a failed CPU.

6. **A.** In the nothing-shared clustering model, two servers share a disk resource, but one of the servers owns the resource, and the other server takes ownership of the resource only if the primary server fails. Answer B is incorrect because in the shared-device model, applications running within a cluster can access any hardware resource connected to any node/server in the cluster. Answer C is incorrect because a client/server model refers to a topology wherein a central control provides services and resources to a client or clients.

7. **B.** Scalability refers to how well a hardware or software system can adapt to increased demands. Answer A is incorrect because redundancy refers to having a backup that can take over in the event of a failure. Answer C is incorrect because fault tolerance refers to the capability to support a failure (or fault). Answer D is incorrect because high availability refers to the designing and configuring of a server to provide continuous use of critical data and applications.

8. **A.** If you have a 24 × 7 × 365 system and require 99.999 percent availability, you can have up to 5 minutes of downtime. Answer B is incorrect because you have up

to 53 minutes of downtime if you require just 99.99 percent availability. Answer C is incorrect because you have up to 44 hours of downtime if you require just 99.5 percent availability. Answer D is incorrect because you have up to 88 hours of downtime if you require just 99 percent availability.

9. **D.** For memory failures, you want to verify that the type of memory is correct. (That is, is it error-correcting memory, non-error-correcting, parity, and so forth?) You should also check the speed of the memory (50 nanosecond, 60 nanosecond, and so on). Finally, check the form factor. Is it a DIMM or the older SIMM type of memory?

10. **D.** In a RAID 5 array, the data is striped across the disks, much like RAID 0, but each block of data has a parity bit written to a parity drive. Answer A is incorrect because in a RAID 0 array, the data is broken down into blocks and each block is written to a separate disk drive. Answer B is incorrect because in a RAID 1 array, each drive is completely mirrored to another drive. Answer C is incorrect because in a RAID 0/1 array, two RAID 0 arrays are mirrored.

Linux+ Sample Test

Questions

Chapter 1: Planning a Linux Implementation

1. Linux is known as _____ software.
   a. Copyrighted
   b. Open source
   c. Proprietary
   d. Single-code

2. In the context of Linux, GPL stands for _____.
   a. General Periodic License
   b. GNU Positional License
   c. GNOME Public License
   d. General Public License

3. The _____ is the core of the Linux operating system.
   a. Kernel
   b. Script
   c. dll
   d. Executable file

4. The interface between the computer hardware and the operating system is controlled at the hardware level using the system _____.
   a. CMOS
   b. BIOS
   c. Interface
   d. PCI bus

5. sendmail uses the _____ protocol to communicate with other MTAs.
   a. IP
   b. TCP/IP
   c. SMTP
   d. POP

6. The _____ command is most commonly used to display the system date.
   a. timedc
   b. time
   c. date
   d. rundate

7. The client component to Samba is known as _____.
   a. smbclient
   b. samba_client
   c. sambacl
   d. cli_samba

8. Which of the following placeholders are not parameters that can be used for setting the time and date? (Choose all that apply.)
   a. td
   b. ii
   c. MM
   d. hh

9. The most common Web server associated with Linux would be the _____ Web server.
   a. Active server
   b. Apache
   c. IIS
   d. Netscape

10. _____ prints the configuration information for the configured serial ports by specifying the serial port you want the information on.
    a. setconfig
    b. serialset
    c. set_IO
    d. setserial

11. The _____ directory holds applications or programs used to operate the system.
    a. /bin
    b. /boot
    c. /dev
    d. /

12. The Debian package management system is known as _____.
    a. **debpackman**
    b. **dpkg**
    c. **debpms**
    d. **dpms**

13. Which directory holds all files necessary for system startup?
    a. /dev
    b. /bin
    c. /boot
    d. /pkg

14. What command lists all name-specified entries?
    a. **man**
    b. **info**
    c. **whatis**
    d. **whereis**

15. _____ are usually found in an online documentation format.
    a. File directories
    b. User manuals
    c. Man pages
    d. Command references

16. What directory would you access to read an external CD-ROM drive?
    a. /etc
    b. /opt
    c. /home
    d. /mnt

17. Which of the following are utilities used for finding files on the system?
    a. **man**
    b. **seek**
    c. **which**
    d. **update**

18. Use the _____ directory if you need space for additional applications in Linux.
    a. /opt
    b. /sbin
    c. /root
    d. /proc

19. You can use the _____ command in order to analyze filesystem structure.
    a. filesys
    b. dir
    c. disk
    d. fsck

20. Which command displays disk usage for files and directories?
    a. fileck
    b. chdsk
    c. du
    d. df

21. The process separating the hard disk into smaller logical sections or drives is known as _____.
    a. Partitioning
    b. Duplexing
    c. Swapping
    d. Dividing

22. Which of the following pieces of information does inode not include?
    a. File type
    b. File permissions
    c. File deletion date
    d. File size

23. The temporary storage location for files is in the _____ directory.
    a. /usr
    b. /root
    c. /
    d. /tmp

24. The _____ directory is the home directory for the root user.
    a. /
    b. /root
    c. /sbin
    d. /proc

25. Linux shared libraries can be found in the _____ directory.
    a. /proc
    b. /root
    c. /user
    d. /lib

Chapter 2: Installation

1. _____ is a common tool used in the partitioning of disks among network infrastructures.
    a. **fdisk**
    b. Directory File System (DFS)
    c. Filesystem Disk Mounting (FDM)
    d. Samba

2. POST is an acronym for _____.
    a. Power On System Terminate
    b. Post Office Self Test
    c. Power On Self Test
    d. Power On System Test

3. What component enables Linux systems to interact with Windows networks?
    a. NetBIOS Message Block (NMB) service
    b. The portmap daemon
    c. Domain Name Service (DNS)
    d. The Network File System (NFS) server

4. Which of the following are examples of dselect menu commands? (Choose all that apply.)
    a. **select**
    b. **write**
    c. **config**
    d. **install**

5. Which of the following is not an example of a generic Linux installation?
   a. Custom
   b. Server
   c. Standard
   d. Workstation

6. Which is not a Debian package priority?
   a. Standard
   b. Required
   c. Optional
   d. Additional

7. Which of the following commands are used with **fdisk**? (Choose all that apply.)
   a. a Toggles a bootable flag
   b. m Prints the partition type menu
   c. x Executes a new partition
   d. s Changes the partition system ID

8. The _____ directory is where the source RPM files are located in regards to directory tree package construction.
   a. /BUILD
   b. /SOURCE
   c. /RPMS
   d. /SRPMS

9. Which command would work best to restore files that may have accidentally been erased while the system was running?
   a. **clear**
   b. **chkalias**
   c. **grpchk**
   d. **rpm**

10. Which **tar** option lists all the contents of an archive?
    a. -v
    b. -q
    c. -f
    d. -x

11. Which of the following is not a component of the TCP/IP model?
    a. Internet
    b. Presentation
    c. Network interface
    d. Transport

12. What component of Linux enables it to coexist with other operating systems on the same hard disk?
    a. Network File System (NFS)
    b. Master boot record
    c. LILO
    d. tar

13. Protocols such as the Simple Network Management Protocol (SNMP) and the File Transfer Protocol (FTP) are found in the _____ layer of TCP/IP.
    a. Internet
    b. Application
    c. Network interface
    d. Transport

14. When dealing with kernel software naming, the x.y.z. of linux-x.y.z.tar.gz is the _____.
    a. Kernel ordination
    b. Kernel designator
    c. Version number
    d. Version name

15. If you have an application that requires streaming video, what protocol would you use to best facilitate this connection?
    a. UDP
    b. TCP
    c. IP
    d. SMTP

16. Which of the following is not an example of a window manager?
    a. Window Maker
    b. iceStep
    c. AfterStep
    d. olwm

17. Data is transported to the application layer through _____.
    a. Ports
    b. Hubs
    c. Bridges
    d. Interfaces

18. Which command should you use when configuring an Ethernet card?
    a. ifport
    b. ifconfig
    c. winipconfig
    d. ping

19. The user who would have the most privileges over the entire Linux network system would be the _____ user.
    a. Directory
    b. Base
    c. Central
    d. Root

20. Which of the following fields can be found in the /etc/passwd file? (Choose all that apply.)
    a. Group ID
    b. User ID
    c. User's domain name
    d. User's home directory

Chapter 3: Configuring the Linux System

1. The command-line interface in Linux is known as the _____.
    a. XFree86 interface
    b. Shell
    c. Root
    d. XDM interface

2. Modules can be loaded in Linux using the _____ command.
    a. modadd
    b. depprobe
    c. groupmod
    d. depmod

3. _____ variables are keywords defined with a value for processing by the shell.
    a. Bourne
    b. Z
    c. Shell
    d. Script

4. The **modinfo** command reports all except which of the following pieces of information?

   a. Author

   b. Module description

   c. Parameters the modules accept

   d. Version number

5. Which of the following are commands for loadable modules? (Choose all that apply.)

   a. **modinfo**

   b. **depmod**

   c. **lsprobe**

   d. **groupinfo**

6. The _____ command is used to display variables that are part of the environment.

   a. **echo**

   b. **env**

   c. **ver**

   d. **path**

7. Which of the following are variables associated with the **env** command by default? (Choose all that apply.)

   a. *HOME*

   b. *FIRST*

   c. *LOGNAME*

   d. *GROUP*

8. A separate option for moving data besides the **ftp** command is the _____ command.

   a. **rcp**

   b. **batch**

   c. **head**

   d. **mov**

9. Which of the following prompts queries the system time?

   a. \#

   b. \$

   c. \t

   d. \ti

10. The _____ command establishes a remote connection to a host that simulates a physical data connection.
   a. netstat
   b. rlogin
   c. ps
   d. traceroute

11. You can transpose a parameter on the command line using the _____ command.
   a. dir
   b. alter
   c. shift
   d. swap

12. What do both the **ruptime** and **rwho** rely on for information?
   a. printtool
   b. ruptime -a
   c. rwhod
   d. uptime

13. Which of the following is not a **test** command option?
   a. -d
   b. -b
   c. -c
   d. -x

14. The _____ is a synonym for the **test** command.
   a. [
   b. ~
   c. #
   d. /

15. Which command stops any and all processing activity within the shell?
   a. stop
   b. exit
   c. ckstop
   d. halt

16. Which of the following is not an example of an **r** command?
    a. route
    b. ruptime
    c. rcp
    d. rlogin

17. Which of the following commands are examples of print options using lp?
    a. -m
    b. -x
    c. -p
    d. -y

18. The _____ loop evaluates the condition at the top of the loop and executes the instructions in the block until the test fails.
    a. for
    b. until
    c. while
    d. next

19. Which of the following tools would be best to use for improving overall network performance?
    a. **nslookup**
    b. **netconfig**
    c. **linuxconf**
    d. **finger**

20. Which of the following command-line options performs IP address resolution?
    a. **ping**
    b. **trace**
    c. **nslookup**
    d. **path**

21. Which of the following components can be used to determine which hosts can be found on the network system?
    a. Subnet mask
    b. Default gateway
    c. IP addressing table
    d. Host determiner

Chapter 4: Administration

1. Which of the following is not an example of a flag that can be used with **usermod**?
   a. -m
   b. -p
   c. -l
   d. -x

2. Which of the following configuration files is used to lock the file for queue control?
   a. printer-name
   b. log.printer.name
   c. active.printer-name
   d. status.printer-name

3. Which of the following options are password parameters under Linux? (Choose all that apply.)
   a. At least one number included
   b. At least four characters long
   c. At least one symbol included
   d. One space per every four letters

4. The _____ command can be used to take jobs out of the active print queue.
   a. lprm
   b. lpstat
   c. lpq
   d. lpremove

5. The _____ command can be used to delete users from the system.
   a. passwd
   b. pathdel
   c. hostdel
   d. userdel

6. Which command would you use with **lpc** if you needed to disable a network printer?
   a. topq
   b. abort
   c. down
   d. holdall

7. Why is group management necessary for the administrator of a Linux-based network?

    a. It enables easier storage of group files.

    b. It is used to control Internet access.

    c. It enables the administrator to see all users as one user.

    d. It enables the administrator to set privileges and options for groups of users.

8. Which of the following is not a field that is listed in the crontab entry?

    a. Seconds

    b. Minutes

    c. Hours

    d. Day of the month

9. Which of the following are part of the grep family of commands? (Choose all that apply.)

    a. **egrep**

    b. **fgrep**

    c. **grep**

    d. **ggrep**

10. Which of the following are formats for running jobs at specified times using **at**? (Choose all that apply.)

    a. 20:15

    b. Now

    c. 7:00 A.M. GMT

    d. Today

11. A _____ is considered an occurrence of a command or application.

    a. Program file

    b. Script

    c. Process

    d. Code source

12. Which of the following is one of the four fields found in inittab?

    a. Runlevel

    b. Long ID

    c. Command level

    d. Stop

13. The _____ are used to disable all characters except for the backstroke, dollar sign, and single quote.
    a. Back quotes
    b. Double quotes
    c. Single quotes
    d. Forward quotes

14. Which of the following commands is not used to shut down the system?
    a. **reboot**
    b. **powerdown**
    c. **poweroff**
    d. **halt**

15. A command that is running attached to the terminal is said to be running in the _____.
    a. Background
    b. X-terminal
    c. Foreground
    d. Processor

16. If you need to switch priority for a currently running process, you would enable the _____ command.
    a. **quotacheck**
    b. **chmod**
    c. **renice**
    d. **switch**

17. The purpose of run level _____ is to provide a single-user mode for the operating system.
    a. 1
    b. 2
    c. 3
    d. 4

18. The _____ option in **shutdown** issues a warning, but does not affect the overall state of the process.
    a. -k
    b. -u
    c. -f
    d. -c

19. The _____ command illustrates the process table for the user.
    a. protab
    b. pt
    c. rmdir
    d. ps

20. The _____ level in Linux consists of levels 2, 3, and 5.
    a. Application
    b. Operational
    c. System
    d. Physical

Chapter 5: Maintenance

1. The system recognizes a filesystem through a process known as _____.
    a. Mirroring
    b. Duplexing
    c. Mounting
    d. Copying

2. Which of the following is the most all-inclusive method of security for a network?
    a. Encryption
    b. Digital certificates
    c. Password protection
    d. Locking the server room

3. Which Linux component keeps track of network devices such as files and folders?
    a. The directory tree
    b. Subdirectories
    c. The file-sharing system
    d. CD-ROM drive

4. Which of the following options is used with **ulimit** to indicate the maximum file size?
    a. -f
    b. -a
    c. -t
    d. -n

5. If an unforeseen problem occurs, which of the following components will most likely help you re-establish your previous network state besides just the backup?
   a. The man pages
   b. The user manual
   c. Your own documentation
   d. Help-desk support

6. Which of the following **mount** command options prints a help message?
   a. -V
   b. -h
   c. -v
   d. -a

7. What can be used as an alternative to **tar** for archiving purposes?
   a. Taper
   b. Amanda
   c. Kbackup
   d. Backup

8. Which of the following properties will **df** illustrate if required? (Choose all that apply.)
   a. Amount of memory taken up
   b. Percentage of memory used
   c. Mount type
   d. Mount designation

9. Which of the following can be used to fix problems associated with the file-system?
   a. **pathck**
   b. **fsck**
   c. **file**
   d. **grpck**

10. **tar** stands for _____.
    a. Target archive
    b. Tape archive reader
    c. Tape archive
    d. Test archive reader

11. Which of the following is not a command that can be associated with a backup process?
    a. tar
    b. gzip
    c. fdisk
    d. cron

12. The two parts of cron consist of the daemon and the application. What is the name of the application?
    a. table
    b. crontab
    c. cronc
    d. cat

13. One alternative to using mirroring for a backup process is _____.
    a. Disk duplexing
    b. Tape backup
    c. RAID
    d. Live update

14. Which of the following options displays the crontab file?
    a. -e
    b. -l
    c. -r
    d. -v

15. What type of backup backs up only files that have altered by changing the archive bit since the last full backup?
    a. Partial
    b. Full
    c. Incremental
    d. Differential

16. In Linux, a major system crash produces a _____ and logs it into the /home directory.
    a. Core dump
    b. Application log
    c. File log
    d. System error

17. Which of the following is an option that is used with the syslog.conf that produces a log message from the printing subsystem?
    a. ftp
    b. kern
    c. lpr
    d. mail

18. The _____ command can stop processes after they've quit responding.
    a. kill
    b. stop
    c. halt
    d. at

19. Which of the following is not an option that can be used with **cpio**?
    a. -i
    b. -o
    c. -p
    d. -j

20. Which of the following network components are needed before invoking a network connection? (Choose all that apply.)
    a. Host IP address
    b. DNS address
    c. IP address
    d. Domain addresses

Chapter 6: Troubleshooting

1. For the network administrator, a very important step to troubleshooting is _____ your procedures and policies for the system.
    a. Publishing
    b. Viewing
    c. Documenting
    d. Autosaving

2. If you run into trouble and cannot bring the machine back up, you may require the use of a _____. (Choose all that apply.)
    a. Boot disk
    b. Kernel disk
    c. Rescue disk
    d. Floppy disk

3. A _____ problem is one that occurs continuously.
   a. Intermittent
   b. Repeatable
   c. Occasional
   d. Discontinuous

4. Which is the two-digit error code for LILO that indicates the wrong media type?
   a. 0x00
   b. 0x07
   c. 0x04
   d. 0x02

5. _____ problems can sometimes lead to problems with missing or corrupted data.
   a. Kernel
   b. Driver integrity
   c. Filesystem integrity
   d. Disk

6. Files in which changes have been made should be _____ periodically.
   a. Modified
   b. Backed up
   c. Deleted
   d. Reinstalled

7. All jobs to be scheduled for Monday and Tuesday at 3:00 P.M. are stored in which file?
   a. kernel
   b. crontab
   c. appendix
   d. directory

8. Which of the following are tasks related to administering the filesystem? (Choose all that apply.)
   a. Designating hard drives
   b. Installing external hard drives
   c. Ensuring data confidentiality by limiting file and system access
   d. Checking for and correcting filesystem corruption

9. Setting software permissions is usually a(n) _____ process.
   a. Scheduled
   b. Reoccurring
   c. Automatic
   d. Intermittent

10. You can use the _____ command to move through a file by each page.
    a. rdate
    b. batch
    c. less
    d. cron

11. If you need to display the contents of ASCII files, use the _____ command.
    a. list
    b. ls
    c. cat
    d. disascii

12. In addition to being a file and print and/or intranet server, Linux can also function as a robust _____ server.
    a. Applications
    b. Domain controller
    c. Backup
    d. ICMP

13. Small offices can use a standard _____ as an interoffice intranet front end.
    a. ftp client
    b. Text editor
    c. Word processor
    d. Web browser

14. Which example indicates that a job should run at 8:00 A.M. on every Tuesday in February every year?
    a. 08> 02 03
    b. 0008> 3 tue
    c. 0 08 * 2 tue
    d. 0 08 * 2 Tuesday'

15. Linux print services can often be found in two configurations on a network: dedicated and _____.
    a. Peer-to-peer
    b. Token ring
    c. Decentralized
    d. Star topology

16. The _____ daemon is responsible for generating the system log.
    a. **syslogq**
    b. **logger**
    c. **syslogd**
    d. **named**

17. Linux is designed to operate in what kind of environment? (Choose all that apply.)
    a. Peer-to-peer
    b. Client/server
    c. Distributed data
    d. Centralized network

18. Which of the following lists shows the correct order of severity for message levels?
    a. alert / crit / err / warning
    b. debug / notice / warning / alert
    c. alert / err / emerg / debug
    d. notice / debug / crit / alert

19. Which of the following is not an example of a facility-level pair?
    a. *.crit
    b. *.info
    c. mail.err
    d. kern.emerb

20. Linux can function as a _____ if you want to connect a small network to the Internet.
    a. Router
    b. Hub
    c. Bridge
    d. Modem

Chapter 7: Hardware

1. Which of the following is not a standard volt power supply?
   a. 9v
   b. 3.3v
   c. 5v
   d. 12v

2. A common name for a server might be a dedicated server or _____ server.
   a. Stand-alone
   b. File
   c. Clustering
   d. Printing

3. Which of the following power supplies available to Linux would be the most current?
   a. AT
   b. ATX
   c. AT-5
   d. Uninterruptable

4. A network that enables sharing of resources by a group of computers is known as a _____ type network.
   a. Star
   b. Ring
   c. Peer-to-peer
   d. Proxy

5. Every internal component inside the PC in some way connects to the _____.
   a. Computer case
   b. Hard drive
   c. Power supply
   d. Motherboard

6. Which network topology is used most often in new installations?
   a. Peer-to-peer
   b. Ring
   c. Star
   d. Bus

7. How is a local area network classified?
   a. Routing procedures
   b. Topology configuration
   c. Configuration parameters
   d. Networking capabilities

8. Which of the following are not contained on the motherboard? (Choose all that apply.)
   a. ROM BIOS
   b. Floppy disk drive
   c. Clock/CMOS battery
   d. Cooling fan

9. Ring topology networks pass data through the network by means of a
   _____.
   a. Token carrier
   b. Token
   c. Token server
   d. TCP/IP connection

10. CD-ROM and DVD are both a removable-media _____ drive type.
    a. Infrared
    b. Optical
    c. Rewritable
    d. Magneto-Optical

11. A star topology network's biggest issue is most likely what?
    a. Amount of wiring required
    b. Specific backup type is required
    c. Tokens are required to pass data
    d. User error

12. Monitor displays are redrawn via what type of memory?
    a. RAM
    b. Video adaptive
    c. Video ROM
    d. Virtual video

13. Standards for communicating to and within computer networks are known as
_____.
    a. Topologies
    b. Fixed codes
    c. Protocols
    d. Addresses

14. What offers the primary storage capacity for a computer system?
    a. Hard disk
    b. ROM
    c. CD-ROM drive
    d. CPU

15. The purpose of the _____ test is to check the availability of various integrated components.
    a. POST
    b. I/O
    c. PCI
    d. System

16. Which of the following memory types requires power to activate it?
    a. Extensible
    b. Dump
    c. RAM
    d. ROM

17. In order to function correctly, a SCSI hard driver requires a SCSI _____.
    a. ID number
    b. Port
    c. Ribbon cable
    d. Interface

18. Traditionally, SCSI drives are usually _____ in cost compared to EIDE drives.
    a. Higher
    b. Lower
    c. Opposite
    d. Similar

19. The time it takes for a disk head to move is known as the _____.
    a. Head rate
    b. Transfer rate
    c. Seek measurement
    d. Seek time

20. A SCSI-1 drive uses a _____-pin _____ connector.
    a. 25, DB-25
    b. 40, IDE
    c. 50, centronics
    d. 9, HD-9

Answers

Chapter 1: Planning a Linux Implementation

1. **B.** Unlike traditional operating systems, it is not necessary to purchase your copy of the Linux operating system. Linux is known as open-source software and is not subject to the rules of proprietary software products.

2. **D.** Linux is free thanks to the GNU General Public License (GPL). The full context of the license is beyond the scope of this book. However, the GPL instructs distributors of GPL-protected programs that they must provide the same rights to the recipients that you have. This means people must have access to your source code, and you must provide the terms of the GPL so that they can understand their rights.

3. **A.** The kernel provides control of the system hardware, memory management, system and process scheduling, and other low-level system management tasks. Every request to access a file or interact with a system on the network is processed through the kernel. Without the kernel, there would be no operating system.

4. **B.** Each computer type has its own system BIOS. The capabilities of today's BIOS have significantly expanded from those of a BIOS one year ago. ISA, EISA, and PCI bus architectures all introduce specific BIOS configurations that are different from each other. Consequently, BIOS configuration can be a challenge and is best performed with a copy of the BIOS documentation specific to your BIOS and system mainboard.

5. **C.** The sendmail daemon is an implementation of a Mail Transfer Agent (MTA), and uses SMTP to deliver mail from one system to another, or to a user on the local system. As an MTA, users do not interact with sendmail; rather, a user interacts with a Mail User Agent (MUA), such as mail or elm, used to handle reading and composing messages.

6. **C.** The **date** command has a wide array of options to print the command in multiple formats or extract specific information from the date. However, the administrator, or root user, has the ability to define a new date and time on the command line, thereby changing the system clock.

7. **A.** Samba also provides a client component, smbclient, which enables the Linux system to connect to other Windows systems and use the resources available, including disks, printers, and other devices. Once Samba is operational, smbclient can access the SMB shared resources in the network (assuming the permissions are appropriate).

8. **A and B.** The parameters for setting the current time and date and their explanations are

   MM Two-digit month

   DD Two-digit day of the month

   hh Two-digit hour in 24-hour clock format

   mm Two-digit minutes

   CC Two digits of the year (century)

   YY Current year

   ss The number of seconds to be applied

9. **B.** The Apache Web server is available for the Linux platforms and is included in several distributions. If you don't have it or want an updated version, you can download it from **www.apache.org**.

10. **D.** Unlike many commands, **setserial** does nothing to validate that the I/O address and IRQ are valid and not already in use. Although **setserial** accepts the values and configures the serial driver, the serial port will still not function due to the invalid configuration.

11. **A.** On today's implementations, the /bin directory holds commands available to all users, whereas the system administrations typically found in /bin on Unix implementations are now found in /sbin. Additionally, application programs or binaries that are not critical to the operation of the system are found in /usr/bin.

12. **B.** The Debian system uses a facility called **dpkg**. The primary method for package management is through **dselect**, which in turn uses **dpkg** to execute the actual commands. **dselect** provides a user-friendly interface, whereas **dpkg** is an entirely command-line-based tool. **dpkg** actions consist of one action and zero or more options to define what **dpkg** is to do and how to do it.

     dpkg maintains information about the installed packages, much like RPM does. However, the information maintained consists of the package state, selection states, and flags, each modified using **dselect**.

13. **C.** The boot directory holds all the files needed to boot the system, except for configuration files. These include the kernel, boot loaders, and message files defining the text printed on the screen at system boot. Most new implementations of Linux store the kernel in /boot, whereas some still place the kernel in the /root directory as a holdover from traditional Unix.

14. **D.** The **whatis** command lists all entries in the man pages with the specified name. The **whatis** command is similar to the **locate** command in that it uses a database to look for entries, created with /usr/sbin/makewhatis.

15. **C.** The man, or manual pages, are online documentation, which is often what you find in the printed manuals shipped with your Unix system. The **man** command displays the online documentation for the specified command. However, Unix was historically not good at having man pages for all of the commands. This has improved dramatically on Linux.

16. **D.** The /mnt directory is used to mount other external filesystems or devices. Although the /mnt directory often contains entries, these are not used to store data directly, but are reference points to external filesystems or devices.

17. **C.** The **which** command does not use a database like **locate**, but searches the directories specified in your *PATH* variable to find the files. When **which** finds a match, it stops searching.

18. **A.** The /opt directory is the storage place for additional or add-on software. Not every application installs itself in this location, but any application that does creates a subdirectory with the application name. There is no definitive standard stating that applications must install in this directory, but it is a holdover from traditional Unix.

19. **D.** The **fsck**, or **filesystem check**, command is a major utility that system administrators are concerned with. This command verifies the filesystem structure and if damaged, repairs it. The **fsck** command uses the entries in the /etc/fstab file to

determine which filesystems must be checked during system startup if **fsck** has been configured to run automatically using the -A option.

20. **C.** Whereas the **df** command displays disk usage information on a filesystem basis, the **du** command displays the disk usage for files and directories. For example, the **df** command reports the amount of disk space used on the filesystem, but does not indicate where the space is actually consumed. The **du** command displays the number of disk blocks used for each file and directory, starting from the specified location.

21. **A.** The process of partitioning the disk divides it into smaller logical sections or drives. The partition itself exists as a set of contiguous sectors treated as an independent disk. All of the disk partitions or divisions are stored in the partition table and describe where the logical partitions are. They also give information about which partition is active and contains the operating system to start.

22. **C.** Every file and directory on the system has an inode associated with it. An inode always includes the following information: the inode number, the type of file, the permissions, the size of the file, the number of links or references, the UID of the file's owner, the GID of the group owning the file, modification and access times, and the locations of the data on the disk. It does not contain file deletion times.

23. **D.** The /tmp directory is used to hold temporary files. Many applications, including compilers, create temporary files for specific purposes. These files are generally short lived; for example, they might not last longer than your current session. By storing them in the /tmp directory, the filesystem can be better managed, as these files are deleted on the next system restart.

24. **B.** Not to be confused with the / directory, which is the top-level directory containing many directories, the /root directory is the home directory for the root user. In traditional Unix systems, the root user's home directory is /. This was changed in later Unix versions and carried to Linux where the root user has his or her home directory as /root. This was done for security purposes, although improved security is achieved by moving the /root directory to an alternate location on the system and by renaming it to something less obvious.

25. **D.** Many of the Linux operating system commands use shared libraries, enabling the executable files to be smaller and use new features in the library without needed to be recompiled. The shared libraries are typically written in the C programming language and found in the /lib directory.

Chapter 2: Installation

1. **A. fdisk** is a system tool used for partitioning hard drives. Commonly found in Unix and Linux implementations, **fdisk** has been ported to other operating systems. When started, **fdisk** reads the contents of a hard drive and reports it. Changes are then made and written to the partition table.

2. **C.** When any machine starts, it first performs a Power On Self Test (POST) to verify that all that should be is internally present. This occurs regardless of the operating system.

3. **A.** Windows networks use NetBIOS names to identify computers that Linux cannot interact with natively. The NetBIOS Message Block (NMB) service resolves the NetBIOS names to actual systems for the resources to be found and used. Linux uses the nmbd daemon to translate the NetBIOS names to something Linux understands, and in so doing, makes the Windows network resources transparent to Linux.

4. **A** and **D.** The dselect menu commands and their definitions are

   access   Selects the method to obtain and install the select packages

   update   Uses the package database and creates a list of updates applicable to your system

   select   Selects the package

   install   Processes and installs all selected packages

5. **C.** The three generic installations of a Linux system are

   Server

   Workstation

   Custom

   You will always fit into one of these categories. The server serves files to workstations. The workstation receives files from the server. A custom system is one designed as a hybrid fit for smaller companies that want the security of a centralized network, but do not have the need or the resources for a separate server.

6. **D.** The Debian packages are prioritized to determine the need for the package in the operating system. The priorities are as follows:

Required   The package must be installed for the system to operate properly.

Important   The package is typically found on all Unix systems.

Standard   The package is part of the text-based Debian system.

Optional   Additional components are not required for the operation of the system. It includes utilities such as the X Window System.

Extra   The package is for a small group of people and is interest-specific or specialized in nature. They are not required for system operation.

7. **A** and **B. fdisk** has a very comprehensive list of commands, but the most commonly used commands are as follows:

a   Toggles a bootable flag

p   Prints the partition table

d   Deletes a partition

l   Lists known partition types

m   Prints this menu

t   Changes a partition's system ID

n   Creates a new partition

d   Deletes a partition

q   Quits without saving changes

w   Writes the new partition table and exits

8. **D.** The build tree is typically defined in /etc/rpmrc or /usr/slib/rpm/rpmrc and can be modified by the package maintainer to suit particular requirements. Most people use the /usr/src directory to construct and build their packages. If necessary, you may need to create some directories for your package construction. The following is a list of other directories:

BUILD   Where the package is built

SOURCE   The location of the source files

SPECS   The location of the spec files

RPMS   The location of the assembled binary RPM files

SRPMS   The location of the source RPM files

9. **D.** From time to time, files get accidentally erased on a running system, and no one notices until a command doesn't work right. The verification options in **rpm**

can identify the packages that are installed and what, if any, components of those packages are missing. Verifying all the packages installed on the system is accomplished with the following command:

```
# rpm -Va
```

10. **A.** The v option to **tar** lists all the files in the archive as they are extracted. If you prefer not to see the files listed, simply omit the -v. The -x option informs **tar** to extract the files, whereas the -f option identifies the file to extract the files from.

11. **B.** While the International Standards Organization (ISO) was developing the Open Systems Interconnect (OSI) protocol suite as a formal standard, TCP/IP surged ahead as the industry-independent de facto standard. The OSI model has seven layers, whereas TCP/IP has four layers: the network interface, Internet, transport, and application layers. These four layers form the basis of the Internet protocol suite and correspond to one or more layers of the OSI model (which the TCP/IP model predates).

12. **C.** LILO enables Linux to coexist on your machine with other operating systems. Up to 16 images can be swapped back and forth to designate what operating system is loaded on the next boot. By default, LILO boots the default operating system each time, but you can enter the name of another operating system at the BOOT: prompt or force the prompt to appear by pressing SHIFT, CTRL, or ALT during the boot sequence.

13. **B.** The highest layer of the Internet protocol suite is the application layer, which maps to the session, application, and presentation layers in the OSI model. Many protocols interact at this layer, providing an interface to text- or graphics-based user interfaces, and an access method to the network. Some protocols in the application layer include the Simple Network Management Protocol (SNMP), the File Transfer Protocol (FTP), and the Simple Mail Transfer Protocol (SMTP).

14. **C.** The kernel software is typically named linux-x.y.z.tar.gz, where x.y.z is the version number. The highest even number is the latest stable version, whereas the highest odd number is considered a test version. If you're expecting your system to be stable, for example, on a production system, then don't use the latest odd numbered kernel.

15. **A.** UDP is the protocol of choice for delivering streaming audio and video. The lack of a delivery guarantee does not affect the experience in this case because retransmitting the packets would be pointless. In most cases, unless the number

of packets lost is severe, the user does not notice. If there is a requirement to use UDP for its speed, but you still require some delivery guarantee, the verification can be included in a higher layer such as transport.

16. **B.** The following is a list of available window managers in Linux:

fvwm	Highly extensible manager
icewm	Window manager capable of emulating multiple environments, including OS/2
amiWM	Amiga workbench window manager
mlvwm	Macintosh-style window manager
dfm	A desktop and file manager that resembles the OS/2 workplace shell
olwm	Sun's Open Look window manager
olvwm	Open Look window manager with a virtual desktop
mwm	Motif window manager from OSF
Window Maker	Provides a NextStep environment
AfterStep	A NextStep window manager
Enlightenment	The default window manager for the GNOME environment

17. **A.** Port numbers or sockets are actually used to transfer data to the application layer. These sockets or ports enable a host machine to support and track simultaneous sessions with other hosts on the network. There are approximately 65,535 definable ports.

18. **B.** Proper configuration of an Ethernet card is done using the **ifconfig** command, which is used to display and change the actual network parameters. You check the operation of the NIC using the **ifconfig** command, which reports and can change the network interface configuration.

19. **D.** During the installation process, the root user, or superuser, is added to the system. As the most powerful user on the system, root can perform any function available and override some of the security features that prevent other users from doing things they should not. Every individual user can't be allowed to use the root account to access the system and run applications, however.

20. **A, B,** and **D.** The following are descriptions of each file found in the /etc/passwd file:

User ID (UID)   This is the numerical representation that the system really knows the user as. The UID must be unique on the system. The root account is always 0; system accounts typically run to 99. The number assignment for user accounts differs from one Linux vendor to another, but generally starts at 500 or 1,000.

Group ID (GID)   The GID establishes the default or login group for the user. The lower numbers represent system groups, which the users should not generally be members of. The regular users are assigned groups starting with the number in the /etc/login.defs file.

User's home directory   This is the location in the filesystem where the user is placed when he or she logs in. The user has permission to add, modify, and delete files in this area.

Chapter 3: Configuring the Linux System

1. **B.** The shell is the command interpreter, or command-line interface to Linux. It accepts commands, interprets them, issues commands to the kernel, starts commands, and provides the results to the user. It also understands input and output redirection, filename generation, variable substitution, and piping. These facilities combined with a built-in programming language make the shell one of the administrators most powerful allies.

2. **D.** Modules can also be loaded using the **depmod** and **modprobe** commands. As there is often a dependency between modules, it is necessary to understand how Linux determines and resolves those dependencies. The **depmod** command determines the dependencies between the various modules, and is run at system startup to create a Makefile type dependency list that is used by the **modprobe** command. Running **depmod** with the -a and -v options instructs **depmod** to touch each module and be verbose about what it is doing.

3. **C.** Shell variables can be used in shell scripts to hold information for processing in the script, or they can form part of the environment, which affects the configuration and operation of the shell. Shell variables are case-sensitive. This means the variable names *STUFF* and *stuff* do not refer to the same variable. Although there are a number of shell variables built-in, the variable that can most significantly affect command processing is *PATH*.

4. **D. modinfo** can report the following information:

The author

The module description

The parameters the modules accept

5. **A** and **B.** The following is a list of commands for loadable modules:

lsmod	Lists the loaded modules
insmod	Installs a module
rmmod	Removes a module
modinfo	Prints information about a module
modprobe	Probes and installs a module and its dependents
depmod	Determines module dependencies

6. **B.** The **env** command is used to display variables that are part of the environment, whereas **set** sets the local variables. Typically, the output of the **env** command is a subset of the variables shown in the **set** output.

7. **A** and **C.** The most common variables displayed using the **env** command and their definitions are as follows:

HOME	The user's home directory. The initial value of this variable is the home directory defined in the /etc/passwd file.
LINES	The number of lines in the display (used by commands like **more** or **less**).
LOGNAME	Who the user is logged in as.
PWD	Where you are currently working—the Present Working Directory.
SHELL	The full pathname of the shell you are using.
TERM	The terminal emulation or type currently used.
USER	The name of the user, which is rarely different from the value of LOGNAME.

8. **A.** Although Linux still offers the **rcp** (remote copy) command, many users choose to move data using the **ftp** command. The **rcp** command copies files from one system to another, much like the **cp** command. It is a much less efficient protocol for moving large quantities of data than **ftp**, however.

9. **C.** The \t prompt queries for the current system time. The following are examples of prompts and their subsequent results:

\d	The current system date
\h	The hostname without the domain
\n	New line
\s	The name of the shell
\t	The current system time
\u	Username
\W	Current working directory
\!	History number
\#	Command number
\$	Default prompt -$ for standard users and # for root
\\	An actual backstroke is to appear (literal)
ABC	ABC (the value of that text)

10. **B.** The **rlogin** command provides functionality by establishing a connection to the remote host as though they were physically connected. The **rlogin** command, however, does not support the same type of terminal-negotiation protocol defined in **telnet**. The advantage of **rlogin** is that it tries to connect to the remote system with the same username as the one you are logged in as on the local system. If the account exists on the remote system, you may be granted access without having to provide a password. If the account does not exist, however, you are prompted for a password. You must then log in as normal.

11. **C.** The **shift** command is used to shift the parameter on the command line or a variable after it is separated into multiple components.

12. **C.** Both the **ruptime** and **rwho** commands rely on the **rwhod** daemon process running on each machine. If the daemon is not running, the two commands won't print any information for that system. The **rwhod** daemon updates the information for the local system, broadcasts its information to the network, and listens for other **rwhod** broadcasts from other systems.

13. **D.** Some of the test options for the **test** command include the following:

   =   True, if the two strings are equal.

   !=   True, if the two strings are not equal.

   -a   (AND) Both tests to be evaluated must be true.

   -b   True, if the file is a block special file.

   -c   True, if the file is a character special file.

   -d   True, if the name specified is a directory.

   -e   True, if the file exists.

   -eq   Two values are equal. Typically used to evaluate numbers.

   -f   True, if the file exists and is a regular file.

   -G   True, if the file belongs to the user's group.

   -g   True, if the file exists and has SGID set.

14. **A.** The **test** command has been around since the earliest days of Unix and exists on every Linux implementation. The [is a synonym for **test**, as most people do not use the **test** command specifically in their shell scripts because of the popularity associated with the [command. Because [is a command, it must be followed by a space, and then the condition to be evaluated, and finally with a]. The closing] signifies that the entire condition has been specified and instructs [to perform the evaluation. This is important because [file is not a command.

15. **B.** The **exit** command enables us to stop processing at the point where the **exit** command is in the script and provide a return code back to the parent shell.

16. **A. route** displays or alters an IP table and is not a member of this command family.

17. **A. -m** identifies e-mail addresses to send error messages to, whereas -p specifies the destination printer. Some other options for printing include the following:

   -K   Specifies the number of copies to print.

   -Q   Specifies the spool queue.

   -R   Specifies the remote account name for remote print jobs.

   -T   Specifies text for the title page (added by pr).

   -w   Defines the page width.

18. **C.** The syntax for the while loop is

```
while {condition evaluates true}
do
     (execute the commands)
done
```

A common use for this type of loop is to continue to process variables as long as variables exist: in other words, to continue to shift while variables remain.

19. **B.** Aside from configuring the networking basics such as IP address, subnet mask, and so on, **netconfig** can also be used to configure the TCP maximum window size for network performance improvements. If you have a low-speed network connection, you might want to decrease your TCP window for smaller packets, whereas a faster, dedicated connection yields improved network performance from a larger TCP window size. **netconfig** is commonly found in /usr/sbin and uses the /etc/netconfig file to store the networking configuration information.

20. **C.** The **nslookup** command is used to query DNS and perform both name and IP address resolution. If started without any arguments, **nslookup** begins an interactive session.

21. **A.** The subnet mask determines whether the network has been further divided into smaller networks (called subnets) or whether all the hosts can be found on one wire.

Chapter 4: Administration

1. **D.** The following are the values associated with -m, -p, and -l:

-l   Changes the user's login name

-m   Creates the new home directory (must be used with -d)

-p   Changes the password

2. **A.** printer-name is used to lock a file for queue control. The rest of the options are as follows:

log.printer-name   The log file

active.printer-name   The active job (This file exists only while a job is active.)

status.printer-name   The current status

3. **A and C.** Passwords should consist of at least eight characters, including upper and lowercase, at least one digit, and a symbol. The Pluggable Authentication Module (PAM) in Linux has a feature to check potential passwords against a list of disallowed words.

4. **A.** You can remove jobs from the print queue by using the **lprm** command. Users typically run it with the job number they want to remove. If they don't provide a job number, **lprm** attempts to remove the last job submitted. If they use the -a option, **lprm** attempts to remove all the jobs listed in the queue. Like the other commands, the -P option instructs **lprm** to process the specified printer queue.

5. **D.** Deleting the user can be done manually by editing the /etc/passwd and, if necessary, the /etc/shadow files directly, or by using the **userdel** command. Regardless of which method you choose, the user's files are not automatically deleted, requiring someone, typically the manager, to review them and determine what should be kept and what deleted.

6. **C.** Using the **down** command either enables or disables the printer. The following are options for the other choices:

topq   Rearranges jobs within a queue

abort   Cancels the active job

holdall   Holds/releases print jobs

7. **D.** Group management is important because it enables the administrator to group users into a set and grant them permissions and privileges based on their group rights. Each of the group file entries has four fields. The first field is the group name, which is limited to a maximum of eight characters. The group name is displayed with a command like **ls -l**. The second field typically is blank, but can contain a password for using the group. The third field is the numerical group ID, which must be unique on the system. The fourth field is used to list the users who are members of the group.

8. **A.** The following are the six fields found in the crontab entry:

Minutes (0 through 59)

Hours (0 through 23)

Day of month (1 through 31)

Month (1 through 12)

Day of week (0=Sunday, 6=Saturday)

Command to run

9. **A, B,** and **C.** The grep family of commands consists of **grep, egrep,** and **fgrep. grep** is really an acronym for Global Regular Expression Print. **grep** takes a regular expression and a filename as its arguments and searches the file for the given pattern or expression. To be proficient with these commands, you must become proficient with regular expressions.

10. **A and B.** You can specify the time in a variety of formats, including

20:15	Runs the command at 8:15 in the evening
now	Runs the command now
now + 5 days	Runs five days from now at the exact same time
09:30 Aug 29	Runs at 9:30 in the morning on August 29
midnight	Runs at midnight tonight. Other special words are today, tomorrow, and noon

11. **C.** A process is any instance of a command or program while it is being executed. When you type a command to the shell, such as **cat**, a program file is loaded into memory and a process created to execute the instructions returns the results to the user. Everything on the system is a process at one time or another. Even the shell is a process.

12. **A.** The four fields for inittab are as follows:

Short ID	Unique identifier in the file.
Runlevel	What run levels is this executed at (blank means all)?
Action	How do we do it?
Command	What is executed?

13. **B.** Quoting is generally accepted as one of the more difficult shell concepts to master, although once you learn it, it is hard to forget. There are three distinct sets of quotes used in the shell, each with a distinct meaning:

Double quotes (")

Single quotes (')

Back quotes (`)

The double quotes are used to disable all characters except for the backstroke (\), the dollar sign ($), and the single quote ('), whereas the single quote disables all characters but the back quote (`). The back quote is used to execute the command specified and place the results in place of the command.

14. **B.** Commands used to shut down the system are as follows:

halt   Implements shutdown -h

reboot   Implements shutdown -r

poweroff The same as **halt**

15. **C.** Commands can be run in the foreground or the background. Running commands in the foreground is the most common method, meaning that the command runs attached to our terminal, and we must wait for it to complete before we can execute the next command. Background processing disassociates process from the terminal, so we can perform other work while waiting for the command to finish.

16. **C.** The **renice** command is used when you need to change the priority of a currently running process. The command uses the same priority numbers as **nice**. The **renice** command can affect a process using the -p option and the PID, a process group using -g, and a user using the -u option.

17. **A.** The available run levels and their corresponding purpose in Linux are as follows:

Run Level	Purpose
0	The systems powered off or down
1	Single-user mode
2	Multi-user mode, no network services
3	Multi-user network mode
4	Differs per implementation
5	The X environment
6	Shut down and reboot

18. **A.** The options that may affect how **shutdown** works are as follows:

-F   Forces **fsck** to run after the reboot, which is the default behavior

-f   Prevents **fsck** from running after the reboot, thus creating a fast reboot

-h   Switches to run level 0 after shutdown

-k   Sends out a warning to all users, but does not really change state

-r   Reboots after shutdown (level 6)

-t   Specifies the number of seconds before the change begins

19. **D.** The **ps** command is the user's view into the process table and lists not only the processes, but specific information about the process status. When executing **ps** with no options, your currently running commands are listed, including the **ps** command. Remember, because **ps** is a process, it is listed in the process table as well.

20. **B.** Run levels 2, 3, and 5 are the operational level. They provide all system services and give users access to the system services. All other run levels are used for maintenance or system shutdown, preventing user access.

Chapter 5: Maintenance

1. **C.** The files that you manipulate everyday on your system are organized into a filesystem. To access files on a device such as a CD-ROM or floppy disk, you attach its filesystem to a specified directory. In this way the system can read and interpret the file. This is called mounting the filesystem. For example, to access files on a floppy disk, you must first mount its filesystem to a particular directory, usually /mnt; other mounted filesystems are listed elsewhere.

2. **D.** A locked door and a secure room are still the best answer to data protection after you have hardened your system to digital attackers.

3. **A.** Linux files are organized in to a filesystem. Linux keeps track of the where the files and filesystems are on your system by the use of a directory tree. The files themselves reside on storage devices such as hard drives or CD-ROMs. The Linux directory tree may encompass several filesystems and storage devices. On a hard drive with several partitions, there is a filesystem for each partition. All of the files and filesystems themselves are organized into one seamless tree of directories, beginning from your root (/) directory. This is called a hierarchical filesystem. If you wanted to look for file on a CD-ROM, the root may be located in a filesystem on a hard drive partition, but a pathname that is listed in the filesystem leads directly to files on the disc itself.

4. **A.** -f specifies the maximum size of files created by a shell. The following are the option definitions for the others:

   -a Shows all current limits

   -t Specifies the maximum CPU time that can be used (in seconds)

   -n Specifies the maximum number of open files

5. **C.** Documentation is always key. Maintain a log of system changes to help you correct them and revert to the original settings should an unforeseen problem occur. Remember to always perform a full system backup, including all your data prior to making any major changes to the system.

6. **B.** -h prints a help message with the **mount** command. The other option definitions are as follows:

   -V   Output version

   -v   Verbose mode

   -a   Mount all filesystems of a given type that are listed in fstab

7. **A.** Taper is an alternative to **tar** for producing tape archives or archive files. The advantage of Taper is that information about the files being stored is placed at the start of the archive so that it is easy to restore a list of files in an archive without scanning the entire archive, as is required with **tar**.

8. **A and B.** The **df** command lists all your mounted filesystems and their properties as follows:

   The name of the device

   How much memory they take up

   Percentage of the memory used

   Where they are mounted

9. **B.** You can use **fsck** to check the health of your system. The **fsck** command is also used to repair the damage done to a filesystem. It is a front end for whichever filesystem checker comes with your flavor of Linux.

10. **C.** The **tar** utility was originally designed to create archives of files on tape devices (hence, the name **tar** for tape archive). However, it also came to be used to create archive files: a number of files and directories bundled together in a single file for archiving and retrieval.

11. **C.** When implementing your backup strategy, you have the choice of building a backup system out of common Linux components and tools such as **gzip**, **tar**, and **cron**, or using backup software that provides an environment for configuring and managing your backups. Ultimately, a homegrown solution can offer just as robust a set of backups, but it may be harder to manage those backups from day-to-day and the process of restoring from the backups may require more effort.

12. **B.** There are two parts to **cron**. The first part is the daemon. The second part is the application crontab, which is what drives **cron** by supplying scheduling information and user files. The daemon crontab should be run only once. When started, it goes out and looks for crontab files in /etc/crontab/, /var/spool/cron, and /etc/cron.d. These crontabs are loaded into memory. From this point on, the daemon wakes up once every minute to see if anything needs to be run. If a job is to be done, it completes the task and sends output results to the owner of the crontab.

13. **C.** A variation on disk mirroring is using RAID. RAID stands for Redundant Array of Inexpensive Disks; there are a variety of levels of RAID, each with different features and disk mirroring is just one type of RAID. The common feature of RAID is that it improves data integrity and disk speed by using multiple disks. RAID can be implemented in software or in specialized disk controllers.

14. **B.** Option definitions for crontab are as follows:

-e   Edits a crontab file

-l   Displays the crontab file

-r   Removes the crontab file

-v   Displays the last time you edited the crontab file

15. **C.** An incremental backup is usually performed one or more times between full backups and backs up only those files that have changed or been created since the date and time of the last incremental or full backup.

16. **A.** Core dumps are the result of system crashes. When a program crashes, it will often dump a core or memory image into your home directory. These memory images contain debugging information and are meant to be a debugging tool. If you do not want to use this information in determining why your system crashed, you may simply get rid of the dumps. If your system continues to crash, you may want to use these to find out why the application breaks.

17. **C. lpr** generates a message from the printing subsystem. The other choices generate messages from the following:

ftp   Messages from the FTP daemon

kern   Messages generated by the Linux kernel

mail   Messages from the mail susbsystem including sendmail

18. **A.** The **kill** command provides a way to stop a process on a Linux system that has stopped responding to your commands. The **kill** command works by sending a termination signal to the process in question. These signals provide a mechanism to interrupt a process and tell it to respond to the signal. Ultimately, though, it is up to a process to decide if and how it should respond to the signal.

19. **D.** The following are the options that can be used with **cpio**:

    -i   Extracts files from an archive

    -o   Creates or copies out to an archive

    -p   Prints the contents of an archive

20. **A and C.** The following are required items for a proper network interface:

    Host IP address

    IP broadcast address of your network

    IP network address

    IP netmask

    Addresses of any routers

Chapter 6: Troubleshooting

1. **C.** Always document a problem. Whenever you discern a piece of evidence, or you figure out something about the current situation your PC is in, document it. Keeping a history of what you discover and what your symptoms are will help you not only with this problem, but also with any future difficulties. A log book is a good idea. The first place I turn for answers is to the file that you have on a certain computer. The motherboard book and any other documentation on hardware such as the video card, network card, modem, and so on are in it.

2. **A and C.** If your system fails to boot, you should have a boot disk handy along with a rescue disk. If you have installed a recent distribution of any popular Linux OS, you should have been asked if you wanted to make a boot disk. If for some reason you didn't, you can use the **mkbootdisk** command to create one.

3. **B.** A repeatable problem is one where the problem occurs all the time or always in response to a specific user action. For example, a PC that has a problem that prevents it from booting will probably always fail to boot no matter how many times you reset it. Or you may have an application that whenever you try to run it, it crashes with an error. You may find that your PC hangs, but only when you move the mouse at the same time that you are communicating using your modem.

4. **D.** 0x02 is the error code that indicates a media problem. The following list illustrates the definitions for the remaining codes:

   0x00   Internal error: usually corrupt LILO install.

   0x04   Sector not found: usually a disk geometry mismatch.

   0x0   Invalid Initialization: BIOS failed, used BIOS overrides for LILO.

5. **C.** Filesystem integrity problems can occasionally lead to data loss. It is important that any problems be caught as soon as possible to minimize the chances of extensive damage. Fortunately, checking for filesystem problems is very quick and easy to do. It is important, and can be set up to run automatically by program schedulers such as cron. Filesystems should be scanned for errors on a daily basis. It can be done less often, but you increase the chances of problems mushrooming exponentially.

6. **B.** Files that you modify should be backed up regularly. When system filesystems need to be completely restored (usually due to hardware problems), some special considerations come into play. There are often two distinct approaches that can be taken:

   - Reinstalling from the original operating system installation tapes or CDs, and then restoring those files that you have modified. This approach may also involve reconfiguring some subsystems.

   - Booting from alternate media, and then restoring the filesystems from full backups that you have made.

7. **B.** Scheduling jobs is an easy matter. All scheduled jobs are stored in an individual configuration file (known as crontab file) for the user, with each line representing a scheduled job.

8. **C and D.** Administering the filesystem includes tasks such as

   Making local and remote files available to users

   Monitoring and managing the system's (usually) finite disk resources

   Protecting against file corruption, hardware failures, and user errors via a well-planned backup schedule

   Ensuring data confidentiality by limiting file and system access

   Checking for and correcting filesystem corruption

   Connecting and configuring new storage devices when needed

9. **C.** Setting permissions for a software package usually occurs automatically during installation. The installation script that comes with your application usually installs each file with the proper ownership and permissions. Only when something goes wrong and a user who should be able to access the program can't do so are you required to find the directory the application was copied to and check the permissions.

10. **C.** One disadvantage to the **less** command is that you can't use an editor on a file being displayed. However, **less** makes up for the deficiency by enabling you to move forward and backward through a file. The **less** command works almost the same way that **more** does. To page through a file, type the command **less** *filename*. One screen of data is displayed. To advance to the next screen, press the SPACEBAR as you did with the **more** command.

11. **C.** For displaying short ASCII files, the simplest command is **cat**, which stands for *concatenate*. The **cat** command takes a list of files (or a single file) and prints the contents unaltered on standard output, one file after another. Its primary purpose is to concatenate files (as in **cat file1 file2>file3**), but it works just as well to send contents of a short file to your screen. If you try to display large files by using **cat**, the file scrolls past your screen as fast as the screen can handle the character stream. One way to stop the flow of data is to alternatively press CTRL-S and CTRL-Q to send start and stop messages to your screen, or you can use one of the page-at-a-time commands, **more** or **less**.

12. **A.** Unlike Windows NT as a server platform, Linux is by nature designed to act as both a file/print/intranet server and a full-fledged applications server. With an applications server, applications actually run on the server and are only displayed on a terminal or workstation, using the X Windows protocol or a terminal connection such as Telnet. In the Windows world, the applications run on the desktop and the data is stored on the server and accessed there.

13. **D.** Even in small offices, an intranet can provide a convenient way to publish information to be read by all employees through a Web browser, and with a little ingenuity and some time, paperwork in your office can be eliminated by introducing Web-based forms for everything from leave requests to expense report submissions.

14. **C.** The following are time-date entry parameters:

- Ranges of numbers can be used. For instance, 1 through 3 in the hour field says to schedule the command for 1:00 A.M., 2:00 A.M., and 3:00 A.M. Similarly, 2 through 4 in the day of the week field schedules the job for Tuesday, Wednesday, and Thursday.

- Ranges can be stepped through the increments greater than one. For instance, to indicate every other hour from midnight to midnight, use the range 0 through 23 and combine it with the step of 2, separating them with slashes: 0-23/2.

- An asterisk (*) indicates the entire range for a field from smallest value to largest value. Thus, * in the day of the month field is the same as 0 through 31 and in the day of the week field is the same as 0 through 7.

15. **A.** It is not uncommon to find print services provided in both a centralized, dedicated fashion and the peer-to-peer method on the same network. Some users who use a printer heavily may warrant their own printers at their desks, whereas others who use the printers less frequently may share a printer located in a common area. Often, a user with a dedicated printer will share it on the network so that other users can print documents for his or her attention directly to the dedicated printer rather than the common shared printer.

16. **C.** System logs are generated by the syslogd daemon, which loads at boot time. The daemon accesses messages at eight levels of severity from various system processes such as the kernel, the mail system, user programs configured to use syslogd, and authentication programs (such as the login program).

17. **B and C.** Linux is designed to operate in a client/server environment. Linux was never designed to work in a peer-to-peer manner. Although there is flexibility to this approach by allowing users to decide what data to share and with whom, there are also drawbacks. Linux can also operate in a distributed data network, which is what a client/server architecture imitates.

18. **B.** These levels of messages are in order of increasing severity:

debug

info

notice

warning

err

crit

alert

emerg

These levels are used in the /etc/syslog.conf file to tell syslogd where to create logs for different types of information. The /etc/syslog.conf file contains multiple entries, one on each line, each containing two fields separated by one or more spaces: a facility-level list and a log file location.

19. **A.** The facility-level list is a semicolon-separated list of facility-level pairs. Facilities are indicated by facility names such as mail, kern (for the kernel), user (for user programs), and auth (for authentication programs). Sample facility-level pairs include the following:

mail.err   Errors generated by the mail daemon

*.info   All information messages

kern.emerg   Emergency messages from the kernel

20. **A.** If you want to connect a network of PCs to the Internet, Linux can be an excellent router. In many cases, it is far less costly to use a Linux computer as a router than to purchase a hardware router to connect your network to the world.

Chapter 7: Hardware

1. **A.** Needed to supply electrical power to every part of the PC, the power supply is very important and the least noticed. Basically, the power supply needs to change the 110v AC wall current into the 3.3v, 5v, and 12v power that the system needs for operation.

2. **B.** To implement a client/server network, one must begin with a server. A server may also be called a dedicated server or a file server. A server is nothing more than a powerful computer. A server does what its name implies; it serves files and applications for client computers. The server contains shared file storage and applications that are accessible to everyone on the network. The server can also share peripherals such as printers.

3. **B.** The newest power supply available that is compatible with Linux is the ATX style. The seemingly innocent power supply can be a common source of intermittent problems.

4. **C.** A peer-to-peer network is composed of computers that share each other's files and resources. On a peer-to-peer network, no one computer is the boss. Each user on the network makes decisions about which files and resources are to be shared with other users.

   Peer-to-peer networks are the easiest to set up. They are easy to maintain if they are small. Linux is not designed to operate in a peer-to-peer fashion.

5. **D.** The motherboard maintains everything in the system. It is the PC. Everything in the working system connects to the motherboard.

6. **C.** The most common type of network topology is the star topology. In a star network, each computer is connected by a cable to a central device called a hub.

7. **B.** A local area network (LAN) is defined as a set of computers connected in a series within a building or other defined space. A LAN is defined by its topology, or how it is connected.

8. **B and D.** The following components are typically found within the motherboard:

   Bus slots

   Memory SIMM or DIMM sockets

   Motherboard chipset

   Processor voltage regulators

   Level 2 cache, usually found in today's CPUs

   ROM BIOS

   Clock/CMOS battery

   Super I/O chip

   Processor socket

9. **B.** Ring networks operate by passing a token around the ring with each computer given a chance to acquire it. The computer then attaches data to the token that is bound for a certain computer. The ring topology is limited.

10. **B.** CD-ROM and DVD drives are removable media optical drives of high capacity. The drives can only read information; hence, data cannot be altered or rewritten on the discs. The more expensive versions are available to be rewritten, but are not included as standard in most PCs. CD-ROMs have become the mainstream of storage for removable media because they can hold a great deal of information and are inexpensive.

11. **A.** The biggest disadvantage associated with the star topology is the amount of wiring needed to connect each computer to the hub. On the other hand, a computer can be disconnected or taken off of the network and reconnected without disturbing the network. Star networks are the most popular network topology to implement.

12. **B.** The display of the screen is redrawn from the contents of the video adaptive memory on an average of 60 Hz or 60 times per second. Higher-quality monitors refresh at 100 Hz. Tied to the functioning of the system video adapter, the monitor controls the resolution and refresh rates (with the exception of portable LCD screens).

13. **C.** What makes a network function is not merely the physical connections, it is a collection of rules and regulations about how the computers can communicate. These rules are called protocols. Protocols are fixed, formalized standards that specify how two dissimilar network components can establish communication. How a network functions depends on how the protocols interact.

14. **A.** The primary storage facility for a system is the hard disk. Spinning platters of aluminum or ceramic, coated with a magnetic medium, hard disk drives contain all the programs and data that are currently active in the main memory. Most desktop systems use drives with three-inch platters, although laptops and notebooks use a smaller size of two-inch platter drivers for obvious space-saving reasons.

15. **A.** The purpose of the POST test is to check various internal parts of the computer such as motherboard circuitry, CPU, ROM, memory, and important peripherals. Errors are detected and the user may note these as they are detected, although the POST system check is not as complete as other disk-based diagnostics.

16. **C.** Everything in RAM is emptied when the computer is turned off because RAM requires power to maintain storage. In order for the processor to run, the memory must be reloaded each time the user turns on the PC.

17. **A.** As with all SCSI devices, a SCSI hard drive relies on a setting called a SCSI ID number. This number uniquely identifies the drive to the system. The hard drive should be a low number as it should be one of the first devices involved in the startup of the system. If the ID of the hard drive is set to the same number as another device, the hard drive will not boot.

18. **A.** EIDE drives are typically less expensive than SCSI drives of the same capacity. This is due in part to the SCSI interface, economic factors, and drive performance.

19. **D.** The time it takes to move the head is known as the seek time. There are several ways to measure the seek time, including the time to seek from the center to the outer edge, the time to seek to the midway point, and so forth. The seek time measurement you will most often see is the average time taken to move the head from one location to a randomly selected second location. Statistically, that usually equals the time it takes to seek one-third of the head's range.

20. **C.** The SCSI-1 connector has 50 pins and is of the type centronics, as compared to the IDE drive's 40 pins.

Linux Internet Resources

This appendix consists of various web pages about, for, and from the Linux community. Because the Linux community is a dynamic and ever-changing group, changes to these sites will most likely be the norm and not the exception. Therefore, some may expire, while new ones may come along to take their place. The following can be found within:

- Linux distributions
- Linux organizations
- Linux projects
- Kernel sources
- Linux documentation
- Pre-assembled Linux workstations
- Linux laptop information

Linux Distributions

Armed Linux

http://www.armed.net/

Armed Linux is a version of Linux that is customized to install on top of either Windows or any version of DOS.

Astaro Security Linux

http://www.astaro.com/products

Astaro is a Linux firewall security solution designed by Astaro of Germany. This version takes care of many security issues such as virus scan, VPN with IPSet, as well as both content and packet filtering. It provides ease of management with Internet updates, as well as a Web-based management tool. The entire distribution is based on a hardened 2.4 kernel version.

Beehive Linux

http://www.beehive.nu/

Beehive is a stripped-down distribution that boasts a "tighter and cleaner" version than most distributions. Beehive is geared to power Linux users.

Best Linux

http://www.bestlinux.net/

Best Linux is a good distribution for use in either home or workstations. It can also be used well as an Internet server. Some of the more interesting features include a graphical boot feature, as well as a multilingual desktop boasting multiple workspaces.

BlueCat Linux

http://www.lynuxworks.com

BlueCat is LynuxWork's distribution of Linux. It is more geared towards embedded development. BlueCat is usually the default Linux distribution standard for development tools and multiple embedded targets.

Caldera OpenLinux

http://www.caldera.com/

Caldera is a Linux distribution more geared for use on a single machine. It boasts multitasking and multi-user functionality. It comes complete with various utilities, graphical interfaces, as well as third-party programs and installation procedures.

Conectiva Linux

http://en.conectiva.com/

Conectiva Linux is a distribution developed in South America. The workstation version comes complete with software such as StarOffice, Netscape, several games, as well as image programs and utilities. The server addition comes complete with network admin and e-commerce applications.

Corel Linux

http://linux.corel.com/

Corel Linux was developed specifically for the desktop environment and utilizes a KDE-based drag-and-drop front end. Easy to install and configure, Corel Linux is a great choice for first-time Linux enthusiasts.

Coyote Linux

http://www.coyotelinux.com/

Coyote Linux is the Linux answer for those needing to share an Internet connection that is provided via an Ethernet link with other machines connected via a LAN. The primary focus of Coyote is to make cable modem, DSL, and leased-line connections easy and configurable.

CRUX

http://crux.nu/

CRUX is a stripped-down Linux distribution that takes away all unnecessary features and packages. Its mantra is to keep everything simple. It was designed by Per Liden.

Debian GNU/Linux

http://www.debian.org/

Debian is a no-cost distribution of Linux. It is comprised totally of individuals who have invested their free time into making it a reality. Some of the features of Debian include packet management tools that provide easy of maintenance and installation. Debian also makes available a public bug tracking system so as to have access to customer feedback.

DemoLinux

http://demolinux.org/en/qui/qui.html

DemoLinux is a specific distribution that is bootable from a single CD-ROM. It is designed as a demo distribution of Linux that works well in learning and training scenarios with individuals unfamiliar with Linux.

Dettu[Xx] Linux

http://dettus.dyndns.org/dettuxx/

With the entire distribution booting from floppies, as well as the need to manually mount the partitions, Dettu Linux is definitely not for the beginner. Created for the *"really* masochistic Linux-geeks out there,"* this one is not for the faint of heart.

Devil-Linux

http://www.devil-linux.org/

Devil Linux is a mini-distribution that is truly utilized at its best as a software firewall solution. It boots straight from the CD; therefore, it takes away the need for any hard disk necessities. It supports Intel 496 and higher machines.

DragonLinux

http://www.dragonlinux.net/

DragonLinux is a quick-and-easy, Internet-ready distribution. Because it has only 20MB installed, it can now coexist on the same partition as Windows, taking up very little space. It comes complete with networking tools and related documentation.

easyLinux

http://www.eit.de/

With easyLinux, everything is GUI-based, making it easy to use for the first-time Linux user. There are a few components that require the use of a text editor; otherwise, this is the choice for individuals new to the Linux OS.

Elfstone Linux

http://www.elflinux.com/linux.html

Built around the OSF Motif 2.1 API, Elfstone is designed for high-end individuals who really know Linux. Elfstone is probably the most Unix-like of all the distributions, and functions as a true networkable OS right out of the box.

EnGarde Secure Linux

http://www.guardiandigital.com/

Created by Guardian Digital, EnGarde is a distribution with advanced security techniques as the core of its distribution philosophy. It can be used as a variety of servers including Web, mail, Internet, intranet, DNS, and e-commerce.

Flight Linux

http://flightlinux.gsfc.nasa.gov/

Flight time was developed by NASA's Advanced Information System Technology (AIST) department, is a variation of the open source, and is used onboard various spacecraft. It was built with the idea of better addressing problems that are faced by various onboard computers employed by NASA.

Freesco

http://www.freesco.org/

Freesco is another single-disk distribution that is intended to replace minor models of Cisco routers. With just one floppy, users can use old i386 machines to function as routers that support Ethernet cards without any odd configurations.

Gentoo Linux

http://www.gentoo.org/

Developed by Gentoo Technologies, this distribution is designed specifically for power Linux users. It comes complete with the latest sources and technologies available in the Linux community.

Gentus Linux

http://www.gentus.com/

Gentus is an interesting distribution of Linux that comes complete with ATA/66 support. Therefore, it takes out the need to install the ATA/33 mode, and then upgrade. It is built from a Red Hat-like template, utilizes many Red Hat features, and should be easy to use for those who have experience with Red Hat Linux.

Grey Cat Linux (GCL)

http://www.greycatlinux.myweb.nl/

This is a smaller distribution based on Slackware 3.5 and BasicLinux. It can be loaded anytime one needs it, or remain permanently on the system. The size is only 2MB, making it easy to obtain. It also comes with browser and word processing software.

Hard Hat Linux

http://www.mvista.com/

Maintained and distributed as an open-source toolkit, Hard Hat Linux is designed from the ground up using complete Linux components. Both source and preconfigured binary packets come in the Hard Hat Linux box. There is nothing proprietary about any facet of Hard Hat, and the entire system is royalty free.

Icepack Linux

http://www.icepack-linux.com/

This is a beginning-level distribution that utilizes a nice user-friendly graphical install routine. This enables icepack to easily run configuration of hardware settings, as well as software. With extensive installation guides, it is definitely one of the easiest to install on the market. It comes complete with software such as StarOffice, Gimp, Netscape, as well as various games.

Immunix OS

http://www.wirex.com

Developed by WireX, Immunix is a distribution that comes with a plethora of security tools and features including StackGuardT, SubDomainT, and CryptoMarkT. Based on Red Hat 6.2, it is fundamentally like Red Hat, only it is specifically designed to shield against the majority of possible Internet security attacks. It was developed as part of technology funded by the U.S. Defense Advanced Research Projects Agency (DARPA).

KRUD (Kevin's Red Hat Über Distribution)

http://www.tummy.com/krud/

This is a distribution created by Kevin Fenzi, who is co-author of the *Linux Security HOWTO*. It is based on Red Hat, and has emphasis on security, which should come as no surprise based on the background of its creator.

KYZO File, Print, and CD Server

http://www.kyzo.com/

KYZO's main function is to work as a file, print, and CD server. Taking only three floppies to contain the entire system, KYZO also offers tape backup, UPS support, and decnet Web management through using it in conjunction with Samba.

L13Plus

http://l13plus.deuroconsult.ro/

This is a large-scale project to develop a distribution that is truly a high-end Linux production. Automatic updates of packages and sources come complete on shippable CDs.

Linux Antarctica

http://www.linuxantarctica.com/

This version, developed by Linux Antarctica, includes its very own configuration tools, as well as other popular Linux applications found with major distributions. It comes complete with KDE, Netscape, and the Apache Web server.

Linux by Libranet

http://www.libranet.com/

Designed by Libranet, this distribution is based largely on Red Hat, and provides all the pluses of the Debian system. Because of Libranet's strong commitment to customer support and online documentation, this is a chance for new Linux users to experience the possibilities of a Debian-type system. Upgrades are free, and with Debian's packet manager, all updates can occur automatically.

Linux Embedded

http://linux-embedded.com/

Linux Embedded is a tight and tiny distribution of the i386 Linux kernel that can provide developers with a small multi-user networked OS framework. It can be utilized with any X11R6 server.

Linux-Mandrake

http://www.linux-mandrake.com/en/

Developed by Mandrake, this LM is a combination of KDE, GNOME, Window Maker, and other GUIs. This makes this distribution very user friendly. It can be used efficiently in both home and home/office environments, as well as in a server capacity.

LinuxOne

http://www.linuxone.net/

What sets this relatively easy-to-use distribution apart from many is its complete collection of device drivers for the OS. Also included in the package is a complete set of application software.

Linux PPC

http://www.linuxppc.org/

Linux PPC is simply a Linux distribution created specifically for PowerPCs. Linux PPC is the native port of Linux to the PowerPC processor.

Linux Pro

http://www.wgs.com/

The best thing you get with Linux Pro is content. The distribution comes complete on six CDs, which include among other things, a 1600+ page reference manual of tutorials and man pages. Information on kernel hacking, setup, installation, and configuration can be found within these pages.

LinuxWare

http://www.trans-am.com/index1.htm

This unique distribution is one of the nicer learning environments for Linux that I have found. It easily installs through most Windows versions, as well as DOS, as long as the CD-ROM drive supports a DOS-based install. It is flexible and easy to use.

LoopLinux

http://www.tux.org/pub/people/kent-robotti/index.html

This is a neat distribution that can be installed over the top of virtually any DOS type and version, including msdos, pcdos, opendos, and any Win9x OS running in DOS mode.

LuteLinux

http://www.lutelinux.com/

This release includes such components as a user-friendly installer and step-by-step book that walks you through the entire setup and configuration of the Linux/X Windows system. It combines the 2.2 Linux kernel with programs such as NS Communicator and StarOffice.

MaxOS

http://www.maxos.com/

With one of the more stable desktop environments, MaxOS has created a platform that provides users with a nice system available to use easily, day in and day out. It comes complete with a variety of different applications and utilities, and is built around the GNU Linux kernel, the KDE desktop, and X Windows.

Midori Linux

http://midori.transmeta.com/

Developed by Transmeta (who as of this writing employs Linus Torvalds), Midori is a project whose focus is to provide smaller devices with a functional operating system. It comes standard with a build system and Linux kernel with memory and storage features, as well as system-level support for various types of Linux software.

MkLinux

http://www.mklinux.org/

MkLinux is a Linux distribution that is designed specifically for Power Mac users. This functions by having Mac platforms run on top of the OSF Research Institute's implementation of the Mach Linux microkernel.

muLinux

http://sunsite.dk/mulinux/

Developed by muLinux, this is a really cool full-configured application-favored distribution of Linux. It can fit entirely on a floppy, and upon install will kick out RAM, UMSDOS, EXT2, and LOOP-EXT2.

Peanut Linux

http://www.ibiblio.org/peanut/

This is a completely operational Linux OS that has a download size of only 48MB and takes up only about 150MB of space after install. It comes complete with TCP/IP support, various networking applications, a text editor, graphics, games, as well as other useable components.

Plug and Play Linux

http://www.yggdrasil.com/

Plug and Play Linux by Yggdrasil, is comprised of two CD-ROMs. The first contains all system programs and packets, whereas the second contains the entire source code. Plug and Play Linux is as simple as running the included boot floppy and CD-ROM, which activates the entire boot process.

Pocket Linux

http://pocket-linux.coven.vmh.net/about.html.en

Created by Pawel Wiecek, Pocket Linux is a small one-floppy Linux distribution. It can turn a PC workstation into a Linux-based workstation in no time at all. It also comes complete with features for dial-up and local networking.

Red Hat Linux

http://www.redhat.com/

Red Hat is likely the most popular distribution of Linux in the world. It is designed to be accessible for all levels of Linux users. For the advanced user, it is a robust and highly configurable environment, while the beginning user will still find it easy to install and configure.

ROCK Linux

http://www.rocklinux.org/

ROCK Linux is a distribution designed specifically for advanced Linux administrators. Though it is a smaller distribution, it still comes complete with over 200 packages, including the X11 and GNOME desktop. It comes complete with manually driven configuration tools.

Slackware Linux

http://www.slackware.com/

Slackware is a great choice of Linux for higher-end PCs, as it includes support for symmetric multiprocessing, PCI, and special code optimizations for 486, Pentium, and Pentium Pro machines. It is compatible with most Intel PC hardware.

SuSE Linux

http://www.suse.com/index_us.html

SuSE is another all-inclusive Linux distribution that was born around June 2001. It comes complete on seven CDs. SuSE is completely easy to install and maintain, and comes in versions available for IA 32, IA 64, PowerPC, Alpha, and S/390. The complete list of SuSE products can be found at **http://www.suse.de/en/produkte/index.html**.

ThinLinux

http://www.ThinLinux.org/

Developed by the Fireplug Consulting Group, this distribution is a combination of select modules and applications. The aim of ThinLinux has been to create a complete line of tools and support that aid with products that use Linux as the embedded OS.

TurboLinux

http://www.turbolinux.com/

Available in a myriad of different languages, TurboLinux delivers many distributions for both the workstation and server markets. TurboLinux is unique in that it is geared towards corporate networks as well as the home market. This is largely due to a specific clustering solution that enables scaleable network creation and construction, based on lower-end hardware and componentry. TurboLinux comes preconfigured with the choice of GNOME, KDE, or TurboDesk.

White Dwarf Linux

http://www.emjembedded.com/linux/dimmpc.html

In a nutshell, White Dwarf Linux is a small (16MB at load out), but powerful Linux distribution that includes such features as a graphical package-based installer, various internetworking tools and utilities, a scaled-down version of Apache, gcc development tools, and other components. It was developed by EMJ Embedded Systems.

WinLinux 2000

http://www.winlinux.net/2001/

Developed by JRCP, WinLinux 2000 is a distribution that is geared towards those who have previously been working with Windows 95/98. It includes such features as Install Shield, the KDE Windows-like desktop, a Windows Configuration Tool, and comes completely ready to load applications such as StarOffice, Gimp, and others.

Yellow Dog Linux (YDL)

http://www.yellowdoglinux.com/

YDL is a distribution specifically designed for PowerPC architecture. YDL comes in two versions: Champion Server and Gone Home. The first is the server side for intranet, development, and other environments. The second type is the home/home office version.

Linux Organizations

Freshmeat

http://freshmeat.net/

Freshmeat is a Linux-related site that keeps track of and submits information on the various software releases that relate to Linux. You can search by date to see the most current versions of products and scripts.

Helsinki Linux Page

http://cs.helsinki.fi/linux/

This is the page for the University of Helsinki's Computer Science Department, which proclaims, "Linux was invented here." The reason for this statement is that Linus Torvalds, the original author of the Linux operating system, studied and worked at the Department of Computer Science, University of Helsinki, from 1988 to 1997. More importantly, this is where new kernels for Linux are generated.

Linus Torvalds

http://www.cs.helsinki.fi/u/torvalds/

This is the home page for Linus Torvalds, the creator of the Linux system. This is just here as an FYI more than anything. It has points of interest for those wanting to know a little about the creator of Linux.

Linux Applications

http://www.linuxapps.com/

This is an all-inclusive site devoted to all things Linux in terms of applications. Here you will find information on all types of Linux applications, from text editors to databases and word processors. This is also a great site for sound and music programs, as well as hardware and devices.

Linux Changes

http://home.datanet.hu/404.html

This site deals primarily with software and applications for system upgrading of various types.

Linux Documentation Project

http://www.ibiblio.org/mdw/index.html

The Linux Documentation Project is an extensive site devoted to all things Linux. Here you can find resources that include book referrals, newsgroups, resources, and news announcements related to changes in the Linux community. HOWTOs and FAQs also make up a large part of this site.

Linux Gazette

http://www.linuxgazette.com/

This is a magazine site published by Linux Journal that covers all public interest issues related to Linux. This site contains a backlog of *Linux Gazette* issues, as well as FAQs and mirror sites.

Linux Information

http://www.linux.org/

Linux Information is the Linux Online site, a site that has been devoted to Linux for the past ten years. Here you will find resources for Linux applications, distributions, and hardware. This site also features an extensive list of Linux vendors, as well as people and user group sections.

Linux International

http://www.li.org/

This is the home page for Linux International, which is a worldwide, nonprofit organization devoted to promoting Linux development and its growth in the marketplace. Here you will find, among other things, information on how to obtain Linux-related development grants.

Linux Library

http://www.redhat.com/apps/support/

The Linux Library is actually a component of the Red Hat Linux site that gives such information as products and services, the current marketplace regarding Linux, as well as Red Hat training programs and sites.

The Linux News Agency

http://www.cdm.com.mx/newswire/LinuxNews.html

The Linux News Agency site deals primarily with product release announcements or updates, as well as various Linux-related security vulnerabilities.

Linux NOW!

http://new.linuxnow.com/library.shtml

Billed as "The Most Extensive Collection of Linux Resources," this site contains an editorial/newsgroup page, as well as Linux documentation, and a pretty decent file library.

Linux Site

http://www.linux.org.uk/

The Linux Site is a U.K.-based Linux resource devoted to Linux news and related events. It boasts an extensive collection of U.K. Linux links, as well as a plethora of Linux archive sites.

Linux Weekly News

http://www.lwn.net/

Linux Weekly News is dedicated to bringing their readers the latest news from the Linux community. It is dedicated to keeping Linux users up-to-date, with concise news for all interests.

LinuxFocus

http://www.linuxfocus.org/

LinuxFocus was the first international Linux magazine. It is managed and produced by Linux volunteers, fans, and developers. *LinuxFocus* is free and available on the Web at this location.

LinuxNET

http://ww.telent.net/linuxnet.html

LinuxNET is an independent IRC network. This is basically a newsgroup portal for a complete newsgroup set relating to Linux topics.

LinuxWare.com

http://www.linuxware.com/index2/index.html

Billed as the "general-purpose Linuxer Hangout Site," this is an all-purpose site for Linux interests and endeavors. More of a personal interest site relating to Linux, it has links for such things as entertainment, finance, health, home, and other related links.

Rootshell

http://www.rootshell.com/

Rootshell is largely devoted to subjects relating to Linux security. There are some good links here in terms of news that relate to security issues and breaches surrounding Linux and Linux-related components.

Slashdot

http://slashdot.org/

Slashdot is a bit more humorous of a resource, which includes articles on Linux as well as other operating systems and technologies. You can find decent interviews with individuals discussing the future of Linux, as well as marketplace trends.

Linux Projects

The 86open Project

http://www.telly.org/86open/

The 86open project is a common programming and binary front end for Unix/Intel. The idea here is to motivate Linux developers to port to the Unix/Intel platform by diminishing the problems associated with support for the myriad of x86 operating systems available.

ATM on Linux

http://lrcwww.epfl.ch/linux-atm/

This site illustrates the current state of ATM with Linux. Currently, they list an experimental release of the software that supports an unrefined ATM connection, as well as IP over ATM, and LAN emulation. Additional information and documentation links can be found here as well.

Full Duplex Switched Ethernet (FDX 10BaseT) with Linux

http://www2.primushost.com/~jeffc/fdse/

This Web page goes into detail about integrating a Full Duplex Switched Ethernet system with the Linux kernel. It offers information on the background of Ethernet, the required hardware, as well as the software side of things.

GGI Project

http://www.ggi-project.org/

This is the homepage for the General Graphics Interface (GGI) project. The goal of this project is to develop an all-inclusive graphics system that can run virtually anywhere. The project was born out of the constraints of graphics in Linux being either available on X or svgalib.

GNOME

http://www.gnome.org/

This is the site for the GNOME project, which is a subset of the GNU project. This organization is responsible for creating the GNOME desktop environment for Linux. In addition to a desktop environment, GNOME can also be used as a complete application creation package.

hardware.doa.org

http://hardware.doa.org/

This site is mainly dedicated to all and any hardware aspects of the Linux operating system. It includes information on special projects, Linux and Unix hacks, as well as Linux polls and other related feedback.

IP Masquerading under Linux

http://www.indyramp.com/masq/

This simple, but effective Web site offers information and tips on IP masquerading with Linux. It also includes an IP masquerading mailing list, which discusses implementation and development ideas and processes.

Ipfwchains

http://www.adelaide.net.au/~rustcorp/ipfwchains/ipfwchains.html

This site is a location for obtaining the generic IP firewall chain ipfwchain. At the time of this writing, version 1.3.8 can be obtained here. It also includes the HOWTO documentation in a text form, as well as a quick reference card.

Itsy

http://research.compaq.com/wrl/projects/itsy/

Itsy is a handheld prototype that claims to deliver more computing power than standard PDAs, and therefore has the capability to run such memory-intensive applications as voice recognition and graphics programs from a PDA. The Itsy software is based in the Linux OS and utilizes the standard suite of GNU tools.

Linux IP Firewall and Accounting

http://www.xos.nl/linux/ipfwadm/

This is a site dedicated to the ipfwadm utility that is used to administer the IP accounting and firewall services that are part of the Linux kernel. The site includes a functional overview of the utility, as well as an ftp location for downloading various versions.

Linux LAN Information

http://samba.sernet.de/linux-lan/

This page is a nice front end to find utilities and scripts that can be used to administer a Linux LAN environment. This site has tools for using Linux as a file and print server, SMB/NFS protocol converter, and a Windows application server as well.

Linux Services for Macintosh and Windows Users

http://www.eats.com/linux_mac_win.html

This is a helpful site if you are running Linux and want to share desktop functions, files, and printers with both Macintosh and Windows users. There is ample documentation for each of these processes.

NeoMagic MagicGraph 128 X Server

http://www.mnsinc.com/js/Neomagic.html

NeoMagic is an X server that can be used with Linux to run on laptops. Site configuration files and technical specifications can be found at this site.

OpenSource

http://www.opensource.org/

OpenSource Open Source Initiative (OSI) is a nonprofit entity that takes up the task of managing and promoting the Open Source Definition through the OSI Certified Open Source Software program. The site includes mailing lists for licensing, as well as press resources, FAQs, and links.

Plug and Play Driver Project for Linux

http://www.io.com/~cdb/mirrors/lpsg/pnp-linux.html

The Plug and Play driver project for Linux is a group founded to create support within the Linux kernel for working with Plug and Play devices (components such as the official Plug and Play doc for Linux, as well as driver alternatives, and other related components).

Project Muscle

http://www.linuxnet.com/smartcard/index.html

This site is dedicated to the task of providing smart card and cryptographic support for the Linux operating system. You can locate drivers here for components for Linux, Solaris, Mac OS X, and other software systems.

RHAD Labs

http://www.labs.redhat.com/

RHAD stands for Red Hat Advanced Development Labs. This group was originally a part of the GNOME Desktop Project, and has now branched off on its own. Their projects include GTK+, Embedded GTK+, and the Inti C++ Foundation Library among others. The site lists all projects currently running, as well as RHAD LAB members.

SEUL

http://www.seul.org/

SEUL stands for Simple End User Linux. The goal of this organization is to produce applications of all types that are usable under the GPL for the Linux platform. Their focus is also developing further uses of Linux for the education and scientific arenas.

Team Linux

http://www.teamlinux.org/

The Team Linux site is also the source of the hpcalc.org site. This site is devoted to software for HP49, HP48, HP28 RPN, HP38G, HP39G, and HP40G programmable graphic calculators. You can find links for applications, complications, and other related programs and utilities.

Kernel Sources

Bit Wizard

http://www.bitwizard.nl/

This site is reserved for a group that is the stopping point for several individuals who will write device drivers on a freelance basis. The site has pages for drivers that deal with TCP/IP networking, firewall components, WAN simulators, as well as other components.

Cross-Referencing Linux

http://lxr.linux.no/

The Linux Cross-Reference project is the testbed program of a general hypertext cross-referencing tool. The idea here is to create a robust and flexible tool for cross-referencing large code repositories.

ftp.kernel.org

http://ftp.kernel.org/pub/

This is the homepage for the Public Linux Archive. This site provides links to such sites as the Linux Repository, as well as links to free software and locally published Linux distributions. There is also a link for Linux site mirrors and the Linux Kernel Archives Mirror System.

Irqtune

http://www.best.com/~cae/irqtune/

This is the page for irqtune, which is a Linux IRQ priority optimizer. Irqtune can change the IRQ priority of devices so that devices which require a faster service can have access to it. This can predominantly be used to increase modem speeds up to three times their normal rate.

Kurt Huwig's Linux Page

http://www.huwig.de/linux/

This is an all-around resource for certain Linux patches.

Linux BusLogic SCSI Driver

http://www.dandelion.com/Linux/

This site is a place in which you can find drivers for Mylex/BusLogic's Multimaster and FlashPoint SCSI Host Adapters. There are also improvements and performance upgrades to the SCSI system.

The Linux EIDE (ATAPI) Multiplatter CD-ROM Project

http://orion.it.luc.edu/~bgallia/cdrom.html

This project deals with CD-ROM drivers on EIDE-based CD-ROM drives. This program was created to increase functionality in this particular format of CD-ROM drive. The site offers information about the project, its current status, as well as information about the EIDE standard, and various related HOWTOs.

Linux Kernel Changes

http://www.crynwr.com/kchanges/

This is a nice, compact site that lists the various Linux kernel changes for the various Linux releases.

Linux Kernel Configuration Help Texts

http://math-www.uni-paderborn.de/~axel/config_help.html

This is a site that publishes the various Linux kernel configuration help texts. They are listed on the site by release version number. There are links to other sources, including HOWTOs.

The Linux Lab Project

http://www.llp.fu-berlin.de/

This is a site dedicated to providing resources for those who develop data collection and process control software for Linux. It is a knowledge pool for application developers and programmers who work in this field in various business and educational arenas.

Linux Modules Home Page

http://home.pi.se/blox/modules/

This site is reserved for FTPing a whole host of Linux loadable modules for various uses and applications.

Linux SMP

http://www.linux.org.uk/SMP/title.html

This is the Web site for Linux SMP, which is Linux for shared memory multiprocessor machines. This site lists the project's current status, a mailing list, FAQs, and required hardware info.

Linux Filesystems

Coda

http://www.coda.cs.cmu.edu/

This is the site for the Coda advanced network filesystem. Originally developed at Carnegie Melon University, it is a distributed filesystem that has many outstanding features including disconnected usage for mobile computing, client-side persistent caching resulting in high performance, as well as server replication.

docfs

http://www.on-line.de/~lutz.behnke/docfs/index.html

This is the site for the docfs unified documentation storage and retrieval filesystem for Linux. The site offers information on the database itself, the system architecture, new docfs features, man pages, as well as a further reading section.

Ext2fs Home Page

http://e2fsprogs.sourceforge.net/ext2.html

This is the official site for the Ext2fs filesystem. Among various other components, the site primarily houses ext2fs utilities, filesystem papers and documentation, filesystem development efforts, as well as links to related sites.

Linux FAT32 Support

http://bmrc.berkeley.edu/people/chaffee/fat32.html

This site is dedicated to providing FAT32 support for Linux users. The site includes a FAT32 overview, technical documentation, as well as kernel patch notes relating to the subject.

Linux Filesystem Hierarchy Standard

http://www.pathname.com/fhs/

This is the site for the Filesystem Hierarchy Standard (FHS). This filesystem has been developed by Linux developers, and is intended to be a reference for filesystems and directory hierarchies. The site contains documents, resources, and links for information related to the Linux FHS.

Linux VFAT Filesystem

http://bmrc.berkeley.edu/people/chaffee/vfat.html

This is the site for the VFAT filesystem that is Windows long filename compatible. Although it can read long filenames, it is not NTFS compatible. The various VFAT distributions can be currently downloaded from this site.

NTFS for Linux

http://www.informatik.hu-berlin.de/~loewis/ntfs/

This site houses an NTFS driver for Linux. Currently, a read-only file system driver for Linux is what is available. You can also download user-level tools that will check the contents of an NTFS volume. There are also links to other NTFS-related sites.

Linux Documentation

BootPart 2.20

http://ourworld.compuserve.com/homepages/gvollant/bootpart.htm

This site is reserved for BootPart 2.20 boot partition utility for WinNT. It is used to add a partition to the Windows NT multiboot menu. BootPart 2.20 is also compatible with NT/2000 as well as XP. BootPart can be obtained directly from this site.

HEPpc

http://hepwww.ph.qmw.ac.uk/HEPpc/

HEPpc is a clearinghouse site dedicated to High Energy Physics projects that either use or involve Linux. The site has general information, a list of HEP projects that use Linux, Linux resources, as well as HEP software for Linux.

Implementing Loadable Kernel Modules for Linux

http://www.ddj.com/articles/1995/9505/9505toc.htm

In this knowledgeable article, the author describes the dynamic-kernel-module implementation, concentrating on the steps required to load a module on a running system.

Linux Applications and Utilities Page

http://home.xnet.com/~blatura/linapps.shtml

Although slightly out-of-date, this site is a good listing of open source, commercial, shareware, and freeware applications, as well as utility programs, development tools, and servers having their own Web pages. All of the programs listed here have either a Linux native binary, or source code available that has been successfully compiled to run under Linux.

Linux Business Applications

http://www.m-tech.ab.ca/linux-biz/

This really neat site offers of list of various businesses that apply Linux in some way. If you click on a link, it gives the company location and information, as well as a comprehensive list of how Linux is applied in that particular business, educational, or military environment.

Linux Java Tips and Hints Page

http://www.parnasse.com/java.shtml

This is a site dedicated to helping individuals integrate Java with Linux for use in various capacities. Some of the more prominent items include a Netscape Java bug list, as well as a link to Blackdown—a source for Java/Linux binaries.

Linux Man Pages—Indexed HTML Version

http://linux.ctyme.com/

This page is exactly what the title indicates. It is an HTML version of the man pages that utilizes a searchable index for the /usr/doc directories. This page also contains a good list of usable Linux books that the author (of the site) advocates.

Linux-Netscape Help Page

http://members.ping.at/theofilu/netscape.html

This site addresses the issue of Netscape not running well with various Linux libraries. This site can be viewed as a small HOWTO in terms of fixing these problems. It offers instructions, as well as information about where to retrieve the latest Linux library.

Linux Parallel Port Home Page

http://www.torque.net/linux-pp.html

This site is dedicated to the development of device drivers that can be used in conjunction with Linux to access a computer's parallel printer port. This site offers excellent resources if you are looking for a driver for a device that will run with Linux through a parallel port connection.

Newton and Linux Mini-HOWTO

http://misf67.cern.ch/~reinhold/Newton/Newton_and_Linux-mini-HOWTO.html

This is a HOWTO that is dedicated to information about running Linux in conjunction with a Newton PDA. The site contains information on connecting, installing the Newton package, and synching up the PDA with the workstation.

The Rampantly Unofficial Linus Torvalds FAQ

http://www.tuxedo.org/~esr/faqs/linus/index.html

This amusing site is a list of FAQs about Linus Torvalds, his background, and physical appearance, as well as info on his taking a job with a non-Linux company.

RPM

http://www.rpm.org/

This site is a documentation resource for information on the Red Hat packet management tool. It offers the latest release, product documentation, and various resources.

Pre-Assembled Linux Workstations

ASL

http://www.aslab.com/

This is the home page for ASL, which is an acronym for Advanced System Lab. This company develops hardware and workstations specifically in mind for Linux. They have a complete line of both servers and workstations.

PromoX Systems

http://www.promox.com/

This is the Web site for PromoX Systems, which is a maker of servers and workstations that come preconfigured with Linux. They offer a complete range of networking and communication systems, as well as systems, software, hardware, and menswear.

SWT UP1000 Alpha Linux System

http://www.swt.com/alpha_linux.html

This is SW Technology's page that is devoted to their SWT UP1000 Alpha Linux System. The SWT UP1000 is their base-configured UP1000 Alpha machine preinstalled with Linux, which includes X11R6, networking and sound support, as well as other components.

VA Research Linux Workstation Supplier

http://www.varesearch.com/

This site is VA Linux's site for SourceForge, which is a software development platform for developing Linux-based applications. Various information can be found at this location, including documentation and technical manuals for SourceForge.

Linux Laptop Information

Linux on Laptops

http://www.linux-laptop.net/

This is the one-stop shopping resource for information regarding running Linux on various vendor laptops. The site provides links to information on just about every laptop type by vendor, as well as documentation on running Linux on laptops, laptops and the X Windows system, as well as utilities, patches, and files.

Linux User Groups

Atlanta Linux Enthusiasts

http://www.ale.org/

This is the home page of the ALE, which is a Linux interest group located in Atlanta, Georgia, USA. They host a monthly meeting that discusses various topics such as PPP configuration, driver writing, as well as other topics. Their group usually hosts anywhere from 40 to 100 people per meeting.

Freenix

http://www.freenix.fr/

This is the home page for Freenix, the French Linux user group organization. If you speak French and are interested in Linux, then this is a good stopping-off point for you.

Manchester User Groups

http://www.manlug.mcc.ac.uk/

This is the site for the Manchester Users Group of Manchester, United Kingdom. They provide a calendar of discussions and meetings on various topics related to Linux.

The UC Berkeley Linux User Group

http://www-callug.cs.berkeley.edu/

This is the home page of the UC Berkeley Linux group. On this site you can find the meeting schedule, as well as the mailing list sign up. Regular meetings are held on campus the first and third Tuesday of each month during the school year. Summer meetings are on the first Saturday of each month.

U.K. Linux User Group

http://www.linux.ukuug.org/

This home page for the U.K. Linux User Group has such information as their newsletter and useful links, as well as a mailing list and other components. This site offers a decent little FAQ devoted to Getting Started With Linux.

Washington D.C. Linux User Group (DCLUG)

http://wauug.erols.com/dclinux/dclinux.html

This is the home page for the Washington D.C. Linux User Group. There is info listed here about meetings, events, previous meeting minutes, as well as a contact and mailing list.

GLOSSARY

! (exclamation mark)   Can be used to rerun commands from the command prompt. Pronounced as a *bang* in Linux.

A
absolute path   The full path to an object, regardless of where you currently are.

Address Resolution Protocol (ARP)   A protocol used to resolve an IP address to a MAC (physical) address.

Advanced Interactive Executive (AIX)   IBM's version of the Unix operating system.

AIX   *See* Advanced Interactive Executive.

Amanda   A Linux backup program that originated with the Advanced Maryland Automated Network Disk Archiver project.

Apache Web server   A Linux-based Web server running the http daemon (httpd).

ARP   *See* Address Resolution Protocol.

authentication   A security measure typically using digital signatures or comparing a username and password combination against an authorized list.

B
background   The place where unattended jobs run without user interaction. Only one job can be running in the foreground, but there can be any number of jobs running in the background.

back up   Copying files to removable media to be able to recover them in the event of a system failure.

bash   The Bourne Again shell (bash) is the most common interpreter in Linux between the user and the operating system.

Basic Input/Output System   The set of instructions stored on a chip that PCs use to handle input/output operations.

BIOS   *See* Basic Input/Output System.

boot   Starting from a powered-down stage and moving to a fully operational stage.

boot loader The software responsible for booting the operating system. In Linux, the most popular boot loader is LILO.

Bourne Again shell *See* bash.

Bourne shell The original—and most limited—shell in the Unix operating system. It is listed as sh.

bus architecture The set of conductors that connect elements within the processor. The bigger the bus width, the faster the transmission speed.

C

CERT *See* Computer Emergency Response Team.

checksum A numerical sum of the bits within the file. Checking this number can quickly identify if any changes have been made to the file.

child Any object that is beneath another. For example, one process (a parent) can start another (the child).

clock drift A slow deviation from actual time over an extended period of time caused by an inaccuracy in timing.

cold boot Starting a computer after the power has been completely removed.

Computer Emergency Response Team (CERT) An organization that tracks viruses, bugs, and other miscreants and helps combat them.

console The primary terminal for the system (usually associated with the root user).

CRC *See* cyclic redundancy check.

critical services Services that must be running in order for the system to be operational.

CSH An interpreter, based on the C programming language, that can reside between the user and the operating system.

cyclic redundancy check (CRC) A number that identifies the amount of data stored in a block that can be used to determine if the data has changed (or been lost in sending).

daemon A service that runs in the background on Linux. Daemons are used to provide services to the system, such as httpd, which provides the Web service.

D

DARPA *See* Defense Advanced Research Projects Agency.

datagram A packet of data that holds its own address information about its intended destination.

Debian package management system A popular system for distributing software and patches originally created by Debian.

Defense Advanced Research Projects Agency (DARPA) The first iteration of the TCP/IP-based network that became the Internet.

device Any physical object that can be accessed with Linux. An example would be a tape drive.

differential backup A type of backup that only gets files that have been added or modified since the last full backup.

directory An object that holds files or other directories (subdirectories). The main directory on Linux is / (known as root).

disk caching A way to improve performance of the filesystem by using a section of memory as a temporary holding place for frequently accessed file data.

disk controller   The electronic interface between a disk drive and the processor.

disk drive   A physical item that stores data.

Domain Name System (DNS)   A method of converting hostnames to IP addresses for large networks.

Domain Name Server (DNS)   A computer running DNS that converts hostnames to IP addresses.

Dynamic Host Configuration Protocol (DHCP)   A protocol/service that assigns (leases) IP addressing information to hosts on a TCP/IP network.

E

echo   Anything that returns back the same value it was sent. For example, the command **echo Hello** will return **Hello** to the terminal (unless it has been redirected).

EISA   *See* Extended Industry System Architecture.

electronic mail (e-mail)   Documents and text messages sent across a network.

encryption   The act of altering data that is electronically sent to make it difficult for a party intercepting the data to be able to read it. Upon receipt by the intended party, it must be decrypted to make it readable again.

Enhanced Integrated Drive Electronics (EIDE)   An interface enabling up to four hardware devices to be connected to the computer.

Enhanced Small Device Interface (ESDI)   An obsolete interface that enabled disk drives to be connected to computers.

environmental variable   A variable holding a value within the user's environment that can be accessed by programs and scripts.

ESDI   *See* Enhanced Small Device Interface.

Ethernet   A protocol for creating networks via a star or bus topology. It was originally developed by Xerox, DEC, and Intel.

execute permission   The permission that must be on a file in order for it to be executed.

Extended Industry System Architecture (EISA)   A PC bus architecture originally designed by competitors of IBM.

extended partition   A division of the hard drive beyond the limits of a primary partition.

F

FAQs (Frequently Asked Questions)   A document holding answers to questions that are commonly asked on a topic.

FAT   *See* File Allocation Table.

FAT16   An early filesystem for Microsoft operating systems that replaced FAT.

FAT32   A filesystem from Microsoft that allows for long filenames. This is the default filesystem for Windows 98, and an option in Windows 2000.

File Allocation Table (FAT)   The original filesystem used by Microsoft with DOS and Windows.

file mirroring   Mirroring an entire filesystem to a second disk to alleviate any data loss.

file permissions   The rights that are placed on a file to specify what can be done with it and by who.

File Transfer Protocol (FTP)   A protocol within the TCP/IP suite that is used for transferring files from one host to another.

filesystem   All the aggregate partitions with which a Linux system can interact.

foreground   Where the user is working and where jobs can run. This is the opposite of the background and only one job can ever run here at any given time.

full backup   A complete backup of all the files on a filesystem.

G

General Public License (GPL)   The license under which Linux is distributed, which, among other things, specifies that the source code must always be included with any distribution of the operating system.

GID   *See* Group ID.

GNOME   A graphical, Windows-like environment that the user can use to interact with the operating system.

GNU   *See* GNU's Not Unix.

GNU's Not Unix   A project whose intention is to create utilities.

GPL   *See* General Public License.

graphical user interface (GUI)   An interface that uses objects and graphics to specify items and actions. Typical interaction is done through a mouse.

group   A collection of users who are grouped together to share the ability to own resources and access items within Linux.

Group ID (GID)   A unique numerical value assigned to each group.

H

hierarchical filesystem   A filesystem in which all objects are interlinked in a hierarchical structure.

High Performance File System (HPFS)   A filesystem originally developed by IBM for use in OS/2.

host   Any device that uses TCP/IP.

host ID   The portion of the IP address that identifies a computer within a particular network ID.

HOSTS file   A text file that can be used to map hostnames to IP addresses on small networks. On large networks, DNS replaces the use of these files.

HOWTO   A tutorial document that addresses an individual topic.

HPFS   *See* High Performance File System.

hyperlink   A link to another document that is reached when a user clicks on a particular tag, or phrase.

Hypertext Markup Language (HTML)   The language used to create documents displayed in a Web browser.

Hypertext Transfer Protocol (HTTP)   The protocol used by Web servers.

I

IANA   *See* Internet Assigned Numbers Authority.

ICMP   *See* Internet Control Message Protocol.

IDE interface   *See* Integrated/Intelligent Drive Electronics interface.

IMAP   *See* Internet Message Access Protocol.

incremental backup   A backup that includes any files added or modified since the last full or incremental backup.

Industry Standard Architecture (ISA)   A bus architecture that was the original de facto standard.

inode   A unique filesystem entry that holds information about every file or directory on the system.

Integrated/Intelligent Drive Electronics (IDE) interface   An interface for allowing devices to be connected to a computer wherein the controller for the device resides within the device itself.

International Standards Organization (ISO)   The organization responsible for creating the OSI networking model.

Internet   A worldwide network that uses the TCP/IP protocol suite.

Internet Assigned Numbers Authority (IANA)   The organization that assigns IP addresses.

Internet Control Message Protocol (ICMP)   A protocol within the TCP/IP suite that handles such items as echoes and pings.

Internet Message Access Protocol (IMAP)   A protocol used to retrieve mail messages from a server. With IMAP, the messages remain on the server after being viewed, as opposed to POP, which actually downloads the messages.

Internet Protocol (IP)   A protocol at the network layer of the TCP/IP protocol that addresses and sends packets over the network.

Internet Protocol Suite   The collection of software utilities running within IP.

interrupt request line (IRQ)   A hardware entity that can be assigned to a device.

intruder detection   Software or other means of noticing when an unauthorized party has entered your system.

IP address   A 32-bit number used to identify a host.

IPv4   The current version of IP, allowing for 32-bit addresses.

IPv6   The next version of IP, allowing for 128-bit addresses.

IRQ   *See* interrupt request line.

ISA   *See* Industry Standard Architecture.

ISO   *See* International Standards Organization.

J

job   Any process that is running and can be moved between the foreground and background, or stopped.

K

K Desktop Environment (KDE)   A graphical user interface similar to Windows.

kernel   A unique file per each machine that is compiled.

kill   Terminating a process.

Korn shell (ksh)   An alternative to bash; an interface that can be used between the user and the operating system.

L

LILO The Linux Loader: LILO is the primary boot loader used to start Linux on a computer.

Line Printer Remote (LPR) A TCP/IP protocol for sending commands to printers.

log files Files that hold data about events.

logging The act of writing messages to log files.

logical partition A division of an extended partition on a hard disk.

login Becoming authorized by the Linux operating system.

logoff Ending a session with the Linux operating system.

M

MAC address *See* Media Access Control address.

man Short for manual pages, it is a set of documentation available in all implementations of Linux.

master boot record (MBR) An area on the hard drive loaded by the computer's BIOS.

MBR *See* master boot record.

MCA *See* Micro Channel Architecture.

MD5 *See* Message Digest 5.

Media Access Control (MAC) address A physical address that is unique for each Ethernet card.

Message Digest 5 (MD5) An encryption algorithm used in the creation of digital signatures.

message spooling The accumulation of messages prior to sending them out. This enables multiple small messages to be sent together and saves bandwidth over establishing connections and sending each small message immediately.

MFM *See* modified frequency modulation.

Micro Channel Architecture (MCA) A bus architecture used in older PCs that was never widely adopted.

modified frequency modulation (MFM) The encoding algorithm used on old hard drives and floppy drives. Newer hard drives use the run length limited (RLL) algorithm.

mount The process of making external resources (such as filesystems) available for local use.

multi-boot Adding more than one operating system to a computer and a means (such as a menu) of choosing which one you want to boot into each session.

N

NetBIOS Message Block (NMB) A service that resolves NetBIOS names to systems, enabling the resources to be found and used.

netstat A TCP/IP utility used to display protocol statistics and connection information.

network Any number of computers (and peripherals) that have the capability to interact with each other across a shared communications link.

Network File System (NFS) An independent means of mounting and then sharing disks among computer systems.

network ID The part of an IP address that identifies a number of computers and devices located on the same logical network.

Network Information Service (NIS) A means of identifying users on a large-scale network.

network interface card (NIC)   A physical card that resides within a computer and connects the computer to a network.

Network Time Protocol (NTP)   A time synchronization service that resets system clocks to the correct time.

NFS   *See* Network File System.

NIS   *See* Network Information Service.

NMB   *See* NetBIOS Message Block.

NT File System (NTFS)   The filesystem created by Microsoft for Windows NT and not used in Windows 2000. The latest version of NTFS is v5.

NTFS   *See* NT File System.

NTP   *See* Network Time Protocol.

O

open-source software   Software that is distributed with the source code.

Open System Interconnection (OSI) model   A model created by the ISO that defines how networking should work across all platforms.

OSI   *See* Open System Interconnection model.

P

Packet Internet Groper (ping)   A TCP/IP utility for testing connectivity between two hosts.

package management   A means of packaging and deploying software, and patches. The two most common and competing types of package management were created by Red Hat and Debian.

packet filter   Software that looks at the header of packets as they pass through and decides what to do with the packet.

PAP   *See* Password Authentication Protocol.

parallel port   A port that is able to receive and send data more than one bit at a time.

parent   The process that starts another. A parent process starts others (children) to be able to complete its tasks.

partition   A workable portion of the hard drive.

password   A word or phrase that is associated with a user. This is a unique string that must be provided by the user before a logon is authorized.

Password Authentication Protocol (PAP)   An authentication protocol that utilizes plain text (non-encrypted) passwords.

patch   A software fix.

PCI   *See* Peripheral Component Interconnect.

PCMCIA   *See* Personal Computer Memory Card International Association.

Peripheral Component Interconnect (PCI)   A bus architecture originally created by Intel that is used to connect devices to a computer.

Perl   *See* Practical Extraction and Report Language.

Personal Computer Memory Card International Association (PCMCIA)   A standard for connecting small devices to computers via PC Cards.

Point-to-Point Protocol (PPP)   A line protocol used in dial-up networking communications.

POP3   *See* Post Office Protocol 3.

POST   *See* Pre-Operating System Test.

Practical Extraction and Report Language   A scripting language created by Robert Wall that is used to automate tasks.

Pre-Operating System Test (POST)   An internal check done by the computer during boot up, and prior to loading the operating system.

Post Office Protocol 3 (POP3)   A protocol used to retrieve e-mail messages from a mail server. An alternative to POP3 is IMAP.

PostScript   A language developed by Adobe for use by printers to offer flexible font capability and high-quality graphics.

PPP   *See* Point-to-Point Protocol.

primary partition   The main, bootable partition on a hard drive.

process   Any instance of an application or service that is running.

prompt   The shell's signal to the user that it is ready to accept input.

protocol   A set of rules defining how data is transmitted between machines.

PS1   The primary prompt shown to a user when he or she is working on the command line.

PS2 through PS4   Additional prompts that can replace PS1 to indicate that more data must be given before the command can be executed.

R

RAID   *See* Redundant Array of Inexpensive/Independent Disks.

read permission   The permission needed to be able to view the contents of a file.

reboot   The process of removing and restoring power to a system.

recursive   Moving through an object and all objects beneath it.

Red Hat package manager (RPM)   One of two popular methods used for package management and distribution.

redirection   Sending output to a file or other location, other than its default.

Redundant Array of Inexpensive/Independent Disks (RAID)   A method of adding fault tolerance to a computer system to be able to prevent the loss of data in the event of a hardware failure.

relative path   The path to an object relative to where you currently are. This is the opposite of an absolute path. For example, if you are in the directory /home/jdurham/files/cyberatlas and want to move to /home/jdurham/files/compression, you could give the relative path ../compression.

removable media   Any resource that can hold files and be removed from the system. This term is usually used in reference to backups and for backup tape.

Requests for Comments (RFCs)   Official documents specifying developments with protocols related to TCP/IP.

restore   The process of recovering data after a failure.

RISC-based processors   Processors that are non-Intel based. RISC is an acronym for Reduced Instruction Set Computer.

root   The main directory beneath which all others directories in Linux are subdirectories. In terms of users, the root user is the system administrator.

RPM *See* Red Hat package manager.

run level A level at which the computer can operate and/or the current level at which the system is operating.

S

Samba An interpreter between the Linux operating system and Windows-based operating systems.

scope A range of IP addresses given to a DHCP server to distribute (lease) to clients.

SCSI *See* Small Computer System Interface.

security audit Any analysis of the current state of your network (or system) security.

Serial Line Internet Protocol (SLIP) An older line protocol used for dial-up networking. This has been replaced in most implementations by PPP.

serial port A port on the computer that can transmit data one bit at a time.

server A computer or program that responds to requests from clients.

Server Message Block (SMB) The default protocol used by Windows, Windows NT, and Windows 2000 for networking between machines.

SGID (Set Group ID) permission A value that is assigned to an executable file to temporarily make the person who executes the file have the permissions of the group who owns the file.

shell The command interpreter that resides between the user and operating system. The most popular shell in Linux is bash, but other options include ksh and csh.

shell script A text file that holds a series of commands to be executed.

shell variable A variable used within a shell script for processing by the shell.

shut down The act of properly closing open files and ending services to bring the system to a powered-down state.

Simple Mail Transfer Protocol (SMTP) The protocol used to transfer mail messages between mail servers.

sliding windows The capability of TCP/IP packets to change size based upon the size of data being sent.

SLIP *See* Serial Line Internet Protocol (SLIP).

Small Computer System Interface (SCSI) A parallel interface standard used for connecting devices to the computer at high data transmission speeds.

SMB *See* Server Message Block.

SMTP *See* Simple Mail Transfer Protocol.

source code The uncompiled code that can be viewed and examined to see how a package or operating system works.

standard error The default location where error messages are sent when an error occurs.

standard input The default location where data is expected to come from.

standard output The default location where output is sent.

sticky bit A value that can be assigned to a file that leaves the file in memory after it has been run once.

subdomain A subset of the entire domain.

subnet mask A value that identifies which subnet a particular host belongs to. An IP network can be divided into multiple subnetworks to make routing easier.

subnetwork   A small network that is part of a larger network and created to aid with routing and other administrative issues.

SUID (Set User ID) permission   A value that is assigned to an executable file to temporarily make the person who executes the file have the permissions of the person who owns the file.

superuser   The root user.

swap   The act of moving data between the hard drive and RAM.

T

tarball   A compressed archive of a number of files. The tarball is created with the **tar** utility and often used to move patches and updates around.

tcsh   *See* Tom's C Shell.

Telnet   A TCP/IP protocol used for remote access of a host on TCP/IP networks.

terminal   A monitor that can be used for logging in to the Linux operating system.

terminal emulation   A program that runs—often within a GUI—and looks as if you are working at a terminal.

text file   A file containing characters that can be viewed on any system.

Tom's C Shell (tcsh)   A possible shell (interpreter) that can be used between the user and the operating system.

Transmission Control Protocol (TCP)   A connection-based protocol responsible for dividing data into packets that the IP protocol then sends over the network.

Transmission Control Protocol/Internet Protocol (TCP/IP)   A suite of utilities and protocols used to connect hosts on the Internet.

U

UART   *See* universal asynchronous receiver-transmitter.

UDP   *See* User Datagram Protocol.

UID   *See* User ID.

universal asynchronous receiver-transmitter (UART)   The standard used by serial connections.

user   Anyone who is given access to resources on the Linux system.

User Datagram Protocol (UDP)   An alternative to TCP that does not require a connection.

User ID (UID)   A numerical value unique for each user and used to identify the user.

Unix   One of the original multi-user, multitasking network operating systems.

unmount   To make an external resource (a filesystem) no longer available for local use.

W

warm boot   Restarting the system without ever taking away the power. This is accomplished by changing to run level 6.

Web browser   The client software used to browse the Web.

Web server   A server responsible for Web content using the HTTP protocol.

white space   A blank used to separate entities in a file (a delimiter). It can be either a tab character or a space.

wide area network (WAN) A geographically widespread network. When LANs are joined together, they typically form a WAN.

wildcard Any character that can represent other characters. The two most common wildcards within Linux are the question mark (?) and the asterisk (*). The former is used to represent any one character, whereas the latter represents zero or more characters.

window manager The front end management component of any X Window-based system.

write permission The permission necessary to be able to create or modify a file.

X

X The X Window System, which provides a graphical interface to Linux.

X Display Manager (XDM) The X Display Manager is an optional part of the X Window System that is used for login session management. This is useful for several types of situations, including minimal X Terminals, desktops, and larger networks.

XFree86 The free Windows X system used in Linux, as of this writing, in version 4.

Z

Z shell The Z shell (zsh) is a command interpreter (shell) usable as an interactive login shell as well as a shell script command processor. Of the standard shells, zsh most resembles the korn shell (ksh), but includes many enhancements. zsh has built-in command-line editing, built-in spelling correction, and programmable command completion.

INDEX

Symbols

!! (bangs), viewing command history, 255

$, keywords as variables, 172

$! variable, 173

$$ variable, viewing current process execution, 172

$* variable, 181–182

$0 variable, 181

$? variable, 172

$a variable, 181–182

%, foreground jobs, 283

& variable, 173

&& operator, 191

* asterisk, 197

[command, 185

|| operator, 191

/ directory, 12

1024-cylinder limit, hard drive systems, 397

A

A records, DNS, 211

accepting input, shell scripts, 180

accounts, users, 93, 97–98

   home directories, 99

   passwords, 93–94

   SKEL variable, 95

   switching between passwd and shadow files, 96

adapters, network, 80

adding

   groups, 246

   user accounts, 242

addresses, IP, 200

admin security, 340–342

administrators, groups, 247

Amanda, 337

Apache Web server, 30

Application layer, TCP/IP, 75

applications

   logs, 359

   version conflicts, 368

Apropos utility, 54

apt-get program, 368

archives, 334

   compressing, 325, 335

   date stamps, 336

   extracting particular files, 336

   tar, 131, 334

   viewing included files, 335

arguments, testing for, 187

arithmetic, 199

ARP (Address Resolution Protocol), 79

arp command, 205

Q–R

INTERNATIONAL CONTACT INFORMATION

AUSTRALIA
McGraw-Hill Book Company Australia Pty. Ltd.
TEL +61-2-9417-9899
FAX +61-2-9417-5687
http://www.mcgraw-hill.com.au
books-it_sydney@mcgraw-hill.com

CANADA
McGraw-Hill Ryerson Ltd.
TEL +905-430-5000
FAX +905-430-5020
http://www.mcgrawhill.ca

**GREECE, MIDDLE EAST,
NORTHERN AFRICA**
McGraw-Hill Hellas
TEL +30-1-656-0990-3-4
FAX +30-1-654-5525

MEXICO (Also serving Latin America)
McGraw-Hill Interamericana Editores S.A. de C.V.
TEL +525-117-1583
FAX +525-117-1589
http://www.mcgraw-hill.com.mx
fernando_castellanos@mcgraw-hill.com

SINGAPORE (Serving Asia)
McGraw-Hill Book Company
TEL +65-863-1580
FAX +65-862-3354
http://www.mcgraw-hill.com.sg
mghasia@mcgraw-hill.com

SOUTH AFRICA
McGraw-Hill South Africa
TEL +27-11-622-7512
FAX +27-11-622-9045
robyn_swanepoel@mcgraw-hill.com

**UNITED KINGDOM & EUROPE
(Excluding Southern Europe)**
McGraw-Hill Education Europe
TEL +44-1-628-502500
FAX +44-1-628-770224
http://www.mcgraw-hill.co.uk
computing_neurope@mcgraw-hill.com

ALL OTHER INQUIRIES Contact:
Osborne/McGraw-Hill
TEL +1-510-549-6600
FAX +1-510-883-7600
http://www.osborne.com
omg_international@mcgraw-hill.com

A HISTORY OF
TECHNOLOGY

A HISTORY OF
TECHNOLOGY

EDITED BY

CHARLES SINGER · E. J. HOLMYARD

A. R. HALL and TREVOR I. WILLIAMS

ASSISTED BY

Y. PEEL and J. R. PETTY

VOLUME III

FROM THE RENAISSANCE
TO THE
INDUSTRIAL REVOLUTION
c 1500—*c* 1750

OXFORD
AT THE CLARENDON PRESS

Oxford University Press, Walton Street, Oxford OX2 6DP

OXFORD LONDON GLASGOW
NEW YORK TORONTO MELBOURNE WELLINGTON
KUALA LUMPUR SINGAPORE JAKARTA HONG KONG TOKYO
DELHI BOMBAY CALCUTTA MADRAS KARACHI
NAIROBI DAR ES SALAAM CAPE TOWN

ISBN 0 19 858107 6

© *Oxford University Press 1957*

First published 1957
Reprinted 1964, 1969, 1979

Printed in Great Britain
at the University Press, Oxford
by Eric Buckley
Printer to the University

PREFACE

THIS third volume of *A History of Technology*, unlike its predecessors, can draw upon contemporary printed sources, which, as the centuries advance, constitute a large and rapidly expanding technical literature. Correspondingly, archaeological evidence, prominent in the first two volumes, becomes of less importance, though no doubt much may yet be learnt of the technical practice of the sixteenth and seventeenth centuries from artefacts, from sites of manufacture, and from old equipment. Studies of this kind, for the period of the present volume, are not yet numerous. However, at this stage the wealth of literary evidence for almost every technique of manufacture and production—often very copiously illustrated, as with such classics as Agricola's *De re metallica* (1556) or the great *Encyclopédie* (1751–72) at the limits of our survey—is already so great that it cannot be adequately summarized even in a massive volume. The Editors have therefore necessarily been highly selective in their choice of topics for discussion, and have perforce imposed on authors restrictions of space that have rendered their tasks far from easy. The Editors have sought to emphasize those changing aspects of technology which were of the greatest social and economic importance, while at the same time illustrating the gradual permeation of technological innovation by the results of scientific inquiry.

Without doubt, the greatest occurrence in the history of Europe and of the whole world in the period treated in this volume was the emergence of modern science, with all its fruitful potentialities. The study of this supremely significant movement falls outside the compass of this *History*, but its repercussions will be felt throughout the present volume and its two successors. At the close of the Middle Ages the points of contact between science and technology were few and tenuous: certain aspects of them are discussed in chapters 19 and 22. It fell within the province of the philosopher to explain the phenomena of nature; their use for practical ends was left to the craftsman. The philosopher was much concerned with books and opinions, and but little with things; he displayed admirable intellectual ingenuity in framing his explanations of the natural world in general terms while largely neglecting their application in detail. The craftsman, on the other hand, knew little or nothing beyond trade methods and processes which he followed because they had been handed down to him and because they brought the results he sought; he was altogether innocent of theories to explain his actions. Only in the seventeenth century (though the idea had been adumbrated in the Middle Ages) was it realized—and even then by few—that science and the crafts were alike concerned with natural phenomena and could aid each other. Gradually it was seen that knowledge of nature conferred power to control its forces. From the time of Francis Bacon, Galileo, and Descartes there have always been men in Europe believing that science must ultimately guide the operations of the technician, and that a scientific technology would shape the future course of civilization.

Despite this, it would be absurd to overestimate the effect of such thinking, or of the achievements of pure science, on the technology of Europe in the period covered by this volume. Some few techniques—those of navigation (ch 20) and industrial chemistry (ch 25), for example—were directly modified by the application of scientific ideas, but in relation to many others premature attempts to rationalize and improve craft methods failed dismally. The gradual penetration of scientific method and discovery into the economic activities of production, and the substitution of analysis and precise measurement for the craftsman's impalpable skill, make a very long story extending through the remainder of this work. Until long after the close of the seventeenth century, industrial progress depended overwhelmingly on craft invention rather than on the fruits of systematic scientific research. The complete ascendancy of the latter, from about the end of the nineteenth century, marks a turning-point in human affairs upon which this *History* will conclude. Hence although great achievements were being made in pure science, the basic elements of technology in the sixteenth and seventeenth centuries were not greatly dissimilar from those of earlier times. The dominance of hand-tools and of natural or animal power, a relatively small use of metals, a vast expenditure of skilled and unskilled human effort, and a small scale of production were as characteristic of these centuries as of those immediately preceding them. Even the character of the inventions and new methods of this inventive age was not novel, for the progressive craftsman or entrepreneur continued to play the leading role.

Il n'y a que le premier pas qui coûte. In the perspective of three more centuries of history the apotheoses of long technological traditions regarded as the marvels of the age—the great wooden ships (ch 18), the ponderous machines for raising water (ch 13), the massive stone buildings (ch 10), and the intricately woven tapestries (ch 8)—diminish in importance as compared with the first humble off-shoots of scientific research. These, for our period, were the pendulum clock (ch 24), inquiries into the properties of metals (ch 2), and, indeed, the very instruments that science invented to prosecute its own researches (chs 22, 23). The former are, like the dinosaur, unequalled products of a line of evolution doomed to extinction; the latter, heralds of a new course of development whose future is still unguessed. In this volume the Editors have sought to give due attention to both.

It has also been their design in this volume to prepare the way for the discussion of the Industrial Revolution which will be the subject of its immediate successor. Chapters 2, 3, 7, and 17 indicate how firmly the foundations were laid for the great changes in production and economic relations of the second half of the eighteenth century, affecting chiefly the use of metals and coal, the textile industry, and transportation. It will be seen that inventiveness was not ineffective before the times of Abraham Darby (the second), Richard Arkwright, and James Watt; that indeed men had long been conscious of the existence of the problems the solution of which made possible the industrialization first of western Europe, and then of the world.

The geographical limitations of this *History*, and the reasons for adopting them, were set out in the preface to volume II and need not be repeated. Following the design there described, the present volume is wholly concerned with the countries of western Europe. Their history is now doubly unique, since it embraces both the birth of modern science and that of industrialism. The relationship of these states to the Near East and the rest of the globe becomes the opposite of that prevailing previously, to which attention was drawn in the epilogue to volume II. Europe is drawing ever more largely upon the rest of the world for raw materials and primary products (ch 1), exporting manufactured goods in return; and this continent is no longer borrowing from the technical heritage of regions more anciently civilized, but is instead establishing among them its own technical hegemony. It is not within our scope to discuss the economic aspects of this changed relationship, as a result of which, by the end of the nineteenth century, Europe held almost all the rest of the world in commercial fee. Its inevitable impact upon European technology through the new problems of manufacture it created is seen throughout the remainder of the work.

A word of explanation on the wide chronological variation of the chapters in the present volume may be required. It arises from the fusion in Europe at this time of the old technology, mainly of ancient Near Eastern origin, with a newer technology in which the scientific element is in the ascendant. Hence certain topics, which particularly illustrate the latter development, such as cartography and navigation (chs 19, 20) or the construction of scientific instruments (chs 22, 23), have been treated here from antiquity onwards. In other cases, as with the use of hand-tools (ch 5) which have altered little in many centuries, it has been convenient to carry the discussion forward and bring it to a conclusion. The history of techniques fits no simple scheme, and the chronological limits assigned to the volumes of this *History* are to be taken only as broad guides to their contents. The present volume is largely concerned with events of the sixteenth and seventeenth centuries, that is, with the technology of the age between the Italian Renaissance and the Industrial Revolution, but it has often proved convenient and indeed essential to cross these limits in either direction.

As the general history and geography of Europe and North America are generally known, and as sources for further information are readily accessible to all, it has not seemed necessary to include in the present volume such chronological tables and general maps as were given in its predecessors. The time-scale of our volumes diminishes rapidly, as the available material grows proportionately. Volume I had a time-span of geological scale; volume II covered roughly two thousand years; the present volume extends over little more than two hundred. As the time-scale is reduced, so the events of political history are, for the historians of science and technology, diminished in significance. In the period of this volume the city-state waned and the nation-state emerged; religious bigotry gave place to economic rivalry; France replaced Spain as the leading power in Europe. But these events, important in themselves, had little effect on the changes in techniques discussed in these pages. It would be more relevant to turn to economic history, to examine the growing ascendancy of the Atlantic seaboard of Europe over the Mediterranean, to study changes in economic organization and the relations of economic groups, and to inquire into the processes of economic growth. But to attempt such a survey would be to embark upon a complete history of modern industrial civilization, and that is not our object.

The Editors record with regret the death of one of the contributors to this volume, Mr J. F. Flanagan. His chapter on 'Figured Fabrics' was passed by him in galley proof and all the illustrations had received his approval. For assistance in the preparation of this volume, special thanks are due to Professors R. J. Forbes, A. W. Skempton, Cyril S. Smith, and E. G. R. Taylor. All the authors have given generous assistance in the preparation of illustrations.

There have again been changes in the editorial staff. With great regret the Editors accepted the resignation of Dr Elsbeth Jaffé, who wished to be free to complete researches of her own. Her learning, scholarship, and painstaking devotion were freely given to the preparation of the first two volumes of this *History*. Miss M. Reeve has joined the staff. The Editors once more express their thanks to the other members of their team—Mrs A. Clow, Mrs E. Harrison, Mrs D. A. Peel, and Miss J. R. Petty. On them has fallen a heavy burden of bibliographical research and routine work, which has been well and cheerfully borne. The Editors have continued to receive at every point the warm assistance of the staff of the Clarendon Press.

The production of such a work as this would be impossible without recourse to large libraries. The Editors once more tender their thanks to the officials of the British Museum Library, the Cambridge University Library, the London Library, the Patent Office Library, the Science Library, and the Warburg Institute. In the present volume, artists' work has been less essential than in its predecessors; the greater part of it has again been entrusted to Mr D. E. Woodall, but we are also glad to acknowledge the services of Mr E. Norman and Mr F. Janca. The indexes have been compiled by Miss M. A. Hennings.

The financial outlay necessary for the completion of this *History* has proved considerably greater than was originally anticipated. The Editors wish to acknowledge the beneficent generosity of Imperial Chemical Industries Limited in making renewed provision for this purpose, by which the completion of the work is ensured. In particular they again thank Mr W. J. Worboys for his unfailing interest, support, and encouragement.

CHARLES SINGER
E. J. HOLMYARD
A. R. HALL
TREVOR I. WILLIAMS

CONTENTS

PART III

MATERIAL CIVILIZATION

PART IV

COMMUNICATIONS

PART V

APPROACH TO SCIENCE

ILLUSTRATIONS

Metallurgical furnaces used for smelting silver. Left, *charging a furnace, while red-hot metal flows from its* base. Right, *removing litharge flowing down the hearth-wall with a crochet. The furnaces correspond to Agricola's descriptions (1556); the long white smocks were presumably worn for protection against the heat. From a painting of 1521, by Hans Hesse, on the 'Miners' Altar' in the church of St Anne, Annaberg, in the Erzgebirge district of Saxony. Annaberg was an important silver-mining settlement early in the sixteenth century.* Reproduced by courtesy of the Gewerkschaft Eisenhütte Westfalia, Wethmar, Post Lünen

* The names at the end of entries are those of the artists who drew the illustrations.

3. COAL MINING AND UTILIZATION *by* J. U. NEF

4. WINDMILLS *by* REX WAILES

5. TRADESMEN'S TOOLS *by* R. A. SALAMAN

6. FARM-TOOLS, VEHICLES, AND HARNESS, 1500–1900 *by* OLGA BEAUMONT and J. GERAINT JENKINS

8. FIGURED FABRICS *by* J. F. FLANAGAN

11. TOWN-PLANNING FROM THE ANCIENT WORLD TO THE RENAISSANCE *by* MARTIN S. BRIGGS

12. LAND DRAINAGE AND RECLAMATION *by* L. E. HARRIS

13. MACHINES AND MECHANISMS *by* A. P. USHER

14. MILITARY TECHNOLOGY by A. R. HALL

20. CARTOGRAPHY, SURVEY, AND NAVIGATION, 1400–1750, by E. G. R. TAYLOR

22. PRECISION INSTRUMENTS TO 1500 by DEREK J. PRICE

PLATES

ABBREVIATIONS OF PERIODICAL TITLES

(AS SUGGESTED BY THE WORLD LIST OF SCIENTIFIC PERIODICALS)

Abh. Ges. Wiss. Göttingen	Abhandlungen der Königlichen Gesellschaft der Wissenschaften zu Göttingen, mathematisch-physikalische Klasse. Göttingen
Acta hist. sci. nat. med., Kbh.	Acta historica Scientiarum naturalium et medicinalium. Copenhagen
Amer. hist. Rev.	American Historical Review. American Historical Association. New York
Ann. Ponts Chauss.	Annales des Ponts et Chaussées. Ministère des Travaux publics et des Transports. Paris
Ann. Sci.	Annals of Science. A Quarterly Review of the History of Science since the Renaissance. London
Ann. Trav. publ. Belg.	Annales des Travaux publics de Belgique. Brussels
Antiquity	Antiquity. A Quarterly Review of Archaeology. Newbury, Berks.
Archaeol. Cambrensis	*Archaeologia Cambrensis.* Cambrian Archaeological Association. London
Archaeol. J.	The Archaeological Journal. Royal Archaeological Institute of Great Britain and Ireland. London
Archaeologia	*Archaeologia* or Miscellaneous Tracts relating to Antiquity. Society of Antiquaries. London
Beitr. Gesch. Tech. Industr.	Beiträge zur Geschichte der Technik und Industrie. Jahrbuch des Vereins Deutscher Ingenieure. (Continued as *Technikgeschichte.*) Berlin
Blackwood's Mag.	Blackwood's Magazine. Edinburgh
Bull. Inst. franç. Archéol. orientale	Bulletin de l'Institut Français d'Archéologie Orientale. Cairo
Bull. Soc. R. Archaeol., Bruxelles	Bulletin de la Société royale d'Archéologie de Bruxelles. Brussels
Burlington Mag.	Burlington Magazine. London
Centaurus	Centaurus; International Magazine of the History of Science and Medicine. Copenhagen
Ciel et Terre	Ciel et Terre. Société Belge d'Astronomie, de Météorologie et de Physique du Globe. Brussels
Clessidra	La Clessidra Associazione degl' Orologiai d'Italia. Rome
Connoisseur	The Connoisseur. London
Dolphin	The Dolphin. Limited Editions Club. New York

Econ. Hist. Rev.	Economic History Review. Economic History Society. Cambridge
Endeavour	Endeavour. A Quarterly Review designed to record the Progress of the Sciences in the Service of Mankind. London
Gaz. Beaux-Arts.	Gazette des Beaux-Arts. Paris
Glastekn. Tidskr.	Glasteknisk Tidskrift. Glasinstitutet i Växjö. Växjö
Hist. Acad. R. Sci.	Histoire de l'Académie royale des Sciences avec les Mémoires de Mathématique et Physique. Paris
Horol. J., Lond.	Horological Journal. British Horological Institute. London
Isis	Isis. History of Science Society. Cambridge, Mass.
J. Brit. astr. Ass.	Journal of the British Astronomical Association. London
J. Cork hist. archaeol. Soc.	Journal of the Cork Historical and Archaeological Society. Cork
J. Hist. Med.	Journal of the History of Medicine and Allied Sciences. New York
J. Instn civ. Engrs	Journal of the Institution of Civil Engineers. London
J. Jr Instn Engrs	Journal and Record of Transactions of the Junior Institution of Engineers. London
J. polit. Econ.	Journal of Political Economy. Chicago
J. Soc. Arts	Journal of the Society [afterwards Royal Society] of Arts. London
Jb. kunsthist. Samml.	Jahrbuch der kunsthistorischen Sammlungen des allerhöchsten Kaiserhauses. Vienna
Mariner's Mirror	Mariner's Mirror. Journal of the Society for Nautical Research. London
Meded. Rijksmus. Gesch. Natuurwet.	Mededeeling uit het Rijksmuseum voor de Geschiedenis der Natuurwetenschappen. [Communications from the National Museum of the History of Science]. Leiden
Min. Proc. Instn civ. Engrs	Minutes of Proceedings of the Institution of Civil Engineers. London
Numism. Chron.	The Numismatic Chronicle and Journal of the Royal Numismatic Society. London
Observatory	Observatory. London
Occ. Publ. Soc. naut. Res.	Occasional Publications of the Society for Nautical Research. London
Phil. Trans.	Philosophical Transactions of the Royal Society. London
Prakt. Akad. Athen.	Praktika tes Akademias Athenon. Athens
Quart. J. Econ.	Quarterly Journal of Economics. Cambridge, Mass.
Relaz. Congr. int. Sci. ist.	Relazione del Congresso internazionale di Scienze istoriche. [International Congress of historical Sciences]. Rome

Rev. belge Philol. Hist.	Revue belge de Philologie et d'Histoire. Société pour le Progrès des Études philologiques et historiques. Brussels
Saml. Svenska Fornskriftsällskap.	Samlingar af Svenska Fornskriftsällskapet. Stockholm
Schweiz. Bauztg	Schweizerische Bauzeitung. Wochenschrift für Architektur, Ingenieurwesen, Maschinentechnik. Zürich
Sprechsaal	Sprechsaal für Keramik, Glas, Email. Fach- und Wirtschaftsblatt für die Silikatindustrien. Coburg
Stahl u. Eisen, Düsseldorf	Stahl und Eisen. Zeitschrift für das Deutsche Eisenhüttenwesen. Verein Deutscher Eisenhüttenleute. Düsseldorf
Syria	Syria. Revue d'Art oriental et d'Archéologie. Institut Français d'Archéologie de Beyrouth. Paris
Tech. Stud. fine Arts	Technical Studies in the Field of the Fine Arts. Fogg Art Museum, Harvard University. Cambridge, Mass.
Town Plann. Rev.	Town Planning Review. Liverpool
Trans. Newcomen Soc.	Transactions. Newcomen Society for the Study of the History of Engineering and Technology. London
V.D.I. Jb.	Verein Deutscher Ingenieure. Jahrbuch. Berlin
Wasserwirtschaft	Die Wasserwirtschaft. Stuttgart
Woodworker, Lond.	The Woodworker. London
Wschr. Arch. Ver. Berlin	Wochenschrift des Architekten-Vereins zu Berlin. Berlin
Z. Ver. dtsch. Ing.	Zeitschrift des Vereins Deutscher Ingenieure. Berlin
Z. Ver. dtsch. Zuckerind.	Zeitschrift des Vereins der Deutschen Zuckerindustrie. Berlin
Z. Ver. lübeckische Gesch.	Zeitschrift des Vereins für Lübeckische Geschichte und Altertumskunde. Lübeck

I

FOOD AND DRINK

R. J. FORBES

I. NEW FOOD FROM A NEW WORLD

THE period now to be considered is marked by a great change in diet, as the combined result of several factors. Such were the acquisition of new food-stuffs; changing agricultural techniques; improvements in milling techniques; progress in testing, preparing, and preserving food; and changing views on diet and the rise of dietetics as a science.

Direct overseas contact with the Indies and the Far East, and the discovery of the New World, confronted Europe with a wide new range of animals and plants. During the sixteenth and seventeenth centuries many new food-crops were adopted by the European farmer. Apart from such important new drugs as ipecacuanha, guaiacum, and quinine, and the narcotics coca-leaf, Indian hemp, and opium [1], four new plant crops—potato, maize, rice, and oil-seed—began to play their part in the agriculture and diet of Europe. Sugar-cane also was soon cultivated in colonial plantations in the tropics and even in parts of Europe, as was tobacco. Sugar acquired added importance when the new beverages tea, coffee, and cocoa were introduced. The only new contribution to the table from the animal world, however, was the turkey, which was introduced from Mexico about 1520 and became common Christmas fare a century later.

The *potato* was the most important addition to European farming, though its introduction took the full span of three centuries [2]. Its cultivation in the Andes region of western South America began at least 2000 years before the Spanish conquest, by which time it dominated the life of inhabitants of the highlands of Peru and Bolivia. They not only ate it freshly cooked, but preserved it as a durable food resisting damp and frost.

The potato was long thought to have reached Europe from Virginia, whereas in fact it was introduced there from Europe late in the seventeenth century. Spain was the first European country in which the potato was grown and eaten, certainly not later than 1570. Probably an independent introduction into England, and thence to Ireland, occurred some years later. In both cases tubers of the species *Solanum andigenum*, native in the northern Andean region, were imported. The plant is first illustrated in Gerard's 'Herball' (1597) (figure 1).

Early confusion between the potato (*S. tuberosum*, *S. andigenum*), the sweet potato (*Ipomoea batatas*—known in Europe since the fifteenth century), the yams (*Dioscorea*), the Jerusalem artichoke (*Helianthus tuberosus* L), and other plants yielded the strangely varied names for it in the European languages (potato, *patata*, *pomme de terre*, *Kartoffel*). The native name seems to have been 'papa'.

By the end of the sixteenth century the potato was common in Spain and Italy, whence it travelled to France and through Burgundy to Germany. As it was used by the Spanish navy it may have come to Ireland from the stores of the wrecked Armada ships; the story that Ralegh introduced it is unlikely to be true. It was preceded in England by the sweet potato (figure 2); hence when the true potato went from Ireland to the new colony of Virginia it was called the Irish potato.

FIGURE 1—*The potato plant. From Gerard's Herball, 1597. He wrote: 'The roote is thicke, fat and tuberous; not much differing either in shape, colour or taste from the common [i.e. sweet] Potatoes.' Gerard was responsible for the mistaken belief that potatoes came to Britain from Virginia.*

In 1616 the potato was still a luxury of the royal table in France. Both there and in Germany it was praised by botanists and poets, and the desirability of cultivating it in less fertile areas was propagated even in sermons. By 1712 it had reached the Bohemian border, but here as elsewhere it proved unpopular with farmers. In 1764 a Prussian edict ordered its cultivation in certain backward areas. The peasants remained recalcitrant, regarding the potato as fit only for the poorest folk, and as liable to cause disease. The cultivation of the potato in eastern Europe owed much to the encouragement of Frederick the Great of Prussia (reigned 1740–86), and, from about 1785, to its use as an industrial source of starch. The manufacture of alcohol by fermenting mixtures of wheat and potato was also begun. This was soon displaced by the distillation of alcohol from fermented potato-mashes alone. Fully developed cultivation of potatoes in central Europe, however, began only in the nineteenth century.

In Ireland, owing to the great indigence of the peasantry, the potato became established in the late sixteenth century. In the next century it dominated Irish agriculture, with the result that Ireland suffered the full disadvantage of a single-crop economy. In the eighteenth century the food of the Irish, consisting mainly of milk and potatoes, became a byword for extreme poverty. The disastrous Irish potato blight of 1845–6 proved the delicacy of the balance between famine and subsistence. In other countries development lay between the extreme examples of Ireland and Germany. In the Lowlands of Scotland the introduction of the potato led to greatly improved methods of husbandry and offered an important source of food to an increasingly industrialized area. In the Highlands it little affected agriculure, and even retarded cultural development. In the rest of Britain, as in France, the potato was not a common article of diet before the late eighteenth century.

FIGURE 2—*The sweet potato. From Gerard's* Herball, *1597. It is often mentioned in Jacobean literature.*

By the close of that century the potato had become much cheaper, and through careful selection good varieties were produced. These won public favour, and consumption advanced steadily. After 1780 in Britain the number of industrial workers grew rapidly, and there was an increasing shortage of wheaten flour. By the end of the century the average man had at his disposal but two-thirds of the wheat he had enjoyed at its beginning. An additional source of food was necessary, for wars and the growth of population caused the price of bread to soar. Within two decades the potato was a necessity in Britain's larder, and was hardly less essential in the rest of Europe. By 1800 it had come to stay as a staple ingredient of European diet.

Maize (*Zea mays*). Columbus records that, during his first visit to Cuba (November 1492), he saw a 'type of grain like millet, which they call *maize*, which tasted very well when boiled, roasted, or made into porridge'. The Indians had cultivated maize for centuries and knew several species of it; they had a host of methods of turning it into palatable foods, and used the rest of the plant for a diversity of purposes [3]. The Spaniards gave it the name of *panizo de las Índias*, from its resemblance to millet, *panizo*.

Maize was soon taken to Europe. The first importations were from the West Indies, others from Mexico and Peru followed. At first the plant was grown in European gardens as a curiosity, but within a few years it had spread over southern France, through Italy and the Balkans, to Asia Minor and north

Africa, in which regions it rapidly assumed economic importance. Though it began to attract attention in southern Europe by the beginning of the sixteenth century, it remained in the north a poor competitor with other cereals, for climatic reasons.

The great navigator Magellan (? 1480–1521) seems to have introduced Caribbean and Mexican varieties of maize into the Philippines and the East Indies, whence they reached the Asian mainland. Varieties from Brazil were brought to west Africa and thence to India by the Portuguese. Maize became an important commodity for the slavers plying from Africa to the West Indies, though it was never a specific unit of cultivation in Africa or Asia. Its rapid spread to Turkey and the Near East caused confusion in botanical circles. Thus Fuchs, who gives the first good picture of the plant in his famous herbal (1542) (figure 3), says that it came from Asia and calls it *Turcicum frumentum* or 'Turkish corn' [4].

FIGURE 3—*Maize. From Fuchs's* Historia stirpium, *1542.*

That in the earlier references to maize little attention was given to its use and preparation was a factor in the tardiness of its acceptance. No mention was made of 'green corn' as food, or of the methods of removing the hulls of the grain with lye and lime, though a few explorers actually recorded these American Indian practices. While European medical and agricultural writers neglected the sound Indian recipes, valuing maize only for its imaginary medicinal properties and treating it as a kind of wheat, it was naturally unesteemed. Thus when the Spanish physician Casal described pellagra (1730), now recognized as a vitamin-deficiency disease, he believed it to be a toxic effect wrought by changes in maize caused by the climate of Europe. Yet maize did become a popular food in south-eastern Europe in the sixteenth century, eaten mostly in the form of a porridge called *polenta*. Its excellent qualities were not fully recognized until late in the nineteenth century.

Rice (Oryza sativa) was a crop well known in the Middle Ages, for the Muslims brought it to Spain in the eighth century. Its cultivation demands irrigation and a hot climate, hence it was successful only in southern Europe. Rice-growing was introduced into Italy during the sixteenth century, and about 1700 it reached South Carolina, whence it spread widely in the Americas.

Buckwheat (*Fagopyrum esculentum*) had been grown on a larger scale since 1400, and its cultivation spread during the sixteenth century when it was found profitable though precarious on peaty soils. *Oil-producing plants* like rapeseed and coleseed (colza), varieties of *Brassica napus*, grew in favour as it was discovered that they yielded not only oil but cattle-fodder in the cakes left after pressing. They did not acquire full importance, however, until well into the nineteenth century.

Tea (*Thea* spp), *coffee* (*Coffea* spp), and *cocoa* (*Theobroma cacao*) were never grown in Europe, but their introduction made an important change in European diet and drinking habits. The oldest of these new beverages, tea, was popular in China about 150 B.C. but did not reach Japan until the ninth century A.D., to become its national drink by 1300 [5].

The first shipment of tea was brought to Europe by the Dutch East India Company in 1609; some of it was sold in London for £3 10s a pound. Ten years later the price had dropped by half. By 1636 tea was drunk in Paris, and by 1646 the English East India Company was importing it. Though heavily taxed its price dropped to about 20s a pound by 1689. In that year imports reached a total of 20 000 lb. By 1750 tea had become sufficiently cheap to be a popular beverage.

Tea was still drunk in the Chinese fashion as a weak infusion, largely for its supposed medicinal qualities. Thus Samuel Pepys writes (28 June 1667): 'Home and there find my wife making of tea; a drink which Mr Pelling, the Potticary, tells her is good for her cold and defluxions.' In Holland the distinguished physician Cornelius Bontekoe (d 1685) prescribed 100 to 200 cups a day and drank tea himself day and night. Tea was never greatly favoured in Italy, France, and Germany, where coffee became the popular beverage [6].

Coffee was first harvested in Ethiopia (1450). It is said that a shepherd noticed that his goats remained awake all night through eating the berries of a certain shrub, and that it was found that an infusion of these berries yielded a drink which did indeed chase away sleep and suppress appetite. Early in the sixteenth century seeds were sent to Aden, whence coffee spread to the Muslim world. The Venetians entered the coffee-trade about the end of the century. Prospero Alpini of Padua (1553–1617) first described the plant.

Coffee-drinking was an established habit in the Near East by this time. It had reached Paris by 1643, and less than fifty years later there were already 250 coffee-houses in the city. In Germany neither staunch opposition nor punishments could stop its advance. In England the first coffee-house was opened by a Jew called Jacob at Oxford in 1650. Others appeared in London, and at Cambridge and other towns, to become meeting-places for literary, artistic, scientific, and commercial groups.

Meanwhile Europe was making herself independent of the Near East for her supplies of coffee by starting plantations in tropical countries. Nicolaas Witsen (1641–1717), burgomaster of Amsterdam, prompted the East India Company to have coffee-shrubs taken to Java. In 1700 they were common around Batavia, and a strong plant was sent back to Amsterdam, whence seedlings went to Surinam to start the cultivation of coffee in the New World. Brazil obtained its first coffee-plants from Amsterdam and Surinam.

Chocolate and *cocoa* were products of the New World [7]. Cortez found the cacao-bean highly regarded by the Aztecs of Mexico as being very nutritious and beneficial to their health. Chocolate reached Spain in 1520 in the form of slabs and tablets. The 'chocolatl' of the Mexicans had been compounded of cacao-beans and other seeds, but the Europeans brewed their new drink from cacao-beans only. It reached Flanders and Italy about 1606. The first chocolate-house was opened in London by a Frenchman in 1657, where the 'excellent West India drink called chocolate' was sold both raw and prepared. Pepys tells us that he first drank 'jocollate' at a coffee-house in November 1664. In England as in France the drink became popular only when abundant supplies of cane-sugar were available, and for a long time it remained a luxury. In the next century Linnaeus (1707–78), knowing the Aztec legend of its divine origin, gave the plant the generic name *Theobroma* ('food of the gods'). As with tea and coffee, Europeans soon began the cultivation of the cacao-bean in their tropical colonies.

These new beverages all demanded sweetening agents. Europe had largely relied upon honey and must (unfermented grape-juice) in the Middle Ages, for sugar remained a rare and expensive importation from the Near East [8]. During the later Middle Ages the consumption of sugar in Europe rose steadily, and honey and must were gradually replaced by it. The cane was introduced into southern Europe, and sugar became an important article in the trade of Genoese and Venetian merchants, who brought it from Cyprus, Syria, and Egypt (vol II, p 372). During the age of discovery the sugar-cane was taken to Madeira and the Canaries; later it reached Central and South America, and in the early seventeenth century it was first grown in the West Indies (figure 4). These islands became in the seventeenth and eighteenth centuries the main sources of supply for the European market, the factories being built on the Egyptian model.

The habit of taking sweetened drinks and eating sweet puddings and pies became more common during the seventeenth century, and by 1700 the price of sugar had fallen to 6*d* a pound, or less. Raw sugar was imported into England, Holland, and other European countries, and there refined for the local market.

FIGURE 4—*West Indian sugar-factory.* (Left) *Vertical roller-mill crushing the canes;* (centre) *channel to the first boiler, where the juice was reduced and skimmed;* (right) *boiler-house. In the second boiler the sugar was purified with lime and egg-white, in the third and fourth it was concentrated to permit crystallization.* 1694.

The original process of making sugar as used by the Arabs[1] was simple. The pieces of sugar-cane were expressed between rollers (sometimes driven by wind-mills or water-wheels) and then often boiled with water to obtain a second extract. The expressed juice was skimmed, filtered, and boiled down to a brown-black syrup, scum and dirt being skimmed off at intervals. From this syrup loaves or cones of raw brown sugar were obtained (vol II, figure 340). The Egyptian refineries, however, introduced more sophisticated methods of treatment.

In the European refineries a solution of the raw sugar was refined by adding lime-water and blood; the mixture was boiled and skimmed until no more scum

[1] The word sugar is derived from the Arabic *sukkar*, cognate with the Greek *sakchar*.

was formed and the boiled solution was clear. It was then filtered through cloth and evaporated as quickly as possible until a sample showed the correct consistency. The viscous mass was transferred to the crystallization-vat, mixed with other portions, and then allowed to crystallize in pottery moulds. Refining was not further improved until the nineteenth century when proper evaporation, heat-economy, and refining with charcoal and decolorizing earths were introduced. By 1800 about 150 000 tons of sugar were consumed annually in England —fifteen times the amount consumed in 1700.

FIGURE 5—*The tobacco plant. From a herbal of 1570.*

Tobacco (Brazilian or Carib *tabaco*) also came from the New World, and its cultivation was soon of economic significance [9]. When Columbus first landed the natives offered him some leaves which they clearly considered very valuable. On reaching Cuba (2 November 1492) he observed men and women smoking 'cigars' of a weed called 'tobaccos' there, but elsewhere known by other names. Before 1560 tobacco plants (*Nicotiana* spp) were cultivated in the 'physic gardens' of the botanists and herbalists in western Europe (figures 5, 6) and tobacco reached England about 1565. The Spaniards brought its cultivation to the Philippines about 1575, whence it spread to north and west. The African natives developed a great appetite for tobacco in the seventeenth century, when it became an important article of currency in the slave-trade.

In Europe, tobacco was first used as a medicinal herb. André Thevet (1502–90) described how the natives of Brazil used it to 'loosen and carry off the superfluous humours of the brain'; he brought seeds to France in 1556 [10]. Jean Nicot (? 1530–1600) observed it at the Portuguese court, and Jacques Gohory (d 1576) of Paris gave tobacco repute as a cure-all. Not until the end of the seventeenth century did it lose its medical interest. Cultivation, first of *Nicotiana tabacum*, then of *N. rustica* (which was better suited to the European climate), began in Spain in 1558. Thence it spread to Italy, Turkey, the Balkans, Russia, and farther east. In Europe it appears here and there as a cash-crop by the end of the sixteenth century. Word of the new plant was brought to England in Thomas Harriot's account of Virginia (1588) after the first abortive attempt to settle there[1] [11]. The emigrants had brought back tobacco plants (*N. rustica*) from Virginia to Gloucestershire in 1586. Success for European pioneers of

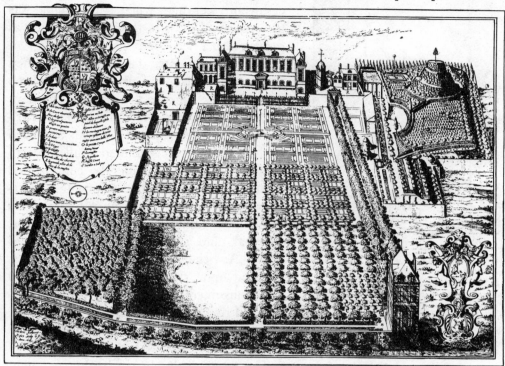

FIGURE 6—*Botanic Garden in Paris, the* Jardin des Plantes, *in 1636. The herbs were grown in the formal beds.*

tobacco-culture in Virginia itself came only in 1612, when John Rolfe (1585–1622)[2] brought seeds from the Spanish plantations farther south and when selection of proper species prevailed. Exports of Virginian tobacco to England, where it was in high demand as a substitute for the expensive Spanish product, soon increased. The English Navigation Acts protected the Virginian tobacco-farmers, who by the early eighteenth century had established an important industry there. Correspondingly, the growing of tobacco in England was prohibited.

The habit of smoking tobacco met with formidable opposition, headed in England by James I's 'Counterblast to Tobacco' (1604). The war against it

[1] Thomas Harriot, mathematician and astronomer, was born at Oxford in 1560 and died at Isleworth in 1621. He was a friend of Sir Walter Ralegh and of the 'Wizard Earl' (Henry Percy, ninth Earl of Northumberland).
[2] Husband of Pocahontas.

raged until 1650 and later in some countries, but neither western nor eastern rulers could eradicate the taste for tobacco which later justified itself in their eyes as a new source of revenue. Smoking went out of favour in polite society in the eighteenth century, when snuff-taking was the rage, and even in the nineteenth it was regarded as a peculiarly masculine vice.

Snuff-taking dates back to 1558, when powdered tobacco-leaf was introduced into Portugal; the practice was supposed to have a medicinal value. Jean Nicot, the French Ambassador there, sent some seeds to Queen Catherine de Medicis, and so snuff came to France. The habit evidently commended itself, for the Papacy had to prohibit snuff-taking in church. The ground tobacco was commonly adulterated with other herbs, charcoal, and soda before it was sold as snuff. An elaborate social etiquette was founded upon the snuff habit, which for a time consumed a large quantity of tobacco and still has numerous votaries.

FIGURE 7—*Distilling-apparatus.* (Above) *Brick-built still in which the alembic head is cooled discontinuously by a water-trough. 1567. (Below) Cask still; to save metal, only a small part of the liquid in the still C is heated directly by the furnace in the copper boiler B. The distillate flows through the worm-cooler D in a cask of water. 1651. Such illustrations were very frequently reprinted for over a century.*

II. ALCOHOLIC DRINKS

There was little change in the manufacture of alcoholic drinks in this period. Beer won the market formerly enjoyed by cheap wines, and imports of wine from Spain and France into northern Europe declined with the imposition of tariffs, navigation acts, and other measures tending to reduce freedom of trade. Such legislation promoted the consumption of locally produced beer, cider, and other drinks. Most imported wines were drunk from the wood, bottling, if desired, being carried out by the consumer or vintner. Cork stoppers were not widely used before the late seventeenth century, when the custom of bottling and laying down special wines began. Apart from the introduction of hops during the late Middle Ages (vol II, p 140) no important change took place in brewing and malting. The ordinary weak home-brewed beer was a harmless and healthy drink in an age when water was commonly impure.

Spirits were now competing seriously with wine and beer in many countries. Many kinds of 'aquavite' were distilled from cheap wine or fermented corn, with secret mixtures of herbs and berries. This gave rise to much abuse until such national organizations as the Distillers' Company (1638) and others drew up regulations for the trade. Gin was introduced into Holland by German soldiers from Hanover serving in the wars of liberation against Spain; thence it went to

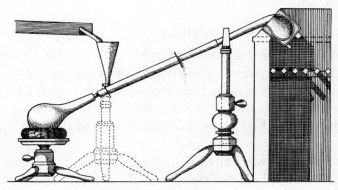

FIGURE 8—*von Weigel's still with counter-current cooling, 1773. The distillate flows down from the retort on the right to the receiver, while the coolant flows upwards through the water-jacket.*

England and Ireland. In early eighteenth-century London the sale of cheap gin under the sign 'Drunk for a penny, dead drunk for twopence' became a social evil, savagely depicted by Hogarth (plate 2 A). Its destruction of the energy and morals of the 'labouring poor' was prevented only by the imposition of an excise. Similar events occurred in other great cities. Whisk(e)y[1]—the usquebaugh[2] of the Irish bogs and Scottish moors—made its way into genteel society in Britain as did schnapps in Holland. Hot punch warmed a cold winter's gathering, and the new practice of fortifying wines with brandy (vol II, p 142) contributed to the popularity of sherry, madeira, and above all port.

There was some empirical but no scientific development of distillation and distilling-apparatus (figure 7) [12]. There were further attempts to develop proper cooling of the alembic and the distillate. Such operations as repeated boiling and rectification received some attention, and apparatus for these operations was developed, but little progress could be made while the theory of heat

---

[1] By a useful convention, whisky is Scotch and whiskey Irish.
[2] Gaelic *uisge beatha*, water of life. Hence 'whisky' equals 'water' (cf *vodka*).

was inadequate to guide design and operation. The principle of continuous counter-current cooling was introduced by von Weigel (1773) (figure 8) and Magellan (1780), and duly led to the famous Liebig condenser (1830). Steam was already used in the distillation of essential oils from flowers and fruit, and distillation techniques were now applied to the manufacture of sulphuric, hydrochloric, and nitric acids, as well as to the preparation of wood-tar (ch 25). The distillation of spirits was still crude. The distillate was highly contaminated unless redistilled several times, but a check on purity was provided by use of the hydrometer (p 22).

III. NEW AGRICULTURAL TECHNIQUES

The employment of new agricultural techniques, notably in the seventeenth and eighteenth centuries, was only partly a result of the cultivation of new crops [13]. It was more often caused by local economic changes, which varied all over Europe. There was an increasing endeavour, reflected in the literature of the time, to encourage the best farming methods and to discover their scientific foundation.

In Germany progress was halted by political causes. The peasant wars of the sixteenth century ended disastrously, and the Thirty Years War (1618–48) again brought devastation to central Europe. Many decades passed before peasant agriculture was as prosperous as it had been at the close of the Middle Ages. In 1700 real wages were still at only about half the standard of those of 1500; much of the population lived on the margin of starvation. Yet the cultivation of winter fodder for cattle profited by the slow introduction of clover and lucerne from Italy by way of Flanders, though 'artificial grasses' remained uncommon until 1750. The many cattle that could not be fed through the winter had to be killed in the autumn and pickled or smoked. Fewer pigs were bred as deforestation proceeded, owing to the reduction of their food-supply; sheep took their place. More pigs were raised again when the potato was introduced. Oil-yielding rapeseed and colza came to central Europe very slowly and were not important crops until after 1750. The farmers of that region, as elsewhere, were usually better fed than the poorer townsmen, who had already suffered through the withdrawal of trade from Italy and Germany to the Atlantic seaboard, following the discovery of America and new routes to the East.

There was little uniformity in European farming methods, for even in France, a more advanced country, striking contrasts could be observed. The neighbourhood of Paris and west and north-west France were areas of *petite culture*. In Picardy the methods differed greatly from those current in Artois and Flanders.

Even viticulture had its traditional local variations of technique. The penetration of the potato was slow, becoming effective only at the end of the period. Maize was cultivated with some success in the south-west. It was not only an important food for the poor but, together with clover and other new crops, was used as cattle-fodder. The eighteenth-century physiocrats, who believed that cultivation of the land was the sole real foundation of wealth, glorified the farmer and his work but directed little effort towards the practical improvement of farming. Most French farmers persisted in the use of medieval methods; improvements were merely local. France thus remained a land of fallows and scattered strips, of scrub animals and clumsy implements. The sound initiation of agricultural writing in the sixteenth century by such original authors as Charles Estienne (1504–64) and Olivier ‘de Serres (1539–1619)[1] was not followed up [14]. The attempt to improve French agricultural technique was begun only just before the Revolution, and in imitation of what had been achieved in England.

The story of farming in the Netherlands is completely different. Treatises on farming were very inadequate, failing even to describe the work of draining and reclaiming farmland for which the region was famous. Here the practice was that of ‘horticulture transferred to the field’. The Netherlands were in this period the most densely populated area in Europe. They flourished on their great carrying-trade—wine and salt from France and Spain were traded for the timber and corn of the Baltic. Regular imports of corn were needed to feed the people. They grew flax for the linen-industry, madder, weld, and woad for dyeing, barley and hops for brewing, hemp for ropes, and tobacco. The industrial crops were mostly grown in the western provinces and some were exported. The United Provinces specialized in horticulture, market-gardening, and fruit-growing. These required extreme care and the application of fertilizers, which were obtained from the stock-raising areas and the towns. Ashes, compost, night-soil, and oil-cakes from the mills were all used as manures. Sheep-manure and pigeon-dung were in heavy demand, notably by tobacco-growers.

Market-gardening, arboriculture, and bulb-growing increased greatly in importance during the seventeenth and eighteenth centuries, during which the old alternation of crops was replaced by a three-year crop-rotation or even by a cycle of nine years in which clover played a part. Bed-cultivation and row-cultivation were typical of these regions. Rapeseed was largely replaced by colza during the sixteenth century, yielding cattle-fodder. Potatoes spread slowly but did not gain much importance until their value as foodstuff and fodder was understood, after the famine of 1740–1.

[1] de Serres introduced the cultivation of the mulberry in France.

Certain improvements in types of plough were made in Flanders and Brabant, and new marking-tools and seeding-horns were proposed. Attempts at constructing a sowing-machine (1770) failed, but a winnowing-mill was introduced (1727) from China. The churn-mill for the manufacture of butter is first men-

FIGURE 9—*The hop-garden.* (Above) *Tying the young hop-vines.* (Below) '*The best and readyest way to take the hoppes from the poales.*' *1574.*

tioned in 1660. Cattle-breeding was not yet rationalized, though the standard was already high.

Sixteenth-century England saw a vigorous development of farming. The 'floating' of water-meadows was introduced, market-gardening began to develop slowly but steadily, and there was a revolution in rural housing. Many new books on farming were published, such as Fitzherbert's 'Boke of Husbondrye' (1523) and Tusser's 'Hundreth good pointes of Husbandrie' (1557). The latter also dealt with gardening, grafting, planting of trees, cultivation of hops (figure 9), and management of poultry and cattle. However, English agricultural literature up to 1700 was wholly empirical and could have no proper scientific basis. Most of the new books led away from subsistence farming and were inspired by the methods used in the Low Countries. The investigations begun by the Royal Society after 1660 failed either to produce a nation-wide survey, or, despite a few experiments with turnips and clover, to promote the general adoption of new crops and methods.

In England as in Holland the East India trade stimulated the rise of a class of gentleman-farmers who had invested their commercial profits in country estates. Rents trebled and purchases of land doubled between 1600 and 1688. Though the price of corn fell, the acreage under it increased. Agrarian conditions improved through the better adjustment between tillage and wool-production, and through greater stability of employment on the new estates. Market-gardening became more important as the size and wealth of the towns increased. The old bailiff-farming practically disappeared.

After this incubation period the early part of the eighteenth century may well be called the age of the innovators. The old forms of crop-rotation with fallow periods had been abandoned by landowners and tenants in favour of legume-rotation and field-grass husbandry, under the influence of late medieval town economy. This was notably the case in the southern and eastern districts of England. Enclosure of the medieval open fields was a cause of rural depopulation, but on the other hand the pioneers of the 'New Husbandry' and scientific rotation were now active. Jethro Tull (1674–1741) invented the seed-drill, pulverized the soil to cultivate without manure, and introduced the horse-hoe from Languedoc. Charles Townshend (1674–1738) introduced the Flemish method of cultivating turnips, clover from Spain, and manuring by marling. Burgundian and other French grasses suitable for pastures were imported. Arthur Young (1741–1820) and William Marshall (1745–1818) sought to improve British agriculture by educating the farmer in the scientific principles of farming. Robert Bakewell (1725–95) and the Duke of Bedford (1765–1805) effected great improvements in cattle by systematic stock-breeding. Famous gentleman-farmers like Thomas William Coke of Holkham (1752–1842), Lord Somerville, and Sir John Sinclair took part in this movement, which was to bear fruit between 1770 and 1850 and attain the finest balance between tillage and cattle-breeding before the introduction of specialized intensive farming later in the nineteenth century.

IV. MILLING

The production of flour was a major industry, employing most of the available water-wheels and windmills [15]. The relatively simple machinery embodied much empirical knowledge. Thus the mill-stones had to be obtained from special quarries. Local stone was used, but English millers preferred those obtained from Andernach on the Rhine, and the French millers those from La Ferté-sous-Jouarre and Bergerac, near Paris, which were even exported to America. Good grinding demanded that the runner-stone be very exactly balanced over the bed-stone. Usually it was balanced by lead poured into four symmetrically sited holes drilled in the top of the runner-stone. Adjustment of the distance between the stones was effected by screws.

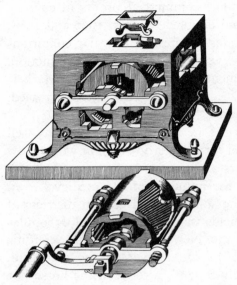

The floury part of the kernel had to be ground to the finest possible powder without overheating. Hence the grooves of a dressed stone served not only in cutting but in ventilating the meal as it passed outwards towards the circumference. As the American Oliver Evans expressed it: 'A dull stone kills or destroys that lively quality of the grain, that causes it to ferment and rise in the baking; it also makes the meal so clammy that it sticks to the cloth and chokes up the meshes in bolting.' The dressing of the stones was done by itinerant craftsmen.

FIGURE 10—*Ramelli's portable iron roller-mill for grinding flour. Both the roller and the interior of the drum are grooved; they are slightly tapering, so that adjustment of the long screws alters the fineness of the grind. The grain is placed in the little hopper and the flour emerges from the spout. 1588.*

During the sixteenth century there were attempts to make milling more simple and efficient. The Emperor Charles V, after his abdication and retirement into a monastery (1556), is said to have invented, with his watchmaker Turriano, a roller-mill 'small enough to be placed in the sleeve of a monk's gown'. Such a roller-mill figures in Ramelli's book on machines (figure 10) [16]. Ramelli's mill has a rotating roller with spiral grooving. The combination of the roller with its suspension inside the casing, the spiral corrugations, the provision of a hopper, and the arrangement for bringing the two grinding-surfaces together, reveal this design as far ahead of its times. Another roller-mill was illustrated by G. A. Böckler in his *Theatrum machinarum novum* (1662) (figure 11) [17]. Its roller was eccentric to the concave block near which it rotated; thus grinding took place along a straight line rather than over the whole surfaces as with mill-stones. The meal passed into a bolter (sieve) agitated by the crank rotating the roller. Böckler's method is that of the modern mill, in which a second rotating roller takes the place of his concave block. We do not know how far these ideas were applied in practical milling before the end of the eighteenth century.

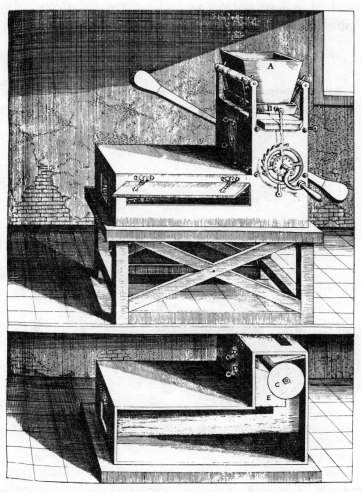

FIGURE 11—*Böckler's roller-mill.* (A) *Hopper;* (B) *sieve agitated from the drive;* (C) *roller;* (D) *adjusting screws;* (E) *fixed concave block. 1662.*

In the second milling-operation progress was also very slow. The meal was crudely sifted to divide the fine flour from the grits, the sieves being square box-like structures shaken by hand. Soon such sieves were fitted into a kind of hand-agitated bolter, as shown by Jerome Cardan in his *De subtilitate* (1550), which permitted four separations.

The mechanization of bolting began with Boller's proposal to use mill-power to shake the sieves (1502). An early illustration of mechanical bolting is given by Verantius in his *Machinae novae* (Venice, *c* 1595) in which a lever is struck by a lantern-wheel and so agitates an inclined trough covered with cloths of different meshes (bolters) (figure 12). Bolting-cloth was an extremely hard

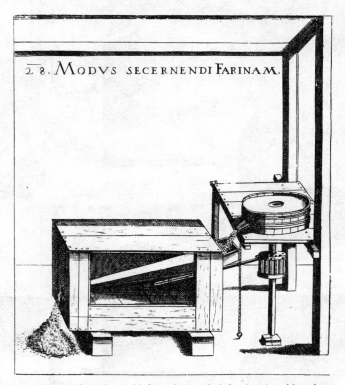

28. MODVS SECERNENDI FARINAM.

FIGURE 12—*Verantius's mechanical bolting-device; the bolter is agitated by a lever struck by a pinion on the mill-stone drive.*

material of even weave. It was originally of linen or cotton, but during the eighteenth century silk was often used with up to 100 threads an inch, and therefore of very fine mesh. These devices were still hand-operated. Cylindrical bolters with power-operation were designed by Ramelli (1588) (figure 13) and Charlemagne (1793). Auxiliary drives were used in many mills to hoist the unground grain, and for other purposes, but the introduction of such mechanical refinements as bolters and hoists was retarded by the slow improvement of gearing and the lack of proper design in water-wheels, windmills, and other machinery. Above all there was still no urge for the large-scale production of flour, which was milled for local use and seldom carried over long distances owing to the great cost of transport. Much grain, however, was carried by sea. As the prime movers slowly developed, the idea of powered factories sprang up here and there; thus the Swedish metallurgist Polhem built (1700) a water-driven factory to manufacture a wide range of metal tools and objects. He employed rolling- and shearing-machines and a variety of specially invented devices. The mechani-

FIGURE 13—*Water-driven corn-mill with mechanical bolting-device* (lower left), *on which the flour falls from the stones. The bolter is actuated by a lever from the main driving-gear. Ramelli, 1588.*

zation of flour-production awaited the work of Oliver Evans (1795), who designed the first automatic mill for the mass-production of flour, using power-driven roller-mills and cylindrical bolters.

V. PREPARING, TESTING, AND PRESERVING FOODSTUFFS

Cookery-books were published soon after the advent of printing, one of the earliest being the English 'Boke of Keruynge' (carving) of 1508. They helped to spread skill in the more refined ways of preparing food for the table, and in the cooking of the newly cultivated vegetables. Changes in eating-habits also occurred. Whereas in the Middle Ages two meals a day were generally considered sufficient, four were not uncommon in the sixteenth century. The main meal was usually at noon, followed by a supper at about seven or eight o'clock in the evening, but by the eighteenth century gentlefolk had their main meal in the late afternoon, a light lunch preceding it and tea following. The use of the spoon spread quickly in the sixteenth century. The fork (normally two-pronged) was used in the Middle Ages to hand pieces of food to guests or table-companions, then the old-established Italian custom spread, in the seventeenth century, of using it to bring food to the mouth. An Englishman who saw this custom in Italy in 1608 and tried to introduce it at home was nicknamed *furciferus* (fork-bearer). At the Austrian court in 1651 food was still eaten with the fingers, but by 1750 the fork had become fashionable through imitation of French manners. Three- and four-pronged forks appeared in the seventeenth century. At the same time the guests were also provided with knives, for in earlier days everybody brought his own knife and spoon or fork. Slices of bread had served as plates for centuries, but wooden, pewter, and pottery table-vessels became common in the sixteenth century. The industries—especially those of pewter, pottery, and glass—supplying table-ware were correspondingly enlarged to meet the growing demand. Glass drinking-vessels became common about 1650.

A few new inventions entered the kitchen. Roasting was a major operation of cooking and therefore spits were important devices. Early handbooks on machinery show weight-driven spit-jacks, which became common. Though many inventors designed clockwork-jacks, the larger spits were driven by dogs turning the 'dog-drum', which was introduced about 1650 and survived into the nineteenth century. The hot air rising in the chimney was also employed to rotate a fan, which then turned the spit by means of gears (figure 14). Such 'chimney-wheels' or 'smoke-jacks' were primitive hot-air turbines. From the time of Leonardo da Vinci many famous engineers tried their hands at such devices, which, however, did not become of practical use until the eighteenth century.

The sixteenth-century fire-grate consisted of bars placed on two fire-dogs, which lifted the fire from the hearth and provided means for regulating the heat. New kinds of trivets were introduced, as were conical mullers; these vessels were filled with drink and thrust into the fire.

Progress in food-testing methods was slow, though it became increasingly important to detect adulteration in the greatly increased number of foodstuffs traded over long distances [18]. The first guardians of the food and health of the public were the 'garbellers'.[1] Garbellers had no knowledge of chemical analysis and relied on appearance, taste, and smell. Their tests were mostly

---

[1] From the Arabic *gharbala*, to sift or select.

empirical and dealt only with the more patent and gross forms of adulteration; rarely could they detect the more subtle impurities. New instruments such as microscopes were not systematically turned to foodstuffs until the nineteenth

FIGURE 14—*Cooking-spit turned by a smoke-jack with a fan in the chimney. Böckler, 1662.*

century. The strength of alcoholic spirits was long determined by the gunpowder test, which consisted in pouring some of the liquid on gunpowder and then trying to ignite it. If the powder burnt, the water-content of the spirit was considered to be sufficiently low. Proof-spirit would just, and only just, allow the powder to ignite.

The idea of using specific gravity as a characteristic of natural substances dates from Archimedes, and Arabic scientists had examined the purity of precious metals and stones in this way. The hydrometer for testing the specific gravity of liquids is also old, for the instrument was known at Alexandria in the fourth century. It was studied by many scientists of the sixteenth and seventeenth centuries. Robert Boyle (1627–91) describes a hydrometer for testing spirits, in a paper in the 'Philosophical Transactions' of the Royal Society [19]. In his *Medicina Hydrostatica* (1690) he proposes that the hydrostatic balance be used to test rain-water, wine, brandy, cider, beer, ale, and so on, using a piece of amber as the weight to be immersed. Boyle's ideas took root in many countries. Roger Clarke's 'Hydrometer or Brandy Prover' (London, 1746) was generally accepted in England. It was adjusted by adding a series of graded brass weights, and was adopted by the excise officers. George Gilpin published a series of tables giving the gravities of mixtures of alcohol and water, which were used with Clarke's hydrometer (1794).

John Dicas's hydrometer (1780) was adopted in America in 1790. In France Antoine Baumé (1768) proposed a hydrometer with fixed points marked on the scale representing the gravities of water and a specified salt solution; for solutions with a density lower than that of water the scale was simply extended below zero. Cartier adapted this idea in his hydrometer, on which the strength of alcohol could be read in 'degrees', and which was officially adopted in France (1771). A few years later (1774) Demachy published the first systematic account of the use of the hydrometer for testing alcohol, acids, and commercial fluids generally. Many other new types of hydrometer were proposed later.

The testing of foodstuffs became more effective with the rise of analytical chemistry after 1790. In 1820 Friedrich Accum (1769–1838) published his 'Adulteration of Food and Culinary Poisons', the pioneer treatise on the subject.

During these three centuries no major invention affected the preservation of food. The ancient techniques of salting, drying, smoking, and so on were hardly improved. One invention of the later Middle Ages did, however, have a marked effect on fifteenth- and sixteenth-century diet, namely an improved technique of gutting and preserving herrings [20]. Herrings had long been preserved by salting, like other fish, but this did not prevent them from going bad after some time. William Beukelszoon, a wholesale dealer in fish living at Biervliet, Flanders, invented the following procedure about 1330. As soon as the fish were caught, an incision was made near the gills. Part of the guts was removed, and the gutted fish were salted and packed in barrels. This technique was the basis of the herring-fishery, for a time a Dutch monopoly, and made possible the long-distance transportation of this cheap food (vol IV, ch 2).

The technique was invented when the fishermen of the Flemish coast were seeking independence of the English shore, and enabled them to clean and pack their fish without landing at some point nearer the fishing-grounds than their home port. Its full value was not attained at first, through the opposition of the Hanse and of the wealthier Flemish merchants.

VI. THE RISE OF DIETETIC SCIENCE

It is impossible to speak of a 'European' diet, for regional and local variations remained very great. Thus in central Europe, so often devastated by war, diet was for several centuries unvarying and barely sufficient, while conditions improved in the countries on the Atlantic seaboard. In the Low Countries, for instance, sixteenth-century diet differed little from the medieval. Meat (except perhaps pork) and milk were still unusual foods for the poorer classes, though fish—fresh, salted, or dried—was common fare. Milk, it is true, was slowly getting more popular, but butter was used by the rich only. Vegetable-growing was increasing, especially the cultivation of cabbages, carrots, turnips, onions, and leeks. Eggs were much eaten and herring was a staple food. Ale was the common drink.

During the seventeenth century several changes took place. Barley bread made way for rye or wheaten bread, the latter being a luxury. Butter became more general. Gin, at first a drink of the lower classes, became more fashionable. The ruling middle classes ate plentiful and well seasoned food; the authorities had to check their over-indulgence. Peasant diet was slightly enriched by greater quantities of milk and pig-meat, but in winter only the rich ate meat, salted or smoked. Pigeons were kept as a source of food. The potato was still virtually unknown. Diet in the army, the navy, hospitals, and almshouses was still badly balanced and generally too low.

During the eighteenth century everyone in the Low Countries ate bread of a better quality, and also potatoes. Rye bread fell into contempt as 'the fare of artisans and labourers', and wheaten bread was preferred. Gluttony was a notorious vice of both Dutch and English. Cheese and butter milk were now consumed in larger quantities, but the poor too often ate salted vegetables even in summer, and the variety was still small. Salted meat was now more common and a taste for rich, greasy food developed. Fish and eggs were still eaten in large quantities, and some fruit was consumed. Sugar became more popular as tea, coffee, and other drinks displaced ale. The diet of prisons, hospitals, almshouses, and other institutions remained inadequate.

This Dutch picture differs little from that of England. During the sixteenth century the meat-supply hardly changed. Between about 1530 and 1640 wages rose in value far more slowly than the prices of food, so that the mass of the people were less well fed during most of this period. Beans, some salted meat, bread, fish, cheese, a little bacon, and some game formed their diet; the precarious balance of their lives was easily upset by famines and epidemics. The towns had fair supplies of butter, meat, white bread, and fruit, and an increasing quantity of vegetables and fresh fish. The army and the navy seem to have been well fed.

After the general improvement in living conditions during the latter part of the seventeenth century, and despite the evil social effects of the enclosure movement and the early stages of the industrial revolution, there was a rapid increase in the population of Britain; this seems to have been associated with a general improvement in public health and diet in the eighteenth century. The death-rate declined, perhaps in part owing to the greater availability of fresh foodstuffs. There were still great distinctions between rich and poor. While the wealthy indulged too freely in rich food and wines, the diets chosen for institutions such as barracks, prisons, and almshouses, though copious enough, were unbalanced through lack of scientific knowledge. Bread, cheese, beef, and beer, nourishing in themselves, do not contain everything required for good health; there was admittedly some carelessness with regard to quality, but ignorance was a worse evil than neglect. This was particularly true of seamen's food, so regularly the cause of deficiency diseases such as scurvy.

During most of the seventeenth century the theory of nutrition was still that of Galen, governed by the idea of the four 'humours', each considered to be 'hot', 'moist', 'dry', or 'cold' in any of one to four degrees. The humoral theory was itself based on the Aristotelian conception of the four elements, which had declined in esteem but was not yet finally renounced. Walter Harris (1647–1732), with others, tried to substitute for the humoral system a primitive chemical notion of disease (1689), but such scientific thrusts were still widely disregarded, and prejudices remained firm. Milk, for example, was believed suitable only for the very young and the very old. Vegetables were distrusted on the grounds that they engendered wind and melancholy.

Sanctorius (1561–1636) and Van Helmont (? 1577–1644), original as their investigations were, did not cast much more light on the processes of digestion, or on the nutritive needs of the healthy individual. Nor were the next two generations of chemists more successful. The usual method of analysing a foodstuff was to submit it to destructive distillation; the 'watery', 'oily', and 'saline' products obtained were then examined, and many erroneous conclusions drawn. Some chemists thought they could distinguish between 'alkaline' and 'acid' foods, and prescribed their use accordingly. Not till the late eighteenth century were new views on the nature of chemical compounds established, as the result of the investigations of Black (1728–99), Priestley (1733–1804), Scheele (1742–86), and Lavoisier (1743–94). They were hardly applied fully to organic substances before another fifty years had passed. Thus deficiency diseases continued unrecognized as such, misunderstood, and (before about 1750) virtually untreated. The victory over the first of them, scurvy, and the remedy, the drinking of fresh fruit-juice, were purely empirical, owing nothing to chemical science or indeed to the prevailing ideas on dietetics.

Digestion in the stomach was still regarded as akin to putrefaction. Réaumur (1683–1757) made experiments in which a young kite swallowed open tubes full of food, and disgorged them after a short while. Similar experiments were made by Stevins of Edinburgh (1777), who found like Réaumur that food was softened and dissolved in the stomach, and also by Spallanzani (1729–99). Lavoisier finally approached modern theories, holding that the products of digestion are carried to the lungs by the blood-stream and oxidized there.

These few examples show how modern views on diet and nutrition were beginning to dawn at the close of the eighteenth century.

We observe the following factors playing an ever-growing role:

1. The New Husbandry with its scientific and intensive agriculture and co-ordinated system of food-production extends over a large part of the world, and involves the mechanization of the farm.
2. The automatic mill and the mechanization of bread- and flour-making herald the mass-production of other foodstuffs.
3. The new analytical chemistry, applied to the testing of foodstuffs, raises the standard of quality.
4. Chemical and physiological evaluation of food makes the scientific study of nutrition possible.
5. Such new methods of food preservation as canning, desiccation and evaporation, and refrigeration permit the world-wide distribution of food-supplies.

REFERENCES

[1] LEWIN, L. 'Phantastica: narcotic and stimulating drugs.' Kegan Paul, Trench and Trubner, London. 1931.
[2] SALAMAN, R. N. 'The History and Social Influence of the Potato.' University Press, Cambridge. 1949.
[3] WEATHERWAX, P. 'Indian Corn in Old America.' Macmillan, New York. 1954.
[4] FUCHS, LEONHART. De historia stirpium commentarii, p. 825. Isingrin, Basel. 1542.

[5] MENNELL, R. O. 'Tea: an Historical Sketch.' Wilson, London. 1926.
    UKERS, W. M. 'The Romance of Tea.' Knopf, New York. 1936.
[6] JACOB, R. J. 'Coffee, the Epic of a Commodity.' Viking Press, New York. 1935.
    UKERS, W. M. 'All about Coffee.' Tea and Coffee Trade Journal Company, New York. 1922.
[7] FINCKE, H. 'Handbuch der Kakaoerzeugnisse.' Springer, Berlin. 1936.
[8] LIPPMANN, E. O. VON. 'Geschichte des Zuckers.' Springer, Berlin. 1929.
    Idem. Z. Ver. dtsch. Zuckerind., **84**, 806, 1934.
[9] BROOKS, J. E. 'The Mighty Leaf, Tobacco through the Centuries.' Redman, London and
    Sydney. 1953.
    CORTI, CONTE EGON CAESAR. 'A History of Smoking' (trans. from German by P. ENG-
    LAND). Harrap, London. 1931.
[10] THEVET, ANDRÉ. 'Les Singularitez de la France Antarctique, autrement nommée Amérique',
    p. 57. Christóphle Plantin, Antwerp. 1558.
[11] HARRIOT, THOMAS. 'A Briefe and True Report of the New Found Land of Virginia.'
    London. 1588.
[12] FORBES, R. J. 'A Short History of the Art of Distillation.' Brill, Leiden. 1948.
[13] PROTHERO, R. E., LORD ERNLE. 'English Farming Past and Present.' Longmans, London.
    1936.
    GRAS, N. S. B. 'History of Agriculture in Europe and America.' Crofts, New York. 1925.
    See also communications in Relaz. X Congress. Int. Sci. Hist., Vol. 4, pp. 139–226. 1955.
[14] ESTIENNE, CHARLES. 'L'agriculture et maison rustique.' Jacques Du-Puys, Paris. 1567.
    (Published in Latin as *Praedium rusticum*, Paris. 1554.)
    SERRES, OLIVIER DE. 'Le théatre d'agriculture et mesnage des champs.' Paris. 1600.
[15] STORCK, J. and TEAGUE, W. D. 'Flour for Man's Bread.' University of Minnesota Press,
    Minneapolis. 1952.
[16] RAMELLI, AGOSTINO. 'Le diverse et artificiose machine.' Published by the author, Paris.
    1588.
[17] BÖCKLER, G. A. *Theatrum machinarum novum*. Cologne. 1662.
[18] FILBY, F. A. 'A History of Food Adulteration and Analysis.' Allen and Unwin, London.
    1934.
[19] BOYLE, ROBERT. *Phil. Trans.*, **10**, 329, 1675.
[20] DOORMAN, G. 'Patents for Inventions in the Netherlands', pp. 55–58. Nijhoff, The Hague.
    1942.

BIBLIOGRAPHY

AINSWORTH-DAVIS, J. R. 'Cooking through the Centuries.' Dent, London. 1931.
BUREMA, L. 'De Voeding in Nederland van de Middeleeuwen tot de twintigste eeuw.' Van
    Gorcum, Assen. 1953.
DRUMMOND, J. C. and WILBRAHAM, A. 'The Englishman's Food.' Cape, London. 1939.
FRANCIS, C. 'A History of Food and its Preservation.' Princeton University Press, Princeton. 1937.
FURNAS, C. C. and FURNAS, SPARKLE M. 'Man, Bread and Destiny.' Cassell, London. 1938.
GOTTSCHALK, A. 'Histoire de l'alimentation' (2 vols). Éditions Hippocrate, Paris. 1948.
HINTZE, K. 'Geographie und Geschichte der Ernährung.' Thieme, Leipzig. 1934.
JACOB, H. E. 'Six Thousand Years of Bread' (trans. from German by R. WINSTON and CLARA
    WINSTON). Doubleday, Doran and Co., New York. 1944. German ed. enl., Rohwolt
    Verlag, Hamburg. 1954.
MAURIZIO, A. 'Geschichte der gegorenen Getränke.' Springer, Berlin. 1933.
VERRILL, A. H. 'The Food America gave the World.' Page, Boston. 1937.

METALLURGY AND ASSAYING

CYRIL STANLEY SMITH AND R. J. FORBES[1]

I. RENAISSANCE WRITERS ON METALLURGY

No spectacular new discoveries or inventions modified metallurgical methods during the sixteenth and seventeenth centuries. This period, however, is important for the large-scale application of metallurgical methods, helped by rising capitalism and mechanization, and is technically significant since it saw the systematization of those methods.

The spread of printing released a stream of metallurgical knowledge codified in carefully prepared treatises. Early in the sixteenth century we have the first modest attempts in the illustrated *Bergwerkbüchlein* ('Essay on Mining') and *Probierbüchlein* ('Essay on Assaying') [1]. Many medieval collections of workshop recipes must have circulated among adepts or pupils in mining and metalworking, from which these first printed manuals descend, and they are certainly reflected in the 'Books of Secrets' (p 33). Traces of them can also be found in J. A. Pantheus's *Voarchadumia contra alchimiam* (1530), a rare work of alchemical interest whose title is explained by the author as 'gold of the two reds' [cementations] [2]. It claims to oppose common alchemy, and contains among other matter a series of strictly practical recipes, probably Latin translations from an Italian workshop recipe-book, concerned with the metallurgy of the more precious metals and materials. Its illustrations of metallurgical processes sometimes have little association with the rather fanciful text of the book (figure 19).

Ten years later (1540) the Italian Vanoccio (or Vanucci) Biringuccio published his *Pirotechnia*, the earliest comprehensive handbook on metallurgy [3]. Its first four chapters deal with smelting the ores of gold, silver, copper, lead, tin, and iron. They contain the first fairly complete description of silver amalgamation, of a reverberatory furnace, and of the liquation process. In its description of mining and smelting Biringuccio's important work is, however, surpassed by that of Georgius Agricola [Georg Bauer], whose *De re metallica* (1556) is one of the great monuments of technology by reason of the comprehensiveness of its text and the detail and intelligibility of its numerous illustrations [4].

[1] Professor Forbes has supplied the greater part of Sections I to III; Professor Smith the remainder of the chapter.

Agricola (1494–1555) was a physician practising at Joachimsthal in one of the most prolific mining districts of Bohemia, and at Chemnitz in Saxony. He became interested in mining and metallurgy, and after extensive travels set himself the task of recording the knowledge he had gained, achieving a clarity and a conciseness well above those of his contemporaries. Two of his other works are important to the metallurgist in particular. In 1546 he published a volume of four essays: the first is on physical geography (*De ortu et causis subterraneorum*), the second is on sub-surface waters and gases (*De natura eorum quae effluunt e terra*), the third is the first systematic treatise on mineralogy (*De natura fossilium*),[1] and the fourth is a history of mining and metallurgy since antiquity (*De veteribus et novis metallis*), to which was added a glossary of mineralogical terms in Latin and German (*Rerum metallicarum interpretatione*). At the same time (1533–53) he was occupied with his main work, which was published posthumously. For two centuries *De re metallica* remained the chief textbook on mining and metallurgy; its frequent reprints prove the continuity of metallurgical traditions.

The third important author of this period is Lazarus Ercker (d 1593) who also worked in the Erzgebirge between Saxony and Bohemia. His 'Treatise describing the foremost kinds of Metallic Ores and Minerals' (1574) [5] is less concerned with mining and smelting, but by giving more precise instructions on assaying it supplements Agricola's work. The growing knowledge of assaying and evaluating ores and metals formed an important factor in the rise of a quantitative chemistry.

Two more works on metallurgy merit our attention. The first, the *Bericht von Bergwercken* ('News of Mines') by Georg Engelhard Löhneiss (1617) has some valuable discussion of the organization of mining and its employees, but the technical information is largely copied from Ercker [6]. The *Arte de los Metales* of Alvaro Alonzo Barba (1640) is mainly concerned with smelting operations as practised in the gold and silver mines of the New World, and contains few important remarks on European metallurgy [7]. Some information can also be gleaned from Johannes Mathesius's *Sarepta oder Bergpostil*, a collection of sermons to miners and smelters, and the manuscript *Bergbuch* of the Swede Peder Månsson written between 1512 and 1524 [8].

As authorities on metallurgy Biringuccio, Agricola, and Ercker dominate the sixteenth and seventeenth centuries. A new period begins in the eighteenth century with Réaumur's essay on the art of converting iron into steel (1722), and Schlüter's metallurgical handbook (1738) [9]. At about this time, too, the

---

[1] In medieval and Renaissance Latin *fossilia* signified not fossils but minerals, 'things that are dug up'.

smelting of ores with coke and new methods of producing iron and steel were introduced. The earlier works were mainly concerned with the smelting of gold and silver ores; copper, lead, and tin were treated more superficially and the metallurgy of iron was given little attention. Indeed Réaumur's is the first reliable treatise on iron metallurgy, which is the more strange because this period was one in which the iron industry expanded enormously, with some notable technical advances.

The growing art of assaying and the attempts at classification of the minerals, ores, and metals, though meritorious, were not yet sufficiently precise to permit the identification and exploitation of new metals. They were to bear fruit in the eighteenth century, when many new metals were added to the 'seven' known to the alchemist and metallurgist of our period [10].

II. THE MINOR METALS

The semi-metal arsenic had long been known. Alchemists of the thirteenth and fourteenth centuries referred to it as *arsenicum metallinum*. Pantheus (1530) gives a recipe for a mixture of realgar, orpiment, quicklime, white tartar, and albumen, which when heated in a closed vessel yielded bright silvery arsenic by sublimation, to be used in alloys for mirrors. The first precise description of its preparation is in Johann Schroeder's *Pharmacopoeia medico-chymica* (1641), translated as 'The Compleat Chymical Dispensatory' (1669). Schroeder prepared the element by either decomposing orpiment with lime or smelting arsenious oxide with charcoal.

Metallic antimony produced by smelting stibnite with iron or copper, or by roasting to yield the oxide and reducing this with charcoal, enjoyed a certain vogue in this period because Paracelsus and his followers claimed miraculous effects for its compounds, and even for medicine drunk from a vessel made of antimony.[1] Antimony is discussed at length by the pseudonymous 'Basil Valentine' [Johann Thölde] in his 'Triumphal Chariot of Antimony' (1604). Agricola mentions the smelting process in his *De natura fossilium*, and attaches some value to the metal as a component in type-metal and in pewter.

Bismuth seems to have been known in the fifteenth century, when it was used in type-metal. Paracelsus vaguely mentioned it as a kind of antimony [11]; both Agricola (in his *Bermannus*) and Barba defined it as a metal differing from tin and lead. However, some metallurgists still believed it to be of a composite nature and give recipes for compounding it. Not until the eighteenth century was it fully recognized as a distinct metal.

---

[1] Wine placed in an antimony vessel dissolves some of the metal, which is a powerful emetic.

Much the same may be said of zinc. Though produced in India and China during this period [12] and imported from the east by European merchants as 'pewter' or 'spelter'[1] we find only vague and distorted passages in the works of Paracelsus, Cardan, and others referring to the occasional production of metallic zinc in lead-smelting. This 'jagged ore' was often considered a 'semi-metal' (Cardan), an 'imitation of tin and silver' (Agricola), or a 'white or red marcasite of the nature of copper' (Libavius). By the early seventeenth century, however, the metal was being collected from furnaces smelting lead-zinc ores. Henckel isolated it in 1721 and described it in 1743, not knowing that in 1742 Anton von Schwab had distilled it from calamine. A. S. Marggraf smelted zinc from calamine in 1746. Hence, like nickel and cobalt, zinc was recognized merely as a freak product, hardly applied before the end of the eighteenth century.[2] See, however, pp 37, 51.

III. THE IRON INDUSTRY

The main features of sixteenth- and seventeenth-century metallurgy are its mechanization and its spread. The works of Agricola and Biringuccio portray and describe improved mining-shafts, hoists and ventilators, stamp-mills, crushing-, jigging-, sieving- and roasting-apparatus all driven by water-power. Certainly, metallurgy profited much from the introduction of the water-wheel as a prime mover, while the rising capitalism of western Europe found the money to build the large apparatus that the engineers designed. All the big banking firms of those days, such as the Fuggers and the Welsers, were heavily involved in the mining projects of the noble landowners, and thus contributed to the world-wide distribution of metals and metal products. Far more attention was now given to the legal aspects of mining, and the rights and duties of miners and smelters were carefully regulated. The state increasingly intervened in the metal industries which, especially in the manufacture of bronze and iron, contributed powerfully to its warlike potential [13].

During the Middle Ages the price of iron had been fairly stable, though wages and the price of raw materials rose steadily; but with the general rise in prices during the sixteenth century iron rapidly became much dearer. Even with larger blast-furnaces, and with better machines for producing blast-air by means of water-power (frontispiece; plate 3), the effects of the increased cost of labour and fuel could not be wholly overcome. The merit of the blast-furnace was that its iron could be cast, while the wrought iron obtained by working the pigs in

---

[1] These two words are cognate but of unknown origin. The name zinc seems to have been invented by Paracelsus.
[2] For the use of zinc compounds in the manufacture of brass, see p 37 and vol II, pp 53-55.

'chaferies' was also of higher quality than that obtained from the older furnaces, owing to proper slagging of the impurities in the ores treated. Its greater efficiency and the higher percentage of iron obtained from a given ore were not in themselves sufficient to balance the quickly rising expenses of the smelting-plants.

The consumption of iron[1] rose steadily with the frequency of wars and the mechanization of armies. The growth of the industry was, however, seriously impeded by the lack of timber, for metallurgy was still dependent upon charcoal. Ironmasters and ship-builders were the great destroyers of forests, and it was often necessary to protect them from the active resentment of the local population. In Britain the rise of the iron industry in the Weald of Kent in the sixteenth century aroused protests against the increased cost of timber, while in the Forest of Dean the use of timber was limited to building and charcoal-burning, coal taking its place as a domestic fuel (p 78).

In these iron-working regions military contracts employed many thousands of men, who in time of peace found an outlet for their cast iron in the form of fire-backs, fire-dogs, pots and boilers, and the like. Armies made away with much cast iron; thus Tilly fired 12 000 to 18 000 cannon-balls into Magdeburg every day during his siege of the town in 1631.

In Britain deforestation was particularly severe, leading to the decline of the iron industry in the Weald and the Forest of Dean. New furnaces were built in south Wales, Shropshire, and the midlands, and a powerful incentive was provided for the discovery of a method of smelting with coal, for which several ineffective patents were taken out in the seventeenth century. In 1720 Britain still produced some 25 000 tons of pig iron and 13 000 tons of bar iron annually, though over 10 000 tons of the latter had to be imported, mostly from Sweden.

A similar increase of iron-production occurred in Sweden, where the blast-furnace was introduced in the later Middle Ages. Sweden, with its rich ores and its wealth of timber, became an important producer of high-quality bar iron and steel. Gustavus Vasa (1523–60) encouraged the building of blast-furnaces, and, to improve the quality of Swedish iron, invited foreigners to assist the young Swedish industry. By 1620 Swedish exports of cast iron cannon already aroused concern in England, which had enjoyed almost a monopoly. In the early eighteenth century two Swedish scientists, Emanuel Swedenborg (1688–1772) and Christopher Polhem (1661–1751), did much to improve Swedish metallurgical and mining methods. As a result, the production of their country rose to 32 600 tons in 1720 and to 51 000 tons in 1739. Similar expansion occurred in

[1] About 60 000 tons in 1500, Germany (30 000 tons) and France (10 000 tons) being the largest producers [14].

other countries, including the British colonies in North America, where there were by 1732 six blast-furnaces and nineteen hammer-forges, besides numerous bloomeries.

This higher production of iron was mainly achieved by using larger furnaces with an increased air-supply. Thus, roughly between 1500 and 1700, the volume of the *Stückofen* (vol II, p 73) rose from 1·1–1·7 cu m to 3·4–4·5 cu m, and the daily output grew from 1200–1300 kg to 1800–2100 kg. Whereas the blast-furnace of 1500 produced perhaps 1200 kg of pig iron a day using double the weight of charcoal, by the eighteenth century the furnaces produced 2000 to 2500 kg a day, and the fuel consumption was greatly reduced. This larger production was attained by adopting a continuous process, in which ore and fuel were fed into the furnace as the pig iron was tapped. In 1600 in the Siegen area of Germany the cycle lasted some 7 to 24 days before the furnace had to be stopped for repair. In the Weald the 'found-day' rose from 6 days in 1450 to 40 weeks in 1700. Hence the large, efficient furnace tended to displace such more primitive forms as bloomeries using batch processes.

Wooden box-bellows invented by Hans Lobsinger of Nuremberg (1550) slowly displaced the older leather ones in the larger furnaces. Mechanization, however, affected mining and the working of iron and steel more than smelting itself. Water-driven hoists for filling blast-furnaces were exceptional; usually men or animals still served. Water-wheels were mainly used in hammer-forges and rolling-mills, and for wire-drawing. Rolling- and slitting-mills developed quickly during this period, though they were not strong enough to produce good sheet iron until 1750. They were mainly used for bar iron, sheet lead, and the like. Originally invented in the Middle Ages for the production of the H-shaped lead ribs for stained-glass windows, they increased rapidly in number in the sixteenth century, spreading to all countries. Power-driven tilt-hammers became common in the sixteenth century, possibly as a result of some Italian improvements, yet the manual hammer retained its position in the lighter branches of the iron industry, such as nail-making, until the nineteenth century.

Most of the iron produced was still wrought iron, though the consumption of cast iron was large, and growing. The fusion of iron, which was rapidly becoming one of the most commonly used metals, so that it could be cast, gave a great impulse to casting techniques. Cast iron could be applied in many ways where stone, wood, or other metals had formerly served, and much wrought iron ware was now made by refining the cast iron pigs. New methods of making steel were investigated, and the number of patents to this end increased notably during the seventeenth century. Anton Zeller of Aschhausen in 1608 proposed to manufacture steel by a cementation process, wrought iron rods being heated with beech-charcoal in 'boxes'. In other processes wrought iron bars were immersed in a bath of molten pig iron, so that their carbon-content was increased and they were converted into steel. Until the structures of iron and steel were better understood such attempts were inevitably inefficient. Lack of proper temperature control was a serious defect in all metallurgical endeavours.

The efficiency and indeed the survival of the iron and steel industry depended on the discovery of a plentiful substitute for charcoal. The cost of fuel was a dominant factor in other types of ore-smelting; these too expanded and spread to many countries without materially changing in character. Certain processes became more popular; thus amalgamation, the extraction of gold and silver from their ores with the aid of mercury, was more commonly used, notably in the New World. The liquation of copper ores with lead provided a most important supply of silver. However, no fundamentally new process was added to the inheritance from the classical world, so well preserved during the Middle Ages. Rapid progress came only in the eighteenth century with new inventions in every field of metallurgy.

IV. UTILIZATION OF IRON AND STEEL

In the sixteenth and seventeenth centuries the craftsman's knowledge was still far in advance of theory, and apart from the few great treatises already mentioned, the writings of purely practical men—mint-masters, locksmiths, jewellers, gun-founders, and the like—give the best insight into the metallurgical equipment and methods of the time. This is especially so for iron and steel, though the new use of cast iron was one of the few real innovations of the period. The literature on the ferrous metals before the sixteenth century is insignificant, and even the Renaissance writers have far less to say of them than of the precious metals, and of copper and its alloys. The recipes in the 'Books of Secrets' [15], and the accounts of Baptista Porta (1589) [16] and Jousse (1627) [17], are somewhat feeble precursors of the first real study of ferrous metals, that of Réaumur (1722) [9].

Here we have to consider the essential differences between the various forms of wrought and cast iron and steel. Before the recognition in the late eighteenth century of the role of carbon the distinction was almost entirely one of furnace operation. Slight modification of iron-smelting processes would produce material with more or less carbon. A shallow fuel bed gave sponge iron. Cast iron resulted from the operation of a high-shaft blast-furnace which would hold the reduced iron in contact with charcoal and produce a high-carbon alloy of low melting-point. Depending on the ore and on the manner of operation a white or grey iron would result, though only the latter would be used for foundry work. Castings were made either direct from the blast-furnace or after remelting.

Saint-Rémy (1697) mentions the casting of iron cannon directly from a blast-furnace in Périgord [18]. The furnaces were 24 ft high and in a single cast yielded enough iron to make an eight-pounder nearly a ton in weight. For larger pieces the products of four blast-furnaces were combined. Musket-balls were cast of iron, though the best, according to Biringuccio, were forged in special dies [3]. Cannon-balls were usually of cast iron, though cast lead and cut stone were not extinct in his day. The moulds were split, cast in either bronze or cast iron, and contained as many as seven cavities. They were dressed with washed wood-ashes and held in specially designed tongs. The furnace was a high built-up forge (essentially a low cupola) arranged for tapping at the bottom. Although the *Feuerwerkbuch* of 1454 had mentioned the addition of antimony, tin, and bismuth, perhaps to improve fluidity, Biringuccio recommends cast iron alone, 'the crude corrupted kind that has been sent through the furnace to purify it of earthiness' [19].

Smiths produced much steel for agricultural tools by direct reduction of the ore in a hearth. A better quality was made either by the carbonization of soft iron or by the decarbonization of cast iron. The production of steel as described by Biringuccio (1540) consisted essentially of dipping blooms of wrought iron sponge into a bath of molten cast iron until sufficient carbonization had taken place, then forging and quenching. Ercker (1574) mentions both carbonization in a charcoal fire and decarbonization by repeated forging [5]. The case-hardening of iron files and other tools is described by Theophilus (vol II, p 63), Biringuccio, and many of the innumerable 'Books of Secrets'. Generally it was a small-scale operation. A single object was plastered with a carbonizing (and often nitriding) compound and protected by an exterior jacket of clay or sometimes of iron. The Neapolitan Giambattista della Porta, in his *Magiae naturalis* ('Natural Magick') (1589), describes the simultaneous hardening of many files or pieces of armour [16]. They were packed in iron chests, interlayered with a compound of chimney soot, glass, and salt or powdered horn. This operation was evidently carried out on a relatively large scale, for provision was made for removing test samples from time to time to check progress.

The complete cementation of bars of wrought iron to give steel for subsequent working into all kinds of objects is first described in detail in Robert Plot's 'Natural History of Staffordshire' (1686) [20]. The process was not very much different from that in use for making blister steel even as late as the present century. The furnace was like a baker's oven with a fire-box 2 ft wide, heating coffers that contained over half a ton of iron in bars up to 5 ft long. Cementation was done with charcoal without admixture, and was continued for between three and seven days and nights.

Though crucible-cast steel did not become important in Europe until Huntsman developed it commercially in 1740, it had been produced in India under the name of *wootz*,[1] and was known to at least two seventeenth-century English writers. Robert Hooke in his diary notes in 1675 that 'steel was made by being calcined or baked with the Dust of charcole, and that bringing it up soe as to melt made the best steel after it has been wrought over againe, that it would be at first porous but upon working and hammering as fine as glasse' [21]. To Joseph Moxon (1677) cast steel was a substance familiar enough to be used for comparison with Damascus steel.

Hardening of Steel. The heat treatment of steel is an ancient art, and the literature of the sixteenth century merely summarizes age-old artisan practice. Though water was no doubt generally used for quenching, the 'Books of Secrets' describe quenching liquors based on vegetable juices, snails, blood, dung, urine, the dew of a May morning, or solutions of inorganic salts. The booklet *Stahel und Eysen kunstilich weych und hart zu machen* (1532) describes the quenching of steel thus: 'Get your iron hot but not too hot. When it is at the correct heat plunge it in the mixture, as far in as is to be hard. And let the heat go out by itself until it takes on little flecks of a gold colour. Then cool it off completely in the water and if it is very blue it is still too soft.' Whatever the nature of the gold flecks, a careful visual control of the quenching temperature is indicated [64].

The best sixteenth-century description of the heat treatment of steel is in Porta's 'Natural Magick' (1589) [16]. He was clearly aware of the possibility of obtaining proper hardness both by direct quenching and by quenching and tempering. He cautions against quenching too hot, and recommends oil quenching to avoid excessive brittleness or warpage. Hardened armour-plate, made by carbonizing in a chest and quenching, is hard and brittle. He recommends a duplex quench for swords, which need softness in the body combined with a sharp edge: the body with an oily, the edge with an acidulated, material. His best description is perhaps that of a tool to cut stone. The English translation (1658) reads:

The business consisted in these difficulties. If the temper of the Graver was too strong and stubborn, with the vehement blow of the Hammer it flew in pieces: but if it was soft, it bowed, and would not touch the stone: wherefore it was to be most strong and tough,

---

[1] Or *wudz*. Kanarese *ukku*, steel.

that it might neither yield to the stroke, nor flie asunder. Moreover, the juice or water the Iron must be tempered in, must be cleer and pure: for if it be troubled [turbid], the colours coming from heat could not be discerned: and so the time to plunge the Tools in would not be known, on which the whole Art depends . . . and because that the Iron must be made most hard and tough, therefore the colour must be a middle colour between silver and gold: and when this colour is come, plunge the whole edge of the Tool into the liquor, and after a little time, take it out; and when it appears a Violet-colour, dip it into the liquor again, lest the heat, yet remaining in the Tool, may again spoil the temper.

Clearly an interrupted quench is described. The first colour is that to which the steel is heated for quenching; the second is the temper colour which appears in the actual operation of quenching in the bath, and is not a result of a second distinct operation for tempering. For other purposes he recommends different colours.

The process of quenching directly to give the desired hardness must have called for extreme skill, but when successful would give a tougher product than quenching and tempering to the same hardness. It would be controlled by observing the temper colours formed during quenching, which would necessitate the removal of scale if they were to be correctly observed. Sometimes it would flake off, but Biringuccio and Porta both mention dressing the hot tool with soap to bring out the colours. Probably the efficacy of some of the various organic nostrums lay in the fact that they would modify scaling of the hot steel. Others might cause transitory deposits on the surface of the hot steel and thus delay cooling enough to enable the internal transformation responsible for hardening to occur at the right temperature.

The actual sequence of colours and their relation to hardness is first described accurately by Biringuccio: 'Because the first colour shown by steel when it is quenched while fiery is white, it is called silver; the second which is yellow like gold they call gold; the third which is bluish and purple they call violet; the fourth is ashen gray. You quench them at the proper stage of these colours as you wish them more or less hard in temper' [3].

Mathurin Jousse describes (1627) the sequence of colours on tempering both in the production of decorative finishes and for softening: 'First it will become the colour of gold, then a blood colour, violet, blue and lastly the colour of water. When it has become the colour you wish, you remove it promptly with little tongs' [17]. He is the first writer clearly to prefer quenching, cleaning, and tempering to the ancient process of direct hardening. He checks the temperature for quenching by melting glass, and the tempering of springs just beyond the temper colour range by rubbing a piece of wood against them.

It was natural that Boyle, in his 'Experiments and Considerations touching Colours' (1664), should pay attention to this interesting phenomenon [22]. He lists twenty-five colours appearing in sequence on the skimmed surface of molten lead, and records interesting experiments on hardening small tools. The steel should not be quenched too hot, and should be tempered to the proper colour. He observed that the succeeding colours indicated changes in the 'texture' of the steel, which when tempered yellow was fit for making such tools as axes, and when blue was softer and could be used to make springs.

Robert Hooke developed (1665) a theory of the hardening of steel on the basis of the colours and related it to the hardening of other materials by cold working [23]. He believed that 'the pure parts of Metals are of themselves very *flexible* and *tuff*; that is, will indure bending and hammering, and yet retain their continuity'. The hardening and softening of steel arose, according to him, from varying amounts of vitrified substance interspersed through it, a view remarkably prescient of the amorphous metal theory of nearly three centuries later; but he thought the vitrified substance was derived from 'certain salts, with which [iron] is kept a certain time in the fire' to convert it into steel.

V. COPPER ALLOYS

Brass, made from copper by a kind of cementation process with calamine and charcoal, has been known and used extensively since Greek times (vol II, p 53), though metallic zinc was almost unknown until the sixteenth century. Savot first reported (1627) that zinc alloyed with copper produced brass [61]. Glauber (1656) studied the alloys in more detail, and they found some use for decorative trifles under the name of 'Prince Rupert's metal' [24]. The process of direct alloying from the metals did not displace cementation until well into the nineteenth century.

Biringuccio (1540) has a good account of the furnaces and processes used in making brass. Ercker (1574) described German practice in brass-founding and casting brass plates for subsequent working. English practice is given best by Merrett (1662) [25]. The brass-makers used a special furnace consisting of a deep conical hole below the working floor. At its bottom was a shallow fire containing eight or ten relatively small crucibles filled with a mixture of roasted and ground calamine mixed with powdered charcoal and copper scrap (figure 15). The time of heating varied from 9 to 18 or 20 hours. The excess of weight of the brass over the copper from which it was made corresponds to a resulting alloy with from 29 per cent zinc (Ercker) to 40 per cent (Merrett).

Bronze (vol I, pp 589 ff and vol II, pp 48 ff) is the oldest of all widely used alloys, but its metallurgy is interesting here for the wealth of technological detail available from the sixteenth century. The alloy for general foundry purposes was copper with from 8 to 20 per cent of tin, according to the use in view. For guns and large statues, additions were made of about 1 per cent of zinc in the form of brass. This improved the casting properties. Small household objects generally contained lead, usually about 7 per cent but sometimes as high as 30 per cent.

FIGURE 15—*Brass-foundry.* (A) *Interior of furnace [dotted line] showing arrangement of crucibles within;* (B) *furnace in operation;* (C) *crucible;* (D) *scoop;* (E) *tongs for handling crucibles;* (F) *draught-holes for furnace;* G, *stone slab mould. 1580.*

Bell-metal contained 20 to 25 per cent tin, and speculum-metal about 25 per cent, often with addition of arsenic and silver.

Biringuccio remarked that on adding more tin to copper the metal changes: 'From red which is the colour of copper it becomes white; from soft and flexible it becomes hard and brittle as glass. This admixture removes copper so far from its original nature that one who does not know that it is a compound material believes it to be one of the metals engendered by nature.' The composition must be adjusted to the specific use: 8 to 12 lb tin per hundred of copper for guns, 23 to 26 for bells (depending on the tone). As a brittle material for explosive bombs he suggests three parts of brass to one of tin.

For casting guns Biringuccio emphasizes the importance of a large feeding-head to prevent porosity in the casting, owing to shrinkage, while to avoid what is now known as inverse segregation he added tin to the last metal to run into the mould.

Before the eighteenth century guns were cast with cores, and the boring-mill was used only for trueing the bore (ch 14). All the old writers mention the use of heavy iron chaplets to centre the core at the bottom of the mould (p 365), although surviving guns of the seventeenth century and later rarely have iron embedded in the appropriate places. Though most of the many writers on artillery say little about the cast iron or bronze alloys used for gun-making, Saint-Rémy (1697) notes that the best metal was that made from 87 per cent copper, 8 per cent tin, and 5 per cent brass, but that some founders used a higher proportion of tin (figure 16) [18]. Some founders, he reports, always added at least a quarter of new metal on re-melting old. Others used a potent flux containing saltpetre, antimony, and other materials moistened with nitric acid and plunged beneath the surface of the bronze in a box; this was supposed to free the metal from blow-holes, and would probably have been effective through its oxidizing effect. Foundrymen and fluxes have always been inseparable.

FIGURE 16—*Bronze gun-foundry in operation, 1697. Reverberatory furnaces like these commonly held about 30 tons of metal, which was melted in 24 to 30 hours.*

Some techniques of casting are described elsewhere. Large castings such as guns, bells (figure 17), and statues were made in loam moulds (p 364); small ones from patterns in boxes, much as today's sand-castings are, but with some finely divided refractory material (bone-ash, tripoli, emery, iron oxide, pumice, or brick dust) bonded together with a salt solution or an organic substance, such as egg-white. The making of medallions and other fine-art castings is well described by Biringuccio and also in the 'Books of Secrets', particularly the pseudonymous 'Secrets of Alexis' [15]. The casting of metal in greensand moulds was unusual in the sixteenth century, though it is mentioned by both Leonardo da Vinci and Biringuccio. At the brass-foundry in Milan described by Biringuccio, mass-production of small objects—as many as 1200 in a single mould—was achieved by stacking together sections of dried loam moulds.

Speculum-metal. The outstanding metallic property of reflection had been used since antiquity in both solid metallic mirrors and as a backing to glass. Månsson describes (*c* 1515) the application of tin to glass with mercury, while Hans Sachs mentions (perhaps with poetic licence) lead (1568), and Biringuccio antimony (1540), as a backing for glass [8, 26, 3]. Porta refers to tin amalgam on glass (1589), and also to a kind of Christmas-tree ornament lined with an alloy of

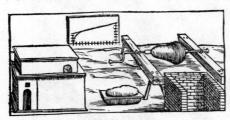

antimony and lead by pouring in the molten metal and draining out that which did not stick [16]. Most mirrors, however, were from antiquity made solid of speculum-metal. Pliny, for example, mentions the use of two parts of brass to one of tin. Biringuccio refers to the 'old' composition of three copper, one tin (sometimes with one eighteenth of antimony or one twenty-fourth of silver), but prefers to use an alloy of three parts of tin to one of copper, with some arsenic added. Though he usually describes casting and polishing from first-hand knowledge, this composition rich in tin would be expensive, brittle, and hard to cast and polish. Leonardo da Vinci, Pantheus, and Porta all give a more normal composition.

FIGURE 17—*Bell-founding, 1540. The size and shape of the bell to be cast were proportioned to the thickness of the rim, which was taken from a traditional scale according to the weight of the bell desired. From a drawing made according to the rules strickle-boards were cut, with which to shape the moulding-clay to the form of the core and the outer mould. The core was formed first on a spindle; then on this, covered with ashes, more clay was built up to the exterior dimensions of the bell, with inscriptions or ornamentation added in wax. This 'case' was coated well with tallow, to receive the outer mould. After thorough firing the outer mould was lifted off, the 'case' was cut away from the core, and then the two parts of the mould were fitted together, now with a space between them which was to be filled with bronze.*

Porta recommends adjusting the composition of the melt on the basis of the appearance of the fracture of a sample of the metal taken on an iron rod.

Glauber (1651) gives the best description of both the casting procedure and of the metal itself [27]. He points out that the harder the metal the better it is for polish, though whiteness is needed also: 'Red comes from too much copper; black from too much iron, or dusky from too much tin.' His composition was essentially a copper-tin-arsenic alloy. Copper plates were packed in white arsenic impregnated with linseed-oil and heated so that the arsenic could diffuse into the plate, like 'oil piercing dry leather', thereby increasing the thickness of the copper two to three times and making it brittle. Two parts of brass were then melted in a quick fire, one part of the arsenic-copper was added, and the alloy was cast into an ingot, which was re-melted with one-third of its weight of the best tin and cast into specula. The alloy could also be made directly by melting three parts of copper, one of tin, and one-half part of white arsenic.

Neri (p 217), a reliable writer on glass, mentions (1612) a composition like Biringuccio's which, when melted, is treated with a flux of tartar, saltpetre, alum, and arsenic [25]. J. H. Cardalucius, in his notes to Ercker (1672), recommends equal parts of copper and tin to which, when molten, are added one part of arsenic, one-half part of antimony, and one-half part of tartar. Since there was no control of mechanical properties in the resulting product, the alloy was ripe for experimentation. Merrett, in his English translation (1662) of Neri, mentions additions of antimony, bismuth, mercury, silver, and zinc.

The Royal Society records a letter (1672) from Isaac Newton, inventor of the reflecting telescope, in which he remarked that speculum-metal often contained small pores, visible only under the microscope, which wear away faster than the rest of the metal during polishing and thus spoil the image. He comments that bismuth mixed with bell-metal makes it white, but its fumes fill the metal full of microscopical pores 'like so many aerial bubbles', while arsenic both whitens and solidifies the metal [28]. Later the Society experimented with steel mirrors, and also received a proposal from Hooke to make reflecting telescopes in great numbers by stamping plates of silver in the screw-press at the Mint between concave and convex dies [29]. Silver had been mentioned as a material for unbreakable mirrors by Pantheus (1530) [2].

Bearing-metals were of surprisingly little concern to writers on metallurgy and engineering earlier than the nineteenth century, though there are many impressive illustrations from the sixteenth and seventeenth centuries of machines that would not operate successfully without fairly good bearings. Nevertheless, they frequently show what appear to be iron shafts running directly on wooden frames, though often with (apparently) a wrought iron plate protecting the wood. A roller, or rather pulley-like, bearing is sketched by Leonardo and Agricola. The latter mentions bronze for cams in the machine for breaking up cakes of copper. Biringuccio (1540) refers to glass or gun-metal grooves for pendent bells as an alternative to iron-on-steel bearings. Zonca (1607) seems to be the first to remark that, when running against steel, any sort of metal other than brass is consumed; he illustrates separate bearing-blocks in his little mill for rolling lead strips for windows [30].

The best seventeenth-century treatment of bearings is by Robert Hooke, who observes, in reporting to the Royal Society on Stevin's 'sailing chariot', that

The less rubbing there be of the Axle, the better for this Effect: upon which account Steel Axes and Bell-Metal Sockets, are much better than Wood, clamped or shod with Iron; and Gudgeons of hardened Steel, running in Bell-Metal Sockets yet much better, if there be provision made to keep out Dust and Dirt, and constantly to supply and feed them with Oil to keep them from eating one another: but the best way of all is, to make the Gudgeons run on large Truckles, which wholly prevent gnawing, rubbing and fretting [31].

Other copper alloys. Arsenic and copper have been closely associated through most of the history of metallurgy. In both the Near East and South America the earliest alloys were of copper and arsenic, soon to be displaced by mixtures of copper and tin. In the sixteenth and seventeenth centuries arsenic was frequently added to other copper alloys to improve castability and colour, but it is mentioned more frequently in the 'Books of Secrets' than in the reputable metallurgical works. 'With arsenic', says Biringuccio, 'fraudulent alchemists blanch copper, brass and even lead to the whiteness of silver.'

Copper alloys containing sulphur, oxygen, and generally iron were inevitably produced during the processes of refining the metal. The copper-lead alloy produced during the desilvering of copper by liquation is of interest in connexion with alloy constitution, for the process depended on the fact that copper and lead are completely miscible in the liquid state at high temperatures, while a molten phase rich in lead and a solid phase rich in copper coexist at a low red heat. Silver is almost entirely concentrated in the lead phase, which can be drained from the interstices of the copper dendrites, carrying with it most of the silver. About 80 per cent of both the lead and silver in the initial cakes could be recovered. This process, developed in Saxony about 1450, deeply affected European economy.

VI. TIN ALLOYS

Tin and alloys rich in tin were used for plating copper and iron, and as solders, while the alloy pewter found many applications. Most old sources agree that the best solder consists of two parts of tin to one of lead, though one-to-one mixtures were most often employed because of their lower cost; five-to-one alloys were used for soldering window-leads.

The name pewter has covered a wide variety of tin alloys at various times and places, and the high cost of tin has encouraged fraudulent adulteration. The best pewter was commonly regarded as that with the highest tin-content, hardened with small amounts of copper, bismuth, and, later, of antimony. Cheaper alloys containing lead were used for large or common objects.

The records of the ancient Pewterers' Company contain a draft ordinance of 1348 which indicates that the chief metals used in the craft were brass, tin, and lead. The Company appointed overseers to supervise the alloys and the work of the pewterers. They were empowered to assay for the detection of fraud. The best pewter vessels should have 'the measure of brass to the tin as much as it would receive of his nature of the same; and all other things of the said craft that be wrought, as pots round that pertain to the craft, to be wrought of tin with an alloy of lead to a reasonable measure; and the measure of the alloy of a hundred tin is 26 pounds lead' [32].

Bismuth as an addition to pewter was mentioned by Bishop Roderick in 1471, but its first appearance in the English records (under the name of 'tinglass') was in 1561, when a member was disenfranchised for revealing the secret of its use. By 1619 $2\frac{1}{2}$ lb of bismuth were added to every thousand of tin. Later, this weight was increased to 3 lb, with a rider allowing more or less as the tin would bear it. Harrison (1577) [33] gives the composition of English pewter as 30 lb of brass to a thousand of tin and 3 to 4 lb of bismuth, while Houghton (1697) [34] says that the copper varies between 3 to 6 lb per hundred of tin, depending on the fineness of the tin, while a few ounces of zinc are added to improve the colour.

The pewterers' casting process was very simple and usually involved permanent moulds of soft stone or metal. Sand- or composition-moulds were used for complicated objects. The tin-rich alloy for plates and high-quality ware was generally hammered to improve its solidity and finish, while the cheaper alloy ('lay') was cast directly into the shape of the desired vessels, which were dressed and used with no further treatment. Continental pewter was similar.

There are many early references to alloying for the purpose of improving the sound of the metal. On the European continent material known in the seventeenth century as *étain sonnant* or *stannum sonans* was composed of 100 lb of tin with 1 or 2 lb of copper and 1 lb of bismuth, contrasting with common pewter of 12 to 15 lb of lead per hundred. The fact that the common adulterant of tin was lead permitted the use of density as a relatively easy method of assay (p 68).

The first mention of antimony for hardening tin is by Biringuccio, but its use did not become common until late in the eighteenth century. Alexis (1555) adds an eighth part of antimony 'to harden it and make it sound well' [15]. Glauber gives more detail [24]. One part of antimony to twenty of tin gives a hard enough alloy, while with less than twelve parts of tin the alloy is brittle and useless. Tin may, he says, also be alloyed with zinc instead of antimony; indeed, it is then easier to melt.

Type-metal. There seems to have been a close connexion between the pewterer's art and the invention of printing. Although, by the seventeenth century, lead-based alloys were being used for casting type, sixteenth-century descriptions imply tin-base alloys. Thus Plantin (1567) says loosely 'tin or lead', while Hans Sachs in his jingle appended to Amman's famed woodcut (1568) (figure 254) says, 'bismuth, tin and lead' [35, 26]. E. O. von Lippmann (1930) believed that bismuth-rich alloys may have played a crucial role in the invention of type-casting, though to the present author it seems that the ordinary pewterers' compositions with only minor bismuth-content would have met all the requirements for the first trials [11].

Biringuccio gives the first description of type-casting, and the best until that of Moxon in 1683 [3, 36]. He states that 'letters for printing books are made of a composition of three parts of fine tin, an eighth part of black lead, and another eighth part of fused marcasite of antimony'. This corresponds to 92·3 per cent tin and 3·85 per cent each of lead and antimony—a tin-rich composition of a kind that would be familiar to a pewterer. When one considers also the close similarity between the type-caster's mould, with its adjustable permanent parts and replaceable matrix, and the pewterer's stone or metal moulds, often with undercut or relief parts arranged to be withdrawn separately, it seems probable that Gutenberg was strongly influenced by the pewterer's art. His genius lay in combining and adapting existing techniques, for he did not need to originate in detail all the many devices and procedures that made printing possible. Movable type could have been laboriously cut by hand or cast from patterns in moulds of sand or clay, as indeed the Chinese seem to have done, but the critical part of Gutenberg's invention was the realization that the pewterer's material and moulds made possible the cheap production of innumerable identical objects that were accurately shaped, sized, and finished (ch 15).

Two centuries later—and probably much earlier—the initial tin-base alloys had been entirely displaced by the harder and cheaper lead–antimony alloys. A lead–antimony alloy like modern type-metal is described by Moxon [36]. He made it by fusing 3 lb of antimony sulphide with an equal weight of iron and alloying the resulting regulus with 25 lb of lead. This would have resulted in an alloy with 7·9 per cent antimony. Moxon mentions the addition of a little block tin to this to render it more fluid for small letters, and Glauber (1656) refers to a silver-bearing antimony used by type-casters to give fluidity [24].

VII. USES OF LEAD

Lead was extensively used in the commercially pure form for building purposes. For general decorative work it was cast in moulds of stone, metal, or clay, and was often gilded. For reinforcing stained-glass windows, pieces of an H section were made, at first by casting [37] and later by rolling [26, 30, 17]. Before the seventeenth century, sheet metal for roofing was made, as described by Biringuccio, by pouring molten metal down an inclined board covered with a flat bed of sand (figure 18). This was replaced by a horizontal mould only when thick castings were needed for the rolling-mill. De Caus mentions (1615) a flimsy hand-operated rolling-mill for making the cast plates uniform in thickness [38]. Later in the century heavier mills driven by water-power or horse-power were in operation in England. By 1691 'milled' lead sheets up to 3½ ft wide were available in thicknesses corresponding to weights of 1 lb, or up to 20 or more, per square foot [39]. Rolled lead rapidly replaced cast sheets because of its cheapness and freedom from defects. Its use for sheathing boats in 1670 brought about a mysterious disappearance of the wrought iron rudder-fixtures. This wonderful

FIGURE 18—*Pouring molten lead or tin upon an inclined sand-bed to form cast sheets of metal. 1624.*

example of electrolytic corrosion resulted in acrimonious debate between producer and consumer, but unfortunately did not lead to scientific investigation.

Lead shot was made by casting into a split mould or, after Prince Rupert's invention (c 1650), by alloying lead with arsenic and pouring the molten alloy through a kind of colander into a tub of water. Hooke describes the process in detail and comments that the skin formed when arsenic is present contracts everywhere equally and gives a spherical shape [23]. Larger bullets, of course, had to be made in split moulds.

VIII. PRECIOUS METAL ALLOYS AND WORKING-TECHNIQUES

The alloys for coinage and jewelry are of more interest for the techniques used in shaping them than for the alloys themselves, which have remained almost unchanged for millennia. The principal European coins of the fifteenth and sixteenth centuries are all of the ternary system gold-silver-copper. The actual composition changed with the relative value of the metals and the honesty of the governments. Gold coins were sometimes made of the pure metal despite its softness. Up to the time of Henry VIII, English coinage contained only 0·54 per cent of alloy, which was allowed to pay the coiner and for a necessary working tolerance [40]. The Italian ducats and Hungarian florins were also nominally pure gold. Even Henry VIII debased English gold only to 20 carats.[1] The crown of the Holy Roman Emperor was $22\frac{1}{2}$ carats. An initial tolerance as to the nature of the alloying metal was replaced by a general requirement that it be silver and copper in the ratio of two to one. The assayer needed to be alert for the various compositions, and his touch-needles (vol II, p 45) were usually made in three series.

Silver coinage has never been made with the pure metal. It was debased partly for fiscal reasons and partly to facilitate the making of small-value coins of sufficient size. On the continent extensive use was made of *billon*, an alloy containing 20 per cent or less of silver, while in England the lowest was 25 per cent silver, in Edward VI's reign. Elizabeth I restored 'sterling', 925 parts of silver per thousand, which had been and was to remain the standard for English coins for many centuries. The debased coinage that Elizabeth recalled from circulation must have been highly adulterated, for not only was the dross bulky enough to use as road-filling, but many workmen died from the fumes emitted during re-melting. The re-establishment of fine coinage was unpopular, for it left no minor medium of exchange except private merchants' tokens made of lead, tin, or copper, and involved a form of deflation. Though Irish coins of brass and copper were made as early as 1461, it was not until 1613 that royal coins were actually made of copper.

The Commonwealth under Cromwell issued a variety of coins of copper, of pewter with a centre of copper, and even of concentric rings of copper and brass around a central silver disk. Tin coinage (to which the Mint had objected as being too easy to counterfeit with zinc, arsenic, or antimony) was issued in 1684 with a round slug of copper in the centre. Copper was the preferred metal for coins of small value because of the relative certainty of its composition. It was tested by being hammered flat when red hot, for most impure copper alloys will not withstand this treatment.

Metallurgically interesting is the process of blanching, which has been used by both legal and illegal coiners since classical antiquity, to give a fine silver-rich surface to relatively base alloys. Oxidation of such alloys produces a layer of nearly pure copper oxide with the equivalent silver-content concentrated in the

---

[1] A *carat* is a twenty-fourth part, so that 20 carats means that 4 parts in 24 are not gold. The word *carat* is of Arabic origin (*qīrāṭ*) and in that language meant a weight of 4 grains.

surface of the residual metal beneath the layer of oxide. The coins (generally after striking) were annealed in a pan filled with burning charcoal and tossed frequently about so that they would heat uniformly. Pickling, to remove the layer of oxide and so reveal the silvery surface, was usually done in a boiling solution of a mixture of tartar, common salt, and sometimes rock alum. Blanching was part of the standard operations on silver coinage on the continent, and is so described by most writers from the time of the *Probierbüchlein* (pp 27, 59).

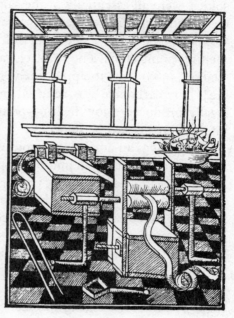

Gold coins seem never to have been given a superficial enrichment, although the process of cementation was a standard one for producing pure gold from gold-silver alloys (vol II, ch 2), and various pickling processes have been used by goldsmiths to give an enhanced colour.

Though a fair idea of the metallurgical aspects of minting may be derived from Biringuccio and other sources, the *Traité de Monoyes* of Jean Boizard (1696) gives the most detail [41]. In the Paris mint at that time clay crucibles were used holding $42\frac{1}{2}$ lb of gold, while silver was melted in iron crucibles holding up to

FIGURE 19—(Foreground) *Rolling-mill turned by cranks;* (background) *draw-plate for forming rectangular bars. The artist has mistakenly combined two distinct processes. 1550.*

650 lb. In the latter the bath was held while a sample was assayed and the composition adjusted before casting. Metallic moulds, dressed with a greasy mixture, had been known to Biringuccio, but the Paris mint was still using the more laborious method of making sand-moulds. The plates were subsequently rolled, but only lightly for adjustment and not for really heavy reductions. Both Leonardo da Vinci and Biringuccio mention a draw-plate with a rectangular orifice, the bar being drawn through with a little windlass. Pantheus (1550) shows a rolling-mill which, despite the seemingly impossible manner of use, is the first realistic figure of the device (figure 19).

The techniques of the goldsmith were so well developed in the Middle Ages that little change has occurred subsequently (vol II, ch 2). The sixteenth-century goldsmith had practical acquaintance with almost all of the problems that interest the twentieth-century scientific metallurgist: change of melting-point and properties by alloying, effects of cold working and annealing, diffusion, surface tension, phase-transformations, and the effects of oxidation and corrosion.

The various solders used for gold and silver, as well as brazing-solder and soft solder, were all essentially of the same composition as at present, and had been described centuries earlier. Amalgams were sometimes used as cold solders. Copper was used as a solder for gold, depending on local alloying to give a low melting-point alloy. The most elegant form of this process, well described by Cellini (1568), was to apply finely ground copper carbonate mixed with a flux [42]. The carbonate was reduced by the charcoal flame used for heating, and locally produced a low melting-point alloy that was carried by surface tension into the crevices to be joined.

For gilding, an amalgam of gold was applied to the object. Wire and plate of silver covered with gold and of copper coated with silver (later to be known as Sheffield plate) were made by preparing a composite ingot before working down. Spun gold (a yellow linen thread covered with metal) was always made with very fine gilded silver tape. Biringuccio made a soldered bi-metal plate with a ducat of gold for every pound of silver; it was hammered repeatedly in the manner of the goldbeater until almost as thin as gold-leaf, when it was cut into narrow strips and applied to the thread. In Boizard's day (1696) the same material was made by flattening a drawn gilded wire between two highly polished steel rolls. The rod for drawing was made merely by cleaning the surface of the silver and rubbing on gold leaves without solder.

The goldsmith made wide use of niello, a low melting-point, black sulphide used as a kind of enamel to fill in incised designs. It was known in Roman times (vol II, p 480) and was described by Theophilus [37]. Pantheus, like Biringuccio a decade later, makes the material by pouring a molten alloy of silver, copper, and lead in the ratio of $1:2:3$ into a clay pot filled with powdered sulphur. The contents are then washed and ground to a coarse powder and mixed with a little sal ammoniac, pressed into the incised design on the silver to be decorated, and fused [2, 3]. Though the metallurgist was very familiar with sulphides in refining and parting processes, the jeweller never seems to have made his niello by direct mixture of the sulphides.

The prodigious extensibility of gold has attracted the attention of both philosophers and experimenters. This remarkable property permits the permanent beauty of gold to be widely utilized despite its high cost. The use of layers of metal, paper, or gold-beater's skin to protect the gold during extension is very ancient, and the process as described by Boizard is practically identical with modern goldbeaters' practice. He states that the goldbeaters first forged the gold to leaves of the thinness of paper. These were cut into pieces about 1 inch square, and hammered in 'books' of vellum or of cow-intestine, using three different sizes of hammers in the process of reduction. The finished leaves weighed as little as nine or ten grains for 4-inch-square leaves (125 to 150 sq ft per oz).[1]

For many uses gold-leaf was in direct competition with the powdered metal applied as paint or ink. Theophilus and many of the 'Books of Secrets' describe the wet grinding of gold, silver, and even brass and tin for this purpose. Coloured 'bronze' powder was made by oxidation of copper-alloy filings to give appropriate temper colours.

The temper colours produced on alloys by oxidation were used in another decorative application—that of foils placed under gems to enhance their beauty. Biringuccio implies that the foils were a recent development in his day, while Cellini and particularly Porta describe them in great detail [3, 42, 16]. The alloys were of various copper-silver-gold compositions, hammered to thin foils and burnished, then exposed to the heat of a moderate and clear fire to develop the colour. Porta

FIGURE 20—*Blast-furnaces for smelting non-ferrous metals. 1556.*

built a special little sheet iron furnace for the process, and sometimes laid goose-feathers or bay-leaves on the coals to obtain special colours.

IX. METALLURGICAL FURNACES

Furnaces can be roughly classified into those for the reduction of ores and those for re-melting the subsequent metal for alloying and casting. Roasting of the ores to remove impurities before smelting was done in open piles, in stalls, or sometimes in reverberatory or open-shaft furnaces, occasionally so arranged that a stream of water could be directed upon the hot ore to quench it, in order

[1] Mersenne (1621) reports 104 sq ft per oz; Réaumur (1713) 146 [43].

to facilitate subsequent crushing. Non-ferrous metals were smelted principally in blast-furnaces of the type described in vol II, ch 2. Sixteenth-century writers such as Biringuccio (1540), Agricola (1556), and Ercker (1574) agree in showing these furnaces built close against a heavy wall separating the furnace-room from the bellows, there being as many as five or six furnaces in a row. The furnaces were rarely more than 5 to 6 ft high, for they were charged directly from the floor. The inside profile was usually rectangular, with sides of about

FIGURE 21—*Italian smelting-furnaces. 1678.*

18 to 24 in and tapering uniformly from top to bottom, although quite complicated profiles were sometimes used, such as the wide middle or double hopper depicted by Biringuccio. The construction of these furnaces is seen in figure 20, from Agricola, and figure 21, from the Marchese della Fratta et Montalbano (1678) [65]. The latter figure shows on the left an unusually high furnace, probably for iron-smelting, with the tuyère (from a *trompe*) inserted in the front. Furnaces for smelting iron were larger than their non-ferrous counterparts. As the utility of cast iron, both for simple castings and as an intermediate step in the production of wrought iron, began to be appreciated between the fourteenth and seventeenth centuries, open hearths (bloomeries) for direct reduction of iron were gradually, though not completely, replaced by blast-furnaces. Furnaces 12 to 16 ft high and $4\frac{1}{2}$ ft wide internally were common by the mid-sixteenth century, and this size had been doubled by the end of the seventeenth (frontispiece; plate 3).

The furnaces were usually built of soft refractory stone with a renewable lining of clay. The crucible was commonly lined with a brasque, that is, a paste of charcoal tempered with clay. Though the iron furnaces were tapped at infrequent intervals, the smaller furnaces for non-ferrous metals were often operated with the tap-hole open, the forehearth (lined with brasque) being depended on to separate slag and metal. Figure 22 shows furnaces for smelting roasted matte to copper and alloying the latter in the forehearth with lead from a little auxiliary furnace to give liquation-cakes. The liquation-hearth itself, to the right of the drawing, had changed very little from the design of a century earlier. This illustration also shows the dust-catching chamber

FIGURE 22—*Furnaces for reducing copper and alloying it with lead to make liquation-cakes in the forehearth. 1574.*

above the furnaces. The deposit collected here, principally zinc oxide, was used in making brass.

The smelting of antimony and bismuth involved little more than melting the metal or mineral away from the gangue, and was done in small pots or even in open fires, as is well illustrated by Agricola. Mercury was distilled from its ores in inverted pots or in simple ceramic stills. The European smelting of zinc is first described by Löhneiss (1617), who refers to it as an accidental condensate in chinks and cracks of furnaces smelting the Goslar lead ores. By 1700 the fronts of the furnaces were made thin and were intentionally cooled to increase the yield, while in 1734 Swedenborg described a special internal stone slab which, inserted as a false front in the furnace, served as a simple condenser for the metal.

Melting-furnaces were far more diverse in form. Furnaces for melting alloys, either for purification or for casting, were relatively simple (figures 23, 24). The most generally adaptable was the smith's forge worked with bellows. With a few

FIGURE 23—*Wind-furnace for melting metal in crucibles by natural draught. 1540.*

FIGURE 24—*Wind- and blast-furnaces for melting metal in crucibles.* (A) *Interior view of brick furnace with crucible standing on grate;* (B) *the same closed;* (C) *crucible;* (D, K) *furnaces of potter's clay. 1574.*

bricks to hold the crucible in place, this would suffice for almost any metal. Next came the wind-furnace depending on natural draught, though usually only that produced by the height of the furnace itself. Relatively tall furnaces were used by the brass-makers. Although hoods and chimneys for smoke-removal were common, the intentional use of a chimney-stack to enhance the draught is not seen until 1648. In that year Glauber illustrated in his 'New Philosophical Furnaces' [27] a wind-furnace with a properly applied chimney-stack. This had a great influence upon subsequent design (vol II, figure 675).

For melting somewhat larger amounts than could be contained in a crucible, ladles were used. These were lined with refractory clay, which was also built up around the top to hold fuel; combustion was urged by blast from the bellows (figure 25). When the metal was ready for casting, the fuel was raked off and the ladle carried to the mould. Still larger amounts of metal were melted in stationary hemispherical hearths in which metal and fuel were piled together. These were actuated by bellows and arranged for bottom-pouring through a tap-hole and channel, either directly into a mould or into a ladle (figure 26). This kind of furnace could be made of almost any size and became a kind of semi-permanent low-shaft cupola.

Bellows were extremely important to the metallurgist. Both Biringuccio and Agricola devote much attention to their construction and operation. The aeolipile—a kind of steam injector pump—was used with small laboratory blast-furnaces (figure 27) and constitutes the first significant use of steam-power. The *trompe*, invented in Italy in the mid-sixteenth century, found wide application in the Catalan forge used by the iron smelters of the Pyrenees. It was essentially a water aspirator feeding into a closed wind-chest from which the expelled air was

FIGURE 25—*Arrangement for melting metal in a casting-ladle. 1540.*

led by a pipe to the tuyère (figure 28).
Giambattista della Porta (1588) seems the
first to mention this device, reporting that
he had seen it in Rome and that its blast
was suitable for brass- and iron-smelting
furnaces.

FIGURE 26—*Stationary melting-hearths, both arranged for bottom-tapping. 1540.*

For baking moulds and many miscellaneous purposes, Biringuccio built a fur-
nace of bricks arranged in open checker-work to hold the fuel and allow ingress
of air. Cellini used a furnace of this kind in preference to a forge even for melting
gold and silver in crucibles. Operations calling for prolonged heating must have
been very tedious before the invention of a self-stoking furnace. In metallurgical
literature it is Ercker who first describes a gravity-stoked athanor which needed
to be filled with charcoal only once a day (figure 29). The principle of a hopper
from which fuel would descend continuously into the combustion zone to keep
a steady fire was possible only for relatively low temperature operations, and

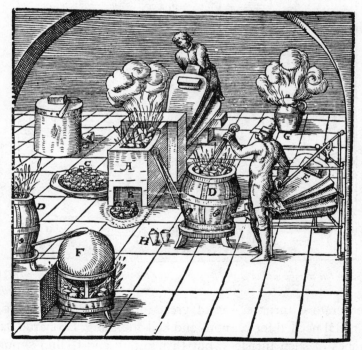

FIGURE 27—*Furnaces for the crucible-assay of copper ores (cf figure 24). (A, D) Furnaces; (C) crushed ore; (E) lever-operated bellows; (F) steam aeolipile used instead of bellows; (G) pot in which flux is prepared; H, assay-crucibles. 1574.*

these furnaces were used for processes like cementation, distillation, and evaporation. Operations demanding slowly increasing heat were effected by placing the crucible in the centre of a ring of coals which was gradually raked nearer and nearer (figure 30).

FIGURE 28—*The* trompe *used to blow a forge fire. Note the tilt-hammer in the foreground. 1678.*

The reverberatory furnace was of great importance for melting the large amounts of metal needed for cannon- and bell-founding. Leonardo da Vinci has several sketches of such furnaces, but Biringuccio and Cellini supply the first detailed descriptions (figures 16, 31). These furnaces were rather like present-day reverberatory furnaces except for the lack of a chimney to enhance the draught; the products of combustion escaped through small vents above the doors. It was recognized that copper could not be melted in a reverberatory furnace but had first to be alloyed with tin in a crucible-furnace of some kind. Biringuccio describes a kind of reverberatory furnace arranged so to carry the flame as to melt the cracked part only of a bell in order to repair it.

Solar furnaces, referred to as scientific wonders in antiquity, had become important possessions of scientific academies by the eighteenth century. Biringuccio mentions a German mirror about a foot in diameter capable of melting a gold ducat. Glauber (1651) specifically relates the amount of heat concentrated to the diameter, and says that a mirror of one span in diameter burns wood, of two spans melts tin, lead, or bismuth, of four or five spans melts gold and silver and softens iron sufficiently for forging [27]. Robert Hooke developed this concept further, and proposed to use the necessary aperture as a quantitative index of the degree of heat necessary to achieve various effects.

The blowpipe is still used by modern primitives to blow a charcoal fire for smelting and crucible-melting operations, as it was in ancient Egypt (vol I, figure 384). Its use for more delicate heating, as an adjunct

FIGURE 29—*Self-stoking furnace used for cementation.* (A, B) *Lower and upper mouth holes;* (C) *line where bottom plate rests on iron bars;* (D) *vents;* (F) *vent-plug;* (G) *scorifier;* (H, K) *pots for cementation. 1574.*

to the hearth in a goldsmith's shop, is depicted in a Pompeian fresco, and it was probably goldsmiths who first applied it to the flame of a lamp to obtain an intense, highly localized heat. Robert Boyle (1685) used 'a small crooked pipe of metal or glass such as tradesmen . . . call a blowpipe' with a lamp or candle to melt not only the more fusible metals but even copper itself [44]. The delightful scientific art of blow-pipe analysis was beginning. A blast-lamp, consisting of an oil-lamp with a jet of air from foot-bellows, was illustrated by Kunckel (1679), who suggested its use for testing ores [45]. Early in the eighteenth century it was well established for local heating, as in soldering and enamelling metals and making coloured glass beads.

The annealing of rolled strip for coining operations, and of coiled drawn wire, was generally done with the simplest of devices, the metal being embedded directly in a pile of glowing charcoal on a flat grid. When closely uniform results were required, as in blanching coins, the fuel and coins were placed together in a kind of warming-pan and tossed frequently in the air to maintain uniformity.

X. METALLURGY AS A SCIENCE

This volume marks the transition from the purely empirical knowledge of processes and materials to the beginning of a scientific understanding of them. The great sixteenth-century works on metals have many quantitative aspects derived from experience, but make no effort to elucidate theory. To discern any

FIGURE 30—*Ring of coals used to increase heat gradually in the pot. 1574.*

theoretical metallurgical considerations of lasting importance we must await the eighteenth century. However, the great physicists and chemists of the seventeenth century consulted craftsmen, and Boyle, Hooke, and Glauber in particular appreciated the two-way interdependence of science and the arts.

Many of the interesting properties of metals and alloys were known in classical antiquity. Constitution diagrams could not, of course, be expected before the invention of a thermometric scale, but the essential phenomena were familiar enough: the depression of the melting-point of mixtures of metals and the proportions that yield eutectics of minimum melting-point, the immiscibility of some molten metals and the partition of solutes between the two liquids, the difference in composition between solid and liquid, the existence of terminal and intermediate solid solutions, and the formation of intermetallic compounds. That cold-working made metals hard and that annealing softened them had been known for millennia. Changes in properties, resulting from transformation or solubility changes, were produced even though not understood. The differing affinities of metals for each other and for non-metals were the very basis of refining and assaying. The existence of something like an electrochemical series was implicit in the knowledge that metals could replace each other sequentially from solutions of their salts. Diffusion in solids was utilized in making steel, cementing gold, and blanching silver. The relations between structure and properties were utilized daily in fracture-tests for quality and as a guide for composition or heat-treatment.

Both the followers of Descartes (1596–1650) and the opposing atomists were deeply concerned with the structure of matter, and their writings contain remarkably prescient remarks concerning the dependence of the properties of metals on the disposition of their component parts. Though there is much confusion as to the nature of the minute structure of matter (for phenomena due to interatomic forces are hopelessly intermixed with those due to microcrystals) there is nevertheless a clear concept of a metal as composed of parts which can slide over each other without losing their attraction, which are agitated by heat, and which can interdiffuse. The physical phenomena, however, were too complex for easy reduction to a quantitative scheme.

The phlogiston theory, which first appeared clearly in a metallurgical work, was the key doctrine of eighteenth-century chemistry. It was in essence an attempt to combine corpuscular theory with the ideas summarized in the theory of elements of the old chemists. By stimulating experiment it resulted in the accumulation of facts that eventually led to its displacement and the revival of atomistic ideas.

FIGURE 31—*Exterior view of reverberatory furnace used for melting bronze. 1540.*

The structure of metals as seen in fractures was commonly used to control craftsmen's operations. Savot (1627) remarks that 'bellfounders judge the quantity of tin which they should put in [bell-metal] by breaking a piece of the material before they cast it . . . , because if they find the grain too large they put in more tin; and if it is too fine they augment the copper' [61]. The learned blacksmith Jousse (1627) devoted several chapters to the recognition of good iron or steel, chiefly on the basis of fracture [17]. Boyle (1672) observed the crystalline facets of a fractured cast lump of bismuth and speculated on the mechanism of solidification [46]. The microscopist Henry Power records (1664) the first observations of metal under the microscope: 'Look at a polished piece [of gold, silver, steel, copper, tin or lead] and you shall see them all full of fissures, cavities and asperities and irregularities; but least of all in lead which is the closest and most compact solid body probably in the world' [47]. His examination of the sparks struck from steel inspired Hooke's discussion of their nature in his *Micrographia* (1665). Despite Réaumur's important efforts to understand the structure of metals on the basis of intercrystalline and transcrystalline fractures, it remained for the nineteenth century to realize the nature of polycrystalline materials.

The earliest physical property of metals to be quantitatively measured was density. There is an eleventh- or twelfth-century list of weights relative to wax compiled in order that the founder might know how much metal to melt. By the seventeenth century extensive tables of similar data become common in mathematicians' works, for example those of Napier (1617) [48] and Mersenne (1644) [49]. Caswell (1693) lists new measurements of the densities of twenty-nine metallic materials to five significant (?) figures [50].

Studies of the density of alloys were used in the first attempts to understand the nature of the interaction of metals. The experiment of Archimedes with the crown of Hiero will be recalled. In the Middle Ages it was assumed that a given weight of metal occupies the same volume in an alloy as when pure. Glauber showed that this was not true for copper and tin alloys, and believed that one metal could fill interstices between the parts of another. Perrault (1680) first

FIGURE 32—*Assay-laboratory, showing balance, muffle furnace for cupelling, ingot-mould, &c. 1540.*

recorded the increase in volume of steel on hardening [51]. In 1679 and 1680 the Royal Society studied 50–50 alloys of the various possible combinations of copper, tin, lead, silver, and antimony, noting their obvious qualities and their densities [29]. The alloy was generally of higher density than the theoretical mixture. This was explained by analogy with a mixture of shot of different sizes. Actually, most of the differences resulted from the varying soundness of the castings.

Metals were used for engineering long before their strength was quantitatively measured. Music inspired[1] the first serious tests of tensile properties, made by Mersenne (1636) [52]. He reports that wires $\frac{1}{72}$-inch in diameter of gold, silver, copper, and iron fractured at 23, 23, $18\frac{1}{2}$, and 19 lb respectively. These are much higher than today's figures, with the possible exception of iron if somewhat carbonized. Mersenne also records the density and natural frequency of hemispherical bells of many metals and alloys, thus giving for the first time a measured property related to elastic modulus. From Galileo (1638) on, those concerned with the formal science of the strength of materials were more interested in mathematical

[1] Thus repaying music's debt to metallurgy, for, according to the medieval *Speculum humanae salvationis*, music itself originated in the forge of Tubal Cain when his brother Jubal contemplated the pleasant rhythmic noise of the hammer on the anvil.

elasticity than in the realities of strength, though Galileo cites as an example a copper wire, a cubit long and weighing 1 oz, which could support 50 lb before breaking—about 6450 lb per sq in [53]. In 1662 Croone carried out before the Royal Society tests on silver wires $\frac{1}{6}$- and $\frac{1}{16}$-inch in diameter, but the experiments were abandoned. Not until Musschenbroek began his important investigations in 1729 was there further study of the problem.

XI. ASSAYING

In the sixteenth century there was no field of applied science more advanced than

FIGURE 33—*Assay-laboratory with furnaces, distillation vessels, and so on.* 1574

that of assaying. By centuries of purely empirical experiment precise methods had been developed for quantitative analysis in circumstances where it was economically justified. The assayer excelled the alchemist in all but the desire for a systematized philosophy. Unlike the alchemist he recorded his procedures in language for all to understand, and was essentially quantitative in outlook. The techniques for the assaying of ores and metals containing gold and silver had so developed that they were changed only in incidental details until the present century. Conversely, assaying for the base metals was relatively unimportant and had been poorly developed.

The printed literature on assaying begins with the anonymous *Probierbüchlein*, (Magdeburg 1524) [1]. There are extensive chapters on the subject in Biringuccio and Agricola, while Ercker's volume is largely devoted to assaying. Thereafter, except for minor works [54], original writing on assaying ceased until Boizard

(1696) reported the practice in the Paris mint [41], and Cramer (1739) for the first time attempted to combine the empirical knowledge of the assayer with growing chemical theory [55].

Assaying had two main functions: the examination of ores to determine the possibility of profitably working them, and the examination of coins and jewelry to determine their quality and to detect fraud. The early assaying methods were not applied, as is modern chemical analysis, to determine the suitability of a material for engineering purposes.

FIGURE 34—*Forge fire adapted for crucible-melting.* (A) *Iron hoop containing fuel;* (B) *lever-operated double bellows.* 1556.

The assayer's equipment. In addition to the wind- and muffle-furnaces (figures 32, 33) the assayer also used the forge fire, adapted for melting metals in a crucible (figure 34). The muffle-furnace for scorification and cupellation was built either entirely of fireclay, reinforced with iron rods or external iron straps, or of fireclay applied to a sheet iron shell. The muffle itself was initially merely a little clay arch with holes in the sides and back (figure 35) resting on a fire-brick, but Schreittmann (1578) shows the modern closed form [54]. Crucibles were moulded from fireclay either in hand-moulds or in a press (figure 36).

The assayer's utensils are notable for their satisfying shapes, which resulted partly from proper adaptation to function. Many are closely similar to those still in use. Though cheap glazed ceramics were used whenever possible for handling liquids, the assayer used glass extensively for distillation apparatus and for the delicate operations of parting (figure 37).

Cupels were very important to the assayer. They were made chiefly of levigated wood-ashes, with a facing of extremely fine bone-ash. The facing ashes are particularly important since they come into contact with the bead of metal. According to Ercker, they are best made of the bones of a calf's head, especially the forehead, although other assay books list various preferences, most commonly the ashes of fish-bone or horn. The cupels, of various sizes, were made by pounding the moistened ashes in brass or wood moulds (figure 38).

FIGURE 35—*Side and rear views of muffle for cupelling furnace.* 1533.

The assayer needed three separate balances, which were usually of the same type but of different capacity and sensitivity, the best showing about 0·1 mg. All three had beam-lifting devices to protect the knife-edges from shock (vol II, figure 678). The assayer had to know how to make his own balances, though he undoubtedly often bought them. There are excellent descriptions of the adjustment of the balances, reflecting a complete understanding of the principles involved, in both Ercker and Schreittmann.

The weights of the assayer were usually not those legal for trade, but miniature sets planned to give a reasonable size of sample for assay. These developed partly because no sufficiently small units existed in the legal systems and a cumbersome fractional designation would have been needed, but principally because the miniature weights avoided calculation since they maintained the proper ratios between the multitudinous units in vogue. The assayer had to have several sets of weights for different purposes (assay of ore, gold, silver, or copper). He usually made his own, either by starting with the smallest piece that his balance could detect and building up from this, or by starting from the biggest weight and successively subdividing by various tricks. A single set of weights usually contained from nine to sixteen pieces.

FIGURE 36—*Mould and screw-press for making crucibles.* (A) *Lower section of two-piece wooden mould;* (B) *the complete mould, showing the shaping of the crucible;* (C) *iron retaining hoop;* (D) *crucible. 1574.*

One assayer, Schreittmann (1578), developed a system of weights that deserves an important place in the history of metrology [54]. It is nothing less than a comprehensive decimal system adapted to give proper equivalents for all the fractional weights—sixteenths, twelfths, quarters, and thirds—that were involved in the various assay systems. He starts logically with weights smaller than can be detected with his assay-balance, and his first actual piece is ten of these units, which he calls *elementlin oder atomi, stüplin oder minutslin*. From this he builds up to 20, 30, and 40, then 100, 200, 300, and 400 and so on in thousands, ten thousands, and hundred thousands. He states that a legal pound is 1 106 920 units, thus one unit equalled 0.42 mg. Schreittmann gives many examples of computing assays in various systems by his new scheme. The fact that assays had to be reported in conventional units meant that the advantage of his system was for a time largely theoretical; nevertheless, it has in it most of the virtues of subsequent decimal systems and is an important precursor of the decimal fractional division of weights and measures proposed by Simon Stevin (*De thiende*, 1585) and the integrated decimal metric units of the French Republic.

Assaying of ores. Relatively little attention was paid by the early assayers to the assaying of base metal ores. Biringuccio, for example, states merely that base metal ores are assayed by fusion exactly as a larger quantity would be treated. Agricola assays lead ore by mixing a crushed sample with borax and placing it in a lump of charcoal in a crucible, while tin ore, after roasting and crushing, is mixed with borax and placed in a hole in a piece of charcoal. Bismuth is merely melted out of its ore, and mercury distilled out. Iron ore is first magnetically separated, then melted with saltpetre in a crucible in a blacksmith's forge.

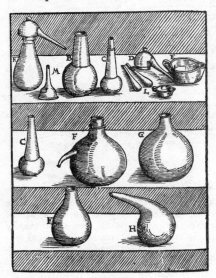

FIGURE 37—*Assayers' glassware and pottery vessels. (A) Coated glass flask, with still-head; (B, C) coated flasks; (D) still-head; (E) pourer; (F) receiver used in fractional distillation; (G) ordinary receiver; (H) earthenware retort; (K) earthenware pot; (L) small flasks; (M) glass funnel. 1574.*

Not until Ercker (1574) is there evidence of proper provision of a reducing agent. In assaying refractory copper ores, he says, it is necessary to roast thoroughly, then grind and mix with black flux (p 63) and some sandiver[1] before melting in a crucible to yield the metal. He assays for matte production by melting the ore with the reducing flux, without a previous roasting. He also describes the assay of copper, tin, and lead ore by smelting samples weighing a pound or so in a little laboratory blast-furnace in direct contact with charcoal, the metal being collected in a blast-hearth at the bottom. All early assayers tend thus to make their methods correspond on a small scale to actual production, and preferred to have results indicating practical yields rather than the true content of metal. Copper matte and black copper were assayed for refined copper by exposing the molten material in a scorifier to a blast of air until the surface showed the proper *Blick* (flash), the practical end-point (p 64).

Galena ores were assayed for lead by Ercker by mixing with the black flux and a small amount of iron filings, the iron removing the sulphur. Intractable lead ores were first roasted before melting with the flux and the iron filings were omitted. A simple assay is described that can be done without any furnace, simply by mixing the roasted ore with saltpetre and charcoal, a mixture which, once ignited, melts by itself.

[1] A neutral salt skimmed off the surface of melted glass. It is sometimes known as glass-gall.

In practice, trial in a smith's forge would be the most important assay of iron ores. Ercker suggests a magnetic assay for iron ores and remarks that some ores become magnetic only after roasting. Schindler (1687) is the first assayer to give a method of assaying iron ore by fusion with reducing material to give a regulus of cast iron [54].

The fluxes for the assay of precious metal ores contained such ingredients as silica pebbles, glass, salt, sandiver, borax, or *caput mortuum*,[1] with a collector which was almost always lead. For many purposes saltpetre was also added. Unless lead was present in the ore, it was added in the form of litharge. The most important single flux was the black flux, made by igniting a mixture of crude tartar and saltpetre with a piece of glowing charcoal. The materials reacted leaving a blackish mass, consisting of a mixture of potassium nitrite, potassium carbonate, and carbon.

FIGURE 38—*Moulding cupels by hand. 1540.*

In no field does Ercker's superiority appear more than in his attitude towards fluxes. The *Probierbüchlein* quotes eight different varieties of fluxes, while Agricola lists no fewer than eighteen. Ercker, however, uses only two, either the standard black flux or a lead silicate glass, adding iron filings for lead sulphide ores.

A fine sixteenth-century English account of assaying copper and other base-metal ores in Cumberland has been found recently in the notebook of Daniel Hochstetter, one of the principal German experts who were brought over to work the deposits there [63]. Gabriel Plattes (1639)—the first man to publish a useful treatise in English on metallurgical matters—describes simple fireside assays of lead and copper ores [56]. Lead ore he merely mixes with iron filings and melts, though he remarks that a quarter of an ounce of sandiver and as much saltpetre will make it melt sooner and give a clean slag. Tin and copper ores are similarly treated but without the iron filings or any reducing agent! As with most of the early assayers, he gives methods for extracting silver from iron, which must have been a rather profitless operation except on objects inlaid or encrusted with silver. Barba (1640) advises the use of litharge alone as a flux for crucible assay, claiming that other additions are unnecessary [7].

Another common method of assay for ores containing gold and silver was by scorification, in which the ore mixed with flux was placed on the top of an open

---

[1] An alchemical name for the earthy residue left in the retort after distillation, usually of materials to give nitric acid. It would consist principally of ferric oxide and potassium sulphate.

bath of lead in a scorifier exposed to air under a muffle. Much of the lead oxidized away, but the residual button contained the whole of the precious metal.

Samuel Zimmerman (1573) suggests, apparently for the first time, a wet method of assay. He says that gold or silver can be extracted from an ore, after roasting with lime if necessary, by extraction with *aqua regia* or *aqua fortis* respectively, the metal being precipitated from the solution with mercury or copper [62].

When assaying base metal ore the metallic product was weighed directly; for the precious metals the lead button from crucible or scorifier had to be cupelled.

Cupellation makes use of the resistance of the precious metals to oxidation, which distinguishes them from all other common metals. If a bath of impure lead is heated in air at a full red heat, the litharge formed by the oxidizing lead will dissolve the oxides of most other base metals, and the surface tension relations are such that the molten litharge will wet and soak into the ash of the cupel, while the metal will remain unabsorbed as a compact molten bead. The base metals continue to oxidize away until there remains nothing but a fine bead containing all the gold and silver originally present in the lead.

Cupellation still remains one of the most accurate assay methods, particularly for low concentrations. Though the process is chemically simple it calls for skilled craftsmanship, and the old writers seem to delight in attempting to pass on their knowledge. In cupellation the cupels were placed under a muffle in a furnace and annealed for half an hour before adding either the lead button from a scorification or crucible-fusion of ore, or a bullet of lead to which a weighed metal sample was added. The largest cupels held about 2 oz of lead.

The importance of temperature control was well realized. The assay was usually started hot and finished cold. The operation was controlled by careful observation of the play of colours and the movement of litharge over the surface of the metal, and the formation of the delicate yellow litharge crystals on the cold parts of the cupel. To protect the assayer's eyes and face he commonly used a board with a slit in it through which he peered into the hot furnace (figure 41). Arphe (1572) thus describes the appearance of the lead on the cupel: 'During the process waters are seen on top of the assay rising from the border of the grain, but when the silver becomes fine it forms a cover of a matte appearance, without any gloss. This is a sign that all the lead has been absorbed in the cupel and has taken with it all the other metals except silver, or gold if the silver contained any. After the assay becomes covered, it uncovers again and remains shining bright and clean' [54]. This sudden brightening or flash (*Blick*) is the end-point of the operation.

In assaying bullion or base metal the operation was essentially the same. The weight of lead varied from four times the weight of the silver, if it was relatively pure, to as much as eighteen times for silver-bearing copper. The assayer knew that his lead contained silver and he prepared silver beads as blanks by cupellation of the amount of lead to be used in an assay, which beads were used as counterpoises during the weighing of the assay beads.

Parting. The beads from cupelling would contain both gold and silver if both were present in the sample. Though on a larger scale these two metals were separated with sulphur or antimony sulphide, for assay purposes nitric acid was always used. Beads containing less than a third of gold were hammered into a little strip and directly attacked with concentrated nitric acid. This left the gold behind in the form of a coherent piece, a loose sponge, or as fine particles, depending on the alloy-concentration and the strength of the acid. If too much gold is present the alloy remains unattacked, and for assay it was

FIGURE 39—*Parting-flask* (B) *and annealing cups* (C, D). *A cornet* (A) *is immersed in the parting-acid.* *1572.*

therefore diluted with silver. This operation, known as *inquartation*, generally aimed at producing a bead containing three times as much silver as gold, though both Arphe and Boizard recommend a 2 : 1 ratio.

If the approximate composition of the gold was not known, it was tested by touchstone or by a trial parting, and silver was then added to give the proper ratio for the gold to remain in a porous but coherent form after acid treatment. The inquarted bead was hammered flat, coiled into a little spiral or cornet, and boiled with three successive lots of nitric acid in a little flask (figure 39), after which the residual gold was washed, transferred to a small crucible or silver cup to be annealed, and finally weighed. The present-day assayer does precisely the same.

Assayers generally made their own parting-acid, and Biringuccio, Ercker, and Agricola all devote pages to its manufacture. It was made by destructive distillation of saltpetre mixed with alum or vitriol in a still composed of a matrass, alembic-head, and receiver (figure 40). Before use in parting, the acid was always treated by dissolving a small amount of silver in a little acid and adding it to the rest until no further precipitate was formed. This was essential to remove chlorides, present as impurities, the presence of which would leave the parted gold heavily contaminated with silver chloride and in extreme cases would, as *aqua regia*, dissolve the gold itself instead of the silver.

Assay by touchstone is mentioned in Greek literature and was common in the sixteenth century, although it was quite properly regarded as only an approximate method (vol II, p 45).

FIGURE 40—*Four types of furnace for distilling parting-acid.* (A) *Tower of 'slow Harry' furnace;* (B) *side chambers in which pots containing reagents are placed;* (C) *glass receivers;* (D) *earthenware vessel;* (E) *furnace used to heat a retort (shown within);* (F) *small receptacle connected to large receiver to make room for 'spirits' driven over from retort;* (G) *long furnace;* (H) *side chamber.* 1574.

Assay by density is not distinctly referred to as a method of assaying (otherwise than for merely checking identity, as by Archimedes, p 58) until the thirteenth century, when the pseudonymous treatise *Liber Archimedis de ponderibus* appeared [57]. Many variations on the principle are described thereafter, usually with confusion between volume- and weight-percentages of the components. A balance with a graduated beam and movable fulcrum for use in this type of study was described in the poem *Carmen de ponderibus* attributed to Priscian (sixth century A.D.; printed 1475) and in modified form in Galileo's first scientific paper

FIGURE 41—*Assay laboratory.* (A) *Furnace;* (B) *iron sheet on to which assays are poured;* (C) *implement with slit used in inspecting furnace to avoid damage to the eyes;* (D) *parting-flask on stand;* (E) *assay by water-displacement method on auriferous silver. 1574.*

(*c* 1586) [58]. Actually such balances would be hopelessly insensitive to small changes in composition.

An exact though tedious method is given by Ercker, who adjusts quantities of pure silver and pure gold granules counterpoising the sample to be assayed, until there is no change on immersing the balance in water (figure 41). He describes another method, using silver weights and determining the overweight on immersion in water, and a third method involving the comparison of the weights of equal lengths of wires of gold, silver, and the alloy, all drawn through the same die. Ercker, however, did not recommend these assays, for he knew that different samples even of a pure metal may differ in density. Porta (1589) [16] has still another variant, erroneously computed, while Boyle developed a simple hydrometer float (1675) for weighing above and below water [59]. He tested coins by direct comparison against standards, and used no assumed relation between density and composition.

The weight of a cast ball made in a standard mould was used by pewterers as a method of assay at least as early as the mid-fourteenth century. This was a simple acceptance or rejection test and although, in its actions against fraudulent pewterers, the Pewterers' Company records the excess weight over the standards, it records no attempt to relate this to actual composition until the comparatively late date of 1710 [32].

Various qualitative assay methods were well known, and are discussed in some detail by Glauber [60]. He uses the colour of both flame and fume as an indicator of metals and makes astute observations on the effect of impurities on the shape of drops of metals, which we now interpret in terms of surface tension. Eight years earlier Glauber had suggested qualitative assay by observing the colours produced by a sample of ore melted with glass, a method that was later to be refined into the borax bead test.

Metallurgy in the sixteenth and seventeenth centuries was much influenced by the wide distribution of printed books recording in detail the techniques and alloy compositions that had been in use for many centuries, for the subject then became of general interest to scholars and other citizens. The special properties of metals and their transformations were not ignored in the general spirit of inquiry that now prevailed.

With the foundation of the great learned societies in the mid-seventeenth century the practical knowledge of artisans attracted the interest of experimental philosophers, but practical knowledge continued far in advance of theory. Not until the eighteenth century was theoretical science in a position to aid practice in any but minor ways. Yet the methods of modern science were being begotten from this conjunction of philosophy with the practical observation and intuitive knowledge of those who actually handled the materials, and in the next century the increased understanding of the nature of metals and their reactions led naturally to improved processes and to materials better suited for the increasingly stringent demands of a more sophisticated engineering.

REFERENCES

[1] PROBIERBÜCHLEIN. Magdeburg, 1524. Eng. trans. in 'Bergwerk- und Probierbüchlein', trans. and annot. by ANNELIESE G. SISCO and C. S. SMITH. American Institute of Mining and Metallurgical Engineers, New York. 1949.

[2] PANTHEUS, JOANNES AUGUSTINUS. *Voarchadumia contra Alchimiam.* Venice, 1530. See also TAYLOR, F. SHERWOOD. Newcomen Society Preprint. 1954.

[3] BIRINGUCCIO, VANOCCIO. 'De la Pirotechnia libri X.' Roffinello, Venice. 1540. Eng. trans. by C. S. SMITH and MARTHA T. GNUDI. American Institute of Mining and Metallurgical Engineers, New York. 1943.

[4] AGRICOLA, GEORGIUS. *De re metallica libri XII.* Basel. 1556. Eng. trans. and comm. by H. C. HOOVER and LOU H. HOOVER. Mining Magazine, London, 1912; Dover Publications, New York, 1950.

[5] ERCKER, LAZARUS. 'Beschreibung allerfürnemsten mineralischen Ertzt- vnnd Berckwercks-arten.' Georg Schwarz, Prague. 1574. Eng. trans. from German ed. of 1580 by ANNELIESE G. SISCO and C. S. SMITH. University Press, Chicago, Ill. 1951.

[6] LÖHNEISS, GEORG ENGLEHARD VOM. 'Bericht vom Bergwerk, wie man dieselben bawen . . . sol.' Zellerfeld. 1617.

[7] BARBA, A. A. 'El Arte de los Metales.' Madrid. 1640. Eng. trans. by R. E. DOUGLASS and E. P. MATHEWSON. Wiley, New York. 1923.

[8] JOHANNSEN, O. (Trans.). 'Peder Månssons Schriften über technische Chemie und Hütten-wesen.' Verlag der deutschen Technik, Berlin. 1941.

[9] RÉAUMUR, R. A. FERCHAULT DE. 'L'Art de convertir le fer forgé en acier et l'art d'adoucir le fer fondu.' Paris. 1722. Eng. trans. by ANNELIESE G. SISCO. Chicago, 1956. University Press, Chicago, Ill. 1955.

[10] WEEKS, M. ELVIRA. 'Discovery of the Elements' (5th ed. enl. and rev.). Journal of Chemical Education, Easton, Pa. 1945.

[11] LIPPMANN, E. O. VON. 'Die Geschichte des Wismuts zwischen 1400 und 1800.' Springer, Berlin. 1930.

[12] DAWKINS, J. M. 'Zinc and Spelter.' Zinc Development Association, Oxford. 1950.

[13] GILLE, B. 'Les origines de la grande industrie métallurgique en France.' Collection d'histoire sociale, no. 2. Éditions Domat, Paris. 1947.

HALL, A. R. 'Ballistics in the Seventeenth Century.' University Press, Cambridge. 1952.

[14] JOHANNSEN, O. 'Geschichte des Eisens' (3rd ed. rev.). Stahleisen, Düsseldorf. 1953.

[15] ALESSIO PIEMONTESE (Ps.-). 'Secreti del . . . Alessio Piemontese.' Venice. 1555. See also DARMSTAEDTER, E., 'Berg-, Probier-', und Kunstbuchlein'. Munich. 1926.

[16] PORTA, G. B. DELLA. *Magiae naturalis libri XX.* Naples, 1589. Eng. trans., London. 1658.

[17] JOUSSE, M. 'La fidelle ouverture de l'art de serrurier.' La Flèche. 1627.

[18] SAINT RÉMY, P. S. DE. 'Mémoires d'artillerie.' Paris. 1697.

[19] FEUERWERKBUCH. 1454. The metallurgical contents are quoted by O. JOHANNSEN. *Stahl u. Eisen, Düsseldorf,* **30,** 1373, 1910.

[20] PLOT, R. 'The Natural History of Staffordshire.' Oxford. 1686.

[21] HOOKE, R. 'The diary of Robert Hooke, 1672–1680' (ed. by H. W. ROBINSON and W. ADAMS), p. 193. Taylor and Francis, London. 1935.

[22] BOYLE, R. 'Experiments and Considerations Touching Colours.' Henry Herringman, London. 1664.

[23] HOOKE, R. '*Micrographia,* or Some Physiological Descriptions of Minute Bodies Made by Magnifying Glasses, with Observations and Inquiries Thereupon.' London. 1665.

Reprinted in GUNTHER, R. T. 'Early Science in Oxford', Vol. 13. Printed for the Subscribers, Oxford. 1938.

[24] GLAUBER, J. R. *Prosperitatis Germaniae pars prima*. Amsterdam. 1656.

[25] NERI, A. 'L'arte vetraria distinta in libri sette.' Florence. 1612. Eng. trans., greatly amplified, by C. MERRET. London. 1662.

[26] SACHS, HANS. 'Eygentliche beschreibung aller Stände . . . mit kunstreichen figuren [by JOST AMMAN]. Sigmund Feyerabend, Frankfurt a. M. 1568.

[27] GLAUBER, J. R. *Furni novi philosophici*. Amsterdam. 1648. Eng. trans. by C. PACKE. London. 1689.
Idem. Opera mineralis, Pt. I. Amsterdam. 1651.

[28] NEWTON, I. *Phil. Trans.*, **7**, 4004, 1672.

[29] BIRCH, T. 'The History of the Royal Society of London for Improving Natural Knowledge' (4 vols). Vol. III, p. 43. London. 1756–57.

[30] ZONCA, V. 'Novo teatro di machine et edificii.' Bertelli, Padua. 1607.

[31] GUNTHER, R. T. 'Early Science in Oxford', Vol. 7, p. 678 (entry for 25 February 1685). Printed for the Subscribers, Oxford. 1930.

[32] WELCH, C. 'History of the Worshipful Company of Pewterers of the City of London Based upon Their Own Records' (2 vols). Blades, East and Blades, London. 1902.

[33] HARRISON, W. 'An historicall description of the Islande of Britayne.' London. 1577.

[34] HOUGHTON, J. (Ed.). 'A Collection for the Improvement of Husbandry and Trade' (rev. ed. by R. BRADLEY, 4 vols). London. 1727.

[35] [PLANTIN, CHRISTOPHER]. 'La première et la seconde parties des dialogues francois pour les ieunes enfans', Dialogue 9. Christophle Plantin, Antwerp. 1567. Eng. trans. by RAY NASH. 'An Account of Printing in the Sixteenth Century from Dialogues Attributed to Christopher Plantin.' Harvard University Library, Department of Printing and Graphic Arts, Cambridge, Mass. 1940.

[36] MOXON, J. 'Mechanick Exercises, or the Doctrine of Handy-works' (2nd ed., 2 vols.). London. 1683.

[37] THEOPHILUS PRESBYTER *Diversarum artium schedula*. Ed. with comm. and German trans. by W. THEOBALD: 'Die Technik des Kunsthandwerks im zehnten Jahrhundert.' Verein Deutschen Ingenieure, Berlin. 1933. Ed. with Eng. trans. by R. HENDRIE: 'An Essay upon various Arts by Theophilus called also Rogerus.' London. 1847.

[38] CAUS, S. DE. 'Les raisons des forces mouvantes.' Paris. 1615. Also another edition with additional figures. Charles Serestne, Paris. 1624.

[39] HALE, T. 'New Invention of Mill'd Lead . . . for Ships.' London. 1691.

[40] RUDING, R. 'Annals of the Coinage of Britain and its Dependencies' (3rd ed., 3 vols.). London. 1840.
CRAIG, SIR JOHN H. McC. 'The Mint. A History of the London Mint from A.D. 287 to 1948.' University Press, Cambridge. 1953.

[41] BOIZARD, J. 'Traité des monoyes, de leurs circonstances et dependances.' Paris. 1696.

[42] CELLINI, BENVENUTO. 'Due trattati, vno intorno alle otto principali arti dell' oreficeria. L'altro in materia dell' arte della scultura.' Florence. 1568. Eng. trans. by C. R. ASHBEE. London. 1898.

[43] RÉAUMUR, R. A. FERCHAULT DE. "Expériences et réflexions sur la prodigeuse ductilité de diverses matières." *Hist. Acad. R. Sci.*, 100, 1713.

[44] BOYLE, R. 'An Essay of the Great Effects of Even Languid and Unheeded Motion.' London. 1685.

[45] KUNCKEL, J. *Ars vitraria experimentalis*. Amsterdam and Danzig. 1679.

[46] BOYLE, R. 'An Essay about the Origine and Virtues of Gems.' London. 1672.

[47] POWER, H. 'Experimental Philosophy.' London. 1664.

[48] NAPIER, J. *Rabdologiae, seu numerationis per virgulas*. Edinburgh. 1617.

[49] MERSENNE, M. *Cogitata physico-mathematica*. Paris. 1644.

[50] CASWELL, J. *Phil. Trans.*, **17,** 694, 1693.

[51] PERRAULT, C. and PERRAULT, P. 'Essais de physique.' Paris. 1680.

[52] MERSENNE, M. 'Harmonie universelle.' Paris. 1636.

[53] GALILEI, GALILEO. 'Discorsi e dimostrazioni matematichè intorno à due nuove scienze.' Leiden. 1638. Eng. trans. by H. CREW and A. DE SALVIO: 'Dialogues concerning two New Sciences.' Macmillan, New York. 1914; Dover Publications, New York. 1952.

[54] ARPHE, JUAN. 'Quilatador de la Plata oro y Piedras.' Valladolid. 1572.
FACHS, MODESTIN. 'Probier Büchlein.' Leipzig. 1595.
SCHINDLER, C. C. 'Der geheimbde Müntz-Guardein und Berg-Probierer.' Frankfurt a. M. [1687?].

SCHREITTMANN, CIRIACUS. 'Probierbuchlin. Frembde und subtile Künst.' Frankfurt a. M. 1578. See *Isis*, **46,** 354, 1955.

[55] CRAMER, J. A. *Elementa artis docimasticae*. Leiden. 1739. Eng. trans., London. 1741.

[56] PLATTES, G. 'A Discovery of Subternaneall Treasure.' London. 1639.

[57] MOODY, E. A. and CLAGETT, M. (Eds). 'The Medieval Science of Weights.' University of Wisconsin Press, Madison, Wis. 1952.

[58] *Idem. Ibid.*, pp. 353, 357.
GALILEI, GALILEO. 'Opere' (Edizione Nazionale by A. FAVARO), Vol. 1, pp. 215–20. Florence. 1890.

[59] BOYLE, R. *Phil. Trans.*, **10,** 329, 1675.

[60] GLAUBER, J. R. *De signatura salium, metallorum etc*. Amsterdam. 1659.

[61] SAVOT, L. 'Discours sur les médailles antiques.' Paris. 1627.

[62] ZIMMERMAN, SAMUEL. 'Probierbuch.' Augsburg. 1573.

[63] DONALD, M. B. 'Elizabethan Copper. The History of the Company of Mines Royal 1568–1605.' Pergamon Press, London. 1955.

[64] 'Stahel und Eysen kunstilich weych und hart zu machen.' Mainz, 1532. Eng. trans. from later ed. by H. W. WILLIAMS. *Tech. Stud. Fine Arts*, **4,** 64, 1935.

[65] FRATTA ET MONTALBANO, M. A. DE LA. 'Pratica Minerale.' Bologna. 1678.

General view of a French ironworks in 1716, showing the water-wheel for driving the bellows, with its chute, the partly-sectioned building around the furnace, pigs of iron being transported and weighed, and men carrying away slag to the tip.

3

COAL MINING AND UTILIZATION

J. U. NEF

I. THE EARLY HISTORY OF COAL

IT is impossible to say when coal was first deliberately burned. What is certain is that this mineral has played an important part in the development of western technology only in comparatively recent times, namely since the Middle Ages. Scientific interest in coal as a source of raw materials, not merely of heat, was a product of the nineteenth century.

All the societies that evolved before the Christian era in the Mediterranean basin and in the Near East had some recourse to the mineral wealth of the sub-soil. But there have never been, at least since the dawn of recorded history, rich coal-seams near the surface in Egypt, north Africa, the Balkans, Asia Minor, Mesopotamia, or India. If coal, or at any rate lignite, was burned at all in these regions before the birth of Christ (and there is little convincing evidence that it was) it had certainly no part in shaping the technical development of ancient peoples. Here its history has to be distinguished sharply from that of metals such as copper, lead, iron, or even silver and gold, for the ores of all of these metals were dug in ancient times, and the technology of metallurgy has a very ancient and interesting history (vol I, ch 21; vol II, ch 2; vol III, ch 2). After the Hellenistic era the extension of Roman dominion beyond the Alps into north-western Europe placed the technology and science of Graeco-Roman societies partly at the disposal both of settlers from southern Europe and other parts of the Roman Empire, and of the inhabitants conquered by the legions of Rome in Gaul and Britain. Both Gaul and Britain are distinguished from other parts of the empire—the Balkans, the Near East, and north Africa—by abundant out-cropping coal-seams. Such seams were to be found to some extent at several places in southern and central France, and in much greater numbers along a strip of territory in the Low Countries that begins just west of Mons and runs in an easterly direction to Liége and onwards to Aachen (Aix-la-Chapelle).

The most abundant outcropping coal-seams were in Britain. It has been suggested by one scholar, on the basis of modern archaeological evidence, that after the Roman conquest coal was fairly extensively worked for a time at many places in England, particularly during the fourth century A.D. [1]. Such a high importance is, however, not usually allowed to the coal-workings of Roman Britain; and even if it were the case that mineral fuel was dug during the Roman occupation in most of those fields where the seams poked their way close to the surface, it is unlikely that coal had any appreciable influence in Graeco-Roman times upon technological processes—upon the structure of ovens, forges, and furnaces, upon the machinery used in industry, or upon the means of transporting commodities by land and sea in any part of Europe.

After the barbarian invasions from the east and north, verifiable historical references to the digging or the use of coal disappear, so far as both the European continent and Britain are concerned. From the sixth to the eleventh century there is apparently no mention of coal in the documents of medieval Europe. Nor have archaeologists, it seems, been able to offer any clear evidence that coal was worked during that period. There is nothing for coal comparable to the records we have concerning metallurgy, and iron metallurgy in particular, during these early centuries of medieval history. Foreigners and visitors from the south of Europe and from the Near East sometimes speak, not without awe, of the iron-work of the barbarians, particularly their weapons of war and above all their swords. They never mention the burning of coal.

In short, coal remained a closed chapter in western Europe until the twelfth and thirteenth centuries—if indeed, which is rather doubtful, it had ever been anything more than a footnote to a chapter.

Farther west still, across the Atlantic, on the huge continent of which the ancient and medieval peoples seem to have been unaware, no chapter was written by coal, not even a footnote, until after the European settlers began to come in during the sixteenth century. The rich early societies of South and Central America, and those particularly of Peru and Mexico, made some use of metal, but apparently none of coal. This is not surprising when we realize how poor these territories were in coal-resources as contrasted with North America, which was still in the hands of primitive tribes.

In the Far East the early history of coal was different. Marco Polo (1254?–? 1324) was much struck when he discovered that in parts of China the natives were burning black stones as fuel. As an Italian, he had never seen this done before. While he probably would have been less astonished had he come from the Low Countries or from England, it appears that coal had been worked in China much more extensively than in Europe for many centuries. The question is how extensively and for what purposes coal had been burned. On these points the historians' answer must still be tentative. Joseph Needham has recently declared, 'It is certain that coal was used directly for smelting iron at least since the fourth century in China.' Needham seems to have compelling evidence that the smelting of iron ore was common in parts of China a great many centuries earlier than it was in Europe, partly because some Chinese ores could be melted at a considerably lower temperature than any European ones. But it does not necessarily follow that coal fuel was commonly used in the process. It has been suggested, on the other hand, that relevant passages in Chinese literature indicate nothing more than the use of coal in the manufacture of iron objects; such a use of coal in producing crude iron wares, for example·horse-shoes, was in other parts of the world frequently that to which coal was first put, coal being mixed with charcoal in the forge [2]. The substitution of coal for other fuels in the working of wrought iron in smithies presented no technical problems commensurable with those involved in the first smelting of the iron from ores. What is certain is that coal has been dug and used as fuel in China for two or three millennia. The Chinese made rather more of their coal resources than other peoples until the thirteenth, and possibly until the sixteenth, century.

In Europe, from the thirteenth to the middle of the sixteenth century, the coal resources of the Low Countries, especially those of the small principality of Liége, were those most exploited. Charles the Bold (1433–77), the fiery Duke of Burgundy, in his fury with the Liégeois, is said to have ordered his soldiers to erase the city from the map, and to have vowed that even its name should not be revived. Yet, in the decades following his death, Liége became one of the great European armouries. During the first half of the sixteenth century the output of coal in the region tripled or quadrupled [3] to provide fuel for the growing manufactures of iron and other metals into finished wares in the town itself and at many places up and down the wide, gently flowing river Meuse (figure 42). Liége coals were not quite carried to Newcastle; but this fuel from the land of 'Luick' did compete at Calais and other Channel ports with sea-coal brought from the Tyne. At Liége, long adits were driven to drain the coal-pits sunk in the hills above the town. They were planned systematically in such a way that the continuous flow from the underground passages, where the miners worked, provided the main water-supply of the city. The town had a double stake in the careful development of the technique of working coal. By the mid-sixteenth century the mounds of black earth thrown up beside the pits were hardly less prominent a sight for travellers than the spires of the churches. They were more portentous of the future that awaited the western people than the city halls, the courts of justice, and the merchant palaces that were rising in profusion [4].

FIGURE 42—*Coal-mine in the Liége district. (Centre) Haulage shaft with galleries leading off; (left) ventilation shaft, with chimney and doors to shafts. 1773.*

II. THE BRITISH COAL INDUSTRY

It was just after this time that a great change occurred in the place of coal in technology, destined to have an immense influence upon the coming of the iron and steel and machine economy. While the reign of Elizabeth II seems to mark the end of English supremacy among the nations of the world in the exploitation

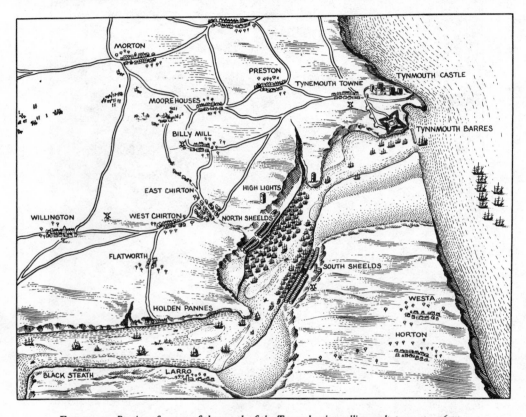

FIGURE 43—*Portion of a map of the mouth of the Tyne, showing colliers, salt-pans, etc. 1655.*

of coal, the reign of Elizabeth I marked its beginning. From the end of the sixteenth century until the middle of the Victorian age, from about 1600 to 1860 or so, Great Britain was without a close rival when it came to the mining and use of mineral fuel. Already during the early decades of the seventeenth century coal came into widespread use, not only in the domestic hearths of the English and Scottish, and in their laundry-work and cooking, but in the extraction of salt and the manufacture of glass, bricks and tiles for building, anchors for ships, and tobacco-pipes. The dyers, the hat-makers, the sugar-refiners, the brewers, who were growing very numerous especially in London and some provincial towns, and even some of the bakers of bread required coal. As early as the reign of James I (1603–25), the expansion of the English manufacture of alum, to supply the native dyeing industry with an essential mordant, came to depend upon the arrival of ship loads of coal from the north of England at ports along the Yorkshire coast, near newly discovered deposits of alumstone. In the year 1563–4 the shipments of coal from Newcastle-upon-Tyne amounted to 32 951 tons. A century later, in the year 1658–9, they had risen to 529 032 tons. Between about 1580, when Shakespeare is said to have settled in the capital, and the Restoration in 1660, the imports at London increased some twenty- to twenty-five-fold (figure 43) [5]. Foreigners who visited the rapidly growing city were astonished at the filthy smoke from tens of thousands of domestic fires and from hundreds of workshops. There was no spectacle like it anywhere else on earth. With its breweries, its soap- and starch-houses, its brick-kilns, sugar-refineries, earthenware works, and glass-furnaces, London seemed to some of these foreigners to have been rendered unfit for human habitation [6]. Even the English virtuoso John Evelyn (1620–1706) was repelled by the fog of smoke belching from the sooty throats of the new manufacturing shops, to hang over the metropolis and insinuate itself along the streets. He compared this new, dark London to 'the picture of Troy sacked by the Greeks, or the approaches of Mount Hecla' [7]. By the Restoration or very soon afterwards the small island of Great Britain, with its expanding mines in Scotland, Wales, and many parts of England, was producing in all probability some 2 m tons of coal annually, perhaps five times as much as all the rest of the world [8].

For the history of technology and science, which have so direct a bearing on the advent of the unique industrial civilization of our times, the great significance of this novel shift from a wood-burning to a coal-burning economy consisted in the new technological problems that were raised in an acute form in three domains: first, in the industrial use of coal; second, in the mining industry; and third, in the transport industry. Upon a solution of these problems the eventual adoption of a machine economy largely depended.

III. NEW USES FOR COAL FUEL

The pressure put upon the supplies of firewood and timber by the expansion of population, and by ship-building and other manufactures in England, had become so great by the end of Elizabeth I's reign that the prices of firewood in London and of many kinds of timber for construction-work had risen more than those of any other commodities for which modern statisticians have gathered the figures [9]. In a number of industries, such as the evaporation of salt water to produce salt, the heating of solutions of alumstone to produce alum, in the making of lime, and in the baking of bricks, the substitution of coal for earlier fuels, particularly for firewood and charcoal, could be effected without any great change in the processes of manufacture. There were also, however, many industries in which the adoption of coal fuel was possible only if new methods of manufacture were invented. Glass-making is an important case in point (pp 220–1). Between about 1605 and 1612 a new type of furnace was devised. In it the raw materials were heated in closed crucibles, and so were protected from the nauseous fumes and flames of the burning coal [10]. While the new furnaces rendered it possible to produce sheet glass—serviceable for such commodities as plain window-panes—in larger quantities than ever before, it made impracticable the blowing of glass in the flames, an art in which the Italians and, under Italian influence, most continental peoples excelled.

Thus the need for substituting coal for wood as fuel tended to encourage a concentration of capital and labour upon types of technology in which the primary purpose of invention was to increase the output of cheap commodities, rather than to improve the quality of more valuable, and often very beautiful, commodities.

The future of an expanding manufacture of iron in the British Isles after about 1600 came to be bound up with the replacement of wood by coal in the furnaces and the forges at which pig iron was converted into bar iron, some of which was reconverted into rods at slitting-mills. Charcoal for iron metallurgy was not rising in price nearly so rapidly as firewood and timber during the late sixteenth and early seventeenth centuries, because, unlike firewood and timber for building, it was not carted for long distances to the centres of population and of industry, but was made and burned mainly at the place where the trees were felled. Parts of Great Britain—for example, the Forest of Dean—had abundant forests, and ironmasters built new furnaces and forges where plenty of wood was to be had for charcoal (figure 416). But this involved a movement away from the centres of demand; it added to the expense of setting up metallurgical plant and of marketing the output. The advantages that would follow the adoption of coal fuel in metallurgy were recognized at the beginning of the seventeenth century, and the very slow growth in the output of cast and bar iron in Great Britain during the later seventeenth and much of the eighteenth century must be attributed in a considerable degree to the stubborn technical difficulties that had to be overcome before coal replaced wood generally in iron metallurgy.

While coal had been used earlier in small quantities for making crude iron wares from wrought iron, no success had apparently been achieved in Europe at the end of the sixteenth century in the substitution of coal for wood in smelting any metallic ores. If, as has been suggested, such progress had been made much earlier in China in the smelting of iron ore, it was not from China that the western peoples learned how to use coal instead of wood in metallurgy.

How, then, did the conquest by coal of the smelting-processes in Great Britain come about? Two men claimed to have solved the problem of substituting coal for charcoal as fuel in the blast-furnaces at which iron ore was smelted and run into moulds, at the very beginning of the seventeenth century. Simon Sturtevant, who was apparently of Dutch origin, and John Rovenzon published treatises on metallurgy in 1612 and 1613 advocating the adoption of coal-burning blast furnaces, which they suggest are feasible though they fail to describe the processes that they profess to have invented to bring it about. Their methods, like those of many other inventors during the decades that followed, proved unsuccessful.

As the technical obstacles to the substitution of coal for wood had been overcome in glass-making at about the time that Sturtevant and Rovenzon published their treatises, and as a method, probably inspired by this success in glass-making, was devised by William Ellyott and Mathias Mersey in 1614 for using coal as fuel in the manufacture of steel from bar iron, it is puzzling why the general success of the substitution in iron metallurgy should have been delayed for several generations.

During the late sixteenth century the production of wrought iron by the indirect process (in which the iron was run in liquid form from the blast-furnace into moulds, known as pigs, to be converted into wrought iron by heating and hammering at forges) was coming into widespread use, particularly in northern Europe, in the Low Countries (plate 3), in Sweden, and in Britain. The problem of substituting coal for charcoal as fuel was complicated because the ore and iron had often to pass through a number of stages before the metal was ready in the form of bars or rods for smiths to forge into finished products. It was necessary for coal to make the conquest of all these stages. Each stage presented its own special problems, and in each the simple replacement of charcoal or wood was impracticable because, as in glass-making, the mineral fuel damaged the material.

Early in the seventeenth century a little coal was certainly mixed with charcoal as fuel for calcining the ore in preparation for the blast-furnaces, and also at both the finery and the chafery—the two types of forge used for manufacturing bar iron from pig or cast iron [11]. But, in spite of the claims of Sturtevant,

Rovenzon, and others, the conquest of the blast-furnace by coal fuel was long delayed. It was finally brought about indirectly, as a result perhaps of efforts to solve the problems of substituting coal for charcoal and wood in the brewing industry. The use of coal at the breweries themselves seems to have presented no serious problems, and some London brewers began to burn coal at least as early as the reign of James I [12]. In 1637 four out of five of the breweries in West-minster were said to burn ordinary coal instead of wood [13].

It was in the drying of malt, necessary for certain brews, that the new fuel transmitted its obnoxious properties indirectly to the taste of the beer. Few persons could bear to drink beer brewed from malt dried with raw coal. The idea of charring coal, as wood was charred to produce charcoal, to purge the mineral fuel of some of its impurities, may have occurred in 1603 to an ingenious promoter named Sir Hugh Platt (1552–1608), who supplied a recipe for making briquettes as a means of sweetening the domestic fires that caused so much distaste to sensi-tive noses in London [14]. But the early efforts to coke the coal failed. It was apparently in connexion with the drying

FIGURE 44—*Coke-burning. 1773.*

of malt that success was first achieved, in Derbyshire about the time of the Civil War (1642–8). Beer brewed from malt dried with what were then called 'coaks' was pronounced sweet and pure (figure 44). The coke was made from a special kind of hard coal dug near Derby; and, as a result of the new discovery, Derbyshire beer became famous throughout England [15].

The same properties of raw coal that transmitted a disagreeable taste to the beer brewed from coal-dried malt caused it when used in blast-furnaces to damage the cast and pig iron, making it brittle and useless. Yet, curiously enough, it seems that half a century elapsed after coke was used in drying malt before it was successfully tried in a blast-furnace. Meanwhile, at the end of the seventeenth century, the invention of a new reverberatory furnace for smelting the ores of lead, and later those of tin and copper, made it possible to substitute raw coal for charcoal in these metallurgical processes. The first recorded successful experiment in using coke for smelting iron ore was at Broseley, in Shropshire, in 1709 [16], but this experiment did not at once bring about any widespread introduction of mineral fuel into iron metallurgy. The problem of using something more than driblets of coal at the forges where pig iron was made into bars and rods remained to be solved. Until it was solved, the iron-works generally had to be grouped about the forests rather than about the expanding coal-mines. As the ironmasters required charcoal in large quantities for converting pig into bar iron, they may have felt that they might as well use it also in their blast-furnaces.

Some seventy years later, about 1784, Henry Cort (1740–1800) invented the so-called puddling process, in which the evolved heat of coal fuel was transmitted by reverberation to make pig iron into bar iron. This invention, combined with Cort's new method of finishing iron by passing it through grooved rolls, ensured the triumph of coal in iron metallurgy. Puddling made it possible to eliminate the deleterious sulphur from the iron.

Some 200 years elapsed, then, between the time at which the technical problem of substituting coal for wood fuel was first raised in an acute form and the actual effective union of coal and iron. It seems to have been, above all, the advent of a coal-burning economy in Britain, beginning at the turn of the sixteenth and seventeenth centuries, which brought about the union.[1] The need that arose about 1600 for substituting coal, cheap near the mines and anywhere near navigable water, for wood, cheap only at great distances from the principal markets for iron, provided an unprecedented stimulus for technical inventions of new kinds. The fact that this need was felt at the same time in a host of other industrial processes focused the attention of inventors on the various problems of substituting coal for wood. In the long run, it provided inventors with a wide range of experience on which they could draw for the knowledge they needed to solve the especially difficult and complicated problems presented by the substitution of coal for charcoal in iron-metallurgy.

IV. COAL MINING AND TRANSPORT

The need for digging and transporting coal in far greater quantities than ever before, caused by the expansion in demand at the juncture of the sixteenth and seventeenth centuries, made acute two other technical problems, whose eventual solution precipitated the industrial revolution 200 years afterwards. One was the drainage of mines at a considerable depth. Flooded pits had plagued the miners of central Europe even before the first Elizabethan age. During the late fifteenth and early sixteenth centuries there was a great increase in the demand for

---

[1] To some extent, however, the advent in seventeenth-century Britain of a coal-burning economy might be represented as delaying the solution of the problems of smelting iron ore with coal. The adoption of coal in so many other industries reduced the pressure on the English forests for wood fuel, and perhaps encouraged ironmasters to persist in the use of charcoal.

copper, and for the silver which was being obtained for the first time from argentiferous copper ores. This led to more intensive mining in central Europe, and ingenious engines for raising water were devised, notably in Hungary. Some of these engines had come into fairly common use in Germany and the adjacent countries to the east and south in the time of Agricola, whose celebrated post-humous treatise on mining and metallurgy, *De re metallica*, appeared in 1556 (vol II, p 13). The machinery for drainage, like the machinery that moved the

FIGURE 45—*Horse-whim haulage machine used at Newcastle-upon-Tyne. 1773.*

most powerful bellows and the heaviest hammers in the metallurgical works, and like that which raised salt water from the brine-springs at the principal salt works, was driven by horses or by the force of moving or falling water.

Until after the Reformation Britain was backward compared with the leading continental countries in the use of such power-driven machines. During the last half of the sixteenth century Englishmen travelled abroad, especially in Germany, in search of technical knowledge that could be used in mining as well as in metallurgy. Foreign mining-experts from central Europe came to Britain to instruct the English and the Scots (p 63). Models of the most ingenious engines known hitherto in Hungary, Bohemia, Saxony, and the Harz were set up for inspection in some mining centres in Great Britain, notably at Wollaton on the outskirts of Nottingham.

By the end of the sixteenth century it was becoming plain that the early sources of power for driving machinery—wind, water, and animals—would prove inadequate to meet the special problems of draining flooded coal-pits which the unprecedented growth of coal-mining in England presented. Silver-bearing ores owed their value mainly to their scarcity. In connexion with these ores, the new horse- and water-driven engines, introduced in mining and especially in metallurgy at the beginning of the sixteenth century in central Europe, proved economical for a time, partly because the silver and copper fetched good prices, until the inflow of American silver during the second half of the sixteenth century depressed the markets. Coal, on the other hand, owed its new-found value mainly to its abundance. Mine-owners in Britain were staggered, as their continental predecessors had never been, by the cost of drainage even when they copied the most advanced continental methods. It was difficult to produce coal for long at a profit when it was necessary to maintain many squads of horses to drive the engines (figure 45), or, in lieu of horses, to divert streams and even rivers from their courses and dam up water to drive such engines. It was more difficult in mining than in metallurgy to make this substitution, because the water-power for driving the hammers at metallurgical works could be concentrated, as the water-power for driving drainage-machinery at coal-mines could not, for a fairly long stretch of time at a single place. In short, the costs of the older sources of power for driving machinery were rendered almost prohibitively high in connexion with such a product as coal, widely considered so objectionable and vile that the greatest English poet made his characters shun Master Seacoal[1] whenever he appeared on the stage. Consequently, the pressure that a coal-economy exercised for the discovery of a new source of power capable of cheapening the costs of machinery was unprecedented.

At their wits' end to deal successfully with the problems of flooded coal-mines, mining-experts began to turn to the knowledge which had long existed that power might be generated by a jet of steam. At the very beginning of the seventeenth century in England, and to a lesser extent on the continent, some persons set about trying to apply this force of steam to solve the new difficulties of draining coal-mines. Attempt after attempt was made throughout the country. As one colliery expert remarked almost a hundred years after the treatises of Sturtevant and Rovenzon were printed, and after experiments with steam were tried, whoever discovered a practical, workable steam-engine to help the mine-owners to drain their pits was sure to be rewarded so handsomely that he could set up in London with his coach and six [17].

[1] 'Much Ado about Nothing.'

He had hardly written those words when primitive steam-engines were in fact installed in collieries, first in Staffordshire about 1712. They spread thence quickly to other parts of the British Isles, and to the continent. It was, however, not until seventy-five years later—not until the widespread application of Watt's invention of a rotary engine in the 1780s—that steam-power began to come into general use for driving machinery in manufactures. The preliminary experiments at the beginning of the seventeenth century brought about by the early, precocious expansion of the British coal industry, were no less essential a preparation for the invention of the steam-engine than for the union of iron and coal.

Similar problems of meeting high costs with a commodity that fetched such a

FIGURE 46—*Horse-tram used at Newcastle-upon-Tyne. 1773.*

small price as coal created a need for cheaper means of transport, especially over land. The relative advantages of water- over land-transport for so bulky and cumbersome a commodity as coal were even greater at the beginning of the seventeenth century than at the beginning of the twentieth. But with the exhaustion of the most favourably situated surface-seams that accompanied the fuller exploitation of coal-mines, it was necessary to mine large quantities of coal some distance from harbours or navigable rivers. This led to the perfection of a new means of transport over land.

Between 1598 and 1606 wooden rails were joined to the ground and a semi-permanent way was thus created from collieries at Wollaton to the river Trent, and from collieries at Broseley to the Severn [18]. These rails were apparently laid along an inclined way so that wagons loaded with coal at the pit's mouth could be run along them to the wharves where the river ships loaded, the empty wagons being hauled back along the rails by horses.

The idea of the railway may have been derived by Elizabethan Englishmen from Germany where, at the time of the silver- and copper-mining boom of the early sixteenth century, blocks of wood had been laid for short distances of some metres at certain metal-mines in central Europe, and wagons with a pin underneath to keep the wheels from slipping off the track had been pushed to the furnaces by hand. But the use of what were called tilting-rails was an English invention. It was prompted by the novel need for moving certain dirty, cheap commodities in ever-increasing quantities. By the eighteenth century, horse-drawn railways were used for hauling coal to the rivers and harbours in all the principal coalfields in Britain (figure 46). At about this time an attempt was made to introduce such rails into Germany, and it is significant that in the Ruhr at the end of the eighteenth century the innovation was known as an *englischer Kohlenweg*. The railway in its modern form was an English idea, developed by long-forgotten special technicians at coal-mines, more than two centuries before steam-engines—likewise invented because of the pressure of coal-mining problems—were introduced to haul the wagons.

V. COAL AND THE DEVELOPMENT OF TECHNOLOGY

As previously mentioned, the rise of the British coal industry at the end of Elizabeth I's reign was of capital importance in raising problems whose solution led almost inevitably to the industrial revolution. The wholesale use of coal in iron metallurgy made possible the utilization of iron and eventually of steel for machinery, and for construction-work of many kinds. Steam-driven machinery, when applied to manufacture as well as to mining, led men a long way in the direction of the machine-economy characteristic of the world in which we live. Traction on rails, when combined with the steam-engine for haulage, transformed both the movement of freight and the movement of travellers over ground. The entire system of canals, developed in England during the second half of the eighteenth century, was planned and executed primarily to permit the transport of coal at a low cost to those parts of the country where it was most needed. While the potential heat stored up in coal could be carried in a more concentrated form than that stored in firewood and other combustible materials, coal was a very bulky material, nasty as well as expensive to handle without the power-driven machinery whose development coal was stimulating. So, as Mantoux wrote fifty years ago: 'The more we study the history of communications by water in England, the more do we realize how closely it was interwoven with the history of coal' [19].

Before the end of the eighteenth century, therefore, coal had entered into the blood-stream of economic life, as a force that was helping to move technological endeavour in novel directions unknown to the technicians of any earlier society.

While the coal industry of Britain dwarfed that of other countries during the seventeenth and eighteenth centuries, coal was by no means without its technological influence at this time in continental Europe. As early as 1638 a tract on canal-building by a man named Lamberville appeared in France [20]. In it the author advocated the construction of canals partly as a means of carrying fuel, particularly coal, from one part of France to another. By the beginning of the eighteenth century the advantages of coal as a fuel, in spite of its nauseous properties, had begun to impress men in all the leading European countries, and overseas in North America. Technological development, in imitation of England —*à l'imitation de l'Angleterre*—became a kind of watchword among the French, and gradually among the Germans, the Dutch, the Belgians, and, finally, the Spaniards. Foreigners—at first especially Frenchmen—paid visits to Britain for the purpose of studying the new technology, which they realized was based in no small measure upon the precocious exploitation of the British coal-mines. Ticquet, whose observations remain in manuscript [21], anticipated to some extent the more celebrated work of Jars, a French government official who travelled all over Europe and published in the 1760s his *Voyages métallurgiques*. It was apparently not until the first decade of the eighteenth century, 100 years after the invention had been made in England, that French glass-manufacturers adopted coal-burning furnaces. In the meantime, the English seem to have greatly improved these furnaces, so that the coal fires were less damaging to the materials than they had been in the beginning. The result had been a new kind of glass, of British invention, called flint-glass (p 221). The French, with their predilection for quality, had been developing the aesthetic aspect of technology, and in glass-making as in other industries a bridge was thrown across the Channel by the attention that British inventors were beginning to pay to substance and appearance in the commodities they turned out in coal fires. During the eighteenth century, and especially during its second half, the continental peoples adopted one English technical process after another. By the end of the century they had in many cases begun to improve upon them. Had it not been for the French Revolution and the Napoleonic wars, it is conceivable that they might at this time have forged ahead of Britain even in the technological development that owed its strength to the use of coal fuel.

When the nineteenth century opened, coal had become a great driving-force in technological development throughout western Europe and overseas in North America. It was at about the close of the eighteenth century and the beginning of the nineteenth that scientific thinking began to concern itself for the first time with problems arising out of the treatment of coal and the saving of fuel. Once science had supplied general principles, the opportunities for technological advance in the mining, the transport, and the treatment of coal—as well as in the saving of fuel—multiplied rapidly.

During the first sixty years or so of the nineteenth century, Britain retained the lead in the development and exploitation of coal resources that she had gained much earlier. With the practical application of the theories of free trade derived from Adam Smith, an immense new market was opened to British coal during the twenties and thirties of the nineteenth century. Exports multiplied fifty-fold, and more, in sixty years. Other countries of Europe were obtaining from England the fuel that their own mines were sluggish in supplying. Meanwhile, Europe and to some extent the rest of the world were overtaking Britain in the development of their own coal-mines and of technical inventions stimulated by the expanding mining industry.

In the 1860s, Jevons, in his book 'The Coal Question', stated clearly that coal was the great resource on which industrial civilization had been reared. He saw that the supremacy of Britain in industry and technology had been based on coal, and that, as a result of the limitations of the natural coal resources of the British Isles, this supremacy was bound to diminish and eventually to disappear. What he failed to recognize was that the world was entering an age in which the resources of scientific discovery would be able to create new sources of power for technological development, alternative to the coal resources. The last century has not only been a period in which British supremacy in connexion with the mining and the use of coal has been lost: it has also been a period in which the place of coal in industrial civilization has steadily diminished in importance.

REFERENCES

[1] COLLINGWOOD, R. G. and MYERS, J. N. L. 'Roman Britain and the English Settlements' (2nd ed.), pp. 231–2. Clarendon Press, Oxford. 1937.

[2] READ, T. T. *Trans. Newcomen Soc.*, **20**, 132–3, 1939–40.

[3] LEJEUNE, J. 'La formation du capitalisme moderne dans la principauté de Liége au seizième siècle', p. 133. Bibliothèque de la Faculté de Philosophie et Lettres de l'Université de Liége, Paris. 1939.

[4] POSTAN, M. and RICH, E. E. 'The Cambridge Economic History of Europe', Vol. 2, pp. 472–3. University Press, Cambridge. 1952.

[5] NEF, J. U. 'The Rise of the British Coal Industry', Vol. 1, p. 21. Routledge, London. 1932.

[6] *Idem. J. polit. Econ.*, **44**, 662–9, 1936.

[7] EVELYN, JOHN. '*Fumifugium*; or, the inconvenience of the aer and smoak of London dissipated. Together with some remedies humbly proposed.' London. 1661.

[8] NEF, J. U. See ref. [5], Vol. 1, pp. 29–30, 123–30. (In saying 'five times as much', I have allowed not only for the coal of continental Europe, but for that of China and North America in the later seventeenth century.)

[9] *Idem. Econ. Hist. Rev.*, **7,** 180, 1937.
     Idem. See ref. [5], Vol. 1, pp. 158–61, 163–4, 192–6.

[10] *Idem. Econ. Hist. Rev.*, **5,** 16, 1934.

[11] PLOT, R. 'Natural History of Staffordshire', pp. 161–4. Oxford. 1686.
     NEF, J. U. See ref. [5], Vol. 1, p. 250.
     JENKINS, R. *Trans. Newcomen Soc.*, **6,** 60, 1925–6.

[12] NEF, J. U. See ref. [5], Vol. 1, p. 215.

[13] Calendar of State Papers Domestic 1636–7, p. 415. Record Commission, London.

[14] NEF, J. U. See ref. [5], Vol. 1, p. 247.

[15] *Idem. Ibid.*, Vol. 1, pp. 215–16.

[16] ASHTON, T. S. 'Iron and Steel in the Industrial Revolution' (2nd ed.). University of Manchester Economic History Series, No. 2. University Press, Manchester. 1951.

[17] J. C. 'The Compleat Collier', p. 22. London. 1708.

[18] NEF, J. U. See ref. [5], Vol. 1, pp. 244–5.

[19] MANTOUX, P. 'The Industrial Revolution in the Eighteenth Century' (rev. ed., Eng. trans. by MARJORIE VERNON), p. 111. Bedford Series of Economic Handbooks, Vol. 1. Cape, London. 1928.

[20] LAMBERVILLE, C. 'Alphabet des terres à brusler et à charbon de forge.' Paris. 1638.

[21] Archives Nationales, Paris, MS. O¹ 1293.

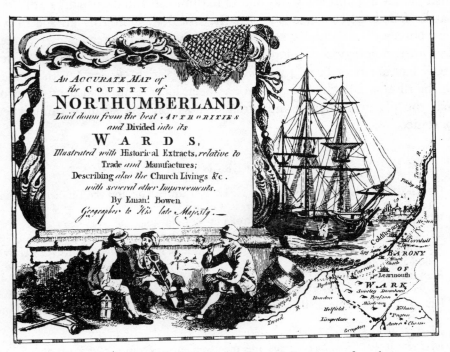

Miners and seamen, with a collier in the background. From a map of c 1760.

4

WINDMILLS

REX WAILES

W ITH the invention of the *wipmolen* (hollow post-mill, p 94) in the Low Countries in the fifteenth century the main types of mill were established, but it was not until the end of the sixteenth century that drawings illustrating the mechanical details of windmills first appeared. They are contained in Ramelli's work of 1588 [1] and show post- and tower-mills for grinding corn and a tower-mill using a chain of pots for raising water, though not for drainage (figures 47, 48). The drawings are a distinct advance over the fanciful sketches in earlier publications purporting to describe machines. Ramelli's designs are practicable and show sufficient detail to satisfy most main questions of construction and mechanism.

Yet it was not until the beginning of the eighteenth century that any specification was published complete and detailed enough to enable a windmill to be built from it. This was contained in the second edition of a work by Mathurin Jousse [2] published in 1702. The plates are poor, but in 1765 Diderot [3] quoted this section of Jousse in full and illustrated it with five fine plates (figure 49), inspired no doubt by earlier publications in Amsterdam [4]. In complete contrast to Jousse, who relied on elaborate verbal description and shows very little detail in his drawings, these Dutch books reduce description to a minimum and all details are included in the drawings (figure 59), from which numbers of mills were built throughout the country. Jousse and the authors of the Dutch books on mills (including Linperch, a Swede) were all practical men, and their books, with that of Ramelli and archaic survivals of mills to the present day, enable us to follow the development of windmill construction and mechanism in detail.

The first mills were crude affairs, driving a single pair of stones (vol II, pp 623–8). Some had their substructures sunk in the earth of an artificial mound and were called sunk post-mills (figure 50). Examples have been recorded in the U.S.S.R., in Lancashire, and in Long Island, U.S.A., and remains have been excavated from time to time in England [5]. Probably the crudest post-mills still extant are the variety known in west Brittany as *chandeliers*, of which a handful remain, while a few survive in the islands of the Baltic, in north Spain, and in the Canary Islands. The post is embedded in a solid masonry base, and the Breton mills are so small that the miller can tend the single pair of stones only with the door open [6].

By the sixteenth century, post-mills were being built to drive two pairs of

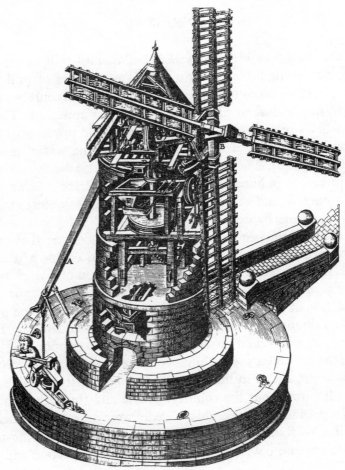

FIGURE 47—*Corn-grinding tower-mill, from Ramelli (1588). Note the threading of the sail-cloth between the sail-bars, the rollers centring and supporting the cap, and the portable winch for hauling round the tail-pole.*

stones placed fore-and-aft in the mill, and a few of that period still survive; before that time a single pair of stones only was driven, placed in the breast of the mill.

The weight of the mill is taken by the upright post which is placed somewhat in advance of the centre-line of the mill and rests on two horizontal intersecting cross-trees supported at their ends by brick or stone piers (plate 5 A). The weight is transferred to the outer ends of the cross-trees, and hence the piers, by diagonal struts or quarter-bars. In England these struts were single, but on the continent they were invariably doubled; that this was so from the earliest times

FIGURE 48—*Corn-grinding post-mill, from Ramelli (1588). The tail-pole has a winch attached and the quarter-bars are doubled as is usual on the continent of Europe.*

can be seen from contemporary manuscripts of English and continental origin. In some cases, as in Picardy, post-mills were provided with four cross-trees and no fewer than sixteen quarter-bars [7], but in England no more than three cross-trees and six quarter-bars were provided, and even that number only seldom.

Very unusual substructures were to be seen in Russia, consisting of an almost solid mass of unsawn timbers (figure 55).

On top of the post of a post-mill rests the horizontal crown-tree spanning the whole width of the mill-body (plate 4 A), whose frame is based upon it. An early method of framing was to attach to each end of the crown-tree vertical struts,

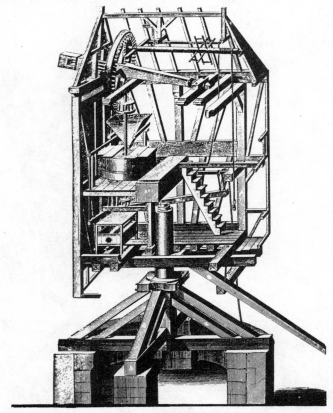

FIGURE 49—*Post-mill as described by Jousse (1702). Note the sack-hoist (in the roof) and bolter* (bottom left).

which extended upwards to the level of the eaves of the roof and downwards to the level of the first floor of the mill; these struts carried horizontal timbers terminating at the corner-posts of the body. In the method of construction seen in most surviving post-mills, however, two heavy horizontal side-girts (French *sommiers*) are supported by the ends of the crown-tree and in turn carry the corner-posts at their ends. The heavy breast-beam across the front of the mill at the level of the eaves and taking the weight of the sails is supported at its ends by the front corner-posts and at the centre by a prick-post. Just below the first floor of the mill are two heavy parallel timbers called sheers, running fore-and-aft the full length of the mill on either side of the post. At their ends they support the horizontal transverse timbers, at floor level, joining the lower ends of the front corner-posts carrying the prick-post. Immediately fore-and-aft of the main post two spacers were fitted and with the sheers formed a vertical steady bearing at this point, which prevented the mill from swaying about on top of the post. An additional framed bearing or collar next below the sheers was often used to form a horizontal bear-ing for the same purpose.

The subsidiary framing of the mill was carried out in accordance with local tradition, vertical members suitably cross-braced being employed in England and diagonal members on the continent, but local variations are numerous. In Flan-ders, mills dating from the Spanish occu-pation can be distinguished by such details [8]. Horizontal weatherboarding was favoured as a cover for the framing in England (figure 51), but shingles were used in France and vertical boarding was preferred elsewhere. In England the boarding was tarred or painted white, and in parts of the Netherlands fancy designs in various colours were, and often are, painted on the vertical boarding; elsewhere the timber was left untreated.

FIGURE 50—*Russian sunk post-mill with buried substructure, and six boarded sails.*

The early post-mills had straight-pitched roofs, but subsequently curved roofs in England, and ogee and mansard roofs on the continent, accommodated the more massive gearing inside. Bodies were at first small, but as mills were built with larger sails the bodies also were made larger, and some of the smaller mills were extended a foot or two at the rear to help to balance the heavier sails, to accommodate an additional pair of stones in the tail, and to provide more storage space.

The substructure in England was in later times frequently enclosed by a round-house, which served the double purpose of protecting the substructure and providing additional space for storage. In eastern and southern England it had no structural significance, but in the north-east and the midlands it was frequently provided on the top of its circular wall with a track on which skids or rollers ran. This arrangement prevented undue pitching in a gusty wind. On the continent the round-house seems to have been much favoured in the Low Countries but less often elsewhere. That it was a comparatively late introduction is evident from old prints; it was frequently added to mills up to quite recent times. There is at present no reliable evidence of a round-house earlier than the

FIGURE 51—*Weatherboarded post-mill, with round-house built round the substructure. Note fantail on tail-ladder and 'patent' sails. Friston, Suffolk.*

eighteenth century, although during and after that time a number are coeval with the mill.

A well designed and well built round-house was an asset and, incidentally, not seldom improved the appearance of the mill. Those built of timber often became shabby, but in England, when local stone or brick and tiles were used, the building was weatherproof and most pleasing.

The *wipmolen* (hollow post-mill), born of the necessity to drain the Low Countries by a power greater than that of the muscles of men or beasts, was a tremendous step forward, for it established the use of an indirect drive from the sails to the water-raising scoop-wheel by means of an upright shaft. This shaft had to pass down through the built-up hollow post of the movable mill-body to the fixed portion of the mill below, where the gears that drove the scoop-wheel were housed. Later this type of mill was developed for grinding corn, and in the Loire valley a distinct variety was developed known as the *cavier* [9]. Elsewhere the *wipmolen* seems to have found scant favour outside the Netherlands.

The most primitive tower-mills are today to be found round the coasts of the Mediterranean (vol II, figure 566), in the Iberian peninsula, and in Brittany. They drive a single pair of stones and are crudely but sturdily built. It is noteworthy that the earliest illustration of a tower-mill (French, fifteenth century) shows one which appears to be of superior external design to those mentioned. The essentials of a tower-mill are a fixed tower and a movable cap mounted on it carrying the sails. Both local and imported materials were used to build the towers; besides being built of brick and stone, they were also of timber where it was grown or could be imported easily. Thus we find timber-built mills in England, northern Europe, the Low Countries, and the United States. The majority of surviving timber-built tower-mills in the Netherlands date from the seventeenth century to the nineteenth, when the Baltic trade was considerable

FIGURE 52—*Octagonal timber smock-mill. Note the gallery, fantail, and 'patent' sails. Cranbrook, Kent.*

[10] and the country wealthy; the lavish use of heavy timber is most marked. Timber-framed tower-mills are typically covered with horizontal weatherboarding in England, reed-thatch in the Netherlands, and wooden shingles in Flanders and the United States.

In England these timber tower-mills were frequently painted white, were usually octagonal (figure 52), and were known as smock-mills from their resemblance to the old countryman's smock-frock. It is difficult to render the corners of such a weatherboarded mill weather-tight, and deterioration was much more rapid than with the reed-thatched mills of the Netherlands. Brick tower-mills in England were frequently tarred to prevent wet from penetrating the brickwork (figure 53), but this practice was not in vogue elsewhere. Round brick towers as well as the octagonal wooden ones were usually given a taper or batter from

bottom to top, although this was by no means invariable. It prevented the tower
becoming unduly distorted and also gave increased room at the base where it was
most needed. In France and the countries of southern Europe this practice was
not followed, and the walls of the towers are proportionately thicker to withstand

the weight of the cap and sails. In Brittany
short two-storeyed stone-built mills of a
type known locally as *petit pied* or *ventru*
[10] actually have an oversailing upper
floor, larger in diameter by several feet than
the ground floor, and walls of a thickness
up to 4 ft 6 in. Some *petit pied* mills are
of great age, one at Paclais (near Savenay,
Loire-Inférieure) dating from 1340, though
it has been largely rebuilt (figure 54). In
south-west Spain towers with equally thick
walls of rubble were built round two
parallel arches which supported the upper
floor.

As the tower-mill became higher it
proved necessary to build a stage round it,
so that the sails could be reached without
a ladder (figures 52, 53, 57) and the length
of tail-poles (in the Netherlands) kept
within bounds. Most stages were of timber,
but a few in England were of iron, where
galleries were also sometimes constructed

FIGURE 53—*Brick tower-mill, with gallery, fantail, and eight sails, at Heckington, Lincolnshire.*

round the caps. While the stages are attractive and useful, the galleries spoil
both the appearance and the air-flow behind the sails.

On the top of all towers is a track or curb on which the cap turns. In primitive
mills this was and is of unfaced wood; the cap slides round on it on wood skids,
being centred by similar skids bearing on the side of the curb. Later types of
these 'dead curbs' were faced with iron on top and side, and iron blocks ran on
them. Ramelli (figure 47) shows an independent ring of rollers inserted between
the cap and the curb, and rollers fixed to the cap centring it, while the Dutch mill-
books show similar roller-rings in use in *paltrok* mills (figure 59 and p 106).
These are known as 'shot curbs'. In the Netherlands fairly large wooden rollers
(about 7 inches in diameter by 7 inches in face) were used, while in England
cast iron rollers of about half this size were normal practice. In England, how-

ever, the 'shot curb' was not very popular, a modified form, the 'live curb', being preferred. In this type, iron rollers were fixed to the cap itself and ran on the track on the curb. The later curbs in England were of iron, cast in segments and held to the tower with anchor bolts.

The caps of tower-mills are often as distinctive of the region to which they belong as are the head-dresses of the countrywomen in Brittany or the Nether- lands. Thus in south-eastern England the typical cap resembles the curved roof of an English post-mill (figure 52); in Norfolk it is of a neat boat-shape; in the north-west it is of a much larger boat- shape, and in the north-east and midlands an ogee, a shape also found in Den- mark, Sweden, and Germany (figure 53). There are similar variations in other parts of Europe, the conical cap being favoured in France and the south generally.

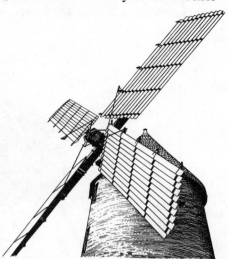

The post-mill was turned into the eye of the wind manually, by pushing against a long tail-pole, which was attached to the body of the mill and extended downwards at an angle, passing through the ladder at the back of the mill (figures

FIGURE 54—*Raised* petit pied *mill with Berton sails (open) at Savenay, Loire-Inférieure, France.*

49, 55). In England the ladder normally rested on the ground and acted as a back stay, restraining the mill from pitching when at work; it therefore had to be raised off the ground before the mill could be turned. This was done by a lever pivoted on the tail-pole, one end of which was connected by chains to the bottom of the ladder. By pulling on the other end of the lever the ladder could be raised, and when this was done the lever was held in place parallel to the tail-pole by an iron pin; the mill could then be pushed round with the tail- pole. An alternative method was to fix a cart-wheel to the tail-pole, leaving the ladder permanently clear of the ground (figure 48). In Flanders two hinged struts on the tail-pole were used to steady the mill, while in Prussia wooden poles were wedged between the rear corner-posts and the ground for the same purpose, the ladder of the continental mill not resting on the ground.

If the mill is well balanced and well maintained it is not difficult to push round by hand, but mechanical aids were not despised. The earliest was a portable ungeared winch, which could be anchored to one of a number of posts set round the mill (figure 47). A chain or rope was run out from the winch to the tail-pole and wound up on the winch, thus turning the mill; later the winch was fitted to the tail-pole itself.

With the introduction of improved metallurgical techniques in the mid-eighteenth century it became possible to cast gears of iron. This opened the way to improvements in turning the mill. Hand-winches were geared, and in 1745 Edmund Lee patented the automatic fantail [11] (figure 51) (erroneously

FIGURE 55—*Russian post-mill on massive timber substructure. The wind-shaft, carrying six boarded sails, is mounted in the lower right-hand corner of the body, and drives upward.*

attributed to Andrew Meikle). This device consists of a jack or fly at first mounted on a carriage at the end of the tail-pole which, through iron gears and shafts giving a very considerable reduction in speed, drives two road-wheels running on a track set round the mill, a subsidiary track being provided for smaller wheels supporting the base of the ladder. As long as the mill faces square into the eye of the wind the vanes of the fantail, usually six or eight, present their edges to the wind, but when the wind changes direction it strikes the vanes at an angle and turns them, thus turning the mill until it faces squarely into the wind once more.

It was found that when the fantail was mounted on the end of the tail-pole it would sometimes act as a weather-vane in strong gusts, so in East Anglia the tail-pole was usually cut short and the fan-carriage mounted on the end of the ladder. A few post-mills had fantails mounted on their roofs, driving down either to wheels on the bottom of the ladder, or to a worm-wheel mounted on the post just below the bottom floor of the mill.

The tail-pole was also used to 'wind' the caps of tower-mills (figures 52, 53). In France, and in southern Europe generally, it is fixed to the inside of the cap without external bracing, and this method is shown in the early illuminated manuscripts. In England, the Netherlands, and northern Europe, however, it is customary for external bracing to be used.[1] Movable ungeared winches and geared winches fixed to the tail-pole were used, and the winch was also transferred to the cap itself, operated either from inside as in the Netherlands, or from the ground by endless chain and gearing engaging with a rack fixed to the curb on the top of the mill-tower as in England. From the latter method the fantail drive was but a step; however, the fantail did not spread from England to Denmark and north-western Europe until about a century after its invention, and is not generally to be met with on the continent south of the two northern provinces of the Netherlands. Its use relieves the miller of much hard work and enables him to leave the mill unattended when not working. Its one disadvantage is the risk of 'tail-winding' if a thunderstorm passes closely over the mill, for it is not an easy matter to turn the cap quickly by hand when any form of reduction-gearing is used.

The early sails [12] were flat frameworks, inclined at an angle, over which cloths were spread or else laced in and out of the bars of the sail-frames (figures 47, 48). Very primitive forms of sail are still to be found in Brittany built of un-sawn timber, in which the absence of a hem-lath, connecting the bars at their outer ends, makes the sail appear like a comb. Another primitive type found in Sweden, and until recently in Germany, had removable boards, instead of sail-cloths, fitted to sail-frames, while in the U.S.S.R. sails were made of a number of light wooden boards running the full length of the sail (figures 50, 55). The Dutch mill-books yield the earliest information on the twist or 'weather' that is a feature of the cloth-covered sails we know, with the cloths spread over the surface of the sail and not laced in and out of the bars.

The sail-cloths are attached to rings running along a bar on the inner end of the sail. When the cloths are not in use they are furled to one side, wound up like a rope, and tied to a sail-bar near the outer end of the sail. To set the cloths each sail is brought round to the bottom position in turn, the cloth is unwound, and looped cords on the selvedge are slipped over wooden cleats on the leading

---

[1] In the Mediterranean area caps are often turned from within by means of a crowbar and a series of holes round the curb.

edge of the sail-frame. The cloth is then pulled across the sail-frame by means of
four cords, called pointing-lines, attached to the selvedge. By them the cloth can
be set to 'sword-point', 'dagger-point', 'first reef', and 'full sail', according to
the wind and the power required.

The sail-frames consist of horizontal bars mortised into a main timber back-
bone called a whip and connected at their outer ends by hem-laths. In primitive
sails there is sail-area on both sides of the whip. In England, the Low Countries,
and parts of northern Europe the single-sided sail was developed, having sail-
area on the trailing side of the whip only and a leading-board on the leading side;
in the Netherlands this design was carried to a high pitch of efficiency. Near the
sea in the Iberian peninsula, and in the eastern Mediterranean, triangular jib-
sails are used. No sail-frame is provided, the cloths being wrapped round radial
poles; the required amount of sail is unwound and braced to the tip of the
next pole. A bowsprit extends forwards from the centre and the tips of the poles
themselves are braced to it, any number of sails from eight to sixteen being used.

John Smeaton (1724–92) first investigated scientifically the design of windmill sails, experimenting with a whirling table and presenting his conclusions
to the Royal Society in 1759 [13]. His recommendations on angles of weather
were no doubt followed by millwrights to some extent, but, in England and the
Netherlands at least, most country millwrights followed their own traditional
practice, attained and modified empirically.

The difficulty of setting and shortening sail-cloths in uncertain weather led
to the invention of the spring-sail in England in 1772 by Andrew Meikle. He set
a number of hinged shutters in the sail-frame, connecting them together by a
bar and controlling the movement of the bar by a spring, the tension of which
could be varied by means of an adjusting mechanism at the tip of the sail. The
spring was adjusted to permit a certain wind-pressure to be used; when this
pressure was exceeded it overcame the resistance of the spring, and the shutters
opened and 'spilled the wind'. Once the spring adjustment had been made individually, the action of each sail was automatic and the sails were self-regulating;
but as the shuttered sail did not provide so much power as the cloth-covered sail,
to whose 'weather' it could only approximate, it was quite usual to drive a mill
with two spring-sails and two common sails to make the best of both methods.

In 1789 Stephen Hooper of Margate, Kent, invented his roller-reefing sail.
In place of the shutters of the spring-sail small roller-blinds were fitted, and all
the operating rods of all the sails were connected by cranks and levers to a
spider-coupling at the centre. A hole was bored through the wind-shaft carrying
the sails and a rod passed through it, connected at the front to the spider-coupling

and at the rear to a rack and pinion and a chain-wheel around which passed an endless chain hanging down to the ground. By this means it was possible to open and close all the roller-blinds in all the sails simultaneously without stopping the mill. The inventor claimed that the blinds operated automatically while the mill was at work, but in practice this did not happen. Such sails were used in Kent, Lincolnshire, and Yorkshire.

In 1807 William Cubitt (1785–1861) combined the shutters of Meikle's spring-sail with the remote control of Hooper's roller-reefing sail, to devise what has always been called the 'patent' sail (figures 51, 52, 53). Its operation is truly automatic, the sails being controlled by hanging weights on one side of the control chain; the heavier the weight the greater the wind-pressure required to open the shutters and spill the wind. By hanging the weights on the other side of the chain the shutters can be held open. Shuttered sails may have shutters on both sides of the whip or on the trailing (or 'driving') side only. If well designed the single-shuttered sails will start more readily at low wind-velocities and some sails have been converted from double to single for this reason.

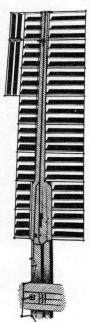

FIGURE 56—*A sail fitted with Catchpole's air-brake. This is formed by the two longitudinal shutters attached at the side of the main frame of the sail. From a post-mill at Gedding, Suffolk.*

About 1860 Catchpole, a millwright of Sudbury in Suffolk, devised the first air-brake (figure 56). He fitted two longitudinal shutters on the leading edges of 'patent' sails parallel to the whip and at right-angles to the main shutters. These when closed gave additional sail-area, but when opened spoiled the air-flow and acted as a brake. The idea was used, though sparingly, in Suffolk, Lincolnshire, and Yorkshire only, but was revived in the Netherlands in the 1920s.

At about the same time a miller at Haverhill in Suffolk designed the first annular sail, of 50-ft diameter with shutters operating like those in a 'patent' sail (figure 57). Four such sails operated successfully in East Anglia and were the precursors of the American wind-pumps, of which a variety of types was produced.

In France, about 1840, the Berton sail was invented [14]. This is a cheaply built, non-automatic sail with remote control which can be operated from inside the mill while it is at work. It consists of a number of wooden slats operating like a parallel rule; when open they present an unbroken rectangular surface with a constant angle of weather and when closed nest up one behind the other. The Berton sail was widely used and is still to be found in France (figure 54).

The wind-shaft carrying the sails is set in the top of the mill-body in post-mills and in the cap in tower-mills [15]. The shaft is normally inclined upwards at an angle of between 5° and 10° so that the sails may clear the lower part of the mill, that they may be more easily balanced on the shaft about the neck-bearing immediately behind the sails, and that a thrust-bearing can be provided at the

FIGURE 57—*Tower-mill with annular sail at Haverhill, Suffolk. The gallery and fantail are visible.*

tail of the shaft. The first wind-shafts were of wood, and at the nose of the shaft mortices accommodated two heavy timber stocks at right-angles. These projected equally on each side; they were wedged in place and each carried two sails, the whips of which were bolted and clamped to them. In the Netherlands whips are dispensed with, and the sail-bars are mortised into the stocks themselves, while the primitive sails in Brittany have the ends of the whips wedged into the wind-shaft and no stocks. Rotting of the nose of the wind-shaft was a constant trouble, not overcome until cast iron shafts were introduced by John

Smeaton. Preferring five sails to four he devised an alternative method of mounting them on a cast iron hub with arms, known as a cross, fixed to the nose of the wind-shaft. The size of the whips was increased and they were bolted and strapped to the cross. The use of this much superior method was confined to the area roughly to the north and west of Cambridge in England and to a few examples on the continent. Elsewhere in England and Europe iron poll-ends, like two boxes at right-angles with their ends knocked out, were fitted to the wooden shafts, or iron shafts incorporating poll-ends were installed.

Since the use of eight to sixteen jib-sails has been mentioned it should also be noted that mills with six common sails (figures 50, 55) were in use in the Mediterranean area and in Russia, while in western Europe the multi-sailed mill had a vogue only in England, and then only where the cross was adopted. Six sails were most favoured, but five-sailed mills were not uncommon, and at least seven eight-sailed mills are known to have been built (figure 53).

The journals of wooden wind-shafts consist of wrought iron strips sunk flush in the timber and looking not unlike the commutator of a direct-current electric motor, but in many cases iron tail-ends as well as poll-ends have been fitted to wooden shafts. The thrust-bearing on a wooden shaft is an iron ring on the back face, and when a cast iron tail-end is fitted the thrust is taken by a small flange at the tip of the journal. The early bearings were of wood or stone and these materials are successfully used today; the neck-bearings have a circumferential contact of about one-quarter to one-third. Brass bearings came to be used with cast iron journals in England, and a neck-bearing is called a 'neck-brass' in England but a *marbre* in France. A refinement to be found in East Anglia is a self-aligning bearing housing on trunnions.

On the wind-shaft of the mill is mounted the brake-wheel (plate 4 B), so called because a contracting brake acts on its rim, and in some post-mills a similar but smaller wheel called the tail-wheel is mounted farther back on the wind-shaft. Where direct drive is employed both these wheels, which are face-gears on an inclined shaft, drive stones from above or 'overdrift' through a pinion called a stone-nut. Where indirect drive is employed the brake-wheel drives the 'wallower' (the first driven wheel in a mill), mounted on the upright shaft, and the stone-nuts are driven by the great-spur-wheel mounted lower down on the same shaft [16]. In the case of indirect drives the overdrift stones are driven by nuts mounted on 'quants', while if 'underdrift' the nuts are mounted on the 'stone spindles' which carry the runner-stone. In the U.S.S.R. some post-mills have the wind-shaft mounted low down in the bottom right-hand corner of the mill-body as viewed from the front of the sails, while the entrance to the mill-body is on the left-hand side and not at the rear. This implies a drive upwards, as in a water-mill (figure 55).

The primitive mills in Brittany have no brake and are stopped by being 'quartered', that is, turned till the sails are at 90° to the wind. Brakes are usually operated by heavy wooden levers, whose weight applies the brake which has to be hauled off. The brakes themselves are usually of wood, built up of curved sections connected with metal plates, but in England hoop iron is also used.

The first gears were 'compass-arm' wheels, two or three arms being mortised right through their wooden shafts. The teeth or cogs were crude pegs meshing with the round wooden staves of lantern pinions, which had wooden flanges top and bottom. Later the upper flange was dispensed with and pegs similar to those in the wheels were used. The bevel was not used until the advent of cast iron gears, and even so Smeaton's designs show no bevels in windmills. The compass-arm wheel weakened its shaft considerably, and at the beginning of the eighteenth century the clasp-arm wheel was introduced. Two intersecting pairs of arms form at the centre a square clasping the shaft, the wheel being centred by means of wedges. Iron brake-wheels are frequently cast in halves for ease of fitting, but iron wallowers at the top of upright shafts are in one piece (plate 5 B). Brake-wheels were also made with iron hubs and arms and wooden cants and rims. Wooden cogs were often sawn off brake-wheels and replaced with iron teeth cast in segments and bolted in their place. Iron upright shafts in tower-mills are almost always in two or more sections connected by dog-clutch couplings,[1] which provide a certain degree of self-alignment.

Great-spur-wheels are as diverse in construction as brake-wheels, while stone-nuts are sometimes made completely of wood, sometimes of iron with wooden cogs, and sometimes wholly of iron. They are disengaged from the great-spur-wheel in a number of ways. In an overdrive the top bearing of the quant is arranged so that the quant or the bearing can move sideways away from the wheel. In an underdrive several cogs of a wooden nut are made easily removable, and in the case of an iron nut a segment of the rim is sometimes detachable. More often, however, an iron nut is lifted clear of the great-spur-wheel by chains, a rack and pinion operating a ring from below, or a screw and ring.

The stone-spindle passes through a greased wooden bearing in the stationary or bed-stone and drives the upper or runner-stone, which is balanced on top of it (figure 58) [17]. It revolves on a thrust-bearing supported by a bridge-tree hinged at one end, which can be raised and lowered to adjust the gap between the stones. As speed varies the runner-stone tends to rise and fall and the bridge-tree is

---

[1] A dog-clutch consists of two opposed flanges carrying projections or slots.

adjusted accordingly by a compound lever, originally operated by hand and later automatically by a centrifugal governor, the initial setting of the gap being made with a hand-operated screw. While there are many exceptions, the governors are usually driven by a belt off the upright shaft in the case of overdrift stones and off the stone-spindles in the case of underdrift ones.

The stones are fed from grain contained in hoppers above their wooden casings, the grain passing to the stones down an inclined trough or 'shoe' agitated either by the quant or by an iron device known as a 'damsel', against either of which it is held by a spring. To warn the miller that the supply of grain in the hopper is low an alarm-bell is usually fitted in England, a sufficient weight

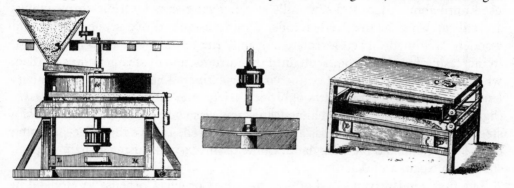

FIGURE 58—*View and partial section of underdrift millstones and gear. Note the weighted lever regulating the gap between the stones, and the hopper bell-alarm.* (Right) *Early cylindrical bolter.*

of grain on a strap in the hopper restraining a bell on a string from falling against some moving part of the machinery.

The hoppers for the stones of primitive mills were filled by hand from sacks or baskets, and before the sixteenth century there is no mention or illustration of a sack-hoist to fill storage bins above the hoppers. While hand-operated sack-hoists are still in use in France, in England power-driven hoists were the rule (plate 4 B). The drive is usually from a belt, normally slack, but tightened by raising one bearer of the hoisting-drum when required. This is effected by a cord passing down through all floors of the mill. The sack-chain, passing through double-flap trap-doors in all floors, is wound up on a drum.

In post-mills the chain-drum is in the ridge of the roof and the belt-drive is either direct from a pulley on the wind-shaft or from a gear- or friction-drive off the brake- or tail-wheel. In the case of tower-mills the belt-drive is usually derived from a countershaft driven by a bevel-wheel on the upright shaft. The common alternative is a friction-drive from below the wallower.

A number of auxiliary machines are to be found in corn-mills: of these the most common are bolters and 'wire-machines' to separate or dress the flour out of the meal. This was originally done by hand by a meal-man, and Jousse is the first to describe a bolter in a windmill (figure 58). Such machines are driven by pinions from one of the main gears of the mill, and usually the final drive is by belt. In the north of England groat-machines and 'jog-scrys' or sifters were used in the production of groats from oats roasted in kilns near by. In America corncob-crushers for extracting the grains of maize from their cobs were to be found, while in the Netherlands barley-mills to produce pearl barley are used. Oil-mills, operating drop-stamps by means of cams on the wind-shaft, were used until about 1940, and saw-mills working gang-saws by triple-throw cranks are still at work in the Netherlands. Drainage-mills drove scoop-wheels and wooden Archimedean screws (plate 20); only the former were used in England, in increasing numbers from 1588 until the introduction of steam-pumps in 1820, when within 130 years they became virtually extinct. The decline in the Netherlands has been less rapid, although one variety, the miniature skeleton *tjasker* (figure 204), in which the Archimedean screw was coupled direct to the tail of a steeply inclined wind-shaft, has already disappeared, as have the brine-pumping mills of England and New England. Some drainage-mills, using a chain of pots, survive in Spain and Aden.

The first wind-driven saw-mill was built by Cornelis Cornelisz in Holland in 1592; it was mounted on a raft which was warped round to face the wind. From this developed the *paltrok* mill (figure 59), the whole of which turns on a roll-ring running on a brick base a few feet high. In appearance it is a square smock-mill with panniers on either side, and a few post-mills in Germany have been converted into *paltroks*. In the Netherlands mills were used for every conceivable industrial purpose, especially on the Zaan, where over 900 were at work at one time before the advent of steam-power.

The horizontal mill, with sails attached radially to a vertical shaft, is still to be found in Seistan, in the north-east of Persia, where it originated and whence the idea was taken to China (vol II, figure 558). In western Europe it has never met with much success on account of its mechanical limitations, which prevent any considerable power from being developed. It has been re-invented many times between 1600 and the present day and, while it was used to some extent in south Russia, the only continuously successful variety is the Savonious S-rotor, which is outside our period.

Thus, in short, the most advanced mechanical devices were found in English windmills—the use of cast iron leading to cycloidal gearing, the use of bevel-gears, fantails, and shuttered sails—and the design of the East Anglian post-mills has never been equalled. The best-constructed tower and smock mills are to be found in the Netherlands; these cannot be rivalled elsewhere, and the Dutch always led in the design of cloth-spread sails.

The millwrights who designed and built these windmills with the aid of

FIGURE 59—*Section of a* paltrok *saw-mill. The wind-shaft is coupled by oblique gearing to a crank-shaft, which causes two frames carrying the saws to reciprocate up and down. The timber body of the mill rotates on rollers upon a brick base.*

axe, adze and auger, pole, block and tackle, and jack were the ancestors of the mechanical engineers who started to transform the world two hundred years ago. Of those who built the early mills we know little; manorial rolls tell us something of the cost of repairs to mills, and from them we learn that, in addition to the stones, the iron portions of the mills were expensive and were correspondingly cared for. The parts most often mentioned are the stone-spindles and the mill-rynds; these are seldom found in old mill-sites, which, when excavated, have yielded mainly nails and charred or rotted timber. The nails held the weather-boards, for the framing of the mills was fastened with wooden pegs.

These millwrights were versatile carpenters, who could also if necessary frame and hang church bells and whose work can be matched in timber-framed barns, which they may well have built. Their early drawings, if any, have not survived, and it is significant that the first technical description of a windmill, already mentioned (p 89), is contained in a treatise on carpentry published in 1702.

The Dutch mill-books printed from 1728 onwards are the first to depict mill-wrights at work and their tools; from that time onwards we can form a clear picture of the operations involved. The broad axe and the adze were widely used, as is evident from examination of timbers in the older surviving mills. Heavy-duty lifting-jacks were also essential; but perhaps the most important element in the millwright's equipment was his rope tackle. The ropes had to be of considerable length and strength to haul up first the heavy wind-shafts, with the aid of a pole, and subsequently the sails, for the repair and renewal of which the tackle was most frequently used.

Besides building the mill and renewing and repairing the sails millwrights undertook running repairs, supplying and fitting new bearings, re-cogging gears, and sometimes dressing the stones. Dressing, however, was more often per-formed by the miller, his man, or an itinerant stone-dresser. The influence of a firm of millwrights could often be seen in the regional design of the mills. This could be traced along the main lines of communication radiating not only from the millwright's home town or village, but also from other centres at which his apprentices had set up as independent masters. Thus national types can be subdivided and the varieties easily recognized as regional and local.

The millwright was usually his own smith or at least employed one, but he let out his bricklaying or stone-mason's work to others, the bricks often being made or the stone quarried on a site adjacent to the mill. He had to be a man of considerable initiative, ingenuity, and resource. With the advent of steam-power it was the millwrights who built, installed, and later designed not only the engines but the machinery that they drove. This can be seen from the history of a number of famous engineering firms; the millwright can indeed justly be regarded as the ancestor of the present-day mechanical engineer.

REFERENCES

[1] RAMELLI, AGOSTINO. 'Le diverse et artificiose machine.' Published by the author, Paris. 1588.

[2] JOUSSE, M. 'L'art de charpenterie' (2nd ed.). Paris. 1702.

[3] DIDEROT, D. and D'ALEMBERT, J. LE R. (Eds). 'Encyclopédie ou dictionnaire raisonné des sciences, des arts et des métiers.' Paris. 1765.

[4] LINPERCH, P. *Architectura mechanica* of Moole-boek.' Amsterdam. 1727.
    VAN NATRUS, L., POLLY, J., and VAN VUUREN, C. 'Groot Volkomen Moolenboek' (2 vols). Amsterdam. 1734, 1736.
    VAN ZYL, J. *'Theatrum machinarum universale* of groot algemeen Moolen-boek.' Amsterdam. 1761.

[5] BENNETT, R. and ELTON, J. 'A History of Corn Milling', Vol. 2. London. 1899.
    WAILES, R. *Trans. Newcomen Soc.*, **15**, 117, 1934-5.

[6] HUARD, M. G., WAILES, R., and WEBSTER, H. A. *Ibid.*, **27**, 209, 1949-51.

[7] WAILES, ENID and WAILES, R. *Ibid.*, **20**, 113, 1939-40.

[8] WAILES, R. and WEBSTER, H. A. *Ibid.*, **19**, 127, 1938-9.

[9] CLARK, H. O. and WAILES, R. *Ibid.*, **27**, 212, 1949-51.

[10] HUARD, M. G., WAILES, R., and WEBSTER, H. A. *Ibid.*, **27**, 203, 1949-51.

[11] WAILES, R. *Ibid.*, **25**, 27, 1945-7.

[12] BURNE, E. L., RUSSELL, J., and WAILES, R. *Ibid.*, **24**, 147, 1943-5.

[13] SMEATON, J. "Experimental Enquiry Concerning the Natural Powers of Wind and Water to turn Mills." *Phil. Trans.*, **51**, 100, 1759.

[14] CLARK, H. O. and WAILES, R. See ref. [9], p. 211.

[15] WAILES, R. *Trans. Newcomen Soc.*, **26**, 1, 1947-9.

[16] CLARK, H. O. and WAILES, R. *Ibid.*, **26**, 119, 1947-9.

[17] RUSSELL, J. *Ibid.*, **24**, 55, 1943-5.

BIBLIOGRAPHY

BENNETT, R. and ELTON, J. 'A History of Corn Milling' (see: Handstones, Slave and Cattle Mills, Vol. 1; Watermills and Windmills, Vol. 2; Feudal Laws and Customs, Vol. 3; Feudal Mills, Vol. 4). Simpkin and Marshall, London. 1898-1904.

JOUSSE, M. 'L'art de charpenterie' (2nd ed.). Paris. 1702. Reprinted in the article: "Agriculture" in 'Encyclopédie ou dictionnaire raisonné des sciences' (ed. by D. DIDEROT and J. LE R. D'ALEMBERT). Paris. 1765.

LINPERCH, P. *'Architectura mechanica* of Moole-boek.' Amsterdam. 1727.

RONSE, A. 'De Windmolens.' Desclée de Brouwer, Bruges. 1934.

SKILTON, C. P. 'British Windmills and Watermills.' Collins, London. 1947.

SMEATON, J. 'An Experimental Enquiry concerning the Natural Powers of Water and Wind to turn Mills and other Machines, depending on a Circular Motion.' London. 1794.

VAN NATRUS, L., POLLY, J., and VAN VUUREN, C. 'Groot Volkomen Moolenboek' (2 vols). Amsterdam. 1734, 1736.

VAN ZYL, J. *'Theatrum machinarum universale* of groot algemeen Moolen-boek.' Amsterdam. 1761.

WAILES, R. 'Windmills in England, a Study of their Origin, Development and Future.' Architectural Press, London. 1948.

Idem. 'The English Windmill.' Routledge, London. 1954.

5

TRADESMEN'S TOOLS
c 1500–1850

R. A. SALAMAN

TOWARDS the end of the seventeenth century the artisan came to be called a tradesman, and it is under this name that we follow him into the centuries after the medieval period (vol II, ch 11).

When considering hand-tools, it will be convenient to have a rough classification of the principal types according to their uses:

Hammering: hammers, mallets, and mauls.
Cutting, splitting, and scraping: knives, wedges, adzes, axes, saws, chisels, and files.
Piercing and boring: awls, drills, and augers.
Measuring and marking: rules, squares, plumb-lines, compasses, and calipers.
Grasping and holding: pincers, vices, and brakes.
Sharpening: grindstones, whetstones, and saw-sharpening tools.

Man began making tools about half a million years ago, and it is therefore not surprising that the design of most ordinary hand-tools attained a final stage of evolution in the classical Mediterranean civilizations and has remained little changed since (figure 60). Indeed, the form of many modern tools has scarcely changed from that of their predecessors in Neolithic times. Thus, the knife of the boy scout of today is very close in form and dimensions to the predynastic flint implement of Gebel el-Arak (Egypt) dating from perhaps 3500 B.C. (vol I, p 667). Another instance is the close resemblance between the modern felling-axe of 'Yankee' pattern and the Neolithic stone axe (vol I, p 601); for both are smooth wedges with swollen sides so that the axe cleaves and cuts at the same time.

As has been shown earlier (vol I, pp 687–703) the tools and products of an Egyptian carpenter of the fourteenth century B.C. would be perfectly recognizable by his modern western counterpart. While we do not know exactly the entire kit of Roman hand-tools, it appears that workmen in even the remoter parts of romanized Europe, such as Britain, possessed most of the ordinary hand-tools except the brace, clear evidence for which does not exist in Europe earlier than the fifteenth century (figure 65 and vol II, p 653).

The form of ordinary hand-tools remained fairly static after *c* A.D. 500, but the increasing number of specialist trades that emerged during and after the Middle Ages led to an increasing differentiation in the design of some tools, which continued until the end of the nineteenth century and after.

From about 1750 attempts were made to increase the wearing properties of wooden tools. Iron plates or boxwood inserts were screwed to the soles of planes, routers, and shaves; wooden braces were plated with brass. Planes made in iron or gun-metal appeared about 1800, leading eventually to a very handsome and still sought-after iron plane of which Spiers of Ayr was one of the foremost makers [66]. The modern cast iron plane was developed in America, and it is now unusual to find a wooden bench-plane employed in a carpenter's or joiner's shop.

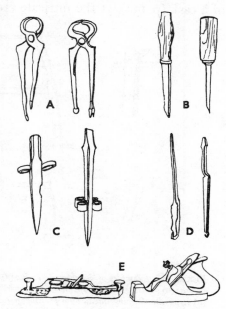

FIGURE 60—*Comparison of Roman and modern tools.* (A) *Carpenter's pincers, from a site in Germany* c 50 B.C., *and modern English;* (B) *mortising chisels, from Italy* c 50 B.C., *and modern English;* (C) *mower's anvils, from Silchester* c A.D. 50, *and modern French;* (D) *hooked reamers, from a German site* c 50 B.C., *and modern Czechoslovakian;* (E) *carpenter's planes, from Silchester* c A.D. 40, *and modern English. Scale 1/18.*

I. THE VILLAGE WORKSHOPS

During the Middle Ages and later most villages supported a blacksmith, a carpenter-wheelwright, and a mason. The blacksmith was also a farrier; the carpenter's shop also carried out millwright's work and the management of funerals; the mason became the village builder. Thus village needs were met from within the village community.

The smithy or wheelwright's shop was sometimes part of a dwelling-house, and often set at right-angles to the road, with a yard in front in which can still be found the apparatus of cart-, wagon- and wheel-making. The scene is admirably drawn by Hennell [7]. Like the tavern, the village smithy became a meeting-place, a centre for business or friendly intercourse. Until recent times everyone was familiar with the thump of the hammer on a piece of wrought iron; with the smell of burning horn as the hot shoe was offered to the hoof; with the steady rhythm of labour in the saw-pit, and the exhilarating smell of sawn timber.

The village tradesmen developed a tradition of skill and an instinctive talent for good design. A very high level of workmanship and design was maintained. Wherever one goes, it is scarcely possible to find a poorly made cart or plough, a badly forged harrow, or shoddy work in saddlery or harness.

On looking at a dished wheel with its spokes and felloes forming a flat cone on the hub (p 124), at the assemblage of staves trussed to form the double-arch of a cask (p 130), at the intricate cross-bracing of a wagon's under-carriage, or

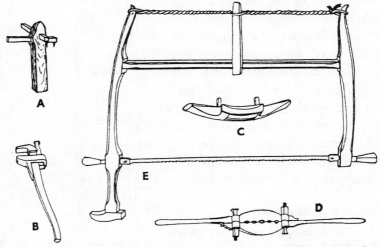

FIGURE 61—*Examples of home-made tools.* (A) *Wheelwright's gauge for scribing outlines of mortises and tenons;* (B) *adjustable wedge-spanner;* (C) *cooper's cross-shave for smoothing inside pails, etc. across the grain;* (D) *screw-die, forming thread by a pressing or rolling action rather than cutting;* (E) *bow-saw made by wheelwright for cutting felloes. Scale* A, 1/10; B, 1/14; C, 1/13; D, 1/15; E, 1/15.

indeed at the cutting of cloth by a tailor to fit the human body, one finds it hard to imagine how the tradesman learns to make or do these things without working-drawings or textbooks. For, so far as we know, there were few if any written sources of trade knowledge.

On the other hand, there existed a number of rhymes that were probably composed to help the apprentice, as was the following lesson (related by a Hertfordshire blacksmith) on how to operate the old pear-shaped blacksmith's bellows:

> *Up high*
> *Down low,*
> *Up quick*
> *Down slow—*
> *And that's the way to blow.*

Or the sawyer's advice to the beginner in one of the most strenuous of all trades:

> *Strip when you're cold and live to grow old.*

Or the horse-bit maker's maxim:

There's a key to every horse's mouth

—a saying that seeks to explain the infinite variety in bit-design [53].

One might imagine that something besides teaching and example existed for handing down complicated techniques; but, if so, this—like many other aspects of the workman's life and thought—is largely hidden from us.

II. HOME-MADE TOOLS

Though towns like Sheffield are known to have been centres of tool-making from medieval times,[1] most of the tools used by farmers and tradesmen in the

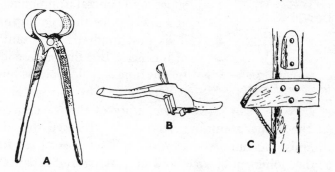

FIGURE 62—(A) *Farrier's shoeing pincers, forged from old rasps by 'Pincher Jack' (scale 1/8); (B) coach-maker's pistol router, for grooving frames to take panels (scale 1/12); (C) wheelwright's post tire-bender (scale 1/24).*

period 1500–1700 were made by village carpenters and blacksmiths. The situation was much the same all over Europe.

As late as the middle of the nineteenth century it was the rule rather than the exception for smiths to make their own tongs, anvil-tools, and even screw dies and taps. Carpenters made their own gauges, saw-frames, and often planes. Millwrights had their outsize slip-wrenches and turnscrews forged by the local smith. Coopers made their own shaves and jointers. But when the mass produced drop-forged hand-tools flooded the markets in the late nineteenth century, tradesmen soon ceased to look upon a factory-made tool as a luxury.

The plates in the eighteenth-century *Encyclopédie* of Diderot [5] show clearly that a large proportion of the hand-tools were home-made. Examples of home-made eighteenth- and nineteenth-century English tools are shown in figure 61.

[1] Sheffield whittles (hand-knives) were familiar in Chaucer's day.

Wooden handles for chisels and augers were nearly always home-made. Some of these handles are not only a pleasure to use even today but are of great beauty. To quote Christian Barman when commenting (B.B.C., 1948) on an exhibition of old English hand-tools: 'Everybody who appreciates the qualities of materials loves wood, and here was wood formed into . . . a special kind of tactile sculpture made to be felt with the hand. . . . I remembered that old craftsmen, when they buy a new set of modern chisels, throw away the handles and carefully fit their own. These were handles . . . polished bright by a lifetime of use, and were part of their owners' lives. . . .'

FIGURE 63—*Smith's beam-drill. The brace is turned by hand under pressure from the weighted lever. Scale 1/45.*

Before the end of the nineteenth century the factories began to produce tools, horse-shoes, and general ironmongery of all kinds at a lower price than could the blacksmith. This put hundreds of country smiths out of business. But the preference and feeling for the home-made tool has lingered on, and is exemplified by the romantic, but often tragic, story of the travelling smiths of the 1890s who, like the former tramping artisans [22], roamed the villages seeking work at the diminishing number of smithies. They specialized in such highly skilled work as the doing-up of vice-jaws or making and repairing screw dies. Famous among them was a remarkable figure, known as 'Pincher Jack', who travelled all over England and Wales, stopping at the forges to make farrier's pinchers out of old rasps (figure 62 A). He is still remembered by countless older smiths as a tradesman of almost magical skill; and his legend illustrates the persistent, though not always justified, belief in the superiority of the hand-made tool over the factory product.

Improvisation played a large part in the village workshop, and influenced the design of future equipment. Examples are the famous stone-weighted beam-drill that operated without a screwing-down mechanism (figure 63); the post tire-bender in which the iron tire or strake was pulled into a circular shape without geared rollers (figure 62 C); and the home-made slip-wrench, an adjustable spanner made without a screw (figure 61 B) and much esteemed by tradesmen for its power to grip a worn nut.

The new factories recruited their craftsmen originally from the country workshops. Their skills survive in the tool-room and pattern-shop which control the factory's production, and among the maintenance engineers (the Jacks-of-all-trades still known as millwrights) who install and maintain the machines.

III. THE TOOL-MAKING TOWNS

Certain towns became centres of tool-making. Toledo and Damascus were famous for their swordsmiths in the Middle Ages (vol II, p 57). Solingen in Germany, Thiers in France, Sheffield in England, and the towns of Styria in Austria are among the places where for centuries a significant proportion of the world's hand-tools have been made. Styrian iron ores contain manganese, and the steel of the district was valued even in Roman times.

It is not definitely known why these places became centres of tool-making. Supplies of ore and wood fuel were to hand, and in some cases—for example, in the Styrian towns and at Sheffield—the streams provided water-power for tilt-hammers and grindstones (pp 32 and 34). But once the trade started, for whatever reasons, tradition would tend to confine it to these centres.

A high percentage of the inhabitants' of these towns was occupied in tool-making. For instance, during the fifty years before 1600, more than half the bridegrooms married in Sheffield parish church were employed in the tool and cutlery trades. They were classed as follows [8]:

cutlers	.	.	.	122	scythe-smiths	.	.	.	.	3
scissor-smiths	.	.	.	42	file-smiths	.	.	.	.	3
sheathers	.	.	.	17	hammermen	.	.	.	.	1
shear-smiths	.	.	.	7					

When steel became more accessible after 1700 (p 34), and following the growing demand for hand-tools of every kind in the eighteenth and nineteenth centuries, Sheffield grew into a vast concourse of forges, operating not only in organized factories but in the back rooms of cottages, where much of the work was put out. Even today, once out of the commercial centre of Sheffield, the visitor can hear the ring of hammer on anvil in almost every side-street.

Many wooden tools—planes, coach-maker's routers (figure 62 B), malt-shovels, spoke-shaves, and saw-frames—were made outside the tool-making centres by small specialist firms such as those of the late Hannah Griffiths of Norwich [35] or Féron of Paris [51]. Tool-handles, flails, rakes, and scythe-shafts are still mainly produced by one-man concerns situated near the woodlands from which the timber is cut [6].

There is a popular notion that no steel is as good as it was before the 1914–18 war. Though it is true that war conditions contributed to the acceptance of inferior quality, the best makers continued to maintain a high standard, and still do so; but there seems no immediate prospect of an improvement in the cutting-life of even the best hand-tools. Indeed, the resistance to wear of such tools has not altered appreciably during the last hundred years.

IV. SPECIALIZATION OF TRADES

Any trade of considerable extent tends to produce specialists in its various branches. Within the primary trades of smith, mason, carpenter, and miller or baker there gradually appeared innumerable specialized crafts. Thus the smiths were divided into blacksmiths, tinsmiths, anchor-smiths, nail-smiths, shear-smiths, chain-smiths, and so forth. There was also a host of the less fundamental but highly skilled tradesmen, such as the spur- and bit-maker, gold-beater, pewterer, violin-maker, and glass-painter.

After the sixteenth century the number and variety of trades became very large. In 1574 the Swiss artist Jost Amman (1539–91) illustrated ninety different trades practised in his time [19]. Two hundred years later in the *Encyclopédie* Diderot described and illustrated over 250 [5]. In the next century Pigot and Company's commercial directory (London, 1826) records no fewer than 846 trades in London alone. It is true that some of the latter are of a very minor type—such as whalebone cutters, mourning-ring makers, hour-glass makers, whip- and stick-mounters—but each trade had its own techniques, and a considerable proportion of the different trades had each its own particular kit of tools, often supplied by a tool-maker who specialized in their supply.

The tool-kit considered necessary for different tradesmen has steadily increased since the sixteenth century. This is indicated in illustrations of a carpenter's workshop or tool-kit from the following sources:

Date	Source	Number of tools in the picture
1568	Jost Amman [19]	14
1703	Moxon [14]	30
1751	Diderot [5]	51
1892	Wynn Timmins's Catalogue [41]	90

V. SPECIALIZATION OF TOOLS

The differentiation of tools matched the rapidly growing multiplicity of trades.

One cause of the great variety in factory-made tools sprang from a desire to satisfy a demand that had been cultivated originally by village smiths, whose products tended to be characteristic of the region where they were made. This tendency is shown by the use of place-names and surnames to distinguish different tool-designs in the early pattern books of firms such as Isaac Nash [61]. Examples of these books are to be found in the Curtis Museum, Alton, Hampshire.

The 1905 catalogue of William Hunt and Son [44], among others, illustrates forty-two different shapes of bill-hook intended for laying hedges, cutting gorse, chopping firewood, and so on, many of which are named after towns or counties. In only a few instances is there a significant difference of function. Obviously this remarkable variety was designed to meet local demands. Farmers and house-holders bought originally from a local tool-smith, whose business could be captured by the factory only if the customer was supplied with the particular shape to which he had become accustomed.

Even in America, where the products of the factories are popularly supposed to have attained a high degree of standardization, the mail-order house of Belknap [42] lists over forty varieties of felling-axe, each made in six or more sizes.

The adze supplies an example of differentia-tion between trades. Thus the shipwright's adze differs from the wheelwright's (figure 64), and both differ slightly from the carpenter's. Yet these tradesmen could exchange adzes without suffering serious inconvenience. Similarly, a cooper demands a different type of wooden brace from that sold to the carpenter, while the chair-maker uses a third variety (figure 65). It may be suspected that such differences, though based on usage, were sometimes stimulated by the tool-

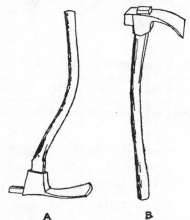

FIGURE 64—*Adzes.* (A) *Shipwright's adze with poll peg for driving in broken nails;* (B) *wheelwright's adze. The carpenter's adze resembles* B, *with the poll peg of* A. *Scale 1/12.*

makers, who sought to extend their business by offering tools intended to satisfy the needs of particular trades.

Firms that made tools for an international market were obliged to carry stock as diverse as it was picturesque. The 1875 tool-list issued by Goldenberg & Cie, of Alsace [38], illustrates the following 'patterns' of adzes, axes, and trowels:

Alsatian, American, Aragon, Asturian, Bavarian, Bayonne, Belgian, Berry, Bessarabian, Biscayan, Bordeaux, Brabant, Bresse, Castilian, Catalonian, Dutch, English, Flemish, Gotha, Greek, Hamburg, Havre, Hungarian, Italian, Kentucky, London, L'Orient, Lyon, Marseilles, Mexican, Moscow, Nantes, Narbonne, Neapolitan, Norman, Paris, Perpignan, Petersburg, Picardy, Pomeranian, Portuguese, Provençal, Saxon, Silesian, Spanish, Strasbourg, Swabian, Tartarian, Toulouse, Turkian, Yankee.

Not only do tradesmen living in different districts demand different varieties of tool but, fortunately or unfortunately for the tool-maker, there are strange

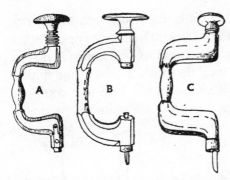

FIGURE 65—*Wooden braces.* (A) *Carpenter's and joiner's brace with latch chuck;* (B) *cooper's dowelling-brace with large head against which he pressed with his chest;* (C) *chairmaker's brace with small head fitting into wooden rest worn on the chest. Scale 1/10.*

inconsistencies. For instance, the cooper's axe used in the Liége district of Belgium [27] is precisely the same shape as the English coach-builder's axe; while the ordinary English cooper's axe is also used in many parts of Europe (figure 66). Yet no English wheelwright or coach-builder would dream of using a cooper's axe for trimming spokes or wedges, although it might serve him just as well as the coach-builder's axe.

A more functional differentiation applies to the chisel. Twenty-four distinct varieties were listed by a well-known London tool-merchant [45] about 1900, each with its own range of styles and sizes:

Firmer, Butt, Buttonhole, Boxing, Coach, Millwright's, Paring, Registered, Barge Builder's, Mortice, Sash, Ship's slice, Mortice lock, Drawer lock, Flooring, Wagon Builder's, Wheelwright's, Ripping, Carving, Turning, Mason's, Bricklayer's, Engineer's, and Smith's.

In 1850 a firm of York plane-makers [34] listed twenty-nine distinct varieties of moulding-plane alone, and each variety was made in five or more sizes.

The following are examples of exceptionally long lists of tools recommended for particular trades:

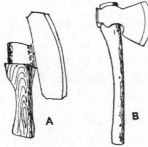

FIGURE 66—*Side-axes.* (A) *Cooper's type;* (B) *coach-builder's and wheelwright's type. Scale 1/12.*

Philipson's 'Coachbuilding' (1897) [17] . . .	275 tools and appliances
Railway list for platelayer's tools (c 1950) . . .	159 ,, ,, ,,
Forestry Commission tool-sheet (1951) . . .	173 ,, ,, ,,
Saddler's tools (1950) [50].	112 ,, ,, ,,

VI. THE ORIGIN OF SPECIALISTS' TOOLS

While the development of basic tools can be followed from the Stone Age, the derivation of the specialist's tool is more difficult to trace. If the etymology of their names can be taken as any guide to the date of origin of the tools, it appears certain that many of them were well known before the twelfth century. The following examples may be given as typical:[1]

The *bruzz* (figure 67 A) is the celebrated three-cornered chisel used by wheelwrights to chop out the corners of deep mortices; the name comes from the Old English word *brysan*, to crush.

The *auger*, the traditional boring-tool of shipwrights and wheelwrights, derives its name from the pre-twelfth-century English word *nafu-gar* which is formed from *nafu*, the nave of a wheel, and *gar*, a piercer. The *f* has been dropped, and the initial *n* was lost through confusion between 'a nauger' and 'an auger'.

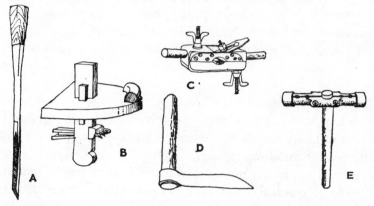

FIGURE 67—(A) *Bruzz or triangular chisel;* (B) *the croze;* (C) *nogg or moot;* (D) *froe or rending-axe, struck with a mallet on top of the blade;* (E) *shipwright's caulking-mallet. Scale 1/11.*

The *croze* (figure 67 B) is the cooper's tool for cutting a groove in the ends of the staves of a cask to receive the edges of the head; the name probably comes from the Old French *croz* meaning a hollow or groove.

The *nogg* or *moot* (figure 67 C) is used in many trades for shaping a rough stick into a round handle or dowel. (*Moot* applies particularly to the shaping of tree-nails for ships.) The origins of these words are obscure and may be much older than the other examples.

Some tool- or trade-names have almost disappeared from English workshop-language but are still in common use in the workshops of America. Examples are the Anglo-Saxon word *speech* meaning a wheel-hub with the spokes driven home but lacking the rim; and the word *froe* (figure 67 D), the name of a splitting-tool used for cleaving staves, spokes, or chair-legs. This tool is sometimes known in England as a *frower* or *frommard*, but is more commonly called a split-axe or rending-axe. The word *froe* probably comes from the Old English word *from-ward*, meaning turned away.

[1] Etymologies are taken from the Oxford English Dictionary.

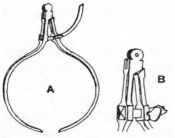

FIGURE 68—(A) *Wing calipers (scale 1/13)*; (B) *detail of stop-chamfering on calipers (scale 1/6).*

There are certain features in the design of hand-tools that have evidently survived for many years and are difficult to explain. For instance, the ball on one foot of the carpenter's pincers (figure 60 A) was possibly put there to provide metal for another claw on the other side. The slot cut through the head of a shipwright's caulking-mallet (figure 67 E) may be easier to explain. The split head deadens sound and gives enough spring to prevent stinging the hand. The old shipwrights liked to hear their mallets 'sing'; several men caulking a deck with ordinary mallets would deafen each other.

VII. DESIGN

Admiration for the artefacts of bygone civilizations should not lead us to overlook the merits of many common tools and utensils of trade in present-day use. Tool-making seldom produces an ugly object, for the design is a culmination of centuries of trial and error; and, as if by instinct, experienced tool-smiths tend to produce tools of graceful appearance. This tendency is apparent not only in conventional tools, such as the hedge-slasher and chisels and axes, but in some of the tools made for newly developed trades—for instance, in the garage mechanic's bi-hexagon ring-spanner (a direct descendant of the coach-builder's wheel-cap wrench) which, with its elegant curves, is an example of good industrial design.

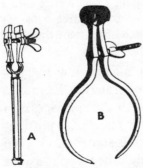

FIGURE 69—(A) *Watch-maker's pin-vice*; (B) *spring calipers with screw adjustment, hand forged. Scale 1/3.*

After about 1750 many of the most beautiful tools were forged in surroundings which pass belief for ugliness and squalor. For such was—and still continues to be—the scene in the overcrowded back-streets of many industrial towns. One such tool is the 'Lancashire' calipers (figure 69 B) shaped with the serpentine double curve recommended by Hogarth in his 'Analysis of Beauty' (1753); another, the all-metal Scotch brace; a third, the watch-maker's pin-vice (figure 69 A) They were produced by tradesmen who lived and worked for the most part in the darkest corners of the industrial towns.

An attractive feature of these metal tools is the custom of stop-chamfering (figure 68 B). This derives from the wain-wright, who applied a draw-knife (figure 70 A) to lighten the wagon's frame, stopping short of the joints where the full thickness is needed. It thus became a form of decoration. Much later this same finishing process can be seen on the connecting-rods of a locomotive, or on the forged frame of early bicycles.

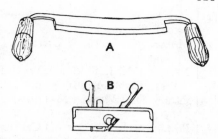

FIGURE 70—(A) *Draw-knife, used for shaping, cutting away, and chamfering;* (B) *trenching-plane for cutting grooves across the grain. Scale 1/12.*

In Italy and elsewhere in Europe during the sixteenth and seventeenth centuries (but not much in England) exquisite decorations and shapes of the kind developed by gun-smiths were applied to metal saw-frames and to surgeons' instruments—particularly the amputation-saw. This was done, perhaps, like the embellishment of sword-hilts, to give some ritualistic dignity to a deadly trade.

Wooden planes with beautiful though sometimes elaborate carvings were made on the continent of Europe during the eighteenth century. Many were imported into England, but, like the baroque in art, outlandish tool-styles never took hold in this country. The English tool-makers held to a tradition of severe but graceful lines (figure 70 B).

The Notes on pp 123 and 128 illustrate in more detail the use of specialized tools in two wood-working crafts which have survived with only very gradual changes of technique into the present century.

REFERENCES AND BIBLIOGRAPHY

[1] 'Boys' Book of Trades.' Routledge, London. *c* 1850.
[2] ASHTON, T. S. 'An Eighteenth-century Industrialist, Peter Stubbs of Warrington, 1756-1806.' University Press, Manchester. 1939.
[3] BARRAS, R. T. 'The Sheffield Standard List.' Pawson and Brailsford, Sheffield. 1862.
[4] CHILDE, V. GORDON. 'The Story of Tools.' Cobbett, London. 1944.
[5] DIDEROT, D. and D'ALEMBERT, J. LE R. (Eds). 'Encyclopédie ou dictionnaire raisonné des sciences, des arts et des métiers.' Paris. 1751-72.
[6] EDLIN, H. L. 'Woodland Crafts in Britain.' Batsford, London. 1949.
[7] HENNELL, T. 'The Countryman at Work.' Architectural Press, London. 1947.
[8] HIMSWORTH, J. B. 'The Story of Cutlery.' Benn, London. 1954.
[9] HOLTZAPFFEL, C. 'Turning and Mechanical Manipulation.' London. 1846.
[10] KNIGHT, E. H. 'The Practical Dictionary of Mechanics' (4 vols). Cassell, London. 1877-84.
[11] LILLEY, S. 'Men, Machines and History.' Cobbett, London. 1948.
[12] MASSINGHAM, H. J. 'Country Relics.' University Press, Cambridge. 1939.

[13] MERCER, H. C. 'Ancient Carpenter's Tools.' Bucks County Historical Society, Doylestown, Pa. 1929.

[14] MOXON, J. 'Mechanick Exercises' (3rd ed., to which is added "Mechanick Dyalling"). London. 1703.

[15] NEEDHAM, N. J. T. M. and WANG LING. 'Science and Civilization in China.' University Press, Cambridge. 1954.

[16] PETRIE, SIR (WILLIAM MATTHEW) FLINDERS. 'Tools and Weapons.' Constable, London. 1917.

[17] PHILIPSON, J. 'The Art and Craft of Coachbuilding.' London. 1897.

[18] ROSE, W. 'The Village Carpenter.' University Press, Cambridge. 1937.

[19] SCHOPPER, HARTMAN. *De omnibus illiberalibus sive mechanicis artibus humani generis*, etc. [Illustrations by Jost Amman]. Frankfurt a.M. 1574.

[20] STURT, C. 'The Wheelwright's Shop.' University Press, Cambridge. 1923.

[21] WOODS, K. S. 'Rural Crafts of England.' Harrap, London. 1949.

[22] HOBSBAUM, E. H. *Econ. Hist. Rev.*, second series, **3**, 299, 1951.

Museum Publications, etc.:

[23] CAMBRIDGE AND COUNTY FOLK MUSEUM. 'Some former Cambridgeshire Agricultural and other Implements' by R. C. LAMBETH. Cambridge. 1939.

[24] CURTIS MUSEUM, AGRICULTURAL SECTION. 'Illustrated and Descriptive List of the Smaller Implements, etc., Formerly (or still) in use on Farms' compiled by W. H. CURTIS and S. A. WARNER. The Curtis Museum, Alton, Hants. 1946.
    CASTLE MUSEUM, YORK. 'Yorkshire Crafts' by C. M. MITCHELL. York Corporation. 1954.

[25] WEST YORKSHIRE FOLK MUSEUM. 'Barns and Workshops' (2nd ed.) [by F. ATKINSON]. Halifax Museums. 1954.

[26] HIGH WYCOMBE MUSEUM. 'Windsor Chairmaker's Tools' [by L. JOHN MAYES. 1948].

[27] MUSÉE DE LA VIE WALLONNE. *Enquêtes du Musée de la Vie Wallonne*, various numbers. Liége 1926-49.

[28] MUSEUM OF ENGLISH RURAL LIFE, READING. Card index of tools.

[29] NATIONAL MUSEUM OF WALES. 'Guide to the Collection Illustrating Welsh Folk Crafts and Industries' (2nd ed.) by I. C. PEATE. National Museum of Wales, Cardiff. 1945.

Trade Catalogues:

[30] Ford, Whitmore & Brunton, Birmingham. Tool-makers. Birmingham Reference Library. *c* 1775.

[31] W. & E. Wynn, Birmingham. List of tool prices. *c* 1810.

[32] Peter Stubs Ltd., Warrington. File- and tool-makers. *c* 1845.

[33] Richard Timmins & Sons, Birmingham. Tools and steel toys. *c* 1850.

[34] Varvill & Sons, York. Plane-makers. *c* 1850.

[35] Hannah Griffiths, Norwich. Price list of planes and coach-builders' tools. *c* 1850.

[36] William Gilpin & Co., Cannock. General tool-makers. *c* 1868.

[37] George Barnsley & Sons, Sheffield. Boot- and clog-making tools. *c* 1868.

[38] Goldenberg & Cie, Saverne, Alsace. General tool-makers for international market. *c* 1875.

[39] Ludvig Peter Schmidt, Germany. General tools. *c* 1875.

[40] Arnold & Sons, London. Surgical and veterinary instruments. *c* 1885.

[41] Wynn, Timmins & Co., Birmingham. General tools and steel toys. *c* 1892.

Trade Catalogues issued 1895–1950:

[42] Belknap Hardware & Manufacturing Co., U.S.A. General tools and hardware.
[43] E. A. Berg Manufacturing Co. Ltd., Sweden. General hand-tools.
[44] The Brades Ltd. (Wm. Hunt & Sons), Birmingham. General tools.
[45] Arthur Collier (Brixton) Ltd. Plumbers' and general tools.
[46] A. Copley, London. Saw-makers and masons' tools.
[47] Bryan Corcoran Ltd., London. Millwrights' tools and equipment.
[48] Coubro & Scrutton, London. Ship chandlers', including sail-makers' tools.
[49] Henry Disston & Sons, Inc., U.S.A. Saws and files.
[50] Joseph Dixon Tool Co., Walsall. Leather-workers' tools.
[51] Féron & Cie, Paris. Planes and other wooden tools.
[52] J. & J. Goddard, London. Organ and piano tools.
[53] Hampson & Scott, Walsall. Harness and saddlers' tools.
[54] Herbert & Son Ltd., London. Butchers' tools and equipment.
[55] Hirst Bros. & Co. Ltd., Oldham. Watch-makers' and jewellers' tools.
[56] C. Isler & Co. Ltd., London. Well-sinking tools.
[57] W. Langley & Co., London. Coopers' tools.
[58] W. R. Loftus Ltd., London. Cellarmen's and coopers' tools, etc.
[59] Lusher & Marsh, Norwich. Wooden shovels.
[60] William Marples & Sons, Sheffield. General tools.
[61] Nash Tyzak Industries Ltd., Stourbridge. Scythes, edged tools, etc.
[62] Peugeot Frères, France. General tools.
[63] Edward Preston & Sons Ltd., Birmingham. Rules and measures, plumbs, etc.
[64] V. Richter, Czechoslovakia. General hand-tools.
[65] C. T. Skelton & Co. Ltd., Sheffield. Spades, garden and contractors' tools.
[66] Stewart Spiers, Ayr. Iron plane makers.
[67] Thomas Tingley Ltd., London. Wheels, coach and cart ironmongery.

A NOTE ON THE WHEELWRIGHT'S TRADE

J. GERAINT JENKINS AND R. A. SALAMAN

IN many respects the craft of the wheelwright is similar to hardwood joinery, but whereas the joiner makes his joints to fit, relying a great deal on glue, the wheelwright relies on tightness of joints alone to hold the work together. He uses many of the same tools as the carpenter, and but few tools peculiar to his craft.

A wheel consists of a central nave, stock, or hub made of well seasoned elm, or less frequently oak, from which radiate an even number of cleft-oak spokes. The felloes, the curved members forming the rim of the wheel, are usually made of ash, but sometimes of beech or elm. An iron tire (or formerly a series of crescent-shaped pieces of iron called strakes) is shrunk on to the felloes to bind the wheel together.

I. THE NAVE

All the timber used in the manufacture of a wheel must be well seasoned, a process taking up to ten years. For the naves, straight smooth elms of suitable thickness are cut into lengths of 14 or 15 in; an auger-hole is bored through the centre to assist in drying, and the naves with the bark still on are stored until they are thoroughly dry. When the seasoning is complete, the dry naves are placed in a lathe and turned to the required shape and diameter. This shape is roughly cylindrical, a diameter of 12 in and a total length of $12\frac{1}{2}$ in being by far the most popular. In the past, when naves had to accommodate a thick wooden axle, the diameter was much greater.

After turning, the nave should have two gauge-marks on it. The first of these, 8 in from the hind end of the nave, acts as a guide for the front end of the spoke-mortises, while the other mark, $\frac{1}{2}$-in back from the 8-in line, allows for the staggering of the mortises. In the more recent type of hand-made wheel the spokes are generally staggered, so that one line of spokes has its front ends in line, while each alternate spoke has its front end a little behind its neighbour. If the spokes on a nave of small diameter were fixed in one line, then the mortises would weaken the nave. In the older, large type of nave this was relatively unimportant, for the dish or convex shape of the wheel was far more pronounced, and the spokes were generally fitted in a line.

Most cart- and wagon-wheels are 'dished' (figure 84), that is, the spokes make an angle of somewhat less than 90° with the hub so that they form a flat cone. As the axle bends down slightly, the lowest spoke (bearing the load) is perpendicular while the upper part of the wheel leans outward. Dishing has been both condemned and advocated: its chief merits would seem to be that it allows greater width in the body above the axle, and that mud is less likely to fall from the upper rim into the bearing. Further, a dished wheel is less likely to be forced out of shape by the sway or lateral movement of the body than a flat wheel.

II. MORTISING

After turning, the nave is placed on a low stool called a mortising-cradle (figure 71 (2)), and compasses are employed to mark out, by trial-and-error steppings, the centres of the required number of spoke-mortises on the gauge line. With a small try-square the centre line of each mortise is marked.

A spoke is now required in order to mark out all the mortises on the nave. By holding the 3 × 1-in foot of the spoke against the gauge line and directly over the centre line, the outline of the foot is marked in. The mortises are then bored with an auger or a 12- or 14-in sweep-brace with a 1-in bit. Three holes are bored, one at the front, one at the back, and one in the centre of each mortise-mark. The wheelwright depends entirely on his own judgement and skill for this operation, for the front hole has to be at a slight angle to allow for the dish of the wheel.

The next step is to chisel out the spoke-mortises, but before this is done a gauge known as a spoke-set gauge is prepared. This merely consists of a piece of hardwood 2 ft 9 in long, about $2\frac{1}{2}$ in wide, and 1 in deep. Some 4 in from one end a hole large enough to take a $\frac{7}{16}$-in coach-screw is bored, while at the other end a series of $\frac{3}{8}$-in holes, an inch apart, is bored. A piece of whalebone 9 in long is passed through the required hole and wedged there. The position of the whalebone depends on the size of wheel being made.

For example, to make a wheel 4 ft 10 inches in diameter, the position of the whalebone should be at half the diameter of the wheel (2 ft 5 in) minus the depth of the felloe (3½ in, for example), which would equal 2 ft 1½ in from the coach-screw pivot of the gauge.

The spoke-set gauge having been prepared, the next step is to plug the central hole

FIGURE 71—*Wheelwright's workshop. He is fitting the felloes on the spokes, using a spoke-dog to strain two spokes together so that their tongues will enter the holes (p 127). (1) Wheel stool; (2) mortising-cradle, for holding the wheel nave (see 3) while the mortise holes are cut to take the feet of the spokes; (3) nave; (4) spoke; (5) felloes, forming the rim of the wheel; (6) spoke-dog; (7) traveller, for measuring the circumference of the wheel and for marking off the same length on an iron bar for the tire; (8) cramp, for holding the wheel steady when fitting the felloes (see further plate 6).*

that runs from one end of the nave to the other. With the compasses the exact centre of the nave-face is found, and at that point a hole large enough to take the coach-screw pivot is bored. The gauge is screwed up close to the face of the nave so that it is just possible to turn it without turning the nave. The main purpose of the spoke-set gauge is to measure the dish of the wheel; since the spokes in a dished wheel emerge from the nave at an angle, the spoke-mortises also have to be cut at an angle. The whalebone of the gauge is set to the point where the spoke will enter the felloe; that is, 2 ft 1½ in from the central pivot in a 58-in wheel. Next, the distance between the gauge and the turner's face-mark at the base of the front spokes on the nave is measured. In a nave 12½ in long it will be 4½ in, as the face-mark is 8 in from the back end of the nave. If one requires a ½-in dish on the wheel, then the whalebone should project 4 in beyond the stick. In cutting the mortise, the slant of the boring must be such that a narrow straight-edge held against the front of the mortise just touches the whalebone. The reason for using a springy whalebone gauge, rather than a rigid stick, becomes apparent when the spokes are being driven into the nave.

A number of tools are required to prepare the mortises. The first of these is a mortising-bruzz; this is a long socket-handled chisel with a V-shaped blade (figure 67 A). The bruzz is used for cleaning the corners of the mortise; a 2-in firmer chisel is required to cut the core. To pare away the front and back ends of the mortises ¾-in and 1-in heading-chisels are required. Lastly the workman requires a heavy mallet, and a pair of inside calipers with which to check the size of the mortise as the work proceeds.

When all the mortises are complete, the nave is taken to the blacksmith in order to have the iron breast- and hind-bonds shrunk on. To prevent these bonds slipping, three nails of special shape are hammered into the nave, resting against the front end of the breast-bond and the back end of the hind-bond.

III. SPOKES

The naves are now ready to receive the spokes. These are of straight-grained oak, cleft from a clean, straight trunk while still green, and seasoned for four or more years. They are roughly shaped with the side-axe (figure 66 B) and finished with a spoke-shave to the required size. The foot of the spoke is then shaped to form a tenon 3 in long and 1 in wide (vol II, figure 505).

The nave is placed over the wheel-pit for the spokes to be driven in. This wheel-pit is rectangular in shape and measures some 6 ft in length and 10 inches in width. To provide a solid base for the nave while the spokes are being hammered in, the sides of the pit are bricked or lined with timber. While one man holds the nave steady and keeps the spoke in an upright position, the other swings a 14-lb hammer to drive the spokes into place. After every two or three blows, the spoke-set gauge is pushed into position, to ensure that the spoke is entering at the correct angle. Since the tenons are tapered, each blow of the sledge makes the spokes tighter in the nave and therefore progressively more difficult to correct. If the spoke is driven in at the wrong angle despite the efforts of the wheelwright to correct it, then it must be left until the adjacent spokes have been fitted. He then places a curved piece of ash, 2½ ft in length, known as a 'crooked stick', behind the spoke that is to be pushed forward and in front of the adjacent spokes. While the misdirected spoke is thus forced against the gauge it is again hammered; hence the use of a flexible 'feeler'. When all the spokes are in place, the wheel is measured with the spoke-set gauge to ensure that it has the right dish.

The next step is to set out the tongues of the spokes. In the days of broad straked wheels—mainly before 1850—the tongues were square and square mortise-holes were cut in the felloes to take them. Round tongues, far easier to make and fit, were used later. A scribe, consisting of a piece of ash 2 ft long and ¾-in square with a bradawl inserted, marks out the shoulder on the face of the spoke. The scribe is placed along each spoke, its foot resting firmly at the point where the spoke enters the nave. The shoulder is then scribed. In a wheel with a diameter of 4 ft 10 in, the shoulder will be 1 ft 7½ in up the spoke from the nave. When this is done a felloe-pattern is placed over the scribed spokes to ensure correct fitting. The front shoulder, then the back shoulder, are cut with a tenon-saw and chisel, and the tongues are trimmed to a slightly oval shape.

IV. FELLOES

In the past, felloes were sawn with a thin-bladed frame-saw (figure 61 E), each felloe conforming to one of the many patterns kept by the wheelwright in his shop. Today they are sawn with a band-saw. After sawing they are trimmed with axe and adze where necessary, and then smoothed with planes. To fix the felloes, the wheel is placed face downwards on the wheel-stool. The correct angle at the ends of the felloes is obtained with a small bevel, and each tongue is marked on it. A gauge is set to mark out the centre of the spoke-holes on the felloes, and these are bored with a 1½-in auger. When all the boring is completed, the next step is to make the dowels joining the felloes. These are short rods of oak, 4½ in long and 1 inch in diameter. When in place each dowel projects 2 in beyond the end of the felloe and each one is slightly rounded at the top, to ease the joining of the felloes.

With the wheel so far prepared, the felloes now have to be fitted to the spokes. The wheel is placed face downwards on the stool, and a felloe tapped some ¾-in down the tongue of a spoke. The second spoke will not at first enter the second hole in the felloe, owing to the radial divergence of the spokes, which causes the tongues to be wider apart at their ends than at the shoulders. To bring two spokes together, so that a felloe can be slipped on easily, a 'spoke-dog' is employed to bend them (figure 71 (6)). As the wheel-wright presses the handle of the spoke-dog forward, the spokes are bent and a felloe can easily be tapped on. When all the felloes have been fitted, wedges are driven into the split ends of the spoke-tongues, which are recessed in the felloe so that they will not touch the tire.

The completed wheel is then placed on the wheel-stool or stand, checked with various gauges, and finished with plane and spoke-shave.

V. TIRING

From the wheelwright's shop, the wheel is taken to the blacksmith for tiring. A bar of iron 16 ft long, 2½ in wide, and ¾-in thick is laid flat on the ground. A chalk-mark is made on the rim of the untired wheel, and another mark on the measuring-wheel or traveller (figure 71 (7)). With the chalk-marks as starting-points, the traveller is pushed round the rim of the wheel and the number of turns noted; then it is run along the bar of iron. This measures the wheel's circumference, but allowance has now to be made for the overlap at the weld and the expansion of the tire when heated. The bar is passed between a series of rollers to be bent to the required shape and the two loose ends are then welded together. In the older country workshops the iron was bent by hand on a post bender (figure 62 C).

The untired wheel is screwed down firmly on the circular iron tiring-platform, which is a permanent fixture in the blacksmith's yard. The tire-hoop is heated on a fire of straw and shavings; when it is sufficiently expanded it is carried with long-handled tongs to the tiring platform and with tire-dogs forced upon the wheel. Water is then poured on the rim, and as the tire shrinks the wheel is tightened under the enormous pressure of contraction.

VI. BOXING

Finally, the cast iron bearing or box has to be fixed in the centre of the nave. A large, tapering hole is cut through the centre of the nave with heavy boxing-chisels and gouges, or more recently with a tool called a boxing-engine, which is a revolving cutter working on a threaded bar. The cast iron bearing is loosely fitted into the nave, and adjusted by trial and error. The axle-arm is temporarily fixed to a bench, and the wheel hung on it so as to turn just clear of the ground. A small block of wood is then placed on the floor, just touching the edge of the tire. Slowly the wheel is turned round, and as it swings clear of the block, small oaken wedges are hammered into the end-grain of the nave around the box. The process is continued until the box is centred and firmly wedged in the nave. All that remains is to chisel off the ends of the wedges, and after smoothing and painting the wheel is ready.

BIBLIOGRAPHY

STURT, G. 'The Wheelwright's Shop.' University Press, Cambridge. 1923.
WELLER, G. W. Articles in *The Illustrated Carpenter and Builder*, June–July, 1950. The authors have drawn heavily on this description, written by a practising wheelwright of Sompting, Sussex, recently deceased.

A NOTE ON COOPERING

J. GERAINT JENKINS AND R. A. SALAMAN

COOPERING is the making and repairing of wooden vessels formed from staves and hoops. The cooper has few written measurements and patterns; tradition is his main guide even when making a vessel of specified capacity and girth. He must know the numbers and dimensions of the staves for a vessel of a particular size, and must shape them to fit accurately. Coopering is one of the few surviving crafts in which machine-techniques have not entirely replaced age-old methods of handicraft.

The craft was developed in ancient Egypt (vol I, figure 500), was well known in Roman times, and survived through the Middle Ages. The growth of trade, especially by sea, increased the demand for casks of standard capacity. On ships almost everything was stored in casks, and the cooper continued to be an important member of the crew until the mid-nineteenth century. On land, coopering was essentially a guild-craft, but by the end of the nineteenth century master-coopers had become few and most of the workshops were in breweries.

The least specialized branch of the trade is that of the dry-cooper, who makes casks for solid materials such as flour, tobacco, sugar, or crockery. His work is far less exacting than that of the wet-cooper, for the staves need not be so tight, and the barrels can be bound with ash or hazel hoops and are far less bulged. Douglas fir is the wood most commonly used for the staves, but elm, spruce, poplar, and beech also serve. In this branch of coopering, machinery early replaced hand-work. The staves are arranged inside a hoop until a complete circle is formed. They are then steamed until pliable, and a windlass is employed to draw together their free ends into a barrel-shape. Thus bent, they are heated to set them. For special purposes the technique of wet-coopering is adopted even for containers of dry goods.

The second branch of the craft, white-coopering, disappeared almost completely in the late nineteenth century. The white-cooper made pails, butter-churns, wash-tubs, and so forth for dairy and household use. He worked almost exclusively in villages and small towns. Some idea of his range of products is given by a rhyming signboard of the early nineteenth century from Hailsham, Sussex:

> As other people have a sign,
> I say—just stop and look at mine!
> Here, Wratten, cooper, lives and makes
> Ox bows, trug-baskets, and hay-rakes.
> Sells shovels, both for flour and corn,
> And shauls, and makes a good box-churn,
> Ladles, dishes, spoons, and skimmers,
> Trenchers, too, for use at dinners.
> I make and mend both tub and cask,
> And hoop 'em strong, to make them last.
> Here's butter prints, and butter scales,
> And butter boards, and milking pails.
> N'on this my friends may safely rest—
> In serving them I'll do my best;
> Then all that buy, I'll use them well,
> Because I make my goods to sell.

Oak was the main material of the white-cooper, but he used also ash and sycamore. The ways of making a tub or bucket were much like those of the wet-cooper, except that the shave was used to cut across instead of along the grain of the wood when smoothing the inside.

The third, the commonest, and the most highly specialized branch of the craft is wet-coopering, that is, making water-tight casks for liquids. It is exacting work, for not only must the staves fit accurately but the cask must be able to withstand the strain of fermenting liquids and rough handling during transport. Moreover the cask must be of an exact capacity. The only timber used is oak: American is preferred for spirits, Mediterranean for wine, and northern European for beer. Different qualities of wood are required for different classes of work; thus porosity is essential for some wines to allow the passage of air through the wood to assist fermentation. For spirits, cleft staves cut along the radius of the tree-trunks are used; this is because, conforming to the natural concentric rings of the tree, the wall of the barrel thus becomes so close-knit that neither water nor alcohol can pass through.

The craftsman's task begins where the woodman's ends (figure 72). Trees of about two hundred years old and of trunk-diameter between 18 and 24 in are cut into the lengths of staves. The logs are cleft into quarters with hammer and wedges, and further broken down to the required shape with a long-handled split-axe (figure 67 D). They are then shaved with a draw-knife (figure 70 A) and cut to the exact length of the required staves with a cross-cut saw. Trees of over 24 inches in diameter are used for headings. The rough staves are dried by piling in the open for a period dependent on climatic conditions, and are then placed in a kiln and further dried to a uniform moisture-content. The final embodiment of these staves into a tight cask involves the following stages.

1. *Preparing the staves.* The roughly shaped stave is clamped in a shaving-horse or firmly fixed in a hook on the cooper's block, which is a tree-trunk about 2 ft high. The smaller staves of casks holding less than 9 gallons are clamped on the sloping table on the front of the horse. The cooper sits astride the horse, regulating the pressure on the clamped stave with his feet. For the larger staves, the wood is merely held in a toothed hook on the top of the block. The outside of the stave is shaped with a draw-knife. The stave is then reversed, and a round-bladed draw-knife is used to shape its inner side.

In a cask the staves are narrower at the ends than in the middle, and the taper is first obtained with an axe sharpened on one side only, with the handle bent towards the sharpened side to prevent the cooper from knocking his knuckles against the stave as he shapes it (figure 66 A). This done he pares down the sides of the stave with a draw-knife, the stave being still held in the shaving-horse.

The sides are then bevelled, according to the radius of the cask, on the long jointer-plane. It stands upside down, one end on the ground, the other on a frame socketed loosely into a mortise at the front. This elevates the plane towards the cooper and enables him to smooth-edge a stave by sliding it downwards over the blade of the upturned sole. This plane may be as much as 6 ft long, while the front end stands some 2 ft high.

2. *Raising the cask.* The staves are arranged inside an iron raising-hoop until a complete circle is formed. An ash truss-hoop, which will be removed later, is driven down to hold the staves in place. The cask at this stage has the appearance of a truncated cone, the staves being held in place at the top by the iron raising-hoop, and splaying outwards to be held at a lower level by the ash truss-hoop. The cask is now said to be 'raised'.

3. *Trussing and bending.* To make the timber pliable for further work it has to be steamed. In large workshops the raised cask is placed in the steaming-chest for twenty minutes. More usually the staves are moistened and the cask is placed over a brazier containing a fire of shavings. This softens the fibres so that the staves can be bent. For wine-casks of the more pliable Mediterranean oak, a rope-and-tackle is passed around the open end of the staves, drawing them together into barrel-form, in which they are

FIGURE 72—*Coopering. The cooper is raising a cask, driving on the truss-hoops (p 130). (1) Block; (2) block-hook, for holding staves while they are shaped with a draw-knife; (3) wooden truss-hoops for holding staves in place during assembly; (4) iron raising-hoop, for holding a circle of staves when raising the cask; (5) stave; (6) drawing-knives and heading-knives; (7) side-axe, used for trimming staves, heads, etc.; (8) holes in jointer to take stool (see 10); (9) jointers, for planing the edges of the staves; (10) stool, on which the jointer rests when in use. The spigot at the top fits into the hole (see 8); (11) cresset or brazier, for holding the fire heating the inside of the cask when bending and setting the staves; (12) trussing-adze, used for driving the truss-hoops when raising the cask; (13) sharp or rounding adze, used for cutting the chiv, in place of the chiv-plane (see 14); (14) the chiv-plane in various sizes, for cutting the shallow channel below the top of the staves, in which the groove to take the head is later cut with a croze; (15) downright, a shave for smoothing the outside of the cask; (16) stoup, a compass type of plane for smoothing the inside of the cask; (17) taper auger, for cutting a tapered hole to receive the bung; (18) flags: dried rushes used for caulking joints between head and croze, and other joints; (19) brace, with shell bit, for boring the holes to take the dowels which join the separate boards of the head (see 21); (20) bick-iron, on which the hoops are riveted; (21) the head of the cask; (22) cap or chime hoop; (23) quarter-hoop; (24) bilge-hoop; (25) bung-hole; (26) tap-hole; (27) hoop-driver; (28) board used for holding head during plan- ing; (29) heading-swift, for planing the heads; (30) letter stencils, for marking the casks (see further plate 7).*

held by iron or sometimes wooden hoops. The staves of beer-casks, on the other hand, are usually too thick and stiff to be thus drawn together. The cooper therefore bends their splaying stave-ends by driving on progressively smaller ash truss-hoops. These are beaten down with a heavy trussing-adze. The cask is then again placed over the brazier for some fifteen minutes to remove moisture absorbed during the steaming. This heating is also said to shrink the fibres of the wood on the inside of the bulge, which helps to set the staves in barrel-form so that when the truss-hoops are removed they will not spring out of position.

4. *Topping*. The ends of the cask staves are now trimmed with an adze to form a bevel (the 'chime'). This special cooper's adze has a short handle, about 9 in long, so that it can be swung within the radius of the cask. The ends of the staves are finished off with a topping-plane having a semicircular stock and a flat sole. A fairly broad but shallow channel (the 'howel') some 2 in below the top of the staves is then made with a special plane called a chiv. For repair-work the channel is cut with a hollow-bladed draw-knife or jigger. A deeper but narrower channel in the middle of the chiv-cut, into which the head fits, is cut with a croze (figure 67 B). Like the chiv, the croze is provided with a large semicircular fence which bears on the rim of the cask. It is more like a giant carpenter's gauge than a plane, the peg which carries the cutter passing through the fence and being adjustable by a wedge. The cutter consists of three saw-teeth set coarsely to cut a wide groove, or of a single hawksbill tooth of the router kind. The fence is placed horizontally on the rim of the cask and the blade set at the required distance below it. As the instrument is pushed around the inside of the tops of the staves, the circular groove to receive the head is cut.

5. *Cleaning down*. Various shaves are taken to smooth both the interior and exterior of the cask. Since the cask is set, all but the end hoops can be knocked off. A small 'downright' shave with its cutting-edge slightly concave is now pushed down the outside and gives the first rough shaping. This is followed by a scraper-shave. For the inside, a tool similar to the downright shave, but with a convex blade, is pulled along the joints towards the operator.

6. *Bunging*. The bung-hole is now bored with a taper-auger and then smoothed with a conical burning-iron. The rough edge inside is trimmed with a hook-like knife oddly called a 'thief'. In beer-barrels a bung of cork is used temporarily, but later a thin wooden cylinder or shive is driven into the bung-hole. When the whole cask has been assembled, another tapered hole is bored through the head, which is stopped by a cork until the tap is fitted to it. Since beer would not flow without an air-inlet to the barrel, after fitting the tap a small hole is pierced through the shive. This hole is stoppered by a tapered peg known as a spile.

7. *Heading*. The heads are of three or more pieces of oak held together by dowel-pegs, and caulked between joints with dry rushes (see 8). The dowel holes are drilled with a brace and hollow bit (figure 65 B). To obtain the approximate radius of the head the cooper proceeds by trial and error, stepping his compasses around the groove at the top of the cask until the circuit is completed in six equal steps or chords. The distance between the compass-points is now equal to the radius of the cask head. The head is rested on the block, being supported by the cooper's left hand and body. It is then shaped with the side-axe, and bevelled along the sides with a draw-knife. The head is planed across the grain with a heavy shave ('heading-swift') fitted with a $2\frac{1}{2}$-in cutting-iron. While the cask-head is being inserted, it is held up by means of a coarse screw twisted into it and removed afterwards. The temporary chime-hoop is taken off, and the head is eased into position. An iron bar, bent at one end, is introduced through the bung-hole to knock up the head if it falls below its groove.

8. *Caulking or flagging.* The dried rushes (or 'flags') for caulking the joints of the head, and the space between the head and its groove, are pushed in with a chisel-like tool. In repair-work, and often in manufacture, rushes are inserted between the staves, but only from their ends down to a point above the bilge. A fork-like tool ('flagging iron') is used to spring each stave in turn, opening the joint sufficiently to receive the rushes. On the continent of Europe other types of tool are used for this purpose. One such is illustrated in a Jost Amman woodcut of 1574 (p 122, reference [19]).

9. *Fitting the hoops.* The iron hoops are cut, beaten into shape, and riveted on the T-anvil. They are driven into place with a hammer and a driver; the latter is a steel wedge-shaped tool with an oaken handle, grooved at the narrow end to prevent it from slipping off the hoop. Finally, graduated sticks called diagonals are used to make sure that the cask will hold the correct volume.

BIBLIOGRAPHY

COLEMAN, J. C. "The Craft of Coopering." *J. Cork hist. archaeol. Soc.*, second series, **49**, 79–89, 1944.

ELKINGTON, G. 'The Coopers' Company and Craft.' Low, London. 1933.

FIRTH, J. F. 'The Coopers' Company.' London. 1848.

FOSTER, SIR WILLIAM. 'A Short History of the Worshipful Company of Coopers of London.' University Press, Cambridge. 1944.

HANKERSON, F. P. 'The Cooperage Handbook.' The Chemical Publishing Company, New York. 1947.

LEGROS, E. "Le tonnelier à la main à Huy." Enquêtes du musée de la Wallonne. Liége. 1949.

6

FARM-TOOLS, VEHICLES, AND HARNESS
1500–1900

OLGA BEAUMONT (I, III) AND J. GERAINT JENKINS (II)

I. FARM-TOOLS

THE majority of the small farm-tools used between 1500 and 1900 were traditional, varying from medieval types only in details of design and in materials of construction. The slow progress of invention before the industrial era is clearly demonstrated by the works of agricultural theorists writing in the sixteenth and seventeenth centuries, such as Thomas Tusser, Gervase Markham, Walter Blith, and John Mortimer. In his 'Five hundreth good pointes of husbandry' (1573) Tusser gave a list of tools necessary for the farmer, including a flail, straw-fork, rake, pitchfork, dung-fork, shovel, and spade. In fact, farms normally possessed, in addition to a plough, a wain, and a tumbril, a small collection of spades, weeding-tongs, forks, sickles, and flails. Subsistence agriculture could scarcely have been practised with less equipment than this.

Digging, harrowing, and drainage. In the sequence of preparing ground for seed hand-tools often had their place between the original ploughing and the final smoothing with a harrow (figure 73). The soil was broken up with spades, mattocks, and clodding-beetles of various shapes. A wooden spade with a two-sided blade and a metal tip was used at the beginning of the period, but blades made entirely of metal came into use later. Tools for breaking clods varied in design from mallet-shaped beetles to flat stampers and hacks with straight or curved blades. As methods improved and harrows and cultivators came into more general use these implements were superseded.

A number of writers after 1660 described the use of the breast-plough (figure 74) for cultivating small areas and paring weeds off the surface of the ground. John Mortimer in 'The whole art of husbandry' (1707) referred to its use for paring and before burning in the counties of south-west England. The most common type had a stout handle 5–8 ft long forking at the top and mortised to a cross-piece. The blade was about a foot long and 18 in wide with a flange or coulter by which the slice was cut. By pushing against the cross-piece the operator forced the blade along under the surface of the ground and cut a thin

broad slice 2 or 3 in thick. In 1802 Sir
John Sinclair, president of the Board of
Agriculture, advocated the breast-plough
for reclaiming waste land in Scotland, but
it was no longer in general use after the
middle of the nineteenth century.

Hand-tools were the only implements
used for drainage until the end of the
eighteenth century, when drainage-
ploughs were invented. The topic was
frequently discussed in books on farming
between 1600 and 1800, and Walter Blith
gave a careful description of drainage
tools in his 'English Improver Improved'
in 1652 (figure 75). Spades of varying

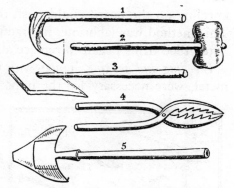

FIGURE 73—*A selection of seventeenth-century farm
tools, from Gervase Markham's 'Farewell to Husbandry' (1620). (1) Hack for breaking clods after
ploughing; (2, 3) clodding-beetles; (4) weeding-tongs;
(5) paring-shovel for clearing ground and destroying
weeds.*

widths were necessary for the different stages of trench-construction. One form
of spade pushed before the worker had two horn-shaped projections at the side,
which cut the turf. Towards the end of the period brush- and stone-filled drains
were gradually superseded by arch-shaped drainage-tiles, and ultimately by
round tiles placed edge to edge to form pipes (vol IV, ch 1).

Sowing. The earliest and simplest way of sowing seed was to broadcast it, a
method still practised by many farmers in the late nineteenth century. The
sower carried the seed in a sheet, basket, or wooden seed-
lip slung over his shoulder; walking up and down the ridges
of the field, he scattered handfuls of grain by rhythmical
sweeps of his arms across his body. Great skill was necessary
to ensure even distribution of seed.

A second method of sowing, known as dibbling, was common
before mechanical drills became popular, particularly for large
seeds such as beans. Holes were made in the ground at regular
intervals by a man walking backwards and carrying in each
hand a pointed iron rod or dibbler (figure 76, right). This tool
was about 3 ft long with a handle like that of a spade and a
tapering knob at the bottom. Women and children followed
dropping seeds into the holes. A wooden setting-board
measuring 3 ft in length and a foot wide with spaced holes
for seeds was described by Sir Hugh Plat in his 'Newe and
admirable arte of setting of corne' (1601). Men standing or

FIGURE 74—*Breast-
plough, 5 ft 3 in high;
the cross-piece is 2 ft
4 in wide.*

kneeling on the board could push their dibblers and seeds through the holes. This method was laborious in practice, and the device was never widely used. After 1800 drills began to replace all other methods of sowing.

Weeding and hedging. Tongs with teeth, originally made of wood and later of metal, were necessary for the important task of weeding. An implement with two large prongs and a third prong curled up behind to give leverage was also used, particularly for docks, a common weed in pastures. Arable weeds could be controlled by the combination of a small knife on a long handle and a forked stick to hold the weed still while cutting. One tool was held in each hand. Thistles were cut with scythes or bruised with thistle-spuds before the formation of seeds.

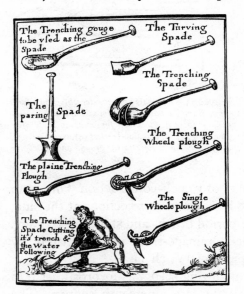

FIGURE 75—*Drainage-tools, from Walter Blith's 'English Improver Improved', 1652.*

Hedges became characteristic of the English landscape as the medieval open-field system gradually disappeared. The enclosure of open fields proceeded throughout the period, and plots were separated from surrounding land by hedges, stone walls, or fences. Large hedging-hooks and smaller-sized bill-hooks were used for the work of laying, cutting, and trimming hedges (figure 76, lower left). Each district had its own pattern. The traditional regional shapes first forged by local blacksmiths are still followed by modern manufacturers (p 116).

Harvesting. Before the invention of mechanical reapers crops were harvested by hand with the aid of sickles, hooks, and scythes. The sickle (figure 76, left) was the earliest implement for reaping corn (vol I, pp 513–14, 541–2; II, p 94), and the form of its continuously curved blade ending in a sharp point several inches beyond the line of the handle remained unchanged from the eleventh century. Some sickles had plain blades, others had serrations along the blade except for the last inch or two at the tip. This tool was intended to cut the corn handful by handful, the stalks being held in one hand by a man stooping or kneeling and cut by a swinging motion of the sickle in the other hand.

Sickles were often replaced by hooks in the mid-nineteenth century. These tools had larger, less curved blades and slashed rather than cut. The man who reaped with a hook carried in his other hand a short wooden crook which he used to draw the crop forward towards himself.

The scythe (vol II, p 95) was a common tool for grass-cutting throughout the period, and its use for reaping oats, barley, and wheat gradually increased. It consisted of a broad metal blade mounted on a wooden pole to which two handles were attached. Medieval illustrations show scythes with straight poles (vol II, figure 62), but curved poles of willow had come into use by the end of the seventeenth century. A light wooden frame or 'cradle' curved parallel to the blade of the scythe collected the stalks during the process of mowing, so that they fell in compact even rows.

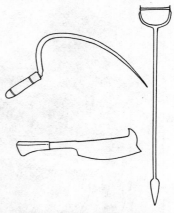

After reaping, the swaths of grass were thrown about with wooden forks or hay-tedders and spread evenly over the ground to dry. When dry, the hay was collected into wind-rows with drag-rakes. It was later pitched into a cart and from cart to stack by forks. Grain was tied in sheaves by women and children (figure 77). It was allowed to stand in stooks before being loaded on to a cart with pitchforks. The continuity in the design of the pitchfork and drag-rake over a long period of years can be seen by comparing eighteenth- and nineteenth-century illustrations with modern examples.

FIGURE 76—(Right), *Dibbler used for sowing seeds;* (left, above), *sickle from Gloucestershire; the strongly curved blade is more than 22 in long;* (left, below), *bill-hook of Northamptonshire design. Scale 1/14.*

Threshing. The flail was the implement in general use in all north European countries before the mechanization of threshing. Its two principal parts were the hand-staff, a straight slender stick of ash or beech 4 or 5 ft long, and the swingle or beater, a shorter, stouter stick of holly, blackthorn, or some other hard wood, about 3 ft long. The two parts were fastened together loosely by thongs, which allowed angular movement in every direction. The proportions between the two parts of the flail and the precise method of joining varied in different areas.

Threshing by flail normally took place in the winter months and was a very skilled operation. The hand-staff was grasped with both hands, at a short distance from one another, and raised so that the swingle flew round the thresher's head and came down with a heavy blow on the ears of grain (vol II, figure, p 102). The work was done in barns, which were often constructed especially for threshing. They had a central strip or threshing-floor where the work was done. The floor was made of hard, beaten earth, oak-planks, or stone. Small compartments were built on either side of this strip, and the barn had a door high enough to drive a loaded wagon through. Sheaves were placed in one compartment and threshed, and the straw was stacked in a corresponding division on the other side of the barn.

To remove coarse material after threshing the grain was sieved through a wide round riddle with meshes of ash or split willow. Corn and chaff were separated

FIGURE 77—*A nineteenth-century harvest scene showing the use of scythes and a drag-rake and the binding of sheaves. c 1840.*

by winnowing, either on the top of a hill or in a barn. The mixture was tossed into the air using wooden shovels or shallow wicker baskets. The wind carried away the chaff and let the grain fall back to the ground or threshing-floor. To assist in winnowing, barns were often built so that the wind blew directly through them. An artificial draught could be created by the use of a crude winnowing-machine, made of wooden arms with sacking attached and mounted on rough bearings. As the handle was turned round by one man a second threw the grain in front of the machine from a shovel or hollow tray made from a single piece of birch or sycamore.

Awners were used to cut the awns or beard off barley. Several varieties existed, the most common consisting of a square iron frame containing parallel blades and a short handle set vertically in the frame (figure 78). The barley was heaped, and struck with this frame. When a rotary awner with blades set round a drum was used the implement was rolled over the grain in lawn-mower fashion.

Agricultural development depended upon dissemination of new ideas, availability of suitable materials for the manufacture of implements, and improvement of transport. The gradual adoption on some farms of new and more complicated implements for all the operations of the farming year did not bring about the complete abandonment of the old tools locally made. The new and the old often co-existed. In Britain machines have now replaced most of the hand-tools, but there are still some survivals on modern farms,

FIGURE 78—*Barley-awner of the early nineteenth century used in Hampshire.*

such as tools for hedging; they are closely related to the medieval types. Farther afield in Europe, in places where mechanization has not completely altered the nature of farming, the scene at such times as harvest is little different from that which might have been witnessed in fourteenth-century England.

II. AGRICULTURAL VEHICLES

Sledges and pack-animals. Despite the general improvement in agricultural transport in the sixteenth century, isolated and hilly districts still clung to the more primitive methods. In those districts human porterage remained very common for short distances, while pack-horses, mules, and asses were used to carry loads for longer distances.

The simplest, and probably the oldest, method of carrying goods was on the backs of men. Nevertheless, the distance that goods could be carried was strictly limited by the weight that the human back could bear. On the farm, ropes of plaited straw, rushes, or horse-hair were used for carrying large bundles of hay or straw from the rickyard to the sheds housing the animals. Deep baskets

FIGURE 79—*Hand-barrow from Glamorganshire, 184 in long by 65 in wide.*

for women to carry peat from the bog to the farm may still be found in Ireland. These burden-creels, as they are called, were slung from the shoulders like a rucksack, leaving the hands of the carrier free for knitting as she walked along. In the Isle of Man burden-creels were generally suspended from a strap passing round the carrier's forehead.

A slightly more advanced aid in carrying material for short distances was the hand-barrow (figure 79). This was made from two parallel pieces of wood joined together by a number of cross-pieces, which formed the carrying-surface

FIGURE 80—*Dorsal-car from Blaencorrwg, Glamorganshire.*

of the barrow. The side-pieces were extended to form handles. As recently as 1850, in Merionethshire, manure was carried to the fields upon these barrows. Each farm in a locality specified a day for dung-carrying, and all the neighbours would congregate at the chosen farm with their barrows. The carrying was performed by means of a shuttle-service, the load changing hands many times before it finally reached the field.

Wheel-less sledges were also very common in hilly districts, where they were mainly used for short-distance porterage around the farm. In the British Isles they persisted until recent times in Cornwall and Devon, Wales, Cumbria, Scotland, and Ireland, as well as in the marshy districts of East Anglia. Sledges were of two types, the dorsal-car and the slide-car.

The dorsal-car (figure 80) consisted of two stout, parallel timbers joined together by a number of cross-bars. The side-pieces extended to form a pair of shafts, which were attached to the horse high up on the collar. The vehicle was dragged along the ground at a tilt, hence it was necessary to fit a wooden framework, or ladder, at the back, so that the load would not fall out. A smaller ladder was also fitted at the front, while the load could be made more secure by tying it down with ropes—a necessary procedure when carrying hay, corn, or wood on steep mountain slopes.

The slide-car (figure 81) differed from the dorsal-car in that the whole base of the vehicle was dragged along the ground like a sledge. Again it consisted of two parallel side-pieces joined by a number of cross-bars that formed the carrying-surface of the car. While the dorsal-car was dragged, with the end of

FIGURE 81—*Slide-car from Llanbrynmair, Montgomeryshire.*

the side-pieces bearing on the ground, the slide-car was equipped with a pair of wooden runners bearing the weight of the vehicle. Generally the body was tilted forwards on these runners, the angle of tilt depending on the slope of the land on which it was used. The vehicle was attached to the horse by a pair of trace-chains rather than by shafts.

These forms of transport, well known from very early times (see vol I, ch 26, and II, ch 15), are still occasionally used in upland districts. They are extremely suitable for the topography of such areas, while the fact that they can be made by the farmer himself, from timber growing on the farm, accounts in no small measure for their continued use. Upland farming is generally difficult and, since the income of the individual farmer is low, tools and implements are consequently primitive and specialized craftsmen rare.

While human porterage and sledge-transport was efficient for short-distance carriage, something more adaptable was required for longer distances. Pack-horse teams, common in medieval times, continued to be used in hilly districts; for example, they were very common in Devon and Cornwall until the end of the nineteenth century. In those counties they were used not only for long-distance transport but for carriage around the farm. Pack-horses were equipped with a pair of baskets (panniers) for carrying peat and similar material; or with a pair of boxes (pots) for dung-carrying; or with a pair of wooden frames (crooks) for harvesting. All these were slung over the animals' backs. In addition, pack-horses were sometimes equipped with an arched wooden saddle, the load being usually in a bag slung over it.

Carts. In medieval times two-wheeled carts were in general use wherever the terrain was suitable for wheeled transport. The carts were either drawn by horses, as seen in the illustration from the Luttrell psalter (vol II, figure 500), or by teams of oxen, and were equipped either with spoked wheels or with primitive solid-disk wheels. Vehicles with solid wheels remained common in

FIGURE 82—*Scotch cart, 1813.*

many parts of the world until recently, and may still be seen in a number of isolated districts. In early nineteenth-century northern Scotland heavy carts with tripartite disk-wheels were numerous, although they were being gradually supplanted by lighter carts designed to be drawn by a single horse. The wheels of the old heavy carts turned in one piece with the axles, and because the vehicles tumbled along they were known as 'tumblers'.

The Lowlands of central Scotland were, however, the centre of a great agrarian movement in the late eighteenth and early nineteenth centuries. English farmers sent their sons as farm-pupils to Scotland, where the most advanced and skilful husbandry was thought to be practised. In that region the design of carts and agricultural implements generally was far in advance of anything then used in other parts of Britain. Through contacts between England and Scotland, the Scotch cart was copied by craftsmen not only throughout Britain, but on the continent as well. It was generally light enough to be pulled by one horse (figure 82), in spite of its long capacious body. A typical cart measured 5 ft 6 inches in length, 4 ft 6 inches in width, and 1 ft 7 in deep at the front. The narrow spoked wheels had a diameter of between 4 ft 6 in and 4 ft 10 in. The body was often made to tip, in which case the cart was known as a coup-cart. The Scotch cart was therefore a general-purpose farm-vehicle, for when it was required for harvesting a wooden framework could be attached to the top of the body, thus considerably increasing its load-carrying capacity. Throughout the nineteenth century one-horse carts of Scottish design replaced the traditional heavy vehicles on the English farm.

The Luttrell psalter of the fourteenth century shows the heavy two-wheeled vehicle in general use in England in the Middle Ages. It was drawn by three horses in tandem, and the massive six-spoked wheels were fitted with iron lugs

FIGURE 83—*Tumbril from north Essex.*

to prevent the vehicle from slipping. The sides of the cart were open rather than boarded, while fore- and tail-ladders were fitted to take the overhanging load. Until the introduction of the Scotch cart in the late eighteenth century, English two-wheeled carts followed this medieval tradition. They continued to be heavy and clumsy, and required at least two horses, or four oxen, to draw them. In marshy districts the wheels were not even shod with metal, while in other districts crescent-shaped pieces of iron, called strakes, were nailed to the wheel to prevent wear. One very important development on the English midland plain, however, was that at some time during the seventeenth and eighteenth centuries four-wheeled wagons replaced the traditional harvest-cart, especially on the larger farms. On the smaller farms two-wheeled vehicles with open sides and fore- and tail-ladders continued in use until fairly recent times. Although these carts were generally light, they were very much in the medieval tradition.

While four-wheeled wagons were used for harvesting on the English plain and the flatter regions of Europe generally, two-wheeled carts of small capacity were retained for special purposes on the farm. For dung-carting two-wheeled vehicles were invariably used. As early as the mid-eighteenth century, tilt-carts or tumbrils were in use throughout western Europe (figure 83). A tumbril had fairly low wheels, and a body sloping upwards to a very high frontboard, which leaned out over the horse's back. Two heavy pieces of oak formed the frame of the cart, and these projected at the back to rest on the ground when the cart was tipped for unloading. An older version of the tumbril was the box-cart with a fixed body that could not be tipped. Its general shape was that of a tumbril, but in order to unload it the horse was unharnessed and the whole vehicle, including the shafts, tipped backwards.

In the hilly districts of Europe, where slopes were too steep for the use of wagons yet not so steep as wholly to forbid wheeled transport, two-wheeled carts were used for all farming purposes, including harvesting. Although box-carts were often adapted for harvesting by the addition of frames at the top, specialized harvest-carts were nevertheless common. The simplest of these was the cart consisting of a flat wooden platform placed on a pair of wheels. The Cornish wain of the eighteenth century and possibly earlier was of this type— a long rectangular platform with arched guards over the low wheels. It had fore- and tail-ladders, while at the back there was a small windlass for tightening the ropes thrown over the load. The Scottish harvest-cart was similar in shape and design, though slightly smaller, while the Welsh *gambo* differed in that it had a pair of rails to prevent the load spilling over the wheels, rather than arched wheel-guards. These Celtic harvest vehicles pulled by either horses or oxen may be regarded as the British equivalents to the Mediterranean ox-carts.

In Scandinavia and north-western Europe generally, the normal harvest-cart was rather different. It had a very long, narrow, rectangular frame. A number of wooden spindles, each approximately 12 in long, was fixed to the frame at such an angle that the spindles overhung the two wheels. The wheels were generally very low, while the cart was again fitted with fore- and tail-ladders.

Wagons. It is not known at what date four-wheeled wagons were introduced into Britain, but it is almost certain that they were extremely rare until the sixteenth century. In the Middle Ages the lack of contact between one region and another, and the communal nature of farming, meant that elaborate wheeled vehicles were unnecessary and rare. The long wagon with its canvas cover, illustrated in the Luttrell psalter, was without doubt a vehicle for carrying people rather than goods: a successor of the Roman *carruca* (vol II, p 540) rather than a predecessor of the carrier's wagon. Four-wheeled vehicles were, however, in general use on the continent of Europe in the Middle Ages, and haulage firms competed to some extent on the main routes. For the limited amount of long-distance transport on English medieval roads two-wheeled vehicles carrying no more than a ton were used. The sixteenth century saw the break-down of the localism of the Middle Ages, which meant that more and better vehicles were required to transport the produce of the agricultural regions to the ever-growing towns. The four-wheeled carrier's wagon became very common in the late sixteenth century, and although at that time the largest wagons carried only four tons, by the end of the seventeenth century wagons able to carry anything up to eight tons were numerous. These large vehicles, each drawn by a team of up to twelve horses, ran on certain routes on days specified beforehand. For example, there was a regular service between some Sussex towns and London, the wagons taking loads of wheat and oats to the metropolis. For the return journey to Sussex they loaded up with old, but sound, ships' timber from London ship-breaking yards. This timber was bought by Sussex landowners for use in building cottages and barns on their estates.

The old stage-wagons were well suited for long-distance haulage, but owing to their great weight they were unsuitable for transport around the farm. During the mid-eighteenth century, the whole aspect of British farming was changing very quickly. More than two hundred private enclosure acts were passed between 1727 and 1760, and enclosed farming became the rule rather than the exception. With this release of initiative, there arose a demand for something much larger than the two-wheeled carts hitherto used on English farms. Village wainwrights took as their model the existing stage-wagons, and adapted them to their needs. Three- or four-ton wagons became the rule; loaded with hay or corn-sheaves, they could easily be drawn by two horses on the journey from the fields to the rickyard.

The general principle on which wagons were built was uniform throughout the country, despite much variation in detail. Counties and districts favoured their own particular designs, the differences being due to the varying demands of soil and topography. For example, the wagons of East Anglia were heavy and box-like, as befitted an area of flat land with large fields. The wagons of the Cotswolds, on the other hand, in use in an undulating region with numerous steep slopes, were much lighter, and excess weight was cut down wherever possible. In general, English farm-wagons may be divided into two distinct types —the box- and the bow-wagon. The box-wagon, as it name suggests, had a deep rectangular body, and where raves or side-boards occurred they were generally narrow (figure 84). This type of vehicle occurred in eastern England, the Midlands, the Welsh border counties, and in south-eastern England.

The bow-wagon had a much shallower body, characterized by side-boards arching over the rear wheels. This lowered the bed of the wagon, without lessening the diameter of the wheels. The bow-wagon was common to the west of England, occurring from the Chilterns in the east to Glamorganshire and Devon in the west.

In general design the wagons of Lincolnshire, resembling those used in the Low Countries and western Europe generally, may be regarded as the simplest of English box-wagons. The typical Lincolnshire wagon was a large vehicle

FIGURE 84—*Box-wagon from Lincolnshire.*

characterized by a deep body, which measured 27 inches in depth at the back, 24 inches in the centre, and 38 in at the front. The lofty, sloping front-board was usually elaborately decorated, and the name of the owner, his address, and the date of manufacture were written on it. Although the body was generally narrow, measuring no more than 42 in wide, it had the considerable length of 12 ft 6 in. The sides of the vehicle were characterized by a large number of wooden pins or spindles acting as supports for the sides, while the bottom frames of the body were notched to form a waist. On turning the wagon, the wheels would enter the waist, and the lock was therefore considerable. The wheels themselves were greatly dished and large, the hind wheels with a diameter of 65 in and the front wheels with a diameter of 54 in. The wagon was not usually equipped with side-boards, thus resembling the continental vehicles, but a wooden framework could be fitted on it to take any overhanging load.

The Wiltshire wagon was probably the parent type of all the west of England bow-wagons, for although in shape it was similar to those used in the Cotswolds, Oxfordshire, and Glamorganshire it was much simpler in design. Wagons from the south of the county had narrow-tired wheels for use on the hard chalk-land of Salisbury Plain, while those from the north of the county had broad wheels, up to 8 inches in width, for the clay land of the vale of Pewsey and the vale of the White Horse. Apart from this variation in the width of wheels, the wagons used throughout the county were remarkably uniform in design. The outstanding features of the Wiltshire wagon were the wide side-boards that curved archwise

FIGURE 85—*Bow-wagon from Wiltshire.*

over the rear wheels. These boards are never found on continental vehicles. Since the bottom frames of the body were straight, the Wiltshire wagon suffered one great disadvantage, in that it required as much as a quarter of an acre to turn in, for the wheels soon rubbed against the frames if the vehicle was turned too sharply. The typical Wiltshire wagon had a very shallow body, no more than 15 in deep. On the other hand, the body was as much as 80 inches in maximum width, and 12 ft 6 in long. Although the actual body of the vehicle was small, the overhanging side-boards added considerably to its load-carrying capacity. The wheels were generally smaller than those of the box-wagon, the hind wheels of the average wagon having a diameter of 55 in and the front wheels of 45 in (figure 85).

All the early farm-wagons were designed for a specific type of soil and country, and were built by village craftsmen who followed traditional methods and designs. In this way distinctly regional styles of wagons came into existence. It was not until the late nineteenth century that standardized vehicles produced by large-scale manufacturers came on the market, and these boat-wagons and trolleys with smaller wheels, greater lock, and sprung undercarriages were used alongside the older village-made vehicles.

III. HARNESS

Information about the history of harness between 1500 and 1900 is very scarce, but the harness now in use has altered little since 1800 (figure 86). Harness varies according to the size and type of horse employed and the work to be done.

FIGURE 86—*Two cart-horses wearing harness as illustrated in a nineteenth-century trade catalogue. The shaft-horse has full cart-harness, but the trace-horse wears only a collar, hames, bridle, and three straps.*

Different tasks, such as carting and ploughing, require different harness: the horses wear full shaft-harness when carting and trace-harness when ploughing. To be fully equipped, a shaft-horse requires a collar, together with hames, saddle, breeching- or back-band, and a bridle. For ploughing only a collar, hames, bridle, and back-band are necessary.

The collar is an indispensable feature of all types of draught harness. Yokes connected to a cart or plough by a long pole called a neb were used when the ox was the common draught-animal on the farm, but even oxen came to be harnessed with collars and hames before they were finally superseded by horses for ploughing and carting (vol II, ch 15). Light wooden hames were used, with a very pronounced curvature to fit the broad neck of an ox.

A horse works by pushing against its collar, and a good collar provides the means of giving a steady draught. Horses used in hilly districts require light collars of close fit because of varied gradients and uncertain draught. The Liverpool collar, common in the northern counties, fits more closely than the collar of midland design, used in flatter land, and is less heavy and thick. Collars normally consist of a stiff leather tube stuffed with straw, but a few early rush-covered collars are in existence. This tube is known as the wale. The main body of the collar is also made of straw, covered with woollen cloth. Collars carry the heavy wooden or metal hames to the hooks of which the trace-chains are attached for drawing the cart or implement. In cart-harness, chains from the shafts also pass over a wooden saddle padded underneath with felt or straw.

Each leather strap in cart-harness supplementary to the collar and saddle has a special name. From the saddle the girth or belly-band goes under the horse to prevent the shafts from rising. The breeching- or back-band is slung across the horse's rump by breeching-straps from the back. The breeching-band is secured to the shafts sufficiently closely to take the forward draught of a cart going down hill and keep it back. From the horse's tail to the cart-saddle a wide strap known as the crupper extends, and between the animal's legs hangs a martingale fastened to the collar and belly-band.

Reins pass over the horse's back and saddle through the hames and are attached to a bit in the mouth. The bridle worn on the head consists of a head-stall, brow-band below the ears, nose-band, and blinkers which limit the range of vision.

Decorative harness was used for cart-horses in town and country throughout the nineteenth century, and was particularly important between 1850 and 1900. Brasses of traditional design were fastened to the martingale, blinkers, and face-piece. As well as brasses some horses wore on their heads disks of brass swinging in brass rings, or plumes of red, white, and blue mounted on brass and known as fly-terrets. Team- or latten-bells fixed in a leather hood above the collar, and often fringed with red wool, gave warning of the approach of a horse and cart. Housen or housings, which were often made in a semicircular shape decorated with brass mountings or painted figures, would be attached to the top of the collar. Wooden housen were used in the eighteenth century, but leather became more common after 1800. This form of decoration has, in common with other trappings, now gone out of use.

The editors and authors desire to thank Mr J. W. Y. Higgs, Keeper of the Museum of English Rural Life, Reading, for his assistance in the preparation of this chapter.

BIBLIOGRAPHY

Farm Tools

BEECHAM, H. A. and HIGGS, J. W. Y. 'The Story of Farm Tools.' Young Farmers' Club Booklet, No. 24. Evans, London. 1951.

COPELAND, S. 'Agriculture, Ancient and Modern.' London. 1866.

FUSSELL, G. E. 'The Farmer's Tools, 1500–1900.' Melrose, London. 1952.

HENNELL, T. 'Change in the Farm.' University Press, Cambridge. 1934.

SLIGHT, J. and BURN, R. SCOTT. 'The Book of Farm Implements and Machinery' (ed. by H. STEPHENS). London. 1858.

Harness

STEPHENS, H. 'The Book of the Farm' (3rd ed., 2 vols). London. 1871.

WOODS, K. S. 'Rural Crafts in England.' Harrap, London. 1949.

Vehicles

BERG, G. 'Sledges and Wheeled Vehicles.' Nordiska Museets Handlingar, No. 4. Stockholm, Copenhagen. 1935.

FOX, SIR CYRIL F. "Sleds, Carts and Waggons." *Antiquity*, **5**, 185, 1931.

LANE, R. H. "Waggons and their Ancestors." *Antiquity*, **9**, 140, 1935.

PEATE, I. C. "Some Aspects of Agricultural Transport in Wales." *Archaeologia Cambrensis*, **90**, 219-38, 1935.

Jethro Tull's hoe-plough, showing the method of harnessing the horses to it. 1733.

7

SPINNING AND WEAVING

R. PATTERSON

I. FIBRES AND THEIR PREPARATION

THE period from 1500 to 1760 is one of the most important in the history of textile manufacture in Europe. The profound effects of the Renaissance were reflected in changing aspirations and higher standards of living, while the spirit of adventure and commercial enterprise led to great expansion of trade in newly developed markets.

Textiles, particularly wool, linen, and silk, were closely linked with vicissitudes in the wealth of nations, and regulation of their manufacture and sale was fundamental to the economic policies of the new nation-states. The religious upheavals of the Reformation and Counter-reformation divided nations and scattered their populations, and amidst international and civil wars the preponderance of power shifted rapidly. A flourishing textile trade was often the basis of national greatness: Spain had a flourishing textile industry in the sixteenth century, when the German trade also was at its height. Holland attained her Golden Age in the seventeenth century, to be followed by Britain's supremacy of the eighteenth and nineteenth centuries.

As the power of the guilds waned the state assumed control of the textile manufactures, regulating each process strictly, safeguarding supplies of materials, and protecting the home market. Spinning-schools were set up in many European countries to foster the trade, and in Scotland a spinning-wheel was presented to each proficient student. Many strange enactments appeared, as in Silesia, where no farm-worker, male or female, was permitted to marry until able to spin. In England from 1666 to 1786 it was unlawful to bury a corpse in anything but wool, whereas the Scots were prescribed the use of linen for their shrouds.

This period saw the firm establishment of the factory system in Europe. At the beginning of the sixteenth century John Winchcombe had a factory at Newbury, Berkshire, thus described by Thomas Deloney:

> Within one room being large and long
> There stood two hundred looms full strong . . .

And in another place hard by
An hundred women merrily
Were carding hard with joyful cheer
Who singing sate with voices clear
And in a chamber close beside
Two hundred maidens did abide . . .
These pretty maids did never lin [cease]
But in that place all day did spin . . . [1]

This factory embraced all the processes of woollen-manufacture. Similar factories were set up before 1550 at Malmesbury, Burford, Lavenham, Newbury, Cirencester, Bath, Halifax, Manchester, and Kendal, but the anti-factory legislation of 1555 attempted to restrict country clothiers to one loom. The seventeenth century saw Colbert's model factory under the management of Van Robais at Abbeville, where 1692 workers were employed, but it was in the second half of the eighteenth century that factories became essential for the application of the new textile machinery.

Sheep's wool, the fibre of greatest economic importance, continued to take pride of place in clothing. The improvement and great increase of the Spanish merino flocks in the sixteenth century produced the finest wools of commerce. The finest Spanish wool came from Segovia, with slightly inferior qualities from Castile, Estramadura, and Andalusia [2]. English wools were considered next in order of fineness, followed by the French wools of Languedoc and Berri. Of the English wools the most expensive came from Norfolk, Suffolk, Sussex, and Herefordshire, second grades from Essex, Wiltshire, Dorset, Somerset, and Gloucestershire, third grades from Cambridge, Kent, Hampshire, Devon, Cornwall, Northumberland, Hertfordshire, and Leicestershire, and the coarsest from Yorkshire, Westmorland, Cumberland, and Lincolnshire [3]. Welsh and Irish wools were coarse, and Scottish wools were unpopular owing to the tar frequently smeared on the sheep as a protection against the weather. The export of English wool was prohibited by statute from 1660 to 1825.

The sheep were shorn with hand-shears unchanged in design since the Middle Ages (vol II, figure 154), the fleece being removed in a single piece and sorted into qualities. In Spain the loins and skirts were removed and the remainder divided into three qualities of descending fineness known as firsts, seconds, and thirds. The quantity of each grade was in the ratio of 12:2:1 [2]. French wools were divided into high wool of long staple and low wool of short staple. In England the fleece was divided into three grades: mother-wool from the back and neck, the wool of the tail and legs, and the wool from the breast and belly.

The fleeces were of three types: (i) finest wool, used for woollens and comprising the majority of English fleeces; (ii) longer pile, used for worsteds; and (iii) medium length, used in the hosiery trade.

Before processing, the wool was washed in a mixture of three parts water to one part of urine, to remove grease and salts, and rinsed in running water, often in a basket attached to a captive raft. The washed wool was dried on a frame in the shade and beaten with sticks on a hurdle or on a framework of cords to open the texture, and was then ready for carding, bowing, or combing. In 1733 John Kay invented a machine for beating wool with spring-loaded laths raised by tappets on a wheel [4].

FIGURE 87—*Carding wool. From an early eighteenth-century engraving.*

In *carding* the short wool-fibres destined for woollen yarn, hand-cards almost exactly of the medieval type (vol II, figure 167) were employed. The three operations of working the fibres into an even layer, stripping from one card to the other, and doffing the loosened fibres in the form of a spongy sliver were followed as in earlier times. To increase the output the cards were made much larger and one of them was mounted at an angle on the end of a bench (figure 87). With this stock-card fixed the carder could use both hands on the free card, which was frequently suspended from the ceiling and balanced by a counter-weight. Stock-carding was often a preparatory loosening process preceding hand-carding. Wool was prepared for carding by sprinkling with olive-oil in the proportion of 1 part of oil to 5 of wool for the weft and 1 part of oil to 9 parts of wool for the warp. Butter was often used instead of oil.

The advent of mechanical spinning foreshadowed by Lewis Paul in 1738 (p 162) led the same inventor to design two carding-machines ten years later [5]. The first was in effect a large stock-card, 3 ft by 2 ft, with the card-clothing attached in parallel strips (figure 88). This was mounted horizontally on a vertical shaft and could be rotated by a foot-lever for stripping. The free card was fitted with two handles, for manual use. The carded slivers, removed with a long needle-comb, were joined end-to-end to make a continuous length which was wound on a cylinder by means of a tape.

In Paul's second machine the card-clothing was attached in strips to the

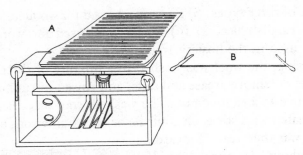

FIGURE 88—*Lewis Paul's rectangular carding machine, 1748. The fibres were placed on the 3 × 2 ft card* (A) *and worked with the hand-card* (B). *The roll was stripped off after turning* A *through 180° by means of the treadles, and wound over a ribbon passing over the two pulleys at the front.*

surface of a cylinder turned by hand (figure 89). The cylinder worked against a concave board lined with card-clothing which could be lowered and rotated for stripping. The process was still intermittent and the separate cardings, removed with a comb as before, had to be joined together.

A more advanced form of carding-machine was patented earlier in 1748 by Daniel Bourn of Leominster [6]. This was a rotary machine in which four card-covered cylinders driven by hand or water-wheel worked against each other (figure 90). The distance between the cylinders was adjustable, and two of the four cylinders had an automatic reciprocating motion along their axes to distribute the fibres evenly over the surfaces. No working details are given, but the doffing would no doubt have been effected with a long comb.

Although not successful this machine was the prototype of later roller carding-machines.

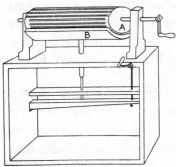

FIGURE 89—*Paul's revolving carding-machine, 1748.* A *is the cylinder covered with strips of card-clothing,* B *a concave card completely covered. To strip off the carded fibres the cylinder was lowered and turned through 180°.*

The *bowing* of wool and cotton (vol II, p 195), as an alternative to carding or in preparation for it, continued to be practised, especially in felt manufacture or where wire cards were not readily obtainable. The bow increased in dimensions and was usually suspended from above. The gut of the 6-ft-long bow was plucked with a piece of wood and the vibrating string passed among the entangled fibres to loosen them and remove small impurities.

Combing of long-staple wool was performed by hand throughout the period. It was essential for the production of worsted yarn, which requires

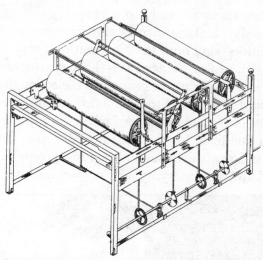

FIGURE 90—*Bourn's carding machine, 1748. The fibres are carded between pairs of rollers rotated in opposite directions by water-power through the shafts and gears.*

parallel fibres from which the shortest ones have been removed. The combs remained almost unchanged, consisting of two or three rows of long, tapering, steel teeth mounted in horn on a wooden handle. They were heated over a stove and attached to a hook on a vertical post (figure 91). The wool, previously soaked in soapy water and wrung out with a winch, was oiled with butter, olive-oil, or colza-oil. Spanish wool which had been washed on the sheep was merely dipped in hot soapy water and combed without being oiled [2]. About 2 oz of wool were attached to the teeth of one comb and worked with the other. The combing, beginning at the tips of the fibres and penetrating deeper at each stroke, was continued until the wool was transferred to the second comb, when the combs were reversed and the process was repeated. The wool was pulled off the comb in a long sliver, and sometimes this was gently recombed with cooler combs before being coiled into a 'top'. The short fibres or noils remaining on the comb were utilized in blanket manufacture.

The teeth were kept very sharp and

FIGURE 91—*Combing wool. From an eighteenth-century engraving.*

were straightened when necessary with a brass tube. A wool-comber could comb about 28 lb of wool a day, and the successful mechanization of this process remained beyond inventors' skill until the nineteenth century.

Flax. The cultivation of flax changed very little during many centuries, but greater care was taken in preparing the ground and selecting the seed. In Holland it was usual to sow seed from heavy soils on light soil and vice versa, although it was found economical in Ireland to use seed taken from the first crop for sowing a second. To obtain fine linen for the extremely delicate cambrics of northern France, the seed was sown thickly and the growing crop was drawn up and sheltered from wind and sun by laying over it branches supported on stakes.

FIGURE 92—*Flax-working.* (Left to right) *Combing the stalks through a ripple; hackling, working the stalks with mallet and scutcher. From an engraving by D. Chodowiecki (1726–1801).*

The flax was pulled before the seed was fully ripe, to preserve its suppleness of fibre. It was laid on the grass, as in Holland, or tied into sheaves and stooked, as in Ireland, for 3 or 4 days to permit ripening of the seeds. The seed-capsules were then removed by drawing bundles of flax through a long coarse comb or 'ripple' (figure 92). This ripple was often mounted on a bench.

The retting process was conditioned by the availability of ponds, lakes, or rivers; ditches and pits were often dug for the purpose. After retting for 1 to 2 weeks the flax was spread out on short grass for 3 to 6 days for partial drying and bleaching and to allow the dew to complete the retting. Dew-retting without steeping was employed in parts of Russia, Germany, and America, but required 3 or 4 weeks to complete the fermentation, while snow-retting in Russia and Sweden lasted through the duration of the snows. In Germany the finest flax was steeped 4 or 5 days in warm diluted milk, and elsewhere lye of wood-ashes and other chemical agents were employed. Steeping unripe flax was a speedy method practised to a large extent in Belgium.

The retted and grassed flax was usually dried artificially. In Holland, specially built ovens were heated to such a temperature that a person inside would not feel uneasy. In Ireland the flax was laid on hurdles over a fire, with resultant unequal drying, discoloration by smoke, and great risk of loss. The drying of flax in domestic ovens was frequently forbidden owing to the fire-hazard.

When dry the flax was ready for braking. The Dutch brake was widely adopted throughout Europe, being fitted with two or three bars to break up the woody stalk or boon. Attempts were made by Abraham Hill in 1664 and by Charles Moreton and Samuel Weale in 1692 to mechanize flax-dressing processes [7]. In 1727 a Scot, David Donald, invented a roller mechanism for beating and scutching flax, and in the following year the machine, driven by a water-wheel, was functioning successfully in Fife. James Spalding invented a machine for dressing flax in 1728, from ideas he gained during a visit to Holland. Similar machines were introduced into Ireland [8] and comprised a horizontal fluted roller engaging with similar rollers above and below (figure 93). The flax was drawn inwards between the two upper rollers and emerged between the two

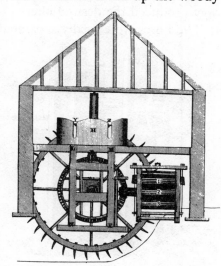

FIGURE 93—*Flax-breaking machine with scutcher (H) above. (Y, Z) Holes for inserting broken flax to be scutched; (1, 2, 3) rolls for breaking the flax.*

lower ones, the process being repeated until the boon (woody portion) was sufficiently broken.

The broken boon was removed by striking the flax over the edge of a board with a rectangular scutching-blade (vol II, figure 158). If the blade struck the flax over the board it damaged the fibres, but the Dutch scutching-board, with a notch in one side to take the flax, eliminated this danger.

Machinery for scutching was introduced in the early eighteenth century; the usual form in Scotland and Ireland was a vertical axle with four projecting arms that rotated in a horizontal drum (figure 93). The flax was inserted through slits in the top and side of this drum and the arms reproduced the action of the scutching-blade and removed the boon.

In Scotland, Ireland, and elsewhere the fibres were then beaten with a ribbed mallet on a block of wood to soften them (figure 92), but in Holland a fining-mill was employed before 1736 (figure 94). This machine was worked by wind, horses, water, or hand, and consisted of a slotted shaft between two wooden uprights, encircled by eight removable spindles. In use, the flax fibres were inserted in bundles through the slotted shafts and then turned alternately backwards and forwards for two revolutions each way. The machine held about 6 lb of flax and as the mass turned back and forth the fibres rubbed against the spindles and were separated into fine filaments. About eighty double turns each way produced the desired effect.

The fibres were finally separated by drawing bundles of flax through a fixed

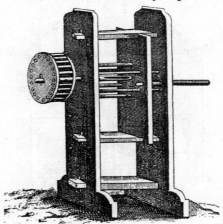

comb or hackle (figure 92). One end was combed and then the other, and the process was repeated with hackles of finer teeth. The Scottish hackles were fitted with stout brass teeth, but in 1728 English and Dutch hackles with long steel teeth were introduced. Hackling was a delicate operation since breakage of the fibres had to be avoided; women were usually employed for the purpose. The short, waste fibres were known as 'tow' and the long, prepared fibres as 'line'. The tow was carded and spun like wool or cotton and made into smocks, underwear, and bed-clothes for everyday use, while the waste

FIGURE 94—*Dutch fining-mill, c 1735. The flax was inserted in the eye of the central shaft.*

from scutching was used to make sack-cloth.

In Holland the braking and scutching processes occupied about 3 months, and one workman could treat 20 lb of flax a day.

The seed, if required for sowing, was separated from the boll by trampling with horses on a barn floor, and finally the husks were removed with a winnowing machine as used for corn.

Hemp also was widely cultivated, particularly in Italy, Germany, Holland, and later in Russia, as a substitute for flax but especially for the manufacture of sails and cordage.

The hemp plant (*Cannabis sativa* L) normally grows to a height of 6 ft, but in some regions up to 16 or even 20 ft. The plants were pulled and retted in standing water for 15 days, after which the bundles were dried. In sixteenth-century Italy the fibres were then separated by hand and passed between fluted rollers before being beaten with mallets and hackled as for flax. A hemp-stamping machine patented in 1721 by Henry Browne comprised vertical timbers which were raised and dropped by tappets on an axle turned by hand, wind, water, or horse power [9].

The *cotton* plant (*Gossypium* spp) occurs in many forms. Linnaeus in 1753 enumerated five distinct species:

1. *Gossypium herbaceum*
2.   „   *arboreum*
3.   „   *hirsutum*
4.   „   *religiosum*
5.   „   *barbadense*

The first is a herbaceous annual growing to a height of 18 to 24 in. It is cultivated in India, China, eastern Mediterranean countries, southern Europe, and North America, and is economically the most important. The second species is a tree attaining a height of 12 to 20 ft. This perennial form is found in Asia, north Africa, and parts of America. The remaining three species are all shrubs varying in height from 2 to 10 ft and are perennial in the hottest countries and annual in the cooler climates. They are found in Asia, Africa, and Central and South America.

Until the eighteenth century cotton was imported into Europe principally from Cyprus, Smyrna, Acre, and Syria. Cotton thread was obtained from Damascus, Jerusalem, and India, the finest being produced in the coastal area of Bengal. During the first half of the eighteenth century cotton of fine quality, known as cotton of Siam because of the origin of the seed, was imported from the West Indies, and before the end of the century West Indian cotton was the main source of England's supply. An unsuccessful attempt was made to grow cotton in Provence at the end of the sixteenth century.

At the opening of that century the weaving of cotton fabrics, and particularly of mixed cotton and linen fustians, was firmly established in Italy, Switzerland, Germany, and Flanders. At this time the fustian industry was reviving in France and was beginning to expand into Holland. Although attempts were made to weave fustians in England with cotton from the Levant in 1430 the first definite mention of a cotton industry there is of about 1621 in Lancashire [10], where it was probably introduced by Flemish immigrants after the fall of Antwerp in 1585.

The large-scale importation of Indian cotton goods by the Dutch and English East India Companies led to the prohibition of such imports in England in 1700, and in many other European countries later, for they were thought to compete with local manufactures. From 1720 to 1774 the weaving of pure cotton calicoes was forbidden in England.

Cotton was picked by hand and passed between two rollers to separate the seed from the fibres. The cotton-gin in India was turned by hand, but in the

West Indies a foot-treadle was incorporated, and one workman could separate up to 60 lb a day. The cotton was tightly packed by treading into wet bags of coarse cloth 9 ft high and 4 ft wide, which held about 300 lb each [2]. Before being carded or bowed as with wool, the cotton from the bale had to be loosened thoroughly by beating with sticks on a hurdle or wire frame.

II. SPINNING

The prepared fibres of wool, flax, tow, or cotton were spun into yarn either with a spindle-and-whorl or a spinning-wheel. The spindle-and-whorl remained in use throughout the period, particularly for the warp and in the more remote areas, but the spindle-wheel

FIGURE 95—*Low Irish spinning-wheel, used for flax.*

(vol II, p 202) was widely adopted in its diverse local forms.

Known variously as the great wheel, muckle wheel, long wheel, or Jersey wheel, the hand-turned spindle-wheel was still employed, particularly for weft-spinning, until comparatively recent times, and its existence was even further prolonged by its use as a pirn-winder.[1] It still remains the standard wheel of the less advanced communities.

The characteristic wheel of the period was undoubtedly the flyer-wheel, which was invented during the fifteenth century (vol II, p 203). Continuous action and the seated position of the operator allowed a foot-treadle to be incorporated. The invention of the treadle is usually attributed to Master Jürgen, a mason of Brunswick, in 1530 [11], but he was anticipated by an illustration of such a mechanism in the Glockendon Bible of 1524 [12], and it is probable that it was an English conception [13]. The treadle was a simple device pivoted between two of the legs and attached at the far end, by a loop of cord, to a connecting-rod, which fitted round a crank at the end of the axle of the wheel, and thus caused the wheel to rotate when the treadle was depressed. This treadle-

---

[1] A pirn is a wooden bobbin fitting the shuttle of a loom and carrying weft.

wheel could be driven by two cords or a single cord. In the former both the bobbin and the flyer are driven, whereas in the latter only the bobbin is driven, the flyer being dragged round by the yarn. An adjustable friction-band rubbing on the flyer-pulley enabled the tension to be regulated to provide the slip necessary for even twisting as the diameter of the yarn wound on the bobbin increased. A similar result is obtained if the flyer is driven and the bobbin retarded by a friction-band, and normal double-drive wheels were often adapted by the spinsters to single-drive with either bobbin- or flyer-lead.

In spite of the many advantages of a treadle-drive, it is remarkable how many flyer-wheels, particularly in France, remained hand-turned by a knob attached to a spoke or a cranked axle. This left only one hand free to draw out the fibres for the yarn, a procedure impossible except with the long fibres of flax or hemp.

The treadle-wheel was a product of the Renaissance and as it spread throughout Europe its technical functions were successfully combined with decorative form, so that various types developed, with the flyer mounted beside or above the wheel. The former are known as Dutch or low Irish wheels (figure 95) and the latter as English or Saxony wheels (figure 96). In addition, the Irish castle-wheel was unique in having the flyer mounted below the wheel (figure 97).

FIGURE 96—*English spinning-wheel, with the flyer mounted above the wheel.*

In North America the spinning-wheel tended to become more utilitarian, and a chair-frame type was produced with a double treadle and an intermediate pulley to increase the speed of the flyer. A flax-spinning wheel with two flyer-and-bobbin units, probably originating in Austria, was introduced into Britain in the eighteenth century.

The distaff became increasingly elaborate. Although usually attached to the spinning-wheel it was frequently mounted on a low stool. A tall distaff is characteristic of flax-spinning; a water-container is often attached for the spinster to wet the fibres as she spins.

Spinning had always been the slowest of the textile processes, and, while the treadle-wheel increased the speed slightly, three to five spinsters were still required to keep one weaver supplied with yarn. The invention of Kay's flying shuttle in 1733 (p 169) increased the disparity, and inventors turned their attention to methods of increasing the rate of yarn-production. Their attempts had been foreshadowed about 1490 by Leonardo da Vinci, who in his *Codice Atlantico* sketched a double flyer to produce two threads simultaneously. He also designed a machine with many such flyer units mounted horizontally, but his ideas were never put into practice. In 1678 Richard Dereham and Richard Haines patented a hand-turned drive to operate 6 to 100 spindles for as many spinsters [14], but it

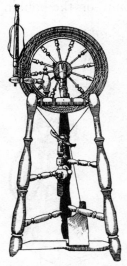

was Lewis Paul of Birmingham, in association with John Wyatt, who attempted the first practical solution to the problem. His patent specification of 1738 [15] describes a system of roller-drafting by means of a series of pairs of rollers, each successive pair revolving faster than its predecessor. He also made provision for one or more of the pairs of rollers to rotate around the axis of the thread to give a slight twist, or for only a single pair of drafting-rollers to be employed. Another patent by Paul in 1758 [16] describes two rollers, on one of which the continuous sliver is wound, feeding a bobbin and flyer revolving proportionately faster so that the sliver is drawn out and spun as it is wound on to the bobbin. His sketch shows about 24 spindles mounted in a circle around a vertical driving-shaft (figure 98).

FIGURE 97—*Irish castle-wheel (mainly used in Antrim and Donegal).*

A frequently overlooked patent of 1754 by James Taylor of Lancashire [17] describes 'an engine to be worked either by men, horses, wind or water, for spinning cotton wool into yarn'. No illustration is attached but the machine is described as having a row of vertical spindles on which are fitted bobbins of roving, and these rovings are spun from the points of the spindles to a reel. The reel is provided with a crank-and-ratchet mechanism so that it winds and stops alternately, spinning 2 ft of thread at each operation and then winding it on.

There is no record of Taylor's patent having been put to practical use, but Paul's machine was in use in 1741 at Birmingham, driven by two donkeys, and in 1743 at Northampton, driven by a water-wheel. Since it was not fully successful, its true value lies in the subsequent embodiment of its principles in the first satisfactory spinning-machine.

III. REELING, WARPING, DRESSING

The spun yarn was wound into a hank for washing, bleaching, sizing, or other treatment. The cross-reel (vol II, figure 173) was widely employed for this purpose and the method of reeling produced a hank twice the length of the reel.

The cross- or hand-reel was, however, subject to wide errors in measurement and its use was prohibited in Scotland in 1695, when the check-reel of fixed dimensions was made compulsory. This was a rotary reel with a chain of gears that produced an audible click after a certain number of revolutions. The circumference of these check-reels was closely regulated in many countries: in England woollen and cotton reels were 1½ yds in circumference and in Scotland the flax reel was 2½ yds and the wool reel 2 yds. Hanks varied in length but became standardized in England at woollen hanks of 256 yds; worsted skeins of 560 yds; linen cuts of 300 yds; and cotton hanks of 840 yds.

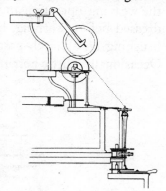

FIGURE 98—*Lewis Paul's spinning-machine, from the patent of 1758. The carded fibres were joined into a long sliver, which was passed between two rollers and compressed, then drawn out by the more rapidly rotating spindle and flyer. A number of pairs of rollers and spindles were mounted in a circle round a central shaft, which drove the lower rollers and the spindles.*

The hanks were washed to remove oil and dirt. Flax and cotton were boiled in soap or potash solution containing a little flour, and woollen yarns were sized with an extract of parchment or rabbit skins.

After treatment the hanks were slipped over adjustable or conical hank-holders and wound on to spools for the warp or quills for the weft. This was often accomplished with a spindle-wheel, but special wheels (both hand-turned and treadle-operated) were in use. An improved hank-holder with two conical cages, known as a 'swift', was introduced in the early eighteenth century.

The warp was still prepared on pegs driven into a wall or on a warping-frame, but during the seventeenth century the warping-mill was introduced and was in use in Scotland in 1687 [18]. This was a large reel (figure 99) about 6 ft high and 3 ft across turned by hand around a vertical axle. Threads from 20 bobbins in a rack were drawn off through a hole-board held in the hand and wound spirally upon the reel. When the required length of warp had been obtained, forming a portee,[1] the threads were passed round a peg at the top and the direction reversed to wind another portee alongside the first. This was repeated, maintaining a cross-over of threads on pegs at each end, until the warp contained the required number of threads. More advanced models of the warping-reel were turned by a handle working a rope and two pulleys, and the hole-board was replaced by a heck-box which was automatically raised by a cord winding round the axle of the reel. The heck-box contained a miniature heddle which served to separate the alternate threads to form the cross-over, and could accommodate forty threads.

[1] A portee is a convenient group of warp threads: in this instance twenty threads.

The warp, looped up into a chain to prevent entanglement, was inserted in the loom by winding it upon the warp-beam through a wooden comb or raddle to space the threads evenly.

Warps of flax, cotton, or woollen yarn are dressed to strengthen them during the weaving operation and to render the cloth smooth. Woollen yarn was usually dressed before warping, but flax or cotton·warps were dressed in the loom by brushing on a starch-paste made by boiling wheat-flour or potatoes in water. Occasionally a little herring- or beef-brine was added to prevent complete drying

FIGURE 99—*Warping-mill. From an eighteenth-century engraving.*

of the yarn. The portion of the warp between the heddle and the warp-beam was treated, and when it was sufficiently dry a little grease was brushed in. This dressing was repeated after each section was woven, and linen-looms were often fitted with an arrangement to extend this section of warp for dressing.

IV. WEAVING

Plain looms. The various types of loom described in volume II (ch 6) continued to be used throughout the present period, but the horizontal frame-loom, or treadle-loom, supplanted all others in the more advanced countries of Europe and Asia. It became the standard loom for all plain and simple pattern-weaving, and was adapted for various types of fabric.

The Dutch loom was extremely heavy, with a device to facilitate dressing the warp, and was suitable only for heavy linen cloths. The French and English looms were less robust, while the low Estille was designed for fine cambrics. Velvet-looms were specially designed (p 204).

The simple draw-loom. Pattern-weaving was limited by the number of heddles that could conveniently be worked between the reed and the warp-beam. This number did not normally exceed twenty-four, and for the weaving of more intricate patterns the draw-loom was employed.

The origin of the draw-loom is unknown but undoubtedly it first appeared in the east for the weaving of silk. In Europe it was naturally first introduced into the silk-working centres of Italy during the Middle Ages and thence followed the silk industry into France. The six-teenth-century draw-loom was much im-proved by the inventions of Galantier and Blache in France (1687), and of Joseph Mason in England in the same year [19]. The improved button draw-loom was employed until the end of the eighteenth century.

The essential features of the draw-loom are described elsewhere (p 187). In the button draw-loom, the simples[1] were united in groups according to the pat-tern and passed through a second comber-board to terminate in buttons or small weights. When a button was pulled down the appropriate leashes were raised to produce the correct shed for that particular passage of the shuttle (figure 124).

The pattern was produced by pulling the cords in the correct sequence while the weaver threw the shuttle through the resultant sheds. The task of pulling or drawing the cords was performed by the 'draw-boy', who was usually an un-skilled assistant working from a squared and coloured chart (figure 128).

FIGURE 100—*Loom invented by the Lyons weaver Claude Dangon, c 1605–20, showing his improvement of the figure-harness.* A, *warp-threads;* B, *couplings;* C, *lingoes;* D, *comber-board;* E, *tail-cords;* F, *pulleys;* G, *rod to which ends of tail-cords are knotted;* H, *simples knotted to tail-cords at* J *and anchored at the base* K. *The leashes are knotted to the simples and each set of leashes to be drawn together is knotted to a single gavacine. The pattern was made by drawing the appropriate* gavacines *before each throw of the shuttle, hence raising the required warp-threads. For further explanation see p 189 and figure 124.*

The button draw-loom was limited in its application by the weight of the large number of lingoes which had to be raised by the draw-boy, until about 1600, when Claude Dangon invented a loom (figure 100) that permitted an increase in the number of leashes from 800 to 2400. The simples extended to the floor and a lever sliding behind the selected cords enabled the draw-boy to lift the additional weight of the lingoes (p 189). This loom, as the lever draw-loom, continued in use for weaving damask until after 1800.

The automatic draw-loom. The inconvenience of employing an assistant, together with the errors it entailed, led to a search for a mechanism that would

[1] Apparatus for raising the warp-threads.

automatically perform the work of the draw-boy, and at the same time facilitate changes of pattern. It took a skilled person about a fortnight to set up the leashes and cords of the simple draw-loom for a particular pattern, work which had to be repeated whenever a major change of pattern was desired.

As France was the land of figured weaves it is not surprising that most developments in shedding-mechanisms originated there. The first notable achievement was that of Basile Bouchon who in 1725 designed a mechanism selecting auto-

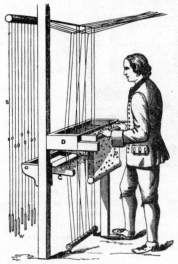

matically the cords to be drawn (figure 101). The cords of the simple passed through eyes in a row of needles sliding in a box. Selection was effected by a roll of paper perforated according to the pattern and passing round a perforated cylinder. When this cylinder was pushed towards the box the needles meeting unperforated paper slid along, carrying their cords with them, while the others passed through the holes and remained stationary. The selected cords were drawn down by a foot-operated comb acting on beads attached to them. Before each shuttle-throw the cylinder was rotated to present the next series of perforations, and the appropriate cords were drawn down.

Three years later Falcon improved the mechanism by increasing the number of needles to several rows and by substituting a series of rectangular cards for the roll of paper. These perforated cards were strung together to form an endless series,

FIGURE 101—*Bouchon's mechanism for selecting the cords, 1725.* (s) *Leashes;* (w) *lingoes;* (D) *needle-box;* (b) *cylinder;* (p) *perforated paper;* (G) *comb-bar acting on knots or beads on vertical simples.*

and the selection was obtained by pressing the appropriate card against the needles with a perforated platten held in the hand.

Looms incorporating these devices were not successful, although they facilitated change of design, eliminated errors, and could be operated by a single weaver. Adaptations of the same principles were, however, successfully applied to multi-heddle looms, where the problems were simpler because the number of cords to be operated was less.

In 1745 Jacques de Vaucanson (1709–82), an inventor famous for mechanical marvels, constructed a loom (cf. plate 8 A) that improved on the ideas of Bouchon and Falcon. He eliminated the simple and the tail-cords and mounted his selecting-box above the loom so that it acted directly on hooks attached to the neck-cords. These hooks passed through needles and were raised as required by a strong metal bar. The needles were selected by perforated cards passing round a complicated sliding cylinder, and the selection was effected without the aid of a draw-boy.

There is no evidence that this mechanism was adopted, for it was unworkable and suffered the disadvantage of a very complex cylinder. It was only rescued from oblivion by an accident, in that it served as the foundation for the successful Jacquard loom.

Power-looms. While improvements in the shedding-mechanism were being sought in France, other inventors were engaged on the design of a loom that would weave automatically. Leonardo da Vinci forestalled them all by working out, about 1490, certain primary principles of such operation [20]. His sketches are neither clear nor to scale, but it is evident that his shuttle was to be carried half-way through the shed by an arm operating from one side of the loom and its travel completed by a similar arm working from the other side. The mechanism was incomplete and the loom remained purely hypothetical.

Anton Möller of Danzig is said to have invented about 1586 a loom that could be operated by an unskilled person who merely supplied power by working a bar

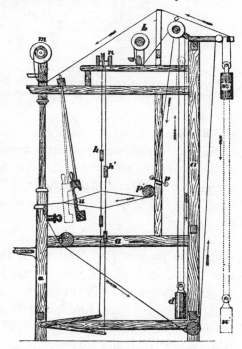

FIGURE 102—*Dutch ribbon-loom.* (b) *Warp-reel;* (c) *pulleys;* (d, w) *weights;* (p) *beam;* (h, h') *heddles;* (u) *reed;* (m) *cloth roller. The warp passes in the direction of the arrows.*

or lever [21]. That such looms did exist is shown by the disturbances provoked by their use in Leiden in 1620, and by Dutch ordinances of 1623 and later regulating their use. Many cities issued edicts against them in the early seventeenth century; the looms and their products were prohibited in Germany from 1685 to 1726. An automatic loom of some kind was introduced into London in 1616 and was the cause of riots in 1675 [22]. Known as the bar-loom or Dutch loom-engine, this was a ribbon-loom capable of weaving four to six ribbons simultaneously. The number of ribbons was increased to 12 by William Dircxz in 1604, to 24 by 1621, and eventually to as many as 50. Until after 1800 it could be used only for plain weaves.

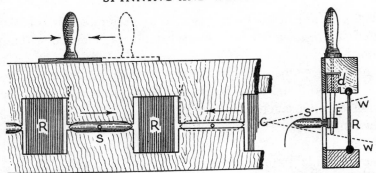

FIGURE 103—*Shuttle-mechanism and batten of the swivel-loom, profile and section.* (R) *Reed;* (w) *warp;*
(c) *cloth;* (s, s) *shuttles sliding in openings between planks;* (d) *shuttle-driver;* (E) *pegs by which the driver impels
the shuttles through the warp.*

The swivel-loom or new Dutch loom was an adaptation of the Dutch loom-engine and could weave 24 laces at once (figure 102). Each shuttle ran in a slot in the batten between the spaces for the individual reeds, and was driven through the shed by a short arm attached to a handle. The shuttles were all driven simultaneously and each took the place of its neighbour to the right or left alternately (figure 103).

In 1745 John Kay and Joseph Stell patented a method of controlling the pedals by tappets [23], and about the same time the rack-and-pinion shuttle was introduced, with a rack on the upper side of each shuttle that engaged a pinion between each shed (figure 104).

About 1730 Hans Hummel of Basel devised a method of operating ribbon-looms by water-power, but was prohibited from using it. In 1760 a factory at Manchester installed water-driven swivel-looms, but failed owing to the unreliability of the invention and the necessity of having a supervisor to each machine. The dream of an automatic power-loom was thus almost realized with respect to ribbon-looms having a warp only a few inches wide, but the problem of dealing with a wide cloth remained.

In 1678 M. de Gennes, a French naval officer, described a loom 'to make Linen-cloth without the aid of an Artificer'. An overhead shaft bore cranks raising the heddles and quadrants operating the spring-loaded beater (figure 105). The weft was inserted by arms that shot in and out of the warp from opposite sides and transferred the shuttle. It was claimed that one water-wheel could drive ten to

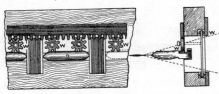

FIGURE 104—*Rack-and-pinion* ʰuttle. *Small racks on the shuttles engage w.. · pinions w. Movement of the large rack proₐ , all shuttles through the sheds.*

twelve such looms and that any width of cloth could be woven, but there is no record of such a loom being used.

The next step was one of the simplest yet one of the most decisive in the search for an automatic loom. This was the flying shuttle patented by John Kay of Bury in 1733 [4]. He had previously, in 1730, patented a machine for twisting worsted yarns or thread [24], but his shuttle-mechanism made him famous. A leather driver or picker slid along a metal rod at each end of the batten, and a loose cord with a wooden handle in the centre joined the two pickers. When the cord was jerked in one direction the picker shot the shuttle through the warp (figure 106). The shuttle was stopped by the opposing picker, and a jerk in the opposite direction shot it back. The shuttle was provided with four wheels and was guided by a shuttle-race attached like a ledge to the batten beneath the lower warp-threads. By this means cloths of any width could be woven by one person, and the rate of weaving was considerably increased. The true value of Kay's invention, however, lay in its subsequent adaptation to automatic weaving.

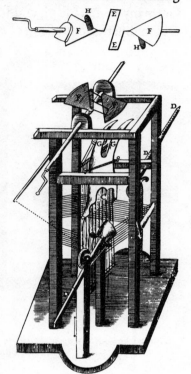

FIGURE 105—*M. de Gennes's 'New Engin to make Linen-cloth without the help of an Artificer'.* (E, E) *Cranks raising the heddles to form the sheds by means of cords;* (F, F) *quadrants acting on levers* G, G, *working the beater* C; (H, H) *cams operating the shuttle-mechanism;* (D, D) *arms transferring the shuttle, meeting at the centre of the shed.*

Vaucanson's improved loom of 1750 (plate 8 A) was also an attempt to produce a broad power-loom with a friction-driven winding-roller. He was apparently unaware of Kay's flying shuttle and adapted the de Gennes shuttle-arms. The fully automatic power-loom remained little more than an aspiration in 1760, and the practical problems were not solved until the following era.

V. FINISHING-PROCESSES

Scouring and fulling. The woven cloth was first washed to remove any oil or dressing. Linen and cotton cloths were soaked in clear water and washed with soap or potash. Soap was similarly used for woollen cloths, but fuller's earth or pig's dung and stale urine continued to be widely employed for reasons of economy.

After repairing weaving-faults woollen cloth was fulled to thicken it and give it a firm structure. This was done in primitive communities until recent times by tramping or 'waulking' the cloth with the feet (cf vol II, figure 186). In more advanced cloth-working centres, however, the fabric was generally fulled in fulling-stocks, first illustrated in Italy in 1607 (vol II, figure 187), but already widely employed in the late Middle Ages. Similar stocks are illustrated in Germany in 1735 [25], and in France in 1733 [2], driven by water-wheels, while Dutch illustrations of 1734 [26, 27] depict stocks driven by windmills. Horse-gins

FIGURE 106—*Kay's flying shuttle, 1733.* (Right) *The complete loom;* (left) *the batten on which the shuttle travels, with the operating-cord; and* (below) *the shuttle.*

were also used to furnish motive-power, and occasionally the stocks were hand-driven.

These early eighteenth-century fulling-stocks were of two types: hanging-stocks with the feet or hammers pivoted at their ends, and falling-stocks with the feet dropping vertically between guides. In both types the feet were raised by tappets on a horizontal driving-shaft and allowed to fall on the cloth bundled in the trough or stock below. The heavy oaken feet were stepped and the stocks so shaped that each time the cloth was pounded it rotated a little to ensure uniform action and prevent damage. In fulling caps and stockings the feet were often equipped with wooden pegs or with horse's or bullock's teeth.

The cloth was treated with hot soapy water with fuller's earth added—soap alone was too expensive. The finest soap was obtained from Castile and Genoa.

In France in 1751, 10 lb of soap was the recommended weight for fulling a piece of white cloth 45 ells long, and 15 lb for coloured cloth. Half the soap was dissolved in two pails of water as hot as the hand could bear, and the solution was poured over the cloth as it was laid in the stock. After 2 hours' fulling the cloth was taken out and smoothed, and immediately returned for a further 2 hours' treatment. It was then wrung out, the remainder of the soap similarly dissolved was added, and the fulling was continued until completed, the cloth being taken

FIGURE 107—*Raising the nap on cloth with mounted teazels, c 1760.*

out and smoothed every 2 hours. Finally the cloth was scoured in the same stock in hot water and rinsed in running cold water. In 1669 French fullers had to use 4 pints of fine oatmeal vat-gruel in every fulling-trough, and not more than two pieces of fustian or four camlets were to be treated at one time. English regulations insisted that not more than one broadcloth or two half-cloths were to be placed in the stocks at the same time [28]. Occasionally cloths were fulled a second time after the first raising.

Stocks were also used for the preliminary scouring process, but scouring-stocks had lighter feet and were so poised that they acted almost horizontally, in order to lessen the pounding. Fuller's earth, from which grit and stones had been carefully removed, was used with a copious supply of cold water. Black soap was also employed, and the final rinsing was carried out on the banks of a stream or from tethered rafts floating in a river, the cloth being manipulated with long poles.

After fulling or scouring the cloth was dried on tenter-frames. These consisted of upright wooden posts with a fixed upper rail and a lower rail whose position was adjustable by pegs or wedges (vol II, figure 184). Both rails were fitted every two or three inches with tenter-hooks—L-shaped double-pointed nails—those in the top rail pointing upwards and those in the bottom rail downwards. The wet cloth was hooked by its lists (selvedges) to both rails and the lower rail adjusted to draw the cloth tight and of even width. Over-stretching on the tenters was a common abuse and consequently their use was at times prohibited; in most European countries the stretch was limited to between 5 and 10 per cent of the length and breadth.

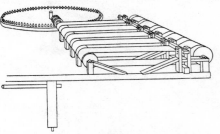

FIGURE 108—*Leonardo's gig-mill. From the* Codice Atlantico.

Raising, cropping, and frizing. The raising of the surface of woollen cloths by hand, by means of wooden or metal implements containing teazel-heads (figure 110, and vol II, figure 189), continued until the nineteenth century. The cloth, sprinkled with water, was hung over a pole or laid on a bench while its surface was rubbed with the teazels (figure 107). The first gentle raising-strokes were followed by a brisker action, and always the cloth was raised first against the pile and then in the direction of the pile. It was dried before being cropped.

Machines for raising cloth were introduced in the fifteenth century if not earlier. Though the use of such 'gig-mills' was prohibited in England by an act of 1551, they were in use at Gloucester before 1640. The earliest illustrations of gig-mills are found in two sketches by Leonardo da Vinci of about 1490 [29]. The first shows a hand-driven device, but the sketch is not readily understood. The second shows a multiple machine to be worked by a horse turning a winch (figure 108). The cloth with its ends sewn together passed round two rollers, one of which was driven, and as it travelled it passed beneath an adjustable beam, the under side of which was covered with teazel-heads. Five cloths could be raised simultaneously.

This proposal for raising with fixed teazels was unusual. In the raising-machines employed throughout this period (and indeed up to the present day) a teazel-covered roller rotates while the cloth passes under it in the opposite direction. This principle was first illustrated by Zonca in 1607 (figure 109).

Coarse woollen cloths were often raised with flatter-cards, which were merely enlarged hand-cards with wire teeth; their use was prohibited in England in 1511 and in France in 1669.

The cropping of woollen cloths after the nap had been raised still furnished

FIGURE 109—*Gig-mill for raising the nap on cloth, 1607.*

work for the shearman. The stirrup-grip, with the hand acting as a lever (figure 110), was employed to the end of the seventeenth century, but during the following century an improved device was introduced. This was a lever that rotated around the rear edge of the upper blade and was connected by a double cord to a block attached to the lower blade (figure 111). When the lever was depressed with the left hand the blades closed, and the spring of the bow-stem reopened them. The lower blade was later curved to fit the padded bench, and the upper blade was tilted to an angle that increased to 30° before 1760. Two shearmen usually worked together, and for close cropping leaden weights were laid on the lower blade to press it deeper into the cloth. Cropping followed each raising operation, and in 1748 woollen cloth in France was cropped four or five times on the face and once on the reverse [2].

FIGURE 110—*Shearmen at work. From a seventeenth-century engraving.*

Cropping was a slow and laborious operation and early attempts were made to mechanize it. The cropping-machines prohibited in England in 1495 may have resembled that sketched by Leonardo (figure 112). This involved little more than a crank-system to open and close the normal hand-shears while automatically progressing over the cloth. Further sketches suggest novel means of using separate blades. Leonardo's designs were abortive and the solution was not found until the end of the eighteenth century.

During the seventeenth and eighteenth centuries the surface of woollen cloth was frequently frized to give a fashionable appearance. This meant rubbing the nap with a circular motion, giving a granular effect; frizing was originally performed by hand by two workmen working a 2 ft by 1 ft plank over the surface of the cloth, which was previously moistened with egg-white or honey [30]. More generally a frizing-mill was employed, driven by water-, horse-, or man-power (figure 113).

The cloth passed between two planks, about 10 ft long and 15 in wide, being slowly drawn along by a spiked roller. The lower plank was covered with a rough woollen cloth and the upper coated on its underside with a cement of glue, gum arabic, and yellow sand with a little *aqua vitae* or urine [30]. By means of a crank at each end the upper plank was given a very small rotary motion which rubbed the long nap into a uniform series of small hard burrs. Black cloths were usually frized only on the reverse, but coloured and mixed cloths were treated on the face.

Bleaching. Linen and hempen cloths from the loom had to be bleached to make them attractive in appearance and texture. In the early eighteenth century the Dutch were esteemed as the best bleachers in Europe; their method was to 'buck' the cloth by steeping it in hot waste lye, followed by fresh lye, for 8 days.

It was then washed with black soap and wrung dry. The cloth was next steeped in a vat of buttermilk, the lengths being treaded in as the milk was added, where it was allowed to remain under pressure for from one to three weeks. It was again washed with soap, wrung, and spread on the grass for two or three weeks to bleach in the sun. During this period it was regularly wetted. The operations of bucking, souring in buttermilk, and grassing or crofting were repeated five or six times, the strength of the lye decreasing each time. The whole process occupied half a year and could be carried out only in the summer.

In 1755 at Haarlem, the centre for the manufacture of the whitest and most lustrous Dutch linen, the cloth was bucked for 10 hours in a lye of various ashes and then wetted on the grass for 24 hours [31]. This procedure was repeated ten or more times before the cloth was soured in buttermilk for five or six days. Rye-meal or bran was sometimes used instead of milk. The sequence of souring, washing, bucking, and watering was repeated as often as necessary for from six to eight months before the fabric was starched and dried.

FIGURE 111—*Cropping-shears, c 1760.*

In Picardy at the same date linen was bucked alternately in cold used lye of wood-ashes and hot fresh lye. After each treatment the cloths were washed and exposed on the fields, being wetted from the river with scoops. When sufficiently white they were soaked in sour skimmed milk and dipped in weak starch and smalt or Dutch *lapsi*. After drying on poles they were finally beaten with smooth mallets on marble blocks.

In Ireland the cloths were washed and boiled in lye for two hours, which was quicker than steeping. This treatment was repeated six or seven times with exposure and watering on the fields between each. The cloths were then soured in warm water and bran or wheat

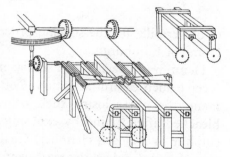

FIGURE 112—*Leonardo's shearing-machine. From the* Codice Atlantico. *The table (upper right) is drawn along the main frame of the machine by a cord winding round the lower rotating shaft. The shears have one blade fixed: the second is actuated by another cord, taken to a lever worked by the toothed wheel on the upper shaft.*

for three days, washed with soap, and rubbed between boards. Finally the linen was well milled in the stocks, starched, dried, and calendered or beetled. In Scotland the use of lime for bleaching was consistently and unaccountably prohibited from 1648 until after 1815, although the slaked lime used by offenders had no deleterious effect on the linen. Richard Holden of Ireland introduced a cheap method of bleaching with kelp, which was successfully employed near Dundee in 1732. In 1756 the duration of the bleaching process was almost halved by the use of dilute sulphuric acid, instead of the lactic acid

FIGURE 113—*Frizing-mill, 1763. The spiked roller driven through gears is at the bottom: the vertical pinions rotate the upper plank.*

of buttermilk, for the souring process. This process was introduced by Francis Home of Edinburgh.

Hemp was bleached in a similar manner, but as it was a coarse cloth it did not receive such careful attention. Cotton fabrics were bleached in a briefer treatment, the fibres losing their colour more readily than flax does. Wool was bleached after fulling by exposing the half-dry cloth to the fumes of burning sulphur in a closed chamber. Chalk and indigo were often added to the final rinsing-water before the treatment with sulphur.

Pressing. Linen and cotton fabrics were smoothed by rubbing with polished stones or wood before being pressed. Woollen cloths were brushed in the direction of the nap and all loose particles were removed by gentle treatment with a board coated on its underside with a putty made of mastic, resin, powdered stone, and sifted filings. Ironing was also employed, using a large metal box containing the iron-heater. The box was lowered upon the cloth by a rope and pulley and worked backwards and forwards by two men holding long pivoted handles.

In certain parts of France woollen cloths were steamed by supporting them, tightly wrapped on rollers, over boiling water in a square kettle or copper. Elsewhere the cloth was sprinkled on the reverse with gum arabic solution and passed over a burning charcoal fire from one tightly wound roller to another, or between a series of polished iron rods to a single roller.

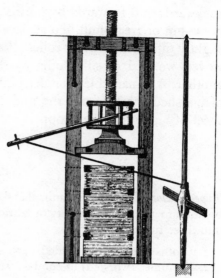

FIGURE 114—*Linen-press, c 1760.*

Most cloths were finally pressed to remove all creases and to impart a gloss. Large screw-presses were turned by levers working in a lantern attached to the threaded column (figure 114). The cloths were carefully cuttled (that is, arranged in suitable folds) and placed between the lower and upper plates with pasteboard, vellum, or wood interleavings. For a greater gloss hot pressing was preferred. The cloth was sprinkled on the reverse with water or dilute gum arabic solution, folded, and interleaved as before, and a very hot brass or iron plate was inserted between every six or seven folds. The cloths were left in the press for from 10 to 12 hours and the process was repeated four or five times with the folds falling in different positions. To obtain great pressure the lever of the press was connected by rope to a winch turned by hand or horse-power.

Calendering was frequently substituted for pressing, or used after pressing to impart extra gloss. The calender was a large wooden box filled with stones cemented together and weighing 10 tons or more, which could roll over two very smooth rollers on a flat table (figure 115). The linen or wool cloth was carefully wound round these rollers and the box moved

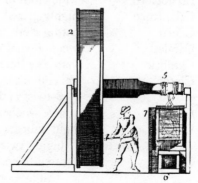

FIGURE 115—*A calender* (end view); (2) *wheel trodden by two men inside it;* (5) *shaft and ropes;* (6) *table;* (7) *box-weight. From an early eighteenth-century engraving.*

backwards and forwards by means of ropes winding on a shaft turned by a horse-gin or tread-mill. To replace a roller the box was wound to one end and slightly tilted on the other roller. Watered effects were obtained on coarse plain woven worsted or silk cloths by the great pressure of one layer of cloth on another. A remarkable calender built in Paris to the order of Colbert had a bed of polished marble, and the underside of the box was covered with a single sheet of highly polished copper.

APPENDIX

Types of cloth. The various animal and vegetable fibres were used separately or in combination to give a great variety of fabrics. Wool gave the greatest scope and was divided into three fundamental types:

1. Cloths (woollen) of carded warp and weft.
2. Tammies (worsted) of combed warp and weft.
3. Serges (mixed) of combed warp and carded weft.

Each of these types was subdivided into numerous varieties according to the spinning, weaving, or finishing techniques employed.

Some of the principal types of cloths are listed below, but the nature of many of them changed with time and imitations assumed false designations.

Barracan	coarse twilled camlet of wool or goat's hair, boiled and mangled to make it waterproof.
Bays	worsted warp and woollen weft, lightly fulled and raised.
Bombazine	silk or linen warp and cotton weft (also a general term for cotton).
Broadcloth	wide cloth of woollen warp and weft, well fulled.
Calamanco	highly glazed woollen cloth, resembling satin in appearance.
Calico	cotton cloth, usually printed, named after Calicut, India.
Camlet	wool or wool/goat's hair mixture, sometimes containing silk threads.
Cambric	very fine linen cloth, named after Cambrai, France.
Cloth	general term for a fabric of woollen warp and weft, the former S-twist and the latter Z-twist, usually fulled.
Cogware	coarse woollen cloth, fulled and raised.
Crepon	light fabric of worsted or silk/worsted mixture with warp more highly twisted than weft.
Diaper	figured linen fabric, named from the medieval Greek *diaspros*, pure white.
Dimity	heavy figured cotton fabric, named from the Greek *dimitos*, of double thread.
Dowlas	coarse linen cloth named after Daoulas, Brittany.

Drugget	figured cloth of silk, silk/cotton mixture, wool or wool/linen/cotton mixture.
Etamine	worsted warp and weft or wool/silk mixture.
Flannel	loosely woven woollen cloth with roughened reverse.
Fustian	linen warp and cotton weft, named after Fostat, the old name for Cairo.
Grogram	coarse silk and wool cloth, after French *gros-grain*.
Kersey	coarse woollen cloth, fulled (carsay).
Linsey-woolsey	coarse fabric of linen warp and worsted weft.
Manchester cotton	originally a coarse woollen cloth, fulled and raised; later fustian.
Mockadoes	pile fabric of goat's hair. (? Italian *mocaiardo*, haircloth.)
Muslin	fine white cotton fabric, named after Mosul, Mesopotamia.
Ratine	closely woven woollen cloth, well fulled and often frized.
Say	cheap fine cloth resembling serge.
Serge	worsted warp and woollen weft, occasionally fulled and usually twill weave.
Shag	pile fabric of goat's hair.
Shalloon	twill woven worsted, named after Châlons-sur-Marne, France.
Stament	coarse worsted fabric.
Stuff	general term for worsted fabrics.
Taffeta	watered fabric of coarse plain-woven silk, from Persian *tāftah*, woven.
Tamis	fine highly glazed wool fabric, from French *tamis*, a sieve.
Tammy	general term for fabric of worsted warp and weft, both with similar twist. Probably also from tamis, sieve.
Velvet	pile fabric of silk or cotton.
Voile	fine worsted fabric of open weave.

REFERENCES

[1] DELONEY, T. 'Pleasant History of John Winchcombe.' London. 1626.
[2] PLUCHE, A. N. 'Spectacle de la Nature; or Nature Display'd' (Eng. trans. from original French), Vol. 6. London. 1748.
[3] LUCCOCK, J. 'Nature and Properties of Wool.' Leeds. 1805.
[4] Patent no. 542, 26 May 1733.
[5] Patent no. 636, 30 August 1748.
[6] Patent no. 628, 20 January 1748.
[7] Patent no. 143, 3 March 1664; Patent no. 288, 22 January 1692.
[8] GRAY, A. 'Treatise on Spinning Machinery.' Edinburgh. 1819.
[9] Patent no. 435, 12 August 1721.
[10] PRICE, W. H. *Quart. J. Econ.* **20**, 608, 1906.
[11] REHTMAIER, P. J. 'Chronicle Brunswick-Lüneberg.' Brunswick. 1722.
[12] This bible, illuminated by Nikolaus Glockendon, is in the Wolfenbüttel Library. SCHÖNEMANN, G. P. C. 'Hundert Merkwürdigkeiten der herzoglichen Bibliothek zu Wolfenbüttel', no. 68. Hanover. 1849.

[13] FELDHAUS, F. MARIA. 'Die Technik der Vorzeit, der geschichtlichen Zeit und der Natur-völker.' Engelmann, Leipzig. 1914.

[14] Patent no. 202, 18 April 1678.

[15] Patent no. 562, 24 June 1738.

[16] Patent no. 724, 29 June 1758.

[17] Patent no. 693, 3 July 1754.

[18] SCOTT, W. R. 'Records of a Scottish Cloth Manufactory 1681–1703.' Scottish History Society Publ. no. 46. Edinburgh. 1905.

[19] Patent no. 257, 3 October 1687.

[20] BECK, T. Z. Ver. dtsch. Ing., **50**, 645, 1906.

[21] BECKMANN, J. 'History of Inventions' (trans. by W. JOHNSTON, 4th ed.), Vol. 2. London. 1846.

[22] WADSWORTH, A. P. and MANN, J. DE L. 'Cotton Trade and Industrial Lancashire 1600–1780.' University Press, Manchester. 1931.

[23] Patent no. 612, 18 April 1745.

[24] Patent no. 515, 8 May 1730.

[25] LEUPOLD, J. and BEYER, J. M. *Theatrum machinarum molarium*. Leipzig. 1735.

[26] VAN NATRUS, L., POLLY, J., and VAN VUUREN, C. 'Groot Volkomen Moolenboek' (2 vols.). Amsterdam. 1734, 1736.

[27] VAN ZYL, J. '*Theatrum machinarum universale* of groot algemeen Moolen-boek.' Amsterdam. 1734.

[28] Statute 7, Anne, cap. 13.

[29] BECK, T. 'Beiträge zur Geschichte des Maschinenbaues.' Springer, Berlin. 1900.

[30] CROKER, T. H., WILLIAMS, T., and CLARK, S. 'Complete Dictionary of Arts and Sciences', Vol. 2. London. 1765.

[31] HOME, F. 'Experiments on Bleaching.' Edinburgh. 1756.

BIBLIOGRAPHY

BAINES, E. 'History of Cotton Manufacture.' London. 1835.

BARLOW, A. 'History and Principles of Weaving by Hand and Power.' London. 1878.

HEATON, H. 'Yorkshire Woollen and Worsted Industries.' Oxford Historical and Literary Studies, no. 10. University Press, Oxford. 1920.

HORNER, J. 'The Linen Trade of Europe.' McCaw, Stevenson and Orr, Belfast. 1920.

LIPSON, E. 'The History of English Woollen and Worsted Industries' (3rd ed.). Black, London. 1950.

ROTH, H. L. 'Studies in Primitive Looms.' Bankfield Museum Notes, Halifax. 1918.

USHER, A. P. 'A History of Mechanical Inventions' (2nd rev. ed.). Harvard University Press, Cambridge, Mass. 1954.

WARDEN, A. J. 'Linen Trade, Ancient and Modern.' London. 1864.

A NOTE ON KNITTING AND KNITTED FABRICS

JAMES NORBURY

THE origin of knitting is completely unknown. Fragments of fabric, a few sandal-socks, and several Coptic caps provide the only evidence we have for its early history. Even the technique applied to producing a fabric built up from a series of loops, instead of on the warp-and-weft basis as in weaving, is obscure.

There are basic differences in structure between woven materials and knitted fabrics. Primitive woven cloths were formed by interlacing warp and weft threads lying at right-angles to each other throughout the fabric (vol I, ch 16). Early woven textiles were made of thick and coarse yarns yielding a fabric bulky in appearance and stiff in texture. This was probably one of the factors that led to the evolution of knitted fabrics, which arose from the purely utilitarian need for a fabric of greater elasticity than cloths woven on primitive looms. The great advantage of the knitted fabric is its readier adaptability to the shape of the human figure.

The first stage in the evolution of knitting was the development of a technique based on netting, to give a finer mesh than could be obtained by use of the shuttle and netting-rod. Evidence of this development is to be found in fragments of early textiles discovered in Egypt and Scandinavia. They are of a meshed fabric, much more elastic than woven material, to which the Nordic term *sprang*[1] has been applied. *Sprang* fabrics probably originated between 1500 and 1000 B.C. They closely resemble knitting, the difference being that the foundation loops out of which *sprang* is built up are interlocked vertically instead of horizontally as in true knitting.

Two techniques appear to have been used in the making of *sprang*. In the first, the fabric was formed with a needle, derived from a netting-needle and in many ways resembling the modern sewing-needle, in the following way:

First the warp was made by arranging a number of closely spaced parallel vertical threads, each as long as the width of the finished material and kept taut by tying their ends to the top and bottom of a large rectangular frame (figure 116). A very simple stitch, consisting of a uniform twist, was worked up the first thread and fastened off at the top. A second row of these twisted stitches was then worked up the second thread, each stitch being interlaced through the side of the stitches twisted on the first warp thread. This action was repeated up every thread of the warp until a meshed fabric had been formed enveloping every thread of the warp. The two ends at the top and bottom of the interlaced threads were fastened off to make them secure; the warp threads were unknotted and withdrawn; and a piece of meshed fabric resembling a very fine piece of netting was obtained.

Once this simple technique of needle-weaving had been mastered, variations in the types of fabric were rapidly evolved. In one of the existing fragments of *sprang* a half-knot technique was employed to keep each loop in place. This gave the fabric a

[1] Icelandic *sprang* means lace weaving.

symmetrical foundation, and upon close examination the resultant material has the appearance of a very fine fishing-net.

Another variant of *sprang* fabric was made by working a chain-stitch up the first warp thread in place of the simple coiled stitch. Chain-stitch was then worked up each of the remaining warp threads, the stitches being interlaced vertically through the side of each chain. The warp threads were withdrawn and a fabric so closely resembling knitting was produced that early fragments of this type of *sprang* were described until recently as the earliest examples of knitted fabric.

In the second technique of making *sprang*, which was more highly developed, instead of using warp threads built on a rectangular frame as a temporary foundation for the fabric, a single continuous warp thread was formed into a plaited mesh on the rectangular frame (figure 117). The work was begun from the centre of the frame. Each time the threads were plaited, two thin sticks were inserted at the top and bottom to hold in place the loops formed by the plaiting action. After the next series of plaits had been made and two more sticks had been inserted, the first two, holding the previous set of plaited loops in position, were withdrawn and could be used again. This action was repeated first from the centre to the top of the frame and then from the centre to the bottom. Thus by working outwards from the centre a piece of fabric was built up having a median axis, on either side of which the stitching was perfectly symmetrical. When the work had been completed the central axis was made secure by knots to prevent the fabric from unravelling when it was taken off the frame (plate 8 B).

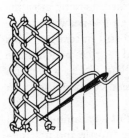

FIGURE 116—*Simple method of making* sprang *by interlacing threads on vertical strands.*

It is interesting that at about the same time as the *sprang* technique was being developed in Egypt, a comparable technique, though on a slightly different principle, was taking shape in Peru. This Peruvian needle-knitting resembled true knitting more closely than did *sprang*. Instead of being worked on warp threads in a frame, a fine woven fabric formed the basis of what is actually a primitive embroidery. The entire surface of the foundation material was covered with a meshed stitch producing a new fabric that could easily be mistaken for a primitive type of knitting. Various colours were used in Peruvian needle-knitting, the resultant fabrics being covered with elaborate patterns not unlike those of Arab colour-knitting.

There is no evidence indicating how the *sprang* and needle-knitting techniques evolved into frame-knitting. There are only sandal-socks from Arabia (figure 118) which may be as old as the seventh century B.C., and a single fragment of Arab colour-knitting found at Fostat (old Cairo) which can be dated between the seventh and ninth centuries A.D. It is worked in crossed stocking-stitch at a tension of 36 stitches to the inch, the patterning being in deep maroon wool on a ground of gold silk. It is one of the finest examples of wool and silk stranded knitting ever found.

In its early stages Arab knitting was worked on frames, and this led gradually to the technique of knitting as practised today. The frames were either circular or rectangular (figures 119, 120) and were fitted with wooden or bone pegs, equally spaced all round the frame. The thinner the pegs and the closer they were together, the finer was the fabric.

Casting on stitches for frame-knitting was very simple. The yarn was tied to the first peg and then wound round each peg in a counter-clockwise direction continuously until every peg on the frame had a crossed loop lying at its base. A second series of twisted loops was then similarly wound round the pegs, the first set at the base of the peg being drawn over the second set of loops that had just been made. Probably this action was originally performed with small sticks, or in coarser fabrics with the fingers. Later a hooked implement was developed to facilitate raising the loops one over the other. When the first set of loops had been drawn over the second, the stitches were cast on and the frame was ready for the knitting to be carried out. This was a repetition of the process of casting-on, the series of loops at the base of the frame being passed over the second set of loops continuously, thus producing a knitted fabric in crossed stocking-stitch. The hooked action led much later to the development of crocheted fabric, probably about the end of the sixteenth century.

Several early investigators of knitted fabrics wrongly assumed that certain woollen caps of Egyptian or north African origin dating from the first century A.D. were crocheted. The fact is that these caps were produced on frames, an early Christian sect having learnt the craft of frame-knitting from the nomads who lived in the Egyptian desert. The rigid frame and hook methods for producing knitted fabrics were to play an important part in the development of knitting on needles as now practised.

In all good knitting-techniques one needle is held completely rigid, the other being used for transferring the stitches from one needle to the other while making the fabric. The earliest knitting-needles were hooked, and this type of needle is still used by the shepherds of the Landes district in France. Once the frame-knitting technique has been completely mastered it is a simple matter to understand how the idea emerged of casting the basic loops for the fabric on to a single needle instead of on a series of pegs built into a frame.

One point of great interest is that as late as the beginning of the present century many

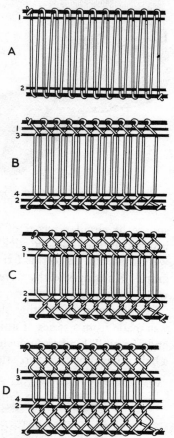

FIGURE 117—*Plaited* sprang. (A) *The first two rods are inserted in the loops;* (B) *two more rods form the first series of loops;* (C) *the first two rods are removed and reinserted nearer the centre, forming more loops;* (D) *the loops are continued towards the centre.*

FIGURE 118—*Arab sandal-sock of red wool.*

knitters in rural districts in all parts of Europe used a similar method for casting stitches on needles as that used in primitive frame-knitting. Twisted loops were passed from the thumb on to the needle. When the required number of loops had been made, the wool was wound over the point of the needle in front of the first loop, the loop then being drawn over the wool with the second needle. This action was repeated until all the loops had been worked off, when the cast-on was completed and the worker was ready to begin knitting.

The series of rigid pegs was thus replaced by a single needle, held firm by pushing one end into a knitting-stick or knitting-sheath (figure 121). Early knitting-sticks were simply square or circular pieces of wood with a hole drilled in one end. With the needle inserted in the hole, the stick was tucked into a belt worn round the waist. The stitches were then cast on to this fixed needle by the method described in the preceding paragraph. Knitting-sheaths developed from knitting-sticks, many of which were carved with very elaborate patterns, some of them being masterpieces of craftsmanship.

Another type of knitting-sheath common among agricultural workers and fishermen was made from a series of quills bound together, the needle being pushed into the open end of a quill. Knitting-pouches consisted of a pad made of fabric or leather mounted on a belt. These pouches were stuffed with straw, wood-shavings, dried grasses, or horsehair,

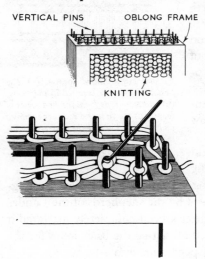

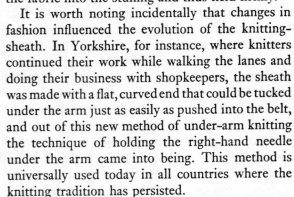

VERTICAL PINS   OBLONG FRAME

KNITTING

the end of the knitting-needle being stuck through the fabric into the stuffing and thus held firmly.

It is worth noting incidentally that changes in fashion influenced the evolution of the knitting-sheath. In Yorkshire, for instance, where knitters continued their work while walking the lanes and doing their business with shopkeepers, the sheath was made with a flat, curved end that could be tucked under the arm just as easily as pushed into the belt, and out of this new method of under-arm knitting the technique of holding the right-hand needle under the arm came into being. This method is universally used today in all countries where the knitting tradition has persisted.

The south of England is an exception to this principle since here a short needle is used, not long enough to tuck under the arm. This exception is accounted for by the virtual disappearance, from the end of the reign of Elizabeth I to mid-Victorian times, of hand-knitting from southern England.

The development of *lace fabrics*, from the simple stocking-stitch of the early knitters, is one of the most fascinating stories in the history of textile development. These fabrics are built up from a series of eyelets, formed by working made loops and decreases on a stocking-stitch foundation. *Cable fabrics*, probably originating with fishermen in imitation of the twist of ropes, are made by passing one group of stitches behind or in front of a second group of stitches. *Coloured knitted fabric* is a patterned fabric in stocking-stitch with two or more colours in each row. The stitches are knitted in the ordinary way, the colour not in use being either stranded across the back of the fabric—the stranding principle was used in all early knitted fabrics—or woven round the strand of fibre that is being used to knit the stitches. Colour-knitting was developed first in the Near East, and appeared later in all parts of Europe. Spain appears to have been first in the European field with this type of fabric, and a very fine example of this type of knitting is seen in a Spanish altar-glove of the eleventh century (plate 9 A).

Florentine knitters of the sixteenth and seventeenth centuries perfected the art of making coloured and brocaded fabrics. Their magnificent knitted and brocaded coats were worn by courtiers in all parts of Europe (plate 9 B).

During the reign of Elizabeth I, William Lee (d *c* 1610), a clergyman and a Cambridge graduate,

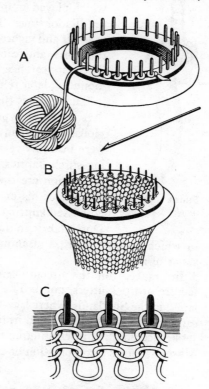

FIGURE 120—*Knitting on a circular frame.* (A) *Casting on;* (B) *formation of the fabric;* (C) *detail of the loops.*

devised the first frame-knitting machine. This employed a combination of Arab frame-knitting and the hooked knitting-needle technique already described. Lee's very ingenious machine had a series of rigid hooks, with a second series of moving hooks at right-angles to them. The stitches were cast on the series of rigid hooks in exactly the same manner as with an Arab knitting-frame. The movable hooks, manipulated by a simple mechanical action, were now inserted into the stitches on the series of rigid hooks. The yarn was then laid horizontally under the rigid hooks, and the stitches were drawn over it by the movable hooks. This simple action is basic to all types of knitting-machines, and Lee's invention led to the establishment of the machine-knitting industry that thrives in all parts of the world today. Lee himself, however, was compelled by lack of support at home to seek patronage from the French king Henri IV. Owing to the

opposition of the hand-knitters the knitting-machine only slowly established itself in the seventeenth century.

One other knitted fabric must be mentioned, namely felted knitting, which played an important part in the development of headgear from pre-Tudor times. The felt was made by soaking a piece of knitted fabric in water and vigorously pummelling it with heavy stones. This loosened the fibres and caused them to mat together, yielding a fabric with a felted appearance used in the Basque country for the production of 'bonnets', later referred to as berets, and for the apprentices' caps worn in Tudor times (figure 122).

A different type of fabric was embossed knitting, a product of Holland, Germany, England, and the Isle of Aran. Embossed fabrics were made by reversing the position of knit and purl stitches in stocking-stitch fabrics, the reverse purl stitches on the stocking-stitch foundation creating elaborate designs. The vest worn by Charles I on the day of his execution (30 January 1649) is a very fine example of embossed knitting (plate 9 c), and a circular piece of eighteenth-century Dutch fabric in the Victoria and Albert Museum, London, has a design

FIGURE 121—*A simple knitting-stick.*

in which flowers, birds, and animals have been used to form an incredibly intricate series of patterns.

In France, from the fifteenth century onwards, lace hose formed the principal manufacture of the knitters' guild. The patterns on these hose were copied from hand-made laces; in the Shetlands, where lace-knitting developed during the nineteenth century, the earliest specimens were copied from a collection of laces taken over to the islands by one Jessie Scanlon. An interesting knitted specimen dated 1840 in the Victoria and Albert Museum shows a combination of embossed and lace knitting. The rectangular centre is a prayer for the High Court of Parliament worked in reverse stocking-stitch foundation. The border is a very fine example of lace knitting.

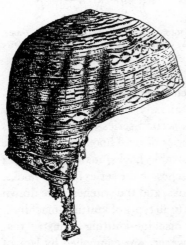

At the present day the domestic art of knitting seems to have returned to its simpler beginnings. Though a great industry manufacturing hose, jersey cloth, and many other knitted fabrics with the aid of complex and expensive machines is now based on the ancient principle of forming a continuous series of loops into a meshed fabric from which hand-knitting originated, millions of women still furnish their families with garments by their skill with knitting-needles, while several makes of simple knitting-machine for home use (of both the circular and the flat-bed types) recall William Lee's invention of three centuries ago and the household stocking-frame industry to which it ultimately gave rise.

FIGURE 122—*Tudor cap of knitted and felted fabric.*

8

FIGURED FABRICS

J. F. FLANAGAN

I. THE DRAW-LOOM

THE term 'figured fabric' is often used to denote any fabric ornamented with design produced by weaving, embroidery, painting, printing, or in some other way. To a weaver, the only figured fabrics are those with a design produced on a loom equipped with a 'figure-harness', an apparatus enabling design repeats to be woven in both the width and the length of the fabric. Before the introduction of the Jacquard machine at the beginning of the nineteenth century, this loom was called the draw-loom (p 165).

There are two main kinds of harnesses, the heald-harness[1] and the figure-harness. The former is used for non-figured weaves, such as plain tabby, twill, and satin, and for small pattern-effects such as those of the traditional peasant weaves of Sweden. The object of the heald-harness is to lift or depress warp-threads, so that a passage (shed) is formed through which the shuttle can be passed. This is called a pick of the shuttle. A figure-harness lifts the warp threads as required for the making of the design in the fabric. The draw-loom had the two kinds of harnesses, the figure-harness for the design, and the healds for the binding-weaves of the fabric (figure 123). The weaver's assistant, the draw-boy, controlled the figure-harness either from the top or from the side of the loom. The weaver sat in front of the loom working the healds by means of foot-treadles. With his hands he threw the shuttle through the warp-shed produced by the healds and the figure-harness, and beat the weft into the fabric with a shed-stick, comb, or reed.

II. THE FIGURE-HARNESS

The figure-harness that was in use at the beginning of the seventeenth century was composed of tail-cords, pulley-frame, neck, comber-board, and couplings with mails and lingoes (figure 124). The pulley-frame was over the top of the

[1] Heald and heddle are two forms of the same word. Heddle is used in Vol I, e.g. p 426, figure 269 and in Vol II, ch 6 for relatively simpler looms. It became the favourite term for this purpose, perhaps because of its assonance with the treadle which sometimes worked it. For the fabrics treated in the present chapter, the term heald is needed.

loom. It contained a few hundred pulleys, which served to divert the tail-cords from a vertical to a horizontal direction. The comber-board was a few feet below

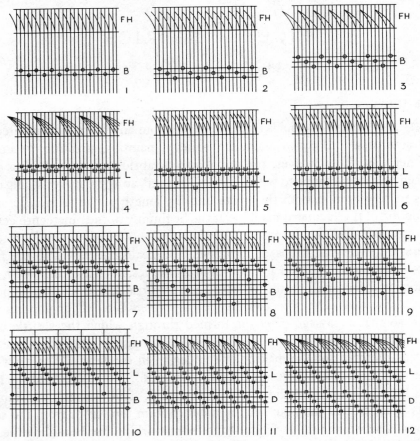

FIGURE 123—*Diagrams showing plan of warp and healds in the loom.* (1) *Weft-faced figured tabby;* (2) *weft-faced figured twill;* (3) *weft-faced figured twill: the drawcords control the figure-harness warp-threads in pairs for 'scaling';* (4) *early tabby tissue, with one binder-heald for tissue-binding;* (5) *tabby tissue with two binder-healds for tissue-binding;* (6) *tabby tissue (diasprum) with two healds and binder-warp for tissue-binding;* (7) *twill ground tissue with four healds and binder-warp for tissue-binding;* (8) *twill ground tissue with six healds and binder-warp for tissue-binding;* (9) *satin ground tissue with two healds and binder-warp for tissue-binding;* (10) *satin ground tissue with four healds and binder-warp for tissue-binding;* (11) *twill damask with four-heald binding;* (12) *satin damask with five-heald twill-binding.* (FH = *Figure-harness cords;* D (⌐) = *Depression-healds;* L (⌊⌋) = *Lifting-healds;* B (○) = *Binder-warp healds.*)

the pulley-frame. It was perforated with small holes, one for each neck-cord to pass through. Its purpose was to extend the harness to the full width of the warp. The converging of the neck-cords between the comber-board and the ends of the tail-cords under the pulley-frame made the 'neck'. The coupling was composed of top and bottom halves, and a metal mail connected them. The top of the coupling was tied to the end of a tail-cord, six inches or more below the comber-board. The warp-ends passed through the eye of the mail. A wire weight, six inches or more in length and usually of lead, was tied to the bottom end of the coupling. This weight is called a lingoe. It served to keep the harness-cords taut, and to bring the warp-threads back to the position of rest after being raised. The neck-cords and coup-lings were more numerous than the tail-cords. If there were four figures in the width of the harness, there would be four neck-cords to each tail-cord. Therefore by pulling a tail-cord one warp-thread of each figure would be lifted. The great advantage of the neck was that the number of cords controlled by the draw-boy was much less than the number of warp-threads in the warp. Thus for a harness with 1600 mails and four figures only 400 tail-cords would be required. The in-ventor of the neck made a very valuable contribution to the construction of the figure-harness.

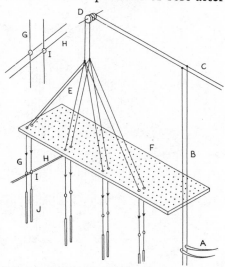

FIGURE 124—*The principles of the construction of the figure-harness with neck.* (A) *Lashes;* (B) *simples;* (C) *tail-cords;* (D) *pulleys;* (E) *neck-cords;* (F) *comber-board;* (G) *coupling;* (H) *warp-threads;* (I) *mails;* (J) *lingoes.*

It is believed that, in 1606, Claude Dangon of Lyons imitated the Italian draw-loom (p 165) and added simples and lashes (*semples* and *lacs*). Simples are cords stretched from the tail-cords to a rod fastened to the floor at the side of the loom. The lashes are loops which were laced round the simples, and agree in number with the tail-cords to be pulled for each figure-pick. The lashes for a single lift of the harness were assembled and tied with a knot. For a long design there were thousands of such knotted lashes. The introduction of the simples made it possible for the draw-boy to stand on the floor at the side of the loom instead of being over the top of it (figure 100).

There is not much information available concerning figure-looms earlier than the seventeenth century. There are no medieval illustrations of them. The fact that simples were added to the harness at the beginning of the seventeenth cen-tury helps us to obtain some idea of the stage in development up to the previous century. Besides the loom with Dangon's simples, there was one with drop-shaped buttons for the controlling of the harness-cords. This is said to have been invented by Jean le Calabrais in the fifteenth century. Lashes were laced round the tail-cords, and a knot of them had a single cord which was passed through a hole in a board. A drop-shaped button was attached to the end of the cord. By pulling a button the warp-threads were lifted for a figure-pick. The number of buttons would agree with the figure-picks required to make the design. This method was not suitable for large designs, as too many buttons were required. It is believed that a neck-harness was used for this loom, but it is doubtful whether the neck was in use much earlier than the fifteenth century (figure 125).

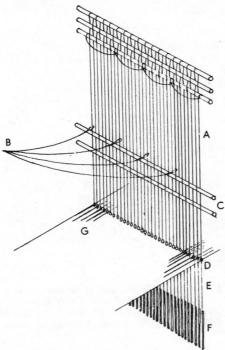

The Chinese draw-loom (figure 126) has a figure-harness without a neck, comber-board, pulley-frame, or tail-cords. The draw-girl sits over the loom behind the figure-harness. The draw-cords pass over her right shoulder. Since the harness has no neck- or tail-cords, a set of loops or lashes would be required for each figure of the harness, instead of only one for a harness with a neck. The figure-harness in use in Europe in the early medieval period must have been similar to that in the Chinese drawing.

FIGURE 125—*Probable arrangement of the early figure-harness without neck.* (A, E) *Harness-cords;* (B) *draw-cords: one cord to each harness figure or repeat;* (C) *cross-sticks to keep the harness-cords in correct order;* (D) *harness-mails;* (F) *wire weights to keep the harness-cords taut;* (G) *warp.*

III. FORMATION OF THE DESIGN ON THE DRAW-CORDS

All figure-harnesses are composed of sections, one section to each repetition of the design. Each section is called a figure, and for that reason the weaver describes the design-repeats as figures. The design, as distinguished from the background, is also called the figure since it is produced by the operation of the figure-harness. In the building or mounting of a figure-harness, alternate figures are sometimes reversed. The kind of harness thus created is called a point-harness, the actual point being the point where the reversing begins and ends. The point-harness produces turn-over designs, such as those with confronting or addorsed animals and birds in roundels on many medieval silks. From the turn-over designs on some early figured silks, we can understand that a figure-harness without a neck was used. The figure-harness with a neck reverses all the details of the design. With a neckless figure-harness it is possible to reverse only a portion of the design. This is clearly shown, on the tenth century Saint-Josse 'Elephant' silk (plate 10 A). This silk has an Islamic inscription giving the name of a ruler of Khurasan. The elephant and other details of the design reverse, but the inscription does not. The same occurs on a thirteenth-century silk at Lyons,

FIGURE 126—*Chinese draw-loom, seventeenth century. Although the weaver (left) is passing the shuttle through the shed, neither the figure-harness nor the healds are forming the shed. There are other technical inaccuracies in the artist's drawing.*

and on other silks without inscriptions some details are not reversed. The loom used for these Islamic silks would be the same as that on which contemporary Byzantine silks were woven. It is therefore certain that the early European figure-harness had no neck.

In the drawing of the Chinese loom two sets of healds are shown in front of the figure-harness, one set of five healds lifted by gibbet-levers, and one of eight depression-healds. The five healds would be used for making satin-ground weave. The eight depression-healds would be used for the binding-weaves of the design. Italian looms of the late fourteenth and the fifteenth centuries had the five lifting-healds for satin-ground weave, and as many as six for the binding of figure-wefts. The depression-healds of the Chinese loom are hung from rods with sufficient elasticity to retract the healds after depression. The European depression-healds did not have such rods. They were hung from weighted levers (figure 127). Spanish looms of the same late medieval period had the five lifting-healds for satin but fewer for the figure-binding.

Scaling. It was possible to increase the scale of the design by controlling the harness-cords in groups of two or more, or by entering two or more warp-threads through each mail. A cloth with 50 warp-threads to the inch, and with a design eight inches in width repeat, would require 400 harness-cords. If the harness-cords were controlled in pairs the width of the design-repeat would be extended to sixteen inches. This principle was understood by Byzantine silk-weavers as early as the seventh century. Scaling produces a horizontal stepping round the design-contours (plate 10 B).

Figure-picks were sometimes repeated in order to economize in the number of lashes. This gives a vertical stepping round the design-contours, a feature that occurs in some of the earliest figured fabrics (plate 10 B).

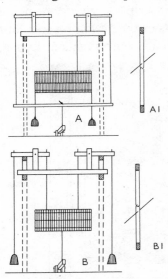

FIGURE 127—*During the last two or three centuries the above methods of lifting and depressing healds have been used, but, as there are no representations of medieval draw-looms, it is not possible to say when they were first used in connexion with figure-weaving. It is certain that similar methods would be necessary for the control of a number of healds.* (A) *Method of lifting healds by wooden levers;* (A 1) *the warp end is entered through the top loop of the heald-harness thread;* (B) *method of depressing healds by wooden levers;* (B 1) *the warp end is entered through the bottom loop of the heald-harness thread.*

Dual control of warp-threads. The warp-threads in the Chinese loom would be entered through the figure-harness mail and through the loops of the five healds, also perhaps through the loops of the eight healds. This method of warp-control was practised in Europe before the middle of the medieval period. It was used for tissued silks and damasks. It is a difficult method, as the warp-threads are lifted and depressed by the figure-harness and the healds. This requires much space between the figure-harness and the cloth, and the shed or passage for the shuttle is thus very limited.

Brocading is the introduction of extra weft into only a part of the warp-shed to enrich some details of the design. Gold thread was much used as a brocade weft.

IV. SETTING THE DESIGN ON THE HARNESS-CORDS

In order to reproduce the design on the cloth by lifting some warp-threads and leaving others down, as required to make the correct shed for the design-pick, it was necessary to select the particular cords to be pulled or drawn. During the past few centuries the design has first been painted on point-paper, the number of squares agreeing vertically with the tail-cords or simples, and horizontally with the figure-picks. The horizontal rows of the point-paper were 'read' by one person and the lashes 'laced' on the tail-cords or simples by another (figure 128). It seems likely that point-paper was used at least as early as the fifteenth century.

For patterns to be worked in cross-stitch embroidery it was certainly used a little later. We can only surmise what method was used in the early period of draw-loom weaving. It is possible that the design was laced directly on the draw-cords without any other aid than the original drawing. Later, but before the invention of printing, the design was probably ruled out in squares by the designer. When draw-loom weaving was first practised in Roman Egypt or Syria, a considerable amount of tapestry-weaving was being produced by direct methods. We know that these tapestries were sometimes woven in conjunction with draw-loom weaving (plate 10 c). In India as late as the present century designs for figured silks were placed directly on the cords without the aid of a point-paper drawing. The

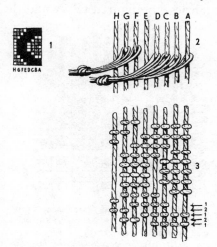

FIGURE 128—*Method of 'reading' or setting the design on the simples.* (1) *A small point-paper drawing for a design in two wefts;* (2) *the lashes on the simples for one line of the drawing;* (3) *the back of the simples showing all the lashes for the design on the paper.*

Indian figured-silk weaving tradition is of Persian origin, and the Persian methods derive from the same early medieval beginnings as the early Byzantine.

V. WEFT-FACED FIGURED FABRICS

The earliest figured fabrics so far known to us, excluding those of China, have a surface mainly of weft, and this is true of both the back and the front of the material. The background and the design on the face of the fabric are of the same weave. They have two sets of warp-threads, and in the beginning both were most probably on the one warp-roller or -rod. One set of warp-threads was controlled by some form of figure-harness, the other by healds or an equivalent. We say some form of figure-harness because in the first place the form must have been very elementary. Also, for the earliest of these fabrics, the weft-faced tabby, a shed-stick might have been used for the making of one of the two sheds required for tabby. The figure-harness warp was used only for producing the design, and the other warp for the binding-weave of the fabric. The figure-harness warp is hidden, sandwiched between the wefts at the back and the wefts at the front. It served to keep at the back the wefts that were not required on the front of the fabric for the design. It cannot be called a ground-warp because it does not make the ground-weave. There were two early weft-faced fabrics, the figured tabby and the figured twill.

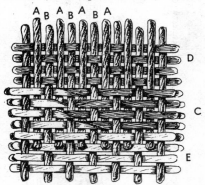

FIGURE 129—*Weft-faced figured tabby weave.* (A) *Warp controlled by drawcords;* (B) *warp used for binding the weft;* (C) *the warp and the two wefts;* (D) *the weave with the face-weft removed:* (E) *the same with the face-weft and binder removed.*

Weft-faced figured tabby (figure 129). It is believed that the earliest fabrics in this weave so far noticed are not earlier than the third century A.D. They are woven in wool, or in wool and linen. A great number have been found in Egyptian graves of the late Roman and early Byzantine periods. Many are ornamented with small designs, resembling in some cases the small filling designs on Roman pavements. The draw-cords for some of these designs would be very few and therefore only a very elementary form of figure-harness would be required. It has been suggested by some writers that the smallest designs might have been woven by a few healds without the use of draw-cords. That is very improbable. It is necessary to take into account the whole group of these fabrics, including those with larger designs, some of which are ornamented with Hellenistic hunting scenes, requiring a great number of draw-cords. It appears that these early draw-loom fabrics, many examples of which have been found in Egypto-Roman graves, were woven by tapestry-weavers using a primitive technique. One of these fabrics, ornamented with a kind of pavement-design in draw-loom weaving, has two panels of tapestry which were woven by the same weaver and at the same time as the draw-loom portions (plate 10 C). The evidence indicating the use of draw-cords lies in the small accidental faults, which recur in each width-repeat of the design. The designs on many of these figured wool-stuffs are so arranged that, to be correctly viewed, the warp-threads must be horizontal and the weft-threads vertical. The cord at the edge of the fabric shown in plate 10 C, which was woven in this manner, is not part of a selvedge, but is the result of twisting the ends of the warp-threads. Tapestry-weavers sometimes treated their designs in the same way, as many Egypto-Roman tapestries show. From the late medieval period it has been the custom to weave most tapestries so that when they are hung the warp-threads are horizontal. This arrangement of design also occurs on a number of figured silks in the weft-faced weave, both the tabby-bound and the twill-bound (plate 12 A). The weft-faced figured tabby was produced in silk for the first time about the fifth century. Chinese weavers wove a figured silk, a multicoloured rep or warp-rib, at least as early as the beginning of the Christian era. Many examples have been found in Chinese Turkestan and southern Mongolia. A few fragments of this Chinese silk have also been found at Palmyra and one or two localities in the west. If the Chinese multicoloured rep and the western weft-faced figured tabby are examined together, one with the warp-threads vertical and the other with the warp-threads horizontal, they appear to be almost identical in weave. This does not signify any technical relationship. The Chinese silk is of warp-effect and the western of weft-effect. The loom used for the one would not weave the other. The technical development was independent. Early in the present century it was assumed, without any consideration of the techniques, that the weaving of figured silks passed from China to Persia

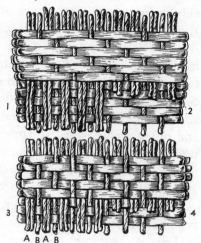

FIGURE 130—*Weft-faced figured twill weave.* (1) *With face-weft removed;* (2) *with face-weft and figure-harness warp ends removed;* (3) *with back weft removed;* (4) *with back weft and figure-harness warp ends removed.* (A) *Figure-harness warp ends;* (B) *binder warp ends. The top drawing shows the front and the bottom drawing shows the back.*

during the Sassanian period (226–651) and later to the Byzantine Empire. This assumption was partly due to the fact that the Persians were the intermediaries in the trade in raw silk between the east and the west, before sericulture began in the Byzantine Empire about the middle of the sixth century. Towards the end of the next century the western weft-faced method passed to China, both the figured tabby and the figured twill. Two important early western weft-faced figured tabby silks are the 'Striding Lion' from Antinoë (Antinoöpolis) (plate 11 A) and the 'Maenad' silk at Sens (plate 12 A). After the sixth century few silks were woven in this weave as it was replaced by the figured twill.

Weft-faced figured twill (figure 130). This was a development of the weft-faced figured tabby. Three healds, instead of two, were used for the binding. In the thirteenth century four healds were used for some silks in this weave. No doubt twill was used instead of tabby because it gave a longer weft-float and therefore the pattern effect was more solid; and because, the cloth being finer in silk than in wool, it required a looser binding-weave. There are some early examples with the twill-binding in wool, but these are coarse fabrics. The weft-faced figured twill (the early Byzantine figured twill) was the chief figured silk fabric during the first half of the medieval period. It began in the Near East, probably in Syria or Egypt. Some of the major works were made in Constantinople about the tenth century. The 'Elephant' silk from the shrine of Charlemagne at Aachen, with roundels 30 inches in diameter, and the great 'Striding Lion', were made there (plates 11 A, B). Later this weave was practised in Spain, Italy, and Germany. After the thirteenth century it was displaced in the older weaving-centres by the new tissue methods, but it survived in Germany as late as the sixteenth century. In the fifteenth, it was employed for the making of orphreys and other ecclesiastical ornaments (plate 12 C). The orphreys have thick linen warp-threads, and their ornamentation includes figures of saints with faces, hands, and so forth worked in embroidery. In some cases the design is so varied and unrepetitive that it is doubtful whether a figure-harness was used.

A very considerable number of fragments of silk in this weft-faced figured twill have survived, many of them in countries where they were not woven, such as France, Belgium, Holland, England, and Spain. Those which have been preserved in Germany are mostly of the kind that were not made there. They served largely for the wrappings of holy relics, ecclesiastical vestments, and royal robes. Many have been preserved made up into seal-bags. At Canterbury there is a large collection of early medieval examples. Durham has a few very important ones. At Westminster Abbey there are many small fragments, mostly of seal-bags and not so early as the earliest of Canterbury and Durham. On the Continent there are more important collections at the Vatican City, Sens, Maastricht, Cologne, Milan, and many other places. No other weave has served for so many major works or for such a variety of interesting motifs.

VI. TISSUED FABRICS

The mature tissued fabrics were first produced about the twelfth century. They have two warps, a ground-warp and a binder-warp. The ground-warp and the ground-weft make the foundation-weave of the fabric. As the ground-warp predominates over the ground-weft, the weave is said to be of warp-effect. For most of the medieval tissues the ground-warp threads are in pairs in the mail. The figure-wefts (called the tissue-wefts) are bound by a binder-warp. Thus there are really two webs, one composed of the ground-warp and the ground-weft and the other of the binder-warp and the tissue-weft. The two webs combine to make one fabric, since the tissue-wefts pass to the front and the back of the fabric as required for the making of the design. The ground-pick is not a figure-pick, as the figure-harness does not help to produce the shed for it. The ground-weave is really a plain foundation cloth of either tabby, twill, or satin. The weaver makes it with the healds alone. If he lifts the whole of the binder-warp when making the ground-pick, a pocket occurs between the two webs.

In making the weft-faced figured fabrics the healds were required only for the control of the binder-warp; for the tissued fabrics, however, an extra set was required for lifting of the ground-warp. The ground-warp threads passed through figure-harness mails and through the top loops of the ground-warp healds. This dual control of the ground-warp was a new principle in figure-weaving, and a very important one. In the weaving centres where it was practised the older, weft-faced method was

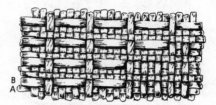

FIGURE 131—*Early tabby tissue with one heald (or its equivalent) for the tissue-binding by every sixth warp thread.* (A) *Ground-weft;* (B) *tissue-weft.*

abandoned. After the thirteenth century, dual control of the ground-warp was more complicated, but the pace of weaving was increased. Its great advantage was that the warp-effect ground and weft-effect tissue gave more variety in texture. The weft-faced fabrics had only weft-effect.

Tabby tissue. The tissue method did not begin in the twelfth century. In an immature form it existed about five centuries earlier. It has its origin in a woollen fabric brocaded with linen, without the use of a figure-harness. The ground weave is tabby. This wool-and-linen brocade fabric is one of the many varieties found in Egyptian graves of the Roman period. About the seventh century A.D. silk was used instead of wool and linen, and the design was made with a tissue-weft instead of brocading. Some of the wool-and-linen brocades have design-binding by every fourth warp-thread, others by every sixth warp-thread. The same occurs on the earliest silk tissues; one at Saint-Moritz, Switzerland, is bound by every fourth warp-thread, and two at Durham and another at Utrecht by every sixth warp-thread (figure 131). The fragments at Durham, found in the coffin of St Cuthbert (? 635–687), are the largest and best preserved. Those at Utrecht were parts of the vestments of St Willibrord (*c* 657–*c* 738), a younger contemporary of St Cuthbert. Examples of about the tenth and the eleventh centuries, mostly Islamic, have the tenth or the twelfth warp-thread as the design-binder. These early tabby-ground tissues had a single warp, and the figure-binding required only one heald. Because there was only one heald for the tissue weft-binding, it was necessary to have two ground-picks to each tissue-pick, otherwise the tabby ground would be imperfect. The single-heald binding produced an unpleasing striped effect, rendering the weave less attractive than weft-faced fabrics. About the eleventh century two healds were used for the tissue-binding, and this gave a satisfactory tabby-binding to the tissue. With two healds only one ground-pick was required to each tissue-pick. In the next century

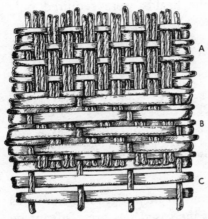

FIGURE 132—Diasprum-*weave*. (A) *Ground-weave with figure-weft at the back of the cloth;* (B) *figure-weave with figure-weft at the front of the cloth;* (C) *showing ground-warp and ground-weft removed from the front of the cloth.*

a second warp, a binder-warp, was introduced to make the tabby-binding of the tissue: a great advantage as it helped to make a more attractive fabric. Previously these tabby tissues were self-colour, the warp and the weft being of the same colour. It was now possible to have tissue-binders of a different colour from the ground-warp. The tabby tissue with a binder-warp, called *diasprum* (jasper), is the first mature tissue (figure 132). One of the earliest *diaspra* is the robe from the tomb of the Emperor Henry VI (d 1197) at Palermo (plate 12 B). The tissue-weft is of gold thread, the ground now a dull rose silk. For some of the early *diaspra* more than one tissue-weft was used, as in a Spanish example (plate 13 A). Most of these fabrics are brocaded (plates 13 C, D).

In the late eleventh and early twelfth centuries some attempts were made to produce the effect of tabby tissue on the loom used for the Byzantine figured twill. For this the whole of the figure-harness warp was lifted to give one tabby-shed, and the whole of the binder-warp to give the other. This made the background weave, the figure-pick being made by the usual weft-faced twill method. Among the silks so woven are a material said to have been part of the robe of the Emperor Henry II (973–1024); part of a vestment supposedly worn by St Bernard of Clairvaux (1091–1153); and a material from the shrine of Edward the Confessor (? 1002–1066). The shroud of Saint Siviard (d 687) at Sens Cathedral is a combination of tabby tissue and Byzantine twill.

Twill-ground tissues (figures 133, 134). With three healds for the ground-weave in place of the two for the *diasprum* weave, the three-heald twill tissue was possible. It is not unlikely that this new European figured weave was inspired by the twill and the satin ground-tissues from China which had spread to Near Eastern Islamic countries about the end of the thirteenth century. Some of these oriental silks were found in a fourteenth-century tomb at Verona in 1921. Secondhand renderings of Chinese motifs and the free treatment of Chinese designs occur for the first time in Europe on the fourteenth-century north Italian twill-ground tissues (plate 13 B). This eastern influence in western design contrasts strongly

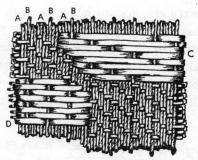

FIGURE 133—*Warp effect twill-ground tissue, with tabby and four-end twill figure-binding.* (A) *Ground-warp;* (B) *binder-warp;* (C) *four-end twill tissue-binding;* (D) *tabby tissue-binding.*

with the more static treatment of pre-fourteenth-century western design. It is believed that many of the Italian twill-ground silk tissues were made at Lucca. They are often referred to as Lucchese fabrics. Twill-ground tissues were also made in Spain. The Italian weavers used more healds for the tissue-binding than were used elsewhere. Four-heald twill tissue-binding was common. Another tissue-binding was a special form of a six-heald weave (plate 14 A). The twill-ground tissue-weave was not much favoured after the early fifteenth century, when satin and velvet fabrics became more popular. The style of the twill-ground tissues, with numerous varieties of fantastic animals and birds, gave place to a bolder and more static form, better suited to the new damasks and velvets. Perhaps the fact that the dyes used for the twill-ground tissues were not very fast to light helped to put them out of favour.

Satin-ground tissues (figure 135). The minimum number of healds required for a satin-weave is five. There is a four-heald weave, satinet, which is half twill and half satin; it is not a true satin. It occurs in some Islamic fabrics. Twilled fabrics have diagonal lines, from which satin is almost free and therefore has a clearer and smoother surface. Five-heald satin was the only one practised in Europe for the weaving of figured fabrics before the sixteenth century. Satin tissues have a warp-effect satin, and for this more warp-threads are required than for other weaves. The earliest satins have about 200 pairs of

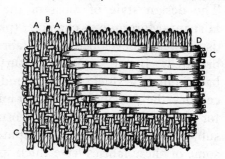

FIGURE 134—*Fourteenth-century Italian twill-ground tissue.* (A) *Ground-warp;* (B) *binder-warp;* (C) *ground-weft;* (D) *tissue-weft.*

warp-threads to the inch. Some European satins woven at the beginning of the present century have as many as 600 single warp-threads to the inch. During the Middle Ages the warp-threads controlled by the figure-harness were generally in pairs. Pairs of threads are not so satisfactory for satins as single threads, but 200 single threads would give a very poor satin. In the fifteenth century Italian silk-weavers, using single threads, increased their number. In the following centuries the number of single ends was further increased in order to make a finer satin.

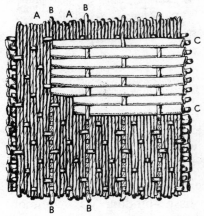

FIGURE 135—*Satin ground-tissue, with tabby tissue-binding.* (A) *Ground-warp;* (B) *binder-warp;* (C) *ground-weft.*

The satin weave is of Chinese origin. Satin tissues and damasks became known in the west about the end of the thirteenth century. The earliest are ornamented with designs composed of a mixture of Chinese and Islamic motifs, including Islamic script. Some have the title *Al-Nāṣir*, appropriated by the late thirteenth- and early fourteenth-century Mameluke sultans of Egypt (*c* 1251–1517). Many of these silks have warp-stripes of various colours, ornamented with Chinese or Islamic motifs including script. The satin-ground tissue-weave was practised in Spain and Italy in the fourteenth and fifteenth centuries. Some of the earliest Spanish examples have the warp-stripes in various colours covered with ornament and script (plate 14 B) showing a continuity of the Chinese-Islamic tradition, but the immediate influence is Near Eastern Islamic and not Chinese. There is none of the freedom of Chinese design which shows so much in fourteenth-century Italian twill-ground tissues. The design style of most of the fifteenth-century Spanish satin tissues is Hispano-Moresque in character (plate 14 C). In northern Italy the satin-ground tissue-weave developed into a fabric which has long been known in Britain as brocatelle. In the sixteenth century, satin made the design and tissue-weft the background, a thick linen ground-weft stiffening the fabric. In the fifteenth century the Italians produced a number of brocatelles with satin backgrounds for use as orphreys. These are ornamented with religious symbols and figure subjects, drawn by artists of repute (plate 14 D). Instead of linen ground-weft, some of these fabrics have thick spun-silk ground-weft. They appear to be the first European fabrics for which spun silk was used.

VII. DAMASKS

Tabby damasks. Damask weaving, especially before the introduction of the Jacquard machine early in the nineteenth century, was a particular method of figure-weaving. Besides the figure-harness and the lifting-healds of the tissue method, a set of healds was required to depress the warp-threads for the binding of the design. In the case of the tissue, the figure was bound by a binder warp. Damasks have only one warp, and therefore the binding of the design as well as the ground was done by the warp, which was also controlled by the figure-

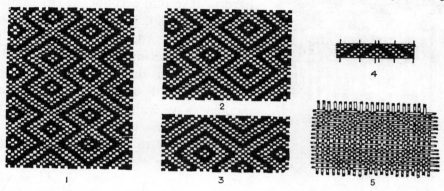

FIGURE 136—*Silk fragments from Kerch (Crimea), probably Chinese, c 100 B.C.–A.D. 100. (1) The main design; (2, 3) variations of the design in the fragments; (4) the unit of the design; (5) diagram showing the interlacing of the yarn.*

harness. The single warp was treble-controlled: by the figure-harness, by the lifting-healds, and by the depressing-healds. This is true of the twill and the satin damasks but not of the tabby damasks. Silks with a single warp and weft, with a ground of tabby and a design in short floats over three, five, or seven warp-threads, may be included as immature damasks, although it is doubtful whether any depression-healds were used in making them.

Advanced tabby damasks were woven in Spain about the end of the twelfth century and early in the thirteenth. Many have been found in the royal tombs at Burgos, including some with bars of Islamic script in an extra weft. One of these Spanish silks, without the bars of script, was used as a lining material for parts of the vestments of Walter de Cantelupe (1236–66), found in his tomb at Worcester in 1861. The Spanish weavers developed a multicoloured silk from the tabby damask, but it did not long remain in favour. The tabby damask is of Chinese origin. Many examples woven in the early centuries of the Christian era have been found in Chinese Turkestan. One of the earliest, found in a Graeco-Scythian grave at Kerch in the Crimea (figure 136), is thought to be at least as early as the beginning of the Christian era. Another, from a tenth-century grave at Birka, Sweden, is believed to be Chinese, but this kind of weaving may have passed to western Asia before that date. It must have reached Spain from some eastern Islamic country.

It is difficult to determine the method of weaving these tabby-ground silks. Some could be produced on a loom with a few healds without the aid of a figure-harness. The Crimean example would have been possible on six healds. However, we have to take into account the large number which could not be woven without some form of draw-cord, such as that from Birka, the Spanish examples, and many of the Chinese. Their designs would be impossible with healds alone. The most probable method was with two healds (or their equivalent) for the tabby ground and draw-cords for the design. By draw-cords we mean some elementary form of figure-harness. The two healds would serve as lifting-healds for the tabby.

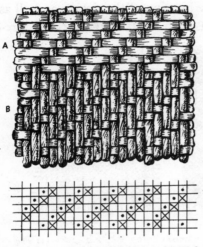

FIGURE 137—*Four-end twill damask.* (A) *Weft effect, for the design;* (B) *warp effect for the ground;* (●) *lifted-ends for the ground-weave;* (X) *lowered ends for the design-weave.*

Twill damasks. There are many kinds of twill damask. Three-heald, four-heald, and six-heald damasks are among the silks found in Chinese Turkestan by Sir Aurel Stein (1862–1943). Four-end twill (figure 137) and tabby occur in the same material; six-end and three-end twills also occur together. Four-end twill ground and four-end twill figure are found in some damasks preserved in Europe. One of these is the silk said to be the dalmatic of St Ambrose (? 340–97), at Milan. Another is in the treasury of the church of St Servatius at Maastricht (plate 15 A). There are also a few fragments, with small designs, in this weave at Sens. The Milan silk has a Hellenistic hunting-scene on it; that at Maastricht has a large roundel setting, with border ornamentation of formal foliage motifs similar to those found on some early medieval silks in the Byzantine figured twill. It is impossible to believe that these western twill damasks were woven at the beginning of the Middle Ages. One cannot but suspect that they are twill-damask renderings of silk designs originally woven in the weft-faced figured-twill weave. Twill damask is a very advanced weave. It must have been considerably more economical to weave than the weft-faced materials, and a more useful fabric. It is most surprising that only these few examples exist. A four-heald damask with a very small design makes the background of the fourteenth-century Catworth embroideries in the Victoria and Albert Museum, London. Another with a similar design is attached to the shield of Henry V in Westminster Abbey. These may be Chinese, for they are similar to some contemporary Chinese examples. There is at least one other with a western design; it is either Italian or Islamic.

Satin damask. Of the many kinds of satin damask only one was made in Europe before the sixteenth century, the five-heald type (figure 138). The method of weaving satin damask was an extension of the twill method, with the use of more healds. Two sets of healds were required, one for lifting the warp-threads and one for depressing. With the use of more healds the distance between the figure-harness and the fell of the cloth became greater. The strain imposed on the warp-threads by the figure-harness, the lifting-healds, and the depression-healds was

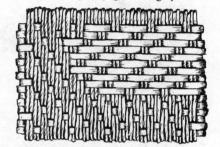

FIGURE 138—*Five-end satin damask.*

considerable, therefore it was more easily possible to weave these damasks with silk warp-yarn than with any other, owing to the great strength and elasticity of silk. No form of weaving called for greater care in the adjustment of the harnesses, for which an elaborate system of lever-control was necessary. Technical knowledge was gained by trial and error.

Like the tabby and twill damasks, satin damask is of Chinese origin. It became known in the west about the end of the thirteenth century. One of the earliest has Chinese cloud forms and Chinese characters for 'felicity' and 'longevity'. Another bears the name of a Mameluke sultan, Muḥammad ibn Qalā'ūn (1293–1341). Since the fifteenth century Italy has been famous for silk damasks. There is no Chinese influence in the designs on the early Italian damasks; they are mainly in the same Italian style as the contemporary velvets. Like the velvets, some of them are brocaded with gold thread. This further complicated the weaving by necessitating an extra set of depression-healds, the brocade-weft being bound in longer floats than the damask-weft (plate 15 B).

VIII. VELVET

Figured velvets. Velvet differs from other silk fabrics in that the whole or part of its surface is of pile, either cut or uncut. The uncut pile or terry is merely a loop. Figured velvets usually have the design of pile and the ground of a tabby or satin foundation-weave (figure 139), but there are many exceptions. The velvet loom has two warps, one for the foundation-weave and the other for the pile. Some brocaded velvets require a third warp for the binding of the brocade-weft. Unlike most figured fabrics, velvets are woven face-up, rendering brocading less convenient. The pile is made by the insertion in the shed of a wire in place of the usual weft-yarn. There are usually three foundation-picks of yarn. This arrangement is necessary to bind the pile firmly in the foundation-web of the fabric. The pile warp-threads are lifted for the insertion of the wire as required to make the design in pile; hence, as only a portion of the pile-warp is lifted, the take-up of the pile-warp into the cloth is uneven. For the weaving of plain velvet it is possible to have all the pile-warp on a single roller, as it is taken up into the cloth uniformly. For figured velvet each pile warp-thread is wound on a separate bobbin, each bobbin requiring a small weight to keep the thread taut; the single roller also requires weights for the same purpose. The small bobbins

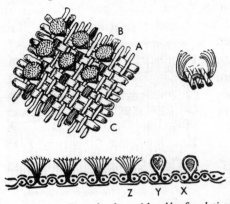

FIGURE 139—*Figured velvet with tabby foundation.* (A) *Foundation-warp*; (B) *pile-warp*; (C) *foundation-weft*; (X) *uncut loop for terry or uncut pile*; (Y) *uncut loop with grooved wire for guiding cutter*; (Z) *cut pile.* (*The pile tufts* (inset) *are reduced comparatively in order to show the foundation weave.*)

are placed on a frame called a creel. The creel is fixed behind the figure-harness, under the foundation-warp. It holds hundreds of full bobbins. The wire for cut pile has a groove in it, that for uncut pile is plain. The groove guides the knife that cuts the loops. The weaver does the cutting while the cloth is in the loom, with an instrument called a 'trevette', and draws out the wires. To roll velvet round the cloth-roller as other fabrics are rolled would damage the pile, therefore a special contrivance for gripping the velvet sufficiently to hold it on the roller is used. The weaving of velvet on the traditional hand-loom is a very slow process.

The invention of figured velvet must have required much imagination and ingenuity. The apparatus was designed to overcome the many difficulties in the making of this rich fabric: the creel carrying the separate bobbins for the pile-warp; the wires for the making of the rows of loops; the trevette for the cutting of the loops; and the special cloth-roller. The apparatus illustrated in excellent engravings in the eighteenth-century *Dictionnaire des Sciences* (1765), although of a much later date, was probably very similar to the fifteenth-century equipment capable of performing exactly the same work. Unfortunately we know of no fifteenth-century illustrations of velvet looms.

It appears that figured velvet was woven in northern Italy during the second half of the fourteenth century. One example is said to have been found in the tomb of the Emperor Charles IV (d 1378). There are others with details of design similar to some on the fourteenth-century twill-ground tissues. Unlike so many of the other figured weaves, velvet was not a Chinese invention. Plain velvet, woven some time before figured velvet, was used for background materials for English and continental embroideries early in the fourteenth century. There is reason to believe that it might have been made in Islam before then. Italian figured velvets of the fifteenth century are magnificent and most luxurious. Some have a foundation weave of tabby, others of satin. The foundation tabby of some examples is covered with gold-tissue weft. Cut and uncut pile, sometimes in more than one colour, and also two levels of cut pile, were used to give variety of effect. Many examples are brocaded with *bouclé* gold thread (plate 15 C). In the fifteenth century Italian velvets and damasks were used in churches and palaces throughout Europe; painters delighted to depict saints, churchmen, and nobles draped with them. In England, painted representations of these fabrics on walls served as substitutes for genuine hangings.

Practically all the basic figured weaves were developed in the Middle Ages. What remained to be done later was mainly to extend established principles and to mechanize the processes of manufacture.

BIBLIOGRAPHY

Cox, R. 'Les soieries d'art depuis les origines jusqu'a nos jours.' Hachette, Paris. 1914.

Falke, O. von. 'Decorative Silks' (3rd ed.). Zwemmer, London. 1936.

Hooper, L. 'Silk, its Production and Manufacture' (2nd ed.). Pitman, London. 1927.

Kendrick, A. F. "Byzantine Silks in London Museums." *Burlington Magazine*, **24**, 138, 185, 1913–14.

Idem. "A 'griffin' Silk Fabric." *Ibid.*, **29**, 225, 1916.

Kendrick, A. F. and Arnold, T. W. 'Persian Stuffs with Figured-subjects.' *Ibid.*, **37**, 237, 1920.

Sabbe, E. "L'Importation des tissus orientaux en Europe occidentale au haute moyen âge (IXe et Xe siècles) [with bibl.]." *Rev. belge Philol. Hist.*, **14**, 811, 1861.

Thurstan, Violetta. 'A Short History of Decorative Textiles and Tapestries' (2nd ed.). Favil Press, London. 1954.

9

GLASS

R. J. CHARLESTON (I–V) AND
L. M. ANGUS-BUTTERWORTH (VI–IX)

IN the later Middle Ages glass-making was roughly divided into two spheres—that of the north (including Germany, France, Belgium, England, and Bohemia) and that of the south (mainly Italy). These divisions were based not on geography but on divergent technical traditions. In the north, in the glass-houses surviving in the forested regions after the break-up of the Roman Empire, glass was made with local sands (providing silica) and with the ashes of burnt inland vegetation (impure potassium carbonate) for flux. In the south, silica was frequently obtained by crushing white pebbles from the beds of rivers, while the flux was a soda (impure sodium carbonate) derived from the burning of marine vegetation. These two spheres of glass-making can be conveniently considered separately for the early part of our period.

I. GLASS-MAKING IN THE NORTH (TO ABOUT 1550)

Fluxes. It is not known when the glass-makers of Gaul and the Rhineland, isolated by the political upheavals accompanying the collapse of Roman power, became cut off from their normal sources of soda and fell back on the use of potash. It is certain, however, that by the time of Theophilus Presbyter, in the tenth or early eleventh century, the use of potash was firmly established in the north. In his *Schedula diversarum artium* (book II, ch 1), he says: 'Prepare ashes of beech-wood.' To our present period belongs the work of Georg Agricola (1490–1555) who deals with glass-making in book XII of his *De re metallica* (Basel, 1556). Although Agricola was fully conversant with contemporary Venetian glass-making, and gives it first place in his work, he also reflects the German and Bohemian methods of his time (figure 140). Having treated of the soda-fluxes, he continues:

But those who have none of the above-mentioned saps take two parts of ashes of oak or ilex or of hard wood (*roborei*) or of turkey oak, or if these are not to hand, of beech or of fir, and mix them with one of gravel or sand, adding a little salt made from brackish or sea water (*aqua salsa vel marina*), and a minute quantity of manganese; but the glass made with these latter is less white and translucent.

In France, bracken-ash was used, and the glass accordingly was called *verre de fougère*.

Furnaces. The use of potash appears to have gone with a predilection for a special type of furnace. The evidence is full of gaps and not wholly consistent, but in general it may be said that a furnace of rectangular plan was favoured, with two to four glass-pots ranged down each side, and with an extension that could be used either for fritting the primary materials or for annealing the finished product. Theophilus, in the work already quoted, prescribes a furnace of rectangular plan, 15 ft by 10 ft, and 4 ft high. This was divided by a wall two-thirds of the way along. Somewhat above the ground was constructed a platform or siege, below which the firing-chamber ran from end to end of the furnace. In the larger chamber there were four holes in the siege down each long side, while holes in the siege in both chambers admitted the heat from below. The smaller part of the furnace was for making the frit. This was prepared with two parts of beech ashes and one of sand, carefully purified from earth and stones; they were mixed together on a clean surface, then roasted over a fire made of thoroughly dried beech-wood. The heated mixture had to be well stirred for a night and a day, to prevent agglomeration. Apart from this, Theophilus prescribes a separate annealing furnace measuring 10 ft by 8 ft by 4 ft.

It is clear, however, that considerable variations of this furnace-pattern were tried in practice. In the work entitled *De coloribus et artibus Romanorum*, attributed to a certain Heraclius, there are in the third book two chapters (VII and VIII) devoted to glass-making. This book was probably added in the twelfth or thirteenth century to the existing tenth-century text. The oven here described has three chambers of unequal size, the central and largest being the working-furnace, with two pots on the siege, the second compartment serving to roast the frit and the third to fire the pots. In a miniature from a fifteenth-century manu-script of 'Sir John Mandeville's Travels', however, a glass-furnace of a slightly different pattern is represented. Here, in the main furnace, there are two pots and two working-holes ('glory-holes') on the side represented, while a smaller, subsidiary furnace is used for annealing, its floor being on the same level as that of the working-furnace (plate 16).

The general arrangement of the rectangular furnace with pots ranged down the two longer sides is confirmed by the ground-plans of late medieval and Tudor furnaces excavated in England, which during this period may be con-sidered a province of France so far as glass-making is concerned. One of the best preserved of these furnace-sites was that at Vann Farm, near Chiddingfold in Surrey, where an earlier glass-house was probably reoccupied in Tudor times.

Here the main working-furnace was an oblong 12 ft by 5 ft 6 in, at the corners of which were four diagonally projecting fan-shaped wings. In these no doubt the heat of the main furnace was utilized for fritting, pot-arching (that is, pre-heating), and annealing. The furnaces were sometimes of stone, sometimes of brick.

Glass-pots. The pots used within these furnaces appear to have been of two kinds. The first was a piriform crucible with an out-turned lip (plate 16), the second a straight-sided pot tapering slightly towards the base. Theophilus (see p 206) gives the following instructions for making a pot: 'Take white pottery clay, dry and pound it carefully, pour water on it, and soften it thoroughly with a piece of wood. Make the pots wide in the upper part, narrow in the lower, and round the mouth form a small lip bent inwards (*labium parvum interius recurvum*).' Fragments of numerous glass-pots of this general shape, but varying in dimensions, have been found on English glass-making sites, and examples with incurved rims attributable to the thirteenth century tend to conform to the description given by Theophilus.

Tools. Of the tools used during this period very little trace is left. The blowing-pipe (plate 16) was rather long, contrasting with the short pipe figured by Agricola (figure 140); like it, however, it has a wooden handle in the upper part, and this seems to be a common feature of the period, as later. Fragments of blow-pipes found on English sites of the fourteenth to fifteenth centuries suggest that the bore varied from about $\frac{1}{4}$ in to about $\frac{5}{8}$ in.

The marver for rolling the glass vesica into a cylindrical form is shown in figure 140. It was no doubt at this period actually made of some smooth stone, if not of marble (as its name suggests).

Moulds for imparting a surface patterning to the glass must already have been in use by the thirteenth century, for vertically ribbed cups and flasks of this century, and even of the end of the preceding one, are known from France and Belgium. In England, many of the glasses of the medieval period are characterized by a close spiral ribbing imparted in the first place by a mould, and in 1535 moulds were among the tools bequeathed by a Sussex glass-maker to his son (figures 140, E, 146, 3).

Otherwise the techniques of making vessel-glass in this period were probably of the simplest, as remaining fragments suggest. Theophilus mentions the processes of blowing, 'warming-in', attachment of the pontil-rod, opening out the vessel, and, for the manufacture of bottles with long necks, swinging of the paraison round the head, the thumb being over the mouthpiece of the blowing-iron (cf figures 140, 147). Threads of glass could be wrought as handles, or trailed on as decoration. These elementary techniques no doubt continued throughout the medieval period. In England, at least, glass of a sealing-wax red was used for ornamentation, and occasionally for complete vessels, probably in the fifteenth century. Blue glass vessels, the colour probably obtained from cobalt oxide, were also being made in England at this date. Until about the sixteenth century, however, vessel-glass was only a by-product of the glass-furnaces of northern Europe, which were mainly occupied with making window-glass (section VIII, pp 237 ff).

II. ITALIAN GLASS-MAKING TO ABOUT 1550

Glass-making in Venice has probably had a continuous existence since Roman times. Little is known of the earliest period there, but in 1090 there is mention of one Petrus Flabianus *phiolarius*, which shows that vessel-glass was already being made. In the thirteenth century the industry was flourishing. By a law of 1291 the glass-works in Venice were moved out to Murano, and it was here that all 'Venetian' glass was made. Enamel glass appears to have been introduced in 1317 and coloured glass for windows by at latest 1330. The most significant of all the Venetian innovations, however, occurred

FIGURE 140—*General view of a glass-furnace at work. Note the blowing-irons* (A), *moulds* (E), *pucellas* (D); (foreground) *a woman haggles over the value of a cullet;* (left) *swinging the paraison;* (right centre) *flattening the paraison on the marver;* (right) *gathering the metal;* (right rear) *blowing.* Agricola, 1556.

over a hundred years later, namely the making of *cristallo*, a clear crystalline glass.

Flux, silica, fritting, and founding. It is clear that by 1450 glass-making in Venice was already highly developed, specialized, and organized on a large scale. Curiously enough, however, the first eye-witness account of Italian glass-making at this period describes processes seen apparently in Rome. This account is the *Glaskonst* ('Art of Glass') written by a Swedish priest, Peder Månsson, who travelled to Rome in 1508 and stayed there until he was recalled to Sweden in 1524. Månsson at the very beginning of his discourse puts his finger on the differences between Italian and northern glass-making:

The art is practised in many lands and with different materials, and glass is not of the same type in all countries. In Rome and Welshland [Italy] glass is made of three sorts of materials: fine white sand, black ashes, made by burning a plant which is there called kali or alkali and in Italian soda, and of a salt which is called sal alkali, the ashes of which are imported from Spain and from Alexandria and France to Rome for the glass-making, and likewise from other countries. The soda-plant only grows on the sea-shore.

He then describes how the soda-plant is burned in a clay-lined pit, water poured on, more plant added, and the process repeated until the pit is full. On top is the black ash in lumps: underneath is the salt called sal alkali, agglomerated into a greyish stone-like mass. The sal alkali is cleansed by being powdered, sifted, and purified by lixiviation. Then equal quantities of fine white sand and of the black ash are mixed on the platform of a low-vaulted furnace fired with dry wood (cf figure 141). They are submitted to the fire for four or five hours, being constantly turned with an iron rake. When cool, the mixture is taken out, pounded, and sifted. This prepared frit is then ready to be put into the pots in the main furnace, where, after two days' intense firing, it is ladled with a long iron scoop from the founding-pot into the working-pot. The glass can be coloured by the introduction of suitable pigmenting substances, or rendered clear and white by the addition of 'manganese' [dioxide].

It will be observed that Månsson does not state how, or whether, his sal alkali was added to the batch. His account is in this respect supplemented by Vanoccio Biringuccio. In his *Pirotechnia* (Venice, 1540) Biringuccio states that the glass-salt ('sal vetro', Månsson's 'sal alkali') is taken and fritted with sand or powdered white river-pebbles in the ratio of one to two, and with a certain quantity of manganese [dioxide], in a reverberatory furnace. Biringuccio is also more explicit about the making of the glass-pots. He says that they are fashioned on the wheel from the refractory clays of Valencia, Treguanda, or elsewhere. The pots are dried in the shade for six or eight months, and are then placed in the fritting-furnace, the temperature being gradually raised until the pots become red in colour. Meanwhile, the wall of one arch of the main furnace (below, p 213) has been opened to allow enough space for a pot to be passed through, and the furnace fired to a red-heat. The pot is then hastily moved with iron tongs to the siege of the main furnace, and placed opposite one of the working-holes. The furnace described by both Månsson and Biringuccio is essentially that of Agricola's account, which, being illustrated and more complete, has been selected for discussion later (p 212). Månsson, however, gives an account of the actual

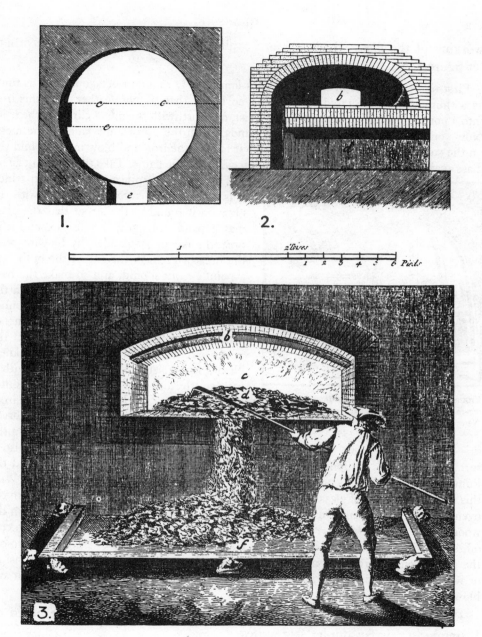

FIGURE 141—*The calcar (Fr.* carcaise) *or fritting-furnace.* (1) *Plan showing the line of the stoke-hole* (c-c) *and fritting-hearth* (e); (2) *transverse section showing the mouth of the furnace* (b) *and the flue* (d) *leading to the fritting-hearth;* (3) *general view showing furnace-mouth* (b, c), *frit on the hearth* (d), *and finished* (f) *ready for mixing with cullet for the founding.* 1772.

working of the glass which is more explicit than that of either of the others (cf figure 147):

First one wants an iron fifty-six inches long, nearly round or octagonal . . ., as thick as a thumb, and perforated with a hole no larger than a goosefeather. Dip this iron into a pot of molten metal and give it a twist, and forthwith the metal clings to the iron. Now you must be brisk . . . with your hands. Turn the iron round, smooth the metal on the stone in front of the furnace, make it fast on the iron and blow into it. Hold the glass again in the furnace, and turn the iron evenly in the flame. Take the glass out again and shape it with pincers to the form which it is finally to have. Swing the iron with the glass on it round in the air so that the glass may expand in length, and also expand it in breadth, like an ox-bladder, by blowing with the breath. Press in the end of the bulb with a point . . . or mould, and so make the base on which the glass is to stand; and with the pincers make it uniformly smooth all round. They now take a piece of wood two inches [fingers] broad, that is fastened from the upper part of the right thigh down to the knee. Next they moisten the iron pincers with a little spittle, and press them against the outer end of the glass where it is fixed to the iron, and place it in front of the opening to break it off. It breaks off at once where the spittle has touched it. The workman has also a second iron 56 in . . . long, shaped like the first, but not hollowed inside, called the Puntellum (puntee). This has always a piece of glass on its end and lies in the fire. With this iron fix the knob of glass on the base: it becomes attached at once, and is held in the oven to warm up. Then take it out and shape it with the pincers while rolling it on the wood bound on the thigh. . . . Then lay the finished glass in the other chamber to cool off, so that it does not get cold too quickly and break. Further, they have shears to cut the glass even, where necessary; and a variety of copper moulds, ornamented inside, or with rims. . . . Into these moulds they first blow the glass, and then take it out and blow it out wider. . . .

FIGURE 142—*The second furnace without the anneal-ing-chamber but with conjoined annealing-furnace. Note the clay tunnels to contain the glasses to be annealed* (H). *1556.*

Furnaces. Agricola's account, although apparently to some extent based on Biringuccio's, is far ampler. He writes:

Some glass-men have three furnaces, others two, others one. Those who use three, cook the material in the first, re-cook it in the second, and in the third cool off the glass vases and other hot articles. Their *first furnace* should be arched over and resemble an oven. In its upper compartment, six feet long, four broad, and two high, the frit is cooked over a strong fire of dry logs until it melts and turns into a glassy mass. . . .

The *second furnace* is round, ten feet broad and eight high, and strengthened on the outside with five ribs . . . 1½ ft thick. This again consists of two chambers, the roof of the lower being 1½ ft thick. This lower chamber has in front a narrow opening for stoking the logs on the ground-level hearth; and in the middle of its roof is a big round aperture opening into the upper compartment so that the flames may penetrate into it. But in the wall of the upper chamber between the ribs there should be eight windows so large that through them the bellied [globular] pots may be put on the floor round the big aperture. . . . At the back of the furnace is a square opening, in height and breadth 1 palm, through which the heat may penetrate into the *third furnace* adjoining. This is oblong, eight feet by six broad, similarly consisting of two chambers, of which the lower has an opening in front for stoking the hearth. On either side of the stoke hole in the wall is a chamber for an oblong pottery tunnel . . . about four feet long, two feet high, and 1½ feet broad. The higher compartment should have two openings, one on either side, high and broad enough to admit the tunnels . . . in which the glass articles now made may be placed to cool off in a milder heat. . . . (figure 142).

FIGURE 143—*Agricola's second glass-furnace, with annealing-chamber; a partially sectioned view showing the glass-pots within. 1556.*

Agricola goes on to explain that some dispense with the fritting-furnace, others with the annealing-furnace. In such cases the main furnace was of slightly different construction (figure 143):

But the second furnace of this type differs from the other second furnace, for it is round, but its open part is eight feet wide and twelve high, because it is composed of three chambers, the lowest of which is not dissimilar from the lower of the other second furnace. In the wall of the middle chamber are six arched openings which, when the heated pots are put in, are blocked up with clay, only small openings being left. In the centre of the roof of the middle chamber is a square opening, a palm long and broad, through which the heat penetrates into the topmost compartment. At the back of the compartment is an opening, so that into the oblong pottery tunnel placed in it the glass articles may be introduced to cool off gradually. . . .

It is clear from this account that a considerable variety of practice obtained in the writer's day. The general type of round furnace described by Agricola, however, remained in use for centuries (figures 144, 145, 423, 424).

Glasses and decorative techniques. To Månsson's account of the techniques in use when he visited the glass-house in Rome, Biringuccio's book adds one or

FIGURE 144—*Interior of a French glass-house making vessel-glass. Note the stoke-hole* (A, B), *and the long annealing-arch* (C) *along which the vessels were moved in 'fraches' (Fr. ferraces = iron trays) to the 'sarosel room'. 1772.*

two points. Thus: 'In addition to colouring [glass vessels] all possible tints, they also make them very clear and transparent like true and natural crystal, and ornament them with paintings and other very fine enamels. . . .' By the date of his book enamel-painting was going out of vogue, except perhaps for the German market, but he clearly refers to another ornamental technique which was at the time reaching the height of its technical accomplishment—the use of drawn-out opaque-white threads (*latticini*). He writes:

Look too at the large things as well as the small, that they make of white or coloured glass and that seem to be woven of osier twigs equally spaced. . . . I must tell you that I have seen glass the colour of pearl or tinted green or blue or formed in various spirals made entirely of a single very slender fibre like a thread, more than 30 *braccia* long, all in one piece like gold or silver drawn through the draw-plate.

To the picture presented by the texts must be added the evidence of surviving glasses. In these the *cristallo* material is seldom completely colourless, having

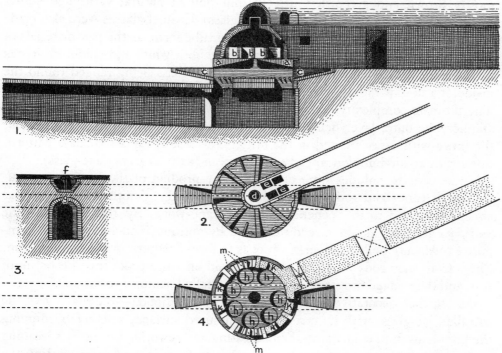

FIGURE 145—*Plan of the glass-house shown in figure 144. (1) Transverse section showing the siege (a) with pots (b) and stoke-hole (c); (2) plan at level of the annealing-arch showing (d), the hole communicating with the arch, and (e) fraches; (3) transverse section showing stoke-hole (f) and entrance to ash-pit (g); (4) plan at level of the siege, showing pots (h, h), working-holes (k, k) and boccarellas (m, m).*

usually a brownish or greyish tint, due presumably to impurities in the materials. Of the coloured transparent glasses, emerald-green, blue, and manganese-purple are all found. No analyses appear to have been made of any of these glasses, and in the absence of such evidence we may at least provisionally assume that they were made by the processes described in the next section (p 218). Enamelling and gilding are both mentioned in the texts, but curiously enough not in conjunction as they are most often found in fact. The gilding was applied before the enamels, which overlay it. None of the sources mention the muffle in which such glasses were refired. Possibly the hottest part of the annealing-chamber or the 'calcar' was used for the purpose, the clay containers shown in Agricola's wood-cuts (figure 142) serving perhaps to shield the glasses from fumes. Opaque-white glass was obtained by the use of tin oxide, and this too was occasionally made into hollow wares.

A further kind of opaque glass was that streaked with a variety of colours, mostly brown and greenish tones, in imitation of natural variegated stones (*calcedonio*, sometimes miscalled *Schmelz* glass). Enamel glasses were also made in many colours for use by goldsmiths, or, in tube form, as the raw materials of the *suppialume* (lamp) workers. In cane-form, both white and coloured, it was used for the *latticinio* decoration, rods of enamel glass being ranged round the inside of a hollow mould, picked up on a paraison of *cristallo* and marvered in. The ultimate complexity of this technique lay in blowing one paraison within another, the outer layer being decorated with canes wrythen in one direction, the inner with canes twisted in the other. The result was a reticulate pattern, often with an air-bubble trapped in each mesh (*vetro di trina*, lace-glass).

These cane-techniques were no doubt a by-product of the Venetian manu-facture of tube- and rod-glass for the bead industry. Another technique was equally indebted to the Venetians' skill in cane-work. By this was made the *millefiori* glass, no doubt directly inspired by antique models, in which com-posite rods were built up in such a way as to form a pattern in the cross-section. Slices from such rods were probably then laid on a fire-proof tray, heated until soft, and then edged progressively together, finally forming a continuous sheet.

One further decorative technique should be mentioned—the making of the so-called ice-glass, with its crackled and fissured surface, whether by dipping the hot paraison in cold water, then reheating and reworking it, or by spreading broken glass on the marver, rolling the paraison on it, and incorporating the fragments.

Venetian metal, being particularly ductile, was usually worked thin. It was therefore not suitable for engraving by the glyptic technique of the lapidary. From about the middle of the sixteenth century, however, it was occasionally engraved by means of a diamond-point, which leaves a whitish spidery line on the surface of the glass. This linear technique was particularly taken up and developed at Hall in the Tyrol, in England, and in the Netherlands.

III. THE DISSEMINATION OF ITALIAN METHODS (c 1550–1615)

The great superiority of Italian glass-making rendered it the envy of all Europe, and princes and potentates everywhere sought to put themselves in control of glass-furnaces working in the Italian manner. Although heavy penalties were imposed on glass-workers absconding from Murano, the rewards were nevertheless sufficiently tempting to seduce many of them. There was, furthermore, a second source of supply of Italian glass-workers. This was the little town of, Altare, near Genoa, where the corporation of glass-makers followed a deliberate policy of disseminating its men and methods. Through the agency of workmen from these two sources, the Italian art of glass was spread throughout Europe, reaching even such distant parts as Sweden (in the 1550s), Denmark (by 1572), and England (by 1570 at latest). Unfortunately, apart from surviving glasses themselves, there is very little evidence as to the methods of glass-making used during this period of intense activity.

There is, however, a wall-painting in the *studiolo* of Francesco I de' Medici (Grand Duke of Tuscany 1574–87) which shows a glass-furnace of Venetian type at work (plate 30). It is clear that at this furnace the finished glasses were annealed in the top compartment of the founding-furnace. The glass-workers or gaffers worked seated, but had not as yet anything but their thighs on which to roll their irons. Particularly to be noted are the shields protecting the workmen, with the crooks (*halsinelle*) in which to rest the irons; the small 'glory-hole' (boccarella) in which the irons keep hot; the pucellas[1] with which the gaffer to the left is fashioning his glass; the shears (*tagliente*) and second pair of pucellas hanging at the right-hand side of his stool, in the time-honoured position; the boy between the gaffers engaged at a mould, and the 'servitor' on the right in the act of blowing; at his feet is the stoke-hole of the furnace: on the right-hand side is apparently a calcar corresponding fairly closely to that described by Agricola.

Little further light on glass-making is forthcoming until 1612, when there appeared Antonio Neri's *L'Arte vetraria*, the first and most famous textbook of glass-making. The greater part of the book is devoted to the coloration of glass, both to imitate gemstones and for the use of enamellers.

Fluxes. Neri opens with several chapters on the preparation of crystal-glass. His principal ingredients are '*Polverine*, or *Rochetta*, which comes from the *Levant* and *Syria* . . . there is no doubt that it makes a far whiter salt than *Barillia* of *Spain*'. The ashes are to be powdered and sifted, and then boiled in coppers until all the salts are extracted from the ashes. The lye is decanted into pans and allowed to stand until all sediment has been eliminated, and the salt-impregnated water is then heated until the salts begin to crystallize, when they may be removed with a skimmer for drying out. Before boiling the polverine, it was necessary to add to each copper about 12 lb of tartar of red wine, obtained as a deposit from wine-casks. The purpose of this was, no doubt, by the introduc-

---

[1] Or procellos, It. *borsello*, special flat-jawed tongs used in shaping glass vessels.

tion of calcium,[1] to produce a more stable glass than would otherwise have been yielded by this highly purified soda. In subsequent chapters, Neri also refers to salt of fern-ashes, and salt from the ashes of bean-stalks, brambles, and other plants.

Silica. Neri mentions a moderate variety of sources of silica, of which tarso is the most important—'the whitest *Tarso*, which hath not black veins, nor yellowish-like rust in it. At *Moran* [Murano] they use the pebbles from Tessino. . . . *Tarso* there is a kind of hard, and most white marble, found in *Tuscany*. . . . Note that those stones which strike fire with a steel are fit to vitrifie . . . and those which strike not fire with a steel, will never vitrifie. . . .' This indicates that the tarso pebbles, although appearing to be marble, must have had a siliceous content; they were probably composed of calcium silicate. Tarso of the latter composition would have the advantage of introducing a further stabilizing dose of calcium into the batch. Neri also mentions, however, Tuscan sand from the valley of the Arno, natural crystal, firestones (presumably flints), and 'calcidonies'.

Fritting and founding. For fritting, the tarso had to be pounded small and sifted, then mixed with the prepared 'salt' in the ratio of 200:130, and placed in the well-heated calcar. The mixture should be heated with a strong fire for 5 hours, being continuously stirred with a long iron rake. When the frits are put in the main furnace, 'then cast in such a quantity of *manganese* prepared as is needful. . . '. Here, as elsewhere, everything is subject to the experience of the furnace-man (*conciatore*).

Colours. The main emphasis of Neri's book is on the colouring of glass. It is impossible here to go into the details of his recipes and processes, but it may be said in general that his blues are based on cobalt, his purple tones on manganese, red on iron and copper, yellow on iron, and green on copper, the metals being introduced mainly as oxides. Variations of tone were achieved by using mixtures of the metallic oxides.

Concerning cobalt, Neri merely provides instructions for its preparation by calcination, trituration, and precipitation; Merrett (1662) knows that it comes from Germany, and says that in England it needs no more than grinding before use. Kunckel (1679), however, is fully aware of its character and preparation, and specifies Schneeberg, near Meissen, as one of the sources of supply. Of manganese, Neri recommends that of Piedmont as the best, that of Tuscany and of Liguria containing admixtures of iron and thus causing a blackish tinge; Merrett adds that good manganese was obtained in his day as a by-product of the

---

[1] Tartar of wine consists mainly of potassium hydrogen tartrate but contains a certain amount of the calcium salt as well.

lead-mines on Mendip. Copper is used in the form of calcined brass, called *ferretto di Spagna* (*aes ustum*), of verdigris, or of various products made by calcination or by solution in acids, and so on. Iron, similarly, was used in the form of *crocus martis* (ferric oxide) produced by calcination or precipitation.

Calcedonio. Apart from his recipes for clear colours, Neri gives instructions for founding a variety of different glasses. Thus in chapters xlii–xliv he gives three recipes for making *calcedonio* glass (with veining resembling agate and other natural stones) which mainly involve dissolving in *aqua fortis* (nitric acid) the various metallic substances already mentioned, mixing these solutions, and obtaining a powder by precipitation from the mixture; this powder is then added to the batch with an admixture of calcined tartar, chimney-soot, and *crocus martis*.

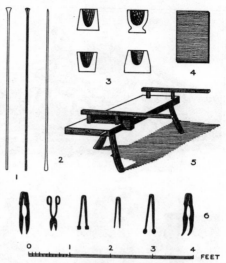

FIGURE 146—*Glassworker's chair and tools.* (1) *Blowing-iron;* (2) *pontil;* (3) *moulds;* (4) *cast-iron marver;* (5) *chair;* (6) *pucellas and shears.* 1772.

Glass of lead. Neri's fourth book is wholly given over to the making of 'glass of lead' or lead-glass, the high refractive index of which admirably suited it for use in counterfeiting precious stones. Neri's precepts, and the observations on them made by Christopher Merrett (1614–95) in his English version of Neri's book (1662), may well have proved highly suggestive to George Ravenscroft in his experiments later in the century (p 221).

Enamel glass. Lastly, in chapter liv, and thereafter in his sixth book, Neri deals with the making of enamel—that is, opaque glasses of different colours. The opacifier is in every case calcined tin, although Merrett, in his commentary on chapters xvi–xix, advocates the use of antimony and saltpetre ground together and mixed with the materials for crystal glass.

IV. DEVELOPMENTS IN THE SEVENTEENTH CENTURY

The glass-maker's 'chair'. Although Neri's remained the standard textbook for the technological aspects of glass-making throughout the seventeenth century, it throws no light on glass-house practice. This is particularly unfortunate in that the period between about 1575 and 1662 saw the evolution of one of the basic appliances of glass-making by hand. This was the gaffer's 'chair' (figure 146), on which he trundles blowing-iron or pontil to preserve the circularity of the vessel as he works (figures 144, 147). This was no doubt a development of the long piece of wood bound to the thigh, as described by Månsson at Rome (p 212), but one can do no more than speculate as to where it was invented. The first written mention of it appears to be in Merrett: 'They sit in wooden

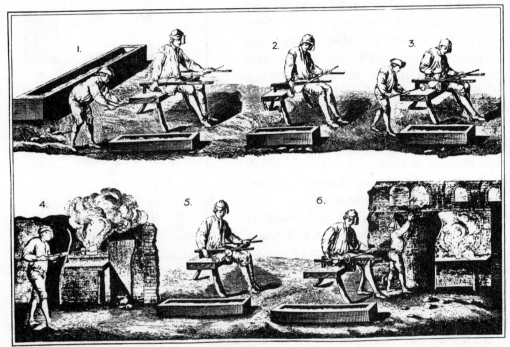

FIGURE 147—*Stages in making a wine-glass.* (1–2) *Shaping the foot;* (3) *attaching pontil and knocking off paraison;* (4) *warming-in;* (5) *trimming the rim;* (6) *shaping the bowl and putting the finished glass to anneal.* *1772.*

large and wide Chairs with two long Elbows.' It seems probable that the chair was evolved by the Italian-manned glass-making centres in the Netherlands. Apart from this innovation, which was probably adopted rapidly all over Europe, the main developments in European glass-making in the seventeenth century took place in England and in the German-Bohemian area.

England: coal-burning. The history of glass-making in England was radically transformed in 1615 by a 'Proclamation touching Glasses' which forbade the use of wood for firing glass-furnaces (p 78). This development had already been foreshadowed both by increasing public concern about the rapidly diminishing national resources of timber, and by the successful application of coal-firing to a number of other industrial processes (ch 3). There is no contemporary description of the English coal-burning furnace of the seventeenth century, but some idea of it can be formed from Merrett's commentary on Neri, and from a remarkable set of drawings made by a Swedish architect visiting London in 1777–8 (figures 148–9). The essential difference between it and the old wood-fired furnace appears to have been that (in the case of the rectangular 'green' glass-furnace) the coal was fired on a grille of iron bars laid longitudinally and supported on a number of shorter cross-bars (figures 149 c, 152 b). Beneath this grille was an ash-pit which could be entered for clearing. Firing with coal seems to have yielded higher temperatures than the older method, and the 'green' glass-furnaces in particular, which Merrett deemed to develop the greatest heat of any then known, had to be built with special materials.

The use of coal seems, in the course of the century, to have prompted the invention of a covered pot of the modern type, with a tubular outlet to the working-hole. It seems clear, however, that such pots were used only in the houses working clear glass, for the bottle-houses illustrated in figures 148–9 and 151–2 used the old open pot. Merrett in 1662 makes no mention of covered pots, and although it has often been assumed that they were part and parcel of the coal-firing process, and therefore introduced early in the seventeenth century, there is no real evidence for this assumption. The compounds of sulphur produced by the combustion of coal, however, would react with any lead in a batch to produce lead sulphide, which is black in colour. To obviate this discoloration, a covered pot might well have suggested itself, and this development may therefore be intimately connected with the epoch-making invention that follows.

The invention of lead crystal. George Ravenscroft is, by common consent, accepted as the inventor of lead crystal. Starting in 1673, he first produced a 'sort of crystalline glass resembling rock crystal'. This, however, had the grave disadvantage of developing gleaming hair-like fissures ('crizzeling' or 'crizzling'), caused probably by an excess of salts. In 1675 Ravenscroft appears to have started to use lead oxide, thus reducing the ratio of salts and stabilizing the glass. By the end of the century the process had become common property amongst English glass-makers, and towards 1700 there was a growing tendency to put more and more lead into the batches, the result being a very heavy metal of a dark and 'oily' brilliance.

Germany and Bohemia: the invention of potash-lime crystal. The same movement that led in England to the production of lead-glass appears to have brought about simultaneously in Germany the evolution of another type of glass which

was much closer than Venetian-type *cristallo* to true crystal in clarity and
brilliance. This was a potash-glass made with an addition of chalk. The exact
date of its introduction is uncertain, but a 'crystal-glass' mentioned in 1677 was
probably already a potash-lime glass. Some glasses of this type probably owed
their lime-content merely to the ash from which they were made, but Johann
Kunckel (1630–1703), in his *Ars vitraria experimentalis* (1679), specifically
refers to the addition of chalk. In the second edition of his book (1689) he gives a

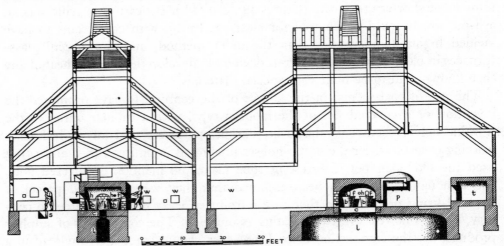

FIGURE 148—*View and plan (figure 149) of a London bottle-glass works, by C. W. Carlberg. 1777–8. The
drawing gives sections along the lines A–B and C–D on the plan. The furnace was 9 ft square inside and 6 ft high.
The pots (b) were 3 ft high, 3 ft 1½ inches in diameter above, and 2 ft 2 in below. Note also the grille for burning
coals (c), working holes (f), boccarella (h), ash-chamber (l), fritting-furnace (o), furnace for heating cullet (p),
linnet-holes (q), hole in ground for blowing bottles in moulds (s), furnace for pre-heating pots (t), annealing-
ovens, each of the two largest taking 800 bottles (u, w).*

recipe consisting of 150 lb of sand, 100 lb of potash, 20 lb of chalk, and 5 oz of
manganese. There were no doubt many other similar recipes current in the late
seventeenth century. Being a solid and colourless glass, this 'crystal' was particularly suited to wheel-engraving, an art that constitutes the chief glory of German
glass during the seventeenth and eighteenth centuries.

Wheel-engraving. It is generally agreed that glass-engraving was a by-product
of hard-stone engraving, the process being merely transferred to the softer,
artificial substance. When this transference originally occurred is not known,
but it is almost certain that glass-engraving was being practised before the end
of the sixteenth century. There is also uncertainty about the tools used for the
work. Sandrart, who is the main source of our information concerning the earliest
engravers, wrote in 1675:

Now although these artists had brought to perfection the art of glass-cutting as far as it depended upon judgment and drawing, yet in consequence of the too powerful and clumsy machinery made use of by them, even they were unable to give grace and charm to their work. When we consider the big heavy wheels that they were fain to employ—turned by those still flourishing weeds, their loutish assistants—we may well marvel at the work they turned out. Since that time the discovery of more convenient and efficient

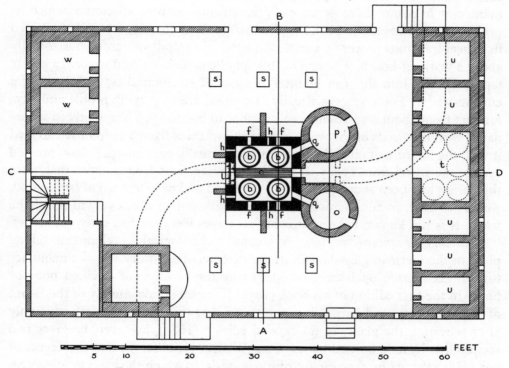

FIGURE 149—*Plan of the bottle-glass works shown in figure 148.*

tools has brought it about that nowadays the art of glass-cutting is no longer a strenuous task, but rather a pastime. . . .

It has been objected that the treadle-operated engraving-wheel was already known in the time of Jost Amman (1568); but the fact remains that in Prague, as late as 1653, the wheels used in the workshop of the Court hardstone engraver, Dionisio Miseroni, were still of the old type—the apprentices turning by hand huge fly-wheels, from which bands ran down to the spindles in which the engraving-wheels themselves were fixed. Later in the seventeenth century water-power was largely used, perhaps as a result of the contemporary demand for glasses carved in high relief (*Hochschnitt*), in which the whole unpatterned surface of the glass was ground down to a depth of some millimetres, at the cost of an enormous expenditure of effort. The date of the general introduction of the treadle-operated wheel for intaglio engraving (*Tiefschnitt*) is uncertain, but it is reasonable to assume that it was to this innovation that Sandrart referred. No early example of such an apparatus appears to have survived, but in the Stockholm city museum there is an early nineteenth-century specimen which is probably in all essentials of the traditional pattern. In this, a treadle-operated fly-wheel transmits power by means of a band to a spindle mounted horizontally above a working-bench. The end of this spindle is hollowed out to form a gently tapering hole. Into this can be fitted a series of steel spindles, each bearing a cutting-wheel. These wheels, usually of copper, are of varying profile and size, ranging from about 1 to 10 mm, and require to be changed frequently in accordance with the needs of the work. Above the wheel is fixed a strip of felt to feed it with the mixture of oil and abrasive which actually cuts into the glass, pressed against the wheel from below. It may be surmised from later practice that, after the design had been roughed out, wheels of lead and pewter, then of fruit-wood, would be used, in conjunction with progressively finer abrasives, to polish the work. It is not known for certain what abrasives were used in early engraving.

Opal and opaque-white glass. A second technological development taking place in the German glass-houses in the seventeenth century was the manufacture of glass made opalescent or opaque by the addition of calcined bone or horn. In the first edition of his book (1679) Kunckel speaks merely of the 'ashes of burned houses and barns', but points out that this opacifier is effective only after reheating the glass; in the second edition (1689), however, he gives two recipes that include burned bones or stag's horn. He observes that the degree of opacity is affected by the amount of warming-in to which the glass is subjected, as also by the proportion of ash in the batch. These glasses could be coloured at will.

Ruby-glass. That gold was already familiar as a glass pigment in the sixteenth century is suggested by a passage in Agricola's *De natura fossilium* (1546).[1] Neri too (1612) speaks of a wonderful red obtained from gold (book V, ch xc). No early glasses of this type are known, and the use of gold chloride did not come into its own until the last quarter of the seventeenth century, in Germany. This development also was due to Kunckel, but he expressed his indebtedness to

---

[1] According to R. Campbell Thompson, the ancient Assyrians (seventh century B.C.) knew how to make ruby-glass by the use of gold. See his 'A Dictionary of Assyrian Chemistry and Geology', Oxford University Press, 1936, pp xxxi–xxxvi.

Andreas Cassius (1640?–?1673), of Hamburg. Cassius discovered that on adding tin chloride to a solution of gold chloride, a purple powder (purple of Cassius) is precipitated. When glass is fused with this powder and annealed, it takes on a fine ruby colour. The powder probably contains colloidal gold. Kunckel left no recipe for ruby-glass, but an eighteenth-century Potsdam formula no doubt reflects his practice. This prescribes taking a gold ducat beaten out thin and cut into pieces, and placing it in an alembic with $\frac{1}{2}$ oz of nitric acid, $1\frac{1}{2}$ oz of spirit of salt, and 1 dram of sal ammoniac. This mixture should be subjected to heat until the gold is dissolved, when the solution is incorporated in a crystal-glass batch.

FIGURE 150—*Detail from a trade-card of the glass-dealers Maydwell and Windle, showing* (left) *a glass-cutter at work.* c *1775.*

This process too required the developing action of reheating before the ruby colour achieved its full strength. The process was rapidly disseminated among the German glass-houses, and was possibly also known to Bernard Perrot at Orleans as early as 1668.

V. THE EIGHTEENTH CENTURY

England. The tendency to add more and more lead oxide to the batch was modified in the early decades of the eighteenth century, and was sharply checked in 1745–6 by an excise levied on glass by weight. English glass-men were thereafter driven to compensate for the reduced bulk and impoverished metal of their glass by adventitious ornament such as enamelling and gilding, which have already been mentioned in the section on Venetian glass, and by wheel-engraving (p 222).

Cutting. Lead-glass was uniquely suited to decoration by cutting, both because of its high refractive index and because of its relative softness in working.

Very little is known for certain about the equipment and materials used for glass-cutting in the eighteenth century. Inferring from later practice, it is probable that the first cuts were made with an iron wheel upon which sand and water fell from a hopper above. The rough cuts were probably then smoothed on a stone wheel running in a trough of water, and finally polished on a fruit-wood wheel fed with fine abrasives. What these were is not definitely known, but the stock of a glass-house at Dudley in 1784 included 'emery . . . pumice stone, &c.', apparently for cutting rather than for engraving. A contemporary illustration (figure 150) shows that the cutting-wheel, here probably of stone, was set in a frame and powered by a hand-turned fly-wheel like the earlier engraving-wheels (p 223). As is shown in the figure, the workman normally presses his glass down upon the wheel. This enables him to exert considerable pressure and to obtain a powerful cutting-action from the wheel, which turns towards him. Such a craftsman was called an overhand-cutter; underhand-cutters presumably worked on the opposite principle, using a wheel that turned away from them, and holding the glass underneath it, like the modern intaglio cutters. This probably permitted a finer type of work.

An examination of mid-eighteenth-century cut glasses suggests that the wheels used were of blunt profile, either flat, rounded, or with an obtuse bevel. With such wheels, over-all patterns of a simple character could be obtained by presenting the glass to the wheel in the axis of its rotation. A richer type of cutting was evolved in the third quarter of the century by combining these elements with cuts made by presenting the vessel obliquely to the cutting edge, thus producing asymmetrical, lunate forms.

The glass-cone. Until the late seventeenth century the glass-house was built up round the furnace like a barn, with a pitched roof, and usually a louvred lantern above the furnace (figure 148). At some time in the century the cone-shaped glass-house was introduced, permitting the concentration of all air-currents in a single upward movement. This structure appears to have given greater efficiency in the use of fuel, and it is singled out by the writer on glass in the great *Encyclopédie* (1751–76) as one of the prime advantages of the English glass-houses (figures 151, 152). A patent granted in 1734 to Humphrey Perrott, of Bristol, for 'A Furnace . . . [which] is contrived in a new Manner with Artificial Draughts to it, whereby to force the Heat or Fire the sooner to perform its office . . .' may be connected with this innovation.

Fluxes. R. Dossie, in 'The Handmaid to the Arts' (1758), states: 'The substances which are used as *fluxing* ingredients in glass, are red lead, pearl-ashes, nitre, sea salt, borax, arsenic, the *scoria* of forges, commonly called *clinkers*, and

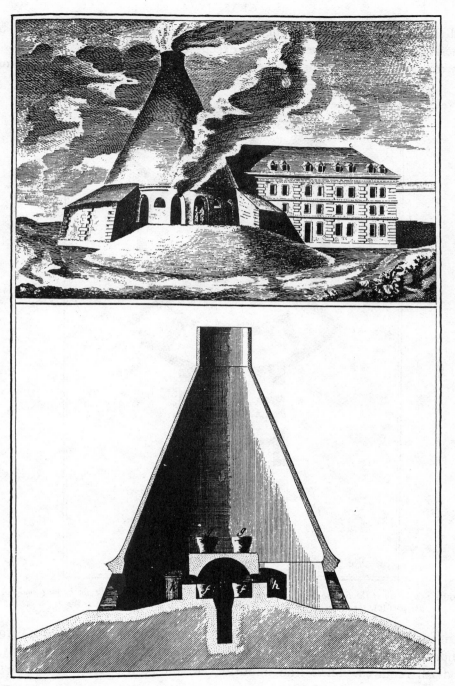

FIGURE 151—*The English type of glass-house cone. Note pots (f, f) on the siege and (g, g) being dried off; and the annealing-arches (h, h). 1772.*

wood-ashes containing the calcined earth and lixiviate salts, as produced by incineration.' There is little new here except borax and clinkers. Borax was imported from the East Indies in the form of tincal,[1] and on account of its exor-

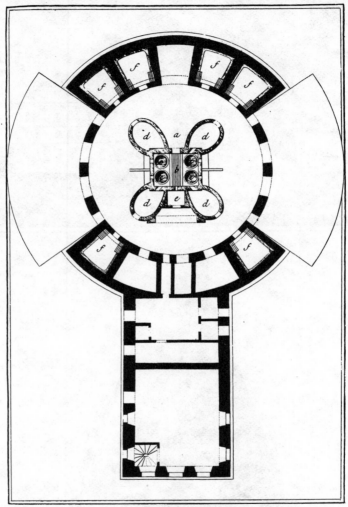

FIGURE 152—*Plan of the English-type glass-house shown in figure 151. Note the grille for burning coal* (b); *the pots* (c); *the pot-arches* (d); *the fritting-furnace* (e); *the annealing-furnaces* (f). *1772.*

bitant price was used solely for looking-glasses. Clinkers, obtained from iron-foundries, were used only in bottle-houses, and served to reduce the quantity of wood-ash required. Their iron impurities would be no objection in making

[1] Malay *tingkal*, Urdu *tinkar*, *tarkar*, crude borax.

dark wine-bottles. At this period, the potash used for the finer kinds of glass was imported in a refined form, known as pearl-ash, from Germany, Russia, and Poland; at a slightly later date it came also from America.

Opacifiers. To the substances prescribed by Neri and Kunckel may be added arsenic, mentioned by Dossie when discussing enamels. Arsenic produces its effects by crystallization during the cooling of the glass, and its effects may already have been familiar to Kunckel.

Transparent ruby lead-glass. On 5 December 1755 one Mayer Opnaim took out a patent for red transparent flint-glass. Opnaim was clearly of German descent, and his achievement lay in applying the German method of making ruby-glass to the English lead-fluxed material. The patent specification is too lengthy to be described here, but Opnaim's method involved the use of both pyrolusite (*Braunstein*) and dissolved Dutch gold.

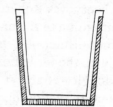

FIGURE 153 — *Section through* 'Zwischengold-glas' *showing outer shell* (diagonal hatching) *and separate base-disk* (vertical hatching): *the etched gold-leaf was laid between these and the inner shell of the beaker* (unhatched).

Decorative innovations on the European continent. Although the Dutch poetess Anna Roemers Visscher (1584–1651) had used stipple-engraving in 1646 on one of her diamond-point engraved glasses, the technique was not fully exploited until in 1722 Frans Greenwood decorated several glasses in this way. One of the most prolific stipple-engravers was D. Wolff, of The Hague. This artist is stated to have stippled 'with the help of a small etching needle driven by a little hammer'. Hardened steel points can make impressions on soft glass, but this account is unsubstantiated and should perhaps not be taken at its face value.

'*Zwischengoldgläser*' (gold-sandwich glasses). During the second quarter of the eighteenth century, in the German-Bohemian area, a decorative technique was evolved by means of which gold-leaf (or silver, or both), etched with a point to the desired design, was sandwiched between the two thicknesses of a double-walled glass—usually a beaker (figure 153).

VI. LENSES AND OPTICAL INSTRUMENTS

Lenses and lens-grinding have played a fundamental part in the history of technology. During their evolution from simple magnifying and diminishing glasses to their use as spectacles, to their combinations in telescopes and microscopes, and to still more complex uses, lenses have transformed some sciences and virtually created others.

The magnifying power of glass spheres filled with water was known to the Greeks. Some of their optical properties were elucidated by Ptolemy in the second century A.D., in his 'Optics'. Islamic writers developed the optical conceptions of the Greeks; foremost among them was Ibn al-Haitham (Alhazen, *c* 965–*c* 1039) whose work has a sound experimental basis. He studied the reflective properties of curved mirrors, and the magnification of segments of glass spheres was well known to him. His study of the rainbow was translated into Latin about 1170, and his 'Optics' in 1269; these translations had a profound effect upon European philosophers.

Among the earliest western scholars to make original contributions to optical theory was Robert Grosseteste, bishop of Lincoln (*c* 1175–1253), who first drew attention to the practical usefulness of lenses in making small things appear large and distant objects near. Grosseteste also developed an important theory to explain the formation of the colours of the rainbow by refraction. His theory of the double refraction of light passing through a spherical lens or burning-glass— one refraction on entering the new medium and another on emerging from it bringing the rays to a focus at a point—was accepted until the sixteenth century. Roger Bacon (*c* 1214–94), a pupil of Grosseteste, followed Alhazen's more experimental trend. Conceiving of an instrument serving the purpose of the telescope, he explored the laws of refraction with the aid of plano-convex lenses, his aim being the practical one of improving vision.

Spectacles were already in use in northern Italy at the time of Bacon's death. A certain Friar Giordano of Pisa, in a sermon preached at Florence in 1306, said:

It is not yet twenty years since there was found the art of making eye-glasses which make for good vision, one of the best arts and most necessary that the world has. So short a time is it since there was invented a new art that never existed [before]. I have seen the man who first invented and created it, and I have talked to him.

This is strong evidence that the invention was made about 1286, but the name of the inventor is unknown. Spectacles were almost certainly not invented at Venice, but they were soon being made at this principal centre of the glass-industry, which had developed in response to the need for window-glass and fine vessels. In 1300 the Venetian guild by-laws relating to *cristalerii* (glass-workers) mention *roidi* (for *rodoli*) *da ogli* (little disks for the eyes) and in 1301 *vitreos ab oculis ad legendum* (eye-glasses for reading). In 1316 'eyeglasses with a case' (*oculis de vitro cum capsula*) were sold for 6 Bolognese soldi. Thereafter references to spectacle-making accumulate rapidly (figure 154). The first portrait depicting spectacles was painted by Tommaso Barisino of Modena in 1352 (plate 1).

Though the Venetian glass-industry was making a product of sufficiently high quality for use in spectacles before 1300, it was much below the excellence afterwards achieved. At first spectacles were provided with convex lenses only, to aid presbyopia; the lenses were ground to curves of small radius, and were comparatively easy to work. No reference to concave lenses for the correction of myopia appears to precede that of Nicholas of Cusa (1401–64) in the mid-fifteenth century. The manner in which lenses correct the natural defects of the human eye began to be studied in geometrical terms in the sixteenth century.

Francesco Maurolico (1494–1575) of Naples showed how the lens of the eye focused light upon the retina, and by 1600 Geronimo Fabrizio (1537–1619) had shown that the lens occurs in the front part of the eyeball rather than in the middle, where error had long placed it.

There are references as early as the mid-sixteenth century to reputedly successful attempts to devise optical instruments whereby distant objects could be seen more plainly, and enlarged. The English mathematicians Leonard Digges (1510–58) and John Dee (1527–1608) both made experiments to this end. Usually, however, it has been thought that the first practical telescopes were the result of fortuitous observations by a Dutch spectacle-maker about 1608, who hit upon

FIGURE 154—*Spectacle-maker's shop, 1568. Note the dividers for marking out the glass, and (on the bench) the little handle for manipulating the lenses during grinding.*

the combination of a convex objective with a concave eye-lens giving an erect image. Certainly at this time the Dutch first made such instruments, which attracted attention and were put to military uses. But according to a reliable record of 1634 Johannes Janssen or Jansen, the son of the fortunate spectacle-maker, declared that his father 'made the first telescope amongst us in 1604, after the model of an Italian one, on which was written *anno* 1590'. Thus the Dutch telescope appears after all to be derived from Italy, the main centre for glass-working and optical study. Moreover, this record gives further significance to the description by Giambattista della Porta of Naples (1536–1605), in the second edition of his *Magiae naturalis* (1589), of ways to improve vision at a distance, including the combination of a convex and concave lens. His account is deliberately obscure. What is puzzling is that Galileo (1564–1642) should have known nothing of this, until he learned in 1609 of the Dutch 'invention'. Galileo was the effective scientific inventor of both the telescope and the compound microscope. His first instrument was a lead tube 2·9 m long and 42 mm in diameter, carrying a plano-convex objective and a plano-concave eye-lens with a magnification of three diameters.

Credit for the invention of the compound microscope has been variously assigned. della Porta again seems to have constructed a compound microscope, but the history of the instrument effectively begins with Galileo's use of what was actually a Galilean telescope with a very short working-distance to discern

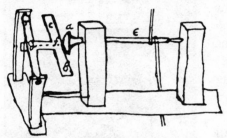

the organs of small creatures. By 1612 (according to Viviani) Galileo had presented such microscopes to various persons. Their tubes were necessarily very long, to permit the short working distance. The combination of two convex lenses (giving an inverted image) was a great advance on the Galilean lens-system, for both telescopes and microscopes; it was first described, as a telescopic arrangement, by Kepler in 1610. In the latter part of the century all

FIGURE 155—*One of Newton's proposed machines for grinding hyperbolical lenses. 'ye glasse a may be ground Hyperbolicall by ye line cb, if it turns on ye Mandrill ε whilst cb turns on ye axis rd being inclined to it as was showed before.'* c 1666.

scientific optical instruments employed the Keplerian combination of lenses, which was further improved by other workers (figure 371).

As experimenters strove after higher magnifications, the defects of existing lenses and their combinations were revealed more sharply. These were of three kinds. First, there were faults of craftsmanship: the glass was not free from flaws, or was poorly figured and polished. Secondly, it is inherently impossible for a spherical lens (or mirror) to bring the light incident upon it to a point-focus, and this spherical aberration causes lack of definition in the image. Thirdly, at more than mediocre powers and apertures the image is surrounded by coloured fringes due to the chromatic aberration of the lens, and these cause further confusion. The first of these defects could be overcome; some scientists—like Huygens and Leeuwenhoek—ground their own lenses with consummate skill. The remedy for the second was revealed by Descartes in 1637; the lenses and mirrors must be given a parabolic or hyperbolic curvature, which renders them capable of reflecting or refracting the light to a point. Descartes suggested various impracticable ways of doing this, and the mechanical problem was further explored by Newton (figure 155), but a solution was impossible. In practice lenses had to be ground as portions of spheres. For telescopes, spherical aberration could be mitigated by making the focal-length of the objective very

great in proportion to its diameter: 48 ft was not uncommon, and tubeless telescopes 200 ft long were tried. Microscopes were improved by using three- or
four-lens systems, stopping down, and renouncing very high powers (figures
370, 372, and tailpiece).

The cause of chromatic aberration was made plain by Newton's investigation,
published in 1671, of the prismatic colours. He showed that a lens does not
refract light of different colours to the same point; therefore a lens, however
figured, cannot form a single image save in monochromatic light. Since white
light is compound, it forms a series of coloured images. Newton, thinking that
this dispersion of the colours was in a fixed ratio to the refraction, regarded
chromatic aberration as incapable of remedy; hence after he had made these
discoveries he turned to the reflecting telescope (figure 369). In fact, by combining convex and concave lenses of suitable refractive indices, a composite lens
can be made which refracts white light without widely dispersing it, and is therefore practically achromatic. This was first discovered empirically by Chester
Moor Hall in 1733, and rediscovered by John Dollond in 1758, who put his
success to commercial use. The achromatic microscope was not manufactured
commercially for another seventy years, again preceded by various ingenious
reflecting instruments.

Thus, by about 1680 the development of instruments using lenses came to a
halt from the optical point of view, though their mechanical properties were
greatly improved and elaborated (p 633). Neither the refracting telescope nor
the microscope was capable of extending its range of vision. In the eighteenth
century astronomers turned increasingly to the reflecting telescope for qualitative work (it was brought to a high pitch of perfection by James Short and the
elder Herschel, who made a 48-in mirror). Biologists mostly employed the simple
microscope, which was easy to manipulate and reliable, but low-powered. None
emulated the genius of Leeuwenhoek, who made and worked with single lenses
having a focal length of 0·05 in, or even less (figure 368).

VII. GRINDING AND POLISHING LENSES

Natural stones and glass have been cut, ground, and polished from early
times, the diamond being used for cutting and sand or emery for abrasion. Lens-
grinding involved no new principle, save that it was directed towards the production of a glass accurately curved, or perfectly plane, and polished free from
scratches. Two aspects of the technique merit special attention: (i) the nature of
the material to be worked, and (ii) the character of the apparatus to be used.

Composition of the glass. It is very remarkable that though the scientific investigation of glass and glass-making is very recent, the composition of the batch still standard for modern bottle- and window-glass is practically identical with that used by the Venetians for their glass in the Middle Ages, having remained unchanged throughout the centuries. The explanation would seem to be that while research has revealed the basis for the ancient empirical formula, it has not been able to improve upon proportions which long experience and trial-and-error proved to be the best for their purpose.

Early lenses were made from a soda-lime-silica glass, the batch being made up of 350–80 parts of soda-ash and 180–230 parts of limestone to 1000 of sand. Modern optical glasses include a wide range of lead, potash, barium, and other compositions then unknown. Extant early Venetian glasses show a slight cloudiness indicative of devitrification, resulting from an excess of sodium oxide which was introduced (as soda) to lower the temperature of fusion. The medieval glass-makers had difficulty in attaining the melting-point of glass, and kept it as low as practicable; as a result their manufactured product was comparatively unstable. In the seventeenth century one of the most serious obstacles to the perfection of lenses, especially telescope-objectives of large size, was the difficulty of obtaining glass of sufficiently high quality. Flaws and bubbles are often seen in extant lenses of this period.

Methods of working. Besides the professional instrument-makers who manufactured lenses, some of whom, like Eustachio Divini (1620–95) in Italy and Christopher Cock (fl 1660–96) in London, became famous for their telescope objectives, many scientists, including Descartes, Newton, Huygens, and Leeuwenhoek were expert lens-workers. In Italy, Galileo and his pupil Torricelli had done much to develop the art of lens-grinding for scientific purposes. Each expert developed his own detailed practice, though the fundamentals of the art remained the same. First, a plate of glass from the glass-house was roughly polished and examined for flaws. If it proved satisfactory, a circle of appropriate diameter was inscribed on it with compasses and a disk was cut and chipped from the plate (figure 154). It was then necessary first to grind this flat disk to roughly the required curvature, and then to polish it while correcting its shape. These operations were either wholly manual, or effected after about 1640 with the aid of simple machines. No power-driven machinery was employed.

In the manual process, the blank was shaped by grinding on a metal tool—a hemispherically concave or convex disk fixed to the bench. White sand, millstone grit, and emery were the abrasives generally used; as the work proceeded it needed a finer grade of abrasive prepared by levigation, and sometimes a fresh tool was employed at each stage of progress. Hence the accuracy of the curvature of the lens depended on the accuracy with which the tool itself was worked, and on the skill of the operator in manipulating the blank so that it assumed the same curvature as the tool. If the tool was made of iron it was forged, and if of bronze

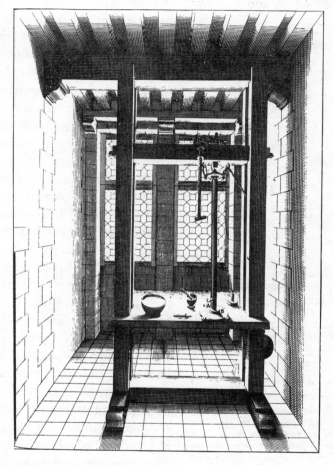

FIGURE 156—*Machine for shaping the forms on which lenses are ground, and working the lenses themselves. By swinging the long vertical rod, which is also rotated by the handle and gears, A and B are ground spherically convex and concave respectively, the radius of curvature being equal to the length of the rod. 1671.*

cast, and then turned accurately on a lathe. The imperfections of the lathe itself (p 336) rendered this a difficult art, especially when the radius of curvature required for the tool might be 40 ft or more (figure 156). The glass blank had to be pressed hard down upon the tool with the fingers, or with a small handle cemented to it, so that the process was laborious as well as lengthy.

To lighten the labour various machines were proposed, similar in principle to machines sketched by Leonardo for use in working metallic mirrors. A simple device used by Huygens involved mounting the blank on a pivoted lever (figure 157) pressed down on the tool by a movable weight. The next stage was to rotate either the tool or the blank—or both—mechanically, as in Huygens's proposed machine of 1665 (figure 157). This principle is employed today. Some seventeenth-century opticians, however, attempted to go farther than this by devising machines that would obviate the need for the dish-like tool and work the glass directly in the manner of a lathe. All these machines were driven by crank-handles, belts, and gearing, thus requiring the services of two men.

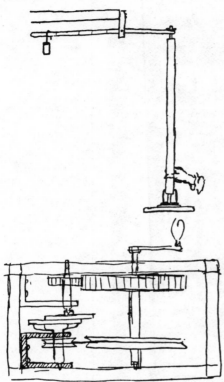

FIGURE 157—*Huygens's lens-figuring equipment.* (Above) *Arrangement for polishing with the* bâton; *pressure is increased by moving the weight to the right, c 1660;* (below) *polishing-machine; the gear drive rotates the polisher, while the belt turns the lens mounted on the lower spindle. 1665.*

The method of working a number of small lenses at once was described by Hevelius (1611–87) as early as 1647. He constructed a kind of vertical lathe, to the mandrel of which a wooden disk could be fitted. The small glass blanks were mounted in pitch on this disk, which had a hemispherical upper surface, and the metal tool was pressed down upon them as they revolved. All were then ground to the curvature of the tool.

After completion of the harsh process of grinding, which removes much of the glass in order to give the blank approximately the required curvature, the very delicate operation of polishing aims at completing the accuracy of the lens and restoring the original smooth, bright surface. A lens without a highly polished surface is quite useless. The lens was still worked in the same manner on a metal tool—either manually or with the aid of a machine—exactly of the required radius; for grinding, the radius of the tool might be slightly greater than that of the finished lens. In the final stages the tool was often lined with pitch, made very smooth and accurately curved while plastic, or with paper after hardening.

The abrasives used for polishing were tripoli powder (kieselguhr), jeweller's rouge (a form of ferric oxide), or tin-putty (tin oxide), levigated to yield various sizes of particle. Towards the end, the polishing was invariably effected by hand; the work must have been exceedingly slow, tedious, and laborious as a heavy pressure was required. Finally, the lens was buffed on a simple form of lathe worked by a treadle—less effort was required, and intimate co-ordination between the hand, foot, and eye of the operator was important.

Special problems arose when, after 1671, mirrors to some extent replaced lenses. They were all cast in a white tin-copper alloy, to which were added small proportions of antimony, arsenic, and other metals supposed to improve the properties of the speculum. Because the alloy was softer than glass, it was easily spoilt by harsh abrasives or excessively vigorous polishing. But the speculum had one important advantage. By considered use of trial-and-error, and repeated examination of the image, it could be brought to a valuable non-spherical curvature. James Short (1710–68) was the first to 'parabolize' a telescope speculum successfully, and it was to such skill in polishing large mirrors—a protracted and arduous labour—that both he and Herschel owed their unparalleled success with the reflecting telescope. The technique was in principle exactly the same as that used for figuring and polishing lenses.

VIII. WINDOW-GLASS

In the Roman Empire window-glass was uncommon before the third century A.D., although a very limited number of glazed window-slits have been found in houses in both Herculaneum and Pompeii. As these cities were destroyed in A.D. 79, its employment must have begun at least as early as the first century of our era. The Roman glass for windows was either cast or rolled, being sometimes polished afterwards. It was thus more nearly related to plate than to sheet glass.

The evolution of Gothic architecture, bringing about an enormous increase in the window-area of ecclesiastical buildings, stimulated a considerable development of the window-glass industry of the district between the Seine and the Rhine. As one might expect, the earliest window-glass used in Britain appears to have consisted of the little pieces of coloured glass inserted in church windows. They could be made comparatively easily because of their small size, and because impure materials would serve when the final result was to be coloured.

The first Lorraine makers of window-glass came to work in England in 1567. In Scotland as late as 1661 the windows of ordinary country houses were not glazed, and only the upper parts of those of even the royal palaces had glass, the lower ones having two wooden shutters to open at pleasure and admit fresh air.

Some advance in the manufacture of plate glass by casting or *coulage* was made at Venice and afterwards at Nuremberg, but the sheets remained small. By the middle of the seventeenth century there was a demand, especially in France, for large sheets of clear glass for mirrors and the *portières* of coaches. Colbert (1619–83), the great minister of Louis XIV, who came into office in 1661, brought glass-makers from Venice, where glass mirrors had been made from early in the fourteenth century. England was not far behind, for mirrors of blown plate-glass were manufactured at Lambeth about 1670, with the assistance at first of Italian workmen brought over by the Duke of Buckingham. Some of the finest surviving examples of this kind of work are in the Hall of Mirrors at Versailles.

The alternative method of producing plate glass by casting had been developed in Normandy, and in 1676 Colbert, expressly to encourage it, placed the French royal glass-works under the control of the Norman glass-maker Lucas de Nehou, who was expert in the art. By 1691 the casting process had been so improved that plates of unprecedented size were being turned out. Essentially it consisted of pouring the glass upon a metal table, spreading it evenly by rollers, and later treating it by grinding and polishing.

The method that de Nehou laid down at the famous Saint-Gobain works was copied elsewhere and soon became standard practice. The main furnace stood in the middle of the glass-house; round it were grouped ovens or annealing-kilns, called *carquaises*, and others for making frit and calcining old pieces of glass before re-melting (figure 141). The furnace seldom lasted more than three years, and even then had to be refitted every six months.

The melting-pots or crucibles, of the size of large hogsheads, contained about 2000 lb of metal. To assist fusion the charge, consisting of fresh materials mixed with scrap glass, was introduced in a number of stages, a fresh layer being added when the previous one had melted, until the crucible was full. Up to this point the furnace had been kept merely at a red heat. There followed the fining or plaining[1] stage, during which the furnace temperature was raised. Just the right temperature had to be maintained, for if the heat was too low bubbles remained in the metal, while if it was too high the walls of the crucible fused and dripped into the glass. The founding proper took twenty-four hours.

When the molten glass was fit for casting there remained the problem of moving it to the casting table. No entirely satisfactory solution was found. One method consisted of ladling out the more or less liquid glass. In another a cistern was filled in the furnace and allowed to remain there for six hours afterwards; it was then withdrawn by means of a hook on an iron chain guided by a pulley,

---

[1] To plain glass means to make it clear and free from bubbles.

and placed upon a frame mounted upon a four-wheeled base for transfer to the casting table. Upon reaching the table the removable base of the cistern was slipped off, allowing the molten metal to pour out.

Ultimately it was found best simply to remove the melting-crucible from the furnace and invert it over the casting table. This drastic procedure was not good for the pot, and demanded strong lifting-tackle, but did result in the maximum amount of glass being delivered to the table in prime condition. A consequence of this method was the use of smaller pots for casting plate glass than the stationary ones used for other kinds of glass, so that their weight could be handled more easily.

Upon the casting table the lateral limits to which the glass could flow were fixed by adjustable iron rulers determining the width of the sheet. On these iron side-rails ran a roller which enabled a man to flatten out the glass to a uniform thickness, this being done within the space of a minute to forestall the effects of rapid cooling. Later, as greater quantities of the molten metal came to be handled, the roller was made larger and heavier, so that a crew of three or four men was needed to turn it.

After annealing, which took about ten days, the glass plate had to be ground and polished. It was laid horizontally upon a flat bed of very fine-grained free-stone, to which it was cemented with lime-stucco to prevent movement. The stone base of the seventeenth century was changed to a copper one in the eighteenth and to a cast iron one in the early part of the nineteenth. The bed was fitted with a wooden frame having a ledge all round rising up rather more than two inches above the grinding-level.

Grinding was effected with a smaller plate of glass—not more than half the size of that to be treated—which was made to slide upon the one being ground. The smaller plate was cemented to a plank, which in turn was fastened to a wheel of hard, light wood. Workmen pulled the wheel backwards and forwards, and sometimes turned it round, thus causing attrition between the two glasses. The introduction of the steam-engine to supply power for grinding and polishing did not take place until the closing years of the eighteenth century.

This early form of grinding-mill had to be supplied with an abrasive. Water and coarse sand were accordingly poured in, to be followed by finer sand as the work advanced, and lastly by glass powder or smalt. After one side of the plate had been ground, it was reversed and the operation repeated on the other side. It was then ready for the polisher.

An ingenious method of polishing plate glass was common to the European continent and England. A board and a small roller, both covered with felt, were used. The roller was moved by a double handle at each end, and was fixed to the ceiling by a strong wooden hoop which acted as a spring. The action of the workman's arms was facilitated by the spring, because this constantly brought the roller back to the same point.

For many purposes thin blown glass formed into sheets could be used instead of cast plate, which was reserved for purposes requiring extra strength, like coach-windows. Blown glass had the advantage of retaining its original fire-polish, so that no grinding or polishing was necessary. Two specialized methods of making sheet glass were developed, known as the 'crown' and the 'cylinder' processes. The former was the earlier.

Crown glass was originally more or less peculiar to Normandy, but later was made in England also. A gathering of molten glass was blown into a hollow sphere on the end of a blow-iron. To the opposite side of the sphere a pontil or solid iron rod was then attached by means of a nodule of the molten metal. The original blow-iron was broken free, leaving an opening in the globe. Rotating the glass rapidly while still in a semi-molten state caused it to open out into the form of a flat disk, adhering to the pontil by the boss in the centre. Crown glass had two characteristics, the small size of the sheet that could be made by this method, and the unavoidable presence of the bull's eye in the centre.

In Lorraine and the German states the hand-cylinder process was employed to make 'broad glass', sometimes known as German sheet. The method probably developed from that used for crown glass, but was a marked advance upon it. If a large globe of glass such as was used in the crown method was made to swing freely it extended into a cylinder; in practice, pits were provided to enable the glass-makers to obtain extra length. The weight of glass used was from 20 to 40 lb according to the size of cylinder required. Cylinders were made from 12 to 20 inches in diameter and from 50 to 70 in long. When blown, their ends were removed and they were slit lengthwise. Finally, by the simple device of re-heating it in a kiln or flattening-oven the cylinder fell into a flat sheet.

IX. STAINED-GLASS WINDOWS

The making of stained-glass windows is a traditional craft which early achieved results of great beauty. Lethaby has spoken of the window of coloured glass as the most perfect art-form known, and declares that the old glass holds the sunlight as it were within it, so that the whole becomes a mosaic of coloured fire.

The craft developed in the Mediterranean lands in the twelfth century. One of its chief aims was to keep churches pleasantly cool by excluding excess of light. Only small pieces of glass could be produced at that time, but they were sufficient to build up mosaic windows. The irregular bits of blue and ruby glass were pieced together by means of grooved lead, the whole being held in a framework of stone supported by iron bars. Harmonious patterns were formed in this way. To soften and subdue the light still further the glass was often shaded with a monochrome pigment of brown, consisting of powdered glass and oxide of iron, with Senegal gum as an adhesive. In England twelfth-century examples of mosaic medallion windows are to be seen at Canterbury, York, Lincoln, Dorchester (Oxfordshire), Wilton, and Rivenhall.

During the next century the glaziers produced larger windows, with freer use of figure subjects. In England, with her grey skies, the need for more light was felt and in consequence the grisaille style was evolved. Grisaille work gave beautiful effects of opalescence and mother-of-pearl, with delicate decoration of foliate designs and geometrical patterns. The Five Sisters window in York Minster is an outstanding example of this kind of work, and there are other excellent ones at Salisbury.

A noteworthy discovery made early in the fourteenth century was that glass could be stained yellow with the oxide or chloride of silver, giving a full range of tones from lemon to orange. As other colours were added to the palette of the glass-stainer, the 'decorated' period (c 1280 to c 1380) proved a brilliant one in stained glass. Heraldry figures prominently in windows, especially in England, Germany, Flanders, and later in Switzerland.

In the course of the fourteenth century magnificent stained glass was made for many of the great churches in France, including Chartres, Évreux, Beauvais, Rouen, Limoges, Carcassonne, and Paris. In England the east window of Gloucester Cathedral is of this period; it is the largest in the country, being 72 ft by 38 ft. Other English cathedrals, and the chapels of the colleges at Oxford and Cambridge, were similarly enriched at this time.

The fifteenth century, in which the distinctively English style of architecture known as 'perpendicular' developed, was a most prolific period for stained glass. Colour-schemes grew ever lighter, and shading was kept luminous. Inscriptions were no longer scratched in enamel brown, but were done in dark lettering on a light ground. The abrading of ruby and coated blue gave new effects. A more natural way of representing flesh-painting was obtained by using a wash of enamel colour upon white. One of the most brilliant uses made of these improved technical resources was in the introduction of an increasing number of coats of arms and other heraldic devices.

The last great period for stained glass was the first half of the sixteenth century, the age of the Renaissance. Designs spread over the whole window, and large pieces of glass were used without regard to the curbs and discipline of leads and mullions. Landscapes were painted with heavy smeared and stippled shadows. The windows of Fairford, Gloucestershire, and the noble glass of King's College, Cambridge, belong to the earlier and better part of this period. By 1550 a severe decline had set in, with the technique of oil-painting eclipsing the true nature of stained glass. The introduction of chiaroscuro and similar devices hastened the fall into a dismal period of abasement.

BIBLIOGRAPHY

The books cited in the first two sections deal only incidentally with the techniques of glass-making.

1. *General:*

DILLON, E. 'Glass.' Methuen, London. 1907.
SCHMIDT, R. 'Das Glas' (2nd ed.). Handbuch der Staatlichen Museen, Berlin. 1922.
VICTORIA AND ALBERT MUSEUM. 'Glass' by W. B. HONEY. H.M. Stationery Office, London. 1946.

2. *Individual Countries:*

America:

HARRINGTON, J. C. 'Glassmaking at Jamestown.' The Dietz Press, Richmond, Virginia. 1952.

Belgium:

CHAMBON, R. 'L'Histoire de la verrerie en Belgique du 11me siècle à nos jours.' Éditions de la librairie encyclopédique, S.P.R.L., Brussels. 1955.

Britain:

POWELL, H. J. 'Glass-Making in England.' University Press, Cambridge. 1923.
THORPE, W. A. 'A History of English and Irish Glass' (2 vols). Medici Society, London. 1929.
WESTROPP, M. S. D. 'Irish Glass.' Jenkins, London. 1920.

France:

BARRELET, J. 'La verrerie en France de l'époque gallo-romaine à nos jours.' Larousse, Paris. 1955.

Germany:

RADEMACHER, F. 'Die deutschen Gläser des Mittelalters.' Verlag für Kunstwissenschaften, Berlin. 1933.
SCHMIDT, R. 'Brandenburgische Gläser.' Verlag für Kunstwissenschaft, Berlin. 1914.

Holland:

HUDIG, F. W. 'Das Glas.' Im Selbstverlag des Verfassers, Amsterdam. Vienna. 1923.

Italy:

CECHETTI, B. and ZANETTI, V. 'Monografia della Vetraria Veneziana e Muranese.' Venice. 1874.
TADDEI, G. 'L'Arte del Vetro in Firenze e nel suo Dominio.' Le Monnier, Florence. 1954.

3. *Medieval and Sixteenth Century:*

A. *Technological:*

Abstracts of the most important passages bearing on glass in works of this period are to be found in S. E. WINBOLT, 'Wealden Glass' (Combridges, Hove, 1933); the translations of this author have been used in the present essay. AGRICOLA's *De re metallica* is available in translation by H. C. and LOU H. HOOVER (Dover Publications, New York, 1950). PEDER MÅNSSON's account of] glass-making in Rome was first published in 'Samlingar af Svenska Fornskrift-sällskapet', ed. by R. GEETE, pp. 557–66 (Stockholm, 1913–15); it was rendered into modern Swedish by HILDING RUNDQUIST in *Glastekn. Tidskr.*, **8**, 81, 1953. See also O. JOHANN-SEN's "Peder Månsson's 'Glaskunst' " in *Sprechsaal*, **65**, 387–8, 1932. VANOCCIO BIRINGUCCIO's 'Pirotechnia' has been translated with commentary by C. S. SMITH and MARTHA T. GNUDI (American Institute of Mining and Metallurgy, New York, 1943). A. ILG edited both HERA-CLIUS ('Heraclius von den Farben und Künsten der Römer', Vienna, 1873) and THEOPHILUS (*Schedula diversarum artium*, Vienna, 1874). THEOPHILUS had a later editor in W. THEOBALD ('Die Technik des Kunsthandwerks im zehnten Jahrhundert', Verein Deutscher Ingenieure, Berlin, 1933), and has been translated into English by R. HENDRIE ('An Essay upon various Arts . . . by Theophilus', London, 1847).

B. *Archaeological:*

DANIELS, J. S. 'The Woodchester Glass House.' Bellows, Gloucester. 1950.
PAPE, T. "An Elizabethan Glass Furnace." *The Connoisseur*, **92,** 172, 1933.

C. *General:*

RADEMACHER, F. 'Die deutschen Gläser des Mittelalters.' Verlag für Kunstwissenschaft, Berlin. 1933.

4. *Seventeenth and Eighteenth Centuries:*

A. NERI's *L'arte vetraria* was translated into many languages: into English, with notes, by C. MERRETT as 'The Art of Glass' (London, 1662); into Latin as *De arte vitraria* (Amsterdam, 1668, and frequently thereafter); into German, with notes, by J. KUNCKEL as part of his *Ars vitraria experimentalis* (Amsterdam and Danzig, 1679); and into French, with the notes of Merrett and Kunckel, by M. D. as 'Art de la Verrerie' (Paris, 1752).

See also:

HAUDICQUER DE BLANCOURT, F. 'De l'art de la verrerie.' Paris. 1697.
J. B[ARROW]. *Dictionarium polygraphicum* (2 vols). London. 1735.
'A New and Complete Dictionary of Arts and Sciences', Vol. 2, Pt II, article: "Glass." London. 1754.
DIDEROT, D. and D'ALEMBERT, J. LE R., *et al.* (Eds). 'Encyclopédie ou dictionnaire raisonné des sciences, des arts et des métiers', Vol. 17, article: "Verrerie". Paris. 1765.
DOSSIE, R. 'The Handmaid to the Arts', Vol. 2. London. 1758.

5. *Optical Glass:*

A. *Histories of Optical Instruments:*

CLAY, R. S. and COURT, T. H. 'History of the Microscope.' Griffin, London. 1932.

DANJON, A. and COUDER, A. 'Lunettes et télescopes.' Éditions de la revue d'optique théorique et instrumentale, Paris. 1935.

KING, H. C. 'The History of the Telescope.' Griffin, London. 1955.

ROSEN, E. "The Invention of Eye-Glasses." *J. Hist. Med.*, **11**, 13–46, 183–218, 1956.

B. *Lens-grinding:*

BEECKMAN, I. 'Journal tenu par Isaac Beeckman de 1604 à 1634' (ed. with introd. and notes by C. DE WAARD), Vol. 3, pp. iii–xiv (between pp. 370–1), and pp. 371 ff. Nijhoff, The Hague. 1945.

CHÉRUBIN D'ORLÉANS. 'La Dioptrique oculaire.' Paris. 1671.

HEVELIUS, J. *Selenographia.* Dantzig. 1647.

HUYGENS, CHRISTIAAN. 'Œuvres complètes', Vol. 22. Nijhoff, The Hague. 1932.

SIRTORI, G. *Telescopium.* Frankfurt a. M. 1618.

Hevelius's 60-ft astronomical telescope, 1673. The rectangular tube is made from wooden planks; the separate eyepiece N from vellum-covered pasteboard with wooden mounts. An objective-glass O, also mounted in wood, lies on the floor. The telescope is adjusted in azimuth by a rack on the stand, in altitude by the suspending-pulleys and others on the stand (pp 233, 634–5).

BUILDING CONSTRUCTION

MARTIN S. BRIGGS

I. ITALY

THE Renaissance revived interest in the classical learning of Greece and Rome, largely forgotten or neglected in the preceding centuries. It had its origin in Italy, particularly in Florence. It made itself felt in literature during the fourteenth century, but in architecture its beginning is usually associated with the visit of the youthful architect Brunelleschi (1377–1444) to Rome about 1402. He was seeking ideas for the design of a dome for the unfinished cathedral of Florence, then the subject of public competition. He certainly studied the ruins of ancient Roman buildings at first hand, and he won the competition. His dome was duly erected and is still standing; but, despite the popular belief that his antiquarian studies accounted for his triumph, his steeply pointed double dome, the first major work of Renaissance architecture (p 248 and figure 158), cannot have had a Roman origin, for there are no Roman or Byzantine double domes, and its prototype is probably Persian.

Brunelleschi acquired an intense interest in Roman architecture, and was among those who spread a fashion for reviving it in Italy, where Gothic architecture had never aroused the keen enthusiasm that marked its development elsewhere in western Europe. In 1414 an ancient manuscript containing the lost text of Vitruvius on architecture and building construction (freely quoted in volume II) was discovered in a Swiss monastery. In 1486 the work appeared in print and increased the interest in ancient building construction.

By the mid-fifteenth century Gothic architecture had gone out of fashion almost completely in Italy, except at Venice, and the forms of ancient Roman architecture, adapted to suit modern conditions, had taken its place. The movement did not affect the buildings of other countries for at least another fifty years, and even then was confined to minor details of design and ornament. In England, small examples of Italian decoration appeared, here and there, early in the sixteenth century, mainly in and around London in churches and mansions erected by the Crown or by noblemen (for example, in Wolsey's work at Hampton Court); but its full effects were not felt until the early seventeenth century. Away from London, traditional Gothic methods of design and

construction continued in all smaller buildings, such as manor-houses and
cottages, right up to the time of Wren's entry into architecture about 1662.

In this chapter, the buildings of the Renaissance, up to *c* 1700, will be treated
in the order in which the new movement penetrated into three important
countries: Italy, France, and England. The new influence was felt mainly in two
directions: architectural design and building construction. It is only with the

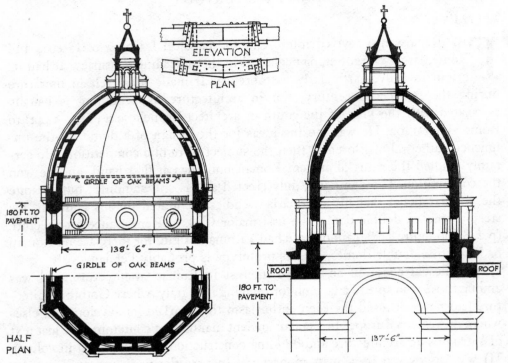

FIGURE 158—*Italian Renaissance dome-construction.* (Left) *The dome of the cathedral at Florence by
Brunelleschi, 1420, with detail of its oak girdle* (centre); (right) *dome of St Peter's, Rome, by Michelangelo,
1546.*

latter that we are here concerned, but, to understand the structural changes, the
sweeping revolution in design must be realized.

In volume II (ch 12) it was explained how the trabeated buildings of the
Greeks, with their various 'Orders' of columns, and the arcuated buildings of
the Romans, with their round arches and domes and barrel-vaults, gradually
came to be succeeded during the Middle Ages by 'Gothic' structures in which
the pointed arch was the characteristic feature and in which thin stone-vaulted
roofs were carried by a system of ribs, slender columns, and bold buttresses.

Thus, by about 1500, Gothic churches in England, France, and Germany had become mere skeletons of masonry with intervening 'walls' or spaces filled with glass. During the thousand years that followed the fall of Rome, the classical orders of columns—Doric, Ionic, and Corinthian, as defined by Vitruvius—had been completely abandoned and forgotten. They were now revived and intro-duced into all new buildings in Italy, but they served a decorative rather than a structural or functional purpose.

At Florence especially the arches of the inner courts of the great palaces, as well as the columns separating nave from aisles in the churches, were supported direct on the capitals of Corinthian columns, a fashion used in some of those old Roman halls of assembly known as basilicas. Most of the façades of the Florentine palaces, however, were with-out columns and were usually crowned with a bold cornice of antique Roman type. One of the finest of these cornices is that of the Strozzi Palace, *c* 1500 (figure 159). It is worth noting that its immense projection over the street, some 7 ft 3 in, is counterbalanced by increasing the thickness of the wall on the inner side, so that the centre of gravity at cornice-

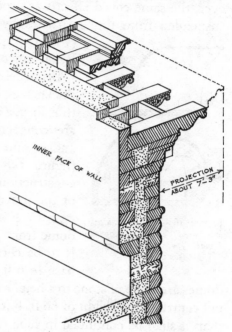

FIGURE 159—*Renaissance masonry. Wall and cornice at the Strozzi Palace, Florence.*

level falls well within the margin of safety. The cornice of the Riccardi Palace at Florence (1430) is 10 ft high and has the amazing projection of 8 ft 4 in. All these great palaces were faced with large stone blocks, often rusticated to pro-duce an illusion of colossal strength, though in fact most of this facing was com-paratively thin, the bulk of the wall being composed of brick or rubble masonry.

Compared with medieval houses, these Italian palaces, built for rich and noble families, were light and spacious. From the baths and villas of Imperial Rome were derived notions of splendour and formality unknown to the Middle Ages. With the end of feudal strife and the development of refined taste, a demand arose for suites of magnificent apartments, usually with lofty vaulted ceilings. Normally, this type of ceiling was flat and constructed of flat bricks in the Roman way, but continued downwards in the form of a curve or 'cove' at each of the walls (figure 160 A). Where it was desired to give more height to the round-headed windows, the cove was pierced (figure 160 B). In these brick or tile ceilings, the flat bricks or tiles were not bonded or overlapped, and complete reliance was placed on the adhesive strength of the mortar. This type of vaulting may be seen in Rome in the Sistine Chapel and the Farnese Palace. Often, however, the same coved effect was produced in lath-and-plaster, the ceiling being suspended from timber trusses by rods or ropes, as described by Vitruvius

FIGURE 160—*Italian vaulted or 'coved' ceiling.* (Above) *Usual type;* (below) *pierced for windows.*

(vol II, p 418). Examples may be seen in many fine Renaissance palaces at Genoa.

Brunelleschi's dome (1420–34) at Florence is of two thicknesses of brick with an intervening space, which thus form a cellular system. The two shells of brickwork are connected with each other at each of the eight angles, and at regular intervals between, by solid ribs (figure 158). His specification (1420) describing the construction may be summarized thus: the brickwork of the inner dome is to diminish from 6 ft 11 in at the base to 4 ft 6 in at the crown, and that of the outer dome from 2 ft 6 in to 1 ft 4 in. The intervening space is to be correspondingly increased from 3 ft 8 in at the base to 6 ft at the crown. The 24 ribs uniting the two

domes are to be of stone to a height of about 12 ft. The dome is to be built without centring to a height of 60 ft, but thence upwards Brunelleschi vaguely states that 'it shall be continued in such manner as shall be devised by those masters who shall have to do with the building; because, in building, practice teaches what one has to do'. It is significant that practice, not theory, is to be the guide.

An Italian writer of 1820 published an older drawing showing scaffolding supported on raking struts springing from the cornice at the base of Brunelleschi's dome, somewhat like Carlo Fontana's seventeenth-century drawing of the centring used at St Peter's in Rome (figure 161); and Brunelleschi may have used the same method. The construction of St Peter's dome, by Michelangelo (figure 158), is surprisingly like Brunelleschi's and shows no significant advance on it. The dome at Florence, incidentally, is very steeply curved, thus transmitting the weight of the lantern effectively on to the supports.

The arched wooden roof of Santa Maria dei Miracoli at Venice (1480) has a coffered ceiling, also arched; and the timber members of the roof are built up in sections (figure 161). As already explained (vol II, p 442), a roof needs a tie-beam at its springing to prevent it from spreading and thus overturning the supporting walls, while a collar-beam half-way up its height is only a palliative and is often ineffective. At Santa Maria dei Miracoli, iron tie-bars have been inserted across each bay of the church. Such tie-bars may be seen across arches in the courtyards of many Italian palaces.

Curved roofs with built-up timbers are also found on the town-halls of Padua (1306) and Vicenza (1560), and in sundry other buildings in north Italy. In France this type seems to have been evolved independently but concurrently. Similarly the double-slope or mansard roof (p 253) appeared in Italy and Eng-

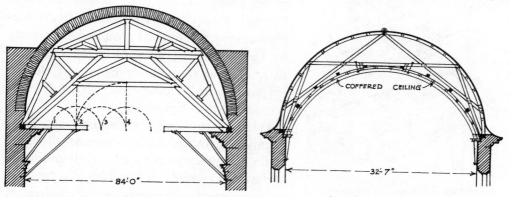

FIGURE 161—*Renaissance carpentry in Italy.* (Left) *Centring for the main arches of St Peter's, Rome;* (right) *roof of the church of Santa Maria dei Miracoli, Venice.*

land at least as early as in France. The designer of the Paduan roof is said to have copied it from drawings he had made of a palace in India.

Many Renaissance churches in Italy, however, had low-pitched roofs with timber trusses, of the type used over Roman basilican churches. In such cases the massive tie-beams are an integral part of the structure. Sometimes these roofs were open, with all the framework visible from below; but many others had elaborately coffered wooden ceilings, another feature inherited direct from ancient Roman times. The example illustrated (figure 162 A), from Santa Maria Maggiore at Rome, shows how the coffering was attached to the coupled tie-beams of the trusses. Here the coffering was painted white, the decorations being gilt.

Instead of stone cornices many Italian Renaissance palaces and churches had very boldly projecting eaves, as at the Pazzi Chapel at Florence (1429), where the immense projection of about 8 ft is obtained by doubling the depth of the rafters at the point where they would be most liable to bend (figure 162 B).

Having glanced at the principal features of Renaissance building construction in Italy, it remains to consider how far these were directly inspired by the revival of ancient scholarship. Round arches, barrel-vaults, and the 'orders' are obviously derived from Roman prototypes. The classical revival, however, went further, and ancient precedent became the rule for processes of actual construction as well as for design and ornament. Vitruvius's book became the architects' bible within a few years from its discovery, and they turned to him for guidance on the burning of lime, the seasoning of timber, or the painting of stucco, with the same complete confidence that they accorded to his pronouncements on matters of taste. Not only Vitruvius but even the Greek Theophrastus (*c* 372–287 B.C.) is quoted extensively by L. B. Alberti (1404–72) in his influential *De re aedificatoria*, first printed in 1485, though his passages on building-materials are descriptive rather than scientific.

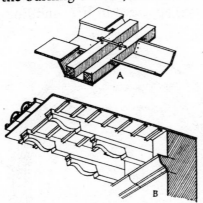

FIGURE 162—*Renaissance carpentry in Italy.* (A) *Coffering of the ceiling, Santa Maria Maggiore, Rome;* (B) *eaves brackets at the Pazzi Chapel, Florence.*

While many architect-antiquarians were rummaging in the Roman ruins in the hope of finding precedents to solve their problems of design, Leonardo da Vinci (1452–1519) was experimenting with every sort of mechanical invention (figure 273); but was he able to contribute anything useful to the science of building, and were there any other pioneers in the same promising field?

Leonardo had no practical experience as an architect or builder, no building or portion of a building being attributable to him, though he made many drawings and sketches of buildings. He does not appear to have made any special study of mathematics or mechanics in early life, but doubtless learnt something from a book on mechanics of the early fifteenth century and from contact with the mathematician Pacioli (1445–1509). Nevertheless, in a manner characteristic of the 'universal man' of his time, his search for knowledge embraced every branch of science. He was not anxious to reproduce antique forms, as were so many architects of his day: flying-machines interested him far more. He experimented with everything that came his way, often abandoning an experiment directly he had shown that its application was practicable.

One such experiment of Leonardo's is illustrated in a drawing showing apparatus for measurement of the tensile strength of wire. On this he makes the comment:

The object of this test is to find the load an iron wire can carry. Attach an iron wire, about 2 *braccia* [roughly three feet] long, to something that will fairly support it; then attach a basket to the wire, and feed into it fine sand through a small hole at the end of a hopper. A spring is fixed so that it will close the hole as soon as the wire breaks.... The weight of the sand and the location of the fracture are to be recorded. Repeat the test several times to check the results.

This simple and ingenious use of sand for tensile tests continued long after his day and, indeed, to our own time—as for cement briquettes.

Many drawings of Leonardo illustrate structural details; but the most important for our purpose is a diagram of loaded beams and struts, one of several in which he attempts scientific solutions of structural problems. These are generally accepted as the first of their kind in modern times. His notes cover the resolution of a single force or velocity into two components, but it is not certain that he had grasped the conception of the resolution of forces as we understand it today.

In dealing with the reactions on supports of loaded bodies, Leonardo approached the problems not only statically as an architect or structural engineer, but also dynamically as in his studies of bird-flight and flying-machines. Examining a rigid structure supported at regular intervals, he argues that 'all bodies which do not bend will exert equal pressures on all of the supports that are equally distant from the centre of gravity, the centre being the middle of the substance of such a body'. The meaning of his phrases is clear, though his manner of expression is often imperfect; lack of a suitable scientific language was his greatest handicap. Elsewhere he considers the effect of applying the load at irregular intervals. His principles are correctly stated, but in some cases his calculations are vitiated by careless arithmetic.

More important, for our purpose, are Leonardo's studies of the strength of loaded struts and pillars, a field in which he had no scientific predecessors. He demonstrates that a bundle of supports bound together is stronger than a single pillar of equivalent sectional area, given adequate strength of the binding material. Again, of two struts of equal height but of different cross-section, he concludes that the strength is directly proportional to the sectional area, and inversely proportional to the relation of height to diameter. Passing then to struts of equal sectional area but of different heights, he argues that their strengths vary inversely as their heights. All this is very sound, but again spoilt by arithmetical errors. In investigating loaded beams, he introduces an ingenious method of demonstration with models built up of several detachable sections. Using this device, he experimented on deflexion. The results he obtained are not accurate, but he did attack such problems of statics scientifically.

Despite Leonardo's pioneering efforts, there is no evidence that architects of his own or the next generation made use of the science of structural mechanics. There was still a gulf between the groping scientist and the actual designers and erectors of buildings. It is known that, by the seventeenth century, bars of metal, wood, and glass were being systematically tested by practical men, but it remains unknown how far the results were transmitted to or used by architects and builders.

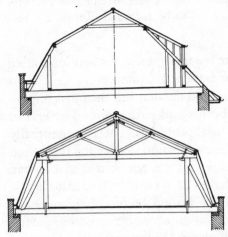

Galileo (1564–1642), who made such important discoveries in mechanics, was the real founder of our modern scientific knowledge of the strength of building-materials, including the principle of cantilevers. However, by the middle of the seventeenth century the chief work in this field was no longer being done in Italy but in London and Paris, and we shall find some of its results in the

FIGURE 163—*Mansard roofs.* (Above) *Simple type, with parapet gutter on left side, and with dormer and eaves gutter on right side;* (below) *trussed type with parapet gutter.*

scientific interests of that remarkable pair of friends, Christopher Wren and Robert Hooke (pp 257, 297).

II. FRANCE

The influence of the Renaissance began to make itself felt upon French building construction in the first years of the sixteenth century. As in England at the same period, it was confined at first to ornamental details in churches and to the country mansions and palaces erected by monarchs and nobles. As in England again, there was a new demand for more spaciousness, light, and dignity in the homes of the wealthy. The change of taste can in large measure be traced to the French military campaigns in Italy between 1495 and 1559, which familiarized the invaders with the novel fashions prevailing there. The actual design and execution of the buildings in France were carried out partly by Italian architects and decorators, and partly by native builders and craftsmen who began to visit Italy for study even before 1500.

Gothic architecture was far more firmly rooted in France than in Italy. Thus it was natural that the first buildings in the new style retained many medieval characteristics, such as steeply pitched roofs, prominent chimneys, gables, and mullioned windows. Vitruvius's work was translated into French and soon became an authority, as in Italy, but it took longer for the introduction of the Roman 'orders' to produce drastic changes of design or structure. The principal innovations in building construction were in roofs, domes, and windows.

For houses and churches alike, the steep medieval roof died hard in France. Indeed, it survived for centuries in a modified form, that of the so-called mansard roof, named from the architect François Mansart or Mansard (1598–1666) who did much to popularize it. This mansard roof, with its double slope (figure 163), was in fact a good deal older than its name would imply. It was used in Italy at least as early as in France, and in England for the great hall at Hampton Court Palace (p 265 and figure 173), constructed between 1530 and 1540. In France it was employed in the portion of the Louvre designed by Lescot in 1549.

The invention of this type of roof, which is still common throughout Europe, had a functional origin. When the Renaissance reached France, there was a vogue

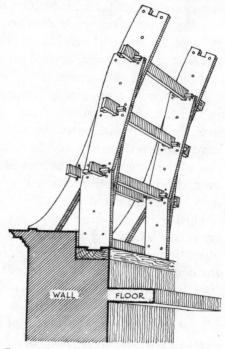

FIGURE 164—*Design for curved roof-timbers built up from short sections, by Philibert de l'Orme. 1561.*

for very high and steep roofs. These provided inadequate space for attics, whereas the mansard, in conjunction with dormers, allowed of good attics with vertical sides, giving an additional habitable room with a considerable saving on masonry walls. For this reason the mansard has remained popular and has led to the semi-bungalow type of house. In America it came to be called a 'gambrel' roof.

Another innovation in roof-carpentry was due to Philibert de l'Orme (1510?–70), who, though he had studied the ruins of Rome, made his reputation in 1561 with his strictly practical book, 'New Inventions for Building well at low Cost'. In it he described and illustrated various methods of constructing curved roofs out of short lengths of light timber, avoiding the use of a tie-beam, an expensive item when spans are large (figure 164). He claimed to be able thus to roof any space up to 300 ft wide, though in one case at least his system failed, the structure collapsing within 20 years.

Most of these French roofs of the sixteenth and seventeenth centuries continued to be covered with slates, as in medieval times. Lead, imported from England, was also used. One of de l'Orme's numerous recommendations was to substitute copper for lead. Slates were also often used for protecting the vertical wooden fronts of timber-framed houses: of this practice there are many examples at Blois. In the royal château of St-Germain, near Paris (c 1540), there are flat terraced roofs of stone, carried on vaults strengthened by iron ties as in Italy, and reinforced with buttresses in the French medieval tradition.

Domes were a prominent feature of many French churches of the sixteenth and seventeenth centuries. Wren, who never visited Italy, studied architecture in Paris in 1665 with particular attention to dome-design, though he cannot then have foreseen that he would be called upon to design St Paul's, for the destruction of the old church in the Fire of London had not yet occurred. He was, however, considering the addition of a central dome to Old St Paul's, and embodied it in his design dated 1666.

During the sixteenth century a few small domes had been built in French churches. There were (a) a dome covered with slates over the Church of the Visitation, later the Calvinist Church, in Paris (1632–4); (b) a high dome over the church of SS Paul and Louis (1625–41) close by; (c) another over Guarini's Théatine Church of Ste-Anne-la-Royale (begun in 1662 and since destroyed), which had the Greek-cross plan that Wren tried to use at St Paul's in 1673; and (d) yet another over the chapel of the huge Hospital of the Salpêtrière (1657), also in Paris. All these Wren could study, but more important than any of them is the dome of the Church of the Sorbonne in Paris (1635–56), which is double, like those in Rome and Florence (p 246). The outer dome is of timber and slated; the inner, or structural dome, of stone. The lantern is of timber. The inner dome is about 44 ft in internal diameter and 94 ft above the pavement at its springing (figure 165).

At the abbey church of Val-de-Grâce in Paris (begun in 1645), Wren could have seen an even finer dome, actually in course of construction. Like that at the Sorbonne, it is double, with a timber lantern; and, again like the Sorbonne, the stone attic (parapet stage) of the outer drum rises as high as the crown of the inner structural dome of stone, thereby helping to resist its outward thrust. This dome is about 56 ft in diameter, and its springing is 105 ft above the floor (figure 165).

The much loftier dome of the second Church of the Invalides in Paris (figure 165) has some affinity with Wren's work, but in this case any traffic of ideas must have been in the opposite direction, for J. Hardouin-Mansart (1646–

1708), grand-nephew of François Mansart, did not begin it till 1693, when Wren was hard at work on St Paul's; it is possible that Mansart may have seen engravings of Wren's 'Rejected Design' (1673), and certainly both architects must have borrowed ideas from the dome of St Peter's, Rome. Mansart's dome differs in many respects from the dome actually built by Wren at St Paul's (figure 166).

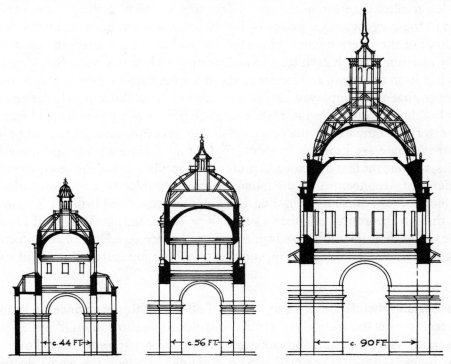

FIGURE 165—*French Renaissance dome-construction.* (Left) *Double dome of the Church of the Sorbonne, Paris, 1635–56;* (centre) *double dome of the Church of Val-de-Grâce, Paris, begun in 1645;* (right) *triple dome of the second Church of the Invalides, Paris, 1693–1706. Drawn to uniform scale.*

The internal diameter is about 90 ft and the height from the floor to the springing is over 140 ft. It is of triple construction, like Wren's. The two lower domes are of masonry, the lowest being pierced by a very large circular opening through which one can see the underside of the middle dome from beneath. The outer dome is of timber covered with lead, like Wren's; but the lantern is of wood, whereas Wren's is of stone and therefore so heavy that his ingenious brick cone was needed to carry it.

Windows in France at this period still retained the medieval subdivision by mullions and transoms. The commonest type was two lights wide and two lights high, divided by a single mullion and transom, forming a cross; hence the French term *croisée* for this kind of window. Gradually, however, the desire for security that had hitherto limited all openings in outer walls to a minimum yielded before the Italian form of large oblong windows. Stone mullions were replaced by wooden ones, and lead cames[1] by wooden bars, until finally the wooden mullions were omitted too. Glass was scarce all through this period. Even in the gorgeous royal palace of Fontainebleau, oiled linen was used in the windows of the inferior rooms almost to the end of the seventeenth century.

Two leading French architects contemporary with Wren were, like him, late converts from science to architecture; yet in neither case have we any conclusive evidence that they employed their knowledge of mechanics in calculations for their buildings. Claude Perrault (1613–88) was trained as a physician, did magnificent work in comparative anatomy, and did not take up architecture until he was 52. At the same age François Blondel (1616–86), formerly a professor of mathematics, became the first director and professor of architecture of the newly founded Academy of Architecture. In the following year he published a book on ballistics and fortification! It is rather in their general intelligence and brilliant inventiveness than in theoretical calculations that these two men, like Wren and Hooke, made use of their scientific training; but in the French Academy of Architecture there were frequent discussions on construction, building materials, and subsoils.

III. ENGLAND

In England, before about 1620, the chief effect of the renaissance of Roman architecture was the addition of Italian ornamental features to buildings of predominantly Gothic design and construction. Between 1617 and 1635, however, Inigo Jones (1573–1652) erected several buildings in which the whole doctrine of Renaissance architecture was proclaimed. Notable among them are the Queen's House at Greenwich, the Banqueting House at Whitehall, and St Paul's Church in Covent Garden. They displayed the Roman 'orders', low-pitched roofs, stone cornices and balustrades, unobtrusive chimneys, regular masonry, large windows, coved ceilings, and indeed all the Italian features already described; while gables, tracery, and other typically English medieval characteristics were generally absent. Such changes as Jones introduced into construction were derived direct from Italy; unfortunately little of his work, so important in the history of English architecture, has survived.

In the time of Inigo Jones, and even later in remote districts of England, old traditions of building lingered on. Not only did Tudor fashions continue in

---

[1] Cames are grooved bars of lead holding and connecting adjacent panes of glass in a window.

many places, but even Gothic persisted here and there, as in St John's Church at Leeds (1634) and the fine fan-vaulted staircase at Christ Church, Oxford (1630). Far more half-timbered houses in England have survived from the sixteenth and seventeenth centuries than from earlier years, although their picturesque construction is essentially in the Gothic tradition; and this is so likewise in France and Germany. Most of the charming stone manor-houses and cottages of the Cotswolds and the Pennines also date from those two centuries, though their appearance is medieval and their construction traditional.

Very few churches were built in England between 1550 and 1660. The number of parish churches was already adequate; many monastic churches became cathedrals or parish churches after the Dissolution of the Monasteries in 1536–9, and the civil wars of the seventeenth century, like the Thirty Years War in continental Europe, created disturbed conditions unfavourable for church-building.

It might be expected that the renaissance in English architecture would have resulted in a more scientific outlook upon building construction, but nothing of the sort is discernible before the time of Wren. Inigo Jones, for all his brilliant gifts, was no scientist, and was not even well educated. He came into prominence as a designer of theatre scenery, and as one who had studied the ruins of ancient Rome first-hand. Wren, on the contrary, had already attained a high reputation as an astronomer, geometrician, and all-round scientist before he turned to architecture about 1663, at the age of 31. He was then professor of astronomy at Oxford, and had held a similar appointment at Gresham College, London. His inventions cover an astounding range and enter the fields of astronomy, meteorology, physics, navigation, civil engineering, anatomy, musical instruments, geometry, mathematics, surveying, and draughtsmanship, as well as a host of miscellaneous practical devices. Among the last were a few related to building construction as, for example, 'A Pavement harder than Marble'; 'New Designs tending to Strength, etc, in Building'; 'Building Forts in the Sea'; 'Inventions for fortifying and making Havens'.

At Oxford, Wren must have met John Wallis, professor of mathematics, who was one of the first mathematicians to study the theory of loaded beams, and who translated into mathematical terms the much earlier published designs of Serlio (1475–1552). Wren's contemporary and close friend, Robert Hooke (1635–1703), was an experimental philosopher who showed skill in many sciences, including astronomy, microscopy, physics, and instrument design, and who is commemorated in 'Hooke's Law' of elasticity. He became an architect even later in life than Wren. Yet in their capacity as architects, there is no evidence that either Wren or Hooke made use of his knowledge of statics to calculate the strength of structural members, even in the form of reciprocal diagrams[1] or other semi-graphical methods. Nothing of the sort seems to have been attempted until the nineteenth century. On the other hand, Wren in particular must have developed an acute intuitive sense, enabling him to adapt basic scientific principles to practical problems, and, like other Renaissance architects, he made some use of geometry in structural design. One of his rough sketches for the dome of St Paul's suggests that he was adopting Galileo's theory of the catenary curve, discovered early in the seventeenth century (p 434).

The dome of St Paul's is a landmark in English architectural history, for it was the first to be built in this country. As we have seen, Wren studied dome-construction in Paris, while other celebrated domes—those of St Peter's, Rome, and of Florence, besides the Pantheon in Rome—must have been familiar to him from engravings. The design finally adopted, after several false starts, can only have been derived, structurally, from those older domes which were capable of supporting the heavy masonry lantern, weighing about 700 tons, that Wren had chosen as the crowning feature of the design. St Peter's had such a lantern, and a double dome of masonry (figure 166).

The purpose of the double dome is primarily for effect. If the curve be very steep, the external aspect is satisfactory but the interior effect is not, because the space is funnel-like and dark. Conversely, if the dome be hemispherical its internal appearance is pleasing but externally it is not bold enough. Wren's double dome, the inner being of brick 18 in thick, the outer of timber covered with lead, meets the case. Between the two he built a brick cone, also 18 in thick, to carry the heavy stone lantern. Around the whole structure, at the level of the Stone Gallery, where the bases of the brick inner dome and the brick cone meet, he provided a massive iron girdle or band to keep them both from spreading. At a higher level he fixed two strong iron chains for the same purpose (figure 166).

Repairs in 1922–30 proved that serious damage to the masonry structure caused by settlement could not have been foreseen by Wren, for it is the result of recent disturbance of the subsoil, to which, however, defects in the masonry contributed. Although the piers consisted of a facing of dressed stone with a rubble core, the masonry was better than the average medieval building of walls and piers. Some fractures were certainly due to Wren's use of iron cramps too near the surface of the stone, so that they became corroded. Here Wren failed to apply his own dictum that 'in cramping of stones, no iron should lie within nine inches of the air'.

[1] Diagrams in which the internal forces in a structure are represented to scale on lines parallel to the members of the structure.

The dome of St Paul's was the chief structural innovation and achievement in English building between about 1500 and 1700. Its erection was not complete till

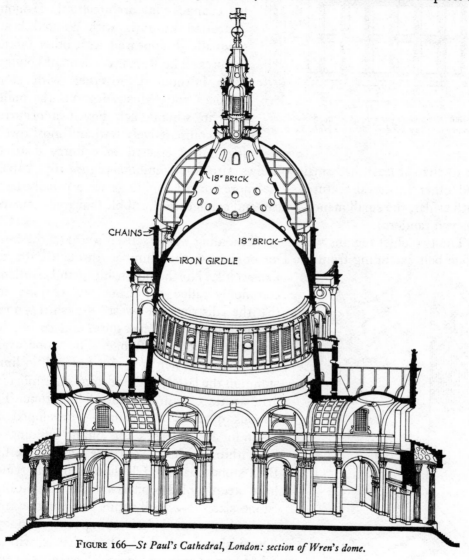

FIGURE 166—*St Paul's Cathedral, London: section of Wren's dome.*

1710, when the work had been in progress for 25 years. Apart from this great monument, however, the development of English building construction from 1500 to 1700 was gradual and unspectacular. It may be treated here most conveniently under the heads of the various 'trades' or crafts.

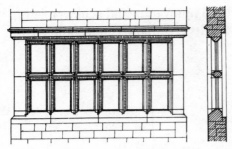

FIGURE 167—*Construction of stone mullions and masonry in a bay window. Swinsty Hall, Yorkshire. 1579.*

Taking masonry first, changes following the Renaissance were mainly due to changes in architectural fashions. Traceried windows with pointed heads gradually disappeared with other Gothic features. The Roman 'orders' of columns were introduced, together with stone cornices and balustrades. Yet the buildings in which such novelties occurred were comparatively few, and most dwelling-houses erected in country districts, up to 1620 at least, had small windows with stone mullions (figure 167), gables, and other medieval features. The more formal buildings were usually faced with ashlar, the small manor-houses and cottages with rubble (squared, coursed, or even random).

The two chief regions where stone building was practised were: (i) the limestone belt extending from the Dorset coast to the Humber, through Bath, the Cotswolds, Northamptonshire, and Rutland, commonly called the 'Cotswold' region; and (ii) the districts of west Yorkshire, north Derbyshire, north Lancashire, and so on, adjoining the Pennine Range. The stone available in the former area is a fine oolitic limestone; in the latter it is sandstone and millstone grit, with a certain amount of limestone. The famous quarries at Portland—developed by Wren for his churches and public buildings—lie within the 'Cotswold' area, as do the fine Bath stone quarries. Old houses in this region have steep gabled roofs covered with so-called 'stone slates'—actually thin slabs of the same stone that is used for walling and chimneys. These 'slates' were laid 'dry'—that is, without a bedding of mortar—on oak pegs driven into holes bored through them, and were often 'torched' or plastered with hair-mortar on their undersides. Valleys were formed of similar 'slates' specially cut for the intersections of

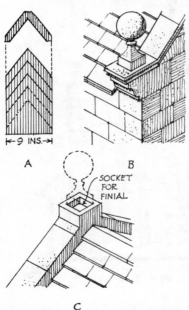

FIGURE 168—*Details of English masonry. (A) Method of sawing Cotswold 'stone slates' from the block; (B) Yorkshire stone finial at the foot of a gable; (C) the same at the apex of a gable, showing the method of jointing.*

roofs, but ridges were made of stones in the shape of an inverted V, sawn out of a solid block (figure 168). Stone for these 'slates' was (and still is) quarried in October in large blocks, which are then allowed to stand out in the open until the winter frosts disintegrate the layers so that they can then easily be split with a hammer. They are laid on the roof in graded sizes with the largest at the bottom, diminishing in size to the ridge.

The walls of these houses are usually 18 to 24 in thick, with stones laid either in ashlar, coursed rubble, or random rubble; but the ashlar is often a mere facing with rubble behind. Inferior buildings, such as barns, were frequently constructed without mortar, as were the fencing-walls between fields. The heads or lintels over windows and doors were of stone, as were the mullions and transoms of windows. Glazing at first was done in latticed or diamond cames (p 256) of leadwork, but this soon gave place to small rectangular lead cames. Sash-windows were hardly ever used before 1700. Lead gutters and down-pipes were seldom provided, the rain-water from the eaves dropping on to the base of the wall and thus often causing its decay.

FIGURE 169—*Brick chimney of an old cottage: the type built in Kent and Sussex during the seventeenth century.*

Old houses in the Pennine region likewise have 'stone slates', but much larger, thicker, and heavier than the Cotswold type. Roofs are of lower pitch, never more than 45°. Walls are somewhat thicker than in the Cotswolds, and may have an ashlar facing or be made entirely of rubble. In other respects the Pennine houses resemble those of the Cotswold area, but they are rougher in finish, since the material is less tractable. Other districts of England where stone building is traditional are West Sussex (sandstone), Devon and Cornwall (granite), and the Lake District (slate).

Brick had come into use in England during the late-Gothic period (vol II, p 438), especially in the eastern counties. In the south-eastern counties and in East Anglia it became very popular during the sixteenth and seventeenth centuries, owing to the scarcity of natural building-stone in those parts. Fireplaces and chimney-stacks were now provided in all houses, even cottages. Logs being the normal fuel, fireplaces were very wide, so that much ingenuity was required to reduce the width of brick chimneys from the base to the stack in a series of stages (figure 169).

Bricks were generally laid in English Bond, but Flemish Bond[1] was introduced during the second quarter of the seventeenth century. The size of bricks was prescribed by charter in 1571 as 9 in × 4¼ in × 2¼ in. Wide mortar joints were used. The introduction from Holland of 'gauged' brick-work, with rubbed bricks and fine white joints, occurred in the second quarter of the seventeenth century, when carved and moulded bricks also came into fashion. Fifty years later, Wren displayed much ingenuity in the use of brick-work, both plain and gauged, notably at Hampton Court. Small yellow Dutch bricks measuring about

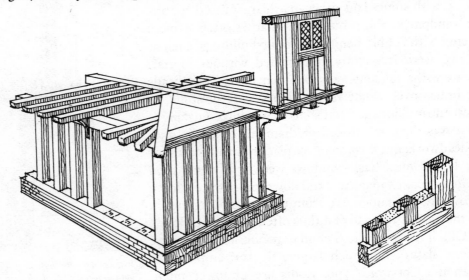

FIGURE 170—*English half-timber construction. (Left) Typical framing of main timbers; (right) the intervals shown filled with stone slabs. Great Chalfield Manor, Wiltshire.*

6 in × 3 in × 1 in were introduced late in the seventeenth century for paving yards and stables.

Buildings entirely of timber were still erected throughout the seventeenth century, and later. The chief difference between French and English practice was that in France curved braces were seldom employed, whereas in England they were common, probably because the tall, straight French oak-trees did not produce curved timbers as freely as the English ones. Elm, beech, and sweet chestnut were also used occasionally for timber framing in England.

Figure 170 shows the main principles of construction. Heavy storey-posts,

---

[1] In English Bond courses composed entirely of headers alternate with courses composed entirely of stretchers. In Flemish Bond each course consists of alternate headers and stretchers, every header being set in the middle of a stretcher in the course below and the course above.

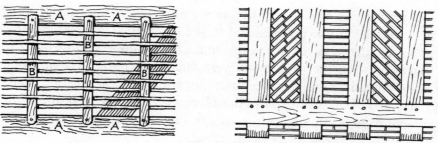

FIGURE 171—*English half-timber construction.* (Left) '*Wattle-and-daub*' *covering.* AA, *framing-timbers;* BB, *laths.* (Right) *panels filled with brickwork.*

8 or 9 in square, were let into a sill-piece resting upon a low brick or stone plinth-wall. The posts at the angles were larger than the others, and were formed from the butts of trees placed root upwards, the top part curving diagonally outwards to carry the angle-posts of the upper storey. Across these were laid beams projecting about 18 inches in front of the framing below, those at the angles being laid diagonally and showing within the house. Into these beams others were connected longitudinally, and to the latter were tenoned floor-joists, projecting the same distance as the main beams.

The framing of the upper storey resembled that of the lower, the plate and the sill being laid upon the ends of the overhanging timbers. The house in its first

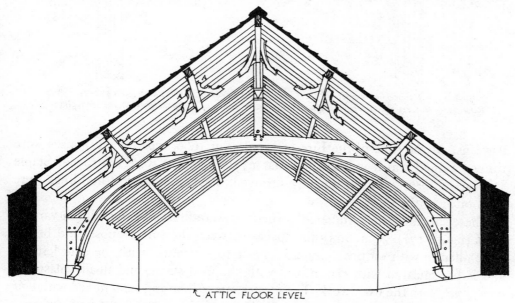

L ATTIC FLOOR LEVEL

FIGURE 172—*Roof-construction in oak; note the wind-bracing* AA. *Swinsty Hall, Yorkshire, 1579.*

stage of construction was a mere timber skeleton which, until the framing was well advanced, had to be propped and stayed externally. In many examples the slots to receive the stays are still visible in the larger timbers of the lower storey. The spaces between the main posts were filled with uprights about 8 or 9 in wide, and about the same distance apart. In later work they were spaced more widely and curved braces were introduced, especially in the west midlands from Worcestershire to south Lancashire, where they formed elaborate geometrical

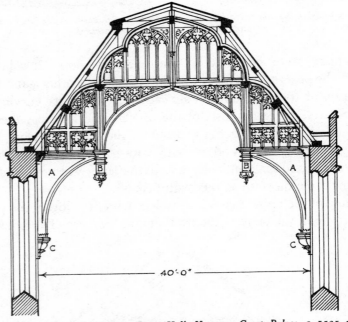

FIGURE 173—*Hammer-beam roof of the Great Hall, Hampton Court Palace, c 1531-5. Typical Renaissance features are the double slope and the ornamentation of the spandrels (AA), the pendants (BB), and the corbels (CC).*

patterns. At the time of the Fire of London in 1666, most of the houses were timber-framed and it is estimated that 13 200 of them were destroyed. Staple Inn in Holborn (1581) fortunately survived. Thereafter timber buildings were prohibited in the City.

These so-called 'half-timbered' structures were finished externally in various ways (figure 171). Sometimes the spaces between the various posts and beams were filled in with wattles (hazel-sticks $\frac{1}{2}$-in to 1 in thick, with the bark left on) and laths, smeared with clay mixed with chopped straw, and finally plastered over, flush with the woodwork. The plaster was of lime and sand mixed with hair or chopped hay or cow-dung; it acquired a tough, leathery consistency. Alterna-

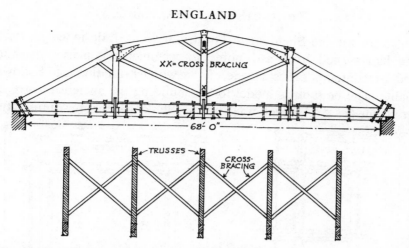

FIGURE 174—*Design for the composite roof-trusses of the Sheldonian Theatre, Oxford, by Wren.* (Above)
Elevation of a single truss; (below) *cross-bracing between the trusses.*

tively, the whole exterior of the building might be covered with vertical tiles.
This method was common in Kent, Sussex, and Surrey; but where the tiles have
rounded ends ('imbricated') they are probably of later date. In Essex, Hertfordshire, and Middlesex, weatherboarding was largely used as
external covering. This practice was carried to America by the
Pilgrim Fathers, becoming a characteristic feature of New
England houses. In England, the boards were of oak or elm,
about 9 in wide, nailed to the intermediate posts of the framing,
each board overlapping the next by 1–1½ in.

Except for the low-pitched roofs introduced from Italy by
Inigo Jones, which might have been designed by Vitruvius
himself, there was no great change in English roof-design
before Wren. Gothic trusses with curved braces continued to
be made, as seen in a Yorkshire farmhouse of 1579 (figure 172),
which also has lateral ornamental wind-bracing of the type
often found in Gothic churches. Hammer-beam roofs, too,
were occasionally built as late as the seventeenth century. That
at Hampton Court (figure 173) was erected in 1531–5 and is
essentially medieval in construction, with Renaissance ornament
in its spandrels, pendants, and corbels. It also has the double
slope associated with the mansard truss.

FIGURE 175—*Chichester Cathedral spire, showing Wren's 'pendulum'.* (A) *'Pendulum',*
80 ft × 13 in × 13 in; (B) *'platforms';* (C) *iron weight.*

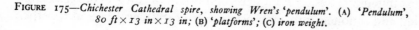

Wren's roof for the Sheldonian Theatre at Oxford, designed in 1663 (soon after he had turned from astronomy to architecture), marks an innovation regarded by contemporaries as one of the wonders of the age. Following the fashionable taste he took as model for his building the ancient theatre of Marcellus in Rome (11 B.C.), which was open to the sky—a manifest impracticability

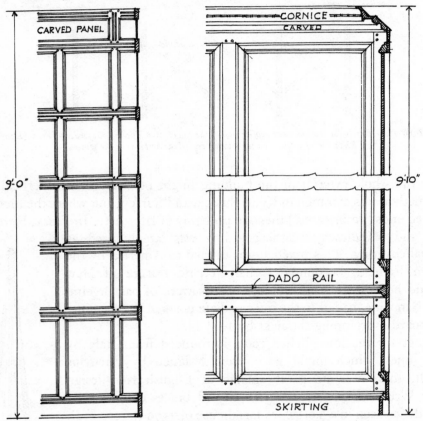

FIGURE 176—*English wall-panelling.* (Left) *From Swinsty Hall, Yorkshire, 1579;* (right) *from Clifford's Inn, London, 1686–8. Note the differences in size, projection, and character of the panels, and the wooden pegs used in the framing.*

in the English climate. Wren's building had the enormous width of 68 ft—far too great to be spanned by any normal form of timber construction. In 1663 he had not yet visited France (p 254), but he may well have seen Philibert de l'Orme's book (p 253) on built-up timber trusses for wide spans. At any rate, he evolved a most ingenious design for a truss composed of timbers of reasonable length, dovetailed and tenoned into each other (figure 174), and bound together by a number of heavy iron bolts, straps, and plates. The trusses were stiffened laterally by a system of diagonal cross-braces. This roof, with its double slope, recalls the mansard type.

In 1694 Wren was called upon to repair the Gothic stone spire of Chichester Cathedral, and showed his scientific ingenuity in a unique structural device. In order to neutralize the effects of frequent gales he suspended a colossal timber pendulum, by means of an iron ring, from the stone finial forming the apex of the spire. This was a single piece of yellow fir,[1] 80 ft long and 13 in square, loaded at its foot with a lump of iron (figure 175). To this pendulum he fixed two stout oaken platforms, the lower one about 3 in smaller, and the upper one $2\frac{1}{4}$ in smaller, than the masonry walls of the spire. When the wind blew hard on one side of the spire, the pendulum touched the masonry on the lee side and the space on the windward side increased; when the wind dropped, the pendulum returned to the perpendicular. This device proved entirely successful until 1861, when the tower and spire collapsed and were rebuilt.

Great changes took place in the craft of joinery during the seventeenth century. The narrow and inconvenient stone spiral staircases of Gothic times gave place to wide, easy, and handsome staircases of wood. Mullioned windows were used by Inigo Jones for the Banqueting House at Whitehall and the Queen's House at Greenwich, but sashes, said to have been introduced from Holland by William III, were installed by Wren at Whitehall Palace in 1685. They had cords and brass pulleys. Wall-panelling during the Elizabethan and Jacobean periods continued to have very light framing (about an inch thick), delicate mouldings, and rather small oblong panels usually about 18 in high by 12 broad. From the time of Inigo Jones onwards, the size of the panels was greatly increased. They had sloped margins, and boldly projecting mouldings were fixed round them instead of the smaller mouldings formerly worked on the edges of the framing (figure 176).

BIBLIOGRAPHY

ADDY, S. O. 'Evolution of the English House' (rev. ed., enl. from the author's notes by J. N. SUMMERSON). Allen and Unwin, London. 1933.
AMBLER, L. 'The Old Halls and Manor Houses of Yorkshire, with some Examples of other Houses built before 1700.' Batsford, London. 1913.
BLOMFIELD, SIR REGINALD (THEODORE). 'A Short History of Renaissance Architecture in England, 1500–1800.' Bell, London. 1900.
Idem. 'A History of French Architecture from the Reign of Charles VIII till the Death of Mazarin.' Bell, London. 1911.

[1] A name variously given to the Scots pine, the Douglas fir, and the white fir (*Abies grandis*).

BLOMFIELD, SIR REGINALD (THEODORE). 'A History of French Architecture from the Death of Mazarin till the Death of Louis XV, 1661–1774.' Bell, London. 1921.

BRIGGS, M. S. 'A Short History of the Building Crafts.' Clarendon Press, Oxford. 1925.

Idem. 'The English Farmhouse.' Batsford, London. 1953.

Idem. 'Wren the Incomparable.' Allen and Unwin, London. 1953.

CHOISY, F. A. 'Histoire de l'architecture', Vol. 2. Paris. 1899.

CROSSLEY, F. H. 'Timber Building in England from Early Times to the End of the Seventeenth Century.' Batsford, London. 1951.

DAWBER, SIR (EDWARD) GUY. 'Old Cottages and Farmhouses in Kent and Sussex.' Batsford, London. 1900.

Idem. 'Old Cottages, Farmhouses and other Stone Buildings in the Cotswold District.' Batsford, London. 1905.

DURM, J. 'Die Baukunst der Renaissance in Italien' in E. SCHMITT *et al.* (Eds). 'Handbuch der Architektur', Pt II, Vol. 5. Bergsträßer, Stuttgart. 1903.

GEYMÜLLER, H. VON. 'Die Baukunst der Renaissance in Frankreich' in J. DURM *et al.* (Eds). 'Handbuch der Architektur', Pt II, Vol. 6 (2 vols). Bergsträßer, Darmstadt. 1898–1901.

GOTCH, J. A. 'Early Renaissance Architecture in England 1550–1625' (2nd ed.). Batsford, London. 1914.

Idem. 'The Growth of the English House from Early Feudal Times to the Close of the Eighteenth Century' (2nd ed.). Batsford, London. 1928.

HORST, K. 'Die Architektur der deutschen Renaissance.' Propyläen-Kunstgeschichte, supplementary volume. Propyläen Verlag, Berlin. 1928.

INNOCENT, C. F. 'The Development of English Building Construction.' University Press, Cambridge. 1916.

JACKSON, SIR THOMAS G. 'The Renaissance of Roman Architecture' (3 vols). University Press, Cambridge. 1921–3.

KNOOP, D. and JONES, G. P. 'The London Mason in the Seventeenth Century.' University Press, Manchester. 1935.

LLOYD, N. 'A History of English Brickwork (new abr. ed.). Montgomery, London. 1935.

MOXON, J. 'Mechanick Exercises, or the Doctrine of Handy-works.' London. 1677–9.

STRAUB, H. 'A History of Civil Engineering. An Outline from Ancient to Modern Times' (trans. from the German by E. ROCKWELL). Hill, London. 1952.

SUMMERSON, J. N. 'Sir Christopher Wren.' Brief Lives, No. 9. Collins, London. 1953.

Stonemasons at work. From a woodcut of 1568.

## 11

TOWN-PLANNING FROM THE ANCIENT WORLD TO THE RENAISSANCE

MARTIN S. BRIGGS

I. THE EARLIEST PLANNED TOWNS

WHEN men first came to dwell together in units larger than the family in Early Neolithic times, their settlements had no recognizable order, the dwellings of each family being sited merely for individual convenience. Even within the limits of Neolithic culture, however, the gregarious habits of men led to some sort of pattern, so that highly developed and very characteristically arranged villages were ultimately constructed (vol I, figure 197). With the early city states, which developed into the ancient empires (vol I, p 44), the pattern became more definite. It cannot on that account be said that the forms of such cities were foreseen by town-planners. These patterns must be regarded as a spontaneous expression of the culture in which they arose. The ancient empires were well established before any of their cities developed along predesigned lines.

Although 'town-planning' was not so described until about 1904, and although the art and science that it implies did not become recognized as special subjects of study until later, it originated in remote antiquity. As a science, it consists in preparing plans to regulate the lay-out of a town with a view to making good use of the natural advantages of a site, and to securing favourable conditions for housing, traffic, industry, and recreation. As an art, it seeks to create an effect of dignity, harmony, and beauty. Here we are concerned with the former aspect, and how it was practised in the ancient empires. The present study begins with examples from each of the ancient river-valley civilizations.

One of the earliest was the model industrial community at Kahun in Egypt, some 60 miles south of Cairo, which was built in Dynasty XII (c 1900 B.C.) to house workmen erecting a neighbouring pyramid. It was laid out in strictly chess-board fashion on about 20 acres, and contained some 300 dwellings of four or five rooms each. There were also some 10 to 20 larger houses for foremen, and ten mansions for the chief officials. On slightly raised ground was a small public meeting-place. One part of the town was reserved for slaves. The straight streets between the square blocks of houses each had a drain running down the middle, providing the earliest known example of street drainage. The little town was inhabited for only 21 years, while the building of the pyramid was in progress.

We still know all too little of the great civilization of the Indus valley which flourished for about a millennium from 2500 B.C. Its best-known cities are Mohenjo-Daro and Harappa. Their culture is characterized by the extreme

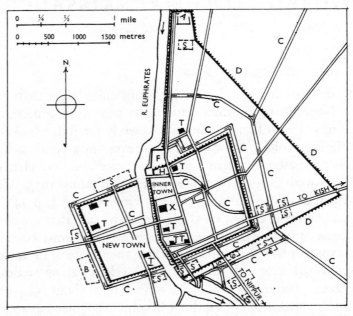

FIGURE 177—*Sketch-plan of ancient Babylon, showing at* A, *Nebuchadrezzar's summer palace; at* B *the burial-ground; at* C, C, C, *canals and moats; at* D, *the outer walls of the city built by Nebuchadrezzar; at* F, *the fortress; at* H, *the 'Hanging Garden'; at* S, *suburban settlements; at* T, *the city temples; at* X, *the 'Tower of Babel'.*

monotony reflected in their city plans. These settlements consisted of a citadel, presumably a royal residence, surrounded by numerous uniform dwellings for workers set out on a rectangular plan with little regard to beauty or dignity (vol I, figure 30).

In the third ancient riverine culture, that of Mesopotamia, we know best the great city of Babylon from the eighth century B.C. onwards (figure 177). It covered a considerable area, and was divided by the river Euphrates. Herodotus, writing in the fifth century B.C., says: 'The city stands on a broad plain and is an exact square. In magnificence no city approaches it. It is surrounded by a broad and deep moat behind which rises a wall of 50 royal cubits wide and 200 high.' He explains how the clay dug from the moat was moulded into bricks for the wall, how these were burnt in kilns, and how the bricks were bedded in bitumen from a source eight miles away, where it was found in lumps in a river-bed. He tells how a layer of wattled reeds was laid in every thirtieth course of brickwork, forming a series of dry-courses. The top of the wall was wide enough for a four-horse chariot to turn. The city being cleft into two parts by 'a broad, swift, deep river', the walls were continued down to the bank on each side. The houses were in rectangles bounded by straight streets closed by brass gates where they reached

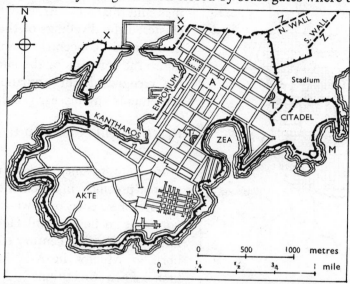

FIGURE 178—*Sketch-plan of the Piraeus, showing the Greek fortifications and the conjectural lay-out of the streets and buildings; A, the agora; M, the munichia (arsenal); T, T, theatres; X, X, X, modern railway-stations; Z, Z, the 'Long Walls' linking the Piraeus with Athens, six miles away. Boat-houses surrounded the zea and the munichia.*

the river-bank. The houses were mostly three or four storeys high [1] (vol I, plate 18).

Much of what Herodotus says of Babylon is confused, but his general description as summarized above has been largely confirmed by excavation (vol I, figure 286). Babylon, like Assur and Nineveh, had a long processional street or avenue. It is thus in contrast to the town of Ur, which, though possessing about 1800 B.C. many spacious houses (vol I, figure 300), yet had narrow, unpaved, winding streets impossible for wheeled traffic.

In these more ancient riverine empires magnificent results were achieved, but it is not yet possible to trace any development of their plans. Some evolution of town-planning can, however, be discerned in the better-explored Mediterranean world. There, every stage has been found from the first irregular settlements of

Early Neolithic farmers to the most grandiose cities of Imperial Rome of the second century A.D., though until the fourth century B.C. the Mediterranean littoral produced no human aggregate much above a city state.

The capital cities of minor states formed naturally by accretion about a central stronghold or acropolis, which developed as a palace, often in relation to a temple, and an *agora* or open space for meetings and markets. Around this nucleus clustered the dwellings of the population in a roughly concentric manner according to the contours of the site. Such was the recognized but unplanned form of settlements in this early cultural phase.

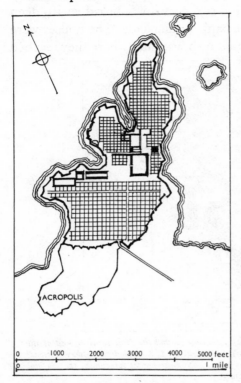

FIGURE 179—*Sketch-plan of Miletos.*

II. THE HELLENIC AND HELLENISTIC WORLD

In spite of magnificent palaces and temple-precincts in the older civilizations, the art or science of town-planning did not come to flower until Hellenic times. Hippodamos (fifth century B.C.), a Greek born at Miletos in Asia Minor, is its first known practitioner. According to Aristotle, who speaks here only of his own Hellenic world, 'Hippodamos introduced the principle of straight wide streets and, first of all architects, made provision for proper grouping of dwelling-houses, and also paid special heed to the combination of the different parts of a town into a harmonious whole, centred round the *agora*' [2]. He laid out the new Greek town of Thurii in southern Italy in 443 B.C. Pericles (*c* 495–429 B.C.) employed him to design the Piraeus, the port of Athens, which he arranged in square blocks so planned that the traffic on the main streets avoided the *agora* (figure 178). This systematic treatment was in contrast to that of Athens, where the splendid groups of buildings on the acropolis and in certain other quarters were very different from the squalid residential districts, planlessly built, with streets narrow, tortuous, unpaved, and unlighted. The *agora*, though surrounded by marble colonnades and fine buildings, served as a market-place and fair-ground, and was normally littered with stalls, shanties, and heaps of goods for sale. These had to be hurriedly removed when a bugle called the citizens to some public gathering. In the narrow streets the shops were open-fronted, as in oriental bazaars today. Similar conditions prevailed in Sparta, chief rival of Athens.

The influence of Hippodamos may, however, be detected in the planning of Selinus in Sicily, which was begun about 408 B.C. There the lay-out is rectangular, in blocks (or *insulae*, as they came to be called in Roman times), regardless of the contours of the site. His share in the replanning of his native town of Miletos (figure 179) after its destruction in 494 B.C. is uncertain, but he must be given some credit for it. Here the *insulae* measured *c* 78 by 96 ft, with some consistency, although the site is irregular in shape. The two main streets were some 25 ft wide, intersecting at right-angles and lined with plain houses of uniform type. Other streets were about 14 ft wide. Several temples occupied the south-east quarter of the city, but they were far older than the gridiron plan of streets and houses, in which no provision was made for monumental vistas.

At Olynthos (figure 180) in Macedonia a new residential suburb was laid out in the same century on a gridiron plan,

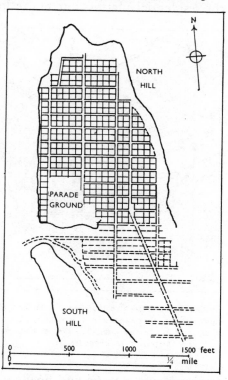

FIGURE 180—*Sketch-plan of Olynthos.*

divided into *insulae* about 283 by 117 ft, with main streets varying in width from about 16 to 23 ft. Each *insula* was bisected by an alley $4\frac{1}{2}$ ft wide, and each semi-block was subdivided into house-lots of some 57 ft square. Each house was planned with a south aspect, and had an internal court paved with cobbles. Most houses were one storey high, with walls of mud-brick on a rubble plinth. A sheltered portico was provided. The main room of the house faced south and was often furnished with a central hearth. There was no provision for sanitation.

The gridiron plan persisted in Hellenistic times. An interesting example is the small town of Priene near Miletos in Asia Minor (figure 181). The site sloped steeply towards the sea from a precipitous rock forming a natural acropolis. Nevertheless, the lay-out was strictly rectangular, with seven main streets running roughly parallel to the slope of the acropolis, crossed by 15 steeply sloping streets. The principal streets were from 18 to 24 ft wide, the others 10 to 15 ft. The whole area was thus divided into *insulae* measuring about 116 by 155 ft, subdivided in the residential quarters into house-lots averaging 58 by 78 ft. Several *insulae* in the central quarter were occupied by public buildings. The total number of dwellings is estimated as between 400 and 500, accommodating a population of about 4000. To keep the plan compact for purposes of defence, no gardens were provided. The normal type of dwelling at Priene, though showing some advance in luxury, resembled that at Olynthos in having a courtyard, a sheltered portico, and one large room. Generally there was a long passage extending through the house from front to back. At Delos, a little later than Priene, many houses had a graceful marble peristyle or colonnade round the courtyard, often with a central water-tank, as in the following Roman period.

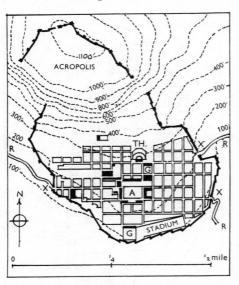

FIGURE 181—*Sketch-plan of Priene, showing at* A, *the agora; at* G, G, *the gymnasia; at* R, R, *roads; at* TH, *the theatre; at* X, *the city gates. The contour-lines show heights in feet above sea-level.*

Better known than these Greek towns is Pompeii, which was destroyed by an earthquake in A.D. 63 and finally submerged in ash from Vesuvius in A.D. 79. The excavation of its buried streets and houses has revealed the complete plan of a Graeco-Roman town, with houses ranging in date from the third century B.C. The lay-out is not strictly rectangular, the *insulae* being slightly trapezoidal, but there was an earlier village on the site, which influenced the plan. The forum measured 500 by 150 ft and contained temples, a basilica, a market, and public latrines. The paving of the main streets was cambered, with gutters at the sides. Pompeii is, however, a more significant example of architecture and decoration than of town-planning. Certain of its houses occupied an entire *insula*, and possessed features not found in their Greek prototypes. Thus planning of the larger dwellings is strictly axial, on either side of a line bisecting the whole block on its longer dimension, namely, from front to back. The famous 'House of the Faun' has a garden surrounded by a colonnade, right across the width of the site, in addition to another peristylar court, and beyond it is the so-called atrium into which the principal rooms faced. Internal gardens were frequent.

Of other Hellenistic cities, one which came to an end in the fourth century A.D. is the frontier fortress-city of Dura Europus, on the Euphrates near Palmyra, which has been well explored. It was on the gridiron plan. The main street was over 36 ft wide; the others were about 20 ft wide, crossed at right-angles by 12 narrow streets.

Ephesus in Asia Minor was monumentally planned around its fine public buildings. It contained large public baths, a theatre, several gymnasia, a stadium, and some imposing open spaces, the great *agora* being about 525 ft square. The long main street, 36 ft wide, was paved with marble, and had deep colonnades on each side, with rows of shops behind them. Colonnaded streets were a characteristic feature, if not an invention, of the Hellenistic period, and the *agora*, a Greek feature, was greatly developed.

Corinth was finely laid out during Graeco-Roman days, with its small but ancient acropolis, and its temple as the focal point. The chief feature of the plan is the enormous double stoa or covered portico, nearly 550 ft long, giving on to a range of 33 shops, each of two chambers. The water-supply of the city was from a perennial source, the poetically famous 'Peirene Spring', in the mountains. It was collected in four parallel reservoirs, discharging through six sluices. Each shop had a square well-pit some 36 ft deep, behind which was a continuous water-channel fed from the spring. It is supposed that the cold running water made the pits cold-storage chambers, as this elaborate system was not applied to dwelling-houses. The date of this remarkable installation is much earlier than the main city plan and is probably fourth or third century B.C.

Antioch was another formally planned Hellenistic city, as was the great port of Alexandria in Egypt, where the chief modern thoroughfare follows the exact line of the old main street running perfectly straight for about four miles. This city was laid out for Alexander the Great by his architect Deinocrates on a sandy strip of land between Lake Mareotis and the Mediterranean. It had a gridiron plan; but of its former glories, which included the celebrated *Pharos* (lighthouse), few traces survive. At Damascus, the 'Street called Straight' was nearly a mile long and was lined with colonnades.

III. ROME AND HER EMPIRE

Town-planning developed rapidly under the Roman Empire, reaching a point of excellence never attained again until the Renaissance (p 285). For various reasons the lay-out of Rome itself (figure 182) did not follow the same evolution as that of other Roman towns, in which the gridiron or chess-board plan was almost universal. It is doubtful whether this very typical Roman plan is due to Greek precedents, or was suggested by ancient Italian towns such as Marzabotto (founded *c* 500 B.C.), or is but the traditional plan of a Roman military

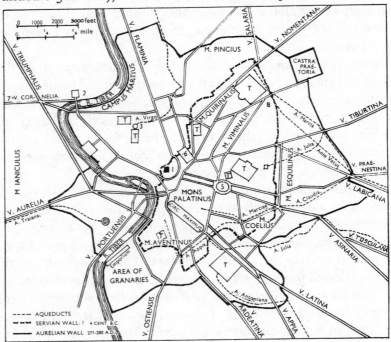

FIGURE 182—*Sketch-plan of Imperial Rome, showing walls, main roads, aqueducts and* thermae (*public baths*). *The area shown is about nine square miles.* (1) *The Capitol;* (2) *the Mausoleum of Hadrian (Castle of S. Angelo);* (3) *the Pantheon;* (4) *the* Forum Romanum; (5) *the Flavian amphitheatre (Colosseum);* (6) *Trajan's Forum;* (7) *the site of St Peter's;* (8) *the site of the modern railway-station;* TT, *thermae.*

camp (figure 183. The Roman camp was square or oblong and divided by two main streets, one running east–west and the other north–south, with the headquarters building close to the point where they crossed). Vitruvius discusses the choice of a site for a new town, giving advice on marshy localities and their drainage, and treats of the planning and erection of fortifications, of suitable aspect for houses, and of the position of public buildings [3].

Roman provincial towns, outside Italy, were either *coloniae*, that is, new settlements for ex-servicemen, or existing towns to which this status had been granted, or *municipia*, the title used for important native towns. In Britain there was only one civil *municipium*—St Albans (Verulamium)—as against four military *muni-*

cipia: Colchester, Lincoln, Gloucester, and York. Of lower rank and much more numerous were the *civitates*, tribal or cantonal capitals. Among the latter were Exeter, Winchester, Caerwent, Canterbury, and Silchester. In general the termination '-chester' in many English place-names stands for Latin *castra*, a camp.

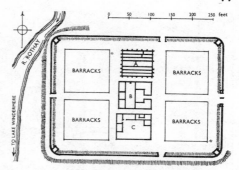

FIGURE 183—*Plan of the Roman fort at Ambleside, Westmorland (second century* A.D.*), showing at* A, *the granary; at* B, *the* principia (*headquarters*); *at* C, *the commandant's residence.*

Typical Roman towns in Britain are Silchester and Verulamium (figures 184, 185). Silchester was originally a tribal capital, retained as an administrative centre by the Romans and rebuilt on chess-board lines, probably within half a century after the Roman conquest. It contained a forum, a basilica, a large inn for travellers, and public baths. The tiny Christian church was built later. The town stood at an important road-junction, where the Bath road from London branched out into three roads leading to Cirencester, Winchester, and Bath. Yet though divided by straight streets into rectangular *insulae*, the actual siting of the houses on these *insulae* was irregular. Presumably Roman surveyors set out the streets but the native inhabitants disposed their dwellings to suit their individual whims. Whereas in most Roman and Greek towns the houses are packed tightly on the *insulae*, at Silchester they were detached, forming an early garden-city. Hence although the area of Silchester (100 acres) was nearly a third of that of Roman London (325 acres), it contained only 80 houses. The colonnaded forum, 310 by 275 ft, contained shops as well as the 'county offices'. The perimeter of the town is irregularly polygonal and the walls were probably sited upon earlier British earthworks.

Verulamium (figure 185), which covered about 200 acres, was the most extensive Roman town in Britain after London (325 acres) and Cirencester (240 acres). It lay on the Watling Street leading from London to Chester. This road entered the city through the fine south gate, which was flanked by projecting towers and provided with arches for two-way wheeled traffic. The massive

FIGURE 184—*Plan of Silchester.*

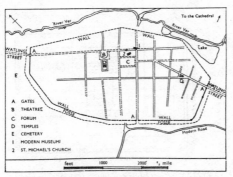

FIGURE 185—*Plan of Verulamium.*

town-walls, strengthened by bastions and a ditch, were of brick and flint and had a total circuit of two miles. They had four gates. Near the forum, which adjoined the intersection of the two main roads, the Watling Street was widened to 35 ft, presumably to provide the equivalent of a car-park. Besides the usual public and domestic buildings of a Roman city, Verulamium possessed the only known Roman theatre in Britain.

Roman London had a population of somewhat under 20 000. Its boundaries are marked by the line of the city wall, much of which is now exposed (figure 186). The landward portion of the wall was probably built between A.D. 60 and 150; the bastions are somewhat later; and the river-wall dates from the latter part of the third century. The wall was of flint, brick, and stone, and its circuit was about three miles. Newgate, the only gate excavated, seems to have had a double carriage-way flanked by two projecting square towers, as at Verulamium (vol II, figure 464). Six main roads converged on London: from Dover (Watling Street), Chichester (Stane Street), Silchester (Akeman Street), Wroxeter and Chester (Watling Street), York (Ermine Street), and Colchester.

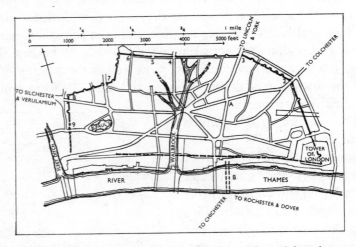

FIGURE 186—*Sketch-plan of Roman London (with the walls in heavy line and the modern streets in thin line),
showing at* A, *the site of the basilica; at* B, *the approximate site of the bridge. The gates are* (1) *Tower Postern;*
(2) *Aldgate;* (3) *Bishopsgate;* (4) *Moorgate;* (5) *Aldermanbury Postern;* (6) *Cripplegate;* (7) *Aldersgate;* (8)
Newgate; (9) *Ludgate.*

The city stood on a plateau of gravel with a maximum height of about 50 ft, bisected by the little stream now known as the Walbrook. The original level of the Roman city was 10 to 30 ft below the present street-level. Timber piles have been found along the bed of the Walbrook. *Londinium* was certainly a flourishing place by A.D. 60. There were two cemeteries within the walls, the larger being close to the site of St Paul's Cathedral. The plan was rectangular, but it cannot be reliably restored owing to lack of adequate evidence. The most important building was the basilica.

Of Roman cities outside Italy very few retain any considerable part of their

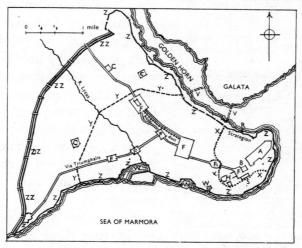

FIGURE 187—*Sketch-plan of Byzantium (Istanbul), showing at A, the acropolis; at B, S. Sophia; at C, C, C, the principal cisterns; at F, F, F, the fora; at H, the hippodrome; at S, the senatus; at R, the modern railway-station; at X, X, X, the land walls of the ancient city and at Y, Y, Y, those built by Constantine; at Z, Z, Z, other fortifications; at W, W, W, ancient harbours; at V, V, modern bridges.*

original plan, though some streets in Treves, Cologne, and perhaps Belgrade follow the old lines. The walls of Treves, founded A.D. 2, enclosed 704 acres, so that it was thus more than twice as large as Roman London and 23 times as large as Timgad (below). Constantinople was rebuilt by Constantine in 330 on the site of the old town of Byzantium (figure 187). Its area was extended by a succession of walls in 413, 447, and later. The latest walls were 100 ft high, and had many lofty towers. Its internal planning was formal but not strictly rectangular, owing to the contours, which formed, as at Rome, seven small hills. These were admirable for the placing of the principal buildings. The main streets were arcaded or colonnaded, and were punctuated by at least six splendid *fora*. The famous hippodrome accommodated 100 000 spectators. The system of water-supply was notable; drawn from various distant streams and springs, the water was conveyed by aqueducts that ran underground except across valleys. It was stored in open reservoirs or in covered cisterns within the city. Some of the latter are still in use; one has a capacity of 6 500 000 cu ft. The roof of another is supported by 224 columns with triple shafts.

Timgad, in Algeria, founded by Trajan in A.D. 100 as a colony for ex-soldiers, has been especially well excavated and shows the gridiron plan in its strictest form (figure 188). It covers only 30 acres, yet is ·divided into 132 *insulae*, each some 75 ft square; nearly 20 of them, in some cases combined together, were occupied by public buildings. The remainder were occupied by houses, of which there were about 400. The principal streets were paved and colonnaded. Near the forum were the basilica, a theatre for 3500 spectators, and public baths. The general effect of this gridiron layout must have been extremely monotonous.

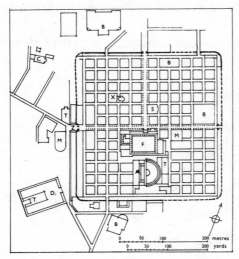

FIGURE 188—*Sketch-plan of Timgad showing at* A, *the theatre; at* B, B, *the* thermae; *at* C, C, *churches; at* D, *the capitol; at* F, *the forum; at* M, M, *market-places; at* S, *the* schola; *at* T, T, *the temples; at* X, *the baptistery; at* Z, *a triumphal arch.*

Palmyra, in Syria, was mostly laid out in the later third century A.D. on the site of an older town, retaining some of the existing buildings. Its chief feature is the magnificent central roadway 3500 ft long and 37 ft wide, flanked on each side by colonnades 16 ft wide. There are ruins of other notable cities of this period in Syria and Jordan—for example, Jerash and Bosra.

In Italy, Aosta, founded as a military colony in 25 B.C., and Turin (figure 194), preserve the original Roman chess-board plan in their older quarters, as do Lucca and Florence to a less degree. Ostia presents some special aspects (figure 189). Lying at the mouth of the Tiber, 15 miles from Rome, it had become the port of Rome, as well as a naval base, by the third century B.C. The original town was planned on conventional military lines. The main road from Rome ran parallel to the river. As the town grew, it was paved with lava and colonnaded. There were, as usual, four gates in the walls, and public buildings round the forum near the centre. The distinctive features of Ostia are the warehouses for grain and other produce, and the large number of commercial offices that occupy many of its *insulae*. Some 70 commercial firms and ship-owners, from all parts of the then known world, had representatives in these offices. Other *insulae* are occupied by shops over which rose blocks of tenements or self-contained flats, some of them several storeys high (vol II, plate 29 A). Here most of the people lived, in contrast to the comparatively low dwellings in the Greek and Roman towns described hitherto. In this respect Ostia resembled Rome, and it contains far more substantial remains of such dwellings than Rome. Its maximum population was about 45 000.

Despite the splendour of its public buildings and its imperial palaces, Rome

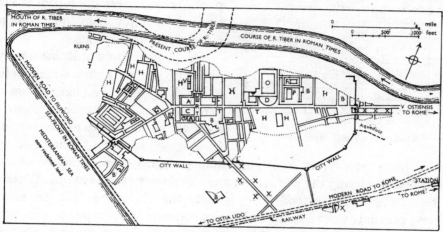

FIGURE 189—*Sketch-plan of Roman Ostia*. (A) *Basilica;* (B) thermae; (C) curia; (D) theatre; (F) firemen's barracks; (G) Christian basilica; (H) warehouses; (J) Porta Romana; (L) Porta Laurentina; (M) Porta Marina (sea-gate); (O) commercial offices; (P) gymnasium; (R) forum; (S) school; (T,T) temples; (V) market-places; (X) tombs.

was never systematically planned (figure 182). Its population in the second century A.D. was between $1\frac{1}{4}$ and $1\frac{1}{2}$ millions, and its area in the following century was over 3000 acres. It had grown gradually, as the tiny settlement near the ford across the Tiber spread over the seven hills that became famous in history. Thus, though the lay-out of the imperial *fora* and several other parts of the city is a model for posterity, the plan of the ancient city as a whole has little significance for town-planning. As at Athens, most of the area within the lofty city walls was covered with a jumble of mean streets and alleys, with ramshackle tenements many storeys high.

During the tremendous expansion of the city, the flat marshy land by the river was gradually drained and its streams were enclosed in sewers, of which the *cloaca maxima* still survives. A series of great roads, constructed at an early date, converged upon the city, and the line of some of them was prolonged within the walls (figure 189).

The lavish provision of public baths and other amenities partially mitigated the lack of sanitary arrangements in the tenements, which had no heating-apparatus, no facilities for cooking, and no chimneys. Some of the larger private houses had cesspools. On some of the roads leading out of Rome there were public conveniences at which a small charge was made. At Timgad, the public conveniences near the forum had 20 carved stone seats, each flanked by graceful dolphins, and a neighbouring fountain flushed out the drains. There were also public latrines near the forum at Ostia, entered by a revolving door and provided with marble seats.

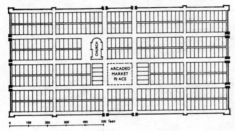

FIGURE 190—*Plan of Monpazier.*

The water-supply of Rome was magnificent (vol II, figure 614). Refuse-disposal appears to have been the perquisite of rag-and-bone men, and there are no references to any municipal scavenging service. Cemeteries were excluded from the city, as from most Roman towns—hence the line of handsome tombs bordering the *Via Appia*, and the numerous catacombs. When the city boundaries were extended to include the Esquiline Hill, an existing cemetery, previously outside the walls, was converted into a public garden and soon became a fashionable resort.

The streets of Rome were unlighted, though there seems to have been a system of communal or municipal lighting at Antioch and Ephesus. The danger of fire in the crowded streets was met, to some extent, by public fire-brigades in continuous attendance at seven fire-stations; but many wealthy private families also maintained private fire-brigades of their own slaves.

IV. THE MIDDLE AGES

Town-planning in its proper sense was largely forgotten or ignored during the thousand years from the fall of Rome to the Renaissance. The growth of towns was fortuitous and spontaneous, not foreseen or regulated. They grew from small villages, or, in some cases, from Roman foundations. Often they clustered round a great church or on the skirts of a fortress.

The need for defence encouraged the crowding of houses and shops within the constricting walls, so that the streets were always narrow; even the market-place was generally congested, and there was no room for gardens. Building by-laws hardly existed. Medieval sanitation is discussed elsewhere (vol II, chs 14, 19).

Despite all this there are some outstanding examples of deliberately planned medieval towns in England and France. The French kings in the thirteenth century established a series of fortified towns (*bastides*) in the newly conquered territory of Languedoc, and their example was followed by leading nobles. Edward I

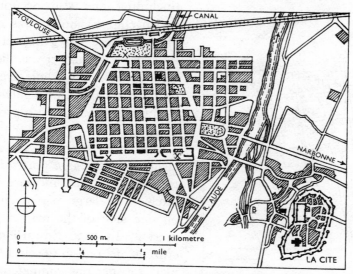

FIGURE 191—*Plan of Carcassonne, the pentagonal shape of the* Ville Basse *being clearly distinguishable. The medieval churches are shown black.* (A) *Railway-station;* (B) Moulin du Roi; (x, x) *remains of medieval fortifications.*

of England (1272–1307), who had received the Duchy of Gascony, laid out some fifty towns in all. Of these, Monpazier in Dordogne (figure 190) is typical. Its plan is monotonously rectangular, the only variations in its oblong housing-units being the spaces for the church and the arcaded market-place, where there was a well. There were ten gates in the enclosing wall. On two sides will be noticed the space within the walls (*pomerium*), represented by streets known as London Wall in London and Back of the Walls at Southampton. Normally this was continued round all the circuit to allow the rapid movement of a garrison. Behind each house in Monpazier was a garden. Another notable example of a French *bastide* is the Lower Town (*La Ville Basse*) at Carcassonne, laid out on chess-board lines by Louis·IX in 1247 to accommodate the inhabitants of the old town which had clustered around the great fortress still known as *La Cité*, their houses having been demolished in order to render the fortress impregnable (figure 191).

In Britain, Edward I laid out, among other towns, Kingston-upon-Hull, Caernarvon, Conway, and Flint. The most interesting is the little town of Winchelsea in Sussex, replacing an older town subject to inundations from the sea. In 1281 he appointed three commissioners to lay out a new town; one of them had helped to plan his French fortified towns. Part of this scheme still remains (figure 192). Originally it comprised 39 square blocks or *insulae*

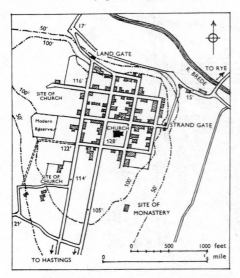

FIGURE 192—*Sketch-plan of Winchelsea. The contour-lines show heights in feet above sea-level.*

(including one still occupied by the parish church), but it was never completed. There was a market-place, and the south-east quarter was allotted to the Grey Friars. The whole area was surrounded by a wall with gate-towers, the landward side being also protected by a moat.

Hull was planned in chess-board fashion in 1293 as a port for York, surrounded on the landward side by a ditch. The large parish church stood on one side of the market-place, as at present. In 1296 Edward ordered the citizens of London to select 'four skilful men . . . persons competent to lay out the plans for towns . . . the most able and clever and those who know best how to devise, order and array a new town' to replan Berwick-on-Tweed, which he had just captured and burnt. Twenty-three other cities were ordered to furnish two planners each, making fifty in all. This remarkable commission is often quoted as evidence of the extensive practice of town-planning in England in the thirteenth century: it would be more prudent to conclude from it merely that the king hoped to enlist the help of fifty competent land-surveyors by his nation-wide appeal.

Germany contains a number of picturesque medieval towns, many of which suffered severely during the 1939–45 war. Many of them (such as Rothenburg ob der Tauber, one of the most beautiful and famous) were mere accidental accretions of houses and other buildings in narrow and tortuous streets, usually grouped around a castle or a great church; others were planned solely with a view to defence; others again, such as Cologne, Coblenz, and Regensburg, developed from a Roman rectangular nucleus. In eastern Germany, however, several new towns were systematically founded and definitely planned during the thirteenth century. A typical example is Neubrandenburg (about 85 miles north of Berlin), which was annexed to Mecklenburg in the fourteenth century. This town was definitely planned in 1248 by the Margrave of Brandenburg on a rectilinear system (figure 193), and laid out in approximately equal blocks, one whole block being now occupied by the Marienkirche, another (the market-place) by the eighteenth-century Town Hall and the Duke's own palace, which was erected in 1774–85. Four remarkable brick gate-towers break the circuit of the walls; and indeed Neubrandenburg possesses in these towers and in its churches some of the finest examples of medieval brick architecture in Germany.

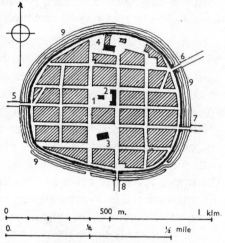

FIGURE 193—*Sketch-plan of Neubrandenburg (with medieval walls drawn in thick line), showing* (1) *the* Rathaus; (2) *the palace;* (3) *the* Marienkirche; (4) *the* Johanneskirche; (5, 6, 7, 8) *gate-towers;* (9) *a dry moat.*

V. THE RENAISSANCE: ITALY

Because the Renaissance originated in Italy, where it made itself felt in architecture during the first half of the fifteenth century, the beginnings of Renaissance town-planning are naturally to be found there too. On the one hand are a number of architects and other writers who developed theories of ideal town-planning in sundry treatises and projects; and on the other is the endeavour to apply such theories in practical examples. Among the theorists, the most notable is that versatile genius Leonardo da Vinci (1452–1519). During his sojourn in Milan from 1481 to 1499 he not only carried out works of military engineering, but made some theoretical study of town-planning. In the 5000 pages of his notebooks there are several memoranda on the subject written between 1483 and 1518.

Some of the notes refer to its aesthetic aspects, treating, for example, 'of cities and other buildings seen in the evening or morning in the mist'; 'of shadows and light on cities'; 'of the smoke of cities'. Others deal with more practical matters, such as 'how to guard against the rush of rivers so that cities may not be struck by them'. One note anticipates a sound rule of modern town-planning: 'let the street be as wide as the universal height of the houses'; another anticipates the modern principle of dispersing the population of overcrowded cities into satellite towns. This memorandum is in the form of an exhortation addressed to Ludovico

Sforza, the ruler of Milan, after the disastrous plagues of 1484–5 in that city, and deserves quotation:

There will be eternal fame also for the inhabitants of that city built and enlarged by him [the ruler]. . . . There will be ten cities, five thousand houses with thirty thousand inhabitants, and you will separate the great congregation of people who herd together like goats one on top of another, filling every place with foul odour and sowing seeds of pestilence and death. And the city will gain beauty worthy of its name, and it will be useful to you by reason of its revenues, and the eternal fame of its enlargement [4].

Even more striking is his scheme for the reconstruction of a town with traffic on two levels. The high-level streets are for pedestrians, the lower for vehicles. The former are approached by viaducts at the entrances to the town. Flights of steps connect the two levels at frequent intervals. All streets are arcaded, the arcades on the lower level being lighted through openings on the upper level.

Many of Leonardo's notes refer to canals and other waterways inside towns, one sketch showing canals in the place of low-level streets, allowing goods to be delivered from boats to the basement storeys of houses normally entered from the upper level. He gives much attention to irrigation, and is believed to have invented mitred lock-gates (figure 282). 'Nothing is to be thrown into the canals, and every barge is to be obliged to carry away so much mud from the canal, and this is afterwards to be thrown on the bank' [5].

Leonardo was employed on irrigation work at Vigevano in 1494, but there seems to be no evidence that he ever actually planned a town.

About 1500 the Italian architect Francesco di Giorgio Martini published a series of curious ideal designs, all for polygonal fortified towns with streets radiating from a central square to the angles of the polygon. In these schemes, he was more concerned to produce a geometrical pattern of streets than convenient housing-lots. Other ideal designs for heavily fortified polygonal towns with bastions were published by Buonaiuto Lorini at Venice (1592), and by Vincenzo Scamozzi, also at Venice (1615). More interesting than any of these, because it was actually carried out and may still be seen, is the town of Palma Nuova (in Venetia, between Udine and Aquileia), designed in 1593 by Giulio Savorgnan. This small town, now housing between 3000 and 4000 people, had the shape of a nine-pointed star, which it still largely retains.

Turin is an interesting example of a once strongly fortified city deriving from a Roman nucleus (*Augusta Taurinorum*), planned on gridiron lines within a rectangular enclosing wall 2526 by 2320 ft. Even at the end of the sixteenth century, its walls and pattern survived unchanged, save for the addition of bastions and a moat. Three major extensions during the seventeenth century spread its boundaries considerably beyond the Roman nucleus, which the great modern city still incorporates in its plan along with the seventeenth-century additions. The elaborate fortifications have long since been replaced by boulevards and streets (figure 194).

Livorno (Leghorn) is an interesting example of a large city with a polygonal fortified town of the sixteenth century as its nucleus, much of the original pattern of streets and the surrounding moat or canal still surviving.

Rome itself, the most notable example of Renaissance and baroque town-

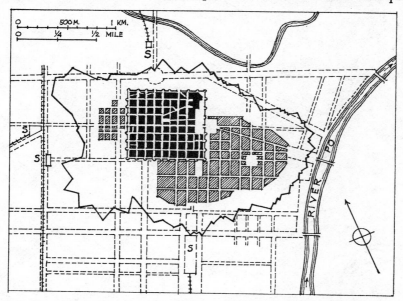

FIGURE 194—*Plan of central Turin, showing the Roman city* (solid black); *the area built up by* c *1700* (shaded); *the fortifications at the same date* (black line); *and the principal streets laid out since 1700* (dotted lines). (s, s) *Railway-stations.*

planning in Italy, and perhaps in the whole world, was completely transformed during this period. During the Middle Ages almost all the splendour of the former capital of the Roman world had departed. The population, estimated to have been between $1\frac{1}{4}$ and $1\frac{1}{2}$ millions in the second century A.D., had sunk to 17 000 while the Popes were resident at Avignon (1309–77). At that period, three-quarters of the area inside the walls was occupied by gardens. Sheep were grazing in the *Forum Romanum* and in the valley between the Palatine and Aventine hills. The people lived mostly in the lower quarters, where the numerous battlemented towers of the nobles rose above crowded hovels and the neglected ruins of antiquity.

Pope Paul III (1447–64) began the remodelling of the city by straightening the Corso (the ancient *Via Flaminia*) from the church of San Marco to the Arch of Marcus Aurelius, afterwards replaced by the Porta del Popolo. Several leading architects—Bramante, Peruzzi, Sangallo—started to study the historical monuments, and Flavio Biondo wrote his book *Roma Instaurata* in 1444–6. Sixtus IV

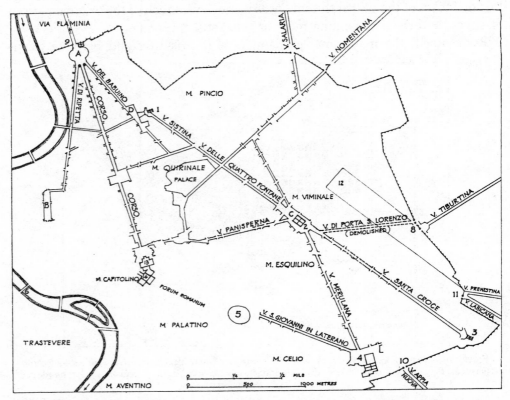

FIGURE 195—*Sketch-plan of central Rome showing streets and buildings mentioned.* (1) *Trinità dei Monti;* (2) *S. Maria Maggiore;* (3) *S. Croce in Gerusalemme;* (4) *S. Giovanni in Laterano;* (5) *Colosseum;* (6) *Ponte Sisto;* (7) *Porta Pia;* (8) *Porta S. Lorenzo;* (9) *Porta del Popolo;* (10) *Porta S. Giovanni;* (11) *Porta Maggiore;* (12) *modern railway-station;* (13) *Vittorio Emmanuele Monument;* (14) *Michelangelo's Piazza,* etc. (A) *Piazza del Popolo;* (B) *Piazza Navona;* (C) *Piazza Esquilina;* (D) *Piazza di Spagna.*

(1471–84) caused a master-plan of the city to be prepared, and in 1473 built the Ponte Sisto across the Tiber. Alexander VI (1493–1503) replanned the Borgo on the east bank. Julius II (1503–13) laid out the *Via Giulia*. Leo X (1513–21) opened the *Via Leonina*, now the Via di Ripetta (figure 195).

The sack of Rome by the French in 1527 interrupted this work of restoration, which was resumed under Paul IV (1555–9) and Pius IV (1559–66). At this period, the Coelian, Viminal, Esquiline, and Quirinal hills were still completely uninhabited. The principal streets converged on the Ponte Sant' Angelo. The disposition of streets and houses was largely determined by the ancient aqueducts. In 1540 Michelangelo planned the magnificent approach to the Capitol.

Sixtus V (Felice Peretti, 1585–90), with Domenico Fontana as his architect, effected more than any of his predecessors. His major achievement was the lay-out of the streets converging on the great basilicas of Santa Maria Maggiore and St John Lateran, namely the *Vie Sistina, Felice, delle Quattro Fontane*, and *di Porta San Lorenzo*. Besides these, he laid out the Lateran and Esquiline piazzas; erected the Lateran Palace; extended the Vatican Palace; and raised obelisks in four of the chief piazzas of the city. Under his rule, the population rose from 45 000 to 100 000, after having previously fallen from 90 000 early in the century to 30 000 after the sack of Rome in 1527.

Sixtus V showed scant respect for historical monuments. He destroyed the *Septizonium* of Severus, but was persuaded to abandon the demolition of the Arco del Velabro and the tomb of Cecilia Metella. His architect Fontana was also

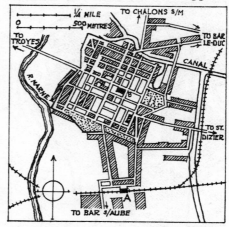

FIGURE 196—*Vitry-le-François. Though the fortifications were demolished in 1891, the original formal lay-out of the town within the line of the polygonal ramparts is clearly seen.* (A) *Railway-station;* (B) *church.*

most successful in planning the Via del Babuino to balance, on the east of the Corso, the Via di Ripetta which entered the Piazza del Popolo on the west of the Corso, so that a traveller approaching Rome from the north on the old *Via Flaminia* was faced by the three converging streets, the Corso being in the middle and continuing the line of the *Via Flaminia*. One of the two churches that stand symmetrically on either side of this entrance to the Corso had been rebuilt in 1472–7, the other (as we now see it) is a work of the seventeenth century. The whole effect of this lay-out of the Piazza del Popolo is most impressive. The popes of the baroque period from Paul V to Alexander VII (1605–67) were also actively engaged in town-planning as a part of their reconstruction of the Papal City. This phase was dominated by the genius of the architect Lorenzo Bernini, whose work included the great colonnaded piazza of St Peter's and the Piazze Navona, Colonna, and Barberini. Rome contains a number of his graceful fountains as well as many of his larger buildings.

VI. THE RENAISSANCE: FRANCE

In France a few towns retain the formal rectangular plan on which they were laid out during this period, especially Vitry-le-François, Charleville, Henrichemont, and Richelieu. Much the earliest is Vitry-le-François (Marne), about 20 miles south of Châlons (figure 196). It was originally planned in 1545 by the Bolognese engineer Ieronimo Marino for François I, to replace the neighbouring town of Vitry-en-Perthois, which had been burnt down by Charles V. Although the ramparts were levelled in 1891 and the adjoining marshes drained, the regular lines of the plan of the town can easily be traced. It is obviously derived from Italian models, with the *place d'armes* as the central feature.[1]

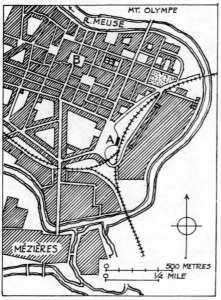

FIGURE 197—*Plan of Charleville, showing formal seventeenth-century lay-out of the old town about the Place Ducale* (B). (A) *Railway-station.*

Meanwhile, Bernard Palissy (1510–90), a potter by trade, who wrote books on gardening and other subjects, devoted some attention to town-planning, advocating 'square and regular planning in every part of the city'. Perret de Chambéry was another writer who concerned himself with the design of imaginary and ideal towns.

The fruits of French and Italian theorizing on this subject are to be seen in three towns laid out during the first third of the seventeenth century. Charleville (Ardennes), a town close to the modern Belgian frontier, derives its name from Charles of Gonzaga, Duke of Mantua and Nevers and Governor of Champagne, who founded it in 1606 (figure 197). It has suffered in many wars. The old fortress on Mont-Olympe across the Meuse was demolished by Louis XIV. The lay-out of the town is strictly formal, the Place Ducale forming the central feature. This is a handsome square surrounded by old houses, with arcades beneath their front walls.

Almost contemporary with Charleville are three of the defensive gateways of Nancy: the Portes de la Craffe (1598), St-Georges, and St-Nicolas; but since much of the fine plan of this city, prepared by an Italian in 1588, was not

---

[1] Vitry-le-François was largely destroyed in the war of 1939–45. It has now been rebuilt on the old plan.

executed until the eighteenth century, a description of it is omitted here. The small town of Henrichemont, about 20 miles north-west of Bourges (Cher) was founded by Sully in 1609. Its lay-out is a combination of the radiating with the rectangular plan.

The model town of Richelieu (Indre-et-Loire), founded by the famous cardinal, was designed by the architect Jacques Lemercier (1585–1654) and laid out between 1631 and 1638 as an appendage to the magnificent château which the cardinal had begun to build in 1620 when he was only 35 years of age. The marshy site was drained by canalizing the little river Mable (figure 198) and diverting it to serve moats surrounding the château and the town. Two thousand men were employed to build the château, which was completed in 1635. Since its decay in the eighteenth century only a single pavilion, known as the *Dôme*, and two small isolated farm-buildings remain, with the foundations of the great mansion and its surrounding moat. John Evelyn recorded his impressions of the château and the adjoining model town, of which he wrote:

The Towne is built in a low, marshy-ground, having a small river cutt by hand, very even and straite, capable of bringing up a small vessell. It consists of one onely considerable streete, the houses on both sides (as indeede they are throughout the towne), built most exactly uniforme, after a modern handsome designe. It has a large goodly Markethouse and Place, opposite to which [is] the Church built all of free-stone. . . . It being onely the name of the place, and an old house there standing, & belonging to his ancestors, which allurd him to build. This pretty town is also handsomely wall'd about & moated, with a kind of slight fortification, two fayre-gates & drawbridges. Before the gate towards the Palace is a most spacious circle, where the faire is annualy kept [6].

Evelyn's words are still faithfully descriptive of the town as it stands today, a rare and even unique example of Renaissance town-planning. The twenty-eight principal houses in its Grande Rue were earmarked from the outset for the chief officials of the cardinal's immense retinue, and some of the lesser dwellings were intended to accommodate others of his household, but the town was never meant to be restricted to his own employees, and indeed he offered inducements to attract others there. The citizens were excused all taxes until 100 houses had been built, and thereafter were granted a special remission; but the freeholders had to use Lemercier's standard designs, and buildings had to be completed within a stipulated period. It has been estimated that the maximum population in the seventeenth century must have been 5000 to 6000; it is now about 1800.

The Grande Rue, running north and south and crossed by transverse streets, is interrupted by the Place du Marché and the Place des Réligieuses, as originally planned. The whole town measures about 600 by 400 yds. It is surrounded by a

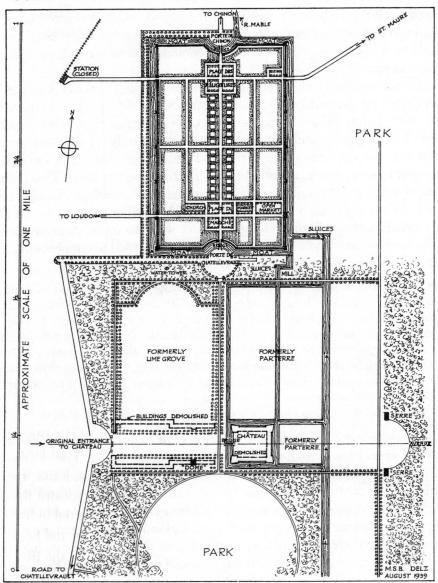

FIGURE 198—*Sketch-plan of the town and château of Richelieu.*

high stone wall with several gateways, by a moat about 70 ft wide and originally
10 ft deep (now filled in), and by enclosing avenues, of which about half remain.
The width of the Grande Rue is about 37 ft, that of the other streets 20 ft or
less. The church stands unaltered. The market-hall, opposite the church, is a

fine example of carpentry, the main posts of the nave (which is about 28 ft wide) measuring 15 by 12 in. The principal houses in the Grande Rue stand almost unchanged, save for the insertion of a shop-front here and there. They are of brickwork, now covered with stucco, with fine limestone dressings. The frontage of each is about 70 ft, the depth from front to back about 30 ft, with a courtyard in the rear and a spacious walled garden behind it.

A good deal of town-planning and town-improvement was also carried out in Paris during the seventeenth century. Henri IV (1589–1610) was the first European ruler since Roman days to undertake building operations on a large scale for political and social reasons, including the provision of employment. Paris in 1600 was in a deplorable state—ill planned, overcrowded, and insanitary. It could boast of but two bridges across the Seine, and five insignificant squares. In 1600, and again in 1608, Henri issued ordinances for the widening, alignment, and paving of streets, forbidding overhanging storeys. In 1600, the triangular Place Dauphine was laid out with middle-class houses and shops, incorporating two islets in the site. In 1604 the unfinished Pont Neuf was completed, and the Place du Pont Neuf followed soon afterwards. The charming Place Royale, now the Place des Vosges, still remains—a square garden surrounded by aristocratic houses with a continuous arcade beneath their façades. A splendid scheme for a Porte and Place de France on the north of the city [7] was prepared under the king's personal supervision, but was abandoned after his death.

His successor, Louis XIII, in 1635 laid out the Île-Saint-Louis, hitherto occupied by meadows and gardens. The scheme consisted of fine houses and streets arranged on a gridiron pattern. Under Louis XIV, the Portes St-Denis (1672) and St-Martin (1674) were erected, the circular Place des Victoires (1684–6) and the Place Louis-le-Grand, now the Place Vendôme, were laid out to the glory of the king, and the Quai Malaquais (1670) was constructed. In 1676, Louis ordered the city architect, Pierre Bullet (1639–1716), to prepare a complete plan of Paris, showing not only existing streets and buildings, but also new works in progress or projected.

VII. THE BUILDING OF AMSTERDAM

One of the most remarkable examples of historical town-planning is the inner, and older, part of the city of Amsterdam (figure 199). The name explains the situation and origin of the city, for it recalls the construction of a castle and a dam on the little river Amstel in 1204, at the point where that stream flows into the Ij or Y, an inlet of the Zuider Zee. At the same time a sea-dike was built to prevent inundation from the Ij. The first houses were erected east of the Amstel, then others followed on the west bank. The earliest defensive ditches (*Voorburgwallen*) were dug outside the new settlement in 1342 and were connected with the Amstel and the Ij by sluices. The western ditch was filled in the nineteenth century, but the street which has replaced it is still called the Nieuwezijde Voorburgwal. A second line of ditches about 60 yd outside the *Voorburgwallen*, and known as the Singel (girdle), was dug in 1383, and was similarly controlled by sluices. Houses were then erected along the canals, on timber piles about 40 ft long. Further extensions followed in 1442, monasteries were established, ship-building and other industries appeared, and in 1481–2 the town was fortified with towers for the first time. One of these, the Schreijerstoren, remains.

In 1593 a more elaborate system of bastions was constructed, and a barrage was erected in the Ij to protect merchant-shipping. In 1610 began the remarkable and ambitious scheme of concentric extension which, in quadrupling the habitable area, produced Amsterdam's unique plan. The new bastions completed in 1593 were demolished, a new canal (Heerengracht) replaced them, and two more canals (Keizersgracht and Prinsengracht) were dug parallel to it. A fourth canal (Singelgracht, 1658, $6\frac{1}{2}$ miles long) surrounded these three, with a new line of bastions. Small radial canals crossing the main concentric canals created a spider's-web pattern. The planning of the outermost ring, between the Singelgracht and the Prinsengracht, was not, however, strictly radial. Except for an area reserved for artisan dwellings on the west, all the canals were lined with trees and with the handsome houses of the wealthier people. A park, the Plantage (since built over), was provided on the north-east; but, except for this public open space, the whole area was filled with houses by 1667. The building of houses was left to private enterprise, though the general lay-out and the canal-construction were done by the municipality. During the seventeenth century, part of the 'Dam' was filled in, and the town hall (now the royal palace) was erected on the site in 1648–55, based on a foundation of 13 659 piles. With the possible exception of Venice, and some modern cities of the east, Amsterdam must surely be built on one of the worst sites in the world. Beneath a top layer of mud, about 50 ft thick, is a belt of sand 10 ft thick, into which the long oak piles had to be driven. The canals divide the old town into nearly 100 islands, crossed by about 300 bridges.

The outer fortifications of Amsterdam were demolished in the third quarter of the nineteenth century, and the ground along the Singelgracht was laid out with gardens. Some of the later alterations to the city are shown in dotted lines on figure 199. Its population had grown from an estimated 50 000 in 1600 to about a quarter of a million in 1859 (nearly all of whom were contained within the fortifications), and numbers over 860 000 at the present day, spread over a much wider area.

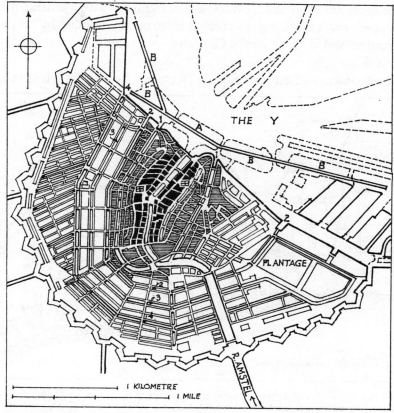

FIGURE 199—*Amsterdam c 1670, showing the stages of the city's growth. The area in black represents the city c 1400; the area horizontally shaded was built between 1400 and 1600; the remaining streets within the fortifications were built between 1600 and 1670 according to a plan prepared in 1612. (B) Breakwater or mole, since demolished. Canals: (1) Singel; (2) Heerengracht; (3) Keizersgracht; (4) Prinsengracht. The dotted line shows the modern foreshore, docks, etc. (A) Central railway-station.*

VIII. THE PLANNING OF LONDON AFTER THE GREAT FIRE

Before the Great Fire of London in 1666 there is little evidence of any conscious town-planning in England. Repeated efforts were indeed made by Elizabeth I and James I to restrict the uncontrolled spread of London beyond the old city walls, and some ordinances were made to regulate the construction of buildings; but the first attempts at formal town-planning were due to the architect Inigo Jones, who had studied in Italy (p 256). In 1618 he laid out Lincoln's Inn Fields with a large open square surrounded by handsome houses, some of which were completed in 1638–9. Two sides of the square were finished by 1641, a third side by 1659, and the fourth a few years later. In 1631 he began to lay out Covent Garden and adjoining streets for the Duke of Bedford, with a central open space, in which sheds for a market were erected in 1632, surrounded by houses standing on arcades, and with St Paul's Church (since rebuilt in its original form) as a principal feature.

The development of Leicester Square (formerly Leicester Fields) began when

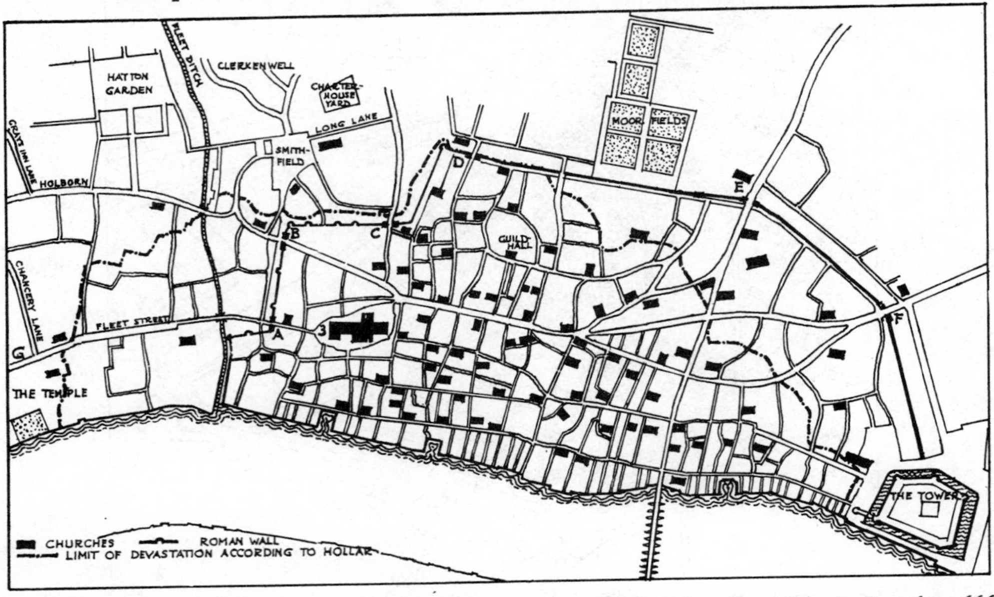

FIGURE 200—*Plan of the City of London, prepared from a survey of the ruins after the fire in December 1666 by order of the City authorities.* (A) *Ludgate;* (B) *Newgate;* (C) *Aldersgate;* (D) *Cripplegate;* (E) *Bishopsgate;* (F) *Aldgate;* (G) *Temple Bar;* (3) *St Paul's Cathedral.*

the Earl of Leicester built his own houses about 1631, but the remainder of the scheme was not completed until after the Restoration in 1660. Bloomsbury Square and St James's Square were both begun in or about 1664. Meanwhile, schemes for building an embankment or quay along the Thames and for embanking the Fleet Ditch had been discussed; while John Evelyn, after his travels abroad, urged the need for replanning London in his treatise on smoke abatement, *Fumifugium* (1661). This was the position when the Great Fire, which broke out on 2 September 1666 and raged for five or six days, destroyed the greater part of the City of London, and opened a new chapter in the history of English town-planning by affording an opportunity such as had never occurred before (figure 200).

The story of the course and results of the Fire may be read in the narratives of Evelyn and Pepys; the ruins were still smouldering when the former virtuoso, with amazing enterprise, submitted to Charles II a plan for rebuilding based upon a hurried personal survey of the City. His diary for 13 September 1666 describes an interview with the king in 'the Queen's bedchamber, her Majesty and the Duke [of York] onely being present', when Evelyn explained his plan to them. 'But Dr Wren had got the start of me. Both of us did coincide so frequently, that his Majestie was not displeas'd with it, & it caused divers alterations; and

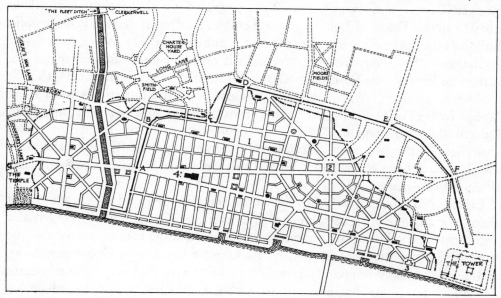

FIGURE 201—*Wren's plan for the rebuilding of the City of London after the Great Fire, hastily prepared on the basis of a rough survey.* (A) *Ludgate;* (B) *Newgate;* (C) *Aldersgate;* (D) *Cripplegate;* (E) *Bishopsgate;* (F) *Aldgate;* (G) *Temple Bar;* (1) *Guildhall;* (2) *Royal Exchange;* (3) *Customs House;* (4) *St Paul's Cathedral.*

truly there was never a more glorious Phoenix upon earth, if it do at last emerge out of these cinders, & as the design is layd, with the present fervour of the undertakers.'

At that time, Wren's career as an architect was only two or three years old, but he had already been consulted about the restoration of Old St Paul's, on the strength of his great scientific attainments. The king's first action after the interview on 13 September was to appoint three Crown commissioners (Wren among them) to organize the rebuilding of London in collaboration with three representatives of the City, including Robert Hooke and Peter Mills. Hooke (p 257) also submitted a plan for rebuilding, as did Mills (whose plan has been lost) and two other persons, one of whom furnished two alternative schemes. Of seven plans in all, six have survived, and of these the designs of Wren and Evelyn are the most skilful as well as the best known (figure 201).

As Evelyn observed, there were many points of similarity between his plan and Wren's. Both showed embankments on either side of a widened and straightened Fleet River. Both treated St Paul's Cathedral (the medieval building) as a focal point at the end of converging street vistas. Both provided a great piazza in Fleet Street half-way between Fleet Bridge (on the site of the modern Ludgate Circus) and Temple Bar. Wren proposed a wide continuous riverside quay from the Tower of London to the Temple; Evelyn offered a range of public buildings facing the river, with a street behind them. He moved the Royal Exchange to the river, whereas Wren left it on its original site and made it a feature of his lay-out. Both plans showed a number of diagonal streets, though differently arranged. Wren's scheme included wide straight streets from Fleet Bridge by way of St Paul's to Aldgate, from St Paul's to Tower Hill, and from Queenhithe to Moorgate. Both designs took account of the numerous parish churches. Of the two plans, Wren's was the more practical, Evelyn's the more idealistic and geometrical; but both displayed some acquaintance with continental town-planning principles.

Either plan would have vastly benefited the City of London, yet neither of them, nor any one of those submitted, was ever carried out. There were lengthy arguments in the House of Commons; but in the end the enormous cost and the legal difficulties involved in settling claims of ownership and compensation, amounting to many thousands, together with the frantic anxiety of shopkeepers and others to resume business at once on their old sites, proved too much for the authorities. All the proposals were abandoned, and the only result of this memorable contest of talent was the canalizing of the foul Fleet Ditch or Fleet River from the Thames up to Holborn Bridge (on the site of Holborn Viaduct) in 1671–4, carried out by Hooke as City surveyor; but that attractive improvement, with its quays, has long been buried underground beneath New Bridge Street and Farringdon Street.

During the last few years of the seventeenth century, several more fine squares were laid out in London, namely Golden Square (1688–1700), Grosvenor Square (1695), Berkeley Square (1698), Red Lion Square (1698), and Kensington Square (1698).

REFERENCES

[1] HERODOTUS I, 178–80. (Loeb ed. Vol. 1, pp. 220 ff., 1920.)

[2] ARISTOTLE *Politica*, II, 8 (1267 b 22 ff.), trans. by B. JOWETT in 'Works of Aristotle', ed. by V. D. ROSS, Vol. 10. Clarendon Press, Oxford. 1921.

[3] VITRUVIUS I, iii; iv, 11; v; vii. (Loeb ed. Vol. 1, pp. 32 ff.; 42 ff.; 46 ff.; 66 ff., 1931.)

[4] McCURDY, E. 'The Mind of Leonardo da Vinci', p. 41. Cape, London. 1952.
DA VINCI, LEONARDO. Codice Atlantico, fol. R. 1203.

[5] McCURDY, E. See ref. [4].
DA VINCI, LEONARDO. Codice Atlantico, fol. 65.v.B.

[6] EVELYN, J. Diary for 15 September 1644. (New ed. by E. S. DE BEER, Vol. 2, pp. 150–1. Clarendon Press, Oxford. 1955.)

[7] LACROIX, P. *Gazette des Beaux-Arts*, **3**, Pl. facing p. 562, 1870.

BIBLIOGRAPHY

ABERCROMBIE, SIR (LESLIE) PATRICK. 'Town and Country Planning' (2nd ed.). Oxford University Press, London. 1943.

DICKINSON, R. E. 'The West European City.' Kegan Paul and Routledge, London. 1951.

GERKAN, A. VON. 'Griechische Städteanlagen.' Gruyter, Berlin. 1924.

GIOVANNONI, G. *et al.* 'L'Urbanistica dall' Antichità ad Oggi.' Sansoni, Florence. 1943.

HACKETT, B. 'Man, Society, and Environment.' Marshall, London. 1950.

HAVERFIELD, F. J. 'Ancient Town Planning.' Clarendon Press, Oxford. 1913.

HIBBERT, A. 'Old European Cities' (with 24 plans reproduced from Braun and Hogenberg's *Civitates orbis terrarum*). Thames and Hudson, London. 1955.

HOMO, L. 'Rome impériale et l'urbanisme dans l'antiquité.' Michel, Paris. 1951.

HUGHES, T. H. and LAMBORN, E. A. G. 'Towns and Town Planning, Ancient and Modern.' Clarendon Press, Oxford. 1923.

KORN, A. 'History builds the Town.' Humphries, London. 1953.

LANCHESTER, H. V. 'The Art of Town Planning' (2nd ed.). Chapman and Hall, London. 1932.

LAVEDAN, P. 'Histoire de l'urbanisme. Antiquité, moyen âge.' Laurens, Paris. 1926.

Idem. 'Histoire de l'urbanisme. Renaissance et temps modernes.' Laurens, Paris. 1941.

RASMUSSEN, S. E. 'Towns and Buildings.' University Press, Liverpool. 1951.

RICHMOND, I. A. 'Roman Britain', ch. 2: "Towns and Urban Centres." The Pelican History of England, Vol. 1. Penguin Books, Harmondsworth. 1955.

SAVAGE, SIR WILLIAM G. 'The Making of our Towns.' Eyre and Spottiswoode, London. 1925.

SITTE, C. 'Der Städte-Bau.' Vienna. 1889.

STEWART, C. 'A Prospect of Cities.' Longmans, Green, London. 1952.

TOUT, T. F. 'Medieval Town Planning.' University Press, Manchester. 1934.

WARD-PERKINS, J. B. "Early Roman Towns in Italy." *The Town Planning Review*, **26**, 126, 1955.

WHEELER, SIR (ROBERT ERIC) MORTIMER. 'The Indus Civilization.' The Cambridge History of India, Supplement. University Press, Cambridge. 1953.

WYCHERLEY, R. E. 'How the Greeks Built Cities.' Macmillan, London. 1949.

## 12

LAND DRAINAGE AND RECLAMATION

L. E. HARRIS

LAND-RECLAMATION comprises essentially the improvement of land for agricultural and other purposes. It involves specific methods of (*a*) embanking submerged shore-lands from the sea, (*b*) training and regulating rivers to prevent flooding, from which arise (*c*) the draining of low-lying lands and marshes, and, at the other extreme, (*d*) the irrigation of arid wastes. With this last, however, we are not concerned here. Our survey is confined to four main European countries, the Netherlands, Italy, France, and England, where there was no extensive irrigation in the sixteenth and seventeenth centuries, and where it is still not practised significantly. But each of these four countries has had its special methods and principles of land-reclamation, characteristic both technologically and historically, and in all of them the sixteenth and seventeenth centuries brought rapid developments, on which their present systems of drainage are founded.

I. THE NETHERLANDS

The real originators of land-reclamation in northern Europe, of sea-defences and polder-formation—or what might be termed assisted accretion—were the Netherlanders, from motives forced upon them largely by self-preservation. The skill which they thus acquired was utilized by other countries certainly as far back as the end of the tenth century when, for example, the bishops of Bremen, the marquises of Brandenburg, and others had employed the coastal Frisians on such works (vol II, p 683). But it is important to note that in this statement we confine ourselves to northern Europe, excluding particularly Italy where, as will be seen later, the influence of the Netherlands, even if to some degree existing, was far from predominant (p 309).

By the beginning of the sixteenth century the Netherlands possessed a well developed system of land-reclamation based on the very early habitations on the *terpen* or clay islands which remained above water in the coastal areas where, thousands of years ago, the sea had broken through the sand-dunes then forming a natural protection on the coast line (vol II, pp 681–5). The primitive but systematic building of embankments and artificial protective works originated some time before the eleventh century, but there is doubt whether the early dike construction was undertaken primarily as a means of protecting existing lands from floods, or as a means of land-reclamation: whether, therefore, it was of a defensive or an offensive character. By the opening of the sixteenth century this comparatively primitive construction had developed into regulated designs, differing in type to suit regional conditions. Thus in west Friesland, where the dikes had to withstand the waves of the open sea, it was found essential to protect the face of the dike by some means. In the calmer estuarine waters of Zeeland the need for protection was not so great. Furthermore, the clay available in Zeeland was much more suited to dike-building than that of Friesland, so that while in Zeeland simple protection by grass and seaweed was sufficient, more substantial materials were called for in Friesland.

The simple making of an embankment with masses of boulder-clay was almost instinctive, but the technique of protecting the face of the embankment or dike could be learnt only from practical experience, often bitter as the sea flooded through breaches. Thus there developed the various forms of dikes:

(i) the *slikkerdijk*, with an earth core, the slopes plastered with clay, later augmented by layers of straw bundles, or bundles of osiers;
(ii) the *wierdijk*, in which seaweed replaced the straw or osiers; and
(iii) the *rietdijk*, where bundles of reeds replaced the seaweed (vol II, pp. 684–6).

Later, in the fifteenth century, more substantial methods of protection were devised, such as the palisade of piles, and later still, towards the end of the sixteenth century, the *krebbingen*, consisting of two rows of short piles a few feet apart, the space between being filled with faggots or fascines held down by straw (figure 208). By the end of the sixteenth century stone pitching had been used experimentally, but this protection was in general found to be too expensive.

About 1578 Andries Vierlingh, a native of Brabant, wrote an important general work on dike-building, which remained unpublished until 1920, when it was given the title *Tractaet van dyckagie* [1]. Vierlingh was for many years bailiff of Steenbergen (Brabant), and in this post he had much concern with drainage and the embanking of polders, while in his youth, in 1530, he had assisted in the work of closing gaps in the harbour-dike at Middelburg, and later in land-reclamation in Zuid Beveland. In 1552 he was dike-master of the Graff-Hendriks polder at Steenbergen, and had considerable experience of such work not only in Brabant but also in Zeeland, South Holland, and west Friesland. The importance of Vierlingh's treatise lies in the fact that here we have for the first time a codification of methods employed in the sixteenth century principally for the construction of dikes, but also for the building of flood-gates and the like. The work is in three books, and Vierlingh had indeed planned the fourth and fifth books in which he intended to deal with the control of rivers and the deepening of harbours, and to treat of the general subject of inundations. His work, there-

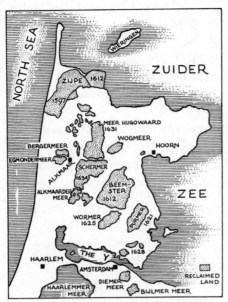

fore, gives us a picture of hydraulic practices before any true science of hydraulics existed. Furthermore, the *Tractaet* demonstrates that comparatively advanced methods of dike-construction and protection were already in use and, indeed, were not very different from those in use today. A close examination of Vierlingh's book, particularly in relation to Brabant, shows that, as compared with the land reclaimed inside the old sea-dikes before the end of the fifteenth century, there had been very considerable expansion by Vierlingh's time, when the new dikes were up to, or even in some cases beyond, the present-day limits. It was also at this period that intense activity began in another direction, the 'laying dry' of inland 'meers' or lakes.

FIGURE 202—*North Holland, showing progress in* droogmakerij *during the sixteenth and seventeenth centuries.*

This 'laying dry' (*droogmakerij*), a new technique essentially different from that of embanking from the sea, started slowly and tentatively in the early years of the sixteenth century. Thus between 1542 and 1548 the Dergmeer, the Kerkmeer, the Kromwater, the Weidgreb, and the Rietgreb, all small meers in the northern part of the Netherlands, were drained and turned into valuable agricultural land (figure 202). Then in 1556 the Count Van Egmond began the greater undertaking of draining the Egmondermeer, quickly followed by, among others, Hendrik Van Brederode in the Bergermeer, and Johann Van Oldenbarnevelt in the Dieps and Tjaalingermeer. The initiative for all this work came from the various 'adventurers' and undertakers, to whom the ultimate agricultural value of the land was of less importance than their immediate profit on their capital adventured. To give some idea of the growth of this *droogmakerij* between 1540 and 1565, the total area of land reclaimed in North and South Holland, Friesland,

Groningen, Zeeland, and north Brabant was 35 608 hectares, of which only 1349 hectares were drained meers, the rest having been obtained by diking from the sea. Between 1615 and 1640 the total was 25 513 hectares, of which no fewer than 19 060 were obtained by the 'laying dry' of meers. The method of reclaiming these drowned lands was to surround the whole area with a strong bank, or *ringdijk*, the earth for which was dug from the outer foot of the dike, so forming a channel, or *ringvaart*. When the *ringdijk* and *ringvaart* were completed then the drainage-mills, generally sited on the *ringdijk*, began their work of pumping out the water from the meer into the *ringvaart*, whence it flowed by gravity, through sluices if necessary, to the river or main canal (figure 206).

Beyond their agricultural importance these *droogmakerijen* have an added significance in the impetus that they gave to the technical development of the drainage-mill. This, the windmill-driven scoop-wheel, was not the child of meer-drainage. It had, indeed, come into use in a somewhat primitive form towards the end of the fourteenth century, much later than wind-driven corn-mills, but its use as a drainage machine could never have been practically successful without the invention about the middle of the fifteenth century of the rotating cap, which enabled the sails to be turned into the eye of the wind without turning the body of the mill, an impossibility with a fixed scoop-wheel.[1] But for this invention the drainage of meers and other low-lying grounds in Holland, formed by natural shrinkage of the land and by the creation of vast flooded pits from which peat had been dug for fuel, might have been indefinitely delayed. Between 1560 and 1700 as many as 102 patents for drainage-mills were granted by the States-General and individual states, besides numerous patents for other forms of pumps such as screw-pumps, spiral pumps, and the like. Not all these were capable of working, but the figures give some idea of the importance of the problem of water-raising in relation to land-reclamation. Furthermore, the drainage-mill introduces two outstanding names in the history of land reclamation in the Netherlands: Simon Stevin (1548–1620) and Jan Adriaanszoon Leeghwater (1575–1650), both of whom were responsible for important developments in the design and construction of drainage-mills.

Stevin's claim to fame rests on a much wider basis for he was, like his contemporary Galileo Galilei, not only an accomplished mathematician but a combination of what we should term today a scientist and a practical hydraulic engineer, with the emphasis on elementary hydrostatics rather than hydrodynamics. Stevin, who was born at Bruges, entered the university of Leiden in 1583, and was later

[1] In this cap-mill (*wipmolen*) the drive was transmitted to the scoop-wheel by a shaft running through the hollow post supporting the body of the mill (vol II, p 625).

employed as an engineer in the army of Prince Maurice. Probably he was responsible for, or adviser on, the construction of the Prinsendijk on the west side of the Grote Wiericke channel, which formed part of the water-defences of the province of Holland in the Spanish war. The first of Stevin's patents was granted to him by the States of Holland in 1584. It covered three inventions: (i) to bring all sorts of ships across shallow waters; (ii) to bring ships across dams; and (iii) to raise water by other means than so far used (to drain polders, harbours, and so forth). Only the last of these concerns us, and this device, according to his son Hendrik Stevin (1613–70), was a special type of piston-pump which, however, was never

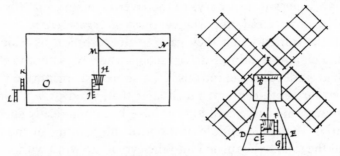

FIGURE 203—*An original drawing by Simon Stevin of the drainage-mills described in his patent of 28 November 1589. (Left) Horse-mill driving scoop-wheel through right-angle gears; (right) turret-mill driving scoop-wheel.*

adopted widely for polder drainage; indeed, a pump of this type is fundamentally unsuited to such work.

In 1588 the States-General, through the Earl of Leicester, granted Stevin a patent for a 'drainage mill of high capacity' which, again according to Hendrik Stevin, included a scoop-wheel with only six blades as opposed to the usual 20 or 24, each blade being provided with leather strips sliding along the floor and sides of the wheel-race (figure 203). That this device was successful appears from a series of testimonials drawn up in the years 1590 and 1591 relating to mills of this type built by Stevin at, among other places, the Duyvelsgat at Delft and the Stolwijksche sluice at Souderak, where it was stated that the new mill 'in one hour lifted as much water as the said Beyer Mill in three hours'. Stevin himself wrote to the bailiff and burgomaster of Delft and showed mathematically that his new drainage-mill there lifted four times as much water as the old mill did. It has been suggested that Stevin's invention was not adopted widely because the Archimedean screw, with or without a fixed casing, was then largely ousting the scoop-wheel. A more likely explanation is that, although the leather strips and reduced number of blades might give a higher hydraulic efficiency, principally by reducing blade-tip leakage, the leather strips must have required frequent and costly replacement. The standard design of scoop-wheel cost little to maintain, and in the larger drainage-mills it outlasted the competition from Archimedean screws, spiral pumps, and other devices introduced into the Netherlands in the sixteenth and seventeenth centuries. But the Archimedean pump for which Dominicus van Melckenbeke of Middelburg was granted a patent in 1598 found many applications in the *tjaskers*, or small inclined wind-mills, particularly in the north-eastern part of the country (figure 204). The logical evolution from the Archimedean screw, the screw with the fixed casing, was the sub-ject of a patent granted to Symon Hulsbos of Leiden in 1634.

Stevin's fame in relation to drainage-mills is firmly based on his treatise *Van de molens* ('On Mills') in which he supports his practical developments by original theoretical studies in statics and hydrostatics [2]. Indeed, this book has claims to be the oldest on the subject, anticipating Smeaton's researches by some 150 years. And if Vierlingh's *Tractaet van dyckagie* is the oldest codified work on em-bankments in general, the first two chapters

FIGURE 204—*A* tjasker *mill, Friesland.*

of Stevin's *Nieuwe maniere van sterctebou, door spilsluysen* ('New manner of Fortification by Sluices'), published in 1617, are, perhaps, the oldest printed treatise on sluices extant in Europe [3].

Jan Adriaanszoon, who in later years adopted the surname of Leeghwater, was a very different type of man from Simon Stevin. A self-made man, he was born in 1575 at a village north of Amsterdam, the son of a carpenter who built the first sluice there in 1594. If, as previously suggested, the development of the drainage-mill was hastened by the expansion of the *droogmakerij*, it is no less true to say that the same factor contributed largely to the creation of Leeghwater, because although he became well known as an hydraulic engineer of wide experi-ence in the planning of drainage-canals, the construction of sluices, and so on, his lasting reputation stands firmly on his skill as the *Molenmaker en Ingenieur van de Rijp* ('Millwright and Engineer of de Rijp'), as he described himself.

The improvements that Leeghwater introduced into the construction of the drainage-mill were not fundamental and he obtained no patents for them. In fact he was granted two patents only, one of them in 1605, in company with

Pieter Pieters and William Pieters, for a device for 'going under water', which attracted the attention of Prince Maurice, and was claimed to have practical value in making possible underwater repairs to bridges, sluices, and the like. But in 1608 the 'laying dry' of the Beemster, the largest of the inland lakes of the north Netherlands (figure 202), was begun, and Leeghwater was appointed

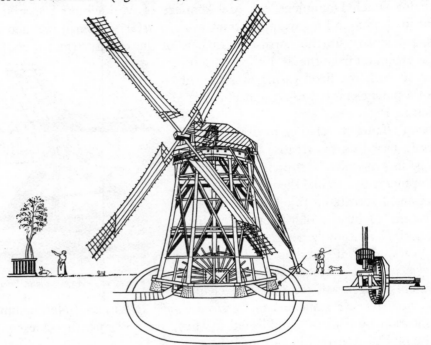

FIGURE 205—*Drawing by Leeghwater of a mill used in draining the Beemster polder. The scoop-wheel rotates clockwise and the outflow is to the left.*

'to undertake the manufacture and erection of the water-mills' (figure 205). Four years later, in May 1612 (forty years after the first plans for the draining of the Beemster had been formulated), the work was completed and Leeghwater's reputation was firmly established.

It was in the Beemster that Leeghwater developed the system of multi-stage water-lifting in which the water was lifted successively by two, three, or four scoop-wheels working in series from the lowest level of the polder up to the level of the *ringvaart* (vol II, figure 627). The system was not his invention, for it was known in the sixteenth century, but it found its full application under Leeghwater in the Beemster, and in many polders on which he was successfully employed.

Leeghwater represents the best type of mill-maker and drainage engineer in the Golden Age of the Netherlands in the first half of the seventeenth century. His fame spread beyond the confines of his own country, and he travelled widely in the Netherlands and abroad (p 319). His best-known monument is a work which he never carried out, the draining of the Haarlemmermeer, vividly des-

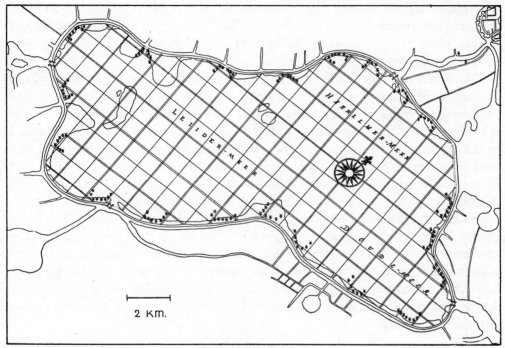

FIGURE 206—*Leeghwater's original plan for draining the Haarlemmermeer, 1629. The area was to be drained by a regular series of channels arranged at right-angles, from which water was to be raised by the windmills closely spaced round the edge of the meer.*

cribed in his *Haarlemmermeerboek* ('Book on the Meer at Haarlem') published in 1641[1] [4]. A striking feature of his plan (figure 206) was his proposed employment of no fewer than 160 drainage-mills; had financial backing been forthcoming (Leeghwater's estimate of the cost was 3 600 000 guilders) the scheme could well have succeeded, as it did in 1852 with the aid of steam pumping-engines. The breadth of the concept gives some measure of the man.

Clearly neither Stevin nor Leeghwater was the inventor of the drainage-mill, and it would be impossible to assign that role to any one individual. One whose part in its development must be mentioned is Cornelis Corneliszoon of Uitgeest,

[1] A thirteenth edition of his scheme was printed in 1838.

who was first granted a patent in 1597 for a design embodying a windmill-driven two-throw crank operating twin reciprocating pumps, a novel but not entirely satisfactory design. His fame mainly rests on the construction of the wind-driven saw-mill, but he has the added distinction of having been granted a patent by the States-General in 1602 for a pump which appears from his obscure description to have been an early design of centrifugal pump, or at least a device for using centrifugal force to raise water. The development of this invention had to wait some 250 years, when the first centrifugal pump for fen-drainage was installed in England.

Too much emphasis, however, must not be laid on the importance of the drainage-mill in land-reclamation at this time. Without it, it is true, the extensive *droogmakerijen* of inland meers might never have been undertaken, but it must be realized that, between 1540 and 1690, 80 per cent of the land reclaimed in the six principal provinces of the Netherlands (some 167 260 hectares) was land embanked from the sea. Thus this extension of the land was mainly achieved by the technology of dike-construction and 'assisted accretion'. In such work the early existence in the Netherlands of administrative organizations for the centralized control of general drainage systems, the *Hoogheemradschappen* (Main Polder Boards), whose foundation goes back as far as the year 1200, and the smaller bodies within their framework, was an important factor. Though these organizations were not creations of the sixteenth and seventeenth centuries, without their existence it is doubtful whether the technological advances made during this period would have occurred. Certainly they would never have been utilized to the full.

II. ITALY

The problem in Italy of *la bonifica*, or land-reclamation in its widest sense, must be considered from a geographical point of view if the special nature of the problem, and its dissimilarity from that of other European countries such as the Netherlands, England, and France, is to be understood. A long, comparatively narrow strip of country separated from the rest of Europe on the north by the great semicircular barrier of the Alps, Italy is divided roughly from north to south by a mountainous spine, down which on either side descend a multiplicity of rivers, often snow-fed mountainous torrents in their upper reaches. Its coast-line is extensive. All these factors combine to create a problem to be solved fundamentally by the training and regulation of the rivers. Regulation of rivers forms the key to *la bonifica*, and to the technology on which it is based. For *la bonifica* always has been, in Italy as in other countries, essentially a hydraulic problem with the double purpose of improving both health and agriculture, an age-long problem of the removal of stagnant waters resulting from the flooding of rivers.

The history of *la bonifica* has three important characteristics. First, it has its roots in the works of the Roman emperors roughly 2000 years ago, even if its development has not been continuous. Secondly, and consequently, it has no clear-cut beginning in the sixteenth and seventeenth centuries as in the case of England and France. Thirdly, land-reclamation in Italy was carried out independently of the skill and experience of the Netherlands, developing in this period an indigenous technology with a scientific basis.

The drainage and irrigation works of the Roman Empire fell into decay with its dissolution, and many centuries passed before the religious houses, particularly the Benedictine and Cistercian foundations, attempted to revive such works. Their attempts, though small and unco-ordinated, provided the pattern for the developments of the sixteenth and seventeenth centuries. Thus in the seventh century the Benedictine abbeys of Palazzolo, Monteverdi, and Salvatori had executed works of drainage in many of the marshes of the plain of Lombardy. In the twelfth century the Cistercian abbey of Chiaravalle had carried out the irrigation of the Vettabia di Milano, and about the same time similar monastic work was done in the Bassa Valle Padana. By the early years of the sixteenth century numerous undertakings of a minor nature were in being, but the initiative was passing from the religious houses to the landed proprietors in the semi-independent states, to the councils of such wealthy and powerful cities as Venice and Milan, and particularly to the Papal State and the successive popes.

At the same time there was a growing recognition of the need for special organizations to study, finance, and control *la bonifica*. Early in the sixteenth century the State of Venice had appointed its *ufficiales supra canales* and *ufficiales paludum* (marsh officers), the city of Verona had constituted its *Collegio per il fiume Adige* for the control of that river, and Florence in 1549 had created *ufficiales di fiumi, ponti e strade* (officers for rivers, bridges, and streets), among whose functions were the regulation of the rivers and the prevention of flooding. The importance of these and similar organizations lies in the incentive that they provided for a scientific technological approach to practical hydraulic problems. Thus, for example, under the control of the *ufficiales di fiumi* of Florence there worked one of the outstanding hydraulic engineers of the sixteenth century in Italy, Bernardo Timante Buontalenti (d 1608), appointed city engineer by the Medici, who carried out much original work of improvement on the Arno.

A significant feature of these official bodies was that they had sufficient authority to ensure replacement of individual and local works of river improvement, and so on, by systematic control of the main river and its tributaries as a single unit. In 1558 Girolamo di Pace, one of the *ufficiales di fiumi*, wrote a general review of the whole Arno situation, and in the forty-five years between 1558 and 1603 masses of reports and schemes for the improvement of the Arno were submitted to that body, all of which had to be sifted and evaluated.

Perhaps the most important hydraulic engineer in Italy at this period was the Florentine Antonio Lupicini (*c* 1530–98), a man whose reputation spread far beyond the bounds of Italy. While his experience was broad, he confined his activities to hydraulics and fortifications, principally the former, and thus became what was indeed rare in those days, a specialist. Lupicini's fame is perpetuated in six books, of which the two most interesting from the hydraulic point of view are: *Discorso sopra i ripari del Po e d'altri fiumi che hanno gl'argini di terra posticcia* ('Discourse on the defences of the Po and other rivers with artificial embankments of earth'), 1587, and *Discorso sopra i ripari delle inondazioni di Fiorenza* ('Discourse on flood-protection at Florence'), 1591 [5]. The former deals with remedial works on the river Po, partly for navigational purposes, partly for flood-prevention. The latter deals exclusively with flooding and its prevention. Lupicini was fully acquainted with methods of dike-construction and the design and building of retaining-walls, groynes, and diversionary banks, the science of which was then as fully developed in Italy as it was in the Netherlands. But it is clear that the mud-dikes, the *slikkerdijk*, the *wierdijk*, and similar constructions employed in the Netherlands for polder-reclamation could not be used for the fast-running and often turbulent rivers of Italy. Thus the Italian engineers had to build pile-dikes, masonry walls, stone pitching, and various forms of mattress protection and fascine-work, with which in consequence they became fully acquainted. It might be said, indeed, that Lupicini had developed original ideas on mattress protection, because in his *Discorso sopra i ripari del Po* of 1587 he discussed in detail the causes of bank-erosion and describes the remedy that he had designed to prevent it.

His method was to employ a 'circular structure' consisting of logs set about 4 ft apart, cross-connected and bound with willow-sprigs, the whole forming a mattress one end of which was attached to the shore and the rest unrolled to fall into place over the point of erosion. The whole was then weighted with stones to keep it in place. As to bank-construction, Lupicini laid it down that in general the height should be 4 ft above the highest ascertained flood-level, with the base three times the height. This, however, might be thought to give too steep a slope, but he specified that the banks should be constructed of alternate layers of earth and straw, the former 10 ft thick, levelled and rammed, and by this means he was able to employ satisfactorily the steep angle of repose. It must be emphasized that Lupicini's constructional principles were devised for river-regulation, not for coastal protection.

The whole story of *la bonifica* in the sixteenth and seventeenth centuries is a complicated and fragmentary one, but perhaps the attempts to drain the Pontine Marshes provide a symptomatic insight into that story, although the problem was a somewhat specialized one (figure 207). The Pontine Marshes, then in the territory of the Papal State, cover an area of some 300 square miles south-west of Rome, and comprise a coastal strip lying between the Tyrrhenian Sea and the Lepini mountains, from which flowed many minor and often turbulent rivers. The efforts of successive emperors to drain the marshes had been partially successful, enabling the Appian Way to traverse the area. Their works had decayed, and by the opening of the sixteenth century, in spite of the well in-tentioned efforts of earlier popes, the region was nothing but a malaria-infested marsh. In 1514 Giovanni de' Medici, Pope Leo X, granted to his cousin, Julius de' Medici, later Pope Clement VII, a concession for the work of drainage, which resulted in the cutting of a canal named *Fiume Giuliano* after the pope's brother, Giuliano de' Medici, in whose service Leonardo da Vinci then was. Probably at this date Leonardo prepared a map showing his scheme for the drainage, in which he proposed to re-cut the ancient Roman canal running parallel to the Appian Way, and to use it (following the Romans) as a cut-off channel for the waters coming down from the Lepini mountains (plate 19). An additional channel was to be constructed at right-angles to the cut-off channel to assist the discharge to the sea of the waters of the rivers Livoli and Ufenti. There was also a second subsidiary scheme for improving the *Rio Martino*, a Roman canal traversing the low ground between the Appian Way and the sea, but, in the end, little or nothing appears to have been done and the whole proposal was dropped on the death of Leo X in 1522.

After this abortive attempt some sixty years had elapsed when early in 1586 Ascania Fenizi, an engineer from Urbino, placed before Sixtus V (1585–90) a plan for draining the marshes with the financial aid of wealthy merchants of Urbino. This pope must be given credit for supporting a scheme that very nearly succeeded. He granted a concession to Fenizi for the laying-dry of all the terri-tory of Terracina, Piperno, and Sezze, $5\frac{1}{2}$ per cent of the drained land to be allotted to the *Camera Apostolica* or papal treasury. Sixtus had already been active in promoting other hydraulic works; thus he had been instrumental in improving the ports of Rimini, Ancona, and Civita Vecchia, and in draining the marshes of Ravenna and the lands at the mouth of the Tiber. Work on the new undertaking began at once, 2000 men being employed, and was completed in January 1589. Sluices were built for the control of the several rivers and streams coming down from the high ground, new minor canals were cut, and a main canal, the *Fiume Sisto*, was dug. After the death of Sixtus in 1590 the works fell into decay, the marshes returned to their pristine state, and malaria again ravaged their inhabitants.

Next on the scene was a Netherlander, Nicolaas Corneliszoon de Witt, of Alkmaar, who presented himself in Rome in 1623 with a scheme for draining the Pontine Marshes. He was granted a concession for the purpose in 1637 by Pope Urban VIII. The undertaking was to be financed by a company of Catholic merchants from both Italy and the Netherlands, but when de Witt died in the following year the scheme collapsed, as did a later one in which another Netherlander was interested.

It was not until near the end of the seventeenth century that the attempt to drain the Pontine Marshes was renewed, again by a Netherlander, Cornelis Janszoon Meijer, perhaps the most important of the engineers from the Low Countries who carried out hydraulic works in Italy. A native of Amsterdam, by 1674 Meijer had made a name for himself in Rome as an engineer of considerable skill. In 1676 he submitted to Innocent XI plans for draining the marshes, on which the pope instructed an Italian engineer to prepare a report. As a result of this report Meijer studied the problem again and in 1678 wrote a memoir ('On the way to drain the Pontine Marshes'); this was published in 1683 and was illustrated by a map made by Giovanni Battista Falda (figure 207) [6]. He did not live to carry out his plans; they were, however, executed by his son, with a lack of success largely due to the active opposition of the inhabitants of the area.

Meijer's more important book, *L'Arte di rendere i fiumi navigabili in varij modi con altre nuove inventioni, e varij altri segreti* ('The Art of making rivers navigable in various ways, with other new inventions and various other secrets') (1696), written when he had become a member of the *Accadèmia Fisicomatematica* of Rome, shows him to have been a man of wide accomplishments. It deals with a variety of subjects and mechanical devices of all kinds, such as boat-lifts, caissons, cranes, mechanically propelled carriages, and so on. While it is likely that in many instances he was acting merely as a reporter, the book does give some idea of the state of certain branches of technology, particularly hydraulic technology, in Italy at that period. He writes of methods of remedying the inundations of rivers, including methods for preventing the inundation of the provinces of Bologna, Ferrara, and Ravenna. He describes the work of pile and fascine construction with which he had repaired the damaged port of Pesaro, discusses the use of dredgers, and discourses on river-training and bank construction that he had carried out on the Tiber in 1696 for Pope Innocent XII (figure 208).

By the end of the seventeenth century the practice of *la bonifica* was highly

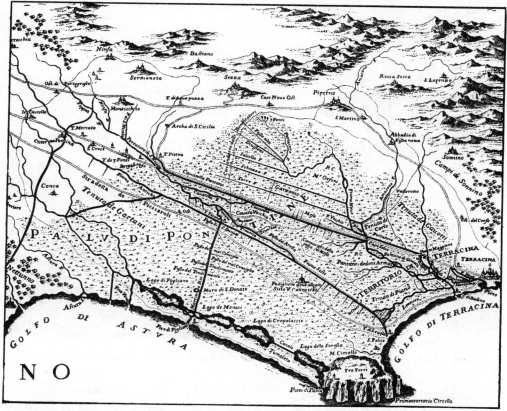

FIGURE 207—*G. B. Falda's map (1678) of Meijer's scheme for draining the Pontine Marshes.*

developed, but we must now mention a most potent factor in land-reclamation and drainage in Italy, particularly towards the latter end of our period, namely the researches of scientists into the behaviour and regulation of rivers, a factor which to a great extent differentiated the conditions there from those in other European countries. If it is true that the work of Galileo Galilei (1564–1642) and, to a lesser degree, of Simon Stevin (1548–1620) in hydraulics represents the first advance in that science since Archimedes, it is equally true that the scientific researches of Benedetto Castelli and his successors into the flow of rivers represent the beginning of a new phase in the art of land-reclamation in Italy. Galileo himself was no mere theoretical worker in this field. Apart from the fact that the State of Venice had in 1594 granted him a patent for the erection of a water-raising machine, he had at one time been superintendent of the waters of Tuscany. There is still extant his report on the river Bisenzio written in January 1630, after an inspection made with the two engineers Bartolotti and Fantoni.

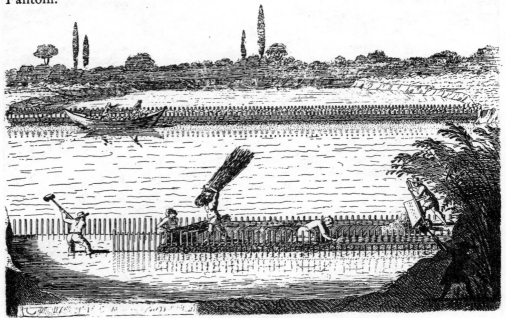

FIGURE 208—*The construction of* krebbingen *as a means of defining the banks of a river. From Meijer, 1683.*

Benedetto Castelli (1577–1643), a student under Galileo at Padua, had been employed in 1623 by Ferdinand, Grand Duke of Tuscany, to remedy flooding in the valley of Pisa between the river Serchio and the Fiume Morto. Then he attracted the notice of Urban VIII and in 1625 was appointed by him to assist Ottavio Corsini, superintendent of the general drainage of Tuscany for the areas around Bologna, Ferrara, and Commachio lying between the rivers Po and Reno. It was during this period that he wrote his book *Della misura dell' acque correnti* ('On the measurement of running waters'), published in 1628 (not posthumously as is often incorrectly stated) [7]. This was not just an abstract philosophical expression of theoretical ideas, but was based essentially on a combination of theory and practical observation applied to the creation of remedies for actual inundations and other hydraulic problems, and thus initiated a sound hydraulic technology. This technology expanded as scientific inquiry was extended.

Vincenzo Viviani, who played a large part in founding one of the first great scientific societies, the *Accadèmia del Cimento*, in 1657, was another of Galileo's most distinguished pupils who did important work as a practical hydraulic engineer. Viviani succeeded Galileo as superintendent of the waters of Tuscany, and successfully executed on the river Bisenzio training-works which Galileo himself, in his earlier report representing a less developed knowledge, had condemned as useless.

Castelli's book was followed by two important publications, the *Della natura de fiumi* ('The nature of rivers') of Domenico Guglielmini (1697) [8], and the complete *Architettura d'acque* ('Hydraulic architecture') of Giovanni Battista Barattieri (1699)[1] [9]. Barattieri was engineer to the Duke of Parma, and his book, based on his own observations and experiments and also on the earlier work of Castelli and Corsini, to both of whom he paid due acknowledgement, is perhaps the best example in our period of a practical and scientific work on the problems of river regulation.

The distinguished Italian mathematician of the eighteenth century, Paolo Frisi (1728–84), wrote with pardonable pride that 'Hydraulic architecture arose, advanced, and almost reached perfection in Italy, where they have written on every point connected with the theory of torrents and rivers, the conducting and distributing of clear and turbid waters, the slopes, the directions, and the variations of channels; and, in one word, on the whole range of Hydrometry and Hydraulics'. What certainly can be stressed is that *la bonifica* was in the sixteenth and seventeenth centuries, as indeed it is today, based fundamentally on river-training and regulation, the science of which was developed so effectively in Italy in the seventeenth century.

III. ENGLAND AND FRANCE

The geographical and economic situation of the 'drowned lands' of England in the sixteenth century was entirely different from that in either the Netherlands or Italy. Some 700 000 acres of fenland, part marsh, part subject to periodic flooding, lay in the eastern counties of Lincolnshire, Cambridgeshire, Huntingdonshire, and Norfolk, forming what might be termed a land bay extending inland on its longest axis some 35 miles from the shores of the Wash (figure 209). There was no imperative need to reclaim the land for purely agricultural reasons, and

[1] The two parts of this treatise had been published separately in 1656 and 1663.

incursions of the sea, on a comparatively limited coast-line, were a danger of restricted extent and infrequent occurrence, largely counteracted by the embankments constructed on the low-lying Lincolnshire coast in pre-Roman days. The four rivers flowing through the Fenland—the Ouse, the Nene, the Welland, and the Witham—were comparatively small and had none of the characteristics of the mountainous torrents of Italy. The development of a systematized reclamation of the Fens in the sixteenth and seventeenth centuries was confined mainly to what was termed the Great Level—later the Bedford Level—between the river

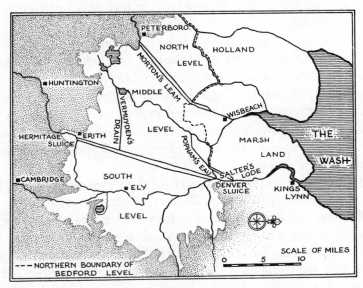

FIGURE 209—*The Great or Bedford Level on the completion of Vermuyden's scheme in 1653. After Badeslade's map of 1724.*

Nene and the uplands of Norfolk, an area of some 302 000 acres, to the exclusion of the Lincolnshire fens. In the Great Level the ancient Fenland abbeys had carried out limited works of reclamation and drainage, but with the final Dissolution in 1540 their influence was removed, leaving behind a vacuum to be filled by the financial speculator and adventurer, whose object was capital gain. Indeed it is to the often despised profit-motive that we owe the initiation and completion of the so-called 'draining of the Fens' in the seventeenth century.

The first positive step towards a draining of the Great Level came from Humphrey Bradley, the Brabanter from Bergen op Zoom who probably owed his name to an English father, an important functionary in the House of the Merchant Adventurers there. He was probably introduced into England by

Joachim Ortell, an emissary from the States-General, and in 1584 submitted to Sir Francis Walsingham an 'Advys' on a scheme for the reconstruction of Dover harbour. In a letter of March 1588 from the Privy Council to the commissioners of sewers of the chief Fen counties, Bradley, John Hexham, and Ralfe Agas were recommended as persons 'able to make viewe and platt [map] for the several fenns, the true dyssentes of waters, and qualities of soile through which waters should be carried', that is, they were skilled surveyors and able to take levels. As a result Bradley submitted a 'Treatise' on the draining of the Fens to Lord Burghley in December 1589.

This 'Treatise' is noteworthy in two main particulars, for it was the first comprehensive proposal for draining the Great Level, as opposed to the piecemeal attempts made hitherto, and it was also a scheme prepared by a man skilled in the arts of drainage and diking (as will appear later), and based, therefore, on sound technological principles and practice. It was, too, founded on a reasonably accurate survey, considering the limitations of instruments and methods of survey at that time (ch 20). That is an important point, because the most essential requirement in a wide region like the Fens was an accurate survey of the whole area. John Hexham and Ralfe Agas, named in the Privy Council letter, were both reputable surveyors. By this date the science and practice of surveying, through its developments during the previous eighty or ninety years, had reached the stage where all the basic items of the modern surveyor's equipment were in use.

Bradley's 'Treatise' gives no figures for the levels on which his scheme was based, but some years later, in 1597, Agas when writing to Lord Burghley stated that in his survey he had levelled throughout the Fens down to the outfalls of the rivers. Bradley himself had said that in the Fens 'practically the entire surface of the land is above high sea-level', and had gone on to point out that 'the only way to redeem the land from the waters is to draw off the waters by directing them along the shortest tracks . . . in canals dug of such width and depth as can serve to make the waters run to the sea'. He emphasized that his purpose could be accomplished by a gravitational scheme without recourse, as he said, 'to embankments, machinery, mills, and inestimable expense'.

Thus the relative land- and sea-levels were such as to render drainage-mills unnecessary in general, but there is little doubt that even in the year 1588, and possibly earlier, such mills were in use in certain individual fens. Whether they were windmills or horse-mills it is impossible to tell. What is known is that even in 1580 Peter Morrice (or Morris), presumably a Netherlander, had been granted a patent for draining 'certaine fens . . . by certaine engines', while applications for similar patents had been made by other Netherlanders about 1578. These, however, were merely individual efforts, and when Humphrey Bradley retired disappointed to Bergen op Zoom, after a further futile petition to Lord Burghley in 1593, a co-ordinated scheme for the reclaiming of the Great Level—the only method by which a true reclamation could be accomplished—receded into a future nearly forty years away. The problem was less technical than financial and human. But Bradley is important in the history of land-reclamation in England for having enunciated a clear-cut scheme in which the Fens, or at least the Great Level, were considered as a single unit. Whatever may have been the solid achievements of Cornelis Vermuyden (p 320), he undoubtedly owed a lot to his predecessor, a fellow Netherlander.

The problem of draining and reclaiming low-lying grounds in France was different again. Fundamentally, as in England, it involved the prevention of the flooding of flat areas by slow-moving rivers, but in France there was no single large 'drowned and surrounded' area such as the Fens. In contrast to the Netherlands, the reclamation consisted principally of draining marshes rather than reclaiming land from the sea. The real establishment of a systematized land-reclamation owes everything to Henri IV (reigned 1589–1610). It is true that some attempts at minor reclamation had been made centuries earlier by the religious houses of the Benedictines, and isolated schemes had been attempted in the years immediately preceding Henri's accession. Thus in 1587 an attempt had been made by the Mareschal de Matignon to drain and cultivate the marshes around Bordeaux, where periodic epidemics of ague or malaria carried off the inhabitants sometimes in thousands. But the initial impetus to Henri's wide conception came indirectly from the claims of war, which constantly pressed upon him for some time after his accession. On 18 June 1596 the States-General of the Netherlands reported that they had received from the French king through his ambassador a request that they should send to France 'four qualified individuals experienced in the art of diking'. In the following month Humphrey Bradley was instructed to travel to France with Jan Gerritszoon from Holland and another, unnamed, diker from Zeeland, there to engage in 'works of diking' on behalf of the king. But the important point lies in the exhortation that they should assist the king 'in all warlike operations'.

This was the reason for Humphrey Bradley's journey to France. What military engineering Bradley and his friends did we do not know, but when major hostilities had ceased Bradley remained in the king's service by royal request. Henri then determined to undertake large-scale land-reclamation as one of the many means of rehabilitating the country, and in 1599 Bradley was appointed *mâitre des digues du royaume* with a practical monopoly to drain low-lying grounds in the whole of France. He had already, on orders from the king in 1597, begun the drainage of low grounds at Chaumont-en-Vexin (Oise).

No particularly novel technological development grew out of Bradley's work in France, and it will suffice here to say that, in due course, he, or rather *L'Association pour le dessèchement des marais et lacs de France* founded by him and largely financed by fellow-Netherlanders, successively drained the marshes of, among others, Saintonge, Poitou, Normandy, Picardy, Languedoc, Provence, and the lake of Sarlièves (Puy-de-Dôme). This *Association* was, perhaps, the most noteworthy and indeed the all-important factor in this work in France. It arose out of the first edict of 1599, was officially constituted by a second edict of 1607, was renewed by a further edict in 1639 until 1655, and continued until the repeal of the Edict of Nantes in 1685. Its importance lies in the fact that it represented a coherent organization, administrative, financial, and technical, of supreme necessity in large-scale and widely distributed undertakings of this nature. It took its pattern from the similar organization, the *Hoogheemradschappen*, of the Netherlands (p 308).

It has been noted earlier (p 307) that Leeghwater visited France in 1628, when he was invited by the Duc d'Épernon to survey and drain the marshes of Lesparre (Gironde). We may guess that Bradley was still alive.[1] The *Association* was certainly still in existence and it is difficult to see why, or how, Leeghwater should be called in to undertake this work and thus encroach on the preserves of the *Association*. The Duc d'Épernon may, of course, have considered a second, independent opinion necessary. Bradley's conceptions were not always right. He certainly had made mistakes earlier in his calculations for the Burgundy canal, but knowledge of hydrodynamics and of the flow and slopes of rivers and canals was at that time still elementary and awaited the developments in Italy of about the middle of the century.

The course of draining the English Fens had Bradley been granted permission to proceed with his plans in 1589 must be a matter of conjecture. Between that date and 1630, when the first undertaking in the Fens came into being, fruitless discussions went on interminably against a background of financial speculation divorced from technical considerations. English financial interests waged a struggle with Netherlands financiers to obtain concessions, the crown balancing the scales somewhat unevenly in its own interest. In 1630, however, Francis, fourth Earl of Bedford, was appointed 'undertaker' for the drainage of the Great Level, being joined by thirteen other Englishmen prepared to 'adventure' their

---

[1] The date of his death is unknown, but it must have been after 1625, and before 1639.

capital on the project. Cornelis Vermuyden (? 1590–1677), a Zeelander from the Isle of Tholen, was appointed director of works or chief engineer. He had first come to England in 1621 and a few years later had been given by Charles I the concession to drain the 70 000 acres of Hatfield Chase in Yorkshire, a scheme financed almost entirely by capital from the Netherlands. The reclamation of the Great Level by Vermuyden, virtually completed in 1653, represents the one great land-reclamation scheme in England of the seventeenth century, and indeed of all time, and some idea of its importance may be gained from the fact that the total area involved, about 307 000 acres, is equal to seven-tenths of the total area reclaimed in the Netherlands in the 150 years between 1540 and 1690.

The original plan and map of Vermuyden of 1630 have not survived (they probably perished in the Fire of London, 1666) but the principles on which he based his later, and extended, scheme are still extant in his 'Discourse touching the Drayning [of] the Great Fennes' written in 1638 and published in 1642 [10]. From this it is clear that the plan was founded on a purely gravitational system, Vermuyden deciding, as had Humphrey Bradley, that there was sufficient fall to the river outfalls in the Wash because, in Bradley's words, 'practically the entire surface . . . is above high sea-level'. Very little is known of Vermuyden's activities before his arrival in England in 1621, but recently there has come to light a map of the area around Steenbergen in Brabant made by him and signed 20 October 1615: 'Map and project of the drowned lands lying in Brabant across from the town of Tholen . . .' (*Caerte ende ontwerp van de verdroncken landen gelegen in Brabant tegens over de stadt Tholen* . . .). This shows that he was a skilled surveyor and even in 1615 could prepare plans for the draining of 'drowned' lands.

When he embarked upon the Great Level undertaking he had behind him not only his experience in the Netherlands but that gained in Hatfield Chase, and it must be admitted that there he had made some mistakes. For such drainage projects as Hatfield Chase and the Great Level, with their treatment of involved river-systems, were somewhat different from, and more complex in diagnosis than, the embanking of a polder or the draining of an inland meer in the Netherlands. There such works were based on an established technology of dike-construction, canal-excavation, the building of sluices, and so on. Vermuyden had the advantage of a knowledge of that technology, almost entirely lacking in England, but his task involved a combination of the Netherlands problems with the Italian problem of river-regulation in a simplified form. He had also to contend with the peculiar river-outfall conditions in the Wash. There was no ready-made solution to this combination; any faults in Vermuyden's general scheme were faults of initial diagnosis, not of execution. His system worked satisfactorily

·for a time after its completion in 1653, and would have continued to work had not the lowering of the land-surfaces through the shrinkage of the peat-lands especially, and of the silt-lands to a lesser degree, destroyed the one simple hydraulic factor on which that system was based, namely gravitational discharge. When this discharge ceased to function a new technology, involving the mechanical raising of water, was bound to be needed just as it had been necessary earlier in the Netherlands for similar reasons.

The extent to which the land shrank through desiccation was itself a measure of the effectiveness of Vermuyden's scheme of drainage. As its effectiveness

FIGURE 210—(Left) *Vertical windmill driving chain-of-buckets in a well;* (right) *fixed horizontal windmill driving scoop-wheel. 1652.*

deteriorated, the need for water-lifting became apparent, even if the true reason for that need was not well understood. When in 1664 William Dodson wrote his 'Designe for the perfect draining of the Great Level . . .' [11] he recognized the fact of land-shrinkage without appreciating the reason for it, yet made no suggestion that pumping had become generally essential in the Great Level. Dodson had worked under Vermuyden when the latter had been director of works and had succeeded him on his retirement in 1655. He had travelled extensively in the Netherlands and had seen how 'the Bempster, the Skermer, and the Wart, &c, . . . are all drained by a multitude of mills, each mill costs near six hundred pounds sterling' (plate 20). Indeed, he had been granted five patents in the Netherlands, relating to drainage-mills, between 1657 and 1660.

About the time of the completion of Vermuyden's scheme in the Great Level Walter Blith published 'The English Improver Improved or The Survey of

Husbandry Surveyed' (1652), and from his comments on the Fen drainage it is quite clear that drainage-mills were fairly common in individual fens although not part of the main scheme of reclamation and drainage [12]. They were, as Blith tells us, either 'wrought by the wind, or by the strength of horse; yea possibly by the strength of two or three men', and could raise the water either by a scoop-wheel 'or else by a good chain pump, or bucket work both of which may be made into a windmill-engine' (figure 210). These various forms of small drainage-mills were of comparatively primitive construction, and when eventually general pumping became imperative the technology of drainage-mill construction was largely borrowed from the Netherlands. Inevitably this technology became naturalized in time, and by the end of the seventeenth century the draining of the Fens as opposed to the initial reclamation had ceased to be the prerogative of Netherlanders. The chief obstacle to its success was the almost entire lack of a central administrative system such as existed in France and the Netherlands. The Fen drainage was at the mercy of commissions of sewers, whose limited powers were less fitted to deal with the wider problems of the seventeenth century than to contend with the simple parochial details facing them in earlier times. Indeed, a major fault was a failure to appreciate that the draining of the Fens was both a technological and an administrative problem.

REFERENCES

[1] VIERLINGH, A. 'Tractaet van Dyckagie' (2 vols), ed. by J. DE HULLU and A. G. VERHOEVEN. Rijks Geschiedkundige Publicatiën, The Hague. 1920.

[2] STEVIN, S. "Van de Spiegeling der Singconst" and "Van de Molens" (ed. by D. BIERENS DE HAAN. Amsterdam. 1884).

[3] Idem. 'Nieuwe Maniere van Sterctebou door Spilsluysen.' Van Waesberghe, Rotterdam. 1617.

[4] LEEGHWATER, J. A. 'Haerlemmer-Meer-Boeck.' Amsterdam. 1641.

[5] LUPICINI, ANTONIO. 'Discorso . . . sopra i ripari del Po e d'altri fiumi che hanno gl'argini di terra posticcia.' Marescotti, Florence. 1587.
Idem. 'Discorso . . . sopra i ripari delle inondazioni di Fiorenza.' Marescotti, Florence. 1591.

[6] MEIJER, C. J. 'L'Arte de restituire a Roma la tralasciata Navigatione del suo Tevere', Pt III: "Del modo di secare le Palude Pontine." Rome. 1683.
Idem. 'L'Arte di rendere i Fiumi navigabili in varii Modi, con altre nuove Inventioni.' Rome. 1696.

[7] CASTELLI, B. 'Della Misura dell'Acque Correnti.' Stamperia Camerale, Rome. 1628.

[8] GUGLIELMINI, G. D. 'Della Natura de' Fiumi, Trattato fisico-mathematica.' Bologna. 1697.

[9] BARATTIERI, G. B. 'Architettura d'Acque.' Piacenza. 1699.

[10] VERMUYDEN, SIR CORNELIS. 'A Discourse touching the Drayning the Great Fennes.' London. 1642.

[11] DODSON, W. 'The Designe for the perfect draining of the Great Level of the Fens.' London. 1665.

[12] BLITH, W. 'The English Improver Improved or the Survey of Husbandry Surveyed.' London. 1652.

BIBLIOGRAPHY

COOLS, R. H. A. 'Strijd om de grond in het lage Nederland.' Nijgh and Van Ditmar, Rotterdam. 1948.

DIENNE, COMTE DE. 'Histoire du dessèchement des lacs et marais en France avant 1789.' Paris. 1891.

DOORMAN, G. 'Patents for Inventions in the Netherlands during the 16th, 17th, and 18th centuries.' Nijhoff, The Hague. 1942.

HARRIS, L. E. 'Vermuyden and the Fens.' Cleaver-Hume Press, London. 1953.

KORTHALS ALTES, J. 'Polderland in Italië.' Van Stockum, The Hague. 1928.

PARSONS, W. B. 'Engineers and Engineering in the Renaissance.' Williams and Wilkins, Baltimore. 1939.

SERPIERI, A. 'La Bonifica nella storia e nella dottrina.' Edizione Agricola, Bologna. 1947.

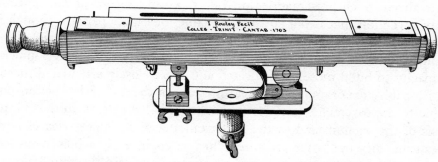

An early surveying level with telescopic sights and bubble, made by John Rowley, 1703.

13

MACHINES AND MECHANISMS

A. P. USHER

I. MACHINES IN GENERAL

THE techniques of machine-building are important in any period, and should not be thought of as involving only problems of mechanics without significance for the prime process of innovation and invention. In the sixteenth and seventeenth centuries, the character of technological change is as clearly revealed by techniques of machine-construction as by specific innovations. New skills in drawing and engraving made it possible to present many novel ideas in the form of sketches and plans, even if they were not at the time capable of being realized. Such presentations provide a positive record of the conceptual stage of invention that is not so fully available for earlier periods, though it is seldom entirely lacking. Outstanding characteristics of this time were the improvement of many well known devices and machines, and the development of the capacity to build more sophisticated and more closely articulated mechanisms. Probably, for example, the great increase in the use of the suction-pump was due to improvements in its construction: this led in turn to the complete analysis of the vacuum and to the understanding of a whole series of power-devices using air- and water-pressure. Thus an engineering achievement led to basic developments in pure and applied science, and laid the foundations for modern power-engineering. Because the full accomplishment came in the eighteenth century, its beginnings are often forgotten.

It is not easy to trace the development of the technique of machine-building accurately. Contemporary accounts do not always give details of construction, and it is unwise to draw inferences from sketches and plans. Fortunately, there is much detail in Agricola's *De re metallica* (1556), at the beginning of the period; while the *Architecture hydraulique* (1737–53) of Bernard Forest de Belidor (1693–1761) provides descriptions over a half-century or more at the end. With these and other works a chronology of machine-construction can be established.

An orderly process can be discerned in the complex array of details, if we can apply to these historical problems the principles of analysis developed by Reuleaux.[1] It is necessary to study the essential mechanical elements and the

---

[1] Franz Reuleaux, 'The Kinematics of Machinery'. London, 1876. (Translation of the German edition of 1875.)

efficiency with which they are employed, singly or in combination, as well as comprehensive trains of mechanism. New proficiencies in engineering are revealed by increased accuracy and definition in the interaction of the parts of machines. In general, the sixteenth and seventeenth centuries are notable for

FIGURE 211—*Agricola's gear-operated chain-and-bucket pump. 1556.*

great progress in the use of gears and screws, and for substitution of positive mechanical action for movements produced by the weight of the apparatus or the muscles of the operative. In this period, the primary achievements lay in the construction of precision instruments (ch 23) and in light engineering. The obsession of the nineteenth-century writers with prime movers long obscured the significance of the engineering and mechanical accomplishments of the sixteenth and seventeenth centuries, but a truer perspective has now been obtained and the earlier stages in technical development should be underestimated no longer.

Despite the great expansion of the iron industry, and the great increases in the skills of working and shaping metals, the use of metals in the construction of machinery proceeded very slowly. Here cost was more important than it was in making luxury goods or armaments, so that wood remained a basic material for machine-construction. Metals were used only for such parts of machines as required great strength or durability.

Agricola's description of the drive for a chain-of-buckets pump represents the most extensive use of iron in a sixteenth-century treatise (figure 211) [1].

First of all [he writes] I will describe the machines which draw water by chains of dippers, of which there are three kinds. For the first, a frame [A] is made entirely of iron bars; it is two and one half feet high, likewise two and one half feet long, and in addition one sixth and one quarter of a digit long, one fourth and one twenty-fourth of a foot wide. In it there are three little horizontal iron axles, which revolve in bearings or wide pillows of steel [K], and also four iron wheels of which two are made with rundles and the same number are toothed. Outside the frame, around the lowest axle [B], is a wooden fly-wheel [C], so that it can be more readily turned, and inside the frame is a smaller drum [D] which is made of eight rundles, one sixth and one twenty-fourth of a foot long. Around the second axle [E], which does not project beyond the frame, and is therefore only two and a half feet and one twelfth and one-third part of a digit long, there is on one side a smaller toothed wheel [F], which has forty eight teeth, and on the other side a larger drum [G], which is surrounded by twelve rundles one quarter of a foot long. Around the third axle [H], which is one inch and one third thick, is a larger toothed wheel [I] projecting one foot from the axle in all directions, which has seventy-two teeth. The teeth of each wheel are fixed in with screws, whose threads are screwed into threads in the wheel, so that those teeth which are broken can be replaced by others; both the teeth and the rundles are steel. The upper axle projects beyond the frame, and is so skilfully mortised into the body of another axle that it has the appearance of being one; this axle proceeds through a frame made of beams [M] which stands around the shaft, into an iron fork set in a stout oak timber [N]; and turns on a roller made of pure steel [P]. Around this axle is a drum [Q] of the kind possessed by those machines which draw water by rag-and-chain; this drum has triple curved iron clamps [R], to which the links of an iron chain [S] hook themselves, so that a great weight cannot tear them away. These links are not whole like the links of other chains, but each one being curved in the upper part on each side catches the one which comes next, whereby it presents the appearance of a double chain.

The figure shows the details of the parts as well as the complete machine, but it is important to note its false scale. The man turning the crank would surely suggest a wheel of 5 or 6 ft in diameter on the main driving-shaft, though it is stated to be only 2 ft. The roller-bearings are noteworthy. There are sketches of such bearings in the notebooks of Leonardo da Vinci, but there are not many indications of their use at this date.

FIGURE 212—*Agricola's water-driven ore-crusher, mill, and mixer. 1556.*

A more characteristic mechanism is Agricola's water-driven ore-crusher, mill, and mixer designed for the mercury-amalgamation treatment of gold ores (vol II, p 42) (figure 212):

This machine has one water-wheel [A], which is turned by a stream striking its buckets; the main axle [B] on one side of the water-wheel has long cams, which raise the stamps [C] that crush the dry ore. Then the crushed ore is thrown into the hopper of the upper millstone [D], and gradually falling through the opening, is ground to powder. The lower millstone [F] is square, but has a round depression [G] in which the round, upper millstone turns, and it has an outlet [H] from which the powder falls into the first tub [O]. A vertical iron axle [I] is dove-tailed into a cross-piece [K], which is in turn fixed into the upper millstone; the upper pinion [M] of this axle is held in a bearing fixed in a beam; the drum of the vertical axle is made of rundles, and is turned by a toothed drum [N] on the main axle, and thus turns the millstone. The powder falls continually into the first tub, together with water, and from there runs into a second tub which is set lower down, and out of the second into a third, which is the lowest; from the third, it generally flows into a small trough hewn out of a tree trunk. Quicksilver is placed in each tub, across which is fixed a small plank [P] and through a hole in the middle of each plank there passes a small upright axle [Q], which is enlarged above the plank to prevent it from dropping into the tub lower than it should. At the lower end of the axle three sets of paddles [S] intersect, each made from two little boards fixed to the axle opposite each other [2].

FIGURE 213—*Improved vertical water-mill described by Besson, making some use of the effect of reaction on the blades of the wheel, which are curved. 1579.*

The figure shows the general features of the wooden construction common in the treatise of Agricola and in his period. The water-wheel and the coarse-toothed wheels were common types. The loose engagement of the toothed wheels was centuries old, and continued with little change for two or three hundred years more. The train of gears for the chain-of-buckets previously described suggests a technique taken over from large clocks, whereas the machine shown in figure 212 is characteristic of the usual prime mover. It presents, however, an unusual feature in the drive-shaft with crown-wheels and lantern-pinions. From the eleventh and twelfth centuries onwards, shafts operating several devices commonly did so by means of tappets (vol II, pp 643–4).

There is little evidence of change in the design of construction of water-wheels and other machines using toothed wheels. The horizontal water-wheel without gearing, does, however, show an important new element. A new type is described by Jacques Besson (1579) as common in southern France (figure

213). This tub or pit-wheel introduced a new feature, which confined the stream and made more efficient use of the force exerted by the moving water on the vanes of the wheel. Thus the hydraulic action was more precisely controlled,

FIGURE 214—*Agricola's simple suction-pump. On the left a man is hollowing out tree-trunks, for pipes, with augers* (P, Q). *1556.*

not enough to make the wheel a true turbine, but enough to improve its performance [3]. This wheel, and other types that developed around Toulouse, undoubtedly set the stage for the invention of the water-turbine. The sixteenth century, however, worked with such loosely articulated machinery that a true turbine would have been inconceivable to the millwrights of the period.

The predominance of wood in the construction of mills is to be inferred from the plate in *Le diverse et artificiose machine* (Paris 1588), by Agostino Ramelli (1531–90), of the turret windmill for grinding grain. This is one of the earliest drawings of the turret windmill, though there is a rough sketch of this type in the notebooks of Leonardo. In his inadequate description, Ramelli states that the mill can be braked by the lever D, which tightens or releases a circular band in contact with a wheel on the main driving-axle of the mill (figure 47) [4].

After 1500 pumping machinery became much more important than during the Middle Ages. No new devices were invented, but many changes in design appeared. Mines and public or semi-public water-works required a progressive increase in the size of the installation. The prime movers involved little novelty of design or construction, whether water-, animal-, or man-power was used. The devices for raising the water reveal many advances in engineering as the suction-pump increased in importance in the sixteenth century. Even at an early date many parts of the pump were of metal, the use of lead, copper, and iron increasing steadily. In details of construction, as in its primary principle, the suction-pump laid the foundations for the steam-engine.

Agricola describes a simple form of suction-pump in which the use of metal was reduced to a minimum (figure 214). His description is particularly interesting because the construction of the piston and valves is shown in more detail than in other early drawings. This is the first of a group of seven suction-pumps.

Over the sump is placed a flooring, through which a pipe—or two lengths of pipe, one of which is joined into the other—is [or are] let down to the bottom of the sump [A]; they are fastened with pointed iron clamps driven in straight on both sides, so that the pipes may remain fixed. The lower end of the lower pipe is enclosed in a trunk [D] two feet deep; this trunk, hollow like the pipe, stands at the bottom of the sump, but the lower opening of it is blocked with a round piece of wood; the trunk has perforations round about, through which water flows into it. If there is one length of pipe, then in the upper part of the trunk which has been hollowed out there is enclosed a box of iron, copper, or brass, one palm deep, but without a bottom, and a rounded valve [F] so tightly closes it that the water which has been drawn up by suction cannot run back: but if there are two lengths of pipe, the box is enclosed in the lower pipe at the point of junction. An opening or a spout [G] in the upper pipe reaches to the drain of the tunnel. Thus, the workman, eager at his labour, standing on the flooring boards, pushes the piston down into the pipe and draws it out again. At the top of the piston-rod [H] is a hand-bar [I] and the bottom is fixed in a shoe [K]: this is the name given to the leather covering which is almost cone-shaped, for it is so stitched that it is tight at the lower end, where it is fixed to the piston rod which it surrounds, but in the upper end where it draws the water it is wide open. Or else an iron disk [L, M] one digit thick is used, or one of wood six digits thick, each of which is far superior to the shoe. The disk is fixed by an iron key which penetrates through the bottom of the piston-rod, or it is screwed on to the

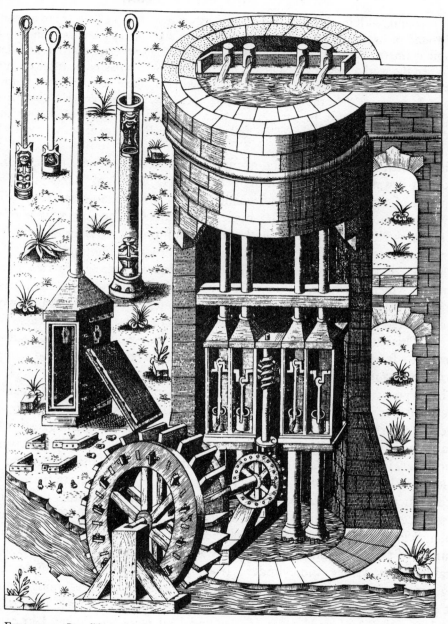

FIGURE 215—*Ramelli's quadruple suction-pump, 1588. Note the worm-drive. The insets show details of the valves.*

rod: it is round, with its upper part protected by a cover, and has five or six openings, either round or oval, which taken together present a star-like appearance; the disk has the same diameter as the inside of the pipe, so that it can be just drawn up and down in it. When the workman draws the piston up, the water which passed in at the openings of the disk, whose cover [N] is then closed, is raised to the hole or little spout, through which it flows away; then the valve of the box opens, and the water which has passed into the trunk is drawn up by suction and rises into the pipe, but when the workman pushes down the piston, the valve closes and allows the disk again to draw in the water [5].

The seventh of the series of suction-pumps consisted of a series of three pumps worked by a water-wheel 15 ft in diameter (vol II, figure 20). Each pump was composed of two 12-ft lengths of wood, with an inside diameter of 7 in. The piston-rods were 13 ft long and 3 inches in diameter. The valves were of the disk type described in connexion with the first pump. The driving-axle was iron, and a crank was used to convert rotary into reciprocating motion [6].

The fourth type of pump was distinctive because there were two pump-cylinders, which discharged into a tightly closed chamber with a single riser-pipe for outlet. The pistons were operated by manually turning a crank, which was connected to a double-throw crank-shaft of iron. The piston-rods also were of iron. This chamber is described as made of beech-wood, 5 ft long, 2 ft 6 in wide, and 1 ft 6 in thick. Because wood is likely to crack, the use of lead, copper, or brass is suggested [7].

This type of pump-action is shown in an elaborate drawing in Ramelli. A battery of four pumps is shown filling a cistern that serves an aqueduct. The valves are of a more advanced design than Agricola's, and there is a suggestion that metal be used for pipes, cylinders, axles, and pump-chambers. The description is, however, incomplete, and we therefore cannot be certain that this pump was constructed by Ramelli or in his time (figure 215) [8], but there can be no doubt that the suction-pump was extensively used, and its operation fully understood, almost a century before the scientific analysis of the vacuum by Galileo, Torricelli, and Pascal (c 1638–48). As the efficiency of the pump depended upon the tightness of the valves and piston, there was an evident advantage in the use of metal for pipes, valves, and cylinders. It would be tedious to follow in detail the progressive substitution of metals for wood in construction. It is enough to note that already in the second half of the seventeenth century cast iron pump-cylinders were employed, while copper and lead were widely used in pump-construction [9]. Pumps for domestic use were commonly made of lead, but the greater strength of copper made it desirable for larger installations. The general character of the engineering of this period is shown by Belidor's drawing of the pumping machine at the Pont Notre-Dame in Paris, which combined suction- and force-pumps (figure 216). The principal features are clearly evident in the draw-

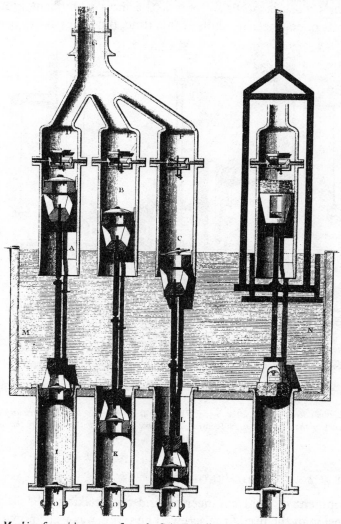

FIGURE 216—*Machine for raising water from the Seine installed at the Pont Notre-Dame, Paris, in 1670 and later reconstructed. The pumps were driven by a triple-throw crank rotated by a water-wheel turned by the river. Four sets of three pumps made up the whole machine.* (I, K, L) *Suction-pumps;* (A, B, C) *force-pumps;* (O, O, O) *supply-pipes rising 16 ft above the river;* (G) *pipe to hydrants.*

ing, notably the device for driving both pistons from one connexion with the power-shaft. The pump-cylinders were castings, but the metal is not named. In the reconstruction by Belidor in 1737 the principles were not modified, but the

dimensions of cylinders and pipes were changed to provide for a better utilization of the capacity of the pumps. There were also revisions in the design of the
pistons. Belidor's work is probably one of the most significant indications we
have of the limits of engineering skills at this time, but it has as yet been too little
studied.

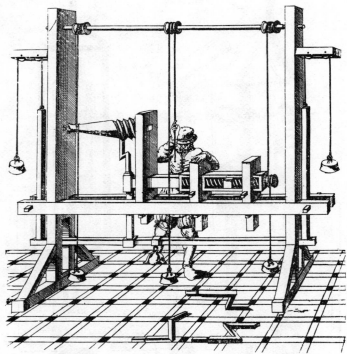

FIGURE 217—*Besson's screw-cutting lathe, 1579. The work is at the upper left. The curiously shaped tool is
traversed by means of the long lead-screw (centre). Screw and work are both rotated by the high shaft and
pulleys.*

II. THE SCREW AND ITS DEVELOPMENT

The development of light engineering and tool-making is closely associated
with the extension of the use of the screw. The screw was well known in antiquity
(vol II, pp 631–3), but its application was limited. Wooden screws were used
in heavy-duty apparatus such as the olive-press, as well as in smaller devices for
wine-making, compressing bales of cloth, and weight-lifting. The use of finer
metal screws in instruments of precision was certainly suggested (p 610).

Although taps and dies were understood and are sketched by Hero of Alexandria, screws were made with the simplest hand-tools. The modern concept of

the use of the screw in tool-making and machine-construction is first recorded by Leonardo da Vinci. In this respect, as in many others, it is not possible to determine the extent of his obligations to predecessors, but his work with the screw seems so far in advance of his time that we assume it to be original. His notebooks contain many sketches of long lead-screws used to control mechanical devices for reproducing the screw itself or for controlling cutting or shaping. The most important sketches show two schemes for reproducing a long lead-screw by mechanical devices. The first system shows a pole-driven lathe with a

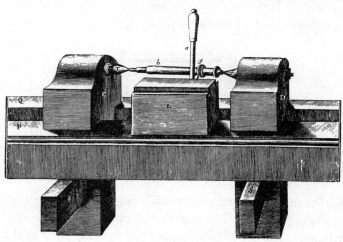

FIGURE 218—*Turning an iron mandrel on a lathe between puppets* (T, T). *The mandrel* (bg) *is rotated by means of a cord looped round it which is attached to a foot-treadle and a pole.* (a) *The cutting-tool;* (L) *the tool-rest.*

traversing-tool. The second system provides for more control of the cutting-tool. It is carried on a frame governed by two master screws, and cuts a thread on a blank spindle set between the master screws (vol II, figure 598). There is, therefore, clear evidence of a complete understanding of the basic principles of the use of a lead-screw. In this instance there are no grounds for presuming that Leonardo attempted to make such a machine. As sketched by him it would probably have proved too light even for cutting screws in wood.

Besson illustrates a screw-cutting lathe with a long lead-screw and a traversing-tool (figure 217). The figure shows a piece of ornamental work in the lathe, but the construction would make it possible to reproduce the lead-screw. The oval-turning lathe of Besson was clearly intended for use in ornamental turning and need not occupy our attention.

Despite the adequacy of these machines in principle, they could not be used in practice, and long screws in wood or metal were cut with chisel or file, much as in antiquity. Short screws, both coarse and fine and in metal or wood, were commonly used for scientific purposes after 1650, for focusing microscopes and on many measuring instruments (ch 23). Long screws were, however, expensive and likely to be inaccurate. The use of a long lead-screw was obstructed by these difficulties in production. It is significant that lathe-work was developed on an alternative principle that presented less technical difficulty. The so-called mandrel-lathe was controlled by one or more short screws which gave the work a traverse of a few inches. Small pieces could be turned with the guidance of these screws supplemented by some form of fixed support for the cutting-tool.

FIGURE 219—*Cutting the screw on the mandrel with the tool* C, *which is fixed by the pins in the block* M. *A guide-screw soldered into the end of the mandrel works in a female thread in the puppet* K; *thus the accuracy of the screw on the mandrel itself depends on the accuracy of the guide-screw.*

The mandrel-lathe is first recorded in a small engraving in Hartman Schopper's book on the crafts (1568) [10]. The engraving is too small to give any idea of the details of construction. It is difficult to trace the development of the lathe in the seventeenth century, before Plumier's detailed account of 1701 [11]. It was used principally for ornamental turning, but it embodied principles that were later to be of industrial significance, especially in clock- and watch-making.

In Plumier's time it was possible to cut the screws for the arbors of the mandrel on a lathe. Plumier was anxious to do so because it was difficult to produce a perfectly cylindrical mandrel with a file; but he found only two work-men in Europe capable of turning satisfactory mandrels in iron and steel. They used lathes of special construction firmly fixed between floor and ceiling and with some backing against the wall. A model of the mandrel was made in wood, somewhat larger in diameter than the finished article. The iron was first forged to this copy and turned to the shape required in the lathe (figure 218). A thread was then cut upon the end of the turned mandrel by the method shown in figure 219. The complete lathe is illustrated in figure 220. The same principle can be used in a centre-lathe, but Plumier gives no plate showing the general assembly of such a lathe. The production of screws by mechanical methods was thus severely limited. Techniques of casting should have been applicable to the production of screws in bronze. Cast iron would hardly have been satisfactory.

When these difficulties and costs of production are considered it is not easy to interpret the sketches of Besson and Ramelli, suggesting a wide application of heavy-duty screws to industry and construction. Yet examples survive to

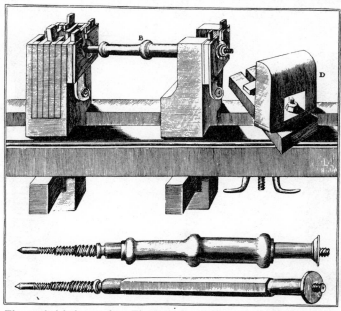

FIGURE 220—*The mandrel lathe complete. The traversing-screw on the mandrel engages in the left-hand puppet, so that it travels to and fro when rotated first in one direction and then in the other by a cord looped round at* B. *The cord is connected by one end to a treadle and by the other to a pole.* D *is the tool-rest. The frames of all these lathes were of wood. When continuous rotation was required a plain mandrel was used on which a pulley was mounted. An endless cord passed round this pulley and a large wheel turned by a crank.* (Below) *Two forms of mandrel with traversing-screws. Note short thread at the other end for attaching the work.*

indicate that their ideas were not wholly visionary, though the elaborate decoration of the door-jack made at Nuremberg *c* 1570 (figure 221) suggests an article of luxury rather than an industrial appliance. The small screws used in scientific instruments and in bench-vices show the quality of craftsmen's skill that had been developed (plate 25) [12].

New applications of the screw-press principle were made in printing and coinage. As is described below (p 382) the early printing-press was an adaptation of one of the lighter presses with a wooden screw, and it is first depicted in printers' devices (figure 250). About 1550, Danner of Nuremberg substituted copper for wood in the screw and secured finer impressions. Other details of the press are not primarily involved in the screw and its action.

The earliest use of a screw-press for die-stamping metals is attributed to Bramante. It is believed that he struck the lead seals of Pope Julius II (1503–13) with such a press. Medals, from dies engraved by Caradosso for Julius II, were also struck on a screw-press [13]. This new method of shaping precious metals, later extended to a wide variety of products, initiated a new type of quantity-production by die-stamping in powerful machines. Other forms of mechanized

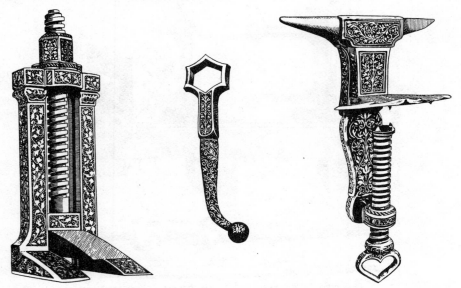

FIGURE 221—*Steel screws in engineering devices.* (Left) *Jack for lifting heavy doors, with contemporary spanner;* (right) *bench-vice with fixing-screw. Nuremberg work,* c *1570.*

metal-working, such as rolling- and slitting-machines, are described below (p 342).

We have no details of the construction of the first coinage presses. Cellini, however, describes a screw-press used by him to strike brass medals for Pope Clement VII (1523–34). Cellini's treatise on goldsmithery gives no drawing of the press, but figure 222 has been reconstructed from his description.

Make a frame of iron as thick and wide as in the method previously described [two fingers thick and four wide] but so much longer as to admit, besides the two [square] dies on which the medal is cut in intaglio, the female screw of bronze which is cast upon the iron male screw.[1] This male screw is indeed what we commonly call a 'screw', and

---

[1] The screw would be cut by hand, but there was no way of cutting the corresponding female thread directly in the iron frame. Therefore a separate bronze nut was made by direct casting on the screw, covering it with a mixture of ashes and fat and enclosing it in a suitable mould. The contraction of the metals would allow the screw to move in the nut after cooling.

the female screw is called a 'nut'. The male screw should be made three fingers thick and its threads should be made [of] square [section], because they are stronger than those made in the other, ordinary way. The frame should be open at the top, and since the dies will be placed in it, and between the dies the metal to be stamped, it is necessary that the size of the nut be such that it does not shift in the frame. And because the dies have to be somewhat smaller, they are firmly fixed with iron wedges so that they do not move at all. Then have prepared a section of beam two *bracchia*[1] or more long, which is buried so that only half a *bracchio* remains above ground. This end is well planed. The lower end of the beam fits into a big piece of timber more than two *bracchia* long, while the frame is fitted into a slot in its upper end, into which [the frame] fits exactly. Then it is necessary to make clamps of strong iron, which strengthen the aforesaid beam where the screw [*read* frame] is fitted into it, so that it is not split.[2] The upper end of the screw is divided, and into this divided part is fitted a big ring of iron, which has two extensions that are pierced and fitted to a long pole, not less than 6 feet long. Then with four men dextrously holding the dies and the blank upright, [the latter] is stamped, which brings about the perfection of the medal. And in this way I struck for Pope Clement more than a hundred all of brass, without casting them, as I observed above is necessary when you choose to strike them like coins.[3] Finally the force of the screw is such when well considered that, although it is more costly and therefore renders this method of striking more expensive than the other way, it expends less money. Because, apart from the medals being better struck, the dies are less rapidly worn out; and, speaking of gold and silver [medals], I struck a great quantity without annealing any of them. In short medals are always properly stamped with two turns of the screw, whereas a hundred blows in ordinary coining would hardly have made one. Whence, for every one struck by the coiners, twenty are stamped with the screw; and of this enough has been said [14].

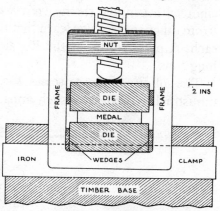

FIGURE 222—*Diagrammatic reconstruction of Cellini's screw-press for striking medals. The lower part of the timber foundation and the 'big ring of iron' (which was presumably attached to the screw in the horizontal plane) are omitted.*

Cellini's remark that the capital expenditure required to install a screw-press was heavy compared with that for the ordinary hand-coiner's equipment, and the fact that the coiners would lose their livelihood, may explain the resistance to the introduction of presses into mints.

[1] A *bracchio* is about 18 inches.
[2] Apparently, bands of iron are fastened tightly round the upper part of the vertical beam, to prevent it from splitting through the torque exerted by the frame when the screw is forced round.
[3] Compare vol II, p 488.

III. BALANCE-PRESSES AND ROLLING-MILLS

The later form of balance-press is exemplified in the press of 1698 in the museum of the Hôtel des Monnaies, Paris (figure 223). The presses described by Abot de Bezinghen (1764) were of iron or bronze mounted on a heavy block of wood, marble, or cast iron. The lead balls at the ends of the balance will be noted. They varied with the length and weight of the bar. In the middle of the eighteenth century the heaviest weighed 150 lb each; the lightest 50 lb each. From other sources, we learn that these balance-presses weighed about 26 000 lb each. A press set up at the Royal Mint in London in 1651 weighed about 13 long tons.

The solidity of these presses was, of course, vital to their success. It may seem unjustifiable to classify such apparatus as light engineering, but the term can

FIGURE 223—*Balance coining-press in the Museum of the Hôtel des Monnaies. 1698.*

best be used to distinguish mechanisms operated by human or animal power from appliances driven by prime movers capable of exerting several horse-power. The balance-press was a truly elegant machine. With the weighted ends to store the energy used in swinging it, the minimum of power was required and none was wasted. It represented a high standard of mechanical design.

The technique of working and shaping metals mechanically was closely associated with the development of coinage by machinery. Rolls and shears came into limited use in the working of copper and brass for other purposes, but the first major application of them is to be found in coinage machinery. The earliest sketches of rolls for working metals are in the notebooks of Leonardo da Vinci. Two devices are shown: relatively broad rolls for preparing sheet metal and narrow rolls for shaping staves [15].

In the second system the rolls were cut to produce a given profile on the staves. There was, therefore, a full awareness of the possible applications of these machines to metal-working. Curiously enough, the set of machines for coinage included a power-driven hammer for preparing the strips from which the blanks were to be cut. Leonardo sketched two types of punches for cutting blank coins, and an ingenious frame with a collar to direct a plunger against the die. Although he was associated with the mint in Rome at one time, there is no evidence that any of these devices were actually used.

The earliest applications of a new process of coinage occurred in France. Cellini had visited France in 1537, and a reform of the methods of coinage was discussed, but nothing was done. A new coinage was proposed in 1548 under Henri II and, on the suggestion of the French ambassador in Austria, mint machinery was purchased from Max Schwab, a goldsmith of Augsburg. There were rolls for reducing the cast plates or bars to proper thickness; draw-benches to adjust the thickness of the rolled product; circular punches for making blanks; balance-presses for striking the coins; and tongs, or appliances for holding the dies under the press [16]. The machines were set up in the Palais du Louvre in January 1552. The *Cour des Monnaies* opposed this project, but coins were produced at the Louvre until 1585, when the *Cour des Monnaies* succeeded in restricting the manufacture at the Louvre to medals and copper. Despite these restrictions on its activity, the technique was perfected and in continuous use.

A different method of using rolls for coinage came into use at Hall (now Solbad Hall) in the Tyrol about 1575. The prepared strips of gold or silver were passed between engraved rolls, which impressed the design on the strips. The coins were then cut out of the strips by punches, and finished. This process was brought to Spain and set up at Segovia, because there was no adequate water-power in Madrid. A somewhat similar process was developed by Nicholas Briot and used in the Scottish mint in 1639. The designs were engraved on portions of two cylinders, which did not make a full revolution. The blanks were made oval, but became round in passing through the rolls [17]. We must, therefore, presume that the Tyrolese system was not likely to rival the balance-press introduced in France with the rolls for preparing the blanks.

The power-driven rolls of the French system were introduced into England in 1561, but the French workman, Mestrell, was condemned to death for counterfeiting. No subsequent use of the rolling-mill for the English coinage can be ascertained before Peter Blondeau was brought over from Paris in 1649. In 1651 he was authorized to issue coins in collaboration with Thomas Simon, the engraver of the Mint. Blondeau added to the equipment of the French system a device for marking the edges of the coins with an incised or raised motto, or with serrations. Coinage began in 1657–8 [18].

The application of rolls to working copper and lead cannot be traced with any assurance in the period immediately following Leonardo's time, nor do we know how the practices he described were related to the techniques current in his time (p 47 and figure 19). The treatises of Zonca (1607), de Caus (1615), and Branca (1629) describe applications of the rolling-mill on a small scale to gold, silver, copper, and lead. These descriptions, however, are of no great importance as rolls were already established in the mints, and early applications to iron-working were described by Esban Hesse in 1532. Rolls were also used for preparatory processes by the wire-drawers and nail-makers of Nuremberg. In the earliest account there is no clear reference to flat rolls; a sheet already prepared was passed through a series of cutting-rolls which produced small bands suitable for drawing. Later, flat rolls were used to give greater uniformity to sheet iron [19].

We have little detail on the use of rolls in the seventeenth century, though it is implied that black sheets for tinning were rolled in Saxony in that period. Substantial information is first available in the 'Political Testament' (1746) of Christopher Polhem (Polhammer) which describes methods of iron-working that can be safely carried back to the beginnings of the century. After a long association with iron- and copper-mining as engineer, director of the mines at Falun, and member of the Swedish commission on mines, he established a manufactory for iron and other metal products at Stjärnsund, about 1704. The works produced a wide array of iron and steel products for industry, agriculture, and general consumption. Copper, bronze, tin, and lead were also worked up. Tinned sheets and articles made from them were especially important [20]. The underlying conception of the establishment was the utilization of water-power wherever possible, even though supplementary manual labour was necessary for finishing processes. There was, therefore, a deliberate and planned division of the processes of manufacture, sometimes using different mechanisms for different stages of the process, sometimes employing machinery and manual work in succession. The works were operated continuously until after Polhem's death in 1751. They were destroyed by fire some years later, and never rebuilt. These new techniques of production exerted an important influence in Sweden and elsewhere. They represent the highest level of accomplishment of an iron industry based on charcoal, and dependent for primary power on water-wheels and horse-driven gins. Unfortunately, Polhem's 'Political Testament' is not illustrated, but many models of his machinery are preserved in the museum of the commission already mentioned.

The machinery at Stjärnsund was of two kinds—hammers and rolls. The hammers, even when worked by power, represent the older technique. The rolls were an advance over contemporary methods of metal-working. According to the water-power available, it was possible to produce on the rolls ten or twenty times as much band iron as could be finished under the hammers. Rolls could be designed to turn out rough knife-blades to be cut apart and finished by the blade-smiths. With the rolls, all kinds of rods and bars were made—square, round, or half-round—as well as strips of steel for files. Sheets were rolled for plates and dishes, and for a variety of tin wares [21]. Polhem was not alone in using rolls for these purposes, but he says that hammers were more commonly employed and that the number of rolls in Sweden was small. This he ascribed to the difficulty of making them.

This process, invented in 1737 and first used in the mint at Cassel, is described carefully in the 'Political Testament'.

All kinds of the smaller rolls up to six or seven inches in diameter can be easily forged out of good iron. The surface is hardened by applying a layer of steel which is welded on and forged. The rolls are then turned on a lathe driven by a small water-wheel. The cutting tool is fastened in a block which is drawn down the length of the lathe by a long screw. This is commonly done by the hand of the turner, but the machine can be arranged so that the water-wheel turns the screw. When the rolls have been turned on the lathe, they are placed in a lathe without traverse which is turned by a wheel. In this lathe they are corrected with small tools and files so that they are round and smooth. They are then tempered. . . . After being tempered the rolls are put back in the lathe and tested to see if they are still as round as they were before, which rarely happens. It may well be that the steel is thinner in some places than in others, so that in cooling the side where the steel is thinnest contracts more. If the rolls are also not defective because they have laminated, which can easily happen in the course of tempering, one proceeds to polish them. This is done by passing a band around the roll and polishing it under a tin or leaden cover with coarse and later fine emery until it is smooth and round [22].

There is a brief reference to the problems of rolling roofing-sheets, and the 'Political Testament' then proceeds with a description of the use of cast iron rolls and of the process of casting them. Polhem also gives directions for making rolls of malleable iron, which were specially treated to make tin-plate.

The whole account is rich in its implications. The general understanding of the use of rolls was not new, but Polhem was doing many new things with them: partly because of his more vivid vision of the advantages of a less direct process of production, partly because his versatility as an engineer made it possible for him to achieve new results by better methods of machine construction. The successful solution of engineering problems is essential if effect is to be given to new modes of motion and new compositions of the elements of mechanisms. Polhem's work provides a fresh standard for measuring the technical accomplishment of the first generation of the eighteenth century. To attain any complete knowledge of the history of technology it is essential to understand the nature of the achievement of such practical engineers of the age before the great industrial revolution as Belidor and Polhem, who prepared the way for its far-reaching economic and social changes. Polhem was an inventor of great fertility of imagination, as well as an engineer of distinction. It is a strange caprice of history that he is so little known.[1]

IV. SCIENCE AND THE ENGINEER

It is important to emphasize the close interweaving of engineering as an empirical practice with science as a systematic investigation of general principles occurring in this period. The sixteenth and seventeenth centuries mark the transition from complete empiricism to engineering techniques fully grounded in mathematics and applied science. Leonardo made great advances in the rigorous analysis of problems of dynamics, and his work was carried to a high level of achievement by the great figures of the seventeenth century, particularly Galileo, Huygens, and Newton. Scientific work was sometimes closely related to practical problems of engineering. The analysis of the vacuum by Galileo, Torricelli, and Pascal was directly inspired by the extending use of the suction-pump. Their results led directly to the study of steam and to the atmospheric steam-engine.

Special problems of dynamics were encountered in the development of clocks and watches (ch 24). Analysis of the properties of the pendulum and of the balance-spring resulted in notable improvements in their performance. These discoveries were not empirical achievements, but the result of the application of mathematics to the study of dynamics begun by Galileo and continued by Huygens and Newton. Increased interest in the determination of longitude by accurate measurement of time rendered the improvement of clocks a question of practical as well as scientific importance, and prevented complacent acceptance of standards that fell short of the precision required in astronomical work.

In the analysis of the pendulum there is an interesting point which illustrates the fact that the attainment of theoretical perfection in a device may not be essential to its practical success. At an early date Huygens recognized that though the pendulum is not (as Galileo had supposed) perfectly isochronous when swinging in circular arcs, the errors introduced are negligible if the arc is small. In his rare work *Horologium* (1658) he described a clock in which the circular error was so reduced by making the pendulum swing through only a

---

[1] For an account of his life (1661–1751), see *Nouvelle Biographie Universelle* (1852–66).

few degrees. It was not until the end of 1659 that he discovered that oscillation in a cycloidal arc is invariably isochronous, irrespective of its amplitude. From this time, influenced partly by the elegance of his mathematical discovery and partly by his belief that pendulums with a large swing would keep time more accurately at sea, he constructed his clocks in such a way that the pendulum traversed a wide cycloidal arc. Although Huygens's work on the cycloid marks an important contribution to dynamical theory, his earlier observation was more significant for practical clock-making. All practical pendulum clocks since then have used a pendulum swinging in a short circular arc, and the cycloidal cheeks devised by Huygens were never generally adopted; they are indeed quite unnecessary complications.

The introduction of the pendulum, which increased the accuracy of time-keeping at least tenfold, gave a great impetus to the attempt to improve the mechanics of the clock, by cutting gear-teeth more precisely and to the most efficient profile, and by devising new escapements, such as the anchor and dead-beat types (pp 665, 671), which would enable the pendulum to oscillate with as little disturbance from the drive as possible. The superiority of epicycloidal teeth was first shown by Roemer and Huygens in 1674 and 1675, their results being communicated to the Académie des Sciences in Paris. Huygens continued the investigation with a study of the form of teeth for crown wheels in 1680. Further studies in this field were made by Camus in 1735, and Thiout in 1741.

The attempt to examine the action and shape of gear-wheel teeth scientifically was, however, limited to the light trains of clocks and watches. Here much advance took place, but it was almost without effect on the design of heavy-duty gears, for example in millwrights' work. In this respect, as in others already discussed (accurate machining of parts by use of the lathe, use of the screw, and so forth), small-scale light engineering led the way towards higher standards of craftsmanship and design. The skill, the machine-tools, and the economic incentive were as yet lacking in the early eighteenth century to transfer to manufacturing machinery the precision and complexity already found in scientific instruments, clocks, and watches; but the basic principles required were at hand, and fully worked out on this small scale.

REFERENCES

[1] AGRICOLA, GEORGIUS. *De re metallica libri XII*, Eng. trans. and comm. by H. C. HOOVER and LOU H. HOOVER, pp. 172–4. Dover Publications New York. 1950.

[2] *Idem. Ibid.*, pp. 295–7.

[3] BESSON, JACQUES. 'Theatre des instrumens mathematiques et mechaniques.' B. Vincent, Lyons. 1579.

[4] RAMELLI, AGOSTINO. 'Le diverse et artificiose machine', ch. 132. Publ. by the author, Paris. 1588.

[5] AGRICOLA, GEORGIUS. See ref. [1], p. 176.

[6] *Idem. Ibid.*, pp. 184–5.

[7] *Idem. Ibid.*, pp. 179–81.

[8] RAMELLI, AGOSTINO. See ref. [4], p. 8.

[9] BELIDOR, B. FOREST DE. 'Architecture hydraulique', Vol. 2, Pt I, pp. 105–8, 114–17, 207–9. Jombert, Paris. 1739.

[10] SCHOPPER, HARTMAN. *De omnibus illiberalibus sive mechanicis artibus humani ingenii* [Illustrations by JOST AMMAN]. Frankfurt a. M. 1568.

[11] PLUMIER, C. 'L'Art de tourner en perfection', pp. 11–12. Lyons. 1701.

[12] TREUE, W. 'Kulturgeschichte der Schraube von der Antike bis zum achtzehnten Jahrhundert', pp. 126–31. Bruckmann, Munich. 1955.

[13] HOCKING, W. J. *Numism. Chron.*, fourth series, **9**, 60, 1909.

[14] CELLINI, BENVENUTO. Opere, Vol. 3, pp. 109–11. Milan. 1811. The quotation on pp. 338–9 translated and the figure reconstructed by A. R. Hall.

[15] UCCELLI, A. 'Storia della Tecnica dal Medio Evo ai Nostri Giorni', figs 73, 74, 83, 84. Hoepli, Milan. 1945.

[16] HOCKING, W. J. See ref. [13], pp. 68–69.

[17] ROBERTS, C. *J. Soc. Arts.* **32**, 811, 1883.

[18] HOCKING, W. J. See ref. [13], pp. 72–95.

[19] BECK, L. 'Die Geschichte des Eisens in technischer und kulturgeschichtlicher Bedeutung', Vol. 2, pp. 513–14. Vieweg, Braunschweig. 1893–5.

[20] *Idem. Ibid.*, Vol. 3, pp. 1101–4. 1897.
SCHREBER, D. G. 'Sammlung verschiedener Schriften, welche in die öconomischen, Policey- und Cameral-, auch andere Wissenschaften einschlagen', Vols 11, 12. Halle. 1763.

[21] BECK, L. See ref. [19], Vol. 3, p. 245. 1897.

[22] *Idem. Ibid.*, Vol. 3, pp. 246 f. 1897.

BIBLIOGRAPHY

HART, I. B. 'The Mechanical Inventions of Leonardo da Vinci.' Chapman and Hall, London. 1925.

PARSONS, W. B. 'Engineers and Engineering in the Renaissance.' Williams and Wilkins, Baltimore. 1939.

TREUE, W. 'Kulturgeschichte der Schraube.' Bruckmann, Munich. 1955.

UCCELLI, A. 'Storia della Tecnica dal Medio Evo ai Nostro Giorni.' Hoepli, Milan. 1945.

USHER, A. P. 'History of Mechanical Inventions.' (rev. ed.). Harvard University Press, Cambridge, Mass. 1954.

14

MILITARY TECHNOLOGY

A. R. HALL

I. STRATEGY AND TACTICS

D URING the sixteenth and seventeenth centuries there was no such violent revolution in the art of war as the invention of gunpowder had wrought in the Middle Ages (vol II, pp 374–82, 726–7). The consequences of that revolution had begun to be of considerable effect during the fifteenth century and were carried progressively farther during the present period until a new position of stability was attained towards its close. Thereafter, though there was a great improvement in the organization of military forces, and a large increase in their size, there was little further change in weapons or the methods of their manufacture for some 150–200 years. The flint-lock musket, the muzzle-loading smooth-bore gun, and common black powder remained the principal destructive agents until well after the Napoleonic wars; only about the middle of the nineteenth century were they rendered obsolete by advances in metallurgy, engineering practice, and chemistry.

Hand-guns and field- and siege-artillery were already prominent in war before 1500. The only major innovation of the next two centuries was the extensive use of explosive projectiles in the form of hand-grenades and mortar-bombs, weapons rarely employed in the fifteenth century and having their greatest scope in the elaborate siege-operations of the seventeenth. But the problem of utilizing fire-arms in the field had not been satisfactorily solved by medieval armies. The administrative problems ranged from high questions of national policy, such as the establishment of powder-works and the control of the armaments industry, to the mobility of artillery in the field and the provision of different kinds of powder, ball, and match. Armies became far more dependent on the organization of their baggage-trains and lines of supply than formerly. By the end of the seventeenth century these matters had been settled as well as the transport and other means of the time allowed—as one may see, for example, from Marlborough's long march before Blenheim (1704). The manufacture of arms was carefully supervised by the state, or even conducted in its own establishments, and facilities for experimentation and inspection had been created. Large quantities of cannon and ammunition could be moved as the commander required, specialist corps of engineers and artillerymen had been formed, and logistics played an important part in the preparation for actual operations.

Thus the greater technical complexity of war stimulated both the growth in power of the state and the enforcement of stern discipline and training within its armed forces. The impetuousness of feudal chivalry had indeed been checked by English archers in the fourteenth century and Swiss pikemen in the fifteenth, but the new weapons demanded high precision in the performance of routine operations, and absolute steadiness at moments when the infantryman or gunner with a discharged piece might seem defenceless in face of an enemy onslaught. For the rate of fire of early guns was very slow, and the hand-gunner especially had to become perfect in the elaborate sequence of motions involved in the loading and firing of his weapon: all modern military drill derives essentially from this fact.

Throughout the period, infantry were divided in their defensive and offensive functions, the pikeman providing the former and the hand-gunner the latter. Various tactical formations were adopted to enable arquebusiers or musketeers to bring their weapons into play while sheltering behind pikes which protected them from enemy cavalry, this enforced combination of arms itself enhancing the need for parade-ground precision in movement and obedience to orders [1]. Only towards the end of the seventeenth century was the solution to this tactical problem discovered, in the attachment to the musket of a bayonet which, without impeding the firing of the piece, rendered it nearly as effective in defence or a charge as the true pike. About the same time, too, the cartridge was introduced, a paper packet containing a measured charge of powder and a ball, so that the operation of loading the musket was simplified and made more rapid.

There are pictures of horsemen carrying hand-guns in the fifteenth century, but the weapon could hardly have been effective in the hands of cavalry before the invention of the wheel-lock pistol (p 355). Thereafter cavalry, like infantry, divided into two classes: those equipped with piercing or slashing weapons (lances and sabres), and those equipped with fire-arms. They had correspondingly different functions, the former being mainly used to destroy a broken or disorderly formation, and the latter acting as mobile musketeers. The tendency for the horseman to lose the pre-eminence he had enjoyed in the earlier Middle Ages, already apparent before gunpowder played a serious role in war, was certainly fortified by the new invention. At the beginning of the sixteenth century the most formidable fighting force in Europe was the Spanish infantry (as the Swiss pikemen had been previously), and military writers pay far more attention to the tactical management of infantry than to that of cavalry. The first half of the next century, however, saw a succession of great cavalry leaders (Maurice of Nassau, Gustavus Adolphus, and Oliver Cromwell especially) who learnt how to combine the impetus of a charge with a deliberate volley from heavy pistols, and to exploit thereby the weaknesses of unmounted troops. In the wars of Louis XIV's reign, the foot-soldier recovered his position with improved weapons and more effective support from field-artillery, while the restriction of mobility by prolonged sieges allowed fewer opportunities for the horseman's dash. Nevertheless, this still had its important place in open warfare until less than a century ago.

Strategy was dominated by three considerations: the desire to bring about or avoid a pitched battle between two armies, destroying the enemy force or preserving one's own; the need to secure lines of communication and, for many states, open avenues between their geographically scattered territories; and the ambition to occupy the enemy's seat of government. From the later stages of the Hundred Years War to Charles VIII's invasion of Italy in 1494 with what was perhaps the first 'modern' army, excellently equipped with artillery, wars had been fought on a minor scale: the Wars of the Roses (1455–85) in England were hardly more than a series of skirmishes, and in Italy fighting was carried out by mercenaries who so arranged matters that battles were decided without much bloodshed.

In the Italian wars between France and Spain in the early sixteenth century, however, the vital issue was the occupation or effective control of Rome and the chief cities; hence war became more bitter as the rival forces sought each other's complete destruction. The same is still more true of the Wars of Religion (c 1540–1648), which were for the most part civil wars involving each religious party in the ambition to secure complete dominion over its opponents. The revolt of the Spanish provinces in the Netherlands (1566–1609) and the Thirty Years War (1618–48) in Germany both show concentrated attention devoted to the technical improvement of arms and fortification, widespread destruction of towns and civilian population, and a growing realization of the significance of economic considerations in determining strategy. As religious fanaticism declined, commercial rivalry took its place, with the Dutch as the main object first of English, and later of French envy; and European wars were now regularly extended to the colonial possessions of combatant powers. For a number of reasons, including the perfection of means of fortification, continental warfare was restricted in violence, moving—apart from the occasional brilliance of such a commander as Marlborough—from siege to leisurely siege. Victories costly in human life, like that of Malplaquet (1709), were avoided by prudent generals.

Something should be said of naval warfare, since the invention of artillery opened the possibility for completely new tactics. In early naval battles a ship might be lost through boarding and capture (the method preferred by the Romans), by ramming, or by the use of incendiary compositions such as 'Greek fire' (vol II, p 375). With cannon it was possible to batter a vessel into an unnavigable wreck, to sink it by shot below the water-line, and not infrequently to blow it up by the explosion of its own magazine of powder. Such tactics, relying on bombardment from very heavy guns, were apparently first fully exploited by English sailors, classically against the Spanish Armada in 1588. Before this, naval commanders had rather aimed at weakening the crews of enemy vessels by light cannon and small shot in preparation for boarding, as at the famous battle of Lepanto (1571); but the numerous small guns and large crews of the Armada were never able to take an effective part in that action. Broadside tactics were paramount in naval battles until after the time of Nelson; ships were little more than platforms for increasingly more massive cannon, and the issue was decided by weight of round-shot delivered at point-blank range. Cannon of the size mounted on the lower decks of first-rate men-of-war were almost immovable on land; hence it was from the sea that the demand came to the foundries for ever weightier and stronger castings.

II. WEAPONS (OTHER THAN FIRE-ARMS) AND ARMOUR

There was little alteration in the art of the smith, and it may well be that the sword-steel of early modern times was inferior in quality to that of the famous blades of Damascus and Toledo. The temper of steel weapons and armour was no longer such a critical matter as it had been in the past. In northern Europe there was some substitution of coal for charcoal in the smith's forge, and his material—bar iron—was wrought for him by water-driven hammers and, later, rolling-mills. It was not yet possible to smelt iron-ore with coal, to roll iron plate, or to make and work steel in large quantities. Weapons and armour were forged by traditional hand-work methods without the aid of power, though Stradanus shows armour being polished by water-driven machinery (figure 224).

Of the types of steel weapons little need be said. The sword with all its variants—claymore, cutlass, sabre, rapier—remained an important arm in the sixteenth and seventeenth centuries and was still carried by pikemen, for hand-to-hand fighting occurred in all serious battles; but by 1750 it had become little more than a symbol of gentility. Apart from the cavalry sabre emphasis tended to be placed on play with the point rather than on slashing strokes: thus the sword became lighter and more flexible. The hilts of special weapons were elaborated with decorative work. Axe-like weapons, such as the halberd, were soon restricted to ceremonial uses. The long, heavy lance of the medieval knight disappeared, to be replaced by a lighter and shorter weapon retained only by some groups of cavalry. The main arm of the infantry was the pike, a stout

FIGURE 224—*Sixteenth-century armourer's workshop: the armour is ground and polished on a series of wheels driven through gearing by water- or animal-power. An attempt is made to prevent the workers from having to inhale metallic dust. From a copper-plate, c 1590.*

shaft 12–18 ft long with a steel head (figure 226), gripped in both hands and presented almost horizontally. It was a clumsy but effective weapon, pre-eminent in days of slow small-arms fire in resisting a determined attack of cavalry.

Although corps of hand-gunners had been raised about the middle of the fifteenth century, and the bow was obsolescent in war by about 1500, it was still considered as a serious weapon for another hundred years. The best-known work on archery, Roger Ascham's *Toxophilus*, was published in 1545, and the Artillery Company which received a charter from Henry VIII in 1538 was originally composed of archers. In England proclamations encouraging the use of the long-bow were issued as late as 1633, but by this time archery had become no more than a sport. The bowman of Elizabeth's reign was supposed to carry eight light arrows among the twenty-four in his leather quiver 'defensible against

FIGURE 225—*Early sixteenth-century armourer's workshop, probably depicting a visit from Maximilian I to Seusenhofer. Forge with bellows on right, complete parts of fluted armour in background. Note the armourer's variety of anvil-stakes, hammers and files, and the large shears.*

the rayne', in order to 'gall or astoyne the enemye . . . before they shall come within the danger of harquebuss shot'. Each bowman was equipped with a 'little cote of plate', a steel cap, 'a mawle of leade five foote in lengthe', and a dagger. In the hands of skilled archers the English long-bow was greatly superior in rate of fire to the primitive hand-gun, and probably equal to it in accuracy and effective range, yet lacking the 'stopping-power' of a heavy ball, especially against armoured men. The cross-bow, which also survived into the sixteenth century, disappeared from war even more rapidly than the long-bow. As an expensive weapon, in whose use men needed careful training, with a poor rate of fire, it had even fewer advantages in comparison with fire-arms. It still found favour in hunting, however, many of the finest examples in museums being made well after 1550; the 'prodd', a type shoot-ing small stones or pellets and used chiefly for fowling, remained fairly common until the end of the seventeenth century.

Armour was virtually laid aside by the end of this period, save for display, though the armourer in his losing battle with fire-arms had continued to produce pistol- and musket-proof plate into the early seventeenth century. The zenith of his craft had been reached about a hundred years earlier, notably in the 'Maxi-milian' or fluted armour said to have been invented by Conrad Seusenhofer, armourer to the Emperor Maximilian I (r 1486–1519) (figure 225). Elaborately jointed plates were provided for the feet, hands, knees, shoulders, and elbows—the last often much enlarged—to allow freedom of movement. The head was

FIGURE 226—*Soldiers aboard a fighting-galley: from a woodcut of 1472. They include pikemen, crossbowmen, and hand-gunners. Note that the gun-stock rests on the shoulder.*

completely enclosed in a helmet with movable face-piece, rigidly attached to the neck-plate (gorget). The head and upper body of horses were similarly protected. In the sixteenth century lavish decorative work embellished the most splendid suits, rendering them quite unpractical in the field or even for fighting in the lists—a sport in which Renaissance monarchs still indulged. By its later decades the complete armour was no longer worn for actual fighting, though the thighs, arms, torso, and head were still protected. The weight required for reasonable protection was already becoming physically unbearable: armour made for the Duc de Guise in 1588, for example, weighs over a hundred pounds, without the leg-pieces. By the mid-seventeenth century infantry commonly wore nothing more formidable than a leather jerkin, and cavalry only an iron cuirass. A round open helmet was still usual.

Since steel was not available in sufficient quantity, armour was worked with the hammer from wrought iron, chiefly on a flat anvil, though a round-topped anvil must have been used for some purposes. Figures 224 and 225 show the equipment of sixteenth-century armourers' shops. The sheet iron was worked cold; this was believed to give it greater strength. Rigid joints were made by rivets, moving-pieces turned on pins, and leather straps were used to fasten the various plates together.

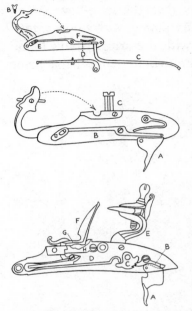

FIGURE 227—*Gun-locks (diagrammatic)*. (Above) *Simple match-lock: the match is held in the jaws of the serpentine tightened by the screw* (B). *On squeezing the trigger* (C) *towards the stock, the sear* (D) *brings the serpentine down by the link* (E) *so that the match fires the priming in the pan. The sear and serpentine are forced back by the spring* (F); *(Centre) trigger match-lock: the trigger* (A), *acting upon a projection from the sear* (B), *forces down the serpentine.* C *is a shield to protect the eye from the flash of the priming (pan-cover omitted); (below) flint-lock: on pressing the trigger* (A), *the sear* (B) *is released from the tumbler* (C), *which rotates under the action of the spring* (D). *On the same shaft as the tumbler is the cock* (E) *carrying the flint, which strikes the steel* (F), *raising the pan-cover* (G) *attached to it. The sparks fall in the pan* (H).

III. HAND-FIREARMS

A variety of different terms—(h)arquebus, caliver (calibre), match-lock, fire-lock, musket, and so forth—are or were applied to the hand-guns of the sixteenth and seventeenth centuries. Technologically it is preferable to ignore the elaborate varieties represented in the larger modern armouries, in order to concentrate upon essential points of difference. A hand-firearm has three parts: a barrel to direct the shot and confine the propulsive force of the charge; a lock, controlled by a trigger, to fire the charge; and a stock to accommodate the weapon comfortably and firmly to the body. Each of these parts underwent considerable modification towards improvement in function. Considering the stock first, the modern type of shoulder-stock appears already in the early seventeenth century, but the modern form of pistol-grip is quite recent. Both have evolved from a straight piece of timber, to which a short barrel was crudely fastened (figure 226). It was clearly impossible to take a careful aim with such a weapon, and indeed the form of modern guns is closely associated with the development of the sporting-piece, for with the growing popularity of shooting as a recreation from the sixteenth century onwards the comfort of the sportsman and his desire to take an accurate sight at his game provided new incentives to the gunsmith. In war, where troops were massed in close formation and ranges were very short, accuracy was of small significance. The developed stock was carved from wood by the carpenter's traditional methods; in fine weapons it was ornamented with inlays and decoration in precious metal or ivory. Stock-making was a distinct trade, subserving that of the gunsmiths who made the metal parts and supplied the market.

While the performance of the gun depended upon the quality of the barrel, its reliability was determined by the lock, and this, the most delicate mechanism of the piece, was also that which was most developed. With negligible exceptions all early hand-guns were muzzle-loaded, and the charge of powder could be set off only by the direct application of fire. Unstable compounds, exploding violently on percussion, such as fulminating gold,[1] were known as chemical curiosities from the early seventeenth century, but they were too dangerous for practical use as detonators. Hence it was necessary to drill a small touch-hole into the barrel near the permanently closed breech through which fire could be applied from without, and to ensure reliability by placing a little fine priming-powder on the firing-pan with which the touch-hole communicated. In the earliest hand-guns, as with cannon, the priming was touched off by a slow-match held in the hand.[2] In the match-lock the action was mechanized, the match being held by an arm which brought its glowing end smartly down on the priming when pulling the trigger released a spring (figure 227).

The two-handed action and open pan of the primitive hand-gun were doubly inconvenient to the horseman, hence the first step towards a fully mechanical lock is found in the single-handed, wheel-lock horse-pistol, often a weapon of fair size. In the wheel-lock (plate 17), probably an Italian invention of about 1520, a spring is placed under tension by applying a key to a squared shaft; on pressing the trigger the spring is released, causing a wheel with a serrated edge to revolve against a piece of pyrites. The sparks so produced ignite the priming. The wheel-lock, though reasonably efficient when in good order and kept dry, had two disadvantages; time was required to fit the key and wind up the spring, and the mechanism could not be operated a second time, after a misfire, until this was done. It was also somewhat delicate. For the infantryman's musket the match-lock was preferred until a little after the mid-seventeenth century, despite

---

[1] There are two or three varieties of this substance; one, according to Raschig, is $HN{:}Au.NH_2,\frac{3}{2}H_2O$, and another, according to Weitz, is $\begin{smallmatrix}Cl\\H_2N\end{smallmatrix}\!\!>\!Au{-}NH{-}Au\!<\!\begin{smallmatrix}Cl\\NH_2\end{smallmatrix}$ with some of the chlorine replaced by $-OH$, hydroxyl.

[2] Slow-match was a kind of coarse twine heavily impregnated with saltpetre so that its lighted end maintained a steady glow. It was not uncommon for troops to keep a tobacco-pipe alight to ignite their matches when required.

the difficulty of keeping the match alight in bad weather. The next important step was the invention of the flint-lock; the flint was held in a screw-clamp, at the end of a pivoted arm, which was cocked by pulling it back against a strong spring (figure 227). On pulling the trigger the arm was released and a sharp edge of the flint struck a roughened plate just above the firing-pan so that sparks flew into the priming.

The flint-lock was far from being a perfect device. Its action was still affected by damp, though less so than that of earlier locks, and it was subject to misfires. But it could quickly be cocked and discharged a second time, and the mechanism was strong and simple enough to resist hard usage. It remained as the standard lock on all hand-firearms until the early nineteenth century, when an efficient percussion-cap was introduced. Incidentally, the 'knapping' of gun-flints (which still survives, for supplying the African market, at Brandon in Norfolk) was the last relic of the old art of shaping flint implements (vol I, figures 57, 58).

Whatever their type, all gun-locks are evolutionary descendants of the cross-bow lock (vol II, figure 656). Etymologically the word is identical with 'lock' as applied to a door-fastening, and the similarities between the two mechanisms are sufficiently obvious, in the frame-plate or -plates, the long U-springs, fixing-pins, and system of levers. Gun-locks were made by the same methods, and with the same tools, as were ordinary locks, and probably originally by the same craftsmen, from whom the gunsmith learnt this part of his skill. In sixteenth-century fire-arms the lock was often set upon the right side of the stock, not inset in a mortice as was the later practice. It was frequently chased and otherwise decoratively treated.

The excellence of a gun is determined by the workmanship of its barrel, which must be perfectly straight and smooth (or uniformly rifled), and of constant internal diameter. The metal must be sufficiently tough to withstand the explosion of the charge without cracking or stretching, even when hot, and rigid enough to resist accidental damage. At short ranges the impact of the projectile at a given velocity will be roughly as the cube of the bore, the charge increasing in the same proportion as the projectile's weight; hence, as muzzle-velocities were low, early military weapons tended to have large bores and weighty projectiles. For sporting purposes a lesser calibre was, and still is, usually adequate. The accuracy and muzzle-velocity of the weapon are to some extent proportional to the length of the barrel; for which reasons some mid-seventeenth century match-locks were made with such massive barrels that the gun could not be managed without the aid of a rest to support some of its weight (plate 17).

For ease in manufacture spherical lead shot was invariably used, cast in a linked two-piece bullet-mould. Since considerable variations in size and shape resulted, it was impossible to hope for an accurate fit inside the barrel, and in any case the ballistic characteristics of a spherical projectile are poor. It was normal to allow a considerable 'windage', so that the shot was loose in the barrel; a wad of paper or other soft material was rammed down on the powder before the ball was inserted, to keep the powder in place. The wad also, by preventing an easy escape of the gases produced, ensured a sharp explosion and a maximum effect on the projectile. A second wad could be used to retain the ball, but it was not uncommon for it to roll out of the barrel before the gun was discharged.

All medieval hand-guns, and the great majority of fire-arms before the nineteenth century, were made smooth-bore owing to the difficulty of cutting rifling, though the ballistic advantages of the rifled barrel were recognized. Various methods of forming the barrel were adopted, all of which, in the days before drawn tubes, involved the welding of seams. Each began with a strip or strips of iron, sometimes forged from old nails. The simplest method was to take a strip, somewhat longer than the barrel was intended to be, bend it longitudinally upon a cylinder into a tube with the edges slightly overlapping, and then weld the edges together (figure 228). The tube might then be twisted so that the joint ran spirally round the barrel. Another was to roll short strips into tubes, with welded joints, and weld these end to end to make a barrel of the required length; in this way the thickness of the metal could be decreased from the breech to the

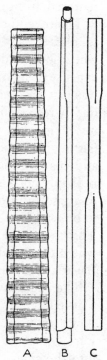

A   B   C

FIGURE 228—*Steps in forging a gun-barrel.* (A) *The iron strip;* (B) *the strip rolled on a rod into a tube;* (C) *partially forged barrel.*

muzzle. A third way, adopted in the eighteenth century, was to form a thin tube by the first method, and upon this to wind a long strip of iron somewhat less than an inch broad and about 0·2 in thick, reduced on each edge, overlapping the turns slightly. The whole was then welded together and bored out so that very little of the inner tube remained. Barrels made in this way were stronger, since the welded joints were transverse rather than longitudinal. In all cases the barrel was bored or reamed out by means of a revolving cutter mounted on the end of a long shaft which was gradually advanced into the barrel; in the eighteenth century, if not before, the boring-machinery was driven by water-power (figure 229). The exterior of the barrel was ground smooth on another machine. Pistol-barrels of brass or bronze were cast hollow before boring. The public 'proof' or testing of gun-barrels before they were sold was commonly required from the early seventeenth century onwards.

The inventor of the rifled barrel is unknown, but examples said to date from soon after 1525 exist (plate 17). The combination of the rifled barrel with the wheel-lock made an accurate and convenient sporting-gun possible, though the expense of such a weapon restricted its use to wealthy amateurs of shooting. This was just becoming popular as a sport: 'so great was the delight I took in shooting', wrote Cellini about 1520, 'that it often diverted me from the business of my shop.' He was a good marksman, bringing down pigeons with ball-shot (sitting birds, however, for the art of shooting on the wing was not yet practised), and his fowling-piece carried two hundred paces point-blank [2]. This was probably not a 'screwed gun' or rifle. The invention of rifling has been attributed to a gunsmith of Nuremberg named Kotter or Kutter, about 1520: this seems to be a mistake since rifles signed by Kotter and dated 1616 are known in Paris. The first use of the rifle for military purposes appears to have been in Germany, where the Landgrave William of Hesse in 1631, and the Elector Maximilian of Bavaria ten years later, armed troops of light horse with rifled carbines.

The usual method of loading a rifle, then and long after, was to make the ball a little larger than the bore within which the rifles had been cut, and hammer it down upon the powder with the aid of a stiff ramrod. (Early Rifle Corps men were equipped with light hammers for this purpose). The lead ball expanded into the rifles, so fitting them exactly. The alternative breech-loading method was well known and even applied to cannon; the difficulty was to apply it with safety. Three sporting-guns made for Henry VIII were loaded with steel cartridges, inserted in the breech, which was closed by a hinged block. A touch-hole in the breech, aligned with another in the cartridge, allowed the charge to be fired.

Unusual weapons of this kind, though they reveal the measure of the gunsmith's skill, were never suitable for production in quantity. Inventors were constantly active, throughout this period, in attempting to render practicable ideas beyond the technological equipment of their time. Thus Pepys was present when 'a gun to discharge seven times, the best of all devices that ever I saw, and very serviceable' was shown to the officers of the Ordnance. If, as he says, there were 'many thereof made', they certainly were never widely used. The attention of the Royal Society was drawn, two years later, to a 'rare mechanician' who claimed 'to make a pistol shooting as fast as it could be presented, and yet to be stopped at pleasure; and wherein the motion of the fire and bullet within was made to charge the piece with powder and bullet, to prime it, and to bend the cock'. Such an 'automatic', if it ever existed, could have been no less of a

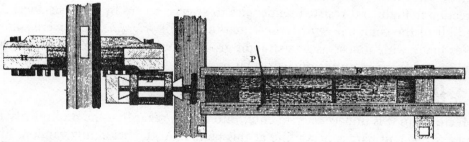

FIGURE 229—(Above) *Machinery for boring gun-barrels, with the outside of a barrel being ground on a stone at the rear;* (below) *plan view of one boring-bench. The rectangular boring-bit of tempered steel, 10 in long, is welded to an iron rod 3½ ft long (N) rotated by water-power through the wooden gearing. Upon the bench (E) slides a carriage holding the barrel, which is forced on the bit by a lever (P) acting upon the fixed pins. Twenty-two bits, successively larger, are used to enlarge the bore of the barrel from $\frac{5}{12}$ in to $\frac{7}{12}$ in. The trough (F) holds water for cooling.*

curiosity than the air-guns with which the philosophers also experimented, and no more useful for military purposes [3].

From the feebleness of the explosive used, the loose fit of the spherical projectile, and the crude methods of making the barrel the military hand-firearms of the seventeenth and eighteenth centuries had poor ballistic characteristics.

Even their locks frequently failed to work properly. Their muzzle-velocity was low, hence the extreme range was short and the point-blank trajectory hardly greater than that of a cross-bow—250 yds would be an optimistic estimate of their effective range, and the useful range was no more than half this. These defects were not of great importance, however, in the prevailing state of warfare when armies engaged closely in dense formations. Marksmanship was little practised until small corps of riflemen were raised towards the end of the eighteenth century. The fine rifled sporting-gun was a far superior weapon, and it was from their private customers, rather than from their mass supply to government departments, that gunsmiths received the incentive towards technical improvements.

There was no scientific study of the interior and exterior ballistics of small-arms until towards the middle of the nineteenth century, though experiments on musket-shot were made by Benjamin Robins ('New Principles of Gunnery', London, 1742). Many misapprehensions, leading to errors in design, persisted until a century ago. For example, it is stated in Diderot's *Encyclopédie* (1751–72) that the benefit obtained from a rifled barrel is due to the tight fitting of the ball, which prevents it flying out easily so that the powder-gases build up compression and act on it with greater force. Yet Robins had correctly pointed out that the function of rifling was to cause the ball to spin, so that it maintained a uniform direction in flight and resisted tendencies to swerve set up by air-resistance. As a result of the common error represented in the *Encyclopédie* rifles were sometimes made with almost useless straight grooves, or with so little twist that the projectile was given an insufficient rotation.

IV. CANNON

Here again it is unnecessary to enter into details regarding the multiplicity of types, sizes, and names prevailing at this period. At the beginning cannon, like small-arms, were known by largely fanciful names, such as serpentine, bastard, culverin, saker, falcon, and the same name was applied to guns of widely ranging weights and calibres. By the end of the seventeenth century the number of types was reduced, and they were known simply by the weight of the projectile (table I). Standardization proceeded rapidly in the seventeenth century, and did much to ease the administrative burdens imposed on commanders in the field, as well as simplifying the task of training efficient gunners. In the earliest history of artillery those who cast cannon had also served them in battle and probably supplied the powder and shot too, and even in the sixteenth century the expert gunner was supposed to know a great deal about the manufacture and

TABLE I

French Ordnance 'of the latest type' in 1697

From Surirey de Saint-Rémy, *Mémoires d'Artillerie*, Paris, 1697

Type	Weight	Length	Range at 45°
24-pounder	3000 lb	6·65 ft	4500 yds
16-pr	2200 lb	6·20 ft	4040 yds
12-pr	2000 lb	6·10 ft	3740 yds
8-pr	1000 lb	4·99 ft	3320 yds
4-pr	600 lb	4·75 ft	3040 yds

The ranges may be regarded as very uncertain. Windages allowed vary from 0·21 inches in the largest guns to 0·11 inches in the smallest.

testing of guns, compositions of gunpowder, and so forth. By 1700 such extensive skill was no longer requisite. The founding of cannon and the manufacture of ammunition were conducted in highly developed establishments, sometimes (as in France) state-owned, and the field-gunner had only to learn the proper handling of standard equipment.

The experimental period in heavy artillery ended before the close of the sixteenth century, from which time the muzzle-loading, smooth-bore, cast-metal gun was that universally employed in all sizes and for all types of service. Iron, bronze, and brass were all cast to make artillery. Iron was the cheapest metal, and would withstand the roughest service, but it was more subject to corrosion than the cupreous alloys, and more liable to dangerous fractures. Hence bronze guns, though more readily worn by iron shot, were generally regarded as superior.

In the age of experiment many strange cannon were produced. In the early fifteenth century, as already mentioned (vol II, p 727), the built-up iron gun or 'bombard' was common for siege-work. Some of these, such as 'Mons Meg' at Edinburgh, were made in two parts, a chamber (of smaller bore than the barrel), containing the powder, being screwed into the breech of the gun. One of the most massive of early cast bronze guns, made by the Turks for the siege of Constantinople in 1453, shows the same principle. Other breech-loaders have the barrel firmly anchored to a wooden frame ending in an upright member: the separate chamber fitted into the breech and was held firm by a wedge placed between it and the upright member of the frame. Small cannon, such as wall-pieces, were made to load at the breech until the sixteenth century was well advanced; in these the iron chamber was wedged into the stirrup extending backwards from the breech. Effective use of breech-loading was, however, utterly impracticable in the existing state of gun-making and metal-working, for not only was there always extreme danger of the chamber being blown from the gun, but the leakage of explosion-gases was so great that the force of the projectile was very much reduced. For naval use admittedly the breech-loader had the great advantage that the gun did not have to be run inboard for loading; this ceased to be of great significance when the size of ships increased, and the bore of guns was enlarged in proportion to their length.

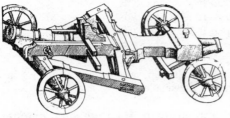

Early illustrations indicate that there was also much experiment in the mounting of guns. At first, relatively small barrels were solidly held to large baulks of timber laid on the ground or supported at a suitable angle, the recoil being limited as far as possible. In an improved form of this mounting the barrel was

FIGURE 230—*Late fifteenth-century gun-carriage; the cannon is mounted on stout timber, and can be traversed by moving the breech end within the framework of the carriage. Note the pivoted front axle.*

made to pivot roughly at its point of balance and the breech end was movable upon a quadrant, so that the angle of elevation could be easily adjusted. Such cannon were transported by loading them into carts. The next step was the construction of a cumbersome wooden gun-carriage upon which the barrel was permanently mounted (figure 230), a development following from the fitting of four wheels to the baulk to which the gun had been fastened. Towards the end of the fifteenth century, trunnions were cast upon the gun-barrel, upon which it could pivot for adjustment in elevation, and the field-carriage with its trail and transom assumed a form essentially similar to that still used (tailpiece). The transom joins the two cheek-pieces of the carriage, under which the axle is slung, and which extends to form the trail supporting the gun in the firing position. The trunnions rest upon the cheeks and are held down by iron straps. The gun is laid by inserting wedges between the breech and a cross-piece of the trail. Early gun-carriages and their wheels were of wood, strongly reinforced with iron; they were rather narrow, with wheels disproportionately large.

Among other experimental artillery there were guns having more than one barrel, cast singly or together, and man-killing weapons consisting of a number of small barrels fired simultaneously by a train of powder mounted on a mobile framework. The device was even attempted of mounting a number of barrels radially on a turn-table, to be loaded and fired in rapid succession.[1] None of

---

[1] Hand-guns of the pistol type, with revolving chambers firing through a single barrel, were known in the sixteenth century.

these inventions achieved permanent success, since all were displaced by the simple cast-metal gun mounted on a suitable carriage.

Naval ordnance was precisely similar to that used on land, though commonly shorter in the barrel and very powerful on the lower decks of great ships. The gun was mounted on wooden trucks running on four rather small wheels. Ropes from the truck to the wall of the ship limited the inboard recoil. Naval guns also were laid with a wedge inserted between the breech and the framework of the truck.

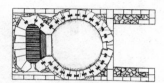

FIGURE 231—*Section and plan of furnace for melting bronze for gun-founding. 1603.*

Large cannon, presumably of cupreous metal, were already being cast soon after the mid-fourteenth century, but a great development in the art of handling masses of molten metal took place in the fifteenth and sixteenth centuries, particularly with the development of the blast-furnace to make iron-casting possible. The surviving evidence indicates that fundamentally the same methods were employed from the beginning until about 1750. Thus an account of the casting of the great cannon used against Constantinople in 1453 could easily be applied to the operations of European foundries in the seventeenth century:

[The founders] take a quantity of very fat clay, the purest and lightest possible, which they make plastic by kneading it for several days. The mass is knit together and prevented from breaking by the addition of linen, hemp and other fibres. The whole is worked into a tough and compact mass. Then they make a long cylinder to serve as the core of the mould. Another [hollow cylinder] to receive the first is made, but larger in order to leave a void space between the two: it is the space intended to receive the bronze pouring into it from the furnace to take the form of a cannon. The exterior [of the mould] is made of the same kind of clay, but entirely surrounded and reinforced by iron, timber, earth and stones built up around it to prevent the immense weight of bronze from fracturing it and spoiling the cannon. Then they erected two furnaces, one on either side and close to [the mould]. These towers were made very strong and fortified internally with brick and a very fat well-worked clay, and on the outside built with large cut stones and cement. And they cast into the furnaces a mass of copper and tin [weighing] about 1500 talents [37 tons]. On it they threw charcoal and wood, arranging that the metal was covered below, above and on all sides. Round about were the bellows, working without intermission for three days and nights until the whole of the bronze, melted and liquefied, became like water. Then the outlets being tapped the bronze flowed through earthen pipes into the mould until it was filled and the interior cylinder covered so that the metal lay 30 inches deep upon it [4].

Biringuccio (1480–1539), who describes methods of casting in bronze in the sixth chapter of his *Pirotechnia* (1540), gives a full account of the manufacture of cannon. This was one of the more difficult applications of the founder's art, though the essential principles were already employed in bell-founding as described by Theophilus in the Middle Ages (vol II, p 64). For cannon the

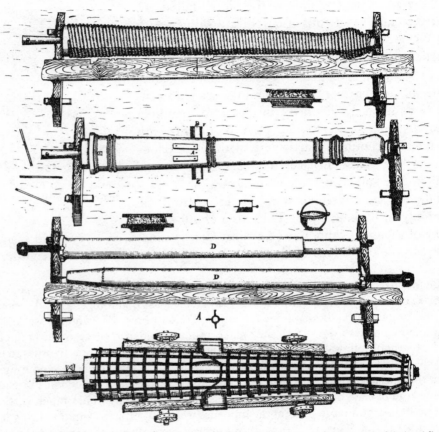

FIGURE 232—*Making moulds for cannon.* (Top to bottom) *Two stages in the preparation of the 'model'; the mould-core; the complete mould, bound with iron, ready to be filled. 1603.*

same furnaces, moulding-clay, and methods of casting were used as for all work in bronze (figure 231), but Biringuccio issues a special warning that cannon-moulds must be filled slowly; the proportion of tin to copper in the bronze was about 1:10, with variations, for the masters used their discretion according to judgement and experience [5]. Nor were there any firm principles of design: 'In every age', writes Biringuccio, 'men have proceeded to make and still today make [cannon] as they think it will be best to use them for their purpose or according to the wishes of whoever has them made or of the masters who make them' [6].

Normally the founder began by making with clay laid on a wooden spindle, or by turning a larger piece of timber on the lathe, an exact model of the exterior of the cannon to be cast, attaching the various prominent pieces of decoration and the trunnions with light pins. This model extended to the breech end of the gun, but the breech itself was made separately. This model was well dried, and covered with a mixture of ashes and fat to prevent adhesion of the thick layer

of clay, forming the actual mould, next spread over it. Fine slip was carefully applied first, then coarser clay with dung and straw added to make it porous as the mould was gradually increased in thickness. When the work was nearly finished iron wires were incorporated in the clay coating to give greater strength, and finally the mould was bound by a reinforcement of iron bars (figure 232).

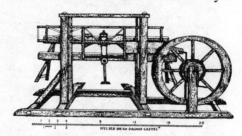

FIGURE 233—*Machine-saw for cutting off the 'gun-head'. 1603.*

When the mould was dry, the spindle within was knocked out, the trunnions and other prominent pieces were removed, and the model was withdrawn from the mould altogether. The mould for the breech was made separately; Biringuccio says that it should be ornamented with some piece of sculpture to make the gun beautiful. This mould was made with a shoulder to fit into a recess cut in the main mould for the barrel; when dry, it was placed in position and fastened to the iron bars enclosing the main mould. The third piece of the mould was the core, formed from clay on an iron bar, which was commonly cylindrical but might be shaped to give a special form to the chamber where the powder would be. The core was held in place by an iron chaplet inserted at the breech-end of the main mould, and by a clay disk or a second chaplet at the mouth of the mould, which was enlarged to form the 'gun-head'. The weight of metal in the gun-head, when the mould was filled, pressed the bronze below it into the recesses of the mould and prevented the occurrence of bubbles in the casting.

With the three pieces of the mould firmly assembled it was thoroughly baked, lowered into a pit near the mouth of the furnace, and filled with molten metal. When cool, the mould was broken up to extract the gun, the gun-head cut off with a saw or chisels, and the exterior neatly finished with hammer, chisel, and file (figures 233, 234). The cannon was now ready to be bored, to have the touch-hole drilled, and to be mounted and proved (figures 235, 236). A good gunner would certainly satisfy himself that the core had been properly placed by the founder, so that the bore was truly concentric with the exterior of the gun; otherwise it would never shoot well.

There is no full description of the methods of making the moulds for iron guns and casting them, but as the techniques of the bronze-founders were

FIGURE 234—*Sixteenth-century bronze-cannon foundry with the furnace, which is being tapped, in the background. (Left) A treadmill provides power for the horizontal boring-bench; (centre and right) finishing a mortar and a cannon with the chisel. The vignettes show the mythical invention of gunpowder by 'Berthold Schwarz', and an attack upon a fortified place.*

certainly imitated by the iron-founders, one may assume that there was little difference in practice. Iron guns, however, were not lavishly ornamented as were those of bronze.

The results of this method of manufacture are obvious. First, since a new mould must be made for each gun, no two could be identical in dimensions and behaviour, and the reduplication of labour was greatly increased. Secondly, as the metal was cast and subjected to no further treatment, it was relatively weak, so that the weight had to be increased to give sufficient strength. Iron guns were commonly cast straight from the smelting-furnace; thus the metal was impure, highly carbonized, and brittle. Prince Rupert in England, about 1678, invented a method of 'annealing' iron ordnance in glass-works, which may have rendered the metal less liable to fracture, but it was not adopted, possibly on grounds of expense [7]. Thirdly, the piece was not accurately bored but reamed out, so that it might be, and often was, extremely erratic. The gunner had to know the idiosyncrasies of his piece at all ranges before he could undertake to lay it with some assurance of hitting the mark.

Since the sixteenth century, and probably earlier, guns had been bored by water-power. Biringuccio (1540) implies that boring was a fairly recent innovation: 'for greater caution, for the beauty and safety of the gun, and to make sure

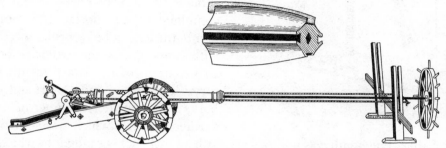

FIGURE 235—*Simple horizontal borer operated by a capstan. The weight acting on the windlass attached to the gun-carriage presses the cannon forward upon the cutter. (Inset) Bronze boring-head, with one steel cutting-blade in place. 1603. In vertical boring-machines the cannon was pressed by gravity upon the cutter, which was turned by animal- or water-power.*

that it achieves its purpose of shooting with perfect accuracy, soldiers and master gunners began to desire that both large and small [cannon] should be bored, as they do arquebuses and iron muskets' [8]. He illustrates a crude horizontal borer, worked by hand- or water-power, with various cutters. The gun is drawn forward against the cutter by a windlass. The vertical borer, however, must have been known not many years later, for it is described in Spain in 1603. An almost exactly similar machine is depicted in Diderot's *Encyclopédie* (1751–72). The bit was mounted upon the end of a long shaft, supported only at its lower extremity, so that it was incapable of cutting a true cylinder or correcting a misalignment of the core made in casting the gun. The practice of boring out a solid cast gun is said to have begun in 1713, but in 1747, when the Dutch authorities abandoned hollow-casting in favour of the new method, they took such careful precautions to preserve the secrecy of their technique and machines that it would seem that hollow-casting was still in general use elsewhere. It was continued in the royal gun-foundry at Woolwich until after 1770. About this time, the English iron-master, John Wilkinson (1729–1808), developed an improved machine for boring cannon, which was also used to cut more accurate cylinders for Boulton and Watt's steam-engines.

Whether cannon were directed against troops, ships, or fortifications they were normally aimed point-blank, or at elevations little above the horizontal. For certain purposes, however, it was desirable to use a high trajectory, with an elevation of 45° or more, in order to bombard the interior of a fortified town, or targets hidden behind a hill or other obstruction. It was realized that greater

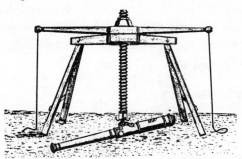

FIGURE 236—*Screw-jack for raising cannon. 1603.*

destructive effect could be obtained if the projectile was not solid, like round-shot, but contained a charge of powder exploded by a fuse. These objects were combined in the mortar and mortar-bomb, the former being probably coeval with cannon, and the explosive bomb an invention of the late fifteenth century.[1] The mortar had a short and wide bore, with a powder-chamber of much smaller diameter which was sometimes detachable. The bomb was hollow-cast, with a touch-hole or plug into which the slow-match was inserted. The earlier practice was for the bombardier, after he had loaded and set his mortar to his satisfaction, to take a linstock in each hand and with one light the fuse in the bomb, immediately afterwards touching off the mortar with the other. The danger was that if for some reason the mortar misfired the bomb would probably burst inside it. In the seventeenth century a safer method was adopted, whereby the bomb was fitted with readily inflammable material at the touch-hole capable of firing a fuse leading through a tube to its charge. It was placed unlighted with the touch-hole next to the propellant explosive in the mortar so that when the latter ignited the flame passed to the combustible on the bomb and so to the fuse.

Mortars were made by the same methods as cannon, first built-up of wrought iron, and later cast in iron or in cupreous metal (figure 234). Later practice was usually to mount them in trunnions, attached low down near the chamber, in a strong wooden frame, without wheels, upon a firm platform. Elevation was given by wedges inserted below the mouth of the piece. Mortars were also mounted in small bomb-vessels in the second half of the seventeenth century, for bombarding port-installations and defence-works from the sea.

[1] According to Biringuccio mortars were 'not esteemed by us moderns': they returned to favour about the middle of the seventeenth century.

During the same period armies adopted a small fused bomb, or grenade, thrown by hand. Corps of grenadiers were first raised about 1670.

TABLE II

Characteristics of French Mortars, 1697

From Surirey de Saint-Rémy, *Mémoires d'Artillerie.*

Calibre	Charge	Elevation	Range	Change of range per degree of elevation
8 in	½ lb	5–45°	210–1890 ft	about 42 ft
,,	¾ lb	31–45°	1922–2790 ft	,, 62 ft
,,	1 lb	34–45°	2870–3690 ft	,, 82 ft
12 in	2 lb	5–45°	240–2160 ft	,, 48 ft
,,	2½ lb	36–45°	2160–2700 ft	,, 60 ft
,,	3 lb	37–45°	2664–3240 ft	,, 72 ft

The characteristics of the high trajectories, 45°–85°, would correspond approximately to those of the low trajectories, 45°–5°.

V. FORTIFICATION

Profound changes in the art of static defence were an inevitable consequence of the introduction of gunpowder and firearms into warfare. Vertical walls and towers, however thick, were vulnerable to shot and mining, and the more massive and complicated defences of the developed late medieval type were, the greater was their tendency to restrict the active operations of the besieged, and even shelter the attackers from missiles and sallies. Sieges raged around fortifications of the old type until the sixteenth century was well advanced, however (figure 234), and even in the English Civil Wars (1642–50) a stoutly defended medieval castle, like Corfe, in a position of peculiar natural strength, could resist small forces for a considerable period. Thus the usefulness of the medieval castle might have diminished less rapidly had it not been that, with larger forces engaged, they could no longer contain a significant fraction of them. A castle holding a few score men could be safely neglected, or neutralized by a small detachment until it could be reduced at leisure, without affecting the main campaign. An effective defence work must be capable of holding some thousands of men and much artillery, stores, and equipment; it requires roads or rivers for supply. For these reasons, as well as the desire to afford protection to the civil population, fortified towns rather than castles became the pivots of the new defensive systems. Of course, many medieval towns had been strongly fortified, as was Carcassonne in the thirteenth century (figure 191).

To guard the perimeter of a town, works less costly than those of medieval castles were desirable. Their function changed, too. The walls and towers of a castle were built to resist entry by battery or scaling: the walls and ditches of a fortified town of the seventeenth century were less conspicuous, but they afforded good protection to troops. The defence relied mainly not on opposing static physical obstacles to the attack, as in the castle, but on its men and guns, to which ramparts and ditches were auxiliary. Thus one of the chief concerns of fortification-engineers was to secure the best possible combination of fields of fire for their own forces, while hampering the enemy's deployment of his guns and restricting their effect as far as possible.

This was achieved largely by adopting a regular geometric plan for the defence-works, which consisted mainly of trenches and low extended parapets. The new

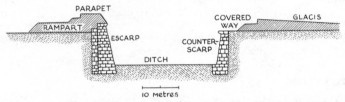

FIGURE 237—*Late seventeenth-century type of fortification, shown in section.*

system of fortification was largely of Italian origin, the problem arousing the interest of some of the best minds of the age, among them those of Machiavelli (1469-1527) and Leonardo (1452-1519). The German artist Dürer also wrote a treatise on fortification (1527). The first step would seem to have been the use of a bulwark, made of earth supported by hurdles, for the protection of gates and extending before long walls, in order to establish gun-positions round the main defences. (The besiegers, too, are often shown sheltering their guns with the aid of gabions, round hurdle-work containers filled with earth.) Ordnance was also mounted on cut-down towers, and in embrasures cut in their bases, but not to great effect.

An improvement was made by substituting for the bulwarks masonry-faced walls, heavily banked behind with earth to lend support and provide firing-platforms for artillery. To make the masonry face more resistant to artillery it was built with arches at the rear running back into the supporting-bank, or rampart. As the wall was lower, a ditch before it as an obstruction to assaulting-parties was a valuable precaution, more necessary than with the very lofty walls of the medieval castle, and the wall could be sunk to form one face of the ditch (the escarp). The outer side of the ditch was also lined with masonry (the counter-scarp) to make it more difficult to enter. Since the defending forces needed ground on which to form for a sally across the ditch, a covered way was built on the far side behind the glacis. Thus emerged the type of defence-work shown in section in figure 237. While every part of the defence from the glacis inwards was covered from shot coming from without, the whole of the work was open to fire from within should the besiegers enter any part of it.

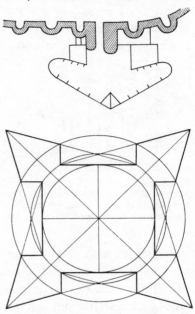

The principal object to be attained in laying out the plan of such works on the ground in relation to topographical features and the development of the site was the provision of the maximum amount of flanking-fire and the opportunity to erect as many batteries and defence-posts as possible. This could best be achieved by interrupting the fairly smooth circular or polygonal perimeter of an ordinary town, that is, by building works projecting from the line of the main inner wall. At first, partly on account of the vast expense involved in completely reconstructing medieval defence-works, this was done by building bastions, fire from which could be directed parallel to the main walls, while the walls of the bastion were themselves enfiladed from the walls (figure 238). To defend long walls many bastions were required, and the area within the bastion had to be

FIGURE 238—(Above) *Modern bastion adapted to a medieval wall: from Troyes;* (below) *trace of a simple polygonal fortification with four bastions making right angles with the curtain.* 1696.

sufficient to hold numbers of troops and guns, so that its walls in turn had to be broken by angles to provide more adequate flanking-fire. The logic of this development led to the complete abandonment of the flat curtain-wall: instead, the site was surrounded by an interlacing system of regular or irregular polygonal defences, the angles made by the bounding-lines being calculated to give the highest concentration of cross-fire.

The possible combinations of triangular elements to obtain the result sought were intensively studied from the end of the sixteenth century by applied mathematicians and engineers, of whom probably the most famous (as a scientist) was the Dutchman, Simon Stevin (1548–1620). The theoretical elements of fortification were commonly taught along with mathematics, and many supposedly impeccable systems, derived rather from familiarity with ruler and compasses than from actual experience of sieges, were propounded (figure 238). In fact the greatest exponents of the art of siege-warfare, offensive and defensive, in the second half of the seventeenth century, Vauban (1633–1707)[1] on the French side and Coehoorn (1634–1704) on the Dutch, did not mechanically apply a predetermined geometrical scheme to each situation, but varied their methods according to the possibilities and the existing works of the place in question. Both devoted much attention to artillery, as well as to earthworks, Vauban inventing the *tir à ricochet* and Coehoorn a form of mortar known by his name. It was only in the eighteenth century that the art of defending places and conducting sieges became for a time thoroughly stereotyped and reduced to rule.

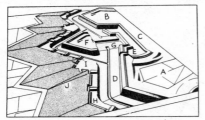

FIGURE 239—*Vauban's 'first system' of fortification.* (A, B) *Two forms of bastion;* (C) *curtain;* (D) *ditch;* (E) *tenaille;* (F) *demi-lune;* (G) *corridor;* (H) *covered way;* (I) *place d'armes;* (J) *glacis.*

The enormous public expenditure on defensive works, particularly in France, is well illustrated by the labours of Vauban. These gave a formal appearance to countless towns— in eastern France especially—which they still preserve, though modern suburbs have since grown up beyond the remains of Vauban's walls and ditches. His methods varied somewhat during his career, for he always maintained that 'the Art of Fortification does not consist in rules and systems, but solely in common sense and experience' [9]. His so-called 'first system' (figure 239) employed the principles commonly adopted by his predecessors, and marked no innovation. The curtain was short and protected by a demi-lune before it as well as by bastions on each side. The dimensions were so chosen that flanking-fire from musketry was available in all parts, for Vauban deplored excessive reliance on the protection afforded by artillery alone. In the more elaborate 'second system' Vauban utilized defence in depth: a second ditch and wall, flanked by two-storeyed gun-chambers (*tours bastionnées*) were erected behind outer works of the same type as in the first system. The low *tours bastionnées* commanded both the inner ditch and the outer bastions, so that even if the enemy forced his way upon the latter, his further way was still barred; and at the same time their thick walls and roof afforded a shield to the cannon in them impracticable for those mounted on the ramparts. Vauban's 'third system', of which few examples exist, was no more than a slight modification of the second.

[1] A French saying of the time ran: *Ville assiégée par Vauban, ville prise; ville fortifiée par Vauban, ville imprenable.*

The engineering work involved in the intense fortification of the seventeenth century was an important prelude to the much greater development of civil engineering—first the construction of canals, then of railways—that came later. Vauban himself acted on occasion as a civil engineer; in 1686 he gave advice, which was adopted, on the construction of the *Canal du Midi* (p 467). Military engineers had to practise accurate surveying, to study soils and their properties, to excavate considerable ditches and construct earth ramparts, to organize gangs of workmen and the transport of materials. Though they worked for the state, their estimates were carefully scrutinized and their disbursements checked. In all this they anticipated the work of canal- and railway-contractors of future generations, so that the military engineer provided many techniques which could be readily adapted to peaceful purposes when the opportunity arose, and when capital comparable to that devoted to war was available.

VI. SCIENCE, TECHNOLOGY, AND WAR

The recurrence of warfare between states from the inevitable conflict of their policies, and the necessity for men to take service leading to suffering and death for reasons of which they understood little, were at an earlier phase of European history more calmly accepted as unavoidable elements in human destiny than they are now. In utter condemnation of war the Quakers stood practically alone, and though others deplored its wastefulness and horror, most men in all countries were comparatively sheltered from them and so felt little. Hence attempts to invent new destructive weapons, or increase the effect of those already in use, were not regarded with such distrust as in recent years: the scale of slaughter sought was, by modern standards, puerile. A new feature of these attempts, in the seventeenth century, was the endeavour to devote scientific knowledge more completely to military ends.

There were, for example, a very large number of works on practical mathematics and applied geometry published in the sixteenth and seventeenth centuries, most of which show, with illustrations, how their methods of survey (measurements of height and distance, and so on) could be applied to military purposes, particularly to the direction of artillery and of mining-operations [10]. Writers on gunnery often teach the rudiments of the same techniques, so that for this and other purposes (such as the calculation of charges of powder in proportion to the bore of the piece) the expert gunner was supposed to have some humble mathematical attainments. Accounts of battles and sieges, unfortunately, are rarely detailed enough to indicate how often they were required in practice.

The most obvious usefulness of science in war was, of course, in military medicine and surgery, where the French surgeon, Ambroise Paré (? 1517–90) had already shown the way. Military doctors have done much to develop preventive medicine and sound hygiene, but control of the epidemic diseases to which armies are peculiarly subject, and of the deficiency-diseases afflicting fleets on the high seas, was not achieved until after this period. As regards the manufactures devoted to war, science could as yet do little, since the chemical and metallurgical industries were still wholly empirical, and indeed governed to a large extent by traditional craft-knowledge: but the Royal Society, for example, showed a desultory interest in explosives and experimented on a number of different compounds. With regard to the mechanical sciences, however, the position was otherwise, for these had advanced with enormous rapidity to a very advanced position by the end of the seventeenth century. As mechanics is concerned with the motion of bodies, its application to the study of the flight of projectiles and the military problems of ballistics was obvious enough.

FIGURE 240—*The 'dispart' of a cannon. As the metal is thicker at the breech than at the muzzle, the line of sight along the exterior is not parallel to the axis of the bore. To correct this, the gunner stuck a piece of wood or straw to the muzzle with wax, to serve as a fore-sight.*

Aristotle had developed certain notions on the free motion of projectiles through the air; his ideas were well known, and considerably modified, in the later Middle Ages. The first to apply these general ideas specifically to the flight of cannon-balls and mortar-bombs was the Italian mathematician Tartaglia (1500–57). Among other things he accounted for the need to 'dispart' a gun (figure 240), he described the trajectory as a continuous curve, and he claimed (probably falsely) to have invented the gunner's quadrant. He asserted, on empirical grounds, that a gun attains its greatest range at 45° elevation, and he attempted as did many others after him to compile tables giving the range at any angle of elevation, the point-blank (0° elevation) range being known. All such endeavours were frustrated by lack of a reliable mathematical theory of motion, and of such concepts as force and acceleration.

The situation was far different when Galileo (1564–1642) enunciated the fundamental laws of motion, and went on to demonstrate in 1638 that a projectile, the air-resistance and other perturbations of its motion being neglected, describes a parabolic trajectory. On the basis of this demonstration he published the first well founded set of range-tables, for he assumed as did many other writers on ballistics until the early eighteenth century that in practice the effect of air-resistance on the flight of military projectiles was slight enough to be disregarded. More careful experiments showed this assumption to be false. The calculation of trajectories with allowance for the effect of air-resistance in reducing the velocity of the projectile was undertaken later by Huygens and Newton: the problem raises enormous mathematical difficulties.

In fact, however, these difficulties were less important than others arising from the state of technology. Neither guns nor propellants were powerful enough to enable long ranges to be usefully employed: and the behaviour of weapons was so unpredictable that calculation of mathematical trajectories was in fact irrelevant and pointless. With an imperfectly spherical shot, fitting loosely in a mere approximation to a true cylinder, at any range but the shortest the shot was distributed in a random manner over a large area about the target. Until the technology of firearms was much improved—as it was only by the development of machine-tools in the nineteenth century—the mathematics of exterior ballistics was a subject that the practical gunner could afford to ignore.

Nevertheless, guns were fired at gradually increasing ranges from the sixteenth century onwards, and there was some demand for instruments to be used for checking the accuracy of the gun's bore, for setting it horizontally on the ground, and for laying it upon the mark. The simplest was a quadrant with a long arm, inserted in the bore of the gun or mortar, showing the angle of elevation: when this had been found by trial-and-error, the piece could easily be relaid on the same mark. A plumb-bob level (or, later, a spirit-level) was employed to make sure that the axle of the gun-carriage was horizontal. More elaborate sighting-instruments were also made, some showing great ingenuity and beauty of workmanship (plate 25), but they can hardly have been of much practical utility. The real gunner trusted to experience, and had more faith in his eye and judgement than in a tangent-scale.

REFERENCES

[1] MACHIAVELLI, NICCOLÒ. 'The Art of Warre' (Eng. trans. from the Italian by PETER WHITHORNE). London. 1588.
   WHITEHORNE, PETER. 'Certain Wayes for the Ordering of Soldiours in Battelray.' London. 1588.
[2] CELLINI, BENVENUTO. Life, ch. 5. (Bohn ed., p. 53. London. 1847.)
[3] PEPYS, SAMUEL. Diary, 3rd July, 1662. (Everyman's Library, ed. by J. WARRINGTON, Vol. 1, p. 271. Dent, London. 1953.)
   BIRCH, THOMAS. 'History of the Royal Society', Vol. 1, p. 396. London. 1756.
[4] CLARK, G. T. *Archaeol. J.*, **30**, 265–6, 1873.
[5] SMITH, C. S. and GNUDI, MARTHA T. 'The Pirotechnia of Vanoccio Biringuccio', pp. 210–11. American Institute of Mining and Metallurgical Engineers, New York. 1943.
[6] *Idem. Ibid.*, p. 222.
[7] HALL, A. R. 'Ballistics in the Seventeenth Century', p. 11. University Press, Cambridge. 1952.

[8] SMITH, C. S. and GNUDI, MARTHA T. See ref. [5], p. 308.
[9] LAZARD, P. E. 'Vauban, 1633–1707.' Alcan, Paris. 1934.
[10] TAYLOR, EVA G. R. 'The Mathematical Practitioners of Tudor and Stuart England.' University Press, Cambridge. 1954.

BIBLIOGRAPHY

A short bibliography on the more technical aspects of military history is given in A. R. HALL, 'Ballistics in the Seventeenth Century', University Press, Cambridge, 1952. Particularly useful works are:

BIRINGUCCIO, VANOCCIO. 'De la Pirotechnia libri X.' Roffinello, Venice. 1540. Eng. trans. by C. S. SMITH and MARTHA T. GNUDI. American Institute of Mining and Metallurgy, New York. 1943.

CARMAN, W. Y. 'A History of Firearms.' Routledge and Kegan Paul, London. 1955.

COLLADO, L. 'Prattica Manuale dell' Artiglieria.' Milan. 1606.

DIDEROT, D. and D'ALEMBERT, J. LE R. (Eds). 'Encyclopédie ou dictionnaire raisonné des sciences, des arts et des métiers.' See: Arquebusier, Canon, Fusil, etc. Paris. 1751–72.

FFOULKES, C. J. 'The Armourer and his Craft from the eleventh to the sixteenth century.' Methuen, London. 1912.

Idem. 'The Gunfounders of England.' University Press, Cambridge. 1937.

GEORGE, J. N. 'English Guns and Rifles.' Small-Arms Technical Publishing Company, Plantersville. 1947.

NAPOLÉON III and COLONEL FAVÉ. 'Études sur le passé et l'avenir de l'artillerie' (6 vols). Paris. 1846–71.

POLLARD, H. B. C. 'A History of Firearms.' Bles, London. 1926.

SAINT-RÉMY, P. SURIREY DE. 'Mémoires d'artillerie.' Paris. 1697.

UFFANO, D. DE. 'Artillerie, c'est à dire vraye instruction de l'artillerie et de toutes ces appartenances.' Frankfurt a. M. 1614.

Laying siege-guns with the aid of clinometers and other instruments. Note the earth-filled gabions used to protect the guns and the wooden platforms prepared for them. The master-gunner holds a lighted linstock. Ramelli, 1588.

15

PRINTING

MICHAEL CLAPHAM

I. ADVENT OF PRINTING

THE development of typographical printing in Europe during the second half of the fifteenth century changed the character of western civilization. A man born in 1453, the year of the fall of Constantinople, could look back from his fiftieth year on a lifetime in which about eight million books had been printed: more, perhaps, than all the scribes of Europe had produced since Constantine founded his city in A.D. 330. It would be natural for such a man, seeing the stream of printed matter widening year by year, to attempt to trace it to its source; and equally natural, at a time when the normal pattern of technological change had not been studied, for him to seek the origin of printing in a single forgetive invention which could be precisely dated and ascribed.

Late in the fifteenth and early in the sixteenth century several writers took this path. They drew their information from the traditions of various printing-houses, either directly or through notes inserted in books by their printers, a practice which did not begin until book-production was already well established; and from this slight and partial evidence established legends that in time acquired the status of history. The resulting concept of a single inventor of printing, and the natural rivalry that developed between the supporters of Johann Gutenberg (c 1400–c 1467) of Mainz and Laurens Coster (fl 1440) of Haarlem, have not only led to some fabrication and much disingenuous interpretation of evidence; they have also tended to obscure the nature of the invention. Only recently have historians inquired exactly what was invented, analysed the techniques involved in early printing, and traced their separate origins.

The beginning of book-production in Europe as an organized industry can be identified with reasonable certainty. There was at Mainz a printing-office which was producing in 1447, and which within ten years had developed to a size requiring substantial capital and employing a number of men. More than fifty printed works are connected with it by the evidence of the type-faces used. Three men were principally involved in its development: Johann Gutenberg and Johann Fust (c 1400–c 1466) in its early years, and Fust's son-in-law Peter Schoeffer (? 1425–

1502) later. How far each contributed technically is unknown; it is not even certain that any of them invented any basic new process. Certainly some of their techniques were of older origin, and were subject to experiment in various parts of Europe at this time. Further, several had been practised in China, Japan, and Korea very much earlier, and though the connexion between the eastern and western technologies is not proved, circumstantial evidence supports it (p 380).

The process: its nature and background. Printing, for our purpose, may be defined as the multiplication of images by applying colouring-matter to a prepared surface and transferring it to a receptive material. The word includes not only typography, or printing from movable types, but also printing from undivided surfaces.

We are not primarily concerned here with decorative printing, but with the multiplication of images conveying ideas. Before analysing the techniques for doing so, it is worth recalling that their widespread development was closely connected with the European Renaissance. At a time of intellectual ferment and a broadening social structure which required easier means of communication, inventive minds were naturally working towards some means of recording and conveying thought less laborious than writing on prepared skins. But without a receptive surface capable of quantity-production there was little advantage in techniques for multiplying images: since a folio of 200 pages required the skins of about 25 sheep, writing was the smaller part of its cost. Thus the initial stimulus to further invention was no doubt the introduction of paper-making from the Islamic Empire to Europe early in the twelfth century. Given a reproducible material like paper, the idea of a reproducible image on it must have occurred to many minds; significantly, we first find signs of printing activity near the early centres of paper-making.

Whether crusaders, merchants visiting the great commercial centre of the Mongol Empire at Tabriz, or missionaries and travellers from the Far East, brought back rumours of the printed books of China as a further stimulus to invention, we do not know. There is no evidence that the art of typography reached Europe from Asia, though the establishment in Korea of a type-foundry and the publication there in 1409 of a book printed from metal types show an interesting parallelism of development. There are, however, strong indications that the idea of printing from a prepared surface came to Europe from the Far East, and the actual technique may have been imported.

The basic techniques. The transference of colour from the printing-surface to the receptive material may be effected in three principal ways. The colouring matter may be applied in viscous form to the raised parts of a partially excised surface, and transferred by contact under pressure to the receiving surface: this is called relief or letterpress printing, and is seen at its simplest when an engraved wooden block is dabbed with ink and a sheet of paper placed on top, rubbed down, and stripped off. The second method, intaglio or gravure printing, also uses a partially excised surface; the colouring-matter, in more liquid form, is applied all over, wiped off the raised portions and then transferred from the excised portions to the receiving surface, which must be absorbent and soft enough to flex some little way into the recesses under pressure (figure 241). The third method, lithographic printing, utilizes a flat printing-surface, parts of which are chemically pre-pared to accept and parts to repel the colouring-matter; but its invention falls outside our period.

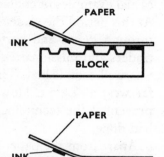

FIGURE 241—*Methods of printing.* (Above) *Relief or letterpress printing;* (below) *intaglio or gravure printing.*

Of the first two processes, relief printing is both older and incomparably more important in this period: it was the fact of a relief printing-surface being divisible into separate components that made possible typographic printing, and led ultimately to large-scale book-production. In comparison, the use of intaglio was small and with few exceptions confined to illustration, decoration, maps, and music printing (p 404).

Development of relief printing. The availability of paper was both a condition of the development of relief printing and a stimulus to it. The complete invention required also a means of preparing a printing-surface, a suitable ink, a means of transferring the ink to the paper, and the creative idea. The originator of the idea, however, and the place and time of its origin, are unknown and probably unascertainable. The use of excised wooden blocks for stamping patterns in plaster and for printing with dye on textiles appears to have been established in the Roman civilization, but since such blocks are highly perishable and generally in very simple forms, few survive and it is virtually impossible to date accurately those that do. One exception is the wooden Protat block, with its engraved picture and inscription, which was found near Dijon and dates from about 1370: it is too big for any sheet of paper then available, and was presumably used for one of the above purposes.

When such techniques were known, the idea of applying them to other than decorative purposes may well have occurred independently to many. The evidence suggests, however, that in practice the idea came to Europe from the Far East. Marco Polo in 1298 had described how the paper currency in Kublai

Khan's empire was printed by a seal dipped in vermilion ink; and the abortive attempt to introduce paper currency in Tabriz (1294) almost certainly resulted in some block-printed notes reaching the home towns of the big Venetian and Genoese colonies there. Twelve years later the missionary Archbishop John of Monte Corvino was writing home from Carambuc (Peking) of the biblical pictures he had had prepared for the instruction of the ignorant. These are casual examples of contact with the art; many more must have been unrecorded. At this period the trade routes into Asia by land and sea were active; southwards through Persia and northwards through Russia there was a regular passage of traders and missionaries to and from the Mongol Empire, where block printing was well established. There is evidence of its use by the fourteenth century as far west as Egypt. However, religious objection to the printing of the Koran prevented the technology spreading westward through Islam, as that of paper had done.

Apart from the paper money of China, the two commonest forms of printing which the traveller to the east might see would be playing-cards and religious charms, the forms in which we find the earliest European block printing. One of the first centres was Venice, whose contacts with the east were particularly close. In 1441 a decree of the Venetian Council laments that the art and mystery of making cards and printed figures has fallen into total decay, and prohibits the importation of such works whether painted or printed. Early in the fifteenth century, printing of this sort was clearly not a struggling new art so much as a lucrative industry. The cause of its decay in Venice is known to have been competition from south German towns. Playing-card makers—and since playing-cards at this time were cheap enough to be within the means of labourers they were probably printed, in outline at least—were registered in Augsburg and Nuremberg between 1418 and 1438, and are known to have operated on a considerable scale. Religious pictures were printed on a similar scale at the same period, in the same centres, and probably by the same men; but this activity became more widely diffused. The earliest surviving European religious prints are very simple productions. The figure of a saint is left in relief on a wooden block and dabbed or brushed with liquid ink; absorbent paper is placed on it and pressed into contact with a brush or a *frotton*, the leather-faced rubbing-pad used for much oriental printing. Later the technique becomes more finished, and inscriptions are cut below the figure: the earliest dated prints of this sort, the 1418 Brussels 'Virgin' and the 1423 Buxheim 'St Christopher' (plate 2B) are highly finished pieces of engraving compared with many extant specimens.

Numbers of these prints have been found pasted into writing-books in monastic libraries; and it is hard to suppose that the idea of producing a series of them in book form did not occur until after typographical printing was invented. In fact, however, though block-books became popular and were extensively produced in the second half of the fifteenth century, none of those surviving can certainly be dated earlier than about 1450. But it is characteristic of these books that one edition was copied from another, often by engraving a new block on to which a print of the old had been transferred, and probably some precursors of the numerous surviving *Biblia pauperum* were circulating before the first typographical books were produced.

Printing-ink. Religious prints and block-books throw light on the development of techniques for preparing and applying colouring-matter, and for transferring it from the printing-surface. The ink used for the early specimens was similar to that used by scribes, an aqueous solution of gum with either lampblack or the more finely divided ferric gallate in suspension as the pigment. Such an ink can, with skill, be brushed or dabbed evenly over a wooden printing-block, and will give a fairly good reproduction if a sheet of paper be laid on it and rubbed down carefully. This method has, however, several disadvantages. Though satisfactory on wood, a water-ink is difficult to apply evenly to metal surfaces, on which it tends to stand in globules; it is not readily transferred by simple impression, while rubbing-down is a slow process; and an absorbent paper must be used, so that the image shows on the reverse. The early block-books were therefore generally made up by pasting one-sided prints back to back.

A major contribution to the art of printing was the invention of an improved ink consisting of a pigment—lampblack or powdered charcoal for the normal black ink—ground in a linseed-oil varnish: it remained the standard printers' ink for more than four centuries. The inventor is unknown: Polydore Vergil, writing in 1499, attributed the discovery to Gutenberg, and a varnish-based ink was certainly used in the Mainz printing-office; but it is also found in some early block prints, and in printed fragments of Dutch origin and probably earlier date. The fact that boiled linseed-oil made a varnish of good binding and drying properties became known to the school of Flemish painters early in the fifteenth century, and the use of paints based on it for inking wooden printing-blocks would be a natural development wherever painters and engravers were working together—for instance, in the playing-card factories of Nuremberg and Augsburg. These factories may also have evolved the technique of applying oil-based ink which became standard among early printers: it was dabbed out thinly on a level surface with a pad made of damped leather stuffed with wool or hair, which in turn was dabbed on the printing-surface.

The press. The origin of the press as a means for transferring ink to paper is as obscure as that of printing itself. Its introduction depended on the availability of the new ink, which was viscous enough to allow the inked printing-surface, with the paper resting on it, to be slid into a press without blurring the impression. Given such an ink, experiments with a press were almost inevitable. Every sizeable household would have a linen-press consisting of a heavy base-board with two uprights carrying a cross-bar, through which a turned wooden screw pressed down a reinforced platen or top board sliding between the uprights. Similar presses (figure 242) were used for various industrial purposes, particularly in paper-factories for flattening the damp sheets (figures 114, 254). Anyone seeking to apply even pressure over a flat surface might well turn to this familiar implement, and several may have done so independently. Certainly by the time of the earliest surviving typographical fragments, about 1440, pressing had superseded manual rubbing or brushing down, though the more primitive technique continued in use for block-books into the last quarter of the century.

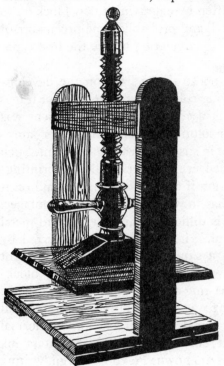

FIGURE 242—*A linen-press.*

In the year or two each side of 1450, when the Mainz printing-office was first printing books, the original screw-down press had probably been improved to make its action more rapid. It would be natural to increase the pitch of the screw, so as to speed the travel of the platen, and to incorporate a board sliding over the base-board on which the pages to be printed could be fixed, thus enabling them to be removed without disturbance for stripping and inking, and slid in again with a fresh sheet of paper and any soft backing-material necessary to get an even impression. Riccobaldi of Ferrara, in a chronicle published in 1474, speaks of the early printers achieving a production of 300 leaves a day; and an experiment in printing with a linen-press will satisfy anyone that a two-minute cycle of operations requires at least these improvements, and possibly some of the further ones described on page 389.

One point in the printing-operation must be noted. The well sized paper used for writing the manuscripts emulated by the early printers had too hard a surface to be printed sharply with the limited pressure available: it had therefore to be printed damp. The damping and subsequent drying increased the labour of printing; the sheets varied in dimension with their water-content, making it difficult to get accurate register when printing the reverse side or a second colour. The compensating advantages, however, were considerable; the impression was clean and sharp, and the pigment of the ink, trapped between the fibres of the paper as it shrank on drying, was securely held, giving an added depth of colour.

II. THE EARLIEST TYPE-FOUNDING

The invention of typography. By the mid-fifteenth century it can be taken that the art of printing, as such, was widely established—at least wherever playing-cards and religious pictures were being produced—probably with the press as an alternative to the *frotton*, almost certainly with a viscous oil-ink as well as one using a gum solution. The next milestone was the invention of typographical printing. The legends are familiar: one tells that Johann Gutenberg, a goldsmith of Strassburg and Mainz, invented movable types and the means of casting them in metal; that he turned to Johann Fust, a fellow goldsmith, for finance; that Fust having secured the technique broke the partnership and combined with his son-in-law, Peter Schoeffer, to exploit it. The other well known version makes Laurens Coster of Haarlem the inventor and Gutenberg an employee who absconded with the secret process.

We are concerned here not with personalities but with the way in which the techniques arose and were developed. There must have been some moment when the idea was first conceived that a type, the mirror image of an alphabetical letter, could be made in metal by a precision casting method: but we do not known when, where, or in whose mind it was; nor who first translated the idea into achievement. If Coster printed at all, there is no evidence of his contemporaries recognizing it; his name is first mentioned over a century after his supposed achievement, and no book bears his imprint. Gutenberg, in contrast, is far from shadowy: his extreme litigiousness has left his existence heavily documented, and he was distinguished enough to receive from the Archbishop of Mainz a sinecure to pension his old age. He too, however, failed to leave his imprint on any surviving book, an omission not in keeping with what is otherwise known of his character; and the clerk who drew up the customary rehearsal of his distinctions in the document, dated 1465, appointing him to the Archbishop's household, makes no mention of printing among them.

On the other hand, Gutenberg's claim to have made some significant contribution to the invention rests on a variety of evidence. A dubiously authentic document of 1436 refers to his partnership with Andreas Dritzehn of Strassburg and to the use of lead and a press. Another document, recording a lawsuit of 1455, claims that Fust had lent Gutenberg money to be employed in their common enterprise, while Gutenberg in reply refers to purchases of parchment, paper, and ink, and to the production of books. Another, dating from after Gutenberg's death in 1467, refers to the disposal of his instruments for printing. Most significant, perhaps, are the facts that Peter Schoeffer, Fust's son-in-law and partner, refers to Gutenberg as Fust's original partner in the invention of printing in the colophon of a book dated 1468—one year after the former's death and two years after the latter's; and that a sixteenth-century transcript of a document dated 1458, in the French Royal Mint, records Charles VII as having heard that Johann Gutenberg of Mainz was adept in cutting punches and characters, and as having decided to send Nicolas Jenson (d c 1480) to learn his art. It is not unlikely that Gutenberg and Fust were in fact independent experimenters in the production of type, who joined forces at the time when Gutenberg returned from Strassburg to his native Mainz about 1446.

But whether one or both conceived the idea of movable types, others certainly did so, probably independently. There survives a range of printed specimens, largely attributable to Holland—the so-called 'Costeriana'—some of which, though undated, are placed on circumstantial evidence earlier than the first productions of Mainz. Both in composition and type design they are cruder than the earliest Gutenberg–Fust–Schoeffer specimens; so much cruder as to suggest a more primitive technique of type-making. And in addition to the craftsmen experimenting with type-casting in Holland and in Germany, we know of one contemporary European experimenter working in southern France.

That many should work simultaneously but independently on the problems of typography is not surprising. With an established industry printing religious broadsheets and playing-cards from wooden blocks, every wood-engraver would learn to repair or correct the block by cutting out and gluing in an individual letter. Again, the economy of assembling up to ten separate blocks of one symbol each, rather than carving a complete block for each numeral card, can hardly have gone unnoticed. Wooden types were probably never used, except for large letters and initials, but, given the idea of the separate symbol or letter blocks, it would be natural to consider reproducing them less laboriously than by carving.

In particular, one can imagine the playing-card maker trying to use a single carved block for each suit as a pattern to press into clay or loam, thus giving a mould into which lead or tin could be cast. Compared with the precision casting of jewelry the technical difficulties would not be great. As a method of producing thousands of small letters, however, it was clearly unsatisfactory. Extreme accuracy of all dimensions is essential if a page of letters, necessarily of varying widths, is to fit together securely and give an even impression, and this could have been achieved with individual castings only by laborious hand-filing.

The key to the further evolution of type-founding, therefore, was the process of die-casting, using an interchangeable matrix in conjunction with an accurate metal mould. Whether or not the early Dutch printers or others anticipated it, this process was certainly first operated on a major scale in Mainz. The first works definitely attributable to the printing-office associated with Gutenberg and Fust—the 'World Judgement' fragment of a poem and the fragment of an astronomical calendar printed not later than 1448—use a type which, though large, is closely set and accurately aligned. It must have been cast in a mould of efficient design, since the same face was later used for the 36-line Bible, requiring a considerable production of type.

'Letter-cutting is a handy-work hitherto kept so conceal'd among the artificers of it, that I cannot learn any one hath taught it any other.' So wrote Joseph Moxon, author of the first full-length manual on printing (1683). We know a little now of sixteenth-century practice: but fifteenth-century techniques can only be surmised by reference to contemporary metallurgy (p 43), and to the appearance of early printing. The earliest Dutch types give rather rough impressions; they may have been cast in moulds impressed by a wooden punch in clay, loam, or one of the special compositions in use for intricate castings. Or matrices may have been made by pressing a wooden punch into lead just as it set; such matrices have been shown capable of casting satisfactorily more than sixty types each. Later, copper punches were used to strike lead matrices (p 392). It is possible, however, that the Mainz printers may have used steel punches initially: as goldsmiths they would know of their use in coining. Certainly the consistency —there is not complete uniformity—of letter design throughout their major works indicates an advanced technique and a durable punch and matrix.

Nothing is known of fifteenth-century type-moulds. Pierce Butler has conjectured that a pair of plates, L-shaped in plan, were slid together to grip type-sized matrices of various widths, but such matrices could equally well have fitted into the end of simple split moulds of fixed size.

The composition of the original type-metal is also unknown. Almost certainly, however, it was an alloy of tin and lead: the casting of this material was already highly developed among the pewterers (p 43).

III. AN EARLY PRINTING-OFFICE IN OPERATION

We may now seek to reconstruct the equipment and methods of working of a printing-office, say that of Fust and Schoeffer about the year 1450. The finishing touches were then perhaps being put to the Constance Missal, the earliest complete surviving book, and a start was being made on the great 42-line Bible whose 1700 folio pages are a masterpiece of both technique and design. The reconstruction necessarily contains speculative elements. The earliest printers were not anxious to divulge the mechanical nature of their process, and, even when the craft was established, its secrets had a commercial value which long kept them unpublished.

The early printing-offices were of necessity self-contained. Although in the experimental stages one or two men may have performed each operation in turn, there must have been considerable specialization of function soon after 1450, when more than one press was in continuous production. Paper would be bought; ink would be made periodically as required. The permanent sections would be the type-foundry, the compositors, the corrector, the pressmen, and—though the bookbinder would be an independent craftsman—a place where printed sheets were collated.

The work of the foundry consisted of making the punches, striking them into the metal used for matrices, and casting the type in the matrices, first, perhaps, constructing a number of moulds in which to do so. All operations except the completion of the type-casting would have to be done before the setting of any type, and the first stage would be the cutting of the punches. Each would be cut on the end of a steel, brass, or copper rod of rectangular section; and owing to the need to imitate all the ligatures and abbreviations of contemporary manuscripts, a set of matrices would run to more than 150 characters for each size of type, without allowing for replacement of breakages. Within the last century, the output of a skilled punch-cutter working on letters already marked out has been put between two and four punches a week, and the accumulation of the punches for each fount must have occupied the fifteenth-century designer and punch-cutter well over a year—perhaps more than two—even if two or three men were working continuously. Without precise measuring-instruments, there would be great difficulty in securing accurate alignment of the type from a series of hand-cut punches struck by hand into matrices, and there is no evidence on how it was overcome. Since, however, we know that a matrix could be of the same size and shape as a finished type, we may guess that the punch was originally a similar blank, on the end of which the 'line'—that is, the line at the foot of the small or lower-case letters—was lightly scratched. With this as a guide, the letter would be drawn in, and the metal round it and inside its outline carefully punched down and chiselled or filed away. The effect would be judged by taking impressions at various stages, perhaps—as in later practice—after blackening the punch in candle-smoke. On completion, the metal would be hardened, and the resulting punch would be identical in face with the type to be cast.

The next operation would be striking the punch with a hammer into a suitable blank of the softer metal used for the matrix. There would no doubt be considerable variation in the depth of strike, but this would not be a serious defect since the type as cast would in any case have to be brought to the right height by filing at the foot.

With the completion of a set of matrices, the preliminary work of the office would be done. The next operation would be typecasting. A single page of the 42-line Bible contains about 2750 letters; and at any time in its production there must have been a minimum of two pages printing, two more being set and corrected, and two more being 'distributed'—that is, being broken up again to individual types for replacement in the type-cases. For these six pages, allowing a very moderate proportion of type unused in the cases, about 20 000 individual types would have to be made. In the later stages of production, when six pages were being printed simultaneously, up to 100 000 types will have been in use at any one time.

In the last days before typefounding was mechanized, four centuries later, 20 000 letters would have been six or seven days' work for a team of two men, one casting and one dressing: but at this time, with a primitive mould probably needing to be taken apart after each cast, with a matrix which would often adhere to the type, with each letter having to be adjusted for height and probably filed down on three sides to get it square and to size, two men can hardly have produced more than 25 dressed types an hour. At this rate there would be two or three weeks of casting and dressing type before such a major work was undertaken, and over twelve months before the quantity ultimately required could be completed. The subsequent replacement of types worn down, damaged, or broken would probably employ one man continuously.

We can therefore imagine the foundry as normally employing at least two men, including one skilled punch-cutter. Of their product, we know little except the design of face, which has been exhaustively studied; but since in an occasional fifteenth-century book we find the impression of types lying on their sides, we can say that in height and shape they were not unlike today's four-sided prism, approximately one inch high (figure 243).

Of the way in which type was stored we lack contemporary evidence; but the Jost Amman woodcuts a century later (cf. figure 244) show that the type-cases—shallow trays partitioned for type-storage—still had compartments of approximately equal size. Presumably this obvious arrangement was adopted early on, and the compositors in Mainz stood before a single case, big enough to hold all the sorts in use. Of the other tools of the trade again we know nothing. The types may have been set into a primitive composing 'stick'. More probably, however,

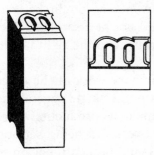

they were too irregular for handling in lines, and were set straight on to a wooden tray, about the size of the printed page, which could be wedged up tightly and transferred complete to the press.

The page would undoubtedly need much attention before it was ready to print. A century later, type came from the foundry so accurate in all dimensions that a page of several thousand letters could be held in a solid block, with a minute variation in the height of the printing-surface, by the pressure at side and foot of wooden wedges—

FIGURE 243—*Type: isometric view* (left), *and plan.*

'quoins'—driven against a tapered 'sidestick'. But the type of the 1450s must have needed careful wedging to keep each line firm and square on its feet. In books of this period the same letter varies in width and height: defective casting or damage when separating the type from the matrix must have meant filing down individual types at the top, bottom, or sides. No doubt the height, too, varied and needed adjustment.

Bearing this in mind, we can assess the speed of working. A nineteenth-century compositor on piecework would have taken three or four hours to set and impose a page of the 42-line Bible, using accurate type in ample supply and a precisely made composing-stick, galley (the shallow tray used to hold composed type), and spacing-material. His fifteenth-century counterpart can hardly have taken less than twice as long, using his highly irregular type and equipment, and a case in whose equal-sized compartments the more commonly used types would soon need replenishing: each page would thus take him about a day. There is bibliographical evidence that in its later stages the book was printed on six presses, each served by its own compositor or compositors, and it seems likely that at this time the composing-room strength was being increased from about three to at least six men.

The first stage of the compositor's work would be completed as each page was firmly wedged together and a proof taken for the corrector to the press, or 'reader'. A printer's reputation for care and accuracy has always reflected his reader's knowledge and acuity of observation: the fifteenth-century reader would normally be a scholar, and would combine with his work of correction the editing of the text. His method of operation has probably not changed much over the centuries; he would compare the original text with the proof, line by line and word by word, using the simple marks and instructions in the medieval scholar's tongue—*dele, transpone, stet*—which a conservative trade retains abbreviated or in full to this day. The corrected proof would go back to the compositor, who would loosen the type and make the alterations, and another proof would be checked before being passed for the press.

FIGURE 244—*The printer. 1568.*

The press used by the early Mainz printers cannot have been far removed from the linen-press. Its slow rate of operation, already mentioned, indicates only minor improvements before 1450: probably a tray in which the type could be wedged, inked, covered with paper and backing-material, and slid under the platen. About this year, however, an important improvement was introduced. This was the 'tympan', a frame covered with parchment on which the paper to be printed was fastened, and which was hinged—at first probably to the tray containing the type—so that the paper came down exactly level with the surface of the type. With this device a sheet could be positioned precisely in relation to the type, in spite of the irregular edges of hand-made paper, by pressing it on to 'press-points' which perforated the margins, leaving holes which were placed over points fixed in the appropriate position to give exact register when backing-up the sheet or printing a second colour. Such points have marked the margin of the 42-line Bible, whereas the earlier Constance Missal, whose register is in comparison a little irregular, was presumably printed by dropping each sheet on to the inked type, and repeating this process for the red printing and for both printings on the reverse: the technique may sound unlikely to achieve reasonably accurate registration, but it is still used successfully in printing-offices where proofs are taken on hand-presses.

About 1450, then, we can suppose the Mainz office to be adding tympans to its two or three original presses and installing three more. Each press would employ two men; one would affix the paper to the tympan, fold it down, place backing material on top of it, slide the assembly under the platen, screw it down, and, after a second or two, screw it open again. The second man would dab out ink on a stone slab, cover the ink-balls with a film of ink, and ink the type while the paper was being replaced. The press-room would also employ one or two men to hold ready the sheets of damped paper, damp further supplies for the following day, and hang up the printed sheets to dry. In addition, there might be one or two men gathering up the dry printed sheets and collating them ready for the binder.

The Mainz printing-office, then, in the early 1450s, must have been a considerable establishment. Our examination suggests a staff of about 25 men; at least 2 typefounders and 6 compositors, a reader, 12 pressmen and assistants, and a few others. It is thus not surprising either that the strain on the working capital of the partners was considerable, as the 1455 lawsuit suggests; or that there were men available to found the various other presses which started in the ten years before the sack of Mainz in 1462, and the numerous ones thereafter.

IV. DEVELOPMENTS: 1462 TO 1730

The improvements in the technique of printing between 1450 and 1730 cannot often be attributed to individuals or even to localities. Printing as an art became widely diffused. By 1500 it was established in twelve European countries; though, of nearly 40 000 recorded editions of books printed in that period, less than a third were produced outside Germany and Italy. By 1600 printing was being carried on in almost every country in Europe, and before 1700 at several places outside Europe, including the Americas. The art, however, retained its international character, recognized improvements in its implements and methods passing fairly rapidly from place to place. It is therefore convenient to examine the progress of the component parts of the process in turn, rather than to attempt an overall chronological survey.

Typefounding. Improvements in the technique of typefounding were rapidly effected. By the middle of the sixteenth century tools and methods had been developed that did not alter greatly over the next 300 years. Progress was aided by the recognition of printing as an art in itself, which enabled printers to dispense with numerous combined letters, known as 'ligatures', and overhanging or 'kerned' letters, which had been appropriate enough to the scribe's pen but added enormously to the labour of casting and composing type. The fount, originally 24 capital or upper-case and 24 lower-case letters, with 10 figures and about 10 marks of punctuation and conventional symbols, was at first supplemented by about 100 variant letters or ligatures, making a fount of up to 170 characters. Some ligatures, such as ff, fi, fl, ffi, and ffl are still used; and the diphthongs and certain ornamental combinations such as ſt, &, and those containing the long ſ, were only gradually eliminated. The standard fount, however, was reduced to about 100 characters during the sixteenth century, in spite of the tendency in its last twenty years to admit the letters J and U to the roman 24-letter alphabet, a practice finally established about 1620 or 1630.

A first brief account of typefounding appears in Vanoccio Biringuccio's *Pirotechnia* (Venice, 1540). Christopher Plantin, the famous Antwerp printer whose equipment survives there, published in 1567 *Dialogues françois pour les jeunes*

FIGURE 245—*The typefounder. 1568.*

enfans containing a simplified but fuller description. A year later the Jost Amman woodcuts illustrating Schopper's Panoplia, *omnium illiberalium, mechanicarum* etc. give us a picture of the typefounder at work (figure 245). We do not get a really detailed account of the typefounder's methods and tools, however, till 1683, when Joseph Moxon published the second volume of his 'Mechanick Exercises', describing a technique of typefounding which did not alter materially till well into the eighteenth century. Its development can thus be followed with some confidence after the *incunabula* period.

The technique of cutting punches and striking matrices changed little from about 1500 till punch-cutting machines were invented. Biringuccio, Plantin, and Moxon all describe the cutting of a letter on the end of a steel rod, which was hardened and struck into a sheet of copper to give the matrix. Moxon mentions the difficulty of positioning the punch exactly while doing so. He further describes the making of counter-punches, with which the unwanted metal inside and outside the letter itself is punched down; and the vice, files, and chisels which were the punch-cutter's main tools in his time, as no doubt 200 years earlier. It is difficult to explain why, since more technically advanced materials were known so early, the use of copper punches and lead matrices also survived. It is, however, recorded that a Dutch foundry was using them about 1500: the matrices are still preserved at Haarlem. In England, type-foundry records show lead matrices in use long afterwards: a set was included in an eighteenth-century sale.

The development of the mould before 1540 can be judged only from occasional impressions, which occur in early printed books, of the side of types pulled out in inking. These differ from modern ones chiefly in lacking the nick, which indicates to the compositor's fingers the right way up to place the type, and in being more roughly formed at the foot (figure 243). Only after several decades was the mould shaped to mark the foot of the type and so enable the tang, or unwanted metal solidified between the foot and the mouth of the mould, to be broken neatly away. Previously, types were apparently cast somewhat longer than required, sawn to length, and filed smooth.

Biringuccio in 1540 describes a mould of brass or bronze, consisting of two flat components sliding together and adjustable for letter-width. It uses flat matrices, which are held underneath the aperture of the mould by small screws. Such a mould might be capable of quite rapid production. The moulds illustrated by Jost Amman in 1568 are still further advanced: the mould shown in the type-founder's hand appears to be a hinged one, which is held closed in use (figure 245). Similar moulds on a shelf near him have a hole near the base, presumably for the transverse insertion of a matrix such as those close to his right hand. The types in a bowl beside him still have the tang attached, but it is not clear whether a break is marked: there is no sign of a nick. Amman, however, may have worked from out-of-date originals. Certainly the mould described by Plantin a year earlier was an elaborate compound construction, mounted in wood, held together by a bow-shaped spring, and containing various parts identifiable with those described by Moxon 126 years later, including a wire to form the nick and a 'break' at the foot; and similar features have been described in a French mould believed to date from the sixteenth century. It seems therefore that a mould not unlike that in use at the end of our period was developed soon after 1540.

The improvement of the mould gradually reduced the amount of manual work in the subsequent operations of typefounding. The earliest types, cast in makeshift moulds and separated with difficulty from the matrices, must each have needed two or three minutes of hand work. First they would be sawn to length, presumably in a simple gauge; then the casting-flash along the sides of the type would have to be rubbed off; and finally the surplus metal round the face itself would need trimming away with the file. In the fifteenth century it was the practice to rub away most of the shoulder, or flat top of the body supporting the face, to ensure that it did not pick up ink and print. Later, when more accurate moulds had almost eliminated any flash except for the tang at the foot of the type, which was marked to break off readily, the main operation of dressing was to run a plane over the feet. Since, however, the number of double letters had been reduced partly by introducing kerned letters, such as *f*, which overhangs its neighbour on either side, these letters had also to be trimmed under the kerns with a special plane, and the shoulders of other letters had to be left square to support them. Kerned letters were a small proportion of the fount, however, and the combined technical improvements in the mould, the matrix, and the type-metal made typecasting a comparatively rapid process; Moxon in 1683 gives 4000 letters a day as the product of a caster and dresser working together, with the aid of a boy to break off the tangs. However, in the following century a rate of 3000 letters a day was thought satisfactory, so he may have put the average too high.

The development of the metallurgy of typefounding is dealt with elsewhere in this volume (pp 43-4). Briefly, the original tin-lead alloy, similar to pewter, was replaced by an alloy in which lead predominated and which also contained antimony, tin, and sometimes other metals. The major step, probably taken early in the sixteenth century, was the incorporation of antimony: it conferred not only increased hardness, but also the attribute of expanding slightly on solidification, thus giving the type sharpness of face and accuracy of body.

Before leaving typefounding, mention should be made of its specialization into a separate trade. Although fifteenth-century printers generally made their own type, there is early evidence of interchange between them. Schoeffer's colophon to his 1468 Justinian implies his readiness to sell type; and the Ripoli Press cost-book records the purchase of matrices from one John of Mainz in 1477, and at other times purchases of founts of type and initials. Typefounding by printers continued to be the normal practice throughout the sixteenth century, and indeed the largest offices retained their foundries until mechanical typesetting transformed them; but there grew up between 1500 and 1600 a number of small offices relying on purchased type, and a class of typefounders who supplied them. The specialist typefounder was recognized before the middle of the century in Holland, which for the next 300 years was to have a high reputation for type and a flourishing export trade; and before 1600 typefounding was established as a separate trade in many European countries, including England.

This specialization, which supplemented the range of type of some offices while supplying others entirely, tended towards standardization of type-heights. At first it was only local, in places where a single foundry was able, or a group of printers was agreed, to enforce the convenience of interchangeable material. In spite of its obvious desirability, the difficulty of getting a printer to replace at great cost his existing stock of types for the sake of future benefits prevented such progress being made until national bodies began to interest themselves in the problem at the very end of our period. Sixteenth–century types certainly varied in height between 22 and 27 mm, and if by 1730 there were considerably fewer type-heights than printers, there were still more than there were countries practising printing.

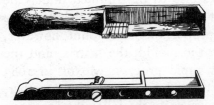

FIGURE 246—*Composing sticks.* (Above) *Fifteenth-century;* (below) *seventeenth-century.*

The compositor's equipment is simple, and has varied little except in material over the past 500 years. His personal tools are a bodkin, a pair of tweezers, and one or more composing-sticks. Plantin's compositor in 1567 holds in his left hand a wooden composing-stick (figure 246) and sets letters into it till he has got a full line, which he then transfers to a galley; and a block in a book published in 1507 shows a stick being used by a compositor in just the same way as his successor used the iron 'stick', with one side sliding to adjust the length of line, which came into general use at the end of the sixteenth century and has altered little since.

Apart from these personal tools, the main equipment of the composing-room consisted of the cases for storing type; the wooden frames on which they were rested; a flat surface on which the type was finally 'imposed', that is, made up into pages, spaced to give the correct margins, and locked up into a metal frame or 'chase'; a supply of chases, wooden spacing-material, and head- and side-sticks narrower at one end than the other; and quoins (p 388) to hold the assembly of pages, or 'forme', firmly in the chase.

The development of the type-case before Moxon's time can be only sketchily reconstructed from the surviving illustrations of printing. The large single sloping case with about 160 divisions shown in a woodcut by Amman was presumably the earliest approach to the problem: it worked adequately so long as a printer possessed only one or two founts, but it was too large readily to move about when a variety of type sizes and styles became normal. Much smaller cases appear in Stradanus's picture of a printing-office (figure 247), dating from about 1590: but this is inaccurate in detail, and serves only as an impression of how a small and not very up-to-date establishment was laid out and operated. The important development was towards a case in which the letters were arranged with the most commonly used ones grouped centrally, and in which the size of the compartments was related to the frequency of each letter's use. It is not known who first departed from the equal-sized, alphabetically arranged

FIGURE 247—*A sixteenth-century printing office.* (Left to right) *Composing the type from copy; correcting the type in the forme; inking type and assembling printed sheets; pressman at work. Note printed sheets drying. From Stradanus, c 1590.*

compartments. It can be inferred that Plantin started by laying his type alphabetically in the cases, which may therefore have been the common usage in the mid-sixteenth century. By 1683, when Moxon wrote, the modern style of case had been established so long that he did not comment on its novelty. In the intervening period there are few illustrations of printing processes, and no surviving type-cases can be placed before 1700 in their present form. Clearly, however, some time after about 1550 there came into general use a pair of cases, the upper case (that is, the one placed higher on the sloping frame) containing the capital letters and figures, arranged alphabetically, in its left half, and either the small capitals or the italic capitals in the right half; and the other case containing the minuscule letters now known as 'lower case', arranged according to the frequency of use, which varied somewhat with the language (figure 248).

Little other notable change occurred in the composing-room before 1730. The frame on which the cases rested came to incorporate racks below, in which additional cases could be stored. The imposing surface was no doubt made of stone in the earliest development of printing, as being readily ground to give a large flat surface, and it was still stone—marble, Purbeck, or some other fine-grained variety—in 1730. The chase, a wrought iron frame inside which type-

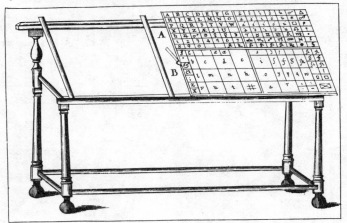

FIGURE 248—*A pair of cases. After Moxon, 1683.*

pages could be locked up for printing, was probably developed between 1450 and 1470, as type became accurate enough to hold in blocks by side and foot pressure alone. By 1499, when the first representation of a chase appears,[1] it has a cross-bar, so that one folio page, or a pair of quarto pages, can be unlocked for adjustment without disturbing the rest of the forme (figure 249). By 1550, when printing in octavo and smaller formats was normal, chases divided into four by cross-bars at right-angles were also in use. The wooden spacing-material and the head-sticks, side-sticks, and quoins were not materially altered from the earliest days until within living memory.

The press and its equipment. After the type-mould, the press is the most important mechanical device in printing. We have no exact knowledge of its development from the simple screw-down wooden press during the fifteenth century, but thereafter it can be followed from numerous illustrations and from the descriptions of Plantin and later writers.

[1] In *La grāt danse macabre*. Lyons, 1499-1500.

The experiment of printing a page of type in a linen-press helps in reconstructing the early stages of development. First of all, the page cannot be inked or covered with paper while under the platen of the press, nor can it be slid in after inking without risking displacement of the type or paper unless it is firmly mounted on a slide which can be introduced into the press complete. It is then found difficult, inserting the slide at random, to get the page centrally under the screw of the press, failing which the platen tilts and applies pressure unevenly; rails are therefore introduced to guide the sliding bed, and the fixed bed is extended to carry them clear of the platen, where the page can be inked. By marking the slide the page can now be centred; but as the screw is held vertical only by passing through the top cross-bar, usually called the 'head' or 'summer', and by the guidance of the side members or 'cheeks', some wobble may occur at the point of impression. The screw is therefore made to pass through a lower member, the 'till' or 'shelf', below the bar that turns the screw. This stage of development can be

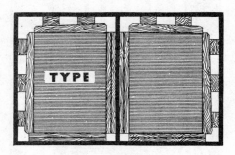

FIGURE 249—*Two-page forme, showing chase with one cross-bar, wooden furniture, and method of locking up with wedges (quoins).*

seen in the Stradanus illustration, the presses in which are more typical of 1490 than of 1590 (figure 247).

The spread of printing throughout Europe in the two or three decades each side of 1500 brought many new minds to bear on its technical problems. Within a framework of established practice, new experiments would be tried wherever printing-offices grew up, though the major items of plant, particularly the presses, would continue in use for many years. There would thus be—as today—differences corresponding to a century's development between the newly established, progressive, and highly capitalized concerns and the old-fashioned ones or those lacking resources to buy new plant. Indeed, to illustrate the next stage in press-design, we turn to a woodcut used about 1507 by the great Parisian printer Jodocus Badius Ascensius[1] (figure 250). The French contributed particularly to the design of the press at this period, and the *Prelum* [press] *Ascensianum* is probably typical of the most advanced practice in the early sixteenth century.

It shows clearly the principal differences between what may be called the improved linen-press and the wooden printing-press which, though refined in detail, was not fundamentally altered until the eighteenth century. The bed has

---

[1] Badius (1462?–1535) was Flemish by birth, but worked for much of his life in Paris.

been made to run in and out on rails; these are not visible, but clearly the bed can be made to travel by means of a handle and winding-gear, or, in the language of the trade, a 'rounce' turning a 'spit' on which is mounted a 'barrel' to which are attached the 'girts' or winding-straps. This woodcut shows a feature that does not appear in the only known earlier picture of a press, the *Danse macabre* woodcut mentioned above (p 396); namely, the 'hose', a hollow block of wood through which the screw passed, and to which the platen was attached. This picture shows it hexagonal, though a square shape later became standard; it passes through an hexagonal hole in the till. The function of the hose was to prevent the platen from twisting as it was lowered, particularly at the moment of impression, and the platen was suspended from it instead of from the screw. It seems here to be fixed rigidly to the platen, having probably developed from the socket in which the base of the screw is held in the press that Stradanus illustrates.

FIGURE 250—*The printing-press of Jodocus Badius Ascensius, used as his device. From the title-page of a book printed in Paris in 1507.*

The tympan, first introduced about 1450, is also visible in Badius's press, as a hinged frame attached to the bed on which the forme is placed. By the middle of the sixteenth century at latest, and probably as early as this illustration, it had developed into an inner and an outer frame, between which was a blanket or other soft material replacing the original loose backing.

Two points about presses of this period should be noted. First, the platen is small, only large enough to print half the forme at once, since with the simple screw-mechanism even the strongest pressman could get only enough pressure for about 240 sq in. Secondly, there is no counterweight to lift the platen after printing.

The minor tools of the pressman are visible in this and the other illustrations; they did not change materially before 1800. The type was inked with a pair of 'ink-balls', the leather covers of which were freed from grease and made supple by long pickling in urine, then carefully stuffed with wool; their basis was a cup-like stock and handle turned from beech wood. The ink on the inking-slab was spread with a flat knife or 'slice', and rubbed out thinly with a wooden 'brayer'. Nearby there would be a trough in which to damp the paper, and a press in which to store it. There would also be a lye-trough in which to wash ink from the forme: it can be seen in the right foreground of the Stradanus picture (figure 247).

Badius reproduced several other presses. In 1520, a more heavily constructed model is shown, with cheeks fully 6 in thick, and the barrel of the screw 8 or 9 inches in diameter; it has a square hose instead of the hexagonal one. Its most notable feature is that instead of a head with the screw passing through it, and a higher transverse member or 'cap' surmounting the cheeks, there is a single massive top member, from which two columns rise to the ceiling to ensure stability. This design was not generally adopted, but later presses were usually designed for greater rigidity.

The Jost Amman woodcut of 1568 (figure 244) shows a further refinement of press-design, the 'frisket'. This was a frame covered with parchment or strong paper, hinged inside the tympan, having the areas to be printed cut out. Its purpose was both to retain the paper in position against the tympan, and to protect the blank areas from contact with any spacing-material that might accidentally be inked. The frisket is first mentioned in 1587, but it must have been used a century earlier. If a pressman did not cut out the printed area accurately, or allow for the play of the hinges, the type might bite on the edge of the parchment, leaving the edge of the page impressed but not printed on the paper below. Such frisket-bites occur in the *Speculum vitae Christi* of 1487, but are uncommon in fifteenth-century books, so it is probable that some other device—perhaps tapes stretched across the tympan—was generally used to retain the paper until about 1500.

No hose is visible on Jost Amman's press, but this is probably a mistake in drawing, since the curved stays from the four corners of the platen no doubt run to the corners of a square hose passing through the till. This method of holding the platen horizontal and preventing it from twisting was by then well established, and is clearly seen in an English press illustrated about 1548; this differs from the Amman press only in having a large square hose and a longer, curved, metal handle. Such a handle became the established form. Its springiness eased the jerk on the pressman's arm when the platen was pulled down, and its rebound when released helped to raise the platen.

Two other points should be noted. First the type bed is clearly no longer the flat wood of the earliest presses, but the polished stone slab, bedded with plaster or bran into a shallow wooden box, the 'coffin', which was later adopted universally. Secondly the system of press-points on the tympan is plainly reproduced for the first time.

With these improvements, the press had completed the most important stage of its development within our period, and it is probable that there were in Europe at the end of the seventeenth century many presses similar to these models of 150 years earlier. A copper plate was being used as backing for the wooden platen before 1567, and towards 1700 brass or iron gradually replaced wood for making the screw, the rails on which the bed ran, and various smaller parts; but the first significant variation in design was not made till the early years of the seventeenth century. Then Willem Janszoon Blaeuw (1571–1638), the Dutch cartographer who as a young man worked with Tycho Brahe on his mathematical and astronomical instruments, and may have shared in his printing activities, introduced what became known as the Dutch press (figure 251). This differed from its predecessors in two ways. One was a minor improvement to the winding mechanism, enabling the girts to be adjusted more rapidly. The other was a radical alteration to the hose, which can best be described by comparing the Blaeuw press with the final version of the 'wooden' press (figure 252). In the latter, the hose is a long wooden box, which encloses the spindle from just below the

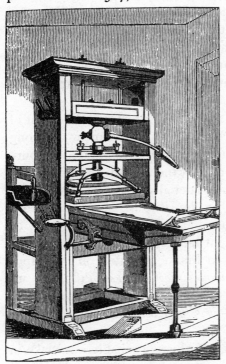

FIGURE 251—*The Blaeuw or Dutch press.*

bar to about 6 in above the platen, where it terminates in a metal cup with a hook at each corner. From these, the platen is suspended by cords running to each of its corners, while the hose itself is hung from a groove in the spindle just below the bar, into which there fit two slides inserted through slots in the side of the hose. The toe of the spindle, passing through the hose, rests in a metal cup at the exact centre of the platen, which is further reinforced by an iron plate below it. When the bar is pulled over by the pressman, the screw at the top of the spindle forces it down, carrying the hose and platen with it: the former is prevented from twisting by the square hole in the till.

In the Blaeuw press, instead of this hose-mechanism the spindle passes directly through circular holes in the till and in a metal plate below it from which the platen is suspended, this plate in turn being suspended from a groove on the spindle by a yoke carrying at each end a square bar passing through a separate hole in the till. This arrangement was perhaps slightly easier to make and to adjust than a well fitted box-hose; certainly it was immediately adopted as an

FIGURE 252—*The improved wooden press.*

improvement in the Low Countries, became almost universal in its use there,[1] and was exported to, or copied in, other countries. The first press to reach North America in 1639 was of the Dutch type. Moxon in 1683 praised the excellence of these presses somewhat extravagantly, contrasting them with the traditional type then generally in use; but, though later writers followed his encomiums, most printers in England and many elsewhere in Europe continued to prefer the square-hose model.

V. STATE OF THE ART ABOUT 1730

It may be easier to appraise the progress of the art if the working of a printing-office at the beginning of the eighteenth century is briefly described. For this purpose we must suppose ourselves to be looking at an office large enough to produce its own type on a substantial scale: an establishment such as that of

[1] The presses preserved in the Plantin–Moretus museum at Antwerp are early versions of the Blaeuw press.

Plantin and Moretus at Antwerp, or of P. and J. Blaeuw in Amsterdam; or one
of the great institutional offices—the *Imprimerie Royale*, the *Stamperia Vaticana*,
or the Clarendon Press at Oxford, which, under Dr Fell, had recently begun to
provide its own type.

In such places the process started with the letter-cutters. They drew the
letters on the end of steel blanks, punching down, graving or filing away unwanted metal; then hardened the punches and struck them into brass or copper
matrix blanks about $1\frac{1}{2}$ in long, $\frac{1}{4}$-in thick, and varying in width to suit the size
of the letter. They then filed away any metal bunched at the side of the impres-
sion, and adjusted the dimensions of the matrix so that the letter would fall in
exactly the right position at the bottom of the mould, after which the matrix
was proved and handed to the caster.

Each caster sat beside a small furnace containing molten type-metal. In his
left hand he held the mould: it was a complex unit, made of steel or brass and
cased in wood, its two main members held together with a spring clip and
positioned together by male and female gauges. Cut in one member and closed
by the other was the adjustable cavity in which the type was cast, with a marked
throat between the orifice and the foot of the type to allow a clean breaking
away of the tang; with one or two wires let in at the side of the body to form
the nicks; and with a hook at each side of the orifice to help to dislodge any type
that stuck to the matrix. Into this mould the caster poured metal from a ladle
picked up in his right hand, giving the mould a sharp twist and shake at the
moment of pouring so as to drive the molten metal into every corner of the face:
this dexterous motion, which varied according to the letter cast, comprised his
main skill. After leaving it a second or two to cool, he opened the mould and
threw the type, tang and all, on to a sheet of paper beside him. His output of
cast types was between 2500 and 4000 a day, according to size and the difficulty
of casting.

The next process was traditionally done by boys, who broke off the tangs,
rubbed down the sides of the shank on a flat stone, and passed the type to the
letter-dresser. He set up a line of types, examined it for defective castings,
wedged it firmly in a 'dressing-stick', scraped with a knife first down one side
of the line and then down the other, and finally, holding the line with the feet
upwards, cut a groove along the centre of the feet with a plough, thus removing
all trace of the broken-off tang. The finished types were then counted into the
quantities of the 'founders' bill', a carefully calculated table giving the numbers
of each letter required for a fount of a given size to print a particular language;
and stored or passed to the composing-room.

The compositors at this period normally worked under a piecework system of elaborate but well understood conventions, and for this purpose were organized in 'companionships', each appointing its own 'clicker', whose main duties were to record the division and performance of the work and share out the earnings. To each companionship the master printer or his overseer gave out the copy to be set, the instructions, and the type—occasionally new type from the foundry, more commonly pages which had been printed and had to be distributed to the cases before re-use. Enough lines having been set for a sheet (two to sixteen pages, according to the size of book), they were made up in pages, laid out on the stone imposing-surface in the order required to bring the pages in sequence when 'backed-up' (that is, printed on the reverse side), and imposed into formes by dressing with wooden furniture to give the correct margins and by locking up with head-sticks, side-sticks, and quoins.

The formes were next proofed, and the proof-sheets sent with the copy to the reader's closet, where they were checked, marked with corrections, and returned to the composing-room. The formes were then unlocked and minor alterations made by changing letters or spaces in the imposed forme, while pages needing major alterations were tied up, lifted out, and reset line by line in the composing-stick. After a further proof—the 'revise'—and final correction, the forme went to the press-room for printing. About the same time, the paper was damped by dipping a number of sheets in water—every fourth, sixth, or eighth according to the thickness and hardness—and stacked under heavy boards until the moisture was fairly even throughout the pile.

The pressmen worked in teams of two, taking it in turn to do the heavy work of running the bed in and out and pulling the press, and the skilled work of dabbing the ink evenly over the pages. One man, having spread ink on the ink-block with the slice and rubbed it out well with the brayer, took his ink-balls from the rack, dabbed them on the ink, and rubbed them together with a circular movement so as to distribute the ink evenly over the surfaces. He then inked the pages of the forme in turn, occasionally rubbing his ink-balls together to redistribute the ink. The other man, who had meanwhile placed a sheet of paper on the press-points fixed to the tympan, and closed the frisket over it, then brought down the tympan, paper, and frisket on to the surface of the inked type with his right hand; gripped the rounce with his left and turned it to bring the first half of the bed under the platen, pulled over the press-handle with his right hand, moved the second half of the bed under the platen, pulled again, and, releasing the press-handle so that it sprang back and lifted the platen, moved the bed out and lifted off the tympan assembly. This cycle of operations continued until all the paper issued had been printed on one side, after which the sheets were printed on the reverse, hung up to dry, and finally collated by the warehousemen and sent to the bookseller or the bookbinder. Meanwhile, the worked-off forme had been washed with lye and sent back to the composing-room for the type to be distributed.

Notwithstanding the laborious double-printing of each sheet, and the difficulty of inking a large forme evenly, two good pressmen would print up to 250 sheets an hour on one side of the paper; say 3000 sheets a day in an office which —like Plantin's—worked from 6 a.m. to 8 p.m. in summer and from 7 a.m. to 9 p.m. in winter. These maximum outputs, however, are not to be compared with the 300 sheets a day which the earliest printers were proud to have achieved, for the average printing in 1700 was greatly debased in quality from that of the astonishing folios turned out at Mainz, on crude appliances but with devoted craftsmanship, two and a half centuries earlier. It is noted that, for large works of the highest quality, production might well fall below 1000 sheets a day even at the end of the sixteenth century. We may conclude that, for a given standard of work, all the improvements tending towards quicker press-work—more even type more rigidly held, improved operating technique, and a much more powerful and accurate press—had raised the productivity of the press by a factor of three, or at the most four, since the days when the first Mainz printers, their plant established and its processes well tested on a smaller book, felt able to embark on so great a work as a printed Bible.

VI. ILLUSTRATION, DECORATION, MAP AND MUSIC PRINTING

Turning from typographical printing to illustration and decoration, we are in a field where technique may vary markedly with the individual artist or with local tradition. It is therefore difficult to generalize, and impossible to trace a consistently developing technology; the metal-engraving processes particularly are capable of numerous minor variations few of which are ever superseded, in that the particular artistic effects they achieve may at any time commend them for re-use. The history of art being well documented, it is necessary here only to outline the main techniques used up to 1730.

Illustration printed in relief. The early woodcuts have already been mentioned. They were used for textile-printing early in the Middle Ages and perhaps in the later Roman Empire. In the medieval guilds, wood-cutters were grouped with carpenters; and their products were simple carvings with knife, gouge, and chisel on the plank—that is, on pieces sawn in the direction of the grain—of fine-grained woods. At first it was necessary to use resinous wood which would not swell or crack through absorbing moisture from aqueous inks, and cherry was considered the most suitable. Later, with the oil-varnish inks of the fifteenth century, apple, beech, pear, and sycamore were also used. Box, a harder and finer-grained wood, later to become the standard material, was widely used well before 1550, and the delicacy of some late fifteenth-century Venetian woodcuts suggests that it may have reached Italy earlier, from Turkey, its principal source.

Long after box came into use as a plank wood, the practice of cutting and planing it across the grain was developed, thus facilitating the use of white engraved lines on a black background. On the end grain very fine lines could be engraved with equal ease in any direction, and the metal-engraver's tools, particularly the graver or burin, could be employed. When this technique of wood-engraving was developed is uncertain, but it probably originated in eastern Europe at the end of the seventeenth century, and is certainly found in some Armenian books printed in Constantinople early in the eighteenth.

Relief blocks were also cut in metal, perhaps as early as the first European woodcuts. Lead, brass, and iron are all mentioned in the fourteenth and fifteenth centuries, but copper was probably the commonest medium. Since the cutting away of large areas of metal was laborious, the early metal relief blocks tend to be of the engraved style, with white lines on a black background, rather than the woodcut style of black lines on white; and to relieve the solid black they were often stippled with punches bearing various dots and ornaments, thus yielding the prints in the *manière criblée* which are characteristic of later fifteenth-century engraving.

Relief-printed blocks were combined with type early in the history of book-printing. The Fust–Schoeffer psalter of 1457, the first book dated by its printers, had ornate initial letters printed in two colours, and wooden or metal blocks were often subsequently used for initials, ornamental borders, head- and tail-pieces, and other large-scale decoration, while for smaller repetitive ornaments the type-casting process was employed. Wood- or metal-cut illustrations in mainly typographical books became common in the 1460s, following the lead of Albrecht Pfister of Bamberg, and soon assumed a special importance in technological history by enabling diagrams, plans, and maps to be incorporated in the text. Early examples of these are the astronomical and mathematical diagrams used by Ratdolt at Venice in the 1480s, and the woodcut maps which, after a first appearance in 1472, illustrated numerous early editions of the ancient geographers.

Woodcut blocks were also used in the fifteenth century to print music, though the earliest example, printed in 1487, is antedated by books containing crude attempts at music type. The design, casting, and composition of movable types to print simultaneously the staves and the notes are, however, exceedingly difficult: the problem was first mastered by Oeglin, of Augsburg, in 1508, though Petrucci of Venice had produced in 1501 an effective system of types requiring two impressions. Meanwhile woodcut music was used for odd phrases in typographical works until much later.

Intaglio printing. The arts of engraving and etching were developed for ornamenting metal surfaces centuries before the availability of paper engendered the idea of printing from them. That this idea coincided in time with the widespread circulation of woodcut prints and with the inception of typography demonstrates the tendencies leading to the rapid development of printing.

Engraving on precious and semi-precious metals has been practised since antiquity by goldsmiths, using a burin to engrave the line and a scraper to remove the burr which curls out on each side of the furrow as the burin is pushed forwards. The simplest form of intaglio print is made by taking such an engraved plate, dabbing ink all over it until every furrow is filled, wiping the ink from the surface, and then rubbing down a sheet of damped paper which sinks into the furrows and picks up the ink remaining there. A line-engraving of this sort in 1446 is the earliest dated one, but its engraver was one of a group working in Germany and the Netherlands about this time, and the earliest engravings of another, the 'Master of the Playing Cards', are probably a decade earlier.

The technique appears to have developed independently soon afterwards in northern Italy, where its first known exponent, Maso Finiguerra of Florence, was working about 1450. It was closely linked with *niello* work, a goldsmith's technique in which lines are engraved on a metal plate and filled with a preparation of metallic sulphides (vol II, p 480). Its original object was to produce a burnished plate bearing an inlaid design in black; but the practice arose of taking a sulphur cast of the engraved plate which, if blackened and rubbed to expose the ridges corresponding to the engraved lines, formed an equally effective plaque. We do not know whether paper was first used to take a proof of the plate by intaglio, or of the cast by intaglio, or of the cast by letterpress: a particular *niello* may be found as plate, or as cast, and in all three sorts of proof. Nor is it known when engraved plates were first made in Italy solely for the taking of prints. The earliest Italian engravers were, at all events, primarily goldsmiths, and their German predecessors may have discovered intaglio printing by the same route.

Three other main forms of engraved plates for printing were used before 1730; dry-points, etchings, and mezzotints. In dry-point work, instead of a burin being pushed forwards to incise the line, a pencil-like steel point is drawn across the plate, leaving the burr all to one side of the furrow, where it is usually left to retain a greater volume of ink and to soften the line. Only a small number of perfect prints can be achieved before the fragile sliver of metal is flattened, so that the technique was not used extensively for book-illustration, maps, or music; and in our period its use was limited to a handful of artists, including, however, two of the greatest. After some early prints by an anonymous German master about 1480, Dürer (1490–1538) used dry-point for three prints early in the sixteenth century. The process was combined with etching by Andrea Meldolla (1522–82), about fifty years later, and more notably in the mid-seventeenth century by Rembrandt (1607–69).

Etching, too, was originally used to ornament metal, and was practised by armourers in the fifteenth century. They reduced the labour of engraving by dabbing a coating of gum, resin, and wax on the lightly engraved metal, and etching the engraved lines not protected by this resist. The idea of making a plate solely by etching may be as late as 1600. The process as eventually established used a relatively soft compound, the etching-ground, which was dabbed out thinly on the heated plate. This surface was then blackened, and the etcher drew on it lightly with a steel point, the etching-needle, to expose the metal below. Etching with acid, generally dilute nitric, removed metal from the exposed lines, and when the required depth had been obtained anywhere it was protected by varnishing. After the first etching the ground could be relaid to add further work; or additions could be made with dry-point or burin. There were no important developments in the process, apart from the transition from etching after engraving to pure etching. The former was practised from about 1500 onwards by German etchers, including Dürer, and their successors in Austria, Italy, and the Netherlands, while between 1600 and 1730 the great development of pure etching is associated particularly with the Netherlands and above all with Rembrandt.

Finally, in the mezzotint process we have an identifiable invention. Ludwig von Siegen, born in 1609, devised an intaglio plate covered with a fine pattern of indentations, which would pick up enough ink to print almost black, except where scraped or burnished away to give lighter tones or white. How he prepared his indented background is unknown: other early mezzotinters—including a notable amateur, Prince Rupert—used a knurled wheel, the 'engine' or 'roulette', but the tool eventually standardized, the 'rocker', was developed well before the end of the seventeenth century. It was a hardened-steel curved head, bearing parallel serrated ridges, mounted on a short handle. Pressed down on a copper plate and rocked, it left a small area patterned with shallow furrows, each with a burr at either side. By repeating this pattern at angles of 90° and 45° to the first one, the engraver broke up the ground into a grained texture, which could be varied in quality by having rockers of different fineness and by altering the angles of rocking. Only two other tools were needed: the scraper, used to remove the burrs where a slightly lighter tone was needed, and the burnisher, with which the indentations could be polished away to give light tones and white.

There were no significant developments of the mezzotint process itself before 1730; but at that date J. C. Le Blon was experimenting in the three-colour process using mezzotint plates, an idea whose later developments were to be extensive.

All four processes of intaglio printing had certain common features: the metal used for plates, the ink, and the method of impression. The metal was commonly copper, which was soft enough to engrave and hammer up for correction easily and could be etched readily, but iron, pewter, silver, and zinc were all sometimes used. The ink was an oil-based one similar to letterpress printing-ink, but rather thinner to ensure that it ran into the finest grooves. The method of printing at first was to ink the plate, wipe the surface, place a double thickness of damped paper on it, and rub down with a rounded tool. Later—probably about 1500— the double-roller press came into use. This simple device is in principle a mangle (figure 253). The early wooden ones had two rollers mounted about $1\frac{1}{2}$ in apart between strong wooden cheeks, on either side of which was a table level with the top of the lower roller. The neck of the upper roller projected beyond the cheek, and had spokes inserted into it. In use, a large wooden board was placed on one side table; the engraved plate was placed to a previously marked position on it, after being inked and wiped; the damped paper, backing sheet, and some soft packing were put on top; and the whole board was slid between the rollers and driven through by the powerful leverage exercised on the spokes of the top roller. Neither the rolling-press nor the printing method altered significantly during our period; iron gradually replaced wood for the spokes, necks, and bearings of the rollers, but the all-metal press is a later development.

Special uses of intaglio techniques. Of the four techniques described, dry-point and mezzotint, because of the short life of the plates, were used mainly by artists for limited reproduction of their works, though the special usefulness of mezzotint for reproducing paintings led it to be used occasionally for illustrating small editions. Both etching and engraving, however, could be used for comparatively large numbers of prints, particularly of simple line subjects. It was not long, therefore, before intaglio plates were used to illustrate books printed from type, particularly where fine lines were needed, as in maps, geometrical diagrams, and mechanical or architectural drawings. Normally they were printed on separate leaves—hence the term 'plates' for illustrations not incorporated in the text—and sometimes by a different establishment; but during the sixteenth century it became common for large printing-offices to have their own rolling-presses and to print intaglio work registered with the text. In the seventeenth century the engraved title-page became fashionable, and in expensive works engraved diagrams, chapter-heads, and tail pieces might be used throughout. Above all, engraved plates lent themselves well to the reproduction of maps. The first two engraved maps are in two editions of Ptolemy (Bologna, 1477, and Rome, 1478).

FIGURE 253—*A primitive rolling-press.*

One other important use for engraving was found, in the reproduction of music. The use of wooden blocks and music type has already been noted: the former were slow to produce, easily damaged, and difficult to repair, while music type is so complex that its use requires specially skilled compositors. Both type and wooden blocks remained in use throughout our period when it was required to combine music and text in one printing, but, once the technique of music engraving was established, its superior appearance and economy soon made it the standard method.

It is curious that the first engraved music-printing to survive is a book published in 1586 by Simone Verovio of Rome and engraved by Martin van Buyten, a Dutchman. It was probably not their first production; and though there are earlier claimants, Verovio almost certainly first developed a commercial process. Others adopted it at once; the Dutch at this time had a lead in the intaglio techniques, and travelling engravers helped to spread this new application of their art. It had reached England by 1598, when Thomas Morley secured a patent, and during the seventeenth century its use extended throughout Europe until by 1730 music printed from type had become unusual.

The process at first was to engrave notes, tails, lines, and all markings on a plate of copper, though pewter may have been used in the seventeenth century for some ephemeral work. Soon after 1700 the Dutch had apparently mastered the annealing of large copper plates well enough to allow the notes to be punched in, and about 1720 this method reached England, where it was found equally satisfactory using pewter, the metal eventually standardized for music plates. With a scoring-tool to rule the staves, and a set of 50 or 60 punches to produce the main notes, tails, and other markings, the music printer had, by 1730, a process which was not to be improved in speed for nearly a century and has not yet been equalled in elegance.

BIBLIOGRAPHY

The literature on the history of printing is extensive, but the historical value of much of it is negligible. Even in the last ten years books have been published reasserting legends that have long since been disproved, and repeating from previous authors information that is demonstrably untrue.

The following list includes only a few of the books which have been of direct value in preparing this article, selected as giving a reliable general review of the subject or as including useful bibliographies, references to documentary sources, or accounts of original research. I am particularly grateful to the Librarian of the St Bride Technical Library, London, for directing me to some of the sources used.

Printing—general works of reference for early printing and its development:

ALDIS, H. G. 'The Printed Book' (2nd ed., rev. and brought up to date by J. CARTER and E. A. CRUTCHLEY). University Press, Cambridge. 1941.

DIETERICHS, K. 'Die Buchdruckpresse von Johannes Gutenberg bis Frederick Koenig.' Gutenberg-Gesellschaft, Mainz. 1930.

HESSELS, J. H. 'Encyclopaedia Britannica' (11th ed.), Vol. 27, pp. 509–41. University Press, Cambridge. 1911.

Illustration and decoration (including map- and music-printing):

BLISS, D. P. 'A History of Wood Engraving.' Dent, London. 1928.

BROWN, L. A. 'The Story of Maps.' Cresset Press, London. 1956.

FLOWER, D. "On Music Printing, 1473–1701." *The Book Collector's Quarterly*, **I**, iv, 76–92, 1931.

GAMBLE, W. 'Music Engraving and Printing.' Pitman, London. 1923.

HIND, A. M. 'A History of Engraving and Etching.' Constable, London. 1923.

Idem. 'An Introduction to a History of Woodcut' (2 vols). Constable, London. 1935.

LIPPMAN, F. 'Der Kupferstich.' Reimer, Berlin. 1905.

Printing—origin and background:

BUTLER, P. 'The Origin of Printing in Europe.' University Press, Chicago. 1940.

CARTER, T. F. 'The Invention of Printing in China and its Spread Westwards.' Columbia University Press, New York. 1925. See also rev. ed. by L. CARRINGTON GOODRICH. Ronald Press, New York. 1955.

McKERROW, R. B. 'An Introduction to Bibliography for Literary Students.' Clarendon Press, Oxford. 1927.

SCHREIBER, W. L. 'Manuel de l'amateur de la gravure sur bois et sur métal au quinzième siècle' (8 vols). Harrassowitz, Leipzig. 1891–1911.

Type, typefounding, and compositors' work:

BERRY, W. T. "Books on Type and Typefounding." *The Book Collector's Quarterly*, **1**, iv, 66–85, 1931.
BIRINGUCCIO, VANOCCIO. 'De la Pirotechnia libri X.' Roffinello, Venice. 1540. Eng. trans. by C. S. SMITH and MARTHA T. GNUDI. American Institute of Mining and Metallurgy, New York. 1943.
REED, T. B. 'A History of the Old English Letter Foundries' (new ed., rev. and enl. by A. F. JOHNSON). Faber and Faber, London. 1952.
UPDIKE, D. B. 'Printing Types: Their History, Forms and Use' (2nd ed.). Harvard University Press, Cambridge, Mass. 1937.

The press and its equipment:

POTTINGER, D. T. "History of the Printing Press." *The Dolphin*, **3**, 323–44, 1938.
WIBORG, F. B. 'Printing Inks: a History.' Harper, New York. 1926.

A NOTE ON TECHNICAL ADVANCES IN THE MANUFACTURE OF PAPER

BEFORE THE NINETEENTH CENTURY

JOHN OVERTON

THE development of the Fourdrinier machine at the beginning of the nineteenth century made it possible for paper to be manufactured on continuous reels. Until then paper was made by hand, sheet by sheet, but the processes involved did undergo some rationalization and changes in technique, all of which anticipated and contributed to the great technical advances that took place subsequently. These advances enabled paper to be manufactured at a greater speed and with greater consistency, and the use of various chemicals made it possible to produce special papers for particular purposes. By these innovations, however, the character of the resulting sheet was considerably altered.

Basically, the paper-making process remains unchanged whether the paper is made by hand or by machine. Raw material consisting of linen, cotton, straw, wood, or other material is reduced to a pulp by a beating process and mixed with water which serves as the carrier of the fibres. When the pulp is spread out over a wire mesh the water drains off leaving the fibres to form the paper. The mesh is given a shake to felt the fibres together. The paper is then dried, and possibly smoothed to give a satisfactory sheet (figure 254).

One of the earliest major technical advances occurred in the beating process. This was the introduction of the stamping-mill, very soon after paper-making was first introduced into Europe; it is thought to have originated at Xativa in Spain about A.D. 1150, and consisted essentially of an elaborate wooden mortar and pestle. Usually the mills were arranged in batches of three or four, although larger assemblies are known to have existed. The pestle was operated by one extremity of a wooden arm, pivoted at the middle (figure 255) rather like a see-saw, whose other extremity was depressed by tappets on a shaft rotated by hand, or later by water- or wind-power. To make the process more effective spiked stampers were made which cut the rags into smaller pieces. The rags were then subjected to a beating by stampers without spikes, which frayed them, as before, the object always being to separate the material into the fibres of which it was composed. During the first stages of the stamping, water was pumped into the stamping-troughs and drained off again, to wash the material being beaten; but the flow of water was usually discontinued during the later stages of the operation.

FIGURE 254—*The first illustration of a paper-maker at work.* (At rear) *Water-driven stamp-mill;* (centre) *press for squeezing sheets;* (foreground) *vat-man using the mould, while his boy carries away finished sheets. 1568.*

This process underwent a further change with the invention of the 'Hollander' by the Dutch in the late seventeenth century (figure 256). This machine stamped or, as it was now termed, 'beat' the rags in an oval-shaped vessel, containing a cylinder on which knives were mounted. This machine was constructed in such a way that the mixture it contained was circulated by the rotating cylinder, so that all parts of the mixture passed underneath the knives. The Hollander itself was subjected to many refinements. One of these machines produced more pulp in one day than did eight stampers in a week.

The linen and cotton rags used to make the pulp were usually thrown into a heap and allowed to disintegrate by fermentation, sometimes after the materials in the bundles had been sorted, in which case the different types were beaten separately and mixed as required. This process was occasionally helped by the addition of lime. Later, the lengthy and wasteful fermentation of the rags was given up, chiefly because it was rendered superfluous by improved beating methods and by the practice of boiling the materials. The yellowish tint of early papers can often be ascribed to it.

When the pulp was ready for the paper-maker it had to be transported to the vat. At first the pulp was carried in buckets, but, by simply rearranging the apparatus, the vat became gravity-fed. Eventually, when the time factor became of importance and the paper had to be made more quickly, the vat had a heater placed against it. This warmed the pulp and increased the rate of evaporation. It could not, however, be made too hot, otherwise the evaporation became too fast and the resulting stresses in the paper-pulp produced a bad sheet, usually one that would not lie flat and on which it was therefore difficult to print. The vat was further improved by the addition of a rest for the mould, so that surplus water could drain off before the sheet was removed by the coucher. The shape of the pole ('hog') used for stirring the pulp in the vat gradually developed to make the stirring more complete, while later still (c 1800) an agitator was incorporated in the vat.

The paper-maker or vat-man dipped a mould into the vat. This mould consisted of a wooden frame to which were fastened a number of tightly strained parallel wires (laid-wires) running the length of the frame. On top of this arrangement was a separate frame,

FIGURE 255—*Manually worked stamp-mill of a simple kind which could be used for beating rags to make paper. 1579.*

the 'deckle', which formed the boundary of the sheet (figure 257). This boundary was not as a rule clean-cut, for the pulp tended to penetrate between the deckle and the wire frame. The frame was traversed from side to side by a number of ribs, and it was to these and to the ends that the wires were fastened. The wires used for fastening the laid-wires to the ribs were called chain-wires and produced the chain-lines in the sheet. This type of mould was improved by the substitution of wire supports for the ribs to which the laid-wires were fastened. This gave a more even sheet of paper. The difference can be detected by the heaviness of the shadow on either side of the chain-line marks on the paper. The heavier shadow denotes a mould of the early type, for the extra width of the wooden ribs tended to retard the heavy drainage of water on either side of the chain-wires, so that more pulp collected there. The number of laid-wires to the inch was gradually increased. Some of the early moulds, particularly the oriental moulds made of bamboo, were very coarse. The paper on which the Gutenberg Bible (p 386) was printed had 28 laid-lines to the inch.

The most easily recognizable distinguishing mark on paper, the watermark, first appeared in paper made in Italy about 1285, in the shape of a cross. The earliest marks were usually very simple in design, but during the fifteenth century they became more and more complicated. They were all made by means of wire bent into the required shapes and then sewn to the mould with finer wire. This practice, and the whole construction of the mould, depended on the development of wire-drawing techniques. Watermarks served to identify the products of individual mills, and often had esoteric significance as well. Some of them, such as the cap and bells of a jester, were the origin of terms now used to describe various sizes of paper.

The coucher, having deposited the sheet of paper from the mould on a felt cloth,

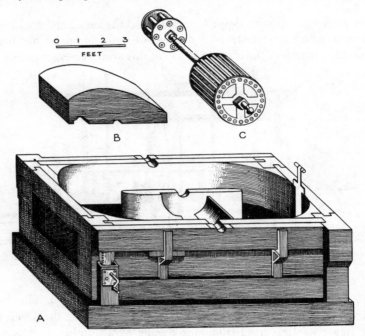

FIGURE 256—*The Hollander.* A, *wooden tub containing water and material to be disintegrated, which flows round the central partition.* B, *cover over cylinder.* C, *cylinder of knives, rotated by a water-wheel so that the blades sweep close to the curved flange in the tub. The clearance is adjusted by the rack which raises and lowers the near bearing for the cylinder. On right of the tub, paddle for running off the contents. The whole device is somewhat like a modern lawn-mower in operation.*

placed another felt over it and upon this another sheet of paper and so on until he had an interleaved pile containing 144 sheets of paper, called a post. This was squeezed in a wooden screw-press to remove surplus water. At first the sheets of paper were hung for drying immediately after pressing; during the sixteenth century, however, the felts, after pressing, were removed from between the sheets and the latter were pressed again, and then again, until the surface of the sheet was of the required finish. This process was called 'sweating'. Another way of giving a higher finish to the paper was to use a smooth stone which was rubbed over the completed sheet. The stone was superseded at the beginning of the seventeenth century by the glazing-hammer; the sheet was moved about under the hammer until its entire surface had been beaten. Wooden glazing-cylinders came into existence in the early eighteenth century, the sheet being passed between a pair of them under pressure.

The paper was then hung in lofts to dry. It was hung in batches ('spurs') of four or five sheets together, because this was found to preserve their smoothness. The sheets were lifted by means of a T-shaped wooden implement and hung on ropes made of horse-hair or cow-hair, usually coated with beeswax. The ends of the ropes were fixed into spars of wood made to slide up and down vertical posts called tribbles, eight or nine of which filled a room. A wheeled table was used after a time to convey the sheets of paper. When the tribble-lines were full the spars were pushed up and retained by wooden pegs.

After the fifteenth century paper was often sized, particularly if it was to be used for writing. This was done by suspending the sheets from a piece of wood and lowering them into a container full of the sizing-material. After squeezing the surplus size out, the sheets were separated and allowed to dry. The material used for the sizing was usually the refuse from tan-yards called 'scrolls'.

The high-lights of the technical advances made in the early European manufacture of paper were: the use of the stamping-mill (1150); the invention of the watermark at Fabriano (near Ancona) about 1285; the use of wind or water as a source of power to

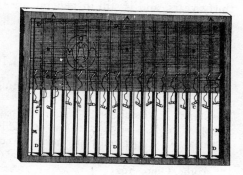

FIGURE 257—*Mould and deckle. The wires of the mould (above) are held down to the wooden ribs by wire passing round them and round nails driven into the sides of the ribs. Note the water-mark symbol wired in position. 1698.*

drive various machines; the invention of the Hollander (1670); and the invention of the wove mould (1750).

Much inquiry was, however, directed to the use of materials other than rags for the making of paper. The search was intensified when the practice of papering walls for decoration was introduced about the middle of the seventeenth century. The patents registered to the end of that century dealing with various aspects of the paper industry do not appear to have passed beyond the beating stage. It is not until 1800 that the name of Matthias Koops appears, with a method of using straw for the making of paper and another of extracting the ink from printed paper, re-pulping it, and using it again. Koops's enterprise failed, but it anticipated the later transition to esparto and wood-pulp fibres. Two years before (1798) Nicolas-Louis Robert (1761–1828) obtained the first patent for a paper-making machine. His ideas, meeting with little encouragement in

France, were developed in England by Bryan Donkin (1768–1855) with the aid of capital provided by John Gamble and the Fourdrinier brothers, stationers in London. The 'Fourdrinier' machine thus evolved was rapidly improved upon during the succeeding thirty years, and is still in general use in the paper-making industry. Variations of it are employed for special purposes, such as making glazed paper.

BIBLIOGRAPHY

'Abridgements of the Specifications relating to the Manufacture of Paper . . . 1665–1857.' London. 1858.

BLANCHET, A. 'Essaies sur l'histoire du papier et de sa fabrication.' Leroux, Paris. 1900.

BLUM, A. S. 'Les origines du papier.' Éditions de la Tournelle, Paris. 1935.

HERRING, R. 'Paper and Papermaking, Ancient and Modern.' London. 1855.

HUNTER, D. 'The Literature of Papermaking, 1390–1800.' Published by the author, Chillicothe, Ohio. 1925.

Idem. 'Papermaking. The History and Technique of an Ancient Craft.' Pleiades Books, London. 1947.

JENKINS, R. "Early Papermaking in England." *Library Association Record*, Vols **2, 3, 4**, 1900–2.

LABARRE, E. J. 'A Dictionary and Encyclopaedia of Paper and Papermaking' (2nd ed., rev. and enl.). Swets and Zeitlinger, Amsterdam. 1952.

LALANDE, J. J. LE F. DE. "Art de faire le papier" in 'Descripiton des Arts et Métiers', Vol. 1. Paris. 1761.

STOPPELAAR, J. H. DE. 'Het Papier in de Nederlanden gedurende de Middeleeuwen, inzonderheid in Zeeland.' Middelburg. 1869.

ZONGHI, AURELIO and ZONGHI, ANGUSTO. 'Zonghi's Watermarks.' *Monumenta chartae papyraceae historiam illustrantia*, Vol. 3. The Paper Publications Society, Hilversum. 1953.

French papermakers of the eighteenth century at work in a factory.

16

BRIDGES

S. B. HAMILTON

I. EARLY BRIDGES

THERE are three main types of bridge. From ancient times trackways have been carried across deep gorges on the China–Burma border and similar places by ropes slung between opposite cliffs. The same device was used early in the thirteenth century, but with chains instead of ropes, when the St Gotthard route was made for pack-horse traffic across the Alps. The suspension bridge was, however, little used in western Europe until in the early nineteenth century it became technically and commercially practicable to forge strong links of wrought iron bars.

In the second type of bridge the arch is in principle an inverted chain (figure 274) with all its links compressed. This has been by far the commonest form of bridge-structure, the links being either wedge-shaped blocks of stone, or balks of timber strutting up a deck from a trestle (figures 266, 268).

The third type of bridge-structure is the beam, in which the top fibres are in compression and the bottom fibres in tension. The beam, however, can be made suitable for long spans only when it takes the form of an open-framed girder. Such girders were actually illustrated in the sixteenth century; Andrea Palladio in designing a truss (figure 265) clearly understood which members were in compression and which in tension, but he had no idea of the magnitude of the forces [1].

The arch was used in ancient Sumeria and Egypt, but for little except work underground (vol I, figures 295, 304). Its use as the main structural feature of monumental buildings and important bridges was first practised by the Romans. The army built wooden bridges on trestles (vol II, figure 467), but if the route remained as an important highway the trestles were in time replaced by great piers of masonry capable of withstanding flood and ice; later a series of masonry arches replaced the wooden decks. The piers were often built half as wide as the spaces left between them. The arch-rings were nearly always semicylinders of large stones so carefully dressed at their radial meeting-faces that little or no bedding mortar was needed. The whole width of an arch might not be completed in one operation; several rings were built successively side-by-side using the same centring.[1] The adjacent rings were commonly fastened together by iron cramps run in with lead. Some Roman bridges have lasted over 2000 years and still stand (vol II, figure 465); but many have fallen, or have been destroyed in the course of military operations.

The maintenance of roads and bridges was sadly neglected after the fall of the Roman Empire. Only strategic routes received the attention of the great rulers. In a few places civic pride or piety led to the building of a fine bridge at a dangerous and busy ford. According to one legend, medieval bridges were the special care of an order of Brothers of the Bridge (vol II, p 525), dedicated to the erection and maintenance of bridges; but this pleasing story finds little confirmation in contemporary sources [2]. The Pont d'Avignon (1177–85) (figure 258) had twenty-one elliptical arches, with a span of about a hundred feet and with the major axis vertical. The arches still standing may, however, date from a fourteenth-century reconstruction.

FIGURE 258—*The Pont d'Avignon. At the foot of one pier can be seen what may have been the springing of one of the original arches (1177–85).*

The Ponte Vecchio at Florence (1335–45) had three segmental arches, one of 95 ft in span and two of 85 ft, with a rise of rather less than one-sixth of the span; but most medieval bridges in Europe were built on the Roman model with semicircular arches. Occasionally in hilly country, where piers in a fast-running stream would have been difficult to construct and perhaps impossible to maintain, bridge-builders of the late Middle Ages and Renaissance constructed single segmental arches of span greater than any built by the Romans. Deep arches were sometimes built in several concentric rings, so that the first ring completed could relieve the centring of part at least of the weight of the next ring.

England, for a good reason, is peculiarly rich in medieval bridges. William the Conqueror, in rewarding his followers with grants of land, gave to each a number of small, scattered estates individually incapable of serving as a solid centre of resistance. To supervise his bailiffs every considerable landlord had to travel; bridges were built by local landowners, lay and ecclesiastical, by corporate boroughs, and by *ad hoc* trusts, the owners looking to tolls to repay the cost. In some places such as London and Bideford the bridge proved a lucrative investment. Most English bridges, being intended only for horse-traffic and pedestrians, were narrow, and many were steep. The individual arches were of

[1] Temporary wooden arch used to support the incomplete masonry arch.

no great span and, particularly if pointed at the crown, exerted but moderate thrust on their wide and massive piers. Usually only the facing-stones of the

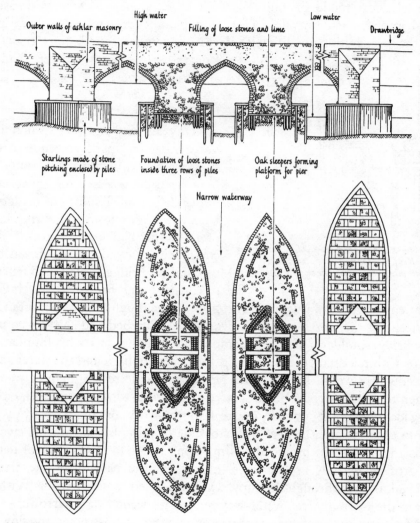

FIGURE 259—*Old London Bridge, after drawings made during its demolition, 1826–31.* (Above) *Elevation;* (below) *plan of the starlings.*

piers (and not always these) were of dressed masonry; the infilling was of rubble and lime mortar (figure 259).

During the sixteenth and seventeenth centuries there were no drastic or fundamental changes either in the materials or in the form of bridge construction. The technique of bridge-building was still largely medieval, though improved tools and mechanical devices such as the crane allowed a reversion to the classical mode of building with large stones accurately dressed. A marked improvement in pile-drivers, pumps, and dredgers also made practicable the preparation in difficult places of sounder foundations than either Roman or medieval builders had been able to construct.

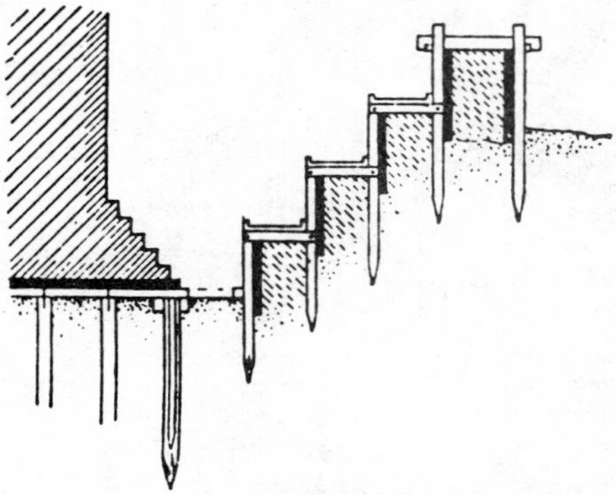

FIGURE 260—*Stepped coffer-dam used in constructing the Pont Neuf, Toulouse. The masonry of the pier, with piles beneath, is shown on the left.*

II. FOUNDATIONS

Many ancient and medieval buildings have either collapsed or required extensive restoration because their foundations have been compressed, or squeezed out, under their load. Failures of bridges have been even more numerous: the designer of a building had some choice of site and could usually avoid one which was always wet, but the bridge-builder had most often to construct his bridge where traffic had already converged towards an existing ford. He might have to contend with flood, ice, and the tendency of the river to scour its bed and shift its course.

The bridge-builder's first consideration was whether to lay his foundations in water or within a drained enclosure. If the bed were hard and the water shallow, as it frequently would be at a ford, he might decide to lay them in water. He had then to raise the river-bed in places up to at least low-water level, either by sinking loads of rubble or quarry-waste in wicker-work containers, or by disposing it within an enclosure, formed by a stockade of piles driven into the river-bed. Each island so formed provided a plinth upon which to raise a pier of masonry. Such artificial islands or 'starlings' obstructed the passage of the river and quickened its pace through the gaps, which often led to heavy scour. With every repair to the piers the free water-way tended to become still narrower.

Old London Bridge (figure 259), begun in 1176, so obstructed the flow of the Thames at a point where the spring tide rose and fell about 16 ft that at half-tide the water-levels above and below the bridge sometimes differed by several feet, making passage by river-traffic impossible. In the sixteenth century matters were made worse by the installation of water-wheels and pumps under some of the arches. When one pier was demolished in the eighteenth century to make a double-width channel for shipping, the race through the widened gap became

FIGURE 261—*A coffer-dam made of interlocking piles. From Ramelli, 1588.*

so fierce that a deep groove was cut in the river-bed, threatening to undermine the two nearest piers. Disaster was averted only by tipping in large quantities of stone with all haste, so forming a submerged weir across the gap.

The alternative to building on artificial islands was to sink the pier-foundations into the ground below the river-bed. To do this the river had to be diverted or part of its bed enclosed within a water-tight coffer-dam, from which water was removed by pumping. The construction of a coffer-dam was no light task. If the water was deep the dam had to be built in steps (figure 260) [3]. The outermost two rows of posts were driven in, horizontal beams were fixed to them and strutted apart, and the space of about 3 ft between the rows was cleared of earth, mud, or gravel as far down as this could be done with a long-handled scoop. The

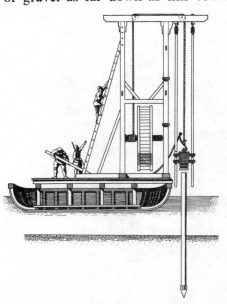

cleared space was then filled with puddled clay up to the high-water level if possible, and at least somewhat above low-water level. The material for puddling had to be most carefully chosen. A soft, sticky clay alone would work into mud; some sand or gravel had to be present or mixed with it to make a plastic mass, which could be worked like putty and well rammed in to form a water-tight barrier. When the dam was complete it was possible to pump out the water and dig down to a firm bottom for the bridge-foundation. Driving large numbers of piles was laborious and expensive; so was pumping great quantities of water. Both required gruelling, repetitive labour by relays of men over long periods. The closer the piles fitted together the better would a coffer-dam keep out water. Interlocking, or dove-tailed, piles were tried. Ramelli's illustration of 1588 (figure 261) [4] might be distrusted as a flight of

FIGURE 262—*Pile-driver mounted on a barge. The hammer is raised by the treadmill, seen end-on. When it is high enough to tighten the rope attached to the end of the shank of the hook, the hook is withdrawn from the eye in the hammer, so that it falls upon the pile.* 1750.

fancy if it were not known that Captain John Perry (1715) used an almost identical form in his work to stop the Dagenham breach in the embankment of the Thames; he had previously seen it used in the royal dockyards [5]. Interlocking piles, however, were seldom used until the twentieth century, when they were made of steel and driven by steam hammers.

B. F. de Belidor (1693–1761), in his *Architecture hydraulique* (1737), showed several ways of driving piles. In one case (figure 262) the pile-driving frame is mounted on a barge, the hammer being raised by men working a treadmill and released by an automatic trip-gear. Similar machines are shown in sixteenth-century books and manuscripts (figure 263) [6]. After the fall of the hammer the rope had to be unwound from the drum and the process repeated hour after hour, day after day. To keep the coffer-dam clear of water some kind of pumping or baling device was needed. In the eighteenth century this would usually be an endless chain, either linking plates that worked in an inclined trough, or carrying cups or balls that nearly filled the bore of a vertical pipe. Sometimes the Archimedean screw was used. Occasionally the current of the river, with half its bed obstructed by coffer-dams, was strong enough to operate a water-wheel to work the pumps.

Once the coffer-dam was made and the water pumped out, mud and loose silt could be removed until the solid bed was exposed. If this were of gravel or stiff clay it would be levelled and a deck of thick planks or balks of timber laid first one way, then across, with a third layer in the same direction as the first. Sometimes a bed of concrete was laid instead of a platform grillage of planks; on this or the grillage the masonry pier could be built direct. It might happen, however, that no firm bottom had been reached by the time the digging was as deep as the engineer cared to trust his coffer-dam. Then piles were driven in the bottom and sawn off level, to be capped with timber or concrete. The Pont Notre-Dame

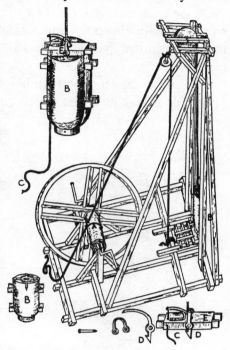

FIGURE 263—*Sixteenth-century pile-driver. The heavy weight* B, *descending in vertical guides, is wound up by the windlass* A, *turned by two cranks with the aid of a fly-wheel. When fully raised, the weight is released by pulling the cord* C. *This, acting against a spring, unlatches the catch* D *from the recess in the weight (see details) so that the latter is detached from the piece* E *and falls upon the pile.* E *is then lowered, attached once more to the weight, and the cycle repeated.*

in Paris, which was built of stone in 1507 to replace a medieval wooden bridge, was founded on concrete on piles. The superstructure was rebuilt in 1853, but the foundations were still sound enough to be embodied in the new work. In 1913–14, however, all except the two shore spans were replaced by a steel arch. The piers in mid-stream were demolished, and the two that remain were widened and strengthened.

The foundations of the celebrated Pont Neuf in Paris (1578–1607) were also dug inside a coffer-dam. They were laid 10 ft above the bed-rock, but the difficulty of sinking that extra distance would have been enormous. It proved unfortunate, however, that no bearing-piles were driven down to the rock, for besides suffering settlement two piers were partly undermined by scour before the superstructure was finished. Sheet-piles had to be driven round the up-stream toes of the piers and strapped back to the repaired masonry. Settlements continued, yet even in 1848 only the superstructure was completely replaced.

The coffer-dam for the foundations of the Santa Trinità bridge at Florence (1567), or at least its lowest stage, consisted of two walls, 7 ft thick and 90 ft apart.

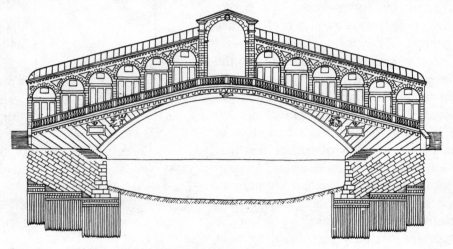

FIGURE 264—*The Rialto bridge, Venice.*

These were of concrete laid between rows of sheet-piles driven right across the river-bed, and were connected by cross-walls to form compartments for the individual piers. They were later left level with the river-bed as a protection against scour. The ground was dug out to 13 ft below the river-bed; piles were driven in the bottom, cut off level, and capped by large foundation-stones.

Somewhat unusual precautions were taken to ensure the stability of the Rialto bridge at Venice (1588–92), a single-arch span of 88 ft. The subsoil was alluvium to a considerable depth, and it was essential to safeguard the foundations of adjoining buildings. The designer, Antonio da Ponte, therefore decided to step the foundations (figure 264). Six thousand piles, each about 6 inches in diameter and 11 ft long, were driven in tight clusters beneath each abutment. This would not now be considered the best way to use piles, since the whole assembly could move as a solid block: fewer, longer piles more widely spaced would have spread the load better. Yet the foundations have not moved. On them the masonry was laid in inclined courses.

The Pont Royal in Paris (1685) was designed by J. H. Mansard (p 254), and supervised by Jacques (IV) Gabriel.[1] An elaborate specification was drawn up for the foundations. The coffer-dams were to be 9 ft thick of puddled clay between a double sheathing of timbers, and the ground was to be excavated to a depth of 15 ft below low water. Timber bearing-piles 10–12 inches in diameter were to be driven at 18-in centres each way over the whole base; the pile-heads were to be cut off level; and a timber platform was to be laid on them to carry the masonry. How much of the foundation-work, if any, was done according to this specification is not known. Until modern methods of site-investigation were developed—from about 1920—elaborate specifications of foundation-work expressed a hope rather than a promise. According to one account, trouble at the Pont Royal began with the first pier on the Tuileries side, and as a result a different procedure for building it was adopted [7]. The site was dredged level, and a great box or caisson floated over it and sunk there, presumably with several courses of masonry already laid inside. For the next stage the caisson served as a coffer-dam. The mortar used in laying the masonry contained pozzolana (vol II, p 407), an Italian volcanic earth forming, when mixed with lime and water, a natural cement capable of setting under water.

If this account could be believed, then the Pont Royal would provide the first instance of the use of caissons in bridge-building, of dredging to provide a foundation, and of the use of pozzolana cement in France. There is, however, reason to regard it as inaccurate [8], and if it be so the first use of caissons in the manner described is correctly attributed to the Swiss architect Charles Dangeau de Labelye (1705–? 1781). Belidor gives good illustrations of the process of dredging at this period [9].

The practice of dredging for bridge-foundations and the use of the caisson were brought to England by de Labelye when in 1738 he was appointed to build a bridge over the Thames at Westminster. The bottom of each caisson was a stout wooden platform 80 ft by 30 ft in plan. The side walls were 16 ft deep, fastened to the base-platform by wedges so arranged that sides and bottom made a watertight caisson, which could be flooded through sluices or pumped dry as required. The platform for each pier remained part of the permanent structure. On withdrawal of the wedges the sides could be released for use in another caisson. There were twelve piers, two abutments, and thirteen arch-spans. The area

[1] The Gabriels were a celebrated family of French architects. Jacques (V) (1667–1742) was principal architect to the king, and Jacques (VI) (1698–1782) designed many of the buildings flanking the Place de la Concorde.

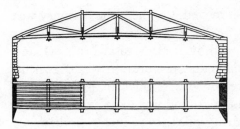

FIGURE 265—*Truss-girder bridge designed by Palladio. 1570.*

within which each caisson was to be sunk was first surrounded by a wall of sheet-piling, within which the bottom was dredged and left level at a depth of 6 ft below the river bed for an area of 90 ft by 40 ft between toes of slopes. No piles were driven below the site of any pier. The caisson, loaded with two courses of masonry, was sunk in position, then re-floated and loaded with a third course, and the sides were strutted from it while the bed received a final trim. The caisson was then sunk in its final position, the top of the masonry being about 2 ft above low water at spring tides. At high tide the caisson was submerged. Pumping began as soon as the top of the caisson appeared above water on the ebb tide, and the building of the pier was recommenced as soon as the masonry was exposed. Even when the sides of the caisson were removed, the masonry piers obstructed one-fifth of the river-passage. It is therefore not surprising that the gravel bed scoured in places, or that one pier settled unevenly before the bridge was completed. That pier and the two arch-spans to which it gave support had to be demolished and rebuilt, a misfortune that retarded the completion of the bridge by several years. Other settlements occurred, and when, about 1840, the roadway was widened a permanent coffer-dam of sheet-piles was left surrounding the lengthened

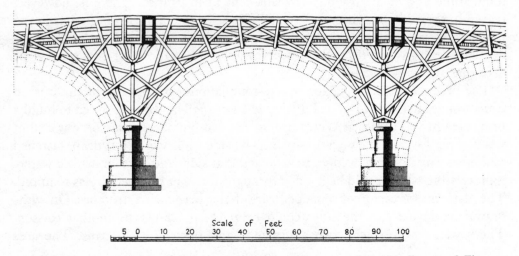

Scale of Feet
5 0   10   20   30 40   50   60   70   80   90   100

FIGURE 266—*The stone piers of Westminster bridge and the wooden superstructure originally proposed. The masonry arches actually built are shown by dotted lines.*

piers. The gap between this piling and the masonry was filled with concrete and capped with slabs of stone [10].

III. SUPERSTRUCTURE

Wood has probably been more widely used than any other material for bridge-building, and still finds much employment in temporary bridges, especially in oversea dependencies. Like its later competitor, steel, timber is strong both in tension and compression, but before the introduction of the toothed-washer type of connector in the twentieth century the making of a neat, economical joint to

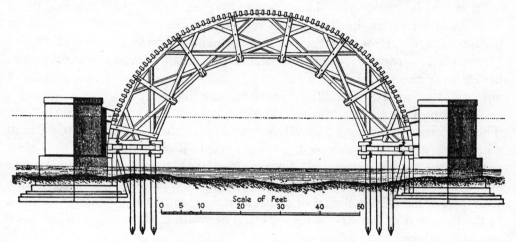

FIGURE 267—*The timber centring for the central arch of Westminster bridge; span 76 ft. 1739.*

transmit a heavy pull from one timber-member to another was difficult. The carpenter, therefore, used most of his material in compression or bending, and tried to arrange that only light loads should be transmitted by joints which put members in tension.

As early as the sixteenth century Andrea Palladio (1518–80) illustrated a true truss-girder bridge of 100 ft span (figure 265) [1]; but this construction was not widely favoured until, nearly three centuries later, it was developed by American engineers.

As late as the 1730s it was proposed to build Westminster bridge with a timber superstructure as shown in figure 266, the framework virtually forming an arch. The centring on which the masonry ring was laid was also an arch (figure 267). The remarkable bridge over the Rhine at Schaffhausen below Lake Constance (figure 268), erected in 1757 by the Swiss engineer Hans Ulrich Grubenmann,

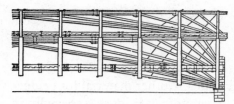

FIGURE 268—*Grubenmann's bridge over the Rhine at Schaffhausen (half of one span).*

was a framework of struts forming a rather complex arch combined near the abutments with a lattice-girder of which the members in tension were iron rods. The bridge was in two spans of 172 and 193 ft. It was roofed and boarded in to protect it from the weather. Grubenmann would have preferred to omit the intermediate pier and throw the two spans into one. Thomas Telford expressed the opinion that he could safely have done so, but the owners were more cautious. Even as constructed the bridge was reported to be very flexible even under pedestrian traffic. How long it might have lasted is uncertain, for it was destroyed by a retreating army forty-two years later. Grubenmann's even more spectacular bridge over the Limmat at Wettingen near Zürich, having a single span of 390 ft and a rise of 43 ft, suffered the same fate (figure 269).

The important bridges during our period were of the masonry-arch type. They differed from most medieval arch-bridges in that they tended to be built with large stones finely worked, as was ancient Roman masonry. The joints between the stones, particularly the voussoirs[1] of the arch, were close. Longer spans with smaller rises than in older bridges were made practicable by the wider use of flattish segmental or elliptical arches, and by a progressive decrease in the thickness of the arch at the crown. The width of the piers between spans was also reduced.

The Ponte Vecchio, or Bridge of the Goldsmiths, over the Arno at Florence was rebuilt in 1345 to an advanced design by Taddeo Gaddi (1300?–66). It was one of the first bridges in which a shallow segmental profile was employed. There were three spans of from 85 ft to 94 ft 6 in; the rise was from 12 ft 10 in to 15 ft, or between one-sixth and one-seventh of the span.[2] The pier-thickness was 20 ft 4 in, between one-quarter and one-fifth of the span. Neither of these ratios was often so low until Jean Rodolphe Perronet (1708–94) and his engineers of the Ponts et Chaussées systematically reduced them in the latter half of the

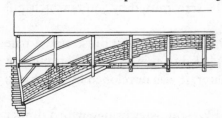

FIGURE 269—*Grubenmann's bridge over the Limmat (half of one span).*

[1] The wedge-shaped stones forming the ring of the arch.

[2] The dimensions of bridges, unless one knows who measured them, should be accepted with caution; they are copied by one author from another. The dimensions of the Ponte Vecchio given above are from Edward Cresy's *Encyclopaedia of Civil Engineering* (London, 1847).

eighteenth century. The keystone was only 3 ft 3 in deep, or one twenty-ninth of the span, below which even Perronet would hardly have favoured a reduction. The Ponte Vecchio was, however, an exceptional bridge.

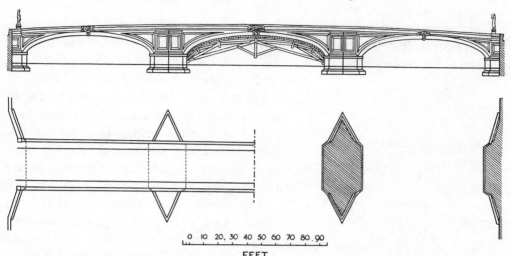

FIGURE 270—*The Santa Trinità bridge, Florence.* (Above) *Elevation;* (below) *plan.*

The usual proportions recommended were as follows:

Span	Rise	Thickness at crown	Width of pier
I	$\frac{1}{6}$–$\frac{1}{3}$ according to relative levels of road and river	$\frac{1}{12}$ (Alberti) $\frac{1}{15}$ (Palladio) $\frac{1}{17}$ (Serlio) $\frac{1}{24}$ (Perronet)	$\frac{1}{4}$–$\frac{1}{6}$

Henri Gautier (1660–1737) realized that bridge-piers were made far larger than was required for the support of their vertical loads, but neither he nor his successors cared to risk making them thinner. It was Perronet half a century later who actually reduced pier-thickness to one-tenth of the span. The end-abutments, and in a long viaduct an abutment-pier at intervals of every five or six spans, were built stout enough to take the thrust. The spans between two abutment-piers were all centred and built simultaneously, the intermediate piers being regarded as columns above which the thrusts balanced one another.

The three arches of the Santa Trinità bridge at Florence (figure 270) were of 87, 96, and 86 ft span. The design was in several respects remarkable. When the bridge was built in 1567 the semicircular arch was still usual, with the segmental arch as an alternative, but, to avoid steep approaches, the designer, Bartolomeo Ammannati (1511–92), gave each arch a rise of only one-seventh of the span, and adopted an unusual profile.

Settlements of the original centring, however, and later of the bridge, made it impossible to tell for certain by later measurements whether the original form was parabolic, elliptical, or multi-centred, or followed an artist's free-hand

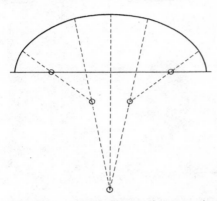

curve. The curve, moreover, was broken at the crown, where the halves intersected at an obtuse angle, giving a slightly pointed profile. The existing bridge is a reconstruction in facsimile, the original having been destroyed by the retreating Germans in the 1939–45 war.

The curvature of a true elliptical arch would vary continuously, and no two adjacent voussoirs could be cut to quite the same radius. To avoid this difficulty, the French engineers came to favour a false-elliptical, or 'basket-handled' form in which the radius of curvature varied discontinuously (figure 271).

FIGURE 271—*Diagram showing the construction of a 'basket-handled' arch by means of arcs of circles struck from five centres. The result approximates closely to a semi-ellipse.*

The bell-mouthing of the openings of arches was a marked feature of later French practice. It was introduced deliberately in the upstream face of the Pont Neuf at Toulouse in 1542, and in both faces of the Pont Henri IV at Châtellerault, Vienne, in 1564. In the second of these bridges the faces of the arches sprang from near the points of the triangular cut-waters, the span of the elliptical arches being increased by about 6 ft while the rise remained constant (figure 272).

A curious feature of certain medieval and later bridges was their secondary use as a site for shops and houses. London Bridge (1209), the Ponte Vecchio at Florence (1367), the Pont Notre-Dame in Paris (1507), and the Rialto bridge at Venice (c 1590) were all so used. To build a bridge to provide a house with a foundation must be the most extravagant method possible! The piers of London Bridge were large; between tides they obstructed about half the width of the river, which at that point was rather more than 900 ft. The starlings (p 420), moreover, were much larger and at low tide obstructed about half the remaining width. They also extended up and down stream far beyond the sides of the bridge, leaving ample room for props to carry the houses. The city was con-

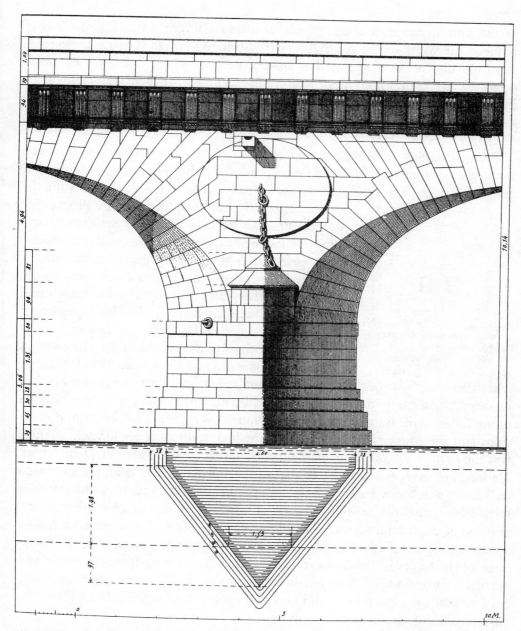

FIGURE 272—*The Pont Henri IV at Châtellerault* (1565–1609); *downstream face of a pier, showing the splay of the arches.*

gested, and the house-sites could be let at substantial rents. Although the houses reduced the width of the roadway over the bridge from 20 ft to 12, these rents were too high to be forgone. The houses were of wood, and were on many occasions partly or wholly destroyed by fire. The last of them was demolished in 1762. The Pont Notre-Dame retained its houses into the twentieth century.

IV. STRUCTURAL THEORY

Bridge-building in Roman, medieval, and even in Renaissance times owed nothing to abstract science. Even for the vaulting of the great abbey and cathedral churches—a far more delicate matter—there is no evidence of theory in the modern sense. By sound deduction from progressive movements and defects in actual structures, and some deliberate experiment, particular problems were solved; but the contemporary statical theory in general terms would have been a quite inadequate guide to anything like the same bold, economical disposition of material. Even for Galileo (1564–1642) the practices of ship-builders and pump-makers presented questions to be studied in the same way as natural phenomena [11]. Craftsmen could tell him

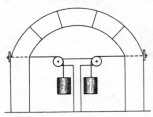

FIGURE 273—*One of Leonardo's drawings, illustrating his study of the horizontal thrust of an arch upon its supporting walls.*

what they did, but they could not explain scientifically why large ships had to be disproportionately massive as compared with small boats, or why a suction-pump failed to lift water from a depth of much over 30 ft. The theory of dimensions and the properties of the vacuum he had to discover for himself. Galileo was the first to discourse in mathematical terms on the strength of materials. He was, however, not the first to make experiments in that field, for Leonardo da Vinci's notebooks contain sketches, accompanied by rough calculations, of tests to measure the tensile strength of wires (p 250), and the strength and stiffness of small columns and beams of given dimensions. Leonardo also showed an apparently novel appreciation of the parallelogram of forces, with the directions of the forces inclined at various angles, and of the moments of forces and of their resultant. On all these points his views were in advance of those generally held at that time. In no case did he reach general conclusions, but neither did anyone else for the next two centuries [12].

On the stability of arches, too, Leonardo seems to have held views far in advance of any known to have been made public until long after his day. He sketched models of loaded arches with cords arranged over pulleys to measure the horizontal thrust (figure 273). He thus disproved the dangerous fallacy that the load on a semicircular arch follows the direction of the arch ring, and so is transferred to the abutment as a vertical force with no horizontal component. So confident was he that in 1502 he proposed in writing to the Sultan of Turkey to build a bridge across the Golden Horn, in a single segmental span of 700 ft and a rise of 180 ft. On plan the sides were to be curved outward to widely spread abutments, the springings situated deep within an excavation of vast size and depth. Leonardo's sketch is small and diagrammatic; but the weight, reactions, thrust, and stresses have been calculated on the optimistic assumption that Leonardo would have made the axis of the rib coincide—or nearly so—with the line of thrust for dead-weight [13]. The thickness at the crown would have been about 30 ft, and the bridge would have taken about three-quarters of a million tons of stone. It would have been impossible to frame the centring required, or to build a coffer-dam to resist a head of perhaps 100 ft of water, nor could such a vast project have been organized and financed. No single-span masonry-arch of such great size has ever been constructed, or is likely to be.

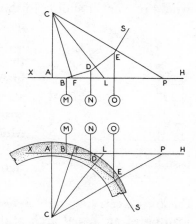

FIGURE 274—*La Hire's force diagram and link polygon. (Above) Forces in a loaded chain; ABDES is the profile of a loaded cord. The rays CA, CF, CL, and CP are at right-angles to AB, BD, DE, and ES respectively, and when produced cut AB (or AB produced) at A, F, L, and P. (Below) forces in an arch.*

The first serious attempt to devise a theory of the arch, one quoted by theoretical writers a century later, was the 'smooth voussoir theory' put forward by Philippe de La Hire (1640–1718) in a little textbook on mechanics (1695) (figure 274) [14]. The sides of the triangles CAF, CFL, CLP represent to scale the forces acting at B, D, and E respectively, and are in fact the triangles of forces for these points. La Hire had developed in ABDES a link-polygon, and in CAFLP a force-diagram, which were reciprocal figures. He had, indeed, laid the foundation of graphic statics; but a century and a half passed before engineers realized the generality and power of the methods of computation that could be based on the use of such diagrams.

Inverted (figure 274), the link-polygon becomes the line of pressure for an arch-ring in which the force acting across each joint is at right-angles to the meeting-faces of the stones, and so causes direct compression without evoking any frictional resistance. This was a simple case to study; it thus assumed an importance it did not deserve and tended to obscure the real problem of the arch. For even ignoring the adhesion at a mortar joint, the friction between two surfaces of stone, however smoothly worked, is high.

It will be noticed that to keep the line of pressure within the profile of a semi-circular arch-rib the loads M, N, O, ... would have to increase rapidly in magnitude as the voussoir to which they apply is farther round the rib from the crown, until, for the last voussoir standing on a horizontal surface, the vertical load that would prevent it sliding in the absence of friction or horizontal restraint would

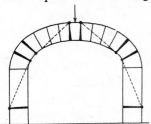

have to be infinitely large. Clearly this in no way represents the actual state of affairs. La Hire realized this, and confined his theory to that part of the arch in which the joints were inclined to the horizontal at an angle greater than 45°. The fact is that the spandrel-filling can exert a considerable resistance. Modern tests have shown that this is so even when the filling is of earth, once it has been packed down tightly by time and traffic.

FIGURE 275—*Diagram illustrating Danisy's study of the virtual hinges in a failing arch.*

The ideal profile for an arch-ring of constant thickness, carrying only its own weight, would clearly be a catenary.[1] The loading of an actual arch seldom approximates to this condition. Nevertheless the idea gained currency in the early eighteenth century, or earlier, that no arch could be considered stable unless a true catenary could be drawn within its profile.

A sounder approach to the problem was made by a Frenchman named Danisy, who reported in 1732 the results of some tests he had carried out with sets of model voussoirs made of plaster. He found no tendency for the voussoirs to slide but noted that, when unevenly loaded, the arch-rib opened at certain joints on one edge, forming a virtual hinge at the other. If loading was increased, rotation about such hinges occurred, and the arch collapsed (figure 275) [15]. It was by the development of this view of the stability of the arch that theory in fact advanced.

V. THE PONT-Y-TY-PRIDD

The history of bridge-building in this period cannot end more appropriately than with the story of the building of a remarkable eighteenth-century bridge, the name of which is perpetuated in that of the Welsh township of Pontypridd. The river Taff at this point was difficult to ford, and impassable in winter. Glamorganshire was being industrialized and Herbert, Lord Windsor, owner of

---

[1] The curve described by a slack rope or chain suspended by its ends.

the land on both sides of the river, was granting leases for mining iron and coal. No local builder was found willing to build a bridge at such a place until William Edwards (1719–89), who combined the occupations of minister of religion and farmer, undertook to build and maintain one for seven years for the sum of £500. He employed local masons to build stout piers in the bed of the river to carry three or four arch spans. The bridge stood for about two years before it was swept away by a flood.

Edwards then decided that he must avoid piers in the stream, and planned to build a single arch with a span of 140 ft, curved to a radius of 175 ft. A fellow

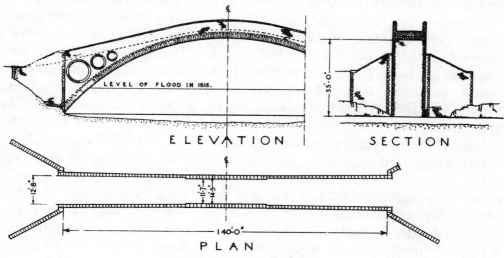

FIGURE 276—*The Pont-y-Ty-Prydd.*

minister-cum-wheelwright, named Thomas Williams, is believed to have shared Edwards's second venture, doubtless erecting the centring. The bridge was built, or nearly so, when a flood carried away the centring and this second bridge collapsed. Edwards made a third attempt, with stronger centring. The bridge was completed and the centring struck while the river was still low; but during flood and storm about six weeks later, in November, 1754, the haunches sank, the crown rose, and the arch collapsed. Edwards seems to have realized why his bridge failed: the haunches were too heavy for the light crown. He started to build the fourth bridge. He formed the haunches with cylindrical voids surrounded by rings of masonry keyed into the spandrel-walls at both sides of the bridge (figure 276). These both lightened the work, where weight had been excessive, and ensured greater firmness. This fourth attempt proved successful.

The bridge was opened in 1756, and still stands. It is now by-passed by a modern bridge, carries only foot-traffic, and has been scheduled as an ancient monument [16].

Although some extra money was collected, Edwards must have lost heavily on his contract. However, having established a reputation as a builder of bridges, he was commissioned to construct others in south Wales; but never again did he attempt anything so bold as the Pont-y-Ty-Pridd.

Whether Edwards had seen illustrations of ancient bridges perforated in the spandrels, or hit on the idea himself, is not known. A drawing of the bridge that he sent with a letter to the Society of Antiquaries in 1760 was later found among the papers of John Smeaton (1724–92) now in the possession of the Royal Society [17]. This find started the false assumption, duly repeated in many histories of bridges, that Edwards had consulted Smeaton, and perforated the spandrels on his advice. Smeaton in 1755, still a maker of instruments, was paying the visit to Holland that preceded his entry into civil engineering as a career. We may be certain that Edwards did not consult him or any established authority.

Edwards's arch-ring is of stones, only about 18 in deep, with wide, wedge-shaped joints, filled with mortar made with a local hydraulic lime. It is probable that the arch-ring, the rubble fillings, the roadway, and the parapet-walls were, once the mortar had hardened, virtually monolithic. Even so, they are the equivalent of an arch-ring at most 3 ft 6 in deep. On Henri Gautier's rule the depth at the crown should have been 9 ft 4 in. Even Perronet, at that period, would have made it 6 ft. It is, therefore, not surprising that later writers often tried out their theories on the Pont-y-Ty-Pridd.

REFERENCES

[1] PALLADIO, A. 'I Quattro Libri dell' Architettura', Book 3. Dominico de Franceschi, Venice. 1570.
[2] GAUTIER, H. 'Traité des ponts.' Paris. 1716. EMMERTON, E. *Amer. hist. Rev.*, **29**, 1–23, 1923.
[3] BELIDOR, B. FOREST DE. 'Architecture hydraulique' (4 vols). Paris. 1737–53.
[4] RAMELLI, AGOSTINO. 'Le diverse et artificiose machine.' Published by the author, Paris. 1588.
[5] HAMILTON, S. B. *Trans. Newcomen Soc.*, **28**, 246, 1951–3.
[6] PARSONS, W. B. 'Engineers and Engineering in the Renaissance', p. 150, fig. 76. Williams and Wilkins, Baltimore. 1939.
   SALZMAN, L. F. 'Building in England down to about 1540', Pl. XVIIIb. Oxford University Press, London. 1952.
[7] GAUTHEY, E.-M. 'Œuvres' (ed. by C. L. M. NAVIER), Vol. 1, p. 69. Paris. 1809.
[8] DARTEIN, F. DE. 'Études sur les ponts en pierre remarquables par leur décoration antérieurs au dix-neuvième siècle', Vol. 2, p. 84. Paris. 1907.

[9] BELIDOR, B. FOREST DE. See ref. [3], Vol. 2, Pt II, Pls XX, XXV. 1753.

[10] WEALE, J. (Ed.). 'The Theory, Practice and Architecture of Bridges.' London. 1843.

[11] GALILEI, GALILEO. 'Discorsi e dimostrazioni matematiche intorno a due nuove scienze.' Elzevir, Leiden. 1638. Eng. trans. by H. CREW and A. DE SALVIO. Macmillan, New York. 1914. Reissued: Dover Publications, New York. n.d.

[12] HART, I. B. 'The Mechanical Inventions of Leonardo da Vinci.' Chapman and Hall, London. 1925.

Idem. Trans. Newcomen Soc., **28**, 1951–3 (in the press).

[13] STÜSSI, F. *Schweiz. Bauztg.*, **71**, 113–16, 1953.

[14] LA HIRE, P. DE. 'Traité de mécanique.' Paris. 1695.

[15] FREZIER, A. F. 'La théorie et la pratique de la coupe des pierres et des bois', Vol. 3, p. 348. Paris. 1769.

[16] WILLIAMS, E. I. and HAMILTON, S. B. *Trans. Newcomen Soc.*, **24**, 121–39, 1945.

[17] [SMEATON, J.]. 'A Catalogue of the Engineering Designs of John Smeaton', p. 105. Newcomen Society Extra Publ. No. 5. London. 1950.

BIBLIOGRAPHY

CRESY, E. 'Encyclopaedia of Civil Engineering.' London. 1847.

DARTEIN, F. DE. 'Études sur les ponts en pierre' (5 vols). Paris. 1907–12.

GAUTIER, H. 'Traité des ponts.' Paris. 1716.

KIRBY, R. S. and LAURSON, P. G. 'The Early Years of Modern Civil Engineering', ch. 5, pp. 133–46. Yale University Press, Newhaven. 1932.

PARSONS, W. B. 'Engineers and Engineering in the Renaissance.' Williams and Wilkins, Baltimore. 1939.

SMITH, H. S. 'The World's Great Bridges' chs 4 and 5. London. 1953.

STRAUB, H. 'A History of Civil Engineering' (Eng. trans. by E. ROCKWELL), chs 3–5. Hill, London. 1952.

## 17

CANALS AND RIVER NAVIGATIONS
BEFORE 1750

A. W. SKEMPTON

I. INTRODUCTION

IT is well known that the English canals of the eighteenth and early nineteenth centuries served as the arteries of the industrial revolution, but even in pre-industrial times the rivers and canals of Europe and Asia played a significant part in trade and commerce. One reason for this is that rivers (and canals are but extensions of river-systems) form the most natural inland routes to and from sea-ports. Moreover, so long as men and horses provided the only practical source of motive power for inland transport, heavy and bulky goods could be carried more economically and efficiently on water-ways than by any other means.

To illustrate this point quantitatively, the loads that can be carried or drawn by a single horse are set out in the table below. The gain in mechanical efficiency was partially offset by the greater capital expenditure required for the engineering works of the canal and river navigations; nevertheless the average cost of carriage by water in eighteenth-century England, for example, was rarely more than half and often only a quarter of the cost by road [1]. And the roads were frequently impassable for commercial traffic in winter.

Typical loads carried or drawn by a single horse

Pack-horse		$\frac{1}{8}$ ton
Wagon { on 'soft' roads		$\frac{5}{8}$ ton
Wagon { on macadam roads		2 tons
Wagon on iron rails		8 tons
Barge { on river		30 tons
Barge { on canal		50 tons

II. TRANSPORT CANALS IN CHINA

The earliest major civilizations were in the valleys of the Euphrates, Nile, Indus, and Huang-Ho, and these great rivers provided a ready means of transport in addition to their life-giving supply of water for irrigation. The Phoenicians and the Greeks were maritime peoples, while the Romans chiefly made use of the many naturally navigable rivers in their empire. Apart from a few notable canals such as that from the Nile to the Red Sea, cut by order of Darius *c* 510 B.C., and several in France, Lombardy, and the Netherlands made during Roman times, the first sustained effort in canal-construction was made by the Chinese [2]. Among the more important of their works are the Ling Ch'u canal in Kuangsi (215 B.C.), the 90-mile-long canal from the Han capital Ch'ang-an to the Yellow River (133 B.C.), the Pien canal in Honan (A.D. 70), the Shanyang canal in Chiangsu (A.D. 350), and the first sections of the Grand Canal completed in 610. This had a total length of 600 miles, and along its banks ran an Imperial road planted with elms and willows. It served to transport grain from the lower Yangtze and the Huai to Kaifeng and Loyang. Under the T'ang dynasty in the eighth century the traffic on the canal was known to exceed 2 million tons annually.

In most cases the land traversed by these canals had a small gradient, and water-levels could readily be controlled by single gates separated from each other by considerable distances. For instance, on the Pien canal in A.D. 70 the engineer Wang Ching built the gates typically some 3 miles apart. They consisted of stone or timber abutments, each with a vertical groove into which squared logs of timber could be lowered or raised by ropes attached to their ends (plate 18). These simple stop-log gates evidently derived from the sluices used on irrigation canals. On the smaller transport canals, and especially in places where an appreciable difference in land-level had to be overcome, a double slipway was usually built, over which the barges were hauled. References to this device occur in Chinese literature at least as early as A.D. 348.

Occasionally a more elaborate gate was adopted, in which a solid door could be raised or lowered by a windlass. Two of these were built by Ch'iao Wei-Yo in 984 to replace a double slipway, during the remodelling of a section of the Grand Canal, and by placing the gates only 250 ft apart he created the first known example of the canal-lock: a device of fundamental technological importance. With single gates widely spaced along a canal or river considerable delays and great losses of water are involved in waiting for the levels to equalize after any particular gate has been opened, unless the difference in level is slight. With the lock, however, only the comparatively small volume within the lock-basin has to be filled or emptied, and the water-level in the long reaches or pounds between two locks is never altered.

It is rather curious, therefore, to find that little use was made of the lock in China. Its later development was entirely due to western engineers. Yet, if the Chinese remained content, in general, with their stop-log gates and slipways, they nevertheless achieved canal-works on a most impressive scale. Outstanding among these was the construction, between the years 1280 and 1293, of the northern branch of the Grand Canal from Huaian to Peking, having a length of 700 miles. Parts of this utilized existing rivers, and other sections were 'lateral' canals; but the section crossing the Shantung foothills, completed in 1283, was the earliest example of a 'summit-level' canal. A lateral canal has a continuous fall in one direction and, with intakes from the river alongside which it runs, there are few problems in water-supply. The conception of a lateral canal is relatively simple, since it is essentially an improvement of an existing river. In contrast, the idea of taking a canal over the summit of a watershed dividing two

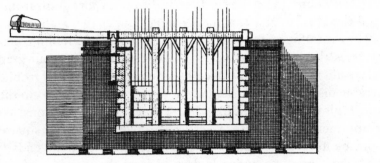

FIGURE 277—*Section of a typical stanch or flash-lock. From Belidor, 1753.*

rivers requires bold imagination and considerable technical skill in providing an adequate water-supply at the summit. The Shantung section of the Grand Canal linked the Yellow River with a group of lakes, situated some 100 miles to the south at approximately the same elevation as the river. But over a short length the intervening land rose to a height of about 50 ft above the river and the lakes. The upper part of the canal was taken in a cutting with a maximum depth of 30 ft, yet this still left a fall of 20 ft to the north and south. To provide for the inevitable losses of water occasioned by operating the gates, two small rivers situated to the east, higher up the foothills, were partially diverted to flow into the summit-level. The engineers of this notable undertaking were Li Yueh and Lu Ch'ih.

III. MEDIEVAL CANALS AND RIVER WORKS

At the time when the Grand Canal of China was completed, water-transport in Europe was still in a primitive state. Few canals had been constructed, and rivers were chiefly used as a source of power for water-mills. On many rivers each mill had its weir, to provide an adequate head of water for the mill-wheel, and these weirs were a serious obstacle to navigation. In the later Middle Ages, however, important developments took place in the Netherlands, as we shall see, while throughout the more commercially active countries of Europe improvements were made in the rivers by building stanches in the weirs and also at intervals along the river, between the mills, to reduce the gradient and increase the depth of water in the shallow places [3].

A typical stanch (also called a flash-lock or navigation-weir) is shown in figure 277. When a boat wished to pass, the wooden boards or 'paddles', with their long handles, were lifted out, and after the rush of water had somewhat abated the balance-beam, with the vertical posts which had supported the paddles, could be turned aside to leave a clear opening. Often the boats had to be hauled through against the flow, by a winch placed on the bank upstream of the stanch; in travelling downstream boats would find the 'flash' of water released by opening the stanch a help in crossing any shoals below it.

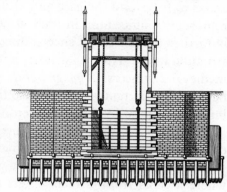

FIGURE 278—*Section of a typical 'portcullis' sluice. From Belidor, 1753.*

The early history of stanches is obscure, but it is practically certain that they were in existence on a number of rivers in Flanders,[1] Germany, England, France, and Italy before the end of the thirteenth century. A reference to the winch for a stanch on the Thames at Marlow occurs in 1306. The oldest complete account of the Thames navigation between Oxford and Maidenhead, in 1585, shows twenty-three stanches; all but four were situated in the weirs of the mills on this 62-mile stretch of river [4]. Many of these stanches were still in place in the mid-eighteenth century, while as recently as the early nineteenth century twenty-two stanches were to be seen on the Marne between Châlons and Paris.

The very existence of Holland depends upon the dikes and drainage canals, and it is not surprising that some of the canals were enlarged and suitably equipped for transport at an early date. Originally the drainage canals had outlets through the dikes controlled by sluices. In some cases goods had to be transhipped over the dike, and in other places boats were hauled over a double slipway similar to those in China.[2] Perhaps the first examples were at Het Gein and Otterspoor, built in 1148 on the Nieuwe Rijn canal near Utrecht. Where

---

[1] Possibly as early as 1116 on the river Scarpe.

[2] The double slipway was used also in Italy, and one was built in 1437 at Fusina where the river Brenta enters the lagoon south of Venice. This slipway, as reconstructed in the sixteenth century, is illustrated by Zonca [5]. The slipway at Fintelle, in Flanders, remained in use until 1824.

hydraulic conditions permitted, an obvious improvement was to make the sluice-gate large enough for the passage of boats. These navigation sluices in Holland were of the lifting-gate or portcullis type shown in figure 278. When the tide in the estuary or river was at the same level as the water in the canal, the gate was raised by a windlass and boats could pass through. At other states of the tide a difference in water-level existed across the gate. To safeguard the sluice from under-seepage the foundations and abutment-walls were extended, typically 20 or 30 ft beyond the gate and also well into the body of the dike. Figure 278 represents a sluice built in 1708; it will be seen that the danger of under-seepage is further prevented by sheet-piling. This was a characteristic feature of construction in the sixteenth century and later, but seems to have been unknown to medieval engineers. A *magna slusa* at Nieuport, mentioned in 1184, may have been of the portcullis type, as also the sluice at Governolo on the river Mincio, built in 1188–98 by Alberto Pitentino, and that at Gouda of *c* 1210.

The next step was of vital importance. It involved building two sluice-gates, one behind the other, enclosing a basin or chamber and thereby forming a lock. The first example that can be dated with certainty was built in 1373 at Vreeswijk, where a canal from Utrecht enters the river Lek [6]. From regulations of 1378 and 1412 we learn that the Vreeswijk lock was operated three times weekly, at 2 o'clock in the afternoon [7]. First the outer gate was wound up, and the boats from the river-harbour entered the large basin of the lock. The outer gate was then closed and the inner one raised, and when a level had been made the boats were hauled through into the canal. The inner gate was then closed again and the outer gate opened, and in due course the boats that had been waiting in the basin could pass into the river. This leisurely procedure was not without advantage to the townspeople of Vreeswijk since it provided the boatmen with ample time for shopping and gossip. It is possible that a similar lock had been built somewhat earlier at Spaarndam, but it was only in the later fourteenth century that this form of construction became widely adopted. Examples include basins at Delfshaven (1389) and Schiedam (1395). At Gouda in 1413 a lock was built by Jan van Rhijnsburch with a triple set of gates.

A large basin was typical of the early Dutch tide-locks and is essential for intermittent working, but in 1394–6 a lock was built at Damme, near Bruges, in which the chamber formed by the two gates and the masonry side-walls was 100 ft long and 34 ft wide. This suggests that the lock at Damme was operated as often as any boat arrived there, and it is the earliest lock with what may be regarded as modern proportions.

By 1400, therefore, important advances had taken place in the construction of locks. But those made in the Netherlands were intended only to overcome differences in water-level, and the first locks to overcome differences in land- as

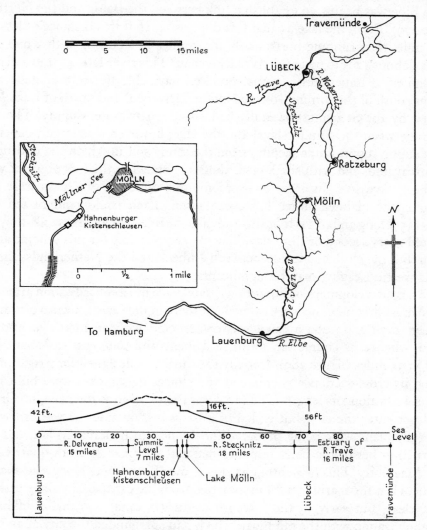

FIGURE 279—*Map and longitudinal section of the Stecknitz canal, 1391–8.*

well as water-level were built on the Stecknitz canal, 1391–8 [8]. This is also the oldest summit-level canal in Europe, and therefore a work of considerable historical interest.

In the early fourteenth century the river Stecknitz had been made navigable from Lake Mölln down to Lübeck, a distance of 21 miles and a fall of 40 ft, with four stanches. In 1391 an extension of this waterway southwards to Lauenburg on the Elbe was begun, to establish a link between the Baltic and the North Sea (figure 279). From the lake a canal was dug, rising 16 ft in a distance of less than half a mile, then running horizontally for 7 miles in a cutting with a maximum depth of about 12 ft to meet the river Delvenau. This river falls 42 ft in a distance of 15 miles to Lauenburg. It was rendered navigable by eight stanches. The sections south of the summit (formed by the Delvenau) and north of Lake Mölln (formed by the Stecknitz) naturally had an adequate water-supply. The steep section between the summit-level and the lake, however, was largely dependent for its supply upon water seeping from the sandy soil in which the cutting had been excavated, and with single-gate sluices or stanches the loss of water would have been excessive. In order to overcome this difficulty two locks were built, known as the Hahnenburger Kistenschleusen. Each could contain ten small barges (35 ft long and of 11-ft beam) and, like the tide-lock at Vreeswijk, they were operated every second or third day. The men responsible for this scheme are not known, but the close connexion between Lübeck and the Netherlands, through the Hanseatic League, may be significant.

The next development of importance took place in Lombardy soon after 1450, but we must first note the work carried out there in the early fifteenth century [9]. Between 1179 and 1209 a canal was constructed with an intake on the river Ticino, whence its course ran south to Abbiate and then east to Milan. It fell 110 ft in 31 miles (figure 280). Initially the canal was designed for irrigation, but in 1269 its cross-section was enlarged and sluices or stanches were built in the various weirs along its length. The canal was then known as the Naviglio Grande. It did not enter the city, but ended in a basin just outside the western wall.

In 1387 plans were being prepared for the new cathedral at Milan, and when construction began the chief building-material was marble from quarries near Lake Maggiore. This was brought down the Ticino and along the Naviglio Grande. How the marble was at first carried from the canal-basin to the cathedral is not clear, but early in the fifteenth century a canal was made linking the Naviglio Grande with the old moat, which had surrounded the city at an earlier date when its area was much smaller. This moat passed quite close to the cathedral. By means of a single-gate sluice in the link canal, situated alongside the Via Arena, boats could pass from the Grande to the mason's yard. But the water-level in the moat, which was fed by the Seveso running in from the north, was several feet above that of the canal. Consequently, whenever the sluice was opened the water-level in the moat had to fall to that of the canal; when the boats had passed the sluice, the moat had to fill again before they could proceed along it. In 1438 this inconvenient arrangement was improved by the construction of a second gate in the link canal along the Via Arena, thus forming the first pound-lock in Italy. The engineers responsible for this work were Filippo da

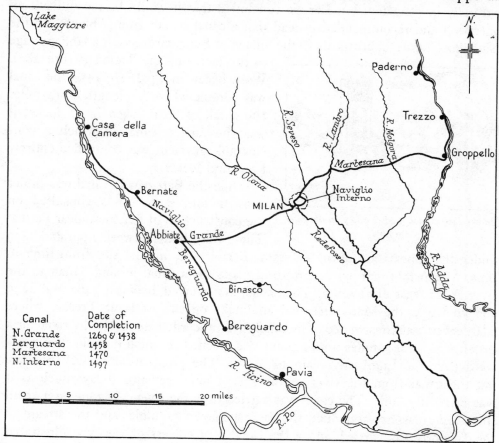

Canal	Date of Completion
N. Grande	1269 & 1438
Berguardo	1458
Martesana	1470
N. Interno	1497

FIGURE 280—*Map of canals near Milan before 1500.*

Modena and Fioravante da Bologna, and it appears that before 1445 they had built a second lock near Sant' Ambrogio on the old moat which, by now, had been enlarged and was known as the Naviglio Interno.

IV. CANALS OF THE ITALIAN RENAISSANCE

The canal-works in Lombardy of the later fifteenth century mark a new epoch in canal-construction. In 1451 Bertola da Novate (*c* 1410–75) was appointed ducal engineer of Milan, and one of his first tasks was to consider the possibilities of building a canal from Milan to Pavia on the river Po [10]. In 1359 a small irrigation canal had been constructed from Milan as far as Binasco, about half-way towards Pavia. The question of enlarging and extending this canal was naturally investigated, but Bertola concluded that it would be too difficult an operation and recommended instead that a canal be cut from Abbiate, on the Naviglio Grande, southwards to the village of Bereguardo, with a land-portage

FIGURE 281—*Sketch of a lock with portcullis gates, c 1470.*

to the banks of the Ticino (figure 280). Work began in 1452. By 1458 the canal was completed, with a length of 12 miles and a fall of 80 ft taken in 18 locks; it was the earliest canal in which a considerable gradient was controlled entirely by pound-locks.

While the Bereguardo canal was under construction, Bertola was consulted on the construction of five locks near Parma. These were built between 1456 and 1459 under the supervision of an assistant, Bertola visiting the site from time to time. Meanwhile in 1457 he prepared plans for a canal joining Milan to the river Adda, east of the city. This canal, constructed between 1462 and 1470 and known as the Martesana, had an intake on the Adda at Trezzo, where a large weir was constructed. The canal then proceeded alongside the river for a distance of some 5 miles until a point was reached at which it could turn west-ward over the Lombardy plain to Milan. The great masonry wall separat-ing the canal from the river in the first 5 miles remains today much as it was originally built. The canal was carried over the river Molgora on a small three-arch masonry aqueduct, the earliest known example, and the stream of the Lambro was carried under the canal in a culvert of the type illustrated in figure 294. By careful planning Bertola was able to lay out this 24-mile-long canal with only two locks. Boats entered a basin or dock near San Marco in Milan.

By this time knowledge of the pound-lock was becoming general in Italy. In his book *De re aedificatoria*, completed during the 1460s and published in 1485, Leone Battista Alberti (1404–72) gives an account of a lock with a pair of gates separated by a distance equal to the length of a boat [11]; it is possible that he was in fact describing the locks built by Bertola, unquestionably the leading canal engineer of his time. In 1481 the brothers Domenico da Viterbo built a lock at Stra on the canal joining Padua to the river Brenta [12], and in 1491–3 several timber locks were built by 'an engineer of Milan' on the canal near Bologna [13]. Few details are known of these early Italian locks, and the only contemporary illustration so far discovered is a sketch in the *Codice Lauren-ziano*, dated between 1460 and 1490 [14]. The drawing (vol II, figure 626)

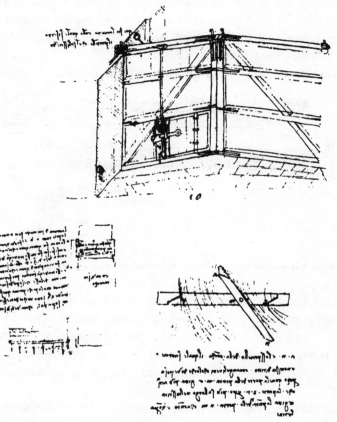

FIGURE 282—*Sketch by Leonardo da Vinci of mitre-gates for the San Marco lock, Milan. c 1495.*

as a whole is difficult to interpret, but a pair of the vertical-lift gates repre-sented may be taken as constituting a lock similar to that described by Alberti (figure 281).

The portcullis type of gate was not ideally suited to navigational purposes. It was superseded in the last decade of the fifteenth century by Leonardo's wonderful conception of the mitre-gate. Leonardo da Vinci (1452–1519) was appointed ducal engineer of Milan in 1482; some ten years later he turned his attention to hydraulics and, in particular, to the construction of six new locks on the Naviglio Interno. These were completed in 1497, and Leonardo's drawing for the gates of the lock at San Marco, situated just below the terminal basin of the Martesana canal, is shown in figure 282. In another drawing (figure 283) Leonardo shows a rectangular masonry lock 95 ft long between the gates and 18 ft wide, having a pile cut-off wall and mitre-gates, in which there are small sluice-doors, identical with those at San Marco. These drawings, which give the first complete design of a modern form of lock, are of the highest importance in the history of canal-construction.

In 1503 Leonardo went to Florence, where he was engaged upon very

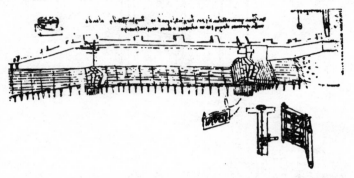

FIGURE 283—*Leonardo's sketch of a longitudinal section of a lock with mitre-gates.*

ambitious plans for a canal from that city to the river Arno near Vicopisano. This was to have been a summit-level canal, and Leonardo gave careful thought to the problem of an adequate water-supply at the summit [14]. His project, however, was in advance of its day, and the first summit-level canal of real importance was not built until the early seventeenth century, in France.

The Martesana canal had successfully linked Milan with the river Adda, but upstream of Trezzo the river was impassable and it was clearly desirable to by-pass this section, to enable navigation to continue up to Lake Como. In 1518 Benedetto da Missaglia designed a lateral canal for this purpose with headworks near Paderno, where there was to be a diversion-weir 14 ft high at a location chosen after borings had been made in the river bed. The canal would then run in an excavation on the right bank, to re-enter the Adda at a point situated 3000 yd downstream and 90 ft lower than the intake. Ten locks were proposed and the amount of water admitted to the canal was to be regulated, all the surplus above a predetermined maximum flowing back to the river over spill-ways in the canal bank. Work began in 1519 and it seemed that this fine example of river navigation would be successfully completed. In 1515 Milan had come under the rule of Francis I of France and it was by his order that the canal had been started. In 1522, however, Francis lost Milan to the Emperor Charles V; the main driving force was thus removed, and work on the canal ceased.

In 1584 plans were prepared for a canal between Milan and Pavia, but in the following year a serious flood damaged the intake of the Naviglio Grande.

FIGURE 284—*Lock at Brandenburg, 1548–50.*

Attention had therefore to be directed immediately towards the reconstruction of this important component of the Lombardy canal-system. The work was entrusted to Giuseppe Meda (*c* 1540–99), who took the opportunity of completely remodelling the old intake, still little changed from its medieval form. He built a weir and control-works similar in principle to those designed by Missaglia on the Adda. Meda's later career was tragic. In 1591 he prepared a new scheme for the Paderno canal, using an entirely novel form of lock, of the type later known as a shaft-lock [15]. After various mishaps and interference from the authorities in Milan his plans were only partially carried out before his death. Meanwhile in 1595 he had drawn up proposals, complete in all details including the locks, culverts, aqueducts, and bridges, for the canal between Milan and Pavia. A year later these proposals were accepted, but work had barely started before the engineer died and this scheme too was abandoned.

V. THE POUND-LOCK IN THE SIXTEENTH CENTURY

The increasing importance of canal and river navigations in the sixteenth century is reflected in the widespread adoption of the mitre-gate pound-lock. The first examples, as we have seen, were completed by Leonardo in 1497 on the Milan canal. These were followed in 1518 by Missaglia's designs for the locks on the Paderno canal, and by three locks near Bologna built in 1548 by Giacomo da Vignola (1507–73). The latter were oval in plan, 100 ft long, 25 ft in maximum width, and 12 ft wide at the entrance [13].

The earliest examples in France that can be securely dated are those designed in 1550 in connexion with improvements of the rivers in the neighbourhood of Bourges. Detailed specifications of these locks still exist in the archives at

FIGURE 285—*Sketch of a lock on the Brussels canal, c 1560.*

Bourges [14]. In all, fifteen locks were required, two of masonry on the river Yèvre, four similar ones on the river Cher, and nine of timber construction on the river Auron. The locks were rectangular with a length of 90 ft between the gates and a width of 13 ft. The floor and side walls extended 15 ft beyond each gate, beneath which sheet-pile cut-off walls were constructed.

In the same period improvements were being made on the Havel and Spree in the Mark Brandenburg [16]. Work began on two locks at the towns of Rathenow and Brandenburg in 1548, at Spaarndam in 1572, and in Berlin in 1578. The lock at Brandenburg, with its large octagonal basin and timber walls, still exists (figure 284), but the type of gate originally used is not known. A sketch by Tilemann Stella (1524–89) of the locks that he built on the Mecklenburg canal between 1572 and 1582 shows mitre-gates and a rectangular chamber 18 ft wide and 90 ft long. He had visited the Netherlands in 1561 to study hydraulic engineering and would have seen the Brussels canal, completed in that year.

This important canal, begun in 1550, is described in the next section (p 452). Here it may be noted that the works included four locks of octagonal shape, 200 ft long and 70 ft wide, with falls varying from 6 ft to 10 ft. One of these locks is shown in figure 285. It can be seen that there were mitre-gates and that the chamber was emptied and filled by means of culverts in the walls. This is the earliest known example of the ground-sluice, a device enabling the basin to be operated more rapidly and with less disturbance than with the usual sluice-doors in the lock-gates.

In England the first pound-locks were constructed in 1564–7 by John Trew on a lateral cut beside the Exe, known as the Exeter canal [17]. Like the locks on the Brussels canal, on the Havel, and the old tide-locks in Holland, those at Exeter had a basin of sufficient size to hold several boats. They were 189 ft

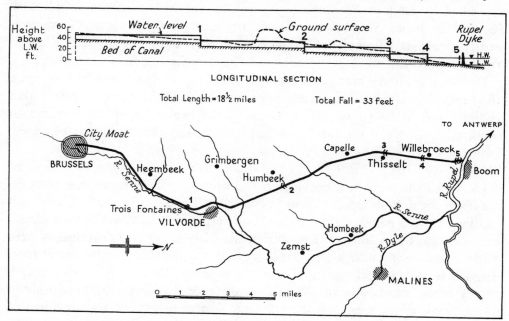

FIGURE 286—*Map and longitudinal section of the Brussels canal, 1550–60.*

long by 23 ft wide. A manuscript sketch shows three vertical-lifting sluice-paddles in each leaf of the mitre-gate at the upstream end of the lock [18]. The lower end, however, was closed by a single gate. This arrangement also occurs in the sixteenth-century Italian lock on the Brenta, illustrated by Zonca (vol II, figure 625).[1] Both upper and lower mitre-gates, however, were provided in the lock built 1571–4 on the Lea, near London, at Waltham Abbey, where

> . . . a rare device they see,
> But newly made, a waterworke; the locke
> Through which the boates of Ware doe passe with malt.
> This locke contains two double doores of wood,
> Within the same a cesterne all of Plancke,

[1] Vittorio Zonca (1568–1602), an architect-engineer of Padua, does not give the location of this lock in his book [5], but says that gates of the type shown are to be found in the locks at Padua and Stra (i.e. on the Brenta canal). There is no reason to assume that the gates built a century earlier in the Stra lock, by the brothers Domenico, were similar to those depicted by Zonca.

Which onely fils when boates come there to passe
By opening of these mightie dores.
(Vallans, 'Tale of Two Swannes', 1577.)

The first mitre-gates in Holland appear to be the triple set built in 1567, and described by Andries Vierlingh (1507–79), at Spaarndam in a new tide-lock (*Grote Haerlemmer Sluys*) 25 ft wide and 122 ft long [19]. There may have been earlier examples, however, for Simon Stevin (1548–1620), writing at Leiden in 1617, says that the mitre-gate pound-lock 'has been in use for a long time' [20].

Finally, it is interesting to note that in Sweden eleven locks were built between 1603 and 1610 as part of the canalization of the river Eskilstuna between Lakes Hjälmar and Mälar (p 455) [21]. Thus, by the beginning of the seventeenth century knowledge of the canal-lock had spread practically throughout Europe.

VI. CANALS IN FLANDERS

Of the canals built in the sixteenth and seventeenth centuries, the Brussels canal was the first of importance to be constructed outside Italy [22]. Navigation had long existed between Brussels and Antwerp along the rivers Senne, Rupel, and Schelde. From time to time during the Middle Ages improvements were made in the Senne navigation, but in 1531 it was decided to cut a canal from Brussels to Willebroeck on the Rupel (figure 286). This would have a length of 18½ miles, which was almost half the distance that boats had previously to travel. Some of the towns on the old route opposed the plan, fearing a loss of trade, but by 1550 agreement had been reached and work was started under the direction of Jean de Locquenghien (1518–74). The fall of 34 ft between Brussels and high-water mark in the Rupel was taken in four locks (p 450). These locks were large enough to hold twelve of the small coasting-vessels using the canal, and the depth of water provided was 5 ft. Seven streams were taken beneath the canal in culverts, four road-bridges were built, and one section of the canal ran in a cutting 2 miles long with a maximum depth of 30 ft. For a distance of about 1½ miles between its entrance on the Rupel and the lowest lock the canal was contained between dikes raised some 10 or 12 ft above the low-lying marshland, and as completed in 1561 the canal was tidal in this reach. But excessive silting occurred, and in 1570 Locquenghien constructed at the debouchment of the canal a tide-lock with three pairs of mitre-gates.

The organization of the undertaking is known in some detail. Locquenghien as director of works received a regular salary during the period 1550–63. Adrien van Bogaerden, the surveyor and principal assistant, was also regularly employed throughout. The day-to-day supervision was carried out by two divisional resident engineers, and there was a treasurer. From time to time expert advice was sought. In this way Willem Maertense came from Holland in 1554 as a consultant on the opening of the Rupel dike at Willebroeck, and two years earlier Gilbert Van Schoonbeke of Antwerp was called in to give advice on the construction of the locks. The canal was not completed without difficulty. The contractor had trouble with the lock at Willebroeck during its construction; the lock at Humbeek failed in 1562, owing to seepage beneath the foundations of one of the gates, and a slip occurred in the canal dike. Remedial measures were successfully carried out in each case. The largest of the culvert aqueducts (all of

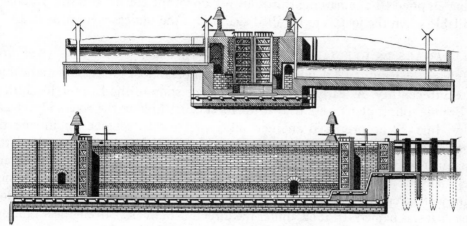

FIGURE 287—*The Boesinghe lock on the Brussels canal, 1643–4.*

which had been built in timber) was not sufficiently strong; it was rebuilt in masonry in 1569 by Georges Rinaldi—a construction said to have been greatly admired by Peter the Great when he travelled on the canal.

The Brussels canal was completed only just before the outbreak of war with Spain. When peace was restored in the early seventeenth century the canal system of Flanders expanded greatly [23]. The more notable works included a 44-mile canal linking Bruges, Passchendaele, Nieuport, and Dunkirk c 1622, the enlargement of this canal in 1641–61, and an extension in 1666 to Ostend, where a very fine tide-lock was constructed in 1669. In 1670 Dunkirk was linked to the river Aa, at the mouth of which, before the end of the century, another great tide-lock had been built at Gravelines. By 1692 the old river navigations near Lille had been improved and extended with a canal forming a connexion between the Lys and Scarpe.

The most interesting technical achievement of the period, in Flanders, was the celebrated lock at Boesinghe built by Maître Dubie. In 1643–6 navigation between Ypres and the river Yser was improved by the construction of a lateral canal, 4 miles long, beside the river from Ypres to Boesinghe. From this point navigation continued along the river to its junction with the Yser. The fall in this 4-mile reach amounted to 20 ft and, instead of building three locks of normal dimensions, the whole of the fall was taken in one great lock at Boesinghe (figure 287). This is remarkable not only for its size but for the use of side-ponds, introduced here for the first time, as a means of reducing the loss of water in operating the lock. Each side-pond takes one-third of the water as the lock is being emptied (the remaining third flowing down the canal), and this volume is available when the lock is to be filled again. Ground-sluices were provided.

VII. CANALS IN GERMANY AND SWEDEN

It has been mentioned that in Germany a number of locks were built in the mid-sixteenth century. As early as 1540, at the suggestion of the Elector Joachim II of Brandenburg, plans were drawn up for a canal linking the rivers Havel and Oder. In 1548 he proposed another, more practicable, scheme for linking the river Spree with the Oder upstream of Frankfurt [24]. Work began on this latter canal in 1558, but it appears that considerable difficulties were encountered and eventually by 1563 operations came to a stop. After many political delays new plans were prepared by order of Frederick William the Great Elector, after whom the canal was named. In 1662, under the direction of the Italian engineer Philippe de Chiese, the earthwork was begun, while construction of the locks and bridges was entrusted to Michael Schmidts, a Dutch engineer who had built a new lock in Berlin five years earlier. The Friedrich-Wilhelm canal, completed in 1669, had a total length of 15 miles and was the third summit-level canal to be built in Europe. As with the early Stecknitz canal the summit was supplied by ground-water from the sandy soil through which the upper part of the canal was carried in a cutting. On the eastern side the canal rose from Neuhaus on the Spree for a height of 10 ft in two locks, and from the western end of the summit-level it fell 65 ft to Brieskow on the Oder.

The construction of the Finow canal, the earlier of Joachim II's schemes, was begun in 1605. After an interruption between 1609 and 1617, for lack of funds, it was completed in 1620. The first reach, 8 miles long, was level with the Havel. The canal then descended the valley of the Finow for 17 miles to Liepe, on a short tributary of the Oder, only eleven locks being provided in the fall of 120 ft. This canal proved to be very unsatisfactory, for the Havel was able to flood down it, and owing to lack of maintenance during the Thirty Years War the works fell into complete decay. By the beginning of the eighteenth century scarcely a trace of them existed. The canal was rebuilt between 1744 and 1751 on a different plan, having two locks up from the Havel to a summit-level, a feeder-channel with an intake several miles upstream on this river, and fourteen locks down to Liepe. The system of water-ways in this region of Germany was completed by the Plaue canal, built in 1743–6, from the Elbe to the Plaue lake and hence to the Havel.

In Sweden, when Telford designed the Göta canal (1808–10), providing water-transport between Stockholm and Lake Väner and thence by the river Göta to Göteborg, he was following in broad principle the scheme first put forward nearly 300 years before in 1526 by Gustavus I, another Renaissance prince with an ambition for canals on a grand scale. It was characteristic of these schemes that they were beyond the technical and financial possibilities of their day. Yet the objective was never forgotten, and in 1596 work began on a much smaller project, which, nevertheless, by canalizing the river Eskilstuna between the Hjälmar and Mälar lakes formed the first step of a route between Stockholm and Göteborg [25]. This was completed in 1610, with eleven timber locks built by Petter von Lübeck, with a Dutch engineer acting as consultant. It was not altogether successful, however, and in 1628 surveys were made by Andreas Bureus for a canal linking Lake Hjälmar and the river Arboga which flows into Lake Mälar. This canal was constructed 1629–39 and entirely superseded the older Eskilstuna route. The fall of 75 ft between Arboga and Hjälmar was taken in ten masonry locks. The works, under the direction of Carl Bonde, included a cutting half a mile long in rock. Trade was considerable and before the end of the century the canal had to be enlarged. The Dutch engineer Tilleman de Moll was in charge of these improvements, which were carried out in 1691–1701. The old locks were replaced by eight new ones, each 24 ft wide and 100 ft long with falls of up to 13 ft, and the depth was increased to 8 ft. Meanwhile in 1635 surveys were made of the country west of Lake Vatter along the course of what was later to be the summit of the Göta canal, and as early as 1607 a lateral cut and lock had been built at Lilla Edet on the Göta river. The subsequent stages in the construction of this great waterway linking the Baltic and the North Sea, associated with Polhem, Telford, and Count von Platen, lie outside the scope of the present chapter [26].

VIII. ENGLISH RIVER NAVIGATIONS

In the British Isles the first summit-level canal was built as late as 1737–45, by Thomas Steers, from Newry in Northern Ireland to Lough Neagh, to bring coal from the Tyrone collieries over the canal and thence by sea to Dublin.

Indeed, canal-construction was not undertaken on a large scale until the days of the industrial revolution, though in the preceding 150 years a great deal had been accomplished in extending and improving the river navigations [27]. To give a measure of this progress, it may be mentioned that by the end of the eighteenth century some 2000 miles of navigable water existed in England, of which approximately one-third was in the form of canals built between 1760 and 1800; one-third was in the form of 'open' rivers which were naturally navigable; and the remaining third had been created as a result of the work of engineers, chiefly between about 1600 and 1760.

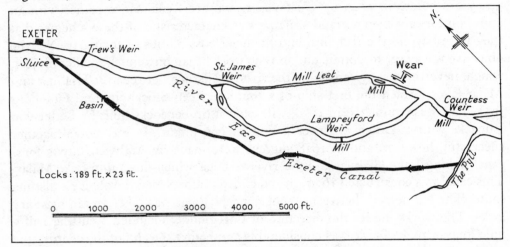

FIGURE 288—*Map of the Exeter canal, 1564–7.*

It will be recalled that during the Middle Ages stanches had been built, usually in mill-weirs. These were works consequent upon the existence of the mills, rather than works designed from the outset to improve navigation. And for small medieval craft navigation was possible on many rivers that would be considered impracticable by modern standards. In the course of time, however, the medieval river system was increasingly felt to be inadequate, and the works at Exeter in 1564–7 (p 451 and figure 288) represent the beginning of a new outlook on water-transport in England.

Shortly afterwards, improvements were undertaken on the Thames and its tributaries. Reference has been made to the lock completed in 1574 on the Lea (p 451), while between 1624 and 1635 three locks were built on the Thames at Iffley, Sandford, and Abingdon. The Wey was made navigable in 1651–3 for a length of 15 miles, with a fall of 86 ft, from Guildford to Weybridge (figure 289).

This work was carried out by Sir Richard Weston (1591–1652) and involved the construction of 7 miles of new cut and ten locks, together with twelve bridges and wharves at Guildford and Weybridge. Seventy years later the Kennet was made navigable from Reading to Newbury. John Hore (c 1690–1762) was the

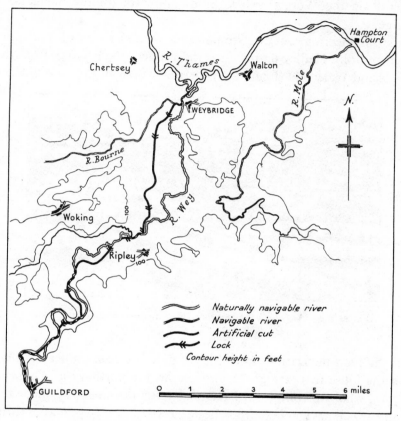

FIGURE 289—*Map of the Wey canal, 1651–3.*

engineer for this work, and for the Avon navigation from Bristol to Bath. On the Kennet, between 1718 and 1723, he built 11½ miles of new cuts 54 ft wide, and in the total length of 18½ miles, with a fall of 138 ft, he provided eighteen locks each having a length of 122 ft and a width of 19 ft. In the west country the Severn was the main artery of transport, the river being an open navigation up to Shrewsbury. It was evident that great advantages would be gained by making some of the larger tributaries of the Severn navigable. Work on the Warwick Avon from Tewkesbury upstream for a distance of 32 miles to Bidford was undertaken by William Sandys in 1636–9. This navigation was extended to Stratford-on-Avon in 1675–7 by Andrew Yarranton (1616–84). In 1662 Sandys attempted to make the Wye navigable from Chepstow to Monmouth, but the technical difficulties proved too great. In the same year, however, Yarranton started work on the Worcestershire Stour and brought the navigation up to Stourbridge.

The first engineering works of importance on the rivers of Yorkshire were carried out by John Hadley on the Aire and Calder (1699–1703), from the Ouse up to Leeds and Wakefield (figure 290). Between 1726 and 1729 William Palmer

FIGURE 290—*View of a lock on the river Aire Navigation near Leeds, c 1702.*

extended the Don navigation up to Sheffield, and he also supervised improvements on the Ouse in 1727–32. Meanwhile, in the north-west, Thomas Steers (1672–1750), who had completed Liverpool's first dock in 1715, made the rivers Mersey and Irwell navigable to Manchester in 1722–5. By 1732, after three years' work, the Weaver navigation was constructed by Thomas Robinson, with eleven locks in a length of 20 miles and a fall of 42 ft from Winsford to the Mersey estuary.

This summary of a few of the English river navigations indicates the scope of the works. Their economic importance is shown by the fact that on the Weaver, for example, over 50 000 tons were carried annually in the period 1750–60. Their construction involved weirs, flood-gates, bridges, and wharves as well as locks and, although individually their technical importance cannot be compared with that of the contemporary canals in France, they represent altogether a considerable engineering achievement.

IX. PROJECTS OF THE FRENCH RENAISSANCE

Inland navigation in France followed a pattern in marked contrast to that in England [28]. It is true that some attention was paid to river improvement, but the principal feature of French work in the seventeenth century was the construction of two great summit-level canals which are so important in the history of engineering that they will be considered separately. Indeed the Languedoc canal (1666–81) was the greatest feat of civil engineering in Europe between Roman times and the nineteenth century; it was largely based upon experience gained from the Briare canal, on which work began in 1604.

The Languedoc canal was conceived in the ambitious and imaginative mind of Francis I (r 1515–47) who clearly foresaw great advantages both to trade and to the prestige of his country if an inland waterway could be established between the Mediterranean and the Atlantic. When Francis returned home from Milan in 1516, accompanied by Leonardo da Vinci, they discussed together the means for effecting this notable enterprise of constructing a *canal des deux mers*. Two possible routes were found. That in the south would link the rivers Garonne and Aude (the Languedoc canal or Canal du Midi); the other, in central France, would join the rivers Loire and Saône (the Charolais or Canal du Centre). The latter was economically more attractive but technically more difficult, and the first detailed studies were made for the southern canal. The survey was carried out by Nicolas Bachelier (1485–1572), who reported in 1539 that the best route would be up the Aude to Carcassonne, then by canal by way of Villefranche to the Garonne just above Toulouse (figure 292). This was essentially the route of the Languedoc canal as built 125 years later but, though locks were mentioned, Bachelier produced no working plans.

After twenty years Adam de Crapponne (1526–76) again investigated this route, and made reconnaissance surveys for the Charolais canal. When the Wars of Religion put a stop to public works further progress had to await the peace of 1598. Then, under Henri IV and his great minister the Duc de Sully, bridges and water-supply schemes were started, land-drainage was initiated on a considerable scale, and a re-examination of the southern canal was ordered. Humphrey Bradley, the dike-master of Henri IV, who in 1584 had acted as a consultant on Dover harbour and in 1589 had prepared the earliest comprehensive proposals for draining the Fens (pp 316, 318), was engaged on this task. A little later he was concerned with a scheme for a canal linking the Seine and Saône, the origin of the Canal de Bourgogne.

The three great Renaissance projects, the Languedoc, Charolais, and Bourgogne canals, were all eventually accomplished, but they were beyond the resources of the early seventeenth century and Sully very wisely decided upon a more practical scheme for a canal linking the Loire and Seine. This was an attractive commercial proposition; it presented few serious technical difficulties; and it would form a branch of the Atlantic to Mediterranean waterway, leading to the Seine valley and the capital.

X. THE BRIARE AND ORLEANS CANALS

Initial plans for a canal linking the Loire and Seine were drawn up in 1603 [29]. The small river Trezée was to be made navigable from its junction with the Loire at Briare for a distance of some 10 miles up to the village of Breteau; then a cutting with a maximum depth of 75 ft was to be excavated in the high land between the Trezée and the Loing, and this river rendered navigable for a distance of 24 miles down to Montargis (figure 291). The rivers and the canal at the summit were to have a minimum depth of 4 ft and a width of 40 ft, and it was thought that 48 locks would be required. These were to be 90 ft long and 16 ft wide, with mitre-gates and a fall varying from 3 to 5 ft. Bids for the contract were made in January and again in February 1604, when Hugues Cosnier was appointed contractor.

Cosnier then examined the site in detail, and found several important errors in the original scheme, which must have been no more than a sketch-plan. For, instead of the rivers Trezée and Loing being at the same level at the points where they were to be joined by the canal in the summit cutting, there was a difference in elevation of more than 40 ft. Provision had been made neither for supplying water to the summit, nor to secure the works against damage from floods. Cosnier was therefore compelled to produce a new design. He proposed to follow the valley of the Trezée only 7 miles up from the Loire and then, striking northwards, to take the canal over a plateau, crossing this with a summit-level 3¾ miles long, from which the canal would be taken down the steep side of the Loing valley to meet this river at Rogny. The new route was nearly 3 miles shorter than the original scheme, it avoided the deep cutting, and it made possible the supply of water to the summit. Cosnier also proposed to construct a true canal along the whole length from Briare to Montargis, realizing that this would prove far more satisfactory than merely making the rivers Trezée and Loing navigable. At the same time he suggested that the locks be enlarged and built of masonry.

These radical alterations were examined on behalf of the king by Jean Fontaine, who found himself in complete agreement with Cosnier's proposals, and the new design was accepted by the royal council in December 1604. Sully drafted 6000 troops to provide the labour force, and himself inspected the works from time to time; in 1608 Henri IV, accompanied by the queen, paid Cosnier the honour of visiting the site. By 1610 about three-quarters of the work had been

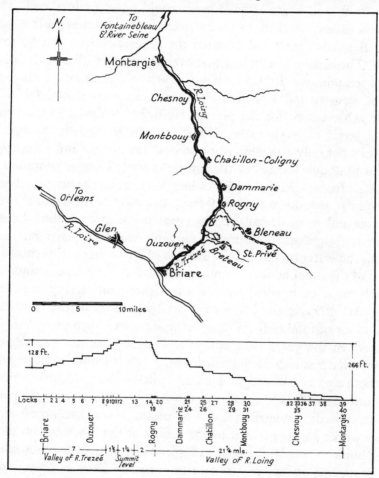

FIGURE 291—*Map and longitudinal section of the Briare canal, 1604-42.*

completed, but in May of that year the king was assassinated and the canal lost its royal patronage. Work nevertheless continued, but in 1611 Sully was forced to resign from the government and under the new régime a commission was appointed to investigate the state of the canal and the cost of its completion. The commission was headed by the Marquis de Rhoissy, who had with him four experts, including Humphrey Bradley (p 459). A careful survey of the works showed that Cosnier had completed 26 of the required 34 miles and that he had built 35 locks, together with many ancillary works such as 15 discharge-weirs and 9 bridges. The locks had masonry walls 6 ft thick, the distance between the gates was 105 ft, and boats of 15-ft beam could be accommodated. The fall of the locks was usually 10 ft, but in some cases was as great as 14 ft. Cosnier had visited the Brussels canal, and adopted the ground-sluices that he saw in the locks there. These were so efficient that even the locks with a 14-ft fall could be operated in ten minutes. In descending from the plateau to the Loing at Rogny, Cosnier had constructed a 'staircase' of six locks with a total fall of 65 ft, a remarkable achievement for the period. He firmly believed in the principle of providing a series of levels each as long as possible, and to this end he built staircase locks not only at Rogny but also near Dammarie and Chesnoy, as well as a number of double locks. For the summit-supply Cosnier proposed, but had not yet built, a feeder-channel $3\frac{1}{4}$ miles long with an intake near the head waters of the Trezée running down to a small lake, the Étang de la Gazonne, which acted as a reservoir and from which the water was taken directly into the canal. To provide further storage a lock had been built without a step but capable of impounding the water on one side to a depth of 8 or 9 ft. By this means a length of $1\frac{3}{4}$ miles of the canal at the summit could act as a reservoir, since the water in this reach could be lowered by 4 or 5 ft without interfering in any way with navigation. At intervals along the canal in the valleys of the Trezée and the Loing a number of intakes from these rivers had also been provided.

Thus between the years 1604 and 1611 Hugues Cosnier had designed and almost completed a summit-level canal, rising 128 ft from the Loire and falling 266 ft to the Loing at Montargis. He had built 35 locks, and had designed the summit-supply as well as looking after the supply of water at other parts of the canal and safeguarding it against floods by means of the discharge-weirs.

All these works are mentioned in the report of the Commission of 1611, in which de Rhoissy wrote '*que ce serait un grand abus de laisser et abandonner une si louable entreprise, qui a esté fort bien entendue, conduite et presque parfaicte.*' Nevertheless, for political and financial reasons the scheme was abandoned. Cosnier made proposals to complete the work partly at his own expense, in return for the right to collect tolls from the canal during the first six years of its operation; but with wars and with the weak government of the Regency nothing was done for seventeen years. During this interval Cosnier naturally was engaged elsewhere, notably in connexion with the Arcueil water-supply to Paris. In 1628 a re-examination of the Briare canal was made by Francini and Le Mercier, who strongly recommended the completion of the work but pointed to the need for additional water-supply at the summit to compensate for the large losses of water involved in operating the six locks at Rogny. For this purpose they proposed a second feeder-channel with an intake on the Loing at St-Privé, leading to a small lake, which would act as a reservoir, at a level just above that of the summit. In order to forward the work to which he had already devoted so much thought and time, Cosnier offered to construct this feeder-channel provided he was paid a part of the money still owed to him since 1611. This offer was accepted, but he was now an elderly man in ill health and he died in the last month of 1629. *Saluons, au passage, la mémoire de ce grand ingénieur!* [30].

Another eight years passed before, in 1638, Guillaume Boutheroue and Jacques Guyon obtained letters patent from Louis XIII to complete the work and to pay the land-compensations still outstanding, in return for ownership of the canal. They formed a company for this purpose and, under the direction of Boutheroue's brother François, the damage of twenty-seven years of neglect was made good, the last five locks down to Montargis were built, and the canal was put into operation in 1642, exactly as conceived by Cosnier. The proposal of 1628 to provide a feeder-channel from St-Privé proved, however, to be well founded, and this channel was duly constructed in 1646. It is notable for having a fall of only $5\frac{1}{2}$ ft in a total length of 13 miles (5 in per mile).

The undertaking was a satisfactory investment and during the latter half of the seventeenth century the company received an annual return of 13 per cent on its capital. The annual trade on the canal in this period was about 200 000 tons. This figure was maintained throughout the eighteenth century, doubled during the nineteenth, and is trebled at the present day.

The goods transported on the Briare canal consisted chiefly of coal and of wine brought down the Allier and the upper Loire to Paris, but part of the trade came up the Loire from Nantes, Tours, and Orleans. To shorten the journey of this latter commerce and to facilitate the export of timber from the forest of Orleans a canal was built in 1682–92 with a length of 46 miles, rising 98 ft from the Loire at Orleans to the summit in 11 timber-locks and descending 132 ft to the Loing at Montargis, in a distance of 18 miles, in 17 locks [31]. The chief technical problem in the Orleans canal was the summit-water supply. The canal crosses an extensive and very flat plateau, and the principal feeder-channel, known as the Rigole de Courpalet, has a length of 20 miles with a fall of only 4 ft ($2\frac{1}{2}$ in per mile). The flow in this channel was therefore very slow, and the system would have been ineffective but for the use of the summit-level as a storage reservoir, in the manner already devised by Cosnier on the Briare. With a length of 11 miles, the summit-level of the Orleans canal had sufficient capacity to store the water flowing from the feeder-channels during the night; this was used to replace the loss of water in operating the canal the following day. The consultant for the Orleans canal was Sébastien Truchet (1657–1729), a well-known *savant hydraulicien* and pupil of the physicist Mariotte [32]. The high degree of accuracy required in surveying the Rigole de Courpalet is remarkable, and calls to mind the achievement of Edward Wright in his survey for the New River water-supply for London as early as 1609 [33]. Here the fall was 18 ft in a length of 39 miles, or $5\frac{1}{2}$ in per mile (almost the same slope as that of the Rigole de St-Privé). The Courpalet feeder is also memorable as having provided a valuable subject for investigation by Antoine Chézy in 1769 during his classic research on flow in rivers and open channels [34].

The Loing between Montargis and the Seine which, after 1692, took the traffic both of the Orleans and the Briare canals, was navigable only by virtue of twenty-six stanches situated in the weirs of the various mills along the river. With the two canals in operation the delays caused by operating these stanches became intolerable, and between 1719 and 1723 a lateral canal alongside the Loing was built by Jean-Baptiste de Règemortes, with twenty-one locks in a length of 32 miles [35]. In 1726 his son Noël rebuilt, in masonry, the locks on the Orleans canal, and thus the canal system between the Loire and Seine was perfected.

XI. THE LANGUEDOC CANAL

It is not surprising that progress was delayed on the Languedoc canal in the south of France since, after the death of Henri IV, the government was reluctant even to complete the Briare canal. It was not until 1662 that the requisite combination of an able administrator in Colbert and an engineer of genius in Pierre-Paul Riquet (1604–80) was found [36]. In the previous year Riquet, with the assistance of François Andreossy (1633–88), had for the first time worked out a scheme for the supply of an adequate amount of water to the summit. For this purpose he proposed a feeder-channel 26 miles long with an intake on the river Sor near Revel. Its flow was to be increased by a second channel taking water from three mountain streams, the Alzau, Vernassonne, and Lampy (figure 292). For the route of the canal, he adopted essentially the line proposed by Bachelier more than a century earlier. The river Lers [now l'Hers] was to be made navigable from Toulouse to a point east of Villefranche (Haute-Garonne). A canal was then to be cut rising over the summit and joining the river Fresquel near Castelnaudary. Below this point the Fresquel would be made navigable to its junction with the

Aude near Carcassonne, and this latter river would in its turn also be made navigable down to its mouth on the Mediterranean coast.

In November 1662 Riquet communicated his ideas to Colbert. Colbert had little difficulty in arousing the interest of Louis XIV, who preferred that even the practical undertakings of his reign should exhibit the quality of grandeur. The king appointed a royal commission to investigate the plans, and during 1663 and 1664 Riquet was busy working out his scheme in more detail, paying visits to Colbert in Paris, and to Hector Boutheroue, the younger brother of

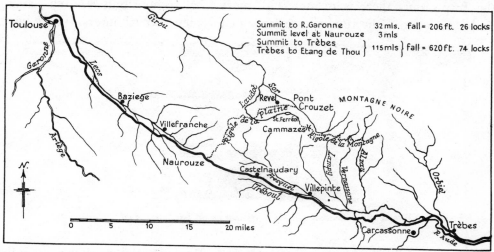

FIGURE 292—*Map of the western part of the Languedoc canal, 1666–8.*

François and one of the directors of the Briare canal, who had been appointed as the principal expert on the commission. In November 1664 Riquet presented his plan formally to the commissioners, who called upon the assistance of Andreossy and Jean Cavalier, Geographer Royal, and two other surveyors. During a period of seven weeks the commission made a detailed investigation of the terrain, approving Riquet's plans in general, but proposing that instead of making the rivers Lers, Fresquel, and Aude navigable, a canal be made along the entire length of the route from Toulouse to the Mediterranean. They also proposed that the canal should end not at the mouth of the Aude but in the Étang de Thau, with a port constructed at Sète.

The commission's report was approved by Colbert and the king, but as a practical demonstration of the validity of the plans for the summit-supply it was suggested that a pilot channel be dug from the Sor to the summit at Naurouze. This work was carried out by Riquet between May and October 1665 with complete success. Meanwhile de Clerville, chief royal engineer, prepared the contract documents for the first section of the canal between Toulouse and Trèbes. In October 1666 Riquet was appointed contractor, and by January of the following year 2000 men were employed, a number doubled by March. In 1668 specifications were drawn up for the second part of the canal from Trèbes to the Mediterranean, and in 1669 more than 8000 men were at work. Riquet had established an admirable organization: the canal was divided into twelve sections each under an Inspecteur-Général, one of whom was Andreossy. Under the Inspecteurs there were men with more local responsibilities, each having under his control the requisite number of foremen and labourers. There were

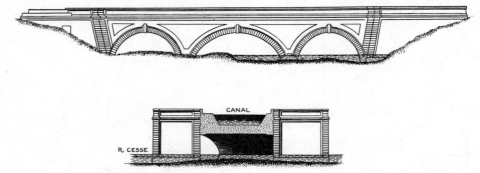

FIGURE 293—*Aqueduct over the river Cesse on the Languedoc canal, c 1688.*

also seven surveyors permanently engaged. By 1680 the work was rapidly approaching completion, but in October Riquet died and so was denied the satisfaction of seeing the opening of the canal seven months later, in May 1681. Riquet was succeeded as director of the works by his son Jean-Mathias, under whom the work continued for a number of years: much had still to be done before the canal was perfected in 1692.

The Languedoc canal excited the admiration of the world. Travellers came to see it under construction and poets celebrated its engineer, Colbert, and the king. Voltaire, in his *Siècle de Louis XIV*, having mentioned the Louvre, Versailles, and other building works of the *Roi Soleil*, said: '*mais le monument le plus glorieux par son utilité, par sa grandeur, et par ses difficultés, fut ce canal de Languedoc qui joint les deux mers.*' Just as the Briare canal had served as the model for the Languedoc in France, so the Languedoc was the prototype for succeeding great canal undertakings in Europe.

From the Garonne at Toulouse the canal rises 206 ft to the summit, in a length of 32 miles and with 26 locks. The summit-level is 3 miles long, and the canal then descends 620 ft to the Mediterranean, with 74 locks in a distance of 115 miles. The whole canal from Toulouse to the Étang de Thau is therefore 150 miles long, with 100 locks. The contract plans called for a channel 50 ft wide at the water-surface, a depth of 8½ ft, and side-slopes of 1:1. These were too steep, and after several slips had occurred the section was modified to a top width of 64 ft, a depth of 6½ ft, and side-slopes of 2½:1, the original base-width of 32 ft being maintained.

The walls of one of the locks collapsed soon after construction, and to prevent any further trouble of this kind the existing locks were rebuilt and the whole lay-out revised to reduce the height of the walls by one-third, to provide stronger foundations, and to curve the walls in plan, the better to resist the earth-pressure. In their new form, dating from 1670, the locks had a length of 115 ft between

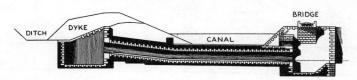

FIGURE 294—*Culvert under the Languedoc canal near Villepinte, c 1680.*

the gates, an entrance-width of 21 ft, and an average fall of 8 ft. The oval shape, though of great solidity, leads to a greater loss of water than from the usual rectangular chamber. Many of the locks were grouped together, the most notable examples being near Béziers, where Riquet built a staircase of 8 locks having a fall of 70 ft. At a distance of about 6 miles upstream of these locks the canal passed through the Malpas tunnel, 180 yds long. There were three major aqueducts. One over the river Repudre with a single arch of 30-ft span was built before 1680. The other two over the rivers Orbiel and Cesse (figure 293) were designed in 1686 by the celebrated engineer Sébastien Vauban (1633–1707, p 372) and built by Antoine Niquet (1639–1724). The countless streams crossing the line of the canal were taken under it in culverts (figure 294). Numerous diversion-weirs, spill-ways, and road-bridges were constructed, as well as the new port of Sète.

This was civil engineering on a grand scale, but perhaps the chief technical interest lies in the scheme for the summit-water supply. The furthermost intake is on the river Alzau (figure 292), situated high up the southern flanks of the Montagne Noire. From this point a feeder-channel, known as the Rigole de la Montagne, runs for a distance of 12 miles, crossing two other streams; then it divides, one short branch leading to the river Sor and the other continuing for 3 miles and passing through a tunnel at Les Cammazes to supplement the head waters of the Laudot.[1] The Rigole de la Plaine, with an intake on the Sor at Pont Crouzet, flows for 8 miles to meet the Laudot and then, carrying the whole supply in a channel 20 ft wide and 9 ft deep, runs for a further 19 miles to the Naurouze summit of the canal. In the valley of the Laudot, at St-Ferréol, Riquet constructed between 1667 and 1671 a large earthen dam with a masonry core wall, 105 ft in height (figure 295), to form a storage reservoir of 250 million

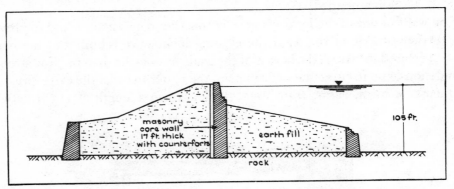

FIGURE 295—*Cross-section at maximum thickness of the St-Ferréol dam, Languedoc canal, built 1667–71. The capacity of the reservoir was 250 million cu ft.*

cu ft capacity [37]. During the summer the flow of the Rigole de la Montagne was directed entirely into the Sor, but in the winter the greatly increased flow in this channel was diverted partially into the St-Ferréol reservoir, the water of which could be used during the following summer. This brilliantly conceived plan proved to be wholly satisfactory, and it was not until 1777–81 that a second reservoir was constructed on the Lampy, with a masonry dam 54 ft high, to provide an additional source of water required by a branch canal to Narbonne.

With the perfection of the Languedoc canal in 1692 civil engineering had reached maturity in this field, and the technical basis had been provided for the vast expansion of the canal system of Europe which took place in the succeeding period of industrial development.

REFERENCES

[1] For extensive data on costs of transport in England see W.T. JACKMAN. 'The Development of Transportation in Modern England.' University Press, Cambridge. 1916.

[2] A general history of Chinese water-ways is given by CH'AO-TING CHI, 'Key Economic Areas in Chinese History, as revealed in the Development of Public Works for Water-control' (Allen and Unwin, London, 1936). Interesting descriptions will be found in LOUIS LECOMTE, 'Memoirs and Observations . . . made in a late journey through the Empire

---

[1] Although part of the original plan, this tunnel was built in 1686–8 by Niquet.

of China . . . translated from the Paris edition' (London, 1697), and SIR GEORGE L. STAUNTON, 'An Authentic Account of an Embassy to China, chiefly from the papers of Lord Macartney and Sir E. Gower' (3 vols, London, 1797). Details of the lock of A.D. 984 and the Shantung summit-canal have been elucidated in discussions with Dr Joseph Needham.

[3] For medieval locks in the Netherlands see G. DOORMAN. 'Techniek en Octrooiwezen in hun Aanvang.' Nijhoff, The Hague. 1953.

[4] THACKER, F. S. 'The Thames Highway: a History of the Inland Navigation.' Thacker, London. 1914.

Idem. 'The Thames Highway: a History of the Locks and Weirs.' Thacker, London. 1920.

[5] ZONCA, VITTORIO. 'Novo Teatro di Machine et Edificii.' Padua. 1607.

[6] TELFORD, T., article on "Inland Navigation" in 'The Edinburgh Encyclopaedia', vol. 15, pp. 209–315, writes: 'The lock at Vreeswyck dates from 1373 and is perhaps one of the oldest on record.' He also recognized that the Stecknitz canal should be 'reckoned amongst the first in which the invention of locks was employed'.

BREWSTER, D. et al. (Eds). 'The Edinburgh Encyclopaedia', vol 15. Edinburgh. 1830.

[7] Private communication from DR FOCKEMA ANDREAE.

[8] REHDER, P. Z. Ver. Lübeckische Gesch., **11**, 339, 1909.

TEUBERT, O. 'Die Binnenschiffahrt.' Engelmann, Leipzig. 1912.

WREDEN, R. V. D. I. Jb., **9**, 130, 1919.

ECKOLDT, M. Wasserwirtschaft, **40**, 255–60, 290–5, 1950.

[9] The standard works on the Lombardy canals are:

BRUSCHETTI, G. 'Storia dei Progetti e delle Opere per la Navigazione interna del Milanese.' Milan. 1821.

LOMBARDINI, E. 'Dell' Origine e del Progresso della Scienza Idraulica nel Milanese.' Milan. 1872.

LECCHI, A. 'Trattato de' Canali Navigabili.' Milan. 1776, 1824.

BASCAPE, G. C. 'Itinerarii della Nostalgia: il Naviglio di Milano e gli antichi Canali lombardi. Tavole di Giannino Grossi.' Delfino, Milan. 1950.

[10] For the work of Bertola da Novate see:

PARSONS, W. B. 'Engineers and Engineering in the Renaissance.' Johns Hopkins Press, Baltimore. 1939.

and also BRUSCHETTI, G. See ref. [9].

[11] ALBERTI, L. B. De re aedificatoria. Florence. 1485.

[12] ZENDRINI, B. 'Leggi e Fenomeni, Regolazioni ed Usi delle Acque correnti.' Venice. 1741.

[13] M——, G. B. 'Notizie storiche . . . del Canale naviglio di Bologna.' Bologna. 1825.

[14] PARSONS, W. B. See ref. [10].

[15] For a description of the modern shaft-lock see McGAREY, D. G. J. Jr Instn Engrs, **49**, 1–28, 1938.

[16] KLEHMET. Wschr. Arch. Ver., Berlin, **3**, 177–81, 191–5, 1908.

ECKOLDT, M. See ref. [8].

[17] DE LA GARDE, P. C. Min. Proc. Instn civ. Engrs, **4**, 90–102, 1845.

[18] TWYNE-LANGBAINE MSS 1, fol. 76 (c 1620). Bodleian Library, Oxford.

[19] VIERLINGH, A. 'Tractaat van Dyckagie' (2 vols), ed. by J. DE HULLU and A. G. VERHOEVEN. Rijks Geschiedkundige Publicatiën, The Hague. 1920.

[20] STEVIN, S. 'Nieuwe Maniere van Sterctebou door Spilsluysen.' Rotterdam. 1617.

[21] NERMAN, G. 'Hjalmare Kanals Historia.' Uppsala. 1910.

[22] ENGELS, H. Ann. Trav. publ. Belg., **1**, 120–73, 1843.

WAUTERS, A. 'Documents concernant le Canal de Bruxelles à Willebroeck.' Brussels. 1882. Personal communication from DR O. GORTEMAN of Brussels.

[23] VIFQUAIN, J.-B. 'Des voies navigables en Belgique.' Brussels. 1842.
RIVE, B. L. DE. 'Précis historique et statistique des canaux et rivières navigables de la Belgique.' Brussels. 1835.

[24] The most convenient general reference for German canals is O. TEUBERT (see ref. [8]). More specialist studies include KLEHMET (see ref. [16]), R. WREDEN (see ref. [8]), and M. ECKOLDT (see ref. [8]).

[25] A detailed history of the Hjälmar canals is given by G. NERMAN (see ref. [21]).

[26] For the Gota canal and the navigation of the Gota river, including the Trollhatten canal, see T. TELFORD (see ref. [6]) and
SKJOLDEBRAND, A. F. 'Description des cataractes et du Canal-de Trollhatta.' Stockholm. 1804.

[27] WILLAN, T. S. 'River Navigation in England 1600–1750.' University Press, Oxford. 1936.
SKEMPTON, A. W. Trans. Newcomen Soc., 29, 1953 (in the press).

[28] Standard works on the French canals of the seventeenth and eighteenth centuries are:
LALANDE, J. J. LE F. DE. 'Des canaux de navigation.' Paris. 1778.
POMMEUSE, H. DE. 'Des canaux navigables . . . avec des recherches comparatives sur la navigation intérieure de la France et celle de l'Angleterre.' Paris. 1822.
DUTENS, J. 'Histoire de la navigation intérieure de la France.' Paris. 1829.
BELIDOR, B. FOREST DE. 'Architecture hydraulique' (Vol. 1, Pt II, Paris, 1750; Vol. 2, Pt II, Paris, 1753) has many valuable drawings of canal works.
An important manuscript, 'Traité de plusieurs sortes de navigations' (Bibliothèque Nationale, Paris, MS fr. 18.954, pp. 47–71), was written by HUGUES COSNIER in 1628.

[29] The history of the Briare canal was first accurately worked out by LÈBE GIGUN, "Cosnier et les origines du Canal de Briare" (Ann. Ponts Chauss., 18, 509–57, 1889). His work has been amplified in the definitive monograph of P. PINSSEAU, 'Le Canal Henri IV ou Canal de Briare.' Houzé, Orléans. 1943.
Earlier books, notably H. DE POMMEUSE (see ref. [28]), contain valuable technical details.

[30] PINSSEAU, P. See ref. [29].

[31] POMMEUSE, H. DE. See ref. [28].

[32] TARBÉ DE ST. HARDOUIN, F. P. H. 'Notices biographiques sur les ingénieurs des ponts et chaussées.' Paris. 1884.
See also "Éloge du P. Sébastien Truchet." Hist. Acad. R. Sci., 93–101, 1729.

[33] DAVIDSON, SIR JONATHAN. Presidential address, J. Instn civ. Engrs, 31, 1, 1948.

[34] CHÉZY, A. 'Mémoire sur la vitesse de l'eau conduite dans une rigole.' (MS 1775). Publ. in Ann. Ponts Chauss., 60, 241, 1921.

[35] POMMEUSE, H. DE. See ref. [28]; for Regèmorte see TARBÉ DE ST. HARDOUIN, see ref. [32].

[36] Illustrated descriptions of the Languedoc canal are to be found in J. J. LE F. DE LALANDE (see ref. [28]), M. DE LA ROCHE, 'Atlas et description du Canal Royal de Languedoc' (Paris, 1787), and A. F. ANDREOSSY, 'Histoire du Canal du Midi' (Paris, 1804). RIQUET DE BONREPOS, 'Histoire du Canal de Languedoc' (Paris, 1805), gives a useful historical account based on original documents. Interesting details of the works, as seen by eye-witnesses, are contained in Phil. Trans., 3, 1123–8, 1670, and LOUIS DE FROIDOUR, 'La relation et la description des travaux qui se sont en Languedoc, pour la communication des deux mers' (Toulouse, 1672).

[37] DEVIC, C. and VAISSETE, J. J. 'Histoire générale de Languedoc', Vol. 14, p. 1088. Toulouse. 1876.

18

SHIPS AND SHIPBUILDING

G. P. B. NAISH

I. OARED SHIPS

THE state of the development of the ship at the opening of the sixteenth century is of particular interest. By then, the great modern voyages of discovery had started, opening up the sea-lanes of the world for trade and the spread of western civilization among the peoples who came in contact with it through sea traffic. It has been claimed that great improvements in ships enabled these voyages to be made. Is this true? And if so, what were those improvements? These are important questions. Also we are often told that the warship became doubly formidable by the introduction on board of heavy guns. Our own Henry VIII is given credit for this step. Can this view be substantiated? First let us survey very shortly the types of ships trading and fighting in European waters at the beginning of the century.

The Mediterranean war-galley. The oared galley was the traditional warship of the Mediterranean, but at the beginning of the sixteenth century the type had changed considerably from the galley of classical times. A typical galley as built in Mediterranean dockyards was about 120 ft long on deck by 15 ft beam amidships. The warship was lightly built with a framework of keel and ribs covered by planking placed edge to edge, called in the north carvel-built. The deck was only 5 or 6 ft above the keel. From 1290–1540 the popular war-galley was called a trireme. There were 25 to 30 benches a side and three oarsmen sat on each bench, every man pulling a separate oar. The thole-pins were on the same level in groups of three.

The typical galley had a single deck and was divided into three parts; a fighting-platform in the bows and a sterncastle and cabin aft with the intervening rowing-space divided down the middle by a gangway. The sides were extended by outrigger frames to give the oarsmen suitable leverage. Thus in a hull with a maximum beam of 15 ft there was a space 22 ft × 106 ft for the oarsmen. The benches slanted inwards towards the after end of the ship. The oars were each 29 to 32 ft long and weighed 120 lb. About one-third of the length of the oar was inboard, and this was weighted to balance the outboard portion.

There were low steps in front of the benches so that the oarsman mounted, placed the blade of his oar in the water, and leaned back, bracing his feet against the step.

A single light mast forward carried a lateen or 'latin' sail, the typical triangular sail of the Mediterranean (vol II, pp 584, 586). This sail allowed the oarsmen to rest when the galley was cruising in fair winds, but was furled and hoisted out of the way in action. One large and some smaller guns were mounted in the bows, firing forward under the forecastle platform. There was also a long beak-head with a ram or spike above water. The galley was steered by a rudder hung on the stern-post. In action the galley was manoeuvred to point at the enemy, the guns were fired, and in the resultant confusion the rowers pulled hard until the spike of the beak-head was rammed into the enemy's upper works, serving as a bridge over which the soldiers were able to board the enemy ship. Unlike the classical galley, the later vessel had no underwater iron ram and its oarsmen were virtually slaves, that is, criminals or prisoners-of-war, not volunteers paid extra wages for their labour. In the wars between Christian and Turk the lot of the galley-slave was unenviable. Yet the officers, sailors, and soldiers (some 50 in all) fared little better than the 150 oarsmen. There was accommodation in the cabin aft for the captain, and his great cabin was used as a mess-room by day. The oarsmen lived on their benches at sea, being controlled by whistle and encouraged in times of stress by extra wine or the lash.

The galley was not eminently seaworthy even within the Mediterranean, and was less so in the Atlantic. Under sail it suffered from the weight of the guns forward and from the effect of the outriggers and oars to leeward. But much was accomplished with the galley fleets, which could be handled in calm weather with the purpose and precision that we associate with the steam navies of today.

There were smaller galleys such as the *fuste*, *galeotte*, *bregantini*, and *frégate* or *fregata*. The names are of interest chiefly from their use again in later times. The war-galleys could also be used to carry light and valuable cargoes and important travellers. There were heavier merchant-galleys designed to carry the rich eastern merchandise which was still brought overland to the Levant and reached western Europe by sea from the eastern Mediterranean.

The Mediterranean trading-galley. In the year 1500 the finest merchant-ships in the world were probably the great trading-galleys, by that date mostly of Venice, which could carry about 250 tons of merchandise below decks (vol II, figure 534). These trading-galleys were built with a length six times their beam, as compared with the eight-to-one ratio of the war-galleys. They had three masts and lateen sails. Indeed, although termed galleys, by 1500 these vessels were rowed only with difficulty, reserving their oars for emergencies or for entering or leaving port. Nevertheless, this arrangement had the advantage of enabling the trading-galleys to run nearer to a time-schedule and so to be more dependable than was possible for ships depending on sail alone. Their oars were arranged trireme-fashion and a trading-galley mustered a crew of 200 oarsmen and gunners. Such galleys carried costly wares, which paid high freights.

FIGURE 296—*A Mediterranean galley, a quinquereme with five men pulling at each oar. Guns are carried in the bow. 1629.*

They were powerful vessels and could be defended against pirates, so that some merchants thought it unnecessary to insure goods carried in them.

At the beginning of the sixteenth century the great merchant-galleys from Venice were at the height of their fame, trading to Alexandria and the Holy Land in one direction and Southampton and Bruges in the other. During the second half of the century, however, they gave way to the round ship, but survived for a time as the galleass, the warship under sail and oars which took part in the Lepanto and Armada campaigns.

Why was confidence in the galley diminished at this time? The chaplain who accompanied Sir Richard Guyldforde (1455?–1506) on a pilgrimage to the Holy Land in 1506, sailing from Venice, has left us a journal that enables us to judge the sea-going qualities of these great vessels. For example, his galley preferred to make harbour at night, and in calms or head winds was reduced to anchoring and rolling about at sea. It was not usually rowed, and was incapable of beating to windward. In trying to beat up a strait between two islands the galley was nearly driven ashore when becalmed and wallowing in the swell, and was saved by using oars, obviously regarded as a desperate remedy. A breeze sprang up but the ship was soon almost in the same plight on the other shore. The owners had avoided the cost of the large crew necessary if trained rowers were to be provided, the use of slaves not being practicable in a ship which usually sailed. The improvement in the round ship, that is the sailing-ship, and the rising cost of large crews enforced the abandonment of the galley for general purposes.

In the mid-sixteenth century there was a change in the method of rowing. All the men on a bench tugged at the same oar and a heavy galley could now be propelled much faster. There were sometimes as many as eight men to an oar, but the usual number was five (figure 296). These big galleys were heavily armed but, whether light or heavy, the galley could not now stand the broadside of the sailing-ship. The new full-rigged ship fitted with naval artillery robbed the merchant- and war-galleys of their special advantages, and could keep the sea. Admittedly in 1509 the Venetian trading-galleys, under threat from enemies, had sailed direct from Southampton to Otranto, 2500 miles, in 31 days, but this was regarded as a remarkable feat. Mediterranean powers, however, retained galley fleets throughout the seventeenth century and even into the beginning of the eighteenth. In rowing, the slaves grasped the handles fixed to the loom of the oars, and had to obey orders conveyed by the boatswain's silver whistle. They have their epitaph: 'If there is a hell on earth it is in the galleys where rest is unknown.'

II. THE FULL-RIGGED SHIP

Traditionally the round ship had been the cargo-carrier of the Mediterranean, but, except perhaps in a strong breeze, this merchantman had been no match either in speed or in battle-worthiness for the fighting galley. In the development of the sailing-ship during the Middle Ages there had been interplay between the Mediterranean and northern ideas of build and rig, and the result of the borrowing of ideas had been a levelling-out of traditional differences (vol II, ch 16).

The great achievement of the fifteenth century had been the rapid evolution —indeed, the almost sudden appearance—of the full-rigged ship (vol II, pp 585–8). The sailing-ship in the Atlantic in 1400 had been the one-masted cog with one square-sail (vol II, figure 530). About 1450 the three-masted ship blossomed in both north and south, and by 1500 many ships had four masts and a bowsprit (figure 297). Thus there was a minimum of five working sails on a three-master: the spritsail under the bowsprit; the foresail; the mainsail and its topsail; and the mizzen-sail. This type is most often called a carack or carrack.

FIGURE 297—*Broadside view of a four-masted ship from the 'Warwick Pageant'—a series of 53 drawings illustrating the life of the Earl of Warwick (1381–1439) probably made between 1485 and 1490. Each of the fifteen large ships shown is of the carrack type, with overhanging forecastles, 3 or 4 masts, and guns firing over the gunwale in the waist. In the figure a short topmast or flagstaff is shown stepped in the topcastle on the mainmast.*

Its hull was distinguished by the aftercastle and poop-deck, and by the forecastle overhanging the stem. In all carracks the after- or mizzen-mast, or, in the case of four-masters, the two mizzen-masts, carried triangular lateen sails, the typical fore-and-aft sail of the south (vol II, figure 536). The mainmast, foremast, and bowsprit set square-sails, the cross-sails of the north. The mainmast and some-times other masts were in two parts; and the top (originally, it seems, a fighting-top from which to shoot arrows and hurl spears and stones) now carried its own mast and sail.

These ships were carvel-built, in the southern fashion, and had the medial rudder hung from the stern-post developed in the north. During the sixteenth century southern ships preserved certain features that were later abandoned in favour of the northern practice. For example, the ends of the deck-beams protruded through the sides of the ship; the shrouds had no ratlines, and access aloft was by a rope-ladder up the mast. Further progress in the design of the sailing-ship was so slow, especially by comparison with this startling sixteenth-century development, that it is necessary to consider what the ship had gained by multiple masts. The change was probably brought about by the increasing size of ships. Merchants wanted bulkier cargoes carried for greater distances with greater security, and big ships were easier to defend against pirates. They could also carry adequate stores for long voyages. For such ships the single square-sail used in the north was unsuitable. A divided sail-plan was stronger, but for long the mainsail and foresail, the 'courses' or 'corps' as they were called, were much bigger sails than the others. They were the driving-sails, with the topsail as a flying kite. The spritsail and mizzen were found valuable aids to the steering. The ship was manœuvred with a smallish, narrow rudder, and by setting or furling the sails at the ends of the ship the rudder was eased or the ship's head forced round.

It should be noticed that the ship could not sail any closer to the wind with many sails than with the original single square-sail, but sail could be more easily increased or taken off and the ship was handier. Thus the new full-rigged ship was fit for the great voyages of discovery: the hull could hold the people and stores, while the divided sail-plan meant that the ship could be managed more safely off unknown shores and was stronger for a long ocean voyage.

Such long ocean voyages are in fact the impressive achievement of the full-rigged ship. Voyages across the Atlantic, to India, and round the world explain how it was that the Venetian galleys sailed no more up Southampton Water. Trade with the east no longer came to northern Europe by sea from the eastern Mediterranean. Even if the Venetian state had not been ruined by wars on land, its old trade would still have become redundant.

It is uncertain as yet whether the carrack, the new armed full-rigged merchant-man, was primarily a northern or a southern type. There is something to be said for calling it an Atlantic type, since many features, especially the greater size which encouraged the improved rig, seem to have come from the ship-wrights around Bayonne, whose work impressed both North Sea and Mediterranean ship-owners. The one-masted square-rigged northern cog had already been copied in the Mediterranean; the lateen mizzen may well have been introduced to the ocean trader from the Portuguese caravels of the type sent by Prince

Henry the Navigator (1394–1460) down the African coast. These little caravels were lateen-rigged on two or three masts and were very suitable for coasting-voyages (vol II, figure 533). They were used for trading and fishing on the coasts of Spain and Portugal, and are often mentioned in the journals of the Elizabethan seamen compiled by Hakluyt. In the second half of the sixteenth century the caravel often carried a square-sail on the foremast. The fore-and-aft rig proved itself more suitable for coasting-voyages and traffic between islands (witness the West Indian schooners of the eighteenth century), while the square rig was more suitable for crossing oceans. For example, in Columbus's voyage in 1492 the *Nina* was a caravel re-rigged at the Grand Canary as a ship. It must be borne in mind that a square-sail, if well set, will point up to windward as close as a fore-and-aft sail.

Official records, such as customs-house returns, prove the general increase in the size of merchant-ships during the fifteenth and sixteenth centuries; the bigger ships during the former century were often out of Spain. From our own Paston letters a correspondent reports in 1458 'sixteen great ships of forecastle' which were Spaniards, and later a correspondent reports the arrival in the Seine of '200 great fore-stages [forecastles] out of Spain'.

By 1500 ships of 600 tons were becoming quite common. Although it is agreed that the development of the full-rigged ship made practicable the voyages of discovery to America and India and the circumnavigation of the world, it must not be supposed that the actual ships in which the great voyages were made were especially fine specimens of the new type. It is well known that Columbus's three vessels were chosen and manned with very little care. In 1518 the five vessels of Magellan's voyage were all bought at Cadiz. 'They are very old and patched', wrote a contemporary, 'and I should be sorry to sail even for the Canaries in them, for their ribs are as soft as butter.' The *Victoria*, the only one of the five that completed the voyage, was a vessel of 85 tons. Little is known about Drake's *Golden Hind* of *c* 100 tons, but she was some 75 ft long over-all by 20 ft beam, and was regarded as a stout vessel by the Spanish captives who reported on her. That Drake could dine off silver plate to music in his own cabin is surprising when one considers that such a small vessel carried some 60 persons. No doubt the new type of ship made long voyages possible, but much human courage and skill were needed too.

To follow the development of the ship, we may consider the navy of Henry VII and VIII, composed of ships of both northern and southern origin.

The full-rigged ship that now held the seas was a combination of Mediterranean and Atlantic shipbuilding practices. Much of the credit for combining the two must go to the ship-wrights of Spain, Portugal, and Brittany. Hulls began to be proportioned on the 'one, two, three' rule of the Spanish caravel, in which traditionally the length of the hull was three times the beam, which in turn was twice the depth. In sailing-ships, unlike galleys, there was no marked difference between the warship and the merchantman, for all ships went armed. Hence the ships that Henry VIII built or bought for his Royal Navy are truly representative of European shipping. He not only employed Italian ship-wrights but obtained ships from Genoa, from Spain, and from the merchants of the Hanseatic league.

Carrack and bark. In 1512 Henry's biggest ship, the *Regent* of 1000 tons, built in 1489 on a French model, armed with 151 iron and 29 brass guns, and manned with 400 soldiers and 300 mariners, grappled the French *Cordelière*, a great carrack of Brest. The French ship caught fire and they blew up together. In Henry's fleet the larger ships, of 800 to 1000 tons, were often called carracks and the lesser, of from 200 to 400 tons, barks. In a contemporary picture of a French carrack two round gun-ports are shown low in the broadside. The other, heavier guns fired over the gunwale in the waist, in the old style.

Henry determined to replace the *Regent* with a larger ship of 1500 tons, called successively while building the *Great Carrack*, the *Imperial Carrack*, and the *Henry Imperial*, and christened or hallowed as the *Henry Grâce à Dieu*, shortened to the *Harry* or the *Great Harry* (plate 21 A). Big ships were a common manifestation of national pride. Henry may have been answering the challenge of the Scottish *Great Michael* of 1506. The *Harry* carried 195 guns and 900 men. One or two of her guns were heavy ordnance. The ship was chiefly armed with 134 serpentines, the common naval cannon; these were small breech-loading guns in which chambers containing the charge of gunpowder were wedged against the breech of the gun. The inventory of the *Harry* shows her to have had four masts, with topmasts and topgallant masts on all save the bonaventure, or after mizzen-mast, which had a topmast only. In 1545 the *Harry* was rebuilt as a smaller ship of 1000 tons, having now a crew of 800 men and 151 guns, 19 of them heavy ordnance with a ball of 60 lb. In 1553 she was accidentally destroyed by fire at Woolwich.

III. HENRY VIII'S ROYAL NAVY, 1546

A pictorial list of 1546 divides the Royal Navy into four categories: ships, galleasses, pinnaces, and barges. There are twenty ships of from 60 to 1000 tons. Although called ships, they are all of carrack type with high castles. Heavy guns fire through gun-ports low in the side. The smallest is the *George*, a four-master of 60 tons.

The fifteen galleasses are drawn without oars, have lower castles, and beak-heads like galleys; their foremasts are stepped farther aft and heavy guns are mounted well up in the bows. They measure from 140 to 450 tons, and the smallest is a three-master. The square transom is a feature of the ships and galleasses. The old-fashioned round stern continued, and in the next century became popular for small merchant-ships called flutes or fly-boats. The ten pinnaces (measuring from 15 to 80 tons) have hulls similar to the galleasses and

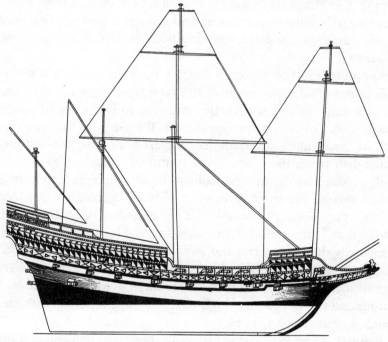

FIGURE 298—*Elevation and sail plan of an English galleon, c 1586. From a manuscript by Matthew Baker (1530–1613), Master Ship-wright under Elizabeth I.*

are three-masters, the fore and mizzen being without tops and the mizzen stepped right aft. The thirteen oared barges of 20 tons each are little galleasses with oars.

The *Subtile* is a typical Mediterranean one-masted galley, fitted out by Venetian ship-wrights. The fifteen ships called galleasses are of a new type, having a galley's beak-head in place of the carrack's overhanging forecastle (plate 21 B). Four of them, the *Antelope*, *Tiger*, *Bull*, and *Hart*, had been built in 1546—as had the thirteen barges. These four represent the latest design for a warship of between 200 and 300 tons. The *Tiger* has a broadside of eight guns, and one or two very heavy guns in the bow firing over the beak-head, as in a galley. The main mizzen-mast has a half-top abaft the masthead, which is also galley-fashion. These four galleasses are flush-decked, in marked contrast to the high-charged carracks. The galley beak-head was a feature of the galleon, an important new type of vessel developed at this time. The so-called galleasses of Henry VIII's navy would thus appear to have been elementary galleons.

The Galleon. The galleon was a type of superior fighting-ship invented by the Portuguese. A large Portuguese galleon, the *São João*, was used in the attack on Tunis in 1535. Contemporary pictures show a four-masted sailing-ship, without oars, mounting a broadside armament and having a galley's beak-head. This beak-head could not be used for ramming because of the bowsprit, which was lashed down to it.

In the second half of the sixteenth century both the Spanish and the English were building powerful men-of-war of this new type, rigged in the same way as the big sailing-ships of the period, but with the hulls longer in proportion to their beam and with lower castles fore and aft. We are told that the galleon had a keel-length of three times the beam, as compared with the old-fashioned twice or two-and-a-half times the beam of the round ship (figure 298).

The galleon was one of the first sailing-ships to be regarded primarily as a warship. She carried her main armament of heavy guns on a gun-deck, firing them through gun-ports in the sides. This gun-deck was not suitable for a merchant-ship, as it interfered with cargo space. Her length and reduction in top hamper made the galleon fast and more weatherly than the carrack. She was described as race-built, while the older ships were known as high-charged. Not all fighting seamen welcomed the galleon, for ships were still carried by hand-to-hand fighting and the castles of a high-charged ship, bristling with small guns, were defended against boarders as castles were defended ashore.

In the Spanish Armada campaign of 1588 there were galleons on both sides. When the Armada sailed from Lisbon it contained 101 vessels of 150 tons and over; the warships included two squadrons of galleons, four Mediterranean galleasses, and four galleys. The galleys were driven into port by stress of weather, and the galleasses proved no match for the English warships. Among the twenty galleons of different sizes were those of Portugal under the Duke of Medina Sidonia and those of Castile under Diego Flores de Valdés. The latter were the galleons of the Indian guard, whose usual service was to protect the treasure-fleets. The *San Martin* and *San Juan* measured 1000 tons and the *Florence* 951, whereas the smallest were of 250 and 350 tons. The dimensions of the larger galleons would have been about 160 ft long over-all, 120 ft on the keel, and 40 ft beam.

An English galleon was the *Ark Royal*, the flagship of the Lord High Admiral, who esteemed her highly and thought her 'the odd ship in the world for all conditions'. Under construction for Sir Walter Ralegh when bought into the Royal Navy in 1587, she was of 800 tons and carried 44 guns. Her ship's company of 425 comprised 300 fighting seamen and 125 soldiers. For comparison, the Spanish *San Martin* had 177 seamen, who were not expected to fight, and 300 soldiers. The *Ark Royal*'s guns included 4 cannon, firing 42-lb balls, and 4 demi-cannon, shooting 30-lb balls. There were 12 culverins (18-pounders), 12 demi-culverins, and 6 sakers (6 lb). The *Ark Royal* was a four-master, with a main topgallant mast (although the inventory of 1588 mentions only the sail). The mainsail and foresail each had two bonnets and a drabbler, which were additions laced on to the body of the sail or course. The main-mizzen and bona-venture-mizzen had two bonnets each. The main tie, that is, the rope hoisting the mainyard, was 40 fathoms of 8½-in rope; the main brace was 70 fathoms of 3-in. The martinets (p 486), for furling the mainsail, were of 1-in rope. The ship carried three bower-anchors weighing 20 cwt each, and a sheet-anchor weighing 22 cwt. She had nine anchor-cables of 17- and 15-in circumference.

The hull was sheathed below water against the ravages of the ship-worm (*Teredo navalis*), probably with elm boards ½-in thick over layers of Stockholm tar and hair of equal thickness. The boards were then nailed in place with broad-headed nails driven in close together. This was the most approved English fashion. The *Ark Royal* sailed no closer than six points off the wind and probably made good seven points.

The average size of the English hired merchant-ships serving against the Armada was 200 tons. The big trading-vessel was still of the high-charged car-rack type, an example being the Portuguese *Madre de Dios* captured by the English and brought into Dartmouth in 1592. She was of 1600 tons, carried 900 tons of merchandise, and had a crew of 600 or 700. We are told that at sea her helm required the labour of 12 or 14 men at once in the steerage. When measured by Robert Adams (1540–95), a 'surveyor of the Queen's buildings', she was found to be 165 ft long over-all, 100 ft on the keel, and 46 ft 10 inches in beam. She drew 31 ft of water when fully laden, but only 26 ft when she entered Dartmouth. Her mainmast was 121 ft high and 10 ft 7 inches in circumference at the deck. Her mainyard was 106 ft long. Her captors admired 'the hugeness of the whole, far beyond the mould of the biggest shipping used among us either for war or receipt'.

The spritsail-topmast. In 1600 the English East India Company chartered four merchant-ships for the Company's first eastern venture. Ships of 600 and 300 tons were chosen, and their inventories show a sudden development in the rigging of ships. Unlike ships of the same size that fought the Spanish Armada, they were all three-masters and carried at the end of the bowsprit the little mast, the spritsail-topmast, and its sail which make the ships of this century so easy to recognize in pictures.

FIGURE 299—*Head of a scale model of an English 90-gun ship, c 1670, perhaps by the ship-wright Sir Anthony Deane (1638?–1721). These earlier ship models were unplanked, but reproduce the beautiful decoration of the period in miniature. The figurehead is a man on horseback. The head-rails, connected by brackets, sweep up to the cat-heads. Five full-length human figures decorate the beak-head bulkhead. The circular gun-ports under the forecastle are surrounded by carved wreaths joined by a painted frieze.*

IV. THE SHIP IN THE SEVENTEENTH CENTURY

The evidence for tracing the development of the ship now becomes much fuller. There are many pictures by good artists, mostly Dutch or Flemish (plates 22, 23). Manuscript sources are more numerous and detailed; good textbooks and nautical dictionaries were published. Sheer-draughts and other plans are elucidated by the fine scale-models which were made in great numbers towards the end of the century, not least by English ship-wrights (figure 299, plate 24 A, B). The new interest in mathematics and science led to attempts to improve the design and build of ships, as well as the sail- and rigging-plan. During this century warships were being built steadily larger, in order to be able to carry more guns. Merchant-ships did not follow this example, 200 tons remaining a general average for ocean-going ships in most trades; yet the great companies, such as the East India Companies of England, Holland, and France, employed larger ships of up to 600 tons or even more.

The galleon type of hull prevailed with a greater length-to-beam ratio than formerly, and low fore- and after-castles. The fore-part of the forecastle ended in a square bulkhead beyond which extended the beak-head, formed by the curved stem and cut-water protruding forwards and finished by the figurehead, with the head-rails on either side (figures 299, 304). It was usual to lay the decks in three sections at different levels, separated by bulkheads under the breaks of the fore- and after-castles. This arrangement allowed more headroom for cabins fore and aft, but the breaks or steps in the decks weakened the hull and it became more and more the custom to have flush decks running from end to end of the ship without break or step. However, in small ships which were more strongly built such breaks to improve accommodation below decks were retained. Reduction of the after-castles made the ships labour less in a sea-way, and it became possible to let in light and air to the officers' accommodation in the stern by fitting stern and quarter galleries and stern windows.

The hulls were strengthened along the sides by the wales, thicker planks running longitudinally, especially at the water-line. Even thicker planks, the chain-wales, were fitted at intervals higher in the side of the hull, and were used to spread the standing rigging, that is, the shrouds and backstays supporting the masts. This standing rigging was set up with dead-eyes and lanyards. The lower dead-eyes were fastened to the chain-wales or channels by means of chains or plates fastened to the hull below. The dead-eye was a round wooden block, with a strop or eye round it and with three holes for the lanyard. Naturally the setting up of the shrouds when the rope had stretched or shrunk was very important to ensure the safety of the masts. Shrouds were being set up with dead-eyes and chains from the first half of the sixteenth century. The masts were set up in three pieces, the lower masts, topmasts, and topgallant masts, and were held together by the tops, trestle-trees, and caps. The forestay and other stays between the masts held them from raking aft. Ratlines up the shrouds made ladders up which the men climbed aloft.

The heavy work of the ship—getting a topmast on end, a gun or the longboat on deck, or weighing the anchor—was done by means of a capstan, a vertical spindle passing through the decks and carrying a barrel or barrels hove round by men pushing capstan-bars fitting into sockets (figure 305). Smaller ships used windlasses, in which case the spindle was fitted athwartships in the bows. The cat-head was a timber sticking out over the bows with sheave-holes in it (figure 299);

through these a tackle was rove and the cat-block at the other end of this tackle carried a great iron hook which was fitted to the anchor ring. A second timber was temporarily rigged out from the forecastle when required, and was called the fish-davit; this was used to hoist and secure the flukes of the anchor, when it was said to be catted and fished.

Wooden ships strained and leaked, especially when old, and rain-water penetrated the decks. Hence pumps were very important. Chain-pumps were fitted to larger ships and the common hand-pumps supplemented the chain-pumps. At the end of the sixteenth century hammocks,[1] first seen by sailors in Brazil, were introduced on board ship. The cook-room was in the hold on a bed of

FIGURE 300—*Fore part of a longitudinal section of a first-rate ship, drawn by Edmund Dummer, Surveyor to the Navy 1692–8, showing the gun-decks, the orlop deck, and the hold below. Under the forecastle are the galley-stove and cook-room. The riding-bitts to which the anchor-cables were attached are on the lower gun-deck beneath the galley.*

brickwork, and as work had to be done by candle-light the danger of fire was considerable. It therefore became increasingly common to locate the galley (as it was later called) under the forecastle before the belfry (figure 300). Ship's time had long been regulated by a bell, and during the seventeenth century the usual position of this bell in important ships was transferred from the break of the poop or after-deck to the break of the forecastle. The large ship was steered below decks by means of the helm or tiller, a wooden beam socketed into the rudder-head. This was controlled by tackles attached to the sides of the ship. In fine weather the whip-staff was used. It was attached to the end of the tiller and passed through the deck above, leading through the rowel, which was a wooden bull's-eye fitted across a hole in the deck in trunnions allowing it to swing. The helmsman standing on a platform could get a glimpse of the deck and sails through a skylight ('hatch') above his head. He grasped the whip-staff and by

[1] Spanish *hamaca*, a Carib word.

pushing it from side to side could work the tiller below, which naturally moved in the opposite sense. In front of the helmsman was the bittacle or binnacle, the box that held the compass and the sand-glass that timed the watch or 'trick' at the helm.

There was little difference in the rig of ships of different nationalities, but very noticeable differences in the style of hull-form and decoration became more pronounced as the century progressed. For example, Dutch ships in order to reach Amsterdam must pass over the shallow and dangerous waters of the Zuider Zee; thus large Dutch vessels were shallower and broader of beam than English and French ships. This is made very clear by a stern view of a Dutch ship. The small merchant-ships of the different countries were very similar. A common type, called a pink, had a broad apple-shaped stern where the planking was worked round to fit the stern-post, and, above, a small square flat transom with stern windows. These pinks were very roomy for their small size.

At the beginning of the century some big ships were still given four masts; one such was the *Royal Prince* of 1200 tons, built by Phineas Pett at Deptford in 1610. A painting, however, shows that she carried a square topsail over both the main- and bonaventure-mizzen sails, which were lateen sails (plate 22). In 1637 the *Sovereign of the Seas* (plate 23, and see p 486), a great ship of 1522 tons built by Peter Pett at Woolwich, had three masts, with topmasts and topgallant masts on all three, topgallant-royal, or royal, masts on the fore and main, and flag-poles above on all three. If not invented by the poets, the names of these new masts were certainly thought poetical. A poet sang of this same *Sovereign*:

> Whose brave Top top-top Royal nothing bars,
> By day to brush the Sun, by night the Stars.

The smaller ships quickly followed the fashion set by the greater, and ships generally, though with only three masts instead of four, gained a great quantity of running rigging to control the more divided sail-plan.

A square-sail was made of lengths of canvas sewn together with the seams vertical. It was roped all round, and rope eyelets or cringles were worked into the corners and other places where ropes must be attached to the canvas. The sail was made fast to the yard by seizings called rope-bands or robins. The yard was hoisted by a halyard, held to the mast by a truss and parrel; its angle to the wind was controlled by brace and lift. The lower corners of the sail were held by sheets, and the courses had both tacks and sheets, the tacks being tapered ropes leading forward while the sheets led aft (figure 306). The sails were furled by men going aloft and tying them down close to the yard, but as a preliminary they were clewed up by clew-lines attached to the lower corners (clews) of the sails, and further gathered up by the leech-lines, running to the leeches or outer edges, and the bunt-lines going to the bunt or belly of the sail. At the beginning of the century ropes called martinets were fitted to the leeches, but the way in which this was done is not quite clear. When sailing close-hauled the weather leech, that is, the leading-edge of the sail, was pulled taut by the bow-line. The square-sail is not necessarily an inefficient one under which to work a ship to windward.

From the middle of the seventeenth century the sail-area of ships was increased by triangular fore-and-aft sails set on the stays between the masts. These were called stay-sails. The area of the square-sails was increased in fair winds by the addition of extensions called studding- or stun-sails. During the first half of the century bonnets and drabblers began to be replaced by a system of reducing sail by reefing. Bonnets were attached to the bottom or foot of a sail; when reefing, the top or head of the sail was gathered up and a strip was tied to the yard by the reef-points, which were lengths of line fitted across the head of the sail at the depth of the reef required. To tie down a reef, men had to climb out along the yard, often in heavy weather, and foot-ropes began to be fitted under the yards as a convenience. The picture of the *Royal Prince* at Flushing, painted in 1623 by Vroom (plate 22), shows reef-points in the spritsail-rigged boats or yachts. Although the rigging of a ship was becoming more complex, this fact is apparently belied by contemporary pictures. The complicated system of crowfeet was largely abandoned; this was a method by which a stay was set up to a mast or another stay by an elaborate arrangement of multiple tackles. These clumsy devices disappear from English ships after the Restoration, which suggests that the cogitations of the Royal Society and kindred bodies had some effect on the thoughts of the humble sailor or ship-wright devising a new sail-plan.

Three-masted ships, large or small, were rigged very much alike and seem to have developed together, with the larger ships slightly in the lead. In fact, it is probably fair to claim that in England the *Sovereign of the Seas*, notorious because the ship-money collected to build her helped to lose for Charles I his kingdom and his head, was a great help to the country's mercantile interests by teaching improved ship-wrightery. The same effect probably resulted from the building of large ships by the state in other countries.

V. SHIPBUILDING

Early shipyards consisted of little more than a storehouse erected on a plot of firm ground near, and with access to, a river or other sheltered water of sufficient depth at high tide to float the vessel to be built. Ships were commonly built as near as possible to the supply of timber and also as far as possible from the open sea, to obtain shelter both from gales and from enemy fleets. The preparations for building the *Henry Grâce à Dieu* (plate 21 A) at Woolwich in 1512 are probably typical of the building of a big royal ship anywhere in Europe. Houses, ground,

and a wharf were leased, and ship-wrights and mariners were brought to Wool-wich from different parts of the country, as were bakers and brewers and quan-tities of provisions. 1987 tons of timber, mostly from Essex and Kent, were given to the king by dignitaries of the church and state to build the ship, with its great-, cock-, and jolly-boats, and three galleys. Ship-wrights, carpenters, and sawyers were sent out to work in the woods. Black-smiths set up forges to make the nails, spikes, chains, and bolts. Cables, hawsers, ropes, ratlines, marlines, and caulking also had to be prepared. The workmen were housed and bedded, and one Robert Bregandyne presided over all, with a house and office. Watchmen were placed on guard over the stores, which now included pitch, tar, and rosin.

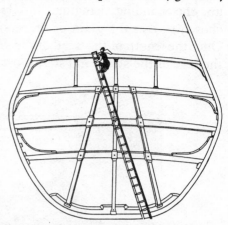

FIGURE 301—*Mid-ship section of a galleon, c 1586, from Matthew Baker's manuscript, showing the 'tumble home' or narrowing of the ship's breadth above the water-line. The figure shows frame-timbers, deck-beams, lodging knees, and struts.*

Then the planks began to arrive and the masts were made, as well as the blocks and parrels, or wooden beads through which were threaded the ropes holding the spars close to the masts. Much money was paid 'for sundry colours, for painting of tops, sails, and images on the *Harry Grâce à Dieu*'. Some of this material arrived in carts and the rest was landed at the wharf from lighters. Hoys, crayers,[1] and other coasters brought guns, anchors, and spars from as far away as Dartmouth, Southampton, and Rye. Thomas Spert, the ship's captain, supervised the mariners who were making the sails and rigging the ships and the three galleys. These galleys were constructed from spare material, left over from building the large ship, which would otherwise have been wasted.

Robert Bregandyne, 'clerk of the King's ships', is believed to have designed the *Henry Grâce à Dieu*, but unfortunately his plans have disappeared. Ship-wrights were not alone in making a mystery of their trade and handing down

[1] Small trading-vessels.

from father to son the secrets of designing and building ships. The first comprehensive textbooks on shipbuilding began to be published at the end of the seventeenth century. In designing a wooden ship the nature of the timber, mostly oak, had to be considered. The planking, perhaps 6 in thick, had to be worked and bent round the bow and stern. The upright timbers had to be built up, the standing, hanging, and lodging knees made from parts of the tree chosen so that the grain of the wood ran with the shape required (figure 301). Once the length of the tread of the keel of a new ship had been decided upon, and the rake of the stem- and stern-post determined (that is, the angle fore and aft at

FIGURE 302—*Drawing-office with Tudor ship-wrights at work designing a new ship. The man on the right is measuring with a large pair of compasses preparatory to drawing the long curves which give the shape of the ship's hull. From Matthew Baker's manuscript, c 1586.*

which these two posts should lean or rake), then the shape of the hull depended chiefly upon the drawing of the mid-ship section. To make this drawing, a number of suitable sweeps or arcs of circles were drawn from different centres and the different curves were reconciled with lines joining them up (figures 302, 303).

The ship-wright's art in the sixteenth century and later lay chiefly in not departing too drastically from the secret and proved mid-ship section of some tried and successful vessel built by the same master ship-wright, his firm, or his family. Few calculations were made, and Samuel Pepys (1633–1703) tells us that his friend Sir Anthony Deane (1638?–1721) was the first naval architect to be able to foretell, from working out the weight of material built into a ship and her volume, the draught of water required to float her ready for launching. To avoid disaster, therefore, one ship was built much like another and the develop-

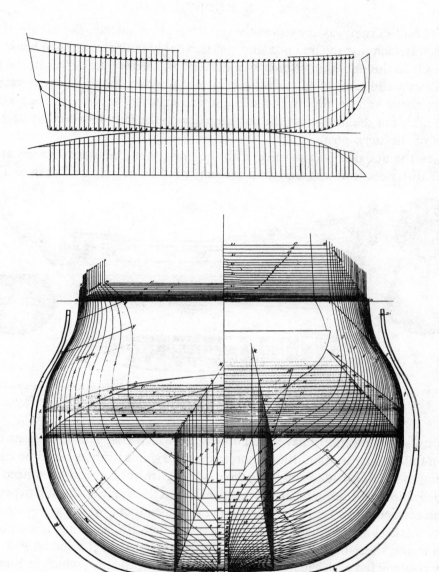

FIGURE 303—Sections for laying down on the floor of the mould-loft. This had a spacious floor, very smooth and even and well lit, which was large enough to contain the curves of the ship's timbers drawn upon it with large compasses called sweeps. The figure represents every timber from stem to stern of a ship of 1000 tons drawn to scale (⅛-in to 1 ft in the original). These curves would be transferred full-size to the floor of the mould-loft.

1711.

ment of hull-design was consequently very slow. Fortunately, the nature of the timber was such that the hull of a ship was inevitably built streamlined below the water. Once the mid-ship section was decided upon, the fair curves of the hull were drawn and reconciled with the help of a wooden spline, taken at various heights above and parallel to the keel and arranged between the three stations of the rabbet of the stem-post, the chosen place on the mid-ship section, and the rabbet of the stern-post.

When the designer was satisfied with the lines, then the other sections at the proper distances from the mid-ship section could be plotted and drawn. Then

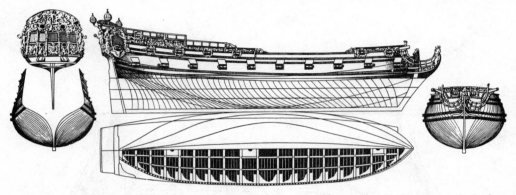

FIGURE 304—*A fifth-rate ship 'of yᵉ largest Dimensions', from a drawing by William Keltridge in a book of plans (1684). Division of naval vessels into 'rates' was introduced by Samuel Pepys (1633–1703).*

a table of offsets seems to have been drawn up, which enabled the sections to be drawn full-size on the mould-loft floor, so that the ship's timbers could be cut according to moulds made from these drawings (figure 303). It will be noticed that wooden ships were designed inside the planking, as the shape of the hull depended on the correct cutting and shaping of the frame-timbers, which were attached across the keel and formed the framework to which the planking was nailed.

From the sheer-draught and body-plan (figures 304, 305) a model was probably constructed with the framework carefully made to scale, which in England was generally ¼-in to 1 ft. The model not only showed the prospective owners what their ship was going to look like, but recorded the decoration agreed, the distribution of gun-ports, and the placing of capstan, cat-heads, and other fittings (figure 299, plate 29 A, B). From before 1700 more models than draughts of ships have survived; these models have not been altered and must therefore be fair copies of draughts, or perhaps rather of the tables of offsets from which ships were built. The offsets were in turn worked out from rough draughts only to be understood by the ship-wrights, who wished to keep secret the exact dimensions of the ships they built.

Models were made of new buildings on shore from very early times. Model

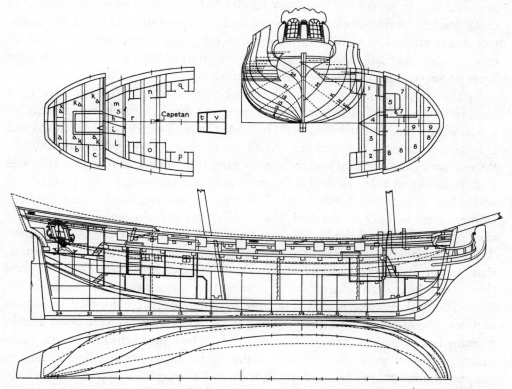

FIGURE 305—*Manuscript draught of the* Shark *sloop, built at Portsmouth in 1732. She was evidently rigged as a brigantine with two masts, that is, like a ship without a mizzen-mast. Often a mizzen-mast was added to a brigantine later. At this time the plans of a ship were commonly drawn on a single sheet of paper. Here are seen a profile of inboard and outboard works, half-breadth plans, body plans, and accommodation plans. Aft; (a) great cabin; (b) bed-place; (c) clerk's office; (k) bread-room below cabin; (l) carpenter's store-room; (m) steward's room; (n, o, p, q) cabins of the surgeons, lieutenants, gunners, and the master; (r) sail-room and (s) fish-room below the platform; (t) shot-lockers; (v) well. Forward; (1) boatswains; (2) carpenters; (3) paymaster; (4) passage; (5) fireplace and (6) stone hearth; (7, 8, 9) boatswains', carpenters', and gunners' store-rooms under the forecastle and fireplace.*

ships for the same purpose are frequently mentioned after 1600, and many survive, especially those of English warships after 1650. In view of the lack of scholarship usual among contemporary ship-wrights, it was probably very necessary to see a model before ordering a new ship. In 1668 John Evelyn (1620–1706) witnessed the launch at Deptford of the *Charles*, 'built by old Shish, a plain honest carpenter, master builder of this dock, but one who can give very little account of his art by discourse, and is hardly capable of reading, yet of great ability in his calling. The family have been ship carpenters in this yard above 300 years.' The French Admiral de Tourville (1642–1701) noted with approval that in seventeenth-century England ship-wrights were accustomed to make models of ships before they were built. Ship-wrights of other countries, too, made models to show a ship's construction, and sometimes models of an existing ship that had become famous. Fortunately many of these models have been preserved and can be seen in museums.

In the sixteenth and seventeenth centuries most ships seem to have been built in docks. These were constructed partly by digging, partly by building up a wall with stakes and stonework. At low tide the dock-gates could be closed and if necessary the dock pumped dry. When newly built or repaired, a ship could be floated out of the dock on a high-water spring tide. The keel of a new ship was laid on blocks in a dry dock and the stem-post and stern-post were erected and scarfed on to the keel at either end. This was the heaviest work. Then the floor timbers were laid across the keel; the keelson was laid along the keel on top of the floor-timbers; and the keelson, floor-timbers, and keel were bolted together. The floor-timbers were straight except at the ends, where they began to compass, that is, to turn upwards. The futtocks were next attached to the floor-timbers; these were the curved or compassing timbers that formed the curved sides of the ship. The timbers were placed very close together, and were doubled amidships and near the masts where a great strain was expected. Clamps were heavy planks running horizontally on the inside of the timbers to support the ends of the deck-beams. Partners were strong pieces of timber bolted across the deck-beams to support the masts, the heels of which were to be stepped on top of the keelson. The frame was further held together with a multitude of standing, lodging, and hanging knees, all made of oak. The ship-wright always searched for crooks of timber, which he cut up most carefully to avoid waste. The elaborate construction of the bow and stern was designed to resist the straining of the rudder and the anchor-cable as well as the battering of the seas.

While under construction the hull was shored up and a staging was built round it on which the ship-wrights could work. The planking was fastened to the timbers by wooden pegs or tree-nails made of heart of oak and driven in with a wad of oakum to stop any leaks. Reckoning the outside planking, the timbers, and the inside planking or ceiling, the sides might be almost 2 ft thick. The outside planking was carefully caulked with oakum between the seams. This heavy construction left unventilated spaces between the timbers, and as ships were built in the open so that rain-water lodged in the hull, conditions were favourable for wood-rot. Fortunately, most ships had much reserve strength in their massive build. It is difficult to realize the amount of wood, mostly oak, that went to build a big ship. A large warship required some 2000 oak-trees, each of them needing a century to reach maturity; wood which had matured more quickly was unsuitable for ship-building because it split too easily. These trees could not have been grown on less than 50 acres of woodland, which would be left stripped.

The weight of timber used accounts for the difficulties always facing the builder in launching a new ship. If the tide was not high enough to float the heavy hull out of the dock it was very difficult to shift it with wedges, screws, and winches. For this reason, though it remained usual to build large ships in docks, all other sizes were constructed above the water-level on hard ground. When the hull was ready a cradle was built round it; launching-ways were laid towards the water; the cradle was supported on the greased ways; the keel-blocks were removed; and the ship was ready to be launched down the greased ways at high water.

The new ship would be taken alongside a sheer hulk to have her masts stepped, after which she would be rigged. The buoyant wooden hull would have to be ballasted before it could be safely sailed.

Tonnage. The tonnage of a ship was an arbitrary figure meant to indicate the carrying-capacity of a ship engaged in the Bordeaux wine trade. The unit was a tun of wine in two butts of 252 gallons, estimated in 1626 to occupy 60 cu ft, allowing for the waste space due to the shape of the casks. In 1626 a ship 63 ft long and of 26 ft beam was calculated to measure 207 tons by the 'old' measurement, which gave her average cargo-capacity or net tonnage, and 276 tons by the 'new' measurement calculated to discover her dead-weight cargo-capacity or gross tonnage. The calculation of tonnage led to the invention of different rules and formulae worked out empirically, for the science of the time was unequal to extracting the exact measurement, which has become possible only in modern times.

VI. DECORATION

The decoration of ships is not functional and may therefore seem to be of little importance, yet it meant a great deal to both the ship-wright and the seaman, perhaps in different degrees. It also had a national significance. Proud ships suggested a disdain of enemies very encouraging to morale. The most costly decorations were to be found upon vessels owned by the king or the state. The fighting-galley of the Mediterranean often sported a profusion of fine works of art in the form of large gilded figures entwined around the stern and quarters. Throughout the sixteenth century the ships in northern waters were principally decked out with paint-work and very little carving: perhaps a series of blind archways or panels along the side and at a height above the water-line to continue under the gunwale at the waist, painted in bright colours. This frieze was sometimes of a geometrical pattern, and often was a design of entwined straps picked out in paint. The figureheads were generally small heraldic beasts crouching at the end of a galleon's beak-head. An example is Drake's *Golden Hind*, renamed after the crest of Sir Christopher Hatton, which one imagines must have adorned this famous ship as a figurehead. A coat-of-arms might be painted on the upper part of the flat stern. On occasion all ships flew many pennants, streamers, and banners.

In the seventeenth century ostentatious display took control. It would seem that the ship-wright wished to embellish his work with heavy gilded ornament for which the sailor had little use. We find naval officers complaining that a heavy figurehead and even heavier quarter-galleries made ships labour at sea. The excellent pictures of the *Royal Prince* of 1610 (plate 22) and the *Sovereign of the Seas* of 1637 (plate 23) show how Charles I surpassed his father in expense; Charles II, although always short of money, was even more extravagant. The ships of all the other European countries reveal the same disregard of nautical convenience. The men-of-war show us elaborate figureheads, such as men on horseback trampling their enemies, women and cherubs being drawn in chariots by eagles, and many other full-length figures disporting themselves both fore and aft, with carved wreaths round the circular upper-deck gun-ports, elaborate belfries like sumptuous summer-houses or well-heads at the break of the forecastle, and with the bulkheads at the break of the poop, quarter-deck, and forecastle richly adorned (figures 299, 304). Merchant-ships were plainer but gallant enough. These ships look beautiful to modern eyes, but the carving must have got in the way at sea and served no functional purpose. Charming features were the hancing-pieces, little figures such as crouching hounds or sleeping babies, which fitted into the step where the rail abruptly altered height at the break in a deck. The originals of this fine carving have all disappeared long ago, but much remains in well executed miniature on contemporary models; the best examples are English. At the end of the seventeenth century the exuberance of ship-decoration was fairly generally curtailed in all European countries, as much because of change of taste as from any real dislike of the great additional expense which all these countries had willingly borne for the last century at least. Nevertheless, the ship-wright continued to place as much carving on a hull as he dared, and the sailor to complain of useless weight on bows and stern of his ship, which should be kept light and seaworthy.

VII. DEVELOPMENT OF THE SHIP, 1700-50

Considering the many signs of an increasing interest in the theory and practice of shipbuilding which showed themselves in the seventeenth century, it is

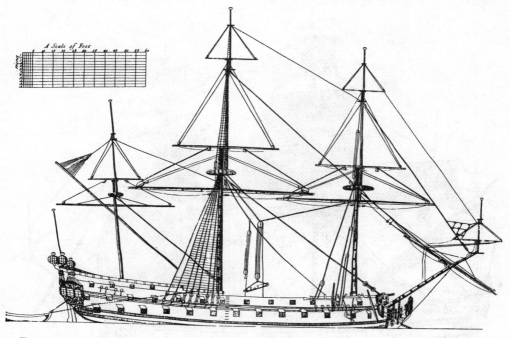

FIGURE 306—*Rigging plan showing masts and spars, with standing and running rigging, from Sutherland's work on shipbuilding of 1711 which names each item.*

somewhat surprising to note how slowly the ship developed during the next. The reason is probably that the wooden sailing-ship had been so far developed empirically by seamen and ship-wrights—naturally conservative when faced by the changeless conditions of the sea—that by 1700 it had nearly attained the peak of perfection then possible. For example, a large ship of some 2000 tons had practically reached the maximum size possible for purely wooden construction. It is noticeable that, when new methods of construction and propulsion took the western world by storm in the nineteenth century, the sailing-ship was for long able to hold her own, even against what proved to be overbearing odds, with minimum changes in her style.

Merchant-ships remained on the whole smaller than warships, a great many being still of about 200 tons to 400 or 500 tons. The finest merchant-ships were those employed by the English East India Company, of some 600 or 700 tons. Popular ships for long voyages were galley frigates, small ships built for speed which could be rowed in calms. They were not so heavily armed because it was hoped that pirates and other enemies would be evaded by superior speed. The

FIGURE 307—*Plan of sails and running rigging from the same work (1711). The two diagrams show fully and clearly the rigging of an English ship (to which that of Dutch and French ships was very similar) in 1700, before the spritsail topmast had been replaced by the flying jib-boom.*

ships of the various European countries had become more and more alike in general appearance, because national differences were being obliterated by the cosmopolitan sailorman.

A few characteristic changes in ship's rig became noticeable at the beginning of the new century (figures 306–9). Square mizzen topsails and topgallant sails were often set. There were now commonly two or three rows of reef-points in the fore and main topsails, and one or two rows in the mizzen topsail and fore and main courses. The heads of the topsails had become squarer, that is, broader, and the sails were deeper in comparison with the courses. The use of fore-and-aft staysails between the masts has been mentioned (p 486); now the spritsail top-mast began to be abolished in favour of the jib-boom, sticking out from the bow-sprit end to boom out the tack of the new flying jib. In England the jib was adopted in the Royal Navy in 1702 and the spritsail topmast officially abolished from the rig of big ships in 1715. The awkward interim period is difficult to

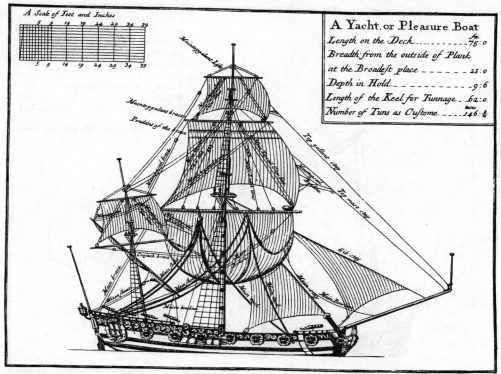

FIGURE 308—*Yachts were vessels of state used to convey kings and their representatives. They were introduced into England from Holland at the restoration of Charles II (1660). His royal yachts were manned by the Navy. By 1700 large yachts were ketch-rigged, that is, like a ship without a foremast. 1717.*

understand, especially as pictures and models show both the topmast stepped and the jib-boom in place, a seemingly impossible combination. The spritsail top-mast, though derided by seamen today, held its own and can be seen in con-temporary pictures—generally of Dutch whaling ships—until well into the century, but probably not after 1750. The steering-wheel was introduced about 1705, according to the evidence of English models in the National Maritime Museum at Greenwich. The cumbersome whip-staff, already described, was effective only in fine weather, for a sudden heavy sea could wrest it from the hands of the helmsman. After 1705, in bad weather the tiller was controlled by tackles led to the drum of a winch which was turned by the steering-wheel on the quarter-deck.

The fashion in decoration also changed at the turn of the century and a figure of a lion, crowned or uncrowned, became very popular. The name of Dutch

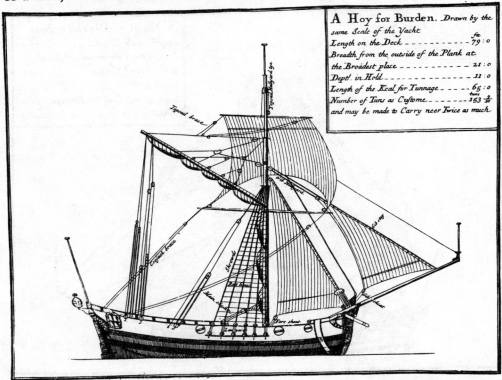

A Hoy for Burden. *Drawn by the same Scale of the Yacht.*
Length on the Deck - - - - - - - - - - - 79 : 0
Breadth from the outside of the Plank at the Broadest place - - - - - - - - - - - 21 : 0
Dept! in Hold - - - - - - - - - - - - - 11 : 0
Length of the Keal for Tunnage - - - - 65 : 0
Number of Tuns as Cuſtome - - - - - - - 153 ½
and may be made to Carry neer Twice as much

FIGURE 309—*During the seventeenth century some coasting-trade was carried on in hoys, beamy fore-and-aft-rigged vessels, with square-sails for running before the wind. 1717.*

ships was indicated by a coat-of-arms or device carved on the upper part of the flat stern. This was called the tafferel or taffrail, meaning a picture. The stern and quarters of ships were decorated with lighter, simpler carvings, which became even more delicate as the century progressed. Heavy gilt carvings were abandoned except by the royal yachts (figure 308) and important men-of-war. The broadside under the rail was decorated with a painted frieze, interrupted by the upper-deck gun-ports.

Merchant-ships still sailed fully armed against pirates and other enemies. Of smaller vessels working on the coasting-trade, the hoys were fore-and-aft rigged (figure 309), and the herring-busses were square-rigged on three masts. Many two-masted brigantines and snows sailed from Baltic and Spanish ports. The snow[1] was the larger type, and was in fact almost a three-master, for a rudimentary third mast, the trysail-mast, was stepped just abaft the mainmast and from it was set the fore-and-aft mizzen-sail of the full-rigged ship.

When we consider the fine voyages of discovery and scientific investigation carried out by Dampier and Halley, or of privateering by Woodes Rogers, we can understand something of the capabilities of the little ships of the period when they were well handled. Big ships also progressed. In 1744 the *Victory*, of 100 guns, was wrecked on the Casquets—a three-decker at sea in November. This loss was attributed by many to folly and lamented accordingly, yet in 1759 Admiral Lord Hawke won the battle of Quiberon Bay, fought in another November gale, with his flag flying in the *Royal George*, a three-decker like the *Victory*. Well handled, well found ships were now invincible, except on a lee shore, where sailing-ships are always vulnerable. Presumably the experienced seaman would shun lee shores, but this precaution was not always possible. It is worth remembering that the sailing-ship, however well designed and constructed, was at sea always dependent on the seaman and the pilot. Without the power of the steam-engine, a sailing-ship was inevitably endangered under certain conditions. The master, caught out on a lee shore, was only reckoned at fault if his ship had driven ashore with an anchor and cable unused.

BIBLIOGRAPHY

ABELL, SIR WESTCOTT S. 'The Shipwright's Trade.' University Press, Cambridge. 1948.

ANDERSON, R. C. 'Seventeenth Century Rigging.' Marshall, London. 1955.

ANDERSON, ROMOLA and ANDERSON, R. C. 'The Sailing Ship.' Harrap, London. 1947.

BLANCKLEY, T. R. 'A Naval Expositor.' London. 1750.

BURWASH, DOROTHY. 'English Merchant Shipping 1460–1540.' University of Toronto Press, Ohio. 1947.

CAMDEN SOCIETY. 'The Pylgrymage of Sir Richard Guylforde to the Holy Land, 1506' (ed. by SIR HENRY ELLIS). Camden Society Publ. no. 51. London. 1851.

CORBETT, J. S. 'Drake and the Tudor Navy' (2 vols). London. 1898.

CRONE, G. C. E. 'Onze Schepen in de Gouden Eeuw.' Patria. Vaderlandsche cultuurgeschiedenis in monografieën no. 19. Amsterdam. 1939.

EAST INDIA COMPANY. 'The Court Records of the East India Company, 1599–1603.' London. 1886.

FALCONER, W. 'An Universal Dictionary of the Marine.' London. 1769.

LANE, F. C. 'Venetian Ships and Shipbuilders of the Renaissance.' Johns Hopkins Press, Baltimore. 1934.

---

[1] Dutch *snaauw*.

LA RONCIÈRE, C. DE. 'Histoire de la Marine Française' (2nd ed.), Vols 2–4. Plon, Paris. 1914–23.

LAUGHTON, L. C. 'Old Ship Figureheads and Sterns.' Halton and Truscott Smith, London. 1925.

NAVY RECORDS SOCIETY. 'The Naval Tracts of Sir William Monson' (ed. with comm. by M. OPPENHEIM), Vol. 1. Publications of the Navy Records Society, Vol. 22. London. 1902.

Idem. Ibid., Vol. 5. Publications of the Navy Records Society, Vol. 47. London. 1914.

Idem. 'Autobiography of Phineas Pett' (ed. by W. G. PERRIN). Publications of the Navy Records Society, Vol. 51. London. 1918.

Idem. 'Life and Works of Sir Henry Mainwaring' (ed. by G. E. MAINWARING and W. G. PERRIN), Vol. 2. Publications of the Navy Records Society, Vol. 56. London. 1922.

Idem. 'Boteler's Dialogues' (ed. by W. G. PERRIN). Publications of the Navy Records Society, Vol. 65. London. 1929.

OPPENHEIM, M. 'The Administration of the Royal Navy, 1509–1660.' London. 1896.

SOCIETY OF NAUTICAL RESEARCH. *The Mariner's Mirror.* The Quarterly Journal of the Society of Nautical Research, London. 1911–.

Idem. 'A Treatise on Rigging *c.* 1625' (ed. by R. C. ANDERSON). Occ. Publ. Soc. naut. Res., No. 1. London. 1921.

Idem. 'Lengths of Masts and Yards etc., 1640' (ed. by G. S. LAIRD CLOWES). Occ. Publ. Soc. naut. Res., No. 3. London. 1931.

SUTHERLAND, W. 'The Ship-builder's Assistant.' London. 1711.

TATO, J. F. G. 'La Parla Marinera en el Diario del Primer Viaje de Cristobal Colon.' Instituto Histórico de Marina, Madrid. 1951.

WILLIAMSON, J. A. "The two ships named *Great Harry.*" *Blackwood's Mag.*, **195**, ii, 205–15, 1914.

Idem. 'Hawkins of Plymouth.' Black, London. 1949.

## 19

CARTOGRAPHY, SURVEY, AND NAVIGATION TO 1400

CHARLES SINGER (I–VI), DEREK J. PRICE (VII), AND E. G. R. TAYLOR (VIII–XI)

I. NUMERICAL NOTATION

IN antiquity all activity in building, engineering, surveying, and many other techniques encountered an obstacle of a kind quite unfamiliar to us. This was the clumsy numerical notation to which the ordinary rules of arithmetic could not be directly applied. Astronomers, it is true, could employ the sexagesimal system which had been in constant use from early Babylonian times (vol I, ch 31). This gave ease of operation without the necessity of expressing any single number greater than 60. In ordinary life, the application of simple arithmetic, especially multiplication and division, was a laborious operation for which the help of the abacus or some other sort of counting-device had to be invoked. Not every intelligent man, even in the educated class, could carry it out; but such simple calculation is of special importance in connexion with surveying and map-making.

The earliest and simplest reckoning-apparatus was a board sprinkled with sand divided into columns by the finger, counters being used in calculation. Cicero, referring to this operation, speaks of an expert calculator as 'clever at handling the sand'. The counters, which could be shifted from column to column, had graven on them figures of the fingers and hand in various positions accepted as representing different numerical digits. These symbols remained in general use till late medieval times, and are still employed as Roman, as opposed to 'Arabic', numerals.

The true abacus began as a board with a series of grooves in which pebbles or *calculi* could be moved up and down: hence our word calculate. The form of the Greek abacus is obscure, but the more developed Roman type is well known and is still in general use in the east. It had an upper row of short and a lower of long rods (vol II, figure 694). Each short rod had a single perforated bead running on it, and each long one had four such beads. The first rod on the right was marked for units, the next on its left for tens, and so on to a million.

Our own decimal system of 'Arabic' numerals, giving each numeral a value according to its position and using a sign for zero, is of Indian origin although the ultimate source of its component inventions is a matter of some dispute. It reached Europe through Islamic channels during the revival of astronomy in the Middle Ages (p 521), but was not generally adopted, except for astronomical purposes, before the sixteenth century. The Greeks, whose numerical use of letters of the alphabet was almost as clumsy as the Roman system, often employed geometrical methods where we employ algebra, but their mathematical developments made little impression on the Romans. How slight was the mathematical knowledge, even of scientific authors, among the Latins may be gathered from the *Geometrica* and *Arithmetica* ascribed to Boëthius (480–524), 'the last of the ancients'. These elementary works represent the immediate mathematical legacy of classical antiquity to the earlier Middle Ages. Even when Rome had world dominion, Cicero bemoaned that 'the Greek mathematicians lead the field in pure geometry, while we limit ourselves to the practice of reckoning and measuring'.

II. TYPES OF MAP

Early maps are broadly divisible into four classes or grades. First there are rough outline pictures of a limited terrain with which the observers were familiar. Children and savages make sketches of this kind. If based on some kind of measurement they may reasonably be called maps. More exact surveys on these lines were constantly made in the ancient empires. Good specimens have survived from Egypt and Mesopotamia (vol I, figures 364, 367, 385). The Greeks regarded the Egyptians as the originators of geometry, or Earth-measuring, which was made necessary by the periodic obliteration of landmarks by Nile floods. Such surveys, of varying accuracy, were also made by the Greeks and Romans for the purposes of town-planning and for the legal establishment of ownership of property, but none seems to have been preserved.

Secondly, there are plans of part of the Earth's surface made on estimates of distances and directions reported by travellers—usually on the basis of time consumed in travelling—and collected by the map-maker. Maps of this kind were necessary to many major officials, especially in the centuries when the Roman Empire was at its greatest. They might be made either with or without a system of projection. True maps of neither type are known from classical antiquity, but we have something which is even more informative. About the middle of the second century Ptolemy (Claudius Ptolemaeus) of Alexandria, who well understood the principles of projection, wrote a 'Geography' possibly provided with maps. This book has come down to us, with the relevant measurements, so that though the original maps are lost they can be reconstructed. Ptolemy's work is considered below (p 508).

Thirdly, we may for the present purpose consider as maps plotted itineraries that act as guides to travellers by recording places and distances graphically but not directionally. We have surviving traces of these, as, for example, in the Peutinger table, to which we shall refer (p 515; figure 320).

Fourthly, and yet more marginal to technology, though sometimes described as 'maps', are attempts to represent the whole Earth, or even the universe. The place of these is in histories of science, of philosophy, or of religion.

III. THE CARTOGRAPHER'S TASK

For measurements on a larger or geographical scale the ancients were much less well equipped than for surveying in the proper sense. The ancient geographer, or rather his informant, could determine latitude by elementary astronomical observations either of the meridian transit of a star by night, or of the Sun's noon height at the equinox by day (ch 22). A very much more difficult problem was the determination of longitude. For this it is necessary to compare the local times of an astronomical event, such as an eclipse, either by having observers in two widely separated places or, by using standard tables, to compare the computed time at the place where the ephemerides were drawn up with the observed time in the place in question. The ancients, having no independent accurate timekeeper, never conceived of the measurement of longitude by using a portable chronometer; this was left for Gemma Frisius (1508–55) to suggest and to John Harrison (1693–1776) to achieve. The astronomical measurement of latitude was therefore reasonably accurate and satisfactory, but the complementary determination of longitude was much more arduous and inherently much more inaccurate (see table, p 583).

Thus for all longer journeys, whether by sea or land, the ancients depended almost entirely on some form of dead-reckoning, a method which is inherently unreliable. This is among the several reasons for the distortion of ancient maps. The principle of triangulation, however, had long been familiar. Trigonometry had been formally inaugurated by Aristarchus of Samos (third century B.C.), but could not be applied for sufficiently great distances. Despite such discouraging obstacles, the general problem of the form of the countries of the Empire urgently demanded some sort of solution. The determination of the frontiers of provinces, the demands of trade, the distribution of the fleet, all made the need of a general map of the Empire evident. None of the Roman maps, however, has survived, though we learn of them from Cicero (106–43 B.C.), Vitruvius (fl A.D. 1), Seneca (d A.D. 65), Pliny (d A.D. 79), Suetonius (c A.D. 121?), and others. Earlier still, Varro (116–27 B.C.) indicates the ancient religious associations of such documents, for he relates that a map of Italy, engraved on marble, had a place in the temple of Tellus at Rome.

Julius Caesar (100–44 B.C.) planned a complete survey of the Empire. Like his calendarial reform, it was perhaps suggested by ideas emanating from Alexandria. In the event, the execution of the scheme fell to Augustus. The survey was finally superintended by Augustus's son-in-law Marcus Vipsanius Agrippa (63–12 B.C.) and was completed in 20 B.C. after nearly thirty years' work. Agrippa wrote a commentary based on this map. It was fairly accurate for the provinces of Italy, Greece, and Egypt, but other countries were only very roughly surveyed. The survey was possible because the Empire was furnished with roads marked out with milestones (vol II, figure 463) and patrolled constantly by a regular service of skilled *agrimensores* or land-measurers. Their work, incorporated in the reports of provincial governors, became available at headquarters. From this mass of material a huge map was prepared, which was exhibited in Rome in a building erected for the purpose. It was perhaps the basis of later strategical surveys, a surviving copy of one of which is known as the Peutinger table (figure 320).

Some idea of the manner in which the main routes of the Empire were surveyed may be gained from certain monuments, notably the inscribed marble pillar of Autun (*Augustodunum*). This gives—or gave, for most of it is now lost—the distances of places on the road from Autun to Rome, such as *Autissiodorum* (Auxerre), *Bononia* (Bologna), and *Mutina* (Modena). Somewhat similar inscriptions have been found in Belgium, Spain, Britain, and elsewhere. Of special interest to English readers is a bronze bowl from Rudge Coppice (near Marlborough) in Wiltshire, around the edge of which are written, in second-century script, the names of a number of sites on Hadrian's wall.

IV. ESTIMATE OF THE SIZE OF THE EARTH

An essential to map-making on the geographical scale is some conception of the form of the Earth. Pythagoras (fl c 531 B.C.) held that it was a sphere, and this doctrine was firmly established by the teaching of Plato (c 429–347 B.C.), Eudoxus (c 370 B.C.), and Aristotle (384–322 B.C.). The spherical form of the Earth was commonly accepted by the educated public from then onward—even, in spite of statements to the contrary, through the Middle Ages (p 518).

This idea once grasped, any major part of the Earth's surface could be represented only by the acceptance of some geometrical operation of projection, as is now familiar through the use of lines of latitude and longitude. It happened that the fourth century B.C. was not only a period of great mathematical advance by the Greeks but a period of rapid expansion of their knowledge of the Earth's surface and of its inhabitants through the activities of merchants, explorers, and military ventures. This widening horizon was especially due to the conquests of Alexander and the journeys and writings of his generals, admirals, and other officers. Good use of this new information was made by Dicaearchus (fl *c* 300 B.C.), a pupil of Aristotle. He sought to make a map of the known world as related to a parallel of latitude through Gibraltar and Rhodes, extending eastwards through the Caspian Gates—not far from Teheran in Persia—and along the base of the Hindu-Kush (figure 311). This line is, on the whole, notably correct.

Eratosthenes (*c* 275–*c* 194 B.C.), librarian of Alexandria, is, however, the real father of projective mapping, basing it on his own brilliant feat of measuring the globe (figure 310). Eratosthenes sought to make geography a science. He adopted the parallel of Dicaearchus but also drew a second, though less accurate, parallel from Ethiopia to south India. In doing this he regarded their latitudes as similar because of the supposed similarity of their climates, plants, animals, and peoples. Between these two parallels he fitted the reported Indian distances, thus twisting the Indian peninsula to point south-east. The over-estimated Indus was supposed to follow a southerly direction, with its mouths pulled far south of the tropic, together with the coast of the fish-eaters (Ichthyophagi) of Baluchistan, and most of the Persian Gulf. Thus the mapping worked along from India, resulting in many errors that were transmitted farther west.

Eratosthenes made his famous measurement of the Earth on the assumption that it was a perfect globe (figure 310). He presumably started with three propositions:

(*a*) That at Syene on the Nile (the modern Aswan) at noon on midsummer day an upright rod casts no shadow, being on the tropic.

(*b*) That Syene is 5000 stades from Alexandria.

(*c*) That Syene is directly south of Alexandria.

Now it is clear that, if we consider the Earth as a sphere, then the ratio

$$\frac{\text{angle at centre subtended by 5000 stades}}{\text{four right-angles}} = \frac{\text{5000 stades}}{\text{circumference}}.$$

The problem is, therefore, to determine the angle at the centre subtended by 5000 stades. But if on midsummer day the shadow cast by an upright rod at

Alexandria is measured, then we shall be able to estimate the angle that the Sun's ray makes with the rod. Since, however, the Sun is so vastly distant from the Earth, the Sun's ray at Alexandria is in effect parallel to the Sun's ray at Syene. Therefore the angle that the Sun's ray makes with the rod is equal to the angle subtended by 5000 stades at the Earth's centre. There is thus but one unknown—the Earth's circumference—in our equation. The circumference of the Earth so obtained is a very fair estimate. The angle to be measured was found to be 1/50 of four right-angles. Since the distance between Alexandria and Syene was 5000 stades, the circumference of the Earth was 50 × 5000 = 250 000 stades. Eratosthenes was aware of various chances of error, and in fact Aswan is not on the tropic but 37 miles north of it, and not on the same longitude as Alexandria but three degrees east of it. Bringing his figure up to 252 000 stades, he reckoned 700 stades to a degree.

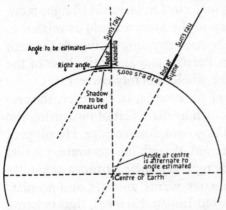

FIGURE 310—*Eratosthenes' method of measuring the length of a degree of the meridian, from which the circumference of the earth was calculated.*

Unfortunately, it is not certain what the stade meant exactly to him or to other geographers. It was 600 'feet', but there were variants according to the foot-standard used, while long distances were not actually measured but interpreted into stades from the time taken to cover them. Writers of Imperial Rome counted at the rate of $8\frac{1}{3}$, or roughly 8, stades to their mile. Assuming that Eratosthenes was reckoning in terms of these ordinary stades his grand total is some 12–14 per cent in excess. At ten stades to the mile it is nearly correct.

On the globe thus measured Eratosthenes proceeded to fit the known world by calculating its north–south breadth and east–west length along two great lines intersecting at Rhodes (figure 311). The breadth extended from the Somali coast —for the torrid zone was known to be habitable so far south—to Thule near the Arctic circle. The length along the great parallel worked out at 70 800 stades from Cape St Vincent to the mouth of the Ganges, or, with allowances for the projection of India and possible islands, at 78 000. This is only about two-fifths of the way round the globe on that parallel. What of the remaining three-fifths? Sailing west from Spain, would there be open sea to India or some 'outer dwellers' on the way?

The work of Eratosthenes was reviewed by the great astronomer Hipparchus, who made observations from 161 to 126 B.C. He attacked the procedure in detail, and stressed the need of a better groundwork of observations. He could add some latitudes from the work of explorers, but the weak point of ancient geography was always lack of longitude determinations (p 503).

Any interest the Romans might have had in science would have found plenty of scope in geography. The Empire, as established by Augustus in 27 B.C., en-

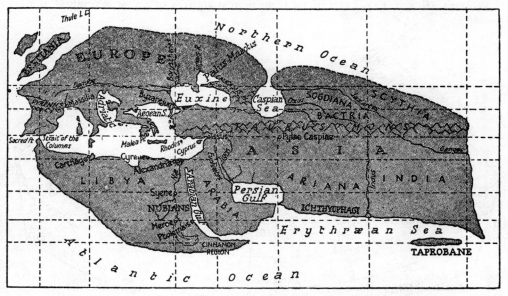

FIGURE 311—*The world, reconstructed according to Eratosthenes' ideas.*

joyed two centuries of almost unbroken peace. Civilization spread, travel was safe, and there was much mingling of races. Writers of the time, impressed by the size of the Empire, often spoke as if there were nothing but a barbarian fringe beyond. Though the Romans did little exploration for its own sake, some of their traders went beyond the legions, while others sailed to India; even of China a little was heard by land and sea. There are several works of Imperial times that add to our knowledge of geography, but very few did anything to advance the technique of map-making.

V. THE PTOLEMAIC MAPS

Important for map-making, however, was Marinus of Tyre (*c* A.D. 120). His 'Correction of the Map' used the latest reports to extend the map far to the east and south. His results were sometimes extravagant because he did not allow for the exaggerations, halts, and divergences of travellers. He had a very simple sort of projection, with parallel meridians drawn at right-angles through degree-points spaced in due proportion along one important parallel—that through the island of Rhodes. His successor Ptolemy, who alone records the work of Marinus, permits this method, but does so only for maps of provinces, because within such small areas the distortion is not considerable.

Ptolemy (fl A.D. 121–51), one of the greatest figures of ancient science, made

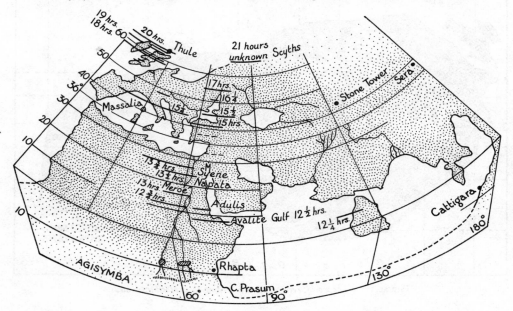

FIGURE 312—*The world according to Ptolemy, using his first projection.*

an elaborate effort to map the known world. His maps are lost (p 510) but he provided ample material for remaking them. They can be reconstructed from his figures of latitudes and longitudes, and are surprisingly detailed and reasonably well shaped (figure 312). Even for the map of Ireland, never reached by the Roman legions, he has many names.

Ptolemy was interested in mapping but not in geographical description. In his 'System of Astronomy'—the *Almagest* of the Arabs and of the later Middle Ages —he explained how to put the known Earth on the globe, half-way round in the north temperate zone and extending southward into the torrid zone. He also tells how 'climates' are determined by their longest day and by the length of shadows at the equinoxes, and defines an elaborate series of such climates by lines of latitude up to the Arctic circle (figure 330). In his 'Geography' he insists that mapping should be based on astronomically fixed points, though practically no longitudes were then so derived. The latter he obtained mostly by computation.

Ptolemy's 'Geography' is basically a list of 8000 places, to each of which is ascribed a longitude and a latitude, but the vast majority of these positions are merely reckoned from itineraries. His data provide material for drawing either a set of 26 land-groups, as he recom-
mends, or another of 63 smaller regions, including, for example, 4 provinces in Gaul. Unhappily Marinus and Ptolemy adopted for the circumference of the globe the poor figure of 180 000 stades on the equator, making 500 to the equinoctial degree or 400 on the parallel of Rhodes.[1] This error only partly accounts for the fact that the Mediterranean is exaggerated as 62°, instead of about 45°, but the error yet further accumulates eastwards.

Ptolemy's task was simplified in that he had only to map the 'known habitable world' of his day, which after a critical examination of the data he considered to cover 180° in longitude, 80° in latitude. Hence he could use a modified simple conic projection, taking as his standard parallel that through Rhodes (36° N), a datum line long in use by his predecessors. It has the advantage that, as just mentioned, the spacing of the meridians along it was at the round figure of 400 stades to the degree. For the scientific map Ptolemy suggests two projections. In his construction for the first projection (figure 313) he drew a great circle of the globe (containing 360 units of one degree), the radius therefore being $57\frac{3}{11}$ units. Drawing a tangent cone at 36° he obtained a radius from its vertex of 79 units for the parallel of Rhodes. His northern limit was 63° N, the parallel assigned to Thule, his southern limit $16\frac{5}{12}$° S, a parallel he chose to correspond with that of Meroë at the same distance north of the equator. All the parallels were correctly spaced, and the standard parallel truly divided, the meridians being ruled from the vertex of the cone through these divisions. The second projection shows both the parallels and the meridians (except one) as curved. The

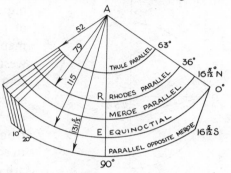

FIGURE 313—*Ptolemy's first method of projection. The scale unit is 1° of the great circle of the globe. The parallel of Rhodes is correctly divided at 5° intervals (each equal to 4 units) and meridians are drawn from A through these divisions.*

[1] See p 506. The accuracy of Ptolemy, as of Eratosthenes, is bound up with the problem of the length of the stade.

same number of meridians is drawn as before, each parallel being correctly divided, that is, spread from four units apart on the parallel of Rhodes to $2\frac{1}{4}$ apart on that of Thule. The improvement is obvious, though there is increasing distortion with increasing distance from the central meridian (figures 314, 315).

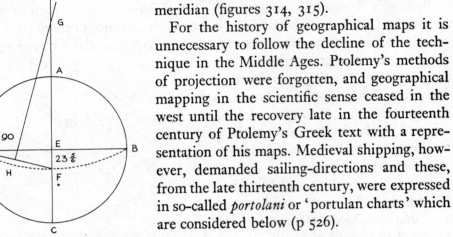

FIGURE 314—*Method of finding the centre for the arcs of the parallels in the second projection. The unit of measurement is 1° of the great circle, that is 500 stades. The radius of the circle ABCD is 90 units; EF is 23 5/6 units, so that E is on the northern Tropic (arc of Syene), and F on the equinoctial (equator). HF (= ½ DF) is calculated as 46 11/20 units. With HG perpendicular to DF, the triangles GHF and DEF are similar, and GF can be calculated as 181 5/6 units. Then G is the required centre and the arc DFB represents the equator.*

For the history of geographical maps it is unnecessary to follow the decline of the technique in the Middle Ages. Ptolemy's methods of projection were forgotten, and geographical mapping in the scientific sense ceased in the west until the recovery late in the fourteenth century of Ptolemy's Greek text with a representation of his maps. Medieval shipping, however, demanded sailing-directions and these, from the late thirteenth century, were expressed in so-called *portolani* or 'portulan charts' which are considered below (p 526).

VI. SURVEY IN CLASSICAL TIMES

For constructing the buildings of remoter antiquity, for much ancient irrigation, and for many other public works, preliminary surveys were obviously needed. None has survived. Mention has been made of land-measurements by the Egyptians (vol I, p 540), and they had ways of determining the horizontal and the difference in height between two points. They are known to have used the plumb-level (vol I, figure 314), the set-square, and several other simple surveying-tools. There still exist an Egyptian sighting-instrument, the *merkhet* (vol I, figure 47), and the remains of a *groma* (figure 316). Such devices passed to the Greeks, Romans, and other peoples.

We cannot discuss all the surveys of classical antiquity, but two famous examples suffice to illustrate the advance in the possibilities of surveying introduced by early Greek science. An inscription records a process of tunnelling by the engineers of Hezekiah, twelfth king of Judah (*c* 715–*c* 687 B.C.). He built the conduit leading water from a spring at Gihon to the Pool of Siloam in Jerusalem *c* 700 B.C. Though the direct distance was only 366 yd, the engineers, to avoid certain obstacles, had to tunnel some 583 yd, with curves in three dimensions.

They had no effective means of mapping their track and were forced to sink shafts to find out where they were. In the end, the two headings nearly missed each other. The completion of the tunnel is commemorated in an early Hebrew inscription (vol I, figure 559).

Greater accuracy was shown in some Greek constructions of somewhat later date. Thus *c* 550 B.C. the engineers of a tunnel at Samos, of about 1200 yd, worked from both ends and met with an error of about 5½ yd (vol II, p 667 and figure 611). Such results could have been secured with the instruments enumerated above (p·510), together with some form of the water-level as described by Vitruvius, who admits that his own methods were of earlier Greek origin. It is probable that the Samos engineers worked on a simple system of triangulation.

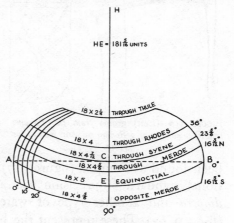

FIGURE 315—*Ptolemy's second method of projection. The projection is centred on the parallel through Syene (the Tropic), the equinoctial (or equatorial) semicircle passing through the points AEB where AB = 180 units, CE = 23 5/6 units. Parallels are correctly spaced on the central meridian HE and correctly divided at 5° intervals. The meridians are curves drawn through the dividing-points.*

Among the Romans the standard of surveying must have been high, as is indicated both by their building achievements and by Vitruvius (ch 10). They held that the art of mensuration was at least as old as Rome itself and that it was first practised by their priests for religious purposes. Familiarity with the processes spread in Imperial times, and a regular school of surveying was established at Rome. The chief instrument in general use was the *groma*, a slight development of the Egyptian instrument (figure 316). One of the lineals was used for sighting, the other to determine the direction in the field at right-angles thereto. Since both agriculture and town-planning were mainly on rectangular lines (ch 11), this instrument was of wide application. It was the custom to erect a *groma* in the centre of a military camp.

The Roman surveyor must have used also an instrument for measuring angles subtended at the eye by two distant points. Its original very simple form was doubtless that of two wooden rods jointed together at one end, each piece provided with a terminal peg or sight at the other. To secure accurate horizontality the surveyor had at his disposal a water-level or *chorobates*. This, as described by Vitruvius, was a straight plank about 20 ft long with supports at the ends,

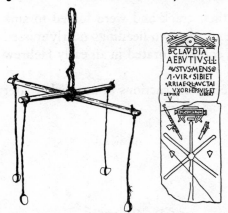

FIGURE 316—(Left) groma *from the Fayum;* (right) *tombstone of a Roman* mensor *found near Turin.*

steadied by cross-pieces. These cross-pieces were marked with lines perpendicular to the plank, which was adjusted till the lines corresponded to plumb-lines. Since wind might disturb the plummets, accuracy was ensured by a groove in the top of the plank, partly filled with water. The height of the water from the level of the plank could easily be measured at either end.

Apart from such instruments as compasses, set-squares, measuring-rods, and chains, these almost completed the ordinary equipment of the Roman surveyor. Some surveying-instruments of the time have been found at Pompeii (figure 317). Whatever the common practice, an exceptional standard of precision was attainable by the use of two instruments, a *dioptra* and another type of water-level described by Hero of Alexandria (fl *c* A.D. 62). These represent the highest development of surveying-apparatus known to have been reached in antiquity (figures 360, 361).

Vitruvius gives a method of estimating the distance from the observer of an inaccessible point on the same level as himself, such as on the opposite bank of a river. A straight line along the near bank is measured by rolling along it a hodometer or 'road-measurer', an instrument consisting of a wheel of measured circumference, the revolutions of which are automatically recorded. From each end of the straight line measured by the hodometer a sight is taken. The angles and the base being thus determined, a triangle, congruent to that formed by joining the point on the far bank to the extremities of the measured line, can be constructed on the near bank. The vertical height of this triangle can be measured, and a simple arithmetical calculation gives the distance of the point from the observer. A comparable device could be used for measuring inaccessible heights (figure 318). The work of Vitruvius was first printed in 1486 at Rome and early circulated in an Italian translation. From it Leonardo da Vinci (1452–1519) doubtless obtained hints that enabled him to design his hodometer (figure 319).

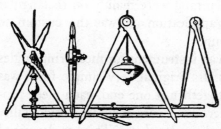

FIGURE 317—*Mathematical instruments found at Pompeii—compasses, calipers, rules, level, etc.*

VII. SURVEY IN THE MIDDLE AGES

During the Middle Ages surveyors continued to use only the most simple direct measurements, with line or rod or pacing for length, and with the *groma*, the plumb-line, and a primitive water-level for setting out right-angles and establishing verticals and horizontals. There are many medieval texts on surveying that describe indirect methods of measuring the height of a tower or an inaccessible wall by the theorem of similar triangles. The most simple of such devices

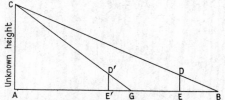

FIGURE 318—*Principle of measurement by similar triangles. If AB, DE, and BE are all known, then*
$$AC = \frac{AB \cdot DE}{EB}.$$
If the distance AB cannot be measured, the staff DE is advanced the measured distance BG and the observation repeated. Then
$$AC = \frac{AG \cdot D'E'}{E'G} = \frac{(AB - BG)D'E'}{E'G} = \frac{AB \cdot DE}{EB}.$$
Hence AB is determined and the first equation can be solved.

is a staff of known height which the observer can use to 'cover' the tower when his eye is in a suitable position. Another simple device is to measure the length of the shadow of the tower at such a time that the Sun is at an altitude of 45°, so casting a shadow equal in length to the height of the tower. More complicated is the use of the shadow-square (p 528), either inscribed on the dorsum of an astrolabe (figure 329), or incorporated into a separate instrument such as a geometric quadrant or a geometric square. Using any of these, it is possible to sight the tower or wall directly, or sight the Sun in order to measure the ratio of shadow-length to object-length at the time of observation. All these indirect methods show considerable ingenuity, and there are many refinements by which the height of the observer's eye is taken into account, or a mirror is laid on the ground so that the viewpoint is accurately established.

Such indirect methods are usually described for measurements in the vertical plane, while similar applications to the horizontal plane are singularly rare. It might be suggested that such technical procedures were too familiar to demand description. A more likely explanation is that nearly all these texts were written by geometers anxious to impress powerful patrons with their skill. But in practice it is seldom necessary to make indirect measurements of heights of buildings. Moreover, such information would have been of little use to the gunner or architect devoid of mathematical skill.

FIGURE 319—*Leonardo's hodometer, counting the revolutions of a wheel of known circumference. The recording by stones dropping into a box is taken from Vitruvius. Similar devices with clock-face recorders were much used in the eighteenth century.*

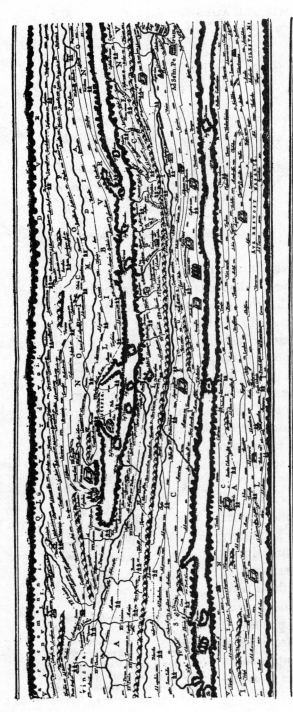
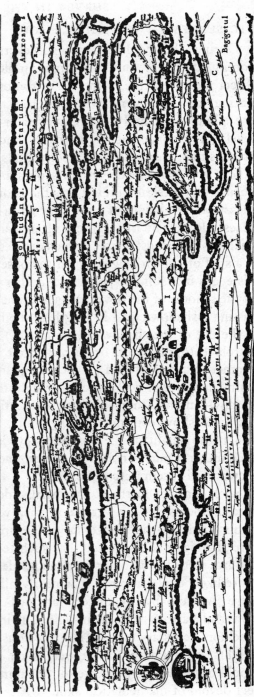

FIGURE 320—A portion of the Peutinger table, showing Italy, the Dalmatian coast (above), and the N. African coast (below). The seas intervening are so schematized that they almost disappear.

One way in which the accuracy of medieval surveying techniques can be assessed is the orientation of churches. Measurement of some 700 of them in Britain shows a standard deviation of the order of $\pm 14°$ about a mean which is 10° N of E. This is a very crude result. It is probable, therefore, that the craftsmen orientated the buildings merely by noting roughly the direction of sunrise at whatever time of year operations began.

Maps prepared by medieval surveyors confirm that only the basic direct measurements of length and right-angles were used. These maps show certain

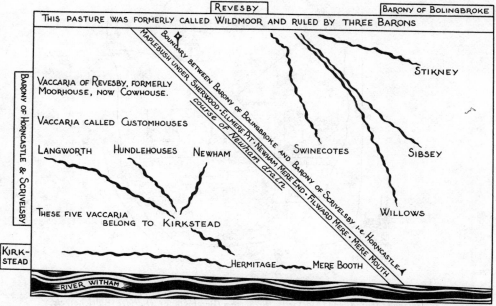

FIGURE 321—*The Kirkstead Abbey Psalter map of cow-pastures* (vaccariae) *north of Boston, Lincs.* c *1300.*

points of similarity with an Egyptian map (vol I, figure 385) and also with the Peutinger table (figure 320). Medieval maps have usually a variable scale, interesting regions being magnified at the expense of the less important. On the whole, however, distances are recorded more accurately than angular bearings. Furthermore, obscurities are often introduced by the addition of views in elevation of buildings, mountains, and other objects of interest which are superimposed on the ground plan (figure 322). Another feature of medieval survey plans is that, although the map may be orientated with E at the top as with *mappae mundi* (p 519), S and W are at the top almost as frequently. In some cases, even, the cardinal points are at the corners of an oblong sheet.

One of the earliest reasonably accurate medieval plans is of the water-works at
Canterbury Cathedral of about 1165 (vol II, figure 628). Such plans are engineers'
drawings rather than surveys proper. The first true survey map—from England
at least—is that drawn up about 1300 on account of a boundary dispute
between two baronies (figure 321). It shows the boundary running along a
ditch leading into the river Witham, with five cow pastures (*vaccariae*) to the
west belonging to one barony and four on the east belonging to the other. The

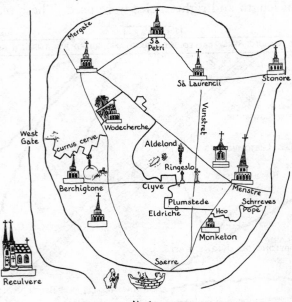

FIGURE 322—*Map of the Isle of Thanet, c 1414. The modern forms of the place-names are easily
recognizable: thus Alland (Aldelond), Birchington (Berchigtone), Oldridge (Eldriche), etc.*

boundary is marked by a shield on a pole which the commission of true and
sworn men set up at the beginning and the end of their survey-walk. All the
vaccariae may be identified from villages and houses marked on the modern map.
The boundary still exists, but the medieval map straightens the course of the
river. The distances on the map are tolerably accurate, but the angles follow the
bending of the river.

A map of the Isle of Thanet of about 1414 (figure 322) shows how greatly
topographical surveying technique had improved towards the end of the Middle
Ages. But despite greater detail and pictorial representation of various buildings
it still shows considerable angular distortion, and the 'island' is almost square
instead of having its length nearly twice its breadth.

It is interesting to compare the features of these topographical maps with those of the navigation-charts, which were drawn with the aid of the magnetic compass. The charts, unlike the maps, render angles of bearings more accurately than distances. Both types were transformed, or rather united, after the development of angle-measuring devices and triangulation-techniques which became necessary in Britain and elsewhere with the sixteenth-century redistribution of the church lands following the Reformation, and with the new geographical knowledge brought by maritime explorations.

VIII. THE WIND-ROSE AND THE CARDINAL POINTS

For survey, cartography, and navigation alike, the underlying techniques rest on a clear understanding of the meaning and measurement of distance and direction, which together establish position. For some purposes, such as drawing a plan or defining a coastwise sailing-route, the correct representation of relative position suffices, but a true map must also show absolute position on the globe. This requires astronomical observations, and the use of a system of terrestrial co-ordinates—parallels and meridians—such as those of Ptolemy.

The decline in the study of astronomy and geography in the Latin world after the separation of the eastern from the western Empire, together with the barbarian invasions, made neglect of such works as Ptolemy's inevitable. Cartography became limited to what may be termed sketch-maps. These were not drawn to scale and were often highly diagrammatic or stylized.

Apart from the Roman mile (1000 paces each of 5 common feet), measures of distance were ill defined, while direction was not precisely determined. It is true that mathematicians since Hipparchus (fl 130 B.C.) had divided the circle of the horizon into degrees, but the layman merely recognized the four quarters of the sky, related to the daily journey of the Sun. The Greeks, however, had early distinguished and used the directions of summer and winter sunrise and sunset, while sailors had given individual names to the most important wind-directions between the four cardinal points.

A scheme which gave to each of the cardinal points two companions had finally evolved as a twelve-fold wind-system or wind-rose. This was current in classical literature, but there was also an eight-fold system mentioned by Pliny, which was probably that used by sailors. It is beautifully illustrated by the octagonal Tower of the Winds at Athens, of the second century B.C. (plate 26 A).

The Germanic peoples who lived in lands where winds were less regular named their winds only from the four cardinal points. When the need arose for indicating intermediate directions they spoke of 'north and east', 'south and west', and so on. These were not thought of as 'points', but as quarters of the sky. The 'and' became elided and we find, for example, Alfred the Great (871–99) using the terms *northan-eastan, southan-eastan* in his translation of the work of Orosius (fifth century A.D.).

It seems likely that there was no further subdivision until the introduction of the magnetic needle in the twelfth century, for only then do we find the terminology that by combinations of the eight wind-names used in the Mediterranean, or of the existing eight compound names of the Germanic languages, gave sixteen-fold and thirty-two-fold systems. Even the thirty-two 'points' or wind-rhumbs had a play of nearly six degrees on either hand, although seamen gradually came to recognize half- and quarter-points.

IX. MEDIEVAL VIEWS ON THE HABITABLE WORLD

The astronomer or the maker of sun-dials could, of course, establish his meridian by the traditional method, that is by marking the position of a pair of forenoon and afternoon shadows of the upright gnomon which had equal length, and bisecting the angle between them. But such knowledge was rare and its application rarer—at sea it was impossible—so that the measurement of direction, like the measurement of distance, remained imprecise. The medieval cartographer therefore did not hesitate to adapt the shape and size of his map, and the position of its particular parts, to the piece of parchment that he was using, or to give prominence, by enlargement, to particular features. The actual shape that he gave to the *mappa mundi*, the world-map, was also a matter of taste. Thus the eccentricities and humours—as they seem to us—of such maps do not carry the implications often nowadays assigned to them. The Christian maps, in fact, were based on those current in the pagan Roman world, and particularly on those accompanying late Latin textbooks, while the general principles of ancient classical geography were accepted.

It is an error to suppose that educated people in the Middle Ages thought the Earth flat. Indeed, the basic fact for the initiated was that the Earth was a sphere, a mere point by comparison with the universe, which itself was bounded by the ever-turning starry firmament. Only one-quarter of the sphere of the Earth was known, and was often itself briefly called 'the Earth'. It comprised three parts, Asia, Africa, and Europe, completely surrounded by the ocean. The suggestion of Crates the Grammarian (c 165 B.C.) was accepted, that it was reasonable to suppose that the three unknown quarters of the globe resembled the known, consisting of inhabited land-masses surrounded by ocean. The people of the southern quarter opposite our own would be 'foot against foot', literally antipodes, to ourselves. There would be an equatorial ocean right round the zone held to be 'unhabitable because of the heat', so that the two southern continental masses could never be reached from ours.

This last point was seized on by St Augustine (354–430) to prove that there could not be antipodes, for it had been promised that the gospel should be preached to 'all men'. The later change in the meaning of antipodes, from a human race to a position on the globe, has here confused an issue and perhaps did so from the first. St Augustine did not reject the spherical shape of the Earth. That matter, however, was deemed to concern the astronomer and geometer

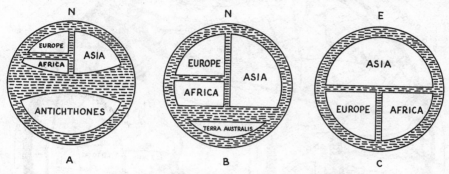

FIGURE 323—*Three types of medieval world map.* (A) *The known hemisphere with two balanced land-masses;* (B) *the* terra australis *has become residual;* (C) *the* Ⓣ *map showing only the known habitable world.*

only, not the geographer and still less the ordinary reader. Thus it was passed over with but slight mention by the Christian encyclopaedists, as for example by St Isidore (? 560–636) in his famous *Etymologiarum libri VII*.

There are three early types of world map: one type gives the whole eastern hemisphere with its pair of known and unknown continents; another shows merely a residual *terra australis*; the third is limited to the known habitable world, variously presented as lenticular, rectangular, oval, or circular (figure 323).

The three-fold division of the world into Asia, Africa, and Europe was effected by the rivers Tanais (Don) and Nile and the Mediterranean Sea, which were stylized into a T of water, giving the well-known OT or Ⓣ map (figure 323 C) after the surrounding ocean had been added. Christian features and symbols were gradually added to this *mappa mundi*, and the orientation was changed so that the east (usually marked by the 'Earthly Paradise') was at the top. As the copying and decoration were entrusted to monastic or professional illuminators, a map was usually embellished with pictures and lively ornaments, especially in large wall-maps, such as the Hereford map (figure 324), intended for royal or ecclesiastical chambers. That many who looked at them, even many who drew them, believed the circle of the habitable world to be the whole world and to be flat, is

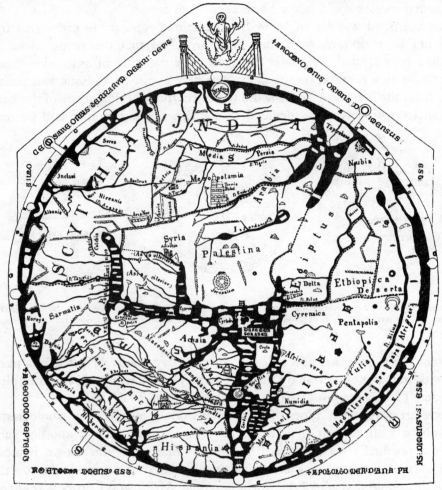

FIGURE 324—*The Hereford* mappa mundi, *much simplified. Jerusalem is at the centre, and the East at the top.* c *1280.*

undoubtedly the case, but the learned clerical world, which had some grasp of mathematics and astronomy, did not lose sight of the truth.

X. MEDIEVAL CARTOGRAPHY

Meanwhile, Greek geometry and astronomy continued to be studied in the eastern Empire, and the leading works were translated into Syriac, or made the subject of compilations in that language. Such, for example, was the oldest surviving treatise on the astrolabe (ch 22), written by Severus Sēbōkht (d 667). The Arab conquest of Mesopotamia, Syria, and Egypt led to the translation of Greek science into Arabic, and to the setting up of libraries and observatories such as those ordered by Al-Ma'mūn (Caliph 813–33) at Baghdad and Palmyra. Learned Muslims and Jews remained settled in the cities of Spain and Sicily after their reconquest by Christendom, and these centres of learning were the principal agencies through which Latin translations of scientific texts were diffused in the western Christian world.

Even more important from the standpoint of technology was the passage to the Latin west of old and new mathematical instruments and tables and, for our immediate purpose, their influence on map-making. The direct Islamic contributions to cartography included modification of the world-map, remeasurement of an arc of the meridian, and compilation of new tables of latitude and longitude. Using the back of the astrolabe the Muslims could determine latitude with precision by taking the mean of the upper and lower meridian-transits of a bright star, or by the noon altitude and tabled declination of the Sun. For longitude they compared the local times of lunar eclipses, using a water-clock.

Since Arabs were settled along the East African coast as far south as Sofala, and traded in the Sudan, they followed Ptolemy in extending the habitable world across the equator, and in placing the lake sources of the Nile in the equatorial region. Their superior practical knowledge also allowed them to open the Indian Ocean towards the Far East, where Ptolemy had closed it (figure 312). They were quite familiar with the idea of a spherical earth, but they were satisfied to sweep a circumambient ocean about the inhabited world as they conceived it, and to place the whole in a circular frame. Their tables of latitude and longitude were used only for astronomical purposes, and covered 90° E and W of an imaginary city (or island) of Aryn, the cupola of the world on the zero meridian and on the equator, treated much as we do the longitude of Greenwich. For convenience, however, the prime meridian was transferred to a point $72\frac{1}{2}°$ W, supposed to be the 'farthest inhabited west', as opposed to the 'true west' in 90°. The earliest tables, those of Ibn al-Zarqālī (known to the Latins as Arzarchel) were compiled at Toledo in the early twelfth century, and translated into Latin later in the same century by Gerard of Cremona (1114?–87). The tables reckoned Toledo as at 11° E, or $28\frac{1}{2}°$ from the 'true west'.

The effect of the impact of the restored Greek and new Arabic learning is well illustrated by the geographical section of Roger Bacon's *Opus Majus* (1264).

Here he points out how much information can be deduced from the latitude of a city or region, and for the first time since Ptolemy he attempts a map in which position is fixed by co-ordinates, although he laments the paucity of data 'among the Latins'. His parallels are set out as straight lines parallel to the equator and at their correct distances as taken from the graduated brass meridian on a globe. They were apparently not chosen at equal intervals, but so as to run through particular cities, where they were intersected by the appropriate meridians, running from the equator to the pole. A red circle round the point of intersection showed the precise position of the city, in striking contrast to their indication by large and vaguely placed vignettes on the ordinary *mappa mundi*.

This map of Bacon's, which he sent to Pope Clement IV, is lost. We know, however, that he considered the general distribution of land and water, and rejected the idea of four 'quarters' in favour of a single land-mass. This stretched eastward so far that, as Aristotle had suggested, the Atlantic Ocean between the confines of Spain and of India was comparatively narrow and might easily be crossed. Bacon also believed, on literary evidence, that both India and Ethiopia extended southwards far across the equator (with a large gulf between them). Nevertheless, the generalization about the five zones, of which the torrid and the frigid were not habitable, was to hold the field in geography textbooks down to the sixteenth century.

The Arab measurement of the circumference of the Earth had been described by Al-Farghānī (Alfraganus of the Latins, fl 861) from whom Bacon takes it. The elevation of the pole star, which (with due attention to its eccentricity) gives the latitude, was taken by Al-Farghānī near Palmyra, by means of an astrolabe or quadrant, and the observers then followed the meridian until their instruments showed that they had moved one degree. This distance was measured and was expressed, says Roger, in great cubits. If so, it works out at 68 miles, which is very close to the truth; but it was generally treated as from the lesser cubit, giving a result of only $56\frac{2}{3}$ miles. When it is recalled that Ptolemy's figure of 500 stades or $62\frac{1}{2}$ Roman miles had been recovered, and that the widely current degree of Eratosthenes of 700 stades (p 506) was reckoned by St Isidore and others at $87\frac{1}{2}$ miles, it is easy to imagine the resulting confusion. The resolution of this confusion was, as yet, no one's business or interest. Moreover, the existence of a 'geometrical' mile of 1000 'geometrical' feet, which measured five-sixths of the common feet of the Roman mile, was quite overlooked. Campano da Novara (thirteenth century) stated that 81 'geometrical' miles went to a degree, and this short mile corresponds closely to the 'little sea mile' which was used on the medieval maritime charts of the Mediterranean Sea.

XI. NAVIGATION-INSTRUMENTS

Meanwhile the detail of the world-map was being improved from two sources —the travel of Europeans across the vast Mongol Empire, and the introduction of the sea-chart. At some time in the twelfth century, and possibly earlier, there was discovered the directive property of the lodestone, of which the attractive property had long been familiar. A needle or steel wire which had been rubbed

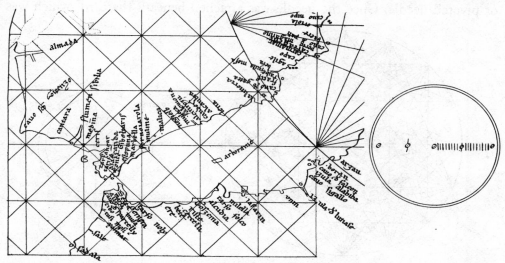

FIGURE 325—*The* Carte Pisane, c 1275. (Left) *A portion of the western Mediterranean, showing the straits of Gibraltar and the Spanish and N. African coasts, with the network of 100-mile squares and diagonals used for transferring detail, and found outside the rhumb-line circles (upper right); (right) the scale of the map: each large division is 50 miles, each small division 5 miles.*

by the stone would, if floated in water, turn towards the pole star. From the days of the Phoenicians—perhaps even of the Minoans—the sailor had steered at night by the northern constellation of the Lesser Bear, and during the day by the course of the Sun. When the sky was overcast he lost his bearings. Now he could recover them by setting the 'touched' needle afloat on a piece of cork or straw.

At first the navigator did no more than this, but by about 1180 Alexander Neckam appears to describe a pivoted needle, and during the first half of the next century we find that the nomenclature of the wind-rose now covers thirty-two points. Sailing-directions, traditionally stated in terms of distance and following wind, could thus take on a new precision, and an accurate chart could be drawn. Such a chart, covering the Mediterranean and Black Seas, survives from about 1275, and it is so detailed, accurate, and stylized that it must certainly have had predecessors (figure 325, the *Carte Pisane*). It carries a scale, being the oldest map to do so, and is drawn upon a set pattern of wind-roses (figure 326), providing a network of rays or rhumbs by which a pilot, furnished with dividers and ruler, could set course between any two ports assigned.

The term 'sailor's compass' originally meant the division of the horizon by the wind-rose, and a compass-card was at first used side by side with the bare floated or pivoted needle. Once the needle was attached beneath the card, which was

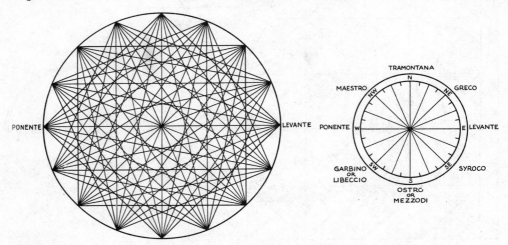

FIGURE 326—(Left) *Scheme of rhumb-lines connecting a wind-rose divided into sixteen points with as many others similarly divided. The* Carte Pisane *was drawn over a pair of such circles;* (right) *the Italian division of the compass or wind-rose into 32 quarters or points.*

perhaps done at the beginning of the fourteenth century, the simple magnetic compass was complete. A contemporary, friend, and teacher of Roger Bacon's, Peter Peregrinus of Maricourt in Picardy, had actually described two boxed compasses in 1269, a floating one containing a lodestone, the other with a pivoted needle. These had scales of degrees marked on their respective lids, and were intended for establishing the meridian for astronomical purposes. That no such use is later reported suggests that the variation of the needle had been discovered —it was certainly known and allowed for early in the fifteenth century by the makers of travellers' sun-dials (figure 354), and possibly also by Flemish compass-makers.

By about 1298, Marco Polo (1254?–?1324) had given an extensive description of China and even of Japan (placed by a misunderstanding 1500 miles from the

mainland), as well as of the East Indies. The fourteenth century saw the incorporation of the Mediterranean sea-chart in the *mappa mundi*. In the famous
'Catalan Atlas' of 1375 we find evidence of a widening topographical knowledge
—of the Atlantic islands, for example, of the negro kingdoms beyond the Sahara,
and of the Far East (figure 327). It is in this 'Catalan Atlas' that we first meet
with a tidal diagram, giving the 'establishment of the port' for a number of Breton

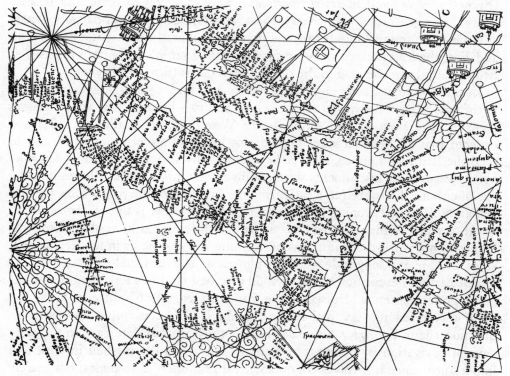

FIGURE 327—*The 'Catalan Atlas', 1375; a portion showing Italy, the Adriatic, and Sicily.*

and English Channel harbours. These are set out on the rays of a compass or
wind-rose, for sailors reckoned hours and days by the thirty-two points, assuming
(incorrectly) that the heavenly bodies moved through equal azimuths in equal
times—that is, they ignored the obliquity of the local horizon. Supposing, for
example, that full sea at a particular port occurred three hours after the new
moon crossed the meridian, they would say 'Moon NE—SW full sea' and mark
the port on the appropriate rhumb. The second high tide of the day would occur
12 hours later, that is, on the south-west rhumb, and low tides on the south-east

and north-west rhumbs. The daily retardation was reckoned at forty-five minutes, or one point on the thirty-two point wind-rose. Hence if the age of the moon was known, the time or rhumb of high tide could be found by the card.

While the seamen of the west and north-west of Europe learnt to make and use tide-diagrams, they had no charts such as were used by the presumably better educated Mediterranean pilots. Sailing-directions, called in English rutters (French, *routier*) and in Italian *portolani*, were common to both, and besides courses these recorded land-marks, rocks, shoals, tide-rips, and dangers generally. Once he found himself in soundings the medieval sailor made use of lead and line, the lead greased to bring up a revealing sample of bottom deposit, as had already been the case in the days of Herodotus (fifth century B.C.).

In addition to magnetic compass, and lead and line, a sand-glass was essential to the navigator. This was to set the watch, and two-hour or 'half-watch' glasses seem to have been in use. Alphonso the Wise (king of Castile, 1252–84) had ordered that all Spanish ships should also carry an astrolabe or quadrant, to read the latitude. This could have been done only very exceptionally, for suitable types of these instruments were not invented until the fifteenth century, the age of oceanic discovery (ch 22). During the fifteenth century, however, we find Italian tables for reckoning the 'course made good', that is to say, the resultant distance sailed in the required direction when the ship has been obliged to tack. This was not worked out in terms of northing and easting as in modern sailing, since latitude and longitude were not plotted on the medieval chart.

The earliest description of the method is to be found in a long memorandum[1] on shipping matters addressed to the Captain-General of Venice in 1428. But as it is referred to very plainly by Ramón Lull (for example, in answer to question 192 in his *Arbor Scientiae*) before 1295, it must date back to the early days of navigation by compass and chart. This gives the method interest and importance, since it involves trigonometrical resolution of triangles, not merely in the mathematician's study, but in the ordinary daily practice of the professional pilot.

The use of the scale-drawn chart and of the Rule and Tables of *Marteloio*, as the method was called, stamp the Italian seaman as the first technician to make use of applied geometry. The academic mathematician had, however, to adapt the Rules to the probable limitations of the user's aptitude and knowledge. The sailor recognized angles only as 'quarters' of the wind, which ran from one to eight between each of the four cardinals, and therefore contained 11° 15′, 22° 30′, 33° 45′, and so on up to 90°, which were tabulated as one-quarter, two-

[1] Egerton MS 73, British Museum.

quarters, and so on up to eight-quarters. Four such quarters made a 'wind' on the Italian eight-fold wind-rose (figure 326). An Englishman would call them rhumbs or 'points'.

A knowledge of multiplication and division was sufficient for the user of the tables, which were arranged so as to answer questions of the following two types. First, 'I wish to sail on (say) the east rhumb, but contrary winds oblige me to sail one quarter (or two, or three, etc) south of east. When I have sailed 100 miles

FIGURE 328—*One method of using the cross-staff to measure inaccessible heights. At the nearer position the transom is adjusted so that its distance from the eye is equal to half its length, at the farther position so that its distance from the eye equals its length. Then (since the tangents of the angles subtended are 1 and 0·5 respectively) the height is equal to the distance between the two positions, added to the height of the observer's eye. For this method to be accurate the height must be vertical, both positions on a horizontal plane, and the cross-staff held horizontally.*

how far have I gone to the east, and how far am I off my course?' The first table sets out the answer in three columns, number of quarters, distance on true course, distance off course. Secondly, the pilot asks: 'I am 10 miles off my true course which is (say) east. How many miles must I sail, and at what distance east shall I meet it, if I turn towards it one (two, three, . . .) quarter(s)?' The required figures are found in the second table. In the memorandum of 1428, to which we have just referred, there are worked examples that show how to proceed when the actual figures are other than the 100 miles or 10 miles to which the tables correspond, but it is difficult to judge what proportion of pilots would have the necessary command of arithmetic. A diagram called 'The Circle and Square', that accompanies the memorandum but is not explained, suggests that a graphical method of solution was also current, for which a quite simple rule would be adequate.

An instrument that was to come into general use among mariners in the sixteenth century was first described by the Provençal Jewish mathematician, Levi ben Gerson, in 1342. This was the cross-staff, designed at first for the use of astronomers and later known as 'Jacob's staff' (p 546 and figure 340). The cross-

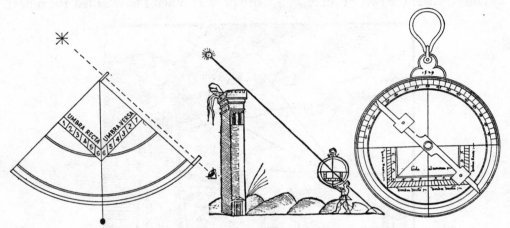

FIGURE 329—*Shadow-scales* (umbra recta *and* umbra versa) *on a quadrant* (left), *on the* dorsum *of an astrolabe* (right), *and shown in use in a work of 1564* (centre).

staff could also be used for geometrical survey, that is, for finding heights and distances by the method of similar triangles, a commonplace of Greek geometry that was beginning to reappear in Latin dress for western use in the twelfth century. Again the principle was simple (figure 328). An astrolabe, quadrant, or geometrical square, or even a measured staff, could be employed instead of a cross-staff, and as there were no tables of tangents a graphical device, the *umbra recta et versa*, was in use to find the required ratios (figure 329).[1] Actually, however, these methods appear to have been used in medieval days for geometrical demonstration only and not for any practical purpose. There is little evidence of precise survey taking place, land-areas being reckoned to the nearest acre (or half-acre) after rough measurement with a perch rod. On the other hand, the erection of large buildings, such as castles, cathedrals, and forts, and the laying-out of new towns could hardly have been done without some preliminary survey.

[1] A graduated square with six or sometimes twelve divisions was drawn on the quadrant, a double square on the back of the astrolabe (figure 329), which gave the ratios $\frac{1}{6}$, $\frac{2}{6}$...$\frac{6}{6}$ (along the side) followed by $\frac{6}{5}$, $\frac{6}{4}$, $\frac{6}{3}$...$\frac{6}{1}$ (along the bottom), i.e. the figures on the scale are to be put over 6 up to an angle of 45°, and under 6 for the larger angles of elevation..

We read that the Arabic writer Messahala of Basra, who wrote on the astrolabe, took part in surveying the site for the foundation of Baghdad in A.D. 762–3.

BIBLIOGRAPHY

FARRINGTON, B. 'Greek Science'. Penguin Books, Harmondsworth. 1953.
FONTOURA DA COSTA, A. 'A Marinharia dos Descombrimentos.' Imprensa da Armada, Lisbon. 1934.
KIELY, E. R. 'Surveying Instruments. Their History and Classroom Use.' Bureau of Publications, Teachers' College, Columbia University, New York. 1947.
KIMBLE, G. N. T. 'Geography in the Middle Ages.' Methuen, London. 1938.
MOTZO, B. R. 'Il Compasso da Navigare.' University Press, Cagliari. 1947.
TAYLOR, EVA G. R. 'Tudor Geography.' Methuen, London. 1930.
Idem. 'The Mathematical Practitioners of Tudor and Stuart England.' University Press, Cambridge. 1954.
Idem. 'The Haven-Finding Art.' Hollis and Carter, London. 1956.

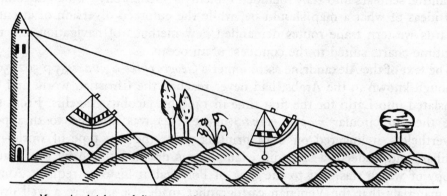

Measuring heights and distances with the shadow-square on the reverse of a quadrant.

## 20

CARTOGRAPHY, SURVEY, AND NAVIGATION
1400–1750

E. G. R. TAYLOR

I. CARTOGRAPHY

THE pressure of Turkish armies upon the eastern Mediterranean lands during the opening decades of the fifteenth century had among its lesser consequences the stimulation of new techniques in the fields of cartography, survey, and navigation. For the Greek manuscripts brought by Byzantine scholars into Italy included Ptolemy's 'Geography', which introduced new ideas of what a map should be, while the enforced diversion of attention towards western trade-routes demanded new methods of navigation and new maritime charts suited to the conquest of an ocean.

The text of the Alexandrine astronomer's *Geographike Syntaxis* (pp 502, 509), although known to the Arabs, had never reached the Christian world and was translated into Latin for the first time in 1409 by Jacobus Angelus. From that date the old circular *mappa mundi* (figure 324) was doomed to disappear. Nevertheless, it lingered on until printing made the new type of world-map familiar, and, indeed, a splendid example was drawn in 1459 by Fra Mauro, a copy of which was sent to the king of Portugal at his own request. Among the materials that the Venetian cartographer made use of were a well drawn Mediterranean sea-chart, charts of the new Portuguese discoveries along the African coast, and much surprising detail about the topography of Abyssinia and eastern Africa. Yet, encyclopaedic as it was, his map was still no more than a sketch-map, one drawn, that is to say, without reference to the mathematics of the globe, but only to an immensely extended horizon.

Projections. A true map must indicate the precise position of each feature upon the sphere of the Earth, and consequently the mutual distances and directions between them. Ptolemy had demonstrated in the second century A.D. how this could be done by means of a system of co-ordinates—the parallels and meridians—assumed upon the globe and mathematically projected upon a plane surface. But whereas celestial co-ordinates for a hemisphere of the stars can be determined by an astronomer from a single point, he can observe the terrestrial co-ordinates only of the place where he stands. Nevertheless, if the length of a degree of a great circle of the globe is known, any measure or estimate of direction and distance can be transformed into latitude and longitude. This laborious calculation was carried out by Ptolemy for all the features of the known world, and from the resulting lists of figures his maps were drawn— *ipso facto* to scale. As previously mentioned (p 503), his original maps have not survived, but they can be and have been redrawn from his data.

Taking 500 stades as the measure of the degree, he devised two plane projections of the spherical co-ordinates for his 'universal' or world map, and these laid the foundation of modern cartography (p 509). The prime meridian on the terrestrial globe must be arbitrarily chosen, and Ptolemy made his calculations relatively to Alexandria. For convenience, however, he numbered the meridians from the farthest known west to the farthest east, so that longitude zero ran through the Fortunate Islands. The Renaissance reader interpreted these as the Canaries, and the prime meridian was taken as running through the most westerly island, namely Ferro.

Later theories about the variation of the compass led to the idea that there was a 'true meridian' of no variation. During the sixteenth century, therefore, many cartographers took this as the prime meridian, assuming that it ran through St Michael Island in the Azores. During the seventeenth century, when observatories were founded in Paris and London, a new practice began of using the meridian of the capital city as the zero for national maps. There was no uniformity until the twentieth century.

The world-map to accompany Ptolemy's text is on his second projection. For maps of separate countries or regions he had written that it was sufficiently accurate to draw a rectangular grid, so long as the parallels were correctly spaced, while the meridians should be correctly spaced along the parallel half-way between the northern and southern edges of the map. Such a rectangular projection, which ignores the convergence of the meridians, distorts scale and distance most markedly in high latitudes—with which the Greeks were little concerned. Rather more than half a century after the 'Geography' was translated one of the most notable of the Renaissance copyists, the miniaturist Dominus Nicholaus Germanus (Donis), greatly improved upon it. This German monk came to work in Italy in 1462, and in the set of Ptolemy's maps that he drew for a noble patron in 1466 he substituted a trapezoidal projection for the rectangular one. This was effected quite simply. The northern and southern bounding-latitudes were each divided correctly and the meridians therefore converged. Both parallels and meridians were rectilinear.

Tabulae novae. The full influence of Ptolemy's text and maps was not felt until the printing-press gave them a wider circulation. The maps were first engraved for an Italian edition in 1477, and the set drawn by Dominus Nicholaus was used for the woodcuts in the Ulm edition of 1482. The great astronomer Johann Müller, generally called Regiomontanus (1436–76), had planned to issue an edition from his Nuremberg press, but his premature death prevented it. He had intended to include in this publication some *tabulae novae* or 'modern'

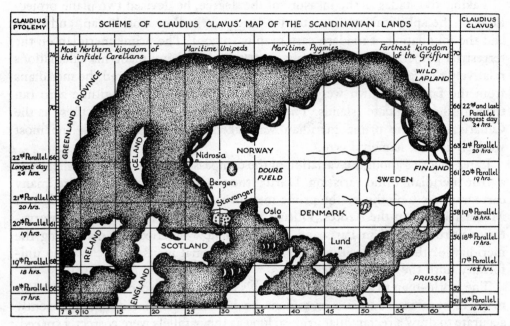

FIGURE 330—*Outline of Claudius Clavus's map of the Scandinavian lands, showing Ptolemy's latitudes* (left) *and his own* (right).

maps drawn after Ptolemy's pattern, and in fact a number of such maps had already been devised. The earliest, so far as is known, had been commissioned by Cardinal Guillaume Filastre of Rheims, one of the first to possess a copy of the precious manuscript. The Alexandrine author had not known the Scandinavian countries, and it was to fill this gap in the contents of the Ptolemaic atlas that the cardinal called upon a Danish cartographer named Claudius Claussøn Swart, usually known as Claudius Clavus (b 1388).

The map (figure 330) included the lands between the Baltic and Norway seas, and is remarkable for being extended to the west of Iceland so as to include the eastern shore of Greenland, a country thus mapped for the first time. The network was, of course, rectangular, and the meridians were correctly spaced along the sixtieth parallel, which was approximately the middle latitude. Following Ptolemy's practice, too, the 'climates' are distinguished in the margins, each defined by the length of the longest day. But the numbering of the parallels differs in the two margins, those on the left running from 55° upwards, those on the right from 51°. The former, the western margin, is headed Claudius Ptolemaeus, the latter Claudius Clavus. Clearly the Dane was correcting the Alexandrine master's figures: and the correction was a just one, for Scotland and Ireland, as copied from the Greek map, were too far north, and the new map was indubitably based upon an actual list of latitudes of Scandinavian towns. Among those accurately placed in this respect, some to within half a degree, are Nidrosia, Bergen, Stavanger, Oslo, Stockholm, and Lund. Yet the cartographer obviously had a very poor knowledge of the general lie of the land, and his longitudes are grossly erroneous. The extension of the Scandinavian peninsula is shown as from east to west instead of north to south, while the Gulf of Bothnia appears to have been unknown. A land-bridge runs from the east of the White Sea to Greenland, and along it are marked the Wild Lapps, griffins, pygmies, unipeds, and the infidel Carelians, names that indicate the vague literary and verbal descriptions on which the map-maker had chiefly to rely. Mountainous Scandinavia had no well travelled network of roads and navigable rivers such as, with the help of latitude-lists, facilitated the making of the *tabulae novae* of other western European countries.

Itineraries and river-systems afforded a framework for the first modern map of Germany, drawn about the middle of the century by Nicholas of Cusa (1401–64), cardinal and mathematician, who, like Filastre, possessed a manuscript copy of Ptolemy. Such great churchmen were among the most frequent travellers of the day, and among the most learned scholars.

As it happened, too, the early fifteenth century saw the introduction of a little instrument that allowed the traveller to determine, if he chose, the direction of each stage of his itinerary. This was the pocket sun-dial, the *organum viatorum* or 'travellers' instrument' made by a guild of the famous Nuremberg metal-workers, and set in the meridian by means of a tiny inset magnetic needle (figure 354). That these dials were early familiar outside Germany is indicated by a passing reference to *os relógios de agulha* ('clocks of the needle') in the *Leal Conselheiro* ('Faithful Adviser') written by King Duarte of Portugal between 1428 and 1437. While, however, the land-traveller thus equipped could draw a map, it is not until nearly the end of the fifteenth century that there is direct evidence of the association of compass-dial and cartography.

In 1492 Erhard Etzlaub, a compass-dial maker of Nuremberg, published a map of his native city and of its environs for sixty miles around. Seven or eight years later he followed this with a road-map, *Das Rom-Weg* ('The Road to Rome'),

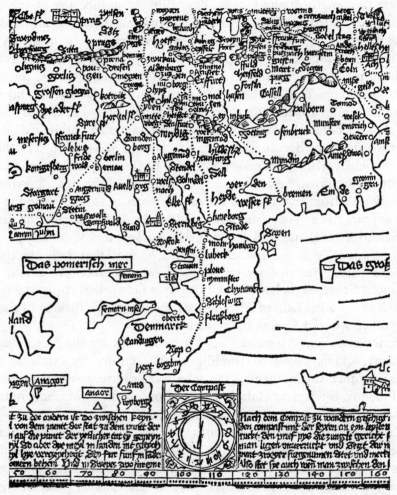

FIGURE 331—*Outline of the lower (northern) portion of Etzlaub's road-map. The scale is in German miles, and the roads are marked by dots spaced in miles. The compass-dial is to be placed as shown on the map, allowing for the NE declination of the needle.*

showing the routes across Germany to the Eternal City. Beneath the map is drawn a compass-dial, and the traveller is instructed to lay his own instrument correctly upon it and so find his way (figure 331). The influence of Ptolemy is shown here by the insertion of latitudes in the margin, as well as the lengths of the longest day, which defined the 'climate'. A new technical device was the representation of the roads by a series of dots placed one common German mile (four Roman miles) apart. Distances were thus immediately apparent. Towns were indicated by open circles, except for capital cities, which were represented by a group of buildings, and places of pilgrimage, where a church was drawn. Mountains were shown by chains or groups of mound-like hills, tinted stone-colour, and colour was also used to distinguish the nations and languages bordering on Germany. All this symbolism was explained in German in a leaflet sold with the map.

An itinerary map of Europe, also planned and explained as specifically for use with the traveller's pocket-dial, was published by Martin Waldseemüller[1] in 1511 and 1513. In 1525 and 1530 a printer and engraver of Augsburg, Georg Erlinger, published road-maps of the Holy Roman Empire, again showing the dial; these maps owed much to Etzlaub. By this date, the idea of a map as showing distance and direction correctly, as well as position on the globe, was thoroughly familiar.

Cosmography. A further impetus to the development of cartography was given by the work of Regiomontanus at Nuremberg in 1474–6, when he published the 'Alphonsine Tables' or *Ephemerides*, issued a calendar, and described the construction and use of astronomical instruments. His pupils and disciples were quickly able to advance the study of astronomy and cosmography at the universities; they published almanacs and extended the lists of latitudes and longitudes. To all this was added the stimulus of the sudden extension of the known world by the great discoveries made during the last decade of the century. Ptolemy's map projections had to be extended likewise. Contarini in 1506 and Ruysch in 1508 made use of modified versions of his conic projection, the latter cartographer, however, introducing the mathematical impossibility of placing the Pole at the vertex of the cone, which is inconsistent with the correct spacing of the parallels. Neither accepted Ptolemy's device for diminishing the latitudes south of the equator, but simply extended the cone. His second projection was developed by Johann Werner (1514) both in latitude and longitude, resulting in a heart-shaped world-map. The same writer made the more useful suggestion of employing the stereographic projection (long known to astronomers) in cartography. This is a true geometrical projection of a hemisphere from an opposite point on the equator or from one pole. A simple modification of it is to divide the central meridian, the equator, and the bounding meridian of each hemisphere

[1] Waldseemüller (*c* 1470–*c* 1518), latinized as Hylacomylus, is credited with being the first to call the New World *America*, in his *Cosmographiae Introductio* (1507).

correctly (that is, equally) and pass arcs of circles between the three points thus obtained (figure 332). This is the globular projection. Waldseemüller in 1506 drew a world-map in which the lines of latitude were parallel straight lines correctly spaced. Each was equally, but not correctly, divided by the curved meridians, since the author wished to diminish the true convergence. In fact the ingenuity of mathematicians can devise an infinity of projections, each producing its own slight distortions, but the first significant novelty was the network for a marine chart invented by Gerard Mercator in 1569 (p 550).

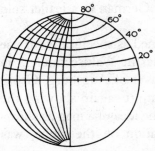

FIGURE 332—*Globular projection. The centre meridian and the circumference are divided into equal parts and the parallels are arcs of circles. The equator is also divided into equal parts, and the meridians are arcs of circles passing through the poles.*

The writings of the new cosmographers contained much that was immediately relevant to cartography, particularly the description of instruments, such as the astrolabe (p 603), quadrant, and astronomers' staff (soon to be adapted to survey, p 528) and the exposition of the mathematics of the globe. They furnished, for example, a detailed table of the diminishing length of the degree of longitude with increasing latitude, and gave a discussion of the measure of the arc of the meridian. Ptolemy's figure for this was naturally generally accepted; converted at 8 stades to the mile, it gave the length of the degree as $62\frac{1}{2}$ miles. But German itineraries (as in Etzlaub's road-map, p 534) gave 15 German miles (equivalent to 60 'foreign' miles) to a degree; this figure found currency in Werner's commentary on Ptolemy (1514) and was subsequently adopted in France and England. It was recognized that the current mile differed in different countries, and that the measure of the stade was uncertain. Conversion tables gave, for example, 68 Italian miles to the degree, and sailors had their own figure (p 547).

The determination of the distance between two places whose latitude and longitude were known was a problem set out in the textbooks, and was at first solved (in Ptolemy's manner) by means of Pythagoras's theorem, assuming the difference in longitude and the difference in latitude as the lengths of the sides containing the right angle, the required distance being the hypotenuse. It was, however, pointed out by Stoeffler in his treatise *De usu astrolabii* (1512) that an error was introduced because the convergence of the meridians was ignored. He therefore substituted for the whole difference of longitude the difference measured along the middle latitude between the cities. This gives an approximately correct answer, but the error introduced by treating a spherical triangle as a plane triangle was not considered. Current textbooks supplied tables of squares and square-roots to assist in solving such problems as this.

II. SURVEY

While it is not until the opening of the sixteenth century that any direct evidence of cartographical surveying or discussion of the appropriate instruments can be found, the general principles had long been familiar to the medieval scholar. A section on the measurement of heights, depths, and distances was a normal adjunct to a treatise on geometry, but its purpose was rather to illustrate the properties of triangles than to persuade readers to take up field-work. The simplest proposition was that, knowing the angle of elevation of the top of a tower and its distance away, its height could be found by simple proportion from the geometrical square engraved (with an alidade at its centre) on the back of the astrolabe (p 528). The exercise could be carried out with a quadrant, or with a cross-staff, or even (using a little ingenuity) with a mirror or a simple rod. Then there was the device, by taking two observations, for finding the distance of an object that could not be reached, as for example a ship at sea (figure 333).

Such a treatise on mensuration was to be found in the *Astrolabii Canones* of Robertus Anglicus, a thirteenth-century writer whose work was first printed about 1478 and reprinted many times subsequently. Twenty years before this, in a manuscript written and illustrated by a gun-founder for a noble patron, the same principles are to be seen related to the military art, for example to range-finding. Whether they were thus early applied in the field is, however, very doubtful. It is certain that the estate-surveyor, in drawing up his maps and terriers (pp 515, 540), long remained faithful to his perch-rod and simple estimates. Yet once printing made them familiar to practical men, these principles provided the actual basis of survey-, plan-, and map-drawing.

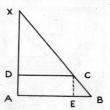

FIGURE 333—*Method of measuring distance to an inaccessible point X from A. The observer erects a mark at A, proceeds at right-angles to the line AX to B, marks it, goes directly towards X as far as any point C, marks it, and then walks to D. When AB, CD, and AD have been measured, then since* AX:AB = CE:BE *the distance*

$$AX = \frac{AB \cdot AD}{AB - CD}.$$

A surveyed regional map. Whatever may be surmised about the town-plans and modern maps that began to be published in the latter part of the fifteenth century, it can be quite definitely stated that systematic field-observations lay behind the chorographical or regional map of the upper Rhineland that appeared in the Strasbourg edition of Ptolemy in 1513. A representation of the earliest modern surveying-instrument had been published a year or two earlier in the

Strasbourg edition of a famous university textbook, the *Margarita philoso-phica*.

The same group of cosmographers and cartographers, Walter Lud, Ringman, and Waldseemüller, can be associated with both instrument and map. They were working at Saint-Dié in the Vosges Mountains under the patronage of

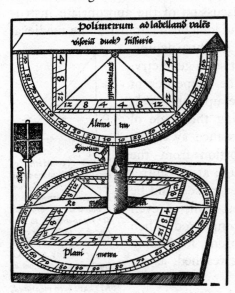

FIGURE 334—*Waldseemüller's* polimetrum, *from a woodcut of 1512. The sight is in the form of two crossed slits. The whole of the upper part of this level-ling-instrument turns in the horizontal plane, with the index-reading on the lower scale. The upper part with the sights turns in the vertical plane and is read on the scale by the plumb-line.*

Duke René II of Lorraine. The map of the Rhineland and another of Lorraine it-self, drawn on a scale of about 1/500,000, were among twenty *tabulae novae* included in the Strasbourg Ptolemy; they are con-sidered to be the work of Waldseemüller. The Rhineland map has been closely examined, and the latitudes of all the chief cities found correct to within 18', while their mutual bearings, or angles of posi-tion, are also true within a few minutes of arc. Such accuracy could not have been achieved except by field-survey. The work, however, appears to have been done in two sections, the north and south halves of the map being faultily assembled.

The polimetrum. The instrument re-ferred to was known as a *polimetrum* (figure 334); it was designed for taking bearings and altitudes, and for levelling. It is found among addenda to the *Margarita philosophica* (which do not appear in the Basel editions) known to have been supplied by Waldseemüller. They include tracts on architecture and perspective. The author of the book, Gregor Reisch, was rector of Freiburg University, at which Waldseemüller had been a student. The first essential feature of the *polimetrum* is the sighting-tube, with twin slits, which turns in a vertical plane on a semicircular scale carrying a plumb-line. The tube can be clamped in a horizontal position by a screw, and then turned with its support in the horizontal plane, thus carrying a pointer or alidade around a horizontal scale furnished with an index. The fiducial line of the alidade corre-sponds to the line between the sighting-slits.

The whole instrument is the prototype of a theodolite. It was presumably oriented by means of a pocket compass-dial, such as Waldseemüller advised for use with his itinerary map. Such an instrument, or even a mere graduated circle and alidade, when carried up into church towers, could have been used for taking the horizontal angles of position plotted in the 1513 map of the Rhineland, which is also remarkable for the unusual fidelity of its physical features—particularly indicating the sharp, parallel edges of the rift-valley, which are scarcely apparent on much later maps.

Tartaglia's survey-instruments. It soon became customary for textbooks on practical mathematics to include one or more chapters on how to survey a region or country. Such a section is to be found in the *Quesiti e inventioni* of the Italian mathematician Niccolò Tartaglia (*c* 1500–57), which was first written about 1524 and published in an enlarged form more than twenty years later. Tartaglia describes two surveying-instruments to an English friend, both of them limited to taking horizontal angles of position and both embodying inset magnetic needles. The first had a large boxed needle in the centre of a circular graduated board or plate, the alidade being turned about on a collar fitted round the compass-box by a rod at right-angles to it. In the second instrument (which was cheaper) the alidade turned directly on a circular scale and the instrument was set by means of a needle from a little German compass-dial, inset at the edge of the board (figure 335). Latitudes, angles of position, and distances (taken from

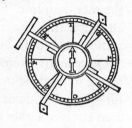

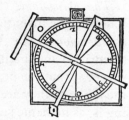

FIGURE 335—*Two surveying-instruments described by Tartaglia, 1546.*

itineraries, from local knowledge, or actually paced) were still the basis of the map. Itinerary-distances were automatically reduced by one-quarter, to allow for the turns of the road. Ptolemy's practice was to deduct one-third from the length of reported routes before converting them to latitude and longitude figures.

Triangulation. In 1533 a notable technical advance was made in survey when Gemma Frisius (1508–55), professor of mathematics at Louvain, explained the principle of triangulation, which eliminated all distance-measurement save that of the base-line. The method involved taking angles of position, that is, bearings, of the same feature from either end of the chosen base-line. This line is then plotted to scale on paper, and rays to the object are ruled in at the correct angle from each end. The point at which the rays meet is the position of the object, and its distance can thus be measured on the scale of the base-line.

Simple as the procedure sounds, it is liable to many errors when applied in the field. Gemma recognized and emphasized, for example, the importance of the precise orientation of the instrument at either end of the base-line, and the need for placing it level, but his instrument was probably only the back-plate of his astrolabe, laid upon a parapet or a stool or stone. His nephew, Walter Arsenius, a notable instrument-maker, later made astrolabes with a little inset compass-needle under the ring, so that they could be used for taking such horizontal angles of position. Alternatively a simple graduated circular plate was used, fitted with an alidade, which had a small magnetic needle inset into the plate on the meridian line. These, too, were merely laid down on some convenient object, although they are also pictured in the latter half of the century mounted on a staff which could be thrust into the ground, or held upright.

Quite apart from errors of observation due to faulty placing of the instrument, errors in plotting must at first have been difficult to avoid. Drawing-instruments, for instance, did not include a protractor. The surveyor is directed to draw a graduated circle at either end of his plotted base-line and rule in the rays accordingly.

The plane-table (figure 338). A great advance in survey by triangulation followed the invention of the plane- (or plain-) table. It is first described in 1551 as the *holometre* by Abel Foullon, a member of the household of the French king (Henri II) and a student of mathematics. The essential feature of a plane-table survey is that the position-lines are ruled directly on a sheet of paper fastened to the table, as they are sighted. The modern sight-rule used in plane-table survey-ing is, as its name suggests, a well made ruler, engraved with plotting-scales and carrying sights. But in the earliest tables two sighting-rods were attached to the edge of the table, one of them moving to and fro along a scale so that it could be set and used for sighting from the second station at the end of the base-line, which had been directly marked off to scale. This was not a very satisfactory arrangement, and Foullon's table had the further disadvantage that it was set by a centrally placed compass-needle which could not be seen unless the paper were removed or torn open. However, a table shown in a contemporary edition of the *Cosmographia* of Sebastian Münster (1489-1552) is oriented by the cus-tomary little compass sun-dial, though, like Foullon's, it has the clumsy pair of attached sight-rods.

Drawing a plan or map by means of the plane-table was so simple a matter, since it required no mathematical knowledge, that surveyors, and in particular estate-surveyors, quickly became numerous. As a consequence, improvements were rapid. Well before the close of the century the separate sight-rule of modern type, with slit-and-wire sights, and carrying plotting-scales, was in use. The table had a frame which held down the sheet of paper; it was mounted on a tripod and oriented by a separate boxed needle. Moreover, the perch-rod, or the knotted rosined cord of the earlier 'land-meaters', had been replaced by a linked steel chain. The front 'chain-man', too, carried a bundle of arrows, to be thrust into the ground at each complete chain and picked up by the rear man, as is done today.

The theodolite. In 1571 the English mathematician Thomas Digges (*c* 1521–95) published under the title *Pantometria* the notes on mensuration written by his father Leonard Digges (d 1558), who had taught the subject in the middle of the century. The older man had given the name *theodelitus* to the bearing-dial, or circular plate with alidade (figure 336), and suggested its combination with another topographical instrument, the sight-rule turning on a vertical scale for

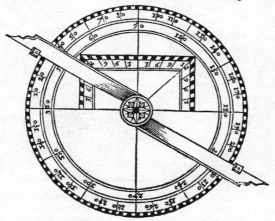

FIGURE 336—*Leonard Digges's 'theodelitus', 1571.*

measuring altitudes. The combined instrument (which was on the pattern of the early *polimetrum*) became known as the theodolite (figure 337). It was made in various patterns, such as that with a central inset compass on the lower plate, round which the upper part turned on a collar; but Digges left all detail to the 'skilfull artificer', only stipulating that there must be somewhere an inset needle, and that the variation (which he put at 11° 15′ E) must be noted. The instrument was mounted on a single leg or staff, and was to be levelled with a plumb-line. Both the vertical and horizontal plates were engraved with the geometrical square, as well as with a scale of degrees.

Mathematical tables. The computation of the areas of fields and estates was a laborious matter for surveyors, who consequently were among the first to take advantage of mathematical devices that simplified their task. This is illustrated by the first comprehensive English textbook on survey, Aaron Rathborne's 'Surveyor' (1616), which can be taken as typical of professional practice from the turn of the century. The author advocates the new decimal arithmetic introduced by Simon Stevin (1548–1620) in 1585, and had himself designed and used a decimal chain. This was, however, shortly superseded by the more convenient chain of 100 links invented by Edmund Gunter (1581–1626) and still in use. Rathborne also made use of trigonometry, a subject on which a general textbook by a German writer had appeared in 1600. Pocket trigonometrical tables had now become available and, only two years after their invention,

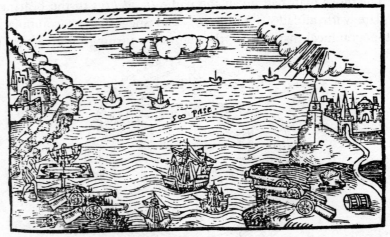

FIGURE 337—*The use of Digges's 'Topographical Instrument' (a precursor of the modern theodolite) to measure an inaccessible vertical distance. Assuming that by a method already described he found the distance BA to be 500 paces, he turns the sights of the instrument upon A. The perpendicular line falls on the tenth division of a linear scale of 120, i.e. tan ABC = AC/BC = 1/12. But AC² + BC² = BA² = 250 000 paces. Hence AC,*

$$\text{the required vertical distance, is } \sqrt{\frac{250\,000}{145}}, \text{ which works out at nearly 42 paces.}$$

pocket-tables of logarithms, of which Rathborne writes enthusiastically. Not many years later Edmund Gunter put a logarithmic scale upon a staff, and 'Gunter's line', as it was termed, was employed for computation throughout the century side by side with the various slide-rules dating from about 1650.

An engraving in Rathborne's book shows surveyors at work with theodolite and plane-table, their instruments mounted on tripods; readings are entered in an orderly manner in a field-book, and plotting is done with a protractor and a mounted needle for pricking points (figure 338). A bearing-dial or circle termed a 'circumferentor' is also in use, and the particular pattern described includes a table of horizontal equivalents (that is, reduction of slopes) on the alidade.

Levelling. An important part of survey had always been precise levelling, necessary in relation to water-supply, drainage works, and building. The Roman water-level or *chorobates* (p 511) was familiar in the sixteenth century through its representation in editions of Vitruvius's *Architectura* from 1486 onwards. The method employed was to sight horizontally forwards and backwards, either with a water-level or with a theodolite, on to graduated staffs held by assistants. Records remain of the survey made between 1609 and 1611 for the New River enterprise designed to bring water to London. This was carried out by Edward Wright (*c* 1558–1615), who combined mathematical learning with great practical experience, both in field-survey and in instrument-making. He went over the ground more than once, for, since the fall of level between Amwell and Islington averages only 5 in to the mile, great precision was demanded. According to a contemporary, Mark Ridley, Wright was accustomed to fasten a 'perspective glass' parallel to the sights of his instrument, and this would have assisted him.

FIGURE 338—*Surveyors at work. Two vignettes from the title-page of Rathborne's 'Surveyor', 1616.*

The introduction into surveying-instruments of actual telescopic sights, carrying cross-hairs to define position, was the most important advance in survey-instrument making of the seventeenth century. In addition, the vernier (often miscalled the nonius) and the micrometer made fine measuring possible, while the bubble-level replaced the plummet. These improvements, however, were costly and were only slowly adopted, even by scientists. A treatise on levelling by the French savant Jean Picard (1620–82) describes the telescopic level which he used to survey the relations of the Seine and Loire, and other waters about Versailles; but he set his instrument with a plumb-line, as did his fellow Academicians Huygens (1629–95), Römer, and La Hire, who all designed somewhat similar levels.

The fact that the Torricellian tube or mercury barometer could give a measure of height was demonstrated by Pascal in 1648, but there are only sporadic experiments to record, such as those of John Caswell (1656–1712) and Edmond Halley (1656–1742), during the period under review.

The arc of the meridian. The French Academicians in 1669 first successfully attacked what is a fundamental problem of cartography, namely the precise length of the arc of the meridian. Willibrord Snell (1591–1626) had obtained an improved figure in 1606 by a triangulation carried out on the level plain of Holland, and Richard Norwood (*c* 1590–1675) got a surprisingly good result from his road-survey of the distance between London and York in 1635. Jean Picard and his assistants were able to adopt methods that inspired much greater confidence. Their base-line of over 11 000 yd was measured with extreme care by means of iron rods, and a system of 17 triangles covered the distance, about 70 miles, between Malvoisine and Amiens. The latitudes of the extreme stations, and of five intermediate points, were taken with a 10-ft quadrant, but it was realized that accuracy could be assumed only to the nearest two seconds of arc. The result accepted was 69 m 783 yd, in English measure. Some years later the triangulation along the same meridian was continued southward by Jean Dominique Cassini (1625–1712), and a rather higher figure was obtained; this gave rise to a controversy about the shape of the Earth which was not decided until the following century (p 553).

III. NAVIGATION

The methods of navigation developed first for the enclosed Mediterranean Sea and for the narrow seas on the continental shelf of north-western Europe (pp 523–9) were inadequate for the new ocean navigation of the early fifteenth century sponsored by the Portuguese Prince Henry the Navigator (1394–1460). The Canary Islands had been occupied in 1402, the Madeira group in 1420, and the Azores, due west of Lisbon, about 1444. All these island groups had already appeared on the fourteenth-century maritime charts, but the charting of the west African coast stopped abruptly at Cape Nun.

Prince Henry sent out ships with the intention of reaching the kingdoms known to lie beyond the Sahara, and under his orders the chart was gradually extended. Meanwhile he consulted expert opinion and took as one of his advisers a Master James of Majorca, probably the Jew Jafuda Cresques, son of the famous Abraham, chart- and compass-maker to the King of Aragon in 1370–80. In effect, the new method of navigation proposed was what is termed 'running down the latitude', that is to say, the latitude of the port of destination being known, the ship sought that latitude by sailing north or south through the open sea, and then set course due east or due west until within sight of land. This involved something totally new. The medieval sailor had relied on compass and chart, on dead-reckoning and soundings. Now the pilot must know how to make an astronomical observation, he must find the *altura*, as it was termed (actually the latitude), and must know the *altura* of each port of call.

The quadrant. The earliest astronomical instrument used at sea appears to have been the quadrant. As used by astronomers the plate was engraved with a geometrical square as well as the marginal scale of degrees, and had sets of curved lines by which the time of day and the Sun's position in the zodiac could be ascertained by means of a bead on the silk thread which carried the plummet. For the sailor, however, only the angle of elevation of a star was to be measured, by observing it through the pin-holes.

The sailor found the *altura*, or height, of the pole star with which he was already familiar, and there is some evidence that the plate was at first engraved with the names of ports at the correct degree at which the thread should fall. This involved making the observations at one or other of the two positions of the star when it was at the altitude of the celestial pole. Fortunately

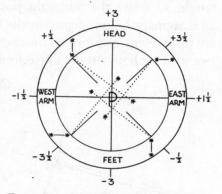

FIGURE 339—'*Regiment of the North Star*', *showing the position of α-Polaris for four positions of the Guards, and the number of degrees to be added to or subtracted from the observed height of the pole star for eight positions of the Guards.*

this was indicated by the position of the Guards, two stars in the Lesser Bear which the sailor was accustomed to observe for time-keeping. He early learnt, too, that 'Guards in the head', that is, towards the northern horizon, meant that three degrees must be added to his observation of the North Star, while 'Guards in the feet', or towards the south horizon, meant that three degrees must be taken away.

Eventually a complete 'regiment of the North Star' was taught, giving the number of degrees to be added or subtracted from the observation for eight positions of the Guards shown on a diagram (figure 339). The maximum correction (that is, angular distance of the star from the celestial pole) was 3° 30′ at that period, and it was more than a century before this figure was reduced in nautical manuals in accordance with the diminution due to the precession of the equinoxes. The concept of 'degrees' is difficult for the non-mathematician to understand, and there is evidence in some extant fragments of early nautical directions that pilots were taught to read a degree as representing a distance of

17½ leagues (or in some cases 16⅔ leagues), sailed north or south of their point of departure.

The nocturlabe. Time-keeping by the meridian passage of the stars goes back to ancient Egypt (vol I, p 123). The medieval European night-watcher, whether shepherd or sailor, was accustomed to observe the circling of the Guards of either the Lesser or the Great Bear. A meridian passage takes place approximately an hour earlier every fortnight, and French and Portuguese sailors were taught to relate the midnight position of the Guards throughout the year to an imaginary human figure in the sky. Early in the sixteenth century, however, an instrument came into use that set the twelve months of the year and the twenty-four hours of the day round a circle in such a way that a pointer directed

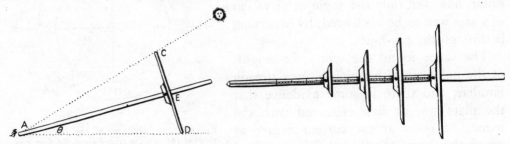

FIGURE 340—*The 'Jacob's staff' or cross-staff.* (Left) *As used in making an astronomical observation;* (right) *fitted with several vertical staves.*

to the date gave also the midnight position of the Guards (figure 363). A second pointer was directed by the observer (who looked to the pole star through a hole in the centre of the instrument) to the actual position of the Guards, when the difference gave him the number of hours before or after midnight. The edge of the circle was toothed so that the hours could be counted round in the darkness, and a refinement was to allow for the eccentricity of the pole star. English nocturlabes or nocturnals of the seventeenth century had two scales, for use with the Guards of the Great Bear or of the Lesser Bear respectively.

Sea-astrolabe and cross-staff. There is no direct mention of the use even of the sea-quadrant until the middle of the fifteenth century, for seamen were seldom writers. Nor do we know when two further instruments came into use. The sea-astrolabe was merely a heavy graduated circle carrying an alidade or sight-rule, and swinging and swivelling freely from a thumb-ring. It performed the one function needed—taking an altitude. The cross-staff, known to astronomers since its description by the Jewish scholar Levi ben Gerson in the fourteenth century (p 528), was a much cheaper instrument serving the same purpose.

Sailors knew it as the *balestilha*, for they were taught to aim at the star like a cross-bowman (*balestier*) aiming at a mark: they 'shot' the star or the Sun, a mode of expression still employed.

The principle of the instrument is very simple. A transversal can be drawn to and fro along a staff, and half the angle which it subtends is given by $ED/AE = \tan \theta$ (figure 340). The staff can therefore be graduated to show the values of 2θ. The seaman, placing his eye at A, moved the cross-piece until D covered the horizon and C the star. He then read off the *altura*. Before the seventeenth century cross-staffs were made with three, or even four, removable transversals of different lengths, each with a corresponding graduation on the staff. One or other was selected and used according as the heavenly body to be observed stood low or high in the sky.

Regiment of the Sun. At about latitude 9° N sailors used to say that they 'lost the star', and certainly, owing to haze on the horizon and the motion of the ship, they would have found it difficult to observe at its lower transit, while at its upper the Guards would fail them. Yet exploration southward continued. By 1474 the equator was crossed, and in 1482 the castle of El Mina was founded in Guinea. A new technique of navigation was urgent, and Prince (later King) John of Portugal, who was responsible for the African ventures, did as his great-uncle Prince Henry had done before. He brought into consultation astronomers and mathematicians, who devised the rules for finding the latitude by the noonday Sun. This involved calculating a table of the daily solar declination from the Sun's position in the zodiac, which was already tabulated in the *Ephemerides* of Abraham Zacuto (1450–1515?), a Spanish Jew whose disciple José Vizinho had been among those consulted. Regiomontanus had already prepared and printed such a table in 1475 with slightly differing figures. To use the table nine rules were necessary, covering the various positions of ship and Sun on the same or opposite sides of the equator, north or south of each other, or on the equator itself. Vizinho probably made the voyage to Guinea in 1485 to test the rules and establish the latitudes of key points.

Raising a degree. Whether the latitude was found by Sun or star it was necessary to relate change of latitude to distance sailed, and sailors were furnished with a table of the distance that must be covered on each rhumb of the compass in order to raise a degree, or the reverse. The degree was taken by the Portuguese as $17\frac{1}{2}$ leagues of four miles each, that is to say 70 miles, and this figure was probably derived from Eratosthenes's degree of 700 stades, since it is also found in Sacrobosco's *Sphaera*, the text prescribed for pilots' instruction. The earliest surviving printed navigating manual is the Portuguese *Regimento do astrolabio e do quadrante*, dated 1509; it is clearly not a first edition, and no doubt also had manuscript predecessors. It contains the rules and tables outlined above, and a list of latitudes from Cape Finisterre to the equator. In a manual of a few years later the declination-table covers the four-year cycle, and the latitudes extend to the Indies.

Christopher Columbus (1446?–1506) appears to have known and used an early Portuguese manual, but after the discovery of America the development of navigation was also fostered by Spain, and pilots were trained at the *Casa de Contratación* or chamber of commerce. Spanish manuals were published in 1545, 1550, and later, and one of them, by Martin Cortes (1532–89), provides the necessary rule to be used with that for raising a degree, namely how much easting or westing is made according to the rhumb on which the ship sailed. This was given in terms of the 'great' or equatorial degree of $17\frac{1}{2}$ leagues, and a table was also furnished of the proportion the degree of longitude in each latitude bore to the great degree. Hence a pilot or chart-maker had the means to interpret the ship's run in terms of latitude and longitude. In fact, however, estimates were often grossly at fault.

The plain chart. Mathematicians commonly decried the 'plain chart' as a major cause of disaster at sea. Based as it was on the pattern of rhumb-lines laid down for the medieval chart of the Mediterranean Sea, it showed all north–south lines as parallel, and hence increasingly falsified east–west distances with distance from the equator. In fact, however, as Cortes states, the scale was usually made correct along some middle latitude of the chart, and hence the distortion was lessened, nor were any lines of longitude indicated. Nevertheless, if two points had been placed the correct distance apart on the chart then their bearings were falsified, and vice versa; yet pilots were accustomed to lay off bearings and distances with confidence from such charts.

In 1537 the Portuguese mathematician Pedro Nuñez (1492–1577) analysed the causes of error at some length and pointed out the true course of a rhumb-line (line of constant bearing), which is a spiral on the surface of the globe. In fact, however, there was no substitute for the plain chart until the chart on Mercator's projection was invented and (much later) accepted by sailors. Meanwhile, some captains took globes to sea, but the size and clumsiness of these devices, not to say their inaccuracy, rendered them of little use. A further source of error in the plain chart arose from the variation of the magnetic needle, causing the bearing which the pilot entered in his journal to be incorrect.

Magnetic variation. The Nuremberg compass-dial makers noticed that the magnetic needle did not lie precisely in the meridian, and scored the dial to show where it should be when the instrument was correctly oriented. Compass-makers, too, noticed the same phenomenon, and fastened the magnetized wire a little askew under the card so as to correct the fault. The correction differed according to the port where the compass was made, and in some cases was not attempted at all; the instrument was then called a meridian compass. Portuguese sailors must have noticed that their corrected needles swung westward as they approached the Azores, and eastward again as they returned to Lisbon. Columbus remarked on the fact that his different needles did not agree, and that there was a marked north-westing when he passed the Azores into the undiscovered hemisphere. In the old world north-easting was the general rule.

Pilots of standing, and their mathematical advisers, urged the regular instrumental observation of the variation. The principle of the methods proposed was to compare the true meridian as found by equal-altitude observations of the Sun with the magnetic meridian as found by simultaneous readings of the Sun's amplitude or azimuth. The earliest instrument was a graduated circular plate carrying a central style and an inset magnetic needle by which the zero reading was set due north. The west and east bearings of the shadow of the style were read when equal-altitude forenoon and afternoon observations of the Sun were taken with the astrolabe. Half the difference between the needle and Sun bearings is the magnetic variation. Alternatively the Sun can be observed at the moments of rising and setting. A later form of instrument was a large magnetic compass, carrying a scale of degrees as well as the ordinary scale of rhumbs, and fitted with a sight-rule or alidade and a thread for casting a shadow. The making of a pair of observations presented difficulties on a moving ship, and most pilots appear to have been satisfied with a rough check on the compass when they took the noon Sun. Mathematicians were aware, however, that the amplitude of the Sun when it rises and sets can be calculated if the solar declination and latitude are known, and all that is then necessary is to compare the true and the magnetic amplitudes at either sunrise or sunset. Amplitude-tables were first used towards the close of the sixteenth century.

The log. The sixteenth-century master or pilot kept his reckoning on a traverse-board hung in the steerage. It was a circular board marked out with the 32 rhumbs, along each of which were equally spaced peg-holes. By means of pegs the number of hours and half-hours sailed along each rhumb in the course of the day was marked off, and from these data, coupled with his estimate of the way of the ship under the prevailing wind, each officer or would-be officer worked out the ship's position when the noon Sun was taken, using the departure-tables in the navigating manual to resolve the course. In England, however, some time before 1573 an instrument was devised to determine the ship's way more precisely. This was the log-and-line, quickly imitated by French and Dutch sailors, although not by the Spaniards and Portuguese. A wooden board, weighted at one edge with lead to make it ride upright, was attached to a length of line on a reel, knotted at equal intervals. The log was thrown overboard from the stern of the ship, and after it was clear of the dead water under the ship a half-minute sand-glass was turned and the linesman counted the knots that ran through his hands until his mate cried to him to stop, as the sand ran out. The knots were so spaced (at about 7 fathoms) that the passage of each one during the half-minute represented a rate of one mile an hour. Hence if three knots passed the ship was 'making three knots' or three miles an hour. When, during the seventeenth century, it was established (in the first instance by Richard Norwood, c 1590–1675) that the measure of the degree was over 69 miles and not the 60 miles accepted by English sailors, the situation was met by re-knotting the log-line at a wider interval using the correct proportion. The sailor's method of reckoning remained unchanged, and there were still 60 sea-miles to a degree, but each of these was equal to a minute of arc of the great circle, and corresponded in length to the best measure made of the latter. Complaints were to be heard, both in England and France, that even in the eighteenth century the old seven-fathom log-line was still in use, but this was often adjusted by the use of a sand-glass running for only 27 seconds instead of the full 30 seconds.

The Mercator chart. Gerard Mercator (1512–94) as a young man was the mathematical pupil and assistant of Gemma (Reiner) Frisius (1508–55), and an able instrument-maker and globe-maker. He became a professional cartographer and, familiar as he was with the strictures on the plain chart, invented a new projection for marine charts in 1569. The essential feature of this projection, upon which he published a large map of the world, was that, unlike the plain chart, it gave true bearings or rhumb-lines between any two points. The ship's course could be found by laying a ruler across the map. On the plain chart north–south distances were kept true, but east–west distances were increasingly exaggerated with distance from the equator, since the convergence of the meridians was ignored. If north–south distances were exaggerated *pari passu* with east–west, then there would be no distortion of bearings. The required exaggeration is in the ratio of the secant of the latitude, but Mercator did not explain this; he merely gave a graphical device showing how his map could be used to solve the nautical triangle, in which the elements are bearing and distance, *d. lat.* and *d. long.* Not until towards the close of the century was Mercator's principle brought in a practical form to the notice of chart-makers and sailors.

Two English mathematicians, Thomas Harriot (1560–1621), working privately for Sir Walter Ralegh, and Edward Wright (1558–1615), a professional 'mathematical practitioner', both making use of the trigonometrical tables now available, drew up the tables of meridional parts, as they were termed, by which the lines of latitude on a Mercator chart should be spaced. This table was built up by the continuous addition of secants of the latitude at minute intervals. Wright explained its use in his text-book 'Certain Errors in Navigation' (1599), which included a map of the north Atlantic on the new projection. Instructors in navigation immediately began to teach sailing by the Wright–Mercator chart, and in 1614 one of them, Ralph Handson, published the six cases of the nautical triangle and their trigonometrical solutions. He pointed out, as Stoeffler had done for cosmographers a century earlier, that for *d. long.* the scale of the middle parallel of the triangle must be used.

Longitude. The problem of finding the longitude at sea remained intractable, although many theoretical methods were known and even attempted. Precise timing of celestial events, such as a lunar eclipse or the occultation of a star by the dark limb of the Moon, awaited improvements in horology, as did the carrying of an exact timepiece recording the time at the point of departure. The measurement of lunar distances, and indeed all measurements involving the Moon, were vitiated by the imperfection of lunar tables; nor were the catalogues of the fixed stars precise. The results obtained by John Flamsteed (1646–1719) at the Royal Observatory were not published until early in the eighteenth century. It has also to be remembered that nautical instruments and tables remained generally coarse, and that while during the seventeenth century some manuals introduced the idea of corrections for atmospheric refraction, for dip of the horizon, and for parallax, the correction-tables were imperfect and the seamen indifferent.

Hopes for the longitude were, however, twice raised during the century. Galileo's telescope had long ago revealed Jupiter's satellites, which are very frequently eclipsed. Both in England and France a beginning was made during the second half of the seventeenth century in tabulating the occurrence of these eclipses, but the 6-ft telescope required for their satisfactory observation could not be successfully used at sea, while the mirror of the short reflecting telescope[1] rapidly tarnished when damp. The second invention that seemed to offer possibilities of success was Huygens's pendulum clock (1659), that is to say, a new, reliable timepiece, but after repeated trials it had to be admitted that such a clock was not trustworthy at sea (p 557). Perfected lunar tables were believed to be the answer.

---

[1] First suggested by James Gregory in 1663, and successfully made by Isaac Newton in 1668.

The back-staff. During the seventeenth century the old nautical instruments—astrolabe, quadrant, and cross-staff—were very generally superseded by John Davis's back-staff, first described in 1595, and known to foreign sailors as the English quadrant (figure 341). The advantage of the instrument was not only that the observer turned his back to the Sun: he no longer had to 'blink' simultaneously at horizon and heavenly body. There were two arcs carrying movable

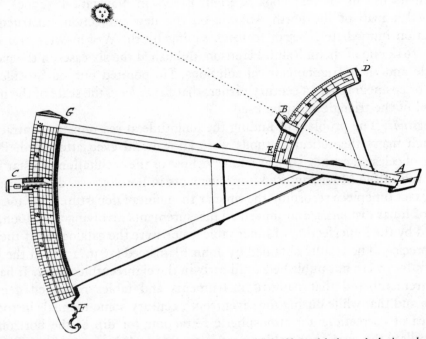

FIGURE 341—*The back-staff. The observer has the Sun behind his shoulder and looks at the horizon through the sight (C) and the slit in the vane (A). Having set the shadow-vane (B) by estimation, the sight (C) is adjusted until the shadow of the upper edge of (B) falls on the upper edge of the slit in (A), with the horizon seen through the slit. Adding the readings of the two scales gives the zenith-distance (complement of the latitude). The larger arc (FG) is divided diagonally so that fractions of a degree may be read more accurately.*

vanes, the upper one being adjusted to the approximate height of the Sun so that its shadow fell on the forward sighting-slit, while with the lower arc the user then sighted precisely on to the horizon. Later patterns had a lens affixed to the sun-vane so that a spot of light cast through it was substituted for the shadow on the forward slit.

Nautical tables. In England a 'Seaman's Kalendar', containing the *Ephemerides* of the Sun and Moon and tables of the most notable fixed stars, was first published in 1600, and was edited by a succession of private teachers of navigation. A rival 'Mariner's New Kalendar' appeared in 1676, and continued to be published for over a century. In France the semi-official *Connoissance des Temps* began to appear annually under royal licence in 1678–9, edited by a member of the Académie des Sciences, and has continued publication ever since. Although not specifically a nautical almanac it included the tables necessary for sailors. A seamen's manual was expected to contain tables of meridional parts, distance and departure tables (for resolving the course) for every quarter rhumb ($2\frac{7}{8}°$) and for every degree, as well as logarithm tables for the natural numbers and trigonometrical functions, and tide-tables.

IV. THE EIGHTEENTH CENTURY

No new principles were introduced into survey and cartography during the eighteenth century, but plane-table, theodolite, and level were used with increasing refinement. This is exemplified in the procedures adopted in France for determining the shape of the Earth by re-measuring the arc of the meridian. The spherical shape had been called in question both by observations made with the pendulum and by Sir Isaac Newton's assumption on theoretical grounds that the globe was an oblate spheroid. This conflicted with the measurements made by the second Cassini (p 544) when he extended the meridian measured by Picard to the south of France. These pointed to an ovoid shape, with the polar diameter exceeding the equatorial. Louis XV ordered expeditions to be organized to make fresh measurements near the equator and near the Arctic circle, the latter being described in detail by a member of the party, the philosopher Maupertuis (1698–1759).

The principle to be employed was that adopted by the Arabs in the tenth century, namely to observe the meridian altitude of a star, to travel north or south until its altitude had changed by one degree, and to measure the distance travelled. The French party went to Finland, then Swedish territory, and set up two observatories (at Tornea and Kittis) approximately in the same meridian and about one degree of latitude apart. In each, the direction of the meridian was laid down precisely by repeated observations of the meridian passage of the Sun and of selected bright stars.

The clock used for timing observations was one made by the famous George Graham (1673–1751) of London, regulated daily by observation of matching forenoon and afternoon altitudes of the Sun, and used in combination with a seconds pendulum. At the moment of their meridian passages, the altitudes of two stars close to the zenith were to be observed, since this would eliminate the errors due to atmospheric refraction. The instrument used (called a 'sector'), also made by Graham, consisted of a 9-ft telescope mounted so as to hang vertically. It was so delicately poised that it could be directed on the star by means of a micrometer screw, the revolutions of which were counted from its initial position. The silver cross-wires in the focus of the telescope had been fixed on springs so that they were held at constant tension in spite of the extreme temperature changes to be expected, for the observations were to take over a year (1736-7). The limb of the instrument had been graduated by Graham personally, and the index-error determined, but the scientists took the precaution of calibrating the divisions by passing the scale under a pair of diverging taut wires over each of which a microscope was fixed. The observed altitudes were corrected for the minute change in stellar positions due to the precession of the equinoxes between the dates of observation at the respective stations, and for the phenomenon of aberration recently discovered by the English astronomer Bradley.

The distance between the two points of observation was measured with equal care. A number of visible hill-top beacons were established, whose positions were to be observed from either extremity of the base-line. This was about 8 miles long, and was pegged out between two signal-posts on the frozen and level surface of the river Tornea. The measuring was done by two independent parties carrying 30-ft measuring-poles of fir-wood. These had been tested under different temperature conditions, when it was found that they expanded or contracted almost imperceptibly, by 'the thickness of a leaf of the finest paper, more or less'. The two sets of measurements differed by a mere 4 in, and the mean values were taken. After the triangulation was completed and the distance between the observatories calculated, the savants were astonished to find that the degree near the Arctic circle was nearly a mile longer than Cassini's theory had predicted, and definitely longer than Picard's degree measured just north of Paris. The Earth was in fact flattened at the poles, a result amply confirmed by the expedition sent to Peru to carry out a similar measurement, whose return was delayed until 1745. The length of the degree at each latitude was thus established with sufficient accuracy for navigational and cartographic purposes.

A map of France, based entirely on triangulation, was begun in 1744 by Cassini de Thury, and took almost forty years to complete. In 1784 the English military engineer William Roy (1726-90), who as a young captain had mapped the Highlands of Scotland after the rebellion of '45, undertook a triangulation in southern England which was to link across the Channel with the French geodetic survey. The necessary base was measured on Hounslow Heath, and a few years later (1791) the Ordnance Survey was officially instituted. During the century much detailed topographical survey was carried out on the continent in various theatres of war by other military engineers, who developed the convention for indicating slopes on maps by precise hachuring. Pen or pencil strokes were drawn downhill, being made thicker on steep slopes, finer on gentle slopes. Towards the end of the century the length, width, and spacing of the strokes were made systematic, so that actual gradients could be indicated. The increasing observation and recording of heights above sea-level also enabled the first contoured map, one of France, to be drawn in 1791. Improvements in instrument-making, such as John Dollond's invention of the achromatic lens in 1758 and Jesse Ramsden's of a scale-cutting machine in 1775, also advanced the accuracy of cartography together with that of other observational sciences.

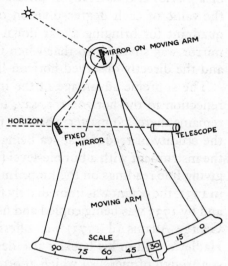

FIGURE 342—*The principle of Hadley's octant. When the included angle of the instrument is D°, the angle of both the fixed mirror and the movable mirror (in the zero position) to the axis of the instrument is (45−D/4)°. When the index is moved d° from zero, the angle of incident light must be raised 2d° to enter the telescope or sight.*

Improvements in the seaman's equipment were foreshadowed by the publication in 1686 of the first wind-chart (trades and monsoons) compiled by Edmond Halley (1656–1742) and by the same author's chart of the variation of the magnetic compass. Including his own recent observations at sea, the figures were expressed by Halley as interpolated isogonic lines[1] drawn over the most frequented oceans at intervals of one degree. This was the earliest isometric map. Users were warned of the secular change in the variation, and about the middle of the eighteenth century the chart was revised by Mountaine and Dodson to include the very large number of observations by then available. These were the more reliable owing to the introduction of improved mariners' and azimuth compasses made under the direction of Dr Gowin Knight (1713–72), who used magnetized steel bars instead of lodestones for 'touching' the needle.

Meanwhile a great advance followed the introduction of John Hadley's quadrant, the principle of which had been anticipated by Robert Hooke and Isaac Newton, but since forgotten. If a mirror is fixed opposite to the sighting-tube or telescope of a quadrant, and a second mirror, parallel to the first in the

[1] Lines of equal variation.

zero position, is placed on the arm of the quadrant which moves across the limb (that is, the scale) at the pivotal point, then an object such as a star can be reflected from one mirror to the other and down the tube so that it appears to coincide with an object seen directly. The angle between the two objects is then twice the angle between the two mirrors (figure 342). The angle of 90° (quadrant of a circle) is thus read off on a scale of 45° (octant) and to facilitate reading the value of each degree-division on the scale is doubled. Hadley devised his quadrant for bringing a star down to the horizon. Only one-half of the fixed mirror was silvered, so that when the movable arm stood at zero the reflected and the directly observed horizon-lines coincided.

The supreme advantage of the instrument is that, once a star is brought by reflection to the horizon (or, say, to the rim of the directly observed moon), it remains there, no matter what the motion of the ship. The principal reason for the crudity of readings at sea being thus removed, it became worth while to fit the instrument with a bubble-level (for it should be held vertically) and a vernier giving fine readings on the limb. Introduced by Hadley before the Royal Society in 1731, the octant was immediately tested and approved by the British Admiralty, and by 1733 was being copied and used in France. In 1738 the instrument-maker George Adams (d 1773) was offering a cheaper form of the instrument than Hadley's, and in his booklet also describes the invention of the artificial horizon —a trough of mercury which affords a horizontal reflecting surface. The star as reflected from the movable mirror is brought into coincidence with the image of the same star reflected from this surface, seen directly. The angle thus found is equal to twice the elevation of the star above the horizon. The advantage of the new device is that the frequent obscurity of the visible horizon is overcome, as well as the uncertainties of atmospheric refraction, while the correction for the dip of the horizon below the observer's eye becomes unnecessary. By 1757 the limit of the octant was extended to cover rather more than 120°, so that its included angle was now rather over 60°, and it thus became a sextant. Besides its daily use for 'taking the Sun' at noon (when a dark glass is turned between the mirrors), and for measuring lunar distances (the angle between a star and the Moon's rim), the sextant can be used for taking horizontal angles. Thus the standard of hydrographical charting was improved, as it was also by the introduction of the plane-table and of the method of triangulation where it was possible for the seaman to work ashore.

Astronomical observations by scientists on shore, based on eclipses, on lunar distances, or on the appearance and disappearance of Jupiter's satellites, taken in combination with the improved time-keeping now possible at a stationary point of observation (ch 24), led to a lengthening list of accurate longitudes and consequent improvement of maps and charts. At sea, however, on a travelling ship, no such accuracy was possible, while the determination of longitude even to a single degree does not provide safety. An Act of Parliament of 1714 offered a reward of £20 000 for a device for determining longitude at sea, the test being that the method was to be accurate to within half a degree during and after a voyage to the West Indies and back. It was generally assumed that the solution lay in a precise time-keeper, that is, a chronometer correct to within two minutes at the end of such a voyage. In France a generous prize was offered with a similar object. Improvements in horology, associated with the names of Thomas Tompion (1639–1713) and George Graham in the one country, and of Sully and Julian Leroy in the other, had still not dealt with the difficulty arising from the expansion and contraction of metal parts with temperature changes (ch 24).

The younger Leroy and John Harrison (p 672) gave themselves to this problem for many years, and the latter was successful with his fourth chronometer (the first was made in 1731) in 1763. The British Admiralty imposed rigid tests on the English time-piece both at sea and at the Royal Observatory, and Harrison did not receive the full award until shortly before his death. A facsimile of his 'No. 4' (a watch-type) made by a clockmaker, Larcum Kendall, was carried by Captain Cook (1728–79) on his second voyage, when it proved its worth. Since, however, the cost of such an instrument ran into hundreds of pounds, there was an interval before it could be cheapened for general use. The Admiralty did not order a general issue to the Royal Navy until 1825. Meanwhile the method of lunar distances had been greatly improved, not only by the refinement of the sextant but by the precise lunar tables published by the Astronomer Royal, Nevil Maskelyne (1732–1811), who first issued an annual 'Nautical Almanac' in 1767; it was later continued by the Admiralty. In France annual astronomical tables are published by the Bureau des Longitudes, continuing those first edited by Picard under the title of *Connoissance des Temps* in 1679.

BIBLIOGRAPHY

DAUMAS, M. 'Les instruments scientifiques.' Presses Universitaires de France, Paris. 1953.
GOULD, R. T. "John Harrison and his Timekeepers." *Mariner's Mirror*, **21**, 115-391, 1935.
GUNTHER, R. T. 'Early Science in Oxford', Vol. 1, Pt II. Oxford University Press. 1923.
MARGUET, F. R. 'Histoire de la longitude à la mer au XVIIIᵉ siècle en France.' Paris. 1917.
TAYLOR, EVA G. R. 'Tudor Geography.' Methuen, London. 1930.
Idem. 'Late Tudor and Early Stuart Geography.' Methuen, London. 1934.
Idem. 'The Mathematical Practitioners of Tudor and Stuart England.' University Press, Cambridge. 1954.
Idem. 'The Haven-Finding Art.' Hollis and Carter, London. 1956.

21

THE CALENDAR

SIR HAROLD SPENCER JONES

A CALENDAR is a method of combining days into periods, such as weeks, months, and years, for the convenience of civil life, the guidance of day-by-day activities, and the fixing of religious feasts and observances.

Attempts to construct a satisfactory calendar go back to the dawn of civilization. It was primarily with this end in view that the observation and recording of the positions of the heavenly bodies, of the phases of the Moon, of eclipses, and of other celestial phenomena were first undertaken.

The three astronomical periods of most importance in everyday life are (i) the period of the rotation of the Earth on its axis, the day, giving the alternation of day-time and night-time associated with the rising and setting of the Sun; (ii) the period of the revolution of the Moon around the Earth, with the sequence of its phases, giving the month; (iii) the period of the revolution of the Earth around the Sun, with the sequence of the seasons, giving the year.

The sidereal revolution of the Moon is the period occupied by the Moon in passing from a given star back again to the same star. Its average length is 27·321661 days. The synodic revolution, generally known as the lunation or lunar month, is the period from new Moon to new Moon, or from full Moon to full Moon. Its average length is 29·530598 days. The actual length is not constant, because the orbits of the Moon round the Earth and of the Earth round the Sun are slightly elliptical and because of the perturbations of these orbits; the extreme range in the true length of the lunar month is about thirteen hours.

The sidereal year is the period of a revolution of the Earth round the Sun, relative to the fixed stars. It is the year determined, for example, by observation of the 'heliacal risings' of stars, that is, by the first appearance of conspicuous bright stars, such as Sirius, in the morning twilight near the eastern horizon. Its length is 365·256360 days.

The natural unit marked out for the use of man is not, however, the sidereal year. It is the period of revolution of the Earth relative to the First Point of Aries (the apparent point in the heavens where the path of the Sun—the ecliptic —crosses the equator from south to north); this period determines the commencement of the seasons and all associated phenomena. It is called the tropical year and its length is 365·242199 days: its length was determined by the ancients by the use of the gnomon. The sidereal year is about 20 minutes longer than the tropical year, this difference being due to the retrograde motion of the First Point of Aries resulting from the precession of the Earth's axis. The difference in the lengths of these two years was determined with fair accuracy about 130 B.C. by the Greek astronomer Hipparchus.

The complexity of the problem of devising a satisfactory calendar is due primarily to the incommensurability of the three natural periods of time: the day, the month, and the year. Thus the tropical year contains 12·368267 lunations. Further, the first attempts at the formation of a calendar were made long before the lengths either of the lunation or of the tropical year were known with any accuracy. The beginning of the lunar month was customarily fixed either by the first appearance of the crescent of the new Moon in the evening sky after sunset, or by the first invisibility of the crescent of the old Moon in the morning sky before sunrise. The first or last visibility of the crescent Moon depends, under clear conditions, on several variable factors; the principal of these are the angles which the ecliptic and the plane of the Moon's orbit make with the horizon; the distance of the Moon north or south of the ecliptic; and the distance of the Moon from the Earth. In the latitude of Babylon the time after new Moon at which the crescent can first be seen may be as short as 16 hours or as long as 42 hours; there is a corresponding range in the times before new Moon at which the crescent can last be seen. Superposed on these variable conditions of visibility is the variable length of the lunation itself.

For the work of primitive man the cycle of the seasons was by far the most important period. Most of his activities were regulated by this cycle, whether, as in northern latitudes, it involved a cold winter, in which the earth was dormant, and a warm summer, in which crops could be raised; or whether, as in lower latitudes, it involved an alternation of dry and wet seasons; or whether, as in Egypt, it was bound up with the annual flooding of the cultivable land. Hunters and fishermen might be dependent upon the seasonal migration of animals and fish. As phenomena dependent on meteorological causes, such as the beginning of the rainy season or the flooding of a river, are too irregular in their recurrence to serve as reliable guides to the proper times for preparing the ground, for sowing, and for harvesting, some more certain guides were needed. The variability of the length of the lunation, as determined from the visibility of the crescent Moon, and the fact that the times of new or full Moon did not recur at the same periods each year, combined to make the Moon an uncertain guide.

From very early times it was known that different constellations were visible at different seasons of the year. As the Sun has an apparent eastward motion relative to the stars of about 1° a day, any given star crosses the meridian and is due south about four minutes earlier each day. Amongst the Babylonians and Egyptians, as also amongst the Greeks and Romans, it was customary to observe the heliacal risings of bright stars to indicate the passage of the Sun amongst the stars. Thus in Egypt the periodic flooding of the Nile usually began soon after the summer solstice and its coming was heralded by the heliacal rising of Sothis or Sirius, in the month of June.

The gnomon, a stick stuck vertically into the ground, served with some peoples to mark the succession of the seasons. Its use is bound up with the northward and southward motions of the Sun relative to the stars in the course of the year. At the summer solstice the Sun rises farthest north of east and sets farthest north of west; at the winter solstice, it rises farthest south of east and sets farthest south of west; at the equinoxes it rises due east and sets due west, directions which are midway between the directions of rising and setting at the summer and winter solstices. These positions could be marked out by stones and, when once marked, were a sure guide to the time of year.

The length of the tropical year exceeds 12 lunations by about 11 days. Consequently when the month was the lunation, whose beginning was obtained by observation of the lunar crescent, it became necessary every two or three years to intercalate a thirteenth month; these intercalations originally took place at irregular intervals when it appeared that the months were deviating too far from their proper seasons. Gradually, with the emergence of a priestly caste, one of whose duties was to ensure that the religious festivals were observed at the proper seasons of the year, the regulation of the calendar became one of their principal functions. Records were kept, regularities were noted, and cycles were determined which facilitated prediction and served as a basis for providing a calendar system. But there was a great variety in the nature and complexity of the various calendar systems that were developed amongst different peoples and at different times. It is the purpose of this chapter to consider some of these early calendars.

1. THE EGYPTIAN CALENDAR

The most important event in the year in the agricultural life of Egypt is the annual flooding of the Nile, as it is upon this flood that the fertility of the narrow cultivated strip of land along each bank depends. The year in Egypt was in early times divided into three seasons—flood time, seed time, harvest time—each containing four months. Though the months were given names derived from the important feasts celebrated in them, they were always designated in hiero-glyphics by their position in the season to which they belonged. The first month of the first season, which began the year, was called Thoth, which is equivalent to Seth or Sothis, the name of the brightest star, Sirius, whose heliacal rising in June foreshadowed the flooding of the Nile. This suggests that the Egyptians, when a rigid time-reckoning was introduced, began the year with the heliacal rising of Sirius.

The day in Egypt began at dawn and was reckoned from one dawn to the next. It was natural, therefore, that the month should begin on the morning of the day when the crescent of the old Moon was no longer visible in the eastern sky before sunrise. The original Egyptian calendar was purely lunar. Some time in the fourth or fifth millennium B.C., when the heliacal rising of Sirius and the start of the Nile inundation were near together in time, Sirius, or Sothis, came to be regarded as the harbinger of the inundation; and its heliacal rising was adopted as the starting-point for a purely lunar calendar, containing three seasons each of four months, the commencement of each month being determined by observa-tion of the invisibility of the crescent of the old Moon. The beginning of the year was the first day of invisibility of the crescent Moon after the heliacal rising of Sirius. It must have been recognized quite soon after the introduction of this calendar that, though the intervals between successive inundations of the Nile were very variable, the intervals between successive heliacal risings of Sothis were practically constant and that they exceeded the length of 12 months by some 11 days. It thus became necessary at intervals of three—or occasionally of two—years to intercalate a thirteenth month. This intercalation appears, from the discussion by Parker of the evidence from various inscriptions and papyri, to have been made whenever the first month began within 11 days of the heliacal rising of Sothis; it was thereby ensured that the feast called 'Opener of the Year', which marked the time of the heliacal rising, was always celebrated in the twelfth month [1]. The intercalary month was dedicated to Thoth and a feast of this god was celebrated in it.

In course of time, as a well organized economic life developed in Egypt, the inconveniences became apparent of a calendar in which the year sometimes had twelve months and sometimes thirteen, the beginning of each of which had to be fixed by observation. The idea of a fixed civil year, based upon an averaged lunar year, was conceived. From records of the actual lengths of the lunar years in previous decades, it could readily be found that the average length was very close to 365 days; records kept for a few years of the heliacal rising of Sirius would also show that the average interval between successive heliacal risings was 365 days. So the introduction of a fixed civil calendar followed: in this calendar the length of the year was taken to be 365 days, and the year was divided into three seasons, each containing 4 months, each month having 30 days. The extra 5 days were intercalary and were placed before the first month of the year, in the same way that the intercalary month of the lunar calendar, when it was needed, always headed the lunar year. The circumstances of the introduction of this civil calendar are uncertain, but Parker has shown that there is a strong probability that it came into use early in the third millennium B.C.

The two calendars were used concurrently. The fixed civil calendar served for the regulation of secular matters, while the lunar calendar continued to be used for religious purposes, such as the determination of feasts. For some time it would not have been detected that the adopted length of the civil year was too short by about 6 hours, causing the fixed calendar to move forward through the seasons by one day every 4 years, for the interval between successive heliacal risings of Sirius was 365 days to a good approximation, while the variability of the lunar calendar was sufficiently large for general agreement between the civil and lunar years to persist for many decades.

But eventually, after perhaps two centuries, it could no longer have escaped notice that the first month of the civil year ended before the first month of the lunar year had begun. The fixed civil calendar and the lunar calendar based on observation had gradually drifted out of phase with one another. The civil calendar had by that time become so well established and had proved so convenient that there was no question of forcing it back into agreement with the lunar calendar.

The difficulty was solved by an ingenious device—the creation of a special lunar year, whose sole purpose was to maintain the parallelism between the lunar and civil calendars that had existed when the civil calendar was introduced. The beginning of each lunar month was still obtained by observation as before, but, by suitable intercalation of a thirteenth month, the new lunar year maintained its general agreement with the fixed civil year. The original lunar calendar, tied, as we have seen, to the heliacal rising of Sothis, continued in use as before, while the later lunar calendar was free to progress through the seasons along with the civil calendar. It is not known precisely when the second lunar calendar was introduced, but Parker considers that it was likely to have been around 2500 B.C. From the time of its introduction, three calendar years were in use in Egypt, all of which continued in use to the very end of pagan times.

At a much later date this second lunar calendar became stereotyped into a schematic form, the lengths of whose months were fixed by definite rules instead of by observation, but in such a way that the beginning of each month fell very close to the true new moon. Most of the details of this schematic calendar are given in the Papyrus Carlsberg 9, which was written in or after A.D. 144 and which is stated by Parker to be the only truly mathematical astronomical Egyptian text yet published (vol I, p 797 and plate 36). There is evidence to prove that this calendar was in use long before A.D. 144 and Parker, from the discussion of this evidence, concludes that it was introduced somewhere about the year 357 B.C.

The complete details of this later lunar calendar have been reconstructed by Parker with very little uncertainty. The calendar was in the form of a 25-year cycle in which each month had a length of either 29 or 30 days, so arranged that there were never more than two consecutive months of the same length. A thirteenth month was intercalated in the 1st, 3rd, 6th, 9th, 12th, 14th, 17th, 20th, and 23rd year of each cycle, these years being known as 'great' years. The rule determining the intercalation was that a month was intercalary whenever the first day of the lunar month Thoth would fall before the first day of the civil month Thoth. In the complete cycle of 25 years there were accordingly 309 months; 145 of the months had a length of 29 days and the other 164 had a length of 30 days. The duration of the cycle was consequently 9125 days, which gave for the average length of a year through the cycle exactly 365 days, in agreement with the length of the Egyptian civil year. The precise length of 309 lunar months is 9124·9517 days, which differs from the length of the 25-year cyclic lunar calendar by not much more than one hour. Thus it follows that the beginning of each month could never deviate by much more than a day from the true new Moon, an amount which is within the uncertainty of the observation of the invisibility of the old lunar crescent.

The Egyptians were the first people to determine the length of the year as $365\frac{1}{4}$ days, although their civil year was given a fixed length of 365 days. Their determination of the length of the year was probably based on observation that the heliacal rising of Sirius occurred on the average a day later every four civil years, causing the civil calendar to progress slowly through the seasons. Taking the length of the natural year as $365\frac{1}{4}$ days, they formed a cycle of 1461 calendar years which were equated to 1460 natural years, this cycle being known as the Sothic cycle. The length of the sidereal year is 365·2564 days and is thus not strictly $365\frac{1}{4}$ days; but Schoch has shown that the heliacal rising of Sirius, a star with a very large proper-motion, recurred after a mean interval of 365·2507 days, giving 1456 years as the precise length of the Sothic cycle, after which the heliacal rising would occur on the same date in the calendar year [2]. Censorinus in the third century A.D. called a year in which Sirius, the dog-star, was first seen in the morning twilight on the first day of the first month Thoth, an *annus canicularis*. Ideler concluded that this occurred in the years 2782 B.C. and 1322 B.C., and supposed that the introduction of the civil year fixed at 365 days occurred in the latter year [3]. Neugebauer and Parker both consider the most probable date to have been *c* 2800 B.C.

But long after the length of the year was known to be 365¼ days, the movable year of 365 days continued to be used, until, in fact, the introduction of the Alexandrian calendar, probably in the year 26 B.C. In the ninth year of Ptolemy Euergetes, 239 B.C., the great assembly of priests at Canopus passed a decree, according to which an additional day was to be inserted every fourth year in order to arrest the forward movement of the civil year. This decree was of no effect at that time and the civil year continued to have a length of 365 days. The first undisputed fixed year in Egypt came with the introduction of the Alexandrian calendar, in which this change—the insertion of an additional day every fourth year—was made; the first day of Thoth in this calendar coincides with 29 August (or in leap year 30 August) in the Julian calendar. But the old calendar still remained in use along with the reformed calendar until well into the third century A.D.

The Egyptian civil calendar is of importance in chronology because, until the Julian reform of the Roman calendar in 46 B.C., it was the only calendar in which the length of each month and of each year was fixed by an invariable rule and not left to be varied at the whim of officials. For astronomical purposes it had the great convenience that the exact number of days between any two observations, whose dates in the Egyptian calendar were known, could be determined with ease and certainty. Thus we find Hipparchus, who observed at Rhodes, reducing Chaldean observations to the Egyptian calendar.

The Egyptians did not use a definite era from which to date events, but referred always to the year of the reign of the king in which an event happened. Both Hipparchus and Ptolemy accordingly used for convenience an era dating from the beginning of the reign of Nabonassar, founder of the kingdom of the Babylonians, known as the era of Nabonassar. This era begins with midday on the 1st day of Thoth of the first year of the reign of Nabonassar, corresponding to 26 February in the year 3967 of the Julian period, or 747 B.C. At the beginning of the era 1 448 658 days had elapsed in the Julian period. This era was of great convenience for scientific purposes, but was never used in ordinary everyday life. The year used for dating events in this era was the Egyptian year of 365 days. By means of the famous Canon of Kings, prepared by Ptolemy, dates in Babylonian and Egyptian history, expressed in terms of the year of the reign of the then king, can be conveniently converted into dates in the era of Nabonassar.

The Egyptians began the day with sunrise; they divided the interval from sunrise to sunset into 12 equal hours, and the interval from sunset to sunrise also into 12 equal hours. The daytime hours were necessarily of different length from the night hours, except at the equinoxes, and both the day and night hours varied in length according to the seasons of the year. The hours so provided were known as temporal hours.

The seven-day week is not an interval of time that is marked out by any celestial motions. It was introduced into Europe from the Assyrians, and then from the Jews it was taken over by the Christians. The Egyptians divided the 30-day month of their civil calendar into three decans, or 10-day periods. There were 36 decans in the year, to each of which corresponded a divinity. There are two series of divinities connected with the year in Egypt; one consists of the 36-decanal divinities of the civil year, the other consists of 59 divinities. Parker has suggested that the 59 deities are made up of 48, each representing one quarter of the Moon throughout the 12 lunar months of the lunar year (which together account for 354 days), the remaining 11 each representing one day, and making with the 48 others the civil year of 365 days. The two different series represent the essential duality of the year.

The seven-day week must have been familiar to the Egyptians, through the Jews, from early times. But the first reference to its use in Egypt is by Dio Cassius (3rd century A.D.). The names for the days of the week which have been adopted throughout western Europe are based on the names of the seven known 'planets', arranged in their supposed order of decreasing distance from the Earth —Saturn, Jupiter, Mars, the Sun, Venus, Mercury, the Moon—and are of astrological origin. There was a great development of astrology in Egypt at about the beginning of the Christian era; according to the current astrological beliefs, each hour in succession was consecrated to a different planet, the sequence following the order of their distance. The planet to which the first hour of the day was consecrated was regarded as the regent of that day. If, then, we start with the day whose regent is Saturn, that planet would control the 1st, 8th, 15th, and 22nd hours; the 23rd would belong to Jupiter, the 24th to Mars, and the first hour of the next day to the Sun. Thus is obtained the succession of regents: Saturn, Sun, Moon, Mars, Mercury, Jupiter, Venus, from which the names of the days of the week are derived. In the Teutonic languages, the names of their divinities Tiu, Woden, Thor, and Freya are used instead of their Roman counterparts, Mars, Mercury, Jupiter, Venus; the latter can be recognized in the names used in the Latin languages.

Though the naming of the seven days of the week after the seven planets started in Egypt, whence it spread to Rome and thence throughout western Europe, there is no evidence that the seven-day week was ever in common use in the civil life of Egypt.

II. THE BABYLONIAN CALENDAR

The earliest observations recorded by Ptolemy in his *Almagest*, going back to the year 721 B.C., were observations of eclipses of the Moon made by the Chaldeans, the hereditary priestly caste of Babylon, who acquired a great reputation for soothsaying and forecasting the future by means of the stars. Astrology was first brought by them to a well developed system, and along with its cult there went the study of astronomy, which was unbroken in Babylon for more than 3000 years. The accuracy with which various astronomical periods were determined by the Chaldeans is amazing; many of their determinations were more accurate than those made later by the Greek astronomers [4].

After Cyrus the Great destroyed the Babylonian Empire in 539 B.C., the caste of the Chaldeans gradually lost its splendour. It was at about that time that the Greeks and other western peoples began to become acquainted with the astrology of the east.

Knowledge of the details of the Babylonian calendar is less precise than that of the Egyptian. The calendar seems to have become fairly well fixed late in the third millennium B.C. Its basis was lunar, the beginning of the month being fixed by observation of the first visibility of the lunar crescent; the day, correspondingly, began with sunset. The year normally contained twelve months, but, in order to keep it in phase with the seasons, a thirteenth month was from time to time inserted by repeating a month. There was no consistency, however, in the method of adjusting the length of the year; the intercalary month was inserted at intervals that were quite irregular, being sometimes as short as six months and sometimes as long as six years, and though normally the month to be repeated was the last month of the year it was not unusual for another month to be chosen.

But for the recording of their astronomical observations and for facilitating calculations the very convenient fixed year of 365 days was used. This year may have been derived from the Egyptians or found independently. It appears to have been used in Babylon from the time of the accession of Nabonassar in 747 B.C. and may have been due to him. It thus became possible to determine with ease the exact interval between two observations; the determination of astronomical periods was thereby much facilitated.

The records kept by the Chaldeans of the times and magnitudes of lunar eclipses enabled them to discover the saros or eclipse period, after which eclipses recur. This period was known to them at least as early as the sixth century B.C. They determined its length as $6585\frac{1}{3}$ days. The discovery of the saros made it possible to foretell with considerable accuracy the occurrence of eclipses, although they had no accurate tables of the Sun and Moon. They found the saros period to be equal to 223 lunations. The precise length of 223 lunations is 6585·322 days, so that the error in the Chaldean determination amounts only to about one day in 1800 years or, expressed otherwise, their determination of the mean length of a lunation was in error only by $4\frac{1}{2}$ seconds. The *anomalistic* period of the Moon—the average interval between successive passages through perigee—is 27·55455 days: 239 anomalistic periods amount to 6585·537 days. The *draconitic* period of the Moon—the average interval between successive passages through the nodes of the orbit (the points at which the orbit intersects the ecliptic)—is 27·21222 days; 242 draconitic periods amount to 6585·357 days. Hence, after the interval of a saros, the position of the Moon in its orbit with respect both to the perigee and the nodes is practically unaltered, which accounts for the very close recurrence of the circumstances of individual eclipses after the lapse of a saros period.

It must also have been known to the Chaldeans that the length of the tropical year was $365\frac{1}{4}$ days, for Ptolemy states that after the saros period of $6585\frac{1}{3}$ days (just over 18 years) the Sun was taken to be 10° 40′ to the east of its position at its beginning. Its motion in longitude during this period was accordingly $(18 \times 360°) + 10\frac{2}{3}°$, from which it follows that its motion in longitude through 360° (the tropical year) is almost exactly $365\frac{1}{4}$ days. It is uncertain whether the length of the year was first obtained in this way or whether, from previous knowledge, this length was used to derive the change in the Sun's longitude of 10° 40′. In either case, the length of the tropical year became known.

In 529 B.C. an attempt was made to provide regular intercalations of months by the introduction of an 8-year cycle, consisting of 99 lunations, in which the intercalary months were inserted at fixed places in the cycle; the beginning of each month continued to be fixed by observation. The mean length of 99 lunations is 2923·53 days, that of 8 tropical years is 2921·94 days, while the then accepted length was 2922 days. The error in the supposed equivalence of 8 years to 99 lunations caused the cycle to be abandoned after 25 years, when arbitrary intercalation was resumed.

In 383 B.C. a 19-year system of intercalations was introduced by the Chaldean astronomer Kidinnu (often referred to by the Greek form of his name, Kidenas) in which 19 years were made equal to 235 lunations, seven intercalary months being inserted at fixed places in the cycle, the beginning of each month continuing to be determined by observation. The 19-year cycle had been announced by Meton at Athens in 432 B,C. It is not certain whether the introduction of this cycle in Babylon was made independently of Meton's discovery. After 235 lunations the phases of the Moon recur on the same day of the solar year and nearly at the same time. Such careful records of lunar phases and eclipses were kept by the Chaldeans that it seems unlikely that they could have failed to discover for themselves the 19-year cycle. It should be noted, moreover, that whereas Meton fixed the length of his cycle at 6940 days, the Chaldeans, by determining the beginning of each month by observations of the lunar crescent, tied the length of the tropical year, through the adopted equivalence of 19 years to 235 lunations, to the true mean length of the lunation and so made the mean calendar year equal to 365·2468 days, as compared with the 365·2632 days of the Metonic cycle. The former value is much more nearly correct.

The 19-year cycle of intercalations, introduced by Kidinnu, remained in use throughout the subsequent existence of the Babylonian calendar. It is of interest to note that the determination of the lengths of the year and of the lunation by Kidinnu, together with the system of seven fixed intercalations in 19 years, were taken over by the Jewish calendar and are still used to this day.

The Chaldeans used in their observations both the system of temporal hours, in which the intervals between sunrise and sunset and between sunset and sunrise were separately divided into 12 hours, and the system of equinoctial hours, in which the whole day was divided into 24 equal hours. If an occultation were observed, for instance, the cock of the water-clock was opened at sunset and the quantities of water which flowed out from sunset to the moment of observation and from that moment to sunrise were compared; the time of observation in temporal hours was thus obtained. From the known variation in the length of the temporal hours through the year, the time could then be reduced to equinoctial hours. Alternatively, the amount of water which flowed out from sunset to sunrise was compared with the amount which flowed out from sunrise to sunset, so that a direct conversion from temporal to equinoctial hours was possible.

III. THE GREEK CALENDAR

The basis of the Greek calendar was lunar. The beginning of each month was determined by the first appearance of the crescent Moon in the evening sky after sunset. The length of the month was consequently equal, on the average, to that of the lunation, and was normally either 29 or 30 days. The days were numbered through the month from its beginning, partly to indicate those days which the superstitious had come to regard as lucky or unlucky and partly to ensure that the festival days should not be overlooked in spells of cloudy weather, for most of the Greek festivals were celebrated at definite phases of the Moon.

From very early times the festivals were associated with definite seasons of the year. It must have been evident soon after the lunar month was adopted that the year of twelve months was appreciably shorter than the year of the seasons, because the day of the shortest or longest shadow of the gnomon shifted rapidly from year to year and in three years by more than a month. So a thirteenth month had sometimes to be intercalated. Whether in early times the additional month was always inserted into the same year by the different communities is uncertain, but it can be assumed that there was common agreement from the time of the inauguration of the Olympic games in 776 B.C.

Different communities, however, kept calendars that differed in the season when the year began and in the place in the year at which the insertion of the intercalary month was made. The public authorities decided the length of each month. There was often considerable neglect in keeping the months adjusted to the phases of the Moon, and the manipulation of the calendar became a public scandal. Aristophanes held it up to contempt in *The Clouds*, acted in 432 B.C., when he made the Moon complain that the days were not being kept correctly according to her reckoning.

The adjustment of the calendar to the seasons was made by observing the heliacal rising and setting of bright stars. The zodiacal sign in which the Sun was at any particular season of the year was known; the heliacal rising or setting of any particular sign gave a rough indication of the time of year.

The most ancient division of the Greek year was into three seasons—spring, summer, and winter—which were marked out by natural phenomena such as the arrival and departure of migratory birds. Autumn was first mentioned about 400 B.C. by Hippocrates and other Greek medical writers. Winter began with the heliacal setting of the Pleiades and ended with the spring equinox; spring continued until the heliacal rising of the Pleiades; summer until the heliacal rising of Arcturus; autumn occupied the remainder of the year until the next heliacal setting of the Pleiades.

With the development of civic life and of culture, the system of movable months and years tied to the phases of the Moon became increasingly inconvenient. A growing need was felt for a calendar in which the months and years were not dependent on observation, which was often hindered, moreover, by the weather. The search began for a cycle that should contain as nearly as possible an exact number of years and months. The first step in this direction was taken by Solon about the beginning of the sixth century B.C. He introduced a regular alternation of months of 29 and 30 days, so that 12 months occupied 354 days. This agrees with the length of the lunar year to about 9 hours. But it is $11\frac{1}{4}$ days short of the length of the year; accordingly, in alternate years a month of 30 days was inserted. The two years together—the short and the long —were $7\frac{1}{2}$ days too long, so from time to time the intercalation was omitted.

A great improvement on the cycle of Solon was effected by the 8-year cycle or *octaeteris* invented by Cleostratus in the 59th Olympiad (about 542 B.C.). In this cycle 8 years were made equal to 99 lunations and to 2922 days. The year contained months of 30 and 29 days alternately. A month of 30 days was intercalated in the third, fifth, and eighth year of the cycle by repeating the sixth month, Poseideon. The average length of the solar year was thus made equal to $365\frac{1}{4}$ days. As the true length of 99 lunations is 2923·53 days the cycle would rapidly have resulted in a large error in the agreement between the beginning of the month and the new Moon.

Geminus records further improvements made to the cycle to give greater accuracy, but does not state when they were introduced. First, 3 days were added each 16 years, which gave a better approximation to the mean length of the lunation, but only at the expense of a larger error in the year. To obtain a better adjustment to the year, one month of 30 days was omitted in 160 years. With these adjustments 160 years (whose true length is 58 438·8 days) were made equal to 1979 lunations (whose true length is 58 441·0 days) and to 58 440 days. There was accordingly an accumulated error of about one day in 160 years both in the length of the lunation and in that of the year.

It is doubtful whether these modifications of the 8-year cycle were ever used in civil life, for the *octaeteris* was superseded by the 19-year cycle published by Meton in 432 B.C. This was a fixed cycle, in which the length of each month and of each year was determined solely by its place in the cycle and therefore became entirely independent of observation. The months consisted of either 29 or 30 days; in some years there were 7 months of 30 days and 5 months of 29 days, giving a total of 355 days; in others there were 6 months of each length, giving a total of 354 days. A thirteenth month was intercalated after the sixth month, Poseideon, in the 3rd, 5th, 8th, 11th, 13th, 16th, and 19th years of the cycle; these longer years were always of 384 days, the intercalated month having a length of 29 or 30 days according to whether the total length of the other 12 months was 355 or 354 days. The cycle of 19 years (whose true length is 6939·60 days) was made equal to 235 months (whose true length is 6939·69 days) and to 6940 days. The error in this cycle consequently amounts to several hours. The calendar based on this cycle was introduced on the day of the summer solstice (the 13th day of the twelfth lunar month, Scirophorion) in the fourth year of the 86th Olympiad, 27 June 432 B.C., but it is doubtful whether it was ever actually employed for civil purposes.

After the Metonic calendar had been in use by astronomers for a century, a slight modification was proposed by Callippus in order to improve its accuracy. He combined four of the 19-year cycles into a single cycle of 76 years and changed one of the full (30-day) months into a deficient month (29 days), thereby shortening the 76-year cycle by one day. The Callippic cycle thus consisted of 76 years, containing 940 lunations and 27 759 days. It will be seen that this cycle gives for the mean length of the year exactly $365\frac{1}{4}$ days, the value earlier obtained both in Egypt and in Babylon, while 235 lunations are made equal to 6939·75 days, as compared with Meton's value of 6940 days and the true value of 6939·69 days. The modification by Callippus therefore was an appreciable improvement in the lengths both of the synodic month and of the tropical year. The Callippic cycle was made to begin at the summer solstice, the beginning of the first month, Hekatombaon, in the third year of the 112th Olympiad, 28 June 330 B.C. The Callippic calendar was used, by astronomers if not by the general public, for dating events for the next two centuries.

About 130 B.C. a further improvement was devised by Hipparchus. Four Callippic cycles were combined and a single day was again omitted by changing a full into a deficient month. The cycle of 304 years was thus made to contain 3760 lunations and 111 035 days. This gives a length of 365·24671 days for the tropical year and of 29·530585 days for the lunar month, as compared with the true values of 365·24220 days and 29·530598 days. The true length of the lunar month is very exactly represented: the true length of the year is not so closely represented but Hipparchus had obtained from observation a length of 365·24667 days, in close agreement with the mean value in his cycle. It does not seem that any use was ever made of this cycle; it remained merely as a suggested improvement.

The Greeks first adopted the Julian calendar when they adopted the Christian religion. Even so, the lunar months appear to have remained in use by the common people to a much later date. The month of Hekatombaon was displaced from the summer solstice to the autumnal equinox. Probably when the Attic months became solar instead of lunar they were given the old names, the Roman September being called Hekatombaon.

The Athenians numbered their years according to the year of the reign of the hereditary king, and later, in the days of the Republic, after the chief magistrate, who at first held his office for life, but the period was subsequently restricted to ten years. When, later still, the chief magistracy became an annual appointment, the election being either by voting or by drawing lots, the year continued to be named after the holder. This office lasted in Athens until the fourth century A.D., although the Republican régime had long ceased to exist and Greece had come under Roman domination.

For the purpose of dating events in Greek history, the era of the Olympic games is most useful. The Olympic games were founded, according to tradition, by Hercules, but it was not until after the victory of Corobus in 776 B.C. that they were regularly held every four years. The dating of this year has been definitely established through the records of the occurrence of an eclipse. The games were celebrated at about the time of the summer solstice; they lasted five days and ended at the full Moon, which was probably the first after the summer solstice. The year in the Christian era of any event whose dating in the Olympic reckoning is known can readily be found: thus Ol. 112. 3 (the third year of the 112th Olympiad) is $111 \times 4 + 2 = 446$ years later than 776 B.C. (Ol. 1. 1) and therefore corresponds to 330 B.C. The celebration of the Olympic games was unbroken for 293 Olympiads until the end of the reign of the Emperor Theodosius, A.D. 394, when it was replaced by the cycle of the indiction (p 581).

IV. THE JEWISH CALENDAR

The ancient Jewish calendar was undoubtedly of the lunar type, though nowhere in the Old Testament is there any mention of the lengths of the months (29 or 30 days). That the day began in the evening (probably at sunset) can be inferred from passages in the Pentateuch, such as 'from even unto even shall ye celebrate your sabbath' (Lev. xxiii. 32). It may therefore be assumed that the month began with the first visibility of the crescent Moon in the sky after sunset. The passage in Psalms civ. 19, 'He appointed the moon for seasons', is an indication that the months were determined by the Moon.

The special feature of the earliest Jewish calendar is the emphasis on the week of seven days, with the seventh day as a Sabbath or rest day. The Mosaic commandment that no work was to be done on the seventh day is tied up with the story of the Creation in six days, with the seventh day as a day of rest (Exodus xx. 10–11; Genesis ii. 2–3), so that it is probable that the seventh day had been observed as a day of rest from very early times and certainly throughout the period of bondage in Egypt. It has been conjectured that the seven-day week was in use not merely among the Hebrews but among all the Semitic peoples. From the Jews it was taken over by the Christians and has secured general adoption. The Jews regard the seven-day week as divinely ordained and going back to the time of the Creation; they are in consequence strongly opposed to any scheme of calendar reform that would break the continuity of the week.

The Mosaic law enacted that Abib, the month in which the Israelites came out of Egypt, was to be observed as the first month of the year. It was in this month that the feast of the Passover was to be celebrated and that green ears of corn were to be brought to the priests as the first-fruits of the harvest. The earliest ripening of barley in Palestine is about April, so that the first month of the year must have opened at about the time of the spring equinox. In order to keep the first month at the correct position in the year, it must have been necessary from time to time to intercalate a thirteenth month. The decision whether or not to do so was made by the priests; if it appeared towards the end of the twelfth month that the corn would not be ready to offer as a sacrifice in the following month, then a month would be intercalated. In such a rough-and-ready but practical way the beginning of the year was prevented from drifting through the seasons.

After the captivity the names of the months were changed, the first month being called Nisan. The names of most of the months are given in the later books in the Old Testament, though usually a month is specified by its number in the yearly sequence. They are of Chaldean origin, mostly agreeing with the Syrian names. The beginning of the month was fixed by the appearance of the crescent Moon in the evening; when two trustworthy men had reported to the Sanhedrin in Jerusalem that at such and such a time the Moon had been seen, the new month was declared to have begun. If by the 30th day of any month the new crescent Moon had not been seen, a new month was taken to start on the following day. As it might well happen that because of cloudy weather two or more 30-day months occurred consecutively, it was decided that the year should contain not fewer than four nor more than eight full (30-day) months. Because religious festivals, sacrifices, and so on were fixed with reference to the beginning of the month, the information was spread throughout the country by means of signal fires on the hill-tops or by special messengers. After the captivity a number of Jews remained dispersed in other lands; as the information could not then reach them in time, they were provided with special instructions for beginning a new month. Also, all the important feasts—such as the first and last days of Passover and of the feast of Tabernacles—were duplicated so that, if elsewhere the month was full when in Palestine it was deficient (29-day) or conversely, the feasts would be celebrated everywhere on either the one or the other of the two days.

After the return from captivity, the civil year commenced with the beginning of the seventh month, Tishri; this time was of special importance, because it was on the first day of the seventh month that the law had been read to the people on their return to Jerusalem and burnt offerings offered up on the site of the ruined temple. This brought the Jewish reckoning of the year into agreement with the system that was already well established in Syria. For a time both beginnings of the year were in use; both are, for instance, used in the Apocrypha, though the months are numbered from Nisan. In books of the Old Testament written after the deportation, the years of the kings and the months of the festivals are generally reckoned from Nisan. The older beginning of the year gradually fell into disuse, however.

In more recent times, after the destruction of Jerusalem by Titus and the dispersion of the Jews, the empirical calendar, in which the beginning of each month was fixed by observation, was replaced by one based on fixed rules. The date of the introduction of this fixed calendar is not known, but it is generally thought to be about the fourth century A.D. Its basis is the 19-year cycle introduced into Babylon by Kidinnu, containing seven intercalary months, and therefore incorporating a mean length of the synodic month of 29·530594 days and a length of 365·2468 days for the year. The beginning of the month of Tishri in this calendar is determined by complicated rules, designed to prevent various festivals and solemn days from falling on incompatible days. The normal ordinary year consists of months of 30 and 29 days alternately, giving a total of 354 days. The normal embolismic or leap year contains an extra month of 29 days, inserted after the sixth month, Adar, and known as Veadar, but the length of Adar is then increased from 29 to 30 days, so that the year contains 384 days. The embolismic years of each 19-year cycle are the 3rd, 6th, 8th, 11th, 14th, 17th, and 19th.

Because of the special rules already referred to, the second month, Hesvan, may sometimes require to have one day more than in an ordinary year and the third month, Kislev, may require to have one day less. Consequently, an ordinary year may have 353, 354, or 355 days and the embolismic year may have 383, 384 or 385 days.

The insertion of Veadar in the embolismic year ensures that the Passover, on the 15th day of the following month Nisan, is kept at its proper season, which is the full Moon after the vernal equinox. It always precedes the following new year by 163 days. Pentecost always precedes the new year by 113 days.

In our present Gregorian calendar, the epact is the age of the Moon of Tebet, the fourth month of the Jewish calendar, and so represents the day of Tebet corresponding to 1 January. The approximate date of the beginning of the Jewish year can be obtained by subtracting the epact from 24 September after an ordinary year, or from 24 October after an embolismic year. It can range from 5 September to 5 October.

The Jews employ an era of the Creation whose date is taken as 7 October, 3761 B.C. In this era the Jewish year 5718 began on 26 September 1957.

V. THE ROMAN CALENDAR

The calendar which is now used throughout the whole of the civilized world had its origin in the local calendar of the city of Rome, the beginning of which is lost in obscurity. It is stated by authorities such as Macrobius and Censorinus that Romulus, at the foundation of the Roman state, instituted a year containing ten months and comprising 304 days. Six of these months, namely April, June, Sextilis, September, November, December, each contained 30 days, and the other four, March, May, Quintilis, and October, each contained 31 days. The year began with March, as is proved by the names of the last six months (Quintilis, Sextilis, etc.).

The origins of the names of the first four months are uncertain: March is supposed to have been named in honour of Mars, the father of Romulus, and April after Aphrodite or Venus, the progenitress of the Ænean race. May and June are supposed to have been named respectively after the *majores* or elders, and the *juniores*. Many other origins have been suggested: April, for instance, from *aperire*, the month when the earth is awakening from its winter torpor though, if the year originally contained only 304 days, the months would have drifted through the seasons so quickly that this derivation could not be correct. Ovid affirmed in his *Fasti* that the original year contained ten months, but was not certain about the derivation of the names of the first four months.

Probably, as Eutropius believed, the Roman year before the time of Numa had no definite system. It is reasonably certain that the months were lunar and did not have the fixed numbers of days mentioned above. Numa is supposed to have added 2 months (51 days) to the year, making a total of 355 days. January (named from the god Janus, facing backwards and forwards) now began the year, and February (from the god Februus, who presided over ceremonies of purification) preceded March, which became the third month.

According to Macrobius and Censorinus, Numa took 1 day from each of the 6 months of 30 days, as the Romans had a superstitious dislike of even numbers;

these 6 days, with the 51 additional days, were divided between January (29 days) and February (28 days). Thus January, April, June, Sextilis, September, November, and December each had 29 days; March, May, Quintilis, and October continued to have 31, while February had 28. The year of 355 days strongly suggests a lunar calendar, as it exceeds 12 lunations by only 0·63 days. The difference between the length of this year of 355 days and the solar year was adjusted by the intercalation of a month, when it was considered necessary. This intercalated month normally alternated between 27 and 28 days, but adjustment to the proper seasons was obtained by omitting the intercalary month from time to time.

The intercalary month was inserted after 23 February. Whatever may have been done in earlier times, in later historical times the last five days of February, which should have followed the end of the intercalary month, were omitted. The actual number of additional days in the intercalary years was therefore either 22 or 23. The calendar had consequently worked free from the Moon and became purely solar. It is uncertain when this occurred, but it was certainly before 400 B.C. The normal sequence of days in four successive years was 355, 377, 355, 378, giving an average length of the year of 366¼ days, about one day too long.

The days of the month were enumerated backwards from the next following Kalends (1st of month), Nones (5th of month, except for the 31-day months when it was the 7th of month) or Ides (13th of month, except for the 31-day months when the 15th of month). Thus the day after the Ides, for instance, would be expressed as 17 days before the Kalends of the next month.

The intercalary month was normally inserted in alternate years. The actual regulation of the calendar was under the exclusive control of the College of Pontiffs, as a matter of religious importance, and was not always done honestly; the calendar was often manipulated for political or personal ends. When Julius Caesar became Pontifex Maximus in 63 B.C. intercalation was so often neglected that by 47 B.C. the months had drifted considerably from their proper seasons, causing the celebration of various festivals to come at the wrong times. January, which should have followed the winter solstice, occupied the season of the year that should have been occupied by October.

Julius Caesar accordingly decided upon a reform of the calendar and called in the astronomer Sosigenes of Alexandria for advice and assistance. The first step was to correct the error into which the calendar had fallen. The year corresponding to 46 B.C. was given the usual intercalation of an additional 23 days, and two further months, amounting together to 67 days, were inserted between November and December, in order to bring the Kalends of 45 B.C. to their proper position, corresponding to 1 January; this year, known as 'the year of confusion', consequently contained 445 days.

On the advice of Sosigenes the mean length of the year was fixed at 365¼ days; to achieve this, it was decreed that the normal length of the year should be 365 days but that an additional day should be inserted every fourth year. The lengths of the months were fixed at the present durations, which have never since been altered. The extra day in a leap year was obtained by repeating the sixth day before the Kalends of March (on which occurred the feast of Terminalia), and so it became known as *ante diem bis sextum Kalendas Martias* or simply *bissextum*, whence we derive our word bissextile for leap year.

In the new calendar the months of March, May, Quintilis (July), and October, which already had 31 days, remained unaltered in length. They retained their Nones on the 7th and their Ides on the 15th day of the month. January, Sextilis, August, and December were increased in length from 29 to 31 days; their Nones remained on the 5th and their Ides on the 13th day, the days that were added being placed at the end of the month so that the religious festivals connected with the Nones and Ides, which took place on fixed days, should not be changed. In 44 B.C. the name of Quintilis was altered to July (*Julius*) in honour of Julius Caesar.

The essential and important feature of the reform was that the calendar year became purely solar. The months were given definite lengths, the same from year to year (except for February) and there was no attempt to relate them to the phases of the Moon. The seasons were expected to retain their places in the calendar without change; farmers could therefore plan their work by the calendar without having to consider the phases of the Moon.

The pontiffs misunderstood the directions for the intercalation and proceeded to add one day every third year instead of every fourth. In consequence the year 8 B.C. began three days too late. When this was discovered, Augustus directed that it should be corrected by suspending further intercalation until the error had been eliminated. From that year, A.D. 8, the Julian calendar remained in force without further alteration until its reform by Pope Gregory XIII in A.D. 1582. The name of Sextilis was changed in the year 8 B.C. to August (*Augustus*) in honour of the emperor.

The years in the Roman calendar were commonly designated by the names of the consuls and changed when the new consuls took up their office. In the early days the date of entering office was frequently changed, but about 222 B.C. it was fixed at 15 March (the Ides of March). March was then the first month of the year. In 153 B.C. the date was changed to 1 January, which then became the first day of the new year; this beginning of the year was never afterwards changed. In the eastern provinces, however, the years were often reckoned from the accession of the reigning emperor, the second year of his reign being counted from the first new year's day (which varied from province to province) following his accession.

The dates of events in Roman history are usually indicated by reference to the supposed date of the foundation of Rome. The letters A.U.C.—an abbreviation of *anno urbis conditae*—are used to express dates in this era. The generally accepted date for the conventional beginning of the era is 753 B.C., corresponding to Olympiad 6. 4. This date, ascribed to Varro, was supported by Cicero and Plutarch and was adopted by Censorinus.

The Christian era, in which years are reckoned from the supposed date of the Incarnation, was introduced by the Scythian monk Dionysius Exiguus about A.D. 530. He based the date of the Incarnation on the widespread tradition that Christ was born in the 28th year of the reign of Augustus; he assumed the beginning of the reign of Augustus to have been 727 A.U.C., which is now known not to be correct. Dionysius constructed a table of the dates of Easter from A.D. 532 to A.D. 626, in which he used the new era. From him it was adopted by Bede, and from Bede by western Christendom generally.

VI. THE GREGORIAN CALENDAR

The mean length of the year of the Julian calendar is 365·25 days, which is 0·0078 days or 11 min 14 sec longer than the tropical year. This difference causes the seasons to drift gradually backwards in the calendar. The discrepancy is small; it first became noticeable in connexion with the observance of Easter.

In A.D. 325 the General Council of Nicea had dealt with the date of Easter to ensure, amongst other things, that the observance by the various Christian communities should be on the same date. In the framing of the tables for the dates of Easter in different years, it was assumed that the spring equinox was on 21 March, though it actually fell on the evening of 20 March. The date of Easter, derived from that of the Jewish Passover, depends upon the date of the occurrence of the first full Moon after the vernal equinox. As the centuries passed, the calendar date of the vernal equinox fell progressively earlier and there was in consequence doubt as to the correct date for the celebration of Easter.

The Council of Trent, which assembled in 1545 and continued its sittings for 18 years, authorized the Pope to take the matter in hand. By that time the vernal equinox had receded to 11 March. When Gregory XIII became Pope in 1572 he found various proposals, which had been submitted to his predecessors, awaiting him. The plan which was most favoured was one proposed by Aloysius Lilius, a Neapolitan physician. This proposal was submitted to various Christian princes and learned academies for comments, and a commission of mathematicians and chronologers was appointed to consider it. In 1582 the Pope published a bull instituting the revised calendar.

It was ordained that the day after 4 October 1582 should be called 15 October, in order to restore the vernal equinox to 21 March, the date assigned by the Council of Nicea. In future the intercalary day was to be dropped in those centurial years that were not divisible by 400, in order to maintain a more exact correspondence between the calendar and the tropical years. Certain changes were made at the same time in the rules for fixing the date of Easter.

In the Gregorian calendar there are 97 leap years in 400 years, so that the average length of the calendar year is 365·2425 days. The cumulative error will amount to 2 days 14 hours 24 minutes in 10 000 years. A more exact agreement between the calendar and tropical years would be obtained if the years divisible by 4000 without remainder were not counted as leap years; there would then be 969 leap years in 4000 years, giving an average length of the calendar year of 365·24225 days, which is too great by about 4 sec.

The new rules for fixing the date of Easter which were incorporated into the Gregorian reform imply a mean length of the lunation that is in error by only the millionth part of a day. These rules determine the date of a hypothetical full Moon, whose motion is closely in agreement with the mean motion of the actual Moon. As the tables ignore the inequalities of the actual motions of the Sun and Moon, the date of the Easter full Moon may differ by a day from the actual date of full Moon. This can occasionally result in the ecclesiastical full Moon occurring after the vernal equinox with the true full Moon occurring before it, and conversely. The tables, which are based on the 19-year cycle, fix the full Moon for a definite calendar date for the whole world, whereas the true full Moon occurs at a definite instant which may not be on the same calendar date all over the world.

The Gregorian calendar was adopted in Italy, Spain, Portugal, France, and Poland in 1582, by the German Catholic States, Holland, and Flanders in 1583, and by Hungary in 1587. Its adoption was long delayed by the Protestant countries. The German and Dutch Protestant states and Denmark adopted it in 1700, Britain and the British dominions in 1752, Sweden in 1753, Japan in 1873, China and Albania in 1912, Bulgaria in 1916, Soviet Russia in 1918, Rumania and Greece in 1924, and Turkey in 1927.

In Britain the Gregorian calendar was officially introduced by the Calendar

New Style Act (1750) under which Act it came into operation in 1752, the day following 2 September being designated 14 September (but without interruption of the continuity of the week). There was considerable opposition from the common people, who rioted with the cry: 'Give us back our eleven days.'

At the same time the official date of New Year's Day in England was changed from 25 March to 1 January, which date had already been adopted in Scotland in 1600. English dates between 1 January and 25 March before 1752 are commonly given with both of the alternative years; it should be noted, however, that, for the purpose of intercalating the extra day in February before 1752, the year had been treated in England as though it had commenced on 1 January. Some customs dependent on the calendar remained unchanged and have persisted to the present day: thus the official date for the ending of the government financial year is 5 April, corresponding to 24 March, the last day of the year in the Julian calendar style.

The different reckonings of the beginning of the year are known as styles. In Italy down to the eighteenth century the years of the Christian era began in the Venetian style on 1 March, in the Pisan style on the preceding 25 March, and in the Florentine style on the following 25 March. In England the Nativity style, beginning on 25 December, was used in the early Middle Ages; it was superseded by the Annunciation style, beginning on 25 March (Lady Day), in the fourteenth century. The style beginning on 1 January is known as the Circumcision style. The word 'style' is also used in a somewhat different sense, dates in the Julian and Gregorian calendars being often referred to as 'old style' and 'new style' respectively.

VII. THE ISLAMIC CALENDAR

Muslims use a calendar for religious purposes that is purely lunar and has no connexion with the solar year. The year consists of twelve lunar months, the beginning of each month being determined by observation of the crescent of the new Moon in the evening sky. Different beginnings of the month may consequently be used by neighbouring communities. As a result there is uncertainty about the precise day of any date given in this calendar unless the day of the week is also specified; this is usually done in important documents.

The era of the calendar is dated from the first month preceding the flight (*hijra*, hegira) of Muhammad from Mecca to Medina, namely Thursday, 15 July, A.D. 622, and the calendar commences on the following day. It is known as the era of the Hegira (A.H.).

The new year of the Islamic calendar retrogrades through the seasons in about

$32\frac{1}{2}$ years. For astronomical purposes the months are fixed by rule and not by observations. The months have 30 and 29 days alternately, except the twelfth month which may have either 29 or 30; in a cycle of 30 Islamic years 19 are common years of 354 days and 11 are intercalary years of 355 days. The years of the cycle numbered 2, 5, 7, 10, 13, 16, 18, 21, 24, 26, 29 are the intercalary years.

This calendar makes 360 lunations equivalent to 10 631 days; their real duration is 10 631·015 days, so that the error is extremely small.

VIII. THE JULIAN PERIOD

For many chronological purposes and for various purposes in astronomy the Julian Period, invented by Scaliger (1484–1558), is very useful. This period is formed by the continued product of the cycle of the Moon (19 years), the solar cycle (28 years, after which, in the Julian calendar, the days of the year recur on the same days of the week), and the cycle of the indiction (a non-astronomical cycle of 15 years, which took its origin in a provincial census for taxation in Egypt about A.D. 300 at 15-year intervals). Its length is thus $19 \times 28 \times 15 = 7980$ years. In this period no two years can be expressed by the same numbers in all three cycles. All these cycles began on 1 January in the Julian calendar in 4713 B.C., so that one Julian period covers all dates in recorded history and is therefore for some purposes more convenient than an era whose epoch lies in historical times.

The year of the Julian period is now little used. On the other hand, the numbering of days in this period continuously from 1 January 4713 B.C. is very convenient and is much used for calendarial purposes and in astronomy. If the Julian days of two events are known, the exact number of days between them is at once ascertained, without complication of changes of calendar and so on that may have intervened. The Julian day begins at noon. Julian day 2 435 840 began at Greenwich mean noon on 1 January 1957.

REFERENCES

[1] PARKER, R. A. 'The Calendars of Ancient Egypt.' Studies in Ancient Oriental Civilisation, No. 26. University Press, Chicago. 1950.
[2] SCHOCH, C. 'Die Länge der Sothisperioden beträgt 1456 Jahre.' Selbstverlag, Berlin-Steglitz. 1928.
[3] IDELER, C. L. 'Handbuch der mathematischen und technischen Chronologie', Vol. I, p. 131. Berlin. 1825.
[4] FOTHERINGHAM, J. K. Observatory, 51, 315, 1928.

22

PRECISION INSTRUMENTS: TO 1500

DEREK J. PRICE

with a section (VII) on Hero's instruments by A. G. DRACHMANN

I. THE IDEA OF THE PRECISION INSTRUMENT

THE development of precision instruments is, in the main, part of the larger story of astronomy. Man's early interest in the regularity of celestial motions and their connexion with seasonal changes of his environment is one of the most important factors in the cultural life of primitive civilizations. There is no need to tell here how the Sun and the Moon, planets, eclipses, the heliacal rising and setting of bright stars, and other astronomical phenomena became endowed with mystical significance. Clearly there was a need to formulate these regularities and to predict the periodic phenomena that were so vital to seasonal occupations in daily life and to ritualistic practice in religion.

To formulate such astronomical theory it is essential not merely that there should be qualitative observation of the heavens: there must also be accurate measurement of the position of stars and planets at definite times. Much is possible without the use of any but the most primitive aids, such as a plumb-line held in front of the eye (cf the *merkhet*, vol I, figure 47), a string held out so that it appears to draw a straight line in the sky from one star to another, and the marking of a shadow cast on the ground by a pillar or a high building. Using such means alone, as far as we know, the Babylonians had by the second millennium B.C. built up an accurate *corpus* of measurements and a series of empirical rules for predicting phenomena with very great accuracy.

The Sun and Moon seem quite large objects, and an error of observation or prediction similar in magnitude to their diameters would be out of the question for even approximate use; this sets a lower limit to accuracy amounting to the angular diameter of those bodies—about 30 minutes of arc. On the other hand the physiology of the eye prevents it from distinguishing objects if they are separated by less than about one minute of arc, and though it is actually possible to sight a single star with great precision, this may be taken as a useful upper limit to the accuracy obtained in naked-eye astronomy. All astronomers from the Babylonians up to Tycho Brahe were imprisoned between these limits of attainment. From Alexandrian times until the end of the Middle Ages one may safely assume that the accuracy attained lay at about 5 minutes of arc for angle-measurements, 20 seconds of time when estimated by the diurnal rotation, and $2\frac{1}{2}°$ of terrestrial longitude when this was found by eclipses or other methods involving lunar positions (table I).

The goal of devising astronomical theories that would agree with observations within such a degree of fineness was eventually attained in most particulars by the Alexandrian astronomers from Hipparchus (second century B.C.) to Ptolemy (A.D. 150). Once the theories had been devised, and even indeed while they were in the course of construction, it became necessary to make observations and measurements of similar accuracy, but in circumstances where the simple techniques of plumb-line, shadow, and string were inadequate. This led to the invention of a series of instruments for the measurement of time and of angular distance. Results obtained by the use of these instruments were fed into the theory, resulting in an increase of accuracy and a demand for instruments of even greater precision and wider variety.

TABLE I
Orders of Accuracy in Astronomical Observation

	Casual estimation Error corresponds to apparent size of Sun or Moon	Reasonably good	Best probable Error corresponds to resolving power of the eye
Angular accuracy (minutes of arc)	30′	5′	1′
Radius of a divided circle on which the angular accuracy corresponds to an error of 1 mm of scale .	12 cm	72 cm	360 cm
Time occupied by a diurnal rotation of the heavens through an angle corresponding to the angular accuracy . . .	2 min	20 sec	4 sec
Accuracy of a determination of terrestrial longitude using lunar measurements made with this order of error*	15°	2° 30′	30′

* This follows from the fact that the Moon revolves only once in some 28 diurnal rotations of the heavens. The error of a determination of terrestrial latitude is the same as the angular accuracy.

Such continuous progress of supply and demand put a great strain on technical skill and inventiveness. An angle of 5 minutes—one-sixth of the apparent diameter of the Sun—is readily discernible in astronomical use, but for terrestrial purposes it subtends a distance of only 1 mm on a divided circle 1½ m in diameter. An instrument must certainly be very large, carefully and closely divided, perfectly jointed, and made quite stable in order to secure this required accuracy. The story of precision instruments is that of a succession of men applying themselves to attaining these ends.

II. SCHOOLS OF INSTRUMENT-MAKERS

The first great wave of instrument-making was due to the Alexandrian astronomers; it reached a peak with the work of Ptolemy, continued to develop slowly for a few centuries, and then perished with the rest of the world of classical science. Very little of the theory or the knowledge of instruments was transmitted to the Byzantine Empire, though a notable exception is provided by the fortunate preservation of two important texts on the astrolabe and a unique specimen of the instrument itself (p 603).

When Greek science passed to the Arabic-speaking peoples, it was astronomical theory, probably more than anything else, that excited them and called forth the greatest activity. More than six centuries had elapsed since Ptolemy's *Almagest* was composed, and the small secular motions of the heavenly bodies had accumulated sufficiently to be perceptible. The need for correcting the newly recovered theory, and the opportunity to make it more perfect by re-estimating the secular terms, must have been a very attractive incentive to further work. One finds indeed a brilliant series of advances, each including the establishment of an observatory with special instruments, and leading to the publication of a new set of astronomical tables with canons explaining their use and improving the existing theory. The most important of these observatories were those founded at Baghdad by Al-Ma'mūn (813–33), at Cairo in 966 by Al-Ḥākim, at Toledo by Al-Zarqālī (*c* 1029–87), at Marāgha by Nāsir al-Dīn al-Ṭūsī (1201–74), and the great observatory founded at Samarkand by Ulugh Beg about 1420. A notable feature of this activity is the appearance for the first time of men who seem to have specialized as instrument makers and designers. There is, for example, Al-ʿUrdī who worked for Al-Ṭūsī at Marāgha, and there are many craftsmen and even dynasties of craftsmen to whom the description *al-asturlābī*, 'the astrolabist', is applied.

The revival of astronomy in Europe dates from the translation of the *Almagest*, first from the Greek in 1164 and then from the Arabic in the popular version of Gerard of Cremona in 1175. The Toledo tables of Al-Zarqālī were translated in 1187, and were in common use from the beginning of the thirteenth century until they were displaced by the Alfonsine tables (1274), which reached the great university centres of Oxford and Paris by the beginning of the fourteenth century. Both these sets of tables with their accompanying canons (that is, explanations, and texts on instruments) gave rise to much activity in the construction and use of astronomical instruments. Many new instruments were devised and probably made by such scholars as John of Linières (fl Paris, 1320–50), and Richard of Wallingford (1292?–1335) (tailpiece) and other astronomers of Merton College, Oxford. By the end of the fourteenth century the second burst of interest had lost its impetus in England and in France, without the establishment of any great observatories or any tradition in the craft of instrument-making. The beginnings of the great renaissance of instrument-making are to be found in Germany during the latter half of the fifteenth century. One of the first indications of the existence of specialist craftsmen is the purchase by Cardinal Nicolas of Cusa (Cues, on the Moselle) of three instruments and fifteen books on astronomy during a visit to Nuremberg in September 1444. The instruments, which are still preserved at Cues, were a large wooden sphere, a *torquetum* (p 593), and an astrolabe.

Soon after this there is more definite information about the pre-eminence of Nuremberg in scientific instruments, for when Regiomontanus settled in the city in June 1471 he wrote that he had chosen the place 'because I find there all the peculiar instruments necessary for astronomy, and there it is easiest for me to keep in touch with the learned of all countries'. Both reasons were due to the fact that Nuremberg straddled the great trade-route of Europe that ran from Italy to the Low Countries and carried the merchandise (and manuscripts) of the world. The structure of the city-state and its highly organized guild craftsmen had already made it a centre for the skilled metal-work needed in the construction of fine instruments. Although Regiomontanus records a favourable state as already existing on his arrival, it was his own life-work that made the city so famous for its scientific craftsmen, and caused the craft to spread to Augsburg and indeed to the whole surrounding area. Throughout the sixteenth century, and until the Thirty Years War, Nuremberg and Augsburg produced instruments of considerable ingenuity and of such exquisite craftsmanship that many have been preserved as fine works of art; they are frequently signed and dated by the maker, and they enable the development of the craft to be chronicled in detail from this period onwards.

In Italy, too, there was some activity, particularly in the latter part of the century, but there does not seem to have arisen any school of workmanship comparable with that in Germany during the same period.

Some of the finest extant specimens of astrolabes and other instruments were made at Louvain by Walter Arsenius and other members of his family. The workshop had been inspired by the astronomer Gemma Frisius (an uncle of Arsenius) and by Gerard Mercator. Unfortunately, after a fairly short life the workshop was dismantled, and unfinished instruments were scattered over Europe owing to the 'Spanish Terror' that devastated the Low Countries in 1578 and thereabouts.

In England, some instrument-making had been introduced by Nicolas Kratzer, a Bavarian who lectured at Oxford on astronomy. Some of his instruments can be seen in the portrait of him by Holbein, and again in 'The Ambassadors' by the same artist. The first regular craftsmen seem to have flourished under the aegis of John Dee (1527–1608) and Leonard Digges (c 1550), and at a time when there was great interest in England's maritime adventures and explorations. The first mathematical instrument-maker here was Thomas Gemini (fl 1524–62) who came from Lixhe near Liége and settled at Blackfriars; he had great skill in the engraving of brass instruments and had indeed already established his reputation by engraving the plates for the 1545 English edition of Vesalius. Soon after him came the first Englishman to take up the craft, namely, Humfray Cole (1530?–91), an engraver and die-sinker who worked at the Mint and was connected with the Mineral and Battery Works (1565) which made sheet brass available in England for the first time. The wide range of Cole's surviving instruments is as remarkable as their fine engraving and ingenious construction. Within a few generations from the time of Cole the number of suppliers of mathematical instruments had increased prodigiously, and the range of their products had extended from astrolabes, sun-dials, and quadrants to include devices for surveying and gauging, as well as a series of instruments designed for the performance of 'philosophical experiments' (p 636).

III. OBSERVATORY INSTRUMENTS

The only full account of the instruments used by the Alexandrian astronomers is contained in the *Almagest* of Ptolemy (second century A.D.) and in the commentaries on this work by Proclus, Theon, and Pappus. In general it is impossible to tell whether the instruments and the minor variations on them described by the commentators were devised by Ptolemy himself or by others. Some forms must have been known by Hipparchus (second century B.C.), and some may be of even greater antiquity. It is clear, however, from the designs of the instruments that they are at best only a stage or two removed from the earliest *ad hoc* devices which replaced the primitive line and plumb-bob expedients. Each instrument has been devised for a specific purpose, a single type of observation. There is no indication of a move towards the economy and convenience of designing an instrument that might be used for a variety of purposes. Furthermore, the limitations of technique in constructing the instrument are everywhere apparent. Wood or stone is used whenever possible, and where metal is employed it takes the form of armillae constructed from strips of bronze rather than sheets or disks which might otherwise have been preferable.

(a) *The equinoctial (or equatorial) armillary.* In the *Almagest* Ptolemy describes how Hipparchus used this instrument to determine the dates of vernal and autumnal equinoxes at Alexandria. It consists simply of a large ungraduated bronze ring, set rigidly on a masonry base and adjusted exactly in the plane of the celestial equator (figure 343 c). When the Sun is north or south of the equator the fore-edge of the ring casts no shadow on the hind-edge, but at the equinoxes, where the ecliptic[1] crosses the equator, the shadow will fall precisely on the inner surface of the lower part of the ring. It is desirable to make the ring as large as convenient (Theon says it should be at least 2 cubits in diameter[2]), and the accuracy depends entirely on the lack of distortion of the ring and the accuracy with which it is set in the equatorial plane. Ptolemy is explicit on this point and mentions that the older and larger of the two equatorial armillaries in the principal palaestra at Alexandria was no longer reliable owing to distortion and the shifting of its placement. He also notes that an error of observation of only 6 minutes (corresponding to a shadow movement of about 1½ mm in a 2-cubit instrument) causes an error of about 15 minutes in the Sun's longitude in the ecliptic; this implies an error of 6 hours in determining the date of the equinox. The public site of the Alexandrian instrument is a reminder of the importance of equinoctial observations for ritualistic and calendrical purposes.

(b) *The plinth.* This is one of two instruments described in the *Almagest* and used to determine the midday altitude of the Sun; such observations made at the periods of winter and summer solstice enabled the astronomer to determine the obliquity of the ecliptic and the latitude of the place of observation. The instrument consists of a single block of stone or wood, set on the ground and carefully levelled by thin wedges driven underneath (figure 343 A). One face of the block in the plane of the meridian is smoothed with set-square accuracy, and two cylindrical pegs are set at the top and bottom of the southern edge of

---

[1] The apparent path of the Sun's annual rotation against the background of the fixed stars.
[2] The cubit originated in the length of the forearm. 1 cubit = about 45 to 55 cm.

this face. The upper peg is used as a gnomon to cast a shadow upon a graduated quadrant of arc engraved on the face. This peg also supports a plumb-line which should fall exactly on the lower peg when the plinth is correctly levelled. Because the peg casts a wide shadow it is necessary to measure both edges on the scale and take the average of the readings. A serious disadvantage of this form of the plinth is that the Sun can cast a shadow on the face of the plinth only before noon or after noon, according to whether the surface looks due E or due W; this makes it difficult to judge the moment of true noon, when readings must be taken. This objection was met in later ages by the replacement of the peg and shadow device by a pivoted arm carrying a pair of sights. In this form, as the 'mural quadrant', it was used by Tycho Brahe (1546–1601).

(c) *The meridional armillary*. As an alternative to the plinth, and for the same purpose of determining the meridian altitude of the Sun, this instrument is described in the *Almagest* and also by Proclus (fifth century A.D.) in his *Hypotyposis astronomicarum positionum*. It consists of an accurately made and graduated bronze ring, mounted on a pillar and set vertically in the plane of the meridian[1] (figure 343 B); Ptolemy does not give dimensions, but according to Proclus the ring should be not less than ½-cubit in diameter and graduated every 5 minutes of arc. Even with a ring one cubit in diameter this would correspond to the very unlikely fineness of marking of about 3 divisions in the space of 1 mm. Inside the fixed ring, a smaller concentric ring fitted closely, its sides flush with the outer ring, but with sufficient play to enable it to turn freely in its meridional plane; small catches prevented it from falling out of its frame. At the opposite ends of a diameter of the rotating ring, little plates serving as sights were mounted perpendicularly to the plane of the rings. Proclus represents these plates as having holes for seeing through, but according to Ptolemy and Theon the plates are whole, and a sight was taken by allowing the shadow of the upper plate to fall exactly on the lower. Pointers at the ends of the diameter enabled a reading to be taken on the graduated arc of the fixed circle, and a plummet suspended from the apex of the ring allowed the instrument to be levelled. It was set in the meridian plane by aligning the sights against a meridian line marked on the ground below the instrument. The usefulness of the meridional armillary must have been severely limited by its comparatively small size; it was also impaired by the unsound mechanical construction. A friction-fit between two rings is particularly sensitive to any deformation, and the necessary free play of the movable ring can cause considerable error in taking readings. It is significant

---

[1] The plane containing the observer, the north and south poles, and the zenith. Hence the meridian altitude of a body is its altitude in degrees as it passes through this plane.

that the use of the alidade[1] with two sights mounted on it—a far superior device —is not employed by Ptolemy in these instruments.

(d) *The parallactic instrument* (*Ptolemy's rulers* or *triquetrum*). This is perhaps the most serviceable of Ptolemy's instruments, and the only one used in

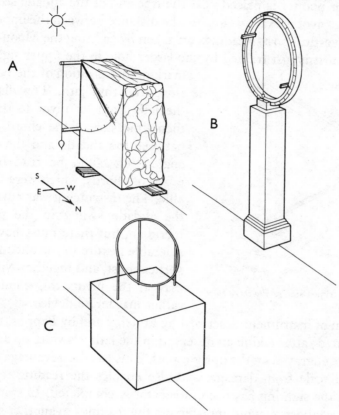

FIGURE 343—*Astronomical measuring instruments described by Ptolemy.* (A) *the plinth;* (B) *the meridional armillary;* (C) *the equatorial armillary.*

similar form by subsequent astronomers. Copernicus (1473–1543) used it for his observations, and his 8-ft-long instrument eventually passed as a cherished relic into the hands of Tycho Brahe. Its use, as described in the *Almagest*, was for determining the zenith[2] distance of the Moon at its meridian passage, but it could also be employed for measuring the meridian transits of the fixed stars.

[1] The diametrical or radial arm of circular measuring-instruments, pivoted at the centre and marking at its ends a position on the circle.

[2] The point on the celestial sphere directly above the observer's head. Hence zenith distance is the complement of altitude.

It consists of a vertical post at least 4 cubits high (figure 344); at the top of the post is pivoted an alidade containing a pinnule at the lower end and a larger hole at the upper; at the bottom of the post is pivoted a thin lath of wood.[1] As with the other instruments, a plumb-line is used to ensure that the main post is upright. A pin or pointer is placed near the free end of the alidade so that its distance from the pivot is exactly equal to the distance between the upper and lower pivots on the vertical post. Readings are taken by sighting the Moon through the pinnule so that it is just framed by the larger hole in the upper sight, and then marking the position of the pin or pointer along the thin lath. The distance along the lath from its pivot to the mark was then a measure of the chord of the angle between the alidade and the vertical; the angle itself could be read off from the tables of chords, which were readily available. The instrument was adjusted so that the alidade swung in the plane of the meridian, but there must have been considerable flexure in the alidade and in the vertical post, and together with any slight play at the pivots this would make it a rather inaccurate device.

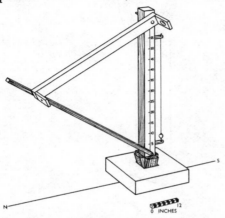

FIGURE 344—*The triquet um, or Ptolemy's rulers.*

In the form of instrument described by Ptolemy and by Pappus, the lath itself is not graduated; after taking an observation the lath is swung up and compared against a scale engraved on the upright post. This has the advantage of protecting the engraved scale from damage, and also enables the reading to be taken at leisure when the sighting has been satisfactorily completed. In spite of this it is clearly more accurate to avoid transferring the readings to another scale, and the step of graduating the lath was taken eventually by Al-Battānī (c 858–929).

The vital point of the parallactic instrument is that it employed only a simple graduation along a straight line and avoided the accurate division of a circular arc, a troublesome and tedious procedure. Even though it was necessary to consult a table of chords for each observation, the use of the parallactic instrument was more convenient and probably more accurate than would have been the graduations of a circular arc of similar size. Furthermore, the parallactic instrument could be folded flat and transported without damage far more easily than any other observational device of similar radius and accuracy.

[1] The post, alidade, and lath are the 'three rods' implied by the name *triquetrum*.

(e) *The four-cubit dioptra.* This instrument is mentioned in the *Almagest* as a device described by Hipparchus and used for measuring the apparent diameter of the Sun or the Moon. Ptolemy does not give a description, but fortunately one is provided in the commentary by Pappus. The instrument consists of a rod (probably wood) rectangular in cross-section and at least 4 cubits long (figure 345). A dove-tailed groove runs the length of the rod on one of its faces, and into this groove fits a small slider carrying a small perpendicular prism. The observer looks through a pinnule in a block fixed to one end of the rod, and moves the slider back and forth until the prism just covers the apparent solar or lunar disk. The angle subtended by the disk can then be found from the known width of the prism and its distance from the sighting-pinnule. It is worth noting

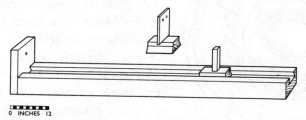

FIGURE 345—*The four-cubit dioptra.*

that the prism, if it is to cover the solar disk at 4 cubits, must be only about $1\frac{1}{2}$ cm in width. In another form of the instrument, the prism is replaced by a plate having two small sighting-holes; this would probably be more convenient as reducing the direct glare when observing the Sun.

In principle this instrument is related to the primitive use of the index-finger or palm held at arm's length as a means of approximate measurement of angles (finger-breadth $= 1\frac{1}{2}°$; palm-breadth $= 6°$). The same principle occurs later in the invention of the cross-staff (or Jacob's staff, *baculus*) by Levi ben Gerson (1288–1344), and its revival by Regiomontanus and employment in navigation by Martin Behaim (p 528). In this later form the cross-staff consists of a set of cross-pieces of various lengths, any of which may be slid along a rod held with one end against the eye. Still later refinements include that due to Gemma Frisius (1508–55), where a single cross-piece is fitted with a scale and a pair of sliding sights so that measurements can be taken asymmetrically.

(f) *The armillary* astrolabon *and associated devices.* The armillary *astrolabon* is the most complex of Ptolemy's instruments, and is also the one that has caused most confusion; through its name it has often been confused with the quite different plane astrolabe (Theon calls the latter the 'little astrolabe'), and through its appearance it has been confused with the armillary sphere, a later device used primarily for teaching and demonstration rather than for observation. Also, as the 'armillary astrolabe', it has been confused with the spherical astrolabe, a calculating instrument described by the Alfonsine astronomers.

The instrument described in the *Almagest* consists of a nest of seven concentric bronze rings, the innermost of which carries a pair of sights in the same fashion as the meridional armillary (figure 346). The whole device may have been mounted on a pillar and set in the meridional plane, but Pappus's words suggest that it was suspended in some way. The purpose of the many rings is that, once the inner sights have been set on the Moon or a fixed star, the ecliptic co-ordinates (latitude and longitude) may be read directly without the extended calculations needed to derive this information from altitudes and azimuths. This is of the greatest importance, since the kernel of Ptolemaic theory is its treatment of planetary motion in which the ecliptic is the prime plane of reference. The three outer rings merely provide a framework

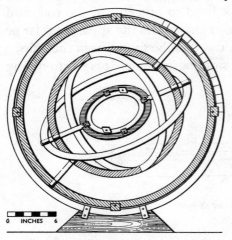

FIGURE 346—*The armillary* astrolabon.

which enables the fourth ring to rotate in the plane of the equator and to follow its diurnal rotation. The framework also carries an axle arranged at the proper inclination to follow the motion of the axis of the ecliptic, and this axle carries near the centre a pair of sights that may be used to determine the latitude from the ecliptic of any star or of the Moon. An extra ring is supplied on the outer portions of the ecliptic axle so that the instrument may be used to make simultaneous observations of two celestial bodies. With so many moving parts, the armillary *astrolabon* would have been subject to considerable error if not constructed with extraordinary skill; nevertheless, it was probably with this type of device that Ptolemy and perhaps Hipparchus took most of the observations for their famous star catalogues.

The need for making observations directly in ecliptic co-ordinates—or, at the worst, of having a geometrical device to transform altitude and azimuth into this form convenient to theory—was very real during the Middle Ages, when trigonometrical computation was a long and tedious process. An ingenious alternative to the armillary *astrolabon* introduced in the thirteenth century, the 'torquetum' or 'turketum' (figure 347), consists of a set of inclined, rotating tables, the lower one being set on a desk-like stand so that it may be slanted according to the latitude of the place of observation and set in the plane of the meridian. On this is pivoted another table representing the plane of the ecliptic, set at an angle of $23\frac{1}{2}°$ to the first. This carries a theodolite-style pair of graduated circles with a sighting-alidade. The usefulness of the instrument is much enhanced by the

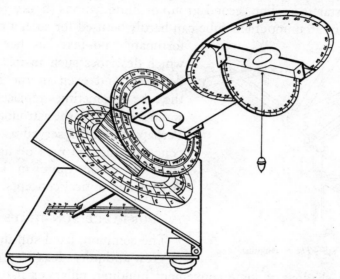

FIGURE 347—*The torquetum.*

addition of a semicircular protractor (*semissis*) and plumb-bob to the alidade; this enables observations and calculations of altitudes to be readily performed.

The *rectangulus* (figure 348), a skeleton version of the torquetum, was invented by Richard of Wallingford, chief of the Merton astronomers, in 1326. It avoids the use of the many divided circles of the parent instrument, but it must have been awkward to use and does not seem to have had any lasting vogue.

(g) *The sighting-tubes.* The modern scholar is so accustomed to seeing an astronomer depicted with his telescope that it has sometimes escaped attention that a number of medieval manuscript miniatures show the astronomer apparently gazing through a long tube held on a stand or by his hands. Such pictures must give rise to the suspicion that the instrument in question is actually some sort of telescope with lenses, and although the evidence is weak, it cannot be summarily discarded merely because of the great improbability of the invention having been made so early.

There appear to be two groups of pictures, in one of which the tube is mounted on a stand, while in the other it is trumpet-shaped and held to the eye. The first type occurs in conjunction with a text by Gerbert (Pope Sylvester II, 999–1003) in a St-Gall manuscript of 982. The instrument (figure 349 A) is designed as an aid to observing the celestial pole; it is directed towards the pole star by a teacher, and his students may then look through and learn without error which star it is. The second group of illuminations (figure 349 B) is more puzzling, since an unmounted tube can hardly be used for such a purpose. Un-

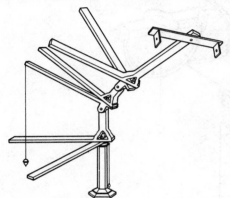

FIGURE 348—*The* rectangulus.

fortunately no text has been discovered which describes such an instrument as is depicted, and even in the illuminations the tube is sometimes replaced by a magic wand suitable for the astronomer-sorcerer. Perhaps the tube served as a funnel for concentrating the rays of light from the stars—a notion quite in keeping with Aristotelian optical concepts.

IV. PORTABLE SUN-DIALS

The common, fixed sun-dial is a device of great antiquity. It is no great step from marking the shadow of some convenient building, pillar, or natural object to the construction of a vertical or horizontal slab with its own little gnomon for casting a shadow of convenient size. Even during the early Middle Ages many Saxon scratch-dials were constructed on church walls. The more primitive of these devices can hardly qualify as precision instruments, but one special form of masonry dial known from classical times as the *skaphe* or hemicycle was sufficiently accurate for all daily purposes and even for the timing of eclipses. Many examples of the instrument have been preserved (figure 350).

More important technically are the numerous and often very ingenious portable sun-dials. Their small size demanded a certain accuracy in construction, and their portability led to problems that do not arise with an instrument rigidly fixed with respect to the meridian and horizontal planes.

(a) *Altitude-dials.* The shadow of a fixed object changes throughout the day both in direction and in length, and either of these variations or any combination of them may be used for the measurement of time. When a portable form of sun-dial is required it is perhaps natural to single out the length-variation, because it need involve no determination of the direction of the meridian and the instrument will not therefore require to be orientated before use. Because of its simplicity, the measurement of shadow-lengths is probably as ancient as any other means of telling the time, and the primitive empirical method of estimating in paces the length of a man's own shadow seems to be as ancient as it is widespread. Shadow-lengths vary not only throughout the day but from month to month through the cycle of the year; they are also dependent on the latitude of

FIGURE 349—(A) *Gerbert's sighting-tube. From a St-Gall manuscript, now lost;* (B) *similar tube used without a stand, from a thirteenth-century manuscript.*

the place of observation. It follows that tables or graduations must be available for various times during the year, and that these data are valid only for the latitude of the intended place of use. Typical of such tables is one given by Bede (673–735), which shows the length of the shadow of a 6-ft gnomon at noon, 9 a.m., and 3 p.m. at intervals of about a fortnight throughout the year; it is constructed for a latitude of about 55°, corresponding to the position of his monastery at Jarrow.

The earliest form of instrument for such measurements seems to have been the Egyptian shadow-clock (tenth to eighth centuries B.C.), and very similar devices are still in use in that country The shadow-clock is nothing more than a horizontal graduated rod, with a vertical projection of some sort used as the gnomon (vol I, figures 44–45). The graduations of the rod seem to have been arrived at empirically, and the annual variation must also have been allowed for by rule of thumb. A later type of Egyptian altitude-dial (probably of the Roman period) illustrates a fundamental improvement in the technique of the instrument. It consists (figure 351 A) of a small wedge with a rectangular block set before it. In use, the device is orientated so that the shadow of the block falls squarely on the slanting face, and the length of the shadow may be then read on one of the scales

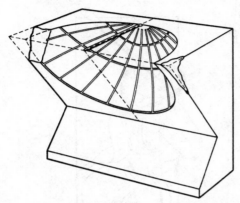

marked lengthwise on this face. Scales are provided for each month of the year, but since the variation is cyclical one scale may be made to serve for two months equidistant from an equinox.

A Roman 'ham' dial from Herculaneum (figure 351 B) shows a marked improvement on the Egyptian forms, in that it consists of a flat plate which may be suspended from a ring so that it automatically takes up a vertical position and does not need to be levelled by independent means. In the 'ham' dial the gnomon protrudes from the surface of

FIGURE 350—Skaphe, *or hemicycle sun-dial, found at Civita Lavinia.*

the plate, which is orientated until the tip of the shadow falls on the graduations of the appropriate column containing divisions for the month of the year.

In practice it is found that the use of a single fixed gnomon leads to inconvenience in graduating the instrument, and this difficulty is removed in the design of the earliest English instrument, a Saxon (ninth or tenth century) dial of exquisite workmanship found at Canterbury Cathedral in 1939 (figure 351 C). A strikingly similar example, this time of Muslim origin, is a dial made in 1159–60 for the Sultan Nūr al-Dīn (figure 351 D). In both dials the gnomon is detachable and may be placed in a socket above any of the appropriate month-columns. Each separate hour of the day is marked on the Muslim instrument, but the Anglo-Saxon dial agrees with Bede in distinguishing only the 'tides' at noon, 9 a.m., and 3 p.m.

The cyclical character of the annual variation is probably responsible for the appearance of dials in the form of a cylinder with the columns for each month arranged around it (figure 351 E). This type of instrument, mentioned by Chaucer as the 'chilindre', and still in daily use in the Pyrenees as the shepherd's dial,

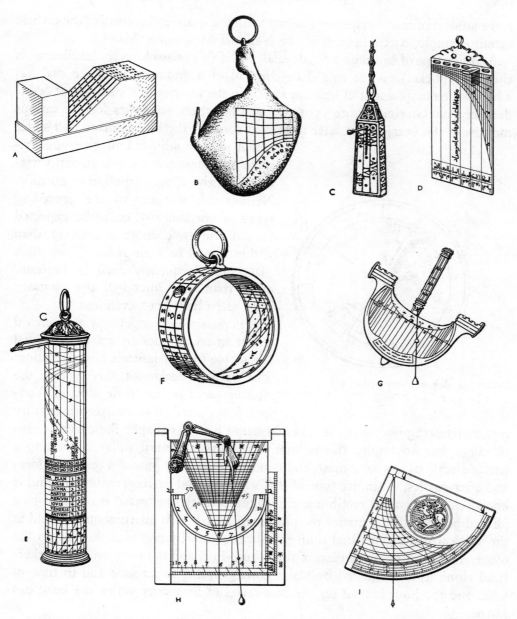

FIGURE 351—*Sun-dials of various types and periods.* (A) *Egyptian wedge-dial;* (B) *Roman 'ham' dial*
(C) *Saxon dial from Canterbury;* (D) *Islamic dial of similar type;* (E) *'chilindre' or shepherd's dial;* (F) *ring-dial;*
(G) navicula *or ship-dial;* (H) *universal rectilinear dial;* (I) *horary quadrant (dated 1399).*

is the subject of manuscript texts dating from the fourteenth century; the earliest extant example, dated 1455, is in the National Museum at Munich.

Another type of common altitude-dial, probably not so old as the 'chilindre', is the poke (pocket) dial or ring dial.[1] Instead of a gnomon, the poke dial has a hole which casts a spot of light on a scale in the interior of a small squat cylinder like a napkin ring (figure 351 F). Sometimes there are scales for the various months of the year, but in later improved versions the hole is made in a slider which can be adjusted to give approximate compensation for the annual variation in the Sun's meridian altitude. Neither this nor any of the preceding types of portable dial could be expected to tell the time more accurately than within about half an hour. Since such dials were frequently used in latitudes other than that intended, the accuracy must often have been even less.

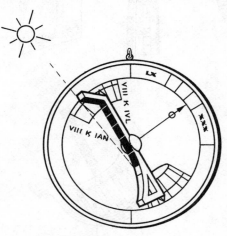

FIGURE 352—*Roman equatorial dial, c A.D. 250–300.*

It is possible, by ingenious geometrical construction, to design an altitude-dial adjustable for any latitude of observation. The earliest design of this type is the *navicula de Venetiis* (little ship of Venice), first described in fourteenth-century manuscripts (figure 351 G). It takes its name from its shape; the curved semicircular plate resembles the outline of a ship, a central pillar containing a latitude-scale passes for a mast, and two projections for pinnules resemble fore- and after-castles. A similar type of dial was designed by Regiomontanus and is known as his universal rectilinear dial (figure 351 H); the 'mast' is replaced by a jointed pointer, which carries the plummet. In use both instruments are held in the vertical plane and tilted until the shadow cast by one pinnule falls on the other. The point of suspension of the plumb-line, and the position of a marker-bead along it, are adjusted by scales corresponding to latitude and to time of year, and the hour is read on one of a series of lines over which the bead can range.

The portable quadrant is included in this section because although it was used as a more general astronomical instrument, and adapted for terrestrial surveying

---

[1] The latter term is to be deprecated as ambiguous; there are 'universal' ring dials, finger-ring dials, and others.

and as a variation on the astrolabe, it is as an altitude sun-dial that it probably had its greatest vogue. The instrument (figure 351 1) consists of a quadrant of metal or wood, furnished with a pair of pinnule-sights along one of its terminating radii and fitted with a plumb-bob suspended from the centre of its arc. The

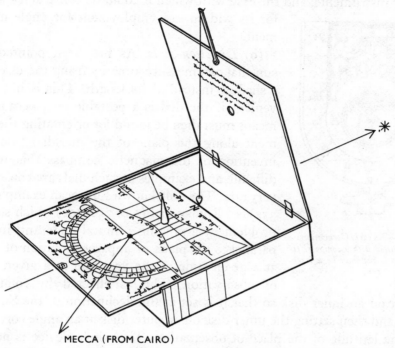

MECCA (FROM CAIRO)

FIGURE 353—*Syrian double-dial, which could be used to determine the* qibla (*direction of Mecca*). *Fourteenth century.*

fundamental idea of the economy of using a quadrant instead of the larger and heavier full circle is apparent already in Ptolemy's plinth (p 587), but whether the portable form of instrument was introduced by the Alexandrians or by the Muslims who succeeded them remains uncertain. The earliest known portable quadrant seems to have contained a shadow-square for surveying (p 528) as well as the divided arc; it is in this form that it receives its first European mention by Leonardo da Pisa about 1220. Soon afterwards Profatius (Jacob ben Tibbon, a Jewish astronomer of Montpellier) mentions the 'old quadrant' (*quadrans vetus*) as containing the divided circle, shadow-square, and a set of horary lines, in contradistinction to his 'new quadrant' (1288, revised 1301) which included an astrolabe projection as well. From the fourteenth century onwards there is a considerable literature on the portable quadrant in its European and Muslim, and old and new, forms. Its economy of size for a given radius of arc, and the scope for ingenuity in devising suitable scales and graduations for various purposes, made it a favourite subject amongst the inventors and engravers of scientific instruments, and the ease with which it could be constructed accounts for its widespread employment for angle measurement.

FIGURE 354—*An early German horizontal dial fitted with a compass. It is dated 1453, but may be a later copy.*

(b) *Direction-dials*. As has been pointed out, a sun-dial can measure time by using the direction of a shadow instead of its length. This is not so convenient if the dial is a portable one, because some means must then be found for orientating the instrument along the plane of the meridian. Before the invention of the magnetic compass this was very difficult, and examples of such dials are consequently very rare. The only known European example (figure 352) is a Roman dial (A.D. 250–300) which solves the problem by arranging a 'mural quadrant' in a plane parallel to the plane of apparent rotation of the Sun at a given time of the year and at a given latitude of observation. This is effected by rotating the quadrant on an inner disk so that it is set at the declination of the Sun in the ecliptic, and then setting the inner disk on an outer disk at an angle corresponding to the latitude of the place of observation. The whole device is next supported in the vertical plane by means of a ring, and twisted until the shadow of the gnomon falls along the arc of the quadrant and indicates the time. An inverted use of such direction-dials is found in Islam; a fourteenth-century dial from Aleppo (figure 353) uses an altitude-dial to find the time and then sets a direction-dial along the meridian by turning it until it reads correctly. The double dial thus acts as a sort of sun-compass and can be used to determine the direction (*qibla*) of Mecca, which Muslims need to know for ritual purposes. To facilitate this operation, the Aleppo dial and others of similar construction are furnished with a special scale showing the direction of Mecca from various cities.

The introduction of the magnetic compass led to the devising of many types of direction-dial orientated by this means. Ships' inventories record 'dyolls' from 1410–12, and *horloges de mer* appear at about the same date, but these are probably sun-dials (without compasses) and sand-glasses. The earliest known compass dials are several of almost identical construction dated 1541–63, in which the shadow is thrown by a style of thread stretched between the base-plate and a vertical pillar which can fold down for ease of carrying (figure 354). The style is set, according to latitude, so that it is parallel to the polar axis. An interesting feature of these dials is that the compass-plate is marked with a line showing the deviation of magnetic from true north. This practice was followed by later instrument-makers, but the deviation recorded is often traditional rather than actual.

V. WATER-CLOCKS

The oldest time-measuring devices independent of astronomical phenomena undoubtedly indicated merely the passage of arbitrarily fixed periods, as does the modern egg-timer. The sand-glass is not known by explicit mention until the second half of the fourteenth century, but its precursor the clepsydra, which used water instead of sand, was known in Egypt about 1400 B.C. and is probably of much greater antiquity. One found at Karnak, and believed to date from the reign of Amenhotep III (*c* 1415–*c* 1380 B.C.). consists of an alabaster bowl with a small hole near the bottom through which water was allowed to leak away. Some extant clepsydra jars from Egypt have scales marked on the inside, but for these to measure equal intervals of time the graduation would have to be made empirically and the water-level at the start would have to be at exactly the right height on the scale (vol I, figure 48).

(a) *The constant-flow clepsydra.* The first technical problem of the water-clock is to make the water flow at a uniform rate. This cannot be done readily with a simple leaking jar, although the sloping sides of the Egyptian clepsydras help to compensate for the decreasing head of water. The most important step in the design of the true water-clock was made by Ctesibius (? *c* 100 B.C.). Vitruvius tells us that he was the first to fashion the leak-hole in a gem or in gold so that it should not get worn away or clogged by corrosion. He also inverted the usual practice by measuring the water flowing out of the jar instead of that which had been poured in or which remained, and, most important of all, he arranged for a continuous flow of water into the jar and an overflow-pipe near the top so that the leak always occurred under a constant head of water. The water was allowed to drip into a cylindrical container, and in the simplest form its height could be read by means of a time-scale on the inner wall. Ctesibius, being of an inventive and mechanical turn of mind, preferred more elaborate devices (figure 355 A) and fitted the cylinder with a float moving a rack and pinion; this provided motive power for working little devices (*parerga*) and making signals to be seen or heard at the end of each hour.

(b) *The parastatic clock*. The next stage was to fit the float with a pointer that could travel along a vertical scale marked in hours. This was not so simple as it sounds, for the hours that it was desired to indicate were not the equal hours of astronomy; they were the unequal hours of which there were always just twelve from sunrise to sunset, regardless of the length of the day (p 565; vol I, p 113). Ctesibius tried at first to adjust the clock by adding a valve to the leak-hole, but this proved too erratic in action. As an alternative, a number of scales

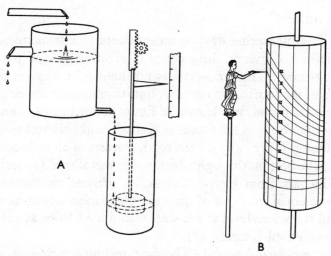

FIGURE 355—(A) *Constant-head clepsydra with float operating pointer on time-scale and (through the rack and pinion) automata; (B) parastatic water-clock.*

varying in length from month to month were inscribed on a pillar (*parastatica*) along which the pointer (in the shape of a manikin) could travel. By making the hour-marks into a set of continuous sloping lines around the cylinder (figure 355 B) the scale could be accurately turned to the appropriate length for any day of the year.

(c) *The zodiac-regulated clock*. Vitruvius gives an account of an ingenious solution to the difficulty experienced by Ctesibius in adjusting the outflow of the parastatic clock so that a single scale might be used throughout the seasons. The device functions by varying the depth of the hole below the water-level rather than by altering the size of the hole or adding a valve. The hole of the clepsydra is placed near the circumference of a bronze disk which can be turned in its setting, and a pointer is fixed on the disk near to the hole (figure 356). This pointer indicates a position on a circular scale marked with the signs of the zodiac and evenly graduated in 365 days. When the Sun is at the summer solstice in Cancer the hole is uppermost and the rate of outflow is small, so that the cylinder fills slowly; at the winter solstice the pointer is in Capricorn and, the hole being lowermost, the rate of flow is greatest and the cylinder fills more rapidly in the shorter day. The construction is in fact only an approximation for other days of the year, but the disk could always be turned slightly to correct empirically for any inadequacy of the time-keeping.

VI. THE ASTROLABE

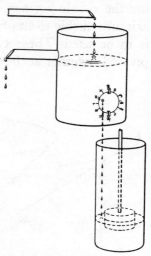

The name astrolabe (Greek *astrolabon*, star-taker) has been applied, at some time or other, to almost every astronomical instrument except the telescope. The confusion with Ptolemy's armillary *astrolabon* has already been noted (p 591) and this, together with a well known but altogether misleading letter from Synesius (*c* A.D. 410) to Paeonius, has led to the ascription of the plane astrolabe to Ptolemy and even to Hipparchus. It is a perfect instance of a correct conclusion being drawn from false evidence, for although the earliest extant text on the plane astrolabe is that of Philoponus (*c* A.D. 530) it has now been conclusively demonstrated by Neugebauer that the

FIGURE 356 — *Zodiac-regulated water-clock, the height of the hole adjusting the flow according to the length of the day.*

instrument was known to Ptolemy, and that the underlying theory of stereographic projection was indeed probably known in the time of Hipparchus.

(a) *Principle of stereographic projection.* Stereographic projection is one of many devices that may be used to map the surface of a sphere on to a flat plane; it has the special property of mapping all circles on the sphere as circles on the plane, and of projecting angles between two lines on the sphere into equal angles between two lines on the plane. For the purpose of the ordinary plane astrolabe, the map is made by projecting from the south pole of the celestial sphere on to a plane perpendicular to the polar axis (figure 357). If one held a sheet of paper directly over the north pole of a transparent globe and looked up from the south pole of the globe towards the paper, the mapping could be performed visually.

A full account of the construction and use of this projection is given by Ptolemy in one of his minor works, the *Planispherium*; but he is clearly making use of earlier material, for Hipparchus was able to solve problems on the sphere without a knowledge of spherical trigonometry, and it is therefore very reasonable to presume that his method was that of stereographic projection. Once the idea of stereographic projection is familiar, it can be only a very short step to the basic principle of plane astrolabic devices. For these, two plates are constructed, one representing the celestial sphere and engraved with the position of stars and the ecliptic in which the Sun moves, and a second representing the visible horizon, zenith, lines of constant altitude, and lines of constant azimuth visible to an observer at the particular latitude at which the instrument is to be used. These two plates are then placed one over the other, and are pivoted together at the north celestial pole in both cases. By rotating one plate

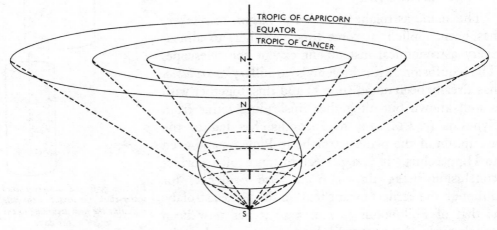

FIGURE 357—*Principle of the stereographic projection.*

with respect to the second the diurnal rotation of the celestial sphere can then be simulated, and many types of calculations may be thus facilitated.

(b) *The anaphoric clock.* It seems very likely that the first application of the principle just described was in the construction of a star-map made to rotate so that it showed artificially the diurnal rotation of the heavens. This was not only effective as an ingenious spectacle, but could also be of practical use in showing the rising and setting of the Sun and the progress of the customary 'unequal hours' between these limits. The difficulty of recording unequal hours with a water-clock of constant flow has already been mentioned (p 602). The anaphoric clock, as described by Vitruvius, is simply a constant-flow clepsydra arranged so that the rising float is connected to a sand-bag counterpoise by means of a flexible bronze chain, which passes round an axle and turns it through one revolution in a solar day. The axle carries a large circular star-map, laid out by stereographic projection (figure 358), and in front of this map is placed a stationary grill corresponding to the projection of the horizon and visible hemisphere for the desired latitude (Vitruvius chooses Alexandria, *c* 31° N). Part of a star-plate from an anaphoric clock dating from the first or second century A.D. has been found at Salzburg; it contains delineations of some constellations, and also part of a circle which originally contained 182 or 183 holes. A little disk representing the Sun was probably plugged into the appropriate hole and moved to the next one every second day, so that it made one complete rotation in the plate during a year.

(c) *Evolution of the plane astrolabe.* The greatest technical difficulty of the anaphoric clock lay in the construction of the grill. If only a few wires were used, the device was too inaccurate; with many thinner wires the grill became fragile

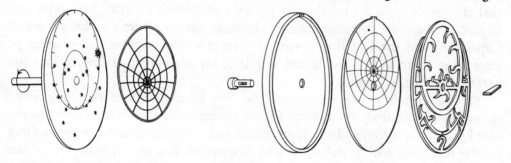

FIGURE 358—(Left) *Rotating star-map and fixed grill of anaphoric clock (reconstructed)*; (right) *mater, plate, and star-map (rete) of an astrolabe, showing the same arrangement reversed.*

and liable to deformation and tended to obscure the underlying star-map. We do not know who made the brilliant suggestion that the grill might be engraved on a solid plate and a 'transparent' star-map rotated above it (figure 358). The important point is, of course, the conception of a transparent disk and its realization by cutting away everything from the star-map except the indispensable circles and a small number of pointers marking the position of only the brightest stars. This improvement transformed the instrument from the realms of demonstration and crude time-indication to the greatest heights of utility, as a calculating device suitable for working with sufficient precision most of the problems of spherical astronomy.

In the *Planispherium* Ptolemy seems to refer to a 'horoscopic instrument' which has the fixed stars marked on the *aranea* or spider. Unfortunately we have no other evidence to support an assertion that this instrument is a true astrolabe, and it is therefore necessary to fall back on the evidence of the earliest available texts on the instrument. In date, the first is a treatise by Philoponus (*c* A.D. 530), but it has now been shown that this is merely a later edited version of a treatise by Theon of Alexandria (*c* A.D. 375) which is preserved with only slight changes in a text by Severus Sēbōkht (before A.D. 660). A useful indication of the evolution of the instrument is the history of its name. For Ptolemy and Proclus, *astrolabon* is always the armillary *astrolabon*. Theon distinguishes the plane instrument as the 'little astrolabe' (p 591); and Philoponus calls it simply the 'astrolabe', in common with all medieval writers on the subject.

An interesting aspect of the early history of the plane astrolabe concerns the circular outer limit of the instrument. In Ptolemy's *Planispherium*, the letter of Synesius, and perhaps also the treatise of Sēbōkht, the outer border represents the Antarctic circle of the celestial sphere—the southernmost limit of stars that are visible from the inhabitable portions of the world. In all later texts and all extant instruments (tenth century onwards) the outer limit is the Tropic of Capricorn, and the instrument cannot therefore always show the position of stars lying south of this tropic and visible to an observer in the northern temperate zone of the Earth.

(d) *Construction of the plane astrolabe.* The basic design of the instrument shows no change from the earliest known examples of the tenth century to the obsolescent productions of the seventeenth and even eighteenth centuries. Only in the techniques of metal-work and decoration has the appearance of the astrolabe altered.

The body of the instrument (figure 359) consists of the *mater*, a thick plate of metal with a circular depression hollowed out of the obverse to contain a set of thin circular tablets engraved with lines of altitude and azimuth for a series of convenient fixed latitudes. Usually the tablets are keyed by a notch and tag so that they will fit in the *mater* only when correctly positioned. At one point of its circumference the *mater* bears a lug or 'throne', to which are attached a swivel and a suspensory ring to hold the instrument; its weight then aligns the *mater* in a vertical plane. Above the tablets, in front of the face of the *mater*, is an open-work metal plate, the rete, containing a set of pointers indicating the positions of the fixed stars, and a circle representing the zodiac.

The whole instrument is fastened together by a removable peg running through the centre of the *mater*, tablets, and rete. It frequently carries also a small pivoted rule on the face of the instrument, and a rule fitted with a pair of pinnule-sights (the alidade) on the dorsum of the astrolabe. In later instruments the peg consists of a screw and nut, but in all the early versions the peg is fixed by a little wedge (the 'horse') which passes through its end.

The majority of astrolabes are made of brass because of the ease with which it can be obtained in good plates and satisfactorily engraved with fine lines.

Sometimes the *mater* is cast in brass or in bronze, but more often it is hollowed out of a thick sheet; sometimes it is built up from a thin plate on which a heavier rim has been riveted or brazed. From the sixteenth century onwards cheap astrolabes, and indeed many other types of instrument, were made by pasting printed diagrams on suitably cut sheets of wood. Islamic astrolabes are sometimes found embellished with precious stones and highly ornate decorative

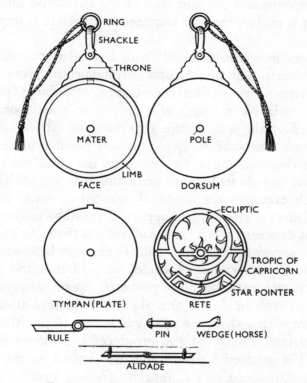

FIGURE 359—*The component parts of an astrolabe.*

engravings; their retes often contain zoomorphic star-pointers and are of great intrinsic beauty.

(e) *The dorsum of the astrolabe.* Essentially the astrolabe is a calculating instrument, but it seems to have been adapted at an early stage in such a way that it could also be used for observing the altitude of the Sun or fixed stars. From such an observation, and using the face of the instrument, one may calculate such things as the time of day or night and the sign of the zodiac which is in the ascendant. This adaptation as an instrument of observation is secondary, in almost the same way as a modern slide-rule may also carry a scale of inches or centimetres. It is most probable that the original form of the device had no sighting-alidade, which was later added so as to take advantage of the divided circle of the instrument. Before the invention of the dividing-engine it was laborious and costly to produce an accurately divided circle by a process of continued bisection of angles and laying off calculated chords. Even the earliest treatises of Philoponus and Sēbōkht refer to the alidade on the dorsum of the instrument, so it is evident that the astrolabe had been thus improved at some very early stage.

At first the dorsum was marked only with a circular arc containing degrees and their subdivisions. The first Muslim astronomers improved upon this by adding many devices for geometrical computation, including a 'shadow-square'; this showed the variation in length of a vertical or a horizontal shadow of a fixed stick—in effect the scale (figure 329) gives the tangent or cotangent of the angle observed. The shadow-square made it possible to use the astrolabe also as an observing-instrument for terrestrial use. One could measure the shadow of a tower or sight its topmost point and deduce its height by means of the device. Such examples are frequently quoted in texts, but the method probably served more as an ingenious application used by teachers of mathematics to show that geometry was a 'practical' subject than as a means commonly employed by any surveyor, builder, or military engineer before the Renaissance. The shadow-square was sometimes included on quadrants, and was even transformed into a separate instrument, the geometric square, which consisted of an open square frame with an alidade or a plumb-bob pivoted at one corner. The portable quadrant with a shadow-square was known to the Muslims from the time of Al-Khwārizmī (c 840) and was introduced into Europe by Leonardo da Pisa (c 1220). The geometric square was also known to the Muslims, but although it was introduced into Europe by Gerbert (940?–1003) it did not become popular until the development of practical trigonometrical methods of indirect measurement by Purbach (c 1450) and the rise of instrumental surveying in the sixteenth century.

The *mariner's astrolabe* can hardly be called an astrolabe at all; it consists only of the alidade and divided circle that compose the observing portion, the whole of the calculating apparatus being omitted. The instrument is made heavier than usual, and as much as possible of the inside of the outer limb is cut away, so that the device may hang in a vertical plane and be little disturbed by wind. As an instrument for taking the height of the Sun or pole star, to derive the latitude, it seems to have been invented about 1535; some earlier mentions probably refer to the use of astronomical astrolabes at sea. After 1600 its popularity declined, as better alternative instruments became available.

(f) *Later history of the astrolabe.* The astrolabe attained widespread use in Islam very soon after its introduction there. The first writer on the subject is reputed to be Al-Fazārī (*c* 800), but his work remains unknown. It was perhaps displaced by that of his contemporary Mesahallah (Māshāllāh), a Jew probably of Egyptian descent. Mesahallah's treatise on the instrument became, in Latin translation, the most popular text on the subject in Europe during the later Middle Ages. Many other Arabic texts are known, and a number of ingenious variants on the astrolabe were evolved by the Muslim astronomers.

The earliest European text on the instrument is the *Sententiae astrolabii* (second half of tenth century), which has been attributed to Gerbert and describes the use but not the construction of the device. Full details of the geometric construction are first given in *De mensura astrolabii* by Hermannus Contractus ('the Lame'), abbot of Reichenau, about the middle of the eleventh century. It is probable, however, that the astrolable did not become common in Europe until the revival of astronomy towards the end of the twelfth century. The earliest extant Gothic instruments come from the second half of the thirteenth century and show great similarity in design and construction.

By the close of the fourteenth century the medieval astrolabe had achieved the peak of its popularity in Europe. Later there was a decline before the rise of the schools of instrument-makers in Germany and other countries. One of the most interesting of the later medieval texts is the 'Treatise on the Astrolabe' composed by Geoffrey Chaucer in 1391; it is one of the earliest technical works on science written in the English language, and is still one of the best and most lucid accounts of the astrolabe.

The revival of the astrolabe by the astronomers and instrument-makers of the Renaissance initiates the new age of craftsmanship and design in the construction of precision instruments. Although by this time the device was beginning to be outmoded by advances in astronomical theory and technique, its complexity and pleasing appearance made it the most popular subject for art metal-work, fine engraving, and the careful workmanship which later became so valuable when instrument-makers were able to turn their hands to the more varied experimental apparatus of the scientific revolution (ch 23).

VII. HERO'S DIOPTRA AND LEVELLING-INSTRUMENT

Hero's dioptra is a surveyor's instrument, a combined theodolite and waterlevel. It stands alone among devices known from antiquity, and is probably

Hero's own invention. It is described in his book *Dioptra*, in which there is a reference to a lunar eclipse that happened in A.D. 62.

The oldest manuscript of this work still extant, which is the source of all later ones, has lost eight pages; thus the description of the instrument is incomplete and has to be supplemented by conjectures and from deductions drawn from the description of its use. It must have had a foot, but whether this was a tripod or a sort of table we do not know. It must, however, have been possible to set the instrument strictly vertical, and a plummet was used for this purpose.

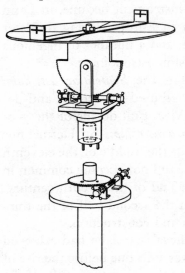

The instrument proper (figure 360) consisted of a column ending in a cylindrical axle, round the foot of which was a circular plate of bronze. A hub with a toothed wheel fitted the axle, and the wheel was engaged by an endless screw carried by uprights fixed on the bronze plate. This screw had a furrow as broad as the toothed wheel was thick, running lengthwise. When this furrow was opposite the toothed wheel the hub was free to turn in any direction; a turn of the screw would fix it and adjust it in any position.

On the upper side of the hub were three holes. The theodolite and water-level were each provided with a socket fitting the axle, and three pegs fitting the holes; in this way they were interchangeable. In the theodolite this cylinder ended in a Doric capital on which were two uprights; between them these carried a toothed semicircle of brass. An endless screw on the capital engaging with the teeth moved the semicircle and held it, just as the other screw did for the horizontal wheel. On the diameter of the semicircle was fitted a disk which carried the sighting-rod; it turned freely round an axle, and had two pointers moving over the surface of the disk. Here were engraved two lines at right-angles, one of them being in the plane of the semicircle. To use the dioptra for astronomical purposes the circle described by the pointers is divided into 360 degrees.

This is the theodolite; its principal use was to stake out lines at right-angles. By this means it was possible to stake out a straight line between two points not visible from each other, to find the distance to a remote point, or to direct a tunnel through a mountain. The theodolite could also be used in measuring the

FIGURE 360—*Hero's dioptra (reconstructed diagram)*. (Above) *The theodolite instrument*; (below) *the upper part of the base on which the theodolite and water-level rest*.

area of a piece of land, or for dividing it, even if it was inaccessible because of vegetation or buildings. By using the up-and-down movement of the sighting-rod it was possible to measure the height of an unapproachable point, such as the top of the enemy's wall, or the depth of a trench.

The water-level also had a cylinder with three pegs (figure 361); on its head were two small uprights to hold a wooden rod some 6 ft long. Into this rod was fitted a tube with upturned ends, to which vertical glass tubes were attached. When water was poured into this system, the water in the two glass tubes would stand at the same level. However, the surface of the water would not serve for

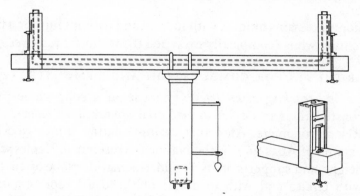

FIGURE 361—*Hero's dioptra: the water-level with* (inset) *one of the two sights.*

sighting. Round each glass tube was built a small wooden housing; a brass plate could slide up and down just in front of the tube, and a slit in the brass could be adjusted exactly at the level of the water. The same brass plate carried the sighting-slits in the form of a cross, and in this way a horizontal line could be determined. To move the plates Hero once more used screws. The vertical screw came through the rod outside the housing and passed through a primitive nut—a smooth hole with a peg thrust in from the side so as to engage the screw thread. It was not possible at this time to cut in metal an internal thread of such small dimensions. The top of the screw was fitted into a cylinder fastened on the brass plate; a peg in the cylinder engaged a furrow in the head of the screw. The water-level was also provided with a plummet to set it vertical.

To use the water-level it was necessary to have two staves consisting of poles with plummets. Upon each a large target, painted half white and half black and sliding in a dove-tailed groove cut along the length of the staff, was raised and lowered by a string. A pointer on the target moved along a scale on the rod. To compare the height of two points it was necessary to set up a staff on each point, and then to place the dioptra on the line between them. When the slits had been adjusted the surveyor sighted one of the targets and had it raised or lowered by means of shouts or gestures, until the dividing-line was exactly on the sights. Then he looked through the dioptra the other way and had the other target adjusted. The difference in height between the targets, as read on the staffs, gave the difference in height between the two points. Then one staff was moved to the next point and the dioptra placed between the two points before repeating the procedure. The idea of turning the dioptra round and sighting many times from the same place does not seem to have occurred to the inventor.

Hero's dioptra remains unique, without past and without future: a fine but premature invention whose complexity exceeded the technical resources of its time.

VIII. INSTRUMENTS FOR COMPUTATION AND DEMONSTRATION

(a) *Globes and teaching-armillaries.* The use of a solid globe marked with stars and constellations to depict the celestial sphere is at least as old as the earliest Greek astronomers. An actual example dating from *c* 300 B.C. is preserved in a statue of Atlas now in the National Museum at Naples; the figure is 186 cm in height, and supports on its shoulders a marble globe 65 cm in diameter, engraved with circles and with diagrams of the usual representations of the major constellations. It seems likely that such globes were first constructed in this fashion merely as solid pictures and without any thought to their possible use for scientific record, teaching, or calculation. The next step is recorded by Ptolemy in the *Almagest* but might well date back to Hipparchus. Ptolemy describes how to make a celestial globe and mark it with the proper set of imaginary astronomical lines and to colour the surface dark, like the night sky, so that the stars will stand out properly in realistic fashion. Most important of all, Ptolemy describes how to mount the globe on an axis supported by a meridian which was in turn supported by an equatorial circle so that it might revolve to follow the diurnal rotation of the stars; and he inclines this axis according to the latitude of his observatory so that the visible celestial hemisphere shows above the plane of the horizon. This in all essentials is the modern celestial globe, and has undergone no major improvement between the time of Ptolemy and the present day.

The celestial globe seems to have had great popularity amongst the Muslim astronomers, and many texts survive to augment the information derivable from extant Arabic spheres. A brass globe made by Ptolemy himself, and a second silver globe made for the Caliph Adād al-Daula, were preserved in the public library at Cairo, according to a statement made by Ibn al-Nabdī in 1043. Unfortunately both these globes have been lost, and the oldest Muslim spheres are examples dated 1080 and a number from the thirteenth century and later. In Europe outside the Muslim region of influence, references to celestial spheres marked with the fixed stars are virtually non-existent until the revival of globe-making amongst the German school of instrument-makers towards the end of the fifteenth century. The subsequent developments belong mainly to the story of cartography.

A simpler type of celestial globe, showing the imaginary circles but not the stars or constellations, is found in a mural (c A.D. 50) from a villa at Boscoreale near Pompeii. This type of globe was developed later as the teaching-armillary, probably much influenced by Ptolemy's observing instrument, the armillary *astrolabon*, with which, however, it must not be confused. The teaching-armillary is known from manuscript miniatures of the thirteenth and fourteenth centuries. In its basic form it consists of a series of wire rings representing the equator, ecliptic, tropics,

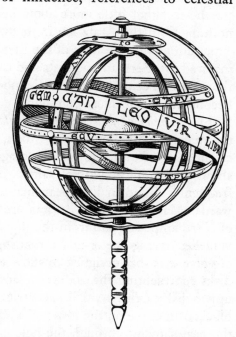

FIGURE 362—*Fifteenth-century armillary sphere, showing the Earth at the centre, the ecliptic (with signs of the zodiac), and other circles.*

polar circles, solisticial colure, and other meridian circles (figure 362). The polar axis is usually extended to form a little handle which may be held by the teacher. In this form, or with slight improvements, it had great popularity throughout the Middle Ages and must have been frequently used as an adjunct to Sacrobosco's 'Sphere', the most-used text on elementary astronomy. During the sixteenth century teaching-armillaries were much elaborated by the addition of movable figures representing the planets, by the marking of star positions with little pointers, and by elegant craftsmanship and embellishment. They were a popular object for instrument-makers working under the patronage of noble and wealthy amateurs of science.

Although the sphericity of the Earth was well known to the Greeks, the knowledge seems not to have resulted in anything more than a passing desire to make a terrestrial globe. Strabo reports that Crates, a contemporary of Hipparchus, made such a globe and exhibited it in Pergamum about 150 B.C.; he adds that such a globe was relatively so small that it did not have much advantage of representation over a flat map of the required accuracy. This probably accounts for the fact that little more about such globes is known from the Greeks, and nothing from the Arabs or from medieval Europe. It is not until the age of explorations that we hear of the first *Erdapfel* of Martin Behaim (1492), which inspired the German scientists and cartographers to follow his example. During the sixteenth century, terrestrial globes of all sizes and degrees of ornamentation become more and more common.

(b) *Calendrical and horary calculators.* The cyclical nature of the days of the week, the lunations of the Moon, and the seasons of the solar year make the calendar a natural subject for diagrammatic representation. Circular charts showing dominical letters, saints' days, and aids to paschal calculation are frequently found in European manuscripts from about the ninth century onwards. Many ingenious devices are used—for example, the annulus of John of Northampton—and from the thirteenth century such tables often consist of volvelles having one or more rotating disks. Probably the most common type of volvelle is that designed to show the phases of the Moon; it consists of two disks representing the zodiacal places of the Sun and Moon respectively. The upper disk carries a small excentric hole through which can be seen part of a blocked-in curve on the lower disk. This curve, often circular, is so placed that the part showing through the hole is similar in shape to the appropriate phase of the Moon for this particular elongation between the Sun and Moon. Using such a device one could easily determine the zodiacal place of the Moon by noting its phase and the known place of the Sun. This knowledge could then be used to tell the time at night. A remarkable instance of a Sun and Moon phase-calculator occurs on the dorsum of an Arabic astrolabe dated 1223–4; it includes a set of gear-wheels which turn the Sun and Moon disks at the correct speed when a calendar circle is adjusted to the date in the year.

The Moon phase-indicator is often combined with a nocturnal, which may consist of nothing more than a pointer added to that disk which records the position of the Sun (figure 363). The nocturnal is used for finding the time at night from the position of the circumpolar stars. The pole star is sighted through a hole at the centre of the disks and pointer, and the arm of the pointer is then adjusted to lie along the 'pointers' in the constellations Ursa Major or Minor.

(c) *Trigonometrical calculators.* Even the earliest Arabic astrolabes include on the dorsum one or more quadrants inscribed with devices to assist calculation by graphical means. A set of curves for determining unequal hours is often included, and even more frequently one finds a quadrant ruled with a series of horizontal and vertical lines. Such a reticulated quadrant is of great assistance, since it enables trigonometrical sines and cosines to be found graphically. This device occurs, but only rarely, in medieval European instruments, and by the fourteenth century one even finds sinical quadrants which contain this aid and nothing else. Later, in the sixteenth century, such calculators were made in larger quantities.

It is very interesting that the technique of computation by geometric construction received much attention from Greek astronomers. The Muslim astronomers, too, seem to have had great enthusiasm for all such devices, and many new forms and variations are known from their texts. The explanation is doubtless to be found in the tedious character of long computations, involving the sexagesimal system of notation, necessary for all astronomical work; the tedium was much increased by the habitual use of even eight or ten places of sexagesimals where two or three might have sufficed.

(d) *Planetary models and calculators.* The *Almagest* represents the apex of Greek attainment in pure science, and it is Ptolemy's planetary theory which

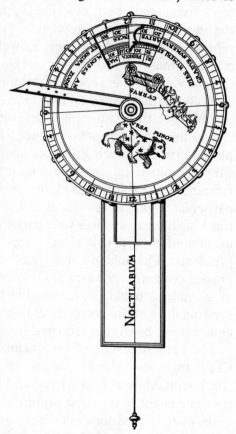

FIGURE 363—*Nocturnal by Georg Hartmann of Nuremberg. 1535.*

forms the greater part of that work. Planetary theory was the most successful instance of the mathematical analysis of natural phenomena until very recent times, and this characteristic aspect of Ptolemaic astronomy reigned supreme and had the largest influence on men's minds until the seventeenth century. It is no exaggeration to say that the existence of this single overwhelming success in the pure sciences determined the whole course of scientific analysis through more than 1500 years.

Since this directing influence sprang from the accuracy of the planetary theory it was natural that much attention should be paid to the construction of models and devices that show the planets behaving according to rule, and reproducing the very courses of those planets as seen in the sky. The anaphoric clock has already been described (p 604) as perhaps the first artificial model of the movements of the heavens; it was succeeded by other models including representations of the planets as well. The mechanical clock indeed owes its origin to the desire to exhibit more complex models, which would demonstrate the glory of God as revealed in the perfection of regularity in the complicated motions of the heavens. The first great public clocks usually showed more resemblance to gigantic planetaria or orreries than to the modern timekeepers.

Another type of planetary device was intended for professional use rather than public gaze. Although Ptolemaic planetary theory achieves its success by fairly simple geometrical construction, it results in lengthy calculations and many references to tables if used for computing the position of a planet at some particular time, say for casting a horoscope. It has already been remarked that the Muslim astronomers were particularly enthusiastic about graphical methods of computation, and it is not surprising that they adapted them to planetary problems. The method used was the straightforward one of simulating the proper geometric construction by circles and straight lines engraved on plates of wood and metal, with movable bars and stretched strings to provide the variable lines of the geometrical figures. Such an instrument is usually called an equatorium, because it 'equates' or computes the positions of the planets.

The earliest texts on the equatorium have come to us through the archaic Castilian of the Alfonsine *Libros del Saber*, which translates Arabic texts by Abulcacim Abnacahm[1] (d 1035) and by Al-Zarqālī (1029–87). The former gives the instrument in the most primitive and inconvenient form possible; a separate brass plate is used for each planet, and this plate is engraved with a number of graduated circles. Al-Zarqālī improves the technique by arranging half the planets on each side of a single plate, but his device still includes a large number of divided circles, made rather confusing by the small space into which they are packed. The equatorium was taken up and further improved by the ablest European astronomers of the thirteenth and fourteenth centuries. John Campanus of Novarra (*c* 1261–92) is said to have been the first to write on the device. A slightly more convenient form was devised by John of Linières (fl Paris *c* 1320–50), who placed all the planetary circles on one side of the plate and reduced the confusion by making one graduated circle serve for all the angles to be laid off. His treatise on the instrument was often included with the canon

---

[1] Abū'l-Qāsim ibn al-Samḥ, of Granada.

to his version of the Alfonsine tables, which was the standard work on the subject from about 1320 until the time of Regiomontanus.

The Merton College astronomers seem to have valued the equatorium as a most important instrument, and as a necessary complement to the astrolabe. The only surviving medieval example of the device is preserved there; it was probably given to the college by Simon Bredon (d 1372), who may have also written a Latin version of an Arabic tract on the subject. Another variation on

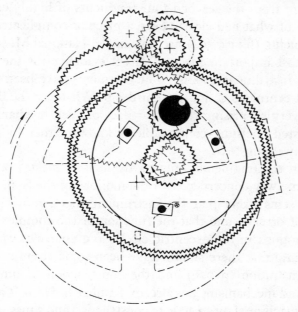

FIGURE 364—*Reconstruction of the fragments of an instrument found at Antikythera in the form of a planetary calculator or model.*

the fundamental design is the albion, invented by Richard of Wallingford in 1326, which reverts to the original design by having a separate plate for each planet, but makes the instrument more manageable by arranging the plates within a *mater* designed in the fashion of an astrolabe.

The most economical and efficient type of equatorium is described in a tract in Middle English, 'The Equatorie of the Planetis', which is dated 1392 and is thought to be a holograph work by Geoffrey Chaucer (d 1400) written to supplement his 'Treatise on the Astrolabe' (1391). In this form there are only two inscribed circles, and the design shows the greatest economy and ease of use.

The Persian astronomer, Al-Kāshī (d 1436), extended the principle of the instrument to the more complicated problems of computing the ecliptic latitude, as well as the longitude, of the planets, and of determining data for eclipses of all degrees. Similar extensions and simplifications were introduced by many astronomers and mathematicians throughout the fifteenth and sixteenth centuries, and indeed the equatorium seems to have provided a favourite target for the exercise of geometrical and mechanical ingenuity of a high order.

(e) *The 'Antikythera' machine.* In 1902 archaeologists, working on the wreck of a treasure-ship off the coast of the island of Antikythera between Greece and Crete, dredged up from the sea-bed four fragments of highly corroded copper showing vestiges of what had clearly been a piece of complicated geared clockwork. The fragments (figure 364) are now in the National Museum in Athens, and present a most important piece of direct evidence for the attainments of Greek science in instrument-making. The fragments have been variously dated between the first century B.C. and the third A.D. Whatever the date within that range, it is still very surprising that an artifact of such mechanical complexity should have existed; nothing comparable is known either by example or by description in any extant text.

Inscriptions on the fragments, only partly legible, make it evident that the device was in some way concerned with the motions of the Sun, the Moon, and the planets. It seems likely that the instrument was a moving model of the planets—a sort of orrery—and that the function of the complex gearing was to reproduce the motions in the excentric circles and epicycles of the Ptolemaic system. It is natural that there should have been some attempt to make such a model for demonstration (p 616) and the construction of quite complicated automatic jacks and mechanisms was already familiar to Hero. The gear-work on this Antikythera machine shows a style of construction and a mastery of technique that would not have been out of place in a good workshop of the seventeenth century. It is one of the greatest enigmas in the history of technology that these badly preserved remains of a Greek machine should present features so far in advance of anything else known from classical times.

BIBLIOGRAPHY

ALFONSO OF CASTILE. 'Libros del Saber de Astronomía del Rey Don Alfonso X de Castilla' (5 vols), ed. by M. RICO Y SINOBAS. Madrid. 1864.

CHAUCER, GEOFFREY. 'A Treatise on the Astrolabe', ed. by W. W. SKEAT. London. 1872.

DICKS, D. R. "Ancient Astronomical Instruments." *J. Brit. astr. Ass.*, **64**, 77–85, 1954.

DRACHMANN, A. G. R. 'Ktesibios, Philon and Heron.' Munksgaard, Copenhagen. 1948.

Idem. "Heron and Ptolemaios." *Centaurus*, **1**, 117–31, 1950.

GÁRCIA FRANCO, S. 'Catálogo crítico de astrolabios existentes en España.' Instituto Histórico de Marinis, Madrid. 1945.

GUNTHER, R. W. T. 'The Astrolabes of the World.' University Press, Oxford. 1932.

Idem. 'Early Science in Oxford' (14 vols), esp. Vols 1, 2. Oxford Historical Society for Publications, Oxford. 1923–.

HARTMANN, J. 'Die astronomischen Instrumente des Kardinals Nikolaus Cusanus.' *Abh. Akad. Wiss., Berlin*, Math.-Natur. Kl., Vol. 10, 1–56, 1919.

KIELY, E. R. 'Surveying Instruments, their History and Classroom Use.' Bureau of Publications, Teachers' College, Columbia University, New York. 1947.

MAYER, L. A. 'Islamic Astrolabists and their Works.' Kundig, Geneva. 1956.

MICHEL, H. "L'Art des instruments de mathématiques en Belgique au XVIe siècle." *Bull. Soc. R. Archaeol., Bruxelles*, 1935.

Idem. 'Traité de l'astrolabe.' University Press, Brussels. 1947.

NEUGEBAUER, O. "The Early History of the Astrolabe." *Isis*, **40**, 240, 1949.

PRICE, D. J. 'The Equatorie of the Planetis.' University Press, Cambridge. 1954.

REDIADIS, F. "Der Astrolabos von Antikythera" in 'Das Athener Nationalmuseum' (ed. by J. SVORONOS), Vol. 1, p. 43. National Archaeological Museum, Athens. 1906.

ROHDE, A. 'Die Geschichte der wissenschaftlichen Instrumente vom Beginn der Renaissance bis zum Ausgang der 18. Jahrhundert.' Klinkhardt und Biermann, Leipzig. 1923.

ROSEBOOM, MARIA. 'Bijdrage tot de Geschiedenis der Instrumentmakerskunst in de Noordelijke Nederlanden.' Mededeeling No. 47, uit het Rijksmuseum voor de Geschiedenis der Natuurwetenschappen, Leiden. 1950.

STEVENSON, E. L. 'Terrestrial and Celestial Globes' (2 vols). Hispanic Society of America, New York. 1921.

TAYLOR, EVA G. R. 'The Mathematical Practitioners of Tudor and Stuart England.' University Press, Cambridge. 1955.

THEOPHANIDIS, J. "Sur l'instrument en cuivre dont les fragments se trouvent au Musée Archéologique d'Athènes et qui fut retiré du fond de la mer d'Anticythère en 1902." *Prakt. Akad. Athen.*, **9**, 130, 1934.

WINTER, H. J. J. "The Muslim Tradition in Astronomy." *Endeavour*, **10**, 126, 1951.

ZINNER, E. 'Astronomische Instrumente des 11. bis 18. Jahrhunderts.' Beck'sche Verlagsbuchhandlung, Munich. 1956.

A medieval astronomer making an instrument. Richard of Wallingford (c 1292–1335), a member of the 'Merton school' (pp 585, 617) and the first Latin writer on trigonometry, is shown dividing a circle. On the table are anvil, hammer, and square. A quadrant hangs in the cupboard. Richard's face is shown spotted because he suffered from 'leprosy'. From a fourteenth-century manuscript.

## 23

THE MANUFACTURE OF SCIENTIFIC INSTRUMENTS

FROM *c* 1500 TO *c* 1700

DEREK J. PRICE

I. THE FIRST SPECIALIST CRAFTSMEN

IT is a truism that the modern scientist is a man of the laboratory. He uses scientific instruments and apparatus to extend observation beyond the range of his unaided senses, and to create powers of manipulation greater than those of his bare hands. It has not always been so; indeed, one of the most significant factors in the scientific revolution of the seventeenth century was the development of new tools for the scientist, which opened new worlds to his experience.

Probably the most interesting link between the histories of science and technology is the way in which science has ploughed back her profits by creating instruments to be used for further scientific work or for the application of science to practical purposes. There are already many accounts of these instruments, which serve to illuminate the history of science by explaining how knowledge led to new instruments and how such new instruments led to the acquisition of further knowledge. It is the object of this chapter to describe the technological factors associated with the rise of the craft of instrument-making in its great formative period in the seventeenth and eighteenth centuries.

Medieval scientists had few instruments at their command. Some devices, like the balance, the furnace, drawing-compasses, and dividers were already ancient and could readily be obtained from craftsmen. Other instruments, such as astrolabes, sun-dials, astronomical observing-instruments, and calculators were more complex and depended on scholarly appreciation of a manuscript tradition. The scientist might be able to employ a carpenter or metal-worker to do the rough construction, but the detailed planning, the engraving, and the graduation he must needs do himself.

The coming of the printed book and the revival of Greek mathematics and astronomy during the last quarter of the fifteenth century had a profound effect on instrument-making. Rapid dissemination of the new-found learning created an intensified demand for the traditional instruments, and texts describing their construction became more readily available. At the same time there was a conscious move by the scientists towards the employment of more specialized artisans, capable of carrying out fine work as well as crude, and able to produce these instruments with the minimum of assistance from the astronomer or mathematician himself, who thus became a designer simply. A craftsman could be shown the scientific principles, or could copy the pattern of any instrument such as a pocket sun-dial or an astrolabe; he could adapt the mechanical and practical design to his materials and to the techniques at his disposal. This done, he was capable of turning out a large number of similar instruments, though of varying size, decoration, and elaboration.

Thus by the beginning of the sixteenth century there were two distinct types of instrument-makers. On the one hand there were scientists (mainly astronomers) whose special interest was in the design and actual making of instruments. On the other hand there were whole dynasties of craftsmen who learned to turn out large numbers of special types of the more popular varieties of instruments. Both forms of activity at first centred on Nuremberg and its surrounding region, including especially the sister-town of Augsburg (p 585). Here the guilds of artists and craftsmen were extraordinarily well developed, and their members possessed in high degree the necessary techniques of fine working and engraving alike on metal and on ivory.

It took about a century for the increased interest in instruments to spread to the rest of western Europe. By the last quarter of the sixteenth century both scholar and craftsman instrument-makers were numerous in England, France, Italy, and the Low Countries, as well as in Germany. It is particularly interesting to trace the diverse stimuli in the transmission of the craft from place to place. Augsburg rose to a prominence comparable with that of Nuremberg partly because of the money poured into its workshops as a result of large orders for special instruments from the Danish astronomer Tycho Brahe (1546–1601). Erasmus Habermel at Prague made a prodigious number of highly original instruments under the active patronage of the erratic Emperor Rudolph II (1552–1612) and Franciscus Paduanius of Forli (1543–16—?), his physician. A refugee, Thomas Gemini (fl 1524–62), perhaps connected with Arsenius's Louvain workshop, brought his craft of engraving to England at just the time when sheet brass was first being made in this country (p 586). The organization of craftworkers in London was particularly well adapted to the master–apprentice method of instruction in the complicated business of instrument-making. The trade flourished here and workshops multiplied rapidly; in other countries the seed fell on less fertile ground or the organization was destroyed in times of war and unrest—as, for example, in Germany itself, where the Thirty Years War brought the workshops of Nuremberg and Augsburg to a meagre end in which only shoddy and stereotyped instruments were produced.

11. TOOLS FOR PRACTITIONERS

The spread of instrument-making from scholar to artisan was quickly followed by a similar spread in the use of instruments. Here again the stimulus was partly due to printed books which, besides explaining the design of instruments, revealed the manner of their use. More important was the influence of social changes, which led to a demand for the survey of estates as they were redistributed, of military techniques, which placed an emphasis on more accurate gunnery, and of the great maritime explorations, which led to a much increased interest in navigational methods and instruments. These stimuli, together with the more general availability of scientific knowledge, produced a new class of men, the 'practitioners'. They were by no means scholars in the normal sense, but they had sufficient technical knowledge to use surveying-, gunnery-, and navigation-instruments, and in many cases they augmented their living by teaching the practice of the instruments and the elementary mathematical principles on which it rested. The practitioners were the first fully conscious exponents and teachers of technical science; they did much to form the idea, so often expressed in the scientific revolution, that science was not only an intellectual pursuit but a potential source of much practical good to the individual and to the state.

A large part of the business of the artisan instrument-maker lay in the production of instruments for the practitioners. Some of them were even practitioners themselves, demonstrating and using the instruments and writing about them, advertising themselves and their wares; they worked hard, but sad personal notes in their writings show that many found little monetary reward and died in penury. They were a close-knit group, partly because of the apprenticeship system necessary for the specialized craft, partly because they congregated their shops and workshops in highly localized districts—a convenient system followed by many older trades. Outside these areas there were even more specialized makers of instruments, who set up business in places dictated by their custom. Thus makers of navigation-instruments were to be found near the shipyards, wharfs, and docks, and gunnery-instruments were made in or near the national armouries. A few fortunate artisans of exceptional skill were patronized by the state or by some eminent scholar, and were wholly or partly maintained to produce instruments for some special purpose.

The chief materials used for instrument-making before c 1650 were wood and brass, though ivory, leather, and vellum might also be employed for the making of an object that was to receive much decoration. Engraved ivory could be coloured, while vellum and leather could be stamped and gilded by bookbinders' methods. There seems to have been a cleavage between the artisans using wood only and those using brass for the greater part of their instruments. Probably the 'makers of instruments in wood' had developed, and were still trained, rather as carpenters, joiners, or turners than as metal-workers or engravers. Apart from the division of their scales, the instruments involved technical methods common to other wood-working of the period. The woods used were the close-grained varieties—box, beech, and pear—normally adopted for all fine work.

The 'makers of instruments in brass' were principally engravers, and fine-metal workers only secondarily. This is particularly evident in the range of instruments produced, and it seems to have had some considerable effect on the

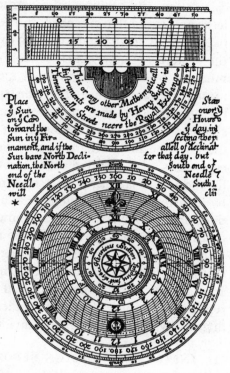

FIGURE 365—*Trade-card of Henry Sutton (1654), showing* (above) *a protractor and* (below) *a sundial.*

evolution of design. Whenever possible, a device was made by shaping a flat metal plate and engraving lines and scales on it; the plate might be combined with others similarly made, but specially shaped or moulded components were avoided unless absolutely essential. The techniques applied to such simple instruments were therefore those of the engraver together with ordinary hammering, cutting, and filing to shape the brass plates (figure 365). All the finest artisans, however, especially those working on instruments for patrons who demanded an object of beauty, prided themselves on their proficiency in the more complex arts of metal-work. In such cases they seem to have borrowed the techniques of the goldsmith and other decorative metal-workers, producing involved shapes, ornamental mouldings, and so forth. This is especially notice-able in the case of pocket sun-dials, astrolabes, armillary spheres, and some of the finer gunnery instruments.

The all-important scales and graduations were determined by measurement, calculation, and geometrical construction, and numerals for the scales as well as lettering were often punched on the plate. Sets of such punches seem to have been handed down from workman to workman, and it is often possible to identify the products of a particular school by peculiarities of the stamped characters as much as by the general style of metal-work and engraving. Undoubtedly the most important feature of any instrument was the careful accuracy with which the graduations and engraved lines were laid out. Here again, only the simplest techniques were used. In addition to the ordinary graving-tools for incising fine lines—there was no broad graver then—they had only scribing-compasses, plain or fitted with a screw opening adjustment, and beam-compasses for the arcs of larger radius. Crude tools could produce high craftsmanship only by the exercise of meticulous care, and it is not uncommon to find trial gradua-tions and constructions faintly showing on the face of the instrument or, more clearly, on the hidden backs of the main plates.

There were no sophisticated methods for graduating rectilinear or circular scales. If elementary geometrical construction would not suffice, marks were set according to calculation or by trial and error. For the division of the circle, repeated bisection of six 60°-angles gave arcs of 15°; these were then sub-divided by trial stepping with dividers.

III. INSTRUMENT-DESIGN BEFORE 1650

To understand the development of instrument-design during the period of the scientific revolution it is essential to distinguish between the three main groups of people concerned with instruments and their use. The first and largest group was that of the artisans with their general, everyday trade of producing instru-ments for the practitioners or making more elaborate, costly, decorated in-struments for their patrons and richer clients. Secondly, there were the scientist instrument-makers embodying their own devices, unaided or with some assistance from a workman in the manual labour. Thirdly, there was a small intermediate class of specialists making, for example, ships' compasses at some particular shipyard, or gunnery instruments at some state armoury.

If one wishes to study the radical improvements in scientific function of the instruments, and the introduction of quite new devices, these may be found in the published works of the scientists. Such information is readily accessible, yet may be misleading because it does not necessarily follow that the instrument was adopted in practice, or even that it was accepted by other scholars. It was quite common for general use to be delayed for several decades, or even for centuries, after the original invention. To investigate the history of instrument-technique it is essential to supplement learned treatises by the writings of the practitioners and, above all, by the evidence afforded by instruments that have been preserved.

The basic selection of instruments produced by the artisans was related to classical designs. Quadrants, astrolabes, armillary and other spheres, besides all varieties of sun-dial, were made in great profusion and elaborated in scientific principle and mechanical construction. More direct improvement was made in the observatory instruments demanded by the great astronomers of the period. General tendencies can readily be seen in the devices used by Tycho Brahe and by Johann Hevelius (1611–87). All instruments had to be divided finely and carefully; they also had to be as large and as rigid as the strength of their materials permitted, compatible with the necessity of providing accurate pivots and bearings for the moving parts. Large instruments were sometimes made of wood covered with strips or sheets of brass in order to avoid serious difficulties of weight, and devices both large and small were rendered lighter by cutting away the redundant areas of metal plate, leaving only struts to support, for example, the divided limb of a quadrant.

Navigation-instruments were sturdily built and of simple design. The cross-staff or 'Jacob's staff' (figure 340) of the astronomer was widely adopted at sea; it possessed the great advantage of using a linear scale, so much easier to graduate than a circle. Towards the end of the sixteenth century the back-staff or Davis's quadrant (figure 341) was introduced, using a similar principle, but enabling the navigator to sight on a shadow cast by the Sun and so avoid the danger and difficulty of direct observation in the Sun's glare. The nocturnal was also taken from the range of astronomical instruments into common use, and became useful as a means of telling the running-time at night from the rotation of the circumpolar constellations. The staffs and nocturnals were all produced by the wood-working instrument-makers; they were reasonably cheap and sturdy, though the accuracy of graduation is sometimes poor. The mariner's astrolabe was a Spanish-Portugese adaptation of the astronomer's (planispheric) astrolabe, probably invented c 1535 and popular for about a century thereafter. It is important as the first scientific device made solely for navigational use, and it seems to have been made by specialist foundry-men and engravers in the shipyards (p 608).

The magnetic compass was much employed, on land as well as at sea. The earliest surviving examples are found on portable sun-dials for travellers (p 600) —the needle serving the double purpose of guiding the traveller and orientating the gnomon—and on miners' dials used for setting underground galleries. There is, however, plenty of contemporary evidence to assure us that some sort of

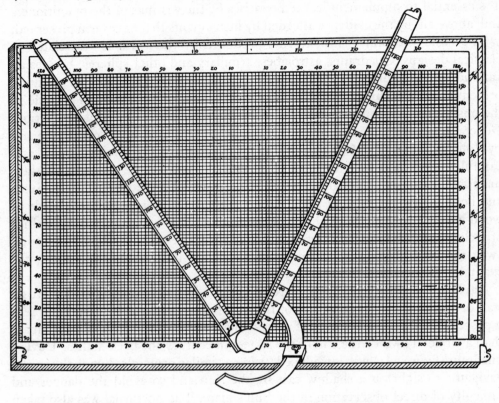

FIGURE 366—*Bramer's* trigonometria (*1617*), *a triangulation instrument. The lengths of two known sides of a triangle (with their included angle) are set out by proportion on the movable, graduated alidades. The length of the unknown side is computed by Pythagoras' theorem from the lengths intercepted on the network of parallels.*

magnetic compass was in early use at sea. Whereas mariners' and miners' compasses were made by specialist craftsmen, compass sun-dials were the work of general artisans. Considerable ingenuity was exercised in the design and mounting of the magnetic needle, all sorts of shapes and pivots being used, successful methods no doubt being handed down as trade secrets together with the lodestones used for magnetizing the needles and retouching them. To seal the compass from dust, and to prevent the needle from jumping off its pivot, it was usual to cover the compass-box with a thin sheet of transparent material—in early times mica, in later ones glass. The mounting of the window and its retention by a circle of springy wire were later taken over and applied to lenses in the first optical instruments. Earlier spectacle- and reading-lenses had been mounted in frames cut from horn or leather.

The first surveying-instruments were again modifications of older astronomical measuring-devices; in particular the makers adopted the alidade and circular angle-scale found on the *dorsum* of astrolabes (p 608), adding to the instrument a socket by which the surveyor could mount it upon a tripod stand or a staff to hold the instrument steady in the field. With the addition of a magnetic compass for taking bearings, this became the circumferentor or 'Dutch circle', a semicircular modification of which—cheaper because only half as much graduation was needed—was called the graphometer. Perhaps by combining circumferentors in vertical and horizontal planes, perhaps as a direct adaptation of the torquetum (p 593), the theodolite was evolved as a universal surveying-instrument (p 541). Yet the development of the theodolite was not the only advance in surveying-instruments; even more important at the time was the invention of a number of devices avoiding the trigonometrical calculations involved in solving the surveyed triangles. Considerable effort was directed to the perfection of such contrivances as the *trigonometria* (figure 366) of Benjamin Bramer (1588–1650), which incorporate a grid or scales enabling the unknown lengths and angles to be read without computation.

Computing- and calculating-devices were most important in an age when mathematical symbolism and arithmetical technique were crude and more difficult to master than the taking of measurements. Several types of measuring-rule were designed for gauging the contents of barrels, the range of shots, the value of bullion, and so on, and such devices as 'Napier's rods' were used to assist ordinary numerical operations. In the seventeenth century geared calculating-machines were invented by Blaise Pascal (1623–62) and others. The most important mathematical instrument was undoubtedly the sector, a hinged and graduated rule which enabled a wide variety of computations to be made by the theory of similar triangles. Graduated drawing-compasses for gauging had been familiar in gunnery and dialling for some decades, but the sector was put into its versatile form by Galileo (1564–1642) (figure 367) and his workman Marcantonio Mazzoleni, towards the end of the sixteenth century. It was used in combination with a pair of dividers, the hinged arms of the sector being opened to a suitable distance and lengths measured on the engraved radial scales. A wide variety of radial scales—natural numbers, squares, cubes, reciprocals, chords, tangents, densities, and many others—is possible, and standard selections became associated with the English, French, and Italian types of instrument. The sector remained very popular for calculations in gunnery, surveying, dialling, and gauging, in spite of competition from the slide-rule after that device had been invented about the middle of the seventeenth century. The logarithmic slide-rule did not completely displace the sector until late in the eighteenth century; indeed, the sector was included as a standard instrument in drawing-sets and in navigation equipment until well into the nineteenth century.

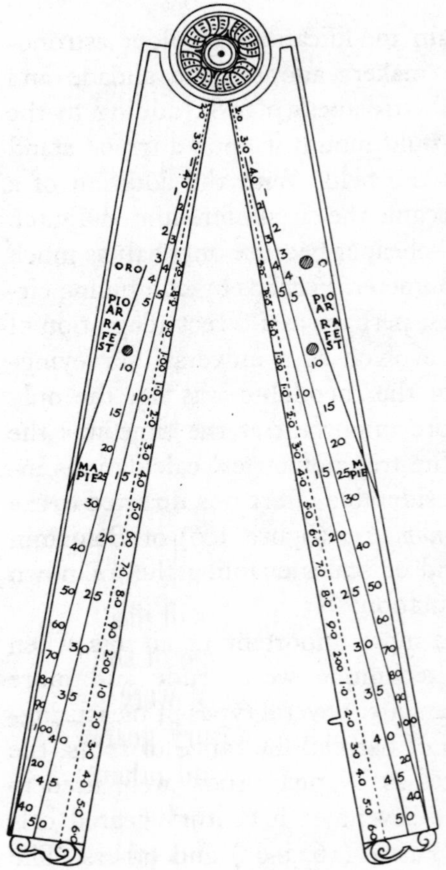

The first instrument of mechanical rather than scientific complexity to become generally available was the hodometer or taximeter. In its elementary form it was merely a click-mechanism for counting the revolutions made by a carriage-wheel of known circumference—a device familiar from the writings of Vitruvius (p 512), though there is doubt whether the instrument was ever actually made and used in ancient times. During the later sixteenth century the hodometer was much elaborated by the addition of a magnetic compass and by a recording-device fitted to the more refined models. This was the first self-registering instrument. It operated by a trident of spikes above the compass-needle; after every 10 or 100 revolutions of the measuring-wheel a trip-lever elevated the needle and pressed the trident into a paper strip which was

FIGURE 367—*Galileo's 'geometrical and military compass', an early form of the sector. The various divided lines permit numerical calculations, calculations involving the densities of the metals, etc.*

then moved on to be ready for the next record of the direction in which the carriage was moving. Theoretically, one could drive round a large estate and subsequently map the path taken. In reality, accuracy cannot have been high, but technically the instrument is important as an indication of the change in practice brought about by the introduction of the methods of the clock-maker.

Perhaps the finest precision instruments were those made by the specialist artisans concerned with gunnery. Quadrants, levels, and gauges made by such craftsmen as Christopher Trechsler (fl 1571–1624) of the Dresden armoury show clearly that much attention was paid to accuracy in the planeness of surfaces and the fit of sliding parts. Another interesting feature was the use of screw-adjustments for fine motion (plate 25); the threaded screw as a fixing-device is a comparatively late development in instruments (p 657). It may have been used earlier for the fastening of jewelry but does not appear otherwise until the middle of the sixteenth century, when crude screws are found in the fittings of armour. Quite probably it was then introduced into other armoury-devices, and from these to general instruments and clockwork. Before the screw came into use, soldering, rivets, and wedge-fittings were the normal means of fixing metal parts together. The screw as a slow-motion device and as a worm-gear is of much earlier, probably Hellenistic, origin (p 610).

IV. THE DIVERSIFICATION OF INSTRUMENTS

From about 1650 onwards the full impact of the scientific revolution manifested itself in the instrument-making trade by great changes in its scale and scope. The rapidly growing group of amateurs of science, and the scientific academies into which they were soon organized, combined with the practitioners to afford a considerable market for instruments. In the past each instrument had been built to order, according to the demands of the patron or the inventive craftsmanship of the maker. During the seventeenth century there was a tendency for new devices or new variants of old devices to achieve sudden popularity through published accounts in books and scientific journals, and through reports that spread rapidly among the ranks of the amateurs. Thus there would arise a large demand for each of these types of instrument, a demand that could be met only by mass-production. Although the trade was expanding as fast as its market, or even faster, the need for a large output increasingly forced the craftsman to specialize in a limited range of instruments at any one time, and to make this range in quantity. During this period the scientific instrument ceased to be an individual work of art-craftsmanship, and there was a noticeable tendency for the maker merely to sign, rather than to sign and date, his products: the artist's subscription was changing into the trade-mark. Although instruments became less artistic, specialization and quantity-production led to a considerable improvement in their technical details and in the precision engineering involved. A secondary effect of specialization was that instrument-makers' shops frequently sold not only the products of the master and his workmen but also those of other craftsmen producing many different types of instrument.

Occasionally, articles were imported from foreign workshops and engraved with the name of the artisan or shopkeeper who acted as an agent.

The greatest effect of the scientific revolution was wrought by new inventions and discoveries that led to the manufacture of instruments radically different from any which had been made before. Conspicuous among these were the optical instruments—the telescope and microscope—but at the same time the evolution of new practitioners' instruments for surveying, navigation, and gunnery was proceeding rapidly, and the wider horizons of physical science led the instrument-maker to produce, for example, thermometers, barometers and air-pumps, magnetic compasses and mounted lodestones, pantographs, and cases of draughtsman's instruments.

The old instruments, based primarily on the astrolabe, quadrant, and the wide range of sun-dials, consisted chiefly of simple engraved plates, but the new optical and physical instruments were widely different in construction and enforced quite new skills upon the trade. Thus the instrument-maker ceased to be a specialist in the art of engraving and had to take upon himself the tasks of more complex metal-working and machining, wood-working and turning, glass-working, and tube-making. In this he was helped by the fact that other trades were already using such techniques and, from the middle of the seventeenth century onwards, instrument-makers are closely allied with the London livery companies of the Clockmakers (chartered in 1631) and the Spectaclemakers (1629), the manufacturers of common measuring-rules, cabinet makers and joiners, glass-blowers, and other craftsmen. The first of these alliances was so strong that in England the principal group of mathematical instrument-makers joined the Clockmakers *en bloc* in 1667, though Elias Allen, 'Doyen of the Mathematical Instrument Makers' Club' (plate 26 B), had been a master of the Company since 1636 and had been regarded as one of its leading members. Later, when many of the makers of telescopes and microscopes had become organized under the Spectaclemakers, there developed considerable friction between them and those of their colleagues who had become master clockmakers or had claimed that neither of the companies was concerned with their craft. During this period a gap seems to have developed between the makers of mathematical and of optical instruments, and this division, together with that already existing between those who worked in metal and those in wood, produced a much disunited trade, served to increase specialization, and prevented the rise of general instrument-shops.

The increase in numbers and specialization of the artisans led them into a new relationship with their patrons and customers, and with designers and scientists.

Instead of being largely supported by a single patron, the craftsman had become a shopkeeper selling his goods to a large clientele. Instead of working under the direction of a single scientist, he had access to many. Special relationships are still evident, as when Elias Allen (fl 1606–54) was taught how to make the new circular slide-rule by its inventor, William Oughtred (1575–1660); and many people were still practitioners devising their own instruments and having them made by their own special workmen. Much more important, however, is the fact that the instrument-makers became a focus for much of the day-to-day scientific activity of the time. Their shops became meeting-places for both scientists and amateurs, and they played a part in the scientific correspondence which was then vital in the dissemination of new ideas. The taverns frequented by the artisans, and later the coffee-houses, played similar roles. The diary of Robert Hooke (1635–1703) records an almost daily visit to some place where instrument-makers and their customers met. It is especially interesting that, in some countries at least, this type of organization around the instrument-makers seems to have been highly active long before the formal meetings of the scientists and amateurs who later constituted the Royal Society and the scientific academies in other lands.

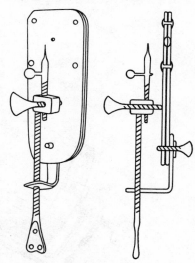

FIGURE 368—*Diagrammatic views of a Leeuwenhoek microscope. The spherical lens is clamped in little pierced recesses between two brass plates. The object is mounted on the point, which is brought into focus by means of the rather coarse screws.*

V. THE NEW OPTICAL INSTRUMENTS

The telescope and microscope were introduced into Holland at the beginning of the seventeenth century, perhaps as a result of casual experiment by practical spectacle-makers.[1] Within a few years Galileo had seized on the idea, probably rediscovering the necessary combination of lenses himself, and soon afterwards he announced very remarkable and entirely unprecedented celestial observations made with his first telescopes. For many years telescopes made in his workshop were greatly prized. Galileo's observations—soon extended by others—aroused enormous enthusiasm and provoked wide controversy; there can scarcely have been another period in the history of science when so much

[1] For a different opinion, see p 231. For applied optics generally, see ch 9, section VI (p 229).

new information came at one time—the discoveries of Saturn's rings, Jupiter's satellites, the phases of Venus, the spots on the Sun, the mountains on the Moon. In view of this great interest it is surprising that so little happened after the first flush of enthusiasm had died away, for a whole generation intervened before the

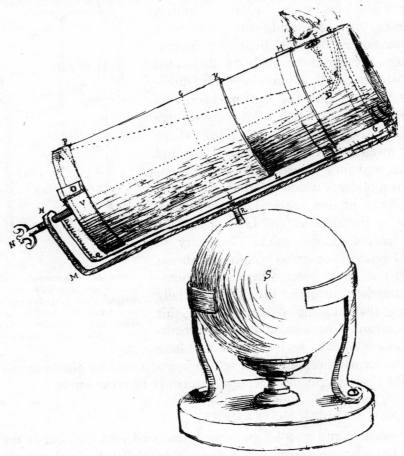

FIGURE 369—*Newton's original drawing of his reflecting telescope, 1672. Light entering the tube is reflected by the concave metal speculum (A) to the flat mirror (D); here it is reflected through the eye-lens (F) to the eye. The telescope is focused by the screw (N) which varies the distance of the speculum from the mirror.*

telescope and compound microscope were accepted as popular instruments. In the meantime they were little more than scientific toys, though Christopher Scheiner (1575–1650) investigated sunspots thoroughly and Francesco Stelluti (1577–1653) used the microscope to produce very fine drawings of insect anatomy. Not until about 1660 does one find instrument-makers beginning to make telescopes and compound microscopes as a regular trade, and even then it took another decade for anything approaching large-scale production to be set on foot. The lack of suitable workmen must have been a not inconsiderable factor in the surprisingly slow acceptance of devices so novel and arresting.

The technical difficulties that faced the first commercial makers of compound microscopes and small telescopes related to the body of the instrument rather than to its optical components. Optical design and the provision of suitable lenses may have been of overriding scientific importance, but by this time reasonably good glass was available, lens-grinding was highly developed in the spectacle-making industry, and the study of geometrical optics was sufficiently advanced. During the seventeenth century there was much progress, especially in the grinding of very small lenses—for example, by the amateur Leeuwenhoek (1632–1723), in his superlative simple microscopes (figure 368) with which he was able to see spermatozoa and even some bacteria—and of very large lenses for the more powerful telescopes demanded. Other important optical improvements were the introduction of an erecting eye-piece for the terrestrial telescope by Schyrlaeus de Rheita c 1645, the use of multiple lens-systems in microscopes after about 1650, and later still the far-reaching invention of the

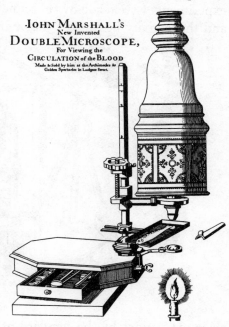

FIGURE 370—*John Marshall's microscope, as illustrated in 1704. The large body contains two lenses; the objectives are fitted in interchangeable brass mounts screwed to it. The arm carrying the body slides on the brass pillar; when locked in position by a set-screw, adjustment is made by the lead-screw turned by the knob. The pillar inclines on a ball-joint fixing it to the box base.*

achromatic lens, thought impossible by Newton, but finally achieved by Chester Moor Hall (an amateur) in 1729 and carried into production by the great optical instrument-maker John Dollond (1706–61) in 1758. Until then, the severe consequences of chromatic aberration could be avoided only by substituting reflecting mirrors for refracting lenses, and from the first construction of a reflecting telescope by Newton there developed considerable activity, soon spreading to the professional instrument-makers. Newton's first reflector (figure 369) shows well the characteristics of prototype instruments made by scientists at this period;

the mechanical design includes novel features, such as a sphere constituting a universal mounting, the sliding tube which gives a crude but sufficient way of focusing, and the method of mounting the all-important mirror. We know from Newton's manuscripts that he spent much time in experimenting to find the best speculum metal and the optimum method of figuring it successfully. Similar experiments were made by subsequent professional makers of telescope-mirrors, and this activity became of major importance, such artisans gaining or losing

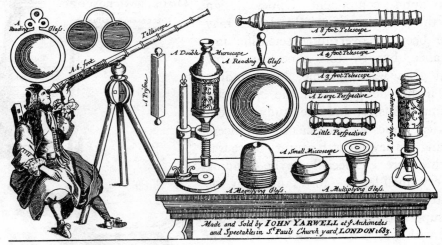

their reputations by the standard of their success in the art of figuring the surfaces to produce instruments with excellent definition and little trouble from tarnishing.

Much more difficult for the artisans were the problems of mechanical design and construction involved in mounting the optical parts. The mounts for the lenses were usually made by wood-turning, which may account for the fact that one of the most distinguished early makers of microscopes in England, John Marshall (1663–1725), entered the trade after apprenticeship as a turner (figure 370). The tubes in which the mounts were centred created greater difficulties; they had to be accurately made so as to slide smoothly for focusing, and in telescopes they had to be reasonably light—though Galileo's first instrument had used a tube of lead. Tubes of rolled parchment or pasteboard were widely employed, and these were frequently decorated by stamping, colouring, and gilding, arts borrowed from the bookbinder (figures 371, 372). Tubes consisting of lengths of wooden moulding were less common, but very long telescopes were sometimes made from four planks fitted together to give a square-section tube to which eyepiece and objective mounts could be strapped (tailpiece, p 244). The excessively long telescopes introduced in an effort to minimize spherical aberration became so ungainly—being a hundred or more feet long—that tubes were abolished altogether, and in an 'aerial telescope' the objective was mounted on a tower or pole and controlled by cords, while the detached eyepiece was mounted near the observer. Needless to say this modification proved equally inconvenient and encouraged the rapid transition to reflecting instruments. Metal tubes occur first in reflecting telescopes, where the sliding action is not essential; for refractors and all compound microscopes they are common only after *c* 1750, the tubes being formed from rolled sheet. Drawn metal tubing was not available until nearly a century later.

Having now considered the optical parts and their mounting in the main body of the instrument, it is important to draw attention to the part played by the stand and accessories that supported the tube, provided for focusing, and enabled the instrument to be suitably directed. In telescopes and microscopes this was generally the weakest part of the design, and the cause of many of the troubles that must have occurred in use. Early compound-microscope bodies were often supported by a long weak arm fixed near the objective, or by a loose, coarse screw; the slightest movement of the eyepiece would have the effect of sending the object out of focus and displacing it in the field (figure 372). An improved

FIGURE 372—*Microscope made for Robert Hooke by Christopher Cock (c 1660). The objective is mounted in a cell at the bottom of the body, which also contains an eye-lens and a field-lens. The body slides on the pillar, and screws up and down in the brass arm for fine adjustment.*

version made by Edmund Culpeper (1660–1738) and his associates mounted the body firmly on a tripod stand, thus securing much better stability. Later instruments reverted to the old arrangement of pillar-support, though towards the end of the eighteenth century more attention was paid to securing mechanical stability.

VI. OTHER NEW INSTRUMENTS

From about 1650 onwards, when the new optical instruments were coming into vogue, there was a corresponding decline in the popularity of traditional instruments. The astrolabe was practically obsolescent by the beginning of the seventeenth century, the plain quadrant lasted for another few decades, and the enormous flow of sun-dials of all shapes and sizes steadily lessened until they were ousted by the pendulum-clock and pocket-watch during the second half of the eighteenth century. Skill in dividing and engraving metal plates ceased to be the central feature of the instrument-maker's craft but remained at a high level. New forms of practitioners' instruments were constantly being made, such as the circumferentor (full circle) and the graphometer (semicircle) used in surveying, the back-staff and the reflecting octant for navigation, and the cases of divided rules and drawing-instruments used by draughtsmen and gaugers. These were augmented by newer devices such as the theodolite and the bubble-level, and improved by the introduction of telescopic sights in place of open pinnules. The old techniques were also applied to instruments for calculation, amongst them Napier's bones, the sector (figure 367), and various logarithmic and other scales.

The physical instruments popularized by the investigations of the learned academies posed quite new problems of instrument-making. The Florentine glass-blowers who had made the first sealed alcohol thermometers for the Accadèmia del Cimento, *c* 1660, were far superior in their techniques to any rivals elsewhere in Europe—surviving instruments show, for example, the degree-markings made by fusing little spheres of black glass to the main tube at closely regular intervals (figure 373). Mercury barometers were perhaps more simple to construct since they did not involve the sealing of a filled tube, but it was not until long after the experiments of Torricelli in 1643 that the barometer and the thermometer came into popular use. Technically, the early history of both instruments belongs to the craft of the glass-blower until late in the seventeenth century, when barometer- and thermometer-tubes were mounted with engraved scales, cursors, and other fittings, so becoming part of the commerce of the instrument-maker.

The history of the pneumatic pump is interesting, not only for the large part it played in science by drawing attention to the physical properties of 'airs', but because it was the first large and complex machine to come into the laboratory. The old astronomical instruments had sometimes been made of great size, and, as has been remarked, the refracting aerial telescopes (p 635) attained stupendous lengths, but in the vacuum pump for the first time there was complexity as well as size and engineering began to invade the province of precision instruments. The first experiments of Otto von Guericke had been described by Schott in 1657, and were quickly seized upon and improved by Boyle, Huygens, Papin, and others. Shortly after the beginning of the eighteenth century, one of the first mechanics of instrument-making, Francis Hauksbee (1687–1763), began to make vacuum pumps in quantity, and to a design that remained essentially the same for about 150 years (plate 27 A). The technical methods developed by such mechanicians stand at the beginning of the direct line of evolution leading to the steam-engine and the internal combustion engine. Although these pumps were made and sold by people calling themselves instrument-makers there is little in common between the techniques they required and those in general use among the makers of other instruments.

Nearer the main stream of development in techniques of instrument-making were the devices made popular by the increased interest in magnetic and electrical phenomena towards the end of the seventeenth century and the beginning of the eighteenth. Hopes of a solution to the problem of determining longitude at sea led to a demand for devices to measure more accurately the magnetic variation and dip, and early in the eighteenth century the general interest in magnetism led some instrument-makers to sell neatly mounted lodestones, miniature compasses,

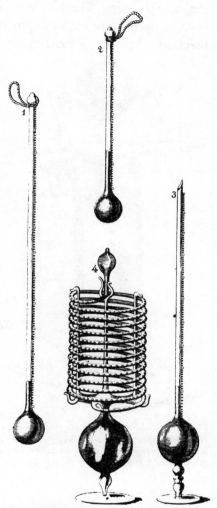

FIGURE 373—*Thermometers designed by the Accadèmia del Cimento (c 1660). They are graduated by small spheres of coloured glass fused to the tubes. No. 4 is a spiral thermometer with a very long scale.*

and magnets of all shapes and sizes designed for the pleasure and edification of the amateur. By this time magnetic compasses, often mounted on crude but effective gimbals, had long been standard equipment on board ship, and there were many specialist compass-makers working in the shipyards or for naval departments. The electrical machine, however, followed a different course, being, like the air-pump, an instrument of large size though not involving such precision in engineering. During the eighteenth century electrical machines became ever larger, and numerous complex modifications were introduced in order to produce more striking effects (figure 374). If the air-pump can be considered as leading to the steam-engine, the electrical machine stands at the beginning of the chain leading to the great machines of modern physics—the electrostatic accelerator, the cyclotron, and the other instruments that are now almost institutions in their own right.

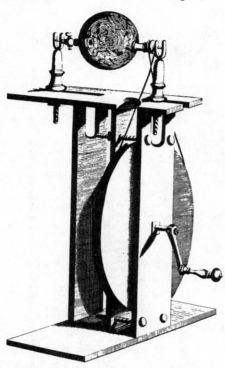

FIGURE 374—*Electrical machine made by Francis Hauksbee, senior, c 1709. The figure shows the luminous effects produced inside an exhausted glass sphere when it is electrified by friction against the hand.*

Shortly after 1700 a new market for instrument-making began to appear. Before then, the majority of instruments had been made for the practical man or for use by pioneering scientists and amateurs. The front line of research was now beginning to recede from the understanding of the amateur and novice, but increased popular attention to science, with little emphasis on mathematics and scientific pedagogy, led to a demand for new types of apparatus suitable for demonstrative experiment. Even during the Middle Ages some teaching devices—such as the demonstration armillary sphere (p 613)—had existed, but now the more popular craftsmen began to sell attractive cases containing sets of apparatus to demonstrate the laws of mechanics or magnetism, boxes of models to illustrate solid geometry, sets of slides and objects for the beginner's microscope, pairs of globes, and such complicated instructional devices as the orrery—an excellent example of the craft of the clock-maker carried into the range of non-horological instruments (plate 27 B). This tendency became more and more marked as the century proceeded (p 642).

VII. THE QUEST FOR ACCURACY

It has been shown how the making of precision instruments was transformed during the scientific revolution by the making of new devices—some instruments

FIGURE 375—*View of part of an observatory (1673) showing the mounting of a large sextant used to measure the angular separation of celestial bodies. Note the counterbalancing weights to relieve strains; the screw-adjusted sights (similar to the adjustment in figure 370); the need for two observers.*

merely employing new adaptations of old principles, better fitted for specific practical uses, others embodying quite new scientific principles. Besides these changes there was a drastic and far-reaching transition in the attitude towards precision and the means of attaining it. New experiments and new measurements constitute only part of the scientist's activity; carrying old measurements to a further place of decimals may be at least as important. Nowhere is this more evident than in astronomy. The work of Kepler (1571–1630) had shown clearly the advantage to be gained by precise knowledge of small fluctuations and secular motions. He had depended on the observations made by Tycho Brahe at the end of the sixteenth century, and the instruments used had pushed accuracy to the limit obtainable by the naked eye. Three main problems are involved in astronomical angle-measuring devices: (*a*) the accurate sighting of the star or other object; (*b*) the accurate alignment and division of the graduated circles; and (*c*) the accurate reading of the graduations. To all of these Tycho Brahe and others, such as the Danzig astronomer Hevelius (1611–87), directed their attention. Special pinnule-sights were designed to avoid parallax and to use the full resolving power of the eye; the instruments were made as large as possible and provided with counterbalancing weights so as to minimize distortion by bending under gravity (figure 375); scales were provided with the nonius or diagonal-scale device (figure 376) which, like the vernier later introduced, enabled sub-divisions of a degree to be estimated accurately without the labour of engraving them to a high degree of fineness all over the limb of the instrument.

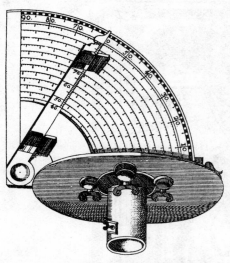

FIGURE 376—*Dudley's quadrant with a nonius for reading parts of a degree (1646). Each graduated arc is divided into a different number of parts, e.g. 90, 89, 88. . . . Observing that the alidade falls on the mth part of an arc divided into p parts, the angle is found to be* 90 m/p *degrees.*

It is ironic that fate should have allowed Brahe and Hevelius to exercise all their powers in seeking the limit of accuracy of the naked eye when their work was to be followed so closely by the invention of the telescope, which made possible an enormous increase in accuracy with much less trouble. The telescope appears to have been used in taking astronomical measurements (as distinct from qualitative observations) within a few decades of its invention, and William Gascoigne had made a micrometer fitting on an eye-piece as early as 1640; but the general replacement of open sights by telescopic ones did not occur until after 1665. At that time Robert Hooke constructed a number of telescopic measuring-devices, and thenceforward very few observations with open sights were made by astronomers. Yet it was not until the mid-eighteenth century that the telescope became common as a component of surveying- and navigating-instruments.

The former limiting factor in the attainment of accuracy having been removed, some attention was next paid to other considerations in instrument-design. In the construction of the body of the instrument it was essential to obtain a greater degree of mechanical precision, and here again (as with the vacuum-pump) instrument-makers were called upon to produce work that would now fall into the province of the precision engineer.

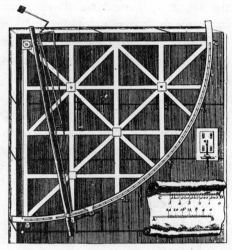

FIGURE 377—*Five-foot mural quadrant of copper, with telescopic sights, made by George Graham (1742).*

Much attention in particular was paid to the construction of accurately centred and true-running bearings and pivots, and divided limbs were carefully designed with cross-strut supports to prevent deformation (figure 377). When all this had been done it rapidly became apparent that the chief remaining limitation lay in the method of dividing and reading the scale itself.

The first steps in mechanical subdivision had already been made by clockmakers, who used a specially marked wheel for laying out the position of teeth on gear-wheels. This method relied on a previous geometrical division of the marked wheel, and it was not until c 1760 that the first steps were taken by the Duc de Chaulnes (1714–69) in France and by Jesse Ramsden (1735–1800) in England towards a completely mechanical original division of the circle (figure 378). By about 1780 the type of device due to Ramsden had swept the board and was in general use, not only for circular arcs but for the division of linear scales of high accuracy when these were required. In essence, Ramsden's dividing engine was a simple enough application of the worm-and-wheel principle that had been used long before, even on Hero's dioptra (p 609), but the mechanical execution of this principle was so exacting that it opened up a new era in precision workmanship and a new concept of instrumental accuracy. Thenceforward the technological problems of instrument-making have been a determining factor in the progress of scientific research, each advance in instruments allowing the scientist to measure to a higher degree of accuracy, and each advance in science posing fresh problems for the ingenuity and precision of the instrument-maker. Although astronomy was the first science to profit from the removal of the old limitations, the process was rapidly extended to other fields. For example, stress was now laid on accurate time-measurement, and clock-driven telescopes began to be widely used in the increasing number of observatories. The observatories themselves exercised a considerable influence on instrument-design since they were perhaps the largest customers for the more complex and expensive devices that acted as prototypes for other products of the artisans. Ramsden's dividing-engines were not only used for astronomical instruments but also for the scales of navigation- and surveying-devices.

During the latter half of the eighteenth century, indeed, instrument-making expanded in scope from fine engraving to take in many quite different techniques needed to produce the new optical and physical instruments invented during the scientific revolution. There had also been an internal revolution, which led to a new approach to the problems of precision workmanship and to the appearance of a new class of artisans whose skill in precision engineering was vital to the progress of science (figure 379).

VIII. FROM INSTRUMENTS TO APPARATUS

In the century following the death of Newton in 1727 there was an increasing acceleration in the growth of the scientific movement and of its importance in national life. At the same time, the research front was steadily advancing, producing more and more exciting knowledge and understanding of the world, but becoming less and less easy for the non-specialist to comprehend. It has already been remarked that this created some demand for those products of the instrument maker which were designed for demonstration and instruction rather than for research or for use by the practitioners of survey, gunnery, and navigation. During the century this type of instrument-making developed so considerably that it began to exercise a major influence on the craft and on the techniques needed by its artisans. The change is, in fact, more important than might be thought, for at the beginning of the modern period, when public laboratories were coming into being, the demand was largely for apparatus for instruction and the performance of routine experiments rather than for instruments needed for original research. Already during the latter part of the eighteenth century it was becoming apparent that the new devices needed by the active scientist had to be specially built for-him by an instrument-maker working to his order, perhaps using sundry components and portions of instruments which were standard products of the trade.

There was a tendency, therefore, for the better and more versatile artisans to

FIGURE 378—*Ramsden's circular dividing-engine (1777). The plate to be divided is screwed to the large toothed circle (CC). The scriber is fitted to the sliding carriage (DD). The circle is turned through a determined arc by depressing the treadle (R) which by means of a cord and a ratchet-device rotates the shaft carrying a worm (seen above (Q)) meshing with the circle. A mark of the scriber following each operation of the treadle produces a series of scratches on the plate at exact intervals.*

be employed in constructing instruments specially designed for a particular piece of work by one scientist, and there was also a move towards the manufacture of standard components and apparatus capable of being applied to several different experimental purposes rather than to one single and definite use. Thus we find lenses and prisms separately mounted so that they can be combined as required; there are reading-micrometers, pressure-gauges, and other measuring-instruments that can be used only in conjunction with other

FIGURE 379—*Workshop of an eighteenth-century mathematical instrument-maker.* (Left) *Pole-lathe;* (centre) *work-bench and stone;* (right) *forge and anvils.*

pieces of apparatus; there are Leyden jars, dischargers, spark-apparatus, and other apparatus for use with the electrical machine.

In addition to making components capable of being variously combined in apparatus for research, the instrument-makers continued to produce an increasing range of instruments for teaching and demonstration. Because the work of Newton had emphasized the fundamental position of mechanics in natural philosophy, many of these instruments were intended to elucidate mechanical principles, such as the laws of force in their static and dynamic aspects, and the laws of impact (figures 380, 381). These demonstration devices were frequently built on a large scale, and many were masterpieces of the work of the cabinet-maker and joiner as well as of the mechanic; they were made like pieces of domestic furniture and ornamented in the style of the period. Many of the best-known instrument-makers of the age specialized in, and were widely famed for, their instructional apparatus, and the books they wrote to explain the use of their wares did much to popularize science and lay the foundations of

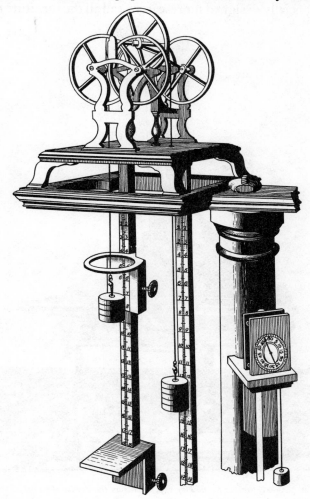

FIGURE 380—*Atwood's machine for demonstrating Newton's law of gravitation.*

the teaching of science outside the universities. George Adams (d 1773), perhaps the best instrument-maker of his day, wrote books of this sort that went through many editions and must have figured in the basic education of a large number of nineteenth-century scientists. His instruments were equally popular, and in a large collection made for George III many of them are still preserved (plate 27 A).

By the time of Adams the craft of the instrument-maker was far removed from that of the early artisans with their astrolabes and sun-dials. The industry now produced standard instruments for the practitioners, standard components and apparatus specially designed for research, and all the furniture of the scientific

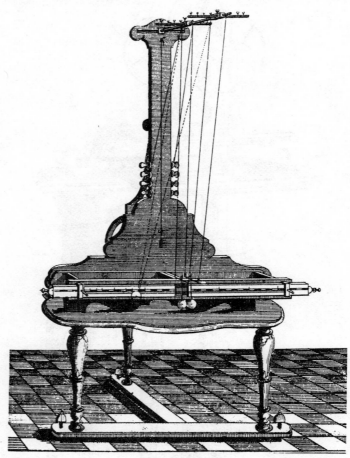

FIGURE 381—*Apparatus for making experiments on the impact of bodies, c 1750.*

school-room. From being principally a group of engravers the makers had joined hands with several other specialist technicians to manufacture optical, pneumatic, magnetic, and electrical devices involving quite new principles of scientific design and mechanical construction.

Most important of all, the quest for accuracy had led them to produce apparatus of large size and of the finest engineering precision, and had forced them to pay special attention to all means of increasing this precision. Such instrument-makers provided the scientist with the tools for his experiments, so that he became increasingly a laboratory worker surrounded by apparatus, a picture quite characteristic by the beginning of the nineteenth century. Scientific instrument-making, moreover, had made its noteworthy contribution to the industrial revolution that was then well under way, as well as to science, for the trend towards precision engineering rendered it natural for great engineers like John Smeaton (1724–92) and James Watt (1736–1819) to learn the elements of their trade in the ranks of the instrument-makers. The steam-engine, the theodolite, the sextant, the planetarium, and the radio-telescope are all descendants of the line starting with medieval astrolabes and sun-dials.

BIBLIOGRAPHY

BOFFITO, G. 'Gli Strumenti della Scienza e la Scienza degli Strumenti.' Con l'illustrazione della Tribuno di Galileo. Facsimile di Primo Benaglia. Seeber, Florence. 1929.

CLAY, R. S. and COURT, T. H. 'History of the Microscope.' Griffin, London. 1932.

DAUMAS, M. 'Les instruments scientifiques aux dix-septième et dix-huitième siècles.' Presses Universitaires de France, Paris. 1953.

KIELY, E. R. 'Surveying Instruments, their History and Classroom Use.' Bureau of Publications, Teachers' College, Columbia University, New York. 1947.

KING, H. C. 'The History of the Telescope.' Griffin, London. 1955.

STONE, E. 'The Construction and Principal Uses of Mathematical Instruments. Translated from the French of M. Bion' (2nd ed.). London. 1758.

TAYLOR, EVA G. R. 'The Mathematical Practitioners of Tudor and Stuart England.' University Press, Cambridge. 1954.

WOLF, A. et al. 'A History of Science, Technology and Philosophy in the Sixteenth and Seventeenth Centuries' (2nd ed., prepared by D. McKIE). Allen and Unwin, London. 1952.

Idem. 'A History of Science, Technology and Philosophy in the Eighteenth Century' (2nd ed. rev. by D. McKIE). Allen and Unwin, London. 1950.

## 24

MECHANICAL TIMEKEEPERS

H. ALAN LLOYD

I. THE EARLIEST MECHANICAL CLOCKS

MECHANICAL clocks were first devised in the thirteenth century. They were designed for controlling the force of a falling weight and, in the fifteenth century, the recoil of a spring, so that they should act slowly and regularly upon a suitable indicator. A very early device (reconstructed in figure 382), perhaps copied from one yet older, appears in the *Libros del Saber Astronomia* [1]. This book was compiled by a group of scholars in 1276–7 for Alfonso the Wise of Castile, a great patron of learning. A weight was attached to a cord wound round a drum; as it fell the speed of rotation of the drum was controlled by mercury in an annular container fixed within it. The drum in turning raised the mercury until it counterbalanced the driving-weight, which could then fall only slowly as the mercury trickled through holes in partitions preventing its free flow in the container. Thus the rate of revolution of the drum depended on the viscosity of the mercury and the size of the holes, and was almost uniform. This controlled slow motion was continuous until the cord was fully unwound.

In all later clocks it was found preferable to interrupt the action of the driving-force regularly and periodically, so that the indicator moved in steps rather than continuously. This is the function of the *escapement*, which periodically checks and releases the driving-train. The accuracy of the clock then depends on the regularity of the escapement's action. The first great step towards modern time-measurement was taken in the later thirteenth century, in the use of an escapement deriving its own motion from the fall of a weight, to control the rate of fall.

Once regulation of the descent of a weight had been achieved, the motion thus obtained could be applied to a variety of purposes—to the rotation of the rete or star-map of an astrolabe (p 604), to the striking of bells at regular intervals, or to the movement of hands over a dial-face. The first record in Europe of a device controlled by an escapement is in the sketch-book of the French architect, Villard de Honnecourt (*c* 1250–*c* 1300) [2]. His drawings were largely of things that he saw in his travels, so that it is unlikely that he himself invented this

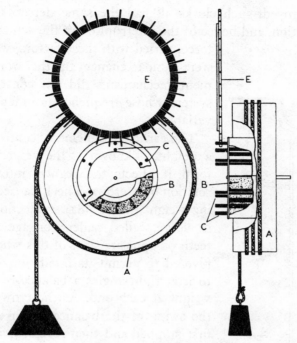

FIGURE 382—*Alfonso X's mercury clock.* A, *the weight-driven drum;* B, *the mercury container divided by perforated partitions;* C, *the studs turning the dial* E.

mechanism (figure 383). No explanation is given, but beneath the sketch is the legend: 'How to make an Angel point with his finger towards the Sun.' This suggests that the figure was intended to revolve once in twenty-four hours. The angel would be mounted on the vertical shaft.

In this sketch of Villard—of what can hardly be called a clock—the descent of the weight and the uniform rotation of the shaft are regulated by to-and-fro oscillation of the wheel round whose axle the driving-cord is wound. The period of the wheel's oscillation is determined by many factors, including its moment of inertia, its friction on its bearings, and the force acting on the cord. Until the seventeenth century all clocks were similarly controlled by the oscillation of a heavy mass, in the form either of a wheel (as here) or of a pair of weighted arms. Although the escapement

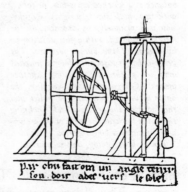

FIGURE 383—*Villard de Honnecourt's rope-escapement.*

was vastly improved, such clocks all had the same defect, namely that the period of oscillation, and hence of the interruption of the action of the driving-force, varied with these factors, which themselves were liable to change. In other words, such escapement mechanisms did not constitute a periodic system whose frequency is independent of these variables.

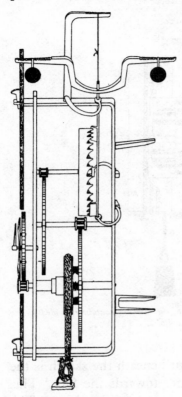

The earliest escapement, controlling the fall of a weight, is known as the verge.[1] In its simplest form it effects the regular interruption of the rotation of a crown-wheel, caused by a descending weight (figure 384). Projections from the rod or verge, called pallets, engage alternately with teeth on opposite sides of this wheel. The verge is pivoted to permit its oscillation and has attached to it at right-angles a balance-rod with an equal weight at each end. As the crown-wheel rotates, the swing of the balance-rod in one direction is first stopped and then reversed, so that it swings back in the opposite direction. Next, as the engaged tooth of the crown-wheel is released from the relevant pallet, the other pallet engages with a tooth on the other side of the wheel, reversing the swing of the balance once more, and so on. The speed of the intermittent rotation of the crown-wheel is therefore dependent on (*a*) the force applied to it by a spring or falling weight through the gearing, (*b*) the friction in the train and escapement, and (*c*) the moment of inertia of the balance. The escapement, linked by gears both to the driving-barrel and to the indicators or hands, forms the *going-train* of the clock.

FIGURE 384—*A fifteenth-century mechanical clock in its simplest form. The balance is a notched cross-bar, or foliot, with two small cursor weights. Regulation was primarily by the size of the weight employed, with a fine adjustment by means of the cursor weights. The verge-arbor is suspended from a notched arm by a thread, affording another means of regulation by varying the angle of impact between the pallet and the tooth of the crown-wheel. Inclining the pallet towards the teeth of the crown-wheel ensured a longer period of contact, hence slower going, and vice versa.*

If a clock is to strike the hours it must also have a *striking-train*, usually driven by a separate weight -or spring, which is released at intervals by the motion of the going-train. The date of the invention of the striking-train is uncertain. The oldest surviving clock striking the hours in sequence is in Salisbury

[1] Probably derived from the Latin *virga*, a wand or rod.

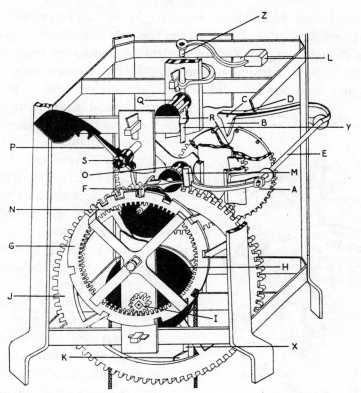

FIGURE 385—*Early form of simple striking-train, c 1550. Once an hour one of the twelve pins on a plate fixed to the hour-wheel (A) carried by the front plate raises the triangular piece (B), which is pivoted at C and has a restoring spring (D). B by means of the arbor (E) raises the locking-piece (F) out of the groove in the locking-plate (G) and another out of the slot in the eccentric cam (N). The striking-train is now free to revolve, impelled by a weight (not shown) attached to a cord passing over the grooved wheel (H). The pinion (I) on the arbor of H turns the locking-plate (G). Twelve pins (not seen) at equal intervals on the far side of the great wheel (J) catch the pallet (K) at the base of the arbor (XYZ) carrying the hammer (L), which, through a restoring spring (not seen), strikes the bell (not shown). The locking-piece having dropped upon the rim of the locking-plate because of the weight (M), the eccentric cam (N), driven by the great wheel (J) through the pinion (O), raises the locking-piece again. The next pin on J then catches K which strikes again, and so until the locking-piece falls into a notch in the locking-plate and a second locking-piece into the notch in the cam. The notches in the locking-plate are so spaced that the hammer may strike one to twelve successively.*

To retard the fall of the weight, a fan (P) is geared through the pinions (O, Q) and the wheel (R), to revolve at a high speed. Attached to the unseen arm of the fan is a click which engages with the ratchet (S) allowing rotation in one direction only. Variations in the design of striking-trains, notably the provision of a 'warning period' of two or three minutes before the strike, when the fan is held fast, are common. In France the locking-plate system is still widely used; elsewhere it is applied only to turret-clocks. It cannot be used to provide a repeating-action.

Cathedral and is of 1386. This, however, has been so modified that it is better to illustrate the Dover Castle clock, which still preserves its original foliot (or verge) escapement (plate 32 A).

In early striking–clocks a wheel, notched at progressive intervals, controls the number of strokes on the bell while revolving blades form an air-brake, limiting the speed of striking (figure 385). This was the only form of striking-mechanism known until 1676 (p 669). The earliest mechanical clocks were probably designed merely to strike bells, warning a monastic officer to announce the appropriate ritual, and they then probably did not indicate time visually. A striking-train,

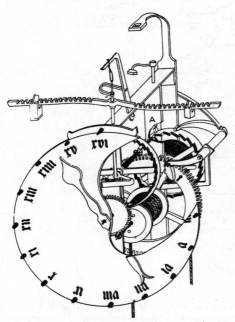

however, would have been meaningless unless a going-train, including the escapement, were available.

There is at Nuremberg an alarm clock of 1380–1400 (figure 386) which has sixteen knobs indicating the time by touch in the dark. It has also a pinion of three leaves driving a wheel of 48 teeth completing one revolution in sixteen hours, thus confirming that the clock was designed for night use only. Until the early seventeenth century, at Nuremberg and in other places, time was reckoned by hours of daylight and darkness, about eight of daylight to sixteen of darkness at midwinter with the reverse ratio at midsummer. The sexton would set the clock each night at the first hour of darkness. Once an hour a lifting device would release the second crown-wheel, that of the alarm, and this, set in motion by its own driving-weight, would oscillate its own verge-staff pallets. At the end of

FIGURE 386—*Early monastic alarm clock, c 1390, recording the hours of darkness to a maximum of sixteen. The stop (A) on the alarm crown-wheel, stopping and re-setting the alarm after one revolution, is an improvement on the design of earlier clocks.*

the verge-staff, on the curved arm, is carried a hammer striking the bell (not shown). On the alarm-wheel is a stud which stopped it after one revolution and reset the alarm. This arrest of the alarm is something new, and eliminated the necessity for rewinding the alarm after each release. From now on the awakening function of the sexton was increasingly replaced by the automatic sounding of a bell, sometimes struck by a mechanical figure or *jaquemart*,[1] whence our English clock-jack. The word 'jack' has been applied to many mechanical devices, such as roasting-jack, screw-jack, and so on.

Quarter-striking was the next development, which is exhibited earliest in the

---

[1] That is, Jack (Jacquème) with a hammer (*marteau*).

great clock at Rouen of 1389. A third train was introduced to provide for this addition, on the same lines as the hour-strike, but with the locking-plate having four divisions only instead of twelve. A quarters bell would be struck 1, 2, 3, and 4 times and, after the last, the hour on its own bell.

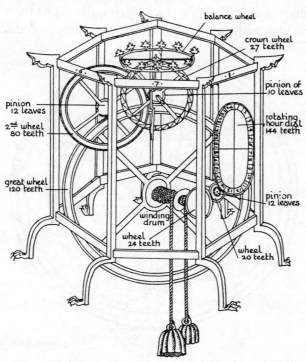

FIGURE 387—*Dondi's incomplete sketch of his going-train, 1364. It contrasts with the very precise details given for other dials and trains. The clock has a verge-escapement fitted with a balance, but no striking-train; it embodies the early practice of combining a fixed hand with a revolving 24-hour dial. As the numbers of teeth shown on the sketch indicate, the winding-drum makes 10 revolutions in a day; the second wheel, therefore, revolves 100 times a day, and the escape-wheel 800 times. Since each revolution occasions 54 oscillations of the balance (1800 in an hour) the balance has a 2-second beat—the standard of Dondi's time. The pinion meshing with the hour-circle was made to slide to allow for daily adjustment. This was essential when, as in Italy where this clock was made, the 24-hour day was reckoned as starting at sunset.*

II. THE FIRST ASTRONOMICAL CLOCK

At a very early date there were attempts to embody the celestial motions in clocks; indeed, the ambition to do this seems to have played a large part in the evolution of uniformly rotating mechanisms. An astronomical clock was first developed in medieval Europe by Giovanni de' Dondi between 1348 and 1362. He constructed a most complete clock (figure 387), which set out the motions of the Sun, Moon, and five planets with surprising accuracy, and included a perpetual calendar for the movable feasts of the church. Dondi left a full description, both of the clock and of his method of construction. He made it with his own hands, entirely of bronze, brass, and copper, an operation that took sixteen years. Because of the astronomical complexities much greater force was required to drive the going-train of Dondi's clock during the night than during the day. He met this difficulty with great mechanical ingenuity, introducing an auxiliary

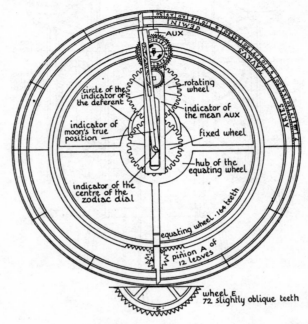

FIGURE 388—*Dondi's lunar train. Note the oval wheels with irregularly spaced teeth, the outer revolving around the fixed inner wheel.*

driving-weight to provide for the extra strain imposed on the going-train when six of the seven planetary dials received their nightly advance at the same time from the drive incorporated in the annular calendar wheel of 365 teeth.

In order to cut 365 (5 × 73) teeth on one of his wheels, Dondi divides the whole circumference into 6 parts, from which he obtains 1/18th and from this 1/72nd. He then divides the remaining 71/72nds of the circumference into 72 parts, thus obtaining 73 nearly equal parts, which he further divides by 5.

To explain Dondi's perpetual calendar for the movable feasts of the church would lead us too far afield, but it may justly be said that he solved the problem mechanically better than any of his successors for 400 years. His ideas were beyond his contemporaries and immediate successors and hardly affected them.

FIGURE 389—*The mechanical cock made for the first Strasbourg clock in 1354. It is of wrought iron, with copper comb and beard, mounted on a wooden base.*

FIGURE 390—*Diagram showing the mechanism for the articulation of the head, beak, and tongue. (Cock of Strasbourg clock).*

Thus the many details of his clock can hardly be treated as an integral part of the history of technology. It is, however, worthy of mention that there was a dial for each planet, and that the trains for those of the Moon and Mercury embodied oval cog-wheels (figure 388). The two oval cog-wheels in the train of the Moon were divided into unequal sectors, each with the same number of teeth. The inner cog-wheel was fixed to the hub of a wheel with regular circular motion and thus provided for a regular increase in the Moon's phase in equal periods of time. The outer oval cog-wheel was carried around the inner, and by reason of the equal number of teeth in the unequal sectors provided for the varying length of arc traversed in successive equal time-intervals.

Almost contemporary with Dondi's great work is the Strasbourg clock of 1354. Its much simpler construction was widely imitated in succeeding centuries.

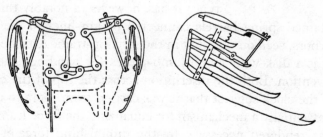

FIGURE 391—*Diagram showing the mechanism for the flapping of the wings and the spreading of the feathers (Cock of Strasbourg clock).*

This clock introduced another feature, namely automata or moving images. Of these the wrought iron cock, recalling St Peter's denial of his Master, is a unique survival. The clock was about 38 ft high and had an annual calendar wheel about 9 ft in diameter. At noon the cock opened its beak, stretched out its tongue, crowed, flapped its wings, and spread its feathers. The crowing was worked mechanically by bellows and a reed. This cock was used again in 1574 by Isaac Habrecht in making a second clock, hence no doubt its survival (figures 389–91).

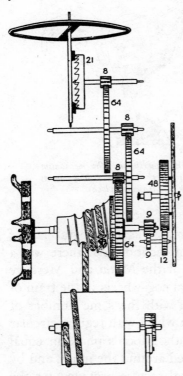

FIGURE 392—*Reconstruction of a clock with fusee from a manuscript of 1477. The number of fusees shown in the manuscript indicates that they were already well known at the time.*

III. THE SPRING-DRIVE AND ITS REGULATION

In a weight-driven clock the motive force remains sensibly constant, but the clock has to be permanently fixed. To make clocks portable the idea was conceived of replacing the weight by a coiled spring. This invention appeared in the fifteenth century or perhaps even earlier.

The earliest timepieces or watches carried on the person were usually drum-shaped. They have been miscalled 'Nuremberg eggs'[1] as they were believed to have originated in that city. This is now in doubt. A letter of 1488 from Milan refers to three watches of which two will strike but not the third [3]. Probably they were small portable clocks or watches carried on the person.

The earliest representation of a spring-driven clock is in a portrait of the middle years of the fifteenth century (plate 32 B). Its shape is in general that of the contemporary weight-driven type; it has, however, a notably thick base which probably contained spring-barrels connected by gut-lines to the drums on the great wheel-arbors, seen on the right in the striking-train. Attached to the arbor of each drum is a disk with four thumb-pieces for winding: the winding-key was a later invention. Both the inscription across the top of the canvas and the suspension of the clock suggest that it was carried from room to room.

The *fusee*, essentially a mechanism for equalizing the force transmitted to the gear-train, was rendered necessary by the diminishing force of the uncoiling

[1] By translating 'little eggs' (= *Eierlein*) in mistake for 'little clock' (= *Uhrlein*).

spring. The invention, which is still in use, is first illustrated and described by Paulus Alemannus in a manuscript written in Rome in 1477 (figure 392). This shows a spring-driven clock fitted with a fusee through which passes a rigidly fixed arbor. At the end of this arbor is a disk with thumb winding-pieces (plate 32 B). The Latin text uses the words *corda* (gut) and *fusella* (fusee) and relates that the great wheel carrying the fusee made one revolution in three hours. Given a half-second oscillation of the balance-

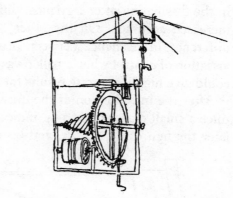

FIGURE 393—*One of Leonardo's drawings of the fusee.*

wheel at the top, that is, with one tooth of the crown-wheel escaping each second and with the number of the teeth of the wheels and pinions given by the text, in three hours the clock would indicate 10 752 seconds, only 48 seconds short of the three-hourly period. A similar mechanism is to be seen in well known sketches of Leonardo da Vinci, of perhaps 1490 (figure 393).

Another method of securing a constant drive despite the continuous weakening of the spring's tension was the *stackfreed* (figure 394). This is a kidney-shaped cam fixed to a wheel and having a stop-piece. The wheel is driven by a pinion fixed squarely to the arbor of the main-spring. Against the cam bears the head of a stiff spring, the pressure from which on the edge of the cam diminishes as the wheel turns during the uncoiling of the spring. The stackfreed also limited the effective number of turns in the spring to those giving the most even results.

Screws are important for the construction of clocks, but the date of their first use in this connexion is uncertain. Leonardo shows the tapping of female screw-threads in metal, and it is generally accepted that screws were adopted in clock-construction about the end of the fifteenth century. At this time, too, hog's bristles began to be used as a fine means of regulation. They served as *banking-pins* limiting the amplitude of the oscillations of the balance (figure 395). They reduced the strain imposed on the train by the reversal of the swing of the balance and so permitted the use of smaller driving-forces. They also damped banking, the factor

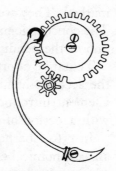

FIGURE 394—*The stackfreed—the term is of unknown origin. With 8 leaves on the pinion and 27 teeth on the wheel only just over the first three turns of the spring—those giving the most equal force—would be effective before the watch stopped and had to be rewound.*

in the dissipation of energy most difficult to control; so this new device greatly increased accuracy. On the other hand, it introduced certain errors, such as difference in resilience between bristles, or the incidence of impact through variation of control when a pallet was not in engagement. Thus bristle-regulation could give highly accurate results for a while, but these were liable to deteriorate.

After the introduction of the quarters strike, it became not unusual to introduce a small dial marked 1–4, indicating the quarters, as well as the hour-dial; later the figures 15, 30, 45, and 60 were added, and soon we find the minutes

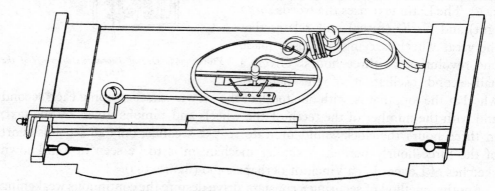

FIGURE 395—*Hog's-bristle regulation. Note the alternative holes and the cranked lever for adjustment.*

marked. They were first indicated without the use of a separate minute-hand. The concentric minute-hand did not come into general use until after the invention of the pendulum.

Tentative efforts were made to indicate seconds about 1550 (figure 396), but the seconds-hand was not regularly employed until after 1670, when William Clement introduced his anchor-escapement (p 665). This made the pendulum with a period of one second fully practicable for domestic clocks.

In 1561 Eberhardt Baldewin, clockmaker to William IV of Hesse, constructed an astronomical clock worthy of consideration as a successor to Dondi's (p 653). It was of great complexity. New features are an endless worm as a means of transmission, roller bearings, and cardan joints (figures 397, 398). This clock was made within about twenty years of Cardan's 'invention' of the universal joint.

At the end of the sixteenth century, astronomers—notably Tycho Brahe (1546–1601) and Kepler (1571–1630)—were well aware of the inadequacy of existing clocks, which were ineffective for astronomical purposes. The Swiss Jobst Burgi (1552–1632), a very skilled instrument-maker, applied himself at Cassel and later at Prague to meet their needs. His first care was to provide a

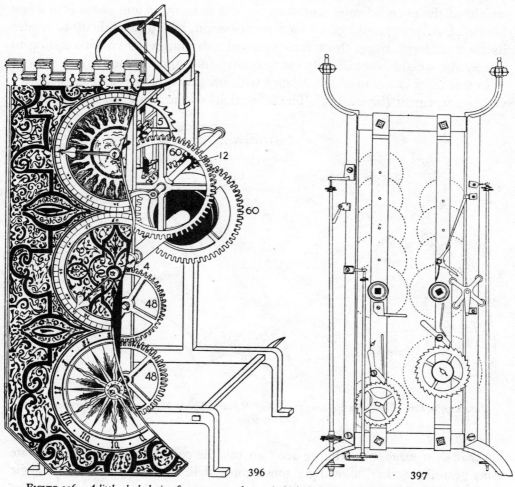

396   397

FIGURE 396—*A little clock dating from c 1550, about 9 in high. It has three dials, showing seconds, minutes, and hours; it would be regulated entirely by varying the weight. The crown-wheels of verge-escapements have an odd number of teeth, so that seconds cannot be recorded exactly.*

FIGURE 397—*Baldewin's clock. Parts of the astronomical trains are fixed behind their respective dials fitted to each of the four sides of the inner frame depicted. The motions are transmitted from the going-train through a series of 24-hour wheels housed below the main trains (these are not shown). These wheels rotate others at the base of the connecting-rods, which are geared to the astronomical trains by endless screws. The eight dials are at two levels on each of the four faces. To enable the distant ends of the connecting-rods to mesh with their associated wheels, many of which are out of line, cardan joints are employed, one of which is illustrated.*

constant driving-force with a long period of action. A weight provided the former but needed frequent rewinding, with a consequent loss of accuracy, since maintaining-power[1] was yet unknown. Further, Tycho complained that the

_____
[1] A device for maintaining the force on the train while the main weight or spring is rewound.

weight of the uncoiled rope caused an error of as many as four seconds in a few hours [4]. A spring could give a long going-period, but it was difficult to render its force uniform. Burgi therefore combined a driving-weight with a spring to restore the weight automatically every twenty-four hours (figure 399).

In this clock Burgi used the balance with bristle-regulation and the ordinary verge-escapement (figure 395). The limitations of the verge led him to design

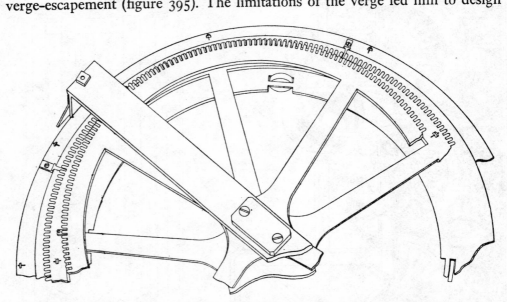

FIGURE 398—*Part of the train operating the dial of Mercury, showing Baldewin's use of roller-bearings as a means of support.*

his *cross-beat escapement* (figure 400). In this the pallets are carried by separate arms geared together, allowing a much more delicate adjustment of the angle between their faces, according to the fineness of the teeth on the gearing. The shape of his escape-wheel teeth also allowed finer adjustment than did the ordinary verge. Its action is, in effect, the same as that of a bristle set to make contact with the balance at the moment of pallet-collision; but since the elastic properties of the metallic arm are more constant than those of the bristle, the period of reversal is shorter and independent of setting; the oscillations are thus more symmetrical. Finally, the flexibility of the arms of the cross-beat lessens the wear on the escape-wheel teeth and pallets. This escapement, although used for only a short period, made a real contribution to the exactness of the clock. With the introduction of the pendulum clock the cross-beat was superseded, and the mechanical time-keeper could be widely applied to astronomical observations.

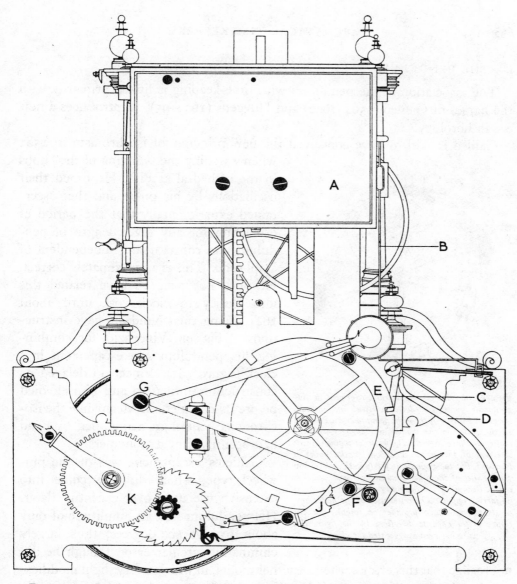

FIGURE 399—*Burgi's remontoire. The weight, a rectangular box* (A), *contains lead pellets, providing a means of fine adjustment. This constant driving-force during its 24-hour descent depresses the lever* (B) *which indirectly moves the catch* (C), *controlled by the spring* (D), *to the right, releasing the spring-driven locking-plate* (E). *This now turns anti-clockwise, carrying with it by means of the stud* (F) *the V-shaped arm pivoted at* (G). *The weight, now resting on the roller at the other end of the V arm, is restored to its higher position, the upper arm of the V being clear of the studs. The end of the lower arm slides off the stud* (F), *the V arm drops back into position, and* D *presses* C *into the next notch in the locking-plate. The lower arm of the V in passing knocks the 7-star wheel* (H) *carrying the day of the week dial one tooth forward. The stud* (I) *depresses the pawl* (J) *and through the ratchet-wheel and pinion moves the wheel* (K), *which carries the dial recording the number of times the remontoire has functioned one tooth forward. The spring will operate for three months and the remontoire counter can record 180 actions. This is the earliest remontoire known.*

IV. THE PENDULUM

The association of the pendulum with time-keeping is linked primarily with the names of Galileo (1564–1642) and Huygens (1629–95). It introduces a new era in horology.

Galileo is said to have conceived the new principle of isochronism in 1581 when watching the swinging of the lamps in the cathedral at Pisa. He timed their oscillations by his pulse, and then ascertained experimentally that the period of oscillation for any given length of pendulum was constant and independent of amplitude. This is approximately correct. He does not seem to have related this idea clearly to clock-work until about 1641. Being then blind, he gave instructions to his son, Vincenzio, for combining his pendulum and escapement in a clock (figure 401). Vincenzio delayed its construction until 1649 and himself died before its completion. Meanwhile the isochronous pendulum maintained by hand had been used by astronomers.

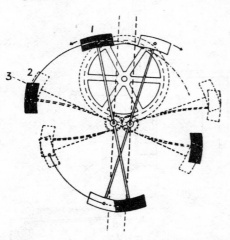

FIGURE 400—*Burgi's cross-beat escapement in diagrammatic form. The dotted vertical lines indicate the mean position of the arms about to cross.* Position 1: *the pallet on the shaded arm engages with the tooth of the escape-wheel, while swinging in the direction of the arrow.* Position 2: *the pallet is liberated and the arms swing freely until at* Position 3 *the pallet of the other arm engages and causes a check. Because of the flexibility of the arms, there is no jarring impact. The restoration of the flexed arm to its normal shape provides an impulse for the return in the opposite direction. In the figure this flexure has been exaggerated for clarity.*

Galileo's escapement was of the pin-wheel type, which did not come into extensive use until over a century later. His pendulum had an amplitude of only about five or six degrees, thus largely eliminating circular error, though he did not realize that this error existed. Another model, in which a very slight modification had been made, was in modern times fitted to a weight-driven clock-train, and showed variations of no more than a few seconds a day. The seafaring Dutch were deeply interested in determining longitude at sea and in this connexion Galileo had approached the States General suggesting the adoption of a pendulum with a recording-device (actually impracticable) for counting the oscillations. Huygens must have been aware of this suggestion but knew nothing of Galileo's escapement.

Huygens's own pendulum-escapement incorporated the much inferior verge mechanism. He started his experiments in 1656 and published the first work on the pendulum clock, *Horologium*,[1] in 1658. It is clear that he then knew that amplitude affects isochronism (figure 402). No clock constructed on these lines has survived. Before introducing his arrangement of pinion and contrate wheel, Huygens had several clocks made with pendulums swinging in an unrestricted arc. Later he reverted to the horizontal crown-wheel and pallets, while controlling the arc of oscillation by curved cheeks, fitted at the point of suspension of the pendulum. The curves of the first cheeks fitted to clocks by Huygens were arcs of circles. The clock claimed to be the first made by Salomon da Coster, Huygens's clock-maker in the Hague, which is now in the Museum for the History of Science at Leiden,[2] has a horizontal crown-wheel and is spring-driven. Coster made many pendulum clocks to Huygens's design and these were the first to be commercially available.

Huygens discovered the importance of the cycloid[3] for horology in 1659 and published his investigations in his second and greater work on time-pieces, the *Horologium oscillatorium* (Paris, 1673) (figure 403). In this he described the theory leading him to the view that the truly isochronous pendulum must swing in a cycloidal arc, which is slightly narrower than the corresponding arc of a circle. In practice the cycloidal cheeks he introduced to this end, though of the greatest theoretical interest and much used by him, introduced more errors than they corrected. Huygens's pendulum was brought to London by the clock-making family of Fromanteel, which was of Dutch origin. One of them learnt the secret of the pendulum from da Coster. The cycloidal cheek was, however, never widely adopted in England, where

FIGURE 401—*Galileo's pendulum escapement. The escape-wheel, bearing on one side twelve pins projecting at right-angles, has twelve small bosses or teeth which are locked by a hinged detent. As the pendulum swings to the left, the unlocking pallet raises the detent and the wheel revolves until a pin strikes the impulse pallet. As the pendulum swings to the right the impulse pallet is freed from the pin; at the same time the locking pallet releases the detent, which then falls upon the rim of the wheel to lock it.*

---

[1] Not to be confused with his *Horologium oscillatorium* of 1673.

[2] The accuracy of this attribution is doubtful. See Drummond Robertson, 'The Evolution of Clockwork', pp 76–78.

[3] A cycloid is a curve traced by a point on a circle as the circle rolls along a straight line. The end of a string wrapped round a cycloid describes a second cycloid (the evolute); this was the property of the curve exploited by Hugyens in designing his 'cheeks'.

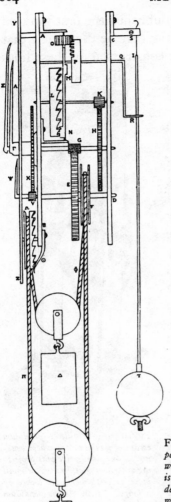

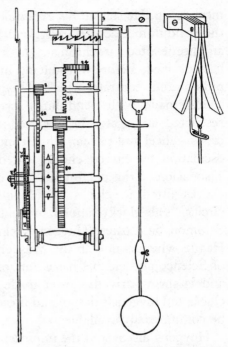

FIGURE 403—*Huygens's clock with cycloidal cheeks. The crown-wheel is horizontal, eliminating the pinion and contrate wheel of figure 402. The pendulum crutch is attached directly to the verge-pallet arbor. Maintaining-power is not shown, but could easily be fitted.*

FIGURE 402—*Huygens's first pendulum clock: the amplitude of the half-seconds pendulum with verge-escapement is reduced by a pinion engaging with a contrate wheel of three times its diameter, fixed to the crutch arbor. Maintaining-power is introduced for the first time. A saw-toothed wheel is fixed to a pulley Ω. A detent Θ allows movement only in the direction raising the weight. A secondary weight Z ensures that the endless rope is taut. In this arrangement half the weight of Δ is always effective in the cord Φ and it will always maintain motion in the time-piece while the weight is drawn upwards by pulling the cord Π.*

it was usual to attach the pendulum rod directly to the verge-pallet arbor. Later the practice was to suspend the pendulum independently and actuate it through a crutch, as originally done by Huygens, but employing a flat spring for the suspension in place of a silk cord.

V. THE ANCHOR-ESCAPEMENT

The anchor-escapement of William Clement (figure 404), invented about 1670, rapidly displaced the verge-escapement in England, except for mantel clocks which were then carried from room to room, since the verge-escapement needs less exact levelling. After the death of Huygens the anchor-escapement was soon generally adopted on the European continent.

In the anchor-escapement the faces of the pallets of the escapement are in the same plane as those of the teeth of the escape-wheel, enabling them to effect clearance within a much smaller arc than was necessary for the verge-escapement. This was of great advantage, because the isochronism of a pendulum is affected by its amplitude; the smaller the arc of circle described, the more closely it approximates to a cycloidal arc. Theoretically these two curves coincide only at the mid-point of a pendulum's swing, but in practice they are indistinguishable mechanically if the swings are of small amplitude on either side of this point: hence the smaller the swing of the pendulum the more nearly it is isochronous (figure 405). Another advantage of the anchor-escapement was that it freed the pendulum from its contact with the escape-wheel to a limited extent, as against the uninterrupted contact of the verge, and so made the first step towards that unattainable ideal, a clock with a perfectly free pendulum. It had, however, the disadvantage that the pallet strikes the face of the escape-wheel tooth, causing a recoil. The effect of this may be seen in an ordinary long-case clock as a slight shudder in the seconds-hand each second.

Despite its inherent imperfections the anchor-escapement was a great advance. Because of its small amplitude it enabled the 39-in seconds-pendulum to be adopted generally for both domestic and scientific use, the long-case clock, as we know it today, immediately becoming popular. In scientific circles the vastly improved time-keeping of the anchor-escapement, with the long seconds-pendulum, was quickly recognized. In an attempt to secure still higher accuracy clocks were made with 5-ft pendulums, beating 1·25 seconds, while Thomas Tompion went yet further and built in 1676, for use in the newly established observatory at Greenwich, two clocks with 13-ft pendulums, beating 2 seconds,

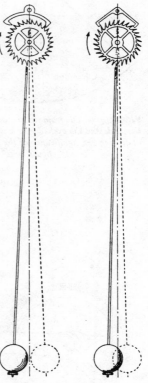

FIGURE 404 — (Left) *William Clement's anchor-escapement. Note the small amplitude of the pendulum and the way in which the pallet strikes the face of the tooth of the escape-wheel, causing recoil. Compare (right) Graham's dead-beat escapement in which the recoil is avoided. The amplitude of the pendulum's swing is here still less.*

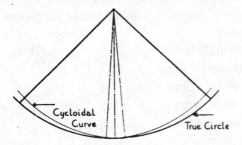

FIGURE 405—*Diagram illustrating the coincidence of the circle and the cycloid over a very limited arc, and indicating the significance of the anchor-escapement, figure 404.*

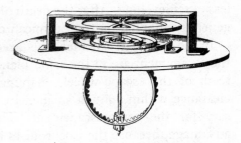

FIGURE 406—*Huygens's balance-spring was a spiral of many turns; acting through a pinion and contrate wheel, it made several revolutions at each beat.*

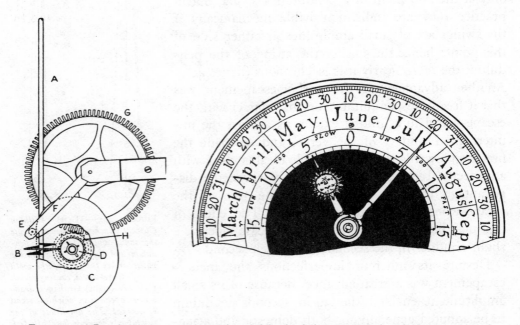

FIGURE 407—*Equation movement. A is a rod rotated by the clock-train which through the worm (B) and wheel (D) turns the equation-kidney (C) once a year. As C turns, the pin (E) on the arm (F) approaches or recedes from its centre, giving a forward or backward motion to the wheel (G), which in turn transmits it to wheel H. This is attached to a friction-tight sleeve arbor carrying the equation-hand with the effigy of the sun. Fixed to the arbor of C, and thus turning once a year, is the annual calendar hand. In wheel G only the lower teeth are shaped, since this sector of the wheel alone is used. The remaining teeth are cut for balance. Sometimes a counterpoised toothed rack is used. When the equation-movement is integral with the clock-movement, the equation is shown either by a second, mobile, minute-ring or, later, by fixing the equation-hand as a sleeve-fit on the arbor of the minute-hand of the clock.*

fitted with maintaining-power, and going for one year with one winding. Except for their maintaining-power these were probably the first clocks to be made incorporating these innovations. They were not an entire success but were a great deal better than those then available in other observatories. They were largely responsible for the accuracy of the stellar tables compiled by Flamsteed (1646–1719), the first Astronomer Royal.

At the other end of the scale we have the astronomer James Gregory, who in 1673 was at St Andrews University, ordering from Joseph Knibb of London

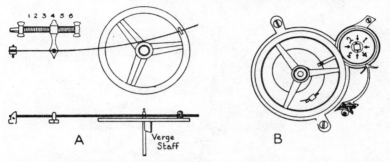

FIGURE 408—*Early forms of balance-spring.* (A) *A straight spring acting on the rim of the balance was used in some early experiments. The figure also illustrates the 'Barrow' screw regulator.* (B) *Early balance-springs usually consisted of $1\frac{1}{2}$ turns only. This drawing shows Tompion's regulator in which a curved sector, corresponding to the outer curve of the spring, and carrying the arm with the curb pins, is controlled by a toothed wheel.*

two long-case clocks with seconds-pendulums and a small clock with anchor-escapement, having 90 teeth in the escape-wheel and beating one-third of a second. This last had only two hands, one for the hour and the other to record thirds of a second.[1] It was the first clock designed to record a split second and so was the first step on the road towards the fractional-second measurements of today: all due to the anchor-escapement.

The higher degree of time-keeping now achieved brought to the notice of the general public the difference between the mean and the solar day throughout the year, known as the equation of time. The difference arises from two facts, (*a*) the inclination of the Earth's axis to the plane of its orbit, and (*b*) the greater velocity of the Earth's revolution in its orbit at perihelion (in winter) than at aphelion (in summer). Only on four days of the year is the solar day of exactly 24 mean hours; the maximum variations of the solar day from the mean day are such that the Sun is 14 minutes behind mean time in February and 16 minutes in advance of the clock in November. The days of equality are irregularly spaced,

[1] These three clocks are still in the library of St Andrews University.

and the daily variation, sometimes fast and sometimes slow on the mean clock, is also irregular. At first, tables were printed and were stuck inside the door of a long-case clock, showing how much a clock going correctly should be fast or

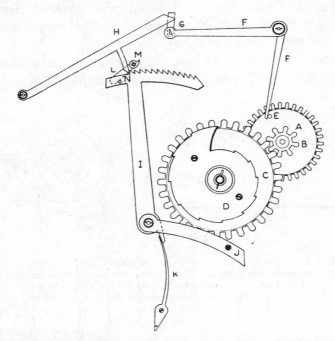

FIGURE 409—*Edward Barlow's rack-and-snail strike (diagrammatic). The minute wheel* (A) *turning once an hour through the pinion* (B) *drives the hour wheel* (C) *carrying the snail* (D) *into which are cut* 12 *progressively deeper steps. Once an hour the pin* (E) *lifts the detent* (F) *and through a pin on the far side* (G), *projecting through the front plate, releases the 'warning' wheel. At the same time the rack detent* (H) *is raised, allowing the rack* (I) *to fall to the left (under the action of the spring* (K)) *until stopped by the pin* (J) *on its far side coming into contact with the edge of the snail* (D). *The number of teeth in the rack* (I) *passing the arm of the detent* (H) *is determined by the depth of the indenture on the snail. When* E *clears* F *the latter falls back, releasing the striking-train, and the arm of* H *will drop into the correct notch in the rack. The gathering pallet* (L) *on the arbor of the wheel operating the hammer will turn about on its pivot* (M), *gathering a tooth at each revolution, the teeth sliding under the arm of* H, *until the rack is moved back to the right to the position shown. Then the tail of* M *is locked by the pin* (N) *and striking ceases. In this striking-mechanism the hour hand is usually only a fairly tight friction-fit on its sleeve arbor, so that if the striking becomes incorrect the hand can be turned to the correct hour without damage.*

slow by the sun-dial on any given day; later, manually operated adjustable dials were sometimes made, until finally the problem of the mechanical recording of the equation was solved—it is believed by Christiaan Huygens, who designed a kidney-shaped cam (figure 407). These mechanical equation-clocks were first made about 1695.

The greatly improved time-keeping of clocks brought about by the anchor-escapement inspired watch-makers to attempt to achieve equal accuracy in watches. In 1675 Huygens described his balance-spring, claiming that it would render a watch sufficiently accurate to enable the longitude to be found at sea (figure 406). Hooke claimed priority, and whatever may be the truth of that, it was certainly Hooke's balance-spring, oscillating through about 120°, as opposed to Huygens's, with its pirouette of several turns, that was generally adopted (figure 408).

Watches with balance-springs were sometimes termed at this time 'pendulum-watches', because their accuracy was supposed to rival that of pendulum clocks. Sometimes the spring-regulated balance of an early watch takes the form of a dumb-bell bar, half of which is hidden by a solid cock, leaving the other half to give the impression of a swinging pendulum. Watches fitted with small pendulums were also occasionally made, the movement being mounted in gimbals, in the manner originally proposed by Huygens for a sea-going pendulum-chronometer.

A lesser advance was the invention by Edward Barlow, about 1676, of the *rack-and-snail* striking-method (figure 409). Since the snail revolves once in twelve hours, each step will take one hour to pass the stud on the end of the lever, so that if the clock be caused to repeat at any time during that hour the stud will fall on the same step of the snail, which will enable the gathering pallet to take in the same number of teeth each time and so correctly repeat the hour.

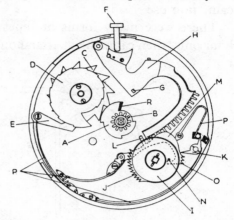

FIGURE 410—*Early repeating-work by Daniel Quare. A is the quarter snail which is turned once an hour by the wheel (B) to which it is secured. On its underside it has a pin which knocks the 12-pointed star-wheel (C), fixed beneath the hour snail (D), forward one tooth each hour. C is steadied by a detent (E). When the plunger (F) is pushed in, the stud (G) on the arm (H) falls upon the hour snail in the correct position. The rack end of H advances by the number of teeth corresponding to the step in the snail and winds the spring, enclosed in the barrel (I), the requisite amount. It also causes the hour-rack (J) to turn anti-clockwise, placing the correct number of its teeth in position for actuating the pallet (K). As I turns anti-clockwise the movement of the pin (N) allows the quarter-rack (M) to advance until its arm (L) reaches a step on the quarter snail (A). When H returns to its original position I turns clockwise, striking the hours by means of J and K; shortly afterwards N impinges on M and restores it to its original position, so striking the quarters through O and K. The pallet (K) is on the arbor of the wheel (not shown) controlling the hammer. P, P, P, P are restoring springs. Shown hatched on A is the 'surprise piece' (R) which operates when the repeat is to function within a few minutes either side of the hour. R is pivoted to A and is held in position by a spring; it carries the pin that actuates the star-wheel. As this pin presses on the star-wheel, R is pushed back level with the edge of the quarter snail (A), returning to its former position when the pin has cleared the tooth of the wheel. This brings the hour and nil quarter into action at the same moment. In this early model the quarter is sounded with one stroke only; later a double stroke, 'ting-tang', was introduced.*

Repeating-clocks remained popular until the nineteenth century, when matches came into use.

There were many forms of repeating-mechanism. The simplest struck the hour only, then came the quarter-hour followed or preceded by the hour, usually

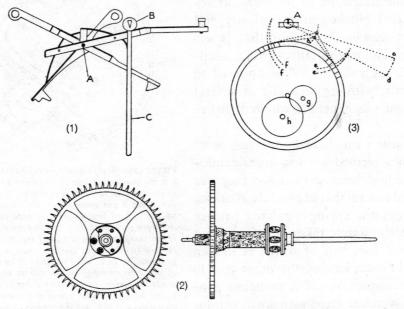

FIGURE 411—*The Harrisons' grasshopper escapement. (1) Shows the pallets, their centre of motion (A) offset from the pallet arbor (B) carrying the pendulum crutch (C). Note the knife-edge arbor finial which rested on a small piece of glass to reduce friction. (2) Shows the brass escape-wheel with its oak arbor and roller pinion of lignum vitae; (3) Harrison's own sketch of the layout of the escapement. A is a small glass plate with a groove supporting the knife-edge of the pallet arbor. c–d is the smallest arc of the pendulum clearing one tooth in the escape-wheel. The offset centre of motion of the pallets will move through the arc a. The extremities of the pallets describe the arcs e–e and f–f, the distance between these arcs at the circumference of the escape-wheel being half the distance between teeth. As the centre of their motion is mobile the friction between pallet and tooth is greatly reduced. g and h are rollers supporting the escape-wheel arbor to reduce friction.*

on a higher-pitched bell; subsequently we find the half-quarter and finally the minute-repeater, of which the earliest known example is about 1705.

In 1688 Daniel Quare and Edward Barlow were contestants for a patent for repeating-watches. The patent was awarded to Quare because his watch repeated both hour and quarter at the pressing of one lever, whereas Barlow's watch required separate actions (figure 410).

Another invention having a great effect on time-keeping was the piercing of jewels with minute holes, serving as almost frictionless and unwearing pivot-holes. A patent for this use of jewels was granted to Nicholas Faccio de Duillier, the inventor, and Peter and Jacob Debaufe, the watch-makers, in 1704. Faccio (1664–1753) was a Swiss who had settled in London in 1687. The jewels commonly employed were rubies and sapphires, the latter being the easier to pierce. The art of jewelling watch-bearings was kept a close secret, and was not

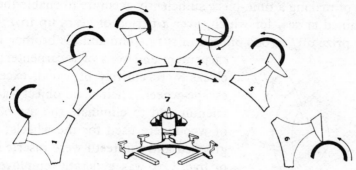

FIGURE 412—*Graham's cylinder-escapement.* (1) *A tooth is about to enter the cylinder.* (2) *Imparting the impulse by the sliding action along the cylinder lip.* (3) *The train is locked by the tooth's impinging on the cylinder wall.* (4) *The balance completes the swing due to the impulse at* (1). (5) *The balance-spring reverses direction and the balance receives an impulse as the tooth escapes.* (6) *Immediately the tooth escapes the next tooth impinges on the cylinder and locks the train during the period of backswing.* (7) *Section of the wheel and cylinder.*

generally practised on the continent until 1798. Nowadays the jewels employed are made artificially.

VI. THE DEAD-BEAT ESCAPEMENT AND ITS SUCCESSORS

The great success of the anchor-escapement led astronomers to seek yet higher accuracy. George Graham, who was as famous both at home and abroad for his astronomical instruments as for his clocks and watches, applied himself to this problem and about 1715 invented a modification of the anchor-escapement known as Graham's dead-beat escapement (figure 404).[1] This found immediate favour, especially in observatories, where it was the standard escapement until Riefler's escapement was adopted after 1893, to be followed by the Shortt free-pendulum clock in the 1920s. This brings home the immense importance of the anchor-escapement which, in its sphere, is equal to that of the pendulum itself.

During the succeeding decade investigations were proceeding, both in this country and on the continent, into the comparative expansion of metals, for variations with temperature in the length of pendulums and of balance-springs seriously affected the accuracy of the finest clocks. George Graham made experiments with brass and iron, but abandoned them in favour of his mercury

[1] A dead-beat escapement is one that operates without imposing any recoil on the train.

pendulum (*c* 1726). John and James Harrison were at the same time experimenting with iron–brass combinations and produced their gridiron pendulum.

John Harrison (1693–1776) is best known for his struggle and final victory in the problem of making a time-piece sufficiently accurate to enable the longitude to be ascertained at sea, for which, over a period of years up to 1772, he was awarded the prize of £20 000 offered in 1714. John and his brother James were

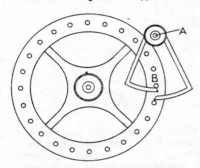

carpenters and sons of a carpenter; their first clocks were entirely of wood, except for the escape-wheel. Their main object was to reduce friction and to eliminate the use of oil. Disks of wood were used for the wheels; these were grooved and the teeth were inserted in groups of five. Oak was generally employed, but for pivot-bearings bushings of lignum vitae (*Guiacum*), a naturally oily wood, were inset. The arbor carrying the escape-pallets sometimes terminated in knife-edges which rocked on small plates of glass, as a bearing-surface, let into the wooden frame. To reduce friction further their pinions were built up of lignum vitae rollers revolving on small brass pins (figure 411).

FIGURE 413—*Amant's pin-wheel escapement (p 674). The pallet arbor (A) is solid with the pendulum crutch. As the pendulum swings to the left the pin (B) on the escape-wheel will slide down the inclined face of the pallet, giving an impulse. B then drops upon the right-hand pallet, and when the pendulum has swung sufficiently far to the right, gives an impulse to the right-hand pallet in the opposite direction. This is a dead-beat escapement, mostly used in France.*

To avoid oiling the escape-pallets, with consequent deterioration in time-keeping as the oil thickened, James Harrison developed the *grasshopper escapement* (figure 411). This had a large circular motion and ensured that the pallet made a practically frictionless contact with the escape-wheel. Very delicate to make and difficult to adjust, this escapement was rarely employed except by the Harrisons; it had a wide arc of swing and had to be used in conjunction with cycloidal cheeks.

That the Harrisons' theories were sound and practical was proved very conclusively in 1955, when a turret clock made by James in 1727 was dismantled and examined. After the oil applied in ignorance had been removed it showed practically no signs of wear after 225 years. Yet Harrison's methods were very rarely imitated, and indeed, except for the bi-metallic temperature-compensation, John Harrison himself abandoned all his pet theories in the making of his 'Number Four', the chronometer with which he actually won the prize. Yet these ideas are so original and so effective that they deserve mention here.

After the advance in time-keeping in clocks resulting from the dead-beat escapement and pendulums with temperature-compensation, the next step was

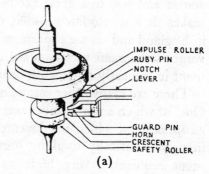

FIGURE 414—*Mudge's lever-escapement.* (a) *The staff carrying the balance and balance-spring shown in relation to the end of the lever. This should be studied in conjunction with* (b), *where* (1) *shows* A, *the escape-wheel, with its 'club-foot' teeth, and the lever with its jewelled pallets and fork or 'horns' at the other end.* B *and* C *are pins to limit lateral movement.* D *is the safety or guard pin.* E *is the impulse-roller, and* F *on the underside of* E *the impulse or ruby pin.* G *is the safety roller with crescent-shaped embrasure. The rectangular space between the horns is 'the notch'. The lever rests against* B, *the ruby pin is pressing the lever to the right.* (2) *The tooth, now un-locked, moves along the impulse-face of the pallet. The ruby pin, receiving an impulse from the notch at the same time, brings the lever against* C. (3) *The first tooth escapes and the next-but-one tooth to the right drops upon the locking-face of the exit pallet. The comple-tion of the balance swing and its reversal until the next unlocking is detached; this free oscillation is the great advantage of the escapement.* (4) *The reversed swing of the balance causes the ruby pin to enter the notch from the other side, unlocking the exit pallet, which receives its impulse as the tooth passes over the pallet-face pressing the lever towards* B. (5) *The balance finishes its swing and on its reversal the ruby pin will again enter the notch as in* (1) *and the whole sequence will be repeated.*

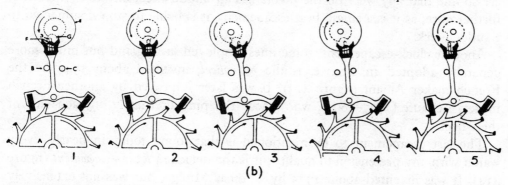

to improve the watch-escapement, which till then was the verge and balance-spring. George Graham invented the *cylinder-escapement* in 1721 (figure 412).[1] In this the escape-wheel is horizontal and in the same plane as the pallets. This allowed the watch to be more slender, but the chief advantage of the cylinder-escapement is that it is a dead-beat, and avoids the recoil inherent in the verge and the anchor. In the cylinder-escapement the escape-wheel remains locked by the cylinder during the supplementary arc of the balance, whereas in the verge it turns backward with it. The cylinder has, however, the same defect as the verge, in that the escape-wheel is never free and there is constant friction between the nose of the tooth and the inner wall of the cylinder. At that time

---

[1] Invented 1721; published 1726.

this was not a severe disadvantage, as the constant friction tended to equalize the irregularities introduced by the somewhat imperfect balance-springs of the day.

The cylinder-escapement was largely, but not wholly, employed by its inventor and was to a great extent the basis of his great reputation as a watch-maker. It was also fairly widely employed by a few of the better watch-makers in England and on the continent. In the main, however, the cheaper and simpler verge-escapement was standard until the general adoption of the lever escapement in the early nineteenth century.

There are many other escapements, but very few ever established themselves. One, of which a fair number was made for better-class watches, was the *duplex-escapement*, of which the inventor and date of invention are unknown. It was first systematically used by Pierre Leroy in Paris about 1750. This escapement requires a very high standard of workmanship; with that, it yields a very good performance, but as it is sensitive to variations in driving-force its use was confined to the more costly watches incorporating a fusee. The clearances are so fine that any wear on the pivots has an undue effect on the escapement; furthermore, as it is a single-beat escapement, it is liable to stop if subjected to a sudden jerk.

Another clock-escapement, sometimes employed in England but much more generally adopted in France, is the *pin-wheel*, invented about 1745 by the French maker Amant (figure 413). It was later improved by another French maker, Lepaute (1727–1802), who placed the pins alternately on each side of the wheel.

The last escapement to be mentioned is that found today in nearly every watch with any pretension to quality; it is the detached *lever-escapement* (figure 414). It was invented about 1755 by Thomas Mudge, but was not extensively used before the early nineteenth century. Mudge does not seem to have realized the importance of his idea, which was that in this design the escape-wheel is free from any connexion with the watch-train, except for the brief periods when the escape-wheel is locked and when it is receiving its impulse. There are many variants in the minor details of this escapement, but they all conform in its essentials. The form adopted by the Swiss manufacturers and now by the leading English firms, with its jewelled pallets and club-footed escape-wheel teeth, is that most widely used and is therefore the one illustrated.

REFERENCES

[1] ALFONSO OF CASTILE. 'Libros del Saber de Astronomía del Rey Don Alfonso X de Castilla' (5 vols), ed. by M. RICO Y SINOBAS. Madrid. 1864.

[2] HAHNLOSER, R. 'Villard de Honnecourt. Kritische Gesamtausgabe des Bauhüttenbuchs.' Schroll, Vienna. 1935. Eng. trans. from French ed. by R. WILLIS. London. 1859.

[3] MORPURGO, E. *La Clessidra*, **8**, viii, 1952.

[4] BRAHE, TYCHO. *Astronomiae instauratae mechanica*. Wandsburg. 1598.

BIBLIOGRAPHY

BAILLIE, G. H. 'Watches.' Methuen, London. 1929.

Idem. 'Watchmakers and Clockmakers of the World' (2nd ed.). National Association of Goldsmiths' Press, London. 1947.

Idem. 'Clocks and Watches, an Historical Biography.' National Association of Goldsmiths' Press, London. 1951.

BRITTEN, F. J. 'Old Clocks and Watches and their Makers' (6th ed.). Spon, London. 1932. Also: 7th ed. Spon, London. 1956.

CAMERER-CUSS, T. P. 'The Story of Watches.' Macgibbon and Kee, London; Philosophical Library, New York. 1952.

CESCINSKY, H. and WEBSTER, M. R. 'English Domestic Clocks.' Routledge and Kegan Paul, London. 1913.

CHAMBERLAIN, P. M. 'It's About Time.' R. R. Smith, New York. 1941.

GORDON, G. F. C. 'Clockmaking Past and Present' (rev. by A. V. MAY). The Technical Press, London. 1949.

GOULD, R. T. 'The Marine Chronometer.' Potter, London. 1923.

LLOYD, H. ALAN. 'The English Domestic Clock.' Published by the author, London. 1938.

Idem. 'Chats on Old Clocks' (2nd ed.). Benn, London. 1951.

Idem. 'Some Outstanding Clocks over 700 Years: 1250–1950.' Hill, London. 1957.

RAWLINGS, A. L. 'The Science of Clocks and Watches' (2nd ed.). Pitman, London. 1948.

ROBERTSON, J. D. 'The Evolution of Clockwork.' Cassell, London. 1931.

SYMONDS, R. W. 'A Book of English Clocks.' Penguin Books, Harmondsworth. 1947.

Idem. 'Thomas Tompion, his Life and Work.' Batsford, London. 1951.

The earliest printed representation of a mechanical clock. c 1490.

25

INVENTION IN CHEMICAL INDUSTRIES

F. W. GIBBS

I. THE DEVELOPMENT OF CHEMICAL ARTS

THE German physician, Cornelius Agrippa of Nettesheim (1486–1535), told of a proverb current in his day that 'every alchemist is either a physician or a soap-maker'. From this we may gather that alchemists earned their livelihood not by making gold from the baser metals but rather by the practice of medicine or the chemical arts (plate 28). By itself, he inferred, the alchemical art would reduce the true chemist to a 'cacochimick' (charlatan), the physician to a 'fewterer' (greyhound-keeper), and the soap-boiler to the mean trade of meat-seller. On the other hand, he noted, there were many inventions that could be credited to alchemy in its more general sense, such as various colours, dyes, and pigments, latten metal (kinds of brass) and other alloys, methods of tinning and soldering, refining and assaying, the invention of the gun—'a fearful instrument', and the art of glass-making.

The introduction of printing with movable type about 1450 led to a vast increase in knowledge and a quickening of the imagination. The first printed books to treat of chemical invention consisted of gleanings from Pliny and other classical authors made by certain 'great and cunning Clearkes' of the Middle Ages, such as the great encyclopaedia of Bartholomew the Englishman (c 1250). These books continued in use throughout the sixteenth century, but the information they contained was largely that of centuries long past. There was little new in them. As Stillman said, the artisans of the Middle Ages were not writers of books; they were busy perfecting their chemical arts, sometimes indulging in alchemy on the side [1].

Until well into the seventeenth century there were two related movements in the chemical field that have a particular bearing on this subject: (a) attempts to rediscover old arts thought to have flourished in classical times and lost during the interval, and (b) attempts to produce new arts and improvements on the old.

The first of these showed itself in two main ways: first, the searching of classical writers and of manuscripts written by monks who were interested in such arts as limning, painting, dyeing, metal-working, and glass-making, and secondly, the travels through Europe, particularly Germany and Italy, of men qualified to inquire intelligently into, and to record at first hand, the techniques in use in various places. The searching of classical authors resulted in a book on lost arts, together with an account of new inventions not known to the ancients, by Guido Panciroli (1523–99), professor of civil law in Padua University [2]. Such books were a challenge to the age, and, when the work was translated into English in 1715, an account of the great discoveries that had been made since Panciroli's day—and particularly since the middle of the seventeenth century—was added to illustrate the fact that in recent years every science had found its Columbus.

One of the best examples of manuscripts on the arts was the treatise of Theophilus (vol II, p 351), copies of which were in circulation, especially in Germany and Italy, long before the age of printing. His work, for example, is referred to by Agrippa. The most famous book of the second type is the *De re metallica* (1556) of Georg Agricola (1494–1555) [3]. It is clear that much, sometimes all, of the information in books of both kinds was new only in the sense that it had not been available to a wide audience before. Thus most of the processes described by Agricola had been followed for some centuries, while writers making use of Theophilus were at times describing arts commonly practised in the Greek Byzantine period. Several countries and cultures had contributed to the information now being collected and distributed in the sixteenth century. Thus it has been said that Greece had been the painter, Tuscany the enameller, Arabia the worker in metals, Italy the jeweller, France the glassworker, and Spain the chemist, while Germany was anxious to acquire dexterity and knowledge in all these arts.

The second movement—the attempt to introduce new arts and to improve old ones—followed logically enough from the first. In general, however, men of different talents were required, inventors rather than chroniclers, men of 'art' rather than men of 'science'. These terms were in common use and signified something close to practice and theory respectively. When a chemist produced a thing 'by art', it was the result of his skill in chemical processes. Art was therefore not applied science, but a combination of techniques together with the special knowledge of materials gained in handling them. By art, attempts were made to bring about improvements in agriculture, which Samuel Hartlib (c 1599–c 1670) called the 'Mother of all other Trades and Scientificall Industries'. The art of metals, said Sir John Pettus (1613–90), was wholly chemistry. Some maintained that chemistry entered into all practical and 'mechanical' arts (as distinct from the liberal arts).

In the fifteenth century, owing largely to greatly increased demands for spirit of wine for other than medicinal purposes, the art of distillation had made rapid strides (pp 11–12, figures 7, 8). Improved methods were designed for the production of brandy, as also for that of the strong mineral acids needed by assayers and metallurgists (figure 40).

By the middle of the sixteenth century Germany led Europe in the practice of mining and metallurgy, and the Nuremberg area was pre-eminent in the manufacture of all types of metal goods. The great prowess of the Germans in these matters was attributed by Hartlib, in the middle of the seventeenth century, to 'their pertinacious industry in manual experiments, and . . . their great courage in daring to haunt untrodden paths in the quest of nature's secrets'.

The Republic of Venice, on the other hand, held pride of place in the manufacture of glass, especially on the island of Murano (plate 30). Processes were jealously guarded and the movements of workmen were often severely restricted. Thus in 1547 the Council of Ten at Venice had the power to execute any workman from Murano who went elsewhere to teach or practise the secrets of his trade. That Italy no longer enjoyed isolated leadership in the seventeenth century is shown by H. de Blancourt's *Art de la Verrerie* (1697), with its tribute to Colbert (1619–83), the great minister of Louis XIV, who was instrumental in bringing about a revival of French arts and manufactures; by the invention of cobalt blue (zaffre, smalt), soon to become a much-prized article of commerce, by the glass-blower Christoph Schürer of Saxony; and by the fact that flint-glass became known in Italy as *cristallo inglese*. (ch 9).

The fifteenth and sixteenth centuries also saw the rise of numerous majolica factories in central Italy, in which *piombo accordato*, a mixture of lead and tin oxidized together, was added to the alkali-silica mixture for the glaze. This technical secret enabled a large export trade to be developed, and more than thirty majolica factories were opened in Faenza alone between 1530 and 1550. Siena (Montalcino) had a reputation for such wares as well. Work on the production of new colours and enamels was also carried out. Success and secrecy often went together, however, and this sometimes led to the loss of important innovations, such as the new colours for ceramics introduced by the Andreolis of Gubbio (*c* 1500–40), the knowledge of which seems to have died with them. Some of the earliest European porcelain was made at Ferrara (see further in vol IV, ch 11).

The monopoly of the Italians in this field inspired men like Bernard Palissy (*c* 1510–89), the celebrated French potter, to emulate them. Through Palissy especially the ceramic industry outside Italy made considerable progress. His observations in this field, together with his appreciation of the value of chemistry and the experimental method, were given in his *L'Art de err e* [4]. The lasting value of his work is shown by the fact that during the nineteenth century Palissy-ware was imitated widely in England and at the imperial factory at Sèvres.

During the sixteenth century also, after new ocean routes to America and the East Indies had been opened up, there was an increased importation of numerous commodities previously unknown or obtained only in small quantities by overland routes. Many of these, particularly indigo and cochineal, had important applications in dyeing. Improved methods of fixing such colours on cloth were introduced—for example, the judicious use of a solution of pewter in *aqua fortis* for fixing cochineal as a scarlet dye. Italy achieved eminence in dyeing also, and the first textbook on the subject, *Plictho dell' arte de' tentori*, was produced by a Venetian, G. V. Rosetti, in 1540 [5].

II. SCIENCE AND INDUSTRY

During the age of Francis Bacon (1561–1626) the impact of science on the arts began to assume some importance. Bacon, who gave a practical bias to scientific learning, was doubtless influenced by the work of contemporary inventors in London, such as Sir Hugh Platt (1552–1611) and Cornelius Drebbel (1573–1633), the latter an arrival from Alkmaar in Holland.

Platt investigated the use of salt and marl in agriculture, produced fire-proof tubs, contrived fire-balls from small coal with loam as binder (p 80), introduced various new distillations, and made recommendations on chemical processes often carried out in the still-rooms of great houses with the aid of books of secrets such as the innumerable editions and recensions bearing the name of Alexis of Piedmont [6]. Platt also paid attention to the needs of navigators; for example, he made available an oily composition to prevent the rusting of iron-work, and his new kind of pitch was used by Sir Francis Drake on his later voyages. Platt looked into the question of keeping food and water wholesome at sea, and advocated the use of dried foods, such as Italian *pasta*, which would keep for long periods.

Drebbel's inventions were extremely varied and attracted attention throughout Europe. Among them were weapons devised for the Royal Navy, such as the floating petards used off La Rochelle in 1628, a more economical method for making spirit of sulphur, thermostatic controls for chemical furnaces and incubators (figure 415), and new processes for dyeing (p 695).

Bacon, holding that learning was too remote from everyday affairs, called for the collection of abstracts and 'patterns' of experiments from all sources and countries and their study by men skilled in discovering 'axioms' and 'aphorisms' for making further advances. Such studies, he thought, by those who combined practical skill to direct their use with mental perception to assess their value, would be of great advantage to mankind. The organization of this work demanded a society or college, where also the collections could be used for the preparation of a descriptive history of trades.

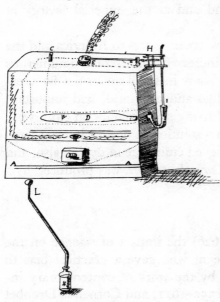

FIGURE 415—*Drebbel's automatic furnace or 'athanor' used as an incubator. The fire-grate (A) is at the bottom, the hot gases passing upwards round the inner box containing the eggs to emerge at E. This inner box is protected by a water-jacket in which is inserted a thermostat (D) filled with alcohol. Mercury fills the U-tube joined to it. As the alcohol expands, the mercury is forced upwards so raising the rod (I), which by means of the levers (H) closes the damper (F). If the heat falls too low, the action is reversed by contraction of the alcohol. The effect of the thermostat is adjusted by a screw at H. Another drawing shows a similar furnace without the water-jacket and with air in place of alcohol in the thermostat. L is an air-thermometer indicating the temperature of the furnace. From a manuscript of 1666. This furnace (not working) was seen by Monconys in 1663. It is perhaps the first example of a 'feed-back' mechanism.*

The 'Verulamian plan', as Bacon's proposals came to be known, stimulated many ideas but led to little immediate benefit. At his death, however, there were at least three young men in their twenties who thought on similar lines. Thus Edward Somerset (1601–67), second Marquis of Worcester, about 1628 employed a German gun-founder, Caspar Kalthoff, to study inventions and to make small-scale models for display to interested people. Sir Nicholas Crisp (c 1599–1666), who almost monopolized the lucrative trade to Guinea, was conspicuous for his interest in the arts and manufactures, giving very large rewards to inventors. He personally studied brick-making and devised a new method that was long used. In 1648 he put forward a scheme for the manufacture of copperas (ferrous sulphate), and introduced economies in the boiling-process. New inventions connected with water-mills, paper-mills, and powder-mills came into use through the knowledge he made available. Third was Samuel Hartlib, the son of a Polish father and English mother, who came to England about 1628 and initiated a kind of mercantile agency and information-exchange, afterwards taking part in many public questions of the day. He also had a plan to publish practical treatises on agriculture and the arts, such as the book by Gabriel Plattes on mines and minerals for prospectors and emigrants to the colonial plantations [7].

During the Civil War Hartlib looked into the possibility of founding a Baconian college, in which John Evelyn (1620–1706), William Petty (1623–97), and Robert Boyle (1627–91) were also interested. All had exceptional talents and the enthusiasm of youth. In 1647 Hartlib approached Boyle about Petty's proposal to found a college of tradesmen and produce a history of trades. A group of men sharing such ideas were then meeting at Gresham College, London, and the time seemed ripe for the venture. However, when Cromwell's army came into London in 1648–9 some of the group moved to Oxford, and before conditions had returned to normal the plan was abandoned.

Nevertheless Petty, the son of a Hampshire clothier, had collected information about textiles and dyeing, and Boyle and Evelyn devoted much time and thought to trade receipts and processes. On the restoration of the monarchy and the foundation of the Royal Society in 1660, many papers on such subjects were read; they were subsequently preserved in the Society's archives.

Several members showed their approval of these inquiries by drawing up lists of manufactures and trades that should be studied. Such drafts were produced independently by Petty, Evelyn, Christopher Merret or Merrett (who translated Neri's *L'Arte vetraria* (p 217)), and Robert Hooke. Of these, Hooke's was the most comprehensive and systematic, and his first item was the 'History of Chymists, either such as make Tryals on Metals, or operate on Mineral, Vegetable, or Animal Substances'. In his manuscript papers Hooke made it clear that he considered the Society's two prime objects to be the improvement of natural knowledge, arts, and manufactures by experiments, and the rediscovery of lost arts and inventions.

Boyle expounded his views on these matters in his essays on the 'Usefulness of Experimental Natural Philosophy' (1663, 1671), and, like Hooke, thought that science and the manufactures both stood to gain from closer contact. Boyle obtained a good deal of information from conversations with craftsmen, and was convinced that much empirical knowledge could thus be collected and used in the development of chemistry as a science. For example, illustrations taken from iron-making, goldsmiths' work, glass-making, soap-boiling, and other similar occupations were used to good effect in his 'Sceptical Chymist' (1661). At about the same time, Otto Tachenius (c 1620–1700), a German chemist who settled at Venice, was among the first to regard salts as formed from acids and alkalis, and he derived his strongest arguments from the practices of glass-makers, soap-boilers, and the like [8].

Books and periodicals assisted the spread of information on the arts and trades that had been brought together during the 1660s. Much of this was published from 1665 in the 'Philosophical Transactions' and in Sprat's 'History of the Royal Society' (1667). John Houghton's collections for the improvement of husbandry and trade (1681–3 and 1692–1703) also helped, for Houghton had the Royal Society's approval and made good use of their material. These news-sheets, he said, were intended to benefit 'not only the Theorical Gentleman, but also the Practical Rustic'. In addition, the first comprehensive dictionaries that set out to include technical information began to appear during this period, such as J. J. Hofmann's *Lexicon universale* (1677) and supplement (1683), T. Corneille's *Dictionnaire des arts et des sciences* (1694), and John Harris's celebrated *Lexicon technicum* (1704).

There were other movements in the chemical field on the continent, and the very influential writings of such men as Glaser (d *c* 1671), Glauber (1604–68), and Lémery (1645–1715) often cast light upon certain processes in the arts; but they also illustrate the close connexion of chemistry with pharmacy and medicine during this period. The works of Becher (1625–82) and Kunckel (*c* 1630–1703), Boyle's most eminent continental contemporaries, contained numerous ideas and observations that were intended for application in the technological field. Both were given to alchemical pursuits, and both were associated with numerous commercial or economic projects, most of which failed. Of the two, Kunckel was the better practical observer, and, like Boyle, made numerous contributions to such arts as engraving, tinning, gilding, varnishing, and glass-making. He spent the years 1679–88 at Berlin in the service of the Elector Frederick William (1640–88) as director of his laboratory and superintendent of the glass-works. His *Ars vitraria experimentalis*, which included the work of Neri and Merret, was published in 1679 (p 222).

In Sweden also the importance of chemistry in the arts was recognized, no doubt through German influence. Attempts were made during the reign of Charles XI to exploit the natural resources of the region with the aid of chemistry. In 1683 the king had a technological laboratory built, which was superintended by Urban Hjärne (1641–1724), assessor and later president of the *Bergcollegiums* in Stockholm. Ores, minerals, soils, and so forth were examined there, and attempts were made to find uses for the various chemical products that could be obtained from them. Charles XI invited Kunckel to Stockholm and created him Baron Löwenstjern in 1693.

One very important result of the widespread study of many manufacturing processes by men of science was the growth of knowledge of ways of testing materials, and this had a considerable effect on the development of chemical analysis. Here Boyle, as well as Kunckel and Homberg (1652–1715), made valuable contributions.

A growing confidence in the experimental method and its beneficent influence on technology was manifested during the second half of the seventeenth century. As Sprat said: 'The genius of experimenting is so much dispersed that . . . all places and corners are busy and warm about this work.' And again: 'This desire of glory, and to be counted Authors [inventors, discoverers], prevails on all, even on many of the dark and reserved Chymists themselves.' In such an atmosphere few important technical discoveries remained hidden for long.

H. de Blancourt admitted that in technological work most improvements resulted from chance observations by men seeking something they could not find. Such discoveries were made, we might say, by 'hazard of Art', for fruitful accidents are fruitful only because those to whom they happen have the knowledge or skill to profit from them. This newly won confidence, however, amounted to a belief that scientific principles could be applied to a great variety of problems. As de Blancourt put it, for those who 'set themselves thoroughly to study the true principles of whatever they undertake, it is not difficult to retrieve lost Arts'.

In the remainder of this chapter selected processes that best seem to characterize the period will be described in greater detail.

III. CHEMICAL INDUSTRIES USING WOOD

Wood, as a source of charcoal, tar, pitch, resin, potash, turpentine, lamp-black, and printers' black, all widely used materials, will be considered first. The favourite trees for these purposes were oak, beech, alder, fir, and pine in the northern countries, and similar processes were employed from the Mediterranean to Norway, from Greece to New England.

In northern Europe three kinds of charcoal (vol II, pp 359, 369) were required, the first, for use in iron-works, being often made from oak and beech. The wood, cut into 3-ft lengths and cleft if necessary to a suitable size, was stacked triangularly about a central pole, smaller pieces being placed around them until the base of the heap was as much as 20 to 30 ft in diameter, the whole being covered with turf, loam, or clay (figure 416). Vent-holes or 'Registers (as our *Chymists* would name them)' were made in the stack with the handles of long-toothed rakes. The central pole was then removed and the 'coaling' begun by building up a fire with burning charcoal added through the central hole. Afterwards the 'coal' was raked into wains, the larger and grosser pieces being taken to the forges, the medium and smoother pieces being sacked by the 'colliers' and taken to the towns. Any 'charked' (charred) roots were reserved 'for *Chymical* fires, and where a lasting, and extraordinary *blast* is required'.

FIGURE 416—*Charcoal-burning.* A, *wood-stack;* B, *preparing the heap of wood;* C, *covering it;* D, *a freshly-lit, and* E, *a nearly burnt-out heap;* F, *uncovering a carbonized heap.*

The second type of charcoal, for use in the gunpowder-mills, was made from alder-wood stripped of its bark and stacked in heaps large enough to provide 60 sacks of 'coal' each. Such charcoal was found to grind best for use in gunpowder. The third kind was made from brushwood and small coppice-wood, which was burnt in the open, the fire being controlled by throwing on water with scoops filled from large tubs standing nearby. This was accounted superior kindling-charcoal and was required in large towns.

Fir and pine were needed especially for the manufacture of tar, pitch, and resin, used as preservatives particularly for timber and ropes and consequently in great demand for shipping. Pieces of wood—the knotty parts of fallen pitch-pine were favoured in heavily wooded areas—of a convenient size were stacked on a hearth built above the ground so that a receiving vessel could be placed underneath, the hearth being shaped somewhat like a shallow funnel ending in a gullet. The wood was then covered with loam or clay and the same procedure followed as for charcoal-making. John Winthrop, who described the process for the Royal Society, pointed out that this was a crude form of distillation *per descensum*, and that it could be done equally well in furnaces (retorts). Though such a furnace—the 'beehive', a simple adaptation of the charcoal-burner's mound—was described by Glauber in 1657, it seems not to have been much used for this purpose, probably because it appeared to be an unnecessary expense (figure 417). When all the tar had run out the remaining charcoal was reserved for the smiths, who preferred this and sea-coal (ordinary coal) to other fuels. Pitch was made by the simple process of boiling the tar until a sample on cooling showed the required consistency. This process, it was found, could be speeded up by adding resin, whereas ship's carpenters sometimes merely heated the tar in an iron kettle, ignited it, and, when the tar had thickened sufficiently, extinguished the fire by covering the kettle.

For resin, the knotty parts of pine were split into thin small pieces and boiled in water, the turpentine gradually thickening and becoming hard on cooling. Tar, pitch, and resin, especially the last of these, were often burnt in a sheltered spot and the soot collected on rags for lamp-black and printer's black.

The use of wood, particularly oak, and of various plants for making potash and soda, will be indicated later, in connexion with glass-making and soap-boiling.

IV. SUBSTITUTES FOR WOOD

During the sixteenth century the widespread consumption of wood for all such purposes created a shortage of timber suitable for ship-building, and this made restrictions imperative. Where coal was abundant, as in parts of England and Wales, attempts were soon made to use it in place of charcoal (ch 3). By 1600 it had been tried in several trades where the presence of acid sulphureous fumes had no deleterious effect, and it had also been used experimentally in Wales for the preliminary roasting of ores. By 1610 coal was sometimes employed as fuel in brick-making, brewing, dyeing, and brass-foundry work. It was also pointed out at this time that coal would be equally satisfactory in boiling and extractive processes, for making copperas, alum, saltpetre, sugar, resin, gum, turpentine, wax, tallow and soap, vegetable oils, and distilled waters. From then on, the use of coal became widespread. Not many years later the coal used by the

FIGURE 417—*Glauber's 'beehive' furnace, and method of collecting wood-tar. 1657.*

brewers, dyers, soap-makers, salt-boilers, and lime-burners of Westminster was creating so much smoke that it penetrated even into the Palace of Whitehall, as John Evelyn tells us in his diary (p 77).

Another approach to the same problem was to economize in fuel. Thus Sir Nicholas Crisp, in Commonwealth times, noted that much was wasted during the concentration of liquids, since it was the practice to pour the cold, weak solution into the tank containing the hot concentrated liquor; he recommended that the steam and waste heat from the latter should be used to warm the weaker solution, which could then be allowed to trickle in without interrupting the boiling. Another help was the inclusion of the fire in a grate surrounded by brick-work, which seems to have been more widely adopted during the latter part of the seventeenth century and enabled some trades previously conducted in the open air to be practised within doors. Fairly early in the next century further improvements in design were suggested; for instance, John Allen or Alleyn (1660?–1741), a Somerset physician and a friend of Newcomen, patented ways of using the hot furnace-gases more effectively and of insulating the boiling-tanks.

Meanwhile various spectacular advances in the use of steam, such as the water-raising machine of Savery and Papin's 'digestor' (a forerunner of the autoclave), caused some technologists to look upon steam-heating as of possible

FIGURE 418—*Desaguliers's scheme for heating boilers, stills, and so forth from a steam boiler.* c *1720.*

use for chemical extractive processes. Desaguliers (1683–1744) and his associates worked out a method about 1720, which showed how useful steam would be for the better control of heating during distillation; for maintaining dyeing-vats at any required temperature; for obviating the very thick and consequently expensive bottoms to boilers used in sugar-refining (figure 4) and soap-boiling, as well as for salt-boiling (during which the bottoms were frequently burnt out) (vol II, figure 324); for the tallow-chandlers, who would welcome a vessel in which steam could mix with the crude tallow; and for reducing hazards in trades where it was necessary to boil such inflammable substances as turpentine, varnishes, and oils. However, from Desaguliers's plan it is evident that much more experience in the manipulation of steam was needed before such projects could be turned to practical use (figure 418).

Among the results of the search for substitutes for wood must be mentioned a unique and successful venture, in which shale was used for the production of 'Oil of Petre' or mineral turpentine, as well as of tar and pitch, first described in

1697 and still being produced as 'British Oil' in the second half of the following century. This was carried out in the neighbourhood of Broseley and Pitchford, near Wenlock in Shropshire (figure 419). The patentee, Martin Eele, collected the bituminous shale found lying over the coal and ground it in horse-mills like those used to grind calcined flints for glass-making. Some was taken to the still-house for the production of oil by distillation, and the rest was boiled with water in large coppers, the bituminous matter separating from it and floating. This was

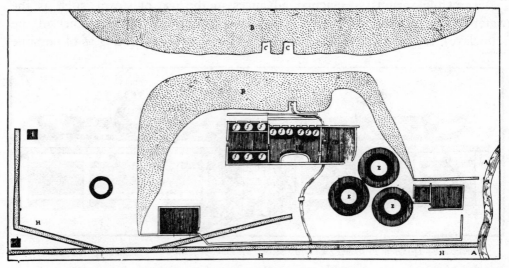

FIGURE 419—*Plant for manufacturing 'oil of petre'.* (A A) *The river Severn;* (B, B) *hills or rocks 'where are coal-pits';* (C, C, C) *the pits whence the stones are taken;* (D) *the storehouse;* (E, E, E) *horse-mills for grinding stones to powder;* (f, f, f) *coppers in which the material is boiled to separate the bituminous material from the stone;* (G) *still-house for distilling the oil;* (H, H) *roads;* (I) *well.*

removed and evaporated until it had the consistency of pitch, when part of it was mixed with the oil already prepared until it had been thinned to the consistency of tar. Eele's pitch and tar were found useful on ships, as they did not crack like wood-pitch and tar but remained relatively soft in use. They were sent by boat down the Severn to Worcester, Gloucester, and Bristol.

Somewhat similar experiments carried out at this time by Thomas Allgood in the Pontypool (Monmouthshire) area resulted in the production of black varnishes that acquired a high lustre after long stoving. These were applied to sheet iron, copper, and tinplate goods, thus ushering in the 'Welsh' lacquer manufacture during the early decades of the eighteenth century.

In the Broseley area further work on the use of coal for roasting iron ore in heaps consisting of alternate layers of ironstone and coal, and on 'charking' coal in mounds resembling those of the charcoal-burners, began probably in the first two decades of that century. These became of considerable importance in the hands of the Darby family (p 80). But the vital progress in this field belongs to a later period, when the coke-oven and the blast-furnace revolutionized iron manufacture. For a considerable part of the century the high sulphur-content rendered coke-iron too brittle to work successfully under the hammer, and it was generally mixed with soft grades of iron before being considered fit for use.

V. MANUFACTURE OF TINPLATE

Another notable advance in the metallurgical field was the British method of production of tinplate, introduced towards the end of this period (figures 420, 421). Early in the sixteenth century the only source of tinned sheet iron was Germany, where it was made on the borders of Saxony and Bohemia by a traditional method. Lengths of bar iron were beaten into sheets under the tilt-hammer, after which scale was removed by long soaking in tubs containing fermented rye-meal infusions of various strengths, the sheets then being rubbed with sand, or filed, and dipped in molten tin covered with grease. In time of war, however, supplies were interrupted and serious attempts were made, particularly in Britain, Sweden, and France, in the 1620s and again in the 1660s, to use home-produced iron and Cornish tin for this purpose. They met with no success, except a partial one in France, where, under Colbert's instructions, a number of Bohemian tinmen and hammermen were enticed to a factory in Nivernais (now the Département de la Nièvre). Here, for a time, by copying the Bohemian process they produced sufficient tinplate to meet the navy's requirements of food-containers and utensils of various kinds. But it was not until the 1720s, some years after Réaumur's inspection of French methods and shortly after his study of the chemical problem of de-scaling, that the French manufacture reached a satisfactory state.

By 1730, however, superior machine-rolled tinplates were being made at Pontypool, a new technological process having been worked out by John Hanbury and his assistant Edward Allgood (p 697). Red-hot bar iron was rolled in several stages to make plates of various thicknesses, this part of the process having been in operation by 1697. It appears that the subsequent stages of de-scaling, annealing, tinning, listing, and cold-rolling were not completely worked out for several years after this. A description of the method as practised some-what later in Yorkshire shows that great care was taken to avoid the production on heating of black scale (which was far more difficult to remove than the red). As the sheet iron came from the rolls it was steeped in a solution of sal ammoniac to remove most of the scale, and subsequently the plates were allowed to stand for some time before tinning in an acid infusion of bran and water (2 bushels to 100 gallons). They were then rinsed, dipped in molten tin covered with train-oil (whale-oil) and resin, and their thick lower edges of surplus tin removed by dipping (listing) in a small quantity of molten tin and wiping with a thumb-

FIGURE 420—*Manufacture of tinplate* (I). (A) *Heating bar iron at a forge with water-driven bellows*, (B) *extending bars by hand-hammering, or at* (C) *by water-powered hammer.* (d, d, d) *Partly extended plates. The extension was continued by long heating and hammering of a stack of plates* (inset).

guard. Irregularities left after handling through a number of stages were evened out by cold-rolling.

VI. MANUFACTURE OF ZINC

Another important and characteristic development of the period was the introduction of metallic zinc. This metal, whose name seems to have been coined by Paracelsus (1493?–1541), was scarcely known until the early seventeenth century, although the name *counterfeht* given to calamine refers to the early use of that ore with copper to make brass, that is, for giving copper the colour of gold (p 37). Because of this property, calamine and zinc itself were for long in great demand by alchemists. During the seventeenth century most of the zinc used was imported by the Dutch from China and the East Indies, and was at first known to them as Indian 'tin' or pewter, whence the English 'spelter'. The silvery appearance of much pewter and tinplate ware after this time appears to have been due to the admixture of a small proportion of zinc with the tin used in both.

The earliest description of the smelting of zinc direct from the ore is said to be that given in the Chinese metallurgical work *T'ien kung k'ai wu* of 1637; the

FIGURE 421—*Manufacture of tinplate* (II). *The plates, roughly cleaned on a grindstone, soak for 24 hours in a solution of fermented rye to remove scale* (C). *They are then cleaned by the women at* (G) *and placed in tubs of water. At* (F) *the plates are dipped in molten tin (covered with tallow to prevent oxidation), first in stacks and then individually. They cool in the rack* (n.)

method was essentially different from that at first developed in Europe. The mineral, presumably mixed with powdered charcoal, was put into earthen pots, which were dried slowly after tight luting. The pots and cakes of charcoal were stacked in alternate layers over wood and the pile was fired to attain a red heat. At the end of the process the pots were broken, the solid masses were removed, and the metal was re-fused and cast into large oblong cakes, in which form it was exported.

Zinc was already associated in the time of Agricola with the mining town of Goslar, west of Halberstadt. A description of 1617 shows that it was regarded as an almost valueless by-product produced during the smelting of silver and lead ores: 'There is formed under the furnace, in the crevices of the walls, where it is not well plastered, a metal which is called zinc or *counterfeht*, and when the walls are scraped the metal falls down into a trough to receive it' [9]. At first it was not much used except by alchemists, but it was known that it made tin more beautiful and that it could be mixed with copper to make brass and other alloys, such as that afterwards known as prince's-metal (pp 30, 37, 51).

The gradual realization of the general usefulness of zinc, however, led to a better method of extraction at Goslar by the early years of the eighteenth century, judging by the first-hand description of the process by Neumann, who pointed out that the metal was obtained not from a zinc ore found at Goslar but from the lead and silver ores of Rammelsberg. During the smelting, zinc vaporized and passed into reservoirs made for the purpose in the front wall of the furnace above the gutter by which the lead was run off. These reservoirs were almost enclosed on the inside by a large flat stone, small chinks being left for the vapour to enter, and by another tightly luted stone on the outside. Throughout the 20-hour fusion the outer parts of these receivers were sprinkled frequently with cold water to cool and condense the fumes. Afterwards the outer stone was hit with an iron rod to loosen the luting, whereupon the molten zinc ran out like mercury. The German zinc was remelted in an iron pot and cast in hemispherical masses. By this time the principles of the process were more clearly understood, and it was realized that the successful extraction of zinc from its ores would depend primarily upon the design of the receivers and on an effective method for condensing the metallic vapour. With this knowledge it became possible, just after the period here considered, to attempt the smelting of zinc direct from calamine.

VII. DYEING AND COLOURING

Another aspect of the search for brighter finishes and livelier colours is shown by developments in dyeing, which has always been regarded as a chemical art. Petty in 1662 made the connexion clear by mentioning in his outline of dyeing such techniques as colouring iron and copper wares black with oil, the varnishing of silver foil to emulate gold, the production of coloured enamels, tinning iron with block tin and sal ammoniac, converting copper with calamine into brass 'and with Zinck or Spelter into Gold', that is, to a golden colour [10].

At this time the favourite dyes were madder, kermes, and cochineal (reds), woad, indigo, and logwood (blues), archil or *oricello* (purple), weld, wood-wax, and 'old fustic' (yellows). Great difficulty was experienced in dyeing a fast green. Petty noted that no simple green dye had in his time come into general use, and the position remained unchanged for another century. The best was 'sap green', obtained particularly by country people from unripe buckthorn (*Rhamnus catharticus* L) berries crushed in water, the infusion being evaporated to the consistency of honey. Otherwise, textiles were first dyed blue and then yellow, or vice versa.

By 1500 instructions for cultivating madder (*Rubia tinctoria*) had been published in Holland, and for the next 300 years the Dutch (Flemish) retained their position as the most advanced growers in the world, meeting little competition

FIGURE 422—*Tropical indigo manufactory. 1694.* (A) *The white overseer;* (B) *cutting the indigo-plant;* (C) *infusing it in water;* (D) *carrying away the dye.*

until the beginning of the eighteenth century when the plant was much grown in parts of France. The use of alum as a mordant for wool, as also for producing the much-favoured Turkey-red colour on cotton, was essential. After dyeing, the articles were immersed in bran-water, the starch of which, according to Petty, helped to fix the colour.

The Dutch imported indigo direct from India, whence they had obtained it since about the fourteenth century. Its production was not well understood, however (figure 422). After 1600 larger quantities were brought to Europe by sea, and it was sometimes known as 'blue ynde' or 'devil's dye'. During the seventeenth century woad (*Isatis tinctoria*) was still widely used as an alternative, or even in preference, as it could produce a variety of shades from light blues to damson.[1] A scale was used to compute the ingredients necessary to produce any required shade. Logwood, like most woods that yield dyes, was chopped and ground before use, and the fabrics were boiled with the dye in rain- or river-water for as long as necessary. This made it unsuitable for wool and for articles that would suffer damage by such treatment. Woad and indigo were popular as they required no alum or other mordant; in fact, Petty stated that alum was not then used with either (vol II, pp 364-5).

Though safflower (*Carthamus tinctorius*) and turmeric (from Indian species of *Curcuma*) are sometimes thought of as the yellow dyes of this period, they had largely been superseded, at least in England, by weld or dyer's rocket (*Reseda luteola* L), much grown in Kent for the London dyers, wood-wax or dyer's green-weed (*Genista tinctoria*), and the misleadingly named 'old fustic' (*Chlorophora tinctoria*), from the West Indies and tropical America. Weld was set with potash to give a deep lemon colour, and wood-wax with potash or urine to give a similar result. Shades as light as straw could be obtained with old fustic used with slaked lime. Safflower gave orange shades with alkalis.

Other plant dyes for which there was some demand included brasil and annatto (or arnotto). Brasil was chopped and ground and used with alum for reds; potash was also added for purples. Annatto, from the tropical American tree *Bixa orellana*, was later known as a yellow-brown dye, but an early variety gave an orange colour when used with potash on silk, linen, and cotton. 'Young fustic' (Venetian sumach) which is not less ancient that the 'old fustic', was also used similarly for orange shades.

Lichens, as well as larger plants, were brought into service. Archil, from species of *Roccella* and *Lecanora*, was imported to Florence from the Near East, and for a considerable time the European trade in it was a monopoly of the Italians. English, Flemish, and German cloth-merchants and dyers were forced to buy it from them in the form of *oricello* dye-paste. Archil lichens were discovered on the Canary Islands in 1703, but even then could not be used until the formula for preparing the paste was divulged, so it is said, by a Florentine cloth-dyer working in London. The powdered dried plant was mixed with stale urine and lime and used with alum for dyeing silk and wool in violet shades. Some other lichens were also used in England and Flanders.

There were several methods for dyeing black, but the most common and perhaps the most successful was to use a solution of copperas (p 680) with added galls, oak-bark, or sawdust. A large amount of copperas was used for this purpose.

---

[1] Woad and indigo plants both yield the same dyestuff, indigo or indigotin ($C_{16}H_{10}N_2O_2$).

Insect dyes (vol II, p 366), such as kermes (*Coccus ilicis*), from Anatolia, and cochineal (*Coccus cacti*), were also in demand, particularly the latter, obtained from Spanish America and named after the Spanish word *cochinilla*. Spain organized its collection under Cortez in the first half of the sixteenth century, and it gradually displaced kermes. The cochineal-culture was centred in Mexico for nearly 400 years until rendered unprofitable about 1880 by the advent of synthetic dyes.

The use of cochineal, by itself somewhat uninspiring though producing attractive 'incarnadines' (pinks) with lemon-juice, received a great stimulus when it was discovered that pewter in *aqua fortis* (nitric acid) turned the red dye into a bright scarlet (p 679). Petty called it a change from 'red rose-crimson to flame colour'. Cornelius Drebbel and his sons-in-law, the Kuffler brothers, developed the process and used it first at Stratford (Bow). The Kufflers' dyeworks dates back to 1607, and cochineal scarlet ('Bow dye' or 'the new scarlet') was already becoming known in the 1620s. The solution was made by dissolving bars of pewter in *aqua fortis*, and the dyeing-kettles were also of pewter. It seems that the effect was ascribed to the *aqua fortis* rather than to the tin of the pewter, for one consequence was that saltpetre (the source of *aqua fortis*) was used by some dyers in an attempt to brighten other colours, by a process of 'back-boiling', though argol (tartar deposited from fermented wines) was also commonly employed to the same end [10].

The Kufflers did not form a company to commercialize their discovery till about 1635. By 1647 Jacob Kuffler was dyeing scarlet in Leiden, the method having been introduced there about 1620 by Van der Heyden, and other members of the Kuffler family formed a company about 1654 to use the process near Arnhem. Abraham Kuffler remained at Bow, and in 1656 Johannes Kuffler left Holland to take over the works. Shortly after 1660 the process was introduced to France at the celebrated *Maison des Gobelins* by Jean Gluck, who is thought to have obtained the method from Gilles Kuffler in Amsterdam. The discovery, which created a deep impression, was regarded as an outstanding achievement.

Further details concerning vegetable and insect dyes are given in vol V, ch 12.

VIII. VARNISHING, JAPANNING, AND LACQUERING

As already noted, dyeing suggested more than the colouring of textiles and in its widest sense the term was sometimes applied to the colouring of metal or wooden objects with varnishes and enamels. The latter, in turn, linked up with the manufacture of glass and glazed pottery, a field where technology and art meet. As in dyeing, so in varnishing and lacquering; a great deal of experiment was carried out with new materials, and from it new methods emerged. Varnishes to protect leather (vol II, figure 146), paintings, and woodwork had been made for a considerable time from drying-oils (turpentine or boiled linseed-oil) mixed with gums or resin and occasionally with colouring-matter. However, the lacquered wares of China, and, to a far less extent, of Japan, were imported in ever-increasing quantities during the seventeenth century, and they showed the possibilities of brilliantly finished and artistically decorated goods of all kinds, from trinkets and snuff-boxes to bedsteads and coaches, to a degree then unknown in the west. The supply, particularly of the Japanese wares, remained far less than the demand, and between 1660 and 1675 the new trade of japanning arose, first in Paris, then in London, and soon afterwards in Holland and Germany. To these developments several men of science contributed, including Boyle, Evelyn, Lémery, and Kunckel.

In the Far East lacquer was prepared from the sap of the varnish-shrub (*Rhus vernicifera*) by a traditional process that remained a carefully guarded secret until the middle of the eighteenth century. The early European wares, on the other hand, though termed 'japan' and imitating goods that more frequently came from Amoy and later Canton in China, were decorated with varnishes based on Indian shellac (vol II, p 362) and other gums in spirit of wine or oils. Boyle directed attention to an account by the Dutch traveller Van Linschoten of the Indian method of lacquering with shellac, and he tested various mixtures of shellac with spirit of wine and colours, as well as yellow varnishes, to give silver foil the appearance of gold, for application either to metals or to leather. The celebrated 'English' varnish, giving the appearance of gold to silver foil used to decorate coaches (vol II, p 174), was later attributed to Evelyn.

Before japanning became common, the favourite decoration was the mottled finish known as 'tortoise-shell', generally produced on yellow, red, or silver grounds. For the yellow and red, ochre and vermilion were ground with a little oil and added to the varnish. The object was given four or five coats of this preparation, drying after each application. Two coats of clear varnish were applied, and the object was then clouded over with darker varnish containing ivory black and dragon's blood, a red resin obtained from the Malayan rattan palm, *Calamus draco*. After anything up to ten applications of thin, clear varnish to give body and transparency, the work was smoothed by rubbing with Dutch rushes and a little water, then polished with tripoli on a wet cloth and, after washing and drying, finished off with a little oil on a clean cloth. For tortoise-shell on a silver ground, the object was first primed with whiting and gum arabic to receive the silver leaf. After silvering, two coats of the purest varnish containing a little dragon's blood and gamboge were applied, giving a golden colour. The surface was then clouded over and finished in the same way as the others.

Such methods were useful on all kinds of furniture and wooden objects, and also for embossed work, in which portions of the surface were raised with a thick cream of whiting and strong gum-arabic water. Apart from this, however, there was a growing demand also for similar effects on metal-work, and here the techniques were not so satisfactory, mainly because the varnish was liable to flake, although high polishes could be obtained. Despite this apparent disadvantage, such methods were practised in France.

In other parts of Europe, those wishing to varnish metals, particularly to imitate the more severe black-and-gilt articles associated with Japan, avoided shellac and spirit of wine lacquers and any form of priming other than polishing the metal surface. For such purposes linseed-oil was boiled with a gum or resin in a glazed pot with cover, through which a broad-ended stick was passed for stirring. Before use, the varnish was strained through a linen bag pressed between boards or iron plates. Lamp-black was frequently added to the varnish for initial coats, and ivory black for final coats. Other ingredients, such as litharge, were added to assist the drying of linseed-oil, at first apparently in making gold size.

By the early eighteenth century the art of lacquering iron and copper with japans that would resist rough treatment, acids, heat, and spirit of wine had come into being. How or when it began is obscure, but the innovations were sometimes attributed to Kunckel and Boyle. Wooden articles were placed in a declining oven, that is, one losing its heat, so as to avoid spoiling the work while at the same time hardening the varnish. Metal objects, however, could be stoved for longer periods and at gradually increasing temperatures, and this was done by the Allgoods in Monmouthshire. According to Kunckel, linseed-oil was boiled with umber until it became very brown and thick. After straining, it was again boiled until it became like pitch. This material could be thinned with turpentine to give a black varnish in a hot stove, or could be laid over a vermilion ground for tortoise-shell. For ordinary black japan, the object could be covered over with drying-oil and, when nearly dry, stoved at sufficient heat to blacken it without blistering. Afterwards the heat could be augmented, and the longer it was maintained the stronger became the coating.

Several of those occupied with the chemical arts were also interested in the preparation of artists' colours from vegetable materials and of coloured enamels for potters and goldsmiths. Two methods are especially worthy of mention—preparing coloured lakes with alum, and the use of calcined lead and tin as a basis of enamels. The former is exemplified by the yellow lake obtained from broom flowers, though many others were similarly treated. Fresh blooms were first boiled with a strong lye of barilla (soda) (vol II, p 354). The remains of the flowers were then removed and the extract was concentrated by boiling in glazed earthen dishes, after which roche alum (vol II, p 368) was added to complete. The mixture was then emptied into a vessel of clean water, and after a time the yellow lake settled at the bottom. The liquid was decanted off, and the colour spread on pieces of white cloth on bricks in the shade to dry.

IX. ENAMELLING

By the seventeenth century jewellers' enamels were made by calcining together a quantity of lead and a slight excess by weight of tin, after which the calx was ground to a fine powder and repeatedly boiled in water and decanted until no more powder was carried away (plate 29). It was then dried and the whole process carried out again. After evaporation to dryness, the finer calx (*piombo accordato*) at the bottom was collected and added to the mixture of white sand and purified alkali used to make crystal glass. The ingredients were mixed well and heated in an earthen pot for ten hours. The frit was then powdered and kept dry. This preparation was used as the basis of coloured enamels, the most common colouring materials being *crocus martis* (anvil scale), calcined brass, zaffre or smalt (cobalt minerals), and manganese dioxide. The pigments, having been powdered, ground, and put through a fine sieve, were thoroughly mixed with the powdered frit and heated in white-glazed pots. After thorough fusion proofs were made on small white-enamelled plates kept for the purpose and placed in a small oven resembling a goldsmith's muffle-furnace (figure 33). The shade was then adjusted as necessary by adding more of the frit or more of the colouring-powder.

X. MANUFACTURE OF GLASS

Numerous recipes for making glass (ch 9) were collected by Neri in his classical book on this subject (1612) [11], which was used until after the middle of the eighteenth century, with some additions by successive English, German, and French translators such as Merret, Kunckel, and de Blancourt [12]. In these books one can see the change from recipe-collection to a search for principles and a more scientific approach to manufacturing problems. During this period the need for better-quality and more transparent glass became acutely felt, for, as Merret pointed out in 1662, glass was then required not only for drinking-vessels, bottles, dishes, sleek-stones for pressing linen, hour-glasses and household ornaments, beads, bracelets, and pendants, but for special purposes, particularly windows, lenses for microscopes and telescopes, glass apparatus for experiments (figure 373), burning-glasses, and triangular glasses (prisms)

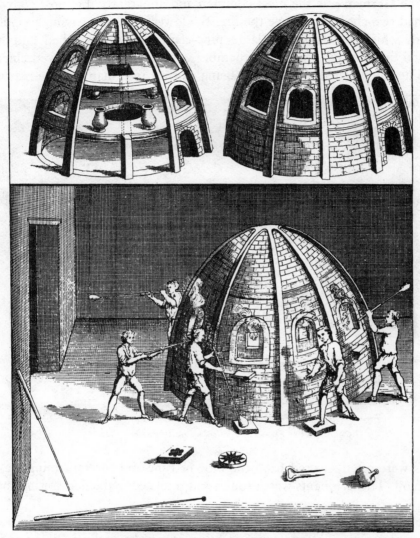

FIGURE 423—*The German glass-furnace. 1752.*

for studying optics (plate 30). Good glass was needed also to provide convex spectacles for the aged and concave for the purblind (near-sighted) as well as transparent eye-shields for engravers and jewellers. Towards the end of that century artificial eyes, coloured with fine threads of enamel, were being made.

Three types of glass-furnace were recognized, the Italian, the Amsterdam, and the German (the last having been described by Agricola) (figures 423, 424). Of these the German was the most common and apparently the most convenient. This had two chambers above the fire, the lower generally having six openings through which the fusion in large pipe-clay pots was watched and 'metal' obtained for blowing; the upper chamber, which was cooler, served chiefly for annealing the finished wares. After being worked into shape by the master, the

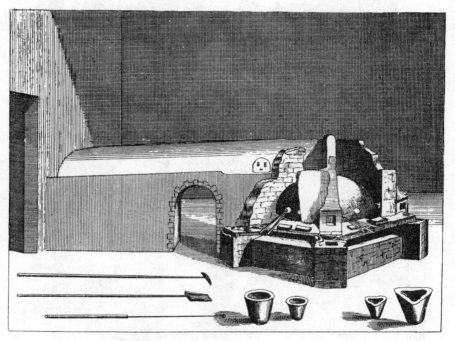

FIGURE 424—*The Amsterdam glass-furnace. 1752.*

objects were often sheared from the pipe or cane and the remaining glass was broken off. The fragments were ground and returned to the pots for use in green glass.

The ingredients of glass were potash or soda, obtained from numerous locations and a great variety of plant sources and thus of various qualities (figure 425), and sand, under which heading were included the stones known to the German miners as quartz, the flints of English glass-makers, and generally any other stones that could be fairly readily powdered after calcination, provided they did not form a soft powder resembling lime. Allowing for all the possibilities of variations under these two heads, and for various colours, it appears that three main

FIGURE 425—*The manufacture of potash.*

kinds of glass were produced, depending primarily on the purity of the materials. The coarsest, green glass, was made from ordinary sand (obtained by the London makers from Woolwich) and unleached ashes, to which were added scrap 'metal' such as ground cullets. On fusion the floating impurities (known as sandiver) were skimmed off, and sometimes the frit was thrown into water to free it from further impurities. The glass was then collected, ground, and re-fused. A better variety, white glass, was made from sand and the best-quality ashes, such as polverine imported from the Levant or barilla obtained from Spain. The resulting white glass, though scarcely transparent, and blue-tinged if made from the Spanish ashes, did not require water-treatment. Special varieties, such as crystal- or flint-glass, were made only with the best materials. Thus in the mid-seventeenth century the London makers used 'salt of polverine' or purified barilla (that is, the alkali obtained by leaching the best ashes, filtering and evaporating, drying and calcining, and finally grinding to powder) mixed with the best white sand (obtained from Maidstone) or with pulverized calcined flint.

The success of the crystal-glass makers depended on their skill in purifying the alkali and on efficient grinding. Ten parts of crude alkali and one of calcined tartar were boiled in copper tanks, preferably lead-lined, like those used by the dyers (plate 31). After half the water was boiled away, the strong lye was left to settle for several days and the clear solution was decanted into earthen vessels. The more careful glass-makers carried this out three times. The solution was then returned to the cleaned boiler and evaporated until it started to 'spit', when the drying was completed in wooden containers. The 'salt' was then dried off completely in the furnace and broken up by grinding. During the seventeenth century the amounts of materials used increased considerably, and the pots were made to hold up to 2 cwt of melt. For this reason stone mortars for grinding gave place to the horse-mill, which consisted of a marble stone about 10 in thick and 7–8 ft in diameter turning on a hard marble floor. One horse turning such a mill could grind as much as 20 men using mortars.

Though there were many special and often secret mixtures, there were in fact relatively few basic colouring-materials. The colours were first ground and put through a fine sieve, and then fusion was carried out in a furnace distinct from that used for crystal. Further, a separate pot was kept for each colour and used only for that. Sea-green, the principal colour, was obtained by means of calcined brass and a fourth part of zaffre. A deeper green was produced by using *crocus martis* in place of zaffre. The principal blue was made by adding calcined sea-salt to the sea-green mixture, and a deep blue by zaffre alone. Darker shades were obtained with more colouring-matter and manganese ore (found near lead ores, such as those mined on Mendip, Somerset). Manganese was commonly known as 'pottern ore', being used by the Delft-ware makers to colour black, as zaffre was to produce blue pottery, glass, and artificial sapphires.

Though smalt and zaffre were so highly prized and widely used, they were obtainable only from Saxony, and their composition was for long unknown. The earliest accurate description appears to be that of Martin Lister, written for the Royal Society and found among Hooke's papers. Lister said that it was made from the ore called cobalt dug up at Schneeberg in Misnia, a province then under the Duke of Saxony. After heating the ore in a reverberatory furnace to drive off the arsenic, it was crushed in a stamp-mill and afterwards calcined, ground, and put through a sieve provided with a cover to hold down the dust. It was then mixed with fine quartz and allowed to harden in barrels. This *zoffloer*, as the miners called it, was broken up with sledge-hammers before sale or export. To make smalt the calcined cobalt was mixed with sand and potash and fused to give a dark glass, which was ground between very hard stones.

XI. SOAP-MAKING

Dyeing and glass-making were not the only trades consuming considerable amounts of potash and soda at this time; the soap-boilers probably used even more, and it is likely that the trade in imported ashes began in order to supply their needs. Kelp and home-made potash, together with lime, were also used. By 1500 the manufacture of soap had already been established for some centuries, a variety of fats and oils being boiled with a lye made from moistened alkali mixed with quicklime (figure 426). Tallow-soaps were more common in northern Europe, whereas olive-oil soaps were made in Spain, France, and Italy. Bristol, Coventry, and London had been early centres for the former, whereas the latter were made and exported particularly by Venice, Savona, Genoa, Castile, and later Marseilles. A black soap was made from the residues of lamp-oil at Amiens and Abbeville in Picardy. Tradition, however, was changing at the beginning of this period, for a London account of the trade in about 1500 shows that the soap of commerce, sold in 30-gallon barrels, was made from tallow and olive-oil from Seville, imported ashes, and unslaked lime. On the other hand, writers like Alexis of Piedmont [6] gave recipes for making soaps from suet and deer's grease heated with caustic alkali.

Soap-boilers were to be found wherever oils, fats, and alkalis were readily available: it was said that every citizen of Bristol was or had been a soap-boiler. The trade also extended to places where native soda could be had from the land merely for the taking. Thus in the seventeenth century it was reported that at Smyrna 10 000 quintals of oil were used annually for soap-making, 1500 camels being used for 8 months of the year to transport 'soap earth' (probably natron or trona, sodium sesquicarbonate) to the boiling-house. This earth was collected in the early morning from the plains near the river Hermus, some miles to the north. The lixivium was formed by mixing three parts of the 'earth' with one of lime and boiling.

In general the lye for soap was made in the way described by Tachenius [8]. Ashes were placed in barrels or troughs, moistened, covered with unslaked lime,

FIGURE 426—*General view of a soap-works. At the rear, the boilers with containers for oil and lye.* (Left) *Weighing and carrying out cakes of soap, and tables on which the hot soap cools and sets;* (right) *splitting wood, making and boiling the lye;* (centre) *packing soap.*

and left for a time. They were then mixed together, water was poured over them, and the lixivium was run off as soon as it was strong enough to float an egg. A second, weaker lixivium was then obtained by adding more water. This second lye was boiled with the oil or fat until a curd formed, when the stronger lye was added, roughly in the proportion of three parts to one of oil, and boiling was continued until the curd became compact and apparently homogeneous. A crude test was then used to ascertain whether or not the proportions had been correct. If the product was sweet to the taste, more alkali was added, and if biting, more oil was poured in to use up the excess alkali. The curd was then set out on platforms or in boxes until it was dry enough to be packed into barrels.

Though the preparation of the caustic lye was conducted with care, the strength of the alkali was not measured with any exactness, nor was there any attempt to determine the relative quantities of alkali and fat to be used in any one boiling. The need for better control of the process was, indeed, realized by the end of the period, but in general chemists were unable to make any considerable contribution until late in the eighteenth century. Thus no great advances could be expected. Nevertheless, other sources of oils were now becoming significant. Whale-oil was obtainable in quantity from the fleets working off Greenland, and fish-oil from other ships sailing to the fishing-grounds off Newfoundland. In earlier centuries supplies of these oils were limited, but when they became cheap enough the soap-boilers were not slow to make use of them; the products were, however, unsuitable for many purposes, such as cleaning wool, owing to their offensive odour. So close did the connexion between these trades become that in 1674 a co-partnership was formed in Glasgow for carrying on both the whale-fishing and the soap-boiling. It also seems to have been known that it was advantageous to add salt to the cauldron towards the end of the boiling-process, thus allowing the soap to separate out better and to become more compact. The true salting-out process, however, with quantitative control, was not introduced until towards the end of the eighteenth century.

Owing to the great variety of materials used, commercial soap varied from white to black, from hard lumps to soft paste, from Castile soap of good quality to the crude product from unpurified whale-oil. Clearly few of these products were suitable for domestic and personal uses without further treatment, but during this period there was a growing demand for domestic soaps, and many recipes were published to enable them to be made in the kitchens or still-rooms of great houses. They appear to have been introduced first at Naples and Venice, common hard olive-oil soap being grated, mixed with scented waters, and rolled into compact balls. Other domestic soaps were made from 2 parts of potash (that from poplar-wood was sometimes deemed best) and 1 part of quicklime, 8 potfuls of lye of the usual strength being employed to every potful of melted strained suet or kitchen grease. The mixture was heated almost to seething in a large-bottomed vessel lined with lead, and was then left in the sun for a week, being stirred at intervals until it formed a paste. Musk-rose water was added, and the mixture left in the sun for a further week, after which it was rolled into balls and kept lying in waste cotton or wool in a wooden box. Other varieties made from olive-oil were frequently perfumed with powder of violets and spices.

XII. CONCLUSION

The types of chemical industry discussed in this chapter have not included the manufacture of basal chemicals, such as acids, alkalis, and salts. At this time such materials were usually made by those who required them as the need arose, or obtained in relatively small quantities from 'chymists', namely, those skilled in chemical preparations. The large-scale production of these raw materials of modern industry belongs to a later period. There were some exceptions, notably alum, saltpetre, and copperas, which were purified by crystallization before sale, but the methods by which they were made had undergone little change throughout the centuries, and they do not afford very instructive examples of advances in chemical technology. Thus some of the fullest accounts of the preparation of acids and salts are to be found in treatises on metals, and that of alkalis in descriptions of soap-boiling and glass-making. Frequently such preparations were regarded as normal parts of manufacturing processes and they were sometimes tedious, particularly if pure substances were required. Improved methods for the distillation of strong acids for use by assayers were introduced, but success often required painstaking care. For example, *aqua fortis* was made by distilling a mixture of nitre or saltpetre and calcined vitriol, but the directions often include the manual separation of salt and similar impurities from the former to avoid producing an *aqua regia* (mixture of nitric and hydrochloric acids). The latter was, indeed, made by adding salt (sal ammoniac was apparently used in Italy) to *aqua fortis* and redistilling. The vitriol was also required to be as pure as possible, and the varieties obtained from Hungary and Goslar were especially recommended. Though alum could be used instead of the various vitriols, its high water-content made the calcination more costly and it was therefore avoided.

By 1730 the point had been reached where science, and particularly chemistry, could begin to give a lead in several manufactures. Before this time one may generalize by saying that trade practices were ahead of the science. Nevertheless, many were already looking to men of science to introduce novel methods and processes, and even the critics of science seem to have assumed that this should be so, though bemoaning the fact that results had not yet come up to expectations. Thus in 1724 Bernard Mandeville (1670?–1733), referring to the 'perfections' that had been reached in several trades, claimed that 'the many improvements, that can be remembered to have been made in them have for the generality been owing to persons who either were brought up to, or had long practised and been conversant in those trades, and not to the great Proficients in Chymistry or other Parts of Philosophy, whom one would naturally expect those things from' [13]. In the later volumes of this work there will be much greater evidence than could be produced here of the power of science to minister to the needs of industry.

NOTE ON THE PAINTINGS FROM THE PALAZZO VECCHIO, FLORENCE

THE paintings from the Palazzo Vecchio reproduced as plates 28–31 are some of the wall decorations in the study of Francesco I de' Medici, planned by Vasari and completed in the period 1570–2. This study is a recess entered by a door from the Great Hall, and two secret passages within lead from it to the treasure-room of Cosimo I, likewise built by Vasari in 1559–62. Francesco, it is said, loved alchemy and the mysteries of nature.

The pictures are held to represent the best work of the late Florentine School. There is a double series of paintings round the room, the lower frieze being movable and arranged so as to conceal cabinets and safes. The four paintings used here are from the upper frieze, and there is some reason to suppose that they were meant to portray the arts as then practised. Cavalori, for instance, who painted the wool-dyeing scene, was the son of a dyer living a short distance from Florence, near Sant' Ambrogio. The much-travelled Dutch artist, Jan van der Straat, painted the so-called alchemist, or maker of distilled waters, extracts, and chemical preparations. This was based on an earlier engraving (vol II, plate 42 B).

REFERENCES

[1] STILLMAN, J. M. 'The Story of Early Chemistry', p. 184. Appleton, New York and London. 1924.

[2] PANCIROLLUS, GUIDO. *Rerum memorabilium sive deperditarum* and *Nova reperta, sive rerum memorabilium recens inventarum et veteribus incognitarum.* Amberg. 1599.

[3] AGRICOLA, GEORGIUS. *De re metallica libri XII.* Froben, Basel. 1556.

[4] PALISSY, B. "De l'art de terre, de son utilité, des émaux, et du feu" in 'Les œuvres de Bernard Palissy' (ed. by A. FRANCE). Paris. 1880.

[5] ROSETTI, G. V. 'Plictho dell' Arte de' Tentori.' [? Venice. 1540.]

[6] ALESSIO PIEMONTESE (Ps.). 'Secreti del . . . Alessio Piemontesi.' Venice. 1555.

[7] PLATTES, G. 'A Discovery of Subterraneall Treasure.' London. 1639.

[8] TACHENIUS, O. *Hippocrates chimicus.* Brunswick. 1668.

[9] LÖHNEISS, G. E. VON. 'Gründlicher und außführlicher Bericht von Bergwercken.' Zellerfeld. 1617.

[10] PETTY, SIR WILLIAM. "An Apparatus to the History of the Common Practices of Dyeing" in T. SPRAT, 'The History of the Royal Society of London' (3rd ed.), pp. 284–306. London. 1722.

[11] NERI, A. 'L'Arte Vetraria.' Florence. 1612. Eng. trans. with additions by C. MERRETT. 'The Art of Glass.' London. 1662.

[12] M. D. [HOLBACH, J. BARON DE]. 'Art de la verrerie.' Paris. 1752.

[13] MANDEVILLE, B. 'The Fable of the Bees', p. 152. London. 1724.

BIBLIOGRAPHY

AGRICOLA, GEORGIUS. *De re metallica*, Eng. trans. and comm. by H. C. HOOVER and LOU H. HOOVER. Dover Publications, New York. 1950.

DAWKINS, J. M. 'Zinc and Spelter.' Zinc Development Association, Oxford. 1950.

EVELYN, J. '*Fumifugium*; or, the inconvenience of the aer and smoak of London dissipated, together with some remedies humbly proposed.' London. 1661. (Old Ashmolean Reprints, Oxford. 1930.)

FORBES, R. J. 'A Short History of the Art of Distillation.' Brill, Leiden. 1948.

JENKINS, R. 'Collected Papers.' University Press, Cambridge. 1936.

LEGGETT, W. F. 'Ancient and Medieval Dyes.' Chemical Publishing Company, New York. 1944.

LI CH'IAO-P'ING. 'The Chemical Arts of China.' Published by the Journal of Chemical Education, Easton, Pa. 1948.

PLATT, SIR HUGH. 'Delightes for Ladies' ed. by G. E. FUSSELL and K. R. FUSSELL. Crosby Lockwood, London. 1948.

SALZMAN, L. F. 'English Industries of the Middle Ages' (new ed.). University Press, Oxford. 1923.

SINGER, C. 'The Earliest Chemical Industry.' The Folio Society, London. 1948.

STILLMAN, J. M. 'The Story of Early Chemistry'; see esp. ch. "The Progressive Sixteenth Century." Appleton, New York and London. 1924.

TIERIE, G. 'Cornelis Drebbel.' H. J. Paris, Amsterdam. 1932.

EPILOGUE

THE RISE OF THE WEST

A. R. HALL

I. CHANGING INDUSTRY

IN the *Epilogue* to volume II (pp 756–71), attention was drawn to the technological superiority of the east over the west throughout the classical period, and during the greater part of the Middle Ages. The eastern, Greek portion of the Roman Empire certainly developed higher skills than did the western, Latin portion; and very possibly the civilization of remote China was more technically accomplished than that surrounding the Mediterranean basin, with which volume II was chiefly concerned. Such broad comparisons between two very different cultures cannot yet be made with absolute confidence, or in great detail; it is certain, however, that before the close of the Middle Ages the balance began to swing, and the technological superiority of western Europe to emerge. Many aspects of the movement, which was founded on the twin processes of transmission and invention, are discussed in the second volume and in various chapters of this one.

In the period treated in the present volume the dominance of the west was confirmed. It is true that political reflection of the economic and technological importance of Europe was delayed: the last Turkish siege of Vienna occurred as late as 1683, and by about the same date Europeans had established their rule overseas only in the East and West Indian islands, at a few points on the coast of India, and sparsely in North and South America. Mass emigration from Europe did not begin until after 1800. In the sixteenth and seventeenth centuries Europeans sailed their ships and carried their trade over the oceans of the world; they left home for South America or the Indies to make their fortunes; but they seldom intended to settle in distant lands, or to establish their industries there. Only in Central and North America was there a considerable population of European descent. Yet if the role of the European in Asia was still limited to that of the merchant, it was one from which he could not be displaced. Conscious of their unassailable position, merchants demanded commercial privileges, and disputes over them often led to wars. From military victories followed the necessity to assume administrative and political authority.

Thus, granted the immense European naval and military superiority, European control of the Far East was an almost inevitable consequence of Europe's commercial intrusion in the fifteenth century. Conquest, like missionary effort, was an aspect of the boundless energy of the west.

It was the western ascendancy in warlike affairs, ship-building, and navigation that first impinged upon the east. Western manufactures could tempt the primitives of Africa and the Americas, but they were as yet neither so excellent nor so cheap as to commend themselves highly to the civilized peoples of India and China. Indeed, eastern wares were acquired with bullion rather than by exchange of goods, and the craftsmanship of the east had greater influence on that of Europe than vice versa. Through their combination of artistic delicacy and technological refinement, certain products of the east—of the past rather than the present—are still unsurpassed. This brings out an important point in the history of technology, which is particularly relevant to the present period, namely that, in certain kinds of work, art and technique are inseparable. We cannot, in appraising a Chinese porcelain dish, divorce our admiration of the potter's sense of form, colour, and line from our wonder at his mastery of the wheel, of pigments and glazes, and of furnace control, without which artistic sense alone would be frustrated. Conversely the most developed engineering, chemical, and pyrometric skills cannot supply a want of artistry in design. While, therefore, it is obvious that many kinds of manufacture of high artistic merit would be unattainable without a certain minimum degree of technical proficiency—such as ancient goldsmith's work (vol I, ch 23, vol II, ch 13), or medieval ceramics (vol II, ch 8) and silks (ch 8)—it is also true that when advance to a yet more developed stage of technology occurs, it is likely to take place (as J. U. Nef has pointed out in chapter 3) in industries where quality is less important than quantity, beauty than serviceability.

There are several good reasons why this should be so. As in the fine arts, at the highest level of craftsmanship—working in gold or ivory or porcelain, for example—the personal contribution of the designer is so great that it is difficult to see how it can be replaced: moreover, the exceptional craftsman is likely to be more conservative in his methods than the ordinary artisan. Technological advances are usually directed towards the standardization and repetition of a good article in large numbers; but the rarity of works of exceptional craftsmanship is part of their virtue. For the same reason there is less significance—and less profit—in discovering an improvement to a manufacture whose products are bought only by a restricted group of wealthy patrons; inventors have always been attracted by large markets. Again, the basic mechanical or chemical processes involved in the making of goods for general consumption are likely to be simpler in nature than those used where the product is more perfect and expensive: hence it will tend to be easier to transform them. For example, it was easier to employ machines in working wrought iron than in working steel. Mass-production, or the substitution of a cheap material for a costly one, may bring about an actual deterioration of quality: thus coke-smelted iron was for long inferior to that smelted with charcoal.

Exceptions brought about by special circumstances naturally suggest themselves. Workers in precious metals first used protoscientific metallurgical techniques (ch 2). The silk industry devised the punched card, since so frequently adopted for 'instructing' machines (ch 7). In the manufacture of scientific instruments precision engineering begins on the small scale (ch 13). Rifling was applied first to sporting guns (ch 14). Where accuracy has been specially required, as by scientists, navigators, governments controlling currency, and so on, there has always been an incentive to devise improvements that might subsequently prove to have wide application, even though the initial market was small. Yet the huge, basic steps in technological progress seem to be linked with the satisfaction of the most elementary and insatiable human needs. Water- and wind-power were first applied to the grinding of corn, then to fulling cloth, then to mining and metallurgy. Steam-power went first to the mines, then to the mills. Mass-production methods appear first in ship-building yards, then in armament factories. Modern chemical industry begins with the 'heavy' chemicals, and so on. In some cases, moreover, where a new technique was initiated in a small way in a comparatively trivial industry—as when powerful presses were used to shape metal for coinage (ch 13)—it is clear that the real importance of the technique begins only with its application in a major industry.

Thus the generally higher level of technical proficiency in Europe in the seventeenth century compared with the rest of the globe is in no way inconsistent with an inferiority in the quality of certain articles, such as silks or ceramics. The superiority of the west lay in its greater use of power and machinery, in its chemical industry, and, in a few respects, in its applications of natural science. These advantages enabled Europe to produce more goods more cheaply, and so gradually to raise its standard of living to an unprecedented level, while dominating the commerce of the world and drawing to itself every necessary raw material.

As might be expected, the rate of technological change varied in different countries and followed somewhat different paths. In the early sixteenth century many crafts were more advanced in southern Europe, especially in Italy, than in the north. Italian metal-workers, potters, and silk-weavers were unrivalled;

many of the machine-books and other technological treatises were the work of Italian writers, who had the skill of the finest printers at their command; and in Italy, too, at this period, science had its most lively progress. The tendency here was towards higher craftsmanship—Cellini (p 338) is perhaps its supreme example—rather than towards radical transformation of the methods of production, and the trades supplying wealthy consumers were those most affected. France followed somewhat the same path later: it is well known how Colbert (1619–83; p 464) encouraged her luxury industries, such as silk-weaving and the manufacture of tapestries at the Gobelins establishment. Gradually, however, the emphasis shifted to northern Europe, where it remains throughout the following volumes of this *History*. Northern France, the Low Countries, northern Germany, Sweden, and Britain become increasingly influential as centres of industry and commerce. The products of this northern industry were often inferior in quality—as may be seen in printing, ceramics, textiles, and glassware, for example—but the scale of operation was larger.

The rise of the north is best exemplified by Britain. In the Middle Ages the position of the British Isles on the northern fringe of Europe, that proved so valuable to their commerce later, had rendered them isolated, uncultured, and of relatively small import in international affairs. Only political and administrative institutions were well developed in England—these, too, contributed to her industrial success; the remaining kingdoms were semi-barbaric. Even in 1500 Britain played but a lowly part in international commerce as the source of wool and unfinished cloth, tin, hides, and a few other materials. Most of her distant trade was in the hands of Venetian and Hanse merchants. By 1700, however, British ships sailed freely on the world's trade-routes, and numerous export industries flourished, especially that of dyed and finished cloth. Britain's need of many commodities, wholly imported in 1500, was now supplied by new manufactures, which were well able to compete with oversea producers. This growth of an industrial economy in Britain was partly effected by direct imitation of foreign methods and with the aid of foreign workmen, but in its later stages especially it owed much to native technical resourcefulness, of which many instances have been quoted in this volume, particularly the use of coal fuel (ch 3).

Now British industry did not thrive because its workers were more skilful than those of other countries: rather, the reverse was true. Even British shipbuilding, the nation's pride, was in many respects inferior in design and practice to that of the French and Dutch. Britain's industrial success, incipient in the eighteenth century and fully assured in the nineteenth, is essentially to be attributed rather to her richness in the two great materials of the age, coal and iron, and to the readiness with which her manufacturers exploited them. To say this is, of course, to simplify a complex process, for the success must be attributed to many social, economic, and political factors, but for the present purpose the technological adaptability of British industry is the outstanding fact (pp 76–80). British manufacturers were constantly active in replacing skilled workers by machinery, in finding substitutes for scarce and costly materials, in hastening or cheapening processes. They steadily resisted attempts to fossilize their business in the supposed interests of their workpeople or of the quality of the product. Those of other nations were moving in the same direction, but less swiftly and less successfully in most branches of industry, and especially in the heavier trades.

The movement was towards a new kind of industry, whose social implications were tremendous. Before the eighteenth century, and later still outside the confines of Europe, productive techniques were of two kinds. Relatively crude methods were used by village artisans and household workers to make the coarse, sturdy articles of common use; more refined and tedious methods were employed by artists, of a different class altogether, to furnish the rich merchants and the landed gentry with their more delicate commodities. Compare, for example, peasant pottery with the products of the kilns of Deruta and Caffagiolo; the harsh stuff of soldiers' uniforms with the dress of a well born officer; the low, earth-floored dwellings of the labourer with the solid masonry and elegant plaster-work of the town house. The difference is not merely that yielded by the contrast between poverty and riches: it is a distinction of technological accomplishment. No social displacement could overcome it. The skilful methods of the exclusive craftsman might be destroyed, but they could never be extended to the supply of the multitude. To overcome it a technological change was required, one that would ultimately destroy the livelihood of most ordinary artisans and domestic workers, though it will probably never wholly destroy that of the exclusive craftsmen—tailor, chef, bookbinder, and the like—whose service to their patrons is almost of a personal nature.

Medieval manufacture was either widespread, crude, and economically inefficient or exclusive, highly dextrous, and likewise economically inefficient. The new technology of the eighteenth century was to be efficient, technically advanced, and yet wide in its markets. It sought to supply from the same establishments and by the same methods not only the more exacting requirements of the wealthy and cultivated classes of society but the needs of those who were less fortunate. Consequently there tended to prevail a condition approximating more and more closely to a state of technological homogeneity—the difference between the methods used to produce cheap goods and those used to produce costly ones tended to disappear, though the latter were made from better materials and more elaborately finished or decorated. In our own time the obliteration of visible social and economic distinctions in dress is a commonplace, but even within the period of the present volume articles made of fine earthenware, metal, and glass entered into more common household use everywhere, whereas formerly the poorer classes had used articles made of wood and horn; this was a result of technological developments already described.

As everyone knows, the disappearance of the village artisan, of the household worker, and of the exclusive craftsman was brought about by the growth of the factory system, and this in turn was promoted by the adoption of new techniques of manufacture. This growth was scarcely evident before the eighteenth century in Britain, and occurred even later in America and continental Europe. It will be discussed further in subsequent volumes of this *History*, but it should be noted here that factors permitting this development of manufacture in large establishments, making extensive use of machinery and power, were forming much earlier. One reason for the occurrence of this development in Europe, rather than elsewhere in the world, would seem to be the operation of these factors in the European economy in a manner that cannot be discerned elsewhere. Something of this development is mentioned below. In connexion with the growth of large-scale industry and the implementation of new processes, however, it is convenient to discuss two of the factors here: the accumulation of capital (without which investment in machinery and plant would be impossible) and the evolution of suitable means for putting capital into service.

There have always been rich men, and partnerships and complex financial arrangements between merchants were not confined to the economic life of Europe. Yet there can be little doubt that the financial systems that had grown up in Europe by the end of the seventeenth century were more serviceable than those known elsewhere. Already in the Middle Ages the currencies of the various states had become fairly stabilized, a rudimentary kind of private banking flourished, and a convenient method of conveying credit from one merchant to another without any actual shipment of money was working. Already, too, there was considerable evidence of a willingness to invest in industry as well as trade —for example, in the construction of water-driven machines for the textile industry of Britain or the metallurgical industry of Germany. By the sixteenth century great banking families like the Fuggers and the Welsers were financing emperors, there was an organized international money-market at Antwerp, and in many parts of Europe the great landed proprietors, following the example of the merchants, were investing in industrial development on their estates.

Oceanic trade prompted still another form of mercantile arrangement, that of the joint-stock company in which many combined to finance an enterprise beyond the resources of an individual. By the end of the seventeenth century an embryonic share-market of the modern type existed—though it was far more concerned with trade than with manufacture—and public banks, such as the Bank of England (1694), had been founded. Thus the old conception of wealth as gold safely locked in a stout chest or as broad acres of rich land was weakening, though not entirely destroyed, and men were accustomed to investing their money at risk in the hope of large ultimate profits. In the years of the notorious South Sea Bubble (*c* 1720) gullible investors were tempted to venture their capital in a host of projected new manufacturing enterprises. That they did so is a measure of a changed attitude, which made possible the private encouragement of the more fortunate pioneers of the industrial revolution and, later, public investment in canal and railway systems. Without the means for raising capital that already existed in 1700 this could have happened only very much more slowly, if at all.

II. TECHNOLOGY IN EUROPEAN HISTORY

In the period of this volume, therefore, the curve of technological history bends sharply upwards, and at its close we are on the threshold of the age of steam and iron. The techniques of the rest of the world (apart from European-settled America), remaining for a long time unaffected by this rapid and conspicuous development as they had formerly been untouched by the less obvious changes that had prepared the way for it, stagnated at the craftsmanship level and indeed yielded works of inferior merit to those of former times. This *History* follows the curve in pursuing the course of events in Europe. The causes lying behind these events, behind the development of power and machinery, are obscure, and it would be inappropriate to discuss them at length here. As with most complex historical processes, causes and effects seem to be inextricably interlocked, each playing upon the other. Expanding markets stimulated technological improvements to facilitate larger production; large production inspired a search for yet wider markets; each step forward in technique encouraged other attempts at invention; and so on.

Medieval Europe began with many advantages. It derived a rich scientific and technical heritage from the ancient world, yet it was not paralysed in initiative by veneration of past glories. Its natural resources in water, wood, coal, metals, salts, and other minerals were large and accessible; its agricultural potentialities were great and its climate varied. The peoples of the west were basically united in religion, had a common language of learning, and enjoyed a relatively easy communication with each other. After the tenth century A.D., though there was much internecine warfare, there was no great barbarian invasion into the heart of Europe. Its population was small enough to offer to all in normal times ample land and opportunity to work; as the population steadily grew the possibility of economic expansion grew with it. Slavery died out, and, though the gross exploitation of human labour did not thereby cease, the value of labour was always recognized. For many centuries Europe has been conscious that the reduction of the labour element in the production of an article usually leads to a reduction in price.

The social system of medieval Europe was in other ways also more liberal than that of any ancient state, or of any oriental civilization. Feudalism was a powerful and conservative force in society, but with growing confidence from the twelfth century onwards riches, comfort, and even political influence could be won through success in trade and manufacture. Long before the end of the Middle Ages some communities—the north Italian states, the Hanse towns, the Rhineland Free Cities, the City of London—were controlled by their merchant class. This class, and the broad development of trade and industry, were encouraged by secular rulers for fiscal and other reasons of prudent policy. Moreover, the society of medieval and of early modern times was tolerably stable: despite wars and minor disturbances it was not shaken profoundly by dynastic upheavals or by widespread revolution. Its rulers were not, generally, tyrannical; they did not seek to force men's lives into a set pattern, or to fossilize their states by an excess of bureaucratic control such as was evident in the last centuries of Rome and the later periods of Chinese history. European society between, say, the twelfth and the seventeenth centuries was far from absolutely free—no society can be without its restraints—but it was probably more free than any before.

These were conditions making for prosperity and expansive development. Many rewards were offered to the ingenious and industrious individual, however humble his origin, and academic learning was relatively freely available to those who could profit from it. In this connexion it is worth emphasizing that although printing is far older in China than in Europe, it was in Europe that full technical advantage was taken of the invention of movable type. The development of literacy in Europe, and from this, that of the book and periodical as vehicles of scientific and technical instruction, are unparalleled elsewhere. Perhaps European civilization could not have progressed so rapidly had it not possessed a remarkable faculty for assimilation—from Islam, from China, and from India. No other civilization seems to have been so widespread in its roots, so eclectic in its borrowings, so ready to embrace the exotic. Most have tended (like the Chinese) to be strongly xenophobic, and to have resisted confession of inferiority in any aspect, technological or otherwise. Europe would yield nothing of the pre-eminence of its religion and but little of its philosophy, but in processes of manufacture and in natural science it readily adopted whatever seemed useful and expedient. From the collapse of the Roman empire onwards there is indeed a continuous history of technological change in Europe, slight at first, but gradually becoming more swift and profound. It would therefore be idle to discuss how this began, for it has always existed.

III. INDUSTRY AND SCIENCE

In the last two and a half centuries, and above all in the last hundred years, a new factor has contributed to the headlong evolution of European technology: natural science. As already indicated in the preface to this volume, science only rarely played such a part earlier. Some of the technical changes of the Middle Ages that might have been attributable to the scientific developments of the thirteenth century—the introduction of gunpowder, for instance, and of the seaman's compass—prove rather to be products of assimilation from outside Europe. The rudimentary scientific knowledge associated with the application of these technical innovations, as in navigation (ch 19 and 20) and the art of war (vol II, ch 20; ch 14), was itself imitative in origin. Medieval science was grounded firmly on ancient classical authors, whose work became known in the Latin-writing west mainly through translations made from Islamic sources. Then, from the fourteenth to the sixteenth century, and especially between *c* 1450 and *c* 1550, European activity in science was again invigorated by renewed attention to its classical origins, now by way of direct translation from the Greek and by the study of authors previously unknown or neglected. Little of the science usually taught about the year 1500 would have been incomprehensible, or perhaps unfamiliar, to a well educated man of the second century A.D. The great age of creative rather than assimilative science in Europe, that in which fundamental conceptual and practical discoveries took knowledge far from its classical foundations, did not begin until about the middle of the sixteenth century. Thenceforward progress was indeed rapid: within another century the pursuit of scientific truth in ancient authors had been quite abandoned. By about 1650, for example, the basic facts of topographical anatomy were securely established, while by 1700 the elements of mechanics were practically complete—and mechanical science could take both heaven and earth within its view. Scientific academies had been founded, and new ideas and methods were making their way even in the traditionalist universities. Everywhere new techniques of mathematics, and new scientific instruments whose number increased yearly, permitted an ever wider and deeper view into natural phenomena. At this time, too, with the first Jesuit missions in China, European science began to displace its equivalent in the older Asian civilizations.

It has been pointed out already in this *History* that the non-speculative bases of science—all derived from experiment, observation, or experience—owed far more to technology and craft-knowledge than technology owed to science. This was largely true at least as late as 1700, and the exponents of the 'new philosophy' of experimental science had been conscious of the fact. As Robert Boyle wrote, about 1659:

'Tis a prejudice no less pernicious than general which natural history and the interest of mankind receive, that learned and ingenious persons should have been kept strangers to the shops and practices of tradesmen [artisans]. . . . Most of the phenomena that arise in trade [industry] are a part of natural history [science]: and therefore demand the naturalist's care . . . they show us nature in motion, and that too when turned out of her course by human power, which is the most instructive state wherein we can behold her.

Boyle, developing an argument of Francis Bacon, is, indeed, arguing that the scientist has not learnt as much from technological experience and practice as he should. Many efforts were made to give effect to this view—for example, by the Royal Society in its early years—and though the direct results were not very illuminating, such efforts did strengthen the attempt to render science more realistic and practical. Most of the great scientific figures of the seventeenth century, from Galileo to Newton, were deeply interested in the double link between science and technology, and in establishing a hopeful cross-fertilization between the two. In this *History* it has been possible to profit from the same interest among the members of the French Académie des Sciences, for many illustrations reproduced here were originally drawn for the comprehensive account of all trades which the Académie projected.

It was argued with equal cogency that, despite its immediate dependence on technology for useful information, the advance of science must in the long run inevitably hasten technological progress towards that 'Empire of Man over Nature' which was contemplated by Bacon. This delightful vision of an existence in which work would be eased by wonderful machines, thought speeded round the world, and life given unimaginable colour and softness by new chemical processes, while men admired the marvellous intricacy and providence of the Creator's work, was portrayed in a score of treatises, many of which have been referred to earlier in this volume. Bacon's 'New Atlantis' (1627) is the most famous attempt to describe a society in this state of scientific-technological bliss, of which, however, its author recognized that the increased power of destructive weapons must be a part:

We have divers mechanical arts [in the Salomon's House] that you [Europeans] have not, and stuffs made by them, as papers, linen, silks, tissues, dainty works of feathers of wonderful lustre, excellent dyes, and many others; we have also furnaces of great diversities, but above all we have heats in imitation of the sun's and heavenly bodies' heats. We have also perspective-houses where we make demonstrations of all lights and radiations; we find also divers means, unknown to you, of producing of light originally from several bodies. We have also engine-houses, where are prepared engines and instruments for all sorts of motions. There we imitate and practise to make swifter motions than any you have, either out of your muskets or any other device. We also represent ordnance and instruments of war, and engines of all kinds; and likewise new mixtures and compositions of gunpowder. We imitate also flight of birds; we have ships and boats for going under water. We have divers curious clocks, and some perpetual motions.

Men had long before dreamed of acquiring such control over their natural environment by magical means, but by the seventeenth century magic had been abandoned. The scientific power over nature was to be of the same kind as the imperfect one men already exercised, one obtained through reason, experiment, and observation. Such a power had been hinted at before. In a famous passage Roger Bacon accurately anticipated many later achievements, c 1250:

Machines for navigation can be made without rowers so that the largest ships will be moved by a single man in charge . . . cars can be made so that without animals they will move with unbelievable rapidity . . . flying-machines can be constructed so that a man sits in the midst of the machine revolving some engine by which artificial wings are made to beat the air like a flying bird . . . machines can be made for walking in the sea and rivers, even to the bottom without danger.

Too much importance should not be attached to such a prophecy. Many men in many periods have dreamed of attaining the seemingly impossible; what is significant, from the latter part of the sixteenth century onwards, is the faith that the seemingly impossible will ultimately surrender to the patient, systematic assault of natural science. By about 1700 this faith was already partially justified by works. Ships were navigated by science; steam was harnessed; the possibility was even open that the most unpredictable of all factors, the weather, might be susceptible of prediction. In the chemical industries especially the preparation of many substances was now notably more scientific than it had been a century before, and practical chemists like Boyle, Glauber, Kunckel, and Lémery were eminently more rational in their outlook than their predecessors. At last, in the ill-fated theory of phlogiston, a temporarily successful attempt was made to explain the phenomena of chemical reactions and combinations in terms consistent with practical experience.

Roger Bacon's words serve also as a reminder of the truth, often demonstrated in this *History*, that in the Middle Ages the ambition to make technical or industrial progress was by no means wholly latent. In the sixteenth and seventeenth centuries such ambition found many opportunities. Geographical discoveries burst open the horizon; American silver wrought an expansive inflation, swamping economic barriers and restraints; a new world of thought and learning was discovered. The idea that men control their own destinies, both here and hereafter, seized their minds. Projects and inventions multiplied: the vast growth of technological literature, much of it filled with suggestive new ideas, has often been mentioned. Most of this flood of invention was devoid of any basis in science or experience, much was wild and ended in disappointment. Even many well planned attempts—for the rapid consolidation of an agricultural science, for example—necessarily failed. Yet some inventors, choosing a propitious subject and persisting in their labours, succeeded, and a pattern of success was established. Still more successful in its parallel course was science itself, and it was perhaps hard to believe that men who could see the hidden corpuscles of the blood, or calculate the forces holding the planets in their courses, could not solve also the more mundane problems of setting steam to work, or making steel cut like diamond. Everyone knew that navigation had called astronomy to its aid, that chemistry promised to subjugate disease: why should not all material problems of civilization yield to the same method, placing in European hands a power and enlightenment such as the world had never seen? Already by 1700 many were proclaiming that the 'moderns' of Europe had at last hit upon the track to boundless knowledge and prosperity missed not only by the Greeks and their predecessors but by the other civilizations with which they were already familiar. Those who sounded this note placed their emphasis on the triumph of science.

It is hardly surprising, then, that starting from such solid achievements, with such ambitions and such confidence, Europe began in the eighteenth century on that tremendously accelerating acquisition of technical mastery which will be traced in the next two volumes. In our own age, when European society seems to be contracting on itself, when its influence in the world declines and Asia eagerly seizes the mechanics of European civilization while repelling its spirit, it is difficult not to be impressed by the thriving, ebullient expansiveness of the Europe of the seventeenth century. It was a brilliant age, yet it looked to greater glories in the future. Within five or six centuries this society of Christian people had risen from fear and barbarism not merely to great achievement in the arts and to domination of the globe but to a position in which it could face Nature, and almost, it would seem, its Creator, on terms of intimacy and understanding. All that was best in the past and present experience of humanity Europe seemed to have drawn to itself and comprehended in itself: and the success of this creative assimilation gave a great impetus to progress. Men looked to the future now, not to the past, and perhaps for the first time in history had some inkling of the road to be traversed in time to come. They saw science as the inspiration of technology, and technology as the key to a life of richness and prosperity: what they could not see, however, was the infinite and tortuous complexity of man himself.

I. INDEX OF PERSONAL NAMES

The dates given for rulers are regnal dates, not years of birth and death

II. INDEX OF PLACE-NAMES

III. INDEX OF SUBJECTS

PLATE I

Portrait by Tommaso da Modena of a Dominican monk, probably Hugh of St-Cher, showing him wearing spectacles. From a fresco at Treviso, 1352. (p 230)

PLATE 2

B. *The Buxheim St Christopher, 1423.* (p 380)

A. *'Gin Lane', an engraving of 1751 by William Hogarth (1697–1764).* (p 11)

PLATE 3

'The Iron Mountain', an oil-painting of 1606 by Martin van Valkenborch (1542–c 1610) of Malines. The picture shows (left to right) tapping a blast-furnace (note water-driven bellows and counterpoise); forge with water-driven hammers; mouth of iron-mine, with rough windlass for raising spoil; chafery for converting cast iron into wrought iron; the 'canteen'; open-cast mining. The scene is supposed to be placed near Huy, Belgium. (pp 30, 56, 79)

PLATE 4

A. *Post-mill at Parham, Suffolk, showing the top of the post and the crown-tree resting on it with an iron 'samson head' bearing. Note the governors in the background.* (p 92)

B. *The same mill, showing the brake-wheel mounted on the wind-shaft. A drive for the bolter (not shown) is taken off-centre from this wheel by means of a skew pinion. The sack-hoist is driven by belt from a pulley in front of the brake-wheel.* (p 105)

PLATE 5

A. *Interior of the substructure of the post-mill at Parham, Suffolk, showing the post, the cross-trees on which it rests, and the quarter-bars running from half-way up the post to the ends of the cross-trees. Above are the sheers supporting the body of the mill.* (Left centre) *An engine-driven sack-hoist.* (p 91)

B. *The same mill, showing the drive to two pairs of stones from the brake-wheel, through the wallower (the horizontal-bevel pinion), the great spur-wheel (mounted on the same shaft), and the stone-nuts (shown disengaged).* (p 104)

PLATE 6

The wheelwright's workshop. (For descriptive details see figure 71, p 125)

PLATE 7

The cooper's workshop. (For descriptive details see figure 72, p 131)

PLATE 8

A. *Vaucanson's loom, showing the selecting device above the sheds with its perforated cylinder. 1750.* (pp 166, 169)

B. *Detail of* sprang *fabric.* (p 182)

PLATE 9

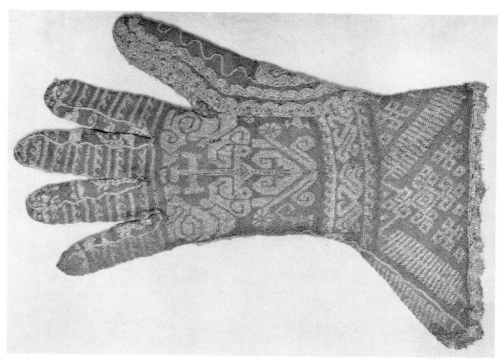

A. *Spanish knitted altar-glove. Eleventh century.* (p 185)

B. *Florentine coat in brocaded knitting. Sixteenth century.*
(p 185)

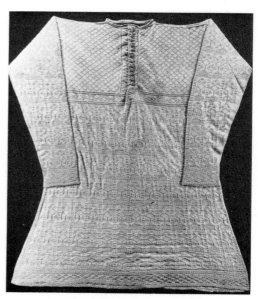

C. *Charles I's vest in patterned knitting.* 1649.
(p 186)

PLATE 10

A. *Shroud of St-Josse in weft-faced figured twill weave. Islamic, tenth century. The inscription does not reverse with the rest of the design. It reads: 'The Glory and Prosperity of the Captain, Abū Manṣūr the Mighty, may God lengthen [his days]'.* (p 191)

B. *Head of a gryphon, worked in weft-faced figured twill. Byzantine, tenth–eleventh centuries. Note irregular scaling and repetition of the figure picks. The roundel was at least 2 ft in diameter.* (p 192)

C. *Design in weft-faced figured tabby weave. Egypto-Roman, probably fourth century A.D. The fabric is mainly drawloom-woven with the aid of an elementary figure-harness. There are fourteen repetitions of the design in the width of the fabric and eleven in the length. The woollen fringe at the side is made from the weft-threads and the cord at the bottom from the warp-ends. The tapestry panel shown in the middle of the fabric was woven with the remainder of the material and not inserted later. Its fine geometrical design is in linen weft.* (pp 193–4)

PLATE 11

A. *Silk with lion pattern from Autinoë. Byzantine work with Persian influences. The Greek inscription, 'Under Romanos and Christophoros, Christ-loving rulers', dates the fabric to A.D. 921-32.* (pp 195, 196)

B. *'Elephant' silk from the tomb of the reburial of Charlemagne at Aachen, with the inscription of the Byzantine factory of Zeuxippos that made it. The weave is weft-faced figured twill.* c 1000. (p 196)

PLATE 12

A. *The 'Maenad' silk from Sens, weft-faced figured tabby weave. Probably Hellenistic, fifth century A.D. The warp-threads are horizontal and the weft vertical. Only two wefts were used, one for the ground, the other for the design.* (p 195)

B. *Fragment of one of the robes of the Emperor Henry VI (d 1197). Sicilian, twelfth century. The weave is tabby ground tissue (diasprum) with a design in gold thread.* (p 198)

C. *German weft-faced figured twill silk. Fifteenth century. There is no repetition of the design. The main warp is of linen and the binder-warp of silk. The background is in gold thread; the faces and other details are embroidered.* (p 196)

PLATE 13

A. *Spanish tabby tissue* (diasprum). *Twelfth–thirteenth century.* (p 198)

B. *North Italian silk twill-ground tissue. Fourteenth century. The design is in gold thread. (Warp-effect three-heald twill ground; design binding four-heald twill).* (p 199)

C. *Italian silk tabby thread.* (diasprum) *brocaded with metallic thread. Thirteenth century.* (p 198)

D. *Italian silk tabby tissue* (diasprum), *brocaded with gold thread and silk. Late thirteenth century.* (p 198)

PLATE 14

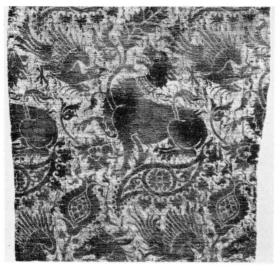

A. *North Italian silk twill-ground tissue. Fourteenth century. The design is in gold thread. (Warp-effect three-heald twill ground; design binding six-heald special twill). (p 199)*

B. *Hispano-Moresque satin-ground tissue. Fourteenth century. Five-heald satin ground, and tabby binding (with binder-warp) for the design. (p 200)*

C. *Hispano-Moresque silk satin-ground tissue. Fifteenth century. Five-heald satin ground and tabby binding (with binder-warp) for the design. (p 200)*

D. *Italian silk brocatelle. Fifteenth century. Christ, Mary Magdalene, and the tree are in gold thread; the faces, hands, and feet in white silk. Five-heald satin ground. (p 200)*

PLATE 15

A. *Four-heald twill damask silk, from the Treasury of St Servatius, Maastricht. Early Byzantine (?). (p 202)*

B. *Italian brocaded damask. Fifteenth century. Warp-effect five-heald satin ground, with design in weft-effect five-heald satin, brocaded in metal thread with special binding. (p 203)*

C. *Italian figured velvet with gold* bouclé *weft enrichment. Fifteenth century. (p 205)*

PLATE 16

Manuscript miniature showing a glass-house at work. Bohemia, c 1420 (cf vol II, figure 310). (pp 207, 208)

PLATE 17

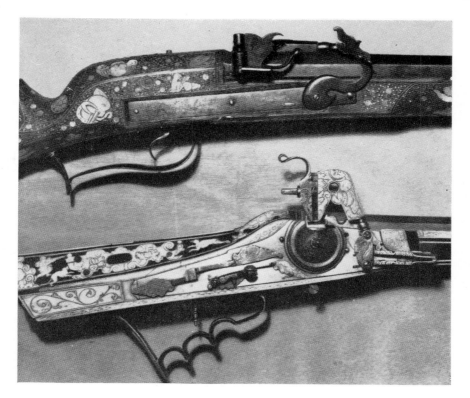

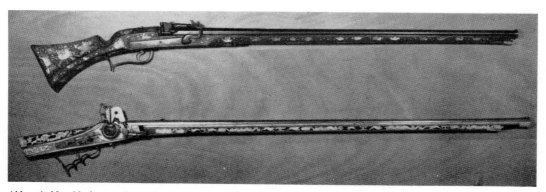

(Above) *Matchlock gun, the stock inlaid with brass wire and mother-of-pearl, c 1600.* (Below) *Wheel-lock rifle, the stock inlaid with ivory. German, 1593. The details show the locks.* (pp 355, 356, 358)

PLATE 18

Chinese barge passing through a stop-log gate on the Grand Canal. From Staunton, 1797. (p 439)

PLATE 19

Leonardo da Vinci's plan for draining the Pontine Marshes. 1515. (p 311) cf figure 207

PLATE 20

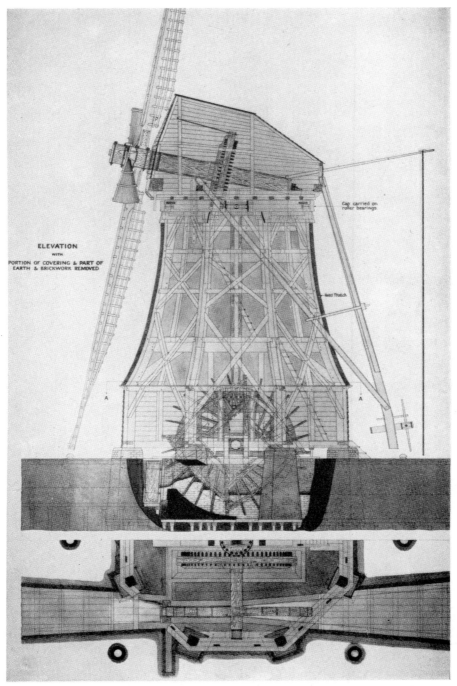

ELEVATION
WITH
PORTION OF COVERING & PART OF
EARTH & BRICKWORK REMOVED

Cap carried on
roller bearings

Reed Thatch

*Sectional diagram (reconstructed) of a Dutch wind-driven scoop-wheel of the early eighteenth century.
(Above)* Elevation; *(below)* plan across the line AA. *The cap bearing the sails is supported on roller
bearings; the main part of the structure is covered with reed thatch. The scoop-wheel rotates clockwise.
Scale 1/134. (pp 106, 321)*

PLATE 21

A. The Henry Grâce à Dieu, *Henry VIII's biggest warship, when rebuilt in 1545, was of 1000 tons. She carried 21 heavy brass guns, 130 iron guns, and 100 hand-guns. Her crew of 700 consisted of 349 soldiers, 301 marines, and 50 gunners. Each of her four masts was in three pieces with two topcastles. Many of her guns fired through gun-ports and her fore- and after-castles were designed to be defended against an enemy boarding the low waist or middle of the ship.* (pp 478, 487)

B. The Grand Mistress, *built in 1545 and classed as a galleass of 450 tons. When building she was described as a 'great galleon'. She has a beak-head similar to a galley's, and a heavy gun in the bow. The fore- and after-castles are much lower than was usual in the older ships.* (p 479)

PLATE 22

The arrival of the Elector Palatine with his bride at Flushing, 1613. The principal ship is the Royal Prince of 1200 tons, 55 guns, built in 1610 by Phineas Pett. She was 210 ft long over-all, 115 ft long on the keel, and of 43½-ft beam. The vessel was a four-master in the tradition of the preceding century, but carried square mizzen-topsails and also the spritsail topmast and sail at the end of the bowsprit. From a painting of 1623 by Hendrik Cornelisz Vroom (1566–1640). (pp 482, 485, 486, 494)

PLATE 23

The Sovereign of the Seas, built at Woolwich by Phineas Pett in 1637, of 1522 tons and 100 guns, was larger than the Royal Prince, being 232 ft long over-all, 128 ft on the keel, and of 48-ft beam. Her guns were mounted on three complete gun decks, so that she was a three-decker like Nelson's Victory. She had three masts only and a very lofty sail-plan with royal sails on the fore- and main-masts. (pp 482, 485–6, 494)

PLATE 24

B. *Contemporary rigged scale model of the Tartar, 20 guns, 1734. The sails and rigging are original. The mizzen and jib are set, the fore and mizzen topsails are loosed. The long-boat can be seen stowed on the booms, the spare spars carried on deck amidships.* (pp 482, 490)

A. *Contemporary scale model of a proposed 90-gun ship, c 1675, showing the elaborate carving decorating the stern and quarter galleries. She was three-decked and would have served as a flag-ship. The scale of the model, ¼-in to 1 ft, was usual in English models at this time. The rigging has been renewed but the spars are original.* (pp 482, 490)

PLATE **25**

PLATE 26

B. *Elias Allen (fl 1606–54), with a variety of instruments: on the table a universal ring-dial, a horizontal dial, and a circumferentor; on the wall a quadrant and a sector.* (pp 630–1)

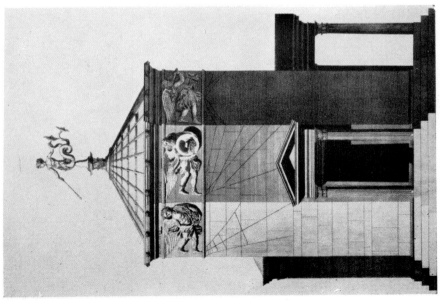

A. *The octagonal 'Tower of the Winds' at Athens. After a drawing of 1762.* (p 517)

PLATE 27

B. *Orrery (model of the solar system) by Benjamin Cole, c 1750.*
(p 638)

A. *George Adams's compressing and exhausting air-pump, 1762. The brass plate to which the receiver was luted is at the top of the instrument; between the pump-barrels is the manometer for measuring the pressure within it.*
(pp 637, 645)

PLATE 28

Alchemical laboratory. (Left) *Press for extracting juices;* (rear centre) *multiple still;* (foreground) *single still. From the*
Studiolo *of Francesco I de' Medici (1541–87), 1570.* (pp 676, 707)

PLATE 29

Jeweller's workshop. From the Studiolo *of Francesco I de' Medici,* c *1570.* (pp 698, 707)

PLATE 30

Painting by G. M. Butteri in the Studiolo *of Francesco I de' Medici,* c *1570, showing a glass-works.* (Centre)
Pounding frit or 'tarso'; (at rear) *blowing in a mould.* (pp 217, 678, 699, 707)

PLATE 31

*Dyers at work. In the right foreground the heated vat is lined with copper or lead. From the Studiolo of Francesco I de'
Medici, c 1570. (pp 702, 707)*

PLATE 32

B. An early spring-driven clock from the background of a portrait of c1440. Note the chain suspension indicating mobility, and the absence of weights. Note also the thumb-pieces for winding, similar to those in figure 392. The winding-key had not yet been invented. (p 656)

A. An early turret-clock with going- and striking-trains, the well known Dover Castle clock. Although for many years wrongly ascribed to 1348, it is of the mid-seventeenth century. Its general lay-out is the same as that of the earliest clocks and it is one of the very few that have not been converted to pendulum control. (p 651)